Fix your eyes on the greatness of medicine as you experience it day by day. Fall in love with the subject, and when you feel its immensity and power, remember that this was attained by men of courage and compassion, with knowledge of their duty, and with a sense of honor in their deeds...

So they gave their minds and bodies to the discipline and received, each for his own memory, praise that will never die, and with it the most magnificent of all sepulchers. Not that in which their mortal bodies were laid, but a home in the minds of men, where their achievements remained fresh to stir speech or action as the occasion might arise. For the whole world is the sepulcher of famous men; and their story is not graven only on stone over their native earth, but lives on faraway, without visible symbol, woven into the very fabric of the lives and actions of other men.

For you now oh reader, it remains but to rival what they have done and, noting that the secret of happiness is knowledge and the secret of knowledge an inquiring mind, not to idly stand aside from the eternal quest to heal.

Adapted from Thucydides, *c.* 460-400 B.C.

The Funeral Oration of Pericles

This book is dedicated to the memory of William Beaumont and his patient Alexis St. Martin. St. Martin owed his survival to the clinical skills and compassion of his physician. Beaumont accrued scientific honor and recognition consequent upon his thoughtful investigation of gastric function and the gift of life that he had conferred upon St. Martin. Their complex relationship epitomizes the eternal inseparability of physicians and their patients.

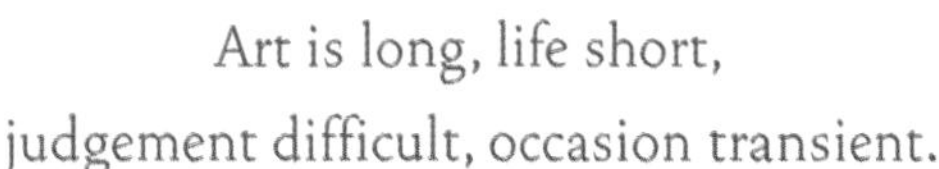

Art is long, life short,
judgement difficult, occasion transient.

Johann Wolfgang von Goethe

(1749-1832)

Veniet tempus quo ista quae
nunc latent in lucem dies extrahat
et longioris aevi diligentia.
Ad inquisitionem tantorum
aetus una non sufficit...
Itaque per successiones
ista longas explicabuntur.
Veniet tempus quo posteri nostri
tam aperta nos necisse mirentur...*

Lucius Seneca, A.D. 45

Thyestes XXV, 4,5

**The day will yet come when the progress of research through long ages
will bring to light the mysteries of nature that are now concealed.
A single lifetime does not suffice for the investigation of problems of such complexity...
It must therefore require long successive ages to unfold all. The day will yet come when
posterity will be amazed that we remained ignorant of things that will seem to them so plain...*

Lucius Seneca, A.D. 45
Thyestes XXV, 4,5

Irvin M. Modlin, M.D., Ph.D., FRCS (Ed), FRCS (Eng), FCS (SA), FACS
Professor of Surgery
Director, Gastric Surgical Pathobiology Research Group
Yale University School of Medicine
Department of Surgery
P.O. Box 208062
New Haven, Connecticut 06520-8062
USA

Editorial Director: Professor Irvin M. Modlin
Art Direction: Wendy Bishop, Sudler + Hennessey Montréal
Index, Line, Copy Editor: Rachel Alkallay
Editing and Coordination: Irvin M. Modlin, Lora-Mae Chartier
Illustration Design and Configuration: Irvin M. Modlin
Illustration Research and Composition: Mark Kidd, Toshi Hinoue, Kevin Lye
Cover Design: Wendy Bishop
Typesetting and Layout: Erich Collar, Centre Typo, Montréal
Production Supervision: Lora-Mae Chartier
Printed by Quebecor World Graphique-Couleur, Montréal

Published by AXCAN PHARMA INC.

ISBN 2-9807504-0-9
Legal deposit – National Library of Canada, 2002
Bibliothèque nationale du Québec, 2002

Irvin M. Modlin

The Evolution of Therapy in Gastroenterology

A Vintage of Digestion

I hav finally kum to the konklusion,
that a good reliable sett ov bowels iz
wurth more tu a man, than enny quantity
ov brains.

Henry Wheeler Shaw (1818-1885)

Josh Billings: His Sayings

Acknowledgements

I am particularly indebted to Léon Gosselin, Dr. François Martin, and Patrick McLean, without whose oversight and amaranthine support this work would never have seen the light of day. They confirmed speculation that the Medici of Montréal have achieved a New World Renaissance no less wondrous than their Florentine predecessors. Isabelle Bourgault provided valuable logistic input and maintained a regal perspective on the subject during the course of our enterprise. The amalgam of their sagacious contributions and the generous support provided by Axcan facilitated the consummation of this felicitous endeavor.

Wendy Bishop and Erich Collar provided artistic and editing input of rare quality and the legacy of their skills, as evident in this book, attests to their exquisite respective talents. Both Eric Capel and Lora-Mae Chartier deserve commendation for their rigorous oversight and support of creative design. All supported the indefatigable Rachel Alkallay in her kabbalistic quest to crystallize a tangle of history, alchemy, science, and clinical comment into a text of perceivable form.

I regret not having been able to accede to the request that the title of the text be "The Axiom of Therapy" or the "Cures for Canada" although the merits of the claims were self-evident, but better judgement prevailed! I am particularly obliged to a number of individuals including Mark Kidd, Kevin Lye and Toshi Hinoue (New Haven), and Christopher Dean and Neil Abbott (Montreal) for their contributions to my current obsession. I believe that prolonged exposure to Gevrey Chambertin fructified the seeds of this endeavor, and that the serenity of the Athenaeum broadened my scientific horizon and honed my etiolated thought processes in a fashion that can only be achieved by adequate Burgundian cortical saturation. I considered the Queen Elizabeth encounters at the Beaver Club to have restored the balance of callosal creativity and vivified the mucosa in a fashion consistent with the creative literary process. Only by dint of serious persuasion was I persuaded not to succumb to the perils of the Tynanian dictum and have abjured from the temptation to *"write heresy, pure heresy – rouse tempers, goad, lacerate and raise whirlwinds."* Consequently this book is sadly lacking in rebarbative comment of which I am particularly fond – believing it to be the one truly definable cause of dyspepsia and disordered gut motility.

A great debt is due to Yale University School of Medicine and in particular, the History of Medicine Library that provided me with the ideal milieu to pursue these studies. In particular, I am grateful to the sagacity of Solly Marks (*amolikke tzeiten*), who has over the years claimed to perceive some obscure merit in my endeavors and whose maieutic skills facilitated my pursuit of the elusive concept of therapy and its evolution.

Numerous institutions and individuals generously provided me with access to material and allowed its usage. These include, but are not limited to, the Yale University History of Medicine Library, the Hunterian Museum and Library of the Royal College of Surgeons of England, the Royal Society of Medicine, the Royal Society of Pharmacy, the Worshipful Company of Apothecaries, the Royal College of Physicians of England, and the Wellcome Institute for the History of Medicine. Innumerable colleagues, scientific collaborators, and friends have generously allowed me to use information emanating from their labors; *Ars Gratia Artis*.

I am entirely responsible for any errors, oversights, and misinterpretations of either historic or scientific data expressed in this text, although the likelihood of any such eventuality is so minimal as to not warrant serious consideration.

Lastly, I wish to acknowledge William Prout and Theophrastus von Hohenheim Bombasticus Paracelsus for exciting in me so monstrous a curiosity regarding muriatic acid, the stomach, and the nature of therapy. Their extraordinary speculations, although centuries old, altered the entire pattern of medical thought and eventually led to the rational treatment of countless millions of patients. Indeed, both labored mightily to succeed in convincing a dubious dogma-ridden medical world of the validity of new knowledge.

Lastly, the most profound acknowledgement is due to the intrepid pioneers of therapy who, in the diverse hospitals and laboratories of Berlin, Breslau, Paris, Lyons, London, Edinburgh, Perth, Vienna, Gothenberg, Capetown, and Los Angeles, so successfully overcame the intellectual obstacles of their times as to vault the boundaries of contemporary therapeutic limitation. By their exquisite delineation of physiology, bacteriology, pathology, pharmacology, and surgery, they mastered the mysterious mechanisms of the cells and like the intrepid maritime explorers of the past, voyaged beyond the acid seas and healed the dyspeptic masses. *Qui genus medici ingenio superavit.*

Léon Gosselin

François Martin

Patrick McLean

Isabelle Bourgault

Mark Kidd

Kevin Lye

Toshi Hinoue

Shelley Robinson

Wendy Bishop

Erich Collar

Eric Capel

Lora-Mae Chartier

Rachel Alkallay

Neil Abbott

Christopher Dean

Foreword

The reader of *The Evolution of Therapy in Gastroenterology* by Irvin M. Modlin will undoubtedly be aroused by a succession of strong feelings.

Feelings of pride for the creative contributions of innumerable physicians and caregivers having resulted in the relief of ailing men and women over so many centuries.

Feelings of gratitude for the work of all the professionals who, day after day, each in their own endeavor, were and are the essential actors responsible for this progress in our constantly evolving therapeutic approaches to disease.

Feelings of humility, nonetheless, for our helplessness and frustration in the continuing quest for the cure of still intractable conditions, despite indisputable and long-lasting achievements in our mechanistic understanding of diseases.

As a gastroenterologist who graduated in the early seventies, I had the privilege of being an active witness and, sometimes, a minor actor in the more recent evolution of therapy in gastroenterology. As a clinician, a teacher, and a clinical researcher, I can measure the need for our continuing efforts in the search of the cure for so many diseases. My recent association with the corporate pharmaceutical world, as a senior officer of Axcan Pharma, allows me to firmly testify that the scientific community should never hesitate to partner with this industry, since we obviously share a common and honorable goal in our search to improve and save human life.

François Martin, M.D., FRCP
Honorary Professor of Medicine
University of Montréal
Senior Vice-President, Scientific Affairs
Axcan Pharma

As a pharmaceutical company dedicated to gastroenterology, Axcan Pharma is proud to celebrate its twentieth anniversary and the contributions it has made to the science and the art of treating GI diseases. We are more than honored to be associated with Irvin Modlin in the creation of this formidable piece of art and history. We would like this book to be an expression of gratitude to the health professionals and patients we serve, and who have helped us inscribe the name of Axcan in the history of therapy in gastroenterology.

Léon F. Gosselin,
President and Chief Executive Officer
Axcan Pharma

Table of Contents

Preface

If somebody were to suggest to you that they had written a text which covered the entirety of the evolution of therapy, you could not be blamed for expressing surprise. Indeed, the concept of attempting to cover a subject that spans almost the entire history of mankind might well be viewed as little more than an exercise in futility or an expression of intellectual hubris. It is therefore with a degree of temerity that one may suggest to the reader that he view this text as a mere distillation, or even a bouquet, of a massive vintage that embraces all the seasons of mankind and their relationship with disease and cure.

While an attempt has been made to focus specifically on the gastrointestinal tract, this goal has not been entirely encompassed, since for thousands of years, bodily disorders and disease were viewed in a holistic fashion and specific symptoms and organs not necessarily defined in the context of suffering and healing. Indeed, the earliest considerations of therapy reflect more a desire of man to return to a state of wellness or well-being, rather than an appreciation of a specific disease. Thus, particular attention was directed at a symptom, and the concept of disease as a unique entity engendering specific symptomatology, was a later notion. Hunger and satiety were amongst the earliest of primitive sensations to be addressed, and the pleasures derived from eating and the sensations of a full belly were probably only exceeded by the exquisite limbic lyrics of physical intimacy. It is therefore little surprise that a considerable early focus of medicine was directed to the satiation of hunger and the process of eating. Lagging only a short distance behind was the appreciation of the fine relief obtained by the expulsion of gas and the emptying of bowel. A profound appreciation of this concept led the Egyptians to believe that the colon was the seat of all diseases and that regular bowel cleansing represented the epitome of health. The Greeks were notable for their focus on herbal remedies and interminable debates on the nature of symptoms, while the Roman militaristic doctrine regarded illness as a weakness and medicine little more than Greek "puffery", and only in times of great plague sought divine intervention. The advent of Christianity led to the consideration of disease as a manifestation of sin, and therapy was considered feasible only if administered under the auspices of religion and as a mechanism designed to facilitate redemption. Suffering, as exemplified by the icon of crucifixion, vied with the healing power of the caduceus as images of the exorcism of sin vied with magic and piety on the path to eternal health and a state of grace.

Much of medicine as it pertained to gastroenterology was folklore, since information regarding diseases of the gut was difficult to obtain. This reflected the fact that access to the organs of digestion from either orifice was limited due to visibility problems, and the peritoneal cavity could not be entered with any degree of safety before the nineteenth century. Information was initially gained by crude animal experimentation, the observation of traumatic wounds, and serendipitous events, while knowledge of disease for the most part reflected postmortem examination. The contributions of the anatomists had defined structure, but it was the physiologists of the eighteenth and nineteenth centuries who laid the foundation for the elucidation of gastrointestinal disease. The advent of endoscopy and radiology in the later part of the nineteenth century essentially breached the portals of the gut and medical knowledge entered a new realm. Advances in chemistry led to the development of drugs capable of ameliorating symptoms, and the introduction of antisepsis and anesthesia imbued surgeons with a zeal to extirpate and cure under circumstances which previously had been fraught with great suffering and mortality.

The access to such information was further amplified by the focus brought to it by great minds such as Ismar Boas, who established the discipline of gastroenterology. The establishment of clinics and departments focused on a particular area of the body led to clarity of thought, as well as advances in

The exploration of time, space, and the unbounded curiosity of the human mind, will ultimately render all disease little more than a distant memory. The difficulty lies with how patients and physicians alike will manage to cope until the advent of this utopian state of existence. Until then we shall be nothing more than a mote in God's eye!

"Ad sapientam pertinet aeternarum rerum cognition intellectualis, as scientiam vero temporalium rerum cognition rationalis."
(To wisdom belongs the intellectual appreciation of things eternal; To knowledge the rational apprehension of matters temporal.)

S. Aurelius Augustinus (*A.D.* 354-430)
De Trinitate, XII, 15, 25

diagnosis and therapy. As the physiological sciences evolved and meshed with biological developments, detailed knowledge of individual organs became available, and the application of agents determined to have specific chemical activities led to the establishment of targeted pharmacotherapy. With this understanding, better concepts of the pathological processes involving the stomach, the liver, the large bowel, and the pancreas, evolved and subspecialization by digestive organ began to manifest itself. By the mid-twentieth century there were experts respectively of the liver, stomach, large bowel, and pancreas, and even surgeons began to subspecialize into gastrointestinal surgery as opposed to pure general surgery. The subsequent further division of the specialty into those who practiced the invasive arts of diagnostic and therapeutic endoscopy further differentiated gastroenterologists from endoscopists and surgeons, and led to the development of substantial expertise in the management of specific disease processes prevalent in the gastrointestinal tract.

While the discipline has evolved considerably from the early days of herbal remedies and elixirs to a world of molecular-targeted pharmacotherapeutic probes and genomics, immense questions still remain unanswered and there is little cause for relaxation. Indeed, as in all explorations, the further one proceeds the more the horizon may be noted to recede. Thus, the causation of gastrointestinal neoplasia remains an intellectual desert. Disorders of the pancreas are inexplicable and the inflammatory diseases of the large and small bowel the source of inspired intellectual guesswork. The mysteries of the liver are as impenetrable as a galaxy and the esophagus for the most part a "*terra incognita*". The stomach, though somewhat better understood, defies regulation of its appetite and the brain-gut axis, though much spoken of, is little charted. The lymphatic system of the gut remains as indecipherable as the circulation before Harvey in the seventeenth century, and the portal system a source of frustration to surgeons as well as hepatologists. The omentum has not even been recognized as a relevant entity, and a discussion of sphincters leads only to an effluvium of intellectual circumlocution. Many remedies, whilst sophisticated in design, have little efficacy and are only supported by the enthusiasm of their proponents. Suffice it to say that though we have made much progress, the road ahead is serpentine and winds far into a misty distance.

In terms of the application of historical perspective to the evolution of gastrointestinal therapy, one may liken the current situation to the early days of maritime exploration. Henry the Navigator, armed only with the knowledge provided to him by the kabbalistic cartographers of Majorca but driven by immense curiosity and certitude of vision, instructed his captains astutely. Their early successful voyages around Cape Bojador in Africa some 500 miles from Lisbon across the turbulent Atlantic were held as the opening of a new era. Little did Prince Henry and his intrepid navigators recognize that the Spice Islands lay a further 6,000 miles away. Unknown to them were the dreaded specters of scurvy, malaria, amoebiasis, dysentery, the Cape of Storms, the Indian monsoons, and the treacherous shoals of Jakarta. Gastroenterology in the palindromic year of 2002 may be viewed as in a comparable position to that of Gil Eanes when he commanded the first caravel to round the great bulge of Africa. An extraordinary voyage, but only a beginning. Nevertheless, it has been a wonderful beginning, with one century encompassing a veritable cornucopia of advances!

This text briefly documents the evolution of therapy in general and broadly addresses its application to the infant science of gastroenterology. There is little doubt that we have traveled far from the days of the Ebers Papyrus. There is even less doubt that the mystic rhythms of the cells, the coding of the regulators, and the inscrutable biologic hieroglyphics of the genomic code await a gastroenterologic Champollion.
Ex Africa semper aliquid nova!

Irvin M. Modlin, M.D., PhD.
March 2, 2002
La Guaira
Venezuela

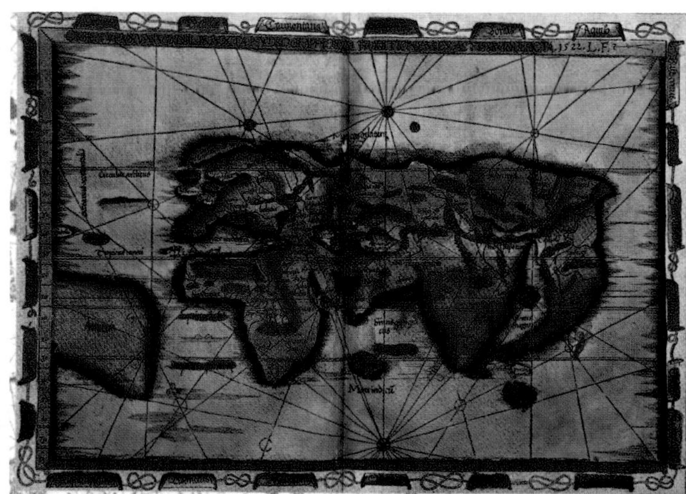

A 1541 xylograph of a classic Ptolemaic planisphere demonstrates the extraordinary advances in the exploration of the earth that had occurred within the century after Gil Eanes of Portugal had first rounded Cape Bojador and opened the path to the East. It is worthy of note that the discipline of gastroenterology was established just over a century ago, when endoscopy and radiology provided the first maps of the interior. We may wonder, what new worlds await to be explored?

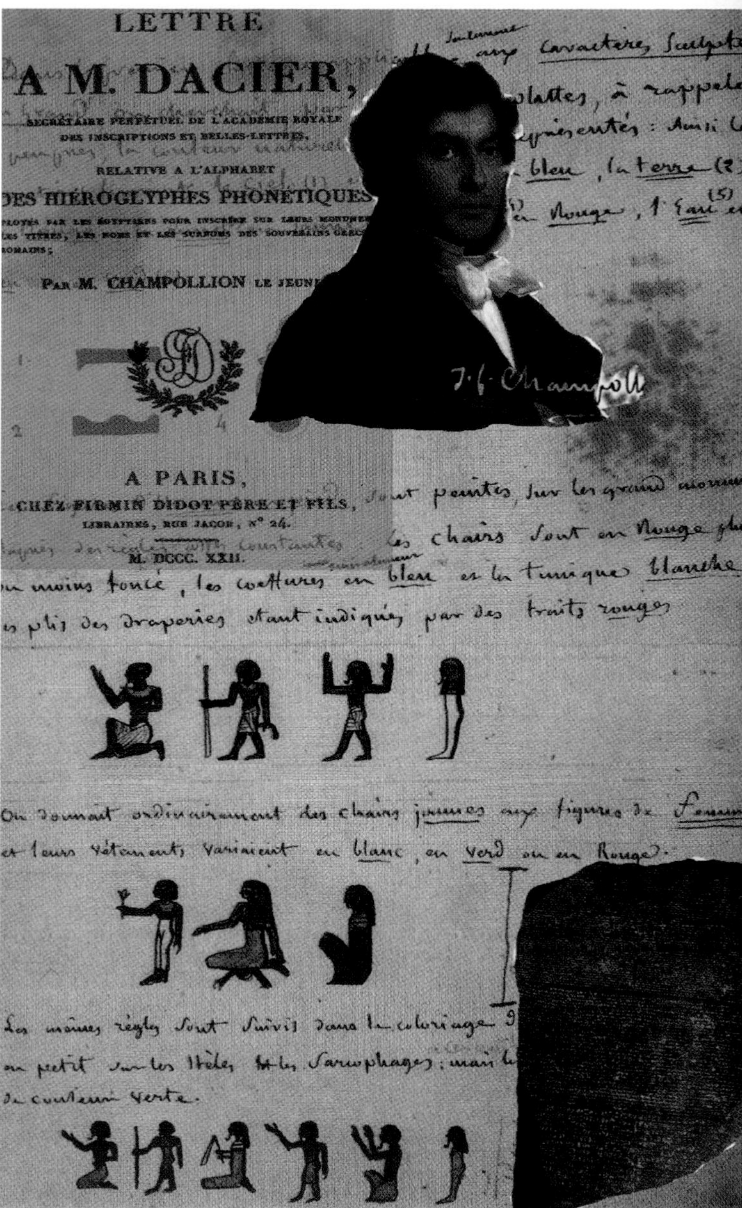

In August 1799, a French officer, Bouchard, discovered an irregularly-shaped stone of black basalt near the town of Rosetta (Rashid), about 35 miles northeast of Alexandria. On September 22, 1822, Jean-François Champollion, in a letter to the Royal Academy of France, revealed how he had utilized the Rosetta Stone to decipher hieroglyphics. In so doing, he unlocked the keys to the history of a civilization and the secrets of the past. Although Watson and Crick defined the double helix of DNA in 1953, and the human genome became available in 2000, the decipherment of the fundamental genetic coding of human health still awaits a scientific Champollion. Therein lies the future of the human race...

Section I

Early Concepts of Health and Disease

INTRODUCTION

In the earliest of times, health was the accepted mode of life, and illness and aberration ill-understood, and as such, felt to be either due to divine providence or fate. Obvious causes such as insect or animal bites could be understood but mysterious afflictions which left people with burning temperatures, loss of appetite and weight were less comprehensible. The relationship between food eaten and subsequent abdominal pain and diarrhea were easily discerned but situations where appetite gradually failed, muscles wasted away and masses appeared in the abdomen were frightening and required help and advice from those skilled in the arts of illness. As such the earliest medical practitioners of any sort would almost certainly have been designated as herbalists. How they acquired such knowledge or became specifically interested in disease is difficult to understand. Possibly a nurturing personality or a random event whereby advice resulted in cure led to a reputation which then was handed down from generation to generation.

While curiosity regarding the use of certain agents or plants may have initiated a skill in early herbalism, it is possible that the healing properties of herbs may have initially been noted by observation of animals. Subsequently, primitive experiments with roots, leaves, and applied ointments led to the development of infusions, decoctions, and ointments. The herbalist and pharmacist among primitive tribes would accumulate facts and experience and note that their skill and service had a market value which enabled them to live in their community by providing a service not involved with manual labor. To further facilitate their position within primitive society they surrounded themselves with an aura of mystery and magic and maintained the secret of their skill within the families. This assured both the awe and respect of their tribes. By further perpetuating theories of supernatural power and its relationship to disease, they were further able to amplify their social standing by suggesting skills of such power that they were enabled to protect their fellow beings from the malign influences of demons and gods. Thus the early uses of therapeutic agents were surrounded with the practice not only of primitive medicine but quasi-religious and supernatural skills involving incantations, exorcism, superstitions, and the development of a priest craft. The subsequent extrapolation of such behavior which fed on the credulities and anxieties of humans who were ill, led to fakery, impostures, and quackery, which have been constant companions of the healing art since its inception.

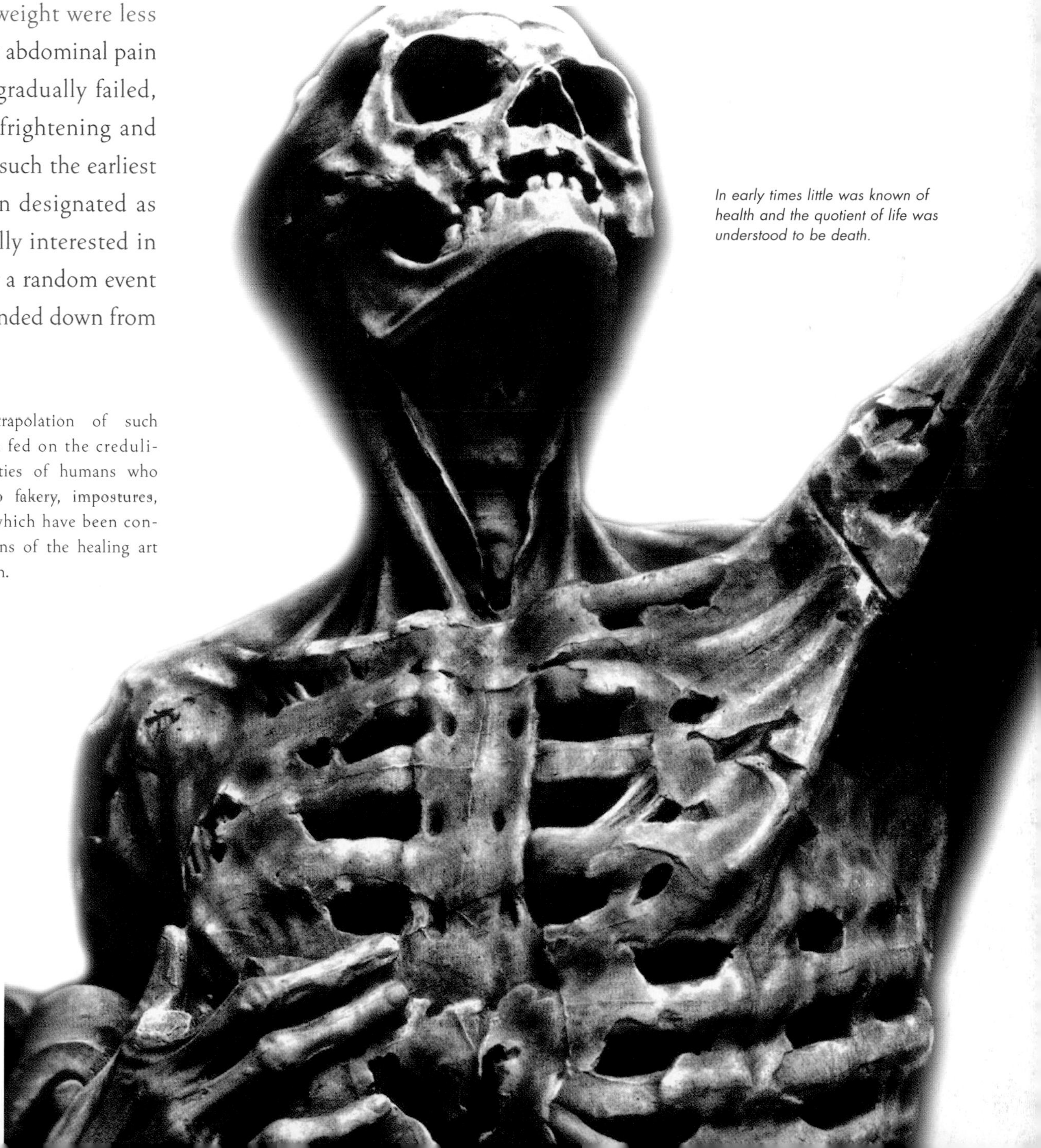

In early times little was known of health and the quotient of life was understood to be death.

Ancient medicine consisted of an amalgam of amulets, sorcery, herbalism and superstition. Since little could be done to ensure health in the present life much emphasis was placed upon ensuring a smooth transit and comfort in the next life.

The concept of therapy cannot be considered without a consideration of early man's notion of health and disease. This in itself has inherent difficulties since it is not truly possible to assess what a person many millennia removed from our civilization may have imagined under circumstances where his feeling of well-being became altered.

Considerations for the cause of the problem must have ranged from the malign influences of his tribe to the designs of an enemy or thoughts of poor food and possibly even the influence of stars, planets or supernatural beings that inhabited the forests and mountains of his environment. Thus, a primitive man's understanding of the human body is unintelligible unless we take into consideration the preconceptions which may have preoccupied the primitive mind. All undeveloped and primitive races possessed what to them must have represented complete "explanations" of the world in which they lived. Such elucidations consisted, in part, like modern scientific rationalizations, of "laws" which would, according to the custom of a particular group, be regarded as invariable. As might be predicted, the tenets which primitive man devolved from contemplation of his life and times were somewhat more inaccurate than represented by current scientific doctrine; and, unlike contemporary scientific imperatives, these explanatory principles were not explicitly stated or formulated in such a fashion as to be normative for the doctrines or beliefs of the time.

For the most part, it has been customary to regard the class of data which primordial peoples developed as an explanation of their world, as falling within the category of magic. Within this context two fundamental principles (the law of contagion and the law of similarity) underlying magical ideas require consideration as regards concepts of health and disease. The concept of contagion states that objects, which at one time have been in continuity or juxtaposition, continue to exert an effect one upon the other, no matter how distantly they may ultimately come to be removed. Thus, if a primal man wounded an enemy, he supposed that he might later exercise an influence over the progress of the healing of the wound by subjecting the weapon that had inflicted the injury to various forms of treatment. Thus, heating the blade of the weapon in a fire would be presumed to result in the wound to becoming hot and inflamed. This law of contagion, although it had little or nothing to do with the science of bacteriology, directed mankind into what at this time might at initial enquiry appear to be a consideration of hygienic pursuits. In fact, observation of primitive tribes reveals that individuals are obsessive at the disposal of their excrement, nail parings, and particles of uneaten food. This does not reflect a preoccupation with hygienic principles but a belief that such preemptive activity will obviate ill-disposed individuals from subjecting him to harm by magically manipulating materials, which were once in contact with him.

The law of similarity states that objects or circumstances which bear some apparent similarity either in form, shape, color, or sequence of events, are considered by the primitive mind to be fundamentally related. Thus certain primitive tribes, for instance, have a belief that a yellow bird is useful in the treatment of jaundice, and being attracted by the similarity of color, capture birds with yellow feathers or eyes. After reciting appropriate incantations over them, they are released in the belief that the bird acquires and carries away with it the agent of the affliction or "illness principle". In the canon of pharmacology this set of "principles" subsequently became adopted under the names of the "doctrine of signatures" and *similia similibus curantur*. A further but alternative extrapolation of this concept led to the belief that objects which possessed certain characteristics directly opposite could be considered to exhibit a sympathetic relationship with one another.

In order to further protect himself from an often hostile and inexplicable reality, primordial man – almost of necessity – developed an alternative set of explanations to comprehend the phenomena of the external world and

Despite the worship of idols and fetishes, the lifespan of primitive mankind was brief and demise as shrouded in mystery as birth. Whether veneration was directed to the sun or moon or a baobab tree, fate and disease soon rendered him to dust.

Whether driven by Cartesian logic (Descartes, top right) or the vision of Blaise Pascal (bottom right), the analysis of structure and function failed to definitively identify the quintessence of the soul or its location.

Death was celebrated rather than feared in ancient Egypt, and preservation of the body was a sophisticated art and ritual. The embalmed viscera removed from a body during the process of mummification were placed in vessels (canopic jars) of wood, stone, pottery, or faience. The earliest, which came into use during the Old Kingdom (c. 2575 – c. 2130 B.C.), had plain lids; but during the Middle Kingdom (c. 1938 – c. 1600? B.C.) the jars were decorated with sculpted human heads, probably representations of the deceased. From the 19th dynasty until the end of the New Kingdom (1539-1075 B.C.), the heads represented the four sons of the god Horus (i.e., jackal-headed Duamutef, falcon-headed Qebehsenuf, human-headed Imset, and baboon-headed Hapy).

within himself, a novel rationale that countermanded the theme of invariability implicit in magical formulae. Such enlightenment was based upon the necessity and assumption that under certain circumstances natural laws could be offset by the influences of supernatural or spiritual power.

It is likely that the concept of a spirit was initiated by the fundamental observation of the stark differences between life and death whereby the deceased were cold, pale, bloodless, and, above all, motionless. In fact, motion became so inseparably identified with life that many primitive cultures even to this time are accustomed to regard anything that moves as "more or less alive." Primitives considered this ineffable "something," which brought about movement during life and, on departing, left the corpse motionless, as an entity capable of traversing space. Despite it being unseen and unheard it was considered pervasive and capable of exerting an influence that might be good or evil depending upon extant circumstances. This concept of a disembodied life principle forms the basis of the primitive idea of spirit that was subsequently extrapolated by prescient philosophers, including Descartes and Pascal, into the concept of the soul. Since they were disembodied such spirits were not considered subject to the limitations of space, time, or the travails of the flesh, and were thus capable of exerting an influence beyond the human sphere. It was divined that a mortal might avail himself of such power by securing the offices of a spirit to intercede on his behalf, and in such a fashion set aside natural law or the fate of the flesh.

In this respect the concept of the vampire is of particular interest in contemplating the principle to which therapy might be applied. Thus the characteristics of cold and pallor, which are associated with death, are direct reflections of bloodlessness, and primitive man noted early that extensive hemorrhage was incompatible with life. From this observation arose an inkling that the life principle in the living might reside within the blood and that assimilation of the blood of another might vitiate the loss of spirit associated with bleeding and death. Further experience in regard to the dramatic loss of blood (and life) in the event of wounds to the heart led to a reasonable belief that the life principle might reside either in the blood or the heart. Indeed, the dramatic excision of the heart as undertaken by the Mayans further supports the early notions of the "spirit" as being a heart-blood related entity. Similarly, the realization of the massive blood content of the liver led to some early magico-medical writings regarding the seat of life as in either the heart or the liver, while also conferring upon the heart various functions consistent with a role in the mentation process.

Such primitive theories of the phenomena of life and disease provided minimal opportunity to embrace a deeper understanding of the mysteries of bodily function, let alone the concepts of miasma and pathology. However,

Torture and human sacrifice were fundamental religious rituals of Mayan society; they were believed to guarantee fertility, demonstrate piety, and propitiate the gods, and if such practices were neglected, cosmic disorder and chaos were thought to result. The drawing of human blood was thought to nourish the gods and was thus necessary to achieve contact with them. The central role of the heart was well-recognized.

with the passage of time, the failure of the primitive scheme of explanations in the face of more complex forms of practical life mandated a more rational consideration of details which had been previously neglected. Initially, attention was directed to structure and early anatomical concepts led to a basic understanding of the fabric of life upon which was slowly grafted a vague appreciation of function. Indeed, the earliest cryptic pictures drawn during the upper Paleolithic era by Cro-Magnon Man indicate that he was not completely without some factual anatomic and physiologic knowledge. Albeit that the cavern walls predominantly reflected magical concepts, presumably superimposed upon this framework of practical topographic anatomy, embodied in the designs are an obvious understanding of structure and function. Nevertheless, prior to the Greek era only the vaguest references reveal any evidence of anatomic information and despite their apparent sophistication, the Egyptians exhibited a profoundly limited grasp of human design, preferring to devote themselves to magic and the attainment of a healthy afterlife.

Birds, animals, and celestial objects such as the moon, sun, and stars were part of a complex system of predicting life outcomes in the ancient kingdoms of the Middle East. In particular, prophetic interpretations based upon the configuration of the liver (hepatoscopy) was a dominant cult in Babylon and Ninevah.

Although certain of the ancient papyri make superficial references to structure, prior to the discovery of Babylo-Assyrian texts dating back to 7000 B.C. in the ruins of the palace of Ashurbanipal, at Nineveh, few writings reflecting ancient medical practices can be identified. This collection, unlike older records, is not the remnant of a mere legal repository, but actually represents a library in the more modern sense of the word, and from them some insight into ancient medicine may be gained. The Code of Hammurabi, which is believed to be based upon a still older source and is a legal document, makes it clear that a definite medical class existed in the valleys of the Tigris and Euphrates at a much earlier period than any medical texts would indicate of themselves. The Code contains material relating to the practice of medicine and describes the physician, or Asu, who was the representative of the healing god Ea, and thus, in a sense, a vaguely priestly individual. Of note even this early in history is the fact that the physician was specifically distinguished from the surgeon and veterinarian, and a separation is established between magical and religious procedures, as well as between these and objective practices in medicine.

Furthermore, the concepts of therapy are defined not only in terms of efficacy but also as they relate to therapy, which might be deemed to be inappropriate, wrong, or to have failed. Thus definite penalties are laid down for the practice of witchcraft, and physicians, necromancers, and priests are also prescribed for malpractice. Although an initial consideration of the Code of Hammurabi might allow for the belief that a very advanced state of medicine existed in Babylonia, subsequent records indicate that this is an illusion. The concept behind the disease in the majority of old Babylo-Assyrian texts represents a transmogrification or modified conception of possession by spirits or devils, of which the Babylonian mythology possessed an overabundant supply. Indeed, suffering was considered by the ancient Babylo-Assyrians as the result of wrongdoing much in the same fashion as is held by contemporary Buddhists. In the face of this ideology it was rational for a sick man to attempt to placate an imaginary, irate deity than to seek out a physician, and it was only in isolated circumstances that the medicine of this civilization attained objectivity.

Although the Babylonians made no distinction between arteries and veins, they did distinguish between venous (blood of the night) and arterial blood (blood of the day). This confusion of arteries with veins was based upon the failure to understand the nature of the circulation of the blood, but allowed for some consideration of the blood as a substance that might harbor the agents of ill health. The Greeks were inconclusive in their understanding of the blood and its conduits. As a result arteries were incompletely differentiated from veins since they noted that some arteries were normally empty of blood after death, thus a precise distinction between arteries and veins was not extant in ancient times. Bleeding to liberate "evil spirits" was not widely practiced and the Egyptians, in particular, believed that the majority of diseases arose in the bowels from the "dirt" contained therein. In consequence much of their medical practice was centered around the anus and the use of enemas to administer cleansing agents or purgatives to eliminate disease. Apart from such notions in the Nile Valley, the inhabitants of the valleys of the Tigris and Euphrates were aware that diseases also afflicted specific organs (lungs, liver), and used this knowledge to seek understanding, as well as to provide portents for the future. This notion was elaborated upon by the Babylonians who supposed that certain animals (sheep) possessed a

Hammurabi, the best-known ruler of the Amorite dynasty of Babylon (c. 1792-1750 B.C.) was noted for his legal code, once considered the oldest promulgation of laws in human history. The medical component of the law held physicians responsible for therapeutic outcome. Thus, the price of therapy was high and could even lead to loss of limb or eye for the caregiver (lex talionis).

War led to penetrating wounds and the primitive understanding of not only the morbid results of trauma but also the early concepts of anatomic structure.

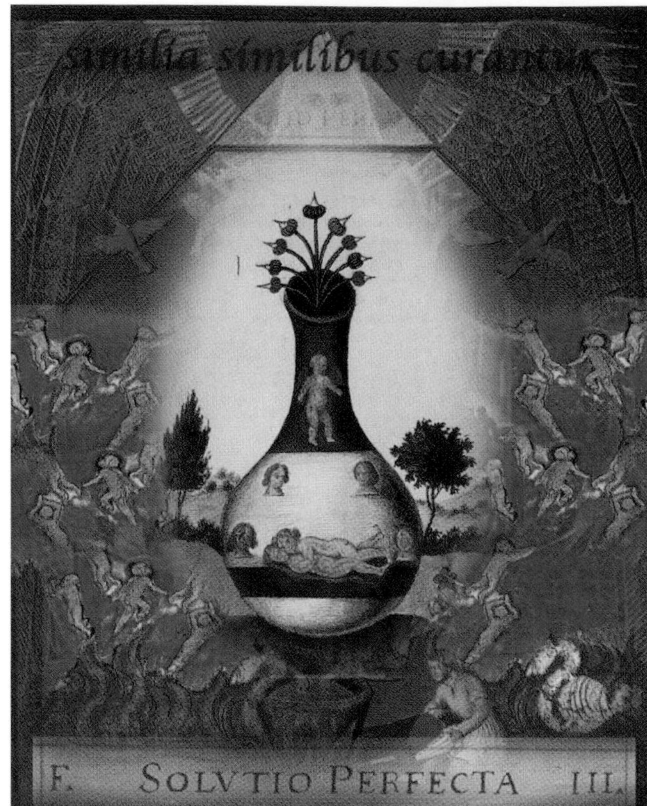

The belief that a cure for the ailment of a particular disease could be provided by a magical property that resided in the afflicted organ, led to the development of mystical notions that later evolved into the "laws of similarity." Procreation was regarded as the cure for all illness – a notion that has persisted from time immemorial.

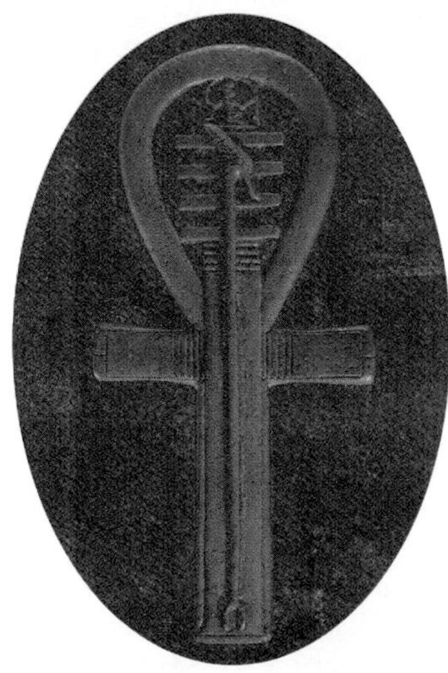

Amulets have been utilized as protection from evil spirits and disease since time immemorial.

knowledge of the future denied to humans and that this understanding was reflected in the shape of their liver. As a result of this quasi-magical-religious medical association, priests developed complex clay models of the liver that bore special designations for the three main lobes and the associated major anatomical structures. The *fossa venae umbilicalis* was designated "river of the liver" and the two appendages attached to the upper lobe – the *processus pyramidalis* and the *processus papillaris* – were respectively described as the "finger of the liver" and the "offshoot", while the depression separating the two lobes from the *lobus caudatus* was referred to as the "crucible" of the liver. In addition, the gall bladder, cystic and hepatic ducts, and the *ductus choledochus* were all specifically mentioned and each structure or aberration thereof (stones, lumps, scars) was accorded a prognostic value for the health of the patient being considered, or the future, if prophecy was the intent of the divination. At a much later time it became the custom to offer to the various deities models of organs or parts of the body which were supposed to be diseased. These models were called votive offerings or "anathemata", and the concept of offering them to the gods represented an expression of the "law of similarity" in magic.

The earliest evidence of a developed medical system in Egypt, as in Babylonia, is indirect and, when apparent as in inscriptions, stele or papyri, offers definite proof that a system was present in an undeveloped form long before the time of the record. Thus the notations of the *Ebers Papyrus* presuppose the existence of a line of thought which must have existed for a substantial prior period of time. As in the case of the Mesopotamian civilization, the Egyptian priestly class was not only of importance politically and economically but also ecclesiastically. Despite the fact that bodily suffering was considered the result of transgression of sacred law and that, to a certain extent the superimposition of Egyptian theology interfered with objective medicine, useful medical remedies and concepts are proposed in the *Ebers Papyrus*. A major issue, however, was the Egyptian restriction against profaning the body, based upon the assumption that unless its form was carefully preserved until the time of resurrection, the spirit would be incapable of incorporation and would become lost in the void. The Egyptians were especially worried about desecration of the body since falling prey to animals or the depredations of worms would result in the body becoming utterly lost to its former spirit. As a result of this belief, an elaborate process of preserving the dead – mummification – became a mainstay of medical and theological practice. Thus the specific prohibition against profaning the dead, as well as a philosophy which stated that suffering and, consequently, disease were due to the intervention of a deity, led to an avoidance of the opportunity to view and comment upon anatomy and disease. Although the Babylonians were concerned about the reunion between body and spirit, the concept never attained the obsessional level encountered in the land of the Pharaohs. Medication was modest and mostly represented by herbal infusions, complex recipes of honey, wine and grains, while administration was for the most part *per anus* although *per os* was possible if the mixture were palatable. Direct physical intervention was usually restricted to repair of broken bones, reduction of dislocations, removal of arrows and javelins. Among the Babylonians the surgeon was a recognized but ignorant craftsman although in Egypt, despite the fact that his function was somewhat better regarded, he was nevertheless restricted by priestly law to mostly reparative and superficial manipulations.

Primitive Therapeutics

Since magical ideas obey the laws of similarity and contagion, it might be predicted that the therapeutic efforts of primitive man would follow such principles. Indeed, primitive pharmacology exhibits numerous examples whereby the law of similarity makes itself apparent.

Thus, a medicine to turn gray hair black may be produced by stewing birds, like the raven, which has intensely black feathers. In a similar fashion, the extrapolation of this process of reasoning allowed for the belief that parts of plants, which resembled organs or portions of the body could be considered to exert an influence over them. Indeed, the subsequent amplification of notions such as this became explicit in the development of the medieval doctrine of signatures and the current usage of an agent such as ginseng, is a modern example of its continued persistence. The antithesis of the theory of cure by the application of the law of similarity (*similia similibus curantur*) also suggested itself, and in this fashion concepts such as the utility of cold remedies for febrile conditions developed. The application of the law of contagion (objects once in juxtaposition continue to exert some mystical power over one another in perpetuity) is also frequently exemplified in medical systems. Thus so-called moonstones, which were believed to have

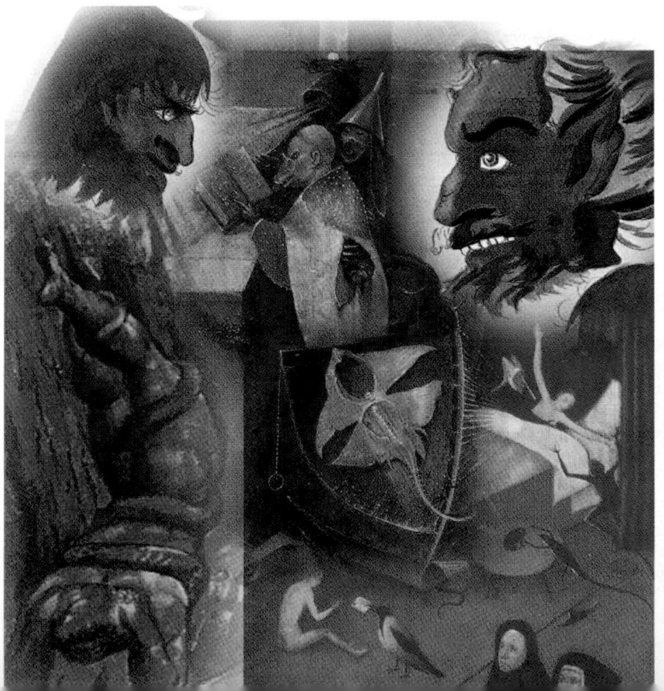

Much disease was felt to be caused by evil spirits naturally present in certain animals or the influence of malignant individuals on such vermin or beasts.

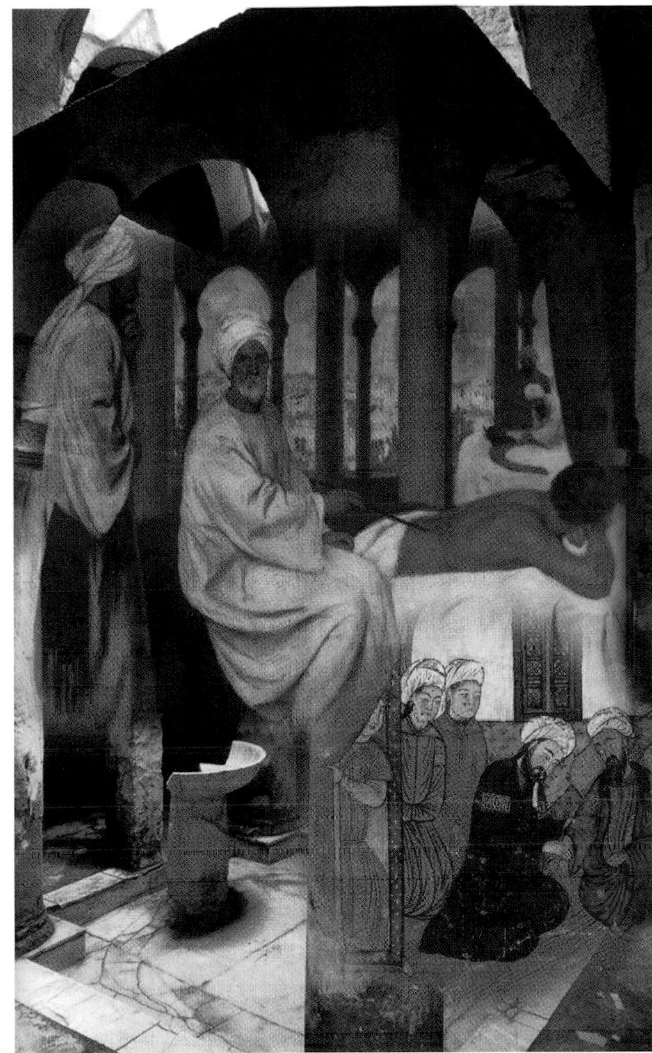

Priests became physicians of the soul as well as the body and interceded with divine authority to effect a cure.

been formed in the earth under the influence of the moon, were long utilized to treat insanity, then held to be consequent upon the malign effects of prolonged lunar exposure.

Despite such arcane notions, primitive pharmacological ideology did not solely reflect theory and some concepts were based upon either observation or personal experience. Thus, abdominal symptoms could be related to the consumption of specific fruits which were then avoided, or noticing that animals, when ill, consumed certain herbs or berries which, when used by the ill person, produced similar beneficial results.

In some circumstances, a misinterpretation of an affliction allowed for the development of a legitimate confusion between magic and disease. Thus, a common primitive concept of the intrusion of an irate deity into the body was that evil spirits would be sent to torment the patient and result in the gnawing pains which accompany many diseases. Given the prevalence of the filth and vermin which were a constant feature of primitive existence, and the presence of maggots in many putrescent diseases, the primitive mind was fortified in its belief that the early pain of the disease was as a result of malignant spirits which were now, in the form of worms, working their way out of the part of the body they had so long tormented. Thus, much of magic cures could be supported not only by prayers and potions designed to rid the body of spirits, but the dramatic demonstration of parasites being passed *per anus* or being extracted from cutaneous sores. As might be expected many complex early pharmacological interventions were steeped in highly developed religious incantations, which were deeply cognizant of demonology and firmly founded upon the belief that the suffering incident upon disease was the result of personal malfeasance. In particular, Babylo-Assyrian remedies were usually accompanied by complex incantations intended as prayers to the putative divinities involved and, in this fashion the two different concepts of etiology and *therapeusis* could be melded into a single beneficial procedure.

BABYLO-ASSYRIAN

Early Babylo-Assyrian *therapeusis* was deeply tinged with religious rituals centering about water, the sacred element of the god *Ea*. Not surprisingly the people of a desert country dependent upon the great river valleys came to regard the life-giving properties of water as synonymous with health.

Indeed, the diversity of balneology with its roots deeply embedded in the dim past of mankind, has been preserved in the public baths, mikvahs, tepidaria, Turkish baths and even the Jacuzzis of this age. Water also played an important role in Greek therapeutics and this belief was common for all people located on rivers or great bodies of water or near springs. The usual procedure was to sprinkle or pour water over the head of the patient and also recite an appropriate incantation so that the demon might be expelled and the patient purified. Among the Babylo-Assyrians, specific demons were considered to preside over special parts of the body and were responsible for generating particular complaints as, for example, *Alu*, for the breast, *Asakku*, for fever in the head and *Utukku*, for throat complaints. Prophylaxis was not unknown to these civilizations and specific amulets and prayers were

The multiplicity of different amulets worn for protection attests to the innumerable agents of disease that required placation.

Isis nourishes her son Horus. In her role as the wife of Osiris, she discovered and reunited the pieces of her dead husband's body, was the chief mourner at his funeral, and through her magical power brought him back to life. Isis hid her son, Horus, from Seth, the murderer of Osiris, until Horus was fully grown and could avenge his father. She and Horus were regarded by the Egyptians as the perfect mother and son and the shelter she afforded her child conferred upon her the character of a goddess of protection. Her chief attribute was that of a great magician, whose power transcended that of all other deities and her intervention was invoked on behalf of the sick.

Horus was the son of Osiris and the opponent of Seth, who murdered Osiris and contested Horus' heritage, the royal throne of Egypt. Horus finally defeated Seth, thus avenging his father and assuming the rule, but in the conflict his left eye (i.e., the moon) was damaged – this became a mythical explanation of the phases of the moon – but was healed by the god Thoth. Subsequently the figure of the restored eye (the wedjat eye) became a powerful amulet. Horus appeared as a local god in many places and under different names and epithets. These included Harmakhis (Har-em-akhet, "Horus in the Horizon") and Harpocrates (Har-pe-khrad, "Horus the Child"). The latter may have given rise to the term Hippocrates.

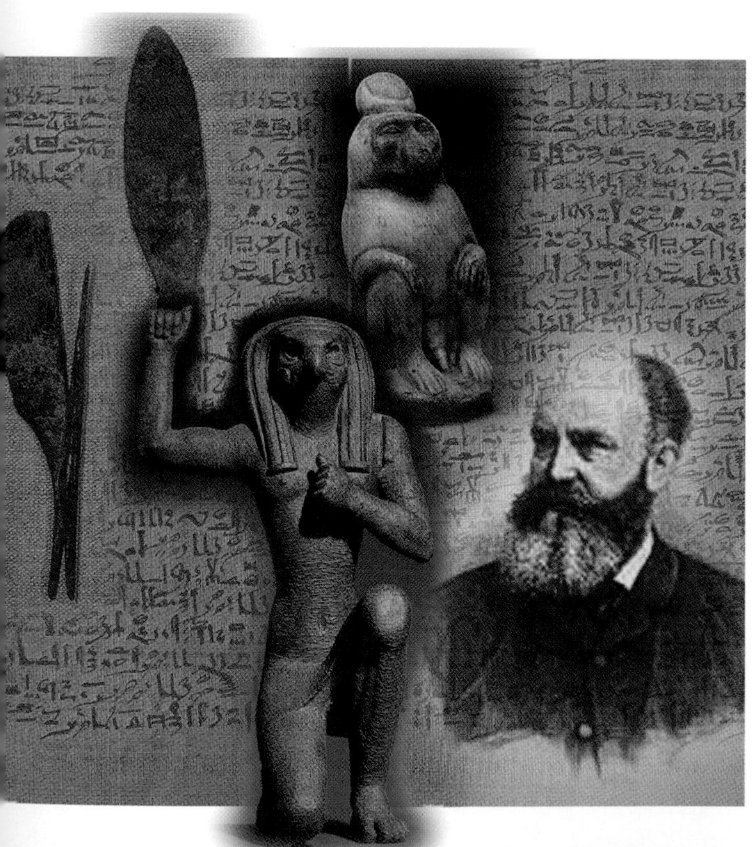

developed for protection or to facilitate demonic expulsion. To support such measures, a variety of medications were developed and Babylo-Assyrian tablets document over 300 drugs (*shammu*) including plants, trees, herbs, roots, seed juices, woods, mineral substances, or precious stones. In some instances the drugs are even listed in special groups, as agents to be employed for particular ailments. Some examples of particularly efficacious incantations and remedies include:

Wicked Consumption, villainous Consumption, Consumption which never leaves a man, Consumption which cannot be driven away, Consumption which cannot be induced to leave, Bad Consumption, in the name of Heaven be placated, in the name of Earth I conjure thee!

If a man's head is affected and the demon in the man cries out, but come not out, is not caught by bandage or incantation, then kill a captured kurku bird, squeeze its blood out, take its … fat and the skin of the crop (?), burn it in the fire, mix cedar with the blood, and pronounce the incantation, "evil finger of man," three times.

Some of the prescriptions of the Assyrian and Babylonian physicians begin with a terse comment on the symptoms to be treated as well as the remedy to be applied. Thus:

Against fever and chills, which is not good for the flesh, fill a shukhurratu jar with water from a cistern, untouched by hand. Add tamarisk wood, mashtkal-plant, shalalu-reed, ukhkhuli (perhaps alkali), cumin, pressed date wine. Add thereto a sparkling rind. Pour the water over that man. Pluck mal kanu-root, pour pure salt with pure ukhkhuli plant, and sweet oil brought from the mountain. Seven times rub the body of that man.

In another prescription that focused on the digestive tract it is stated:

If a man's inside is swollen and inflamed and he is nauseated, then for his life, mix onion with cumin seed; let him drink it in wine without food and he will recover. If ditto, take the green rind of the IL plant, mix with pig's fat, let him drink it with Du-Zab unmixed wine and sweetened water, and he will recover.

Egyptian Concepts

Since medicine and magic were intermittently associated practices, superstitions, facts, and conscious and unconscious deceptions soon became blended into a mosaic which formed a fixed and reverent system known broadly under the rubric of medicine.

In 1872 Georg Ebers (bottom right) discovered in Thebes a papyrus (background) that provided vivid insight regarding the basis of Egyptian medical practice.

Supernatural powers were invoked, and the credit of the revelation of the art was attributed to either a divine being who had brought it from above, to some gifted and inspired creatures who as a consequence of their gift to mankind, had been admitted into the family of the deities. Thus in Egypt, Isis and Osiris, sister and brother and at the same time wife and husband, were worshipped as the relievers of medical knowledge amongst most other sciences. Thus formulas initially credited to Isis were existent as late as the time of Galen. Indeed, the ancient Egyptian priests claimed that all secrets of medicine in their position had been afforded to them by Isis, whom they regarded as the founder of their science. It was believed that Isis acquired this knowledge from an angel named Amnael, one of the sons of God, of whom the Book of Genesis speaks. In return for the passion of her body, Amnael conferred upon her the knowledge of the sciences and medicine. The result of their union, a son, Horus, was identified by the Greeks with Apollo and as a consequence was held by them as the discoverer of medicine. The legend which associated "the sons of god" with the daughters of men before the Flood and the suggestion that they imparted a knowledge of medicine to the habitants of the earth is traceable in a number of different societies including the Egyptians, the Assyrians, and the Persians as well as in Jewish literature. Thus in the sixth chapter of Genesis it is stated: *"They saw the daughters of men that they were fair; and they took them wives of all they chose."* From these unions came the race of giants and the wickedness of man so "great in the earth," that destruction of the race by the Flood resulted. The apocryphal Book of Enoch composed, it is agreed, about one hundred to one hundred and fifty years before the birth of Christ, is definitely in regard to this legend demonstrating that it was current amongst the Jews of that period. Enoch states, *"They (the angels) dwelt with them and taught them saucery, enchantments, the properties of roots and trees, magic signs, and the art of observing the stars."* In a tart comment which echoes over the millennia it is noted of one of the angels, *"He taught them the use of the bracelets and ornaments, the art of painting, of painting the eyelashes, the uses of precious stones, and all sorts of tinctures, so that the world was corrupted."* Suffice it to say that the criticism of behavior and of those that practice medicine and pharmacy appears to have originated at the very dawn of time and with the inception of the written word.

A further important personality in early medicine is the Egyptian deity, Thoth, also described as the friend and secretary of Osiris. The Greeks referred to Thoth as Hermes and also identified him with Mercury. Other societies claimed Thoth to be a Venetian, a Canaanite, the son of Ham, and an associate of Saturn. Despite the diversity of his speculative origins, he was noted as the presumed author of the six secret books which the Egyptian priests were bound to follow in their treatment of the sick. One of these books was specifically devoted to pharmacy. He is also proposed to have invented alchemy as well as medicine, the art of writing, arithmetic, laws, music, and the cultivation of the olive. Jamblicus, who wrote extensively on the mysteries of Egypt in the reign of the Emperor Julian, noted that the Egyptian priests recognized forty-two books as the genuine works of Hermes. Six of these dealt specifically with anatomy, diseases in general, women's complaints, eye diseases, surgery, and the preparation of remedies. No less an authority than Galen uncompromisingly declared the books of Thoth to be apocryphal whereas other writers such as Seleucus considered Hermes to have written twenty thousand books, and Manethon claimed the number to be in excess of thirty-eight thousand. Despite the controversy over the publications of Hermes, the Alexandrian writers of the first century held him in high regard and accorded him the surname, Trismegistus (thrice great). Such were the hour of his writings that if priests who followed his papyrus inscriptions lost a patient they were held null and harmless. If, however, they deviated from the written instructions they were liable to be condemned to death, even if the patient survived!

The majority of information regarding ancient Egyptian therapeutic methods has been obtained from the *Ebers Papyrus*, which was discovered at Thebes, in 1872, by Georg Moritz Ebers (1837-1898). The document dates from about 1550 B.C. and consists of 110 columns of hieratic script describing more than seven hundred drugs. Although many of them bear unfamiliar and fanciful titles such as *heart of Bubastis* (wormwood) and *the blood of the ibis* (fresh dill juice), Egyptologists have been able to identify the majority of these substances. A large number, such as opium, olive oil, honey, and saffron, are still in use although the mode of application has become somewhat more sophisticated. In addition, the lexicon refers to a variety of animal parts, precious stones, and amulets, which should be used under specific circumstances or combined with other agents of medicinal or religious utility. Most of these substances continued to be used until the seventeenth century and frequently commanded handsome prices since they were often difficult to obtain or only available in minute quantities. The papyrus provided detailed information regarding aural and ophthalmologic diseases since these have along been prevalent in the valleys of the Tigris, Euphrates and the Nile. In fact, the sections relating to the eye and ear are generally regarded as amongst the finest portions of the *Ebers Papyrus* and the descriptions of the ailments as well as the proposed remedies demonstrate a fine balance of clinical commonsense and acumen. Of particular interest is the observation that a number of the formulas include agents of an anesthetic nature and indicate a clear recognition of the importance of alleviating pain and suffering. Nevertheless, despite such fundamental principles, there was still much magic involved and the widespread use of distasteful substances, such as crocodile fat, was designed to render the affected part so objectionable that the spirits responsible for the disease would be unable to remain *in situ*.

Greek Medicine

The terms pharmacology, pharmacy, and pharmaceutical are all derived from the Greek word *pharmakon*, which was used indiscriminately by Homer to describe a drug, whether healing or noxious in nature.

Early Greek therapeutic practice was a modification of transplanted Egyptian herbal polypharmacy, modified by indigenous beliefs of magical nature and embellished by local deities. The mythological creator of the Greek *materia medica* was Apollo, himself a modification of an Egyptian deity. In the Greeks' medical hierarchy herbal medicine ultimately became closely identified with Chiron the Centaur. The RX, with which contemporary physicians begin their prescriptions, is in fact an ancient sign that was used to designate the pagan symbol for Jupiter, and was originally written as an invocation to Zeus. It is thus a modern remnant of the incantation that an ancient Greek physician would have recited when he administered a drug.

Apollo, the reputed god of medicine amongst the Greeks, was the son of Jupiter and Latona. His divinity was associated with the sun and his arrows, which often caused sudden death, according to the modern expounders of ancient myth, represented the rays of the sun. Most of his attributes were similar to those which the Egyptians had credited to Horus, and it is

Mythology, mysticism and herbal practicalities were all interwoven into the pantheistic yet intellectualized structure of Greek medicine. Oracles at Delphi (background) divined the future, while chimeras (the physician, Centaur Chiron) promulgated remedies as Aesculapius (bottom right) utilized serpents (shedding the skin of disease) to promote recovery.

The attributes and powers attributed to himself by Apollo were subsequently incorporated into the arms of the Society of Apothecaries and are described in Burke's Encyclopedia of Heraldry *in 1851 as follows:*

"In shield, Apollo, the inventor of physic, with his head radiate, holding in his left hand a bow and his right a serpent. About the shield a helm, there upon a mantle and for the crest upon a wreath of their colors, a rhinoceros, supported by two unique wands, armed and ungulate. Upon a compartment to make the achievement complete, this motto, "*Opiferque per orbem dicor*", the Latin quotation for the newly incorporated Society of Apothecaries was chosen and inserted by William Camden, the famous antiquary and "Clarenseux King at Arms" in the reign of James I.

Whether an individual or part of the collective consciousness of medicine, Hippocrates has remained not only a man for all seasons but a physician for all times.

likely that the Egyptian became incorporated into the early Greek mythology. As well as being the god of medicine, Apollo was the deity of music, eloquence and poetry, and was honored as the inventor of all these arts. The supposedly benign and balanced nature of a physician was not always apparent in the behavior of Apollo. Possessed of the jealousy of artists in an abundant degree, he was ill-prepared for reverses of fortune. Thus, in a musical competition with Pan (flute), Apollo, who was playing the lyre, was recorded the loser by Timolus, whereupon Midas, who disagreed with the opinion, was punished by being provided with a pair of ass's ears. Similarly Marsyas, another flute player who unsuccessfully challenged Apollo, was to be burnt alive lest his skill prosper further. Pion, who is sometimes identified with Apollo, was regarded as the first physician of Olympus and is said to have practiced in Egypt. Thus the fifth book of the *Iliad* by Homer describes how he cured the wound which Diomed had given to Mars:

Pion sprinkling heavily
balm around, Assuaged the glowing pangs and
closed the wound.

Aesculapius, son of Apollo and Corins, had a more immediate connection with medicine than his father. He was taught its mysteries by Chiron the Centaur, another of the legendary inventors of the art who had also taught Achilles and numerous others. Aesculapius became so successful that Castor and Pollux insisted on his accompanying the expedition of the Argonauts. Such was his expertise that Aesculapius ultimately acquired the power of restoring the dead to life but in acquiring such skills and achieving the ultimate perfection of his art, he incurred his own demise. Pluto, the god of the underworld, alarmed for the future of his dominions, complained bitterly to Jupiter and as a result the Olympian ruler slew Aesculapius with a bolt of thunder. As a consequence of this dramatic intervention, Apollo in anger, killed the Cyclops who had forged the thunderbolt and was thereupon expelled from Olympia by Jupiter. During the nine subsequent years that he spent on earth as a part-time Shepherd in the service of the King of Thessaly, he met Daphne, whose story is so elegantly related by Ovid. Thus Apollo, meeting Cupid, laughed at the child's bows and arrows as mere playthings. In revenge Cupid forged two arrows, one of gold and the other of lead. The golden one he pierced Apollo with excited desire and the lead one, which repelled desire, he aimed at Daphne. The subsequent sad ending to this early relationship resulted with the nymph being metamorphosed into a laurel, which Apollo henceforth wore as a wreath on his head. Ovid narrates the gods' introduction to the nymph as follows:

Possessed of inquiring minds and ever seeking to further their understanding of the vagaries of existence, Greeks delighted to contemplate the tragedy and joy of life whether in theaters (background – Athens) or discourse in the groves of Academe. The mosaic inset depicts Aristotle, Plato, Socrates, Hippocrates, Dioscorides and Galen debating issues that may well have related to the efficacy of the herbal remedy (Codex Dioscorides) pictured in the foreground.

"Perhaps thou knowst not my
superior state And from that ignorance proceeds
thy hate." To further ingratiate himself
with Daphne, Apollo states *"inventum medicina*
maium es, opiferque per orbum, dicor, et
herbum subjecta potenta novice." †

†(Medicine is mine, what herbs and simples grow In fields and forest, all their powers I know, and am the greatest physician called below)

Such attributes and powers were subsequently incorporated into the arms of the Society of Apothecaries.

The Hippocratic Concept

With time the provision of medical services shifted from a place of domicile to centers, usually temples (Aesclepium) devoted to the healing gods. With the increase in temple medicine the physicians at the individual Aesclepieae, in an effort to increase the reputation of their own particular temples, introduced more and more "simples". Thus each temple sought to attain fame for a unique cure. By the time of Hippocrates a reaction had already set in against this mass of unwieldy information and, although the Hippocratic physicians were familiar with the properties of a great many drugs, they preferred to confine therapy to practical, corrective measures. Indeed, their principle advice lay in directives regarding the use of proper types of food or exposure to a more salubrious climate (to avoid the all-prevalent malaria), or to prescribe hydrotherapy and massage.

An examination of the *Corpus Hippocraticum* reveals that the universal purgative of the period was white hellebore (*Veratrum album*) that was employed with caution and practitioners were admonished to be wary in its use: *Hellebore is dangerous to persons whose flesh is sound, for it induces convulsions. When you wish the hellebore to act more, move the body, and when to stop, let the patient get sleep and rest. A spasm from taking hellebore is of a fatal nature.*
("Aphorisms" iv. 16-15; v. 1)

In the *Regimen in Acute Diseases* it is apparent that ptisan, especially barley ptisan, was a favorite dietetic remedy of Hippocrates, and specific directions were provided for its preparation to ensure maximal therapeutic effect.

Ptisans are to be made of the very best barley, and are to be well boiled, more especially if you do not intend to use them strained. For, besides the other virtues of ptisan, its lubricant quality prevents the barley that is swallowed from proving injurious, for it does not stick nor remain in the region of the breast; for that which is well boiled is very lubricant, excellent for quenching thirst, of very easy digestion, and very weak, all which qualities are wanted.

Hippocrates was also particularly enamored of the properties of hydromel (honey boiled in water) in acute disease and described its effects as follows: *Hydromel,... increases thirst less than sweet wine; it softens the lungs, is moderately expectorant, and alleviates a cough; for it has some detergent quality in it, whence it lubricates the sputum. Hydromel is also moderately diuretic,... And it also occasions bilious discharges downwards,...*

A variant of hydromel, namely oxymel (honey in vinegar) was strongly recommended by Hippocrates in the treatment of acute diseases. Oxymel, he wrote: *... promotes expectoration and freedom of breathing.... It also promotes flatulent discharges from the bowels, and is diuretic,... and otherwise it diminishes the strength and makes the extremities cold; this is the only bad effect worth mentioning which I have known to arise from the oxymel.*

In contrast to the Egyptians and Babylo-Assyrians, it is evident that Hippocrates decried the efficacy of multiple drug usage and magical remedies. Indeed, a careful perusal of his entire corpus of work leaves a definite impression that he was akin to a pharmacological nihilist. Furthermore, his writings contain no mention of the utility of precious stones, amulets, or even alvine discharges. Overall, Hippocrates was convinced that the gods did not produce disease and this view is particularly strongly expressed in his treatise *On the Sacred Disease*. A physician of such sound judgment would be unlikely to propose either that drugs contained the quintessence of the gods or that evil-smelling compounds would drive away demons whose existence he denied.

A page from the Codex Dioscorides.
A detailed knowledge of herbs enabled the identification of those with specific therapeutic efficacy.

Theophrastus first studied philosophy at Lesbos (his birthplace) and then under Aristotle at the Lyceum in Athens. He succeeded his teacher at the Lyceum and at his death Aristotle willed his botanical garden to his pupil. An individual of uncommon perspicacity and broad learning, all nature aroused his interest and his writings are quite similar to those of Aristotle. In two treatises of the Peripatetic School attributed to Theophrastus, *On the History of Plants* and *On the Causes of Plants,* he collected all the botanical knowledge then available. These texts indicate clearly that knowledge of drugs was far more extensive than is apparent from the Hippocratic books themselves. Another interesting feature of the Peripatetic botanic treatises is the relative paucity of folklore and strange concepts that were often associated with literature of that time. Thus the Hindu collector of herbs, Lynn Thorndike, referred to Theophrastus as follows: *Theophrastus regards some of the ceremonial observances of pharmacists and root cutters in digging or plucking plants as farfetched. Standing to the windward to avoid injury from the effluxions of the herb he admits may be reasonable, and also the instructions to gather some herbs by night, others by day, or even to bray while cutting feverwort.*

Theophrastus described about 500 drugs including silphium (*ferula tingitana*), the source of African ammoniacum, which he notes, grew especially abundantly in Cyrenaica. This plant, now of no serious importance, once enjoyed a very high reputation and was responsible for much of the economic prosperity of the city of Cyrene. Similarly he was the first to mention mistletoe, which he believed was spread by birds. Mistletoe has a long history, which constantly changes from a belief in its efficacy to fear of its poisonous qualities. Pliny the Elder mentions its medicinal virtues and Galen prescribed it as an antidote for its poison. Theophrastus also included a description of madder (which he termed *ereuthedanon*) and alluded to its diuretic and analgesic properties.

Much of the sophistication and knowledge that had originally resided in Athens shifted to Egypt after the founding of Alexandria in 331 B.C. This was accentuated by the encouragement extended to scientists and, as a result of the liberal academic environment that flourished, pharmacology, like anatomy and physiology, underwent a metamorphosis into an experimental science. Unfortunately, in this early phase, most of the experimentation was focused upon the intricacies of the art of poisoning. Nicander (*fl.* second century B.C.) a Greek poet, grammarian, and physician, was the author of two hexameter poems, the *Alexipharmaca* (which particularly dealt with poisons and their antidotes), and the *Theriaca*, which dealt with the bites and stings of venomous animals. In an age where unknown disease wreaked havoc, the concept of known agents of harm, such as poisons, led to an abnormal preoccupation among the general population with toxic material and their antidotes. This neurosis was especially amplified among the aristocratic classes who felt themselves particularly vulnerable to threats of this

Although knowledge of specific ailments was modest, the Greeks understood cleanliness (inset from a Greek krater: depiction of man with water and washing) to be fundamental to health. Relief of suffering was a key issue and the effects of the poppy (top right) were well-known. Remedies derived from herbs were stored in glass jars (inset) and used to protect not only against illness but poisons such as incurred by the attack of snakes, insects, and wild animals. Theriaca or antidotes remained a prominent part of medicine for the two millennia and their details were meticulously documented in illuminated manuscripts well into the Middle Ages (background).

A centaur beguiling a damsel with a lyre. In Greek mythology these were a race of creatures, part horse and part man, dwelling in the mountains of Thessaly and Arcadia. In later times they were often represented drawing the chariot of the wine god Dionysus or bound and ridden by Eros, the god of love, in allusion to their drunken and amorous habits as depicted in this painting. Their general character was that of wild, lawless, and inhospitable beings, the slaves of their animal passions. One of the Centaurs, the son of the god Cronus and Philyra, a sea nymph, Chiron lived at the foot of Mount Pelion in Thessaly and was famous for his wisdom and knowledge of medicine. Numerous of the Greek heroes, including Heracles, Achilles, Jason, and Aesculapius, were instructed by him and he was regarded as a physician of unique skill. Accidentally pierced by a poisoned arrow shot by Heracles, he renounced his immortality in favor of Prometheus and was placed among the stars as the constellation Sagittarius.

kind. According to legend, the most notorious of royal dabblers was Mithridates VI (120-63 B.C.), king of Pontus, who had acquired an unenviable reputation as a poisoner. Haunted by a fear of his own art and paranoid that a similar fate might befall him, he labored for years to concoct a universal antidote. The compound he created was called *mithridatium*, which consisted of 20 leaves of rue, 1 walnut, 1 grain of salt and 2 dried figs. In order to be effective, it was recommended that the *mithridatium* be taken each morning before breakfast, which seems sensible given the fact that most poisons were administered with food or fluid!

Machaon and Podlarus – The Sons of Aesculapius

The noble physician, Aesculapius, sired two sons and four daughters somewhere in the range of 1250 B.C. As such he would have been a contemporary with Gideon, a judge of Israel, about two centuries before the reign of King David. The sons, Machaon and Podlarus, were immortalized in the islet among the Greek heroes who fought at Troy. They exercised their surgical and medical skills on their comrades. Thus, when Menelaus was wounded by an arrow shot by Pandarus, Machaon was sent for and *"sucked the blood and thereafter infused sovereign balm which Chiron gave and Aesculapius used."* At the culmination of the Trojan War, both brothers continued to exercise their art and some of their cures have been recorded for posterity. Their sons, like them, practiced medicine and the earliest Aesculapian Temple is believed to have been erected in memory of the grandfather by Spyrus, the second son of Machaon, at Argos. It is possible that this was only intended as a home for his patients or, alternatively, it may have been nothing more than an advertisement. Thereafter, however, the worship of Aesculapius spread and the temples proliferated in regions as diverse as Titane in Peloponesia, Tricca at Thessaly, Trithorea at Corinth, and at Epidaurus, Kos, Megalopolis in Arcadia, Drepher, Adrope at Corona on the Gulf of Macina, at Egrum, at Delos, at Cyllene, at Smyrna, and at Pergamus in Asia Minor. The Temple of Epidaurus was for a long time the most important, but, before the time of Hippocrates that of Kos appears to have been the predominant site of Aesculapian practice.

The Daughters of Aesculapius

There is considerable controversy as to the precise number of daughters but Hygeia and Panacea are probably the best known. Egrea and Jaso are little known. The former, whose name signified the light of the sun, married a serpent and as a consequence, was changed into a willow, while Jaso, in the only known monument on which she appears, is represented with a pot, probably of ointment, in her hand. Hygeia, however, was widely worshipped by the Greeks and when rich people recovered from an illness they often had medals

Aesculapius and his daughter Hygiea. Aesculapius, the Greco-Roman god of medicine, was the son of Apollo (god of healing, truth, and prophecy) and the nymph Coronis. The Centaur Chiron taught him the art of healing but such was his skill that Zeus, afraid that Aesculapius might render all men immortal, slew him with a thunderbolt. Although Homer, in the Iliad, mentions him only as a skillful physician, in later times, he was honored as a hero and eventually worshipped as a god. Because it was supposed that Aesculapius affected cures of the sick in dreams, the practice of sleeping in his temples became common. Aesculapius was frequently represented standing, dressed in a long cloak, with bare breast; his usual attribute was a staff with a serpent coiled around it. This staff is the only true symbol of medicine. A similar but unrelated emblem, the caduceus, with its winged staff and intertwined serpents, is frequently used as a medical emblem but is without medical relevance since it represents the magic wand of Hermes, or Mercury, the messenger of the gods and the patron of trade. It might however be argued by some that the latter emblem is now appropriate!

struck with her figure on the reverse. Pliny comments that it was customary to offer her a simple cake of fine flour to indicate the connection between simple living and good health. Panacea was likewise well-known and regarded as the divinity who presided over the administration of medicine.

Prometheus

Even more mystical and mythical than the story of Aesculapius or even Orpheus, who was also alleged to have discovered some of the secrets of medicine, is the legend of Prometheus who stole fire from heaven for the benefit of mankind. According to the older mythologists, Prometheus was the same as Magog and was the son of Japhet. Aeschylus is the principle authority on his transition and after describing many of the wonderful contributions that Prometheus had undertaken for humanity, he acclaims, *"One of the greatest subtleties I have invented is that when anyone falls ill and can find no relief; neither eat nor drink, and knows not with what to anoint himself; when for want of the necessary remedies he must perish; then I show to man how to prepare a healing medicine which would cure all maladies."* Or as subsequently rendered by Dean Plumtree: *"If anyone fell ill There was no help for him nor healing balm, Nor unguent, nor yet potion; but for want of drugs they wasted till I showed to them The blending of all mild medicaments Wherewith they ward the attacks of sickness sore."*

Prometheus chained to a rock for eternity while an eagle eats his endlessly regenerating liver. Zeus, having been tricked by the artful Prometheus into accepting the bones and fat of sacrifice instead of meat, hid fire from man and deprived him of light and heat. Prometheus, however, stole it and returned it to Earth once again. As a result of this insubordination and as punishment for mankind in general, Zeus created the woman Pandora and sent her to Epimetheus (Hindsight), who, though warned by Prometheus, married her. When Pandora removed the lid off the jar she carried, all evils, hard work, and disease flew out to wander among mankind forever. Hope alone remained within. As vengeance on Prometheus, Zeus had him chained and sent an eagle to eat his immortal liver, which constantly replenished itself. This tale was incorporated into Prometheus Bound *by Aeschylus, who made him not only the bringer of fire and civilization to men but also their preserver, giving man all the arts and sciences as well as the means of survival.*

Thus, in essence, Prometheus may be regarded as the first pharmacist of mankind as well as his better-known attribute as the donor of fire to mankind.

The innocence of a sleeping child and its freedom from the worries and cares of the world provided the basis for mankind's desire to find an agent capable of producing a similar state. It was believed that Morpheus, one of the sons of Hypnos (Somnus), the god of sleep, sent human shapes (Greek morphai*) to the dreamer, while his brothers Phobetor and Phantasus transmitted the forms of animals and inanimate things, respectively. It is possible that the name Morpheus originally derived from the Greek word* "morphnos" *meaning "dark".*

Morpheus

According to the Roman poets, Morpheus was the son or chief minister of the god of sleep, Somnus. The god himself was represented as living in Cimmerian darkness and his name derived from Morphea (form or shape) and his supposed ability to mimic or assume the forms of an individual he desired to pose as in dreams. Thus Ovid relates how he appeared to Alcyone in a dream as her husband who had been shipwrecked and narrated to her all the circumstances of the tragedy. Morpheus is generally represented with a poppy plant in his hand and bearing a capsule with which he was supposed to touch those whom he desired to put to sleep. An alternative depiction of him represents a man with the wings of a butterfly to indicate his likeness and the evanescent nature of thought, dreams, and sleep. When Serturner

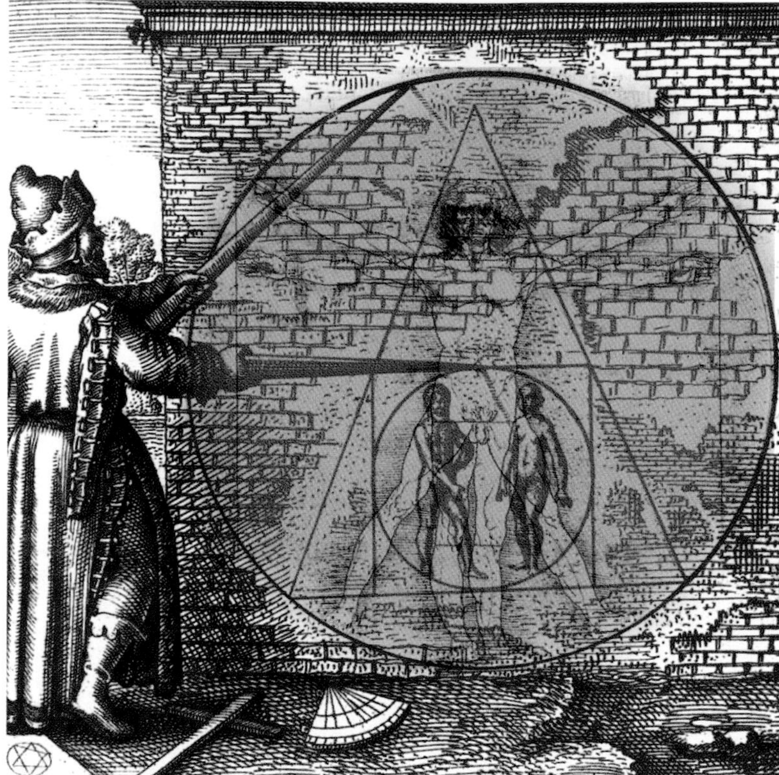

Pythagoras migrated to southern Italy about 532 B.C., to escape the tyrannical rule of Samos, and established his ethico-political academy at Croton. He achieved fame as a philosopher, mathematician, and founder of the Pythagorean brotherhood that, although religious in nature, formulated principles that influenced the thought of Plato and Aristotle and contributed to the development of mathematics and Western rational philosophy. Many of the concepts attributed to him are indistinguishable from those of his disciples since none of his writings survived. He is, however, credited with the theory of the functional significance of numbers in the objective world and in music. Other contributions that were popularly attributed (e.g. the Pythagorean theorem for right-angled triangles) were probably developed later by the Pythagorean school. Indeed, the bulk of the intellectual tradition originating with Pythagoras himself more rightly reflects mystical wisdom rather than scientific scholarship.

identified the first opium alkaloid, he named it "*morphium*" to honor the old Roman mythological figure of sleep.

Chiron

Chiron was a Centaur, famous for his knowledge of simples, which he had learned on Mount Pelion while hunting with Diana. His great merit accords to the fact that he taught his knowledge of medicines to Aesculapius, Heracles, Achilles, and to the various of the other Greek heroes represented by Homer in the *Iliad*.

Thus, it is recorded when Eurypilus was wounded by an arrow he asked Patroculus:

With lukewarm water wash the gore away,
With healing balms the raging smart
allay such as sage, Chiron, once taught Achilles.
(Iliad Book 11, Pope translation)

Heracles subsequently shot Chiron in the foot using an arrow which had been dipped in the blood of the hydra of Lerna in order that the noxious humors of the beast might intensify the agony of the wound. It is held that Chiron healed this wound by applying to it the herb which subsequently bore the name of centaury. An alternative version is that his grief at his rash act was so great that Heracles induced Jupiter to transfer the gift of immortality to Prometheus, and that the spirit of Chiron transcended mortal entropy into the heavens, forming the constellation of Sagittarius. In actuality the fable of the Centaurs has some basis in fact, and refers to the wild nomads who inhabited Thessaly. As a consequence of being such skillful horse-tamers and riders, the reality of their appearance was transmuted from the relationship of the men to their work.

Pythagoras

While it is difficult to separate the philosophy of Pythagoras from the patina-like description of his many legends, it is clear that he was a man of exquisite skills. Living in the sixth century before Christ, he is reputed to have tamed wild beasts with a word, to have visited hell, to have recounted his previous stages of existence from the siege of Troy to his own life, and to have accomplished many diverse miracles. Like many great men, fact and myth often swirl around their person and it is certain that from him or from his disciples in name much exact learning, especially in mathematics, has been handed down to us. He was, however, also famous in many other sciences and in the area of pharmacy was reputed to have been the inventor of *Acetum Scillae*.

According to Pliny he wrote a treatise on squirrels, which he believed possessed magic virtues. But Pliny also noted that he attributed the same virtues to cabbage, although it is possible that in translation this may have been another vegetable. Pythagoras held that aniseed was a magic plant and holding aniseed in his left hand, he recommended it as a cure for epilepsy and prescribed an anisette wine as well as mustard to counteract the poisonous effects of scorpion bites. The *Antidotum Pythagoras* is presented in numerous old texts but there is no certain authority that this was devised by the philosopher himself. It was composed of orris, 18 drachms, and 2 scruples; gentian, 5 drachms (ginger), 4 1/2 drachms (black pepper); and honey qs.

The Hindus

Indian medicine was particularly sophisticated and the ancient Hindu medical text called the *Susruta* not only described more than 760 herbs that could be used as remedies but also enumerated the localities where particular herbs or, more properly, simples were to be found as well as detailing the opportune time to collect them. Of interest is the Hindu belief that drugs would be inefficacious or even dangerous unless they were gathered by a person specifically trained in the art – presumably this concept was maintained in order to protect those in the pharmaceutical business. Despite their focus on illness and its cure, the Hindus did not confine their activities to this area and the *Susruta* exhibits considerable attention in poisons, aphrodisiacs, and antidotes for the

The earliest concepts of Indian medicine date as far back as the 2nd millennium B.C. and are set out in sacred writings called the Vedas whose usage lasted until about 800 B.C. The system of medicine called Ayurveda was received by Dhanvantari from Brahma, and Dhanvantari subsequently became deified as the god of medicine. The Vedas are rich in magical practices for the treatment of diseases and in charms for the expulsion of the demons traditionally supposed to cause diseases.

bites and stings of various animals. Whether this was specifically a Hindu preoccupation, or reflected Greek and Roman influence, is much debated since the latter civilizations had been in contact with India via Alexander's armies and Roman coastal expeditions.

The Chinese

Confucius, the great sage of China, set up in his *Book of Rites* the ideal: *"To gather in the same places where our fathers before us gathered; to perform the same ceremonies which they before have performed; to play the same music which they before us have played: to pay respect to those whom they honored; to love those were dear to them."*

To a large extent until very recently, this spirit permeated much intellectual activity. Thus Chinese medicine for the most part presents a current picture that has changed little in thousands of years. Because of its changeless and ageless character, it is, however, particularly interesting as a voice from past.

The early Chinese, like primitive people elsewhere, believed that the sun, moon, stars, clouds, storms, and fire were the outward manifestations of gods, demons, and spirits. Diseases were the result of demons in possession of the human body, each disease having its particular demon. In the earliest times, healing was entirely in the hands of priests and sorcerers who employed divination, incantations, and magical herbs in the treatment of disease. During the Chou Dynasty (1140 B.C.), the functions of the priest and doctor were separated, the former being assigned duties of a supernatural nature while the latter assumed responsibility for all matters relating to medicine and to the preparation of drugs.

The long-standing historic relationship between religion and healing was particularly evident in China with its three dominant religions of Taoism, Confucianism (indigenous), and Buddhism (transplanted from India about A.D. 67). Taoism was embraced in part by Confucius, and many of its ideas formed an integral part of Confucianism while Buddhism, at first, grew very slowly, but, during the T'ang Dynasty (A.D. 619-907), became a powerful force. Magic was an important adjunct to the Taoist religion, while faith healing, hypnotism, and autosuggestion were dominant in Buddhism. Li Tan, later known as Lao Tzu (the Venerable Philosopher), the founder of Taoism, lived during the middle of the Chou Dynasty (*c.* 600 B.C.), thus antedating Confucius by a century. His philosophical thinking dominated most phases of Chinese thought from that period until the present time. According to Lao Tzu, there existed two cosmic forces, *Yin* and *Yang*, the negative and positive principles of the universe. *Yin* is the passive or female element and typifies cold, darkness, disease, and death while *Yang* is the active or male element and typifies warmth, light, health, and life. This harmonic doctrine underlies all Chinese philosophy, metaphysics, arts, crafts, religion, astronomy, magic, science, and medicine.

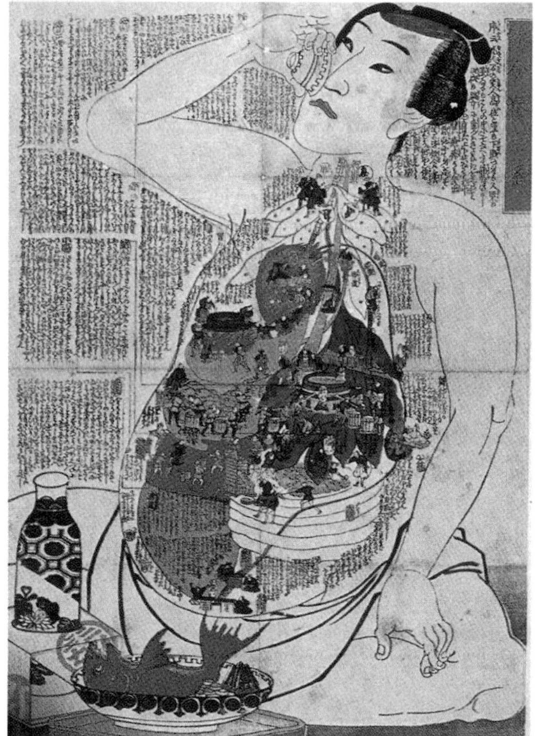

A Chinese depiction of the internal anatomy of a man. Much information was derived from animal sources since desecration of the body after death was forbidden and hence information from human dissection not easily available.

The icon of the principle is represented by a circle, which is divided into two pear-shaped bodies by a double curving line representing the two principles of *Yin* and *Yang*. On the periphery of this circle are eight symbols made up of combinations of triple lines, broken and unbroken, enclosed in an octagonal frame, the whole forming the symbolic diagram, the *Pa Kua*.

This symbol is regarded as a powerful talisman, capable of protection against calamity and disease. It signifies cooperation with the universe and has been the theme of innumerable books and essays. According to tradition it was revealed to Fu Hsi, the first emperor of China, who lived *c.* 2953 B.C. Confucius was greatly enamored of these figures and said that, if he could devote fifty years to the study of these lines, he might attain wisdom.

These two cosmic forces give rise to the five elements: wood, fire, earth, metal, and water. Everything animate and inanimate is composed of the same five elements controlled by *Yin* and *Yang*, which are ethical principles. Thus, ethical forces control the whole universe, animate and inanimate. Similarly, the body is composed of

Three Chinese physicians each of a different philosophic persuasion (Buddhism, Confucianism, Taoism). The many different philosophies of China each gave rise to a slightly modified interpretation of medicine and therapy.

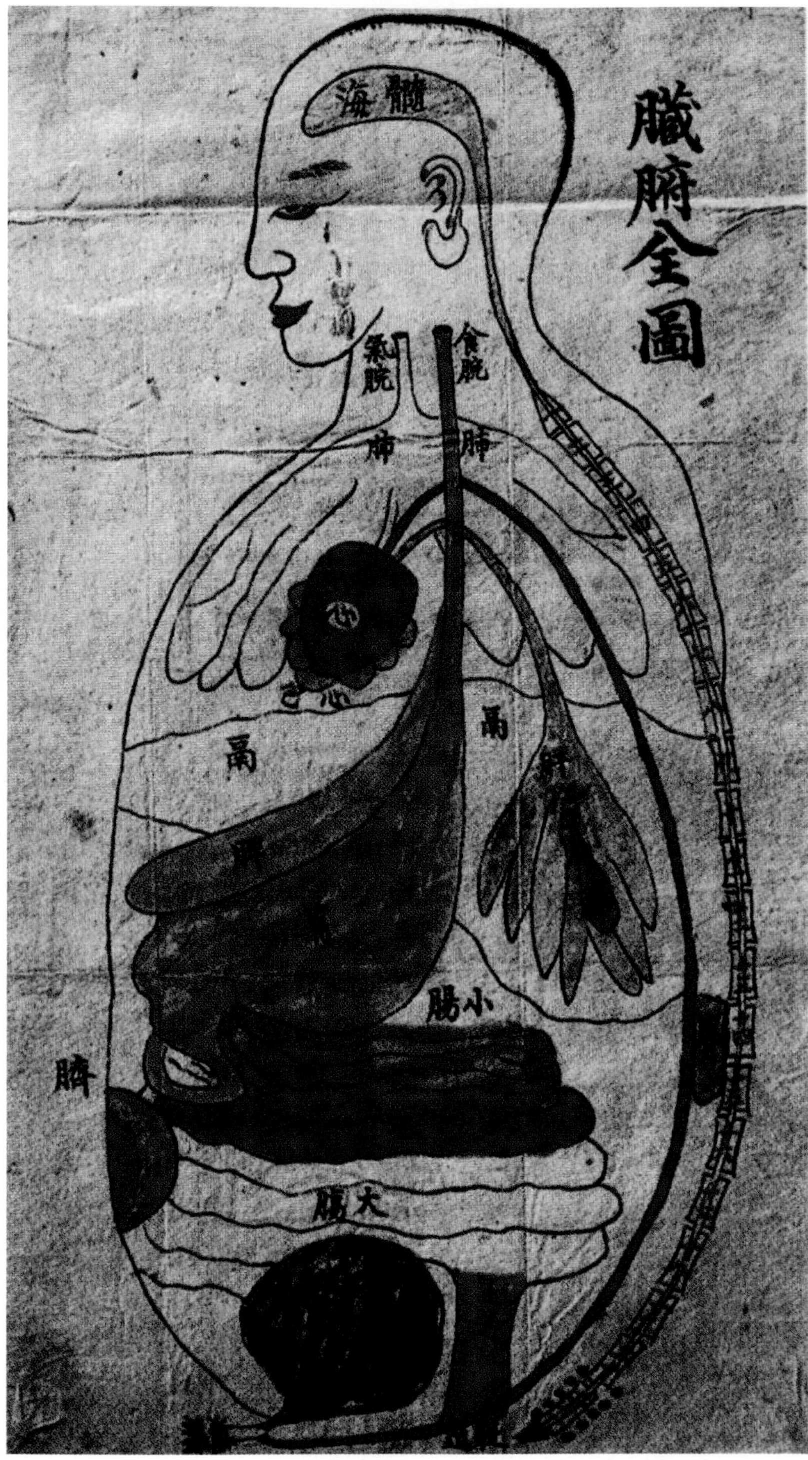

A 17th-century Chinese depiction of the internal organs of the body.

these five elements, and, as long as they maintain their proper proportions, health is present; when their balance is disturbed, disease results. Corresponding to these five elements are the five organs – spleen, liver, heart, lungs, and kidneys, which are related in a very complex arrangement to the planets, tastes and climates. Much like the Kabbalah the mystical properties of numbers is evident. There are three souls – one each in the head, abdomen, and feet. There are four methods of examination – observation, hearing, enquiry and palpation. Physicians were divided into sects: the *Yang Yin* sect who believed the *Yin* was weak and needed constant stimulation, the *Wen Pu* sect who maintained that the *Yang* required most attention; the *Radical* sect that believed evil influences caused disease and should be expelled; the *Conservative* sect who sought to restore the old methods of treatment and the *Moderate* sect who attempted to substitute a compromise between the former two groups. In general, all sects agreed that there were five kinds of afflictions. Five kinds of pain, five kinds of various diseases, such as dyspepsia, gonorrhea, and jaundice, five kinds of injuries, six kinds of weather and seven kinds of emotions. A fundamental tenet of Chinese natural philosophy remained the doctrine of the macrocosm, the universe, and the microcosm, man, or the little universe. Heaven was regarded as round, the earth square; thus a man's head might be round but his feet were considered square. Just as the heavens possessed a sun, moon, stars, rain, wind, thunder, and lightning, so man had two eyes, teeth, joy, anger, voice, and sound. There are nine provinces on earth, and thus man possessed nine openings. The earth has four seas, man has four reservoirs – brain, blood, air, and water. There are twelve rivers, man has twelve pulses. The heart has seven orifices to agree with the seven stars of Ursa Major, and the body has 360 bones, which is the same number as the degrees in a circle.

The legendary father of Chinese medicine was Shen Nung, who is reputed to have lived 2838-2698 B.C. He was reputed to have the head like an ox, taught the people the art of agriculture, discovered the medicinal properties of herbs, and founded the science of medicine. Of particular relevance was his *Herbal*, which enumerated 365 drugs, of which 340 belonged to the vegetable kingdom. Such was the fame of Shen Nung that he became worshipped by the native drug guilds as their patron god.

The Chinese physician and Emperor Fou Hi holds the symbol representing the elements controlled by yin and yang. His clothing contains the herbal elements considered vital to Chinese therapeutic doctrine. The icon of the principal is represented by a circle divided into two pear-shaped bodies representing the two principles of yin and yang. The combinations of the triple broken lines form the symbolic diagram known as the Pa Kua.

One of the most famous doctors of ancient times (Chou Dynasty) was Pien Ch'iao, (*c.* 255 B.C.) also known as Ch'in Yueh-jen. According to tradition, he was given a package of herbs by a fairy and having taken them, found that he could see through the human body and all its ills. Tales of his uncanny predictions and amazing cures were widely circulated in this period. Indeed, one tale reported that he had made two patients insensible with a narcotic wine and while they were under narcosis, opened their chests, removed their hearts, and then exchanged them, producing complete recovery. According to tradition, he traveled throughout the kingdom healing the sick, until he was assassinated on the order of Li His, the court physician, who had become jealous of Pien Ch'iao's success.

The greatest Chinese medical classic was the *Canon of Medicine* (*Nei Ching*), which even at the present time, 3,000 years after it was initially written, is regarded by contemporary Chinese physicians as the highest authority in medicine. This work, which essentially represents the official medical teaching of China, was written, according to tradition, by Huang Ti, the Yellow Emperor (2698-2598 B.C.). However, it was probably actually composed in its present form during the close of the Chou Dynasty (*c.* 300 B.C.) although certain parts are of much earlier origin. The *Canon* consists of two books, *Plain Lions* (*Su Wen*), which record the conversations between the Emperor Huang Ti and his minister Ch'i Pai, and the *Mystical Gate* (*Ling Shu*), a special treatise on acupuncture.

The anatomical section of the *Canon* contains the statement of Ch'i Pai that *"after death the human body may be dissected and observations made as to the size of the organs, the capacity of the intestines, the length of the arteries, the condition of the blood and the amount of pneuma."* This practice was checked by the teaching of Confucius and other religious leaders, who taught the sanctity of the human body and the prohibition of its mutilation in any way.

Since the anatomy of the *Canon* was not based on dissection, it remained mainly a product of the imagination. The weight and length of the tongue, esophagus, stomach, intestines, and rectum are given. The small intestine and large intestine have 16 convolutions. There are 365 bones in the male, 360 in the female, and 365 articulations. The vascular system consists of 12 main vessels corresponding to twelve months of the year, and of 4 main arteries corresponding to the four seasons.

The anatomy and physiology of the *Canon* were not based upon either observation or experiment, but more upon the Chinese theory of cosmogony. In fact, the physiology of the *Canon* is largely a product of the imagination. The heart is the prince of the body, the seat of the vital spirit; the lungs are his ministers, the origin of breath, and the dwelling of the animal spirits; the liver is a military leader and the dwelling place of the soul, or the spiritual part of man that ascends to Heaven; the gall bladder is an upright official and the seat of courage; the kidneys are the seat of vigor and strength; the stomach acts as official of the public granaries. The heart rules over the kidneys, the lungs over the heart, the liver over the lungs, the kidneys over the spleen.

The passages regarding the circulation of the blood have attracted the attention of many observers. *"The heart regulates all the blood of the body... The blood current flows continuously in a circle and never stops."* This statement and similar ones have suggested to some that the *Canon* anticipated Harvey's discovery of the circulation of the blood. The *Canon* did not distinguish between arteries and veins, and later writers and commentators on the *Canon* presented no clear perception of the circulation, one even going so far as to assert that *"the blood stream starts from the foot."*

The liver, according to the *Canon*, was the seat of anger; the heart, of happiness; the spleen, of thought; the lung, of sorrow; the kidney, of fear. The liver forms tears; the heart, perspiration; the spleen, saliva; the lungs, nasal secretions; the kidneys, spittle.

Diseases were divided into two groups: those from external influences, such as wind, cold, dryness and moisture; and those from internal emotions, such as joy, grief, anger, and fear. The importance of the atmospheric changes of the four seasons in the causation of disease was particularly emphasized. The section on therapeutics in the *Canon* is mainly a treatise on acupuncture, although venesection is mentioned.

Although Wang Ping (A.D. *c.* 762) is responsible for the present form of the *Canon*, medical writers have constantly made annotations upon it to the extent that by the end of the Ch'ing Dynasty (1912), forty-nine such commentaries had appeared.

The *Canon* mentions four methods of examination: observation, bearing, inquiry, and palpation of the pulse. At first, the importance of these four methods was in the order named, but, in time, the first three lost much of their importance, and diagnosis was based entirely upon palpation of the pulse. The first exponent of this view was Pien Ch'iao, who lived *c.* 255 B.C., but the most authoritative work on the subject was the *Pulse Classic*, a work of ten volumes written by Wang Shu-ho about A.D. 280.

Chinese pulse lore was an extremely complicated process and enacted with the solemnity of a religious rite. The pulse should be felt at sunrise, the physician placing his right hand on the left pulse and his left hand on the right pulse. The first three fingers are placed over the pulse on either side, each finger feeling a distinct pulse: the inch pulse, the bar pulse, and the cubit pulse. Each of these pulses was subdivided into an internal and an external pulse,

An ivory rendition of Huang Ti and his minister Ch'i Pai conversing on the subject of acupuncture. The two books of the Canon *purportedly written by the Emperor himself consisted of* Su Wen *(Plain Lions) and* Ling Shu *(Mystical Gate).*

The Chinese emperor Huang Ti. The Yellow Emperor composed the greatest of the Chinese medical classics, the Canon of Medicine (Nei Ching) in approximately 2500 B.C.

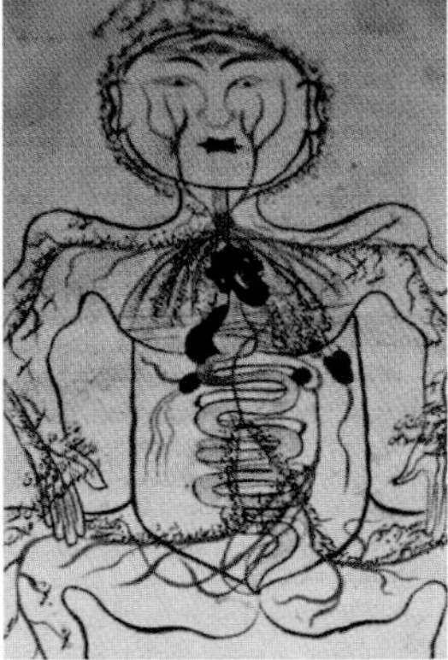
The Chinese were disinclined to desecrate human remains, with the result that their understanding of the internal organs was rudimentary as opposed to their sophisticated concepts of therapy.

making in all twelve pulses. Each of the twelve pulses indicated the condition of twelve internal organs. The "inch" pulse of the right hand revealed the condition of the lungs and large intestine; the "inch" pulse of the left hand, the condition of the heart and small intestines. Similarly, the right "bar" pulse referred to the spleen and stomach; the left "bar" pulse, to the liver and gall bladder. The right "cubit" pulse indicated the condition of the "gate of life" (the space between the two kidneys); while the left "cubit" pulse signified the kidneys and ureters. In all, the physician in his practice needed to be familiar with fifty-two chief types of pulses. Some have condemned Chinese pulse lore as a system of solemn quackery while others have suggested that intense study of the pulse enabled the development of an uncanny skill and perception in the Chinese physician.

The Chinese developed three characteristic methods of treatment: acupuncture, moxa and massage. According to tradition, acupuncture was devised by Huang Ti. It consists in introducing hot or cold metal needles into the body at various points. The needles were of silver, gold, brass, copper, steel, or iron and either fine, coarse, short or long. The overall object of the procedure was to puncture at certain definite points the twelve hypothetical, invisible channels, which contain the *Yang*, the active or male element, and *Yin*, the passive or female element. In health, these two forces are in equilibrium; but, in disease, this equilibrium is disturbed and acupuncture was believed to allow an excess to escape thereby restoring health. To be effective, acupuncture needed to be practiced at the proper points of which 365 such points were recognized. Physicians learnt from models precisely where to puncture for various diseases of the different organs. The art is still widely practiced and considered a panacea for all diseases, especially cholera, colic, sprains, arthritis, and various aches and pains. Acupuncture was introduced into Europe *c.* 1683 by a Dutch East India Company surgeon, Ten Rhyne, and became widely accepted, especially in France.

Moxa, or moxibustion, is another Chinese method of treatment, and of very ancient origin (for details see Section 7). It is carried out by burning combustible cones of the powdered leaves of mugwort (*Artemesia vulgaris*) at various points on the skin, especially in the epigastrium. The subsequent blistering produced effects resembling those of counter-irritation or cauterization but was more painful.

Massage is one of the oldest remedial agents known to Chinese medicine. It is mentioned in the earliest medical works, reached a high state of development in early Chinese history, and, during the T'ang Dynasty (A.D. 619-906), became recognized as one of the branches of the healing art. Although acupuncture, moxibustion and massage seemed to dominate the field of therapeutics, the Chinese developed through the ages a very rich *materia medica*. According to tradition, the earliest herbal was written initially by the legendary emperor Shen Neng and enlarged in A.D. 502. It originally consisted of three volumes and described 365 drugs classified as superior, medium, and inferior. The subsequent revision filled seven volumes and described 730 drugs. During the Ming dynasty, one of the most glorious in Chinese history, the *Great Herbal* of Li Shi-Chen was compiled over a period of twenty-seven years, beginning in A.D. 1552 and being finally completed in A.D. 1578. The work consists of fifty-two volumes and described 1,871 different therapeutic agents including waters, fires, earths, metals, minerals, plants, grains, vegetables, fruits, trees, insects. mollusks, birds, beasts, and organs of animal bodies.

A series of pictures from an illustrated Chinese medical text demonstrating a physician and different herbal elements used in the preparation of drugs.

Among the drugs that have found their way into the Western world are the China root *Smilax pseudo-china*, a relative of sarsaparilla; camphor; eumenol; and more recently, ephedrine, which is derived from *Ma Huang*, a Chinese herb that had been employed in practice for more than four thousand years. Among the substances derived from organs, it is noteworthy that the ancient Chinese physicians employed ground sheep thyroid for goiter and in cretinism. Li Shi-chen commented, "*The liver stores blood and is therefore beneficial for all diseases of the blood*." His comments preceded the work of Minot in the treatment of pernicious anemia by a mere five hundred years.

Among the famous Chinese physicians of antiquity, three are invariably singled out as the Great Trio: Ts'ang Kung, Chang Chung-ching and Hua T'o. Ts'ang Kung began the study of medicine *c.* 180 B.C. and was held in such respect by the people that they called him Ts'ang Kung, or Father Ts'ang. He is remembered especially for his twenty-five case histories, which are the only records of the kind in Chinese medical literature for the next fifteen hundred years. Although not of the same high quality as those of Hippocrates, he recorded failures as well as successes and described cancer of the stomach, cystitis, urinary retention, arthritis, paralysis, aneurysm, hemoptysis, and renal disease. It is to be noted that he usually employed drugs rather than acupuncture in treatment. He did, however, recommend baths, massage, and acupuncture for certain cases.

Chang Chung-ching, the second of the trio, is considered the greatest physician China has ever produced and often called the Hippocrates of China or the Sage of Medicine. The biographical details of his life are lacking beyond the facts that he graduated as doctor of literature in A.D. 168 and became mayor of Changsha about A.D. 196. His reputation reflected not only his clinical acumen, but also the loftiness of his views on medicine, which he considered a noble calling. As such he criticized the superstition, ignorance and venality of physicians of the time. Chang Chung-ching wrote a medical classic, *Essay on Typhoid*, which was in effect a treatise on fevers and miscellaneous diseases. This work appeared in sixteen volumes and was lauded both for its medical point content and for its style and language, such that it became considered as a literary classic. Chang studied disease from a clinical standpoint, describing the symptoms, physical signs, clinical course, methods of treatment, and action of drugs. Unlike others, he disregarded the fantastic theories of disease which had preoccupied his predecessors, and abjured the usage of magic or the supernatural in either treatment or causation.

The last of the trio, and a contemporary of Chang Chung-ching, was Hua T'o, the most famous surgeon in Chinese history, who was born *c.* A.D. 190 and became surgeon to Ts'ao Ts'ao, King of Wei. Despite an initial comfortable relationship the latter subsequently ordered his execution because he absented himself from court without leave. Hua T'o, in marked contrast to most physicians whose prescriptions were very complicated, employed only a few drugs and was a strong advocate of systematic physical examination, although he occasionally employed acupuncture. His fame rests chiefly upon his employment of anesthetics for which he used an effervescing powder in wine to produce insensibility, and upon his great surgical skill. On one occasion, he removed a gangrenous spleen in a patient who was under the influence of this anesthetic but the composition of this agent remains speculative although it may well have been *Cannabis indica*. Subsequent Chinese physicians employed *Datura alba, Rhododendron sinense, Jasmine sambac*, and *Aconite*, plants containing atropine, hyoscyamus, gelsemium aconitin, and other principles with unquestioned anesthetic and analgesic effects. With Hua T'o's death, progress in Chinese surgery ended and the doctrine of Confucius, that the human body should not be mutilated in any way, effectually halted further progress. Operations involving cutting were banned, and dissections, essential to a knowledge of anatomy, were forbidden, and Chinese medicine progressed as a non-invasive discipline apart from acupuncture.

As with many of the earlier cultures, the Chinese attached unusual significance to the color and shape of plants and were firm believers in the doctrine of signatures. Thus yellow flowers were held to cure jaundice and kidney-shaped beans used as effective treatments of renal diseases. Despite such odd notions there was considerable sophistication and iodine (in the form of calcined seaweed), rhubarb, aconite, cannabis, iron (used for anemia), sulphur, mercury, alum, musk, and numerous other drugs, among them camphor- and ephedrine-containing substances were also used in what is, by contemporary standards, prescient application. Some fascinating other usages include toad's eyelids (toad skin contains bufagin, bufanin and bufotalin – substances producing digitalis-like effects as well as bombesin-like peptides) which were employed for the cure of coryza. For reasons that are unclear the Chinese believed that earthworms, rolled in honey, would relieve gastritis and that human semen would obviate dyspepsia. The latter observation has achieved some considerable credibility given the known efficacy of prostaglandin-containing compounds in the amelioration of gastric mucosal disease!

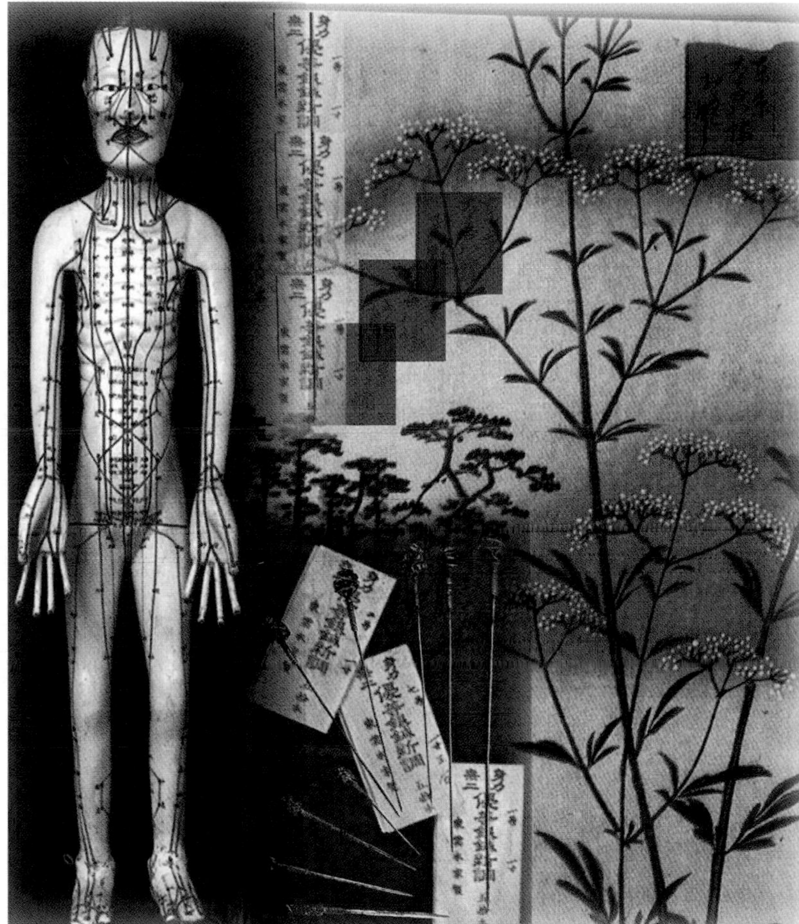

Acupuncture derived from the ancient Chinese philosophy of a dualistic cosmic theory of the yin and the yang. The yin, the female principle, is passive and dark and is represented by the earth; the yang, the male principle, is active and light and is represented by the heavens. It was believed that the forces of yin and yang act in the human body as they do throughout the natural universe, thus disease or physical disharmony represents an imbalance or undue preponderance of these two forces in the body. An imbalance of yin and yang resulted in obstruction of the vital life force, or ch'i, in the body, thus the goal of Chinese medicine was to rebalance the yin and the yang and thereby restore health (harmony).

SECTION 2

ROME and its PHYSICIANS

As a nation initially preoccupied with military matters, early Roman medicine was rudimentary until the assimilation of Greek culture. Nevertheless, even at the time of the Emperor Nero, *mithridatium* was an important item in the *materia medica* and no self-respecting physician could be anything other than expert in its manufacture and usage. Andromachus the Elder (*fl.* A.D. 60), the archiater or royal physician to Nero, achieved fame by the addition of squills, viper's flesh, and a generous amount of opium to the original prescription of mithridates and administered it, in honey, to Nero.

No doubt its efficacy was greatly enhanced by the liberal addition of the narcotic since the other substances presumably would have had marginal effect. Emboldened by his success and no doubt handsomely remunerated by Nero, Andromachus subsequently composed 175 Greek iambic verses in honor of the medicament now named *theriaca*. Furthermore, lest its efficacy be considered limited, Andromachus also strongly recommended it for treating blindness, rabies, dropsy, and phthisis and maintained that it was not only a universal antidote but also a prophylactic medication of the greatest reputation. Roman skepticism of such claims is reflected in the eighteenth satire of Juvenal (*c.* A.D. 60-120) who advised that, *"If your liver is getting impatient seek Archigenes [a Roman physician of the second century] as fast as you can, and buy of him the composition of Mithridates,"* and you will live to eat figs and gather roses another year. Nevertheless the *mithridatium* held a prominent, if not honorable, place in the physician's armamentarium until the middle of the eighteenth century and was at that time widely revered under a variety of names including *Theriaca Andromachi* or Venice treacle.

Amongst the greatest of the medical writers of the time was Celsus who, although not a physician, compiled an encyclopedic text detailing medicine of his time. The fifth book of Celsus', *De Medicina,* was devoted to therapeutics and consisted of twenty-eight chapters preceded by the usual *Prooemium*. Of these, the first sixteen chapters were devoted to the virtues of unmixed substances when used externally, while chapters 17 through 22 dealt with prescriptions for use upon the surface or in the orifices of the body. Antidotes, anodyne salves, and pills were reviewed in detail in chapters 23, 24, and 25 respectively, while chapters 26 to 28 provided an appraisal of surgical procedures. Despite the fact that perusal of the text reveals Celsus to have been a conservative individual who continually admonished his reader to employ drugs with reserve in several instances, he recommended lead and opium as a topical application for the relief of pain. Nevertheless, he practiced much in the same fashion as Hippocrates and placed more emphasis upon careful dietary management stating: *"But his best medicament is food opportunely given..."*

The concept of a universal cure from disease or protection from poisoning has been as pervasive a dream of mankind as flying. In this respect one of the most notorious dabblers in pharmacology was Mithridates VI (120 – 63 B.C.), King of Pontus, notoriously paranoid in regard to the possibility of his own demise by poisoning. Sublimating this concern, he developed a reputation not only for the liberal use of poisons on his enemies but his devotion to the concoction of a universal antidote. This illusionary substance became known as mithridation and its precise ingredients varied dramatically depending upon the maker. One formulation consisted of twenty leaves of rue, one walnut, one grain of salt, and two dried figs whilst yet others comprised more than two hundred bizarre ingredients including goat dung, cat penis, and peacock eye. In order to have the greatest efficacy, it was recommended that mithridation be administered each morning prior to eating, and so compelling was its putative effect that by the time of the Emperor Nero, it was regarded as a significant item in the materia medica.

Andromachus the Elder, who was the Archiater or Royal physician to Nero, added to the mithridation viper's flesh, large quantities of squill, and opium. The regular use of the latter dissolved in honey may well have contributed to some of Nero's more bizarre behavior. Convinced of the extraordinary effectiveness of his drug and enthusiastically supported by Nero (a balanced and thoughtful opinion), Andromachus recommended it widely for the treatment of a wide variety of illnesses.

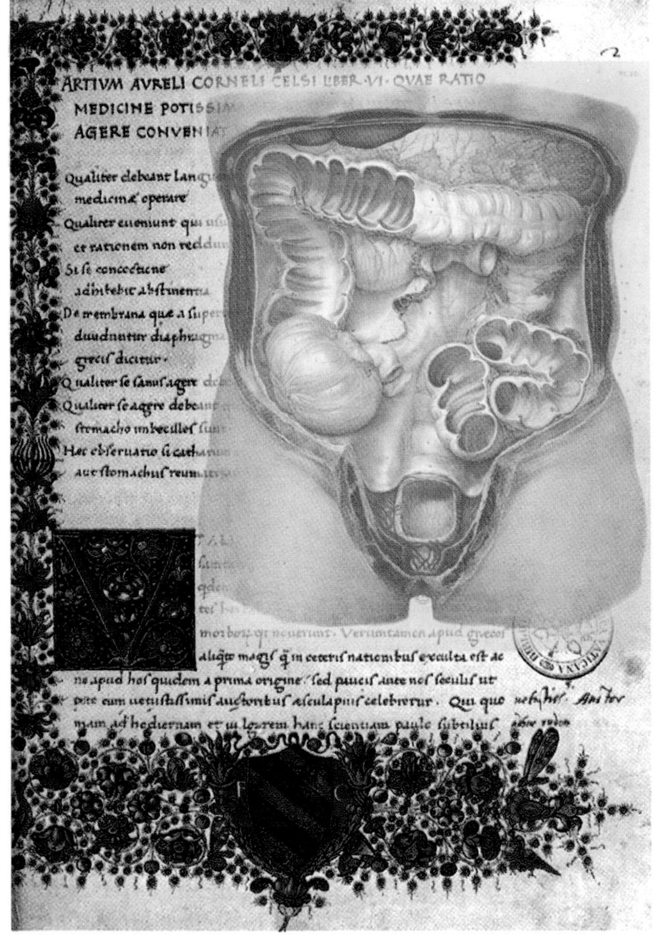

A page from an illustrated text of De Medicina *(background) by Aulus Cornelius Celsus, one of the greatest Roman medical writers. His encyclopedia dealt with agriculture, military art, rhetoric, philosophy, law, and medicine, but only the medical portion has survived. Written in the 1st century A.D., in Rome,* De Medicina *is considered one of the finest medical classics, although it was largely ignored by his contemporaries. The text was subsequently rediscovered by Pope Nicholas V (1397-1455) and became one of the first medical works to be published (1478) after the introduction of the printing press. Of particular interest is the apparently advanced state of contemporary medical practice. Thus Celsus recommended cleanliness and instructed that wounds be washed and treated with substances now considered to be somewhat antiseptic, such as vinegar and thyme oil. In addition he established the four cardinal signs of inflammation: heat, pain, redness, and swelling. Anatomical knowledge (Bougery inset) only achieved viability in the 16th century and attained its acme with the work of Vesalius.*

Despite a focus on the usage of oral medication Celsus provided one of the most detailed early accounts of the usage of enema:

*But medicaments generally irritate the stomach;
a motion when excessively liquid, or a clyster often repeated,
weakens the patient. Never, therefore,
in illness is a medicament, which causes such a motion
rightly given, unless when that malady is without fever,...*

Still, for the most part the bowel preferably is to be clystered;... this remedy should not be tried often, and yet we should not omit to use it once, or at most twice: if the head is heavy; if the eyes are dim; if the disease is in the larger intestine, which the Greeks call colon; if there are pains in the lower belly or in the hips; if bilious fluid collects in the stomach, or even phlegm or other water-like humor forms there; if wind is passed with undue difficulty; if there is no spontaneous motion, and especially if the faeces remain inside although close to the anus, or if the patient who fails to pass anything perceives a foul odour in his breath, or if the motions have become corrupted;... there should then be introduced into the bowel simply water when we are content with a gentle remedy, or hydromel as one a little stronger; or as a soothing enema a decoction of fenugreek, or of pearl barley, or of mallow [or as an astringent clyster a decoction of vervains, but a drastic one is sea-water or ordinary water with salt added; and the better in both instances for boiling. A clyster is made more drastic by the addition of olive oil or soda or honey.... The fluid injected should be neither cold nor hot, lest either way it should do harm. Following upon the injection the patient ought to keep in bed as long as he can, and not give way to his first desire to defaecate; then go to stool only when he must.

In addition to detailing the use of the enema for the administration of drugs, Celsus is generally credited with the introduction of the nutrient enema although Pliny the Elder and Oribasius credit the introduction of this concept to Lycus of Neapolis (*fl.* first century B.C.). It is stated "*The last resource is the introduction into the bowel from below of barley or spelt gruel since that too supports the patient's strength.*" Learned debate argued for centuries that this type of enema had no truly nutrient function, but more recent work indicates clearly that Lycus and Celsus were prescient in their observations.

Pliny

Like Herodotus and Aristotle, the Roman historian Pliny was more a commentator and good faith purveyor of second-hand information. He produced an important text, *Historia Naturalis*, that contained not only knowledge obtained from current books and general hearsay but also added his own observations and prejudices regarding the material. Although it is believed that this originally contained 160 books, only 37 have survived the ravages of time and their contents range from mathematical analysis of the globe to gardening and modeling. Pliny devoted Books XX-XXVII of this work to medical remedies derived from plants and trees. Although many of his pharmacologic ideas are regarded as erroneous, even for the period in which he lived, he often outlined a logical approach and, for example, expressed considerable skepticism in regard to mithridatics:

A version of the Theriac of Nicander. The plant Echium rubrum, *an antidote to snake venom, is depicted. The diversity of herbal medication available reflected not only local superstition but also unproven claims of efficacy often based upon the powers of suggestion, placebo effect or quack-induced beliefs.*

The Mithridatic antidote is composed of four and fifty ingredients, none of which are used in exactly the same proportion and the quantity prescribed is in some cases so small as to the sixtieth part of one denarius! Which of the gods, pray, can have instructed man in such trickery as this, a height to which the mere subtlety of human invention could surely never have reached? It clearly must emanate from a vain ostentation of scientific skill, and must be set down as a monstrous system of puffing off the medical art.

Pliny was a Roman of the old mold and decried the influence of the Greek world on Rome, thus the use of the word "puffery" connotes a subtle slur to Grecian physicians!

Aretaeus (top left) was a widely acclaimed physician of such note that some authorities have described him as the greatest after Hippocrates himself. Having studied medicine in Alexandria, somewhere between the second and third century A.D., he subsequently practiced both there and in Rome where he published two important treatises: The Causes and symptoms of acute and chronic diseases *and* The Treatment of acute and chronic diseases. *Aretaeus believed that digestion took place not only in the stomach but the intestine. He inferred that the process of coction that had been promulgated by Hippocrates and was associated with the development of warmth occurred in the intestines since they were felt to be warm on palpation. He regarded the liver as the source of veins and described it as a solidified blood mass whose function was to produce both blood and bile. Thus, digestion was effected by food being brought by the portal vein from the stomach and intestine to the liver, whence it was transmuted into blood and thereafter conveyed by the vena cava to the heart. In this respect Aretaeus was obviously familiar with the connections of the portal circulation and its tributaries.*

Aretaeus

Aretaeus the Cappadocian (*fl.* second century A.D.), was one of the most judicious physicians of this period. A Greek physician from Cappadocia who practiced in Rome and Alexandria, he was responsible for a revival of Hippocrates' teachings, and ranked second only to the father of medicine himself in the application of keen observation and ethics to the art.

In principle he adhered to the pneumatic school of medicine, which believed that health was maintained by "vital air," or *pneuma*. Although Pneumatists felt that an imbalance of the four humors – blood, phlegm, choler (yellow bile), and melancholy (black bile) – disturbed the *pneuma*, a condition indicated by an abnormal pulse, Aretaeus practiced as an eclectic physician and utilized the methods of several different schools. After his death he was virtually forgotten until 1554, when two of his manuscripts, *On the Causes and Indications of Acute and Chronic Diseases* (4 vol.) and *On the Treatment of Acute and Chronic Diseases* (4 vol.), both written in the Ionic Greek dialect, were discovered. These works not only include model descriptions of pleurisy, diphtheria, tetanus, pneumonia, asthma, and epilepsy but also indicate that he was the first to distinguish between spinal and cerebral paralyses. He gave diabetes its name (from the Greek word for "siphon," indicative of the diabetic's intense thirst and excessive emission of fluids) and rendered the earliest clear account of that disease now known. Unfortunately the medical texts that he authored were mostly destroyed but in those fragments remaining, such as the *Therapeutics of Chronic Affections,* there is clear evidence of a rational use of the *materia medica*. As cathartics, Aretaeus used the juices of fenugreek, linseed, and a decoction of mallow roots. Hiera, a universal purge in general use, composed of aloes and some aromatic ingredient is also described. Writers of the classic period described two varieties of "hellebore," white and black. With regard to the white variety Aretaeus wrote:

But also of all chronic disease when firmly rooted, if all other remedies fail, this is the only cure. For in power the white hellebore resembles fire; and whatever fire accomplishes by burning, still more does hellebore effect by penetrating internally…

For ointments, Aretaeus used castor, resin of the turpentine tree, euphorbium, lemnestis, pellitory, pepper, galbanum, Egyptian natron, and wax, while for sternutatories he advised pepper, root of soapwort, castor, and euphorbium. As evacuants of oral phlegm (ancient medicine described a number of different varieties) he employed mustard, mastic, pepper, and stavesacre. In respect of the production of cataplasms he proposed a variety of agents, including fenugreek, barley meal, oil in which rue or dill was boiled, linseed, and root of mallows. In discussing inunctions he noted in the *Therapeutics of Acute Diseases*:

Inunctions are more powerful than fomentations, as being more easily borne, and also more efficacious; for the ointment does not run down so as to stain the bed-clothes (for this is disagreeable to the patient), and adheres to the body until, being melted by the heat thereof, it is drunk up. Moreover, the persistence of their effects is beneficial, whereas liquid applications run off.

An illustration from the Codex of Dioscorides. *The detailed and accurate drawings coupled with the thoughtful text descriptions enabled other physicians to identify the herb and prepare the appropriate remedy.*

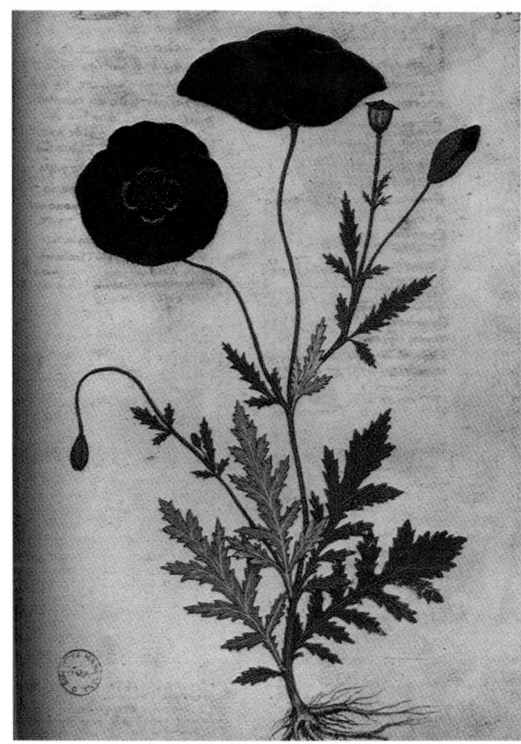

An ancient depiction of a corn poppy.

Like Hippocrates he was a firm believer in the use of the poppy and freely prescribed opium as a soporific:

> *But poppy boiled in oil is particularly soporific when applied to the fontanelle of the head, or with a sponge to the forehead. But the poppies, if recently plucked and green, may be applied whole under the pillows; for they thicken and humectate the spirit (pneuma),... and diffuse over the senses fumes which prove the commencement of sleep. But, if greater applications are needed, we may rub in the meconium (expressed juice of poppy) itself on the forehead with water, and also anoint the nostrils with the same, and pour it into the ears.*

Similarly, in regard to diet, Aretaeus held strong Hippocratic views and a notable example of this tendency is evident in his treatment of phthisis, in which he advocated milk as an important remedy:

> *For milk is pleasant to take, is easy to drink, gives solid nourishment, and is more familiar than any other food to one from a child.... If one, then, will only drink plenty of this, he will not stand in need of anything else. For it is a good thing that, in a disease, milk should prove both food medicine.*

While in many respects such an admonition would be well-accepted even in contemporary society, it is likely in an era prior to pasteurization such advice may likely have even advanced tuberculosis.

The narcotic and sleep-producing qualities of the poppy have been known to humankind throughout recorded history. Thus, Sumerian records from the time of Mesopotamia (5000 to 4000 B.C.) refer to the poppy, and medicinal reference to opium is contained in Assyrian medical tablets. It is apparent from the Homeric text that Greek usage of the substance was well accepted by at least 900 B.C. and Hippocrates (c. 400 B.C.) made extensive use of medicinal herbs, including opium. The Romans probably learned of opium during their conquest of the eastern Mediterranean and the Greco-Roman physician Galen (A.D. 130-200) was so enthusiastic an advocate of the virtues of opium that his books remained the primary authority on the subject for hundreds of years. The art of medicinals was preserved by the Islamic civilization following the decline of the Roman Empire and opium was subsequently introduced by the Arabs to Persia, China, and India.

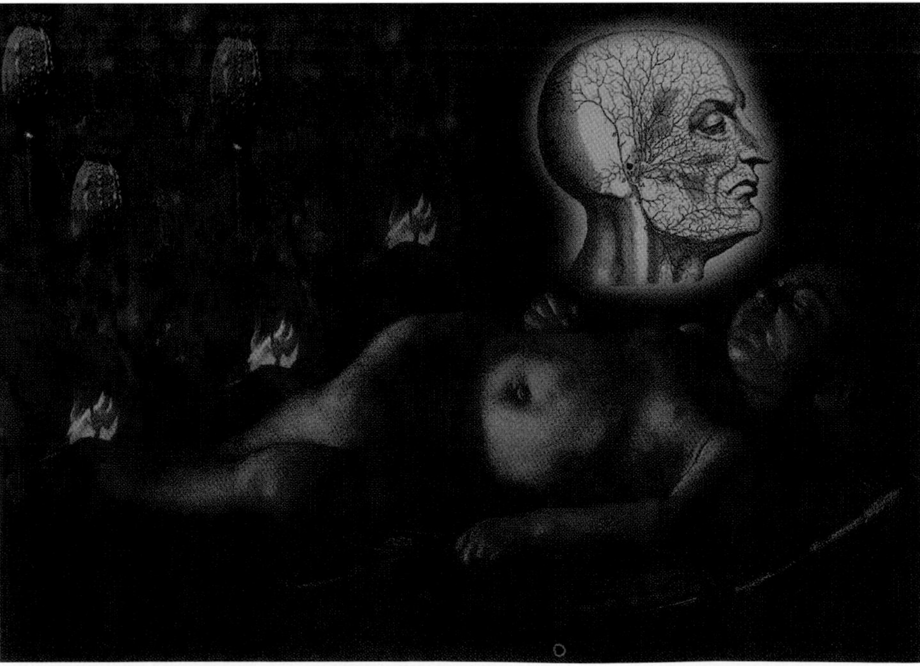

Dioscorides

Although few who have studied the art and science of therapy have left the impact of Dioscorides, considerable controversy still exists regarding the details of his life. Indeed it has been a subject of lively dispute whether Dioscorides lived before or after Pliny.

This is of some interest since it seems certain that one of these authors copied from each other particular matters, and in neither case provided credit to the other. Pliny was born A.D. 23 and died A.D. 79, and would therefore have lived under the Emperors Tiberius, Caligula, Claudius, Nero, Galba, Otto, Vitellius, and Vespasian. Suidas, the historian, whose work was probably undertaken in the tenth century, dates Dioscorides as contemporary with Anthony and Cleopatra, about 40 B.C., while some Arab authorities claim that he wrote at the time of Ptolemy VII, which would be a hundred years earlier. Further confusion is generated by the fact that Dioscorides dedicated his great work on *Materia Medica* to Areus Aesculapius, who is otherwise unknown, but mentions as a friend of his patron, the consul Licinius Bassus. Since it is well documented that a consul, Lecanius Bassus, lived in the reign of Nero, it is therefore generally supposed that Dioscorides was in his prime at that period, and would consequently be a contemporary of Pliny's. It is possible that both authors drew from another common source.

Dioscorides was a native of Anazarbus in Cilicia, a province where the spoken and written Greek was proverbially provincial. Of interest is the belief that the word solecism is believed to have been derived from the town of Soloe in the same district. The written Greek of Dioscorides is alleged to have been far from classical, and Galen with his usual lack of subtlety remarks upon it. In fact, Dioscorides in his preface goes so far as to apologize for it. Although Galen complained that Dioscorides' work was inadequate in many respects and despite his apparent lack of sophistication, Dioscorides maintained for at least sixteen centuries a premier position among authorities on *materia medica*. Galen argued that he was sometimes too indefinite in his description of plants, that he did not indicate exactly enough the diseases in which they are useful, and that he often failed to explain the degrees of heat, cold, dryness, and humidity, which characterize them. As an illustration of one of his other criticisms Galen mentions the *Polygonum*, of which he notes that Dioscorides says "*it is useful for those who urinate with difficulty*." Galen complained that he failed to particularize precisely the cases of which this is a symptom and in precisely which circumstances the *Polygonum* might best be utilized. Nevertheless, despite cataloguing these shortcomings and defects, Galen grudgingly acknowledged that Dioscorides was the foremost authority on the subject of the materials of medicine.

Although it is generally accepted that Dioscorides was a physician, there is no certain evidence of this fact. According to his own account he was devoted to the study and observation of plants and medical substances generally, and in order to study them in their native lands he accompanied the Roman armies through Greece, Italy, and Asia Minor (probably the easiest and safest method of visiting foreign countries at that time). During such travels it is not unlikely that he was employed as an assistant to a military physician, perhaps to the one to whom he dedicated his book. Suidas reports that Dioscorides was nicknamed Phocas, because his face was covered with stains of the shape of lentils.

In his definitive treatise on *materia medica*, *Peri Ules Iatrikes*, or, according to Photius, originally *Peri Ules* (*On Matter*), only, he describes some six hundred plants, limiting himself to those, which had or were supposed to have medicinal virtues. In addition to herbal agents he also alluded to the therapeutic properties of many animal substances including roasted grasshoppers for bladder disorders; the liver of an ass for epilepsy; seven bugs enclosed in the skin of a bean to be taken in intermittent fever; and a spider applied to the temples for headache.

Dioscorides also provided a formula for the *Sal Viperum*, which was a notable remedy of the time and persisted in widespread usage for a thousand years thereafter. The process he described included roasting a viper alive in a new earthen pot with some figs, common salt, and honey and reducing the entirety to ashes prior to the addition of a little spikenard. Although Pliny felt inclined to only add fennel and frankincense to the viper, Galen and his followers insisted upon the need to make the salt a far more complicated mixture.

Despite enormous zeal and application to the subject, the botany of Dioscorides is, as might be expected, defective by contemporary standards. Thus plants are sometimes classified in the crudest way, often only by a similarity of names. Of many his only description is simply that it is "well-known," a habit which resulted in much difficulty for contemporary investigators who have examined his treatise searching for historical evidence to validate the records of herbs named in other works. A classic example is provided by hyssop, whose existence has been virtually impossible to identify, despite the several references to it in the Bible. Dioscorides contents himself by remarking that it is a well-known plant, and then proceeds to enumerate its medicinal qualities. It seems clear, however, the hyssop of Dioscorides was not the plant known to us by that name since in the same chapter he describes the "*Chrysocome*," and notes that it possesses flowers in racemes like the hyssop. Similarly he writes of an *origanum*, which has leaves arranged like an umbel, similar to that of the hyssop. It is evident, therefore, that the hyssop of Dioscorides may refer to a different species. In addition to documenting the herbal remedies available Dioscorides paid considerable attention to mineral medicines in use in his time and included descriptions of such in his treatise. Thus argentum vivum, cinnabar, verdigris, the calces of lead and antimony, flowers of brass, rust of iron, litharge, pompholix, several earths, sal ammoniac, nitre, and other substances are all covered in some detail. Other treatises, one on poisons and the bites of venomous animals, and another on medicines easy to prepare, have been attributed to Dioscorides, but it is not generally accepted that he was the author. Matthiolus of Sienna made the best-known translation of Dioscorides into Latin in the sixteenth century and the sixth century manuscript from which Matthiolus derived his text is still preserved in Vienna. While recognizing the defects in the *Materia Medica* of Dioscorides, it is appropriate to note that he recorded many valuable observations and the descriptions of myrrh, bdellium, laudanum, asafetida, gum ammoniacum, opium, and squill were particularly useful. From a historical perspective, the accounts provided of treatments since abandoned (some of which are mentioned above), are of special interest, while many remedies rediscovered in modern times were originally referred to by Dioscorides. Among these are castor oil, though Dioscorides only alluded to the external application of this substance; male fern against tapeworms; elm bark for eruptions; horehound in phthisis; and aloes for ulcers.

It is generally rumored that he became a surgeon in Nero's army in order to further pursue his study of the flora and fauna of different countries. Thus in the course of his army career he traveled through Italy, Greece, Asia Minor, Spain, and France, collecting a vast number of botanical, mineralogical, and biologic specimens. In addition to merely compiling a collection, Dioscorides actively pursued information of the local usages, medicinal virtues and beliefs regarding such agents from the native-born people. This newly acquired knowledge, as well as the information he obtained from the extant texts, formed the basis of his famous treatise on *materia medica*. This extraordinary work was first published in Greek, arranged upon an alphabetic basis by Aldus Manutius (1450-1515) of the Aldine Press at Venice, in 1499. Its contents were a summation of almost all the current knowledge of

As a medical physician in the Roman army, Dioscorides traveled widely and was exposed not only to diverse diseases but the herbal remedies developed by the local populations in each area. The inset (top right) from Trajan's columns is the first depiction of military surgeons tending the wounded.

A mythical mosaic composite from Pompeii of the seven (note the Kabbalistic numeration) great classic philosophers. In an era of academic diversity, such individuals included medical expertise in their intellectual armamentarium, not regarding it as a separate discipline but as an inseparable component of a broad field of knowledge. Plato is center and surrounded by Zeno, Aristotle, Pythagorus, Epicurus, Theophrastus and Socrates.

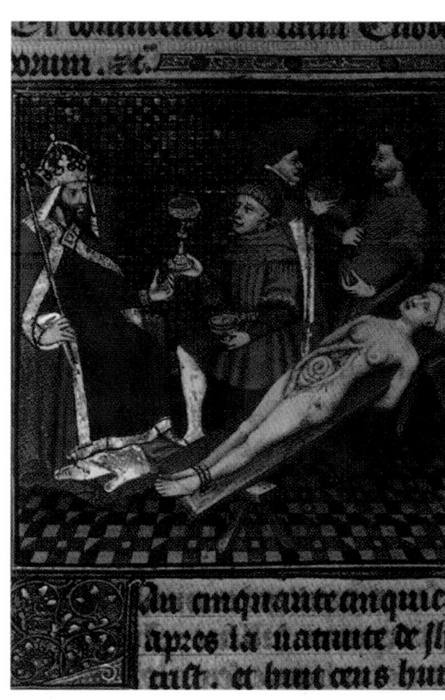

Nero undertaking the autopsy of his mother. Originally known as Lucius Domitius Ahenobarbus, he was the fifth Roman emperor (A.D. 54-68) and stepson and heir of the Emperor Claudius. Although infamous for his personal debaucheries, persecutions of Christians, and sundry extravagances, the evidence that he burnt Rome is doubtful. In his service, Dioscorides profited medicine for all mankind.

herbal remedies and remained the pharmacological *vade mecum* for approximately sixteen hundred years.

An ancient print depicting Dioscorides amongst the great classic philosophers (left). A later copy of his works (right) reveals the detail and beauty of his depictions of herbal remedies.

Despite the fact that information was not always precise, the very detailed assessment was of considerable utility. Thus acacia was recommended as an astringent gum in hemorrhage, agaric for the treatment of gastric disorders and aconite as an anodyne and collyrium. Much attention was paid to the therapeutic value of various salts, and brine was strongly advocated for the cleansing of ulcers. Dioscorides was amongst the first to describe aloes and he recommended its external usage for hemorrhoids and ulcers and internally as a tonic. In addition, he detailed a variety of ammoniacal substances, obtained from plants that could be used for the treatment of asthma. More worrisome was his suggestion that old boiled oil could be therapeutically employed for urethral, vaginal, and rectal injections. Dill, anise, bitter almond, urine, and juniper were proposed as diuretics, and a special starch preparation described for usage in cases of hemoptysis. A particular favorite was bitter almond, which was promoted both as a laxative and soporific while when compounded in rose-oil poultices, it could be used for the relief of headaches. Dill was sometimes employed in nausea and was recommended as a hip bath for hysterical women, while the more dangerous arsenic was in considerable vogue as a depilatory. A home product such as soot was favored for application to burns but wild licorice was preferred as the topical application for indolent ulcers. The latter when mixed with wine was also useful for diarrhea. Licorice was recommended for sore throat and ulceration of the bladder. Jew's pitch, or bitumen, obtained from the surface of the Dead Sea, was applied to fresh wounds, and balsam was placed upon sores.

Wormwood, which later provided the basis for absinthe, was suggested in the treatment of ascites and toothache, while lichens were made into cataplasms and used in inflammatory conditions. He recommended gentian for diseases of the liver and stomach, pennyroyal as an aid in obstetric cases and elaterium as an abortifacient, emenagogue, and for enemata. The dreaded hemlock was employed as a cataplasm in the treatment of erysipelas and herpes and, when applied as a cataplasm to the testicles, it was purported to induce temporary impotence (this property was of considerable social value as well as in religious circumstances such as the Eleusian Mysteries). Mint dissolved in vinegar, was used for the cure of round worms as well as for the relief of hiccough and vomiting, while its aphrodisiac assets enabled its usage as a "pessary" or tampon with contraceptive properties. The humble lettuce much favored by Pliny as a medicament was suggested by Dioscorides as a mild sedative and even Galen claimed to have cured himself of insomnia by the use of *lactucarium*. Tumorous growths could be vitiated by use of a plaster composed of bird lime and caustic lye, whereas cantharides were employed in cutaneous diseases, especially in ulcerative and cancerous conditions. The rare substance verdigris was a fundamental remedy in the treatment of trachoma and other eye diseases, while the more mundane fish glue was valued for the removal of wrinkles from the face. A strange substance – the burnt ash of the hippocampus – was used topically to treat alopecia, while the expensive spice, cardamon was recommended for the eradication of intestinal worms and stones in the bladder. Conversely cumin was utilized to diminish flatulency and the common, or garden buckthorn, prescribed for the cure of various intestinal conditions.

An alcoholic extract of the root of the mandrake *Mandragora officinalis* (*Atropa mandragora*) was widely used in the treatment of ocular disease and as a soporific or primitive anesthetic to facilitate surgery. Indeed, such was the medicinal value of this plant that until the nineteenth century it held a prominent place in European pharmacopoeias. Its irregular roots are not unlike human limbs in appearance and some authors distinguished between the "sexes" by the shape of the roots whose very appearance suggested many applications of the magical law of similarities. Dioscorides distinguished between a black, "feminine" mandrake, *tridacia*, and a white, "masculine" variety, *morion*. A further bizarre notion of the Middle Ages was the German belief that the mandragora plant grew under the gallows (it was

A Roman female pharmacist (left) ensconced in her modest dispensary seems to bear little relation to the grandeur of Imperial Rome (background). Indeed the classic Romans cared little for physicians and medicine, regarding them as "Greek puffery" for the effete and not befitting a race of rulers. The snake images reflect the intrusion of the cult of Aesculapius introduced to Rome in a desperate attempt to avert decimation (skull motif) by a plague.

consequently called *Galgenmännlein*) and was fertilized by the gore which dripped from the executed corpses. Peasants were convinced that anyone digging up these plants would die insane as a result of the shrieks of the spirit which dwelt within the plant, and a black dog was therefore tied to the plant and then lured away with food in order to uproot the mandragora. This belief may have predated its Germanic origins since it is encountered in the Syrian text, *al-Jami'fi al-Adwiyah al-Mufradah* by Abdullah ibn-Ahmad ibn-al-Baytar (d. 1248), and is also mentioned by Flavius Josephus (Joseph ben Matthias (*c.* A.D. 37-95). Surprisingly, the erudite Theophrastus of Athens, who described a variety of superstitions in his *History of Plants,* failed to describe this technique, whereas the prolific and well-read William Shakespeare (1564-1616) penned verse to the effect that the plant could shriek and causes madness:

And shrieks like mandrakes torn out of the
earth, that living mortals, hearing them, run mad.
(Romeo and Juliet iv. 3)

Despite much skepticism as to the efficacy of mandrake as late as 1790, the imitation of the drug was a profitable pursuit and it still sold at a fashionable price to unsuspecting and superstitious patients. Such was the power of the folklore surrounding its efficacy that in addition to its soporific virtues, mandrake was widely employed in the treatment of lameness, cramps, epilepsy, madness, and sterility, being especially used in the compounding of a love philter or *amoris poculum*.

Galen

Given the basis of knowledge at the time that he was educated, it is predictable that Galen's theory of pharmacologic action reflected an extrapolation of the humoral hypothesis. Thus, he maintained that "*It is the business of pharmacology to combine drugs in such a manner-according to their elementary qualities of heat, cold, moisture and dryness-as shall render them effective in combatting or overcoming the conditions which exist in the different diseases.*"

Despite his erudition and intrinsic creativity, it is difficult to comprehend precisely how Galen thought drugs operated in the treatment of disease according to the humoral theory. With characteristic versatility, he produced a long and awkward explanation of which Aetius provided a briefer version although almost as obtuse and arcane in its complexity: "*There are differences in the particular actions of medicines, arising from each of them being to a certain degree hot, or cold, or dry, or humid, or consisting of subtile or of gross particles, but the degree in which each of them is possessed of the above-mentioned properties cannot be truly and accurately determined. We have endeavoured, however, to define them in such a manner as will be sufficient for all practical purposes, laying it down that there is one class of medicines possessed of a similar temperament to our bodies, when they have received a certain principle of change and aliation from the heat in them, and that there is another which is of a hotter temperament than we. Of this temperament I have thought it right to make four orders, the first being imperceptible to the senses, and only to be inferred from reflection; the second being perceptible to the senses; the third strongly heating but not burning; and the fourth, or last, caustic. In like manner of frigorific or cooling things, the first order requires reflection to demonstrate its coldness: the second consists of such things as are perceptibly cold; the third is perceptibly cold, but does not occasion mortification; the fourth produces mortification. So it is in like manner with humectating and desiccant articles. Let such an order of degrees be laid down to render clearer the course of instruction, rose oil or the rose itself being placed in the first order of cooling things; the juice of roses in the second, and in the third and fourth those things which are extremely cold, such as cicuta, meconium, mandragora, and hyoscyamus. In regard to hot things, dill and fenugreek belong to the first order; those which are next to them, to the second; and so of the third and fourth, until we come to the caustic. In like manner, respecting moistening and desiccant medicines, beginning with those of a moderate degree, we may arrange them until we come to their extremes. Such knowledge is of no small importance for the purpose of medical instruction.*"

The mandrake has long been known for its poisonous properties. In ancient times it was used as a narcotic and an aphrodisiac, and it was also believed to have magical powers. Its forked root, seemingly resembling the human form, was thought to be in the power of dark earth spirits and was thus utilized by necromancers and those dealing in the occult. The fact that it was believed to grow best under gallows provided further evidence of the dark powers of the agent. It was believed that the mandrake could be safely uprooted only in the moonlight, after appropriate prayer and ritual. This could only be undertaken by a black dog attached to the plant by a cord, since if human hands came in contact with the plant, the individual would perish. In medieval times it was thought that as the mandrake was pulled from the ground it uttered a shriek that killed or drove mad those who did not block their ears against it. After the plant had been freed from the earth, it could be used for beneficent purposes, such as healing, inducing love, facilitating pregnancy, and providing soothing sleep.

Although the curiosity of Galen extensively embraced anatomy and physiology, he devoted considerable attention to pharmacology and is credited with some thirty books on this subject. Of particular interest was the Latin

A medieval illustrated frontispiece of a Galen text. The writings of Galen achieved wide circulation during his lifetime, and copies of some of his works survive that were written within a generation of his death. By A.D. 500 his works were being taught and summarized at Alexandria, and his theories preempted those of others in the medical handbooks of the Byzantine world. Greek manuscripts were collected and translated by enlightened Arabs in the ninth century, and in about A.D. 850, Hunayn ibn Ishaq, an Arab physician at the court of Baghdad, prepared an annotated list of 129 works of Galen that he and his followers had translated from Greek into Arabic or Syriac. Learned medicine in the Arab world thus became heavily based upon the commentary, exposition, and understanding of Galen.

translation of *De Simplicibus*, which listed its contents in alphabetical order and was widely employed for centuries. Galen's principal characteristic as a pharmacologist was that his "fussy" attention to detail and, in the written as well as spoken word, he always stressed the importance of the purity of drugs and the necessity to handle them with extreme care. Thus he admonished his readers that *"in order to know drugs, inspect them not once or twice, but frequently, for though twins look alike to strangers, they are easily distinguished by friends."* In addition, he wisely cautioned against the excessive use of water from lead pipes, being familiar with Greek teaching regarding the toxicity of lead. With the exception of questionable pharmaceutical items, such as fox oil (obtained by boiling foxes) which he recommended as a bath in the treatment of arthritis, or dried camel brain, drunk in vinegar for the cure of epilepsy, his *materia medica* is generally comparable to that of his predecessors.

Having been appointed by Marcus Aurelius as physician to his son Commodus, he took personal care of the royal drugs, and it is recorded that he was especially gifted in the detection of poor ones and never used any new sample without first submitting it to a meticulous examination in order to determine whether it was of the correct variety and of the right age. Although there was an "apothecary" shop on the Via Sacra which conformed with Galen's conception of standards, he maintained a vast supply of drugs and herbs at his own residence and devoted much time to the acquisition of novel drugs in order that he possess the most current of remedies available. Thus, when he left Rome in A.D. 166, he visited the copper mines at Cyprus to obtain diphryges (probably a by-product of zinc oxide), misy, sory, or chalcanthos (terms employed for crystallized iron sulphate), which was used as an astringent, cadmia (zinc oxide?), copper ore, and pompholyx ("flowers of zinc").

> *When washed, pompholyx [Galen said] is an excellent remedy for drying out in an un-irritating way, and is especially useful in cancerous or other malignant ulcers. On account of its non-irritating quality it is used in collyria for inflammations of the eye, like phlyctenulae and corneal ulcers.*

During his peregrinations he visited the Dead Sea to acquire asphalt, which he required as an agent to control hemorrhage. The method employed involved the use of sponge dipped in asphalt which, when placed on the site of hemorrhage was ignited, thus forming an eschar which effectually prevented further hemorrhage. In addition to the drugs which he himself collected he obtained material from diverse sources: *"drugs are thus sent to me from Syria, Palestine, Egypt, Cappadocia, Pontus, Macedonia, Spain, Gaul and Africa."*

Overall he was a conservative physician and his prescriptions generally reveal a cautious use of hellebore, wine, honey, colocynth, ptisan, hyoscyamus, and opium. With regard to the latter he wrote:

> *In case of severe pain we narcotize ... with opium, mandragora and hyoscyamus, for as Hippocrates teaches, moderate narcotism ... relieves pain. Yet it is not to be forgotten that too powerful narcotics ... may cause death.*

For opium poisoning, he recommended warm water and oil until vomiting occurred. This procedure was to be followed by enemata.

An agent of particular interest to early physicians was the plant squill, which was even known to the writers of the *Ebers Papyrus*. Hippocrates employed it as a detergent for ulcers and also as an electuary in the treatment of empyema, while no less an authority than Pythagoras wrote a treatise on squill and is credited with the introduction of *vinegar of squill*.

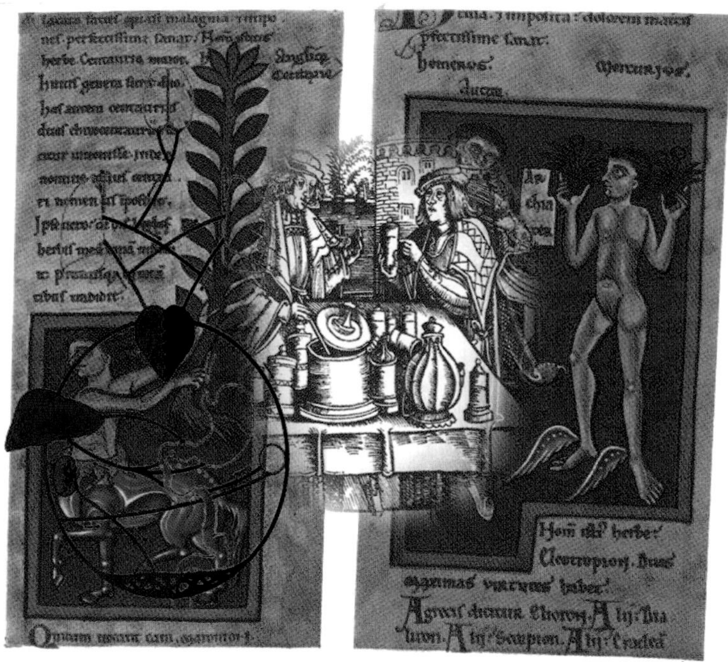

Herbal medicine as represented by the plant centaury (bottom left) was admixed with the use of certain metals best known to alchemists (center) in the treatment of disease. Mythological components also participated in therapy and the co-mingling of mercury (right) with a medicinal plant indicates the complexity of early pharmacology.

In the foreground Galen and Hippocrates debate a therapeutic dilemma, while in the background apprentices collect ingredients necessary to ensure the efficacy of the infinitely complex medication – theriac. The sum of its ingredients clearly far exceeded the quotient of its efficacy!

Pliny recommended its anthelminthic properties and Galen employed it as a medication in the care of epileptics. *"Having broken down squills with your hands into small pieces, put into a vessel used for containing honey, and having covered it up properly, put it in a place exposed to the midday during the heat of the dog-star; forty days after the rising of the dog-star loose it, and you will find that the body of the squill is melted down. Taking, then, its juice, sweeten it with some very fine honey, and give every day a spoonful of it, if to children, a small one, but if to adults, a large one."*

Almost two thousand years later Francis Home (1719-1813) of Edinburgh became the first to demonstrate the cardiac inhibitory action of squill, although it was not until 1879 that E. von Jarmersted identified the active material in squill as a glucoside (which he named *scillain*).

In contradistinction to the position of the somewhat cynical Pliny, a strange aberration was provided by Galen's continued belief in the efficacy of theriac that had been inculcated into him by his teacher, Satyrus.

> *Antidotes are remedies not applied externally, but are taken internally for the purpose of curing obstinate diseases. In general there are three kinds: For deadly poisons, for the bite or sting of animals, and for conditions arising from improper nutrition. Some antidotes are used for the triple purpose as that of Mithridates and these are called theriacs by the physician Andromachus.*

Indeed, this episode represents Galen at his worst as it is difficult to reconcile the sage authority with the wild polypharmaceutical debauch represented by the theriac prescription concocted for Marcus Aurelius. This premise was further supported by the orders of the Emperor Marcus Aurelius, who insisted that a major responsibility of Galen should be the compounding of theriac. Although Andromachus' prescription already called for over fifty ingredients, Galen desired to outdo this venerable physician and included one hundred substances in his preparation, which was to be taken in honey and wine. Convinced of its almost universal efficacy, he believed his prescription to be of therapeutic value in all internal affectations, especially gastric disturbances, as well as being effective against poisonous drugs, animals bites, gout, nervous disorders, tremors, menstrual disturbances, and as an aid in expelling a dead fetus.

Of especial note were the mystical and medicinal properties conferred by snakes, and Galen was particularly enthusiastic about the antidotal virtues of the viper. Its efficacy in a variety of dermatologic affections was suggested by the animal's characteristic of shedding its skin. For those utterly desperate with earache and toothache he prescribed its skin boiled in wine or vinegar. Viper pastilles were also recommended. Of these, he said:

> *The vipers ... should be taken neither while they are hibernating, nor in the middle of Summer, but at the time between the two, despite the fact that the noisy festival of Bacchus (celebrated in the woods) in March tends to disperse them. Pregnant vipers should not be employed. The head and tail are cut off, and thrown away, the former because it contains the concentrated poison, the latter because there is so little flesh. The animal is skinned, the flesh is dried in the sun under special conditions, carefully cooked with many precautions, and then kept in a glass or gold vessel till eventually put up in pastilles.*

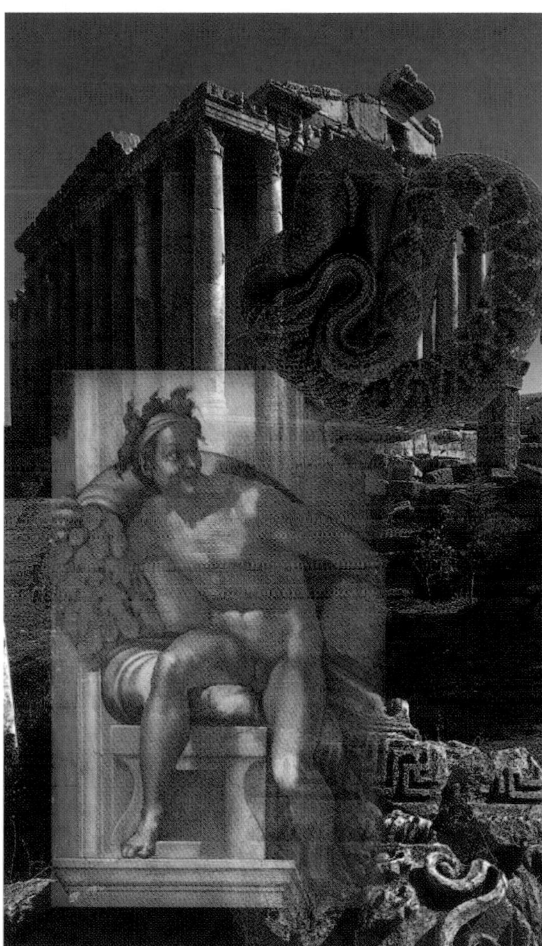

The cornucopia of fruit born by the youth is representative of the herbal polypharmacy of the ancient Greeks and Romans. Despite the magnificence of their architecture (background – Acropolis) and the lucidity of thought, Greek medicine was more theory than practicality and the snake icon of Aesculapius embraced more the concept of a cult than science.

The Galen medal of the London Society of Apothecaries venerates the memory of a man whose contributions to medicine have transcended the passage of time.

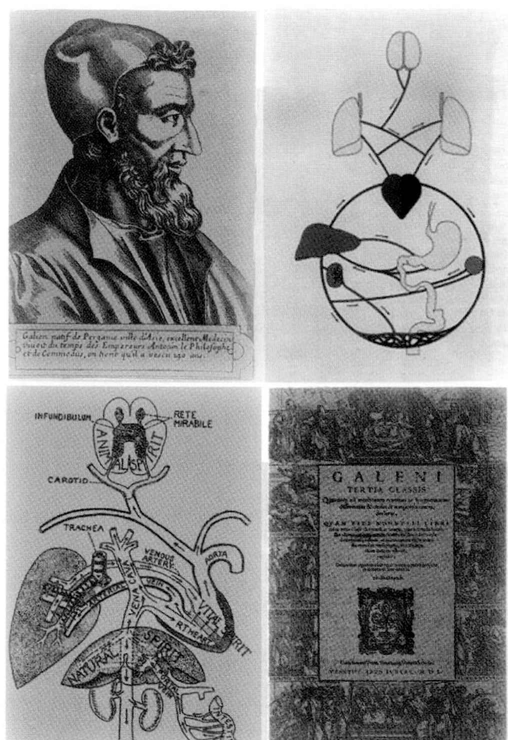

Galen (top left) wrote more than a hundred books (frontispiece bottom right) and may rightly be regarded as the intellectual father of medicine. As might be predicted, some concepts that he promulgated were erroneous. Thus, his dogmatic belief in the liver as the source of blood and pivotal organ led to his failure to grasp the principles of circulation and hindered the elucidation of cardio-pulmonary function until the advent of Vesalius and subsequently Harvey.

The Four Elements and Humors

With the passage of time the originally diffuse humoralism of the Hippocratic period acquired a more rigid formulation and, by the time Galen had reached his formative years, was inseparably associated with the theory of the four elements.

Thus, although initially the humoral theory had been essentially independent of the theory of the elements, these hypotheses eventually became associated to the point that they finally mutually fortified each other. While neither reached its complete, formalized stage until medieval times, the ultimate formalization of the quartenary system seems to a large part to reflect the activity of the early alchemists. It is of note that although the term alchemy came to be regarded as tainted by mystical connotation, there was nothing fundamentally occult in the contributions of the early alchemists.

Although Alexandria lost much of its original vigor after the rise of Rome, there had arisen and flourished in that city, a class of artificers in metal who were the forerunners of the later chemists. To the alchemists of Alexandria the incidental mythologic references accruing to their trade had no more profound significance than similar ones had to contemporary physicians. There was nothing essentially mystical about their writings except their inability to express their concepts lucidly and a commercial desire to keep private processes secret. This secrecy was natural to their occupation, for they were engaged in the art of making artificial gems, of plating low-grade metals to look like gold, and preparing formulas for physicians who had the greatest desire to keep their remedies secret. Just as the physicians in their attempt to understand the working and constitution of the human body had been thrown back upon philosophic speculations on the nature of matter, so these relatively unlettered artisans were forced to draw upon philosophic explanations in order to discourse about the processes involved in their art. The quaternary theory became to them a sort of inspired doctrine and through them served to reinforce the original theory among the physicians. Thus, individuals who pursued the occupation of jewelers and metallurgists predictably, during the course of their development, evolved a body of magical formulae as a remnant of their very early days. Vestiges of these formulas were also seen in the rituals of many other trades, the members of which were required to work with inanimate objects. This pattern reflected the tendency of primitive man to regard all matters as sentient and, in working with metals, these artificers, who were often frustrated by the peculiarities exhibited by the materials, were inclined to regard the failure of their processes as due to a deliberate perversity on the part of their metals and reagents. At times such as these, old magical customs were thought about and, almost in desperation, one suspects, invoked in an attempt to conjure success out of failure.

Aetius

Aetius lived either in the fifth or sixth century A.D. and was also a great compiler although he was, in addition, a great authority on plasters, which he discusses and describes at enormous length. Being of Christian persuasion, he was adept in providing word formulas to be recited when making medicinal compounds. Thus the incantation *"O God of Abraham, of Isaac, and of Jacob, give to this remedy the virtues necessary for it"* was a particular favorite in ensuring a satisfactory outcome. Also contained in his works are several nostrums famous in his time and for which fabulous prices were charged. Thus the *Collyrium of Danaus* was sold in Constantinople for 120 numismata (the unit being the *nummus aureus* of Roman money) and being currently worth approximately $1,000. Aetius notes that even at this price the *Collyrium* was scarce and could only be acquired with difficulty and by paying a further premium. An additional medication of the "why pay less variety" described by Aetius was the *Colical Antidote of Nicostratus* which was so efficacious as to be presumptuously labeled as *Isotheos* (equal to God), and thus sold for two talents of gold.

Not content with purely documenting therapy, Aetius himself devised a remedy for gout called *Antidotos ex duobus Centaureae generibus*. This compound was subsequently popularized in England almost a thousand years later under the salubrious title of "Duke of Portland's Powder." Aetius' cure consisted of a year-long regimen to be taken with the medication prescribed. Thus in September, the patient was to take milk; in October, garlic; in November to abstain from baths; December, no cabbage; in January to take a glass of pure wine every morning; in February, to eat no beet; in March to be allowed sweets in both food and drink; in April, no horse radish; in May, no polypus (a favorite dish); in June, to drink cold water in the morning; in July, no venery; in August, no mallows.

As mentioned previously, in the mid-eighteenth century the old Aetian medication surfaced once again as the Duke of Portland's Powder and achieved a great reputation that lasted well on into the nineteenth century. As such it was composed of *aristolochia rotunda* (birthwort root), gentian root, and the tops and leaves of germander, ground pine, and centaury, of each equal parts. One drachm was to be taken every morning, fasting, for three months, and then half a drachm for the rest of the year. Particular directions in regard to diet were given with the formula. The compound was evidently only a slight modification of several to be found in the works of the later Latin authors, Aetius, Alexander of Tralles, and Paul of Aegina, which were variously entitled

Tetrapharmacum, *Antidotus Podagrica ex duobus centauriae generibus* or *Diatesseron*. The "duobus" remedy was an electuary prescribed by Aetius, and it was necessary that a piece the size of a hazelnut had to be consumed each morning for a year. Hence it was called *medicamentum ad annum*. This, or something very like it, was in use in Italy for centuries under the name of *Pulvis Principis Mirandoloe*, and spread from there to the neighboring countries. An Englishman long resident in Switzerland had compiled a manuscript collection of medical formulae, and his son, who became acquainted with the Duke of Portland of the period, persuaded him to give this gout remedy a trial. Such was the success of the medication that the grateful Duke printed both the formula and diet directions on leaflets and instructed that these were to be offered to anyone who requested them.

Alexander of Tralles

This writer, who acquired considerable celebrity as a medical authority, lived a little later than Aetius, towards the end of the sixth century. He was a native of Tralles, in Lydia, and is much esteemed by the principal medical historians, Sprengel, Leclerc, Freind, and others who have studied his writings. Especially notable is his independence of opinion; he does not hesitate occasionally to criticize even Galen. He impresses strongly on his readers the danger of becoming bound to a particular system of treatment. The causes of each disease are to be found, and the practitioner is not to be guided exclusively by symptoms. Among his favorite drugs were castorum, which he gave in fevers and many other maladies; he had known several persons snatched from the jaws of death by its use in lethargy (apoplexy); bole Armeniac, in epilepsy and melancholia; grapes and other ripe fruits instead of astringents in dysentery; rhubarb appeared as a medicine for the first time in his writings, but only as an astringent; and he was the first to use cantharides for blisters in gout instead of soothing applications. His treatment of gout by internal remedies and regimen recalls that of Aetius and is worth quoting. He prescribed an electuary composed of myrrh, coral, cloves, rue, peony, and aristolochia. This was to be taken regularly every day for a hundred days. Then it was to be discontinued for fifteen days. After that it was to be recommenced and continued during 460 days, but only taking a dose every other day; then after another interval 35 more doses were to be taken on alternate days, making 365 doses altogether in the course of nearly two years. Meanwhile the diet was strictly regulated, and it may well be that Alexander only provided the medicine to amuse his patient while he cured the gout by a calculated reduction of his luxuries. Alexander of Tralles was the author who recommended hermodactyls, supposed to be a kind of colchicum in gout; a remedy which was forgotten until its use was revived in a French proprietary medicine. His prescription compounded hermodactyls, ginger, pepper, cumin seeds, aniseeds, and scammony. He said it would enable sufferers who take it to walk immediately. He is supposed to have been the first to advocate the administration of iron for the removal of obstructions.

As Rome disintegrated into an Eastern (Byzantine) and Western Empire, the intermingling of pagan beliefs, Christianity, and Greco-Roman medicine became further obfuscated by the fascination with magic, astrology, and the occult. Therapy was a curious admixture of rational thought tinged with mysticism and guided by the abstruse.

Mesue and Serapion

These names are often met with in old medical and pharmaceutical books, and there is an "elder" and a "younger" of each of them, so that it may be desirable to explain who they all were. The elder and the younger of each are sometimes confused. Serapion the Elder, or Serapion of Alexandria, as he is more frequently named in medical history, lived in the Egyptian city about 200 B.C., and was the recognized leader of the sect of the Empirics in medicine. He is credited with the formula that medicine rested on the three bases, Observation, History, and Analogy. No work of his has survived, but he is alleged to have violently attacked the theories of Hippocrates, and to have made great use of such animal products as castorum, the brain of the camel, the excrements of the crocodile, the blood of the tortoise, and the testicles of the boar. Serapion the Younger was an Arab physician who lived towards the end of the tenth century A.D. and wrote a work on *materia medica* which was much used for some five or six hundred years. Mesue the Elder was first physician at the court of Haroun-al-Rashid in the ninth century. He was born at Khouz, near Nineveh, in 776, and died at Baghdad in 855. Under his superintendence the School of Medicine of Baghdad was founded by Haroun. Although a Nestorian Christian, Mesue retained his position as first physician to five Caliphs after Haroun. To his teaching the introduction of the milder purgatives, such as senna, tamarinds, and certain fruits is supposed to be due. His Arabic name was Jahiah-Ebn-Masawaih.

Mesue the Younger is the authority generally meant when formulas under his name, sometimes quaintly called Dr. Mesue in old English books, are quoted. He lived at Cairo about the year A.D. 1000. He was a Christian, like his earlier namesake, and is believed to have been a pupil or perhaps a companion of Avicenna; at all events, when the latter got into disgrace it is alleged that both he and Mesue took refuge in Damascus. At Damascus Mesue wrote his

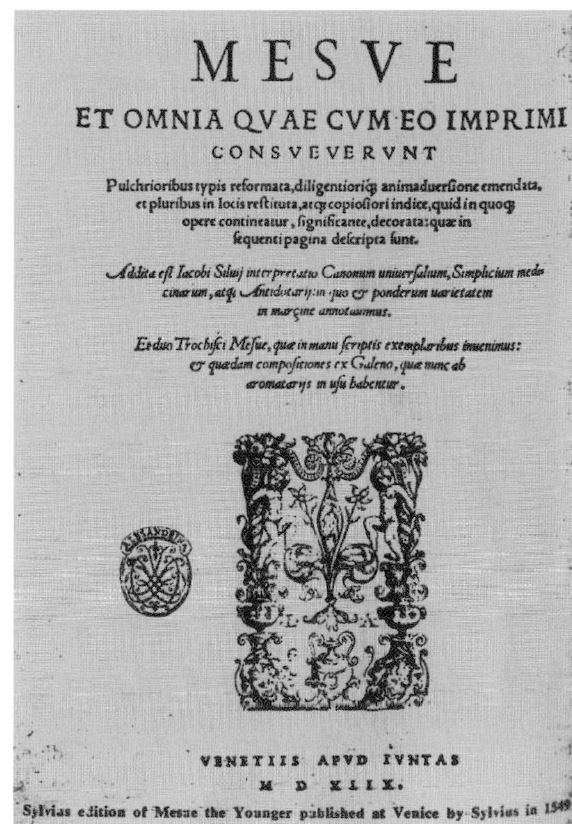

MESVE

ET OMNIA QVAE CVM EO IMPRIMI CONSVEVERVNT

Pulchrioribus typis reformata, diligentioriq; animaduersione emendata, et pluribus in locis restituta, atq; copiosiori indice, quid in quoq; opere contineatur, significante, decorata: quae in sequenti pagina descripta sunt.

Addita est Iacobi Siluij interpretatio Canonum uniuersalium, Simplicium medicinarum, atq; Antidotarij: in quo & ponderum uarietatem in margine annotauimus.

Et duo Trochisci Mesue, quae in manu scriptis exemplaribus inuenimus: & quaedam compositiones ex Galeno, quae nunc ab aromatarijs in usu habentur.

VENETIIS APVD IVNTAS

M D XLIX.

Sylvius edition of Mesue the Younger published at Venice by Sylvius in 1549

The text written by Mesue about A.D. 1000 passed through more than 70 editions and was regarded as the forerunner of the printed pharmacopoeias of the 17th century.

great work known in Latin as *Receptarium Antidotarii*. From the time of the invention of printing down to the middle of the seventeenth century, when pharmacopoeias became general, more than seventy editions of this work, mostly in Latin, but a few in Italian, have been counted. In some of the Latin translations he is described as *"John, the son of Mesue, the son of Hamech, the son of Abdel, king of Damascus."*

This dignity has been traced to a confusion of the Arabic names, one of which was very similar to the word meaning king. Nearly half of the formulas in the first *London Pharmacopoeia* were quoted from him.

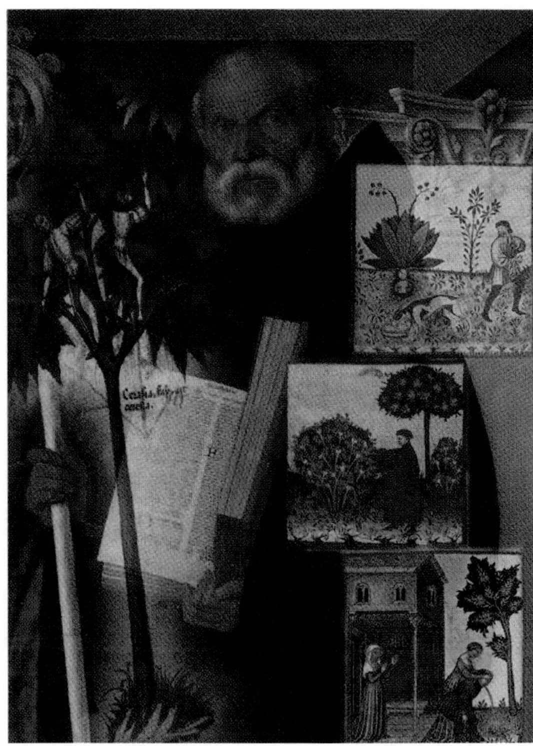

An idealized representation of Mesue the Younger holding a version of the Receptarium Antidotarii. *For seven centuries (10th – 17th A.D.), it remained the definitive compendium of therapy, listing all medicinal agents from herbal to animal, including elephant penis, boar testicles, salamander eyes, and lion teeth.*

Nicolas Myrepsus

For several centuries before the era of modern pharmacopoeias, the *Antidotary* of Nicolas Myrepsus was the standard formulary, and from this the early dispensatories were largely compiled. This Nicolas, who was not the Nicolas Praepositus of Salerno, is sometimes named Nicolas Alexandrinus.

He appears to have been a practicing physician at Constantinople, and as he bore the title of Actuarius, it is supposed that he was physician to the Emperor. He is believed to have lived in the thirteenth century. Myrepsus, which means ointment maker, was a name which he assumed or which was applied to him, probably in allusion to his *Antidotary*.

This was the largest and most catholic of all the collections of medical formulas which had then appeared. Galen and the Greek physicians, the Arabs, Jews, and Christians who had written on medicine, were all drawn upon. A Latin translation by Leonhard Fuchs, published at Nuremberg in 1658, contains 2,656 prescriptions, every possible illness being thus provided against. The title page declares the work to be *"Useful as well for the medical profession and for the seplasarii."* The original is said to have been written in barbarous Greek.

Sprengel, who has hardly patience to devote a single page to this famous *Antidotary*, tells us that the compiler was grossly ignorant and superstitious. He gives an instance of his reproduction of some Arab formulas. One is the use of arsenic as a spice to counteract the deadly effects of poisons. This advice was copied, he says, down to the seventeenth century. It was Nicolas' rendering of the Arabic word *"Darsini"*, which meant cannella, which they so named because it was brought from China.

The compounds collected in this *Antidotary* are of the familiar complicated character common to the style of Myrepsus. Many of the titles are curious and probably reminiscent of the pious credulity of this period. Thus there is a discussion of the Salt of the Holy Apostles (obtained by grinding together a mixture of herbs and seeds [hyssop, wild carrot, cumin, pennyroyal, and pepper] with common salt), which, taken morning and evening with meals, was purported to preserve sight, prevent hair from falling out, relieve difficulty of breathing, and keep the breath sweet. The Salt of St. Luke was similar but contained a few more ingredients.

Similarly he described a *Sal Purgatorius* (which could also be made into an electuary with honey) prescribed for the Pope Nicholas, which consisted of sal ammoniac, 3 oz., scammony, 3 drachms, poppy seeds, 2 drachms, orris root, 3 drachms, pepper, 13 grains, 1 date, pine nut, 25 grains, and squill, 2 drachms.

Antidotus Acharistos, which means un-thanked antidote, is stated to be so named because it cured so quickly that patients were not sufficiently grateful. They did not realize how bad they might have been without it. An electuary said to have been prescribed for King David for his melancholy, was composed of aloes, opium, saffron, lign aloes, myrrh, and some other spices, made up with honey. A *Sal Sacerdotale* (salt combined with a few spices) stated to have been used by the prophets in the time of Elijah, had come down to this *Antidotary* through St. Paul.

*Alexander of Tralles (c. A.D. 525 – c. 605) was a Byzantine physician who also practiced and taught in Rome. He is best remembered for his treatise on pathology and therapy (in twelve books), which served as a basis for instruction long after his death. Such was the popularity of the work that it was translated into Arabic and Latin (*Libri duodecim de re medica*) and thereafter printed in Greek, Latin, and Greco-Latin editions until the late 16th century.*

Herbs and their Usage

Herbs	Usage
Acacia	Astringent gum used in hemorrhage
Aconite	Anodyne and collyrium
Agaric	Gastric disorders
Brine salt	Cleansing of ulcers
Aloes	Hemorrhoids and gastric ulcers
Ammoniacal plant substances	Treatment of asthma
Old boiled oil	Injection in urethra, vagina or rectum
Starch preparations	Hemoptysis
Dill, anise, urine, juniper	Diuretics
Bitter almond	Laxative and soporific
Almond plus rose oil	Relief of headaches
Arsenic	Depilatory
Wild licorice	Topical application for indolent ulcers
Wild licorice plus wine	Diarrhea
Licorice	Sore throat and ulceration of the bladder
Jew's pitch or bitumen	Treatment of skin ulcers or wounds
Wormwood	Ascites or toothache
Gentian	Diseases of the liver and stomach
Pennyroyal elterium	Abortifacient
Hemlock	Cataplasm for erysipelas and herpes
Hemlock on the testicles	Induction of temporary impotence
Mint in vinegar	Cure of round worms and vomiting
Mint and wine	Aphrodisiac
Mint as a pessary	Contraception
Bird lime plus caustic lye	Disruption of tumorous growths
Cantharides	Ulcers and cancerous conditions
Verdigris	Trachoma and eye diseases
Fish glue	Removal of face wrinkles
Burnt ash of hippocampus	Topical treatment of alopecia
Cardamon	Intestinal worms and bladder stones
Cumin	Abolition of flatulence
Mandrake	Eye diseases and as a soporific

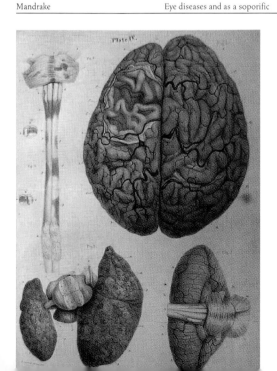

A brain from Robert Carswell's (1793-1857) pathology text of the 19th century. Although ancient medicine had little knowledge of cerebral function, many medications were directed at epilepsy and headache. Burnt ash of the hippocampus was used as a treatment of alopecia.

Byzantine and Arab Medicine

After the demise of Galen, medicine generally declined in Rome as the diverse texts of the earlier Greek physicians were ignored, and the works of Galen gradually assumed the position of not only the greatest but the sole authority in medicine. The subsequent dissolution of the Roman Empire led to its division into a Western and Eastern segment in Byzantium, where, although medical practice became static, several physicians labored vigorously to maintain extant medical knowledge.

Oribasius was born either at Pergamos or Sardis and studied medicine under Zeno of Cyprus (*fl.* A.D. 335) at Alexandria to such good effect that, upon the completion of his studies, he was recommended to the Emperor Julian who he subsequently accompanied on numerous expeditions. At the suggestion (sic) of the Emperor, Oribasius compiled a work (*Synagoge*) on the writings of the ancients that was first published in 1556 in Paris. The text originally consisted of seventy books and although only seventeen survive, they are of considerable value, since they preserve fragments of the writings of medical authors whose original material did not survive. Unfortunately, Oribasius, while providing much text on the authors of treatises on *materia medica* failed to describe the drugs in detail and neglected to give directions for their collection or preparation. Soon after the completion of this encyclopedic text, Oribasius wrote a *Synopsis* that was first published at Venice in 1554, for his son, Eustathios (*fl.* A.D. 350), who had followed in the footsteps of his learned father in the study of medicine. Not content with this monumental achievement, Oribasius then penned a text (*Euporista*, published at Basel in 1529) for laymen that was confined to discussions on diet, hygiene, and therapeutics.

Theodorus Priscianus, the second of this group, was the author of a treatise entitled *Imporiston* which although it displayed a marked preference for simple remedies, was not free from the superstitious beliefs of the period. Thus advice such as, "*If a person wears,*" he said, "*during the waning of the moon, a wreath of a polygonum on his head, he will obtain relief from his headache*" demonstrated a somewhat retrogressive stance. Nevertheless the text of Priscianus, together with one by Theophilus Protospatharius (*fl.* A.D. 630), remained a standard source throughout the Middle Ages and in so doing, contributed substantially to the static nature of medical thought.

Alexander of Tralles, also known as Alexander Trallianus (*c.* A.D. 525 – *c.* A.D. 605), a Byzantine physician who practiced and taught in Rome, is best known for his treatise on pathology and therapy (in twelve books), which served as a basis for instruction long after his death. It was translated into Arabic and Latin (*Libri duodecim de re medica*) and was printed in Greek, Latin, and Greco-Latin editions throughout the sixteenth century. The son

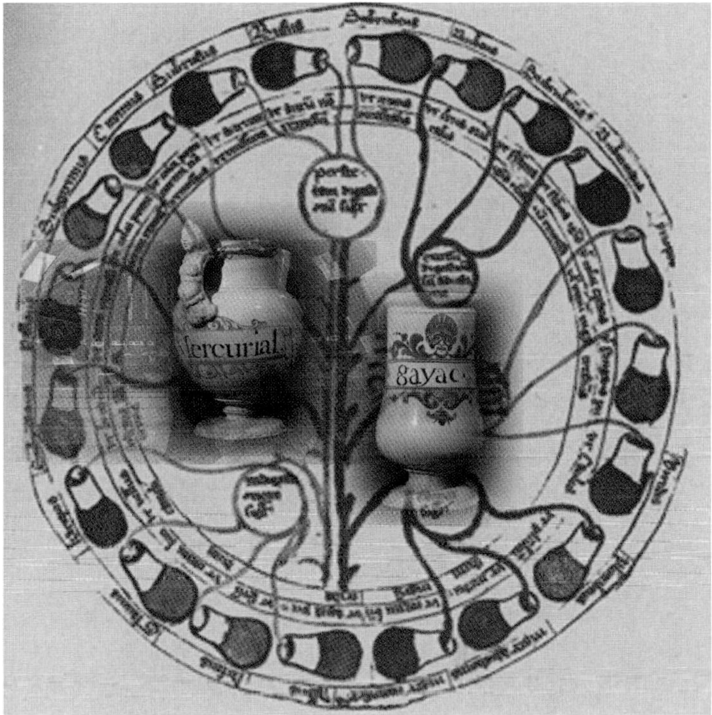

Uranoscopy – the study of the urine – was an early diagnostic tool used by physicians to determine the nature of illness and served as a guide to prescription. The chart depicts the different colors of urine, indicates the disease responsible and provides therapeutic recommendations of either a herbal (guiac) or metallic (mercury) nature.

The eleven great sages of medicine from antiquity to the Middle Ages including Hippocrates, Albertus Magnus, Dioscorides, Aesculapius, Rhazes, Serapion and Avicenna discuss the finer points of herbal preparation on the frontispiece of Giohanne Cademosto's text. Astrology, the body, and the patronage of rulers are noted to influence the decalogue.

The Emperor Justinian (reigned A.D. 527-555), and his wife Theodora (c. A.D. 497-548) of Constantinople. Together they presided over the Eastern segment of the Roman Empire and provided an intellectual haven for medicine as Rome faltered under the onslaught of barbarians and internal decadence. Theodora was probably the most powerful woman in Byzantine history and her intelligence and political acumen made her Justinian's most trusted adviser. Her father was a bear-keeper at the Hippodrome (circus) in Constantinople and Theodora became an actress while still young, leading an unconventional life that included giving birth to at least one child out of wedlock. When Justinian met her, she had been converted to monophysitism, a non-orthodox doctrine. Attracted by her beauty and intelligence she became his mistress and after raising her to the rank of patrician he married her in 525. Theodora is remembered as one of the first rulers to recognize the rights of women, passing strict laws to prohibit the traffic in young girls and altering the divorce laws to give greater benefits to women.

of a physician studied medicine and thereafter settled at Rome where, at the request of his friend Cosmas Indicopleustis (*fl.* sixth century), he wrote a text on medicine. As such it was clearly one of the most lucid treatises of the period, and although Alexander (as did almost everyone) relied upon Galen as one of his principal sources, he unlike his colleagues, did not hesitate to disagree with Galen's authority when personal experience revealed that the theories of the Pergamene were erroneous. Amongst his contributions were the criticism of astringent substances and their replacement with fruits, as well as the use of rhubarb for the treatment of dysentery. Despite evidence of sound commonsense, Alexander has been criticized for his superstitious faith in magical procedures. Thus in describing a remedy for colic, he suggested that the physician:

> *Remove the nipple-like projection from the caecum*
> *of a young pig, mix myrrh with it, wrap it in the skin of a wolf*
> *or dog, and instruct the patient to wear it as*
> *an amulet during the waning of the moon. Striking effects*
> *may be looked for from this remedy.*

Unfortunately the entire pharmacology section of his texts is disfigured by such practices and as a result his work has often been cited more as a source of ridiculous superstitions and tiresome jokes than as a serious repository of medical information.

Aetius of Amida studied medicine at Alexandria prior to relocating to Constantinople where the Emperor Justinian I appointed him both royal physician and commander of the royal bodyguard. Although these dual responsibilities clearly occupied a substantial amount of his time, Aetius was able to write a treatise on medicine. His views on *materia medica* were comparable to those of Galen and he explained the action of drugs according to their physical qualities. Of all the ancients, Aetius provided the most complete account of earthworms and described in detail their utility. Thus, when pounded, they were applied to divided nerves; after boiling in goose grease, they were of use in aural diseases and, when drunk in wine, were reported to have diuretic properties. Aetius employed hellebore for the evacuation of phlegm and bile but cautioned that it might produce convulsions or hypercatharsis. He was the first to prescribe smaragdus (not only emerald but also other green stones) as an amulet to stop bleeding and, in addition, noted that when roasted and levigated with Attic honey it was also of utility in the treatment of vision. When administered internally or externally he further recommended it in the treatment of elephantiasis. As was customary for the time, the views of Aetius were not free from his religious superstition and during the compounding of plasters, of which it should be noted that he recommended numerous foul ones in the treatment of surgical cases, he admonished the physician to recite, *"The God of Abraham, the God of Isaac, the God of Jacob, bestow virtue on this medication."*

Paul of Aegina (A.D. 625 – A.D. 690) was an important member of the Byzantine compilers and the author of a large text in seven books. Originally an Alexandrian physician and surgeon, he was the last major ancient Greek medical encyclopedist, who wrote the *Epitomes Iatrikes biblio hepta*, better known by its Latin title, *Epitomae medicae libri septem (Medical Compendium in Seven Books)*, containing nearly everything known about the medical arts in the West in his time. Based largely on the works of such earlier Greek physicians as Galen, Oribasius, and Aetius, the *Epitome* greatly influenced the medical practice of the Arabs, who considered Paul among the most authoritative of Greek medical writers. The Persian master physician Al-Rhazi (Rhazes) drew extensively from the work in writing his *Kitab al-Mansuri* (*Book to al-Mansur*) and Abu-al-Qasim, one of Islam's foremost surgeons, borrowed heavily from the *Epitome*'s sixth, or surgical, book in compiling the thirtieth chapter (*On Surgery*) of his *al-Tasrif* (*The Method*). Thus, Paul's work exercised a lasting influence on Western medieval medicine when the Arab works were adopted as primary references in medieval Europe. Besides his descriptions of lithotomy (surgical removal of bladder stones), trephination (removal of a disc of bone from the skull), tonsillotomy (removal of part of the tonsil), paracentesis (puncture of a body cavity in order to drain fluid), and amputation of the breast, Paul also devoted much attention in the *Epitome* to pediatrics and obstetrics. He dealt extensively with apoplexy and epilepsy, distinguished sixty-two types of pulse associated with various diseases, and rendered one of the first known descriptions of lead poisoning.

The last volume of the *libri septem* is particularly voluminous and devoted to *materia medica*. Of especial interest are the first two sections that express in detail the ideas of the period in regard to the so-called temperaments of substances.

SECTION 1: ON THE TEMPERAMENTS OF SUBSTANCES AS INDICATED BY THEIR TASTES

Astringents, then, contract, obstruct, condense, dispel, and incrassate; and, in addition to all these properties, they are of a cold and desiccative nature. That which is acid, cuts, divides, attenuates, removes obstructions and cleanses without heating; but that which is acrid, resembles the acid in being attenuant and purging, but differs from it in this, that the acid is cold, and the acrid hot; and, further, in this, that the acid repels, but the acrid attracts, discusses, breaks down, and is escharotic. In like manner, that which is bitter cleanses the pores, is detergent and attenuant, and cuts the thick humours without sensible heat. What is watery is cold, incrassate, condenses, contracts, obstructs, mortifies, and stupefies. But that which is salt contracts, braces, preserves, as a pickle, dries, without decided heat or cold. What is sweet relaxes, concocts, softens, and rarefies: but what is oily humectates, softens, and relaxes.

Section II: On the order and degrees of the temperaments

A moderate medicine which is of the same temperament as that to which it is applied, so as neither to dry, moisten, cool, nor heat, must not be called either dry, moist, cold, or hot; but whatever is drier, moister, hotter, or colder, is so called from its prevailing power. It will be sufficient for every useful purpose to make four ranks according to the prevailing temperament, calling that substance hot, according to the first rank, when it heats, indeed, but not manifestly, requiring reflection to demonstrate its existence: and in like manner with regard to cold, dry, and moist, when the prevailing temperament requires demonstration, and has no strong nor manifest virtue. Such things as are manifestly possessed of drying, moistening, heating or cooling properties, may be said to be of the second rank. Such things as have these properties to a strong, but not an extreme degree, may be said to be of the third rank. But such things as are naturally so hot as to form eschars and burn, are of the fourth. In like manner such things as are so cold as to occasion the death of a part are also of the fourth. But nothing is of so drying a nature as to be of the fourth rank, without burning, for that which dries in a great degree burns also; such are misy, chalcitis, and quicklime. But a substance may be of the third rank of desiccants without being caustic, such as all those things which are strongly astringent, of which kind are the unripe juice of grapes, sumach, and alum.

In his discussion of the pot-herbs, Paul stated that lettuce was soporific, nutritive, and capable of forming a good quality of blood, while beets were detergent and softened the "belly" as did cabbage that had been boiled once. On the other hand if cabbage was boiled twice it bound the "belly." He cautioned that mustard was of a hot and purgative nature and suggested the root of centaury for amenorrhea, expulsion of a fetus, for the agglutination of wounds, and for the relief of various chest conditions. The root of pellitory was recommended for pain in the teeth, and, as an ointment, was of use in paralysis. A variety of spurges were employed for easing the pain of toothache by dropping a little of the juice into the cavity. There is also a formula which suggests that teeth can be extracted without pain by compounding a plaster of spurge and packing it around the defective tooth.

Paul appears to have been especially interested in the subject of blood. As regards the blood of animals, he had comments:

Sanguis, Blood: no kind of it is of a cold nature, but that of swine is liquid and less hot, being very like the human in temperament. That of common pigeons, the wood pigeons, and the turtle, being of a moderate temperament, if injected hot, removes extravasated blood about the eyes from a blow; and when poured upon the dura mater, in cases of trephining, it is anti-inflammatory. That of the owl, when drunk with wine or water, relieves dyspnoea. The blood of bats, it is said, is a preservative to the breasts of virgins, and, if rubbed in, it keeps the hair from growing; and in like manner also that of frogs, and the blood of the chameleon and the dog-tick. But Galen, having made trial of all these remedies, says that they disappointed him. But that of goats, owing to its dryness, if drunk with milk, is beneficial in cases of dropsy, and breaks down stones in the kidneys. That of domestic fowls stops hemorrhages of the membranes of the brain, and that of lambs cures epilepsies. The recently coagulated blood of kids, if drunk with an equal quantity of vinegar, to the amount of half a hemina, cures vomiting of blood from the chest. The blood of bears, of wild goats, of buck goats, and of bulls, is said to ripen apostemes. That of the land crocodile produces acuteness of vision. The blood of stallions is mixed with septic medicines. The antidote from bloods is given for deadly poisons, and contains the blood of the duck, of the stag, and of the goose.

The use of blood in medicine dates back to the most primitive of medical times and has been a consideration from the period of primal man until current time. Although Paul used the word "injected," in the context of his time this meant nothing more than a "pouring in." Although transfusion is a much older practice than is generally realized, it was repeatedly attempted before the principles instituted by Karl Landsteiner (1868-1943) enabled its practical application.

Both Paul and Alexander of Tralles wrote long passages on the medical properties of stones which provided a full account of the various stones employed in the treatment of disease. Paul proposed that all kinds of stones were desiccative prior to pursuing a discussion of the medicinal virtues of a number of them. He advised bloodstone for hemorrhages, fungous ulcers, hemoptysis, and trachoma (*similia similibus curantur*). Jasper was used as an amulet for gastric complaints. The Judaic-stone (*tecolithos* of Pliny, bitumen of Dioscorides) was employed as a lithotriptic and the gagate was administered both in the treatment of emphysema and as a restorative from hysterical fits. Sapphirus (usually lapis lazuli) was recommended for ophthalmic diseases and for internal ulcerations.

Paul of Aegina (c. A.D. 625-690) was an Alexandrian physician and surgeon and the last major ancient Greek medical encyclopedist. He wrote the Epitomae medicae libri septem *(Medical Compendium in Seven Books) that encompassed almost the totality of contemporary Western medical knowledge.*

The value of blood as a medicine was a source of continued debate. Paul of Aegina was profoundly convinced in regard to the efficacy of different types of animal blood as therapeutic agents. He noted that bat blood was useful in preserving the breasts of virgins and that frog blood was similarly essential to obviate hair growth on these objects of pulchritude. Galen, who repeated these studies, was less impressed with its effects on Roman breasts (possibly a control group was lacking) and indicated that either bull or boar blood were more effective.

With the decline of the West, the iconic figures and knowledge of Greek and Roman medicine were translated into Arabic and became enshrined for the most part in Persia.

An examination of Paul's compound medicines reveals several classifications which may be listed as follows:

	Type	Action	Target
1	Simple	Purgative	Biliary, black bile, phlegm evacuant
2	Compound	Purgative	Gout, epilepsy, indigestions, fevers
3	Antidotes	Preventive	Poisons
4	Liniments	Soothing	Limb pain
5	Emetics	Expulsion	Stomach
6	Troches	Emulsion, enemata	Diarrhea, melena, anodyne
7	Powders	Dry	Dermatologic affections (parasitic)
8	Gargles	Soothing	Throat
9	Collyria	Irrigation	Eye wash, douche, fistula irrigation
10	Counter-irritant plasters	Skin	Ulcers, boils, tumors, fractures, contusions
11	Malagamata/emollient plasters	Chest, skin	Epithemes, pleurisy, indurations
12	Acopa	Stimulating ointments	Paralyses/Tremors
14	Oils	Ranging from bland to irritating	External and internal usage
15	Oenanthari	Toilet water + smelling salts	Skin conditions
16	Perfumes	Odorific	Hygiene
17	Pessaries	Medicated tampons and suppositories	Infection, fertility
18	Propomata	Cordials (absinthe)	Digestive disturbances, heart problems

Arab Writers

For the most part, Arab medical knowledge was initially derived from the Byzantines. Although their primary source was Dioscorides they became prolific in their descriptions of drugs introducing many new substances. The rationale for the intense Arab interest in drugs reflected their early dominance of the dye, spice, and drug trade. Vessels traveling to India and the east coast of Africa needed to traverse the Red Sea, which had from time immemorial been subject to Arab control. In order to regulate commerce they insisted that all material transported via the Red Sea ports should be conveyed in their ships. Thus, at the northernmost tip of the Red Sea, cargoes were originally transshipped to the Phoenicians, who dominated the Mediterranean traffic and upon arrival on the Arabian shore at the southernmost tip of the Red Sea, goods were carried by caravan half-way up the west coast of Arabia to a location adjacent to Medina, where they were once again placed on ships and ferried across the Red Sea to Egypt. Since few ancient physicians possessed a thorough knowledge of drugs, the Arabians circulated the most extravagant stories concerning their origin and charged exorbitant prices for material which might originate from locations as close as the island of Socotra (frankincense and dragon's blood). Alternatively, in many instances, they adulterated or sophisticated the substances before they sold them, such that some drugs were diluted with inert agents and others rendered entirely spurious.

The Arab pharmacists were adept at the acquisition and amplification of Western medical thought. In addition, their extensive mercantile trade allowed the introduction of unusual and novel remedies from India and the Far East. Their early development of the science of chemical processing enabled considerable progress to be made in the identification of new agents and the refining of previously impure substances for medicinal purposes.

Among the numerous novel agents introduced by the Arabs, castor oil figured prominently. The castor or *castoreum* referred to by the Greeks was erroneously considered as beaver testicle (castor), although in reality it was the musky product of the scent gland and different to the substance described in Arabic literature. The castor oil of the Arabs was the well-known derivative of *Ricinus communis* which is still employed as a cathartic. In addition the Arabs also introduced musk (for cerebral and ophthalmic diseases), ambergris (cramps, heart disease, and brain disorders); camphor (vertigo, cholera, hemorrhage, and inflammation of the brain); senna (cathartic, anti-seizure); mace (cardiac diseases and indigestion); sandalwood (gout and headaches); picrotoxin for arthritis; nux vomica as an emetic; borax, gum, and sandarac for dental complaints; and tamarind, hops, and spinach as laxatives.

In addition to spices and drugs, the commercial Arabs had long been interested in alchemy, since they were to some extent agents of the gold trade and, thus, the elaboration of a variety of metals was another source of considerable commercial trade and profit.

Prior to Geber (Jabir ibn-Hayyan, *fl.* A.D. 776), the Arabs, themselves, had contributed little or nothing to theoretical alchemy, although even before his time, it had been proposed that all metals were essentially the same thing, but simply existed in varying degrees of purity. This notion enabled alchemists to consider gold as the purest and noblest of all metals which "ripened in the earth" and led them to dream that their destiny lay in identifying a manner by which they might hasten this supposititious natural process. Amalgamation was a process that was long considered as a viable route and the idea that mercury was very closely related to gold but lacked the addition of a mysterious "something" to give it the proper color and solidity was clearly exciting. Among the agents proposed to represent the missing "something" was sulphur since in color it suggested a mercury-like association. Driven by an obsession with the resolution of this conundrum, the search for the appropriate tinctorial substance, or tincture of metal, or "philosopher's stone," (the Arabic name for the "philosopher's stone" [*al-kibrit al-ahmar*] is translated as "the red sulphur") as it was more commonly called, preoccupied innumerable chemists and physicians for centuries.

Unfortunately the passage of time has clouded the precise contributions of Geber and, although over one hundred works have his name attached to them, it has proved extremely difficult to determine those which he authored. In fact, it is certain that nearly all these were the product of Pseudo-Geber (one or more later authors masquerading under Geber's name). There is little evidence that Geber had any notion of the preparation of medicines, or that he thought of the "philosopher's stone" as an elixir of life. This concept does however appear in the works of Pseudo-Geber, Roger Bacon, and Albucasis, thus the most that can be said about the true, eighth-century Geber is that he placed chemical experimentation on a sound basis, improved the methods of evaporation, sublimation, melting, and crystallization, and could prepare sulphuric and nitric acids, a mixture of which seems to have been the original *aqua regia*.

Rhazes was a Persian physician and alchemist who wrote in Arabic and lived in that period of Arab medicine when most of the work of translation had already been completed. He wrote numerous texts, among which were the *Liber Almansoris* and the *Continens*. Probably the most important pharmacologic contribution attributed to him was the introduction of mercurial ointments. Although mercury had long been known, it has proved difficult to determine precisely just what part it played in early medicine because the terminology employed resulted in some degree of obscurity. Thus while mercury occurs in nature in the form of a red sulphide (HgS) called cinnabar, the word cinnabar was used by the classicists to connote several other agents. When Theophrastus wrote of cinnabar, he referred to native vermilion, although Dioscorides was talking about dragon's blood and the term *sal Atticum* was employed by the Romans while Pliny (*Historia Naturalis xxxiii. 38*) referred to it as a resinous exudate (the *m'soilo* of the island of Socotra) also called dragon's blood (*sanguis draconis*).

Dioscorides was well acquainted with mercury, and Paul, following him, accepted the Greek belief that it was a deadly poison. He said: "*Mercury, when swallowed, brings on the same symptoms as litharge, and the same remedies are to be used in this case. A copious draught of milk seems to be beneficial, and vomiting ought to be produced.*" The Arabs were, however, better acquainted with its properties, having ascertained that it might be taken in its metallic state with impunity. Thus Rhazes noted, "*I do not think that any great harm will result from drinking mercury when it is pure, unless it be pains in the stomach and intestines. It afterwards passes out in its natural state, especially if the person who swallowed it moves about. I gave a draught of it to an ape, nor did I perceive any inconvenience arise from it, except, as I have mentioned, that it appeared to be pained in its belly for it often bit it with its mouth and grasped it with its hands.*"

Later Arab authors made a clear distinction between the effects of mercury in its metallic and combined states and pointed out that the latter were extremely poisonous. Indeed, it is apparent that these later authors employed mercury vapors and inunctions. Serapion Senior (*fl.* second half ninth century) claimed that the former produced nervous affections and paralysis (*De Simplicium*, A.D. 385), while Al-Zahrawi (Albucasis, Alsaharavius, Abu-al-Qasim, Khalaf ibn-Abbas al-Zahrawi, 936-1013), a native of Cordova and author of an *al-Tasrif*, reported that mercurial inunction produced gingivitis and glossitis. One of the main sources of knowledge regarding Arab pharmacology is the *Grabadin* of the eponymous or pseudonymous Mesue junior, now called "pseudo-Mesue," a mysterious Latin compilation of the tenth or eleventh century which was long used as an apothecary's manual and of which the Arabic originals have never been identified. Pseudo-Mesue's ideas on therapy differed very little from those of Galen and he also evaluated drugs according to their physical qualities. His instructions for the preparation of extracts were the most lucid of his period and he distinguished mild from drastic purgatives, opposing the employment of the latter.

Avicenna (Abu-Ali al-Husayn ibn-Sina, 930-1037), author of the estimable philosophical treatise (*Kitab al Shifa*) was born at Bukhara and studied medicine under a Nestorian physician. Prior to his compilation of the important medical *Canon* (*al-Qanun fi al-Tibb*), the *Liber regius* of Haly Abbas had remained the favorite therapeutic text of the Arab medical world. Indeed, from the twelfth to the seventeenth centuries this text served as the chief guide to

The frontispiece of Antidotarium Medico-Chymicum Reformatum *by Johann Daniel Mylius (1585-1628) of Wetter in Hesse. A prolific writer on the subject of Spagyrical Medicine and Hermetick Philosophy, Mylius sought to bridge the gap between pure chemistry and medicine. Depicted in the margins are the six great alchemist physicians of the ages: Hermes, Lully, Bacon, Paracelsus, Morien and Geber. The central inset cameos represent the mining of raw elements (above) and after processing their sale in a pharmacy (below).*

Avicenna (right) represented the epitome of Arab medical intellectualism. Many of his recommendations were transmitted back to Europe in his text (The Canon) and formed the basis for medical practice as depicted in a Jewish medical text (left) of the Middle Ages.

Despite different religious beliefs and ethnic backgrounds, physicians, whether Jew, Christian, or Moslem shared a common interest in resolving medical problems.

medical science in the West. The *Canon* is essentially a summary of Greco-Arab medicine and its *materia medica* considered 760 drugs that included practically all the drugs which previous writers discussed, including not only those of Byzantium, but also those of Persian compilers of Hindu systems. On the subject of cannabis, Avicenna is much more specific than the Greeks, describing several varieties variously considered as carminative or desiccative. In regard to mandragora he recommended its usage as a narcotic and soporific that might be used as a suppository. Although he believed that the berries were dangerous, causing amnesia, purging, and perhaps death he felt that the milky juice was of use in evacuating phlegm and yellow bile while mandrake seed mixed with sulphur was recommended for menorrhagia. Mandragora is still used in the Moslem East as a narcotic and in the time of Avicenna, was sometime employed in the same connections as hellebore. A specific variety of black hellebore called *gilbenec* was recommended by him as an emetic for menstrual disorders, although he considered it somewhat unsafe. In speaking of white hellebore, the Arabs followed the Greeks almost exactly as to preparation, dose, and indication, and in general Avicenna reviewed almost everything contained in the preceding literature. In addition, he mentioned some unusual items including guinea grains, betel nuts, methel nuts (a narcotic stramonium), rhubarb, and cubeb. Opium was also well-known to the Arabs and they regarded the lethal dose as two drachms. For an overdose of emetics, irritating enemas, strong smelling things, baths, massages, sternutatories, and various other measures were recommended to prevent sleep.

As regards to poisons, they adhered to the ancient postures and most texts included a separate section dealing with the bites and stings of so-called venomous animals. The manner in which such animal venoms were supposed to act was not very different from the imagined *modus operandi* of the poisons of the *materia medica* and F. Adams in commenting upon the subject stated: "*Aristotle taught that the prime cause of all operation of life is mind, and that the prime instrument, by which it performs them is heat, which, therefore, he denominates the co-cause. He illustrates his meaning by comparing the mind to the artificer, and heat to the wimble or saw by which he performs his work. Having remarked, no doubt, that the heart is the warmest part of the body, he appears to have considered it as the spring which turns the whole machinery of the animal frame, the brain and nerves deriving their origin and influence from it.*"

Based upon concepts of this type Avicenna and, long before him, Galen, had proposed that poisons exerted their primary cardiac influence by impairing the vital heat and that further diminution of this resulted in the loss of sensibility and muscular energy. As a result of this rationale narcotics were referred to as either frigorific or congealing and the action of poisons on the neural system was considered only a secondary effect. Later, in the eleventh century, Albucasis took issue with this theory stating: "*Sometimes, he says, poisons act upon the heart, and thereby prove instantly fatal; sometimes upon the liver, producing jaundice and phthisis; sometimes upon the brain, when they occasion delirium; and sometimes the action is local, giving rise to corruption and lividity of the part.*" A vast list of putative agents, insects, animals and reptiles comprise the list of potential poisonous vectors but it is noteworthy that the concept of rabid animals was included. Some chimeric and fictional beasts were considered, as well as odd substances such as shark's bile, the tail of stag and the "sweat" of various animals.

Given the extensive catalogue of potentially poisonous agents it is not unexpected that the list of substances recommended to repel poisonous animals, exterminate them when present, obviate the ill effects of their bite or sting, and cure persons afflicted by their venom or by pharmacologic poisons, is long, diffuse, and varied. Predictably the majority of these substances were absolutely useless as might be supposed from the nature of two of the most

An Arab pharmacy of the 12th century. The triumvirate of medicine is represented by the learned physician (left), the young apprentice (centre) and the skilled pharmacist (right).

prized remedies, *mithridatium* and bezoar stone (*padzahr*, or *pa-zahar*). Surprisingly Alexander of Tralles makes no mention of the bezoar stone in his list of lapidary remedies and it first appears in the writings of the Arabs, who presumably learnt of it from the Persians.

Bezoar

The name Bezoar stone referred to gastro- or enteroliths and although gall-stones were included among the bezoars, the calculi of the urinary tract were not considered to possess their properties and regarded as separate entities. The mechanism of action as outlined by Rhazes was based upon the heat-dissipating effects of venoms as follows:

The evill Venoms that doe offende
the heart and worke their effects, O how
little prolite doeth any cure prove
in them, if the Bezoar be not taken, for
that doeth resist it. Moreover I myself saw
that it did resist the venome called
Napelo which is the venome that doeth
penetrate more than al venoms.

A great deal of confusion developed around bezoar stones, based upon the diversity of the nature of these materials and the great esteem in which they were held. Thus mysticism, crass commercialism and a desperate demand culminated in the development of a thriving trade in both real and spurious bezoars. Such was the fiscal value of bezoars that the earlier habit of grinding them up and applying the powder to the poisoned site was soon abandoned and stones were merely rubbed on these areas. Ultimately, they became more valued as a preventive than as a cure, and officials who suspected that others might profit by their demise had bezoars permanently set in the dishes and goblets from which they habitually ate and drank. The entire concept eventually became a farrago of nonsense, as confusion reigned regarding not only the authenticity of the stones but even the validity of the theory of their action. Thus, Nicolas Monardes (1493-1588), in 1574, provided a somewhat different account of the bezoar which promoted a viewpoint of the action of venoms which is the direct opposite of the earlier notion that such substances cooled the vital heat of the heart.

Harts, which for the great heat of the Sommer goe into the
caves and hollowe places, where the adders and snakes and
other vermin being of poyson are, which in that country be
many, and verie venomous, because the country is so hot: and
with their breth they drive them out, and tread upon them,
and kill them, and eate them, and after they are filled with
them, they goe as speedily as they can, where water is, and
they plunge themselves therein, in such sort that they leave no
parts of their bodies out, but their snowt, for to fetch their
breath: and this they do, that with the coldties of the water
they may delay the greate heate of the venome, which they
have eaten: and there they remaine without drinking a droppe
of water, until they have alayed and cooled, that fervent heat,
wherein they were by feeding upon the venomous vermine.
And being in the water there doth ingender in the places
where the drops of water commeth foorth of their eyes, a
stone, which being come foorth of the water, falleth from
them, and it is gathered up for the use of medicine.

Although two types of the stone, oriental and occidental, were generally distinguished in each group, there were a number of subtypes, each of which was presumed to have specific properties. Overall their therapeutic value was initially considered solely that of an antidote or preventive, but bezoars were subsequently employed until well into the eighteenth century in the treatment of epilepsy, smallpox plague, and certain fevers. Thus John Quincy, writing as late as 1757, said:

There are two principal Kinds of what is supposed
natural Bezoar, the oriental and occidental, both being a Sort
of Stones of a round or oval Figure, and said
to be found in the maw or Stomach of particular Animals,
as some Species of Goats, Porcupines etc.
The Oriental Bezoar is most esteemed and bears by much the
highest Price; for those who have been at most Pains to
examine it, will by no Means allow that its medicinal
Virtues are answerable to its Price. And to say
the Truth, as t'is now generally among the Apothecaries
reputed of little Significancy in Medicine, they
have a Way to counterfeit its fine tinging greenish Colour
so artfully, as to impose upon very discerning Persons.

Embraced in the same concept of mythical cure and prophylaxis was the "unicorn" horn which was also greatly prized for its prophylactic properties. The legend of this animal and its fabled powers originated before the time of Pliny when tales of mythical beats and chimeric animals ranged from the sublime to the ridiculous. In particular, visitors returning from India referred to the rhinoceros which, in Greek, was called a *monoceros* and from this compilation of myth and reality arose dreams of the white unicorn and its fabled horn.

Despite their much vaunted protective powers neither the camel bezoar (right) nor the bezoar goblet (bottom left) appear to have saved the young woman.

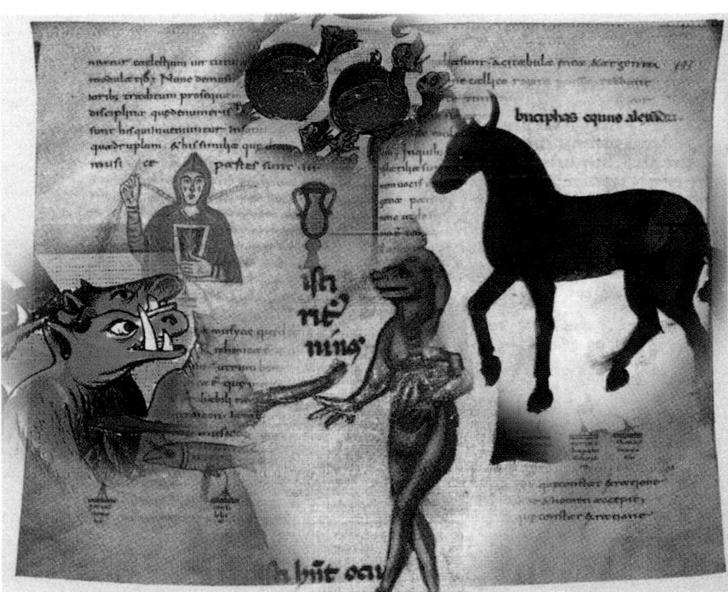

In an attempt to protect against poisoning and disease, arcane incantations, mythical animals, amulets, and exotic substances were sought from the farthest ends of the earth.

Section 3

Medieval Pharmacology

There has emerged an erroneous concept that the Middle Ages constituted a period of time when the medical knowledge of the West was obliterated and that all activity resided among the Byzantine and Arab medical communities. In fact, the Greco-Roman tradition was not only preserved in various localities, but it even diffused northward, intermingling with the primitive systems of medicine which it encountered during its dissemination.

As the Roman grip on Europe waned and Christianity supervened, the practice of medicine evolved into a strange admixture of pagan beliefs, magical invocations, and monastic injunctions against sin and its penalty of illness.

To a certain extent, this degradation reflected the fact that most physicians evinced little or no attention to the poor and this group began to seek information on self-medication by the composition of texts referred to as layman's pharmacopoeia or herbals. Credit for the development of this public resource lies with an unknown writer usually designated Apuleius Barbarus (Pseudo-Apuleius, Pseudo-Platonicus, Apuleius Platonicus), who is believed to have flourished in the fourth or fifth century. This work was subsequently published by J.F. de Lignamine at Rome, and was subsequently extensively copied, thus becoming the precursor of a long line of popular pseudo-medical writings which, although they run parallel with the regular literature, are not usually referenced by the responsible authors. Indeed, this so-called "bastard literature" included a wide variety of contributions such as the receipt-books, books for midwives and nurses, and, more recently, the so-called *"Almanacs"* or more pretentious texts generically entitled, though scarcely less ludicrous, *"Family Physicians."*

As might be predicted, the spread of the Greco-Roman medical tradition was to a large extent closely linked with the diffusion of Christianity, although, in certain areas where the old habits lingered, conflict with the pagan association between medicine and the religious aspects of the Aesculapian cult persisted. Hybrid situations developed in accordance with local needs and thus, some of the characteristics which had been formerly attributed to pagan gods became appropriated for saints and a degree of confusion in therapy developed. Thus, Dioscorides remained the authority of the West, as of the East, a religious cloak impeded the acquisition and development of new information. The failure of medieval Europe to develop any notable secular centers of medical training further reflected the role of the Church as it sought to retain control of knowledge and thus thought. As a result of the relative lack of forward thinking, degradation of the classic pharmacologic tradition occurred and its principles became diffused by the introduction of superstitious practices, derived from ancient pagan residues.

Aurelius Cassiodorus (A.D. 480 – A.D. 575), who had been in the employ of Theodoric the Great (454?-526) and who was later connected with the Benedictine Monastery at Monte Cassino, spent the last years of his life copying and translating manuscripts. Since he was interested in all types of manuscripts, he preserved numerous medical treatises. The Rule of the Benedictine Order included the care of the sick and, in time, the medical knowledge of those monks entrusted with the care of patients dramatically exceeded that of the local practitioners of the period. In his commentary of pharmacology, Cassiodorus opined with no uncertain degree of patronization as follows:

Hildegard of Bingen and her vision of the perfect man redeemed by the almighty physician. With the advent of Christianity, medicine acquired a specific deity that might be invoked on behalf of the patient, and the influence of the innumerable gods of the field and woods waned. The zealotry of prayer and vision inspired a new order of priests and nuns to assume responsibility for both the soul and the body while espousing the doctrine that all ills were the product of sin.

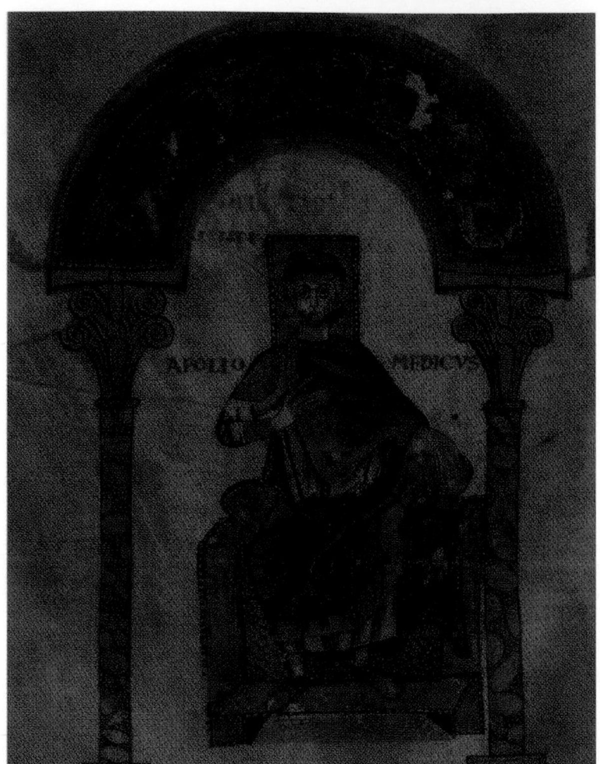

Isadore of Seville (c. A.D. 570-636) was the most learned man of his time. He authored an *Etymologia of Origins and Etymologies*, the fourth book of which contained a vast survey of medicine but was unfortunately replete with many false and far-fetched derivations of medical terms.

The Spanish Inquisition deemed that certain medical texts were seditious and as a result, information was often suppressed and knowledge lost, as physicians and priests alike feared the iron heel of the moral mediocrity.

Learn to know the properties of herbs and the blending of drugs, but set all your hopes upon the Lord, who preserves life without end. If the language of the Greeks is unknown to you, you have the herb-book of Dioscorides, who has described and depicted the herbs of the field with astonishing accuracy. Afterwards read Hippocrates and Galen in Latin translation, i.e. the Therapeutics of the latter, which he has dedicated to the philosopher Glaucon and the work of an unknown author, which, as would appear from investigation, is compiled from several writers. Study further the Medicine of Aurelius [Aurelianus], the Hippocratic book upon herbs and healing methods, as well as a variety of other treatises upon the healing art which I have brought together in my library and have bequeathed to you.

A contrary opinion was expressed by the Spanish Inquisition in the early seventeenth century, where it was decreed that only the *fraile* in charge of the convent pharmacy might read the medical works of condemned authors and then, only such passages of these as were necessary for the preparation of medicines. Such differences highlight the difficulty in either crticizing or supporting censure of the Church in its relation to medicine, since clearly the times and personality of the individual leaders involved resulted in considerable variance in the expression or acquisition of medical knowledge. One important characteristic of patristic medicine that evolved was the production of encyclopedias whose perusal has enabled an excellent insight into the medical opinions of their authors. One such was provided by Isidore of Seville (Isidorus Hispalensis, *c.* 560-636) who left an *Originum sive etymologiarum*, that revealed that in pre-Moslem Spain, the text of Dioscorides was still the official pharmacologic work. A similar observation can be derived a century later in Germany when Hrabanus Maurus (Magnentius, 780-856), Archbishop of Mayence, wrote his *De universo libri XXII sive etymologiarum opus*. Walafrid Strabo (807-848), a pupil of Hrabanus, was the author of a poem called the *Hortulus* in which he described the flora of the monastery of which he was abbot and in so doing, initiated the development of a genre of versified herbals. Thus Otto of Morimont (Odo Moremendensis, Otto Frisingensis, 1114-1158), Abbot of Beauprai, under the *nom de plume* of Macer (Floridus or Aemilius Macer) was inspired to compose a poorly written Latin work, *De virtutibus herbarum* (published at Naples in 1477) comprising no less than 2,269 hexameters. Two further medical treatises (*Liber simplicis medicinae* and *Liber Compositae medicinae*) of this type were also provided by "Saint" Hildegard (1098-1179), the mystic Benedictine abbess of Rupertsberg. The first of these dealt with herbs, plants, minerals, precious stones, and food substances and contained Hildegard's obsession with the use of fern against all types of "deviltry," as well as admonitions regarding the utility of herring in the treatment of the itch, vetch against warts and mint water for asthma.

Subsequent to the demise of Cassiodorus, the influence of Salerno upon pharmacology was perpetuated by Nicholas of Salerno (Nicolaus Salernitanus, *fl.* 1100-1150), who composed an *Antidotarium* based upon the classic Arab tradition. This treatise, considered to be the first formulary, consisted of 139 prescriptions arranged in alphabetical order and, of particular importance, contained the fundamental basis of the system of weights that were used by apothecaries. A later Salernian writer on pharmacology, Matthias Platearius (*fl.* 1150) composed *De simplici medicina*, (also known as the *Circa Instans*, the opening words of the text) which represented an alphabetically arranged description of 273 of the most important drugs. Although the compositions of Nicholas and Platearius do not notably depart from the classic tradition, the thirteenth-century *De vegetabilibus* prepared by Albertus Magnus provides indication of close personal attention to the actual plants and betrays a degree of impatience with the worn, and all but meaningless, conventional, descriptive format previously employed. The text of Magnus as well as the *De Virtutibus Herbarum* of Rufinus (*fl.* 1290) both give evidence of the return to objectivity even before the discovery of the New World initiated a resurgence and renewed interest in the drug trade.

A second motivating influence in therapeutics and pharmacology was provided by the rise of Scholasticism which, despite being primarily interested in supporting theologic position by argument, rather than by objective evidence, found it necessary to establish supreme authorities in a variety of fields. Thus, in the writings emanating from schools such as Chartres,

The School of Medicine of Salerno (c. A.D. 1000), (top right) initially under the influence of Cassiodorus and later Nicholas, promulgated a code of health that was widely accepted. Its practitioneers and graduates were for centuries regarded as the pre-eminent physicians of Europe and the name Salerno epitomized the art of medicine.

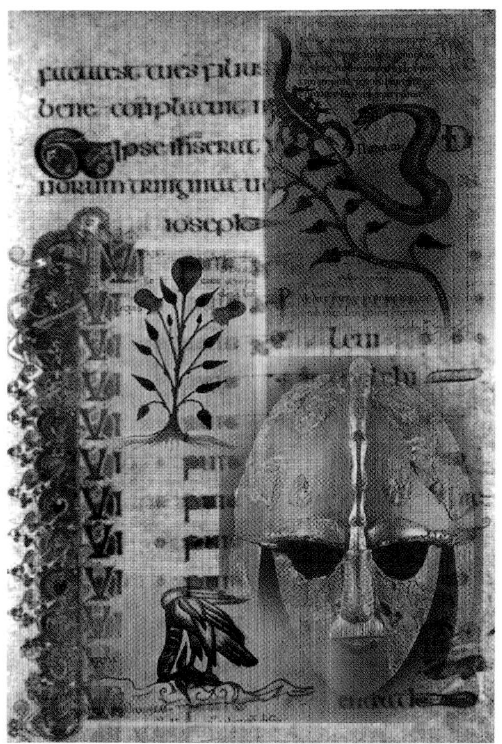

English medicine at the end of the first millennium was characterized by a mélange of Anglo-Saxon herbals, Druidic superstition, and even some Arab culture derived from the University of Paris. Their physicians were known as leeches!

Dioscorides and his vast fund of information became once again elevated to a position of first importance. Of further importance was the Moorish occupation of the Iberian peninsula and that as a result, medieval Europe was exposed to Arab influences. Thus from the tenth century onward, Moslem culture slowly filtered into medieval Europe and individuals such as Nicholas of Salerno and Platearius, although they represent a continuation of the classic tradition advocated by Cassiodorus, actually derived their information not from him but from Arabic translations. Furthermore, the Islamic centers of learning at Cordova, Seville, Malaga, and Granada, which all date from the first half of the tenth century, were especially active in training men, some of whom carried their pharmacologic and chemical knowledge to the courts and monasteries of Europe. In particular the port of Salerno and the island of Sicily, which were predominantly Moslem in culture, became major sources of the pharmacologic and chemical literature that disseminated through Europe during the tenth to thirteenth centuries.

In 1240, the Emperor Frederick II, who was described as the second of the two baptized sultans of Sicily, promulgated a law for the regulation of the practice of medicine (which included drug control) within the Kingdom of the Two Sicilies. As a semi-oriental in his personal habits, he followed the laudable Islamic practice of forbidding physicians to have any business relations with apothecaries or to own apothecary shops. *"Apothecaries must conduct their business with a certificate from a physician, according to the regulations and upon their own credit and responsibility, and they shall not be permitted to sell their products without having taken an oath that all their drugs have been prepared in the prescribed form, without any fraud..."*

In founding the University of Naples, Frederick not only stocked its library with translations he had commissioned from the Arabic writings but provided copies to the libraries of Paris and Bologna. As a result, English students who later congregated at Oxford and Cambridge were exposed to transplanted Arab culture in Paris, and also, to some extent, as a result of travel in Spain. However, even prior to this period, Arab influences were clearly apparent in the Anglo-Saxon herbals of eleventh and twelfth century England which are decorated with pictures of animals, such as the scorpion, and plants which did not exist in the British Isles. Bartholomaeus Anglicus (*fl.* 1225), while a professor of theology at Paris, wrote a general encyclopedia, *De proprietatibus rerum* (a manifestation of the ecclesiastic tendency to produce encyclopedias of the type produced by Isidorus Hispalensis and Hrabanus Maurus) which, although neither original nor a herbal, was characterized as *"the only original treatise on herbs written by an Englishman during the Middle Ages"*!

Pharmacology was an extremely corrupt discipline (*sic*) within the British Isles, and complicated by a variety of local prejudices, including the legacy of Greco-Roman material as well as ancient Druidic superstitions. English practitioners did not trouble themselves greatly about the efficacy of their prescriptions and, indeed, many practiced in a fashion that would currently be regarded as highly irregular if not unethical. Examples of such instances are evident in the writings of Gilbert of England (*fl.* 1245) and in John of Gaddesden's (1280-1361) *Rosa Anglica, practica medicina acapite ad pedes. Emendatum per Nicola Scyllatium*. Gilbertus was a leading exponent of Anglo-Norman medicine and the author of several medical treatises. Although his writings abound with the superstitious remedies and polypharmaceutical prescriptions of the day, he was aware of the folly of these and lamely excused himself by saying that while it was his preference to follow simple remedies, fear of criticism led him to popular compliance. A long line of anecdotes stem from Gilbert's method of treating lethargy by placing a sow in the patient's bed.

The occupation of the Iberian peninsula by the Moors returned Galenic medicine and Arab chemical and mathematical sophistication to a Europe that had for centuries languished devoid of scientific enquiry.

Gilbertus Anglicus was a leading exponent of Anglo-Norman medicine and the author of several medical treatises, some of which contained bizarre therapeutic suggestions. For the expulsion of calculi, he employed the blood of a goat that had been fed on break-stone and parsley and advised a prescription (containing ant eggs, oil of scorpions, or flesh of lions, for the treatment of apoplexy. On the other hand, he appeared capable of sensible work and gave detailed instructions for the preparation of numerous solutions, among which were ammonium acetate and distillation as a means of purifying water. Much humor has arisen from Gilbert's method of treating lethargy by placing a sow in the patient's bed!

The power of alchemy was considered as intimately related to that of the sun and fire. The influence of the male and female principles was similarly regarded as a vital consideration in the successful union of any chemical agents.

A Pharmaceutical Vocabulary

Name	Origin	Description
Acetabulum	Roman	Vinegar vessel
Acetum Philosophicum		Honey vinegar
Acopon		Stimulating liniment
Adept		An alchemist who "had attained"
Adust		Dried up condition of the humors
Aggregatives	Mesue	Mesue's pills to purge humors
Alabaster	Egypt	Lime carbonate used for ointment containers
Album Rhasis	Rhazes	White lead ointment
Alembic	Arab	A still
Alembroth	Chaldaic	"Salt of wisdom" (mercury/ammonium chloride)
Alexipharmic	Greek	Poison remedy
Alexitria		Remedy against venomous animal bite
Alhandal	Arab	Colocynth
Alkahest	Paracelsus	Universal solvent
Alkali	Arab	Plant ashes
Alkekengi		Winter cherry (kidney/urinary)
Alkool	Boerhaave	"Purest inflammable principle"
Aloedarium		Aloe purgative medicine
Aludels		Sublimation pot
Amalgam	Arab	Mercury metal compound
Amphora		Seven to Nine gallon earthenware vessel for wine or oil
Analeptica		Restorative remedy
Anoyntment		Ointment
Antidotary		Book of formulas or ideas
Antidote		"Given against"
Apozem	Greek	"Boiled off", decoction or infusion
Aqua Mirabilis		Water distilled from cloves and spices
Aquila alba		Calomel
Arcana		Secrets
Athanor		Self-supplying furnace
Balm/Balsam	Semitic	Spices
Basilicon	Celsus	Royal ointment
Baths		For digesting substances
Bezoards		Diaphoretic antimony
Blisters	Venice	Introduced during the plague
Bolus	Greek	"Lump of earth" – a stiff medicine
Calx		Burnt lime
Caput		Retort residues
Carminative		Medicine to expel wind
Cataplasm	Greek	"To apply over" – perfumed powders
Catholica		Electuary to purge humors
Cerates		Wax solidified ointments
Cerevisiae	18th C	Medicinal beer
Ceruse	Latin	White lead
Cochleare	Latin	Prescription term – a spoonful
Cohobation		Repetition of distillation
Colcothar		Rust of iron
Collutories		Mouth/gum medicine
Collyrium	Greek	"Roll of bread" – powders
Conserves		A sugared medicine
Crocus		Metallic combinations of a saffron color
Crucible		A vessel in which metals are melted
Cucupha		Cap with aromatic drugs for headaches
Cucurbit		Retort gourd-shaped vessel of glass or earth
Cyathus	Roman	A wineglass measure (1/12th of a pint)
Decocta	Nero	Boiled water with ice and fruits
Deliquium		Deliquiescence
Despumation		Removal of froth from boiling honey/syrup
Dia	Greek	"Through" or "from"
Diagredium		A modifier of purgative action
Dropax	Greek	"Pitch plaster" – a depilatory
Drug		Ingredient
Eclegma		Thick syrup to relieve coughs
Ecussons		Plasters of theriaca
Edulcorate		Deprive substances of acrid taste
Electuary	Greek	Something that could be licked
Elixir	Arab	Essence or quintessence
Emplastra	Celsus	Lead plaster
Emulsion		Milky liquid extract
Enchrista	Celsus	Liquid liniment

Name	Origin	Description
Enema	Greek	"something sent"
Ens		Essence
Epithema		Alcoholic fomentation applied to heart or stomach
Errhines	Latin	Sneeze exciting substances
Gas	Van Helmont	"Chaos"
Gilla Vitriola		White vitriol
Gutteta		Epilepsy
Hepars		Chemicals of a liver color
Infusions	1720	Distillation of an agent – usually by boiling
Julep	Arab	Clear, sweet liquid
Katapotia	Greek	Little balls of bitter medicinal antidotes
Lac Virginale		Dilute solution of lead acetate for complexions
Lapis Infernalis		Nitrate of silver
Lapis Medicamentosus		Astringent, with iron oxide
Lapis Mirabilis		Application for wounds made with green vitriol
Looch	Arab	"To lick" – thick liquid for throat/lung irritation
Maceration		Digestion of a solid in a liquid
Magdaleon		Cylindrical plasters
Magistery		A potent conversion of a substance
Magma		Substance of soft consistence
Magnes Arsenicalis		Sulfur/arsenic/antimony plaster for syphilitic sores
Malagamata		Skin softening substance, a poultice
Malaxation		Process of softening a pill or plaster
Manica Hypocratis		Bag to filter pharmaceutical preparations
Manipulus		Handful measure of herbs or flowers
Manus Christi		Rose flavored sugar tablet
Manus Dei		Myrrh and frankincense containing plaster
Marmalade		Conserve of a fruit
Masticatory		Chewable substance to excite saliva
Matrass		Vessel to digest or evaporate liquids
Mellites		Syrup made with honey
Mensis Philosophicus		Forty days (a Philosophic month)
Menstruum		Solvent
Moxa		Oriental cauterization
Notulica	Boyle	Phosphorus
Nutrition		The act of combining substances in a mortar
Nychthemeron		Maceration for 24 hrs
Obolos	Greek	Weight of half a scruple
Oenalaion		Wine and oil mix
Oenogala		Wine and milk mix
Oenomeli		Wine and honey mix
Oesypus	Dioscorides	Wool fat
Ointment	Greek	Liquid
Opiate		Electuary containing a narcotic, toothpaste
Oxycorceum		Vinegar and saffron plaster
Panchrest		Remedy for all complaints
Panchymagogon		Medicine to purify all humors
Pedilavium		Herb decoction applied to feet to induce sleep
Pelican		Redistillation vessel
Periapt		Amulet to drive away contagion
Pessary	Greek	"Little round stone" – for vaginal complaints
Pill	Pliny the Elder	Drug
Poison		Draught/potion
Polychrest		Medicine of many virtues
Pomatum		Apple ointment to beautify the face
Populeum		Ointment from black poplar, a narcotic
Poultice	Greek	"Pottage", something beaten
Propomata	Galen	Drinks made of wine and honey (4:1)
Psilothrum		Depilatory
Salamanders' blood		Red vapors of nitrous acid
Salia		Salt
Sinapism		Mustard poultice used as a counter-irritant
Smegma		Skin application
Sparadrap		Adhesive plaster
Suffumenta		Inhaled aromatic to fortify the brain
Supplantalia		Remedies applied to soles of feet
Suppository		Anal medication – replacement enema
Syrup	Arab	Sherbert
Tisane	Celsus	Infusions of herbs
Troches	Greek	"A cone", lozenges or pastilles

The legend of the "Quest for the Golden Fleece" was reconstituted in the relentless alchemical search for the philosopher's stone or the ultimate remedy for all disease.

William Caxton (1422-1491) was a translator and publisher as well as the first English printer. "The Recuyell of the Historyes of Troye" was the first book printed in English in 1475. Johann Gutenberg (bottom left inset) (c. 1396-1468), the German craftsman and inventor who originated a method of printing from movable type that was used without any significant change until the 20th century.

An early 16th-century printing press. The publication of medical information led to a widespread dissemination of knowledge. In particular it enabled rapid awareness of the properties of drugs recently acquired from the New World to be transmitted throughout Europe.

Printing and Evolution of the Pharmacopoeia

Printing

Gutenberg and Caxton's invention and application of the process of printing exerted an important effect upon the literature of therapeutic substances. Thus, the previously daunting prospect of preparing illustrations and descriptions of plants by separate processes had discouraged the production of really accurate, illustrated, botanical works.

Not surprisingly, the 1477 edition of *Odo Moremendensis* text was not illustrated but the *Lignamine* edition of Apuleius, although poorly done, demonstrated that printing could maintain reproductive accuracy within practical limits of cost. Full advantage was taken of this process by Peter Schoffer, the partner of Johann Gutenberg (Gensfleisch, 1400?-1468) in 1484, when he produced a Latin *Herbarius*, also commonly known as the *Aggregator* and entitled *Herbarius Maguntie impressus* (i.e., "The herbal printed at Mainz"). The publication of this Latin *Herbarius* appears to have provided the stimulus for a subsequent book work commonly referred to as the *German Herbarius* and entitled *Herbarius zu teutsch*. Far more elaborate in design and structure than its predecessor, its preface proudly proclaimed its title as the *Ortus sanitatis* or *Gart d'Gesuntheyt*. The editor, Johann Wonnecke Kalb (*fl.* 1460-1503), directed its publication by the Schoffer press in Mainz in 1485, including figures which, unlike the conventional diagrams in the Latin *Herbarius*, were drawn from nature and were not surpassed until the time of Brunfels, Bock, and Fuchs. About 1485, the German *Herbarius*, or the *Circa Instans* of Platearius, was translated into French and published under the title *Arbolayre contenat la qualitey et virtus proprietey des herbes gômes et siméces extraite de, plusiers tratiers de medicine coment da vicene de Rasis de Constatin de Ysaac et Plateaire selon le conu usaige bien correct* (Lyons, 1485). In 1491, Jakob Meidenbach (Meydenbach), another Mainz publisher, brought out a greatly enlarged *Ortus (Hortus) Sanitatis* which contained a large amount of non-botanical material and was furnished with an unusual number of fanciful illustrations.

The first published English herbal was printed by Richard Banckes (London, 1525), and known as *An Herball* or alternatively as the *Banckest Herbal*, since it had not been provided with a formal title *per se*. This work is arranged in alphabetical order and, though possessing some of the characters of the earlier Anglo-Saxon leech-books and manuscript recipe-books, does not derive from contemporary material. It began with the opening words: "*Here begynnyth a new mater, the whiche sheweth and treateth of ye vertues & proprytes of herbes, the whiche is called an herball.*" Although not illustrated and often lacking in description of the plant whose medicinal virtues were listed, it was considered to provide more information than the more popular *The Grete Herball* published in London the following year. The latter represented a direct translation of *Le grand herbier* that had been published in Paris by Pierre Sergent some time between 1491 and 1526, and which itself drew its material from the inferior *Ortus sanitatis* of 1491 as well as the much earlier *De simplici medicina*, attributed to Platearius. In actuality the preface of *The Grete Herball* bore a strong resemblance to that of the German *Herbarius* and its illustrations were for the most part simply inferior copies of those in later editions of that work.

The so-called "herbals" were in fact somewhat misnamed in that they did not confine themselves to herbs, but were in effect "*pharmacopeias for the poor which described, for the benefit of the reader, useful substances from each of the three natural kingdoms*; . . ." Thus the "herbal" included not only herbs but also minerals and chemical materials. Relatively pure chemical substances, introduced by the Arab writers, played an increasingly important role from the thirteenth century onward and, during the next two centuries, a particularly relevant change in the focus of pharmacology was provided by the growing popularity of alchemic experimentation. Ultimately, however, the major event that transfigured pharmacology at the end of the fifteenth and the beginning of the sixteenth century was the discovery of the New World. The identification of a diversity of novel botanical agents transferred by exploring vessels back to the botanical gardens of Europe temporarily carried therapy in the direction of treating diseases by means of herbs rather than chemical substances.

Some estimate of the vast influence of American botanical products upon European therapeutics is evident in the work of the successful Spanish practitioner Nicolas Monardes, although his list fails by any means to cover all the substances brought to Europe and which ultimately influenced the *materia medica*. As a physician during the height of Spanish maritime power, the intellectually alert Monardes was in the fortunate position to examine samples of most of the vast number of new Indian and American drugs, herbs, and substances. His treatise of 1574, describing the drugs and medicines of the Indies and the Occident, was literary culmination of these investigations and described substances as diverse as sarsaparilla, bloodstones, and various gums, which, although well-known were most illuminating. His accounts of guaiac, sassafras, and bezoar stones are of particular interest. His comments on tobacco reflect the early history of the agent that had been first brought to Europe, in about 1558 by Francisco Fernandez (Hernandez, 1514-1587). (It is worth noting that Sir Walter Raleigh (1552-1618), who is claimed by some to have "*first brought tobacco back to Europe*," was a mere child at the time!). Some years later, Jean Nicot (1530-1600), the French ambassador to the Portuguese court, (eponymously remembered by the genus *Nicotiana* and nicotine), upon his return to France

DE HISTORIA STIRPIVM COMMENTARII INSIGNES, MAXIMIS IMPENSIS ET VIGILIIS ELABORATI, ADIECTIS EARVNDEM VIVIS PLVSQVAM quingentis imaginibus, nunquam antea ad naturæ imitationem artificiosius effictis & expresis, LEONHARTO FVCHSIO medico hac nostra ætate longè clarissimo, autore.

Regiones peregrinas plerique, alij alias, sumptu ingenti, studio indefesso, nec sine discrimine uitæ nonnunquam, adierunt, ut simplicium materiæ cognoscendæ facultatem compararent sibi: eam tibi materiam uniuersam summo & impensarum & temporis compendio, procul discrimine omni, tanquam in uiuo iucundissimoque uiridario, magna cum uoluptate, hinc cognoscere licebit.

Accessit ijs succincta admodum uocum difficilium & obscurarum passim in hoc opere occurrentium explicatio.

Vnà cum quadruplici Indice, quorum primus quidem stirpium nomenclaturas græcas, alter latinas, tertius officinis seplasiariorum & herbarijs usitatas, quartus germanicas continebit.

PALMA ISING▸

Cautum præterea est inuictissimi CAROLI *Imperatoris decreto, ne quis alius impunè usquam locorum hos de stirpium historia commentarios excudat, iuxta tenorem priuilegij antè à nobis euulgati.*

BASILEAE, IN OFFICINA ISINGRINIANA, ANNO CHRISTI M. D. XLII.

The frontispiece of De Historia Stirpium *by the herbalist Leonhard Fuchs. Texts such as this provided much-needed information in regard to the identification of plants for medicines.*

successfully cultivated tobacco and sent some of the plants to Catherine de Medici (1519-1589). It is to a large extent due to Nicot that the dissemination of the knowledge of its value was promulgated throughout Europe. Thus, during the sixteenth century, innumerable healing powers were attributed to the substance and it was frequently referred to under a variety of salubrious terms including *herba panacea, herba santa*, or *sana sancta Indorum*. A prescient individual, Monardes was not irrevocably committed to the doctrine of vegetable drugs and the last part of his second volume contains a serious evaluation of iron and its medical applications.

During the Renaissance, the scholar commentary of Petrus Andreas Matthiolus (Pietro Andrea Mattioli, 1500-1577) upon Dioscorides evolved as the absolute epitome of botanical information. His text systematically discussed in considerable detail and with great accuracy the characteristics and uses of each of the plants enumerated by Dioscorides as well as providing illustrations of the highest quality. Indeed the contribution of Mattioli would remain the standard reference until well into the nineteenth century and the development of modern botanical science.

While it is difficult to precisely determine who might be credited with the formal establishment of the science of botany F. Greene has proposed that the "fathers" were four German herbalists: Otto Brunfels (1488-1534), Leonhard Fuchs (1501-1566), Hieronymus Bock or Tragus (1498-1554) and Valerius Cordus (1515-1544). These men differed from Mattioli in that, although they discussed medicinal virtues of plants, they were more focused on their correct identification and a minute description of their characteristics than the diversity of the potential pharmaceutical usages. All four separately and virtually contemporaneously, perceived that no accurate identification of botanical specimens could be achieved by the simple descriptive processes previously employed and engaged in a serious attempt to develop a system of precise and meaningful classification. Unfortunately the scientific limitations of the period and the simplicity of their methodology hampered the development of a reasonable system and the resolution of the matter awaited the later attentions of Andreas Cesalpinus and, more particularly, the Swede, Linnaeus.

Pharmacopoeia

Although the evolution of therapy has followed a long and complex route in evolving to its current state, even more difficult has been the task of maintaining structure and order in cataloguing the diverse variety of agents that have been employed over the ages as drugs. As might be expected, some of the earliest compilations were produced by the educated monks of the churches that served as hospitals in the Middle Ages. A number of institutions were particularly active in this respect and the texts that have been handed down represent an extraordinary example of erudition and medical skill. Of these, a small church, the Santo Spirito in Sassia, is sited outside of Rome close to where the Tiber winds its way southward around the Janiculum hills. The church is an integral part of what is considered as one of the earliest hospitals in the world. It was founded almost thirteen centuries ago by some Saxon priests and was the center of the *Schola Saxonum*, a hospice and refuge for pilgrims traveling to Rome from England. The institution had been well supported by England over many centuries because of its interest in having its own hospital in Rome and thus provided for its maintenance, defense, and restoration. In addition, considerable aid was provided to it by a succession of popes who not only defended it in times of travail but also, on a number of occasions, provided finance to rebuild it. The hospital was given a new lease of life when Innocent III invited Guy de

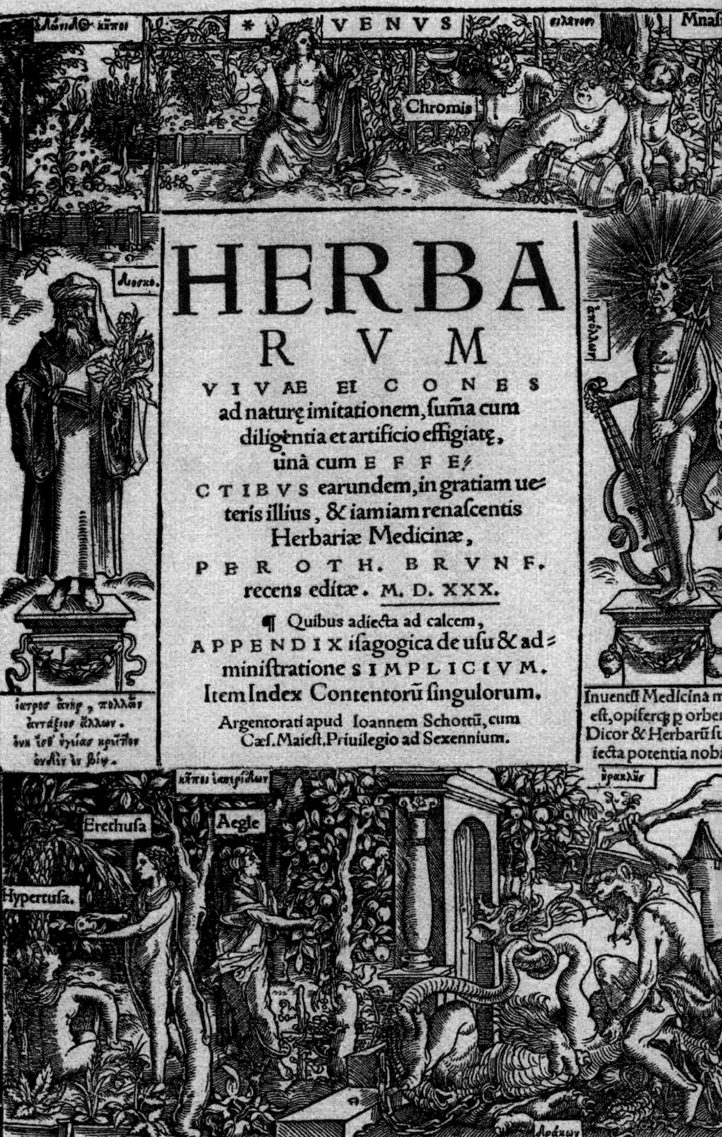

VENVS

Chromis

HERBARVM VIVAE EICONES ad naturę imitationem, sum̃a cum diligentia et artificio effigiatę, unà cum EFFECTIBVS earundem, in gratiam ueteris illius, & iamiam renascentis Herbariæ Medicinæ, PER OTH. BRVNF. recens editæ. M. D. XXX.

¶ Quibus adiecta ad calcem, APPENDIX isagogica de usu & administratione SIMPLICIVM. Item Index Contentorũ singulorum.

Argentorati apud Ioannem Schottũ, cum Cæs. Maiest. Priuilegio ad Sexennium.

Erechusa

Aegle

Hypercusa.

The frontispiece of Herbarum Vivae Icones *by Otto Brunfels. The text marks an epoch in the art of botanic illustration and consisted of 135 configurations of plants executed by Hans Weydiz, the finest wood engraver of Strassbourg.*

The church of Santo Spirito in Sassia outside of Rome, where one of the earliest texts of pharmacology was assembled.

Montpellier to take over its administration, and further support was provided by the decree of King John that the revenues from Writtle Abbey, near London, should be used to maintain the hospital. As a result of this significant support and the substantial individuals to its mission, it developed one of the first hospital pharmacies and in addition a catalogue of its contents. This compilation became known as the *Antidotarium Romanum seu de modo Componendi Medicamenta* (1583) and later, the *Codice Farmaceutico Romano* (1869). As such it achieved important status as one of the earliest documented texts of pharmacology.

Each country, and even city, sought to generate its own pharmacopoeia in an effort to codify drug usage and instill order into an area that heretofore had been characterized not only by confusion but also charlatanry and outright dishonesty.

History of Texts

The evolution of pharmacopoeias is an interesting and fascinating story of the documentation of knowledge. As therapy evolved and the delineation of substances and their usage became more complex and important to physicians, it became even more important to define and document substances and their usage. It is possible to follow the progress of pharmacopoeias, from the first treatises written by individual authors, through collective works officially accepted, first by a city then by country, finally to international pharmacopoeias. The word "pharmacopoeia" comes from the Greek, meaning to make or to prepare drugs. However, the term did not come into use until the sixteenth century, since before that such texts were variously referred to as *antidotaria, electuaria, dispensatoria* or even *ricettari*. Although the first prescriptions for the preparation of medicines with special reference to plants are contained in the texts of Hippocrates, Galen, and Dioscorides, a manuscript dedicated exclusively to drugs, *De Compositione Medicamentorum*, was written in the first century A.D. by Scribonius Largus and constituted the primary source of knowledge during the Roman period. As such it consisted of a list of formulas for compounded medicines and of descriptions of certain drugs to be used for particular diseases.

Unfortunately, much knowledge of medicine and pharmacy was lost during the barbaric Middle Ages in Europe. As a result, knowledge of this area of history is to a certain extent limited, and little is known of the evolution of pharmacy between the fourth and the tenth centuries. Thus, much of the information is fragmentary and as a result, considerable speculation has occurred. It is, however, clear that during this time pharmacy flourished in the Near East as a result of the information which had been transmitted to the Arab lands during the period of the ancient Greco-Roman and Byzantine civilizations. Among the men who contributed to it were Mesue of Damascus, Rhazes (d. 923-4), a Persian, author of *Liber Continens*, and Avicenna (980-1037), also a Persian, author of the famous *Canone*.

The Ricettario Fiorentino, *produced in Florence in 1497, was the first pharmacopoeia ever published.*

Thus, information obtained from Arab texts comprised a predominant part in the first European texts on drugs, such as the *Antidotarium Nicolai* (1150) that was compiled and subsequently annotated in Salerno. This book was widely used throughout the entire Kingdom of the Two Sicilies. A subsequent text which appeared in the thirteenth century was almost certainly the work of a Westerner, although of Arab culture, and was attributed to

John Mesue, who had been dead for more than two centuries. All the subsequent contributions, up to the nineteenth century, from the *Ricettario Fiorentino* to the *Pharmacopoeia Londinensis*, attest to the names and inspiration of the great Arab scholars of the art of pharmacology.

In the period between the tenth and thirteenth centuries, there appear to have been three fundamental texts for the preparation of drugs. The first of these was the *Antidotario Parva Nicolai* of Salerno, the second the *Pseudo Mesue* (as detailed above) and the third a work of Byzantine origin known as the *Antidotarium Nicolai Myrepsi*. All of these texts documented lists of compounded preparations as well as descriptions of some simple drugs. As such they were little more than vast collections of prescriptions that ranged from the simple to the complex, and even included the famous theriacs and mithridates.

Legal recognition

While anybody could in theory prepare a text and publish it, authenticity and validity were guaranteed if the work received official recognition. In this respect, the first legal and certified recognition of a text on the preparation of drugs came from Frederick II of Hohenstaufen who, in 1240, through his *Novae Constitutiones* of the Kingdom of the Two Sicilies, separated the medical and the pharmaceutical professions, the latter being called the "*confectionarii*" or apothecaries. They were ordered to make the preparations *iuxta formam constitutionis* (according to the law). To consolidate this prescient declaration, the *Antidotario Parva Nicolai* of Salerno, revised by Matthaeus Platearius of the Salernitan School, was selected as the authoritative text. As might be expected for the times, it was composed in Latin and as a result almost all subsequent pharmacopoeias until the nineteenth century used this as their common language.

The interior of a medieval pharmacy.

The first official pharmacopoeia was produced in republican Florence, in 1497, by apothecaries at the College of the Art of Medicine, who on the instructions of the university, compiled the *Ricettario Fiorentino*. The work, based broadly on the *Antidotario Parva Nicolai,* was written in Italian, and thereafter translated into Latin. It contained a diverse number of preparations of various drugs and the descriptions of plants, minerals, and organs to be used in treating patients. The subsequent editions, beginning in 1550, appeared during the rule of the Medici and, as well as descriptions of drug preparations, contained a general section on the needs of a pharmacy and the methods to be followed in its organization and maintenance. In addition, they also included all the laws and regulations laid down by the Medici rulers governing the practice of the arts of medicine and pharmacy.

The Florentine *Ricettario* proved to be the gold standard of pharmacology and its influence in Europe was as great, if not greater than, the works of Mesue and of Nicolaus of Salerno. As a result, the *Ricettario* became the text most widely used as the pharmacopoeia of the countries beyond the Alps, or was used as the model on which each developed its own pharmacopoeia. Among these, one of great importance is the *Dispensatorium* of Valerius Cordus, who was born in Erfurt and widely recognized as a great connoisseur of the plants known in his day. He was famous among his contemporaries because of his exceptional knowledge in this field, and traveled widely throughout Germany and Italy, where he completed his studies. Valerus was highly regarded of in Venice, but on reaching Rome, died prematurely in 1544 at the age of twenty-nine years. In the *Dispensatorium* he amplified the original text model provided by the *Ricettario* and added his own original observations and critical annotations on the use of the medicines described in the text. In so doing, he also established a new character to the traditional pharmacopoeia, based on subdivisions of the individual preparations according to their pharmaceutical type. The *Dispensatorium* was adopted by the city of Nuremberg as its official pharmacopoeia in 1546, and revised and edited by Peter Coudenberg of Antwerp (1564), before transmogrification into many different languages and about forty editions in Latin. As a result of its lucidity of style and medical as well as pharmaceutical utility, it became the official text in Germany and in numerous cities in the Low Countries. Indeed, its success can only be compared with that of the Florentine *Ricettario*, whose last editions were published as late as the nineteenth century.

A subsequent work of major import was the *Enchiridion pro Reipublicae Augsburgensis of Occo* (1564), which later, after numerous revisions, became the *Pharmacopoeia Augustana*. In 1653 the Viennese school of medicine represented by Zwelfer, a physician at the Viennese court, amplified this text by producing an edition that contained a series of "*animadversiones*" observations and added "*mantissae*" in an attempt to modify pharmacopoeias such that they might represent critical works rather than a simple books of prescriptions alone.

A selection of pharmaceutical storage jars surround a ceramic mortar and pestle. With the advent of pharmacopoeias the precise constituents of all remedies were documented.

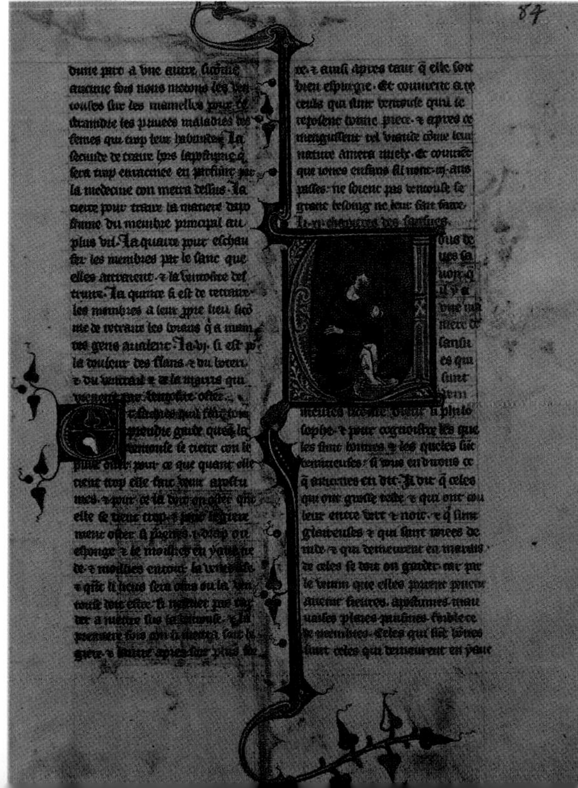

A page from the Antidotarium *of Aldobrandini of Sienna. Despite the magnificence of the text, such documents were impractical for general usage and the introduction of printed pharmacopoeia led to their relegation to the libraries of scholars.*

Medical knowledge was influenced by factors outside of medicine. In particular, the growth of commerce, the new learning of the Renaissance, Johann Gutenberg's invention of a printing press using movable type, and a substantial expansion of lay literacy, widened the circle of book collectors to include wealthy merchants whose libraries contained herbals, books of law and medicine, and books of hours and other devotional works. Italian humanists, such as Petrarch and Boccaccio, searched for and copied manuscripts of classical writings to establish their scholarly libraries while scholars such as Niccolò Niccoli (librarian to Cosimo de Medici) and Gian Francesco Poggio Bracciolini shared this enthusiasm for the classics. Notable collections of books were made outside Italy, too (though Florence remained the center of the rising book trade): by Diane de Poitiers; by Jean Grolier, a high French official and diplomat; Henry VIII of England; and by many others.

In 1618, the initial attempts at formalization of medical practice in England resulted in the publication of the *Pharmacopoeia Londinensis*. Although at first little more than a simple formulary, it was subsequently amplified by the introduction of other information into the later editions. Thus, in conjunction with the classical prescriptions of Mesue, such as the *pilulae de agarico*, or the *pilulae aribicae* of Nicola, can be found the *valentia scabioae* of John of Arderne, surgeon to Edward III. Of note is the foreword penned as a decree by James I in announcing the basis of the text of the *Pharmacopoeia Londinensis* in 1618, which sum up the true purpose and spirit of every pharmacopoeia:

tending to the public good of our subjects
and we minding that the falsehood, differences, varieties
and uncertainties in making compositions of
medicines... hereafter be utterly taken away and abolished,
and that in the time to come the manner and form
by the said book should be generally and solely practiced
by apothecaries for the common good of our subjects...

Modifications and Innovations

Although by the eighteenth century the general pharmacopoeias had acquired a critical character that included general methods and observations, they still basically conformed to the classical style of medieval formulary. Thus, at the end of the eighteenth century almost all the pharmacopoeias, from the *Londinensis* to the *Antidotarium Bononiense*, or to the *Pharmacopoeia Taurinensis*, still contained preparations such as theriac or the mithridates. However, in some situations innovations were beginning to enter the formulaic approach, thus, in the *Antidotarium Bononiense*, it can be noted that details of a chemical pharmacopoeia are evident. Similar examples are evident in the *Augustana* and in the work of Aldrovandi. A further innovation and amplification was provided by the inclusion and commentary provided in respect of new plants and herbs such as ipecacuanha and quinine that had been acquired in the Orient and the Occident.

When considered in terms of their publication rather than content, the various pharmacopoeias fall into the following order: the *Londinensis*, in 1618, *Brandenburgensis* of 1698, the *Edinburgensis* of 1699 for Scotland, the Austrian *Pharmacopoeias*, derivation and integration of the *Augustana* in 1729, the *Portuguese Pharmacopoeia* in 1794, in 1778 the *Russian Pharmacopoeia* and the Prussian or Borussic text in 1744. Thus, by the end of the eighteenth century, the majority of pharmacopoeias were vast collective works compiled by commissions of scholars qualified in the various subjects that comprised the huge body of material that they covered.

In 1818, the *Codex Medicamentarius Gallicus* was finally completed after a long process of preparation. At that time, official pharmacopoeias of individual cities and regions, numbering about one hundred, were substituted by about twenty-seven national pharmacopoeias that corresponded to the delineation of the various European nations in the nineteenth century. Common standards of preparation were introduced in the various countries, and led to the incorporation of a mature and reasonably balanced scientific approach that included the botany of Linneus, the chemistry of Boyle, Scheele, Lavoisier, Dalton, Gay-Lussac, Avogadro, Faraday and Volta. Overall this represented a

The content of modern day pharmacopoeia has expanded to cover diverse medications as well as the advances of molecular medicine.

victory of the scientific method over the empiricism that prior to this time had dominated the *Antidotaria*.

As a result of this readiness to adopt a more rigorous scientific approach, it became possible to introduce precise chemical terminology into the new texts, as well as a logical system of classification of the botanic material according to Linneus. The authors of the pharmacopoeia adapted themselves rapidly to such innovations and gradually eliminated a certain number of formulae while accepting a series of simple chemical products. Nevertheless the pharmacopoeias of the period comprised for the most part innumerable prescriptions and lists of plants and chemical products. In order to remedy this obsessive focus on purely descriptive material, a critical section dealing with methodology was added. Thus, major sections detailing techniques of plants recognition, chemical analysis and compound determination were added. Despite these significant advances and improvements in including all the aspects of a new formulation, the pharmacopoeias were still essentially designed for the use of pharmacists who primarily needed methods that defined the official preparations and the basic ingredients for other medicinal preparations.

The scientific evolution of Pharmacopoeia

From the end of the last century to the present day, the pharmacopoeias of the world have been considerably influenced by the scientific and industrial evolution of the period. Up to the end of the nineteenth century, drugs were prepared almost exclusively in the pharmacies from chemical or vegetable raw materials. Gradually, the work was taken over by specialized pharmaceutical laboratories and finally by the large industrial companies. The development of chemistry, microbiology, technology and scientific research has resulted in many new products – hormones, vitamins, antibiotics – whose preparation is complex and can only be undertaken using complex industrial equipment. Consequently, the pharmacopoeia has acquired the characteristics of a codex of quality control. In addition, as novel medicinal agents are introduced, the number of official preparations has decreased while the pharmaceutical form of the drugs – for example, injectants, intravenous infusions, depot agents, inhalants, suppositories, capsules, tablets – has increased. The rigorous standardization of methods necessary implies the introduction into the pharmacopoeias of general methods of chemical, biological, physicochemical and microbiological analyses and control tests of the drugs, as well as of the characteristics of the materials and containers and of the reagents. As a result, the modern pharmacopoeias contain, in addition to the individual monographs, general methods and specifications for reagents together with appendices describing the various analytical determinations and control tests. Notwithstanding this transformation, the pharmacopoeia must remain a guide for the pharmacist and constitute a code for the producers and analysts by means of which the purity and quality of a drug can be determined. Today, there are various criteria for the selection of drugs for inclusion in a pharmacopoeia of which the most important are the therapeutic effect, the commercial aspect, and the degree of safety. For these reasons modern pharmacopoeias have become far less focused on plants, crude drugs and various extracts as the latter become replaced by the active principles.

J. Bowring. First degree board (1819) is an allegory of the ascent into the mysteries of Freemasonery and based on the three great lights (Bible, compass and square). With the advent of chemistry and the introduction of science, pharmaceutical knowledge passed from herbalism and alchemy into a body of information separated from alchemy and mysticism and governed by more rigorous and defined laws of objectivity. Data replaced belief and mysticism was transcended by rationality.

Bohme's system of the Seven Properties of Nature. The early origins of therapeutics vested in astrology, incantation, and the Kabbalah were supplanted by the introduction of chemistry, an understanding of physiology, and finally the recognition that there was a discrete separation between religion and science.

Section 4
Dogmas and Delusions

The consideration of therapeutics in its entirety requires assessment not only of the period where rational applications of herbal medicine were beginning to evolve, but also a consideration of the persons and agents involved in the application of chemical doctrine to remedies. In this respect one of the most erudite medieval philosophers was the Dominican monk, Albertus Magnus (Albert of Cologne, Count of Bollstadt (1193-1280). Although his text *Physica* was based to a relatively large extent upon the natural history of Aristotle, his *De vegetabilibus* which derived, in part, from the Peripatetic, Nicholas of Damascus, included much of his own botanical observations. Magnus was far more than a herbalist and, in fact, scorned taxonomy. It is likely that the chemical knowledge he exhibited was based upon the perusal of earlier Arabic, alchemical texts. He is credited with providing the most intelligent description of the concentration of alcohol by distillation up to his time, as well as the introduction of the word vitriol to designate metallic sulphates.

Albertus Magnus, Geber, and Roger Bacon each contributed greatly to philosophy and alchemy but all maintained a religious background to their science.

In many respects Roger Bacon (1214-1294), who was trained at Paris, may be looked upon as the successor of Magnus. Bacon was clearly a remarkable individual, well-versed not only in theology and philosophy, but also in certain aspects of physics, thus reflecting a considerable Arab influence on his education. Apart from an extraordinary intellect and a diverse appreciation of science and philosophy, his principal contribution reflected a profoundly systematic thought process capable of not only assimilating a large mass of material but imbued with the capacity to interpret in such a way as to explain what otherwise might have appeared to be inconsistencies. As such, he was thoroughly familiar with all the important operations of alchemy and believed not only in the possibility of transmutation of metals but also that the philosopher's stone, when and if found, would fulfill the role of a universal medicine or elixir of life. Although this notion was somewhat older than Bacon, it probably cannot be traced much farther back than Pseudo-Geber and Albucasis. Despite this vain hope in the development of a single remedy, Bacon did not demur from the investigation of the action of individual drugs and was a firm adherent to the "doctrine of signatures." An unfortunate preoccupation with the belief that disease might be produced as a result of astrologic principles led to the establishment of a set of therapeutic concepts that failed to ultimately culminate in any definite or practical results.

Empedocles and Elements

Although Empedocles was the original author of the ancient theory that earth, air, fire, and water were the elements of Nature, the concept was subsequently adopted by Aristotle and remained the pervasive view of chemists until the eighteenth century.

Some speculative philosophers, however, taught that all of these were derived from one original first principle; some held that this was water, some earth, some fire, and others air. Paracelsus, who was not averse to this notion, contributed an alternative and fantastic one to accompany it, in proposing that everything was composed of sulphur, salt, and mercury. In this respect he did not use the terminology as currently accepted but referred to some sort of refined essence of these. The three essentials, according to Beguin, who also accepted the concept of Paracelsus, could be tabulated as below:

Salt	Sulphur	Mercury
Unpleasant – bitter	Sweet	Acid
Body	Soul	Spirit
Matter	Form	Idea
Patient	Agent	Informant
Art	Nature	Intelligence
Sense	Judgement	Intellect
Material	Spiritual	Glorious

In this schema the mercury, sulphur, and salt are not those *"mixt and concrete bodies such as are vulgarly sold by merchants"* but represent the refined essences of the elements themselves. Thus Mercury combines the elements of air and water, Sulphur represents Fire, and Salt, the Earth. According to Beguin, *"But the said principles, to speak properly, are neither bodies; because they are plainly spiritual, by reason of the influx of celestial seeds, with which they are impregnated: nor spirits, because corporeal, but they participate of either nature; and have been insignized*

The alchemical insignia of Albertus Magnus, a Dominican friar. His contributions were of vital importance for the development of medieval philosophy. An individual of immense erudition and intellectual curiosity, he recognized the value of the newly-translated Greco-Arabic scientific and philosophical literature. His encyclopedic writings included everything he considered valuable in them and he taught this literature to his contemporaries. In particular, he sought to promulgate the philosophy of Aristotle and proposed to write original works to complete what was lacking in the Aristotelian system. In no small measure, the triumph of Aristotelianism in the 13th century can be attributed to his contributions.

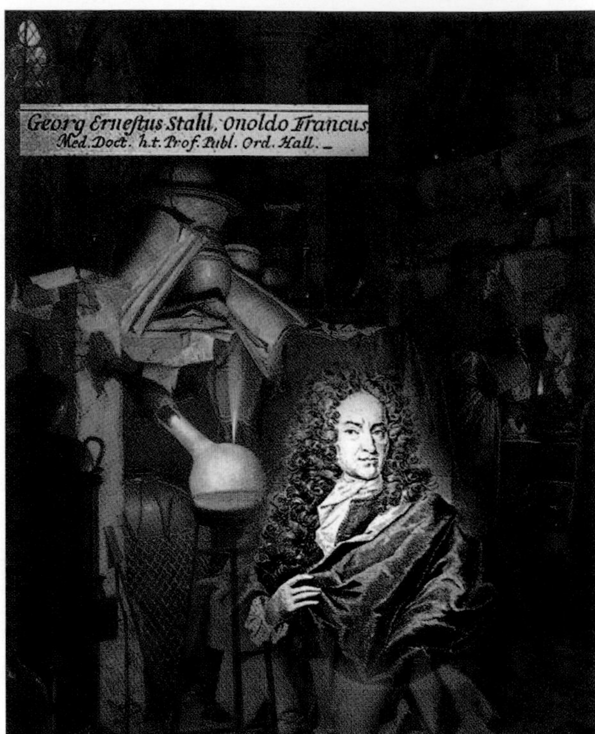

Born at Anspach, 1660; died at Berlin, 1734. Stahl was the originator of the "phlogiston theory," which generally prevailed in chemistry until Lavoisier disproved it in the last quarter of the 18th century. Stahl's contributions to science to a certain degree reflect his personality, which was contemplative, melancholy, and deeply inclined toward the inner-directed religious Pietism of the late 17th century. His intellect, on the other hand, was analytical and sweeping and compelled him toward large abstractions, more a feature of the 18th century. As such he bridged two ages, as did his phlogiston theory, which was the first systematic account of chemical transformation – although he lacked the concepts of atom or element. The roots of his ideas lie not in the prior use of the word phlogiston by Jean Baptist Van Helmont (1577-1644) or in the vaguer theories of Johann Joachim Becher (1635-1682) but in Aristotelian thought: phlogiston is the property of being combustible that is lost in the process of combustion but that may be regained by contact with materials especially rich in phlogiston, such as coal. On an ancient philosophical foundation, Stahl built a practical theory that clarified fundamental chemical concepts.

by Phylosophers with various names, or at the least unto them they have alluded these." He then proceeds to provide examples of the various combinations: If you burn *green woods*, you first have a wateriness, mercury; then there goes forth an oleaginous substance easily inflammable, sulphur; lastly, a dry and terrestrial substance remains, salt. *Milk* contains a sulphurous buttery substance; mercurial, whey; saline, cheese. *Eggs*: white, mercury, yolk, sulphur, shell, salt.

Stahl and Phlogiston

Becker, the predecessor of Stahl, was not quite satisfied with the orthodox opinion, and improved upon it by limiting the elements to water and earth; but he recognized three earths, vitrifiable, inflammable, and mercurial. The last yielded the metals.

Stahl was inclined to go back to the four elements again, but he expressed some doubts in regard to their precise elementary character.

Stahl, however, concentrated his attention on fire, out of which he evolved his well-known phlogiston theory. He proposed that this substance (if it was indeed a substance) was conceived as floating about all through the atmosphere, but only revealed itself by its effects when it came into contact with "material bodies". There was doubt as to whether it possessed the attribute of weight at all, but Stahl believed that its properties were quiescent until united with a substance which thereafter became "phlogisticated". At this point, the putative agent was regarded to exist in a passive condition and required excitation in some special way before its activity could be restored. A confusing and somewhat inexplicable feature of the phlogiston theory developed when it was realized that after the phlogiston was "expelled" from a body, as in the case of the calcination of a metal, the residual calx was heavier than the metal with the phlogiston! The first, and most creative, explanation of this phenomenon was that phlogiston not only possessed "no heaviness", but was actually endowed with the unique faculty of lightness. As might be predicted, seventeenth-century chemists dismissed this notion as fanciful in the extreme. Boerhaave provided a more acceptable proposal, declaring that the phlogiston escaped, it attacked the vessel in which the metal was calcined, and combined some of that with the metal. Unfortunately this notion did not withstand experimental scrutiny and was supplanted by the singularly ingenious explanation of Baume, who insisted that phlogiston was appreciably ponderable. Thus, when it became absorbed into a metal or other substance it did not combine with that substance, but was constantly in motion in the interstices of the molecules. His metaphor was that of a bird in a cage which does not add to the weight of the cage so long as it is flying about. Thus phlogiston did not add to the weight of the metal in which it was similarly flying about in, but when calcination took place the "dead phlogiston" (as he referred to it) combined with the metal, and thus an increase of weight occurred.

Alchemy and Fire. The juncture of the 17th and 18th centuries led to an attempt to evolve beyond alchemical mysticism and reconcile chemical observations with rigorous science.

Temperature and Humors

Hippocrates is usually attributed with proposing the doctrine of the "humors," or humoral pathology and his book, the *Nature of Man,* details his views on the subject. Many have, however, supposed this text to have been written by one or more of his disciples or successors, although Galen regarded it as a genuine treatise by the Physician of Kos himself.

The arcane concepts, as initially proposed, were subsequently elaborated in detail and thereafter Galen provided it with a more dogmatic form. In essence, the concept proposed that the human body was composed not exactly of the four elements, earth, air, fire, and water, but of the "essences" of these elements while the fluid parts, the blood, the phlegm, the bile, and the black bile, were regarded as the four humors. In addition to these constituents there also existed three kinds of spirits, natural, vital, and animal, which were responsible for activating the individual humors.

The blood was the humor which nourished the various parts of the body, and was the source of animal heat, while the bile kept the passages of the body open, and served to promote the digestion of the food. The role of phlegm was to maintain the nerves, the muscles, the cartilages, the tongue, and other organs supple, thus facilitating their movements. The black bile (the melancholy, as Hippocrates referred to it) served as a link between all the other humors and thereby sustained them. In terms of placing this in the context of disease and thereby providing a therapeutic direction, it was considered that the proportion and balance of the individual humors occasioned the temperaments (this concept is still current medical idiom) and sanguine, bilious, phlegmatic, atrabilious or melancholy natures are familiar descriptions to this day.

Each humor exhibited a different character, thus the blood was naturally hot and humid, the phlegm cold and humid, the bile hot and dry, and the black bile cold and dry. As a consequence, alterations of the humors were believed to cause disease conditions or distempers, as they were termed. There might be a too abundant provision of one or more of the humors such that a plethora of blood would cause drowsiness, difficulty of breathing, or fatty degeneration, while a plethora of either of the other humors would have the effect of causing "corruption" of the blood. For example, a plethora of bile was considered to result in a jaundiced condition, bad breath, a bitter taste in the mouth, and other familiar symptoms. Similarly an excess of melancholic humor was considered to culminate in hemorrhoids, leprosy, and cancer, while colds, catarrhas, rheumatisms were occasioned by a superabundance of the phlegm.

To their credit it must be stated that neither Galen nor any other authority proposed that the humors were the sole causes of disease, rather using them as a schema to provide some rationale for drug therapy. Indeed, the theory of the humors provided an excellent framework to enable some degree of logic, albeit fanciful, to not only explain the action of drugs but legitimize a particular prescription. Thus, individual therapeutic agents were each, to a greater or lesser extent, attributed hot, humid, cold, and dry qualities. Galen was quite objective and even classified them in four degrees, such that a specific drug might be hot, humid, cold, or dry in the first, second, third, or fourth degree. In order to prescribe satisfactorily, a physician was required to initially estimate which humor was predominant, and in what degree, and thereafter select a drug which would counteract the disproportionate heat, cold, humidity, or dryness. Since this process could become enormously complex, detailed manuals were compiled to guide him. Thus Nicholas Culpepper of London noted that horehound, for example, was *"hot in the second degree, and dry in the third"* while the herb trinity, or pansies, on the other hand, *"are cold and moist, both herbs and Flowers"* etc. Medicines such as mustard which when applied to the skin, would raise a blister would be considered as hot in the fourth degree, while those which provoke sweat abundantly, and thus *"cut tough and compacted humors"* (Culpepper) could be regarded as hot in the third degree. An interesting example is provided by opium which was classified as cold in the fourth degree, and therefore should only be given alone to mitigate violent pain. The admonition being *"in ordinary cases it is wise to moderate the coldness of the opium by combining something of the first degree of cold or heat with it."*

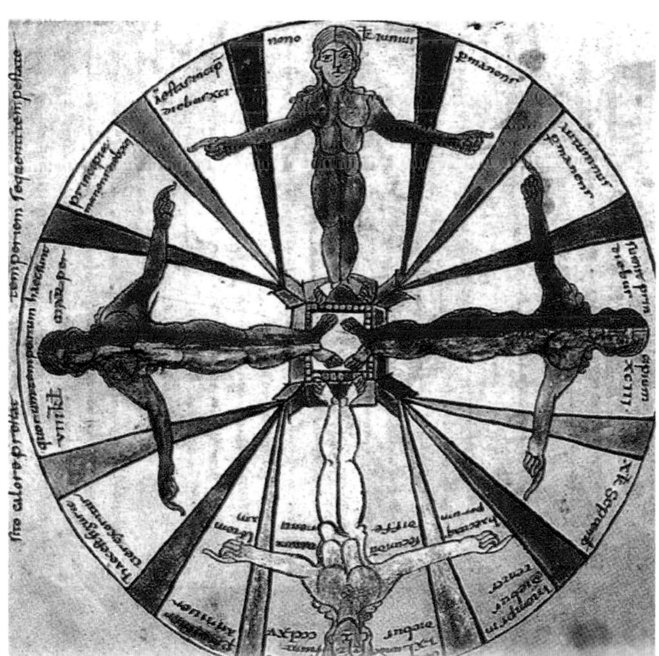
A macro-microcosmic diagram from Isadore of Seville's De Natura Rerum. The four figures represent the seasons of the wheel of twelve months. The microcosmic equivalents are the four humors. Autumn is black gall (Melancholia – Earth) summer – yellow gall (Cholera – fire) spring to the sanguine (Air) and winter to the phlegmatic (Water). The human temperament was thought of as a blend of different humors and temperatures as well as degrees of dryness and moisture. Thus disease and health became considered as a quotient of different components that required a perfect balance to maintain a state of salubriety.

Such complexities were taken to an extreme degree by the Arab physicians who were, in addition, mathematical adepts. Thus Jacob-Ebn-Izhak-Alkhendi (*c.* ninth century), one of the most celebrated philosophers who cultivated mathematics, philosophy, and astrology as well as medicine, extended Galen's theory to compound medicines, explaining their action in accordance with the principles of harmony in music. He proposed that each degree could be regarded as progressing in a geometric ratio, so that the fourth degree counts as 16 compared with unity. The mathematical proposition was expressed as: $x = b^{n-1}a$ where a was regarded as the first, b the last, x the exponent, and n the number of the terms. An example of such a formulation would be as follows.

Medicament	Weight	Hot	Cold	Humid	Dry
Cardamoms	3i	1	1/2	1/2	1
Sugar	3ii	2	1	1	2
Indigo	3i	1/2	1	1/2	1
Myrobalans	3ii	1	2	1	2
Total	3vi	4 1/2	4 1/2	3	6

Such a preparation would thus be deemed to form a mixture exactly balanced in hot and cold properties, but twice as dry as it is humid, thereby rendering the concoction dry in the first degree. If the total had shown twelve of the dry to three of the humid qualities, it would have considered to be dry in the second degree. If one then considers that in addition to these calculations, a physician needed to be cognizant that drugs adapted for one part of the body might be non-functional in another, it becomes evident that the early art of

The Arab physicians and philosophers of the 9th and 10th centuries A.D. embraced Galenic concepts, and in addition amplified them to include mathematics, thus providing some objectivity (albeit abstruse) to an abstract conceptual system

Herbal components remained an important part of Arab medical science but each agent was also considered on a numerical basis rather than as a plant alone.

A Rosicrucian manuscript illustration. In the green mountains of "prima materia" the signs of the relevent materials are assigned to the magic square of Saturn's numbers. At the top, the sun and moon raise their "imperial son" (tintcure of mercury) from its baptism in the retort of chemical knowledge.

prescribing was probably as complex and difficult in the past as it is now, except for different reasons.

Mysteries of the Rosicrucians

There are few groups in history whose arcane beliefs have engendered as much interest and speculation as the Rosicrucians, whose name derives from the order's symbol, a combination of a rose and a cross. Although there is little belief that the Rosicrucian mystics of the Middle Ages did anything for the advancement of pharmacy, they are worthy of mention since they claimed the power of curing disease, and because the fiction which created the legends concerning them was almost contemporaneous with the not dissimilar one (if the latter is fiction?) which created the historical figure of Basil Valentine.

In addition, it seems apparent that many of the thought leaders of chemistry, alchemy, and therapeutics were likely Rosicrucians. Their members were regarded as part of a worldwide brotherhood claiming to possess esoteric wisdom handed down from ancient times, and the teachings of Rosicrucianism combine elements of occultism reminiscent of a variety of religious beliefs and practices. The precise origins of Rosicrucianism are obscure, although the earliest extant document that mentions the order is the *Fama Fraternitatis* (*Account of the Brotherhood*), first published in 1614, which may have given the movement its initial impetus. The *Fama* recounts the journeys of Christian Rosenkreuz, the reputed founder of Rosicrucianism, who was allegedly born in 1378 and lived for 106 years. Although now generally regarded to have been a symbolic rather than a real character, the story provided a legendary explanation of the order's origin. According to the *Fama*, Rosenkreuz (*c.* 1378) acquired his secret wisdom on trips to Egypt, Damascus, Damcar in Arabia, and Fez in Morocco, which he subsequently imparted to three others after his return to Germany. The number of his disciples was later increased to eight, and these much in the same fashion as the Christ disciples traveled to different countries. It is of interest to note that Paracelsus, the Swiss alchemist who died in 1541, is also regarded by some as the actual founder of Rosicrucianism. Others, however, view sixteenth- and seventeenth-century developments as simply a revival of the order and contend that Rosicrucian doctrines not only flourished in ancient Egypt but were espoused by such outstanding philosophical and religious figures as Plato, Jesus, Philo of Alexandria, Plotinus, and others. There is, however, no reliable evidence to date the order's history earlier than the seventeenth century.

To the Reader, Whoever has doubts about the Fraternity of the Rosy Cross, let him read this and having read the poem, he will be certain. ANNO CHRISTI 1617. Written by a Brother of this Fraternity first in Latin, then translated into German and printed by I.S.N.P. & Poet Laureate. Printed at Neuenstadt by Johan Knuber 1618.

Between 1614 and 1616, three works were published professing to reveal the precise (*sic*) history of the brethren of the Rosy Cross. The first was known as *Fama Fraternitatis*, the second was the *Confessio Fraternitatis*, and the third and most important was the *Chymical Marriage of Christian Rosenkreutz*. The treatises were written in a mystic jargon, and have been interpreted as alchemical or religious parables, though vast numbers of learned men adopted the records as statements of facts. It was asserted that Christian Rosenkreutz, a German, born in 1378, had traveled in the East, and from the wise men of Arabia and other countries had learnt the secrets of their knowledge, religious, necromantic, and alchemical.

On his return to Germany he and seven other persons formed this fraternity, which was to be kept secret for a hundred years. The brethren, it is suggested,

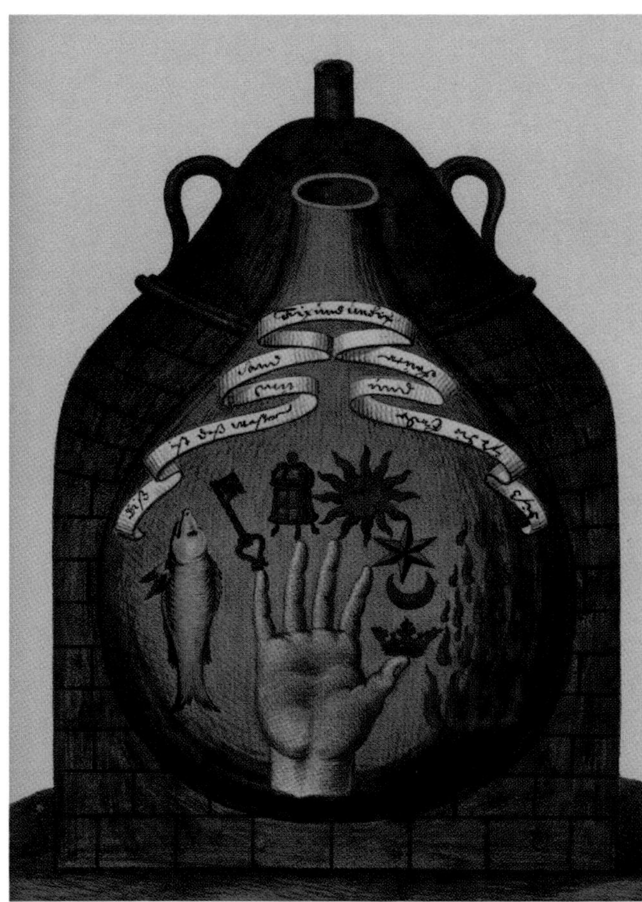

The Rosicrucian sect embodied an extraordinary complexity of alchemy, mysticism and the occult in its creed. The hand of the philosopher (imbued by divine power) contains the seven secret signs to which the ancient sages were bound. (Thumb – saltpetre, Index – vitriol, middle – sal ammoniac, ring – gold, ear finger – common salt, palm – fish of mercury, fire – sulphur). The hand is superimposed upon the elements of chemistry (retort, flask and kiln) while each finger denotes contact with a unique elemental symbol capable of transmuting all into gold. The fire in the palm represents the ultimate power and is vested in the mythical properties of an ageless fish which is mucal-moist Mercury, the copulator or male seed that brings all together.

The entire history of Rosicrucianism remains an enigma within an enigma obfuscated by a paradox. The blend of mysticism, philanthropy, alchemy, and obscure religious beliefs have conspired with the passage of history to produce a shadowy image of a brotherhood, part of whose mission was to alleviate suffering and disease.

communicated to each other their discoveries and the knowledge which had been transmitted to them, to communicate with each other. The precepts of the order were to treat the sick poor free, to wear no distinctive dress, and use the letters C.R. to indicate their allegiance. Although it was well accepted that they had mastered the art of making gold, this was regarded as of no value to them, for they did not seek wealth. In perpetuation of the mystery and secrecy inherent in the order, it was ordained that should only meet once a year, and each member was obligated to appoint his own successor, but leave no memorial of his existence such as tombstones or relics. Christian Rosenkreutz himself is reported to have died at the age of 106, and long afterwards his skeleton was found in a house, a wall having been built over him. Although their primary responsibility was to heal the sick poor, their writings contain little medical or therapeutic information despite the fact that they must have known much about medicine. In this respect they claimed to acquire their knowledge not by study, but by the direct illumination of God and while their theories – such as they were – were Paracelsian, the fraternity, though mystic, was Protestant.

The most curious feature of their legend is that the almost obviously fictitious character of the documents which announced it, should have been so widely believed. Indeed, within a short time of their publication, German students were fiercely disputing the authenticity of the revelations, and the controversy continued for more than two centuries. Much learned investigation into the origin of the first treatises has been made, and the most usual conclusion has been that they were written by a German theologian, Johann Valentin Andreas of Wurttemberg (1586-1654). He is said to have declared before his death that he wrote the alleged history expressly as a work of fiction!

The Doctrine of Signatures

Despite being an arcane concept in itself, the Doctrine of Signatures was to a certain degree intelligible and not completely saturated with mysticism, although much associated with the pious utterances frequent among the medieval teachers and practitioners of medicine. The basic theory held that the Creator, in providing herbs for the service of man, had stamped on them, at least in many instances, an indication of their special remedial value. The roots of certain plants, for instance, were thought to represent the male genitalia, thus the adoption of ginseng root by the Chinese as a remedy for impotence, and of mandrake by the Hebrews and Greeks in the treatment of sterility, have been cited as evidence of the antiquity of the general dogma. No less an authority than Hippocrates also stated that diseases are sometimes cured by the use of "like" remedies although this assertion was not considered adequate to enable him to be considered as the founder of homeopathy. The signatures of some drugs were undoubtedly observed after their virtues had been discovered, thus poppy under the doctrine was designated as related to brain disorders, on account of its shape like a head. However, its reputation as an agent capable of soothing the anxious brain was, in fact, far more ancient than the inference.

The frontispiece of Basilica Chymica *(first published in 1608), written by Oswald Croll (1580-1609) of Wetter in Hesse depicts the great alchemist – philosophers of the time. Croll was a Paracelsian physician who studied at Marburg, Heidelberg, and Geneva. He devised numerous remedies and was a firm believer in the doctrine of signatures.*

The rebis or philosophical egg was a concept as arcane as the doctrine of signatures. The androgynous angel holds in his right hand the mirror of the world through which all illness can be seen and understood. In his left hand he holds the egg which contains all the solutions to disease. Its four elements – the shell, the white, the membrane, and the yolk – which represents the quintessence of life, together represent the ultimate cure. Strange that the stem cell concept of disease cure can be traced back to occult philosophy.

It is more likely that the belief in a special indication of the virtues of specific remedies grew up slowly in the monasteries, and was probably originated by noticing some curious coincidences. It certainly met with wide acceptance in the sixteenth century, largely due to the confident belief in the doctrine expressed in the writings of Paracelsus. Although the mystical medical authors, Oswald Crollius and Giovanni Batista Porta, both taught the idea with enthusiasm, it failed to maintain its influence to any appreciable extent beyond the seventeenth century. In fact, the noted author J.A. Paris was so outraged by the concept that he utilized considerable spleen in describing the doctrine of signatures as "*the most absurd and preposterous hypothesis that has disgraced the annals of medicine*." Why he should have expended much outrage over the use of some therapeutic experiments with a few valueless herbs is difficult to understand.

Good evidence exists for the inductive reasoning involved in the doctrine of signatures as evident in the old herbal manuals. Thus, the saxifrages were supposed to break up rocks and their evident medicinal value in stone in the bladder was considered a logical application. Similarly, roses were recommended in blood disorders, whereas rhubarb and saffron were preferred in bilious complaints and turmeric in jaundice; all on account of their color. The notable pharmacist William Coles in his *Art of Simpling* declared, "*Trefoil defendeth the heart against the noisome vapour of the spleen, not only because the leaf is triangular like the heart of a man, but because each leaf contains the perfect icon of a heart and in the proper flesh color*." *Aristolochia Clematitis* was called birthwort, and from the shape of its corolla was believed to be useful in parturition. *Physalis alkekengi*, (bladderwort) owed its reputation as a cleanser of the bladder and urinary passages to its inflated calyx. *Tormentilla officinalis* (blood root) with its red root, was used to cure bloody fluxes while *Scrophularia nodosa* (kernel wort) possessed kernels or tubers attached to its roots, and was consequently utilized for the treatment of scrofulous glands of the neck. Canterbury bells, from their long throats, were allocated to the cure of sore throats while thistles, because of their prickles, were deemed capable of inflicting a cure.

Oswald Crollius, who described himself as *Medicus et Philosophus Hermeticus*, in his *Tractatus de Signaturis*, wrote a long and very pious preface explaining the importance of the knowledge of signatures. Although his inferences from the plants and animals he mentions are often far-fetched, he provides conclusions as if they had been mathematically demonstrated and never intimates that a signature may be capable of two interpretations. In this respect a few examples from his text are useful. Walnuts have the complete signature of the head, thus from the shell, therefore, a salt can be made of special use for wounds of the pericranium while the inner part of the shell will make a decoction for injuries to the skull; the pellicle surrounding the kernel makes a medicine for inflammation of the membrane of the brain; and the kernel itself nourishes and strengthens the brain. The lemon indicates the heart, ginger the belly, *cassia fistula* the bowels, *aristolochia* the womb, plantago the nerves and veins, *palma Christi* and fig leaves the hands.

The signatures sometimes simulated the disease itself, thus lily of the valley has a flower hanging like a drop and was therefore considered good for apoplexy. The date, according to Paracelsus, cures cancer; dock seeds, red colcothar, and *acorus palustris* cured erysipelas; red santal, geraniums, coral, blood stones, and *tormentilla*, were indicated in hemorrhage; rhubarb in yellow bile; wolves' livers in liver complaints, foxes' lungs in pulmonary affections,

The crowning of the son of Edward II of England. His physician, John of Gaddesden, was a staunch advocate of the doctrine of signatures. When the young prince appeared about to die from smallpox he achieved a miraculous cure by draping his entire room in red.

and dried worms, powdered in goats' milk, to expel worms. The fame of vipers as a remedy was largely due to the theory of the renewal of their youth.

Color itself was a very usual signature and widely regarded as of considerable medicinal influence. In this respect medical books strongly advocated red hangings for the beds of patients with smallpox. John of Gaddesden, physician to Edward II, noted, "*When I saw the son of the renowned King of England lying sick of the smallpox I took care that everything round the bed should be of a red color, which succeeded so completely that the Prince was restored to perfect health without the vestige of a pustule.*"

Planets and Metals

There are no clear historic records of the origin of the association of the seven metals with the seven planets, nor of the connection of either with the deities of antiquity. While it is evident that Greece transmitted the mythological connection to Rome, it is not so certain whence the Grecian concepts emanated, although more than likely they evolved out of the astrological and alchemical mysticism of the priest cults of both Persia and Egypt. Indeed, it is not unreasonable to suppose that the circle of imagery may have developed from the early worship of the sun, thus signifying the solar orb as the heavenly body of supreme divinity, or as the residence of such a being. A natural extrapolation of this concept would thereafter assign to the moon and the five principal planets apparently in attendance on the earth similar, though lower, dignities. The tendency to group gods and planets and metals into sevens would be an obvious link between the last two, and the characters of the deities named would naturally be extended to the materials named after them.

Claude Berthollet (1748-1822) and Antoine Lavoisier. Educated in medicine at Turin, Italy, Berthollet later became associated with Antoine Lavoisier, whom he assisted in reforming chemical nomenclature. His researches with hydrocyanic (prussic) acid and hydrogen sulfide led him to disagree with Lavoisier's contention that oxygen was an essential element in all acids. Berthollet was the first to note that the completeness of chemical reactions depended in part upon the masses of the reacting substances; he thus came close to formulating the law of mass action. Though he incorrectly concluded that elements unite in all proportions, the resulting controversy with the chemist Joseph-Louis Proust led to the establishment of the law of definite proportions. In addition to the above, Berthollet discovered the composition of ammonia (1785), introduced chlorine as a bleaching agent and developed colored fireworks.

Berthollet considered that Babylon and Chaldea were the localities where imagination was first most abundantly applied to the elucidation of science, and both there and elsewhere in the East the mystic relations of the number seven was promulgated. The logic of the numerical extrapolations can be defined with some degree of accuracy. Thus the regular appearance of the seven planets, visible to the naked eye, facilitated the development of these early notions, as did the four equal periods of the moon's phases, each of which consisted of seven days. Similarly there were seven stars in the Great Bear, the seven colors, the seven tones in music, the seven vowels in the Greek alphabet, the seven sages, and, naturally also, the seven known metals – all providing obvious irrefutable evidence of this order of the universe. Out of this concept arose the Chaldean and Persian ideas of seven heavens, each with its gate of a different metal; the first of lead, the second of tin, the third of brass, the fourth of iron, the fifth of a copper alloy, the sixth of silver, and the seventh of gold.

It was thereafter a natural assumption for the ancient Chaldean philosophers to attribute to the heavenly bodies, or rather to the deities who had made these their homes, extensive control over the products of the earth. Thus the sun-god could be deduced to produce gold, the moon-god silver, the deity of mercury – mercury and so on. Such was the obvious logic of this view that the doctrine remained prevalent until well into the sixteenth century. The need to depict intellectual concepts of this kind in a pictorial fashion, produced the early crude attempts at communication using symbolic interpretation that subsequently evolved via ideograms into alphabets. Thus sun and gold were represented by ☼ or ◙, and are still represented by similar signs. Water was indicated 𓈖 in the papyri and as recently as three or four hundred years ago the alchemical books of the times still used the same sign ♀ for the planet and the metal mercury. In effect, it differs little from the hieroglyph of Thoth, whom the Greeks called Hermes and the Romans Mercury, although some students of Greek claim this sign was derived from the caduceus or winged staff of the god, while Egyptologists claimed it as a picture of the "sacred ibis".

It is unlikely that any definite table of the planetary symbols was ever drawn up and agreed to, but with the passage of time a degree of uniformity ultimately became apparent. In fact, the oldest known table is one provided by Olympiodorus in the fifth century and in it, electron is associated with Jupiter and tin with Hermes (Mercury). Initially the association of the planets and

The Seventh Key of Basil Valentine. The salt of the philosophers is an igneous water (Aqua within the triangle of fire) which leads chaos to the perfection of the Wise. The four seasons are thus encircled and held in balance by the Sigillium Hermetis *that dissolves the metal and lends body to the soul.*

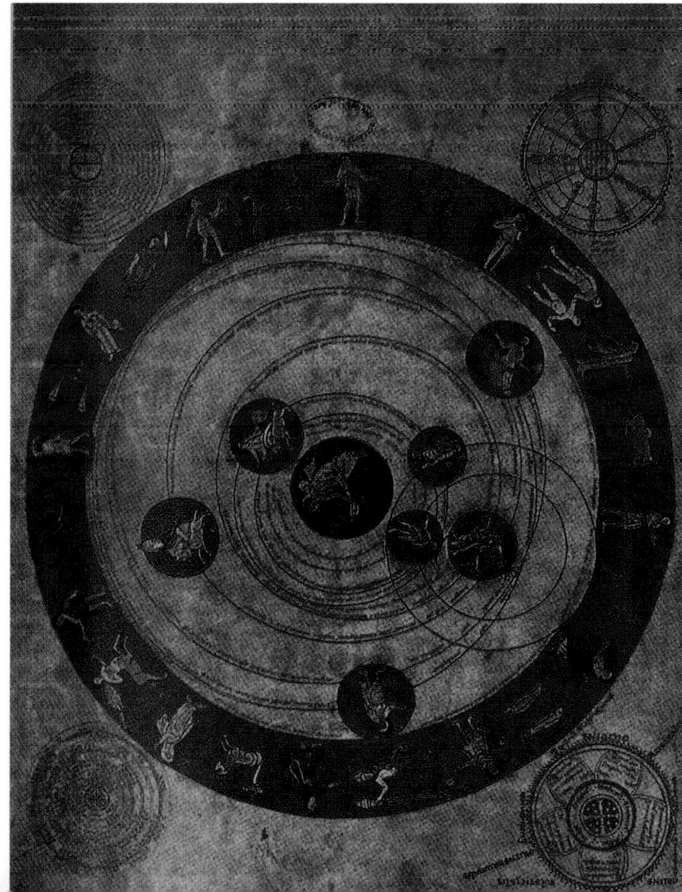

The Zodiac, planetary relationship, and a variety of mystic symbols have been utilized since time immemorial to attempt to provide some rational framework to explain the frightening mystery of disease and the unpredictability of life.

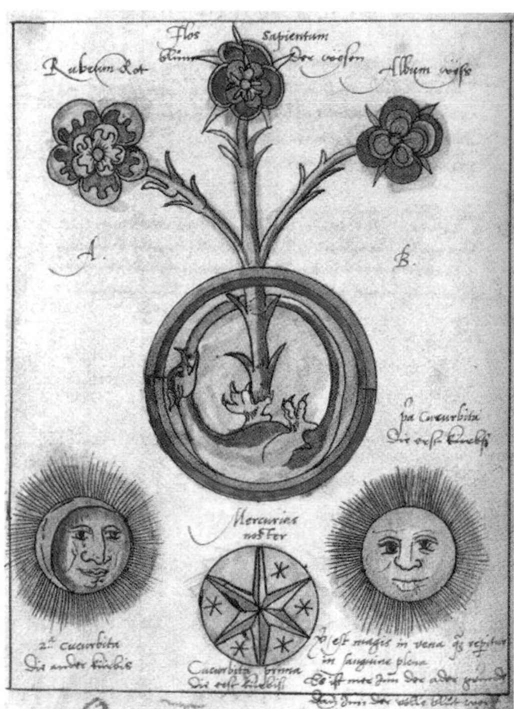

The relationship of alchemical elements to the maintenance of the quintessence of life represented by the drop of primordial water (center). The Gnostic Ophite cosmologic symbol of the Ourobouros (Leviathan eating its tail in the waterdrop) is inaccessible to the divine world of love and light (below).

Alchemists and kabbalists variously ponder the heavens and diverse symbols in search of wisdom. In a world lit only by fire, the desire for the light of knowledge spawned exotic thought.

the metals was by no means invariable in different nations, thus, among the Persians, for example, copper was assigned to Jupiter; while the Egyptians dedicated a compound of gold and silver called electron to him, and in even more recent systems Jupiter and tin became allied. Although Venus was originally believed to control tin according to Persian lore, eventually the Egyptian attribution of brass or copper to her has prevailed. Similarly, iron first belonged to Mercury before quicksilver was recognized as a metal, and at that time Mars was the godfather of an alloy similar to bronze.

The laborious researches of Berthollet into the origin of alchemy, and his reproductions of ancient manuscripts, demonstrate that while signs were used by the ancient Greek writers of about the first century A.D., they were not used by the Latin authors, but were fully adopted in the Middle Ages. Berthollet recorded that the manuscript of St. Mark at Venice (written about the year A.D. 1000), probably for some prince, contained a multitude of these symbols. Strangely enough, there is scarcely any allusion to the symbols in the Arabic manuscripts, given the Islamic discomfort of all forms of Greek paganism. It is, however, worth noting that Arab physicians made a superstition of the practice of bleeding on Tuesdays and Wednesdays only, unconscious perhaps of the origin of this ritual, which depended on the fact that Mars, the god of blood and iron, superintended Tuesday's operations, and Mercury, who had the management of the humors, was in charge on Wednesdays. In fact it would remain confusing until the fifteenth, sixteenth, and seventeenth centuries, when the European alchemists, in seeking a mechanism to transmute the baser metals into gold, developed a code that became "conventionalized".

Although the signs for the seven metals have not been invariable, for many centuries they were distributed thus:

O *Sol, the Sun, Gold*
☽ *Luna, the Moon, Silver*
μ *Jupiter, Tin*
♀ *Venus, Copper*
♂ *Mars, Iron*
☿ *Mercury, Quicksilver*
c† *Saturn, Lead*

It is of course worth noting how these ancient concepts have influenced our language, our literature, and especially our medicine. Thus lunatic, jovial, saturnine, martial, venereal, and mercurial, are etymological reminiscences of a past time when temperaments and diseases were associated with the heavenly bodies. Similarly, the extent to which metallic compounds acquired their medical reputations from their artificial relationship with the powers which were assumed to have adopted them, provides further evidence of the cultural interface of alchemy, chemistry, and medicine. Thus, silver nitrate was administered in brain disorders originally because of the belief in the control of the mental faculties by the moon. The administration of iron for the purpose of invigorating the constitution was largely due to its connection with Mars, whose fame for virility assured the possession of similar virtue in his metallic godson.

To the ancient planetary symbols the alchemists added a number of other signs such as earth, air, fire, and water as well as chemicals of later discovery. Thus their jargon became even more incomprehensible than previously.

Mysticism was a subject much appreciated by the alchemical fraternity, some of whom truly believed there was some hidden meaning in the symbols, for there were among the adepts, brilliant men who were *bona fide* true investigators and not involved in fraud. Nevertheless, under certain circumstances a clearly poetic vision entered their science. Thus Glauber, a contemporary of James I and Charles I, claimed that symbols were invested with a special mysterious meaning and portrayed each in a square:

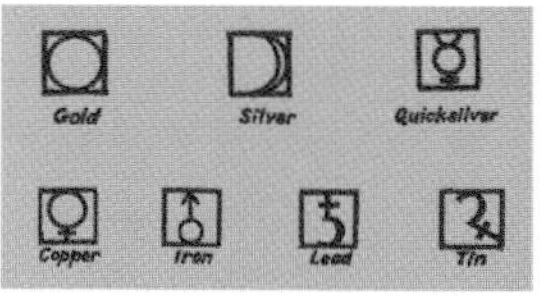

Explaining that the extent to which each symbol touched the four sides of the square indicated how near it approached perfection. Since gold touched all four sides, silver three, and the other metals only two each, it was apparent that the rank order of their value was obvious.

The precise interpretation of these symbols has been much attempted, but they are for the most part mere guesses. Those representing the sun and moon are reasonably obvious, but the others may generally be read in a variety of ways. Thus the sign for Jupiter is alleged to represent one of his thunderbolts; that for copper is supposed to illustrate the looking-glass of Venus; the iron sign is the shield and spear of Mars; the caduceus of Mercury and the scythe of Saturn are likewise traceable back to their respective signatures. It has also been proposed that the three signs of which a circle forms part – namely, those for quicksilver, copper, and iron – were intended to suggest that gold could be formed from them, while the cross or spear attached, being in fact the Egyptian phallus, or organ of generative vigor. Similarly in tin and lead, there are evidences of the presence of silver. Perhaps more probable is the concept that these signs were originally combinations of letters – monograms, in fact, indicating the name which the planet bore in the country where the symbol was first adopted. Thus, in the sign for Jupiter, the Greek initial for Zeus, may traced; in that of Venus, Φ can be found the initial of phosphorus; similarly ♂ may represent *t* and *r*, the first and last letters of Thouros, one of the names of Mars; while ♄+ represents the first and second letters of Chronos (Saturn) welded together. Nevertheless, the interpretation depends to a large extent on the period when the signs were first used, since clearly pictures preceded alphabets and were in fact the originals of the phonetic sounds which ultimately became indicated by the letters.

The mysteries which made up so large a part of the science of alchemy passed from its votaries to the practitioners of physic and pharmacy, and still exist in those professions. Pretended solutions of gold, vaunted as universal cures, were sold under the title of solar elixirs; the popular name of nitrate of silver until the mid-twentieth century was lunar caustic; a black oxide of iron is called Ethiops martial; a solution of sugar of lead is extract of Saturn; sulphate of copper was once known as vitriol of Venus; muriate of tin was famous for the expulsion of worms under the name of Salt of Jove; and ointment of quicksilver is still universally known as mercurial ointment.

Metals, too, were credited with medicinal virtues corresponding with their names or with the deities and planets with which they had been so long associated. Thus it was held that the sun ruled the heart and, since gold was the metal of the sun, therefore gold was especially a cordial. Similarly, since the moon was associated with silver, the head and silver were associated therapeutically. Iron was regarded as a tonic because Mars was strong. Culpepper stated, "*Have a care, you use not such medicines to one part of your body which are appropriated to another; for if your brain be overheated and you use such medicines as cool the heart or liver you may make mad work.*" But it was not quite so simple to select the proper remedy, because there were conditions which made it necessary to follow an antipathetical treatment with due regard for any conflict in therapy. Thus Saturn by ruling the bones could be held responsible for toothache but if Jupiter happened to be in the ascendant, then the appropriate drug to employ was that known to be associated with an opposing planet such as Mercury. Of course such notions seem esoteric in contemporary therapy, given that modern astronomy has sited the heavenly bodies at so distant a place in our pantheon of cures that we no longer view them in the quasi-mystical fashion of the astrologer physicians of yesteryear. Nevertheless, the prescient words of Culpepper are worth considering as we constantly seek for the next pharmacotherapeutic probe: "*It will seem strange to none but madmen and fools that the stars should have influence upon the body of man, considering he being an epitome of the Creation must needs have a celestial world within himself; for.... if there be an unity in the Godhead there must needs be an unity in all His works, and a dependency between them, and not that God made the Creation to hang together like a rope of sand.*" Strange that the people of the century that sang "*This is the dawning of the Age of Aquarius...*" may have to a certain extent lost sight of their miniscule place in the macrocosm as they self-assuredly contemplate ion structures and proton pumps with a hubris born of presbyopia.

A lexicon of arcane chemical symbols in different ancient languages. Each column of symbols was proposed to represent their evolution during the progression of language development.

The Remedy of Sympathy

The concepts embodied within the doctrine of sympathetic remedies are amongst the oldest of medical superstitions. Although utterly arcane and illogical, it found widespread acceptance and was seriously adopted by many highly sophisticated physicians. The earliest record of the perception can be traced as far back as the commandment in the Pentateuch "*Thou shalt not seethe a kid in its mother's milk,*" to an ancient prejudice against the boiling of milk in any circumstances, on the ground that this would cause suffering to the animal which yielded the milk. If the suffering could be thus conveyed, it was logical to believe that healing was similarly capable of transference.

Pliny the Elder (quoted by Cornelius Agrippa) noted: "*If any person shall be sorry for a blow he has given another, afar off or near at hand, if he shall presently spit into the middle of the hand with which he gave the blow, the party that was smitten shall presently be free from pain.*" Paracelsus similarly developed the notion with his accustomed confidence in the face of bizarre theories and produced a formula for *Unguentum Sympatheticum*: "*Take 4 oz. each of boar's and bear's fat, boil slowly for half an hour, then pour on cold water. Skim off the floating fat, rejecting that which sinks (the older the animals yielding the fat, the better). Take of powdered burnt worms, of dried boar's brain, of red sandal wood, of mummy, of bloodstone, 1 oz. of each. Then collect 1 drachm of the moss from the skull of a man who died a violent death, one who had been hanged, preferably, and had not been buried. This should be collected at the rising of the moon, and under Venus if possible, but certainly not under Mars or Saturn. With all these ingredients make an ointment, which keep in a closed glass vessel. If it becomes dry on keeping it can be softened with a little fresh lard or virgin honey. The ointment must be prepared in the autumn.*" Paracelsus describes in exquisite detail the methods of applying this ointment, the precautions to be taken, and the manner in which it exerted its influence. Thus the weapon

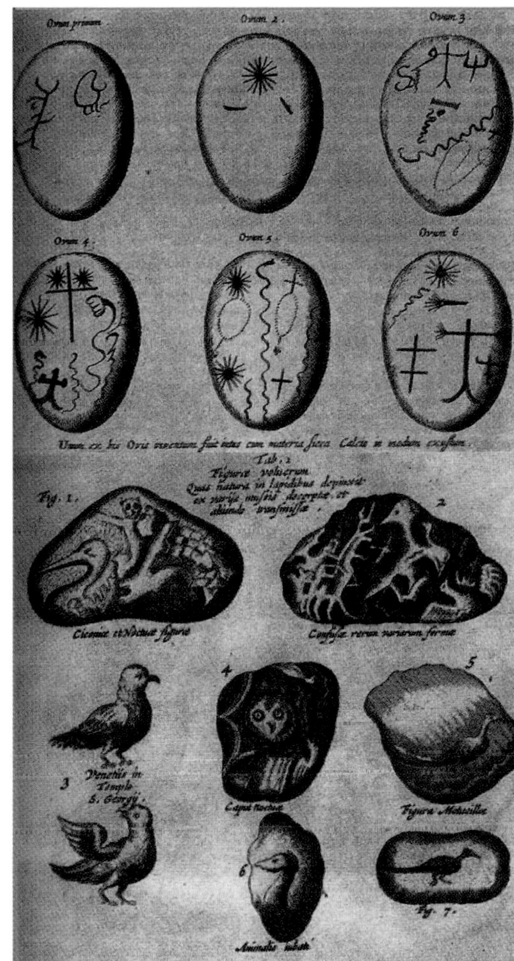

Signature stones and eggs from A. Kircher in Mundus Subterraneus. *Philosophers felt that nature was an artist and that her inscriptions could be found in diverse sites such as stones. Thus even Johannes Kepler noted that he was "confirmed in my view of assigning a soul to the earth... and that the events of human history are played out in the the frangible stone." Thus ciphers could be identified in clouds, stones, eggshells and ice and that each represented a key to understanding the grammar of life.*

GASPARIS
TALIACOTII
BONONIENSIS
De Curtorum Chirurgia per
insitionem.
LIBRI DVO.
AD SERENISSIMVM
PRINCIPEM D.
VINCENTIVM
GONZAGAM
Mantuae, & Montis Ferrati
DVCEM

Gasparro Tagliacozzi (1546-1599) of Bologna and Rhinoplasty. Tagliacozzi in 1597 revived the operation of rhinoplasty that had been in the hands of a Sicilian family of plastic surgeons (the Brancas of Catania) during the 15th century. As a consequence of this innovation, he was abused not only by physicians such as Ambroise Paré and Fallopius, but also by the Church. In the next century Butler satirized both Tagliacozzi and the concept of the operation in Hudibras *while the blessed church expressed serious criticism since they regarded such operations as meddling with the "handiwork of God." Such was the disdain with which Tagliacozzi was regarded that his mortal remains were eventually exhumed from the cemetery of the convent in which they had been placed and reburied in unconsecrated ground. Concern was unabated in Europe in regard to this technique and in 1788 the Paris Faculty utterly interdicted face repairing, declaring it to be immoral, unethical and anti-Christian. As a result of such strictures plastic surgery fell into disrepute and disuse until 1840 when Johann Friedrich Dieffenbach of Konigsberg became the Chair of Surgery at the Charité Hospital in Berlin.*

which inflicted the wound was anointed, and it would be effective no matter how far away the wounded person might be. On the other hand, it would not be effective if an artery had been severed, or if the heart, the brain, or the liver had suffered the lesion. It was of particular importance that the wound be kept properly bandaged, and even more relevant was the requirement that the urine of the patient be poured on the bandages. The weapon was to be anointed daily in the case of a serious wound, or every second or third day if the wound was not so severe. In the intervening time particular care of the weapon was required, such that after the ointment had been applied, it was mandatory to wrap it in a clean linen cloth, and kept free from dust and draughts, or the patient would experience exacerbation of his pain. The Paracelsian explanation of the efficacy of the remedy proposed that the anointment of the weapon acted on the wound by transmitting a magnetic current through the air directly to *"the healing balsam which exists in every living body, just as the heat of the sun passes through the air."*

Robert Fludd, a physician and Rosicrucian, who fell under the displeasure of the College of Physicians on account of his unsound views (he did not adhere to Galenical doctrine), was a ardent proponent of the Paracelsian Weapon Salve. In reply to a contemporary doctor who had ridiculed the theory he waxes earnest, and at times sarcastic. His explanation is a curious mixture of zealotry and quasi-science: *"an ointment composed of the moss of human bones, mummy (which is the human body combined with balm, human fat, and added to these the blood, which is the beginning and food of them all, must have a spiritual power, for with the blood the bright soul doth abide and operateth after a hidden manner. Then as there is a spiritual line protracted or extended in the Ayre between the wounded person and the Box of Ointment like the beam of the Sun from the Sun, so this animal beam is the faithful conductor of the Healing nature from the box of the balsam to the wounded body. And if it were not for that line which conveys the wholesome and salutiferous spirit, the value of the ointment would evaporate or sluce out this way or that way and so would bring no benefit to the wounded persons."*

Lest it be thought that this absurd remedy was only considered by fringe physicians, it should be noted that contemporary authorities including Van Helmont, Descartes, Batista Porta, and other leaders of science in the seventeenth century espoused the theory with enthusiasm. Indeed, the comments of Van Helmont provide good evidence of his commitment to the subject. In his text *De Magnetica Vulnerum Curatione*, written about 1644, he relates that a citizen of Brussels, having lost his nose in a combat in Italy, consulted a surgeon of Bologna named Tagliacozzi, who provided him with another by using a strip of flesh from the arm of a servant. Although the operation was an initial success, after thirteen months the nose became cold and began to putrefy. Van Helmont noted that the explanation for the failure was that the servant from whom the flesh had been borrowed had died

An image from an ancient Greek krater depicts Achilles bandaging the arm of his friend Patroclus. The recognition that sepsis followed penetrating wounds was early apparent to Greek physicians and Hippocrates dealt in detail with the appropriate use of cleansing salves and clean dressings.

and added that, *"Superstites sunt horum testes oculati Bruxellae"*(there are still eye witnesses of this case at Brussels).

The name of Sir Kenelm Digby is probably more closely associated with the *"powder of sympathy"* than that of any other person, and indeed he is often credited with the invention of the concept, although such was not the case. Digby was an extraordinary individual who played a prominent role in the stirring days of the Stuart family. Despite the fact that his father, Sir Everard Digby, had been implicated in the Gunpowder Plot, and duly executed, such were the personal attributes of Kenelm that he not only survived the taint on his pedigree, but rose to great prominence.

Dissatisfied with the idle life of the court, Digby obtained permission from the king to become a privateer and as such achieved immense success. On his return home after thus distinguishing himself, Digby embarked on an exotic and peripatetic life. He was knighted, changed his religion occasionally, was imprisoned, intermittently banished, dabbled in science, or shone in society in London, Paris, or Rome, visiting the two last-named cities frequently on real and pretended diplomatic missions. During his residence in France, in 1658, he lectured to the University of Montpellier on his sympathetic powder, and the fame of this miraculous compound soon reached England. On his return to London, he modestly professed that he had been shy of using it lest he be accused of wizardry. Fortunately, opportunity to doff this feigned reluctance soon arose when he was compelled to take the risk for the sake of his friend, Thomas Howel, the Duke of Buckingham's secretary, who had been seriously wounded in trying to prevent a duel.

Since the physicians involved prognosticated gangrene and probable death, the wounded man appealed to Sir Kenelm, who generously consented to do his utmost. Instructing the attendants to bring him a rag on which was some of the sufferer's blood, they brought the garter which had been used as a bandage and which was still thick with blood. Digby soaked this in a basin of water in which was dissolved a handful of his sympathetic powder and an hour later the patient said he felt an agreeable coolness. The fever and pain rapidly abated, and in a few days the cure was complete. It was reported that the Duke of Buckingham testified to the genuineness of the cure and that the king had taken a keen interest in the treatment!

Digby asserted that the secret of the powder had been imparted to him by a Carmelite monk whom he met at Florence, and his faithful laboratory assistant, George Hartman, published the nature of it in a *Book of Chymicall Secrets*, in 1682, after the death of Sir Kenelm. The text explained that the *powder of sympathy*, which was then made by himself (Hartman), and sold by a bookseller in Cornhill named Brookes was prepared "*by dissolving good English vitriol in as little warm water as will suffice, filter, evaporate, and set aside until fair, large, green crystals are formed. Spread these in the sun until they whiten. Then crush them coarsely and again dry in the sun.*" Sir Kenelm's scientific explanation of the action of his sympathetic powder was similar to others, and proposed that the rays of the sun extracted from the blood and the vitriol associated with it the spirit of each in minute atoms. At the same time the inflamed wound was exhaling hot atoms and making way for a current of air. The air charged with the atoms of blood and vitriol were attracted to it, and acted curatively.

Clearly Digby was a larger than life character and in certain respects one is even reminded of Paracelsus, although the latter seemed to have predominantly focused his intellect on medical matters. Inscribed on the plate attached to the portrait of Sir Kenelm Digby in the National Portrait Gallery, it is written, "*His character has been summed up as a prodigy of learning, credulity, valor, and romance.*" Other testimonials to his character and reliability are to be found in contemporary literature. Thus Evelyn alluded to him as "*a teller of a strange things,*" while Clarendon described him as "*a person very eminent and notorious throughout the whole course of his life from his cradle to his grave. A man of very extraordinary person and presence; a wonderful graceful behavior, a flowing courtesy, and such a volubility of language as surprised and delighted.*" Lady Fanshawe, who had the pleasure of his company at Calais with the Earl of Strafford and others, wrote, "*much excellent discourse passed; but as was reason, most share was Sir Kenelm Digby's who had enlarged somewhat more in extraordinary stories than might be averred.*" At last he told the company about the barnacle goose lie had seen in Jersey; a barnacle which changes to a bird, and at this they all laughed incredulously. But Lady Fanshawe says "*this was the only thing true he had declaimed with them. This was his infirmity, though otherwise of most excellent parts, and a very fine-bred gentleman.*" In John Aubrey's *Brief Lives* (written between 1669 and 1696) Digby is described as "*such a goodly person, gigantique and great voice, and had so graceful elocution and noble address, etc., that had he been drop't out of the clowdes in any part of the world he would have made himself respected.*"

Despite the popular support for his powder, Lemery, in 1690, had the courage to express some doubts about it and almost a century later in 1773 Baume delivered the coup de grâce by declaring its pretensions to be absolutely illusory!

The healing of wounds attained in civilian affairs led to a medical focus on dueling. Trial by battle was the earliest form of dueling and Tacitus reported that the Germanic tribes settled their quarrels by single combat with swords. Subsequent to the Germanic invasion, the practice became established in Western Europe early in the Middle Ages. In Germany duels of honor were authorized by the military code up to World War I and were legalized again (1936) under the Nazis and by the Fascist regime in Italy. The Mensur (student duel) was until quite recently a feature of German university life and most German universities had long-established Verbindungen *(fighting corps) with strict rules, secret meetings, distinctive uniforms, and great prestige. The method of swordplay differs from that of normal fencing, and students obtained scars on head and cheek that were much prized as marks of courage.*

Sir Kenelm Digby. Despite the ignominious execution of his father, after the thwarted "Gunpowder Plot," Digby rose above his genome and became a success. Having inherited an income of £3,000 a year, he flourished at the court of James I (a monarch of dubious character) and was popular with all. Dissatisfied with the sybaritic court life he persuaded James to provide a commission to become a privateer (license to attack and go forth and steal Spanish galleons). Although James consented, the commission was delayed and James therefore simply granted the buccaneer a license to undertake a voyage "for the increase of his knowledge" (sic). With this privateer's license Digby scoured the Mediterranean, capturing French, Spanish, and Flemish ships, and defeating a French and Venetian fleet at Scanderoon in the Levant. This exploit was celebrated by Digby's friend, Ben Johnson, in verse, which can only be termed deathless on account of its puerile ending:

"Witness his action done at Scanderoon
Upon his birthday, the eleventh of June."

Digby's epitaph plagiarized the essence of this "brilliant" strophe as follows: "Born on the day he died, the eleventh of June, and that day bravely fought at Scanderoon. It's rare that one and the same day should be his day of birth and death and victory."

The work of Mesmer (top left) was repudiated to such an extent in his home city of Vienna that he was forced to transfer his practice to Paris. Although the science of magnetism was well known (background), the use of the phenomenon to cure disease was regarded as of dubious value. Despite a critical official investigation Mesmer remained for years the darling of Parisian society and was believed to be capable of effecting extraordinary cures.

A satirical depiction of the efficacy of Magnetism by the Parisian artist Boilly.

Mesmerism and Magnetism

It was Aetius, in the early part of the sixth century, who first alluded to the application of the magnet as a cure for disease. In his commentary on the subject, he noted that holding a magnet in the hand is recognized as useful in providing relief for gout, although he professed to having not tested this treatment himself. Writers of the fifteenth and sixteenth centuries recommended it strongly for toothache, headache, convulsions, and nerve disorders. Indeed by the end of the seventeenth century magnetic toothpicks and even ear-picks were commercially available.

It was claimed that such magnetic devices were effective in both preventing and relieving pains in those organs. As with so many novel therapeutic concepts, it was Paracelsus who initially originated the theory of animal magnetism. According to him, the mysterious properties possessed by the loadstone were transferable from that body to iron and represented an influence drawn directly from the stars and possessed by all animate beings. The central mechanism of this phenomenon resided in a fluid which he called *Magnale*, and its properties explained the movements of certain plants which follow the course of the sun, as well as forming the basis of the hypotheses that supported the action of sympathetic ointment and the actions of talismans. Paracelsus believed that the magnet was particularly effective in epilepsy, and also prepared a *magisterium magnetis*. The celebrated chemist, Glauber, professed to have a secret magnet which would draw only the essence or tincture from iron, leaving the gross body behind, and employed this technique to produce tincture of Mars and Venus, thus "*robbing the dragon of the golden fleece which it guards.*" This has been interpreted to mean that he dissolved iron and copper in *aqua fortis*. Thus, as the fabled Argonaut Jason restored his aged father to youth again, so would this tincture prove a wonderful restorative. It is reported that Glauber actually tested the elixir on one occasion and soon noted the appearance of black curly hair on his bald head. Unfortunately he had insufficient tincture to permit him to pursue the experiment, and although he greatly desired to produce more he procrastinated until it was too late!

Magnetism as a treatment was widely esteemed and Van Helmont, Fludd, and other physicians of mystic instincts were major protagonists of animal magnetism, commonly using pulverized magnet in salves, plasters, pills, and potions. Unfortunately, a report in 1660 by Dr. Gilbert of Colchester, noted that, when powdered, the loadstone no longer possessed magnetic properties. Ultimately, therefore, it became understood that the powder of magnet was incapable of producing effects any different to that of any other ferruginous substance. Nevertheless, the belief in the therapeutic efficacy of magnets applied to the body was by no means dissipated and in fact, at various times, notably towards the latter part of the eighteenth century, acquired considerable vogue. The theory was variously exploited by a number of practitioners, but achieved its apogee during the time of the Viennese physician, F. A. Mesmer. Such was the level of the controversy in Paris that the court, the government, the Academy of Sciences, and aristocratic society were generally ranged in pro- and anti-Mesmer factions. Benjamin Franklin, then resident in Paris, declared that at one time Mesmer alone was being paid more money in fees than the entire regular physicians of Paris put together. Such is the ebb and flow of therapeutic passion that the explanations provided by Mesmer of the phenomena attending his performances were little more than an amplification of the doctrines which Paracelsus had first imagined.

Franz Anton Mesmer (1714-1815)

Born in Itznang, Switzerland, Mesmer's graduating dissertation dealt with the influence of the planets on man. His subsequent fascination with magnetism and hypnosis was founded on the belief that humans shared similar powers to the planetary bodies. His conviction that medicine could become an exact science by adapting cosmology to the physiology of the human

Mesmer casts his eponymous spell (note the position of the hands and feet) over the neurotic desires of a young French damsel. Subsequent to his contributions physicians regarded it as obligatory to "lay their hands on patients" to effect a cure.

body was investigated in his dissertation titled *Dissertatio physico-medica de planerarum influxu*.

As a prominent figure in Vienna, his practices and philosophy attracted much attention. Whilst the society of the time held him in awe, some were not as impressed and at one stage, Maria Theresa's *"commission"* sought to investigate his activities with the result that he was forced to flee Vienna. In Paris, his hypnotic séances were immensely popular and he soon accumulated a fortune. During his séances he would wear a lilac suit, play on a harmonica, and touch his patients with a magnetic wand whist staring at them. Some would be cared for in a private room lest they suffer a "crisis". A prominent feature of Mesmeric therapy was the presence of numerous tubs or *"baquets"* containing a mixture of hydrogen sulphide and other ingredients and provided with iron conductors from which a ring allowed contact to be made with the patients who stood in a circle holding hands.

Several medical and royal commissions were formed to test the scientific methods and physical agent behind Mesmer's theory. One such Royal Commission examined his claims, and reported *"that Mesmer had obtained remarkable cures but [they] declined to regard them as being due to animal magnetism."* They concluded by stating *"the action of man upon the imagination may be reduced to an art, and conducted with method, upon subjects who have faith."* Thus, in their statement, they described hypnotism of the future, while denying it Mesmer's contribution. Having once again been investigated by a committee, Mesmer was ostracized and with the advent of the French Revolution, faded into obscurity.

The eighteenth century, an age of political upheaval during which Mesmer lived, was energized by revolutionary idealism. Where mysticism had once flourished, natural science settled in to create order, thus causing *"the increasingly violent attack against scholastic dogmatism."* Those like Mesmer who attempted to discover more about the psycho-physiological relationship and correlation of mental function with disease were highly criticized.

With his love for music (he had commissioned Mozart to compose for him), Mesmer incorporated the powers of music in not only his dissertation and theories, but also his clinical practice. He expounded upon the notion of maintenance of equilibrium between the heavens and the body in his dissertation. *"The harmony established between the astral plane and the human plane ought to be admired as much as the ineffable effect of UNIVERSAL GRAVITATION by which our bodies are harmonized, not in a uniform and monotonous manner, but as a musical instrument furnished with several strings, the exact tone resonates which is in unison with a given tone."* Physicians contemporary to Mesmer were unable to detach themselves from the dogma of the past and refused to believe the validity of his experiments. In correctly denying the existence of a magnetic fluid, the unbelievers failed to see the potential merit of the practice behind his theory, and as Mesmer himself states, *"while they may forget the good I have done and prevent the good I wish to do, I will be vindicated by posterity"*...

Mesmer's introductory steps into the unconscious and the science of early hypnotism opened doors for future practitioners to use his work as the link between ancient spiritual healing and modern psychotherapy. Thus Puyégur, one of the physicians who practiced during and after Mesmer's time, explored the trance and animal magnetism, and James Braid used Mesmer's ideas to take even further steps forward replaced the term *"Mesmerism"* with *"hypnotism"*. In his theories, Braid specified that hypnotism is a subjective, psychological experience as opposed to Mesmer's objective physical view. Freud, another product of Mesmer's initial inquiries into the mind, emancipated psychological problems from moral judgments and was able to discover and explore the subconscious. Thus Mesmer, despite the initial opprobrium associated with his work, was the first of a succession of physicians who progressively established the basis for modern psychotherapy.

The excitement failed to effect any great response in England, but at about the same time, an American named Perkins created a great deal of stir with his metallic tractors, which sent the nation tractor-mad for the time. Unfortunately this delusion was laid to rest by Dr. Haygarth, of Bath, who undertook a series of experiments on patients with pieces of wood painted to resemble the tractors from which equally wonderful relief resulted! Cure was once again proven to rest greatly on the consequence of faith and trust in the physician.

The Tractors, *by Charles Williams, 1802. A satirical depiction of the curative effects of magnetic therapy on a garrulous woman.*

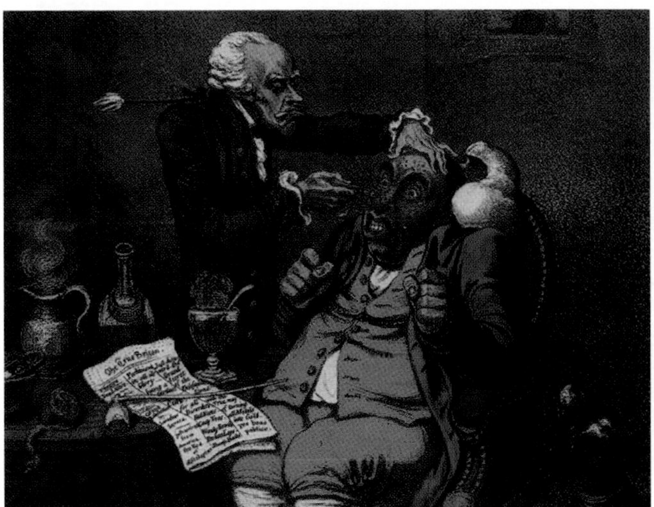

Metallic Tractors *by James Gillray, 1801. The American quack, Benjamin Perkins, treating the carbuncle-ridden nose of an obese patient. The newspaper (foreground) announces… "just arrived from America the Rod of Aesclepius, Perkinism in all its glory being a certain cure for all disorders Red Noses, Gouty Toes, Windy Bowels, Broken Legs, Humpbacks…"*

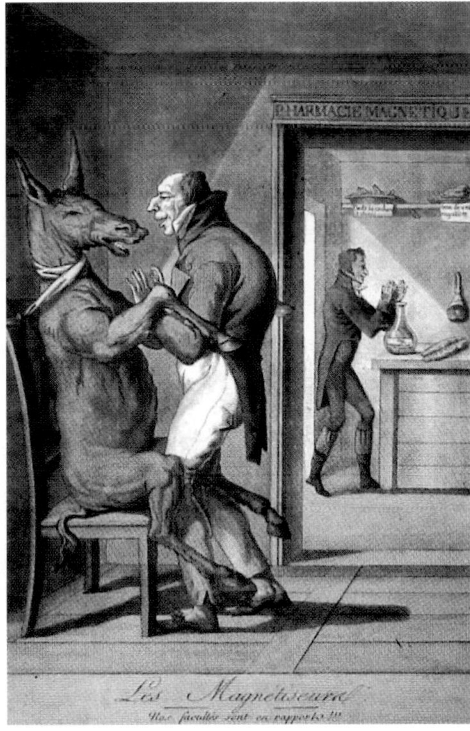

A satyric depiction of Mesmer and a patient. Despite wide popular acceptance many physicians (especially those chemically inclined) remained sceptical of the medicinal effects of magnetism.

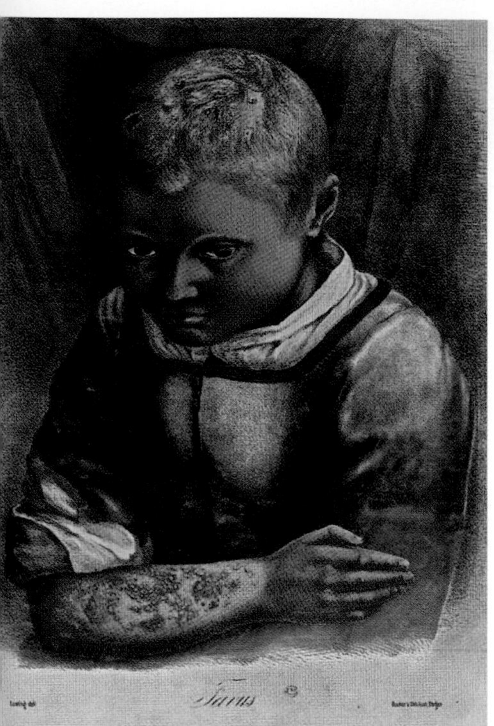

The treatment of skin disease was completely empiric until the identification of microscopic parasites and the recognition of the role of bacteria.

The Treatment of Itch

The history of the treatment of itch is a curious instance of the blind acceptance of authority through many centuries, such that although the explanation was in fact within reach, none could perceive it as dogma blinder their appreciation. It is likely that the disease was known to the Chinese some thousands of years ago as *Tchong-kiai*, meaning "pustules formed by a worm," indicative of their basic understanding of the entity. Similarly, some authorities have supposed that certain of the "uncleannesses" alluded to in the Book of Leviticus have reference to this complaint; and it is quite possible that in ancient times, due to neglect or improper treatment, it had acquired a far more severe character than currently. "*Psora*", in Greek, and the equivalent term "scabies", in Latin, probably encompassed the itch; though in all probability those words included a number of skin diseases which are now more precisely defined. Ultimately the Roman classical writers, including Cicero, Horace, and Juvenal, utilized the word scabies to indicate something unnatural; indicating a transformation that encompassed a more metaphoric concept of the perceived affliction.

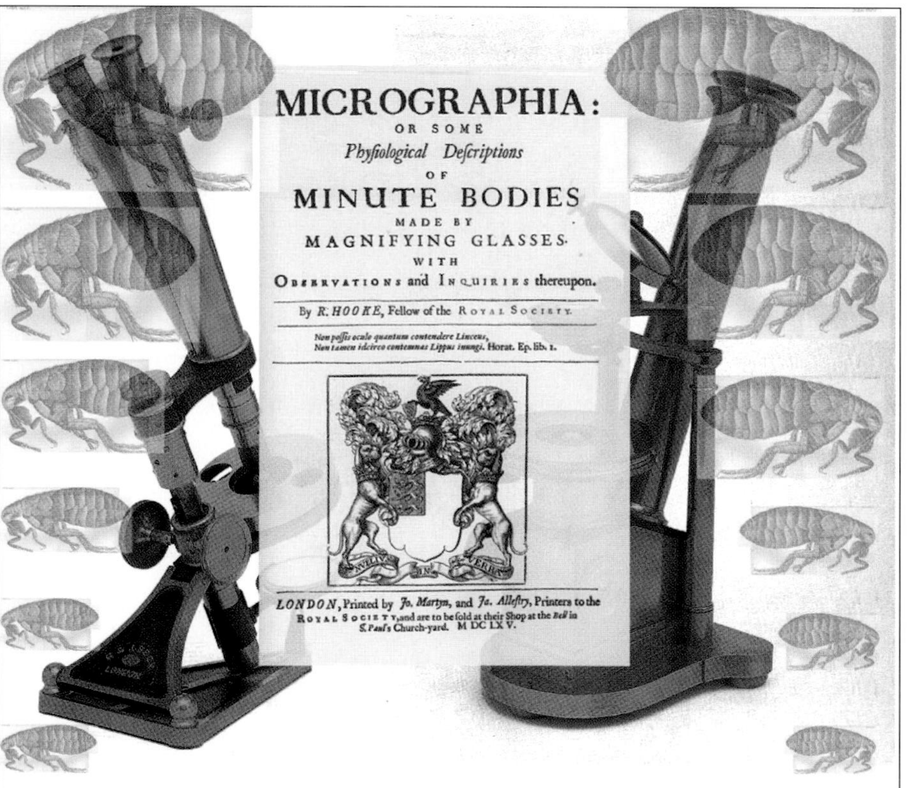

MICROGRAPHIA:
OR SOME
Physiological Descriptions
OF
MINUTE BODIES
MADE BY
MAGNIFYING GLASSES.
WITH
OBSERVATIONS and INQUIRIES thereupon.

By *R. HOOKE*, Fellow of the ROYAL SOCIETY.

Non possis oculo quantum contendere Linceus,
Non tamen idcirco contemnas Lippus inungi. Horat. Ep. lib. 1.

LONDON, Printed by *Jo. Martyn*, and *Ja. Allestry*, Printers to the ROYAL SOCIETY, and are to be sold at their Shop at the *Bell* in S. *Paul's* Church-yard. M DC LX V.

The medical utility of the microscope as applied by R. Hooke enabled the identification of an entire new world of worms and parasites that infested the human body. Mysterious complaints such as the "itch" were thus removed from the realms of wild speculation and supplanted with rational explanations as fleas, mites and larvae became visible to physicians.

Hippocrates mentions *psora*, and for the most part preferred to treat it solely by the internal administration of diluents and purgatives. Aristotle referred not only to the disease but the insects found in the blisters, while Celsus advocated the dermal application of ointments composed of a miscellaneous group of drugs, including verdigris, myrrh, nitre, white lead, and sulphur. The ultimate authority, Galen, alluded to the danger of external applications which might drive the disease inwards.

The Arab writers were far more explicit, and Rhazes, Haly Abbas, and Avicenna provided specific descriptions of the nature of the complaint, and how it could be transmitted from one person to another. Avicenna regarded it as a serious ailment and promoted an extreme treatment directed at the expulsion of the purportedly vicious humors from the body using bleeding and purgatives (*Hamech*). At the same time he advised that the constitution should be reinforced by suitable diet and astringent medicines.

Avenzoar of Seville, a remarkable observer who lived in the twelfth century, clearly grasped the basis of the disease. Thus he alludes to a malady of the skin, common among the people, and known as *Soab*. This, he says, is caused by a tiny insect, *"so small that it can scarcely be seen, which, hidden beneath the epidermis, escapes when a puncture has been made."*

By the sixteenth century there appears to have been a much clearer appreciation of the problem and the language, this effect is evident in the writings of Ambroise Paré: *"Les cirons sont petits animaux cachés dans le cuir, sous lequel ils se trainent, rampent, et rongent petit par petit, excitant une facheuse demangeaison et gratelle"*; and elsewhere *"Ces cirons doivent se tirer avec espingles ou aiguilles."* However, the complaint was regarded as a disturbance of the humors, which required treatment by appropriate internal medicines. Thus in a standard work of the time, *De Morbis Cutaneis*, by Mercuriali, published at Venice in 1601, the author attributed the disease to perverted humors, and affirmed that the disease was communicable since the liquid containing the contagious principle was deposited on or in the skin.

This view remained the prevailing orthodox opinion at least up to the seventeenth century, and the description of Van Helmont's personal experience with the itch was so frustrating that it led to his conversion from Galenism to Paracelsianism as a consequence of his cure. Nevertheless, despite his personal genius, even he never progressed beyond the concept that the cause of the complaint was a specific ferment.

The earliest serious scientific contribution to the study of this disorder may be credited to Thomas Mouffet, of London, who, in a treatise published in 1634, entitled *Insectorum sine Minimorum Animalium Theatrum*, demonstrated

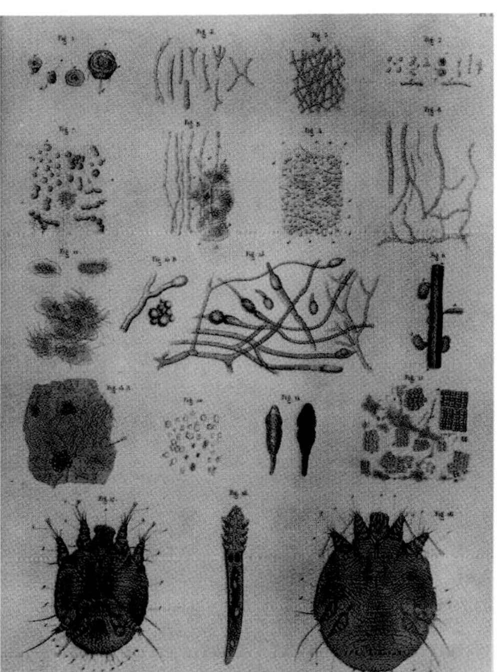

The application of microscopy to medicine allowed the identification of diverse parasites that infested not only the skin and muscles but also the bowel and urinary bladder.

Jean-Louis Alibert (1768-1837) (center) worked at the Hôpital St-Louis (background), Paris, where he became the founder of the French school of dermatology. In addition to classifying many novel skin diseases (mycosis fungoides, keloid) he was an early advocate of vaccination (foreground).

that the animalculae were constantly associated with the complaint. In addition, he clarified the observation that they were not only to be found in the vesicles, but in the connected tunnels to the blisters. In elucidating this critical point, Mouffet resolved the problem that had baffled previous investigators who were unable to explain the disease when the parasites were absent from the vesicles. Although his exposition should have led to a correct understanding of the cause of the complaint, it was practically ignored.

Fortunately at about this time, the microscope came into use and in 1657 a German naturalist, Hauptmann, published a rough drawing of the insect, which was improved upon a few years later by Etmuller. In 1687 Cestoni, a pharmacist of Leghorn, induced his colleague Dr. Bonomo to collaborate in a series of experiments to prove that the acarus was the cause of itch. They had both observed the women of the city extracting the insects from the hands of their children by the aid of needles, and the result of their research was a treatise in which the parasitic nature of the complaint was confirmed, and the uselessness of internal remedies emphasized. As a consequence of their studies, they recommended sulphur or mercury ointment as the essential curative application.

Nevertheless, despite the overwhelming evidence, many eminent physicians remained wedded to their theory of humors. Thus great medical authorities of the eighteenth century, such as Hoffmann and Boerhaave, still recommended general treatment, and compiled a long list of drugs which were suitable for the treatment of itch. Fortunately some parasiticides were included, such that some cures occurred, although in many instances a curative agent was incorrectly attributed. Others, such as Linneus, supported the view of Bonomo and Cestoni, although the former made the error of identifying the itch parasite with the cheese mite. The subject became even further confused at the end of the eighteenth century when Hahnemann promulgated the theory that the *"psoric miasm"* of which the itch eruption was the symptomatic manifestation, was the cause of a large proportion of chronic diseases.

Some observers thought there were two kinds of itch, one caused by the acarus, the other independent of it, while even bolder theorists proposed that the insect was in fact the product of the disease. This dispute continued until 1834, when Francois Renucci, a native of Corsica, and at the time assistant to the eminent surgeon d'Alibert at the Hôpital St-Louis, Paris, undertook to extract the *acarus* in any genuine case of itch. He had learnt this skill as a child on Corsica by observing the peasant women treating their children by needle extraction of the parasite. Although d'Alibert remained skeptical for years it became apparent by the middle of the nineteenth century that the parasitic character of itch was an unequivocal fact.

ESPERIENZE
INTORNO ALLA GENERAZIONE
DEGL' INSETTI
FATTE
DA FRANCESCO REDI
ACCADEMICO DELLA CRVSCA,
E DA LVI SCRITTE IN VNA LETTERA
ALL' ILLVSTRISSIMO SIGNOR
CARLO DATI.
IL PIU BEL FIOR NE COGLIE
IN FIRENZE.
All'Insegna della STELLA. MDCLXVIII.
Con licenza de' Superiori.

Francesco Redi (1626-1697) was the Italian physician and poet who demonstrated that the presence of maggots in putrefying meat was not a result of spontaneous generation but actually from eggs laid on the meat by flies. In so doing he initiated a major advance in the understanding of infectious disease. His interest in the subject was aroused by a book on generation by William Harvey that speculated that vermin such as insects, worms, and frogs do not arise spontaneously (the current belief), but from seeds or eggs too small to be seen. In 1668, in one of the first examples of a biological experiment with proper controls, Redi set up a series of flasks containing different meats, half of the flasks sealed, half open, and subsequently repeated the experiment but, instead of sealing the flasks, covered half of them with gauze so that air could enter. Although the meat in all of the flasks putrefied, he found that only in the open and uncovered flasks, which flies had entered freely, did the meat contain maggots.

Section 5

Alchemist physicians

Given the lack of any real divide between expertise in medicine, disease and therapy, physicians were perforce required to be knowledgeable in all. For the most part, this required a working knowledge of herbs and diverse remedies as well as, in some instances, a serious dedication to the alchemical as well as even the mystical arts. To a greater or lesser degree, many early physicians thus practiced an admixture of clinical discipline interlaced with expertise, which today would be more regarded as in the province of either pure chemists or pharmacists. In many instances, the application of this eclectic medical knowledge was even further amplified by unique personalities that might be variously characterized as ranging from the exotic and iconoclastic to the truly philosophical and genius variety.

RAYMOND LULLY

Raymond Lully is particularly famous in pharmaceutical history for the general use of the "*aqua vitae*" or aqua gardens, which he introduced. He had learned the process of distilling it from wine from Arnold of Villanova, who had himself probably acquired it from the Arab chemists of Spain, but Lully discovered the art of concentrating the spirit by means of carbonate of potash. Of the aqua vitae which he made, he declared that "*the taste of it exceedeth all other tastes, and the smell of it all other smells.*"

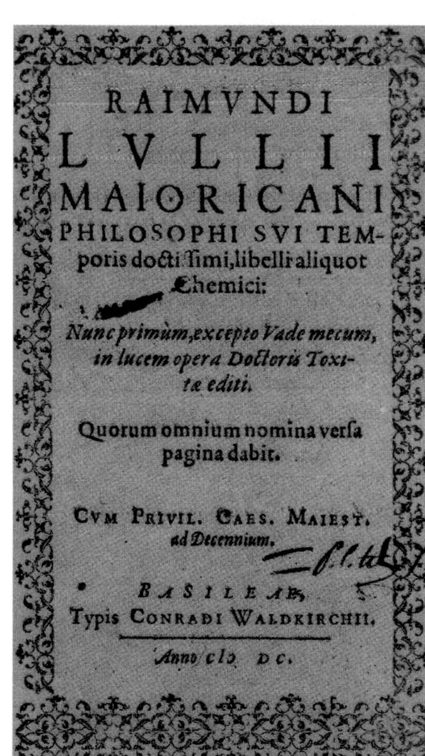
RAIMVNDI
LVLLII
MAIORICANI
PHILOSOPHI SVI TEMporis doctiſsimi, libelli aliquot Chemici:

Nunc primùm, excepto Vade mecum, in lucem opera Doctoris Toxitæ editi.

Quorum omnium nomina versa pagina dabit.

CVM PRIVIL. CAES. MAIEST. ad Decennium.

BASILEAE,
Typis CONRADI WALDKIRCHII.
Anno clↄ Dc.

Ars Magna, *the alchemical text written by Raymond Lully of Majorca, documented medicine and the alchemical arts. Lully was an exotic persona whose significant contributions to alchemy were only exceeded by his religious zeal in attempting to persuade the world of the follies of Islam.*

Despite this notable pharmacological contribution, the life of Lully was also exotic and peripatetic, encompassing romance, vision and tragedy. He was born at Palma, in the island of Majorca, in 1235, of a well-to-do family and, having married at the age of twenty-two, had two sons and a daughter. Unfortunately domesticity did not suit his needs, and he pursued a life of unrestricted pleasure that embraced the concepts of hedonism in the most extreme form, with the result that his fortune was soon decimated. This lifestyle would have continued unhindered but for a unique encounter with an object of desire. His intense desire for a beautiful and virtuous married woman named Ambrosia de Castello, who was living at Majorca with her husband, was abruptly terminated when she displayed her breast that had been mutilated by cancer. Lully claimed that this episode so affected him that he determined to study medicine with the object of discovering a cure for the cruel disease. Clearly there were more complex psychological events at play since once he had engaged upon the study of medicine and of alchemy, he also developed a fixation that it was his responsibility to deliver the earth from Mohammedan error. To this effect he therefore renounced the world, including his wife and children (though it is recorded that he first shared his possessions with his wife), and went to live on a mountain in a hut, which he built with his own hands. After a period of reflection he thereupon began to travel intensively, residing at Paris, Rome, Vienna, Genoa, Tunis, and in other cities, preaching new crusades, importuning the Pope to establish new orders of missionary Christians, and at intervals writing books on medicine. A particularly important tactic in achieving his end was the development of complex mathematical schema, which in his opinion absolutely proved the truth of Christianity. Indeed, he was convinced that by the use of a series of diagrams and formulae it would be possible to persuade the Saracens of the validity of his beliefs. The basic precepts of the concepts underlying his thoughts are enunciated in a great text, *Ars Magna,* that he composed. In the course of his extraordinary life he visited numerous countries and cities including Palestine and Cyprus. It was, however, at Naples in 1293 that he

Arnold of Villanova (1235-1311) was of Catalan extraction and the physician to Peter III of Aragon. He is credited with the introduction of brandy (aurum potabile) to medicine and was opposed to the footloose therapeutic empiricism of Parisian physicians. Although considered as a copious, elegant, and uncritical writer he was a fine teacher and Lully was much influenced by him.

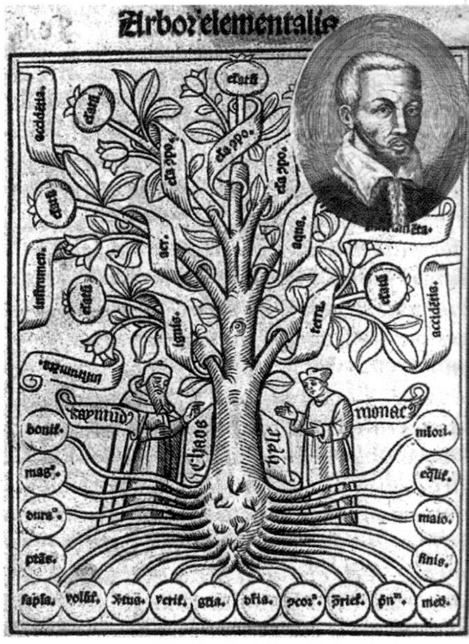

Raymond Lully (inset) and a page from his book Ars Magna*, representing the branches of knowledge, which constituted the tree of alchemical philosophy.*

Hieronymo Frascatoro of Verona achieved immortality for his interminable poem documenting in exquisite detail the ravages of the dreaded affliction for which he coined the term syphilis.

HIERONY
MI FRACASTO-
RII VERON.
LIBER I,
De Sympathia & Antipathia rerum.
De Contagione, & Cōtagiosis Morbis, & eorum curatione, Libri Tres.
Γίνεσθε φρόνιμοι ὡς οἱ ὄφεις.

Estote prudentes sicut Serpentes,

Apu... zeium.

The frontispiece of Syphyllides, sive Morbi Gallici *by J. Frascator with an inset of a medallion cast in his honor.*

made the acquaintance of Arnold of Villanova, who not only taught Lully much medicine and alchemy, but also found a fervent disciple in him.

At the age of seventy he traveled to London with the object of urging Edward I that he wage a new war against the Saracens. As was common for monarchs, Edward alleged lack of resources, but Lully was prepared to meet the difficulty, and historians of the science of the period assert that by using his alchemical skills he produced adequate gold for the purpose of the new crusade. Unfortunately Edward promptly used this money for a war with France, in which he was more interested, with the result that the disgusted Lully left England. Undaunted by this perfidious English behavior, at the age of seventy-eight he set forth to visit Jerusalem and thereafter visited several of the cities of North Africa. At Bougia, after preaching with his usual vehemence against the Mohammedan heresy, he was cruelly stoned by the Moors and grievously injured to the point of death. Fortunately some seafaring merchants recovered his body and determined to return his mortal remains to his native Majorca. His wounds, however, proved fatal and in his eightieth year, 1315, he perished at sea. Nevertheless, this strange man finally returned to the land of his birth and his tomb is still present in the church of San Francisco in the City of Palma.

Hieronymo Frascatoro

Hieronymo Frascator (1483-1553), generally known as Jerome Frascator, was a physician and poet of Verona who acquired high repute in the early part of the sixteenth century. As a physician of considerable influence he aided Pope Paul III, in persuading the Council of Trent to move from Germany to Bologna in Italy by alarming the delegates into believing that they were in imminent danger of an epidemic. Frascator especially studied infectious diseases, and his celebrated *Diascordium*, which is described in the section entitled *The Four Officinal Capitals*, was invented as a remedy for the Plague. Despite his obvious medicinal skills, his great literary fame depended principally on his somewhat bizarre and extensive Latin poem (three books) with the title of *Syphillides, sive Morbi Gallici*, published in 1530. Indeed, the finest classical scholars of the age regarded the poem as the most excellent Latin work written since the days when that language was in its full life, and they compared it appreciatively with the poems of Virgil (wielder of the stateliest measure known to man). The following lines will serve as a specimen:

... nam saepius ipsi Carne sua exutos
artus, squallentia ossa Vidimes,
et foedo rosa era dehiscere hiatus Ora, atque
exiles renentia guttura voces.

In Frascator's extraordinary versified description of the disease, he proposed that the malady had been imported from America and proposed that it had been known in ancient times, and was in fact caused by a peculiar corruption of the air. The mythical "hero", Syphilis, had given offence to Apollo, who, in revenge, had poisoned the air he breathed. The name of the disease was acquired from this poem, and though it has a Greek form and appearance, no ancient derivative for it can be suggested. As relevant to his thoughts on the disease are his proposal for a cure, which held that syphilis could be cured by *"plunging three times in a subterranean stream of quicksilver."* Lest he be considered an individual of marginal talent, Frascator also wrote a poem on hydrophobia, thus unwittingly encompassing both the rabies virus and the treponeme in one brief life!

In 1546, Fracastor outlined his concept of epidemic diseases in *De contagione et contagiosis morbis* (*On Contagion and Contagious Diseases*), stating that each is caused by a different type of rapidly multiplying minute body and that these bodies are transferred from the infector to the infected in three ways: by direct contact; by carriers such as soiled clothing and linen; and through the air. Although the Roman scholar Marcus Varro had mentioned microorganisms as a possible cause of disease in the first century B.C., Fracastor's was the first scientific statement of the true nature of contagion, infection, disease germs, and modes of disease transmission. As such his theory was widely praised during his time, but its influence was soon obscured by the mystical doctrines of the Renaissance physician Paracelsus, and it fell into general disrepute until it was effectively resuscitated and proved by Koch and Pasteur in the late nineteenth century.

Basil Valentine

According to some of his biographers Basil Valentine was born in 1393, whereas others are judiciously vague and have variously suggested the twelfth, thirteenth, or fourteenth century. The text of his work indicates that he was a Benedictine monk and historians have proposed several monasteries where he is supposed to have lived and labored without any authentic proof having been forthcoming. Indeed, many have doubted whether such a person as Basil Valentine ever existed and although his writings are said to have been circulated in manuscript, no one has ever pretended to have seen one of those manuscripts. Of note is the fact that the earliest known edition of any of Basil Valentine's works was published about 1601, by Johann Thölde, a chemist, and part owner of salt works at Frankenhausen in Thuringia. Since it is unlikely that Thölde was himself the author of the works attributed to the old monk, or that he devised the entire fiction of the alleged discoveries, chemistry and all, it seems possible that some degree of authenticity must be accorded the origin. In the light of the known

The frontispiece of the works of Basil Valentine, the mythical monkish chemiatrist of the 15th century. His proclamation of antimony as the cure for syphilis (and almost every febrile disease) attained an apogee of acclamation when in 1657 its usage cured Louis XIV of typhoid.

propensity of alchemists and other writers of the Middle Ages to represent their books as the works of someone of acknowledged fame (as ancient theologians were wont to credit one of the apostles or venerated fathers with their inventions), it was not uncommon for a pioneer to veil himself behind a fictitious sage whose existence he had himself invented. Basil Valentine, meaning the "valiant king", has assuredly an alchemical ring about it, and is precisely such a name as might be invented by one of the scientific fictionists of the Middle Ages. It is impossible, too, to read *The Triumphal Chariot*, at least when suspicion has been awakened, without feeling that the character of the pious monk is somewhat overdone. It seems unlikely that a seriously devout monk would be proclaiming his piety on every page with such vehemence! The last straw of belief is provided in the legend which accounts for the long lost manuscripts and explains that they were revealed to an unidentified person when a pillar in a church at Erfurt was struck and split open by lightning (Selah!), thus disclosing the manuscripts buried in that pillar!

It is unlikely that the "real" Basil Valentine was as ancient as he was generally believed to be, since syphilis is referred to in *The Triumphal Chariot* as the new malady of soldiers (*Neue Krankheit der Kriegsleute*), as *morbus Gallicus*, and *lues Gallica*. Given the fact that the disease was not known by these names until the invasion of Naples by the French in 1495, the life and times of Valentine would seem therefore to have been in the early to mid-sixteenth century. Further confusion is provided by another allusion in the same treatise to the use of antimony in the manufacture of type metal, which was certainly not adopted at any time at which Basil Valentine could have lived. Finally, his entire existence has been cast in doubt by the fact that the most diligent search has failed to discover his name either on the provincial list or on the general roll of the Benedictine monks preserved in the archives of the order at Rome. Indeed, no less an authority than Boerhaave asserted that the Benedictines had no monastery at Erfurt, which was generally assigned as the home of Valentine!

The name and works of Basil Valentine are inseparably associated with the medical use of antimony although adepts of the "gastric faith" believe he may have been involved in the original work on hydrochloric acid. His *Currus Triumphalis Antimonii* (*The Triumphal Chariot of Antimony*) is avowed in all textbooks to have been the earliest description of the virtues of this important remedy, and of the forms in which it might be prescribed. Indeed, much of Valentine's writings provide considerable evidence of not only a sophisticated understanding of a diversity of chemical knowledge but a tincture of significant mysticism. Thus, in the explanation of the process of fusing iron with stibium (antimony) and obtaining thereby "*by a particular manipulation a curious star which the wise men before me called the signet star of philosophy*" can be identified elements of both serious chemistry and alchemical formulation.

As regards the allegation that Thölde was involved in the Valentine work, Kopp's *Beitrage zur Geschichte der Chemie*, asserts that he could only be regarded as an editor of Basil Valentine's works, because at publication they provided such a plethora of novel chemical information that it was impossible to accept that Thölde would have denied himself the credit of the discoveries if they had been his. In *Die Alchemie*, which Kopp published in 1886, he refers to Basil Valentine, and says that there is reason to think that the works attributed to him by Thölde in 1875 were an intentional literary deception perpetrated by the latter.

Valentine's famous text commences by explaining that he is a monk of the Order of St. Benedict and that this "*requires another manner of the spirit of Holiness than the common state of mortals exercised in the profane business of this World.*"

The 1618 text of Johan Mylius was 3,000 pages long and documented much of what was known about contemporary medicinal chemistry including the contributions of Basil Valentine. The frontispiece (background) has Hermes and Hippocrates (right) worshipping the Adamic earth and four emblems (above) representing the elements: fire, air, water and earth. The androgynous being (inset) represents Lucifer and the Antichrist whose roots are the seven deadly sins. This fusion of spagyrical medicine with religious emblems and occultism was pervasive even amongst knowledgeable chemists.

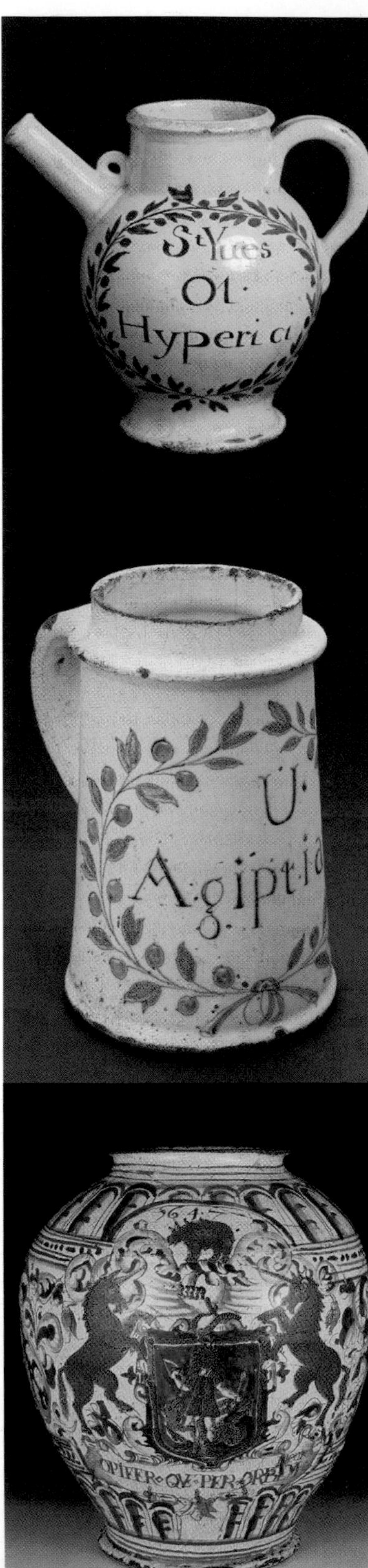

After thus introducing himself, he proceeds to mingle chemistry, piety, and abuse of the physicians and apothecaries of his day with much repetition though with considerable shrewdness, for about fifty pages. At last, after many false starts, he expounds the origin and nature of antimony, thus:

> *Antimony is a mineral made of the vapor of the Earth changed into water, which spiritual sidereal Transmutation is the true Astrum of Antimony; which water, by the stars first, afterwards by the Element of Fire which resides in the Element of Air, is extracted from the Elementary Earth, and by coagulation formally changed into a tangible essence, in which tangible essence is found very much of Sulphur predominating, of Mercury not so much, and of Salt the least of the three. Yet it assumes so much Salt as it thence acquires an hard and unmalleable Mass. The principal quality of it is dry and hot, or rather burning; of cold and humidity it hath very little in it, as there is in common Mercury; in corporal Gold also is more heat than cold. These may suffice to be spoken of the matter, and three fundamental principles of Antimony, how by the Archeus in the Element of Earth it is brought to perfection.*

It requires some practice in the interpretation of alchemical writings to elucidate this rhapsody, and there is little advantage in the interpretation of the mysticism. The Archeus represented a species of friendly demon who worked at the formation of metals in the bowels of the earth; that all metals were supposed to be compounds of sulphur, mercury, and salt in varying proportions, the sulphur and the salt, however, being refined spiritual essences of the substances; and that it was a necessary compliment to pay to any product which it was intended to honor to trace its ancestry to the four elements.

Basil Valentine's scathing contempt for contemporary medical practitioners is worthy of quotation:

> The doctor, he says, *knows not what medicines he prescribes to the sick; whether the color of them be white, black, grey, or blew, he cannot tell; nor doth this wretched man know whether the medicament he gives be dry or hot, cold or humid… Their furnaces stand in the Apothecaries' shops to which they seldom or never come. A paper scroll in which their usual Recipe is written serves their purpose to the full, which Bill being by some Apothecary's boy or servant received, he with great noise thumps out of his mortar every medicine, and all the health of the sick.*

A collection of apothecary jars used to store medicaments. The bottom one is embellished with the seal of the London Society of Apothecaries – two unicorns flank Apollo who is surmounted by a rhinoceros. The inscription "Opifer que per orbem" attests to the pledge of Apollo to spread his healing throughout the world.

Valentine then concludes his *Triumphal Chariot* by thus apostrophizing contemporary practitioners:

> *Ah, you poor miserable people, physicians without experience, pretended teachers who write long prescriptions on large sheets of paper; you apothecaries with your vast marmites, as large as may be seen in the kitchens of great lords where they feed hundreds of people; all you so very blind, rub your eyes and refresh your sight that you may be cured of your blindness.*

NICHOLAS CULPEPPER

Culpepper was a well-known writer, whose *Herbal* was familiar to many generations as a family medicine book. Culpepper lived in the stirring times of the English Civil War, and fought on one side or the other, it is not certain which, although judging from the frequent pious expressions in his works, he was a Parliamentarian. He was severely wounded in the chest in one of the battles and it is probable that it was this wound which caused the lung disease from which he died. Such information as we have of Culpepper's career is gathered from his own works, and from some brutal attacks on him in certain public prints. He describes himself on the title-pages of some of his big books as "M.D.," but there is no evidence that he ever graduated. He lived, at least during his married life, at Red Lion Street,

Nicholas Culpepper, the herbalist and quacksalver, who in 1649 translated the Pharmacopoeia Londinensis *into English. An enigmatic intellect possessed of an admixture of sound commonsense, prescience and a substantial tincture of entrepreneurial skill.*

Spitalfields, and there he carried on his large medical practice. Although many of those who studied his works formed the idea that he was a bent old man with a long grey beard, who eternally busied himself with the collection of simples, he was, in fact, a soldier, and died at the early age of thirty-eight from the sequela of a military wound. The portraits and descriptions of him by his astrological friends represent him as a smart, brisk young Londoner, fluent in speech and animated in gesture, gay in company, but with frequent fits of melancholy, in extraordinarily good conceit of himself, and plenty of reason for it.

Culpepper evidently understood the art of advertising himself and claimed to have been the only doctor in London at the time who gave advice gratis to the poor. Indeed, his frequent comments on the cost of the pharmacopoeia preparations suggest that the majority of his patients were not of the fashionable class.

As a physician he was highly regarded for the freedom, and the occasional sharpness, with which he criticized the first and second editions of the *London Pharmacopoeia*. Indeed, a specimen of his sarcastic style provides good evidence for this. The official formula for *Mel. Helleboratum* was to infuse 3 lbs. of white hellebore in 14 lbs. of water for three days; then boil it to half its bulk; strain; add 3 lbs. of honey and boil to the consistence of honey. This is Culpepper's comment (in his *Physicians' Library*):

"What a monstrum horrendum, horrible, terrible recipe have we got here: A pound of white hellebore boiled in 14 lbs. of water to seven. I would ask the College whether the hellebore will not lose its virtue in the twentieth part of this infusion and decoction (for it must be infused, forsooth three days to a minute) if a man may make so bold as to tell them the truth. A Taylor's Goose being boiled that time would make a decoction near as strong as the hellebore, but this they will not believe. Well, then, be it so. Imagine the hellebore still remaining in its vigor after being so long tired out with a tedious boiling (for less boiling would boil an ox), what should the medicine do? Purge melancholy, say they. But from whom? From men or beasts? The devil would not take it unless it were poured down his throat with a horn. I will not say they intended to kill men, cum privilegio; that's too gross. I charitably judge them. Either the virtue of the hellebore will fly away in such martyrdom, or else it will remain in the decoction. If it evaporate away, then is the medicine good for nothing; if it remain in it is enough to spoil the strongest man living. 1) Because it is too strong. 2) Because it is not corrected in the least. And because they have not corrected that, I take leave to correct them."

The Hellbore plant whose indiscriminate medical usage excited violent rebarbative comment from Culpepper.

This passage is not selected as a favorable specimen of Culpepper's pharmaceutical skill, but more as a sample of the manner in which he often berated "the College." His own opinions are open to quite as severe criticism since a large part of his lore was astrological and he expressed complete confidence in regard to the doctrine of signatures. Nevertheless he possessed a good knowledge of herbs, and his general advice was sound.

Nicholas Culpepper was apprenticed to an apothecary in Great St. Helen's, Bishopsgate, and at the same time a certain Marchmout Nedham was a solicitor's clerk in Jewry Street. Nedham became the most notorious journalist in England, and founded and edited in turn the *Mercurius Britannicus*, an anti-royalist paper, the *Mercurius Pragmaticus*; violently anti-Commonwealth, and the *Mercurius Politicitis*, subsidized by Cromwell's government, and supervised by no less a personage than the eminent poet, Mr. John Milton. Probably Nedham and Culpepper were friends in their early days, and they may have been comrades in arms when the war broke out but thereafter became fierce enemies. In *Mercurius Pragmaticus*, Nedham, pretending to review Culpepper's translation of the official Dispensatory, took the opportunity of pouring on him a tirade of scurrilous abuse. The translation, he says, "*is filthily done*," which was certainly not true and represented the only piece of criticism in the article of which the rest consisted of a personal diatribe against the author. After making further vile insinuations about Culpepper's wife, Nedham states that by two years' drunken labor Culpepper had "*gallimawfred the Apothecaries' Book into nonsense*"; that he wore an old black coat lined with plush which his stationer (publisher) had got for him in Long Lane to hide his knavery, having been till then a most despicable ragged fellow; "*looks as if he had been stewed in a tanpit; a frowzy-headed coxcomb*." He was aiming to "*monopolise to himself all the knavery and cozenage that ever an apothecary's shop was capable of*."

Culpepper's works themselves answer this spiteful caricature, for he was a man of considerable attainment, and of immense industry. That his writings acquired considerable popularity is best proven by the fact that after his death it was regarded as good business to forge materials to resemble them and then pass them off as Culpepper's work.

Alchemical imagery, including the salamander of fire representing the fusion force of life, is surmounted by the igneous water (firewater of life) bounded by chaos against a background of distillation apparatus and zodiacal emblemata. Men such as Culpepper inhabited an ephemereal world where mysticism commingled with chemistry and alchemy as physicians sought to use all disciplines to combat disease.

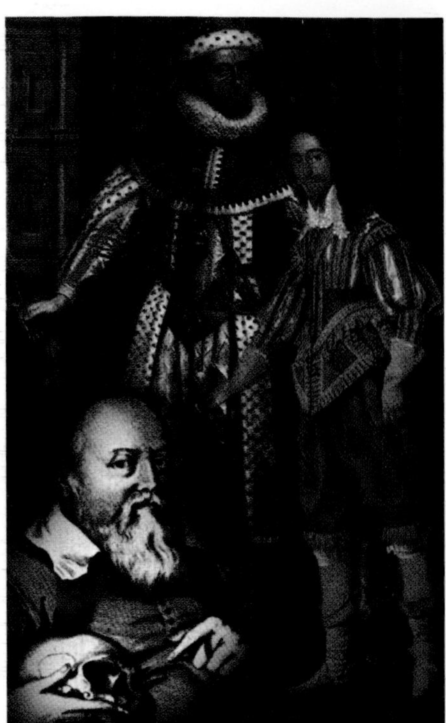

Theodore Turquet de Mayerne (1573-1655) of Geneva (left) studied medicine at Montpellier in France before becoming a teacher and physician in Paris. As a result of his liberal usage of mercury and antimony he was vilified by the Paris faculty and finally fled to England, where he became royal physician to James I (1566-1625) (back) and later to Charles I (1600-1649) (right).

THEODORE TURQUET DE MAYERNE

Sir Theodore Turquet de Mayerne, Baron Aulbone of France, was born at Geneva in 1573 of a Calvinistic family, and studied for the medical profession first at Heidelberg and then at Montpellier. Thereafter he moved to Paris, where he acquired popularity both as a lecturer on anatomy to surgeons as well as on pharmacy to apothecaries. His inclination towards chemical remedies soon became well recognized and brought him to the notice of Rivierus, the first physician to Henri IV, with the result that he was appointed one of the king's physicians. Unfortunately his medical heterodoxy offended the faculty while his Protestantism invited enmity at the royal court. In an attempt to retain his services, the king, who valued the services of Turquet de Mayerne, exerted considerable effort in an attempt to persuade him to conform to the Church of Rome as he himself had done, and to moderate the rancor of his professional foes. He was unsuccessful in both efforts. Nevertheless Henri tried his utmost to retain his services and sought to ignore his heresies (perhaps even sympathizing with them). Unfortunately his wife, Marie de Medici, insisted on Turquet's dismissal, and the Faculty of Paris was delighted to support this regal intolerance. In a well-orchestrated smear campaign they linked his name to a quack named Pierre Pena, a foreigner then practicing medicine illicitly at Paris and issued a decree forbidding all physicians who acknowledged their control to consult with Turquet. Lest this be deemed insufficient, they further exhorted practitioners of all nations to avoid him and all similar pests, and to persevere in the maintenance of the doctrines of Hippocrates and Galen.

In addition to being a fine physician, Turquet de Mayerne meticulously documented all his cases to the degree that on his demise, twenty-three volumes of such material were deposited in the British Museum. Thirty-five years after his death, these manuscripts, which documented his treatment of acute diseases, were collated into a text, *Praxeos Mayernianae in morbis internis praecipue gravioribus et chronicis syntagma, ex adversariis, consiliis ac epistolis ejus, summa cura ac diligentea concinnatum,* and published in London in 1690. Apart from his medical contributions Turquet de Mayerne was instrumental in instituting some regulatory order to the chaos of early British pharmacology. Thus, he managed to have the guild of apothecaries separated from that of the grocers, and he aided in the preparation of the early editions of the *Pharmacopoeia Londinensis*, commonly called the "P. L." Despite local claims to the contrary, the *London Pharmacopoeia* was not the first work of its type. The evolution of the *London Pharmacopoeia* was part of a more complex series of issues and basically was published hurriedly as part of an attempt to prevent grocers from compounding drugs. As a result of the official separation in 1618 of the guild of grocers and apothecaries, the purpose of this pharmacopoeia was ostensibily to introduce a set of recognized standards by which medicines could be compounded. In fact, most of this first edition of the "P. L." was a direct copy from the sixth (1613) edition of the *Augsburg Pharmacopoeia* and on its initial appearance in May, 1618, was so poor that it was canceled and a new edition appeared in December of the same year. Although further editions were published in 1621, 1632, 1639, and 1677 it was not until the edition of 1721 that the *London Pharmacopoeia* acquired any real significance.

Indeed, the evolution of pharmacopoeias is an interesting tale in itself. The first work in the nature of a pharmacopoeia was the *Antidotarium Florentium*, published in 1498 by the medical college of Florence. Subsequently a more extensive book was compiled by Valerius Cordus acting upon government authority at Nuremberg in 1535 and a quarter of a century later in 1561, Anuce Foes (Anutius Foesius, 1528-1595) of Basel first employed the word pharmacopoeia as a title. However, by the beginning of the seventeenth century the expansion of the *materia medica* by Asiatic and American substances had rendered the older therapeutic works too incomplete to be of much use.

As a result of this French persecution, Turquet de Mayerne moved to England where his considerable reputation led to his initial appointment as first physician to the king (James I) and queen, and thereafter to the same position under Charles I. Although he maintained a low profile, during the Commonwealth in 1628, it appears from his manuscript records (*"Ephemerides Anglicae,"* he called them) that he was consulted by a "Mons. Cromwell" whom he describes as *"Valde melancholicus."*

A 16th century apothecary's laboratory with an inset of the Pharmacopoeia Londinensis *and the coat of arms of the London Society of Apothecaries (right).*

CROMWELL y^e 2^d EXALTED or the POISON BAG outdone by the HALTER

A caricature Turquet Oliver Cromwell. As the former personal physician to the late Charles I, de Mayerne thought little of Cromwell who had sought his medical advice.

Turquet de Mayerne died at Chelsea in 1655 at the age of 82, having exercised a considerable influence on both English medicine and pharmacy. Indeed, the Society of Apothecaries owed to him their separate incorporation, and the first *London Pharmacopoeia* was compiled and authorized probably to some extent at his instigation. He certainly wrote the preface to it. Paris quotes him as prescribing among absurd and disgusting remedies *"the secundines of a woman in her first labor of a male child, the bowels of a mole cut open alive, and the mummy made of the lungs of a man who had died a violent death."* The principal ingredient in a gout powder which he composed was the raspings of an unburied human skull – a remedy that he presumably had inherited from Paracelsus. In addition, he devised an ointment for hypochondria which was called the *Balsam of Bats* and contained adders, bats, sucking whelps, earthworms, hog's grease, marrow of a stag, and the thigh bone of an ox. While certainly disagreeable such remedies were commonplace to almost all practitioners in England and France at the time. Despite his sympathy with exotic cures, Mayerne is also credited with the introduction of calomel and black wash into medical practice and the legitimization of their usage.

Jean-Baptiste Van Helmont

Jean-Baptiste Van Helmont was born at Brussels in 1577, and died at Vilvorde near that city in 1644. Less exotic and visible than Paracelsus, he was nevertheless an erratic genius whose writings and experiments, although sometimes astonishing in their lucidity and insight, are often riddled with mysticism and naiveté.

Jean-Baptiste Van Helmont (left) and his son.

Van Helmont was of wealthy aristocratic Flemish descent, a voracious student and a brilliant lecturer. At the University of Louvain, however, where he spent several years, he refused to take any degree because he believed that such academic distinctions only ministered to pride and resolved to devote his life to the service of the poor. With this in mind he made over his property to his sister, and set himself to the study of medicine with the belief that he could provide care for those less fortunate than he. It was soon apparent to the faculty that his gift of exposition was so formidable that they persuaded the authorities of the University to insist that he accept the Chair of Surgery, although that was the branch of medical practice he knew least about, and though it was contrary to the statutes of the faculty to appoint a person as Professor not formally qualified.

Despite his initial success, Van Helmont soon tired of medical teaching and came to believe that the entire system was a fabrication of vanity perpetuating credulity. The particular event that culminated in his final discomfort with medical science was that he contracted the itch, and though he consulted many eminent physicians could not get cured of it.

As a result of this negative experience he came to the conclusion that the pretended art of healing was a fraud, and consequently resolved to shake the dust of it from his feet, after he had recovered from the weakening effects of the purgatives which had been prescribed for his complaint. Determined to seek knowledge elsewhere, he thereupon embarked on a period of travel, during the course of which he met with a quack who cured him of his itch by means of sulphur and mercury. Convinced of the moral turpitude of his peers, he became a violent anti-Galenist and studied the works of Paracelsus, returning after some years to his native country imbued with novel ideas and fantasies. Nevertheless, some commonsense prevailed and he married a wealthy woman, thereby achieving enough independence to embark upon a scientific career. Having established and erected a well-equipped laboratory at Vilvorde, he devoted his time and skill to the study of chemistry, medicine, and philosophy, describing himself as *"Medicus per Ignem."* As such he became one of the most earnest believers in the possibility of discovering either the philosopher's stone or the elixir of life. Such was his purported success that he claimed to have actually transmuted mercury into gold! Similarly, the efficacy of his medical compounds led to such miraculous cures that it is alleged that the Jesuits actually brought him before the Inquisition.

Despite this exoticism, the advance in chemistry for which he is most famous was the discovery of carbonic acid gas, which he named carbon dioxide *"gas sylvestre"* and in so doing provided the first use of the term gas. What suggested this name to him is not certain, but his words reflect his recognition of the new territory of chemistry that he was entering *"Hunc spiritum, hactenus ignotum, novo nomine gas voco."* (I call this spirit, heretofore unknown, by the new name gas.) Some have supposed that it was a modification of the Flemish, *geest* (spirit), but others have traced its origin to the verb *gaschen*, to boil, or ferment, while yet other scholars have assumed that the derivation from chaos is the explanation for his choice.

Nevertheless, whatever his motives, his observations in this area of chemistry represent the first steps in the recognition of the existence of various

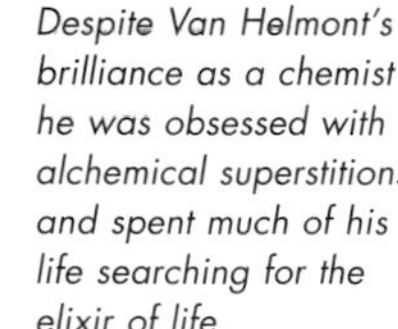

Despite Van Helmont's brilliance as a chemist he was obsessed with alchemical superstitions and spent much of his life searching for the elixir of life.

Nooth's apparatus for making carbonated water had initially been proposed by J. Priestley, who was regarded as "the father of the soft drinks industry" for his experiments on gas obtained from the fermenting vats of a brewery. In 1772 he demonstrated a small carbonating apparatus to the College of Physicians in London, suggesting that, with the aid of a pump, water might be more highly impregnated with fixed air. Antoine Lavoisier in Paris made the same suggestion in 1773 to Thomas Henry, an apothecary in Manchester, England, to whom is attributed the first production of carbonated water, which he made in 12-gallon barrels using an apparatus based on Priestley's. Jacob Schweppe, a jeweler in Geneva, read the papers of Priestley and Lavoisier and determined to make a similar device. By 1794 he was selling his highly carbonated artificial mineral waters to his friends in Geneva but later moved the business to London. Although Van Helmont discovered carbon dioxide and coined the term gas he had little concept of its physiological role.

kinds of gases. Previous to his discovery, chemists had no clear perception of a distinction between the various gases and regarded them all as permutations of air. Although Geber and other predecessors of Van Helmont had observed that certain vapors were incorporated in material bodies, they regarded these as the spirits, or souls, of those bodies, whereas Van Helmont was the first to actually separate and examine one of these vapors. Driven by intuition as well as a significant intellect, Van Helmont examined this gas through many of the compounds in which it is combined or formed, and noted its presence in limestone, potashes, burning coal, and certain natural mineral waters, as well as a fermentation product of bread, wine, and beer. He demonstrated that it could be compressed in wines and thus yield the sparkling beverages that have become so well-known. In addition he observed that it extinguished flame, and asphyxiated animals. Although he alluded to other kinds of vapor, he failed to define them precisely and confused some of his work with bizarre references to spirits and gases purported to have divine properties.

Overall, his physiology was a modification of that of Paracelsus in that he accepted that an archeus within ruled the organism with the assistance of sub-archei for different parts of the body. Ferments stirred these archei into activity and in so doing, activated the processes of digestion which Van Helmont believed to be a central component of the function of the Soul of Man that resided in the stomach. The exact locality of this important adjunct was a subject of intense discussion among the philosophers of that age, and conclusive argument for the stomach as its habitation was the undoubted fact that troublesome events or bad news had the effect of destroying the appetite. As a result of digestion, agents became available to the body and were merged into the vital spirit, a kind of gas that was responsible for the pulsation of the arteries!

Johann Glauber

Johann Glauber, who was born at Karlstadt, in Germany, in 1604, contributed largely to pharmaceutical knowledge, and is remembered by his many investigations, and perhaps even more for the clear common sense which he brought to bear on his chemical work. For though he retained a confident belief in the dreams of alchemy, he does not appear to have let that belief interfere with his practical labor; and some of his processes were so well-devised that they have hardly been altered to this very time.

A collection of astrological symbols from the chemistry texts of the 17th century.

Unfortunately, little is known of his history except what he himself wrote or what was related of him by his contemporaries. According to his own account, he acquired an interest in chemistry when as a young man, a troublesome stomach complaint was cured by drinking some mineral waters. Eager to identify the essential chemical in the waters to which he owed his health, he set to work with the result that he soon identified sulphate of soda, which he called "*Sal admirabile*," but which subsequent generations have referred to as Glauber's Salt. Of note is the fact that Glauber was himself unimpressed by his own observation, believing that he had only obtained from another source Paracelsus' *Sal enixon*, which was in fact sulphate of potash. His own account of this discovery is of some pharmaceutical interest and provided in his work *De Natura Salium*, as follows:

> *In the course of my youthful travels I was attacked at Vienna with a violent fever known there as the Hungarian disease, to which strangers are especially liable. My enfeebled stomach rejected all food. On the advice of several friends I dragged myself to a certain spring situated about a league from Newstadt. I had brought with me a loaf of bread, but with no hope of being able to eat it. Arrived at the spring I took the loaf from my pocket and made a hole in it so that I could use it as a cup. As I drank the water my appetite returned, and I ended by eating the improvised cup in its turn. I made several visits to the spring and was soon miraculously cured of my illness. I asked what was the nature of the water and was told it was "salpeter-wasser."*

Glauber was twenty-one at that time, and knew nothing of chemistry. When he afterward analyzed the water by evaporation he produced long crystals,

Johann Rudolph Glauber (top left) was born in 1604 in Karlstadt, Bavaria and died March 10, 1668, in Amsterdam. Although primarily a chemist his skills were supported by the usual amalgam of astrological and kabbalistic arcana common to the profession of his time. Glauber's chemical skills were so prestigious that he was colloquially referred to as the German Boyle, i.e., the father of chemistry. Having settled in Holland, he prospered chiefly by the sale of chemicals and medicinals that he prepared under conditions of extreme secrecy. Of particular medical importance was his preparation of hydrochloric acid from common salt and sulfuric acid, although it remained for William Prout of England, almost two centuries later, to identify it in the human stomach. Glauber was more impressed with the virtues of the residue of his preparation, sodium sulfate – sal mirabile, or Glauber's salt, which subsequently obtained wide popularity as a laxative. In addition he also noted the formation of nitric acid from potassium nitrate and sulfuric acid. Glauber prepared many substances, made useful observations on dyeing, and described the preparation of tartar emetic. In 1715 his collected writings were reissued as "Glauberus Concentratus."

which, he noted, *"a superficial observer might confuse with saltpetre"* although he soon satisfied himself that it was something quite different. Subsequently he obtained an identical salt from the residue in his retort after distilling marine salt and vitriol to obtain spirit of salt. As already stated, Glauber believed he had produced the *"sal enixon"* of Paracelsus but in memory of the benefit he had himself experienced from its use, he gave it the title of *"sal mirabile."*

This distillation of sulphuric acid with sea salt, which yielded spirit of salt, or as it is now called hydrochloric acid, was probably Glauber's principal contribution to the development of chemistry. In addition, he observed the gas given off from the salt, and it is puzzling, given his astute mind, that he did not at that time isolate and describe the element chlorine. In his text he referred to it as the spirit of rectified salt, and described it as a spirit of the color of fire, which when passed into a receiver would dissolve metals and most minerals. Similarly he noted that if digested with dephlegmated (concentrated) spirit of wine, his spirit of salt formed a layer of oily substance which was the oil of wine, *"an excellent cordial and very agreeable."* In addition to these observations he distilled ammonia from bones, and showed how to make sal ammoniac by the addition of sea salt (*Sal ammoniacum secretum Glauberi*). This subsequently became highly regarded as a fertilizer. Glauber also made sulphate of copper, and his investigation of the acetum lignorum, subsequently called pyroligneous acid, was of the greatest value. Outside the realm of medicine and pharmacy, Glauber produced artificial gems, made chlorides of arsenic and zinc, and added considerably to the chemistry of wine and spirit-making.

Given his genius and proclivity, Glauber worked at many subjects for manufacturers, and was comfortable in selling his information. His enemies asserted that he traded the same secret several times, and that he not infrequently sold secrets which would not work. While such assertions are not easy to prove, it is more likely that they represent allegations made against him by those who were not as skilful as he. Of interest is the record that there was one secret which he claimed to have discovered he would neither sell nor publish. It was that of the *Alkahest*, or universal solvent. To make this known might, he feared, *"encourage the luxury, pride, and. godlessness of poor humanity."* Oliver Cromwell wrote in an old volume of *Glauber's Alchemy*: *"This Glauber is an errant knave. I doe bethinke me he speaketh of wonders which cannot be accomplished; but it is lawful for man too the endeavor."*

Despite his enormous industry and widespread fame Glauber complained that he was not appreciated: *"I grieve over the ignorance of my contemporaries and the ingratitude of men. Men are always envious, wicked, and ungrateful. For myself, faithful to the maxim,* Ora et labora, *I fulfil my career, do what I can, and await my reward."* Elsewhere he writes, *"If I have not done all the good in the world that I should have desired, it has been the perversity of men that has hindered me."* Filled with despair at the venality of his employees, he noted that they were unfaithful and having once learned his processes, became inflated with pride, and left him. Apparently there was a good business to be done in chemical secrets at that time! But Glauber did not give away all he knew, and he found it best to do all his important work himself. *"I have learnt by experience,"* he wrote, the truth of the proverb, *"Wer seine Sachen will gethan haben recht, Muss selbsten seyn Herr and Knecht."*

Patin and Oporinus

Despite the influx of novel botanical products from the New World during the late fifteenth century and the massive increase in interest in the subject of vegetable remedies, those involved in the practice of alchemy were that more medical progress could be predicted from the exhausted residues at the bottom of their alembics than from the combined efforts of all the misguided root-pullers and leaf-pickers. As a result of these two dramatically divergent concepts, bitter acrimony arose that initially centered around antimony, a substance which had been known to the ancients as stibium and which had been listed by the Arabs, Latins, Greeks, and Egyptians, among the latter of whom it had been used as a cosmetic. Constantinus Africanus is said to have been the first to use the term "antimonium" while Basil Valentine popularized antimony in his classic text, *The Triumphal Chariot of Antimony*, and Paracelsus initiated the medical applications of the metal. Antimony had long been a familiar substance to the alchemists who were searching for the

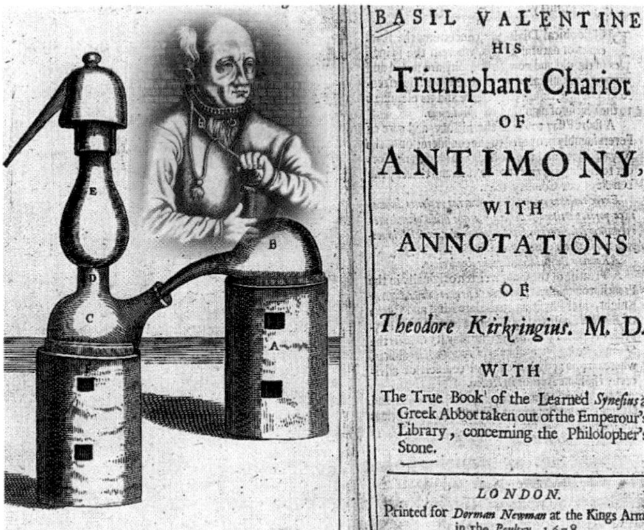

BASIL VALENTINE
HIS
Triumphant Chariot
OF
ANTIMONY,
WITH
ANNOTATIONS
OF
Theodore Kirkringius. M. D.
WITH
The True Book of the Learned *Synesius* a Greek Abbot taken out of the Emperour's Library, concerning the Philosopher's Stone.

LONDON.
Printed for *Dorman Newman* at the Kings Arm in the *Poultry*. 1678.

Paracelsus (center) reviled the majority of current medical practice as nonsense but was an ardent supporter of the use of antimony, which had originally been proposed by Basil Valentine.

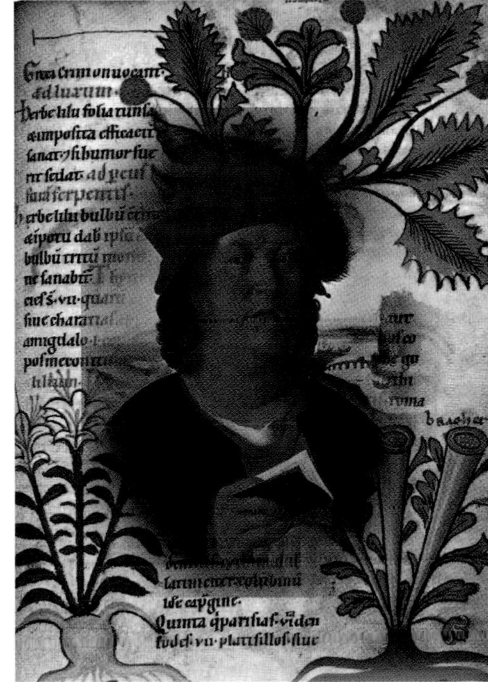

The portraits of Paracelsus found in old books, as well as some celebrated paintings, are curiously various as likenesses. The oldest and by far the most frequent representation of him on title pages of his works are all more or less similar. This particular painting (inset) is in the Bodleian Library at Oxford. There is a similar painting, in the print room of the British Museum. In the year 1875, at an exhibition of historical paintings held at Nancy (France), a painting attributed to Albert Durer, and bearing his name in a cartouche, was exhibited and described as "Portrait presume de Paracelse." Since Durer died in 1528 (thirteen years before the death of Paracelsus) and there is no mention of this likeness in any of his letters, it may have been the work of one of his pupils. A third portrait which is unlike either of the others professes to have been painted from life ("Tintoretto ad vivum pinxit") by Jacope Robusti, more commonly known as Tintoretto. The original has never been found, and the earliest print from it was a copper-plate engraving in a collection issued by Bitiskius of Geneva in 1658. Since Tintoretto scarcely left Venice all his life, it has been proposed that he may have become acquainted with Paracelsus when the latter was an army surgeon in the Venetian army in the years 1521-25. It has pointed out that if Tintoretto was born in 1518 or even 1512 as has been suggested, the painting from life was unlikely. Moreover, the gentle-looking person represented could not possibly have been the untamable Paracelsus if any reliance can be placed on the art of physiognomy.

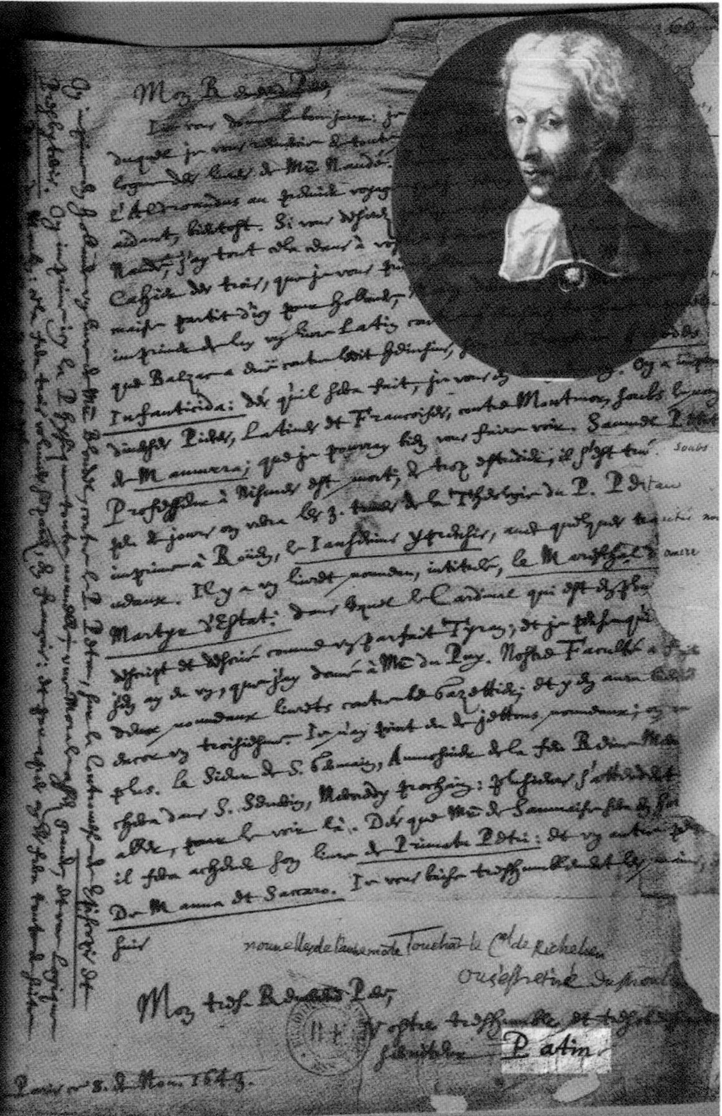

Guy Patin (1601-1672) was the Dean of the Paris Faculty and responsible for the condemnation of almost every advance in medicine of his time. He abjured the use of antimony in extreme terms (vide letter) and was an outspoken critic of Paracelsian medicine. The cure of Louis XIV of typhoid by the use of antimony did little to moderate Patin's prejudice to the agent! His especial disdain was however directed towards surgeons who he described as "a race of evil, extravagant coxcombs who wear mustaches and flourish razors!" When the royal surgeon Felix cured Louis XIV of his fistula in ano, Patin was, however, briefly silenced.

philosopher's stone and the elixir of life. Indeed, as early as the fourteenth century John of Rupescissa (*fl.* 1350), the author of a treatise, *On the Consideration of the Fifth Essence*, had written of it: *"Pulverize the mineral antimony until it is imperceptible to the touch and put it in the best distilled vinegar until the vinegar is colored red. This done, remove the colored vinegar in another vase and pour on it more vinegar until, over a slight fire, it too is colored, when it should be removed. And keep that up until the vinegar no longer is colored. Then put all the vinegar which has colored into a still, and first the vinegar will rise. Then you will see a stupendous miracle, because through the beak of the alembic you will see as it were a thousand particles of the blessed mineral descend in ruby drops like blood.*

Which blessed liquor keep by itself in a strong glass bottle tightly sealed, because it is a treasure which the whole world cannot equal. Behold a miracle! forsooth the great sweetness of antimony so that it surpasses the sweetness of honey. And I declare by God's love that the human intellect can scarcely believe the virtue and worth of this water or fifth essence of antimony. And Aristotle in the book, Secret of Secrets, *says that it is lead. Believe me that never in nature was there a greater secret. For all men have toiled to sublimate the spirits of minerals and never had the fifth essence of the aforesaid antimony. In short I never would be able to express the half of this discovery. For it takes away pain from wounds and heals marvelously. Its virtue is incorruptible, miraculous, and useful beyond measure. Forty days it needs to putrefy in dung in a sealed bottle and then it works marvels."*

It is probable that the conflict between the botanical and chemical therapeutists might have long been delayed or possibly avoided had it not been for Paracelsus. However, his almost rabid espousal of chemical remedies had antagonized the pharmacists to a point that approached a virtual frenzy of indignation. He is generally credited with the introduction of quintessences and advocated the use of alcoholic extracts in prescriptions. In addition he was the first to employ tincture of hellbore, tincture of compound aloes and tincture of metal or *Lilium Paracelsi*. This latter was administered as cordial and was prepared from alloys of antimony and iron, antimony and tin, and antimony and copper. In addition to its use as a cordial, *Lilium Paracelsi* was a constituent of theriacal elixir. Although Paracelsus believed in specifics he also hoped, somewhat paradoxically, to be able to identify a medicine of medicines, an elixir of life. All these ideas were distinctly noxious to those interested in the herbal drug trade and those who had wagered their careers and often fortunes on the possibilities inherent in the influx of American botanicals.

J. Oporinus (1507-1568), the assistant of Paracelsus, said that he *"always kept several preparations stewing on his furnace – as, for example, a sublimate of oil or of arsenic, a mixture of saffron and iron, or his marvelous Opodeldoch [a plaster]. He never prescribed a special diet nor any hygienic measures. As a purge he gave a precipitate of theriaca or of mithridate, or simply the juice of cherries or grapes, in the form of granules (about the size of the droppings of mice), and he was careful always to give them in uneven numbers (1, 3, or 5). He was bitterly opposed to the polypharmacy which prevailed so widely in his day."*

J.Oporinus (1507-1568), assistant to Paracelsus. A complex individual who although apparently a faithful companion and trusted friend, painted a somewhat barbed portrait of the mortal failings of his master. He subsequently became a printer in Basel and published the immortal texts of Vesalius.

Although Paracelsus successfully established antimony as a therapeutic agent, it was not long before some physicians became convinced that the substance was a dangerous poison. The center of this "antimonial" controversy raged in the city of Paris, where the dispute over its efficacy lasted for more than a century until 1566 when its usage as a drug was finally prohibited by Royal decree. Astoundingly enough, when a century later Louis XIV was supposedly cured of typhoid fever by a huge dose of antimony administered by a quack after the treatment of the royal physicians had proved futile, the drug was reinstated! During the decades in which the medical dispensing of the metal was prohibited, advocates of its use found that they could evade prosecution and obtain the desired results and still stay within the law by placing white wine in cups made of antimony. This method of administration came under the category of *pocula emetics*. Pierre Pomet (1658-1699) in his *Histoire générale des drogues traitant des plantes et des animaux* advised patients as follows:

> *to throw away the three or four first wines you make with the Cups, lest they should produce some ill Accident. Whereas most people who have Occasion for the Goblets or cups of the Regulus find difficulty to come by them, let them apply to a Founder, they will have what Sorts and Sizes they will at a cheap Rate, without troubling themselves with Moulds, as several have done to their Labour and Cost, who have at last been obliged to give over the Attempt not being able to make one Cup without a Hole or some other Defect. You may also get these same Founders to make you the perpetual Pills, or you may easily make them yourself with a Musket Ball Mould.*

Louis XIV of France. The curious isolation and the sterile inefficiency of the French internists of the 17th century is most strikingly revealed in the letters of Guy Patin (vide page 80). To a large extent this represented the extraordinary hierarchical system and the dogma of its adepts. A classic example was provided by the treatment of the anal fistula of the King. Louis XIV suffered from a fistula in ano which, after remaining obdurate to the exhibition of innumerable ointments and embrocations (provided by Patin), was successfully healed by operation at the hands of the royal surgeon, Felix. The latter received for his endeavors a farm, 300,000 livres, (three times more than the honorarium of the royal physician) and was ennobled, becoming the Seigneur de Stains. Felix was succeeded by Mareschal, and to Mareschal is due the elevation of the French surgeon's social condition in the 18th century. It is worthy of note that Louis XIV influenced French medicine in three curious ways: His attack of typhoid fever (1657) provided an immense vogue for the use of antimony; his anal fistula (1686) resulted in the rehabilitation of French surgery; and the fact that his mistress was attended by Clément, the royal accoucheur, in 1663, did much to further the cause of midwifery.

While of great attraction in terms of infinite usage, the esthetic disadvantage of such perpetual pills lay in the relatively indecorous and incommodious method of retrieval.

Without doubt the most vitriolic opponent of antimony in Paris was the satiric Guy Patin (1602-1672). Patin's therapy was usually limited to bleeding and the administration of syrup of roses or senna and he exhibited little patience with the therapeutic beliefs of his contemporaries. Indeed, an apt quotation from the correspondence of Patin attests most effectively to his position as well as paying tribute to his classically Gallic insouciance:

> *The reputation of theriaca is without effect and without foundation, it comes only from the apothecaries who do all they can to persuade people to use compositions and would take from them if they could the knowledge and use of simple remedies which are more useful. If I were bitten by a venomous animal I would not trust in theriaca, nor in any cardiac, external or internal, of the shops. I would scarify the wound deeply, and apply to it powerful attractives, and only have myself bled for the pain, fever or plethora. But by good fortune there are scarcely any venomous animals in France. In recompense we have Italian favorites, partisans, many charlatans, and much antimony.*

PARACELSUS

There are few who in history have exercised such a revolutionary influence on medicine and pharmacy as the iatrochemist and erratic genius Philipus Aureolus Theophrastus Bombast von Hohenheim (1493-1541). The name Paracelsus is believed to have been coined by himself, probably with the intention of somewhat Latinizing his patronymic, von Hohenheim, and also perhaps as an attestation of his belief that his skills should be regarded as similar to the celebrated Roman physician and medical writer, Celsus. Although the Bombast family was an old and honorable name that originated in Wurttemberg, Paracelsus' father finally settled at Maria Einsiedeln, a small town close to Zurich. The father was a physician and after years of work in Switzerland finally died at Villach, in Carinthia, in 1534, aged seventy-one. Although the young Paracelsus (an only child) was initially taught classics at a convent school, and at sixteen studied at the University of Basel, it is likely that his early exposure to medicine and alchemy influenced his subsequent career.

Basel had little attraction for Paracelsus and he soon departed for Würzburg where he studied in the laboratory of Trithemius, an abbot and a famous adept in alchemy, astrology, and magic. It is here that much of his early knowledge of chemistry and his mystic views began to shape themselves.

The peripatetic genius and medical revisionist Paracelsus atop a frontispiece of one of his texts: "Prognostication."

A medieval pharmaceutical laboratory by Johannes Stradanus of Flanders, 1570. On the left a worker prepares an extract from an herbal press. A young (and possibly tuberculotic-kyphoid) apprentice in the foreground uses a mortar and pestle while on the right a precipitate is prepared over a furnace. A flask is held by a trainee (center) prior to pouring it into an alembic for distillation. Wearing spectacles (an emblem of erudition, or given the times an indication of a luetic choroid retinitis) the apothecary himself supervises the complex tasks and admonishes, with a raised finger, his minions to exert due diligence in their noble tasks.

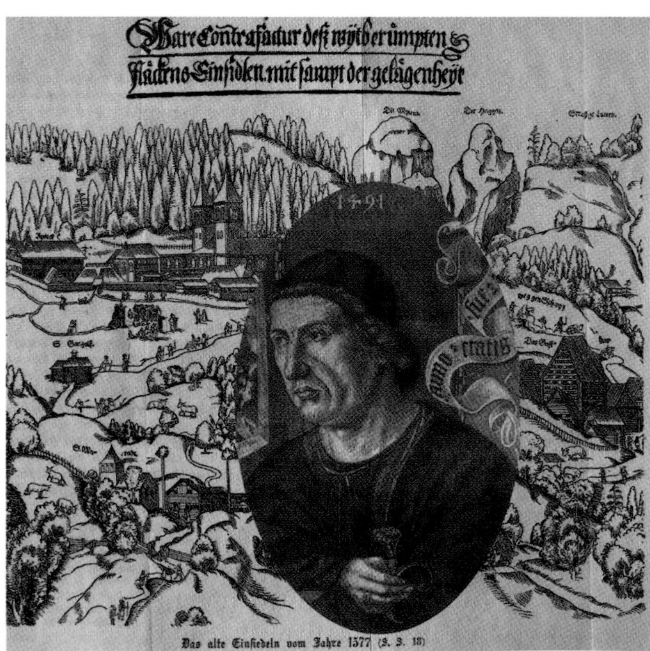

However, Paracelsus was dissatisfied with the artificial ideas of the alchemists and soon sought the acquaintance of the wealthy Sigismund Fugger (the Fugger family were the equivalent of the Rothschilds of Germany), a mine owner in the Tyrol. Such was their wealth that it is reported that the Fugger who entertained Charles V at Augsburg, during the famous Diet at which the Emperor was to crush the Reformation, made a cinnamon fire (an incalculably expensive spice at that time) for the Emperor, and lighted it with a bond representing a large sum which Charles owed him.

In the Tyrolese mines Paracelsus learned much about minerals, diseases, and men, while in his free time he traveled widely throughout Europe, paying his way by his medical and surgical skill, or, as his enemies said, by conjuring and necromancy. Indeed, in his writings Paracelsus claims that as an army surgeon he had participated in the wars against Venice, Denmark, and the Netherlands and thereby had learned to cure forty diseases of the body! It was his unabashed assertion that he had gained his knowledge from gypsies, physicians, barbers, executioners, and peasants. More fanciful are his claims that he had visited Tartary, and accompanied the Khan's son to Constantinople. Nevertheless the celebrated and much revered Van Helmont reported that it was in this city that Paracelsus met an adept who had given him the philosopher's stone. Other chroniclers relate that this adept was a certain Solomon Trismensinus, who also possessed the elixir of life, and had been met with some two hundred years later!

Although Paracelsus in his writings appeared to believe in the transmutation of metals, and in the possibility of producing medicines capable of indefinitely prolonging life, he expended little energy in fantasizing about these, as did most other alchemists. Similarly the production of gold appealed little to him, and his aims in medicine were always eminently practical. Although he variously described his medicinal compounds as catholicons, elixirs, and panaceas, they were all real remedies for specific complaints; and judging from his reputation in the treatment of these he must have been marvelously successful.

Whether he ever went to Tartary or not, and whether he served in any wars or not, may be doubtful, but it is certain that for at least ten years, his life was peripatetic and ranged widely through Germany.

When, therefore, Paracelsus arrived at Basel, in the year 1525, in the thirty-second year of his age, his fame had preceded him and he was duly appointed to the Chair of Medicine and Surgery as well as being ensconced as the city physician. Such recognition reflected not only his skills but the backing of persons of high influence, since according to his own account he had cured no less than eighteen princes during his travels.

Paracelsus' father (inset), a physician himself, and the village of Einsiedeln where the family lived c. 1500.

His lectures were such as had never been heard before at a university and he began his course by burning the works of Galen and Avicenna in a chafing dish, and denouncing the slavish reliance on authority which at that time characterized medical teaching and practice. In a style unusual for the time he taught from his own experience, and he gave his lectures in German rather than the formulaic Latin. Much of the commentary that has survived reflects boastful utterances that are repeated in his writings. Thus he opined that all universities had less experience than he, and that *"the very down on his neck was more learned than all the authors."* He likened himself to Hippocrates, the one ancient whom he esteemed, and criticized the doctors in white gloves who feared to soil their fingers in the laboratory. He declaimed with characteristic zeal and hubris *"Follow me, not I you, Avicenna, Galen, Rhazes, Montanan, Mesue, and ye others. Ye of Paris, of Montpellier, of Swabia, of Cologne, of Vienna; from the banks of the Danube, of the Rhine, from the islands of the seas, from Italy, Dalmatia, Sarmatia, and Athens, Greeks, Arabs, Israelites. I shall be the monarch, and mine shall be the monarchy."*

Similarly in respect of the apothecaries he wrote, *"The apothecaries are my enemies because I will not empty their boxes. My recipes are simple and do not call for forty or fifty ingredients. I seek to cure the sick, not to enrich the apothecaries."*

A broadside proclaiming the medical views of Paracelsus.

Martin Luther was a contemporary of Paracelsus and attacked the dogma of contemporary religious belief with the same vigor that Paracelsus directed against the physicians.

His career at Basel was finally brought to a close by a dispute with a prebendary of the cathedral named Lichtenfels, whom he had treated. The canon, in the midst of his pain, had promised Paracelsus two hundred florins if he would cure him. The cure was not disputed, but as Paracelsus had only provided a few little pills, the clergyman relied on the legal tariff with the result that Paracelsus sued him, and the court awarded the legal fee, which was six florins. Not surprisingly the good doctor published his comments on the case, and it can readily be supposed that they were of such a character as to amount to contempt of court and prompted a swift departure from Basel.

The memorial in a Salzburg church, St. Philip Neri commemorating Paracelsus. The poet Browning (top left) memorialized Paracelsus in a poem that was widely acclaimed for its insight and sensitivity.

Smitten with the peripatetic zeal of his early days, Paracelsus between 1528 and 1535 lived and practiced at Colmar, Esslingen, Nuremberg, Noerdlingen, Munich, Regensburg, Amberg, Meran, St. Gall, and Zurich as well as Carinthia and Hungary. Finally in 1541, the Prince Palatine, Duke Ernst of Bavaria, took him under his protection, and settled him at Salzburg where a few months later he died. His enemies claimed that his passing reflected dissipation and exhaustion although his friends averred that assassination was responsible. A German surgeon who examined his skull when the body was exhumed thirty years after death, noted a fracture of the temporal bone, which, he declared, could only have been produced during life, because the bones of a solid but desiccated skull could not have separated in such a fashion. It was suggested that some hirelings of the local doctors whose prospects were endangered by this formidable invader had "accidentally" pushed him down some rocks, thus causing the fracture. In the chapel of St. Philip Neri, at Salzburg, a monument consisting of a broken pyramid of white marble and his portrait is surmounted by a Latin inscription commemorating his cures of disease and his generosity to the poor in the following terms:

Conditur hic Philippus Theophrastus, insignis Medicina;
Doctor, qui dira illa vulnera, lepram, podagram,
hydroposim, aliaque insanabilia contagia mirificu arte sus-
tulit; ac bona sua in pauperes distribuenda
collocandaque honoravit. Anno 1541, die 24 Septembre.
Vitam cum morte mutavit.†

It is appropriate to note that such novel thought as expressed by Paracelsus was as much a reflection of the time, as the long-suppressed energy of the human intellect was at that period emerging. Thus, listed among the contemporaries of Paracelsus were Luther, Columbus, and Copernicus whose names reflect perhaps the greatest emancipators of the human race from the chains of slavish obedience to authority in the past thousand years. Although Paracelsus was not, so far as is known, a Lutheran Protestant, he was sympathetic to his heroic countryman and probably identified with his common travails. "*The enemies of Luther,*" he wrote, "*are to a great extent fanatics, knaves, bigots, and rogues. You call me a medical Luther, but you do not intend to honor me by giving me that name. The enemies of Luther are those whose kitchen prospects are interfered with by his reforms. I leave Luther to defend what he says, as I will defend what I say. That which you wish for Luther you wish for me; you wish us both to the fire.*" There was, indeed, much in common between these two independent and often wayward souls.

Such details of the personality of Paracelsus as are available were for the most part written by his enemies. Thus Erastus, a theologian as well as a physician, who may have met Paracelsus, and who fiercely attacked his system, depreciated him simply on hearsay. On the other hand Operinus, a disciple who had such reverence for him that when Paracelsus left Basel, he accompanied him and was with him night and day for two years, wrote a letter about him after his death which provides considerable insight into the life of the man. In this letter Operinus expresses the most unbounded admiration of Paracelsus' medical skill; of the certainty and promptitude of his cures; and especially of the "miracles" he performed in the treatment of malignant ulcers. But, adds Operinus,

†("Here lies Philippus Theophrastus, the famous Doctor of Medicine, who by his wonderful art cured the worst wounds, leprosy, gout, dropsy, and other diseases deemed incurable and to his honor, shared his possessions with the poor.") A fitting monument to the greatest of the medical revolutionaries!

An idealized compilation of images of a medical chemiatrist pondering the causes of disease and the nature of cure. Light (truth) shines on his dusty tomes while thoughts of alchemy (background) cloud his lucid enquiry. In the background the skull bears mute witness to the futility of life and embraces the "vanitas" theme. The magnitude of the problem is exemplified by the terrestrial globe and the disarray (the realities of existence) of the study.

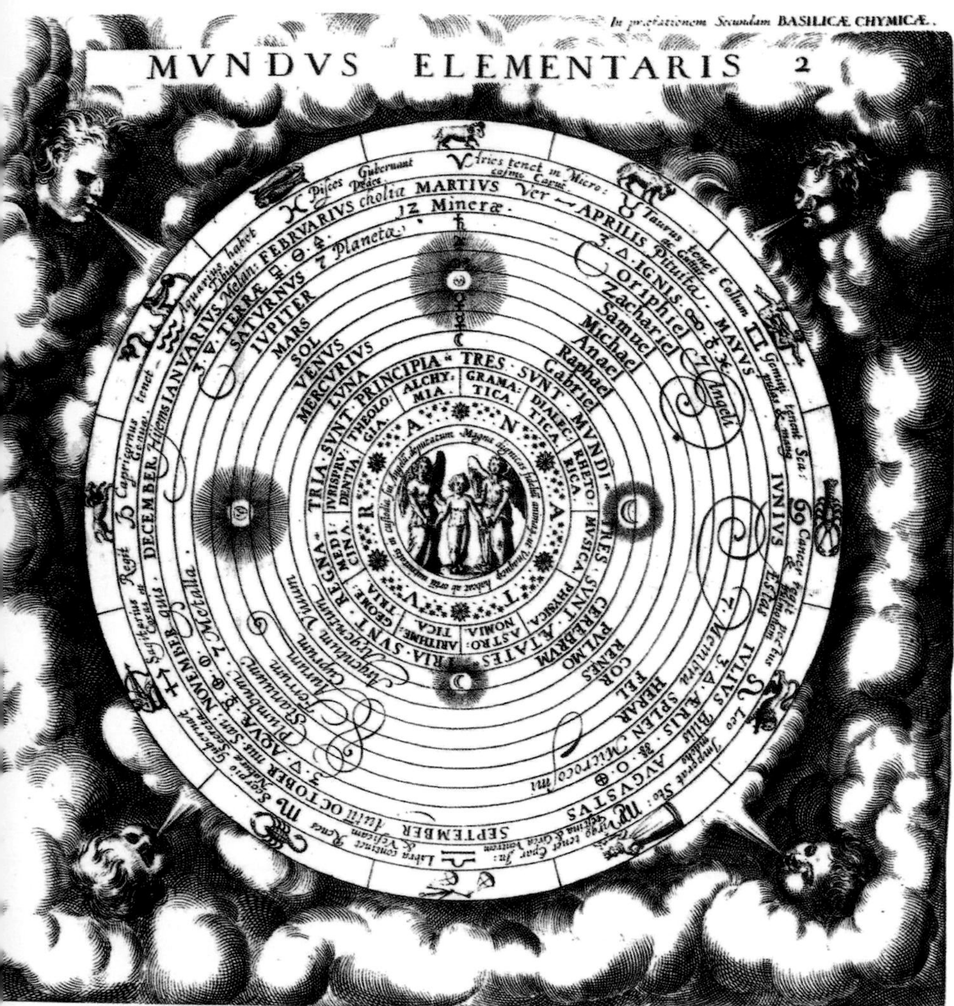

The World of Elements (Mundus Elementaris). *Paracelsus alleged that if we could compile a complete "herbarium spirituale sidereum" all disease could be adequately treated. It was also apparent to him that star influences also form our soul-essences and thereby accounted for our varying temperaments and talents. Of most particular interest was his belief that the material part of man, the living body, is the Mumia which was managed by the Archaeus, which rules over everybody and was regarded by him as the ultimate vital principle providing the internal balsam which heals wounds or diseases, and controls the action of the various organs.*

"I never discovered in him any piety or erudition." He had never seen him pray. Paracelsus was as contemptuous of Luther as he was of the Pope and maintained that no one had discovered the true meaning or actual spirit of the Scriptures. During their two years together Operinus declared that Paracelsus was almost constantly drunk and *"was scarcely sober two hours at a time."* With some degree of distaste he recorded that Paracelsus would go to taverns and challenge the peasantry to drink against him and when he had taken a quantity of wine, he would put his finger in his throat and vomit. Then he could start again. And yet Operinus also reports how perpetually he worked in his laboratory, noting, *"the fire there was always burning, and something was being prepared, some sublimate or arsenic, some safran of iron, or his marvelous opodeldoch."* Moreover, no matter how drunk he might be, he could always dictate, and Operinus says *"his ideas were as clear and consecutive as those of the most sober could be."* Ultimately shocked by his religious sentiments Operinus left his master and returned to Basel where he died in poverty, having established a printing business that failed.

Robert Browning's dramatic poem of *Paracelsus* has been much praised by the admirers of the poet. It was written when Browning was twenty-three, and represents in dramatic form the ambitious aspirations of a youth of genius who believes he has a mission in life; has intellectual confidence in his own powers; and the assurance that it is the Deity who calls him to the work. *In some time, His good time, I shall arrive; He guides me.* His bitter disappointment with his professorship at Basel, and his contempt for those who brought about his fall there, are depicted, and the effect which the realization that his aims had proved impossible had on his habits and character is suggested; and at last, on his deathbed in a cell in the Hospital of St. Sebastian at Salzburg, he tells his faithful friend, Festus, who has all his life sought to restrain the ambitions which have possessed him:

You know the obstacles which taught me tricks
So foreign to my nature, envy, hate,
Blind opposition, brutal prejudice,
Bald ignorance – what wonder
if I sank to humour men
the way they most approved.

(Robert Browning)

The poem of Browning has been referred to as little more than *"a study of intellectual egotism."* Although it is clear that Paracelsus was an egotist, egotism alone seems a ludicrously insignificant term to apply to his exotic self-appreciation. Nevertheless, the Victorianism of Browning's verse somewhat obscures the wild untamable energy of this astonishing medical reformer hidden within the description of the prolix preacher represented in the poem.

The mystic views of Paracelsus, or those attributed to him, are curious rather than useful, and he appears to have had as much capacity for belief as he had disbelief in the speculations of other philosophers. Thus he believed in gnomes in the interior of the earth, undines in the seas, sylphs in the air, and salamanders in fire. These were the Elementals, beings composed of soul-substance, but not necessarily influencing our lives. He believed that the Elementals knew only the mysteries of the particular element in which they live; that there is life in all matter and that every mineral, vegetable, and animal possesses its own astral body. That of the minerals is called Stanuar or Trughat; of the vegetable kingdom, Leffas; while the astral bodies of animals are their Evestra. The Evestrum may travel about apart from its body and of considerable import – it may live long after the death of the body. Thus ghosts are, in fact, the Evestra of the departed such that if suicide was committed the Evestrum would not recognize the act and would continue as if the body were going on also until its appointed time. He believed Man to be a microcosm and the universe a macrocosm. Thus they were not comparable to each other but were one in reality and divided only by form. As regards plants he believed that each plant on earth possessed its own star and noted for example a *stella absinthii*, a *stella rorismarini*. Although his early comments on mercury, sulphur, and salt, as the constituents of all things, seem at first likely to lead to something conceivable if not credible, the influence of his spiritual concepts muddy his initial thoughts and the concepts are lost in notions of an intermingling of sidereal mercury, sulphur, and salt, spirit, soul, and body.

The composition of Paracelsus' laudanum, the name of which he no doubt invented, has never been satisfactorily ascertained and Paracelsus himself made a great secret of it, and probably used the term for several medicines. It was generally, at least, a preparation of opium, sometimes opium itself which he is believed to have carried in the pommel of his sword, calling it the *"stone of immortality."* Next to opium he believed in mercury, and was largely

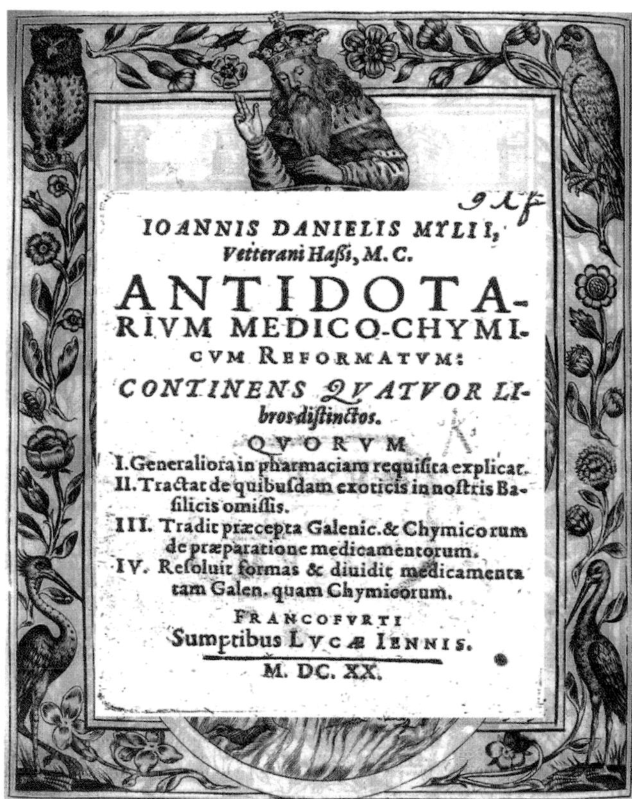

IOANNIS DANIELIS MYLII,
Vetterani Haßi, M. C.
ANTIDOTA-RIVM MEDICO-CHYMI-CVM REFORMATVM:
CONTINENS QVATVOR LI-bros distinctos.
QVORVM
I. Generaliora in pharmaciam requisita explicat.
II. Tractat de quibusdam exoticis in nostris Basilicis omissis.
III. Tradit præcepta Galenic. & Chymicorum de præparatione medicamentorum.
IV. Resoluit formas & diuidit medicamenta tam Galen. quam Chymicorum.
FRANCOFVRTI
Sumptibus LVCÆ IENNIS.
M. DC. XX.

The frontispiece of J.D. Mylius' Antidotarium. *Many of the remedies prescribed were obscure and irreproducible. It is likely that many of the formulas of Paracelsus were purposely unclear in many cases, although obvious obfuscation by magic or the carelessness or ignorance of the copyists may also have been responsible. Nevertheless much of his chemical and pharmaceutical advice is clear enough.*

influential in popularizing this metal and its preparations for the treatment of syphilis. Prior to his suggestions, it had been principally employed externally and he openly derided *"the wooden doctors with their guaiacum decoctions, and the wagon grease with which they smeared their patients."* In addition he used turpith mineral (the yellow sulphate), and alembroth salt (ammoniochloride), though he did not invent these names, and it is possible that his work does not refer to the same substances as the alchemists. Operinus states that he prescribed precipitated mercury (red precipitate, apparently) in pills with a little theriaca or cherry juice as a purgative. Paracelsus was particularly impressed with antimony and highly praised the "magistery of antimony", the essence, the *arcanum*, and alluded to the virtue of antimony.

Besides mercury and antimony, of which he made great use, iron, lead, copper, and arsenic were among the mineral medicines prescribed by him and he produced an arsenate of potash by heating arsenic with saltpeter. He had great faith in vitriol, and the spirit which he extracted from it by distillation. This "spirit" he again distilled with alcohol and thereby produced an ethereal solution. His *"specificum purgans"* was afterwards said to have melded sublimed saffron of Mars in worms.

Paracelsus made balsam from herbs by digesting them in their own moisture until they putrefied and then distilling the putrefied material, and as such obtained a number of essential oils which he prescribed as quintessences having obtained the term from Aristotle. Quintessence was defined as follows: *"Every substance is a compound of various elements, among which there is one which dominates the others, and impresses its own character on the compound. This dominating element, disengaged, is the quintessence."* Thus oil of eggs, which was recommended against scalds and burns, was obtained by boiling the eggs very hard, then powdering them, and distilling until oil rose to the surface. Oil of aniseed was prescribed for colds and the instructions stated that it be put in the nostrils and applied to the temples on going to bed. Oil of tartar was rectified in a sand bath until it acquires a golden color and thereafter used to cure ulcers and stone. Coral would quicken fancy, but drive away vain visions, specters, and melancholy. Oil of a man's excrements, twice distilled, was claimed to be of use when applied to fistulas, and also in baldness. Oil of an unburied man's skull was obtained by distillation and prescribed in 3 grain doses for epilepsy.

Thus his *"Confectio Anti-Epileptica,"* as formulated by his interpreter, Oswald Crollius, was prepared as follows: *"First get three human skulls from men who have died a violent death and have not been buried. Dry in the air and coarsely crush. Then place in a retort and apply a gradually increasing heat. The liquor that passed over was to be distilled three times over the same faeces. Eight ounces of this liquor were to be slowly distilled with 3 drachms each of species of diamusk, castorum, and anacardine honey. To the distilled liquor 4 scruples of liquor of pearls and one scruple of oil of vitriol were to be added."* Of the resulting medicine one teaspoonful was to be taken in the morning fasting by epileptic subjects. An *Arcanum Corallinum* of Paracelsus, which was included in some of the earlier London Pharmacopoeias, was simply red precipitate prepared in a special manner. The Committee of the College of Physicians which sat in 1745 to revise that work rejected this product with the remark that an *arcanum* was not a secret known only to some adept, but was simply a medicine which produces its effect by some hidden property. With the infinite superiority of their British heritage they did, however, recognize that *"Paracelsus, whose supercilious ignorance merits our scorn and indignation,"* had used the term in the sense of a secret remedy.

The translation of the "Seals of the Philosophers" provides some understanding of the complex interpretive world of chemistry and alchemy that Paracelsus dealt with. Left to right: Hermes Trismegistus, the Egyptian: That which is above is as that which is below. Adfar the Alexandrian, teacher of Morienus: The Sun is the Father of our spouse, but the Mother is the white Moon. Calid, Saracen King of Egypt, disciple of Morienus: A third, who is the ruler of Fire, succeeds the Father and Mother. Mary the Jewess, sister of Moses: A smoke embraces a smoke, and the grass of the mountain absorbs them both. Cleopatra, Queen of Egypt: The Divine is hidden from the people according to the Wisdom of the Lord. Medera, the woman Alchemist: Whoever does not know the rule of truth does not know the Flask of Hermes. Thaphuntia, the woman Philosopher: A marriage is made between two Gums, the White and the Red. Euthica, the Arab woman Philosopher: What fights against Fire is Sulphur, what sustains it is Mercury. Calid the Jew, son of Gazichus: The creator's magistery is derived from adoration of God, not from your strength. Musa, from the school of Calid: The teachers of the devout are the middlemen of the Divine Wisdom. Democritus, the Greek Alchemist: The shadow of the solid Body is removed by the fiery medicine. Pythagoras, the Greek Philosopher: In Nature you must study that from which God created all. Anaxagoras, the Chazomoenian Philosopher: The burning Sun, the Soul of the Moon, the Spirit in the center, are nothing but Mercury. Zamolxis, the companion of Pythagoras: With God and Piety as my companions I come from narrow straits to glory. Heraclitus, the Philosopher: Fire is the beginning of all things. Apollonius of Tyana, the Philosopher: No Prophet is ever born wise in his own country.

Section 6

MAGIC, FRAUD and THERAPY

It is not unsurprising that healing and magic have been related from time immemorial, given the value placed upon the ability to restore good health. Any person, object or incantation possessed of such power was by necessity either in contact with deities or spirits. Thus charms, enchantments, amulets, incantations, talismans, phylacteries, and all the armory of witchcraft and magic have been intimately associated with pharmacy and medicine in all countries and throughout recorded history. In many instances the borderline between magic and medicine became hazy as was evident in the degradation of the Greek term *"pharmakeia"* from its original meaning of the art of preparing medicine, to sorcery and poisoning. Such fluctuations in therapeutic practice provide evidence of the prevalence of debasing superstitions in the practice of medicine among the cultivated Greeks.

Thus each civilization and culture developed individual icons (Egypt-Hermes, Persia – Zoroaster, Hebrew – Solomon) who achieved status among the early practitioners and teachers of magic and became legendary names to conjure with. Although originally such individuals were probably sagacious men and above trickery, their skills and knowledge were often transmogrified to suit the purpose or the business of those who might profit from superstition by pretending to trace their practices to mystic cult heroes of a dim past.

While some distortion of integrity occurred, not all magical rites associated with the art of healing were based on conscious fraud. Indeed, in many instances the beliefs of a savage or untutored race of demons which cause diseases is perfectly natural, and might be considered under certain circumstances to be almost reasonable. Thus, a member of a tribe seized with an epileptic fit might justifiably be deemed to have been assaulted by a demon or other invisible foe. Similarly, the dramatic onset of plague or other contagious disease such as smallpox or fever, could conceivably be interpreted as consistent with angry spirits having attacked the tribe, or as punishment for some unrecognized offence. From such a basis the idea of sacrifice to the avenging fiend follows obviously. In some primitive peoples, among the New Zealand natives, for example, it is believed that a separate demon exists for each distinct disease; one for ague, one for epilepsy, one for toothache, and so forth. This reasonable concept was extrapolated to the conclusion that each individual demon would have specific items which would either placate anger or repel it and thus amulets, talismans, and charms were developed for this purpose. On the contrary, the North American Indians generally attributed all disease to only one evil spirit and consequently, their treatment of all complaints was for the most part the same.

Whether pagan, Jew, Moslem or Roman, all early medical belief was suffused with superstition and magic.

The respected physician, Burton, aptly summarized his views on the issue of superstitions by citing a wide variety of such practices.

> *Amulets and things to be borne about I find prescribed, taxed by some, approved by others. Look for them in Mizaldus, Porta, Albertus, etc. A ring made with the hoof of an ass's right fore foot, carried about, etc. I say, with Renodeus, they are not altogether to be rejected. Piony doth help epilepsies. Pretious stones most diseases. A wolf's dung carried about helps the cholick. A spider an ague, etc. Such medicines are to be exploded that consist of words, characters, spells, and charms, which can do no good at all, but out of a strong conceit, as Pomponatius proves, or the devil's policy, that is the first founder and teacher of them.*
>
> Robert Burton, *Anatomy of Melancholy*

Magic and mysticism were part of all primitive medicine whether practiced in the enervating climate of the Euphrates or the iciness of the Arctic. An Inuit Eskimo shaman prepares to exorcise an ice demon from a patient, bound (lest he seek to resist the terror of the therapy) and kneeling (respect for the priest-doctor). The rachitic stance of the healer attests to the vicissitudes of medical practice in a sunless environment devoid of bovine dietary supplementation.

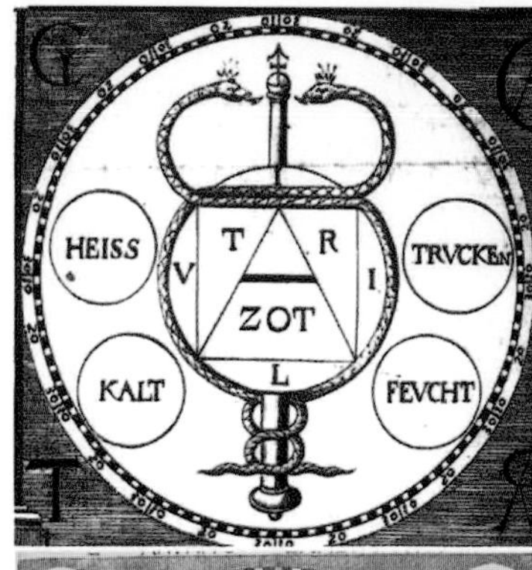

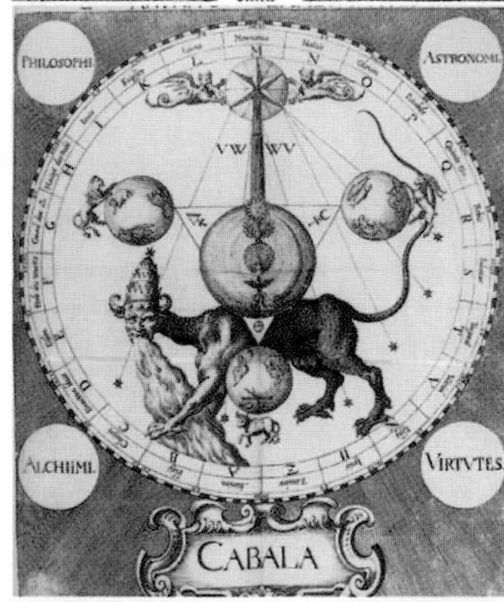

The Kabbalah was an important part of early medical mysticism given the substantial grounding of most intellectuals in Hebraic wisdom. As such, it represented Jewish mysticism as it appeared in the 12th and following centuries. The earliest roots of Kabbalah are traceable to Merkava mysticism, which flourished in Israel in the 1st century A.D. and had as its main concern ecstatic and mystical contemplation of the divine throne, or "chariot" (merkava), seen in a vision by the prophet Ezekiel. The earliest known Jewish text on magic and cosmology, Sefer Yetzira (Book of Creation), appeared sometime between the 3rd and the 6th centuries and sought to explain creation as a process involving the ten divine numbers (sefirot) of God the Creator and the twenty-two letters of the Hebrew alphabet. Taken together, they were said to constitute the "thirty-two paths of secret wisdom." A major text of early Kabbalah was the 12th-century Sefer ha-Bahir "Book of Brightness", whose influence on the development of Jewish esoteric mysticism and on Judaism in general was profound and lasting. The Bahir not only interpreted the sefirot as instrumental in creating and sustaining the universe but also introduced into Judaism such notions as the transmigration of souls (gilgul) and strengthened the foundations of Kabbalah by providing it with an extensive mystical symbolism.

Egyptian, Jewish, and Arab Magic

The Egyptians, according to Celsus, believed that there were thirty-six demons or divinities in the air, to each of whom was attributed a separate part or organ of the human body. In the event of disease affecting one of these parts, the priest-physician invoked the demon, calling him by his name, and requiring him in a special form of words, to cure the afflicted part. Solomon was credited among many Eastern people with having discovered many of the secrets of controlling diseases by mystic processes and, according to Flavius Josephus, he composed and bequeathed to posterity a book of these magical secrets. Given the concerns of the Hebrews with idolatry, Hezekiah is said to have suppressed this work since it led the people to pray to powers other than Jehovah. Nevertheless, it is held that some of the secrets of Solomon were conveyed to certain families by tradition. Thus Josephus relates that a certain Jew named Eleazor *"drew a demon from the nose of a possessed person"* in the presence of the Emperor Vespasian and a number of Roman officers, used a magic ring and a form of invocation to achieve this beneficial result. In order to confirm to those who might doubt his skills and demonstrate that the demon thus expelled had a real separate existence, he then successfully ordered it to upset a vessel of water which stood on the floor.

Much like the philosopher's stone and the elixir of youth, books professing to provide Solomon's secrets were not uncommon among Christians as well as Jews. Even the refined intellect of Goethe was attracted to such a notion and alluded to such a treatise in *Faust* in the line,

Für solche halbe Höllenbrut, ist Salomoni's Schlüssel gut.

Throughout their history, the Jewish people have studied and practiced magic as a means of healing, and the Book of Enoch recounts how the daughters of men were instructed in *"incantations, exorcisms, and the cutting of roots"* by the sons of God who came to earth and associated with them. Given their reputation for wisdom and their reputation as people with significant divine connections, the Greeks and Romans held Jewish sorcery in the highest esteem, and even the Arabs accepted their teaching with implicit confidence. Thus the accumulated wisdom of the sages and the commentaries of the Talmud are replete with magical formulas and injunctions, while the Kabbalah, a mystic theosophy representing an amalgamation of Hebraic religious intellectualism with Alexandrian philosophy that began about the tenth century, was unquestionably the foundation of the sophistry of Paracelsus and his followers. In the Middle Ages, and in some communities until quite recent times, belief in the occult powers of Jews, which they had themselves inculcated, was firm and universal, and became the reason, or at least the excuse, for much unwarranted persecution. For the punishment of sorcery and witchcraft was not based on a belief that fraud had been practiced, but resulted from a conviction both of the terrible truth of the claims which had been put forward, as well as the inherent anxiety of those fearful of being children of a lesser God.

Although assimilation has resulted in the Jews of Western Europe having lost or abandoned many of the traditional practices associated with their popular medicines from time immemorial, in the East, especially in Turkey, Ethiopia, Iran, Iraq and Syria, quaint prayers and antiquated *materia medica* are still associated as they were in the days of the Babylonian captivity. Thus until the mid-twentieth century, dogs' livers, earthworms, hares' feet, live ants, human

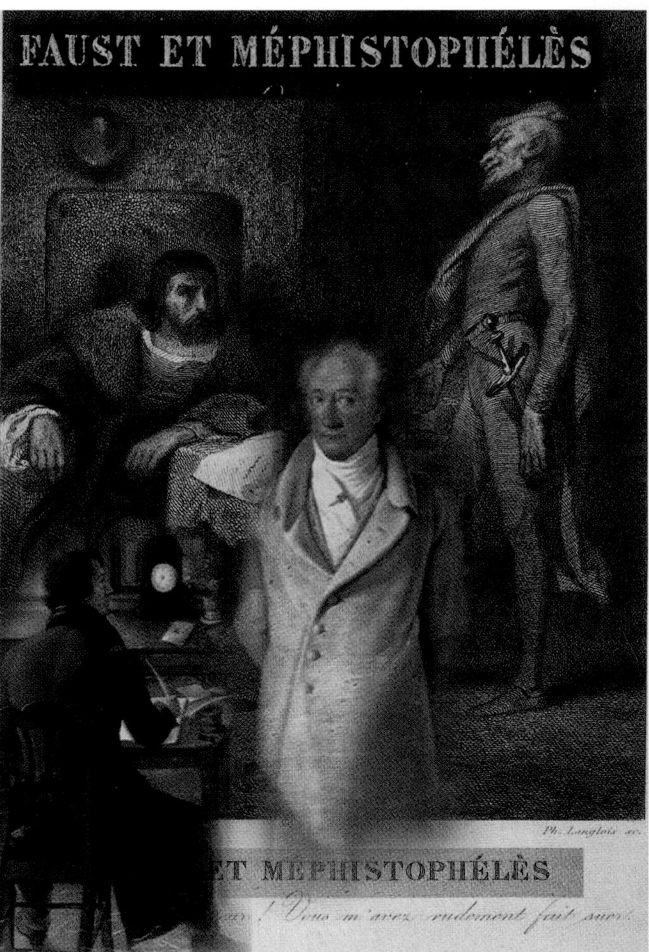

Goethe (foreground) and his secretary (left) respectively face and ignore the dilemma of the doctor (health and good) and the devil (disease and evil). A peripatetic polymath of exquisite sensitivity and radiant genius Goethe bestrode his world as an intellectual colossus. As such his play epitomized the complex interface between Faust (alchemist physician [c. 1540] seeking knowledge and hence power over life) and the arcane support that might be needed by physicians to transcend human frailties and the vale of sorrow that was existence.

bones, doves' dung, wolves' entrails, and powdered mummy were still considered as acceptable remedies. For those of the wealthier sects, such precious products as dew from Mount Carmel or water from Galilee are prescribed. In addition invocations, prayers, and superstitious practices provided the whispered remnants of an ancient coherent refrain of the *"Gabbetes"*, the generally elderly persons who attend on the sick and in so doing projected the multitude of infallible cures included in their age-old repertoire.

The variety of remedies was infinite and reflected millennia of accumulated folklore, wisdom, and commonsense based upon observation. Thus, powdered, freshly roasted earthworms in wine, or live grasshoppers in water, were given for biliousness. For bronchial complaints, Hebrew letters were written on a new plate and washed off with wine to which 3 grains of a citron which had been used at the Tabernacle festival were then added and administered as a draught. Under desperate circumstances, dogs' excrements made up with honey were used as a poultice for sore eyes, while mummy or human bones ground up with honey was regarded as a precious tonic, and wolves' liver was a cure for epileptic fits. Of note was the fact that all administration of such remedies should be accompanied by the necessary invocation, generally to the names of patriarchs, angels, or prophets. In some circumstances such incantations appear to have been mere gibberish, such as *"Adar, gar, vedar, gar,"* which is the formula for use with a toothache remedy, although it is still possible that complex numeric formulations of Kabbalistic background are represented by such words.

Of particular interest are the phylacteries still worn by Jews during certain portions of their prayers, in accordance with inveterate custom. This practice was based upon instruction by the Lord, and has been in all ages esteemed as protecting them against evil and demoniac influences, as well as a necessity in following the Law. They are leathern receptacles, which are bound on their left arms and on their foreheads in literal obedience to the Mosaic instructions in the passages transcribed, and contained in the cases, from Exodus *c.* 13, v. 1-10, and *c.* 13, v. 11-16, Deuteronomy *c.* 6, v. 4-9, and *c.* 9, v. 13-21. While these passages may appear to protest against superstitions and heathenish beliefs and practices, the rabbis and scribes taught that these and the mezzuzoth, the similar passages affixed to the doorposts, would avert physical and spiritual dangers, and they detailed minute instructions for the preparation of such inscriptions. A scribe, for example, who had commenced to write one of the passages, was not to allow himself to be interrupted by any human distraction, not even if the king asked him a question. Such is the belief in the power and efficacy of the ritual and the incantations that despite the passage of thousands of years many of even the most sophisticated of contemporary Jewish thinkers don such regalia and insist that the doors of their homes be so marked!

The practice can be better understood in the context of the historical recognition that all the eastern nations placed a great trust in amulets of various kinds for the prevention and treatment of disease. Thus, Galen quotes from Nechepsus, an Egyptian king, who lived about 630 B.C., who wrote that a green jasper cut in the form of a dragon surrounded by rays, applied externally, would cure indigestion and strengthen the stomach. Among the books attributed to Hermes was one entitled *The Thirty-six Herbs Sacred to Horoscopes*. Of this book Galen says it is only a waste of time to read it. The title, however, as Leclerc has pointed out, rather curiously confirms the statement attributed to Celsus which is found in Origen's treatise, *Contra Celsum*. Indeed, amulets are still in general use in the East and Bertherand in *Medicine of the Arabs* noted that the uneducated Arab, when troubled by an affliction of any sort will see his imam and pay him a fee, in return for which the imam provides a little paper about two inches square on which certain phrases are written. This incantation is then placed in a leather case, and worn as close to the affected part as is possible. Similarly, wealthy Arab women wear silver cases with texts from the Koran in them although for maximum efficacy it is essential that the paper be inscribed on a Friday, a

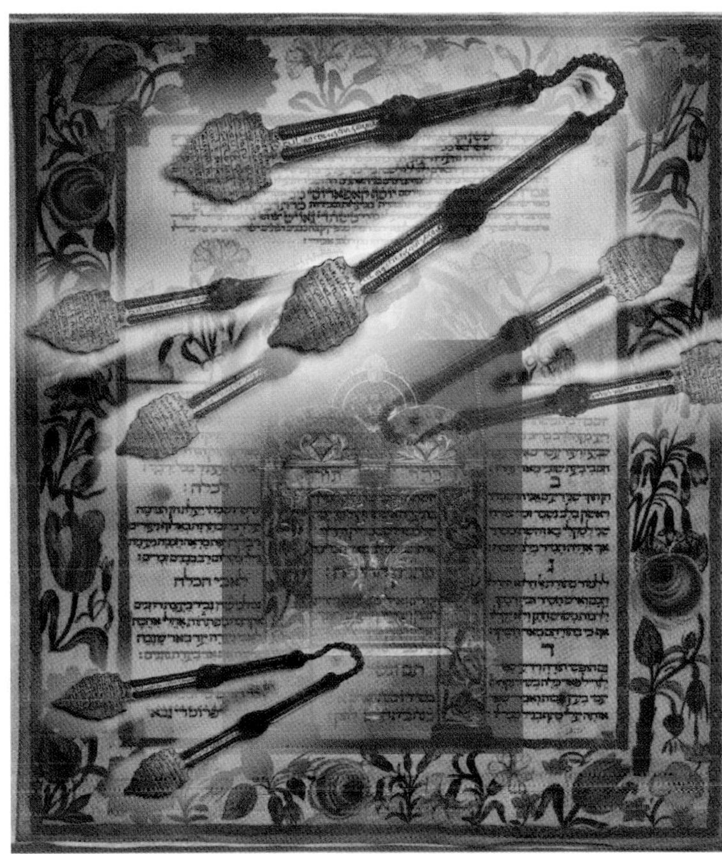

The mystical inscriptions that surround the Book of the Laws represent ancient incantations to a divinity.

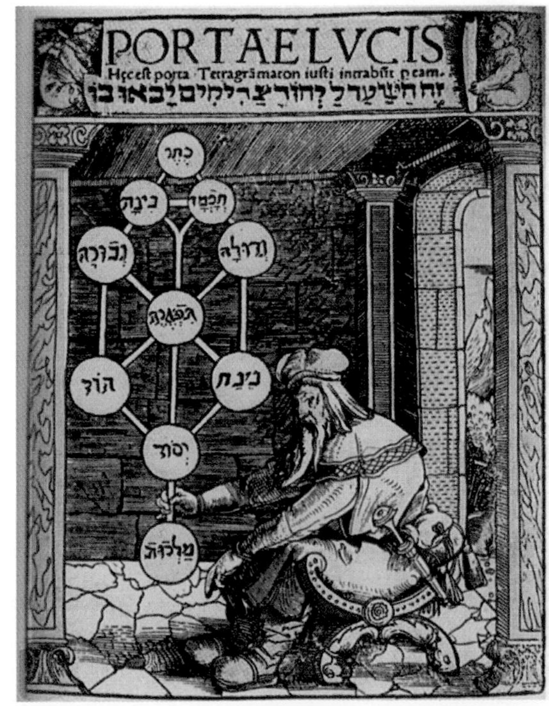

Endless contemplation of the mystic elements of the Kabbalah might take the adept through the gate of light (Portae Lucis) or clarity into the peace of a life eternal enshrined in perfect health.

The mystical elements of the Kabbalah embody the intellectualization of arcane and incognoscible information suffused with esoteric and often inscrutable religious belief.

Individual societies each developed their own array of mystical objects and icons in the belief that their powers would shield them against disease and ill health. The list of such major and minor arcana ranged from virgins to monsters and was liberally interspersed with mystic mantra or diverse objects of genitive potency.

little before sunset, and with ink in which myrrh and saffron have been dissolved.

In the *Third Report of the Wellcome Research Laboratories* at the Gordon Memorial College, Khartoum, R. G. Anderson provided an interesting chapter on the medical superstitions of the people of Kordofan, and included a number of illustrations of amulets and written charms in use by the local Arabs. Anderson noted that *"To the native no process is too absurd for belief, and often, within his limits, no price too high to accomplish a cure"* and that almost all wear talismans of some kind. It is considered perfectly appropriate to spend much of their scanty earnings on charms to ward off chronic disease, such as stone in the bladder. The son of the late Mahdi presented Anderson a charm designed to ward off evil spirits, which consisted of a square case containing a written incantation, and a bag filled with a preparation of roots that his father had worn round the arm above the elbow. The incantations themselves generally consist of quotations from the Koran, often repeated many times and with signs of the great prophets interspersed.

An alternative method of ensuring protection was provided by the use of a *"Lohn"*, or writing board, on which Koranic phrases and mystic inscriptions had been written by *Fikis* (holy men). When the writing was dry, it could be washed off and the fluid then administered as a medication that could be either taken internally or applied externally.

An extraordinary list of absurd objects and agents have been or are being used by people, civilized and savage, as charms, talismans, and amulets. These range from the teraphim which Rachel stole from her father Laban to the magic knots of the Chaldeans and the gold and stone ornaments of the Egyptians, which they not only wore themselves but often attached to their mummies. Such items range as far back as the flint amulets of the pre-dynastic period and include the precious stones whose virtues were discovered by Orpheus, the infinite variety of gold and silver ornaments adopted by the Romans with superstitious notions, the fish (*ichthys*) being the initials of the Greek words for Jesus Christ, the Lord, our Savior, engraved on stones and worn by the early Christians, the Gnostic gems, the coral necklaces, the bezoar stones, the toad ashes, the strands of the ropes used for hanging criminals, the magnets of the Middle Ages and of modern times, and a thousand other things credited with magical curative properties. Besides these there are myriads of forms of words written or spoken, some pious, some gibberish, which have been used and recommended both with and without drugs.

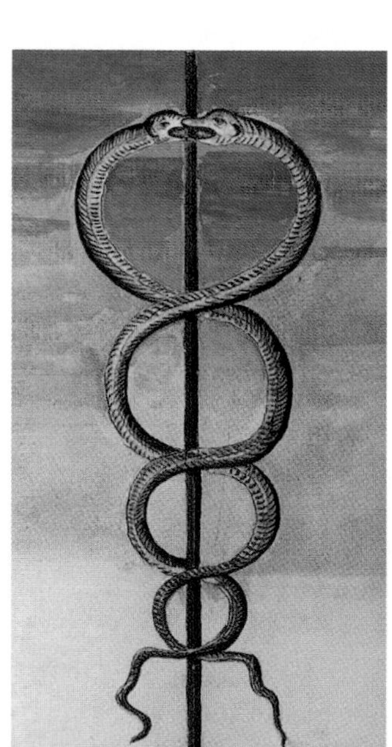

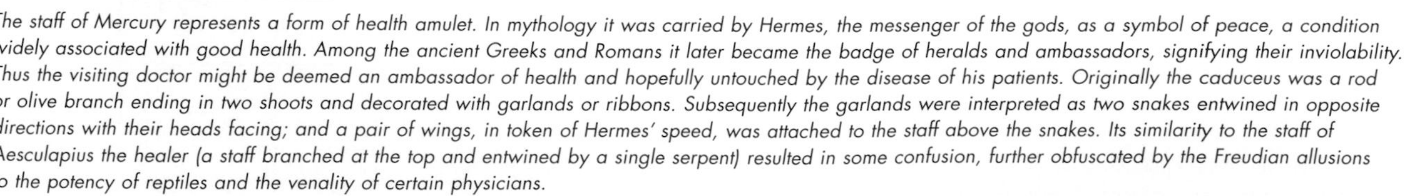

The staff of Mercury represents a form of health amulet. In mythology it was carried by Hermes, the messenger of the gods, as a symbol of peace, a condition widely associated with good health. Among the ancient Greeks and Romans it later became the badge of heralds and ambassadors, signifying their inviolability. Thus the visiting doctor might be deemed an ambassador of health and hopefully untouched by the disease of his patients. Originally the caduceus was a rod or olive branch ending in two shoots and decorated with garlands or ribbons. Subsequently the garlands were interpreted as two snakes entwined in opposite directions with their heads facing; and a pair of wings, in token of Hermes' speed, was attached to the staff above the snakes. Its similarity to the staff of Aesculapius the healer (a staff branched at the top and entwined by a single serpent) resulted in some confusion, further obfuscated by the Freudian allusions to the potency of reptiles and the venality of certain physicians.

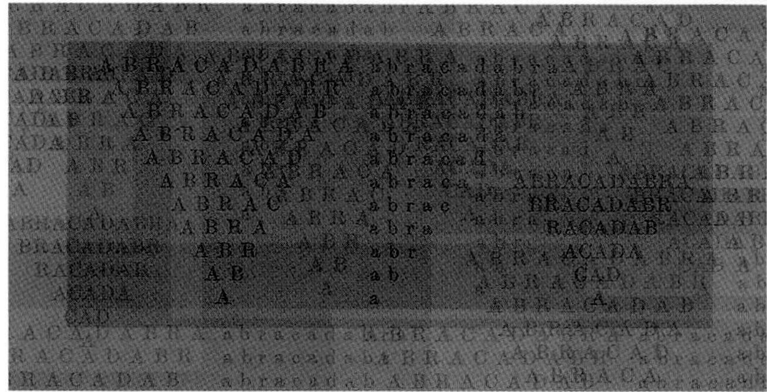

The Abracadabra mantra as originally intoned by Quintus Samonicus (Roman physician of the Emperor Severus A.D. 208) was probably little more than Roman plagiarism of an ancient Hebraic injunction: "Abrai, seda, brai".

Schelenz in *Geschichte der Pharmacie* (1901) quotes from Jakob Maerlant of Bruges, "the Father of Flemish science" (born *c.* 1235) the recommendation of an "Amulett ring" on the stone of which the figure of Mercury was engraved, and which would make the wearer healthy, *"die maect sinen traghere ghesont."*

Cure and Abracadabra

Abracadabra was the most famous of the ancient charms or talismans employed in medicine and although its mystic meaning has been the subject of considerable ingenious investigation, even its derivation is controversial. The first mention of the term is present in the poem *"De Medicina Praecepta Saluberrima,"* penned by Quintus Serenus Samonicus, a noted Roman physician of the second and third centuries. Highly regarded by the Emperor Severus, he accompanied him on his expedition to Britain A.D. 208 but was incapable of preventing the demise of his employer at York in A.D. 211. Having lost his patient he soon thereafter lost his own life when in the following year, Caracalla, the son of Severus, assassinated his brother Geta and twenty thousand other people (including Serenus Samonicus) supposed to be favorable to Geta's claims. The poem, which is the only existing work of Serenus, consists of 1,115 hexameter lines which illustrate the medical practice and superstitions of the period when it was written. The lines in which the word "Abracadabra" and the way to employ it, are introduced as these:

Inscribis chartae, quod diciturAbracadabra,
Saepius: et subter repetas, sed detrahe summae,
Et magis atque magis desint elementa figuris
Singula, quae semper rapies et coetera figes,
Donec in angustam redigatur litera conum.
His lino nexis collum redimire memento. *

This text actually discusses a semi-tertian fever of a particular character and can be translated as follows:

**Write several times on a piece of paper the word*
"Abracadabra," *and repeat the word in the lines below, but*
take away letters from the complete word and let
the letters fall away one at a time in each succeeding line.
Take these away ever, but keep the rest until
the writing is reduced to a narrow cone. Remember
to tie these papers with flax and bind them round the neck.

The charm could be written in several ways, all in conformity with the instructions.

Although there is debate regarding the meaning of the incantation, it is likely that the triangular form of the charm represented a significant icon reflective of the Trinity in Unity. After wearing the charm for nine days, it had to be thrown over the shoulder into a stream running eastwards. In situations where the disease was so virulent as to resist this talisman, Serenus recommended the application of lion's fat (not readily available in York), or yellow coral with green emeralds tied to the skin of a cat and worn round the neck.

The precise derivation of the word abracadabra remains a source of speculation and may relate to the background of Serenus Samonicus, since he was believed to have been a disciple of a notorious Christian heretic, Basilides, who lived in the early part of the second century, and was himself the founder of a sect branching out of the gnostics. Basilides had added to their beliefs some fanciful notions based on arcane areas of the teachings of Pythagoras and Apollonius of Tyre, especially in regard to names and numbers. In particular he is credited with having invented the mystic word *"abraxas,"* which in Greek numeration represents the total 365, thus: *a-1, b-2, r-100, a-1, x-60, a-1, s-200*. In actuality the word is purported to have been a representation of a numeric permutation of the Persian sun god, or if invented by Basilides, to be a symbolic mantra iterating the 365 emanations of the infinite Deity.

As might be expected there are, however, numerous other interpretations. Thus Littré associated it with the Hebrew words, *Ab, Ruach, Dabar*; Father, Holy Spirit, Word, while Ring, an authority on the curious gnostic gemstones well-known to antiquarians, considered this explanation as fanciful and opined that abracadabra was a modification of the term *Ablathanabla*, a word commonly encountered on such jewels, and meaning "Our Father, Thou art Our Father." Yet others held that *Ablathanabla* was little more than a verbal corruption of Abracadabra, while an ingenious correspondent of *Notes and Queries* proposed that a more likely Hebrew origin of the term than the one favored by Littré would be *Abrai, seda, brai*, which would signify "Out, bad spirit, Out", although this theory also required that the word should be pronounced *Abrasadabra*. Another likely origin, suggested by C. R. Conder in 1908 in his text *The Rise of Man*, is *Abrak-ha-dabra*, a Hebrew phrase meaning "I bless the deed."

Greek and Roman Magic

The mystic aspects of Greek and Roman medicine reflect the widespread assimilation of these two civilizations of the cultures that they had absorbed or conquered. Many odd and often inexplicable magical or superstitious responses to disease abound. Thus Pythagoras taught that holding dill in the left hand would prevent epilepsy, while Serapion of Alexandria (278 B.C.) prescribed for epilepsy the warty excrescences on the forelegs of animals, camel's brain and gall, rennet of seal, dung of crocodile, blood of turtle, and other animal products. Pliny the Elder alludes to a tradition, that a root of autumnal nettle would cure a tertian fever, provided that when it is dug the patient's name and his parent's names should be pronounced aloud to assure specificity of action; that the longest tooth of a black dog should be worn as an amulet and would assuredly cure quartan fever; that the snout

Breasts and snakes have long been part of medicinal practice, the former for their deep psychological associations of well-being as well as nutritional support, the latter due to their identification with eternal life (casting off of the skin) and procreation.

The King's Riddle from "Buch der Heiligen Dreifaltigheid," 15th century. A complex representation of an androgynous deity holding aloft the serpents of disease (desire) in a chalice of gold. Emblems of power including the sun as a flower, the subservient dragon and lion as well as an eagle feeding its young pose the question as to what constituted the ultimate protection against evil (disease).

The Egyptians associated the phoenix with immortality, and that symbolism had a widespread appeal in late antiquity. The phoenix was compared to undying Rome, and appeared on the coinage of the late Roman Empire as a symbol of the Eternal City, having transcended paganism and become acceptable in a Christian era. It in addition became widely interpreted as an allegory of resurrection and life after death, ideas that also had particular appeal to emergent Christianity. In Islamic mythology, the phoenix was identified with the "anqa" a huge, mysterious bird (probably a heron) that was originally created by God with all perfections but had thereafter become a plague and was killed. Its identification with the sun and health was consistent with its appeal to physicians.

and tips of the ears of a mouse, the animal itself to run free, wrapped in a rose-colored patch, also worn as an amulet, would similarly cure the same disease; the right eye of a living lizard wrapped in a piece of goat's skin; and a herb picked from the head of a statue and tied up with red thread, are other specimens of the amulets popular in his time. But Pliny, with his usual skepticism, appears to doubt whether all these treatments could be trusted and describes one in particular as a portentous lie.

Namely, that if the heart of a hen is placed on a woman's left breast while she is asleep, it will make her tell all her secrets. One wit commenting on this dramatic repudiation by Pliny, remarked dryly, "*Perhaps he had tried it*." Alexander of Tralles recommended a number of amulets, some of which claimed to have proof of their efficacy. Thus for colic, he names the dung of a wolf with some bits of bone in it in a closed tube worn on the right arm or thigh; for bilious disorders he considered an octagonal iron ring on which are engraved the words "*Flee, flee, ho, ho, Bile, the lark was searching*" to be excellent therapy; for gout, he instructed that henbane should be gathered before sunset with the thumb and third finger of the left hand, when the moon was in Aquarius or Pisces, while reciting an invocation inviting the holy herb to come to the house of e.g. Sachs and cure Winston or George.

Mythical Animals

The Phoenix

The alchemists initially adopted this mythical entity as their emblem and thereafter became a sign frequently used by pharmacists. According to Herodotus, this bird, which was worshipped by the Egyptians, was of about the size of an eagle and lived a solitary life in the Arabian desert. Its head was characterized by a purple crest and its eyes sparkled like stars while the body was majestic and possessed purple and gold plumage. It either came to Heliopolis (the city of the sun) to die and be burned in the temple of that city, or its ashes were brought there by its successor. In accordance with ancient concepts of succession, only one phoenix could exist at any one time and its life span was prodigious. Although legends vary as to its precise longevity, five hundred years is the period usually assigned. When the phoenix knew that its mortal existence was due to end, it made its own funeral pyre out of spiced woods, which were then ignited by solar rays. Subsequent to immolation its bone marrow yielded a worm, which rapidly transformed into a new phoenix, which, after burying its parent in Egypt, returned to Arabia.

No less a text than the Talmud relates some curious legends of the phoenix, which the Jews believed to be immortal. Of particular interest is the relationship of the bird to purity. Thus, when Eve had eaten of the forbidden fruit and offered some to all the animals in the Garden of Eden, it was the phoenix alone that refused. In consequence it escaped the curse of death, which overtook the rest of the animal in creation! An alternative legend is that at the time of Noah's Ark, when all the other animals were clamoring to be fed, the phoenix alone was silent. Noah, observing its unusual demeanor, asked if it was not hungry, to which the phoenix replied, "*I saw you were busy, so would not trouble you*." This response so pleased Noah that he blessed it with eternal life. In the Book of Job, xxix, 18, recalling his earlier glory, the patriarch says, "*Then I said I shall die in my nest, and I shall multiply my days as the sand*." Many Hebraic scholars believe that the word translated "sand" should read phoenix, and in fact the Revised Version actually provides "phoenix" as an alternative rendering of the passage. Indeed, it is easy to appreciate how aptly this alternative translation would express the crux of Job's idea. A further example of the Hebraic veneration of the medicinal powers of this mythical bird is provided by the translation of the verse in Psalms, ciii, 5, "*So that thy youth is renewed like the eagle*," by substituting phoenix for eagle.

The Unicorn

The perceptions of the glorious mythology of the unicorn had not quite passed into the region of fable when Pomet produced his *History of Drugs* in

The unicorn was a mythological animal resembling a horse with a single horn on its forehead. Those who drank from its horn were thought to be protected from stomach trouble, epilepsy, and poison. The earliest description in Greek literature of a single-horned animal (Greek: monokeros; Latin: unicornis) was by the historian Ctesias (c. 400 B.C.), who related that the Indian wild ass was the size of a horse, with a white body, purple head, and blue eyes; on its forehead was a cubit-long horn colored red at the pointed tip, black in the middle, and white at the base. The actual animal described by Ctesias was the Indian rhinoceros. As a biblical animal the unicorn was interpreted allegorically in the early Christian church. One of the earliest such interpretations appears in the ancient Greek bestiary known as the Physiologus, which states that the unicorn is a strong, fierce animal that can be caught only if a virgin maiden is thrown before it. The unicorn leaps into the virgin's lap, and she suckles it and leads it to the king's palace.

the early eighteenth century. Although claiming to have no belief in the existence of the animal, he quotes from other authors not long antecedent to him, who did. Pomet reported that what was currently sold as the horn of a unicorn was in fact the horn or tusk of the narwhal, a tooth that extends to the length of six to ten feet. The unicorn, or *Monoceros,* was variously referred to by Aristotle, Pliny, Aelian, and other ancient writers, and in later times was described by numerous travelers who, if they had not seen it themselves, claimed to have met with persons of undeniable probity who described in detail the attributes of the fabled beast.

The details provided by Aristotle are supposed to have been initially derived from Ctesias, whose description of the Indian wild ass (with many embellishments) was adopted and conferred upon the fabulous unicorn. Aristotle was the first to note the marvelous alexipharmic properties long attributed to the unicorn's horn. Thus drinking vessels made of the horn were purported to protect those who used them against poison, convulsions, and epilepsy, provided that either just before or just after taking the poison they drank wine or water from the goblet made from the horn. In the Middle Ages the horn of the unicorn was esteemed a certain cure for the plague, malignant fevers, bites of serpents or of mad dogs. Such protection was assured if the horn was prepared as a jelly to which a little saffron and cochineal were added! A further powerful application of unicorn horn was its alleged utility in the management of poisoned wounds. Mere apposition of the object to the site of trauma resulted in a dramatic cessation of all symptoms and the rapid onset of healing. Unfortunately the item was difficult to acquire and generally worth about ten times the price of gold. As a result, few were able to derive benefit from its powers and many worthy sufferers could not avail themselves of the remedy.

Given the widespread belief in the unicorn it is not surprising to note its mention several times in the Old Testament. Indeed the translators of the Authorized Version having followed the Septuagint rendered the Hebrew word *Re'em* as the Greek term *Monokeros*, which corresponds to the subsequent usage of the descriptor as consistent with the commoner usage of the word unicorn. The translators evidently found a difficulty in associating the unicorn with the Hebrew *Re'em* in Deut. xxxiii, 17, where it is written as "the horns of the unicorns." Thus in the original Hebrew, the horns are the plural but *Re'em* is singular despite the obvious fact that the horn of the unicorn would have been a contradiction in terms. In fact, it is now accepted that the word in the original text had no reference to the fabulous animal, but actually referred to the wild ox, or ox antelope. This animal is believed to have been the *Urus* mentioned by Julius Caesar as existing in the forests of Central Europe, and not entirely extinct until some five or six hundred years ago. This strong untamable beast was also well known in biblical Palestine and was almost certainly the intended source of the description and as a result in the Revised Version, wild ox was thereafter uniformly substituted for "unicorn".

With the passage of time, the belief in the existence of the unicorn and the efficacy of its horn appear to have waned. Thus, allusions to the unicorn in Shakespeare all indicate considerable disbelief in the legends. In *The Tempest* (Act 3, sc. 3) Sebastian says when music is heard in the wood, *"Now I will believe that there are unicorns."* In *Julius Caesar* (Act 2, sc. 1), Decius Brutus, recounting Caesar's superstitions, comments, *"He loves to hear that unicorns may be betrayed with trees"*; and Timon of Athens raves about the unicorn among the legendary animal beliefs (Act 4, sc. 3). No less an authority on heraldry than Guillim in 1660, however, comments thus on the skepticism of his contemporaries: *"Some have made doubt whether there be any such beast as this or not. But the great esteem of his horns (in many places to be seen) may take away that needless scruple."*

Despite concerns raised by men of science and learning regarding the efficacy of the unicorn in medicine and the very existence of the animal, its unique and special value was still held in wide esteem. Thus the unicorn was introduced into the British royal arms by James I, who substituted it for the red dragon with which Henry VII had honored a Welsh contingent, which helped him to win the battle of Bosworth fighting under the banner of Cadwallydr. In fact, the unicorn had been utilized as a Scottish emblem for several reigns before that of James I, to the extent that even the Scottish pound of that period was known by the name of a unicorn from the device stamped on it.

Despite the later incredulity at the existence and medical properties of the unicorn horn, Pomet in his *History of Drugs* (1723) reported that in 1553 a unicorn's horn valued at £20,000 sterling had been presented to the King of France and that a similar specimen presented to Charles I of England, supposed to be the largest one known, measured 7 feet long, and weighed 13 lbs. It is also related that Edward IV gave to his guest, the Duke of Burgundy, who visited him, a gold cup set with jewels whose value was regarded as inestimable given the piece of unicorn horn that had been skillfully worked into the metal. A further example of the

An ornate drinking cup with a narwhal horn. Such vessels were believed to provide absolute protection against poison or illness.

St. George slays the dragon and saves the Virgin, albeit dressed in red (vide Chris DeBurgh, Lady in Red). Overall the concept was the triumph of good over evil or health over disease, although the virile St. George and his dangerous lance inserted into the jaws of the dangerous animal have long raised questions amongst the cognoscenti. In general, in the Middle Eastern world, where snakes were large and deadly, the serpent or dragon was symbolic of the principle of evil. The evil reputation of dragons remained the dominant belief, and in Europe it outlasted the more benign interpretation. Christianity confused the ancient, benevolent, and malevolent serpent deities in a common condemnation and in Christian art, the dragon came to be symbolic of sin and paganism and, as such, was depicted either prostrate beneath the heels of saints and martyrs or vanquished by knights in shining armor as they saved the purity (Virgin Mary icon) of the world.

The dragon's blood much favored in ancient remedies was in actuality red resin obtained from the fruit of several palms of the genus Daemonorops *and now mostly used in coloring varnishes and lacquers. Once valued as a medicine of great efficacy in Europe because of its astringent properties, dragon's blood is now preferentially used as a varnish for violins and in photoengraving for preventing undercutting of the printing surface during etching. The primary commercial source of the agent is* Daemonorops draco, *a rattan palm native to Malaysia and Indonesia, although other sources include* Dracaena cinnabari *of the island of Socotra, east of Somalia;* Dracaena draco *of the Canary Islands; and* Croton draco *of Mexico, where it is still used locally to heal wounds and as an astringent.*

preciousness of this resource is provided by the record that in the mid-sixteenth century, the city of Dresden acquired one large unicorn horn for medical purposes and that whenever a piece was required (to be sawn off) it was a city regulation that no less than two persons of princely rank be present to monitor the operation. As final evidence of its healing and fiduciary values, the unicorn was employed as a frequent insignia used by the apothecaries and was also adopted by the goldsmiths. Indeed, to this very time unicorns support the venerable Arms of the Society of Apothecaries.

The Dragon

The mythical beast itself was regarded to be of little medicinal value *per se* but was held in repute by the ancients on account of the "blood" which took its name and was at one time popularly supposed to be obtained by "slaughter" of the dragon. Although there is little data to support this statement, it is a recurrent theme in ancient literature. According to *Pharmacographia* dragon's blood was first obtained from Socotra and taken with other merchandise by the Arabs to the Orient. It is quite likely that it was there that it acquired the name of dragon's blood, since the dragon has since time immemorial been a much revered beast in China. Dioscorides called this product cinnabar and proposed a wide variety of medicinal uses for it. An alternative explanation for its derivation is the reference in ancient texts to the fruit of the *calamus draconis* on which the resin collects along with scales. When stripped of its skin this fruit is purported to exhibit a design of a dragon. Lemery in quoting from "*Monardes and several other authors*," states, "*When the skin is taken off from this fruit there appears underneath the figure of a dragon as it is represented by the painters, with wings expanded, a slender neck, a hairy or bristle back, long tail, and feet armed with talons. They pretend,*" he adds, "*that this figure gave the name to tree. But I believe this circumstance fabulous because I never knew it confirmed by any traveler.*"

It is more probable that the shrewd Arab traders invented the name dragon's blood to please their Chinese customers, and it may be therefore that the tree actually acquired its name from the resin, rather than the reverse, whereby the resin was afforded the name of the tree.

Dragon's blood was utilized in old pharmacy as a mild astringent, and was one of the ingredients in the styptic pills first described by Helvetius. An alternative usage was as an inclusion in the formula for Locatelli's balsam although more recently it has become chiefly used as a varnish coloring, as for example in varnishes employed to add luster to violins. In some parts of the world, it acquired a reputation as a charm to restore love and maidens whose swains had become unfaithful or neglectful were urged to procure a piece, wrap it in paper and throw it on the fire, saying:

May he no pleasure or profit see
Till he come back again to me.

[Cuthbert, *Bede in Notes and Queries. Series 1, Vol. II, p. 242.*]

Dragons are mentioned many times in the Authorized Version of the Old Testament. In most of these instances jackals were subsequently substituted in the Revised Version, and in one instance the alternative of crocodiles is even suggested in the margin. It has been whimsically pointed out by numerous scholars that it would obviously be a better rendering in many of the circumstances described.

Superstitions

There exist in all societies a multitude of silly superstitions which make up the medicinal folklore and to recount all would be tedious. Indeed, the diverse methods for curing warts, toothache, ague, worms, and other

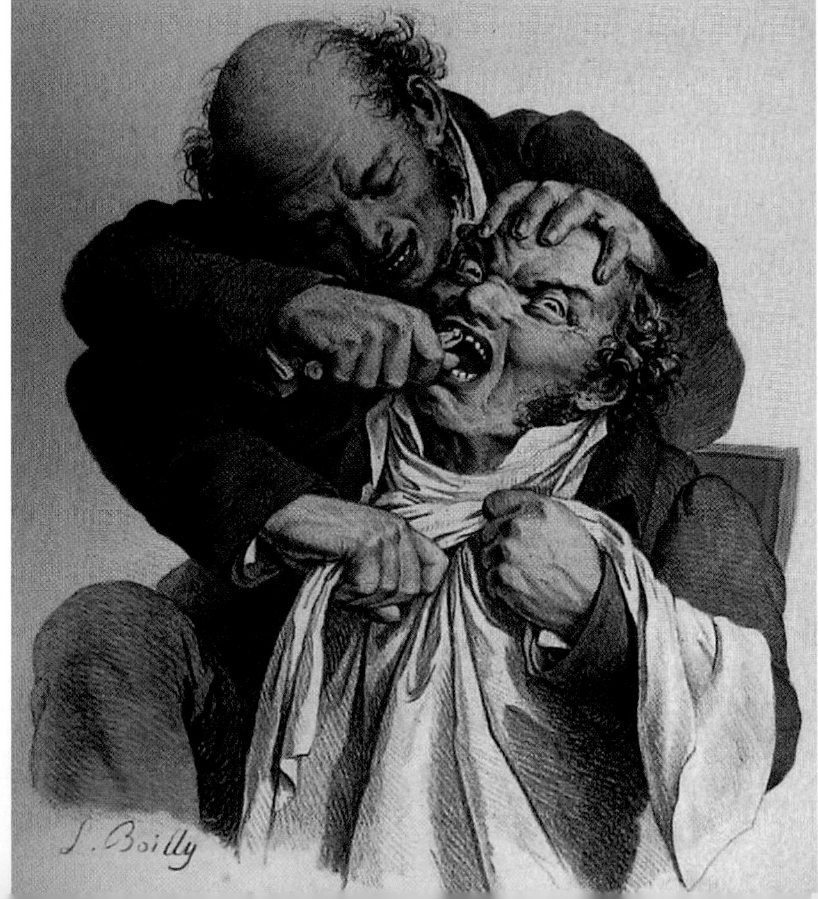

A Parisian etching by J. Boilly depicting a tooth extraction. Innumerable tales exist regarding the beliefs associated with the treatment of the common complaint of toothache. They range from the use of henbane to the insertion of iron nails but none tops the suggestion that spitting into the mouth of a frog would lead to instant amelioration of the pain. Gallic vigor espoused such nonsense and violent extraction was deemed an admirable therapy consistent with Napoleonic policy.

common complaints are familiar. Nevertheless, odd concepts such as the notion that toothache is caused by tiny worms which can be expelled by henbane, is ancient and still exists. A process from one of the *Anglo-Saxon Leechdoms* converted into modern English by the Reverend Oswald Cockayne may be quoted:

> *For tooth worms take acorn meal and henbane seed and wax, of all equally much, mingle them together, work into a wax candle and burn it, let it reek into the mouth, put a black cloth under, and the worms will fall on it.*

Marcellus, a late Latin medical author whose work was translated into Saxon, gave a simpler remedy that relied on more spiritual events for success. He claimed that it was necessary to recite "*Argidam, Margidum, Sturdigum*," thrice, then spit into a frog's mouth and set him free, "requesting him" at the same time to carry off the toothache. Another popular cure for toothache in early England reflected the preoccupation with religious cure and consisted of wearing a piece of parchment on which the following charm was written: "*As St. Peter sat at the gate of Jerusalem our Blessed Lord and Savior, Jesus Christ, passed by and said, What aileth thee? He said Lord, my teeth ache. He said, Arise and follow me and thy teeth shall never ache any more.*"

Sir Kenelm Digby's method presumably drew upon his experience as a hard-bitten pirate and was somewhat less tempting. He directed that the patient should scratch his gum with an iron nail until he made it bleed, and should then drive the nail with the blood upon it into a wooden beam. After such management he adumbrated that the patient would "*never have toothache again.*" For warts, the cures were, if not, more innumerable than for toothache. For the most part they followed a relatively prosaic formula: "*Steal a piece of meat from a butcher's stall or basket, bury it secretly at a gateway where four lanes meet. As the meat decays the warts will die away. Alternatively an apple cut into slices and rubbed on the warts and buried is equally efficacious. So is a snail which after having being rubbed on the warts should be left impaled on a thorn and allowed to die.*"

An alternative to the bizarre use of animal parts was the use of specific colors. Thus a room hung with red cloth was esteemed to be effective against certain diseases, smallpox especially. John of Gaddesden relates how he cured Edward II's son by this device. Indeed, the prejudice in favor of red flannel, which still exists, for tying a piece of it around a sore throat is probably a remnant of the notion that red was especially obnoxious to evil spirits. This belief may be found as far back as Roman times where it is recorded that red coral was hung around the necks of infants to protect them from the evil eye. Among other charms and incantations quoted by Cockayne in his

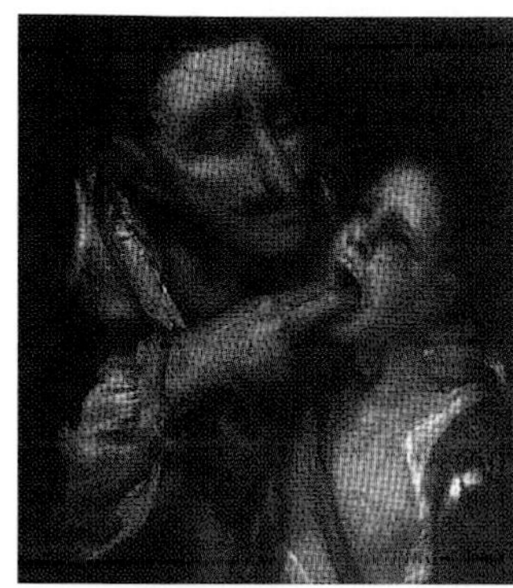

The fear of diptheria as depicted by Goya initiated many abstruse remedies to deal with the dreaded lurgy of "sore" throat!

account of *Anglo-Saxon Leechdoms* was that for a baby's recovery "*some would scrape a hole in the ground and stop it up behind them with thorns*," or if cattle have a disease of the lungs, burn feathers on a midsummer's day, add holy water, and pour it into their mouths and recite over them Psalms 51 and 17 and the Athanasian Creed.

Transferring Diseases

In a world of disease where cures were few and far between, the concept of ridding a patient of illness by means other than curative intervention was an attractive and very ancient notion. Thus amongst those desperate to alleviate illness, it became widely accepted that disease could be transferred by means of undertaking certain formalities. Almost two thousand years ago, Pliny could explain how stomach pains could be transferred to a duck or a puppy. Similarly, a prescription of about two hundred years ago for the cure of convulsions, was to take parings of the sick man's nails, some hair from his eyebrows, and a halfpenny, and wrap them all in a clout which had been round his head. This package should then be laid in a gateway where four lanes intersected, such that the first person to open it might acquire the illness thereby relieving the patient. So certain were the laity of the efficacy of this treatment that in Edinburgh in 1695, John Dougall was actually successfully prosecuted for prescribing this treatment. A more gruesome but probably less immoral or unjust proceeding was to attempt to transfer the disease to the dead. An example of this extraordinary therapy as directed against "boils" can be identified in G.W. Black's *Folk Medicine*.

> "*It is detailed that the boil should be poulticed for three days and nights, after which the poultices and cloths employed were to be placed in the coffin with a dead person and buried with the corpse. In Lancashire matters were less dramatic and it was felt that warts could be transferred by rubbing each with a cinder which must thereafter be wrapped in paper and laid where four roads meet. As before, the person who opened this delightful parcel would acquire the disease from the present owner. Presumably the four road symbolism represented the four humors, although the concept of a cross roads may well have had some Christian symbolism pertaining to suffering. In Devonshire a child could be cured of whooping cough by putting one of its hairs between slices of bread and butter and giving these to a dog. If the dog coughed, as was probable, the whooping cough was deemed to have been successfully transferred.*"

Sir Kenelm Digby provided more than his fair share of bizarre remedies. Supported by an ebullient personality, he convinced many of the efficacy of wound salves, iron nails and exotic powders.

It was not surprising that strange remedies and superstitions regarding cure abounded in a time when the average life expectancy was less than forty years of age and the infant mortality close to 50 percent. All paths led but to the grave, and desperation bred credulity while hope succored charlatanry.

Lord Byron (rear), who was always fond of having the skin of others close to him, and Catherine de Medici (left) both wore a piece of infant skin as a charm against disease. Samuel Pepys (right) supported his wife's endeavors to stay away overnight in order to collect morning dew for her complexion. A notorious philanderer, it is likely he would have encouraged any activity that provided him the opportunity to be "home alone."

Intellectual and Aristocratic Superstition

Lest it be thought that such superstition was only the province of the less educated or privileged, it is interesting to note that even the highest in the land harbored such fanciful notions. Thus, no less a personage than Lord Bacon was convinced that warts could be cured by rubbing lard on them and transferring the lard to a post with the result that the warts would die when the lard dried. Similarly, the great chemical intellect of Robert Boyle quite comfortably attributed the cure of a hemorrhage to wearing some moss from a dead man's skull. The father of Sir Christopher Wren relates that Lord Burghley, the Lord Treasurer of England in Queen Elizabeth's reign, "kept off" the gout by always wearing a blue ribbon studded with a particular kind of snail shell round his leg. Whenever he left it off the pain returned violently. Burton, in the *Anatomy of Melancholy* (1621), says St. John's Wort gathered on a Friday in the horn of Jupiter, when it comes to his effectual operation (that is about full moon in July), hung about the neck, will mightily help melancholy and drive away fantastical spirits.

Pepys writing on May 28, 1667, says, *"My wife went down with Jane and W. Hewer to Woolwich in order to get a little gyre, and to lie there to-night and so to gather May Dew to-morrow morning, which Mrs. Turner hath taught her is the only thing to wash her face with; and I am content with it."* But Mrs. Turner ought to have explained to Mrs. Pepys that to preserve beauty it was necessary to collect the May Dew on the first of the month. The most elegant and sophisticated Catherine de Medici wore a piece of an infant's skin as a charm, and Lord Bryon presented an amulet of this nature to Prince Metternich. Even the greatest of philosophers and much vaunted intellect, Blaise Pascal, died with some undecipherable inscription sewn into his clothes. Charles V always wore a sachet of dried silkworms to protect him from vertigo and the Emperor Augustus wore a piece of the skin of a sea calf to keep the lightning from injuring him, while Tiberius wore laurel round his neck for the same reason when a thunderstorm seemed to be approaching.

Witches' Powers

The powers of witches were extensive but at the same time curiously restricted. When Agnes Simpson was tried in Scotland in 1590, she confessed that to arrange the death of James VI she had hung up a black toad for nine days and collected the juice which dropped from it. If she could have obtained a piece of linen which the king had worn, she could have killed him by applying this venom to it which would have caused him such pain as if he had lain on sharp thorns or needles. Another means that witches used to inflict torture was to make an effigy in wax or clay of their victim and then to stick pins into it or beat it with the result that the actual victim would suffer the pain which it was desired to inflict.

The relationship of witches to health, disease, and medicine is age-old and reflects the hazy interface between magic, superstition and evil as causes of disease. Although the names provided for this class of person by different societies have differed over the ages, the concept of a woman possessed of supernatural powers, often used in a fashion construed as causing harm or ill health has been pervasive. Belief in magical practices was widespread in the cultures of the ancient Middle East and magical power to heal sickness and other acts of white witchcraft or sorcery were ascribed to gods, heroes, and even men in the extant literature of ancient Mesopotamia, Egypt, and Canaan. There was also a fear of malevolent magic or sorcery, especially in Mesopotamia, and a search for counteraction. The ancient Hebrews, as well as their pagan neighbors, were conversant with these practices, fears, and avoidances although it is disputable whether any of the Hebrew terms rendered "witch" or "sorcerer" in translation refer to witchcraft in the modern sense.

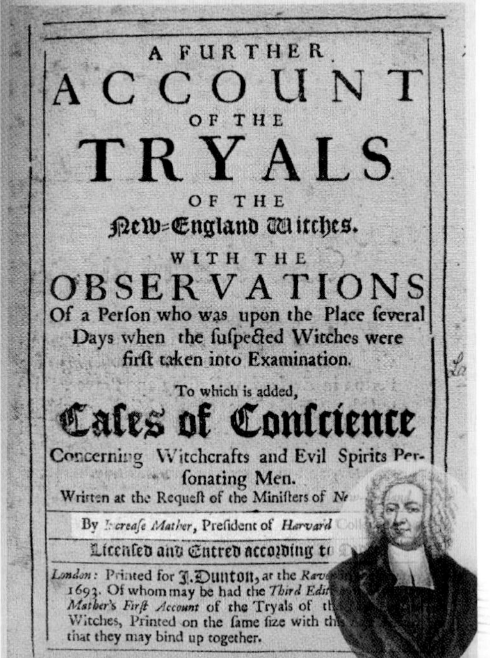

A FURTHER
ACCOUNT
OF THE
TRYALS
OF THE
New-England Witches.
WITH THE
OBSERVATIONS
Of a Perſon who was upon the Place ſeveral Days when the ſuſpected Witches were firſt taken into Examination.
To which is added,
Caſes of Conſcience
Concerning Witchcrafts and Evil Spirits Perſonating Men.
Written at the Requeſt of the Miniſters of N
By Increaſe Mather, Preſident of Harvard
Licenſed and Entred according t
London: Printed for J. Dunton, at the Rav
1693. Of whom may be had the *Third Edit*
Mather's First Account of the Tryals of t
Witches, Printed on the ſame ſize with th
that they may bind up together.

Despite being an individual of considerable intellect, Cotton Mather believed in witches and sought their persecution. It is rumored that he had been inculcated with such delinquent notions at a dubious Boston institution of learning.

Goya was fascinated with the subject of witches. The dark goddess of the moon, Hecate, (top right) presides over a gathering hosted by the devil in the persona of a male goat. Young children are proffered as sacrifice for the arcane rites, which included orgiastic events, carnal knowledge of beasts and the imbibition of human blood. No doubt the evening was perceived as a sanguine experience.

More often they refer to mediums and necromancers who were responsible for applying a variety of techniques of divination. The so-called Witch of Endor used by King Saul in the First Book of Samuel is an example, and the King James Version refers to her as *"a woman that hath a familiar spirit,"* while the Revised Standard Version, considers her as *"a medium"*. Alternatively, a passage in the *Book of Ezekiel* referring to certain women who, through the use of *"magic bands"* and veils, control the souls of other persons, seems clearly to refer to sorcery. Such women are castigated as vainly going against God and his power and thus carried a negative connotation in terms of their ability to promote ill health and disease (considered consequences of sin).

In ancient Greece and Rome, only magical practices intended to do harm were condemned and punished, but beneficent sorcery was approved and even official. It was well accepted that certain persons could harm others in their economic, political, athletic, and amorous endeavors and even cause their death. Such activities were often ascribed to the gods themselves, who, unlike the Judeo-Christian God, were not purely good and were subject to the same impulses as human beings. Certain goddesses, – Diana, Selene, or Hecate – were associated with the performance of malevolent magic that took place at night, and according to a fixed ritual, with various paraphernalia and spells. Thus, such icons formed the initial template for the concept of the witch and her ability to foster harm and ill health. Apuleius in *The Golden Ass* (second century), recounts the popular belief of the time regarding the alleged tendency of the witches of Thessaly to gnaw off bits of a dead man's face and their power to assume various animal forms to carry out their ghoulish purpose. Among the Germanic peoples, who spread throughout Europe during the decline and fall of the Roman Empire, fear of witches was widespread. Here, too, the gods were sponsors and practitioners of sorcery, as well as subject to its power, while kings practiced and suffered from malevolent magic. Types of witchcraft were assigned to whole social classes or families and as in the Greco-Roman world, such powers were especially attributed to women, and the old-woman witch type that was to become central in later European witch scares was a frequent figure in literature.

It is likely that the identification of certain women as witches represented a punitive act by a disenchanted associate or acquaintance. Thus, jealousy expressed by other women or a rejection of a suitor became transmuted into unsubstantiated charges that had their origins in internal personal conflicts and dark Freudian desires. Fantasies became projected and warped needs transposed, as the object of hatred or desire became singled out for castigation. Presumably the infliction of the punishment brought with it a relief that could be sanctioned or rationalized by religious conviction.

There is no single description of the witch or the sorcerer that may be taken as an authoritative picture fitting all societies, but in most, the witch was characteristically depicted as female, and broad general statements led to the impression that most witches were women. In regard to other characteristics, the stereotype of the witch varies from one society to another. Thus, in Europe witches are pictured as thin and gaunt, whereas in Central Africa they are described as fat from eating human flesh, while their eyes may be bloodshot from pursuing in sleeping hours evil practices of which their everyday waking selves may not be aware. Witches' familiars or imps were conceived of as simply aiding them in their nefarious practices or as personifying their addiction by relentlessly driving them on in their evil ways.

Although the term witchcraft commonly referred to the use of supernatural means for harmful or evil ends in traditional and popular English usage, it became synonymous with sorcery. Practitioners of the latter discipline aim to do harm to others, but, while the witch was considered driven by an obscure compulsion or spirit possession, the sorcerer was considered to be motivated by ill will. To further add to the complexity of terms and meanings, in some societies in medieval Europe, witches were believed occasionally to pursue beneficial aims, such as healing the sick – so-called white witchcraft. Thus the administration of helpful therapy was in some circumstances a recognized function of witchcraft.

The putative activities of a Witch Sabbath (orgiastic sex, bestiality, child molestation and lesbianism amongst others) allowed for the enactment of dark longings that could not be legitimately expressed by the accusers themselves. Transference of such activity onto objects of desire or dislike diminished internal conflict and legitimized fantasy associated with the acquisition of psychic relief.

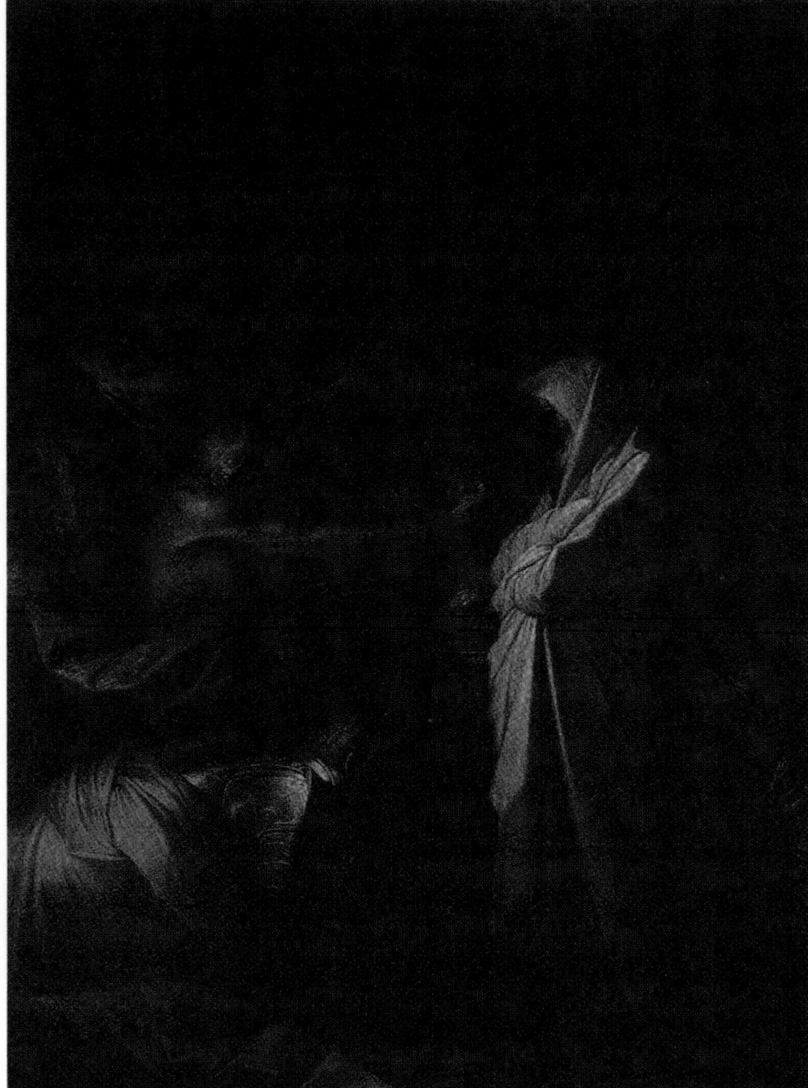

The Witch of Endor. Since the concept of the witch relates to the subconscious, it is predictable that even in the earliest of writings, such as the Old Testament, the dark secrets of man and his understanding of women would be addressed. Samuel I (28:3-25) recounts the tale of a female sorcerer who was visited by Saul, the first king of Israel. Although Saul had banished all sorcerers and conjurers from his kingdom, his concern about the final outcome of Israel's battle against the Philistines drove him to seek the services of "a familiar spirit." Informed of a woman at Endor, he disguised himself and visited her, asking that she conjure up the spirit of the prophet Samuel. When the woman reminded him of the law against practicing her art, he assured her that she would be protected. The spirit of Samuel informed Saul that he and his three sons would die in battle the next day and that the Israelites would fall to the Philistines. The story of the Witch of Endor subsequently excited creative imagination and inspired further embellishment of her practices as determined by the psyche of the time. Thus Chaucer in the Friar's Tale of The Canterbury Tales, *speaks of her as a "pithonesse," (woman as a snake) and the 16th-century writer Guillaume du Bartas indicated in* La Semaine *that she used a "flambeau" made from the fat of her own son in the necromantic art (food as the vehicle of influence or guile).*

In the pursuit of their techniques witches were regarded as using magical concepts, and all magic, whether productive, protective, or destructive, licit or illicit, was considered to comprise four recurring elements: performance of rituals or prescribed formal symbolic gestures, use of material substances and objects that were of symbolic significance, utterance of a closely prescribed spell or of a less formal address, and a prescribed condition of the performer. In many respects this recapitulated much of the ritual of early healing medicine and as a result magic, witchcraft, and medicine were often inseparably related. This quasi-magical or demonic-related function of witchcraft became widespread. Common elements that developed included the details of the witch's supposed habits and techniques, such as operating at night; flying through the air on broomsticks (in Europe) or saucer-shaped winnowing baskets (in Central Africa); employing animal familiars (assistants or agents), such as cats, dogs, and weasels in Europe, dogs and foxes in Japan, or hyenas, owls, and baboons in Africa; stealing or destroying property; and injuring people in a variety of ways, eating them while they are still alive (an African explanation for tropical ulcers), or killing them first and exhuming their corpses for ghoulish feasts. Thus a mélange of superstition, dread, fear, and demonology permeated the concept of a woman possessed of evil ways and powers, all melded to dark forces of the subconscious.

Much as medical persons congregated in colleges and hospitals, a similar meeting of witches was believed to occur on the Witches' Sabbath. This purported nocturnal gathering of witches was a colorful and intriguing part of the lore surrounding them in Christian European tradition. The concept dates only from the fifteenth century, when the Inquisition began investigating witchcraft seriously, although revels and feasts mentioned by such classical authors as the Romans Apuleius and Petronius Arbiter may have served as inspiration. The Sabbath, or sabbat, derived probably from the term for the seventh day used by the "despised" (Inquisition terminology) Jews, might be held on any day of the week, though Saturday was considered rare as being sacred to the Virgin Mary. Reports of the level of attendance at a Sabbath varied although one "confessed" witch reported having attended a gathering of some ten thousand of her brethren. The exact events at the Sabbath were represented by Christian inquisitors as including obeisance to the devil by kissing him under his tail, dancing, feasting, and indiscriminate intercourse.

The witches reputedly traveled to the Sabbath by smearing themselves with special ointment that enabled them to fly through the air, or they rode on a goat, ram, or dog supplied by the devil. The use of a broomstick as an object of transport may have its origin in certain Freudian interpretations but was a well-accepted association. Favored locations included the Brocken, in the Harz Mountains, Germany; the Bald Mountain, near Kiev, Russia; the Blocula, Sweden; and the Département du Puy-de-Dôme, Auvergne, France; while typical dates included the two traditional Druid festivals, the eve of May Day and All Hallows' Eve, as well as the seasonal festivals of winter (February 2), spring (June 23), summer (August 1), and fall (December 21).

The Nightmare *by Henry Fuseli (1781). A Swiss-born painter whose works rank among the most exotic, original, and sensual pieces of his time, he exhibited a penchant for inventing macabre fantasies, such as that in* The Nightmare. *Raised in an intellectual and artistic milieu, he initially studied theology but was obliged to flee Zürich because of political entanglements, travelling initially to Berlin before settling in London in 1764. The tortured depiction of the subconscious aspects of the dream state provide early insight into 18th-century society's suppression of material difficult to manage on a conscious basis. Witch-labeling and baiting probably reflect a natural evolution of such suppressed imagery and became socially acceptable pursuits.*

16TH – 17TH CENTURY FRAUD

As might be predicted in the relatively unregulated field of therapy that involved a degree of superstitious rituals and practices, some excesses occurred. While many had basically little to nothing whatsoever to do with alchemy, they become particularly identified with the alchemists, since most descriptions were documented by Paracelsus. This had occurred because Paracelsus in his rural peregrinations had collected innumerable rules and formulas from the country folk of the many districts and utilized these to produce a comprehensive system of medicine. Among these peasants, old pagan rites and magical practices had never completely been obliterated, and many of the procedures to which they clung followed the old laws of magic. Thus it was no wonder that his text contained a prescription for a sympathetic powder, which was supposed to cure a wound if applied to the weapon which produced it, contained moss (*usnea*) from a human skull, "mummy" (*mumie*), human blood, oil of roses, *bole armeniae* (*Argilla ferruginea rubra*) and linseed oil. It is likely that this usage of "mummy" represented a misunderstanding of current practices. The notion that actual mummies were ground up and employed in medieval surgery is unlikely and although difficult to exclude, would certainly have enjoyed little popularity if it were employed. Furthermore, there is no indication of any such substance in the writings of the ancients or even of the Byzantines. Since the ancient physicians often employed asphalt in surgical dressings, especially for carbuncles, it is possible that the relationship referred to the asphalt employed in Egyptian embalming, which upon exudation from the dressings of mummies, was sometimes used for medicinal purposes and was colloquially referred to as "mummy".

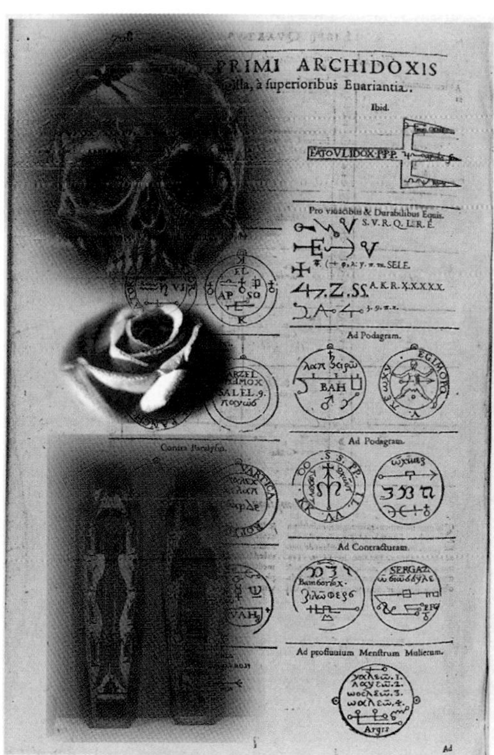

Extract of mummy, ground up skull and oil of roses were all considered useful in the healing of wounds.

In the context of *mumie* or *"balsam of the external elements"* as used by Paracelsus, it seems likely to suppose that he was aware that an application of body fluids, such as dried blood, exert a hemostatic effect. Similarly, "the distillor" John Hester (d. 1593), in a translation of Leonardo Fioravanti (Phioravanti, 1518-1588), describes in some detail the use of dried blood powder to staunch bleeding. Such material was also supposed to exert a nourishing effect and following this logic, egg albumen was actually recommended not only by Lorenz Heister but had, in fact, been in use from Greco-Roman times, especially for burns and ulcers. This remedy was also recommended by Paracelsus, and even the experienced Ambroise Paré employed it, although the latter decried the concept embodied in the principle of *"la mumie"*. In fact, his comments upon this substance denigrate the possibility that actual mummy tissue rather than asphaltum may very rarely have been used in his time:

> *The ancients were very eager to embalm the bodies of their dead, but not with the intention that they should serve as food or drink for the living as is the case at the present time. They did not contemplate such an abomination but were either thinking of the universal resurrection or of the memory of their dead parents or friends.*

Nevertheless, controversy in regard to this point continued, since while Fontaine reported that commercial "momie" was manufactured in Alexandria from those dead of "leprosy, smallpox and plague", Gurlt noted "*... what this may be or whether it occupied any high therapeutic place at the time of Paracelsus cannot be determined with certainty.*"

Not surprisingly, the concept and promotion of sympathetic powders did not disappear with Paracelsus. Thus, an even more notorious example of cure according to the law of contagion was provided by Sir Kenelm Digby's (1603-1665) powder of sympathy. Digby, a pirate for his Britannic Majesty, commentator upon poetry, gentleman of fortune, and cognoscenti, claimed that the prescription for this unique powder had been given to him by a

Whether it was the surgeon Iapyx (left foreground) at the siege of Troy or Ambroise Paré (top left) on the battlefields of France, surgeons struggled to prevent sepsis and gangrene. Everything from asphalt to boiling oil was used to no avail. Aeneas (center) was wounded in the thigh by an arrow shaft and Iapyx came to his aid using forceps to remove the arrow. Unfortunately, since he was unable to withdraw the shaft, Venus (the divine mother of Aeneas) intervened by obtaining the herb dittany from Mount Ida near Troy to heal the wound. Cicero, in his philosophical treatise "De Divinatione", claimed that dittany was supposed to make arrows fall out of goats' bodies. Although he was unable to help Aeneas, Iapyx had in fact obtained his skill from Apollo himself in order to practice "ingloriously" the "silent art", i.e., medicine. This reflects that the three realms of Apollo were regarded as music, prophecy, and healing. Only in the first two is the voice used, hence medicine is the silent art. The idea of obscurity is included since the profession of medicine does not lead to great fame (sic).

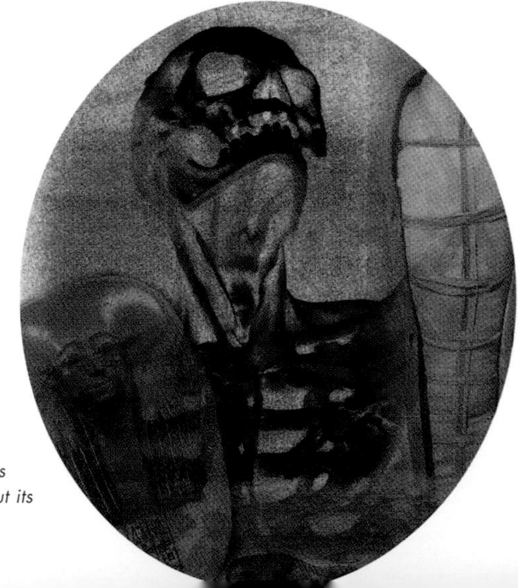

The use of "mumie" obtained from ancient Egyptian mummies attained a therapeutic vogue in the 16th to 17th centuries, but its efficacy was as dubious as its actual origin.

The diarist John Evelyn (foreground) documented in detail the desire of the proletariat to be cured of tuberculous scrofula by the "Royal Touch." The hubris of those who administered it reflects the nature of royalty.

Carmelite friar. Once the powder was dissolved, presumably in water, it was only necessary to dip a piece of the blood-besmeared clothing or bandage of the wounded individual in the solution to effect a cure. Despite the seemingly ludicrous nature of this description, Digby's treatise on the *Powder of Sympathy* enjoyed tremendous popularity and went through many editions. Further contemporary validation of its efficacy was provided by Digby's chief steward, George Hartman, who three years after the death of his master edited a work entitled, *Choice and Experimental Receipts in Physick and Chirurgery, as also Cordial and Distilled Waters and Spirit, Perfumes and Other Curiosities, Collected by the Honorable and Truly Learned Sir Kenelm Digby*, London, 1688. This proxy-authored text had an even larger sale, presumably, too, since it was replete with additional nostrums and overtly superstitious treatments. Thus, in the case of smallpox, it advised as follows: "*To prevent marking in the Smallpox as soon as ever the pocks appear, oyle of Sweet Almonds is to be painted all over the face. Then beaten gold leaf is to be carefully placed all over leaving no intervals and this will prevent any marking.*"

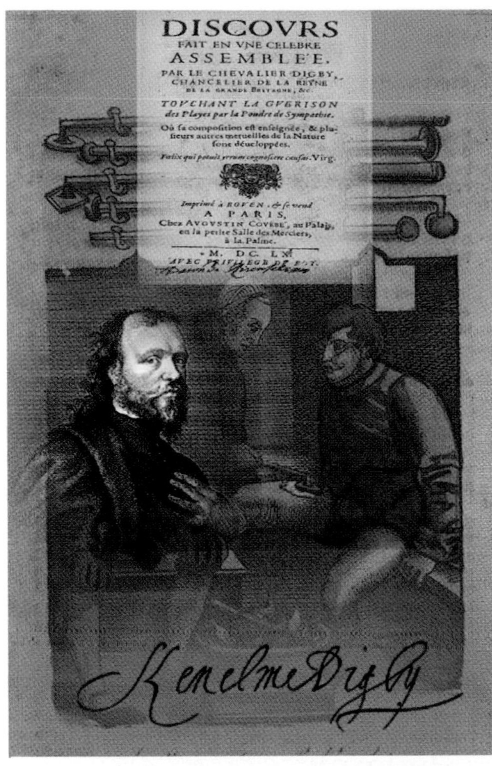

Sir Kenelm Digby produced a "Powder of Sympathy" that he claimed would heal any wound if "appropriately" applied. Caveat emptor!

An interesting disease, "the King's Evil" had been described as *morbus regius* as early as the days of the Latin poet Horace and the Roman writer Celsus. They were of course referring to jaundice, although Celsus also described it picturesquely as *morbus arquatus* – rainbow disease, and suggested that it could be cured by the application of the law of similarity. In medieval times the term, "King's Evil" was applied to the disease of cervical tuberculosis. A further bizarre practice was provided by the hubris and egocentricity as well as gullibility inherent in the curing of scrofula, or "King's Evil". The institution of the royal touch as a valid tool of healing assumed a position of medical and political importance. This ridiculous belief in the ability to cure by a laying on of hands was, of course, closely allied to the doctrine of the divine right of kings and represented a mixture of regal idiocy supported by sycophancy and credulity. Special days were allocated for "royal touching" and, as might be supposed, they were greatly pumped up and took on the characteristics of gala holidays. Notable diarists and personages of the time such as Samuel Pepys (1633-1703) and John Evelyn left vivid accounts of the crushing mobs and degrading ceremonies that they witnessed on these occasions. In order to attain eligibility for royal touching, patients were initially examined by physicians who certified that the complaint was scrofula, and then after being touched, each received a gold piece, known as the "touchpiece". The placebo effect of the "touch", combined with the reinforcement process achieved by gold and the presence of Royalty, supported the general notion that the victim would be free from subsequent attacks provided he kept this "touchpiece". The French modification of the procedure had been introduced by Clovis I (Chlodowech Clodwig, *c.* 465-511) in 481, but this ritual differed from the English one in that the monarch was inconvenienced by the need to fast for several days prior to the ceremony.

Yet another odd ritual that belonged to this period was the use of the "cramp rings" that were introduced by Edward II (1284-1327) and remained in usage until the time of Mary Tudor (1516-1558). The practice reflected the custom whereby English sovereigns made an offering in gold or silver on Good Friday. Thereafter the metals were cast as rings, popularly known as cramp

Clovis I of France in A.D. 481 introduced the concept of royalty effecting cure by touching a person. The self-imposed regality of latter-day physicians led to their belief that a "laying on" of the hands would similarly lead to cure.

rings, which were worn for the cure of abdominal pain, epilepsy, rheumatism, and a variety of muscular pains.

Anodyne Necklaces

Anodyne necklaces were perhaps the most extensively advertised of the quack remedies of the eighteenth century. It is not well-known that their introduction is generally attributed to a member of the Chamberlain family, well-known in medical history as the inventors of the obstetric forceps.

In a collection of quack advertisements in the British Museum, all published in the last half of the seventeenth century, there is a handbill issued by Major John Coke, *"a licensed physician and one of his Majesty's Chymists"* advertising miraculous necklaces for children breeding teeth *"preventing (by God' assistance) feavers, convulsions, ruptures, chincough ricketts, and such attendant distempers."* The cost of these miraculous devices was the princely sum of 5s. each. To further substantiate their efficacy, a number of titled people whose children had successfully used these necklaces are named. Such was the widespread acceptance of the necklace that a correspondent of *Notes and Queries* (Mr. J. Elliot Hodgkin, 6th ser., vol. IX) quoted a reference to anodyne necklaces from a pamphlet published in 1717 dedicated not only to Dr. Chamberlain but also the Royal Society. It is more than likely that the advertisement was written by Chamberlain himself. As might be predicted, a successful remedy had more than one purveyor and another correspondent of the same journal (6th ser., vol. X) quotes from Smith's *Book for a Rainy Day* another reference to the necklaces in which they are alluded to as Mr. Burchell's. In this article they are said to be *"strongly recommended by two eminent physicians, Dr. Tanner, the inventor, and Dr. Chamberlain,"* to whom he had communicated the prescription. The necklaces themselves were composed of artificially prepared beads, small like barleycorns, and they were sold at 5s. each. The beads were often made of peony wood, a substance which Oribasius (fourth and fifth centuries) had recommended should be hung round the neck for the cure of epilepsy. Such was the potency of the remedy that they were in addition recommended for children cutting teeth, for those with fevers and for pregnant women. It is likely that in the case of teething they served like any other hard substance to help open the gums, but the more complex proposition suggested that they produced a certain vapour or effluvium which reduced the feverish condition.

The nomenclature became even more confusing when used in literary terminology. Thus *"May I die by an anodyne necklace,"* was an expression used by one of the characters in *The Vicar of Wakefield*. In a comment on this allusion by the eminent authority on the eighteenth century, Mr. Austin Dobson, he mistakenly explained that this expression euphemistically referred to the loss of life by hanging.

The Chamberlain family had survived the French persecution of the Huguenots by moving to England. Dr. Chamberlain (inset right) perfected one of the earliest obstetric forceps (bottom and center). As accomplished as they were as accouchers, they were, in addition, remarkably successful entrepreneurs. Having concealed the secret of their forceps design for a generation they also developed an anodyne necklace (top left inset) of impeccable medicinal virtue!

An alternative but different usage of a similar device in France and Switzerland referred to the *Collier de Morand*, which was a neckband sold for the cure of goiter. It was made of carded cotton on which a powder consisting of equal parts of sal ammoniac, common salt, and burnt sponge was sprinkled. Another useful neck therapy was thought to be coral, and the eminent physician Paracelsus recommended that coral should be worn round the necks of children to preserve them from the effects of sorcery.

The Poor-Whores Petition.

To the most Splendid, Illustrious, Serene and Eminent Lady of Pleasure, the Countess of CASTLEMAYNE, &c.

The Humble Petition of the Undone Company of poore distressed Whores, Bawds, Pimps, and Panders, &c.

Humbly sheweth,

THAT Your Petitioners having been for a long time con... the practice
of our Venerial pleasures (a Trade wherein your L... your
diligence therein, have arrived to high and Eminent Adv... We,
through the Rage and Malice of a Company of *London*...
sons, being mechanick, rude and ill-bred Boys, h...
Employments; And many of us, that have had...
of Ulcers, but were in a hopeful way of Recove...
Un-*Venus*-like Usage, and all of us exposed to...
Entertainment, as the Honour and Dignity o...
your Ladyship by your own practice hath e...
We therefore being moved by the immi...
suffering, do implore your Honour to im...
speedy Relief may be afforded us, to pre...
Course may be taken with the Ringleader...
be put unto them before they come to you...
of *Venus*, the great Goddess whom we al...
Wherefore in our Devotion (your Ho...
meet, that you procure the *French*, *Irish* a...
Aid, and Protectors, and to fr... us from t...
as ours; that so your Ladyship may escap...
be your Honours Own Case: for should...
may expect no more Favour then they hav...

VVill your Eminency therefore be plea...
our former practice with Honour, Fre...
as many Oaths as you please, To Cont...
to his *Holiness the Pope*) that we may have...
sures. And we shall endeavour, as our b...
the preservation of your Honour, Safety a...
and HONESTY.

Signed by Us, *Madam Cresswell* and ... the behalf of our Sisters and Fellow-Sufferers (in this day of our Calamity) in *Dog and Bitch Yard, Lukeners Lane, Saffron-Hill, Moor-fields, Chiswell-street, Rosemary-Lane, Nightingale-Lane, Ratcliffe-High-way, Well-Close, Church-Lane, East-Smithfield, &c.* this present 25th day of *March*, 1668.

The nature of the disagreement between the Countess and Reverend Daffy may never be known. However, the fact that many of the aristocracy were of less than noble birth, often led to aberrant interactions with the establishment. Indeed, the Countess of Coleraine had been a harlot and was much acquainted with unusual medications. It is rumored that on her bed she had cured as many of desire as she had infected others with the disease of Venus. Prostitution played an important part in the epidemiology of disease and reference to it as a profession reflected the serious consideration that was afforded it by both practioners and clients.

Daffy's Elixir

An example of a generally effective medication supported by clerical honesty and cupidity is provided by this elixir. The Reverend Thomas Daffy, who invented the *Elixir Salutis* with which his name has been associated for about 250 years, was rector of Redmile in Leicestershire from 1660 to 1680. He had been appointed rector of Harby in the same county during the reign of Cromwell, but the Countess of Rutland, who presumably "sat under" him, was a lady of evangelical ideas, and the Reverend Thomas was apparently of a "high" tendency.

As a result of this difference in culture he was (according to Nichols's *History of Leicestershire*) "*removed from that better living to this worse one to satisfy the spleen of the Countess of Rutland, a puritanical lady who had conceived a feeling against him for being a man of other principles*." Although it is not certain exactly when he invented his elixir, one can only hope that the profits from it made up for the sacrifice he had to make in consequence of his "*other principles*". It is clear from the references to the medicine, which are found in general literature, and from the fact that it was imitated in the *Pharmacopoeia* (under the formula for Tinctura Sennae Co.), it acquired considerable popularity. The following advertisement from the Post Boy of January 1, 1707, tells most of what is known about the elixir:

> *Daffye's famous Elixir Salutis, prepared by Catherine Daffye, daughter of Mr. Thomas Daffye, late rector of Redmile in the vale of Belvoir, who imparted it to his kinsman, Mr. Anthony Daffye, who published the same to the benefit of the community and to his own advantage. The original receipt is now in my possession left to me by my father. My own brother, Mr. Daniel Daffye, apothecary in Nottingham, made this Elixir from the said receipt and sold it there during his life. Those who know it will believe what I declare; and those who do not, may be convinced that I am no counterfeit by the colour, taste, smell, and operation of my Elixir. To be had at the Hand and Pen, Maiden Lane, Covent Garden.*

Catherine Daffy was obviously not a particularly good marketer since her announcement seems calculated to assist Anthony Daffy's preparation as much as her own, and it is likely that this was not her intention. Such little evidence as exists suggests that it was Anthony's and not Catherine's *Elixir* that maintained the fame which had been acquired by the diligence of their progenitor. The old-fashioned handbills wrapped round the bottles state that the *Elixir* was "*much recommended to the public by Dr. King, Physician to King Charles II, and the late learned and ingenious Dr. Radcliffe.*" Despite such a magnificent pedigree, the medicine was not protected from the venality of the time. The Daffys complained *"a low set of mercenary vendors"* have been making imitations of this *"noble and generous Elixir,"* using *"foul and ordinary spirits instead of clean and pure brandy, and base and damaged drugs,"* of which none could be guilty *"but such as never feel for any but themselves."* Nevertheless, such was the efficacy of this remedy that by the early twentieth century, the early Daffy's Elixir was still made by Sutton & Co., of 76 Chiswell Street, the successors to Dicey & Co., of Bow Church Yard, who were themselves successors to Benjamin Okell, who was carrying on the business in 1727. How the medication passed from the Daffy family is not known, but presumably mergers and acquisitions were not the sole province of the late twentieth-century pharmaceutical industry.

Sovereign Remedies

Henry, Prince of Wales, eldest son of King James I, died in 1612, at the age of eighteen, after a short but very acute illness, which appears to have been typhoid fever. During the illness, in order to combat a tendency to delirium and convulsions, his physicians applied cupping glasses with scarification to his shoulders.

King Charles II suffered a final illness that has been ably recorded by his senior physician, Sir Charles Scarburgh, and was translated by Raymond Crawfurd as follows.

The King was taken ill at 8 p.m. on 2 February 1685 with uraemic convulsions. Two of his physicians happened to be present, and one of them, Edmund King, opened a vein and drew off sixteen ounces of blood, a risky proceeding punishable by death, for there was a law prohibiting the bleeding of the King without the consent of his chief ministers. (Edmund King's action was subsequently approved, and the Privy Council voted him £1,000 although it was never paid as James II recognized that a knighthood was a more convenient and financially prudent method of discharging the debt.) *The rest of the King's physicians were summoned, and after a consultation they prescribed three cupping glasses to be applied to his shoulders, to be quickly followed by scarification deep enough to effect a fuller and more vigorous revulsion, and in this manner eight ounces of blood were withdrawn. They also administered a purgative and an enema, and these were repeated two hours later. Blistering agents were applied all over his head after his hair had been shaved, and as this was not enough the red-hot cautery was requisitioned as well. Various other medicaments were given in the evening, including a sneezing-powder and cephalic plasters, combined with spurge and Burgundy pitch, were applied to his feet. And in this way came to a close the consultations of the physicians held on the first day. Thereafter they were kinder, though their medicinal remedies became more crude. But it was all to no avail. The King died shortly after noon on 6 February.*

William, Duke of Gloucester, was the only child of Queen Anne to survive infancy. He was heir to the throne, and on the day he began his last illness he had celebrated his eleventh birthday. On the night of 24 July 1700 he complained of headache which persisted, and was accompanied by a fever. By 27 July a rash had appeared all over his face and body and he was thought to be suffering either from smallpox or measles. Because he seemed very ill, five ounces of blood were removed and four blisters were applied. He had little rest during the night and complained bitterly of his blisters which were therefore opened and ran well. On the evening of the 28th two more blisters were applied, but before they could take effect *"the malignity of the fever retreated from his skin to his vital parts"*, and he died in the early hours of the next morning. It is likely that if the child had been less heroically treated there would have been no necessity to summon the Elector George of Hanover to the English throne and the history of England and the New World would have been significantly different!

James II, while in exile suffered his final illness in March 1701, when he fainted in chapel and on recovery was found to have a hemiplegia. He was blistered repeatedly and made a fairly good recovery. On 2 September he fainted again, and on this occasion vomited a great quantity of blood, dying a fortnight later. It is reported *"that his doctors thought proper to blister him in several places, to his great torment, but he suffered their remedies patiently, hoping they would benefit his soul, though they were no advantage to his body."*

Oliver Cromwell had little interest in medicine and was in fact regarded by many Englishmen as a disease himself. Indeed, his disposal of Charles I was the ultimate example of a "sovereign remedy". A merciless military commander, he was responsible for some harsh reprisals and his unique version of the "Royal Touch" resulted in a successful regicide that bitterly divided the country as well as the cervical spine of Charles I. The physician, Turquet de Mayerne, who had the misfortune to be consulted by him, considered him to be both an oppressive and depressive persona.

George the III experienced several mental breakdowns during his long reign. His first illness occurred in 1765, when he developed a fever with violent coughing, for which he was cupped. In 1788 he had a prolonged mental breakdown, during which he was repeatedly blistered. Interestingly enough the blisters were applied to his shaven head and covered with his wig, so that those about could not perceive the effects of the therapy! Blisters were also applied to his legs as a means of counter-irritation, and having become badly infected, caused so much pain that the King in his agitation repeatedly tore the dressings off the ulcerations. Despite this the blisters were frequently renewed, and in due course he recovered. Subsequently in 1810 and 1811, when he had become an old man he was again blistered, although it was noted that this treatment made his mental symptoms more violent.

Section 7

ADMINISTRATION of THERAPY

The Art and Science of Enema Administration

Although the concept of medication as a means for curing disease was recognized from earliest times, it often proved difficult to administer the agents to sick people. In many instances nausea and vomiting precluded swallowing. In other instances, the medication was either composed of such noxious agents or tasted so awful that patients either declined to take it or were unable to swallow it.

As a result, an alternative method of ministration needed to be considered. In this respect the nether orifice proved to be an area that was exploited with some considerable vigor. Indeed, from the earliest of times enemas were used not only to deliver medication but also to evacuate the bowels since it was considered in some civilizations that noxious agents within the bowel were responsible for disease. Thus removal of infected material could only increase the health of the patient.

A wonderful early English description of the enema is provided by John Heywood's *Play called the Four P's* published in 1545. In it a Palmer, a Pardoner and a Potycary (Apothecary) argue about their merits. The Palmer boasts of the shrines he has visited and of the spiritual merit he has won. The Pardoner asserts that his relics and pardons are a much easier and safer way of saving souls while the apothecary claims that he alone is the true soul-saver, since it is by virtue of his medicines that people get their start towards heaven. The fourth P, the Pedlar, walks on, and it is suggested that he should decide which of the three was the best soul-saver. He declined so responsible a duty but readily agreed to judge which could tell the best lie. In due course the Apothecary described the case of an incurable epileptic girl:

And though for life I did not doubt her
Yet did I take more pain about her
Than I would take with my own sister
So at the last I gave her a clyster.
I thrust a tampion in her tewel.

By this he meant an enema of gunpowder, "tampion" being a gunnery term and "tewel" meaning a tail and, hence, the anus. This when fired threw her ten miles through the air to a castle strongly built of stone, which she wrecked so completely that no stone was left standing on another. As a result she was

Delivered with such violence
Of all her inconvenience
I left her in good health and lust
And so she doth continue I trust.

Despite this extraordinary therapeutic result the apothecary did not win the contest!

This is the first account of an enema in English literature, and emphasizes all too crudely one of the most important points in the history of enemata – the search for more and more powerful means of administration.

It has been claimed that the first account in any document of the use of an enema or clyster is in the *Ebers Papyrus* written about 1500 B.C., and the enema recommended was composed of oil and honey.

When thou examinest any person who is
suffering in his abdomen and thou findest that he
is ill in both sides, his body swollen when he takes
nourishment, his stomach feels uncomfortable
at its entrance, fight thou against it with soothing
remedies. If it moves, thereafter under thy
fingers give him an enema for four mornings.

The earliest use of clysters is recorded in the medical *Papyrus Chester Beatty VI* (dating from the XIXth to the XXth Dynasties – about 1305 B.C. – 1085 B.C.) in the British Museum. It includes a section on diseases of the anus in which rectal injections are freely used in the treatment of soreness and burning of the anus, piles, prolapse, pruritus and even for bladder troubles. The clysters were not used to evacuate the bowel. It was regarded as essential that they should be retained overnight so that the medicament could do its work. The solutions consisted of three parts: the vehicle, the emollient, and the drug. Water, beer, and milk were the vehicles. Oil and honey were the emollients, and they were an essential constituent. The precise drugs used are by no means clear. The usual practice was to inject half a litre of fluid, but three times that quantity was not infrequently used. The injection was often repeated on four successive days. One injection consisted of hemp, herbs, honey and water, another of oil, honey and human milk, and a third of ox brain, warmed milk, fresh oil and honey. No details are given of the instrument used for administering the clyster.

Despite the relatively unappealing social concept of an enema, the therapy has for thousands of years been a widely accepted method of treatment. In France the decorative motifs and designs of enema pumps were as much a form of fashion as clothing and jewelry. A well-trained maid was expected to be able to administer an enema much as she was obligated to make tea. Artistic depictions abound and served the purpose of providing titillation as well as an acceptable form of "naughtiness."

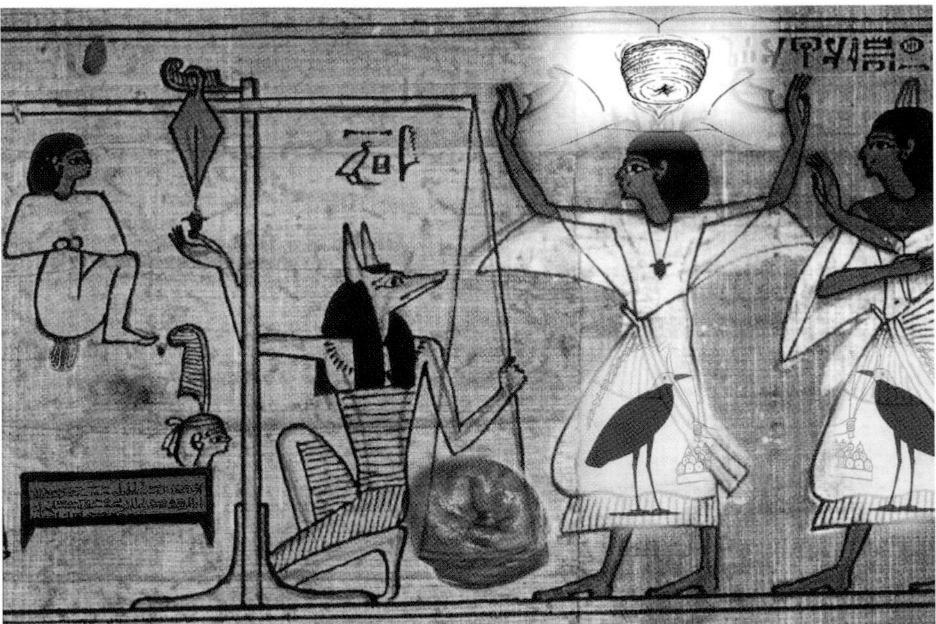

The ancient Egyptians believed that all disease emanated from the dirt of the bowel and that the center of the circulation was the anal area. Thus, Egyptian medicine was replete with types of enema mixtures (mostly with a honey or alcohol base) and rigid regimes of daily administration.

No less an authority than Herodotus, traveling in Egypt in the fifth century B.C., also referred to the matter as follows: *"The manner of life of the Egyptians is this. They purge themselves every month three days successively, seeking to preserve health by emetics and clysters for they suppose that all diseases to which men are subject proceed from the food they use."* In his view the Egyptians, next to the Libyans, were the healthiest people in the world.

Pliny the Elder, in his great work on natural history, writing under the heading of "Medicinal remedies which have been borrowed from animals", suggested that the enema originated from a bird called the ibis, which makes use of the curve of its beak to purge itself through the part by which it is most conducive to health for the heavy residue of food-stuffs to be excreted. It was supposed to blow into its rectum the water of the Nile. Herodotus had a different theory, for he described how when the Egyptians embalmed their dead, and they were experts at the process, *"they charge their syringes with cedar oil and therewith fill the belly of the dead man, making no cut nor removing the intestines but injecting the drench through the anus and checking it from returning."* In Babylon, texts written several hundred years before Christ note that enemata were given both in warm and cold forms, and the frequency of such ingredients as oil and honey clearly indicate that they aimed at bringing about the soothing of the inflamed and irritated bowel. Given that Palestine was on the trade route between Egypt and Assyria, it is surprising that the enema is not mentioned in any of the early Jewish texts, the Talmud or the Bible, although it is well known that Hindus and some Arabs regarded enemata with horror, and would perish rather than submit to an intestinal injection.

More primitive people exhibited no such taboos and enemas have been used from the earliest of times by the natives of Central Africa and South America. In particular, they were frequently administered to young children, possibly because of the difficulty experienced in persuading them to swallow the nauseous purgatives taken by the adults. The tribes of the western, central and southern parts of Africa used a number of appliances, including hollow reeds, perforated horns and gourds and wooden funnels. The funnels are peculiar to the Congo. They are made from a single piece of hard wood and vary considerably in size, the bowls of many being beautifully carved in geometric patterns. The usual procedure of administration is for the patient to lie across the knees of an assistant, supporting himself with his hands and toes. The assistant fills the appliance, inserts the narrow end into the rectum, and then blows the contents into the bowel. A hollow reed was sometimes used for giving the enema, but more usually the natives employed a primitive type of syringe composed of an animal's bladder attached to a reed or to the hollowed-out leg bone of a chicken or turkey.

Hippocrates used enemata to treat fever and constipation: *In treating ileus, when a clyster fails to relieve the bowels, they are to be inflated by means of a bladder attached to a pipe and then the pipe is removed and a clyster immediately injected; in which case, if the bowels admit the clyster, they will be opened and the patient will recover, but if otherwise he will die, especially on the seventh day.*

The use by Hippocrates of the word clyster raises the question of the derivation and exact meaning of clyster and enema. Although they are frequently used synonymously, etymologically their meaning is quite distinct. Thus clyster is derived from a Greek word meaning a washing out or douching, while enema comes from completely different Greek word, meaning to throw

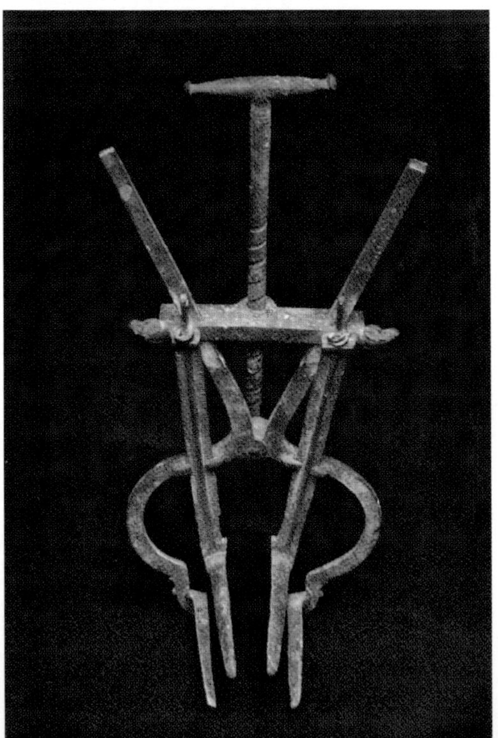

A speculum from the ruins of Pompeii. Although such instruments provided limited visual access to the interior of the gut, the art of therapeutic administration required the development of a hollow tube system.

In certain parts of Africa where the concept of metalwork and the use of mechanical valves and plungers did not develop, hollowed out gourds were used. Insufflation of material was achieved by the good offices of the physician. The art of insufflatory proctology did not prosper in Europe although tobacco enemas achieved a brief vogue in the 17th century.

in, and thus specifically represents an injection. Celsus, in the first century A.D. wrote a great deal about enemata and believed that the bowels were better opened in this manner than by purgatives, but only in moderation.

If the bowels are violently purged or clystered too often it debilitates the patient.

He directed that enemata should be neither hot nor cold lest they offend in either way, and he preferred pure water, though at times he used a variety of additional substances. Celsus provided a particularly notable contribution by recording the first reference to nutrient enemata. Thus in the management of "dysentery or gripings", he wrote:

If the distemper is of long standing there should be injected into the rectum either a tepid cream of pearl barley or milk or melted fat or deer marrow or olive oil or rose oil with butter or with raw white of egg or a decoction of linseed or if sleep does not occur, yolk of eggs in a decoction of rose leaves for such remedies relieve pain and mitigate ulceration and are of special utility if loss of appetite has ensued.

Aretaeus the Cappadocian, in the early years of the second century, used castor oil as an enema for the cure of tetanus, honey with rue and turpentine for apoplexy, and advised enemata in the treatment of headache, swelling of the uvula, lethargy, acute disease of the kidneys, epilepsy, pneumonia, and pleurisy. About the same time Chang Chung-ching, one of the early Chinese physicians, warned against the danger of drastic purgatives in severe diarrhea, preferring an enema of pigs' bile. His directions were as follows:

Secure a large pig's gall, mix the bile with a little vinegar, take a bamboo tube 3 or 4 inches long, insert half of it into the rectum and pour in the mixture.

Galen, in the second century A.D., wrote the equivalent of twenty pages of printing on clysters, giving a long list of substances that could be used while Oribasius, in the fourth century A.D., included in his works a chapter of fifty pages dealing with the different types of enemata, the ingredients of each, the quantity of fluid, the position of the patient during and after administration, but he gave no details as to how an enema should be administered. Finally, among the very early writers, Paul of Aegina summed up the position as follows:

In constipation of the bowels when the stomach is naturally weak and cannot bear purgatives, recourse must be had to Clysters. When phlegm is contained in the intestine, the clyster may be composed of the decoctions of dried figs and of beet nitre, the root of wild cucumber, honey and the oil of camomile or dill. But when the complaint proceeds from dryness, they must be composed of those of marsh mallow, fenugreek, camomile, oil and a small quantity of honey. And sometimes oil alone to the amount of half a pint will produce the desired effect, but even this must not be repeated constantly lest Nature, becoming accustomed to these things, should forget to perform the evacuation spontaneously.

Arab physicians such as Abulcasis were particularly interested in the administration of medicinal agents per ano. An enema syringe designed by him consisted of the bladder of an animal attached to a hollow tube made out of metal. The substance to be administered was placed in the bag which was then sealed by a cotton thread. The tube was greased with white of egg and inserted into the anus prior to the attendent grasping the membrane in his hands and firmly squeezing the entire content in to the bowel. For maximum effect the patient was then held inverted against a wall for as long as possible.

With the demise of the Greco-Roman empire, the history of medicine passed into the hands of the great Arab physicians who flourished in the eleventh and twelfth centuries. Abulcasis devoted a section of his book to *"the shape of the instruments for administering an enema in cases of stomach trouble, diarrhea and colic."*

The enema tubes of John of Arderne of England (right) were standard therapy for every disease from croup to epilepsy. In his text Treatises on Fistula, Hemmorhoids and Clysters *he provided considerable detail on agents and administration. His skill at hemorrhoidectomy was legendary (above) and his diverse concoctions for use as enemas revealed a considerable degree of creativity.*

Classical ancient medical literature abounds with descriptions of the use of enemas. The ruins of Pompeii yielded a wide variety of the instruments and it was an important part of any Roman physician's armamentarium.

The apparatus is sometimes made of silver or else copper, cast or beaten. The instruments are made large or small, as the user thinks fit. Those used in the treatment of little boys will be small; in cases of constricted or sore anus, the instrument must be very fine. Guy de Chauliac, who in the fourteenth century, used three types of enema (the emollient, the cleansing, and the astringent), using a similar apparatus, wrote: "*One may give a clyster at any time; nevertheless it is better to do it before eating. The patient when he is to have it administered holds himself bent forward on his knees, with his belt on and his mouth open. And after he has taken it let his belly be rubbed and let him turn on to the painful part and let him hold the clyster for an hour or two, or even for as long as possible.*"

About the same period, John of Arderne of England wrote his *Treatises on Fistula in Ano, Hemorrhoids and Clysters*. He used enemata for the treatment of constipation and colic, for diagnosis and prognosis as well as nutrient enemata "*nourishing liquors as of any potage or milk of almonds*." In addition, he prescribed enemata to prevent illness, prescribing them three or four times a year: "*Twice in winter, once after Lent and once in summer and often time if need be*." John used a pipe made of wood – he advised box or hazel six or seven inches long with no other holes, but recorded that although old men used pipes holed in the side, his simpler form "*availeth more*." "*Then take a swine's bladder, blow it and allow it to dry. Put therein a spoonful of water, a spoonful of common salt and a spoonful of honey. Leave them to dissolve in the bladder two days, shaking the bladder twice or thrice daily that it may be wet of the liquor on every side.*"

The bladder was then emptied, reblown, and tied "*that the wind go not out*", and hung in a shady place. For the enema itself, he advised salt and water for constipation, with the addition of honey, herbs and camomile. Half a quart at the most of the decoction was put into the bladder. The great end of the pipe was inserted and bound fast and the farther end of the pipe was anointed with swine's grease or with butter or honey. The finger was inserted into the anus and the pipe alongside it. The bladder was then compressed and the patient instructed to hold the enema as long as possible. "*And when he may no longer hold it, go he to a sege (privy) made ready with a basin standing underneath and there do his needs.*"

In Spain the clyster was regarded as an emblem of medical skill and devotion to the well-being of the patient.

In Galen's writings, among the illustrations adorning the capital letters, are two showing different methods of giving enemata, one by the use of a funnel and the other a very clumsy type of bladder. There is also a picture in an early edition of the travels of Ludovig Vartomans published in 1506 supported by a description. "*How I acted as if I were a physician. It happened once that a rich merchant at Calicut fell ill and his bowels would not open. He sent to my companion who was his very good friend, to complain of his illness and to ask if he or someone known to him could help him. So we went together to the patient's house and asked him about his illness, and he said all my illness is in my stomach and I have great trouble around my chest.*"

Then Vartomans related that his father was a highly regarded physician, much of whose practice he had seen. As the patient complained of headache and his bowels had not moved for three days, Vartomans thought the patient must be treated urgently and accordingly prepared a mixture with eggs, sugar, salt and certain herbs, but as this proved ineffective after five doses, he made a clyster. A cord was attached to both feet and the patient was hoisted up until he touched the ground only with his hands and his head, so that the mixture should penetrate farther. After the injection Vartomans left the patient hanging and screaming "*No more, no more. I am killed! So we, standing there to comfort him, whether it were God or Nature his bowels began to act like a fountain and we immediately let him down and truly he was relieved to the extent of half a vat full, and he was well pleased.*"

A woodcut (1506) detailing the therapeutic exploits of Ludovig Vartomans. In many circumstances it seems likely fear of the administration of an enema by a physician might well have been sufficient to induce cure!

Although at some time during the fifteenth century a piston syringe seems to have been used for the first time to give an enema, piston syringes had been known and used for other purposes for many hundreds of years. Thus the Egyptian embalmers had used them, and syringe for irrigating the external ear had been found at Pompeii. In the textbook of surgery written by Hieronymus Brunschwig in 1497, a syringe is clearly pictured among the tools of the surgeon of the period while in the Archaeological Museum of Bruges, a wood-carving of fifteenth-century date clearly demonstrates the administration of an enema by means of a piston syringe. Some authors have given credit to an Italian, Marco Gatinaria, who died towards the end of the fifteenth century and whose work was published posthumously in 1506, as the inventor of the piston enema. This is probably incorrect since Gatinaria used the tube and bladder, but with a modification. His anal tube was doubled, so that while fluid was passing into the rectum through one tube, wind could escape through the other.

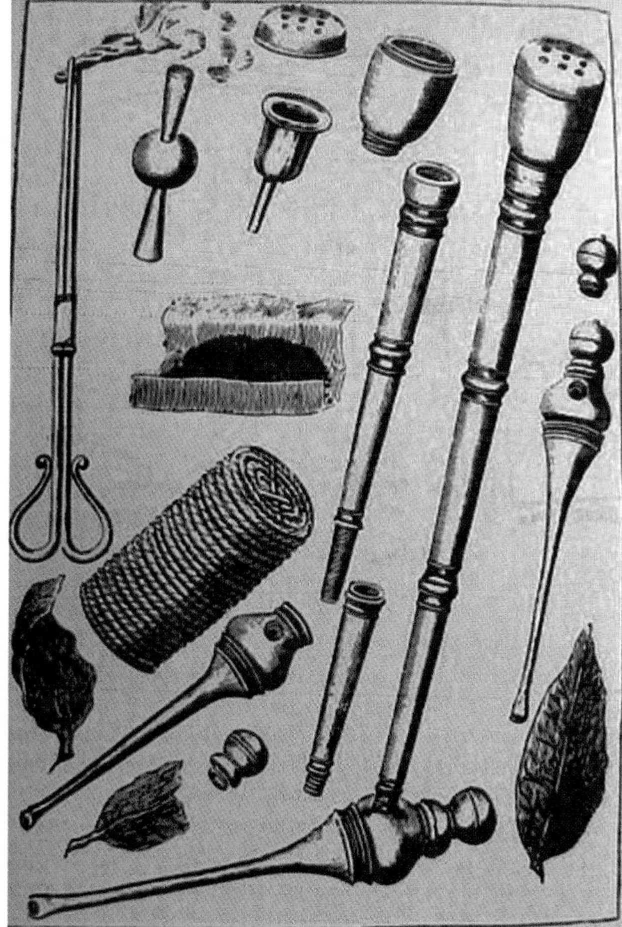

John Woodall was a naval surgeon and wrote extensively on enema. Of particular interest was his description of the usage of tobacco enema. The apparatus for administering such "fumous clysters" took a number of forms (see above). In principle the tobacco was placed in a perforated cup and a bellows used to blow the smoke northwards.

Ambroise Paré, the great French surgeon, wrote in 1580 that the syringe was in common use in every country, and for this fact doctors have thought it more befitting to their dignity not to sully their hands with it so that it had become an instrument most used by the surgeons! Some patients were also shy:

> *There are many who cannot by any reason be persuaded to show*
> *their buttocks to him that should administer*
> *the clyster a foolish shamefastness hindering them.*

Paré therefore devised an instrument "*With which one may give a clyster to himself by putting the pipe into the fundament.*"

In the second edition of John Woodall's textbook for naval surgeons, *The Surgeon's Mate*, published in 1639, there are several sections dealing with enemata. Woodall included in his surgeon's chest a large syringe containing one wine pint, "*commonly called the Glyster Syringe*" and used it to treat both diarrhea and constipation.

> *This worthy and well-devised instrument so needful in the Surgeon's chest, I wish each surgeon's mate was perfect in the use thereof, for it is so necessary and so comfortable an instrument to him that hath need thereof and so ready, neat and easy for the workman as surely no instrument in the Surgeon's chest in my opinion is like to it. Provide therefore that you be sure to have one at hand, and that it is always ready, also that you have several pipes thereto, that you arm it well with good tow and when you have used it you wipe it clean and hang it up in your cabin in two parts being drawn out, namely the staff and the barrel each by itself, for if it be kept close it will be musty and the tow rotten. There is also to be in readiness a crooked neck much like an elbow belonging to the same instrument, so that however crooked the patient lie the medicine may be administered to him; and therewith also any man may give himself a clyster very easily without the help of another.*

The syringe was filled by pouring in the fluid from a clyster pot through a small hole. The hole was corked, the syringe pipe passed through the anus, and the clyster delivered "*with some reasonable good force.*" Referring to the clyster bag and pipe, "*so good and ancient a work,*" Woodall preferred the syringe because it was "*cleanlier for the surgeon, easier for the patient, and could be used with greater or lesser force as the Artist pleaseth and this instrument will last when the other will stink and putrefy and yet I deny not the other to be good, but not to be trusted at Sea.*"

Fabricius Hildanus (top left) also turned his mind to the invention of a simple syringe that could be worked by the patient. When the enema had been prepared and poured into the bladder and the bladder closed by taps B and C, the patient was told to lie on his right side and insert the cannula A into his anus. After these preparations the patient turned the tap B to open the pipe, and pressed and twisted the bladder with his hands. In this way the enema reached the bowel with no difficulty.

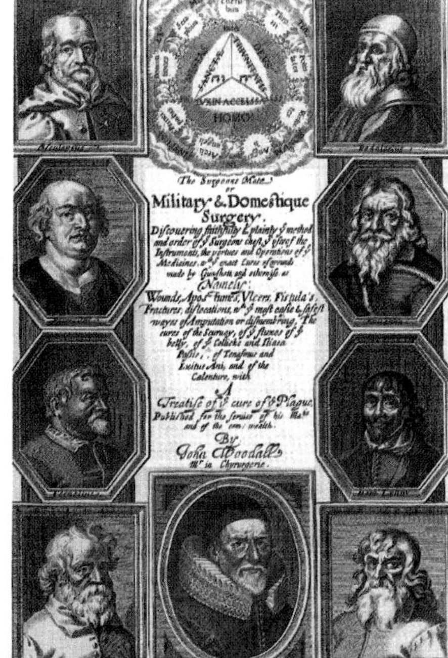

The frontispiece of The Surgeon's Mate by John Woodall, 1639.

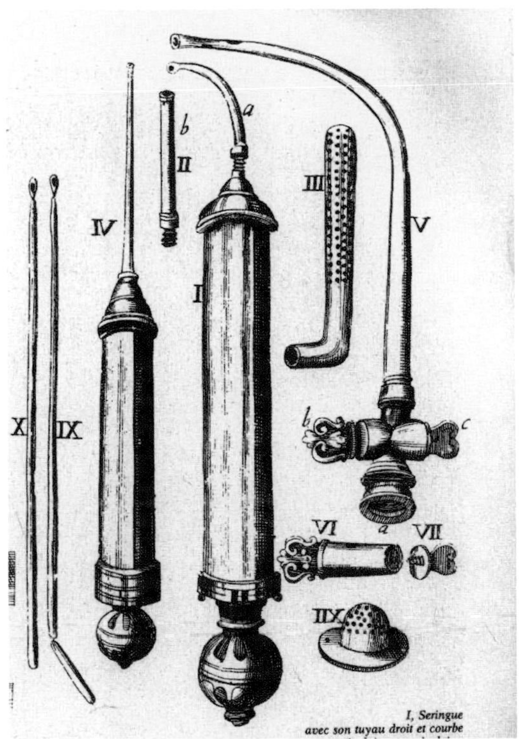

The design of enema syringes was an important part of medicinal instrument-making and well-to-do households each possessed their own. Since many herbal therapies were vile-tasting or patients were vomiting, the use of an enema syringe to administer a drug was an important function of the device.

The technique and apparatus used by Woodward for the administration of smoke enema on board ship. The tedium of the long voyages would certainly have been relieved by such diversions.

Burton referred to clysters in his *Anatomy of Melancholy* published in 1621:

> *Averters and purgers must go together as tending all to the same purpose to divert this rebellious humour and turn it another way. In this range clysters and suppositories challenge a chief place to draw this humour from the brain and heart to the more ignoble parts... For without question a clyster opportunely used cannot choose in this, as in most other maladies, but to do very much good.*

Burton also recorded that for a hypochondriacal person tormented with wind, a pair of bellows could be attached to a clyster pipe in the fundament and the wind could thus be drawn forth.

Although James Primrose is better known as one of Harvey's principal detractors he also left an amusing little book entitled *Popular Errours or the Errours of the People in the Matter of Physick*, published in 1651. The title page showed the guardian angel of the patient preventing error and superstition, in the form of a woman, from hindering the work of the physician. He was eloquent in his support of clysters:

> *Many reject clysters as being perilous and dangerous physic but they are grossly mistaken, for clysters are the most gentle and innocent physic of all, for they never touch any noble part in that they go not beyond the great guts.*

Primrose pleaded for the more general use of the syringe in comparison to an ox-bladder tied to a pipe, for the former sent fluid farther into the bowel while bladders had another disadvantage in that they were apt to burst at inconvenient moments.

Despite all such commentary and inventive contributions the first individual to consider the subject of enemata in a scientific fashion was the Dutch anatomist and physiologist, Regnier de Graaf. Born at Delft in 1641, he achieved renown for his original and accurate observations on the testicle, the ovary with its Graafian follicles, and the pancreatic juice which he collected from an experimentally-produced fistula in a dog. In 1668 he published a short book full of wisdom and sound advice on clysters, which was translated into French in 1878 under the title *L'Instrument de Moliere*, and adorned with illustrations that are curiously inappropriate though typically French.

Further illustrative information was provided by Jan Steen, the great painter of Dutch peasantry who clearly depicted how an enema was given at this period. The syringe was probably made of pewter holding "*one wine pint*" of fluid, and in the hands of a person unskilled in its use it could be most unpleasant to the patient, as in the following personal case note recorded by a doctor, James Scott in 1832:

> *Under an attack of dysentery many years since, the medical friend who attended me administered an opiate injection from a pewter syringe about a foot in length and the size of one's leg with a long stem which was pushed up the rectum. The severe pain occasioned by the passage of this rude pipe and the poking of its point first against one side of the bowel and then the other from the unsteadiness of the operator, compelled me to refuse to have the injection repeated and was such as I can never forget.*

De Graaf's book begins with the following words:

> *Inasmuch as it has often come within my experience as a medical man practicing in this land that patients who are suffering from near and well-nigh insupportable pains in the bowels and other organs who could have obtained quick, safe and pleasant relief by the injection of a clyster or perhaps two, could under no circumstances be induced to expose their buttocks for the injection of a clyster in the presence of a servant, I have made careful investigations whether or not someone has discovered a method by which each of us with due modesty and without danger could give himself an injection by means of a clyster, but all to no purpose, for every method (that is, as many as I know have been discovered thus far) are attended by many dangers and difficulties.*

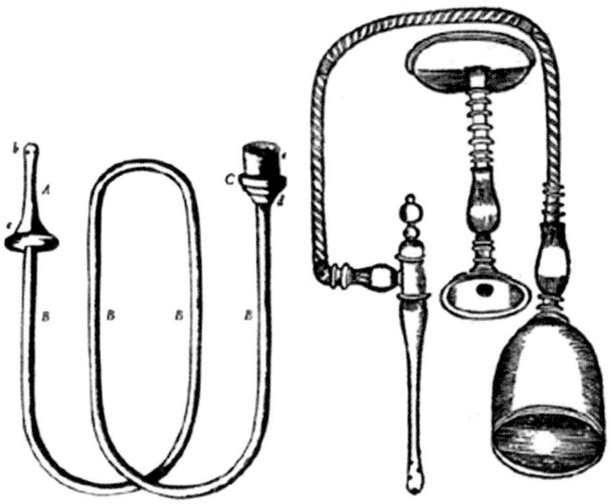

The flexible enema device developed by Regnier de Graaf. The advantage of this design modification allowed for self-administration and flexibility conferred comfort.

This is quite obvious when we have recourse to that method which is usually practiced with a syringe, to which is attached a curved pipe made of ivory, wood, or silver-lead, so that it can be inserted into the anus, for the clyster cannot be ejected from the syringe without moving it. The pipe inserted into the anus follows this movement, so that the rectal intestine is easily damaged or else the clyster leaks past the side of the nozzle. These things easily happen when sick men cannot use both hands to guide the clyster. Just as much difficulty and trouble are wont to be caused when the clyster is injected from a bladder, as described by Hildanus. To this instrument is attached a pipe for insertion into the anus. Now a clyster cannot be ejected from a bladder so accurately that nothing of its quantity remains and the bladder is easily destroyed or torn when it is attached to the pipe. Thus it happens that this method is favored by very few, especially when the patients cannot use both hands, as I pointed out before, so that they cannot properly keep the pipe in place in the anus. For these reasons and because an instrument to my liking has not been furnished by another I have toiled and made every effort my ingenuity can suggest and at last, after much hard work, I have produced an instrument which satisfies my requirements from every point of view. It is of such a description that anyone can give himself an injection with a clyster with all modesty, safety and speed – or allow another to make the injection without any exposure of his privy parts or change of position.

An elegant physician accompanied by the patient's daughter approaches the bed carrying the clyster syringe. At left the maid prepares the toilet anticipating an excellent outcome of the therapy. The rigid device was subsequently replaced by the flexible tubing developed by de Graaf.

De Graaf was also quite critical of the innumerable ingredients then commonly in use and decried the polypharmacy employed: "*There have been times when I have seen a clyster compounded of a quantity of different elements with electuaries, oils and other ingredients of no effect, but one composed of water, honey and salt most efficacious. This has been considered by many a secret not to be divulged.*" In particular he thought little of the value of nutrient enemata, pointing out that the valve of *Bauhinus* prevented the fluid leaving the caecum. He also discussed the size of the enema and its optimum temperature, the best time for administration, how long it should be retained, and the correct position of the patient at the time of administration and afterwards. He listed the indications for enemata:

In addition to my earlier remarks a clyster has an even greater advantage. Generally speaking, this type of treatment frees the bowels without excessive effort, causes no damage to health, no debility, and does no harm to the bowels. Likewise after its use there is not that constipation we see after the use of purgatives, for the more patients are moved by cathartics, so much the more constipated do they become on the following days. Hence Galen in cases of prolonged illness made use of gentle and soothing injections into the bowels. For example, in the case of old men he writes that an injection of oil can be of the greatest benefit, since they were naturally cold and dry.

Therefore, since the clyster can often be a swift and safe remedy in great pain and can give instant relief to sufferers, I have done my best to find a means by which patients with all due modesty can give themselves an enema. At last I have devised an instrument by which not only can injections be given into the anus but also by a mere change of the nozzle can very easily be given to the uterus and other parts of the body without fear of pain or damage.

Regnier de Graaf (top right) developed an ingenious flexible device for administering enemas. Together with cautery and seton placement, enema administration became part of the standard medical armamentarium. The preparation of the different agents to be instilled became in itself a specialized branch of pharmacy.

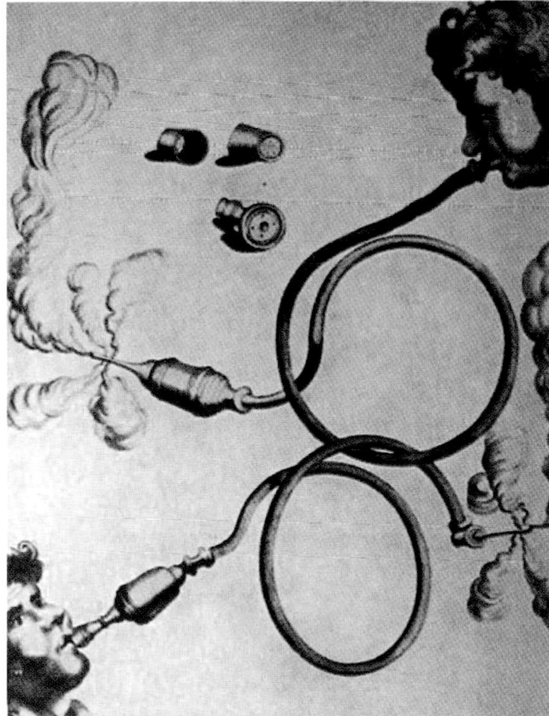

The technique of administering a smoke enema as described in detail by the naval surgeon Woodall. Its usage gave rise to the popular vernacular phrase "Don't blow smoke up my ..."

"Do it yourself enemas" were designed for those seeking both privacy and pleasure.

"Nobles and people of substance keep a sort of little chest supported on four legs like a chair. Into this they place a long pipe in a horizontal position: to its upper end, which has a hollow thread, is fitted the solid thread of an enema syringe in an upright position, so that the syringe itself stands up out of the chest like a column. The lower end of the pipe, which has a solid thread, received the hollow thread of the ivory tube. This tube projects above the box and goes into the anus. In this way the patient can sit on the box as on a horse and insert the piston into the syringe, which has one end standing up in the air like a column, as already mentioned: by pressing with his hand he can easily introduce the fluid into his anus by himself. The box need not have legs for their place can be taken by an ordinary chair."

Another form of apparatus was designed so that pressure on the piston could be applied from a wall or the post of a bed. These latter must have been very dangerous to the anal regions.

In France the subject of enema was referred to as *le Lavement,* and clysters were an important facet of French medical history long before the time of de Graaf's sojourn in Paris. In 1480, Louis XI was believed to have survived a stroke solely due to the beneficial effects of an enema prescribed by his Italian physician, Angelo Catho. After his recovery, Louis was so enamored of this new modality of treatment that whenever even his dogs were ill they were given enemata by means of special copper syringes. Since French aristocracy was closely adherent to the whims of the monarchy, enema administration subsequently became highly popular throughout the country and to ensure maximal effect instruments of great beauty made of porcelain, gilded silver and mother-of-pearl were designed. Louis XIII, who had been trained very unwillingly in the method from childhood by his father, Henri IV, possessed a large and beautiful collection. Such was his passion for the procedure that it is recorded that in one year he received 212 enemata and 215 purgations as well as 47 venesections. By the time of the first years of the reign of Louis XIV, the enema had become an absolute vogue such that even the playwright Molière was driven to comment upon it in *Le Malade Imaginaire* where Argan reads his apothecary's bill: *"So that this month I have taken one, two, three, four, five, six, seven and eight remedies and one, two, three, four, five, six, seven, eight, nine, ten, eleven, twelve enemas and the other month there were 12 remedies and 20 enemas, I am not surprised that I am not so well this month as the other."* Molière, by his ridicule, made the enema a fashionable procedure and a matter of general conversation such that once royalty adopted it as a popular practice, almost all persons of substance followed suit. French art became full of clyster pictures, and French literature abounded with innumerable references to the treatment. In addition cartoonists reveled in the possibilities. Thus in one glorious example King Louis Philippe is shown bleeding a sick working man who typifies the French people, while the Duke of Orleans holds in his hand a flask bearing the inscription "The King's Medicine." On his knee, with the ribbon of the Legion of Honor on his breast and a nurse's apron tied about his waist, General Soult, minister of war and president of the Council, is waiting to administer an enema to the unfortunate patient. Such was the fascination of the population that a celebrated legal case concerned the charge of administering 2,190 enemata over a period of two years to a priest of the city of Troyes. This was not surprising, for the treatment had passed out of medical hands and was administered by all and sundry. Thus by the eighteenth century most people partook of a daily enema and it had become a household ritual much as is the cleaning of the teeth.

Similarly, the English cartoonists at a rather later date took great interest in enemata, and lost no opportunity of including a syringe in their pictures, caricatures and cartoons. Rowlandson showed Dr. Gallipot laying the instruments of his trade at the feet of his betrothed. He also drew a group of physicians attacking the proprietor of a very successful patent medicine. Even in Gillray's, who was particularly crude in his use of the syringe and commode in political caricature, included an enema syringe in his famous cartoon of the surprising effects of vaccination. During the eighteenth century the medical profession began to evince interest in enema apparatus as the utility of the elastic bottle became apparent. The first reference in Europe to these novelties was made in 1743 although the Brazilian Indians had long been aware of the properties of the elastic gum substance *caoutchouc* that they obtained by tapping a tree. Since the gum in its natural state was destroyed in transit to Europe, the elastic bottles were made in South America and consequently not widely available. In fact, the first detailed description occurs in Brambilla's *Atlas of Surgical Instruments*, published in Austria in 1780. *"Truly that type of container which comes to England from America and is made of rubber blown up like a bladder is much more useful, but it rarely comes our way as it is very difficult to obtain. This is the way to use it. The bladder is squeezed with the hand and the air is expelled. Then the tube is placed in the water meant for the enema and the hand loosens its grip so that the fluid of its own accord fills the bladder by entering the vacuum. However, it is a property of the common syringe that it can send the enema with greater force into the intestines, for better results can be expected from fluids which penetrate further. But some people cannot stand up to this and it is for their benefit that the present syringe has been invented."* Brambilla did not picture the new apparatus, but there was a reproduction in Savigny's instrument catalogue published in London in 1798, where it was described as *"a singularly useful machine, surgery has received very few more important acquisitions."* William Cullen, in his textbook of medicine published in 1784, advised that colic should be treated in the first instance by means of clysters composed of any of the following

The beneficial effects of enema were regarded as so substantial that even pet dogs were exposed to this Salubrious treatment.

In France itinerant apothecaries carried enema syringes with them and would provide therapy on demand.

ingredients: warm water with or without some mild oil, common salt, infusion of senna, antimonial wine or turpentine. Although it was the opinion of Cullen that hardly any clysters were more effective than those made with properly prepared turpentine he advised that when all other injections were found to be ineffectual, recourse should be had to injections of tobacco smoke. This remedy appears to have been highly regarded and tobacco enemata seem to have been a popular and successful means of resuscitating drowned persons such that in the first report of the Royal Humane Society "fumigation" (filling of the large bowel with tobacco smoke) was adjudged equally as effective as warmth and artificial respiration and was extensively used. But in 1811 the report of Brodie describing nicotine as cardiotoxic, and that four ounces of a strong infusion of tobacco administered as an enema could kill a dog and one ounce a cat, brought the practice to an abrupt end. The Society became alarmed by these experiments and relegated fumigation to the list of forbidden methods, although in the previous forty years it had apparently succeeded in hundreds of cases. A further advance in the administration of enemas was provided in the early years of the nineteenth century by John Read, a gardener and a man of considerable mechanical ingenuity. His invention of a two-way syringe with ball valves led in 1820 to the filing of a patent for a surgical syringe for removing poisons from the stomach and administering enemata. It was simple and most effective in its action since it could be used to either aspirate the stomach or to blow tobacco smoke into the rectum. In addition, Read's syringe could also be used for drawing milk from a breast, for removing air from cupping glasses, and for dealing with blown cattle. Despite numerous copies of this ingenious device a genuine Read's patent enema syringe was easy to identify, for it alone bore the Royal Arms on its barrel. Other similar instruments such as Patey's hydraulic injector, holding two or three pints, and Jukes's flexible clysmaduct were also available. The latter consisted of a long and gently tapering funnel of from four to six feet in length prepared with a waterproof composition. It was four inches in diameter at its upper extremity and half an inch at its lower, where it was attached to a tube supplied with a tap, the other end being adapted for introduction into the anus. The funnel was filled, with the stopcock closed and hung on a hook in a convenient part of the dressing-room. The tube was then introduced and the stopcock opened. Possibly the most villainous of all the mechanical irrigators was designed by a Frenchman, Eguisier, in 1848. In this model the piston was controlled by a spring that could be wound tight in a container on the top of the cylinder. The piston having been wound to its upper limit, pressed on the fluid with all the strength of the spring, and the jet was controlled by the tap at the base of the cylinder. No more powerful method of injection was ever invented!

Medical therapy has long been focused on the posterior. The development of clysters simply provided further access to the interior.

Cupping and Leeching

The operation of cupping was performed by applying to the skin a glass or other form of cup after the air within it had been removed by heat or by suction. In the dry method, the cup was applied to the unbroken skin, causing local subcutaneous trauma and acting as a counter-irritant. In the wet method, the skin was scarified immediately before the cup was applied, and was a recognized method of blood-letting, but even in this form cupping acted in some measure as a counter-irritant. Both methods probably had considerable psychological value as well. It is not clear when cupping first began although is mentioned in the writing of Hippocrates and was practiced by the Greeks in the fourth century B.C. The earliest instrument used was a gourd, and from this fruit was derived the Latin name for cupping, *cucurbitula*. In the primitive regions of the world, cupping has been practiced for hundreds, if not thousands, of years, and it can still be seen in these parts in its earliest form. The American Indians use the upper end of a buffalo horn about two-and-a-half inches in length with a hole at the tip, through which a vacuum was produced by suction and thereafter plugged. The medicine men used the method for extracting the poison from snake bites and for relieving pain and cramp in the abdomen.

The primitive concept of removing evil spirits causing disease led to the development of numerous creative therapeutic concepts. These ranged from the intercession of a shaman, to the smoking of hallucinogenic substances and the induction of fugue states and the invocation of the spirits of fearsome animals possessed of mystic powers.

Hippocrates and Galen were strong advocates of the use of cupping, believing that it removed noxious agents from the body. Both believed that the site of application was critical in ensuring cure.

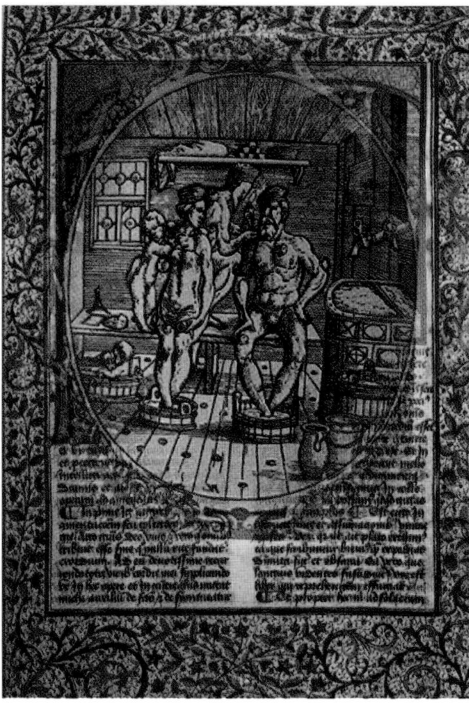

The application of cups in a medieval bath house.

Hippocrates used both dry and wet cupping, in the main to treat menstrual disorders, instructing large cupping glasses to be applied to the breasts of women suffering from menorrhagia. He also prescribed for the same condition and for a yellow vaginal discharge, long-continued cupping to different parts of the thighs, in the groin and below the breasts. Since he was anxious to prevent sepsis after wet cupping he provided the following advice: "*When in cupping the blood continues to flow after the cupping instrument has been removed, and if the flow of blood or serum be copious, the cup must be applied again before the part is healed so as to abstract what is left behind. Otherwise coagula of blood will be retained in the incisions and inflammatory ulcers will rise from them. In all such cases the parts are to be bathed in vinegar after which they must not be wetted. Neither must the person lie on the scarifications but they are to be anointed with some of the medicaments for bloody wounds.*"

Celsus, who wrote on the subject at some length in the first century A.D., thought that the subcutaneous edema produced by dry cupping consisted partly of flatus derived from the breath.

Therefore, when it is some matter inside which is doing the harm, wet cupping should be employed, when it is flatulency then dry cupping. Now the use of a cup is the rule for a disease not of the body as a whole but of some part, the sucking out of which suffices for the reestablishment of the health.

Celsus also advised cupping for both acute and chronic maladies, including attacks of fever, and he particularly stressed that if there was danger in blood-letting, recourse should be had to cupping. He advised dry and wet cupping for edema, dry cups in several places to treat paralysis, cups to the temple and occiput in cases of longstanding pain in the head, wet cupping for pain in the neck, dry cups applied under the chin for faucial angina, cups to the chest for cough, dry cups for pain in the chest if the patient was not strong enough for blood-letting, dry cups – dry in particular – to treat flatulence, dry cups applied to the abdomen in two or three places to treat indigestion and abdominal pain and scarification with cups to the groins and even to the breasts in cases of excessive menstruation. He also advised local cupping for abscess and as a means of extracting the poisons from bites made by man, apes, dogs, wild animals or snakes.

Similarly Aretaeus in the early second century A.D. used both wet and dry cupping, but preferred the former, reserving dry cupping extensively to treat prolapse of the uterus. He based his notion on the idea of attracting the uterus, and for this purpose he cupped the loins, ischial regions, groins, spine and even between the scapulae. For cholera he cupped the back and the body, shifting his instruments rapidly, "*for it is painful when a cup remains on a place and exposes it to the risk of blistering.*"

Galen was a great advocate of the method and described a variety of cups of glass, horn and brass, the latter being the most commonly employed, though he commended glass cups, for they enabled the physician to see the amount of blood discharged. He also felt that it was most important that the patient should have his bowels well opened before cups were applied. He used cupping to abstract what he called "matter" to allay pain, diminish inflammation, disperse swellings, induce appetite, restore energy to a weakened stomach, cut short delirium, transfer morbid afflux from parts deep seated, restrain hemorrhage and benefit menstruation. Application was not always made over the affected area "*thus in promoting revulsion from the chest or belly the application is to be made to the hands: and to the lower parts when a revulsion is to be made to arrest vomiting.*" He added to the indications for cupping, lethargy, frenzy and eye diseases but regarded plethora as a contra-indication. For ocular disease he advised the application of cups to the back of the neck after scarification, and it was regarded as important that a good deal of blood should be removed. Aetius, in the early sixth century, disapproved of the application of cups to the breasts, for they were not easy to detach, and it was sometimes necessary to make a hole in the cup. Rhazes, in the tenth century, cupped children exposed to smallpox if they were less than fourteen years old, but not younger than five months. About the same period Serapion wrote, "*If the strength of the patient allow there is nothing better in the smallpox than to bleed him until he faints: but if not, then let him be cupped.*" Avicenna preferred wet cupping, reserving dry cupping for cold swellings, and whenever cups were to be moved about in various places. He refused to cup infants during the first year of life, and preferred not to cup until they were in their third year. Cupping was contra-indicated after the sixtieth year of life. Magic and astrology were most important factors in the treatment and cups were best applied in the middle of the month, when the humors were in a state of agitation and during the time when the moonlight was increasing. Avicenna advised cupping as follows: "*to the nape of the neck in heaviness of the eyelids, itch of the eyes, fetor of the mouth, tremor of the head and lesions of the teeth, eyes, ears, nose, throat and face;... under the chin for toothache, sore throat, loss of countenance and to cleanse the head and jaws;... between the shoulder-blades.*"

Maitre Henri de Mondeville, surgeon to King Phillipe of France, wrote a textbook on surgery somewhere between 1306 and 1320 including a long and significant section on cupping, containing some interesting admonitions: "*Never cup in foggy weather or when a south wind blows. The humours are most abundant at full moon, so cup then. Do not apply cups after the patient has had a bath. The cupped person can eat one hour later. Never do a cupping with scarification until you have done one without scarification on the same spot. If we wish to deflect a tumor we cup on the opposite side in a straight line or in a region in relation to the tumor.*"

Among the indications he listed for cupping with scarification were these: *Near the navel to bring back a displaced uterus; over the navel itself to reduce a hernia or stop excessive menstruation in girls; over the liver if the right nostril is bleeding; over the spleen if the left nostril is bleeding; on both liver and spleen if both nostrils bleed; on the path of a renal stone coming down to the bladder – a little below the pain so as to draw the stone downwards.*

His instructions regarding technique are interesting:

Shave beforehand when necessary. Keep the skin loose. When cupping the occiput throw cold water in the face so as to send back the spirits and blow towards the back of the head. Stroke the blood from the front to the back of the head with the hand. For bleeding in the head you apply one cup at a time each below the other and overlapping but without incision until you reach the shoulder blades. There you cut and cup.

The skin was prepared by warming, rubbing, and greasing and then a lighted tow was thrown into the cup. The moment it burnt out, the cup was clapped on the prepared area and left until it came off of its own accord.

The earliest picture of cupping occurs in an early fourteenth-century manuscript in the British Museum. It portrays the dry cupping of a gentleman's gluteal region by a rather grim-looking woman. Another amusing picture occurs in a German calendar (*c.* 1483), and depicts the patient as being cupped in a bath by an attendant who is performing the operation while holding a lighted lamp in his left hand.

Cupping was believed useful for a wide variety of disorders and efficacy determined by the precise site of application. Thus a kidney stone could be drawn down or a uterus replaced if the cups were inserted at specific points.

With the passage of centuries, both dry and wet cupping remained in steady use with the indications being little changed from the days of Celsus until the time of Paré, who, although using much the same indications listed, developed a variety of cups and of especial importance, two mechanical scarifiers which were used in the treatment of gangrene. His comments on the subject are worthy of quotation: "*Cups should be applied to the belly when any gross or thick windiness is shut up in the guts. When cupping glasses are too big you may fit horns for the same purpose.*"

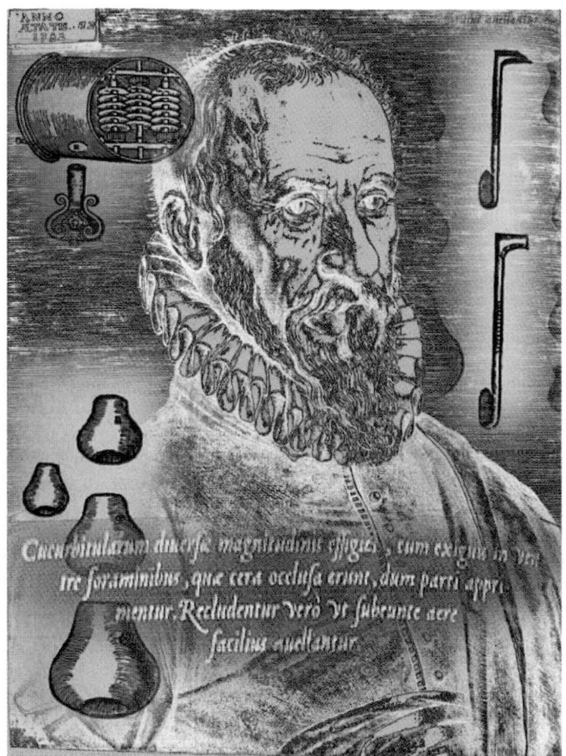

John Woodall's book for naval surgeons published in 1639 is one of the classical books on surgery and contains much information as well as some interesting points of view.

"There are many necessary works in surgery performed by cupping. Some set cups on with tow, some with a small wax light set under them. Some only with the flame of a great candle which I myself use and is not offensive or painful at all. I use my candle close to the place where the cups should be set, the place being first wet and rubbed well with hot water and a sponge and the cupping glasses also wet. Hold your cupping glass over the flame a little and then clap it quickly on the place whilst yet the steam of the light is in it and it will be fast and draw hard, but you must have your cups fit and not too wide for the place you would set them on or else they will not take any hold. Further, when you perceive they have drawn well, which by the blackness and rising of the skin you may easily see, then if you hold it fitting you may lightly and quickly scarify it with a fine lancet which truly is the best and profitablest instrument for that use, and then wetting your cupping glasses again and heating with the flame of the candle, set them on where they stood before, setting as many cups and drawing as much blood as you see good; and when no more blood will come and you think it time to take them away."

If the skin be scarified it draws blood, but if the skin be whole it draws spirit.

The scarifier introduced by Paré consisted of:

A box wherein are fastened many round wheels as it were, sharp as phlemes (lancets) which by a handle fitted into the side of the box are made to strike all together so that with this instrument you shall make as many scarifications at once as the phleme will do at many times and beside all of one depth.

Unfortunately, the art of cupping changed radically in that it moved from the province of the qualified and the wealthy to a service available for all and sundry. Thus in 1750, Heister noted the following:

Scarification and cupping was an operation frequently performed by the most ancient physicians and surgeons, notwithstanding the moderns have, by their pride and neglect, turned the business over to those who attend the baths and hothouses.

A medieval woodcut demonstrating a professional cupper in action. Such cupping salons functioned in much the same way as a nail or hair salon of the 21st century.

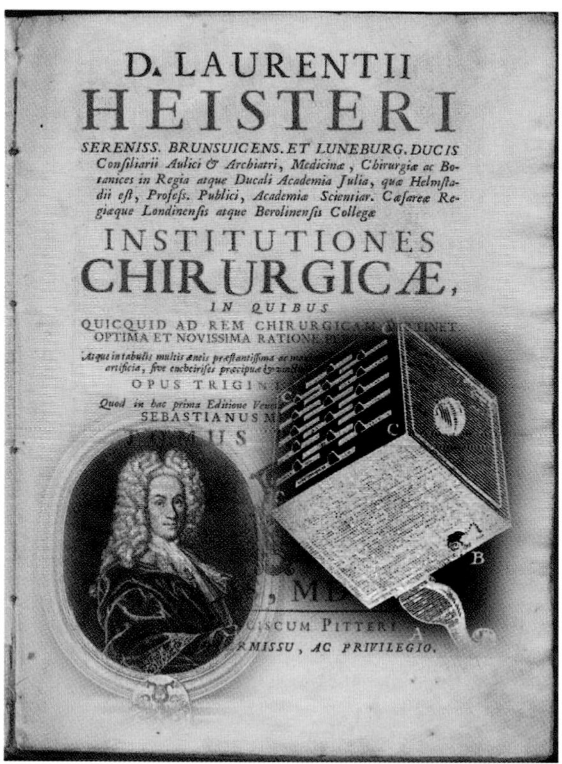
D. LAURENTII
HEISTERI
SERENISS. BRUNSUICENS. ET LUNEBURG. DUCIS
Consiliarii Aulici & Archiatri, Medicinæ, Chirurgiæ ac Botanices in Regia atque Ducali Academia Julia, quæ Helmstadii est, Profess. Publici, Academiæ Scientiar. Cæsareæ Regiæque Londinensis atque Berolinensis Collegæ
INSTITUTIONES
CHIRURGICÆ,
IN QUIBUS
QUICQUID AD REM CHIRURGICAM
OPTIMA ET NOVISSIMA RATIONE
OPUS TRIGIN
SEBASTIANUS
MISSU, AC PRIVILEGIO.

The Heister mechanical scarificator used in wet cupping. This machine consisted of sixteen small blades fixed in a cubical brass box with a steel spring. The base of this instrument was applied to the skin and the spring set by a lever. "Then, by depressing a button, it was suddenly let loose as by its force to strike the points of the sixteen blades out of the case at once in their regular order over which the cupping glass is to be applied." Heister used the machine with benefit for many diseases and as a firm believer in the principle of revulsions, he cupped at some distance from the seat of the disease. Thus, in cases of severe hemorrhage from the nose or lungs, he scarified and cupped the legs and the feet, particularly about the ankles and the knees. Heister admitted that there were physicians and surgeons who regarded the method as useless and even dangerous!

Thus scarification, which possessed obvious dangers, as opposed to the relatively benign practice of cupping, became widely available and Heister noted his concern that in this manner a patient might be infected with leprosy, the pox or the itch:

But that the patient may have no uneasiness in this quarter it may not be improper for him to see that his cupper's scarificator and apparatus are very clean or else he may keep a scarificator of his own, which being kept clean and dry can give no room to make any scruples of this nature.

Cupping was widely used by most of the best physicians, thus Boerhaave dry-cupped for pneumonia while Richard Mead treated apoplexy by cupping the nape and sides of the neck with deep scarifications. In particular, he cupped with deep scarifications under the occiput to treat eye disease and with slight scarifications round the navel for the iliac passion, a diagnosis which probably embraced several acute abdominal conditions, including appendicitis. Similarly, John Huxham strongly advised wet cupping in any feverish condition and wrote in 1788 to this point:

Drawing off blood by cupping on the shoulders may be done with safety and frequently gives good relief in pneumonia and diseases of the breast as well as of the head, though the reason may not be so very obvious or assignable – also for asthma.

William Heberden cupped for menstrual disorders and in the case of persistent headache he cupped the shoulders, removing as much as six ounces of blood.

Despite concerns regarding the safety of the technique, by the end of the eighteenth century, scarificators had become considerably more complex and were available in different sizes containing six, ten, twelve or sixteen lancets, which could be shortened or elongated by a screw, so that the depth of the wounds could be controlled. Unfortunately, since the lancets were fixed in the box, considerable difficulty was experienced in keeping them clean and free from rust. By the early nineteenth century this was altered and the boxes so constructed that the pivots holding the blades could be taken out for cleaning, although this process was somewhat arduous. Aware of these problems, alternative methods were considered, in particular, consideration was given by Baron Larrey, Napoleon's army surgeon, to the use of an exhausting syringe. This method, however, proved inconvenient, given the excessive weight of the syringe, as well as from the necessity of glasses that required the insertion of copper screws. Furthermore, the absence of no local heat was felt to be a disadvantage. An ingenious modification of the concept, which attained some popularity, was provided by Monsieur Demours' introduction of what he termed an "artificial leech." He proposed that after the cup had been applied and its air evacuated by means of the syringe, and the skin had risen well into the cup, the introduction of a lancet to whatever depth was desirable, facilitating a free flow of blood. Despite the use of numerous instruments and the modification of many techniques, some physicians preferred to use more natural means and held firmly to the belief that leeches were the best therapy for the removal of noxious products from the body.

Mr. George Orwell was cupped for pneumonia in a Paris hospital in 1929.

They only put on six glasses in my case, but after doing so they scarified the blisters and applied the glasses again. Each glass now drew out about a dessertspoonful of dark-colored blood. As I lay down again, humiliated, disgusted and frightened by the thing that had been done to me, I reflected that now at least they would leave me alone. But no, not a bit of it. A mustard poultice was applied (more counter-irritation) and strapped tightly to my chest and left there for fifteen minutes while some men who were wandering about the ward in shirt and trousers began to collect round his bed with half-sympathetic grins.

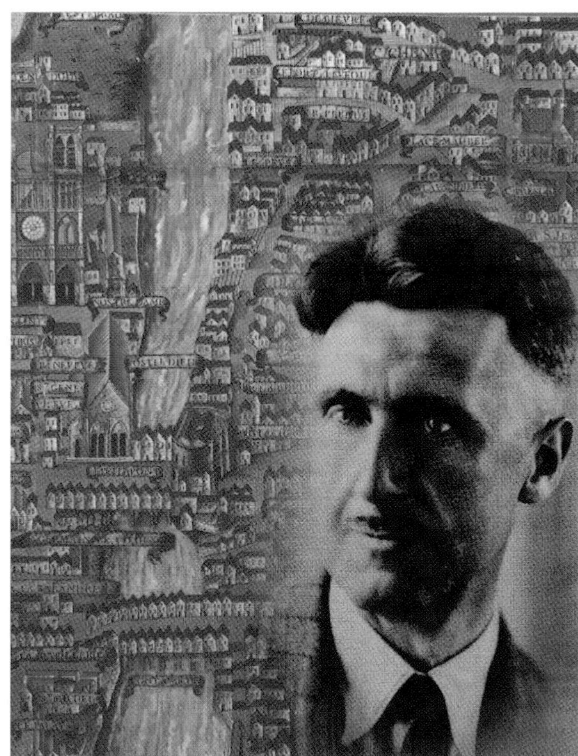

George Orwell (1903-1950), born Eric Arthur Blair in Bengal, India, underwent cupping as treatment for his pneumonia in Paris in 1929 and considered it a frightening event. Orwell never entirely abandoned his original name, but his first book, "Down and Out in Paris and London," appeared as the work of George Orwell (the surname he derived from the beautiful River Orwell in East Anglia). There is little truth to the rumor that the cupping incident inspired his anti-Utopian sentiments expressed in Animal Farm *(1945) and* Nineteen Eighty-four *(1949).*

Orwell later wrote, *"I learned later that watching a patient have a mustard poultice was a favorite pastime in the ward. These things are normally applied for a quarter of an hour and certainly are funny enough if you don't happen to be the person inside. For the first five minutes the pain is severe, but you believe you can bear it. During the second five minutes this belief evaporates, but the poultice is buckled at the back and you can't get it off. This is the period the onlookers enjoy most. During the last five minutes, I noted, a sort of numbness supervened."* After that he was left alone. But he did not sleep at all that night, not even for a minute!

The Art and Science of Leeching

For many years cupping and leeching were closely related and it was not surprising that the cupping machine invented by Demours was called an "artificial leech". Leeches are extensile aquatic creatures, members of the *Hirudinea* division of *Chaetopod* worms that can contract their body from a plump pear-shaped form to a long thin wormlike shape. The two varieties that have been used in medicine are the horse leech and the species known as *Hirudo medicinalis*. They possess chitinous jaws capable of producing a triangular or triradiate bite through which they can suck blood into a vast expanding stomach that can fill the whole body. Of particular relevance is the oral injection of an anticoagulant hirudin into the wound to prevent coagulation, with the result that when the leech is fully gorged and has fallen off, the blood continues to flow freely.

The history of leeching does not appear to extend as far back in medical practice as that of cupping and indeed, the majority of ancient authorities, including Hippocrates, being the most notable, make no reference to the subject. Nicander of Colophon, in Ionia, a hereditary priest of Apollo during the second century B.C., was the first writer to mention the therapeutic use of the leech. Similarly Themison, the Roman physician, who flourished in the beginning of the Christian era, advised the application of a cupping glass after the leech had fallen off the patient, while Antyllus used leeches if the patient feared the lancet or if the area to be treated was too rough for cups. If the hands or feet were the points for application, they should be immersed in the water in which the leeches were kept.

Pliny's great book on natural history, *Historia Naturalis*, contained a short chapter on the subject:

In cases where it is desired to let blood, the kind of leech used is known by the name of sanguisuga. These leeches are used as an alternative to cupping glasses, their effect being to relieve the body of superfluous blood. Still, however, there is this inconvenience attending them. When they have been once applied they create a necessity for having recourse to the same treatment at about the same period in every succeeding year. Many physicians have been of the opinion that leeches may be successfully applied in cases of gout. Leeches are apt to leave their head buried in the flesh; the consequence of which is an incurable wound which has caused death in many cases that, for instance, of Messalinus, a patrician of consular rank, after an application of leeches to his knee. When this is the case, that which was intended as a remedy is turned to an active poison, a result which is to be apprehended, using red leeches particularly. Hence it is that when these last are employed it is a practice to snip them with a pair of scissors while sucking. The consequence is the blood oozes forth through a syphon as it were, and the head, gradually contracting as the animal dies, is not left behind in the wound.

The polymorphous forms of the phylus to which the leech belongs, as depicted by Ernst Haeckel, the eminent scientist and scholar of Jena.

Galen paid little attention to the blood-sucking abilities of the leech but was particularly concerned with what should be done if a leech was swallowed, an emergency which is constantly referred to during the succeeding fifteen hundred years.

Some people advise a draught of urine, others of snow to detach a leech which has been swallowed. But Aesculapius taught that we should wash it out and insert a soft sponge dipped in cold water into the throat and extract the leech when it seized upon the sponge and then he used to give the juice of a lentil. He advised the covering of the outside of the neck with cold water. Appolonius Mys administered a drench of extremely bitter vinegar mixed with urine. He also used a lump of edible snow with edible and drinkable purges

A Dutch woman applies leeches to her young patient. The leech (above) has a sucker-like mouth, secretes an anticoagulant and sucks blood until satiated, leaving a characteristic suction mark on the skin (inset).

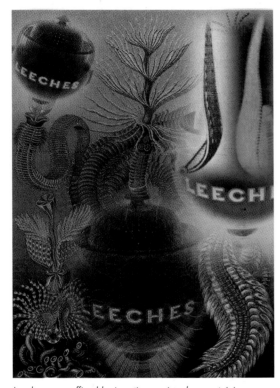

Leeches were affixed by inverting a wine-glass containing as many as were required, but there was the disadvantage that some of them retired to the upper part of the glass, defying all attempts to dislodge them without disturbing those already fastened. Tail snipping was still continued, and it was recorded that the victims did not seem to object, but went on sucking as hard as ever. It had also been found that if the engorged leeches were made to vomit by rubbing salt or vinegar on their mouths, they would bite four or five times in succession, coming off each time completely engorged with blood. At the end, on being put into clear water, they were as lively as when they were first employed.

in order to detach the leeches, for he states that they are often expelled together with what is ejected from the bowels.

Galen did, however, provide details of the best method of applying a leech. He advised the snipping off of its tail to increase the flow of blood, and he applied cups after the leech had been detached. If the bleeding continued over-long, he applied burnt galls and heated pitch. He regarded leeches as a simple substitute for cupping, for they took only the superficial blood from the skin and flesh. Avicenna gave details of the best types of leech and warned against using leeches with large heads of black or green color, leeches with down on them or with streaks of bright color. All these were poisonous and gave rise to inflammation, hemorrhage, fever, syncope, paralysis and intractable ulcers. Nor was it wise to employ leeches whose excrement was black or muddy and whose movements immediately darkened the water and rendered it offensive. He detailed the procedure of their application as follows:

Leeches should be kept a day before applying them. They should be squeezed to make them eject the contents of their stomachs. If feasible they should be given a little lamb's blood by way of nourishment. The slime and debris should be cleansed from their bodies with a sponge. The place of application must be shaved, washed and rubbed until it is red. Dry carefully and moisten with sugar-water or milk or scratch with a needle until blood appears. To ensure that they will not crawl into the gullet, nose or anus, one must draw a thread through the tail end from above down, not from side to side, otherwise one would injure the large blood vessels of the animal. When leeches are full and you wish them to come off, sprinkle a little salt over them or pepper or snuff or ashes or nitre or burnt bristles or burnt sponge or wool. They will then fall off. The place should then be sucked by cupping it in order to extract some of the blood at the spot and thereby get rid of the toxic substances left in the wound. Do not leave the patient until the bleeding has quite stopped. If it is a child, watch it in the following night.

Henri de Mondeville advised the use of leeches for most kinds of skin diseases, delirium, madness, melancholy, for all tumors which had difficulty in coming to a head, and for all conditions suitable for cupping. He thought the best type of leech was small, thin and slender, like a rat's tail, having a small head, a red belly, a dull blue-green back marked with a small number of yellow lines, and caught from clear stony water containing many frogs, and that they were especially beneficial if applied around the joints of the hands in scabies, around the anus [in particular] and on the heel and sole of the foot for madness.

When leeches swell they can be held up with spoons so that they will not fall off.

To remove a leech, thread a horse-hair between the head of the leech and the patient's skin.

Leeches were advised for temporal headaches arranged in groups of ten or twelve in a circular manner on each temple. For retention of the menses, four leeches fastened by a thread were applied as closely as possible to the uterus. There was no disease that would not benefit from their application to the vessels of the anus, particularly cases of epistaxis, hemoptysis and hematemesis and in extreme circumstances they were also of use in treating obesity.

Great value was laid on the snipping off of the tail. By this means one leech answered the purpose of several, for it continued to draw blood as before, which flowed drop by drop from its wounded extremity. There was surprisingly little added to the subject of leeching in the sixteenth, seventeenth, or eighteenth centuries, and it remained an extremely popular therapeutic measure, such that in 1775 Richard Mead wrote that leeches were often of vast service in delirium, and he used them in fevers if the patient was too weak to bleed. Similarly Lettsom in 1815 described the case of a patient who had suddenly become delirious and unconscious. Lettsom shaved his head and applied cold applications before resorting to cupping and leeching. When these failed he tried cathartics and finally blisters but despite his ministrations, the fever increased for a further four days before recovery!

In France it was said that the use of leeches to treat children was of national importance, for it increased the population by cutting down the infant mortality. Gallic leeching was widespread and the demand for the creatures so enormous that they were imported from Eastern Europe to meet the demand. A particular utility was in the treatment of colic where as many as fifty leeches were applied to the abdomen simultaneously.

Leeching had become a substantial trade that centered on France. Five kinds of *Hirudo medicinalis* leeches were described according to their size, varying from "thin" to "enormous". They were called after their color or their country of origin – grey, green, blonde, dark, Hungarian, Syrian, Turkish – all. Their weights were a most important factor. In general, a thousand small leeches weighed from 325 to 500 grams while a thousand large leeches weighed nearly ten times as much. The largest were found in the Bordeaux area, and weighed as much as 33 grams each and measured 25 cm in length. It was calculated that a leech weighing 3 drachms sucked 3 drachms and 1 scruple of blood and a further $3\frac{1}{2}$ drachms escaped from the wound. A leech weighing half a drachm sucked half a drachm of blood with a little oozing and that twenty-four large leeches could take 20 ounces, whereas twenty-four small leeches removed only 3 ounces of blood. Thus leech size was an important therapeutic variable!

At the start of the nineteenth century, France could support herself with home-grown leeches, but with excessive usage supplies diminished and once the resources of Spain and Portugal had been exhausted, Italy and Bohemia were used. By the middle of the century the vast marshes of Hungary were beginning to fail, and Poland, Russia, Syria, and Turkey were utilized for further supplies. Between 1827 to 1844 an average of twenty-seven million leeches were imported into France annually at a cost of 830,000 francs. Transportation was a problem since even if sent in barrels, stone jars, leather or close-woven bags dipped frequently in water, it was inadvisable to put too great a weight together, otherwise the animals crushed one another. Imaginative strategies were devised and they were sent from Budapest to Paris in large numbers, in bags laid on hammocks stretched across a wagon drawn by relays of post-horses. Often leeches made a journey of six or eight days dry, but in hot weather it was advisable to moisten them once daily and it became apparent that spring and autumn were the best seasons. Strassbourg was a large collection center, and there they were emptied into zinc baths until the time came to repack them for transport to Paris. Sixty to eighty thousand were at one period sent on this journey daily. As a result of this huge demand, the prices began to rise such that in 1806 a thousand leeches cost 12 to 15 francs; in 1815, 30 to 36 francs and by 1821 the apogee of 150 to 280 francs was reached before a twenty-year market plateau developed. A million-and-a-half leeches were sent to England and America in 1823 and the next year England alone received five million. In 1846 the price of a single leech in London had ranged from 1s. 2d. to 1s. 6d.

Given the therapeutic importance of leeches it became the practice to attach to hospitals individuals responsible for the leeching, and pay them enough to maintain themselves and their families by furnishing and applying leeches throughout the year at a stated price. A good example is provided by the records of the Manchester Infirmary which was founded in 1752, before moving to a new site in Piccadilly in 1755. On its south side a lunatic hospital was erected in 1766, and on its north side, some public baths under the charge of Mr. Haworth. All three were governed by the Board of Trustees of the Infirmary, and the Board's minutes make interesting reading. "*No agreement having been made with Mr. Haworth upon the subject of cupping, the Board of today have entered into an agreement with him that he must attend the patients of both hospitals gratis and what emoluments are derived from the patients cupped in the baths or at their own houses shall be divided equally between the Infirmary and Mr. Haworth, deducting first the expenses of the cupping instruments.*" In addition, they include frequent references to both cupping and leeching and to the economics of the therapy.

1791: "*Ordered that a sufficient quantity of leeches shall be constantly kept in the Infirmary and that the Apothecary takes care of this order.*"

A specific item for leeches first appeared in the hospital accounts in 1782, when there was a charge of £1 10s and 4 pence; in the 1790s the figure averaged £10 a year, increasing to £20 in the next decade when the hospital had been enlarged by sixty beds. There was a marked increase in the annual cost of leeching in 1810 and in successive years it rose: £50, £80, £90, £129, £144, and £209 in 1816.

By 1831, Mr. Gaylor having represented that the price of leeches had now risen to £7 per thousand, it was resolved unanimously that in consideration of the increased price of leeches, the price for Mr. Gaylor be advanced to one penny three farthings per leech according to his offer. Nevertheless by the mid 1820s it had reached £230, by 1829 it was £328 and in 1832 it had reached £361, no less than 4.4 per-cent of the total annual expenditure of the hospital. The last mention of these subjects in the Minutes occurred in 1840, when Mr. Gaylor's successor wrote: "*I have the pleasure to inform you that my charge for leeches will be reduced from threepence half-penny to threepence a leech from the first of the month.*" The cost of leeching remained over £300 until 1842, when it dropped to £243 and £150 in the next two years, despite a further increase of beds to 191. In 1850 it was £94; in 1860, £16, despite yet a further increase of beds to 277. The last entry was in 1882, and demonstrated a mere 5s. 10d. It is worth noting that the Dispensary's aquarium persisted until the 1930s!

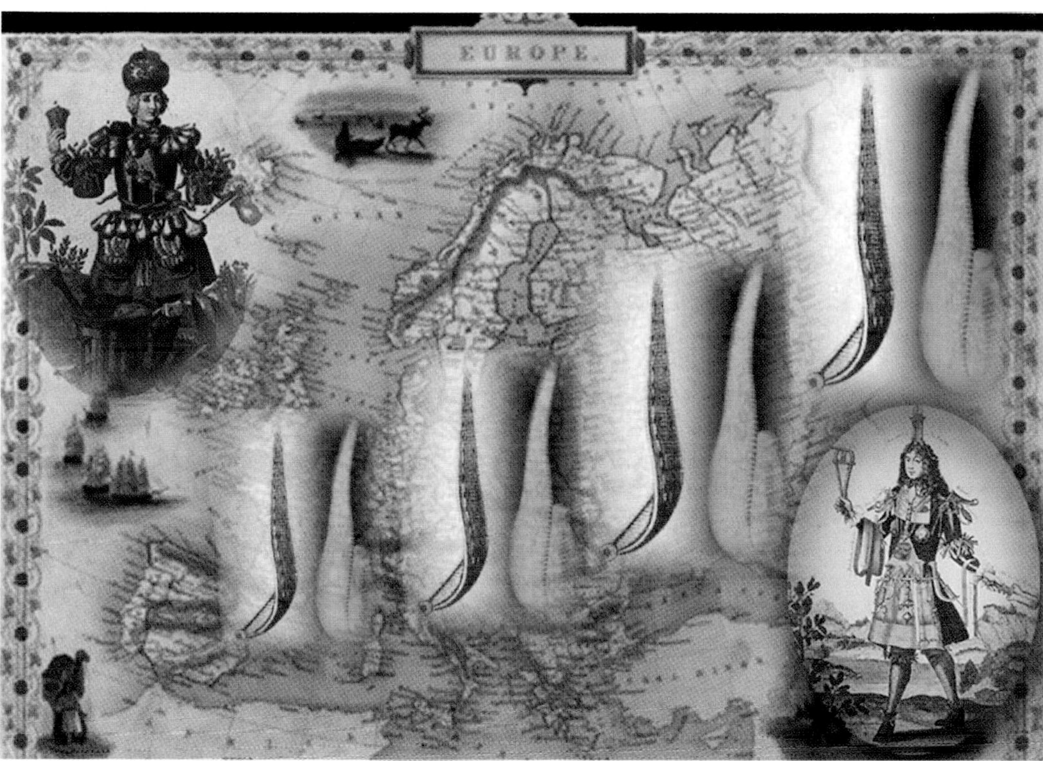

In the 18th century, the use of leeches as medicinal therapy reached extraordinary levels of popularity. Itinerant French pharmacists and physicians (inset) further disseminated their use outside the major cities and no pharmacy was without a leech jar. Trade in the animals rose to such an extent that massive imports from Bohemia, Hungary, and Czechoslovakia were necessary to satisfy popular demand.

François Broussais was a soldier prior to becoming an army surgeon and subsequently one of the great forces in French medicine. He believed "gastroenteritis" to be the basis of all pathology and his detractors claimed that in medical teaching his methods were Napoleonic while his therapeutic strategies sanguinary. He advocated the use of leeches to such an extent that the annual French usage of 2 to 3 million per year in 1824 had risen to 42 million by 1833 at the height of his influence. His protracted death due to intestinal obstruction from a rectal carcinoma so distressed his friend and colleague, Amussat, that he determined to improve the technique of colostomy.

Beetle and insect bites were known to produce pain and inflammation. The use of extracts of blister beetles was considered an excellent method of producing counter-irritation and was in certain areas as popular as the fashionable French remedy of using mustard plasters.

Diverse insect extracts were available for use as counter-irritants and each physician had his own special selection in much the same way as different herbalists favored different drugs.

Counter-Irritation

From the earliest times to the start of the twentieth century, and even into it, counter-irritation was considered an important method of treatment. It ranked with blood-letting in popularity and it was widely used. The concept was based upon the need to produce inflammation since it was long considered that the instigation of an inflammatory reaction, which could be maintained indefinitely if desired, was an important therapeutic technique. The running sore thus created was thought of as a means by which the body could be drained of noxious humours. To achieve this end, various means were employed, including blistering agents, wet and dry cupping, setons, issues and the cautery being the most important, with the moxa as an alternative and exotic addition. The method persisted in the form of blistering agents, and cantharides still finds a place in some textbooks of pharmacology. Many blistering agents were used, but cantharides, being the most potent and powerful, was the most popular. It was prepared from a special variety of beetle known as blister-beetles of whom it was believed that the most effective were those possessed of the greatest diversity of color. Dioscorides recorded that they were collected from corn or from pine trees in an unglazed vessel, the mouth of which was closed with a clean linen cloth. This was held in the fumes produced by warming strong vinegar until the beetles were stifled, at which point they were pierced by a thread and stored.

Cantharides was used internally by the ancients, who were well aware that it produced hematuria even when applied externally. It seems first to have been used for blistering purposes by Aretaeus in the early years of the second century A.D. For headache he advised that a suitable preparation should be applied to the shaved head, also such rubifacients as pitch, lemnestis, euphorbium, pellitory or the juice of thapsia (Gerard in his *Herball* called thapsia the stinking carrot). When rubbed into the skin these agents produced violent inflammation and a pustular rash resembling smallpox. They had, however, a considerable reputation for allaying the pain and eradicating the evil. If anything more powerful was required, cantharides was used, but only after the patient had been given milk to drink for three days to protect the bladder from injury. This treatment was also used for epilepsy and vertigo. It persisted through the centuries. A note in a Bradley's English textbook on *materia medica* published in 1730 comments as follows:

Cantharides or Spanish flies are gold and green shining together on the greatest part of their body with here and there a mixture of yellow and red. Being broken or powdered they are corrosive and are used to raise blisters, but in many constitutions the stranguary will ensue, especially where the discharge of serous juices is too great. But, however it be, such applications are necessary when a patient proves delirious, as frequently happens in high fevers and then we ought not to spare them especially about the arms and legs and even the top of the head itself.

Setons and Issues

Of the methods of producing counter-irritation, the seton was probably the most curious and, though not the most ancient, is worthy of serious consideration. The word seton means a bristle (although horse hairs were also employed) and was one of the earliest forms of foreign body to be used as a source of counter-irritation. As such, the seton was a running sore made deliberately by threading through the skin strands of twine or silk or some other material and leaving them in place indefinitely. If a more bulky foreign body was used, the sore was known as an issue.

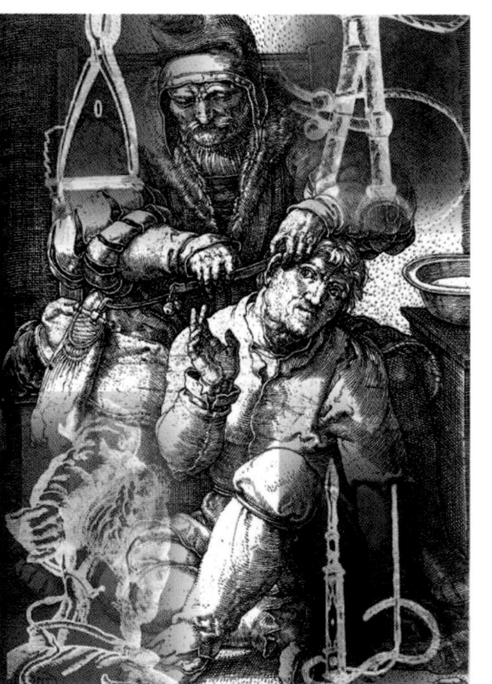

Although believed to function as counter-irritants, setons in probability worked effectively as tissue drains and facilitated the drainage of infected matter, thus facilitating cure.

An article published in 1832 in *The Doctor* provides a succinct description of the "*Modus operandi: Setons may be employed whenever it is required to keep up a discharge from the surface of the body. Their use is twofold – to prevent disease and to cure it. A man gets worse of a local complaint. His head becomes twice as heavy as it ought to be – at least it feels so. He gets a seton made in the nape of his neck and feels as light as if his head had been relieved from a cargo or a crown. Some persons from predisposition to disease are never in health without a seton or issue (for they act in the same principle). Dry up the discharge and they are immediately affected with pain in the head, inflammation of the lungs or eye, disease of the skin, or the blue devils beyond bearing.*"

Issues are generally preferred to setons when it is desirable to set up counter-irritation in a part of the body. In disease of the joints of the spine they are found to be of the greatest service and in what is called hip joint disease they are one of the most efficacious of remedial agents. The discharge produced by a seton or an issue, if produced unnecessarily or neglected or improperly attended to, may weaken the constitution and lay the foundation of many diseases.

Setons

The history of the seton goes back to the seventh century, when it was known as a "hypospathismus", from the Greek word meaning "to push forward a spatula." At this period, it was in its most vicious form and was used to treat certain eye conditions. Paul of Aegina provided a fine account of its usage:

This very formidable operation was soon abandoned, and Abulcasis in the tenth century referred to it as an operation performed by the ancients. The school of surgery at Salerno in the twelfth century used setons in the left hypochondrium to treat splenic disease and for pain in the spine, three setons were applied. One at the seat of the pain and the others three finger-breadths above and below. For pain in the testicle a seton was placed in the scrotum.

Similarly Ambroise Paré is informative on the subject and used a method of insertion that he described as follows: "*Pluck up the skin of the neck with a pair of perforated pincers and pass through the holes a sharp pointed cautery. Then, keeping the clamp in place, pass through the cautery hole a needle threaded with silk or cotton detach the silk, leave it in place and remove the clamp.*" Paré was of the opinion that "*a seton in the neck is a singular remedy against defluxions into the eyes. For we know by daily experience that many who have had the sight dulled by a long and great defluxion so that they were almost blind, have by little and little recovered their former splendour and sharpness of sight when matter once began to be evacuated by a seton.*" At a later date Paré found by experience that a long, thick, triangular needle was less painful, and he therefore advised young surgeons to use it in preference to the cautery.

Ambroise Paré, surgeon par excellence. A stained glass window from the Hôtel Dieu, Lyons. A notable innovator in surgical therapy, Paré not only advocated the use of setons but devised special needles for their insertion.

Fabricius Hildanus pictured the instruments he used and provided detailed case notes as did Matthew Glandorp, a surgeon working in Bremen in 1632 who wrote a whole book on the use of setons and issues. In 1583, Bartisch, an unlettered barber surgeon, published a curiously illustrated book on eye diseases, *Augen Dienst*, which showed the use of the seton to cure a running eye. As the official ophthalmic surgeon to the Elector of the ancient city of Dresden his books did much to lift ophthalmology above what the author calls the "*couchers and eye destroyers*" of the time. Matthew Purmann, an able and courageous surgeon in the Brandenburg army, recorded in 1706 that setons were used against defluxions, "*rheum in the eyes*", pains in the head, cataract of the eyes, if timely used . . . sciatica – applied to the hips and calves – all distempers of the head (particularly deafness), pains in the neck and limbs and the falling sickness. The technique generally used was to pluck up the skin with the forefinger and thumb of the left hand, pulling it well away from the muscles. A three-sided, sharp-pointed, slightly-curved needle was then thrust through the fleshy pannicle and half a skein of silk drawn through and left "*being afterwards moistened by a digestive or oil of roses. This must be done at every dressing. Twice or thrice a day the silk must be drawn from one side to the other, as long as it is desired to continue the seton.*" The result was a double ulcer which discharged freely.

The method was proposed to have three important functions. Thus, it acted as a counter-irritant, it established areas of passive hyperemia, and it built up an active resistance to bacteria. Not surprisingly some physicians disapproved of setons and Blankaart, a Dutch physician of the late seventeenth century, referred to it as "*this nauseous operation which causes a self-created disease without benefit!*" Despite considerable opposition, some significant physicians such as Percival Pott, used setons extensively, albeit with a different and much more scientific purpose. Indeed, Pott was convinced that the use of the seton for the radical cure of hydrocele was "*the most successfully efficacious*" treatment of any that he wrote *An account of the method of obtaining a perfect radical cure of the hydrocele by means of a seton, because some few gentlemen of consequence who have by this means been cured, requested its publication.*

Pott's method was to pierce the hydrocele with a trocar of tolerable size, draw off the fluid and introduce into the cannula a sharp needle armed with a seton, consisting of ten or twelve strands of candle-wick cotton. The needle was passed as high up in the sac as possible, being protected by the cannula, and pushed through the skin. The threads were then detached and usually by the next day the seton was adherent. Within forty-eight hours the scrotum and testicle began to swell and inflame and with the addition of poultices the seton was left in place until it became loose, after the first fortnight. By this time the cavity was completely obliterated and the seton could be withdrawn, allowing the wound to heal rapidly with resultant

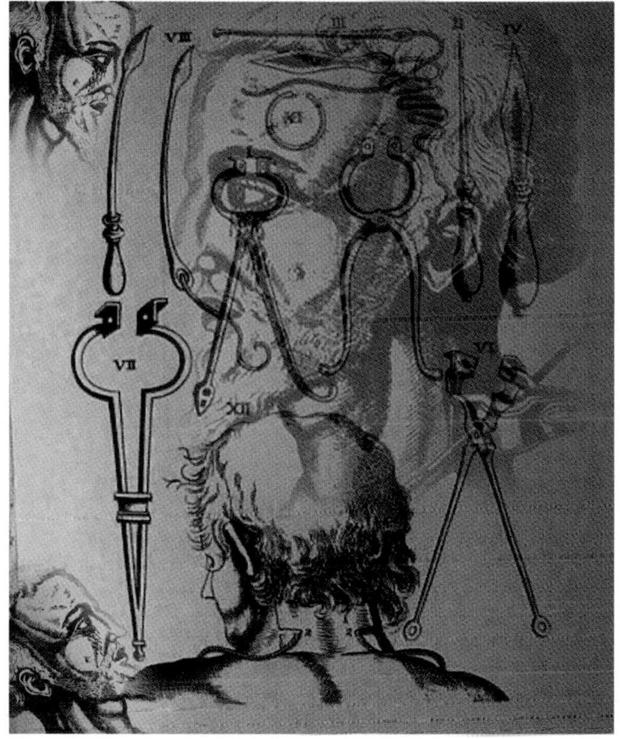

Examples of the various surgical devices available for the insertion of setons.

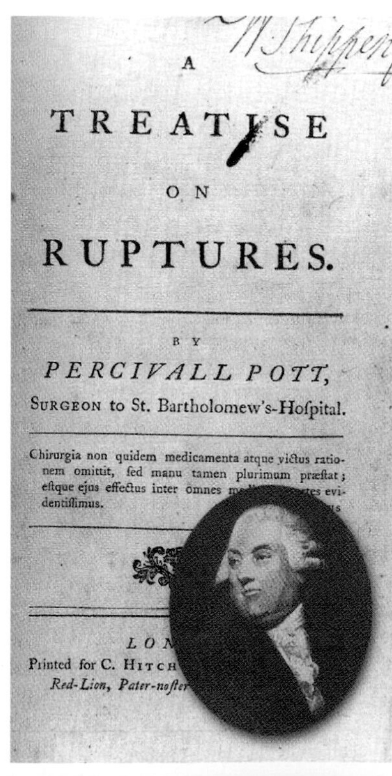

A

TREATISE

ON

RUPTURES.

BY

PERCIVALL POTT,

SURGEON to St. Bartholomew's-Hospital.

Chirurgia non quidem medicamenta atque victus rationem omittit, sed manu tamen plurimum præstat; estque ejus effectus inter omnes m[illegible]tes evidentissimus.

LO[illegible]

Printed for C. HITCH[illegible]

Red-Lion, Pater-noster[illegible]

Percivall Pott of London, who is better remembered for his focus on orthopedic matters, advocated the use of setons in the treatment of hydroceles and even abdominal pain.

The insertion of a seton was regarded as having the effect of a counter-irritant. The site of placement determined the location of its effect and therefore special techniques were described for each site. "Having first shaven the hairs about the forehead we must permit the lower jaw to move and avoiding the place where the temporal muscles seem to act, we are to make three straight parallel incisions descending to the bone. After the incision we apply the instrument called the hypospathister, dividing all the intermediate substances down to the pericranium." A knife was then inserted from the central incision in turn to the lateral incisions and then, with the cutting edge upwards, all structures were divided except the skin. This was intended to destroy the blood vessels, descending from the head to the eyes. A twisted thread was then passed under the skin and a compress applied, soaked in water.

cure of the hydrocele. Pott concluded his essay in these words:

When a seton of any kind is used for the purpose of making or continuing a drain of matter, it is right to move it daily and frequently to shift it. But in this case, as the intention is different so should our conduct be. The intention is merely by the residence of the seton to excite such a slight degree of inflammation as shall occasion an adhesion of the tunica albuginea testis to the tunical vaginalis. Let it remain unmoved for a week or ten days, at the end of which time it will have accomplished its end.

In the mid-nineteenth century, Dr. Marshall Hall had recourse to setons, with the most marked success, in a variety of cases of internal inflammation including hepatitis and nephritis. He laid particular stress on the value of the method in cases of albuminous urine or of disease of the spinal marrow with paraplegia, provided the setons were applied at the level of the disease.

These setons were larger than usual, three-quarters of an inch in breadth, and extended two inches in length. He proposed that they should be inserted on a level with the seat of the disease and be four or six in number, two or three being instituted on each side of the spinal column. There were two further refinements. The threads could be impregnated with drugs, an early method of hypodermic medication or else the two ends of the threads could be tied tightly together.

Issues

The word "issue" was derived from the Latin *ex eo*, meaning "to go out." Issues or, as they used to be called, fontanelles (a little fountain), were similar in many ways to setons. A small scarification was kept open by the use of a pea or some similar form of foreign body although the more elegant Paré used a tiny ball made of gold or silver. He considered that *"To make an issue is no considerable art but to set it in the proper place is all the skill."*

The ancients made them between two muscles on the outer sides of the arms or legs. They could be made either with a needle or a cautery. If the former was used, the skin was pierced and then cut under the needle with a pair of scissors, so that the orifice was big enough to allow of the insertion of a pea, but in the first instance a white peppercorn was inserted for two or three days. In this manner the issue was made with little more pain than the prick of a pin, but if the cautery was used, it was painful and sometimes dangerous. If the issue ran well, it was dressed morning and evening with a fresh pea, but if not, a globule of cantharides or other counter-irritant drug could be used.

Issues were used to treat the same disorders as setons, but in addition they were indicated in

cases of gout, old ulcers, fistulae and in all manner of copious
defluxions of humours to what part so-ever;
for though they do not always free the patient from his
distemper yet they give some ease by carrying off
a great mass of acrid and acid humour.

Heister, in 1750, recorded that though most surgeons considered the method to be of some use, he himself frankly believed a cure was not to be expected, though issues provided some small relief. Van Helmont thought they served only to torment and trouble a patient and Thomas Willis was similarly scathing in 1684. He opined the general belief that issues were the best form of treatment for convulsions in infants and youths, for sore eyes, King's Evil, headaches, vertigo, and cramp-like distempers, and continued:

Neither is it less celebrated against
diseases of the breast. And who suffers from a
cough, bloody or consumptive sputum,
or an asthma that long enjoys his skin whole?
In like manner issues are commended
in affectations of the lower belly, scarce any
hypochondriacal person or hysterical
woman, no gouty or cachectical person but hath his
skin pierced in many places like a lamprey.

Nonetheless, the eminent Boerhaave advised the use of setons and issues for many complaints, applied both locally and at a distance, insisting that their application to the feet in cases of apoplexy was of certain considerable benefit.

The indiscriminate insertion of setons and issues led to a widespread misuse of the technique. For a small payment, diverse quacks, barbers and charlatans could be found at any fair who would claim to relieve obscure pain by inserting a seton made of some wondrous curative substance.

The Cautery

Of the methods under consideration for producing counter-irritation, the cautery was the most important and the most drastic over the longest period of time, though it was the first to fall into disrepute. One of the aphorisms attributed to Hippocrates deals with this method. *Those diseases which medicines do not cure, iron cures [the knife]. Those which iron cannot cure, fire cures, and those which fire cannot cure are to be reckoned wholly incurable.*

Celsus in the first century wrote at length on the subject of cautery and proposed that in cases of long-standing pain in the head or severe pain in the neck, the cautery should be applied to the seat of the pain to produce ulceration. In cases of ophthalmia it should be applied to the skull after a preliminary incision, whereas in cases of edema, ulceration should be established in many places by means of the red-hot cautery. In cases of phthisis the cautery should be applied seven times, once under the chin, at two places on the neck, on each breast and below the shoulder-blades, and the ulcers prevented from healing until the cough had ceased. Similarly, the cautery was also applied to the head and neck in cases of epilepsy and apoplexy, while Rufus of Ephesus also claimed it was efficacious when applied over a gouty joint. Aretaeus, in the early second century A.D., treated epilepsy by burning through the skull as far as the diploe but also cauterized for cephalgia, either burning superficially or, if he wished to burn to the bone, he claimed to carefully avoid the muscles, *"for muscles when burnt occasioned convulsions."* Paul of Aegina, in the seventh century, wrote in detail on the use of the cautery and used the word eschar to denote the artificially-produced sores that developed as a consequence of cautery. He also used the cautery freely to treat elephantiasis (regarded by ancient authors as a form of cancer), which was probably a form of dermal fungoid disease whereby the skin of the face became hard, rough and discolored. The treatment was to burn five scars in the head in the following specific locations. Whether magical in design or representative of some specific therapeutic consideration, such lesions were thought to procure the evaporation and discharge of the collection of thick humors in the deep parts of the head, and prevent the vision from being impaired.

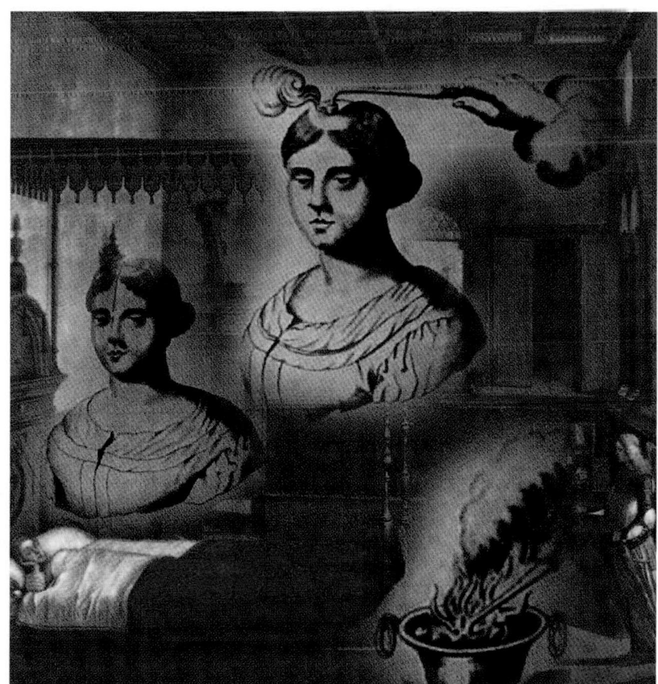

The concept of the use of cautery application for treating disease originates from the times of Hippocrates. Its usage was further supported by the religious concepts of the "cleansing fire" and the belief that disease was sin and that penance was necessary to obviate the latter. The pain inflicted by cautery was therefore considered to both cleanse the soul and the wound.

Avicenna seems to have had rather more sensible ideas on the use of the cautery, but even he used it to produce an invigorating effect on a member whose cold temperament we wish to rectify. He advised that the cautery was best made of gold, and added, *"If the cautery is applied to the skull the application must be gentle, so as not to risk roasting the brain or shriveling up its membranes."* The School of Salerno in the twelfth century cauterized cases of sciatica over the hip joint, making a triangular burn, whereas for gout the soles of the feet were cauterized.

Henri de Mondeville gave many details concerning the use of cauteries in his textbook of surgery written in the early part of the fourteenth century. He was careful to burn only at the precise spot, using a funnel when cauterizing the inside of the nose. He particularly stressed that cauteries should not be used with trembling hands. He liked to dress the wounds with leaves, preferably ivy leaves, but if none were available he used cabbage, sorrel or vine leaves. With the passage of time the use and abuse of the cautery extended and the early texts of surgery contain drawings of cauteries of all manner of shapes and sizes for use in many different disorders. Not all were swayed by their use and John Woodall reflected with some balance on their usage, writing in *The Surgeon's Mate*: *"The ancient surgeons of former ages used cauteries far more than in our own times. The necessary use of them in many cases is now foreborne by reason that the terror thereof to the patient is great, yet the use of them is very needful. In epilepsy or the falling sickness they are used with good success."*

Dekkers, in 1695, pictured the cautery applied to the head, with the victim looking remarkably placid, but he also demonstrated quite vividly the use of the cautery to treat sciatica. Almost half a century later Heister, in 1750, included among the diseases benefited by the cautery, amaurosis, epilepsy, sciatica and pains in the teeth or other parts, yet there seems to have been considerable difference of opinion among the surgeons of the time as to whether the cautery was of any real use, and some condemned it out of hand. By the early nineteenth century it was not considered as standard or acceptable practice.

The site of application of cautery was of course a critical determinant in determining its efficacy. In addition, the degree of injury induced was important in ensuring maximal effect. The religious maxim of inducing suffering to effect cure formed a considerable part of the philosophy of this therapy. In some instances, the actual physical extirpation of a lesion by incineration was actually effective.

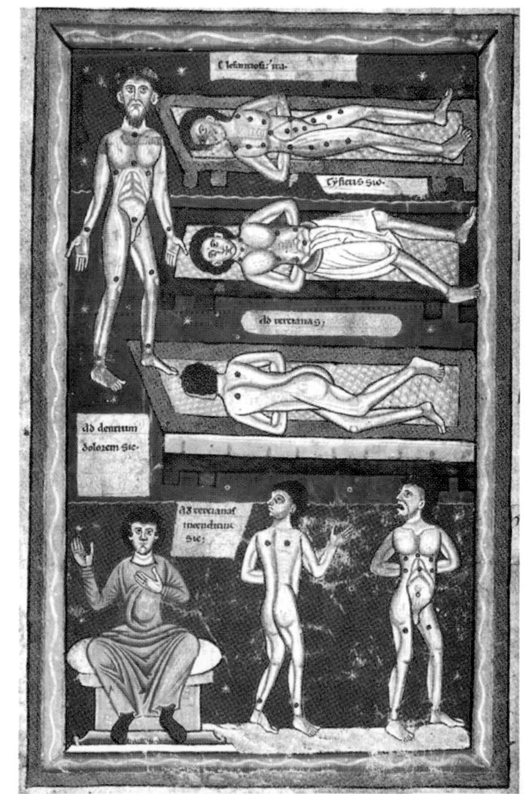

A medieval diagram depicting the various sites at which cautery could be applied for therapeutic effect.

The frontispiece of Herman Busschof's text detailing his appreciation of the value of moxa in the treatment of gout. The title, with its observation regarding the management of women during travel, suggests that his joint disease may have been Reiter's syndrome rather than a uric acid problem.

The physicians of the Dutch East India Company gained enormous experience in the management of novel disease as well as exposure to numerous novel remedies including the use of moxibustion.

Moxibustion

An alternative method to producing a running sore by burning involved the use of moxa.

Moxibustion (or the burning of moxa) was a method that originated in ancient China and consisted of the application of combustible cones of *artimesia moxa*, or common mugwort, to certain areas of skin. On application the cone was ignited and allowed to smoulder until it had burnt itself out, leaving behind a blister, although often times the blisters became infected, and under such circumstances the remedy was often worse than the disease. Such cones could be placed at any site on the body, and moxibustion charts abound in the ancient Chinese medical texts. In the main they were applied in a geometric design, with the sites most frequently used being the epigastrium, the upper part of the sternum and the front of the ear.

As the method spread to various parts of the world, the substance forming the cone was much dependent on the location of the practioneer. Thus nomads used the wool of their flocks as well as certain spongy substances growing upon oak or hazel trees, while Indians used the pith of a reed, and flax or hemp impregnated with a combustible material. The Persians used the dung of a goat, the Thessalians dried moss and the Egyptians cotton. It seems likely that none of these substances was as effective as the genuine Chinese moxa which comprised dried leaves, beaten and rubbed until the harder parts had separated, so that the soft remains could be formed into a pyramid the size of a pea. In applying the moxa the base of the cone was placed on the part to be burnt and the top set on fire, or if the cone failed to burn satisfactorily, a blow-pipe was used. Once the moxa had burnt out the eschar was thereafter treated.

Paul of Aegina, in the seventh century A.D., referred to the method. *Others do not burn with iron but with the substance called Iscae. The Iscae are spongy bodies forming on oaks and walnuts, being mostly in use with the barbarians.*

Despite considerable popularity in the Orient, moxa was not used much in Europe until the seventeenth century, when an attempt was made to popularize it in the treatment of gout.

Its introduction to Western medicine reflected the medical experience obtained by the Dutch merchants who traded with the East. Herman Busschof, a Dutch layman living in Batavia in the service of the Dutch East India Company, was a victim of the gout of fourteen years standing, *"laboring under extraordinary pain in both feet, not knowing whither to turn himself with pain. To him came an Indian woman doctor employed in the treatment of his slaves. She demanded a candle and solicitously searched for that part of the place affected where the greatest pain was and thereupon she burned with her moxa upon my feet and my knees about twenty little scars which looked like little grey specks without raising any blister or causing any after pain whereupon all the pain of the gout vanished."*

Unfortunately the cure was not quite complete, and after twenty-seven months freedom, some symptoms returned but were ameliorated with moxa,

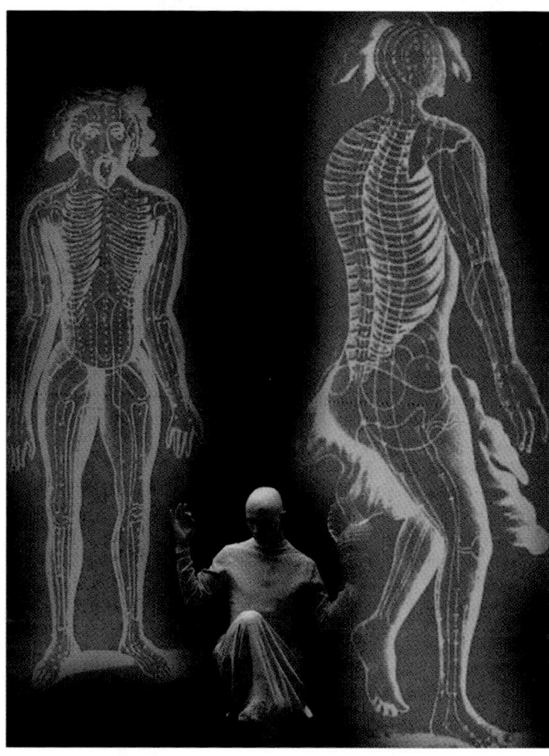

European exposure to Oriental concepts of the harmony of the body first occurred during the trading ventures of the Portuguese, Spanish and Dutch to the Spice islands. Prior to this, acupuncture, moxa, and pulse meridians were unknown.

"thanking most heartily Almighty God for this goodness." Impressed by the efficacy of the treatment, he decided to bring this marvel to the notice of his countrymen by means of a book, which, in 1676, was *"Englished out of the Dutch by a careful hand"* (translated).

Sir William Temple, a statesman and man of letters, who carried through the Triple Alliance between England, Holland, and Sweden against Spain in

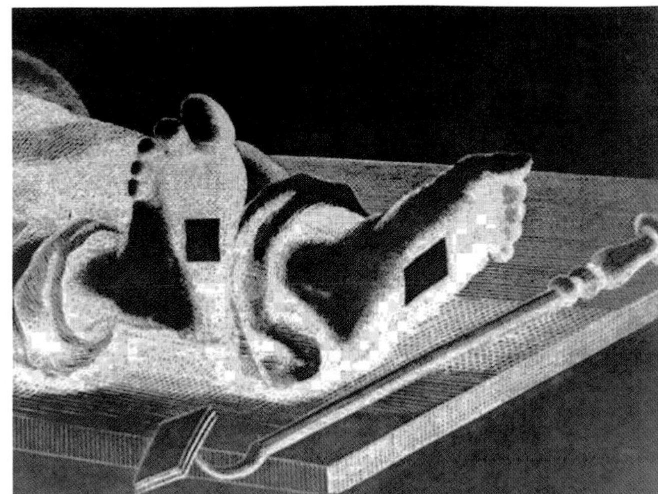

The technique of moxa application to the feet.

1668, and subsequently arranged the marriage between Princess Mary of England and William of Orange, thought so highly of the value of moxa in the treatment of gout that he wrote an essay on the subject in 1677.

For the pain of the burning itself the first time it is sharp so that a man may be allowed to complain. I resolved I would not but that I would count to a certain number as the best measure how long it lasted. I told six score and four as fast as I could and when the fire of the moxa was out all pain of burning was over. The second time was not near as sharp as the first and the third a good deal less than the second. The wound was not raw as I expected but only scorched and black. I would rather endure the whole trouble of the operation than half a quarter of an hour's pain in the degree I felt it the first night.

Sydenham believed the moxa relieved the pain of the gout but did little else, while Heister in 1750 considered that the use of rather larger cones of about a thumb's breadth in length, were more effective, although overall he thought the method of little or no benefit, and added, "*It is now quite in disuse.*"

In 1822, an attempt was made to revive the treatment in England and Dunglison, a Fellow of the Royal College of Surgeons, complained that "*although the indiscriminate use of the metallic cautery had been properly banished from medical and surgical practice, yet the moxa had never met with a fair and judicious trial.*" Baron Larrey, the premier surgeon to Napoleon's Grand Army from 1812-14, was so impressed by the results he attributed to the moxa, that he was moved to write a treatise on the subject:

During my campaign in Egypt and Syria, having had an opportunity of confirming the observations of authors and travelers respecting the great advantages which the people of these countries derive from the use of moxa in several morbid affections, I have availed myself of every occasion which occurred in my practice of making a trial of it.

Larrey used the moxa to cure blindness, deafness, epilepsy, hydrocephalus and phthisis, in which disease he was particularly impressed with its benefit. Of particular interest was his report of a patient with liver abscess who recovered under treatment with moxa when the abscess burst into the colon. Similarly the report of a nineteen-year-old girl "*upon whom Nature had lavished all her favors*" with a severe case of advanced phthisis is fascinating. "*It had even been declared, at the last consultation held upon her case, that nothing more could be done for her in consequence of the advanced state of the disease and her extreme weakness.*" Larrey yielded, with some difficulty, to the entreaties of her parents, and undertook her treatment in September 1817. "*The young patient was in a state of slow continued fever, with flushing of the cheeks, painful and frequent cough – and the expectoration of yellow purulent sputum. She had extreme debility, slight aphonia and pain between the shoulders and in the sides. The tongue, the roof of the mouth, and the inside of the throat were covered with aphthae, or excoriations, which appeared to extend into the air passages, and the nails of the fingers were crooked. Twenty moxas, preceded by a few cuppings and a seton, placed in the left side, had removed the symptoms and conducted the patient by degrees to an unexpected cure. The treatment had continued eighteen months, and she enjoyed perfect health. After a whole year had passed in this satisfactory condition, she was attacked with an inflammation of the bowels, of which she died, notwithstanding the most assiduous and attentive treatment.*" Larrey claimed that despite this relapse "*She did not, however, exhibit a single symptom of her former disorder.*"

A Chinese woman collecting herbs. In addition to acupuncture, massage, and moxa, the Chinese possessed a sophisticated knowledge of herbal medicine and numerous detailed texts were available for consultation. Assessment of the diverse pulse meridians played a large part in defining diagnosis and prescription. Ivory figurines (inset) were often used in lieu of physicial examination since modesty often forbade palpation.

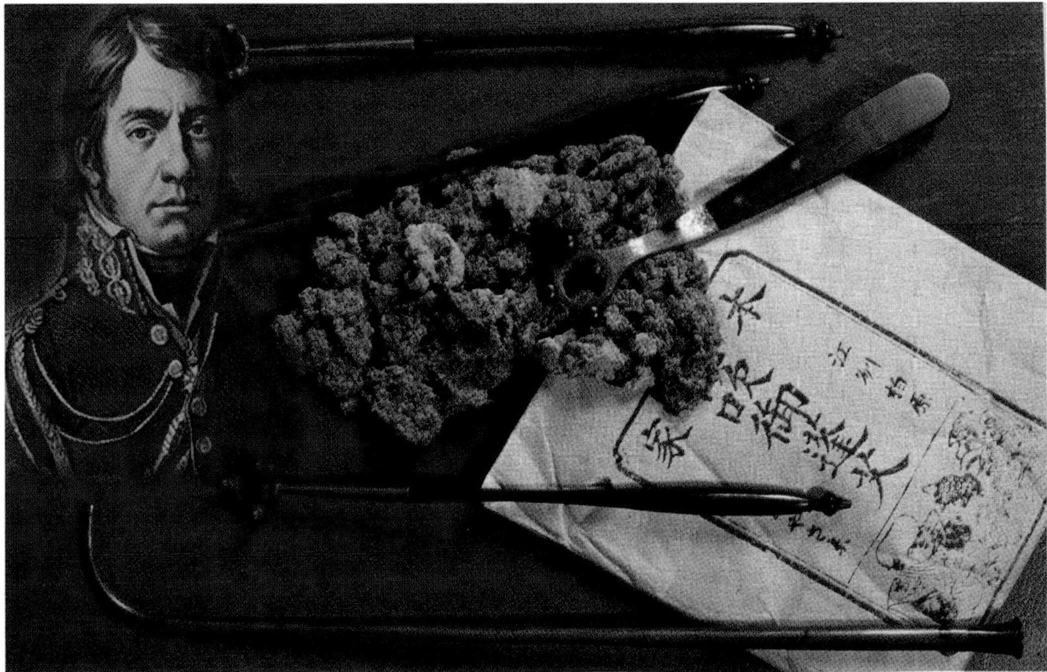

Baron Larrey (inset), the premier surgeon of the army of Napoleon and the inventor of the ambulance, was a firm believer in moxibustion. His original instruments (right) reside in the medical history collection of the Sorbonne, Paris.

Wren was born in 1632 and by the age of 14 years, such was his obvious mathematical genius that he was sent to Oxford where he was admitted as a gentleman commoner at Wadham College c. 1645. He took his degree of Bachelor of Arts in 1650 at the age of 18, and three years later was elected a Fellow of All Souls College. There he became a leading member of a society which met at Oxford for the improvement of natural and experimental philosophy. In recognition of his extraordinary astro-mathematical skills, he was subsequently elected Savilian professor of astronomy at Oxford in 1661. His philosophical demeanor attracted him to many other areas and in 1656, at the age of 24, Wren, in the words of the historian of the Royal Society, "became the first author of the noble and anatomical experiment of injecting liquors into the veins of animals."

Despite the excitement expressed by Larrey in his text, a Dublin physiologist five years later wrote, "*A very striking difference between medical practice in France and Britain is the use of the moxa. On the Continent it enjoys a high character. In Britain it is hardly used at all.*"

Intravenous Therapy

There is little doubt that the discovery by William Harvey of the circulation of blood represented one of the most significant events in the history of medicine. The publication of the text *De Motu Cordis,* in Frankfurt in 1628, laid the basis for the consideration of intravenous medication, although almost thirty years would pass before the first substantitive studies were undertaken. Nevertheless, it was soon apparent that use of the venous system as a therapeutic conduit was clearly of great medical import and by 1664 the procedures of infusion and transfusion were considered of such magnitude that a serious dispute arose between Dr. John Daniel Major, professor of physic at Kiel, and Dr. Elsholz, the King of Prussia's physician at Berlin, as to their legitimate primacy in establishing this therapy. Although the acrimonious dispute was widely aired in the medical periodicals for three years, their respective claims were to no avail, since the inventor was Dr. Christopher Wren, the mathematical professor at Oxford. Dr. Michael Ettmuller, a distinguished German physician practicing in Leipzig in 1668, stated categorically that primacy was the due of Wren, and that following his contributions, the technique and concepts had been improved by Dr. Clarke, physician-in-ordinary to the King of England. Thereafter Major had begun to use it, followed shortly by Dr. Charles Fracassatus, professor at Pisa, and last of all by Elsholz and Dr. Hoffmann, professor at Altdorf.

The medical degree (right) of William Harvey and his coat of arms or "Stamma" (top left) from the wall of Padua medical school. Trained as a physician in Padua, he returned to England and after much experimentation, enunciated the words that have echoed down the years: "It must therefore be concluded that the blood in the animal body moves around in a circle continuously, and that the action or function of the heart is to accomplish this by pumping. This is the only reason for the motion and beat of the heart."

Although it is not well-known, Dr. Wren was none other than the eminent architect Sir Christopher Wren, who built St. Paul's and numerous other magnificent edifices that grace the cities of London and Oxford.

The events that led to the investigation of accessing the bloodstream were detailed by Robert Boyle, who himself was a scholar of considerable repute. Since Wren had indicated to Boyle that he thought he could easily contrive a way of conveying any liquid immediately into the bloodstream, Boyle, being interested, provided a large dog, and the demonstration was carried out in the presence of some eminent physicians and other learned men.

Wren exposed the large vein in the hind leg and applied a small brass plate, half an inch long, a quarter of an inch broad, the sides being bent inwards. This plate had four little holes in the sides near the corners through which threads could be passed, allowing it to be fastened to the vein. In the middle of the plate there was a large slit parallel to the sides and almost as long as the plate. This allowed the vein to be exposed to the lancet and kept it from starting aside. The vein was ligatured below the plate and then opened through the slit sufficient to allow of the introduction of the slender pipe of a syringe. A small quantity of a warm solution of opium in sack was injected. The effect was dramatic. No sooner had the dog's leg been untied than the opium began to show its narcotic qualities. Almost before the dog had scrambled to its feet its head began to nod, it faltered and reeled and became so stupid that wagers were offered that its life could not be saved. Boyle, however, took the dog into the garden and caused it to be whipped up and down, thereby keeping it awake and in motion, whereby it gradually came round and, being carefully tended [for a change], it not only recovered fully but grew so fat so manifestly that 'twas admired.

Thus is recorded for posterity the initiation of intravenous access! Subsequent experiments revealed that the plate was unnecessary if the fingers were skillfully used to support the vein. It was also found that a slender quill fitted to a bladder was more convenient than a syringe.

Seeking to disseminate this knowledge as well as obtain patronage, Wren next experimented before a learned nobleman, the Marquis of Dorchester, who was a Fellow and Benefactor of the Royal College of Physicians of London, using a moderate dose of infusion of the purgative, crocus metallorum (antimony based). Unfortunately it had little effect, but repetition of the experiment on a second dog using an increased dose resulted in a dramatic effect with such violent vomiting and diarrhea that the animal perished. Details of further studies were recorded by Wren in a letter to a friend, and clearly detail the extent to which he recognized the significance of his observations:

> *The most considerable experiment I have made of late was this. I injected wine and ale into the mass of blood in a living dog by a vein in good quantities 'til he became extremely drunk but soon after voided it by urine. It will take too long to tell you the effect of opium, scammony and other things which I have tried in this way. I am in further pursuit of the experiment, which I take to be of great concernment and which will give great light to the theory and practice of physic.*

Subsequent to these studies, Wren's intellectual interest turned more towards astronomy and mathematics and, although he maintained a medical interest, he pursued physical science with considerable effect at Gresham College in London (1657) and subsequently as a professor at Oxford in 1661. While holding these posts he not only continued to participate in medical discussions but actually illustrated Willis's classical treatise on the anatomy of the brain, published in 1664. His subsequent ventures into architecture and the magnificent contributions of his genius to that area are a subject of a separate discussion.

In these early experimental years Boyle recorded that he was informed by an *"ingenious anatomist and physician"* that he had obtained very good success with diuretics. Boyle therefore proposed that if it could be done without either too much danger or cruelty, trial might be made on some human bodies, especially those of malefactors. This was arranged in 1657 in the house of a foreign ambassador, *"a curious person"* residing in London at the time. *"Infusion of crocus metallorum was injected into the veins of an unruly domestic servant who, it was recorded, deserved to be hanged."* The man, as soon as the injection was given, did either really or craftily fall into a swoon whereby, being unwilling to prosecute so hazardous an experiment, the ambassador desisted. The only other effect was that it wrought once downward with him which yet might be occasioned by fear or anguish.

Dr. Timothy Clarke, physician-in-ordinary to King Charles II, recorded in the *Philosophical Transactions of the Royal Society* in 1668, that during the previous ten years he had *"diligently labored at mixing various fluids with blood drawn from living animals and had not only caused fluids of various kinds to be infused into the living body but had also demonstrated the effects of emetics, cathartics, diuretics, cardiacs and opiates in that way."* After examining the subject of "injections" (water, beer, milk, broth, wine and spirits of wine) in both animals and humans for almost five years, he expressed doubt as to whether the technique would ever be of benefit in the cure of disease, but thought it might have potential in the study of anatomy or for the better demonstration of the nature of blood. Unfortunately Clarke failed to document the results of his experiments – possibly because of disappointment at the poor results – and stated that he did not consider the observations sufficiently worthy to enter into controversy regarding primacy. In consequence, others recorded Clarke's experiments, and subsequently claimed them as their own.

Amongst these, the first was Johann Sigismond Elsholz, who published an interesting little book entitled *Clysmatica Nova* or *The New Clyster Art*, which described the method by which a medicine could be administered via an open blood vessel *"so that it has the same effect as if it had been taken orally."* The initial experiments that Elsholz undertook were in 1661 on the body of a woman drowned in Berlin. Having tightly bandaged the right arm above the elbow, he exposed and opened the artery distal to the bandage with a small cut and used a syringe to inject a pint of warm water. At this point he noted that the collapsed vessel in the forearm and hand expanded again as might be predicted in a living subject tied for venesection. Thereafter he opened the median vein and observed that initially blood mixed with water flowed out, but on injecting more warm water into the artery, clear unchanged water flowed out of the vein in the same quantity as injected. He then turned his attention to the veins, which were much easier of access than were the arteries.

Just as if a jug of wine is poured into a river, the wine flows with the river into the sea, a liquor injected into a vein must flow with the circulating blood into the heart. When the liquor enters the heart, necessarily an alteration will follow in the heart, corresponding to the nature of the liquor. And as the heart communicates this change to all limbs by the arteries, there is no doubt that the whole body will feel something of it. But as it is dangerous to test this proposition in a human subject, I decided to start the experiment on dogs. How far I have succeeded can be judged from the true account which follows.

Elsholz then described how he with ease exposed the crural vein of a dog, opened it with a lancet, and using a syringe injected a few spoonfuls of plain

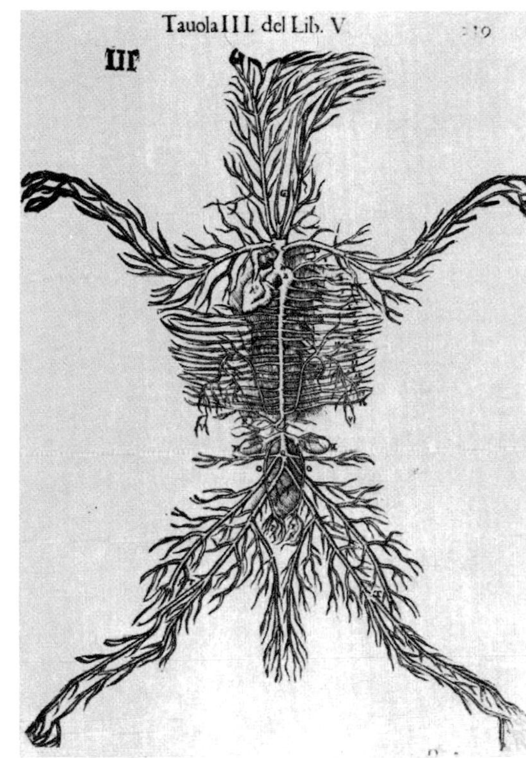

The arterial system of a horse by William Cowper (1666-1709).

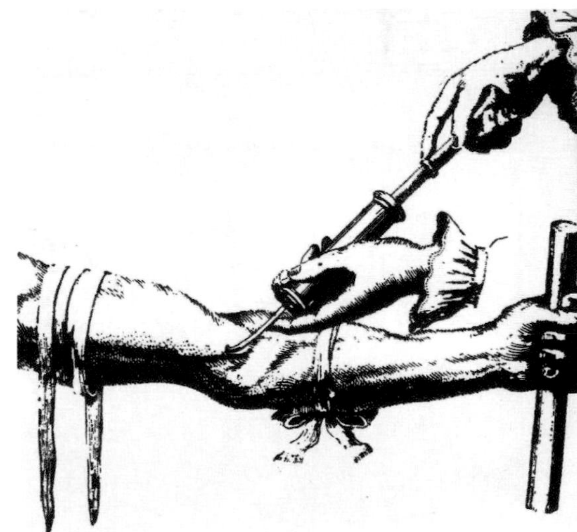

The infusion of an agent into a vein using a primitive syringe.

Robert Boyle (1627-1691) was the 14th child of an Anglo-Irish family of wealth and influence. In 1635 he was sent to Eton College, after which he spent the years from 1639 to 1644 with a tutor on the European continent, for the most part in Switzerland. As a chemist and natural philosopher, he was noted for his pioneering experiments on the properties of gases and his espousal of a corpuscular view of matter that was a forerunner of the modern theory of chemical elements. From 1645 to 1655 Boyle lived partly in Dorset, where he began his experimental work and wrote moral essays, some of which ("Occasional Reflections upon Several Subjects") appeared in 1655. One of his essays is reputed to have inspired the writing of Gulliver's Travels *by Jonathan Swift. Although he spent some time in Ireland in connection with his estates, because laboratory apparatus was unobtainable there, he could only engage in anatomical dissection. From 1656 to 1668 he resided at the University of Oxford, where he had the good fortune to secure the assistance of Robert Hooke, the inventor and subsequent curator of experiments to the Royal Society, who helped him construct an air pump. Recognizing at once its scientific possibilities, Boyle conducted pioneering experiments in which he demonstrated the physical characteristics of air and the necessary role of air in combustion, respiration, and the transmission of sound. Boyle described this work in 1660 in* New Experiments Physio-Mechanicall, Touching the Spring of the Air and its Effects.

The transfusion of blood had long been considered as a therapeutic option but technical difficulties (lack of thin needles and flexible tubes) and catastrophes relating to incompatibility had led to disenchantment with the concept.

water. Having covered the vein with a small piece of lint to stop the bleeding, he sutured the skin with a few stitches, and was delighted to note the complete lack of any adverse effect on the animal. A second animal received a few spoonfuls of Spanish wine, with the intention of making it drunk, but this had no obvious effect (inadequate dose). A third dog was infused with *extractum opii*, in the morning at ten o'clock. Although wild and unrestrainable while receiving the clyster, after the injection it immediately became tame, and after half an hour it fell into a deep sleep with glazed half-open eyes and drooping tongue.

Richard Lower, a physician practicing in Oxford, was an early pioneer in developing the concepts and techniques of blood transfusion. Initially he used simple goose quills for uniting the blood vessels, but soon progressed to the use of silver flanged (to facilitate a ligature) tubes connected by a piece of ox cervical artery that could be more securely fixed to the emitting and receiving of blood vessels.

At almost the same time in 1667, John Daniel Major, professor of physic at Kiel, published his book, *Chirurgia Infusoria*, asserting angrily that the work confirmed his contributions as foremost in the new field and repudiated others who falsely claimed the credit. It is uncertain whether Major undertook any experimentation himself, and although the book resembles a compilation of the studies and opinions of others, it contains useful descriptions of the procedures as well as the earliest illustration known of an intravenous injection.

The next paper of importance was published in 1623 by a professor of anatomy at Pisa, who injected into the vein of a dog some diluted *aqua fortis*. Unfortunately the animal perished almost immediately and on autopsy, the blood in the vessels was found to be coagulated, and some of the greatest blood vessels had burst in a fashion remindive of who perished of apoplexy. In a remarkably prescient interpretation, Fracassatus concluded that as an "apoplexy" was often caused by a similar coagulation of the blood, it might be cured by the *"timely infusion of some dissolvent into the veins"* (a premonition of the later use of anticoagulants). Subsequently Fracassatus experimented with injections of *spirit of vitriol* and *oil of tartar*, and as might be predicted his animals perished in considerable distress. On the contrary, when he administered *oil of sulphur* the dog not only survived despite repeated infusion but also demonstrated evidence of a considerable appetite *"by searching all the corners for meat and having found some bones, it fell a-gnawing of them with strange noises."*

Feeling somehow that his contributions had been ignored or even plagiarized, Robert Boyle of London was critical of this work, pointing out that three years earlier he had conducted similar experiments before the Royal Society at Gresham College (*not by chance but by design upon blood yet warm as it came from an animal*). He described mixing the blood with a small amount of *"aqua fortis or oil of vitriol or spirit of salt. These being* acid menstrums, *the blood would not only presently lose its pure color and become a dirty one but in a trice was also coagulated; whereas if some urinous spirit abounding in volatile salt, such as spirit of sal ammoniac, were mingled with the warm blood, it would not only curdle it or imbase its color but make it look rather more florid than before, and both keep it fluid and preserve it from putrefaction for a long time."*

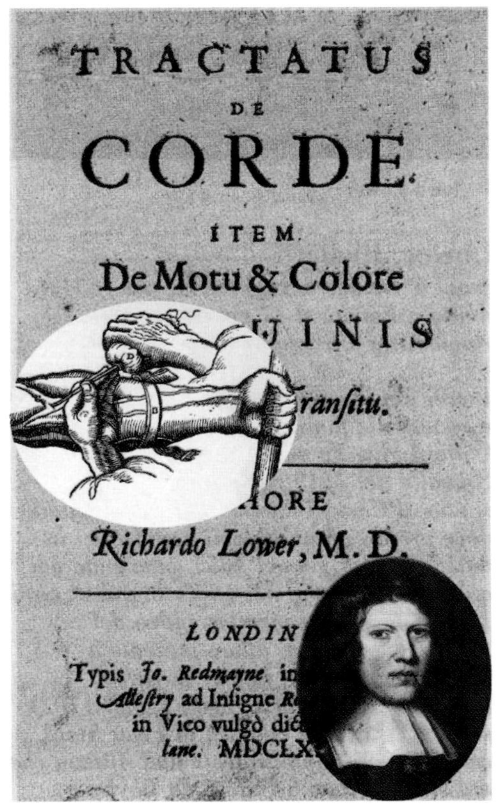

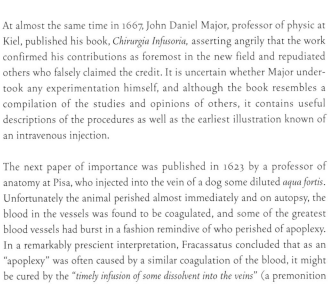

Richard Lower (1631-1691) of Cornwall and subsequently Oxford, was the first to perform the successful transfusion of blood from one animal to another in February 1665 and on November 23, 1667, repeated the procedure on one Arthur Coga in the presence of the Royal Society. After Robert Boyle had shown that air is essential to animal life, it was Lower who traced the interaction between air and the blood. Eventually the importance of oxygen, which was confused for a time by some as phlogiston, was revealed, although it was not until the late 18th century that the chemist Antoine-Laurent Lavoisier discovered the essential nature of oxygen and clarified its relation to respiration.

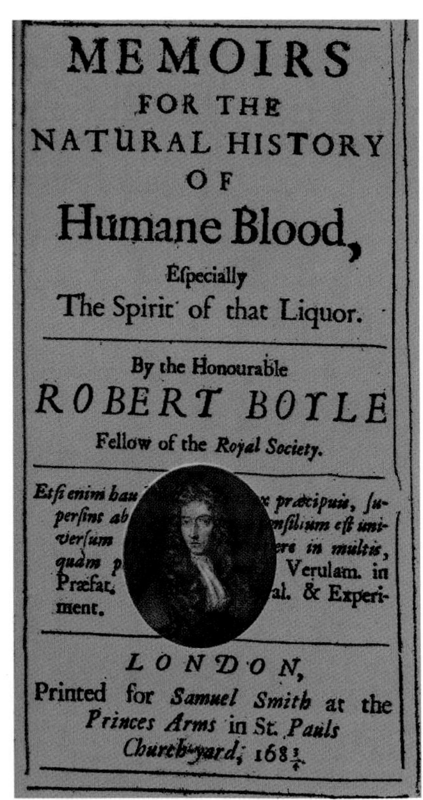

MEMOIRS
FOR THE
NATURAL HISTORY
OF
Humane Blood,
Especially
The Spirit of that Liquor.

By the Honourable
ROBERT BOYLE
Fellow of the Royal Society.

Etsi enim hau ... præcipuis, superfint ab ... nsilium est universum ... re in multis, quàm p ... Verulam. in Præfat. ... al. & Experiment.

LONDON,
Printed for Samuel Smith at the Princes Arms in St. Pauls Church-yard, 1683/4.

A publication by Robert Boyle detailing his thoughts on the subject of blood.

The next account of experimental intravenous injection into human beings comes from Dr. Vincent Fabritius, physician-in-ordinary to the city of Danzig, who recounted the events surrounding his decision to inject two drachms of a laxative mixture into three fit subjects in the city hospital. *"One of the patients was a lusty, robust soldier, dangerously infected with venereal disease and suffering grievous protuberatings of the bones of his arms. He, when the purgative liquor containing scammony was infused into him, complained of great pains in his elbows and the little valves of his arms did swell so visibly that it was necessary by a gentle compression of one's finger to stroke up that swelling towards the patient's shoulders. Some four hours after it began to work not very troublesomely, and so it did the next day, insomuch that the man had five good stools after it. Now here is the great point. Without any other remedies those protuberances were gone, nor are there any signs left of the above-mentioned disease."*

It is likely that not all the results were as spectacular as those described in the literature, and one can be certain that many fatalities were never recorded. An editorial in the *Philosophical Transactions* of the Royal Society referring to experimental work on intravenous injection and blood transfusion taking place on the Continent explained the cultural differences in experiments as follows:

> *"why the curious in England make a demure in practicing this experiment upon men… The philosophers of England would have practiced it long ago if they had not been so tender in hazarding the life of men (which they take such pains to preserve and relieve) nor so scrupulous to incur the penalties of the law which in England is more strict and nice in cases of this concernment than those of other nations are."*

As a result of diligent pursuit of this technique and the accumulation of considerable experience Dr. Ettmuller of Leipzig in 1668 was able to opine as follows:

It is now obvious from these examples that this operation is not only possible but is quite easy, especially so in the case of man, for he does not die so easily as does a beast. Consider, then, all the operations a surgeon has to perform – trepanning, laryngotomy, tapping the chest, cutting for hernias, etc. In comparison with such practice I would call infusory surgery a pleasant pastime which neither endangers the patient nor causes him suffering.

Purmann writing on the same subject almost a decade later in 1679, provided a more balanced analysis of the subject and a more thoughtful commentary:

That this Chirurgia Infusoria is beneficial in dangerous disease where the patient must be speedily helped, or all is lost, is very reasonable to believe; because the injected liquors speedily mix with the blood and are quickly conveyed to the heart and so through the whole body without suffering any alteration by the stomach or the several fermentative juices, but work immediately upon the diseases against which they are leveled. Wherefore I once again admonish the surgeon to inject the liquor leisurely, for otherwise it will not mix so well with the blood as it ought to do, but continue about the orifice and cause an apostema, which mismanagement has contributed not a little to the decrying and disuse of this admirable method. What liquors ought to be injected is the next particular, and therein the surgeon should take advice from an able physician to prevent any accidents that may happen. Purging and vomiting fluids are to be avoided, for they generally leave a malignity behind them, and for the same reason you must forbear the use of diuretics

Of particular interest was the concept embodied in the remedy referred to as the Spirit of Human Blood as described by no less an authority than Robert Boyle. It was an uncommon remedy, for blood was not only a commodity that was not freely available but healthy blood was in especially short supply, "being drawn from persons that parted with it out of custom or for prevention." To be safe and efficacious it was essential that the blood was obtained from healthy individuals since that acquired from persons of dubious health was clearly unlikely to be salubrious. The blood was dried, put in a retort and heated on a sand bath and the material distilled in this way was the spirit (spirit in this context was interpreted as the volatile salt of human blood). Boyle regarded it as an alkaline material similar to that obtained by distillation of hartshorn, urine or sal ammoniac; rather a disappointing substance compared to its name.

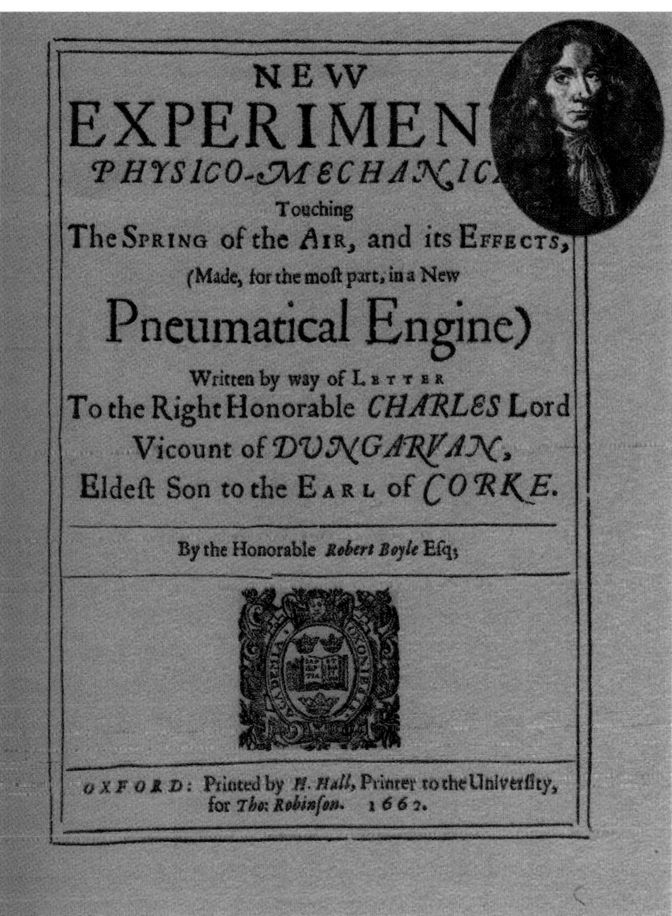

NEW
EXPERIMEN[TS]
PHYSICO-MECHANIC[ALL,]
Touching
The Spring of the Air, and its Effects,
(Made, for the most part, in a New
Pneumatical Engine)
Written by way of Letter
To the Right Honorable CHARLES Lord
Vicount of DUNGARVAN,
Eldest Son to the Earl of CORKE.

By the Honorable Robert Boyle Esq;

OXFORD: Printed by H. Hall, Printer to the University,
for Tho: Robinson. 1662.

Robert Boyle conducted pioneering experiments in which he demonstrated the physical characteristics of air and the necessary role of air in combustion, respiration, and the transmission of sound. He described this work in 1660 in New Experiments Physio-Mechanicall, Touching the Spring of the Air and its Effects. In 1662, in the second edition he appended his report of 1661 to the Royal Society on the relationship, now known as Boyle's law, that at a constant temperature the volume of a gas is inversely proportional to the pressure. In The Sceptical Chymist, *Boyle in 1661 attacked the Aristotelian theory of the four elements (earth, air, fire, and water) and also the three principles (salt, sulfur, and mercury) proposed by Paracelsus. Instead, he developed the concept of primary particles which by coalition produce corpuscles.*

Lorenz Heister described the technique and produced his own apparatus – a tube and bladder (bottom left) – for injecting liquors into the veins. He added a novel suggestion of his own, namely that the morbid blood should be removed and the patient "transfused with warm milk and broth in its stead".

and nephritics but alexipharmicks (antidotes to poisons) comforting and sweating fluids may be used with safety and success.

Heister in 1750 produced the best overall evaluation of the situation, and commented that he believed that intravenous medication was in theory likely to be most useful in patients who could not swallow. Overall the results were not only disappointing but even dangerous, with the therapy often worse than the disease. He noted "*...almost all the patients who have been this way treated have degenerated into a stupidity, foolishness or a raving or melancholy madness or else have been taken off with a sudden death either in or not long after the operation. These lamentable and fatal consequences have brought the art of injections and transfusions into neglect at present so that being suspected and condemned by proper judges at Paris, where they most flourished, we are told they were in a little time prohibited by public edict of that Government.*"

James Blundell, lecturer in physiology and midwifery at Guy's Hospital in 1818, had been interested for some years in the possibilities of successful blood transfusion in cases of post-partum hemorrhage. To this effect he had undertaken numerous animal experiments and having perfected the technique, wished to attempt a blood transfusion on a suitable human being. Fortuitously at this time "a poor fellow named Brazier," between thirty and forty years of age, was admitted to Guy's Hospital with what was subsequently proved to be "a scirrhosity of the pylorus." Vomiting had reduced him to a helpless and hopeless appearance, and Blundell considered that transfusion alone might restore the quality of his life and enable his survival. The patient was agreeable! Three physicians, five surgeons and several other gentlemen were present at the operation and supplied the blood. An ounce-and-a-half was taken by the syringe and immediately injected into the median vein, which had been opened by a lancet and into which a cannula had been placed and held in position by a finger. The operation began at two o'clock in the afternoon of 27 September 1818 and the procedure was repeated ten times in the course of thirty to forty minutes. Although no obvious change in the condition of the patient was evident during the transfusion, it was thought there were slight signs of improvement by the evening. Unfortunately, on the next day there was a dramatic deterioration in his condition and he died fifty-six hours after the start of the experiment. Blundell tried again without success on several occasions, but it was not until 7 December 1828 that he managed to produce a successful blood transfusion. The patient, a woman aged twenty-five years, was suffering from the results of a postpartum hemorrhage. Eight ounces of blood were injected during a period of three hours and the patient expressed herself very strongly on the benefits of the transfusion, saying that she felt as if "*life was being infused into her whole body.*"

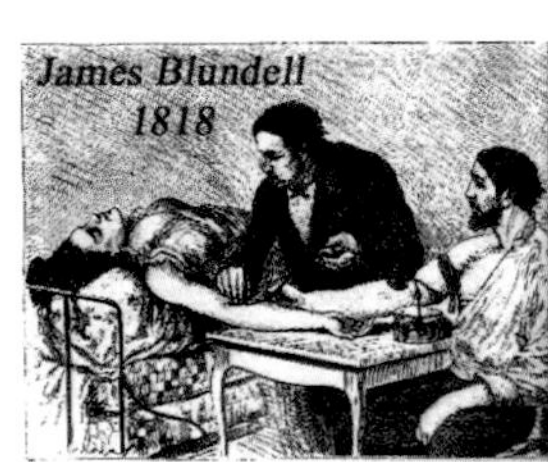

James Blundell of Guy's Hospital in London on Dec. 7, 1828 successfully transfused a woman with postpartum hemorrhage.

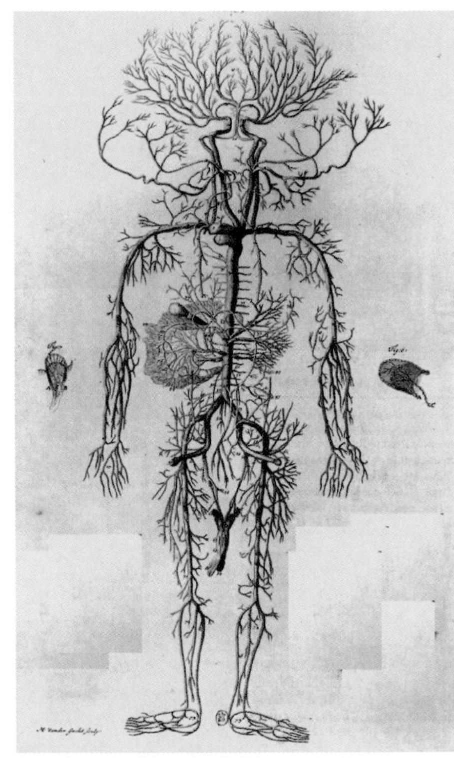

The anatomist William Cowper (1666-1709) produced a detailed description of the arteries of the horse. The elucidation of the circulation excited considerable interest as therapeutic possibilities became apparent and similar studies of the anatomy of the human circulatory system were undertaken.

During studies performed in the early 1820s, François Magendie of Paris had found on frequent occasions that the injection of warm water into the veins of a mad dog would make it quiet. Thus in October 1823, when asked to see a man in the Hôtel Dieu suffering from hydrophobia, who despite copious venesection still had violent paroxysms and was clearly dying, Magendie elected to give an intravenous injection of water. Despite the help of six of the strongest students to hold the patient down, Magendie had difficulty in

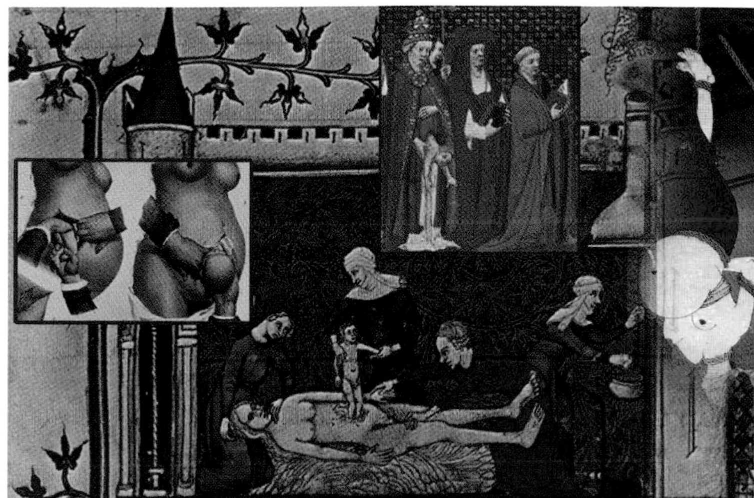

Loss of blood and its replacement had long been perceived as major medical problems, particularly in pregnancy. The first desperate attempts to operate on the abdomen were inspired by the desire to save the child of a dying mother. In the reign of the Roman king, Numa, the Caesarean operation was supported by law. Thus the Lex Regia stated: Si mater pregnas mortua sit, fructus quam primum caute extrahitur *(if a pregnant mother die the child [fruit] must first be removed). The procedure was thus legally obligated in order to save the child in the case of death of a pregnant woman. Although it is reported that Julius Caesar was born in this manner it is highly unlikely since even at the time of the Gallic Wars it is noted that he was writing letters to his mother. The first successful attempt at a Caesarean section on a living woman was reported to have been undertaken by Jacob Nufer, a sow gelder, in 1500.*

getting his cannula into the vein, but finally succeeded in injecting two pints of warm water. The recovery of the patient was dramatic but, unfortunately, complications supervened and nine days later he died of septicemia, probably caused by the two lancets that had broken off and remained in his body after the process of bloodletting. Further unsuccessful trials of Magendie's method by other physicians were made elsewhere in Europe and England before it became clear that the method was a failure.

Nevertheless, such was the reputation of Magendie's in America that it prompted a dramatic medical experiment in intravenous medication in Boston. In 1824 a young physician named Hale allowed half an ounce of castor oil at a temperature of 70°F to be injected into the vein of his left arm by a friend who did not do the job very skillfully and engendered the loss of eight ounces of blood. Hale initially noted an oily taste in his mouth, which was followed by nausea and belching, trismus, and dizziness, and then a major bowel evacuation. Although the experiment resulted in a month of illness, the arm in particular being swollen and inflamed, his strong constitution permitted recovery and he was rewarded for his courage with a prize.

FORMULAIRE

POUR

LA PRÉPARATION ET L'EMPLOI

DE PLUSIEURS

NOUVEAUX MÉDICAMENTS,

Tels que la Morphine, la Codéine, l'acide Prussique, la Strychnine, la Vératrine, l'Éther hydrocianique, le Sulfate de Quinine, la Cinchonine, l'Émétine, la Salicine, le Brôme, l'Iode, l'Iodure de Mercure, le Cyanure de Potassium, l'Huile de Croton tiglium, les Sels d'or, les Sels de Platine, le Chlore, les Chlorures de chaux et de Soude, les Bi-Carbonates Alcalins, la Grenadine, le Phosphore, l'acide Lactique, l'Huile volatile de Moutarde, etc., etc.

PAR F. MAGENDIE,

Membre de l'Institut, titulaire de l'Académie royale de Médecine, Médecin de l'Hôtel-Dieu de Paris, Professeur de médecine au Collège royal de France, etc., etc.

NEUVIÈME ÉDITION.

A PARIS,

CHEZ MÉQUIGNON-MARVIS, PÈRE ET FILS,

LIBRAIRES-ÉDITEURS, RUE DU JARDINET, N° 13.

MAI 1836.

François Magendie (1783-1855). The French experimental physiologist whose pioneer studies of the effects of drugs on various parts of the body led to the scientific introduction into medical practice of such compounds as strychnine and morphine, was also the first to prove the functional difference of the spinal nerves. Magendie was one of the first to observe anaphylaxis when he noted (1839) that rabbits able to tolerate a single injection of egg albumin often died following a second injection. In 1822 he confirmed and elaborated the observation by the Scottish anatomist Sir Charles Bell (1811) that the anterior roots of the spinal nerves are motor in function, while the posterior roots serve to communicate sensory impulses. In 1821 he founded the first periodical of experimental physiology, Journal de Physiologie Expérimentale, *and was appointed professor of medicine at the Collège de France, Paris, in 1831. Magendie greatly influenced (1841-43) the intellectual development of his student, Claude Bernard, who subsequently became a renowned physiologist. In 1821 Magendie was elected to the French Academy of Sciences and became its president in 1837.*

Cholera was regarded as a virtual death sentence since the sequelae of fluid and electrolyte loss were irreversible without intravenous access. To avoid contamination strange measures were taken and every magical and herbal remedy conceivable was employed in an attempt to ward off the disease.

In 1832, during the cholera epidemic, an Edinburgh surgeon, Thomas Latta, had been impressed by an article on the postmortem findings in that disease. It recorded *"that there was a very great deficiency of the water and saline matter of the blood, on which deficiency the thick, black, cold state of the vital fluid depends, which evidently produces most of the distressing symptoms of that fearful complaint and is doubtless often the cause of death."* Latta attempted to replace the fluid loss by means of copious enemata of warm water, holding the requisite salts and by administering fluids by mouth. Finding these methods useless, and even harmful, he decided *"to throw fluid immediately into the circulation."* The osmotic

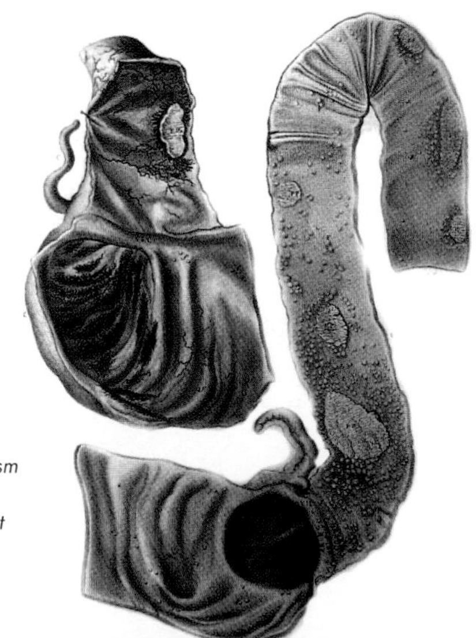

Small Bowel Cholera. The dramatic damage caused by the organism cholera to the bowel was only exceeding by the devastating loss of life as a result of fluid and electrolyte disturbances that could not be adequately remedied.

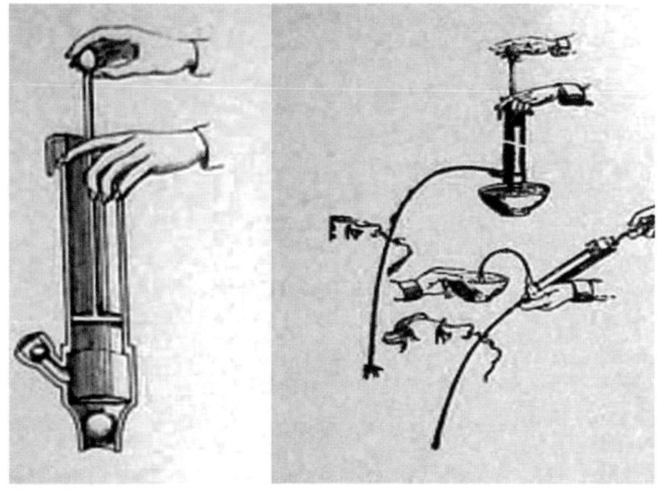

Latta used a modification of the enema syringe that had been patented by Read of Guy's Hospital to administer the intravenous replacement fluid.

pressure of his solution was about one-third of that used today and it was very slightly alkaline in reaction. His first patient was an old woman on whom all the usual remedies for cholera had been tried without effect, with the result that she was almost moribund, and that even a dangerous experimental treatment could not be deemed to harm her further. Latta inserted a tube into the median basilic vein and slowly injected six pints of water containing two or three drachms muriate (or chloride of soda and two scruples subcarbonate of soda at a temperature of 112°F. The injection took half an hour, at the end of which time she expressed in a firm voice that she was free from all uneasiness, actually became jocular and fancied all she needed was a little sleep. Her extremities were warm and every feature bore the aspect of comfort and health. Delighted with the outcome Latta departed but soon thereafter the vomiting and diarrhoea recurred, and she died six hours later. As a result of this sad event, Latta realized that despite any degree of improvement the patient should never be left, and everything held in readiness for a second or a third injection. As a result of this continuous therapy a *"very destitute woman of fifty"* was given sixteen-and-a-half pints of fluid in twelve hours, and her life was saved. In yet another case, nineteen pints were injected in fifty-three hours with a similar success and Latta was able to present a convincing argument in favor of the early use of intravenous injections of saline in cases of cholera. Indeed, the principles of his therapy instituted in 1832, still remain in contemporary usage.

The apparatus he utilized consisted of Read's patent syringe, already in use for giving enemata, washing out the stomach, and a number of other modifications. A silver tube was attached to the extremity of the flexible injecting tube and the syringe had to be of perfect design in order to avoid the risk of injecting air. The fluid was never injected more than once into the same orifice, and the vein was treated with delicacy to avoid phlebitis. If the wound did not heal by first intention it was "poulticed" and carefully watched. As might be predicted, given the circumstances, the injections were by no means always successful, and out of fifteen cholera patients so treated, ten died. Nevertheless, a 30 percent survival was a considerable improvement over the previous 95 percent mortality.

As a consequence of what was perceived of as a remarkable piece of work, Latta's method was tested throughout the United Kingdom. Its success may be judged from a survey of the literature a decade later that revealed that out of 282 patients (some of whom lived in destitute conditions) in whom intravenous saline had been used, 61 (approx. 22 percent) recovered. Apart from demise due to the disease, it was noted that several instances of air embolism and venous thrombosis had occurred. The largest amount of fluid utilized

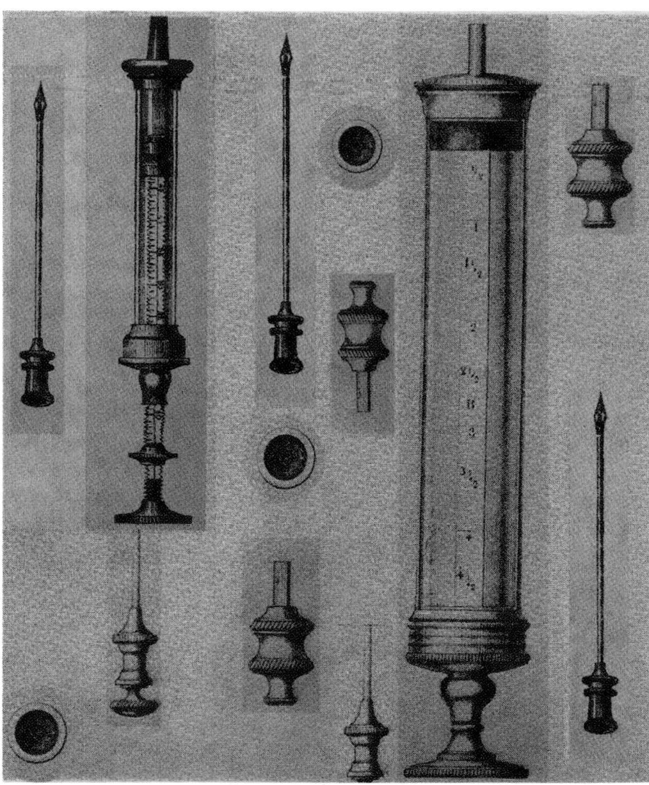

The Bruns syringe was regarded as a major advance in the evolution of therapy since it provided a safe and reliable method of transdermal or intravenous access.

The devastating morbidity and mortality of cholera were a source of considerable anxiety and frustration to both the public and physicians. Unusual garments festooned with amulets, herbs, and charms were used as a desperate attempt to ward off the ill effects of the disease.

was the twenty-four pints given (with complete success) at seven operations in the space of thirteen hours to a twenty-nine-year-old blacksmith. A notable benefit of the treatment was recorded. Namely, that even if the patient ultimately died, the temporary recovery engendered in almost all instances by the fluid might allow him, if he so desired, to execute a will! Over the next fifty years the solution was modified such that its constitution was as follows: chloride of sodium, 60 parts; chloride of potassium, 6; phosphate of soda, 3; carbonate of soda, 20; of which mixture 140 grains were dissolved in 2 pints of distilled water and filtered. This was about twice the strength of the solution used by Latta. It corresponded in osmotic pressure to about 0.67% of sodium chloride, and therefore was about 75% of the tonicity of solutions currently in use.

An interesting diversion in the development of intravenous access was the use (1850) of syringes to inject varicose veins with sclerosants.

One of the main problems of this therapy was the absence of an adequate device to administer the fluid. Syringes were large, cumbersome, unreliable and difficult to use; in particular the concept of an ideal needle remained unfulfilled. The early design of an adequate device was initiated in 1844, when Francis Rynd, an Irish surgeon working in the Meath Hospital, Dublin, reported giving a hypodermic injection to a woman of fifty-nine, complaining of trigeminal neuralgia. "*On 3 June a solution of fifteen grains of acetate of morphia dissolved in one drachm of creosote was introduced into the region of the supra-orbital nerve and along the course of the temporal, malar and buccal nerves by four punctures of an instrument specially made for the purpose.*" Rynd claimed that the relief from pain was instantaneous and when a slight recurrence occurred a week later, a further two punctures were undertaken. Thereafter the patient was completely relieved of her symptoms. Rynd was secretive about his instrument and delayed publishing a description for seventeen years until 1861. The device was, in fact, a trochar and cannula, designed in such a fashion that the former could be retracted by means of a spring operated from the handle allowing the fluid to be injected through the hole (E), using "*a common writing pen,*" presumably a quill.

A somewhat different angle was provided by French physicians, who in the early 1850s endeavored to obtain a cure of varicose veins by the injection of sclerosing solutions. The use of perchloride of iron and iodotannic acid led to some early enthusiasm, but the procedure was soon abandoned due to local pain and ulceration, sepsis and a recurrence of the varicosities. However, in 1853 Alexander Wood, an Edinburgh physician, greatly advanced the study of hypodermic medication by developing a technique that led essentially to the concept of local anesthesia. While endeavoring to remove a nevus by injection with a solution of perchloride of iron, using a small syringe constructed for this purpose by Mr. Ferguson of Giltspur Street, London, it occurred to Wood that such a syringe might easily enable

Francis Rynd (1801-1861) (inset) was one of the leading members of the Dublin School of Medicine and together with John Cheyne (Cheyne-Stokes respiration) and Robert Graves (Graves disease) made important contributions to medicine. In 1845 Rynd published in the Dublin Medical Press a detailed report of the instrument he had devised for hypodermic injections (background).

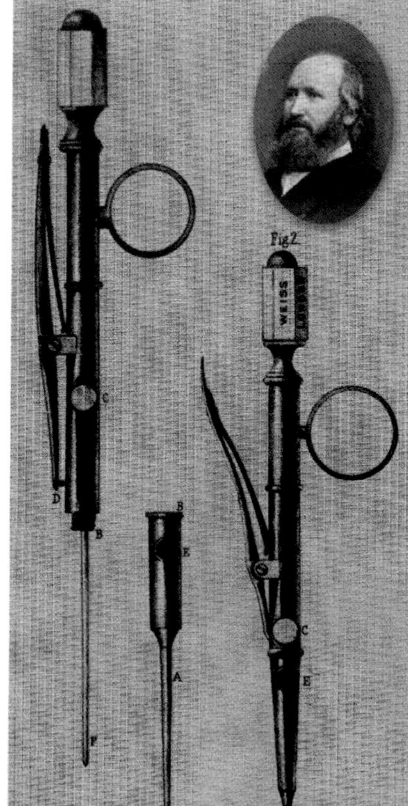

In 1853, Alexander Wood (inset) of Edinburgh developed a syringe that enabled him to produce local anesthesia by injecting muriate of morphine into the acromio-clavicular joint to remove cervico-brachial neuralgia.

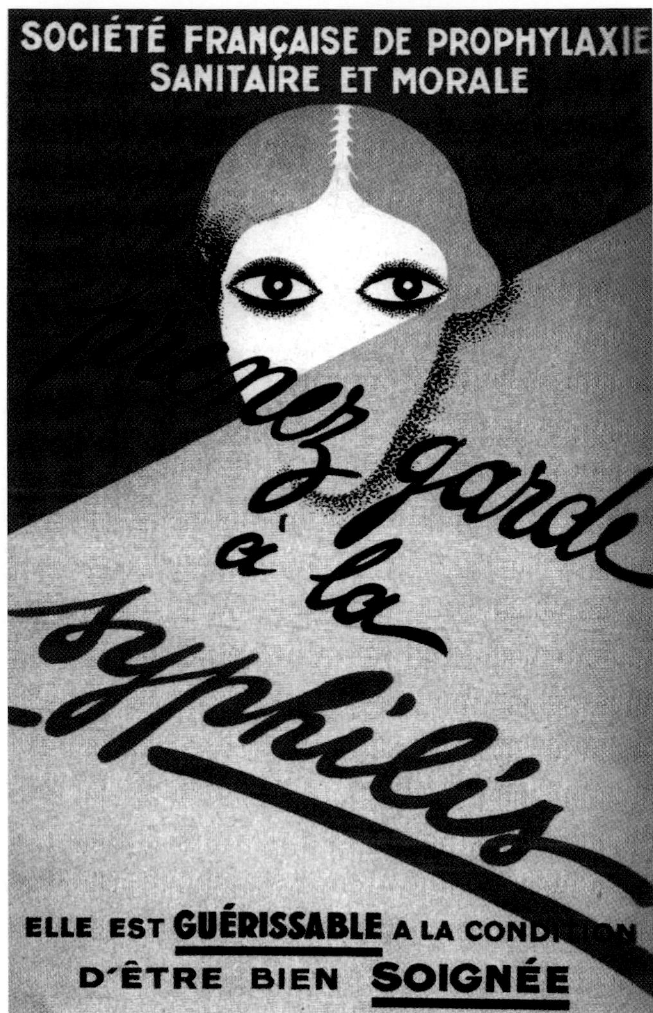

SOCIÉTÉ FRANÇAISE DE PROPHYLAXIE
SANITAIRE ET MORALE
ELLE EST GUÉRISSABLE A LA COND
D'ÊTRE BIEN SOIGNÉE

Public admonitions against the dangers of syphilis reached their peak in the early 20th century once it became apparent that the disease was due to a treponeme and communicated by sexual contact; guilt and its association with disease being a prevalent theme that had prevailed since the advent of religion. The advent of an intravenous therapy – Salvarsan – despite its toxicity, proved to be a major therapeutic advance.

him to inject a narcotic into the region of the affected nerve in cases of neuralgia. Thus on 28 November 1853, while treating an elderly spinster suffering from cervico-brachial neuralgia, he determined to evaluate his idea. Having ascertained that the most tender spot was in the region of the acromio-clavicular joint, he inserted the syringe in that region and injected twenty drops of the solution of muriate of morphia of a strength of about double that of the official preparation. This was equivalent to about two-fifths of a grain of morphine. *"In about ten minutes after the withdrawal of the syringe the patient began to complain of giddiness and confusion of ideas; in half an hour the pain had subsided and I left her in anticipation of a refreshing sleep. I visited her again at eleven next morning and was a little annoyed to find that she had never wakened. The breathing also was somewhat deep and she was roused with difficulty. Under the use of somewhat energetic stimuli, however, these symptoms disappeared, and from that time to this the neuralgia has not returned."* One of Wood's syringes still remains in the Museum of the Royal College of Surgeons of Edinburgh. It is 90 mm in length and the barrel is 10 mm in diameter. The piston is wrapped round at its extremity with cotton wick to make the plunger fit the barrel, and at its apex the syringe is drawn into a conoidal extremity to fit a metallic cap. Wood modified Ferguson's original design, evolving a small glass syringe graduated like a drop measure, and to this he attached a small needle, hollow, and having an aperture near the point like the sting of a wasp.

Despite considerable experimentation and some novel uses, textbooks of medicine prior to 1890 still for the most part, *"referred to the saline treatment of cholera"* as the only example of intravenous medication. In 1890 Baccelli used quinine successfully to treat malaria and four years later he used mercury to treat syphilis and carbolic acid to treat tetanus. Sodium cinnamate, under the trade name of *Hetol*, was given intravenously in 1892 to treat tuberculosis, and although even colloidal metals were injected successfully, little serious progress was made. Indeed, in 1905 Allbutt and Rolleston's great *System of Medicine* stated: *"intravenous injection is practically only used for the introduction of large quantities of saline fluid, though ammonia has been given."* There was, however, a note in the chapter dealing with malaria, of the value of quinine given intravenously and, by 1907 the intravenous use of diphtheria anti-toxin had gained some degree of acceptability. The arsenic preparation atoxyl (40% arsenic) was first used intravenously in 1905 to treat trypanosomiasis and was advised that high doses should be administered for a long period, pushing the injections to the maximum amount that the patient could stand without headache or nausea. Salvarsan was used intravenously to treat syphilis in 1910 and, two years later, neo-Salvarsan was similarly administered. Thereafter the rapid improvements of technique and device resulted in major advances in the intravenous administration of drugs.

Transfusion

The use of blood in the treatment of disease dates back to the time of primitive man. The history of this phase of human thought is very extensive and complicated, involving such apparently diverse notions as vampirism and the bloody lintel of the Passover. There is a certain amount of evidence to indicate that the practice of phlebotomy itself grew directly out of magical beliefs. Blood, as far as the primitive was concerned, was the seat of life and was used in magical practices. It is a common practice of some of the tribes of Africa and the Australian aboriginals to give human blood to the sick and aged for the purpose of strengthening them. In order that the blood may have this effect, it need not always be drunk by the infirm person; it is enough to sprinkle it on his body. Some of these rituals endured surprisingly long and a few have even persisted into modern times. The practice of circumcision has its origin in blood magic and, even in Christian times, infanticide was suggested in order to obtain pure blood by which the life of a dying monarch might be supported. In the seventeenth century it was hoped that the transfusion of blood might be a useful accessory to the practice of phlebotomy. Since phlebotomy was originally employed for the purpose of eliminating some supposedly noxious humor which had entered into the blood and was causing the disease, a natural extension of the idea of evacuating polluted blood was the concept that its replacement by healthy blood would be beneficial.

The earliest known form of elective surgery (top right) was the operation of circumcision. Blood loss, "although usually minimal", could be dramatic if the "mohel" or priest was unskilled. Such catastrophes provided an early focus on the critical role of blood in life and the therapeutic power conferred by transfusion.

An 18th-century depiction of intravenous technique explored the concept of transfusion. The pioneer of the technique, Richard Lower (top right), was an original thinker whose association with Thomas Boyle and Christopher Wren at Oxford University embraced a triumvirate of the greatest scientific thinkers of their generation.

Although it is not exactly clear how early this notion arose, early in the fifteenth century Pope Innocent VIII (1432-1492) was transfused, and Marsilio Ficino (1433-1499) mentioned transfusion as a possible therapeutic procedure. At the beginning of the seventeenth century many writers suggested its use, including Andreas Libavius (1546-1616), who mentioned that a previous operator brought about a double fatality as a result of transfusion. In 1615 Libavius gave a full description of the technique of the operation, which involved the use of silver tubes inserted into the arteries, and in 1628 Giovanni Colle (1558-1631), professor of medicine at Padua, described a similar method of transfusion. In 1653, Robert Des Bagets designed a perfusion apparatus which differed from that originally described by Libavius by virtue of the fact that it included a pumping machine. Francesco Folli (1624-1685) demonstrated the technique of transfusion on August 13, 1654, in the presence of Ferdinand II, and between 1657 until 1669 an English group including Christopher Wren, Boyle, and, later, Lower, performed some experiments on the transfusion of blood and the intravenous injection of drugs. In 1661 Moritz Hoffmann (1622-1698) and also Johann Sigismund Elsholtz (1623-1688) wrote on the subject of transfusion. Subsequent writers were John Daniel Major (1634-1693), in 1667, Jean-Baptiste Denis (d. 1704), in 1668, Paolo Manfredi (*fl.* 1660), in 1668, and many others both before and afterward.

Despite widespread interest and prolific usage, both transfusion and intravenous injection had met with such poor success that by the end of the seventeenth century they were almost completely abandoned and preserved only as experimental procedures, and even in this respect they had fallen into disrepute. Nevertheless the concept of transfusion remained as the last refuge of the intellectually and therapeutically destitute, such that even the venerable Malpighi was transfused in his final illness during 1694. Textbooks of surgery, such as Heister's *Large Surgery*, usually listed the methods and reviewed the literature, but injection techniques were not destined to be re-employed for therapeutic purposes until the nineteenth century, when they made their re-entry not as intravenous but as hypodermic procedures. Transfusion of blood did not return until still later, after bacteriology and pathology had developed a partial appreciation of antibody formation and Landsteiner and Weiner had defined blood groups. The critical phase of the development and introduction of hypodermic injection and the development of the Pravaz syringe (Charles-Gabriel Pravaz, 1791-1853) awaited significant advances in the purification and concentration of drugs.

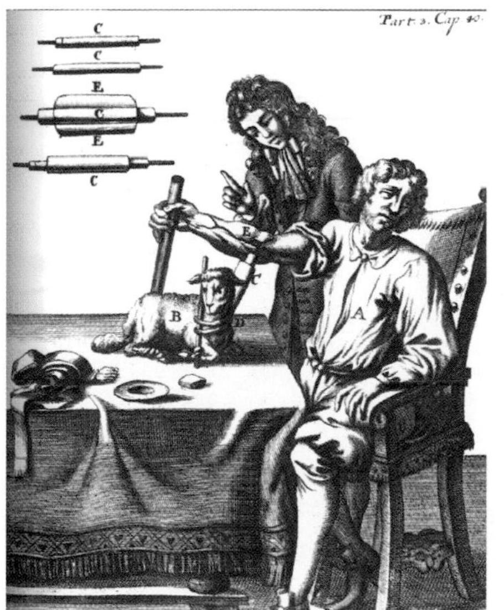

Although the theoretical value of blood replacement was evident to early physicians, the inherent incompatibility issues were unappreciated. Thus the early use of lamb's blood with its predictable consequences led to disappointment.

[illegible]benschrift, 1901, Nr. 46.
[illegible]1, Wickenburggasse 13.

Aus dem pathologisch-anatomischen Institute in Wien.

Ueber Agglutinationserscheinungen normalen menschlichen Blutes.

Von Dr. **Karl Landsteiner**, Assistenten am pathologisch-anatomischen Institute.

Vor einiger Zeit habe ich beobachtet und mitgetheilt[1]), dass öfters Blutserum von normalen Menschen rothe Blutkörperchen anderer gesunder Individuen zu verklumpen im Stande ist. Ich hatte damals den Eindruck, dass in manchen Kr[illegible]llen diese verklumpende Eigenschaft des Bl[illegible] Blutkörperchen gegenüber besonders [illegible]te, dass sie mit dem von M[illegible]chteten starken Lösungsver[illegible]le Körperchen in Zusamm[illegible] und Lösungsvermögen [illegible]ich ändern. Gegen d[illegible]agliano mit der [illegible]chen Reactionen [illegible] nicht Erwärmen [illegible] Gehalt, der de[illegible]ögen der Sera a[illegible]ne Beobachtung [illegible] Hämolyse durch a[illegible] Fall das Hämoglo[illegible] wird. Ein wesentlich[illegible]nd der von Maragli[illegible]aragliano das Serum a[illegible] selben Individuum stammen[illegible] nur mit krankhaftem Blut gel[illegible] zeigte aber gerade Unterschiede recht [illegible]wischen Blutserum und Körperchen verschiedener anscheinend völlig gesunder Menschen.

Die Beobachtung von Shattock[3]) gehört dagegen nach der Beschreibung und Abbildung des Autors zweifellos hieher, wenn er auch die Reaction nur bei fieberhaften Krankheiten nachweist und sie bei normalem Blut vermisst. Shattock bringt

[1]) Centralblatt für Bacteriologie, XXVII, S. 361, v. 10. Februar 1900.
[2]) XI. Congress für innere Medicin. Leipzig 1892.
[3]) Journ. of Pathol. and Bacteriology. Februar 1900.

1

Karl Landsteiner (1868-1943). In 1930, Landsteiner received the Noble Prize for medicine for his discovery of the four major human blood groups, which he had initially identified in 1901. In 1927, he identified the M and N groups and in 1940, he discovered the Rhesus (Rh factor).

Section 8

AGENTS and REMEDIES

The Magistery of Bismuth

Bismuth has been known since the earliest of times, although it had not been clearly recognized as a separate metal and was often confused with others such as lead, antimony, and tin. In the Middle Ages miners even considered bismuth to be nothing more than a stage in the development of silver from baser metals.

Indeed, this belief was so prevalent that considerable dismay was expressed at the discovery of a vein of bismuth, since it was believed that the process of conversion of bismuth to silver had been interrupted. The miners referred to bismuth as *"tectum argenti"* or roof of silver since it was often found above a layer of this metal. In the fifteenth century the chemiatrist, Johann Thölde, who wrote under the pseudonym of the mythical monk, Basil Valentine, discovered hydrochloric acid and argued powerfully on behalf of the use of antimony in the treatment of fevers (*The Triumphal Chariot of Antimony, 1504*).

A 15th-century distillation apparatus.

Somewhere between 1450 and 1470, Thölde referred to the antimony-related element (bismuth) as *wismut*, a name probably derived from the German word *wis mat or Wissmuth* meaning white mass. It has, alternatively, been suggested that the real origin of the word bismuth may be derived from the Arabic phrase *"bi smid"* which means, *"to have the properties of antimony."* Additional explanations propose that the origin of the word is from "*Wiese*" meaning meadow, since a meadow is often covered by red poppies much like bismuth, which may exhibit a red hue from a thin layer of bismuth oxide.

The first formal assessment of bismuth's properties was provided by Georgius Agricola (1490-1555), the founder of mineralogy, born Georg Bauer in Claucau, Saxony (March 24, 1494). He studied classics, philosophy, and philology at the University of Leipzig and following the custom of his times, latinized his name to Georgius Agricola. Although highly educated as a classicist and a humanist, he became one of the first individuals to establish a natural science based upon observation as opposed to speculation. His text, *Bermannus, sive de Re Metallica*, dealing specifically with the arts of mining and smelting, was one of the first of its kind. His second publication, *De Natura Fossilium*, considered the first mineralogy text book, represented the first scientific classification of minerals based on their physical properties and described many new minerals, including bismuth, as well as their occurrence and mutual relationships.

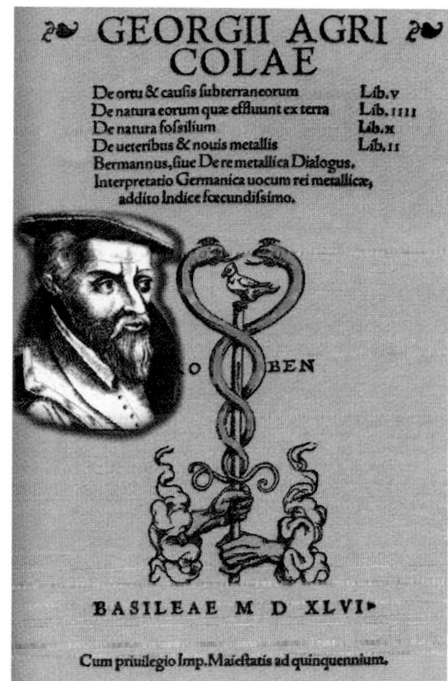

GEORGII AGRICOLAE

De ortu & causis subterraneorum Lib. v
De natura eorum quæ effluunt ex terra Lib. IIII
De natura fossilium Lib. x
De ueteribus & nouis metallis Lib. II
Bermannus, siue De re metallica Dialogus.
Interpretatio Germanica uocum rei metallicæ, addito Indice fœcundissimo.

BASILEAE M D XLVI

Cum priuilegio Imp. Maiestatis ad quinquennium.

A compendium of the diverse works of Georgius Agricola (inset).

Having taught Latin and Greek from 1518-22 in a school in Zwickau, he returned to Leipzig and undertook the study of medicine. Unfortunately, given the theological disarray of the times, Agricola sought the more congenial surroundings of Padua and Bologna in 1523, where he continued his study of medicine, philosophy, and natural science before completing his medical training with clinical experience in Venice. During his time in Venice he prepared an edition of Galen's work of medicine (published 1525) at the Aldine Press and collaborated with John Clement, who had been Thomas More's secretary during the writing of Utopia. During this time he became a friend of the scholar, Erasmus, who subsequently wrote the introduction to Agricola's first book, the mineralogical treatise *Bermannus, sive de Re Metallica*. In 1526, Agricola returned to Saxony and became the town physician of Joachimsthal, a major city in the richest metal mining district of Europe. Agricola was, however, not a particularly talented physician and preferred to devote his energies to the study of minerals. The choice of this location reflected Agricola's interest in seeking to identify medical agents among the new ores and minerals of the area. Although he failed in this quest, his interest in mining resulted in substantial contributions to the

BASIL VALENTINE HIS Triumphant Chariot OF ANTIMONY, WITH ANNOTATIONS OF Theodore Kirkringius, M. D.

LONDON

CVRRVS TRIVMPHALIS ANTIMONII

THEODORI KERCKRINGII DOCTORIS MEDICI COMMENTARIUS IN CURRUM TRIUMPHALEM

AMSTELODAMI,

Theodore Kerckring's commentary on The Triumphal Chariot of Antimony, purported to have been originally written by Basil Valentine.

A 15th-century alchemical laboratory presents a picture of industrious labor admixed with scholarship.

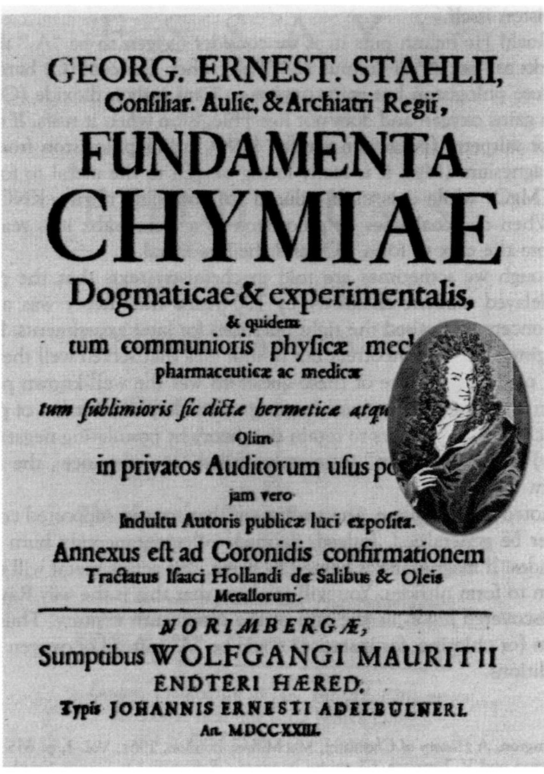

GEORG. ERNEST. STAHLII,
Confiliar. Aulic, & Archiatri Regii,
FUNDAMENTA
CHYMIAE
Dogmaticae & experimentalis,
& quidem
tum communioris phyficæ mec[...]
pharmaceuticæ ac medicæ
tum fublimioris fic dictæ hermeticæ atq[...]
Olim
in privatos Auditorum ufus p[...]
jam vero
Indultu Autoris publicæ luci expofita.
Annexus eft ad Coronidis confirmationem
Tractatus Ifaaci Hollandi de Salibus & Oleis
Metallorum.
NORIMBERGÆ,
Sumptibus WOLFGANGI MAURITII
ENDTERI HÆRED.
Typis JOHANNIS ERNESTI ADELBULNERI.
An. MDCCXXIII.

The frontispiece of George Stahl's text "Fundamenta Chymiae."

scholarship of the area of metallurgy. In 1533, he became the town physician of Chemnitz and remained there until his death in 1555. One year thereafter his classical text, *Bermannus, sive Re Metallica*, was published, which apart from containing detailed descriptions of the geology of ore bodies, surveying, mine construction, pumping and ventilation, included the first substantial description of bismuth and the methods utilized to mine and purify it. He is credited with Latinizing the older terminology to *bisemutum* and described both its distinctive qualities and how it could be refined from its ores.

Thus, by the middle of the eighteenth century, bismuth was accepted as a specific metal and texts on its chemistry were published in 1739 by the German chemist, Johann Heinrich Pott, and subsequently in 1753 by the Frenchman, Claude-François Geoffroy. Subsequently Georg Ernst Stahl studied bismuth and established definitively its characteristics. In 1850, the synthesis of triethyl bismuth by C. Löwig and E. Schweizer inaugurated the study of the chemistry of organo-bismuth compounds. Unfortunately, the spontaneous inflammability of these trialkyl derivatives limited investigation in the field until A. Michaelis and A. Polis prepared triphenyl bismuth in 1887. This aromatic compound was stable in air and could be converted to a pentavalent dichloride or dibromide that possessed unusual stability. In 1913, F. Challenger reported investigations on the preparations of organically optically active organo-bismuth compounds including bismuth trisulfide.

Properties and General Applications

Bismuth is the heaviest non-radioactive element, possesses two stable isotopes and has an atomic number of 83 and an atomic weight of 209. It has a valence of 3 and is in the same periodic table group (Va) as antimony, arsenic, and phosphorus. Bismuth is the most diamagnetic of all metals (exhibits the greatest opposition to being magnetized) and has the lowest thermal conductivity except mercury. It is hard, brittle, lustrous, and coarsely crystalline and can be distinguished by its color – gray/white with a reddish tinge.

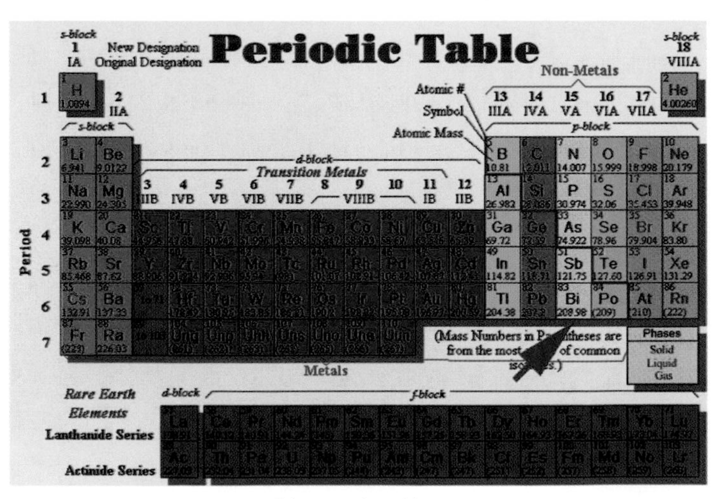

A contemporary representation of the Periodic Table.

A variety of bismuth salts are derived from bismuth nitrate, which in turn is produced by the action of nitric acid on free bismuth or bismuth ores. Following the separation from the acid, bismuth nitrate is hydrolyzed to bismuth subnitrate, which can then react in solution with soluble basic salts to form bismuth subcarbonate, subgallate, subsalicylate, or subcitrate. In medical preparations bismuth subsalicylate and bismuth subcitrate are the two most frequently used bismuth compounds. The salts of bismuth salts are relatively insoluble in water but increase somewhat (but not completely) in hydrochloric acid. Thus, the majority of ingested bismuth is converted in the stomach to the insoluble oxide, hydroxide, and oxychloride forms. Most bismuth salts thus form a precipitate mainly of bismuth oxychloride in the stomach and only trace amounts of bismuth are absorbed in the gastrointestinal tract. The mechanism is probably via localization on the brush broader, glycocalyx, of intestinal enterocytes and subsequent phagocytosis. In the colon, bismuth salts are converted to black bismuth sulfide by the action of bacteria producing hydrogen sulfide, and as a result of this chemical reaction the stools become black. The salts of bismuth are frequently used in the manufacture of "*soothing agents*" for the treatment of digestive disorders, in outlining the alimentary tract during x-ray examination, and in treating injuries and infections of the skin. The oxychloride (BiOCl) has been used to impart a pearlescent quality to lipstick, nail polish, and eye shadow.

Medical Applications

General

It is not certain when the medical properties of bismuth first became apparent, but the early works of Thölde and Paracelsus (sixteenth century) dealt in detail with the use of many metals. Prior to that, considerable emphasis had been placed upon the evaluation of diverse herbal remedies and most pharmacopoeia were little more than extrapolations of the second-century works of Galen, Dioscorides, and their followers. Although the therapeutic properties of bismuth were considered as early as 1660, there exist vague references prior to that to its use in oils and salves. In 1733 it was first documented as use in a salve but before 1786, there may actually have been internal usage. In 1794 Ernst Anton Nicolai (1722-1802) produced one of the earliest medical thesis on the subject. "*De Usu Magisterii Bismuthi Medico Interno*" described in detail the diverse uses of "Magistery of Bismuth" available to the medical profession.

Over the subsequent three centuries, a diverse variety of bismuth medications have emerged, and the popularity of the agent has waxed and waned with the vagaries of therapeutic fashion. Traditional medications containing bismuth have ranged from ointments and salves to injectibles, liquids, colloidal suspensions, and tablets. Topically, it has been employed as an emollient, an astringent, and an anti-infective; peripherally as an anti-syphilitic, and orally for the treatment variously of amoebiasis, diarrhea, abdominal colic and dyspepsia. As a result of considerable publicity and widespread acceptance in the public domain, bismuth has been extremely popular as a medication and was widely used. In 1918, it was marketed under the name of "Bismosol" by the Norwich Pharmacal Company, and thereafter as "Pepto-Bismol" by the Procter and Gamble group. After 1950, the use of bismuth was for practical purposes limited to over-the-counter preparations and A.C. Ivy (1893-1978) and M. Grossman (1919-1981) had noted that, despite its efficacy, it was ineffective as an antacid. Indeed, the advent of antacids considerably decreased the use of bismuth in the United States, but elsewhere in the world the agent continued to be widely used. In France, bismuth salts were highly regarded as a panacea for a wide variety of gastrointestinal disorders, although little was known regarding their precise mode of action. Similarly in Australia, bismuth in its subgallate form became widely utilized as a stool deodorizer for patients who had undergone a colostomy. Thus, despite the passage of time and the advent of numerous alternative therapeutic agents, the usage of bismuth remained widespread. In fact, in 1950 it was estimated to be a component of the medical cabinet of as many as 60 percent of American households and regarded by the layperson as an indispensable agent in the management of abdominal pain, diarrhea, and dyspepsia. Nevertheless, the fear of harmful effects (encephalopathy in particular) somewhat inhibited investigation of the serious medical usage of the agent.

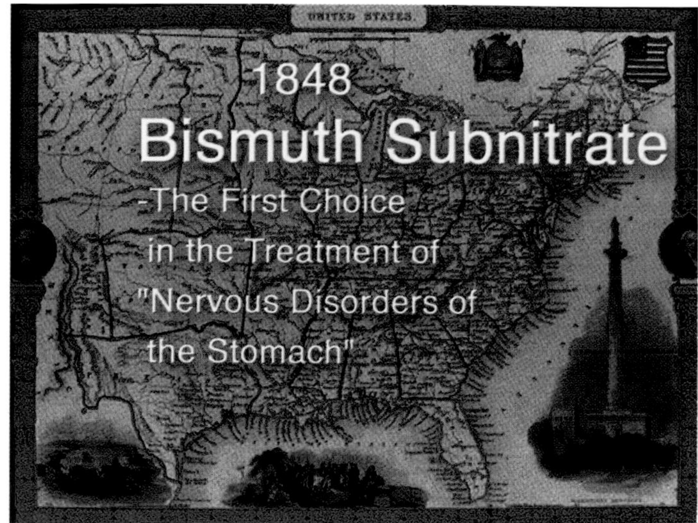

A mid-nineteenth century advertisement for the use of bismuth subnitrate.

Gastric

The use of oral bismuth for gastroenterological purposes dates back to Britain during the late eighteenth and early nineteenth centuries, when bismuth subnitrate was considered a major therapy in the treatment of "*spasmodic pain of the stomach and bowels.*" Subsequently, bismuth subsalicylate became regarded as an important treatment in "*cholera infantum*" and became widely used for conditions afflicting the large bowel, particularly dysentery. By 1848, bismuth subnitrate was widely used in the United States and claimed to be particularly effective in the treatment of "*nervous disorders of the stomach.*" In the British Medical Journal of 1864, J. W. Ogle wrote convincingly on the efficiency of "*effervescing bismuth water*" and proposed that bismuth subcitrate should be regarded as the primary remedy for non-ulcer dyspepsia. Professor Louis Odier (1748-1817) of Geneva, however, studied the medical usage in detail and in 1786 published a monograph documenting the numerous diseases for which the white oxide of bismuth could be used to great advantage. Just over a decade later, the editors of the *London Medical and Physical Journal* (July 1799) concluded that bismuth was a medicine that had either been neglected or forgotten. They opined that despite the fact that it was considered a powerful remedy in a number of different situations, particularly in individuals suffering from spasmodic pains of the stomach and bowel, the medical profession exhibited some reluctance to take advantage of its benefits. This reflected the concern that the prescription of bismuth in large doses was dangerous, since it was frequently found in combination with lead or arsenic and might therefore be toxic. In an attempt to allay such anxieties Samuel A. Moore, in 1810, described a method for the preparation of the white oxide of bismuth which was "*purer and whiter than that form by any other process.*" His dissertation delivered on the subject referred to the situation noting "*I hope, nevertheless that my readers can, at this time entertain, neither doubts nor fears on the subject.*"

A manuscript published by Alexander Marcet (1770-1822) of Guy's Hospital, London, published in 1805, further lauded the medical advantages of the oxide of bismuth. "*Being at Geneva about 12 months ago, I heard that this substance had for many years passed been brought into medical use by Dr. Odier, Professor of Physik in that town, and employed there with considerable zest, not only by him, but also by several of his colleagues in the treatment of a few spasmodic disorders, and more especially in the cure of a particular symptom of dyspepsia.*" Marcet spoke of "*the white oxyd of bismuth,*

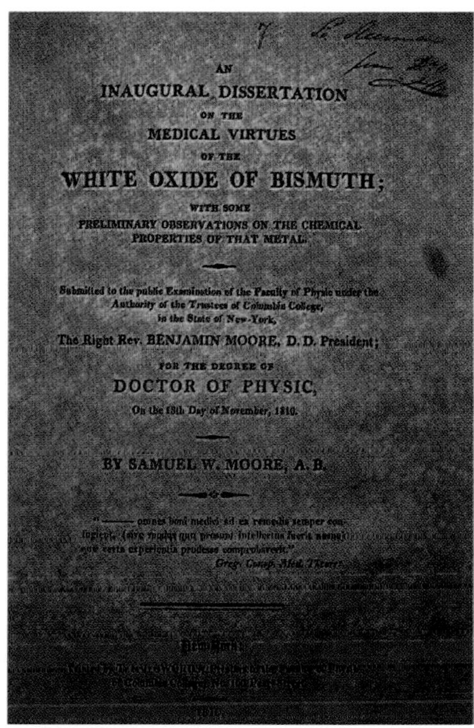
AN
INAUGURAL DISSERTATION
ON THE
MEDICAL VIRTUES
OF THE
WHITE OXIDE OF BISMUTH;
WITH SOME
PRELIMINARY OBSERVATIONS ON THE CHEMICAL
PROPERTIES OF THAT METAL.

Submitted to the public Examination of the Faculty of Physic under the
Authority of the Trustees of Columbia College,
in the State of New-York,
The Right Rev. BENJAMIN MOORE, D. D. President;
FOR THE DEGREE OF
DOCTOR OF PHYSIC,
On the 13th Day of November, 1810.

BY SAMUEL W. MOORE, A. B.

The frontispiece of the inaugural dissertation (1810) by Samuel Moore on "The Medical Virtues of the White Oxlde of Bismuth."

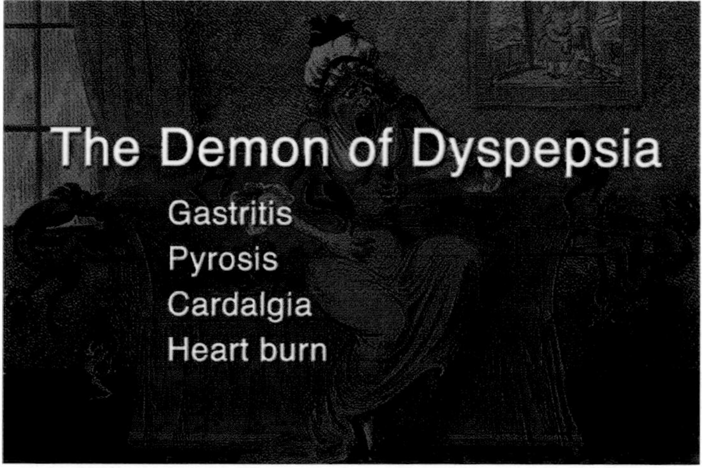

A mid-nineteenth century English cartoon by Rowlandson documenting the diverse agonies of acid peptic disease. The use of whalebone corsets to maintain the sylphine waists of the high-born may have contributed to discomfort and even induced visceroptosis (Glenard's disease).

Adolf Kussmaul (inset) was the first to use bismuth for the treatment of dyspepsia. He also developed a variety of stomach pumps to alleviate the discomfort caused by gastric outlet obstruction consequent upon untreated acid peptic disease.

commonly known by the name of Magistery of Bismuth, and sold chiefly to perfumers as a paint for whitening the complexion." He noted that its diverse medical properties *"are yet but little known, and have never, I believe, been submitted in this country to any regular investigation."* Marcet thereafter proceeded to quote Odier on the preparation of the oxide: *"The Magistery of Bismuth is prepared by dissolving a quantity of very pure bismuth in nitric acid and precipitating it by water, or by a solution of pot ash. But if the bismuth is not very pure, for instance it is mixed with nickel, the precipitate is not perfectly white, it is then mixed with a greenish precipitate, which is nothing but an oxyd of nickel which water will not precipitate; for which reason we are more certain of obtaining a pure precipitate of bismuth by water than by pot ash."* Marcet thereafter detailed his experience with six patients whom he had treated circa 1800 and concluded: *"...if it be permitted to draw any inference from so small a number of trials, it would appear that oxyd of bismuth is a remarkably successful medicine in spasmodic affectations of the stomach; for in four cases out six in which it was tried, a complete cure was almost immediately obtained; and in the two instances in which it failed, the affection, which was at first suspected to depend upon a spasm of the stomach, has since appeared to be of a complicated, and probably, of a very different nature."* Marcet subsequently stated that since his first opportunity to use the agent he had a number of opportunities at Guy's Hospital to try the *"oxyd of bismuth in spasmodic affectation of the stomach, and those trials have fully confirmed an opinion which I offered three years ago on the utility of this medicine."*

Armand Trousseau (inset) of Paris was one of the first physicians to recognize the efficacy of bismuth in the management of gastric disorders.

The strong endorsement of Marcet was subsequently pursued by Samuel Argent Bardsley of the Manchester Infirmary. Thus in 1807, in the *Medical Report,* he noted in regard to the effects of the white oxyd of bismuth, *"in pyrosis (burning sensation), cardialgia (heart burn) and other local affectations of the stomach the oxyd of bismuth seems well calculated to afford relief...it may be proper to mention that the oxyd of bismuth is justly entitled to the attention of practitioners, on account of its safety as well as its utility. For in no one instance did I find it prove injurious to stomach or general systems; nor as a medicine was it disgusting to the palate... Since the above reports were sent to press I have treated five further cases of pyrosis, accompanied more or less with spasmodic pains of the stomach, with uniformed success. In all these instances the bismuth, with occasional aperients was solely employed."*

Despite such powerful endorsements by well-recognized practitioners there still, however, remained considerable opposition to the use of bismuth as a medication and the agent required further champions. Thus in 1845, I.P Garvin, the Professor of *Materia Medica* at the Medical College of Georgia, further supported the cause of bismuth. He noted: *"the utility of the subnitrate of bismuth in certain painful affectations of stomach have been known to the profession ever since the first publication of Odier of Geneva, who was the first to employ it internally... Our sole object is to invite attention to a most valuable remedy which we think is too much neglected... Considerable fear is entertained by some lest poisonous effects should follow the use of bismuth. It is true, that when imperfectly prepared it may contain a small proportion of arsenic in the form of arsenate of bismuth and to the presence of this substance must any ill consequences be attributed which may follow ordinary doses, for when the subnitrate has been prepared from the pure metal, precipitated and well washed, no danger need be apprehended."* In seeking to explain the general lack of understanding regarding the action of bismuth, Garvin noted the comments of the well-known Parisian clinician, Armand Trousseau (1801-1867). *"If we endeavor to ascertain the action of the subnitrate of the bismuth, we will be much embarrassed; no intermediate effects between the employment of the medicine and its curative results can be perceived. Not withstanding the attention we have given to it, we have not been able to perceive the least influence on the general functions. When an individual in good health takes the subnitrate of bismuth, the only phenomenon to be noticed is constipation, but the nervous functions, the animal heat, the movements of the heart, the urinary and cutaneous secretions, are not influenced in any appreciable manner."* Quick to find support for his position as to the merits of bismuth, Garvin thereafter added: *"We can therefore only infer the nature of its action, from the character of the derangement in which it operates beneficially."*

W. Jaworski of Poland failed to receive recognition for his observation that there were bacteria in the stomach, which he believed responsible for gastritis and ulceration.

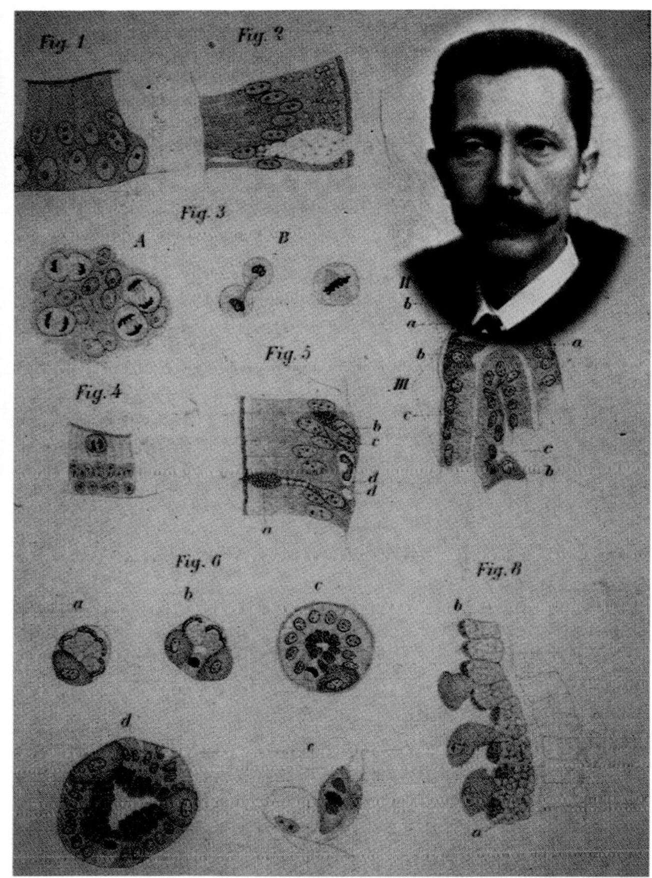

G. Bizzozero (top right) working with C. Golgi, noted the presence of spirochete organisms in the gastric glands at the turn of the 19th century but both failed to recognize their significance. Bizzozero's identification of the platelets of the blood proved to be of more enduring value than his gastric investigations while Golgi subsequently cast his intellectual gaze northwards and shared the Nobel Prize with Ramon y Cajal for his contributions to neurohistology.

Apart from a general sense of its efficacy as expressed by physicians, by 1868 no less an authority on the gastrointestinal tract than Adolf Kussmaul (1822-1902) became one of the first to advocate large doses of bismuth as the treatment of choice for gastric ulcer. His views were widely accepted and gained further weight when towards the turn of the century I. Boas (1858-1938) founded the first clinic dealing specifically with gastrointestinal complaints and directed further attention to the elucidation of gastric problems. Indeed, the description at the turn of the century by Oppler and Boas (Berlin) of gastric organisms, as well as that by W. Jaworski of Poland, raised the issue of whether gastric disease might not have an infective origin. Additional support for an etiologic role of spirochete organisms came from numerous quarters. Thus, the Italian anatomist G. Bizzozero (1846-1901) engaged in the extensive study of the comparative anatomy of vertebrate gastrointestinal glands with his adept and capable pupil, the future Nobel Prize winner, Camillo Golgi (1844-1926). In the specimens of the gastric mucosa of six dogs, Bizzozero noted the presence of a spirochete organism in the gastric glands and both in the cytoplasm and vacuoles of parietal cells. He commented that this organism affected both pyloric and fundic mucosa, and its distribution extended from the base of the gland to the surface mucosa. Although he neglected to ascribe any clinical relevance to these observations, he did, however, remark upon their close association with the parietal cells.

Three years later, in 1896, in a paper entitled "*Spirillum of the mammalian stomach and its behavior with respect to the parietal cells*"; H. Salomon reported spirochetes in the gastric mucosa of dogs, cats and rats, although he was unable to identify them in other animals, including man. In this early paper, Salomon tried to transmit the bacterium to a range of other animal species by using gastric scrapings from dogs, but was only successful when he fed gastric mucus to white mice, which resulted in a spectacular colonization within a week, as evidenced by the series of drawings of infected gastric mucosa reproduced in the original paper. The lumen of the gastric pits of the mice was packed with the spiral-shaped bacteria and invasion of the parietal cells was also noted. Indeed, the successful usage of bismuth to treat the spirochetes causing syphilis excited considerable conjecture regarding the potential role of gastric spirochetes in the genesis of the ubiquitous diagnosis of gastritis and stomach ulcers.

Nevertheless, the role of organisms in the stomach was unclear. Freedberg and Barron in 1941 investigated the presence of spirochetes in the gastric tissue of patients who had undergone partial resection surgery, but in spite of their familiarity with the latest staining techniques, were not able to identify the organisms. They did, however, demonstrate that spirochetes were more frequently present in ulcerating stomachs as compared to non-ulcerated stomachs (53% vs. 14%). In spite of these findings, they concluded that no absolute etiopathologic role for these organisms could be defined. It is with almost tragic irony that one reads that, in the report of the discussion of this paper, Frank D. Gorham, of St. Louis, Missouri, noted:

> *I believe that a further search should be made for an organism thriving in hydrochloric acid medium (and variations of hydrochloric acid are normal in all stomachs) as a possible factor of chronicity, if not an etiologic factor, in peptic ulcer.*

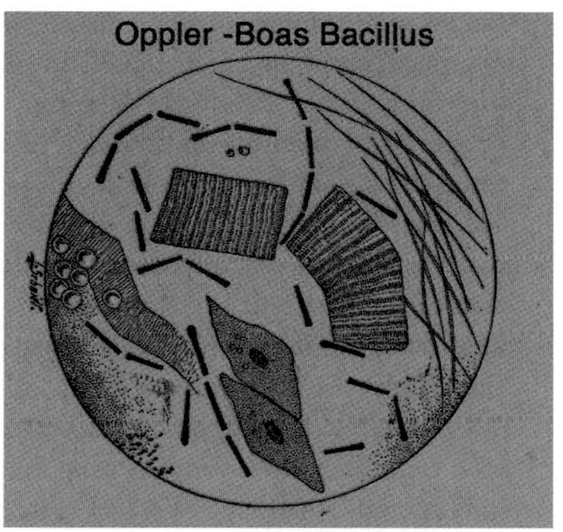

Ismar Boas and his colleague, Oppler, identified bacteria in the gastric lumen (c. 1900) and considered the possibility of their pathological relationship to ulcerative disease.

Frank D. Gorham of St. Louis, Missouri, in 1938 proposed the existence of an organism that would thrive in the low pH environment of the stomach and cause gastric disease. His prescience was lost in the mists of time and the dogma of the day until Barry Marshall in Perth, Australia, confirmed the profundity of the suggestion.

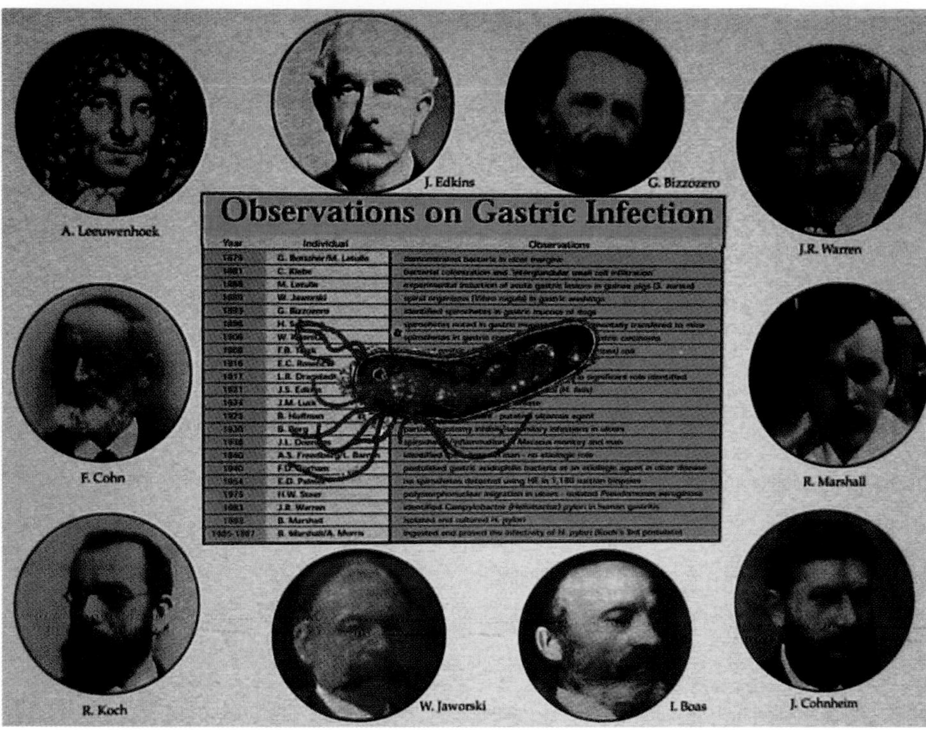

The numerous physicians and scientists who over time noted the presence of organisms in the gastric mucosa. R. Warren and B. Marshall of Perth, Australia, undertook the studies, which fulfilled Koch's criteria and implicated H. pylori *as a gastric pathogen. It should be noted that the "postulates" as propounded by Koch had actually been proposed and taught to Koch by his mentor Jacob Henle of renal tubular fame!*

Of interest is that Gorham also wrote that he had, over the previous ten years, successfully treated patients who had refractory ulcer disease with intramuscular injections of bismuth! R. Sazerac and C. Levaditi, who in 1921 had used it to cure experimental syphilis in rabbits, had already successfully exploited the antibacterial properties of bismuth, which may or may not have been known to Gorham. With the advent of antibiotics after the Second World War the use of bismuth declined, and the focus of attention on acid-induced ulceration further induced physicians to look towards antacids and acid suppression as treatment for peptic ulceration. Thus the introduction of antacids and the demonstration of their efficacy, coupled with the reports by the magi, Ivy and Grossman, of the ineffectiveness of bismuth as an antacid, resulted in a drift of therapeutic inclination away from bacteria and towards acid suppression. The introduction of the histamine receptor antagonist class of drugs and the subsequent advent of the proton pump inhibitor agents appeared to provide convincing proof that antibacterial agents such as bismuth were legacies of a bygone era in which the pathophysiology of the stomach had been misunderstood. The discovery of *H. pylori* by R. Warren and B. Marshall in 1983 resulted in a dramatic reconsideration of antibacterial therapy!

Among the earliest studies of the use of bismuth compounds with metronidazole and tetracycline to cure *H. pylori* infection were the reports of T. Borody and his colleagues in 1987. This therapy was considered so effective that at the World Congress of Gastroenterology in 1990, bismuth triple therapy was advised for *H. pylori* infection by the working party convened to study the subject. As a result of published data and similar recommendations, physicians have used it so successfully in the treatment of *H. pylori* that by 1995, 40 percent of the gastroenterologists in either The Netherlands or the U.S.A. used bismuth-based therapy. Despite its efficacy, the complicated treatment regimens, the large number of pills that were required, and the side effects, indicated the need to seek other combinations. It was recognized that the development of a cheap, simple effective therapy with minimal side effects was required.

Bismuth was widely used as a medication for everything from hemorrhoids to luetic disease. Such were the claims for its efficacy that it was even purported to cure bullet wounds. A 19th-century wound salve!

Trivalent bismuth preparations have therapeutic properties, and a number of these products have been marketed worldwide. Bismuth subsalicylate (BSS; Pepto-Bismol, Norwich, N.Y.) and colloidal bismuth subcitrate (CBS; De-Nol, Gist brocades, The Netherlands) are perhaps the most familiar products. In addition, however, bismuth subcarbonate, bismuth subnitrate, bismuth subgallate, and a variety of other bismuth compounds are available in different countries. Colloidal bismuth subcitrate is a complex bismuth salt of citric acid which forms BiOCl and various structures containing three carboxyl groups and positively charged Bi^{+} when the bismuth citrate bonds are exposed in the stomach. Bismuth oxychloride is poorly soluble whereas bismuth irons (Bi^{3+} and Bi^{2+}) have physiological properties. BSS is a highly insoluble complex of trivalent bismuth and salicylate and reacts with HCl in the intragastric environment (pH less than 3.5) to form bismuth oxychloride (BiOCl) salicylate acid. Some intact bismuth passes unchanged at the duodenum where it can react with other anti-irons such as bicarbonate and phosphate to form bismuth subcarbonate and bismuth phosphate salt. The salicylate release from the hydrolysis of BSS is absorbed in the stomach and small intestines while remaining unreactive. BSS, BiOCL, and other bismuth salts react with hydrogen sulfide in the colon to produce bismuth sulfide, the black salt responsible for the darkening of stool that occurs with BSS use.

The Colon and Cholera Infanticum

As previously observed, the effect of bismuth on abdominal colic and diarrhea had been noted and the agent broadly prescribed for such complaints. Indeed, the medical profession adopted a somewhat empirical approach to the use of bismuth and produced information *"that apart from its use in nervous derangement of the stomach, bismuth was particularly effective in the management of the vomiting of teething children and in the frequent diarrhea of feeble infants and those diarrheas accompanied by fevers following acute disorders."* In 1863, John B. Trask, studying a group of soldiers with acute and chronic diarrhea at Camp Downy, California, in the Finley Hospital, Washington, D.C., provided a glowing report of the efficiency of bismuth in the treatment of dysentery. As a result of his recommendations, bismuth was widely prescribed for many afflictions of the colon, particularly those associated with diarrhea. The black color that the medication conveyed to the stools provided *"ample proof"* of its efficacy and was interpreted as evidence of its potent action. Proprietary compounds containing bismuth thus became widely utilized in the management of the *"upset stomach"* (an early twentieth-century euphemism for diarrhea) and the nostrum enjoyed widespread lay popularity.

Some concerns for bismuth toxicity, particularly in the form of the subnitrate or subgallate, arose during experiences in France and Australia in the late 1970s. In France, bismuth had become a widely-used gastrointestinal panacea during this time and bismuth subcarbonate, subgallate, and subnitrate were commonly consumed in doses up to 20 g of elemental bismuth on a daily basis. As a result, an epidemic of bismuth encephalopathy occurred in that country between 1973 and 1977 resulting in some fatalities. In Australia, where high doses (3 - 20 g per day) of bismuth subgallate were widely used by patients with colostomies, twenty-nine cases of encephalopathy were reported in patients who had taken the drug for between six months and three years. An assessment of the Australian and French data indicated that prolonged use (months to years) of high doses (greater than 1.5 g of bismuth metal per day) were necessary for bismuth toxicity to occur. Serum levels of bismuth in toxic patients often reached 150-4000 ug per liter, while the usual therapeutic dose of bismuth (less than 1.5 g per day) in normal persons provided levels of 15-35 ug per liter after two months of use. The subsequent restriction on the use of bismuth in France, and the banning of the use of bismuth subgallate in Australia, eliminated further cases of bismuth toxicity. Indeed, there have been no documented cases of bismuth toxicity with the recommended acute dosages of either bismuth subsalicylate or colloidal bismuth subcitrate. It appears that only in conditions of over-dosage or individuals with significant mucosal gut damage is excessive bismuth absorption likely.

During the Middle Ages syphilis was regarded as one of the great scourges of the populace. Its recognized relationship to licentious conduct led to widespread speculation regarding the association between pleasure, guilt, and suffering. Religious intervention proved of minimal benefit in the management of the disease but bismuth and mercury were recognized to be of considerable use in treatment.

Syphilis

The pioneering work of R. Koch and L. Pasteur in establishing the bacterial basis for disease led to the urgent search for therapeutic agents. Given that the medical scourges of the early twentieth century in Europe were tuberculosis and syphilis, considerable focus was directed at the management of these diseases. The history of the treatment of syphilis is replete with exotic cures and the use of the metals, mercury and arsenic, had become widespread. Although bismuth compounds had been utilized since 1750 for the treatment of gonorrhea and as early as 1779 for syphilis, they enjoyed wide popularity in the treatment of syphilis at the beginning of the twentieth century. Although they were ultimately replaced with the advent of penicillin, bismuth was still utilized as a preliminary treatment in syphilitic patients with gummatous laryngitis lest the inflammatory reaction induced by the intake of penicillin cause laryngeal obstruction and death.

In 1941, Henry Gilman and Harry L. Yale commented that it had not been until 1921 that the research in the field of bismuth therapy attained a new level of intensity. The pioneer work of Levaditi and his co-workers introduced what became known as "The French School of Bismuth Therapy." So dramatic was the interest in the agent that in the six years after their initial publication, 1,916 articles on bismuth therapy were published and by 1935 the number had risen to almost 5,000. In 1932, a review of the nature of bismuth compounds available for therapy disclosed that no less than 250 organic and inorganic compounds had been prepared and investigated for potential therapeutic utilization. Gilman commented that *"although the actual value of organic bismuth compounds in spirochetosis had long been debated, their value in the intermittent treatment of syphilis by arsenicals was widely acknowledged."* Gilman and Yale were of the opinion that bismuth was more toxic than arsenic and acted more slowly. This was refuted by Dr. R.A. von Derlehr, (Assistant Surgeon General, Division of Venereal Diseases of the United States Public Health Service) who stated: *"it is the general consensus of opinion of experts in this country and particularly of the Cooperative Clinical Group that when all factors are taken into consideration, bismuth subsalicylate, suspended in oil is probably the most practical bismuth preparation for the treatment of syphilis."* Intramuscular injections of bismuth compounds were reported to form "depots" followed by slow release of bismuth into the blood and absorption was so gradual that after 400 days there was still evidence of bismuth at the site of injection. W. Kolle (1868-1935) noted that a depot injection in the ear of the rabbit

Henry Gillman (inset) undertook detailed investigation of the use of bismuth in the treatment of syphilis but remained sanguine as to its long-term efficacy.

A demon inflicted with syphilitic skin lesions by St. Anthony, presumably as a divine punishment.

prevented the appearance of scrotal lesions following intra-testicular injections of the syphilis organism. Following amputation of the ear three months later, the scrotal lesions redeveloped within a period of a few weeks. This was interpreted as evidence that virulent organisms were not destroyed by bismuth, but their multiplication inhibited. Nevertheless, Gilman noted that complete cures of syphilis by the exclusive use of organic bismuth compounds had been reported. Of the more than 5,000 papers published in the field of bismuth therapy between 1921 and 1935, few dealt with the use of organo-bismuth compounds. G. Giemsa, however, documented the healing properties of triphenylbismuth in experimental canine syphilis, relapsing fever, and Nagana (Trypanosomiasis). Based on its lipoid solubility, Giemsa went so far as to propose that triphenylbismuth should be used in the later stage of syphilis since this would facilitate its penetration into the "undecomposed" central nervous system and hence offer a protective effect. A number of contradictory reports regarding the efficacy of this bismuth preparation in the treatment of syphilis emerged (Albrecht and Evers, Schlossberger) but Sollman and Seifter thereupon undertook the study of alkyl bismuth compounds as anti-syphilitic agents. They determined that trimethylbismuth could be handled safely and was sufficiently soluble in water to produce marked effects in experiment animals when administered either intravenously, by inhalation or by skin. Although it exhibited a definite healing effect in rabbit syphilis, it demonstrated "*no extraordinary therapeutic activity.*" In respect of the higher alkyls, trilaurylbismuth, tricetyl-bismuth, and acetyl bismuth dibromide were poorly absorbed and inactive. At this stage the consensus of opinion was that little information was available on organo-bismuth compounds and the principle objection to their usage appeared to be high toxicity. It was proposed that if organo-bismuth compounds of low toxicity could be synthesized, more effective therapeutic agents would be forthcoming. Gilman and Yale noted in 1941 that intramuscular bismuth was apparent in the blood two hours after injection and the vast majority was excreted by the kidney, liver, and intestinal mucosa. They commented on the local necrosis of the muscle fibers in the vicinity of the intramuscular injection of bismuth, but calculated that an individual of normal gluteal muscle mass could tolerate from fifty to one hundred or more injections without serious difficulty. In further studies of bismuth toxicity they demonstrated that massive over-dosage resulted in tubular nephritis, similar to that produced by mercury poisoning. They recommended the use of peanut oil as a bland and non-irritating depot agent while olive oil was particular painful and poorly tolerated. Overall, they commented that the administration of bismuth compounds in therapeutic dosage at weekly intervals was remarkably free from toxic effects. The one exception appeared to be the development of a bluish gray pigment line on the gum margins of the mouth after a half dozen injections. In rare instances (thirty-five in the period from 1922 to 1935) death resulted from bismuth therapy but such events reflected accidental intravenous injection. Nevertheless, the French experience documented that massive, sustained, and unregulated oral intake resulted in toxic levels, encephalopathy and death.

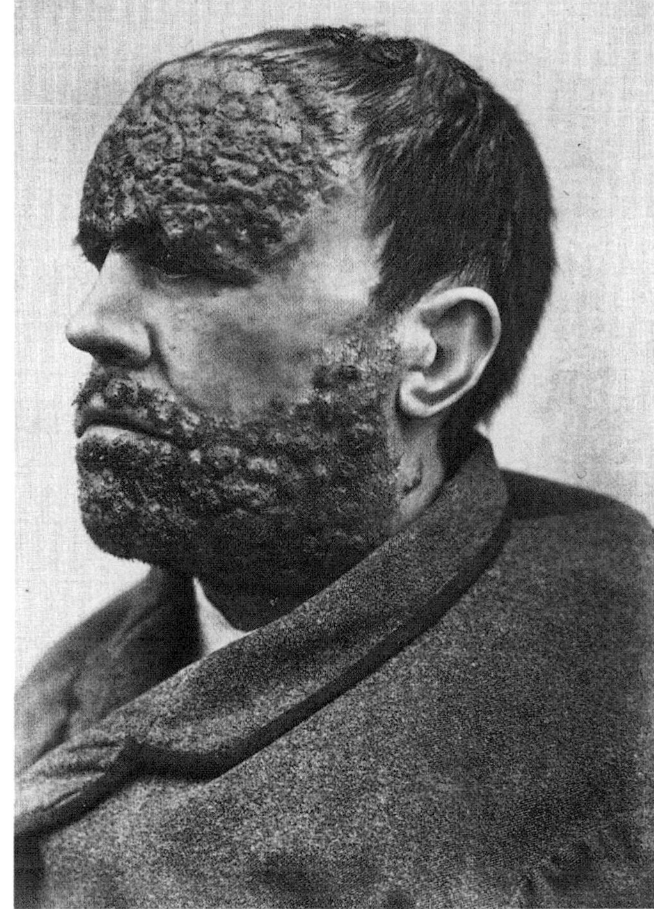

A young man (c. 1912) afflicted with the cutaneous manifestations of syphilis.

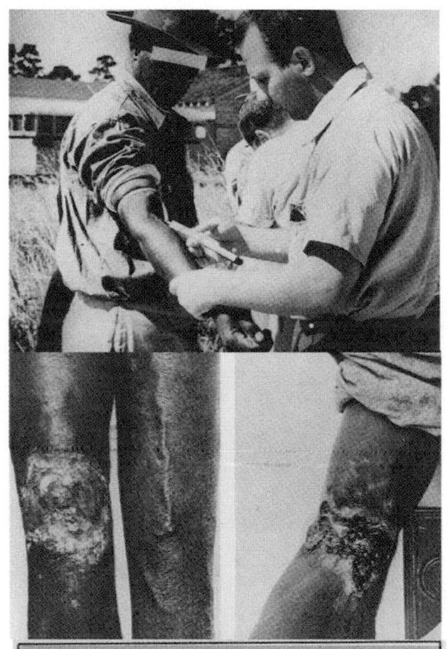

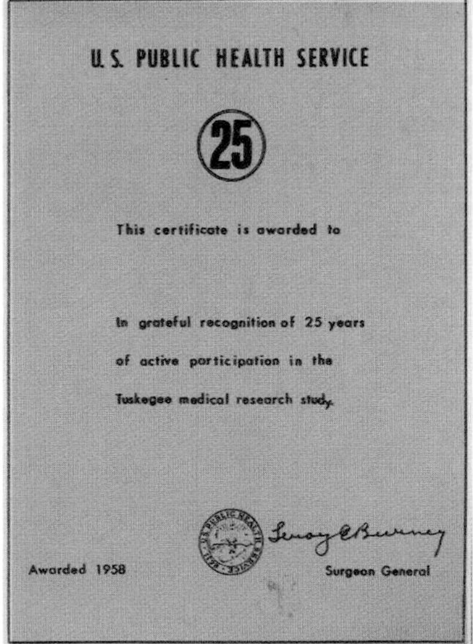

U.S. PUBLIC HEALTH SERVICE

25

This certificate is awarded to

In grateful recognition of 25 years of active participation in the Tuskegee medical research study.

Awarded 1958

Surgeon General

The Tuskegee syphilis study was conducted by the U.S. Public Health Service from 1932 to 1972. It examined the natural cause of untreated syphilis in black American men. The research was intended to test whether syphilis caused cardiovascular damage more often than neurological damage and to determine if the natural course of syphilis in black men was significantly different from that in white. A group of 412 infected patients and 204 uninfected control patients were recruited for the program with the support of Tuskegee University in Macon County, Alabama. The subjects were all impoverished sharecroppers from Macon County. The participants were neither informed that they suffered from syphilis nor that the disease could be transmitted through sexual intercourse. They were in fact advised that they suffered from "bad blood" and treated with arsenic, bismuth, and mercury. After the original study failed to produce any useful data it was decided to follow the subjects until their deaths and all treatment was halted. Of particular note was the fact that penicillin was denied to the infected men after the drug had became available in the mid-1940s. It was withheld from them for a further 25 years in direct violation of government legislation that mandated the treatment of venereal disease. Approximately 100 of the subjects died of tertiary syphilis and the study was ended in 1972 when the Washington Star Newspaper exposed the unethical methods employed in the study. The class action suit against the federal government was settled out of court for $10 million in 1974 and in the same year the U.S. Congress passed the National Research Act requiring institutional review boards to approve all studies involving human subjects. No doubt the survivors framed and proudly displayed their certificate, awarded in grateful recognition of 25 years of active participation!

Quinine-cinchona

The introduction of cinchona to the medical world was fraught with controversy and characterized by considerable acrimony between physicians and Jesuits. Unfortunately, its initial adoption was not universal and its usage was the subject of heated disagreement since many physicians refused to prescribe it simply because it was not mentioned in the texts of the ancients and some obstinate religiose patients preferred death to a medication which was known by a "popish" appellation. In the midst of this altercation, Robert Talbot (*c.* 1642-1681), a notorious quack, did much to popularize the drug by advertising a secret remedy for the cure of febrile conditions. Capitalizing on the repugnance of physicians and the laity to accept the drug, and realizing that it was useful in the treatment of fevers, his usage of the agent under a different name resulted in his achieving widespread medical and financial success. Indeed, so effective was the medication in England that even the French sought its benefit. In a great financial coup for Talbot following the cure of the French Dauphin, Louis XIV purchased the formula, for the public good, on the understanding that it would not be published until the latter's death. Talbot died soon after and his remedy was revealed to consist of a large quantity of Jesuits' powder in a good grade of claret wine.

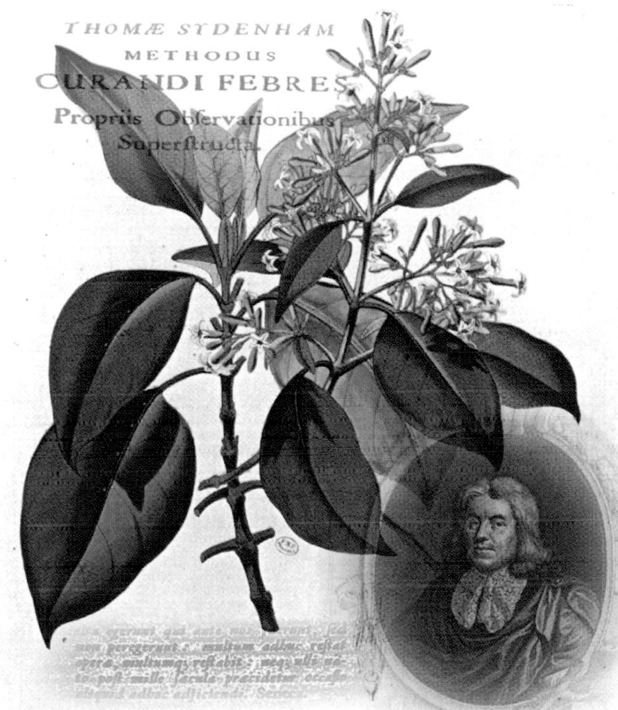

It is generally agreed that Peruvian bark or cinchona made its appearance in European drug markets during the first half of the 17th century and that it was known as Cardinal's or Jesuit powder. Cinchona was one of the most important of the New World drugs whose worth was initially recognized by the Jesuit priests, although exotic tales concerning the introduction of quinine by the Countess of Chinchon were long part of medical mythology. Cinchona was introduced in England about 1655 and although Thomas Sydenham (1624-1689) (inset) was one of the earliest clinicians to use it, it was not until 1676 that he considered it as a specific for fevers. The bark was listed in the 1677 edition of the London Pharmacopoeia under the term Cortex peruanus and, in 1724, Carl von Linne (Linnaeus, 1707-1778) officially designated the plant Cinchona quinquina. The alkaloids, quinine and quinidine, were first isolated in 1820 and 1853, respectively.

The seventeenth and eighteenth century legends regarding the history and identification of the cinchona trees and their usage as a medicine by the natives of Peru before its virtues were ascertained by Europeans, provides interesting reading and much controversy. Although Peru was discovered in 1513, and became subject to Spain about the middle of the sixteenth century, no reference to the bark as a febrifuge has been found earlier than the beginning of the seventeenth century. The apocryphal tale refers to the Countess Ana of Chinchon, wife of the Spanish Viceroy of Peru, who was cured of a fever by the bark in 1633, but there is evidence that its medicinal value had been experienced by some of the Spanish before that date. Indeed, it appears from the reports of La Condamine, and others who acquired their knowledge *in situ*, that the Indians had long used the bark primarily as a dye. It is told that when the Countess became ill and all the usual remedies had been found ineffective, the Corregidor of Loxa, Don Juan Lopez Canizares, who had himself been cured by the bark of a similar illness, brought some of the remedy from Loxa to Lima and staked his reputation on its infallibility.

After her cure the Countess became an enthusiastic advocate of the medicine, administering it with uniform success to her dependents and others in Lima, and on her return to Spain in 1640, proclaimed its efficacy. An alternative version of the story is to the effect that a native maid in the employment of the Countess had made known the virtues of the bark to the Viceroy out of affection for her mistress, though until then the Indians had concealed the secret from their cruel rulers. Despite these exotic rumors, it is most likely that the medicinal value of the bark had initially become known to the Jesuit missionaries who had already been in the country for half a century before the Countess of Chinchon was cured.

The Le Condamine version of the story, related in 1738, detailed the Indian legend that they had become acquainted with the properties of the bark in consequence of an earthquake in the neighborhood of Loxa which had resulted in a number of the trees surrounding a lake near the city to be

The Spanish conquests of the New World yielded considerable riches in terms of gold and silver. It is often forgotten that an additional great benefit was the introduction of the cinchona bark used for the cure of malaria. Ironically the acquisition of the gold and the lives lost in assuring its retention were probably responsible for as many deaths as malaria.

Leopold William, Archduke of Austria and Governor of the Low Countries, was cured by treatment with cinchona and as might be predicted became an ardent supporter of the curative effects of the cinchona bark. Similarly Louis XIV (top) of France supported its public distribution.

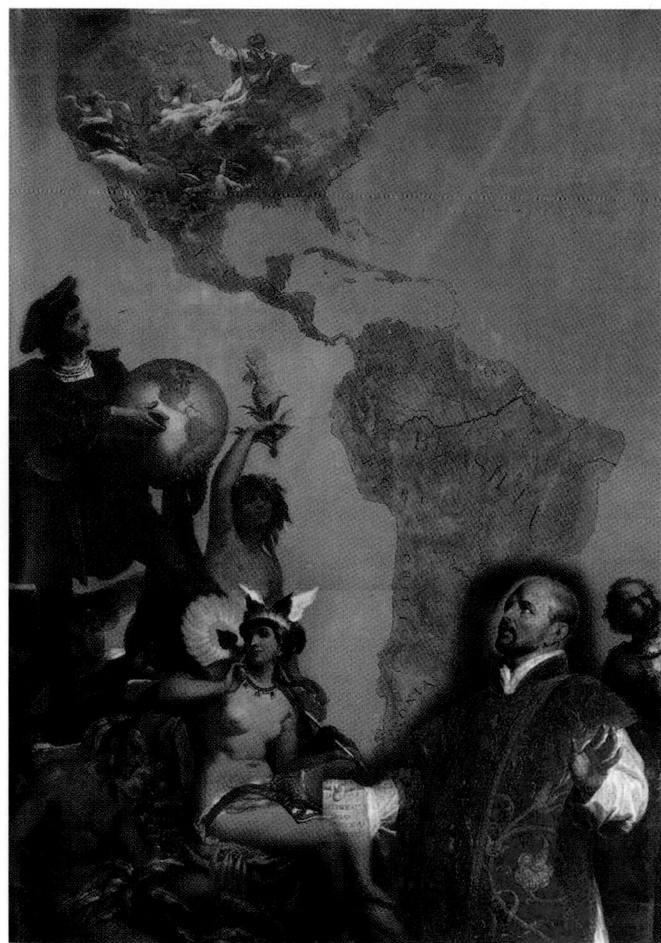

Ignatius Loyola (inset) confronts the bounty of the New World. The Jesuit fraternity was instrumental in identifying the medicinal use of cinchona and introducing it into Europe. Although primarily focused on religious conversion, many priests were well versed in cartography, medicine and philosophy. While aware of divine authority they also were pragmatic enough to recognize the power of knowledge and hence guarded the secret of cinchona.

thrown into the water. An Indian, violently ill with a fever and consumed with thirst, had drunk water from this lake and had been rapidly cured. Yet another tradition held that the pumas of the country had been observed to eat the bark when they were ill, and that the Indians had learned its value from this circumstance.

In 1640 the Count and Countess of Chinchon, accompanied by their personal physician, Juan del Vego, returned to their Spanish estate at Chinchon Castle, about forty miles from Madrid. Del Vego had been astute enough to return with a considerable quantity of the bark from Peru, and during his residence at Seville, sold it for one hundred reals per pound. Although it is uncertain whether Vego's bark was the first importation of the medicine into Spain, a Spanish physician named Villerobel (quoted by Badus in 1663), in a work on the Peruvian bark, stated that a quantity was received in 1632, but was not tried until 1639. The patient was an ecclesiastic of Alcala de Henarez, near Madrid. Neverthless, Vego's reports and the experiments with his bark excited lively interest throughout Spain and thereafter began a controversy almost as bitter as that between the Galenists and Paracelsists.

Thus, many practitioners could believe in any medicine which Galen had not described. Furthermore, it was also alleged by some cynics that a prompt cure of intermittent fevers was not by any means desired by a large number of medical men and apothecaries, who consequently allied themselves in opposition to this very effective bark. Fevers were at that time regarded as caused by some morbific principle in the humors which occasioned effervescence, and which it was essential first of all to expel. The patient was, therefore, treated with evacuants and debilitating medicines while the fever continued, and the vital spirits were afterwards restored by a course of cordials and bitters, such as wormwood, chamomile flowers, mace, carduus benedictus, angelica, and valerian. Emboldened by such theory, the opponents of the bark insisted that if it palliated the fever it "fixed the humour" and ensured either a relapse or the emergence of some more other more dangerous disease.

In 1652 Leopold William, Archduke of Austria, and Governor of the Low Countries, who had become a supporter of the curative effects of the bark, fell ill with a quaternian fever and having been treated for, recovered. A deterioration occurred, but the complaint again yielded to the remedy. Unfortunately he suffered a further relapse, but this time, having succumbed to the views of physicians in regard to the problems with the bark, he refused the remedy and died! With classic illogic, this outcome was regarded as direct evidence of the dangerous character of the medicine!

Despite such poor press, the Jesuits had actively propagated the new remedy and proved its virtues wherever it had been used. Having brought a large

Ignatius Loyola was initially of high birth and became imbued with religious zeal after suffering a serious cannonball injury. During his recovery he was inspired by a divine vision and became the founder of the Jesuit order. The use by the Jesuits of the cinchona remedy for malaria proved a remarkably successful method for assuring the spread of their influence as well as a lucrative commercial venture.

supply to Rome, they explained the method of using it to a congress of Jesuits, then assembled in that city, with the result that the fathers administered it all over Europe, giving it gratuitously to the poor and to their own order, but charging its weight in gold to the rich. As might be predicted from the Jesuits, it is rumored that they endeavored to maintain it as a secret medicine, and would only supply it in powder so that its origin was difficult to identify. The Procurator-General of the order, Father (afterwards Cardinal) de Lugo, during the course of a visit to Paris in 1649, noted Louis XIV to be suffering from an intermittent fever and recommended the bark with an excellent result. As a result of such publicity the bark became variously known as "*the powder of the Cardinal, the Powder of the Fathers and the Jesuits,*" and became highly sought after. Unfortunately this nomenclature was largely responsible for the adverse religious reaction which almost removed cinchona from practice as Protestant fears and prejudices were added to the orthodox opposition of the Galenists. In addition, poor medical practice whereby many practitioners either administered the bark inappropriately (incorrect dosage), or sold it at excessive prices, which led to fraudulent substitution and resulted in disavowal of the bark as a medicine. Thus Jesuits and physicians alike alleged that the Spanish merchants were sending into Italy instead of the true Peruvian bark, other astringent barks devoid of any aromatic taste, but *"flavored up"* to the necessary bitterness by aloes.

Although Sydenham in England, and a number of eminent physicians on the Continent, studied the proper methods of administration and the suitable doses of bark, it fell to a practitioner whose methods were little short of charlatanry to firmly establish cinchona as a serious medication.

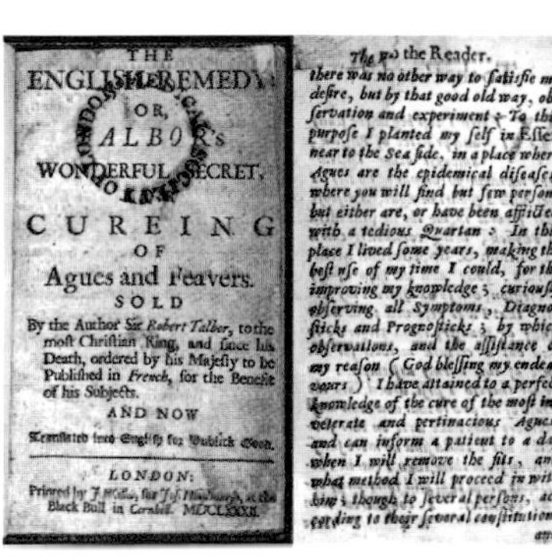
THE
ENGLISH REMEDY:
OR,
TALBOR'S
WONDERFUL SECRET,
FOR
CUREING
OF
Agues and Feavers.
SOLD
By the Author Sir Robert Talbor, to the most Christian King, and since his Death, ordered by his Majesty to be Published in French, for the Benefit of his Subjects.
AND NOW
Translated into English for Publick Good.

LONDON:
Printed by J. Wallis, for Jos. Hindmarsh, at the Black Bull in Cornhill. MDCLXXXII.

To the Reader.
there was no other way to satisfie my desire, but by that good old way, observation and experiment: To this purpose I planted my self in Essex near to the Sea side, in a place where Agues are the epidemical diseases, where you will find but few persons but either are, or have been afflicted with a tedious Quartan: In this place I lived some years, making the best use of my time I could, for the improving my knowledge; curiously observing all Symptoms, Diagnosticks and Prognosticks; by which observations, and the assistance of my reason (God blessing my endeavours) I have attained to a perfect knowledge of the cure of the most inveterate and pertinacious Agues, and can inform a patient to a day when I will remove the fits, and what method I will proceed in with him; though to several persons, according to their several constitutions and

The manuscript of Robert Talbor documenting his "unique" cure for fever.

In about 1663, Robert Talbor was assistant with an apothecary named Dear at Cambridge, where he had enrolled as a sizar at St. John's College for five years, although there is no indication that he took a degree. Talbor acknowledged that he was largely indebted to a member of the University of the name of Nott for suggestions relative to the administration of bark. In 1672 he wrote a book, *Pyretologia,* a rational account of the cause and cure of agues, in which he referred to his own secret remedy, which consisted of four ingredients, two indigenous and two exotic. In his discourse, although Talbor discussed Peruvian bark and intimates that it is an excellent remedy, he disingenuously noted that it should only be employed with prudence, since in the hands of inexperienced doctors it might occasion serious evils. Somehow Talbor failed to mention that it was contained in his specific!

As his reputation increased, Talbor moved to London and opened an office at Gray's Inn Gate, in Holborn, where one of his most successful cures was the daughter of Lady Mordaunt. As a result he was recommended to Charles II, who he also cured of "the ague", thus earning a knighthood and the appointment as a royal physician with a salary of £100 a year. In addition the king formally notified the College of Physicians that they cease and desist from any further interference in Sir Talbor's practice. Such was the fame of Talbor that even the French court sought his skills, although in the elegant circles of Paris he chose to practice under the name Talbot. Given his social skills, he soon became a favorite amongst the aristocracy and the letters of Mme de Sévigny refer to him several times in 1679. In one she notes, *"Nothing is talked of here but the Englishman and his cures."* Finally in November, 1680, fate delivered ultimate fortune into the hands of Talbor when the Dauphin became dangerously ill with a fever. Mme de Sévigny wrote, *"The Englishman has promised on his head to cure monseigneur in four days, although if he fails he will be thrown out of the window."* King Louis XIV was so smitten with the promise of an English cure that he insisted on watching Talbor prepare his wine! To his great credit Talbor cured the Dauphin and Mme de Sévigny noted with malicious glee the discomfiture of the king's head physician, Antoine d'Aquin. The latter, as well as numerous other French physicians, wrote bitterly against Talbor, insisting that his treatment of the Dauphin and of other persons had been based on a mistaken diagnosis, and that in the case of the Dauphin he had made a bilious fever into a dangerous disorder. Yet another of his multitudinous critics claimed that a remedy given to the Duke of Rochefoucauld, who suffered from arthritic asthma, had culminated in a fatality.

Despite the professional rancor that abounded, Louis agreed to buy Talbor's formula, but agreed that the ingredients should not be published during the lifetime of the physician. As a result of this arrangement, two thousand guineas and an annual pension of £100 were granted to the Englishman as well as the title of Chevalier. Thereafter Talbor traveled to Spain where he cured the queen of a fever before returning to London where he died in 1781, at the early age of forty.

Antoine D'Aquin, the personal physician of Louis XIV. Elegant, arrogant and dogmatic, he exerted considerable influence over his monarchial patient.

Talbor's official formula, published after his death, directed six drachms of rose leaves to be infused in six ounces of water with two ounces of lemon juice for four hours. A strong infusion of cinchona was added to the above, together with some juice of persil. He also made alcoholic tinctures and wines of cinchona, to which some malicious French physicians claimed he even added opium.

Aloes

The peripatetic military physician, Dioscorides, was the earliest of the medical writers to mention aloes as a therapeutic agent. According to him, it should be given in doses of from half a drachm to one drachm as a gentle purge, or if a full cathartic effect were required, then the amount could be increased to as much as three drachms. Surprisingly, neither Hippocrates nor Theophrastus mention aloes as a drug, whereas Celsus described it as specially valuable for

The medicinal uses of the aloe plant were first described by Dioscorides and held in high regard by Alexander the Great (cameo inset). The health of soldiers was a source of paramount concern and military medicine became an important discipline.

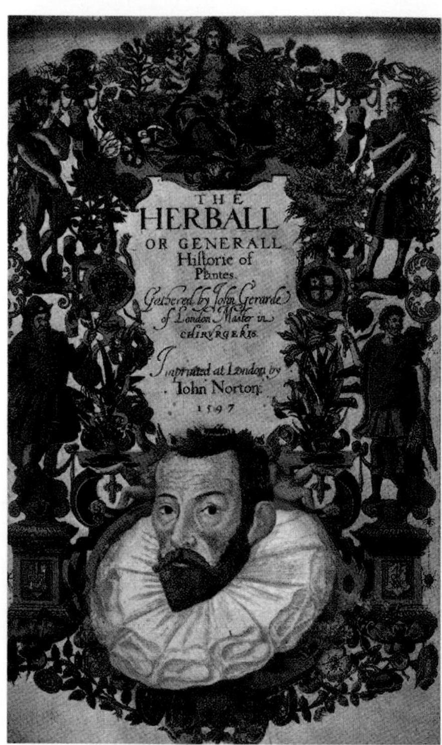

The Herball written by Gerard of England, opined positively on the efficacy of castor oil. Indeed, it was grown by Gerard in London very close to the current site of the Royal College of Surgeons of England in Holborn.

John Tradescant (1608-1662), an esteemed botanist and medicinal herbalist of England, cultivated the castor oil plant in 17th-century London. The remains of his original garden still exist in Lambeth and are directly opposite the Royal Society of Pharmacy. As the son of Charles I's naturalist and gardener (also John Tradescant), whom he succeeded in the same post, Tradescant added to his father's collection of natural history objects, ultimately forming a significant collection acquired principally from Algiers and Virginia. After the younger Tradescant's death, the collection was eventually given to an acquaintance, Elias Ashmole, who in turn donated it to the University of Oxford in 1683, founding thereby the Ashmolean Museum, the first scientific museum in England.

city and men of letters (*urbani et literarum cupidi*). Indeed, he believed it to be a critical component of all purgatives, and subsequent Greek and Roman writers also commented as to the high esteem in which they held this remedy. Such was the presumed virtue of aloes that in *Pharmacographia*, Hanbury refers to the legend of Alexander the Great visiting the island of Socotra at the insistence of Aristotle, particularly on account of the aloes grown there. In order to ensure a constant supply of the purgative, it is believed that Alexander went so far as to leave a loyal colony of Ionians on the island. The fame of aloes was well-maintained by the Arab physicians, and the old Greek and Roman formulas for aloetic compounds were passed on to the physicians of the Middle Ages by Mesue of Damascus, together with some new ones. Its much vaunted effects were considered of such benefit that it was one of the drugs recommended to Alfred the Great by the Patriarch of Jerusalem!

Raymond Minderer of Augsburg was one of the most famous physicians of his time and his notable skills were deemed so especial that he was not only the medical adviser to the Duke of Bavaria and the great house of the Fuggers, but also the Rothschilds. In 1622 he published a treatise *Aloedarium*, on a special compound of aloes which he had devised, and describing in exquisite detail each of the nine ingredients of the medication that was the lineal ancestor of our modern compound rhubarb pill. The components were: *Aloes 3 ounces, Marum (herb mastic, and Saffron, of each 3 scruples, Agaric, Costus, and Myrrh, of each 3 half-drachms, Ammoniacum, 3 drachms, Rhubarb, 3 two-drachms (3vi), and Lign Aloes, 3 half-scruples*. These drugs were each separately macerated in appropriate liquids, the aloes in rose water, the myrrh in rue vinegar, and so forth. Minderer recommended these pills not only as a purgative, but as a general tonic that would prove to be of specific benefit to strong, fair, well-fed persons. A subsequent text entitled *Aloe Morbifuga*, that further embellished the work of Minderer, was produced by William Marcquis of Antwerp. Its main contribution was to stress the importance of the water-soluble component of aloes as the constituent of the drug in which the purgative properties reside. Indeed, to Marcquis must be granted the distinction of being the originator of contemporary aqueous extract of aloes.

Castor Oil

The purported identity of the Palma Christi tree, from the seeds of which castor oil are obtained, was known as "*kikaion*" in Hebrew and originally referred to as Jonah's "gourd" in Biblical times. It is probable that the plant was the same as the "*kiki*" of Herodotus, and the "kiki" or "kroton" that were described by Dioscorides. Avicenna quotes a Dioscorides reference to the seeds from which, he says, "*the oil of kiki which is the same as the oil of Alkeroa can be pressed*." The latter terminology ("*al-keroa*") was that used by other Arab authors as equivalent to the term for the Greek "*kiki*." These terms were subsequently Romanized such that the frequent Latin name utilized to describe Palma Christi was "*kikinum*," or "*cicinum*."

The earliest allusion to the oil is found in Herodotus (*Hist. Euterpe*), where it was noted, "*The inhabitants of the marshy grounds in Egypt make use of an oil which they term the (kiki), expressed from the Sillicyprian plant. In Greece this plant springs spontaneously without any cultivation; but the Egyptians sow it on the banks of the river and the canals; it there produces fruit in great abundance, but of a very strong odour. When gathered they obtain from it, either by friction or pressure, an unctuous liquid which diffuses an offensive smell, but for burning it is equal in quality to the oil of olives*."

From this and other references, it is clear that the Egyptians held the Palma Christi plant in high esteem, and Ebers, in referring to the commentary of the papyrus, ventured to suggest that an aperient medicine made from the fruit of the kesebt tree may have meant the ricinus seeds. Since the seeds of the Palma Christi have been frequently found in sarcophagi, there is good evidence that they had acquired a significant reputation (presumably medicinal).

There is much ancient commentary regarding the use and efficacy of the seeds. Thus Hippocrates sought to reduce the acridity of the seeds so as to

A Dioscorides depiction of the castor oil plant. It was well known even to the soldiers of the Roman legions that castor oil taken with warm water was a fine purgative. Military wisdom recognized that while an army marched best on a full stomach it fought best on an empty bowel! Thus a "bowel prep" for battle long preceded the same concept for or abdominal surgery!

An almost elegiac advertisement supporting the beneficial effects of castor oil.

make them more useful as purgatives, while Dioscorides alluded to their purgative properties, but only theorized on the possibility of the external usage of the oil as a medication. Pliny the Elder, however, was more explicit. Chapter xli., of Book 23 begins with the sentence: *"Oleum cicinum bibitur ad purgationes ventris cum pari calidae mensura."*

The translation of the entire passage is of even further interest. *"It is said, too, that as a purgative it acts particularly upon the regions of the diaphragm (precordia). It is useful for diseases of the joints, all kinds of indurations, affections of the uterus and ears, and for burns, employed with the ashes of the murex; it heals itch, scabs, and inflammations of the fundament. It improves the complexion also, and by its fertilizing tendencies promotes the growth of the hair. The cicus or seed from which this oil is made no animal will touch, and from these grape-like seeds wicks are made which burn with a peculiar brilliancy. The light, however, that is produced by the oil is very dim, in consequence of its extreme thickness. The leaves are applied topically with vinegar for erysipelas. Fresh gathered they are used by themselves for diseases of the mamilloe and defluxions. A decoction of them in wine with polenta and saffron is good for inflammations of various kinds. Boiled by themselves and applied to the face for three successive days they improve the complexion."*

In Egypt and Rome, therefore, Ricinus was evidently esteemed; and though as a medicine their popularity declined, it is clear from old English physic books that a traditional reputation was always associated with both the seeds and the oil. Gerard of England, in his *Herball*, and Piso of Holland, in an account of the natural history of the West Indies, both recommend them, the former in broth, the latter in the form of a tincture made with brandy for colic and constipation. Gerard states that the Palma Christi "of America" grew in his garden (in Holborn) and in many other gardens likewise. The seeds, however, came to be regarded as dangerous, and were little used in orthodox medicine. Thus Quincy in 1724 refers to them as *"hardly ever met with in practice, unless amongst empirics and persons of no credit."*

In 1764, however, Dr. Peter Canvane, of Bath, who had practiced for seven years in the West Indies, published a treatise entitled *A Dissertation on the Oleum Palmae Christi, sive Oleum Ricini, or (as it is commonly called) Castor Oil*, in which he warmly recommended the oil as a gentle purgative, particularly in cases of *"dry belly ache."* His advocacy soon took effect, for in the second edition of his treatise published in 1769, he declared with considerable enthusiasm that it had now become *"officinal"*! By this he meant that it was publicly available, *"at Apothecaries Hall and several other shops in London and Bath,"* and it was admitted into the London Pharmacopoeia in 1788. Dr. Odier, of Geneva, who visited England in 1776, became acquainted with the medicine, and subsequently brought it to the notice of Continental physicians.

The name *"Ricinus"* was in Latin the name of the parasite known as the dog-tick, *Ixodes Ricinus*, and was transferred to the Palma Christi seeds because of their resemblance to the insect. In Greek the same insect was called the kroton, and Theophrastus and Dioscorides describe the Palma Christi seeds as kroton seeds. Of some interest is the observation that in America the name kroton was applied to the cockroach, not from any association with ticks, but from a mistaken belief that the insects came from the Croton River when water from that source was brought to New York in 1842. The name of castor oil itself was similarly mistakenly applied to the oil in consequence of an erroneous idea in the Western Indies that the plant which yielded the seeds was *agnus castus*. There was, however, a castor oil and compound castor oil in medicinal use in England and other countries until the eighteenth century. This simple oil was made by digesting castorum in oil and boiling it with wine until the latter had all evaporated. In addition to its known ingredients this compound oil also contained a number of aromatic gums and spices which were remindive of the taste of the oil from the Palma Christi.

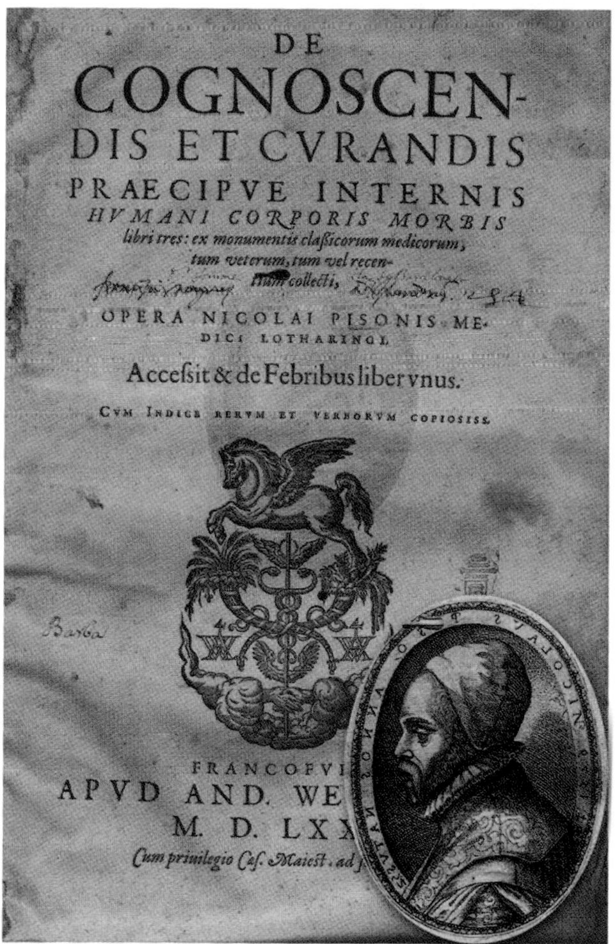
DE COGNOSCENDIS ET CVRANDIS PRAECIPVE INTERNIS HVMANI CORPORIS MORBIS libri tres: ex monumentis classicorum medicorum, tum veterum, tum vel recentium collecti,

OPERA NICOLAI PISONIS MEDICI LOTHARINGI.

Accessit & de Febribus liber vnus.

CVM INDICE RERVM ET VERBORVM COPIOSISS.

FRANCOFVR
APVD AND. WE
M. D. LXX
Cum privilegio Caes. Maiest. ad

The eminent and peripatetic Dutch physician, Nicholas Piso, explored the medicinal products of the West Indies in great detail as a physician to the Dutch West India Company. His important text on diseases of the New World contains useful information regarding novel medications, in particular the use of castor oil, as well as the first descriptions of previously unknown parasitic diseases and the condition of hepatic abscess.

William Withering and the purple foxglove. The observation by Withering in 1779 regarding the efficacy of extracts of the foxglove in the management of dropsy proved to be one of the seminal pharmacological discoveries of his time. Although he learned the secret from local folklore in Shropshire, he rightly deserved the credit for scientifically defining the nature of the remedy.

Digitalis

The purple foxglove was first described by Leonhard Fuchs (1501-1566), although later in the sixteenth century it was also commented upon by Hieronymus Bock and John Gerard who discussed it in his *Herball*. In the seventeenth century the *Theatrum botanicum* prepared by John Parkinson (1567-1650), London, 1640, featured it as did *The New London Dispensatory*, London, 1678, edited by William Salmon (d. *c.* 1700). It was not, however, commonly employed until William Withering (1741-1799) popularized it in the eighteenth century. The son of a successful practitioner, Withering studied at Edinburgh and practiced in Birmingham where in 1776 he published the first complete text on indigenous flora in English, *A Botanical Arrangement of All the Vegetables Naturally Growing in Great Britain*, Birmingham, 2 vols. Withering listed the various English names used by earlier herbalists, described the dietetic and medicinal uses of the plants, and provided a description of the poisonous characteristics they possessed. In 1755, Withering, having learnt of the diuretic value of the purple foxglove (rumor has it from an old woman of Shropshire) began to investigate its medicinal value. Although he gave a preliminary report of his findings at a meeting of the Medical Society of Edinburgh, in 1779, it was not until 1785 that he actually published his classic *An Account of the Foxglove*, Birmingham.

Although the studies undertaken by Withering were excellent, they were incomplete, since he failed to appreciate that the site of action of the drug was on the heart and not the kidneys. Nevertheless, he was cognizant of the toxic qualities of digitalis and warned physicians that when the drug showed evidence of disturbing the kidneys, stomach, or pulse, the medication should be withdrawn. Despite such admonitions and unaware of the mode of action of the drug, physicians ignored Withering's exhortations, and the subsequent fatal results of negligent administration resulted in a temporary decline in the use of foxglove. As a result of these early adverse events digitalis therapy remained in disfavor until the mid-nineteenth century, when physiologic animal experimentation enabled investigators such as Karl Ludwig (1816-1895) and Hermann Friedrich Stannius (1808-1883) to more precisely define the actions of the drug. By application of appropriate chemical techniques, Augustin-Eugene Homolle (1808-1883) and T.A.J. Quevenne (1805-1855) in 1844 discovered the active principle, amorphous digitalin, and in 1868 C. Adolph Nativelle was able to isolate crystalline digitalin.

Guaiacum

There is no clear understanding as to how guaiacum entered the medical armamentarium although its relationship with the treatment of syphilis appears to be the most likely explanation. Legend holds that a Spaniard, Gonsalvo Ferrand, having acquired the disease and finding no cure for it, determined to travel to the countries from which the infection had come, confident that he would there identify the remedy which the natives themselves employed. Having traveled to St. Domingo in 1508, the myth claims that he discovered that wood, Huaiacon, which was regarded as a specific remedy. Having procured a supply he was cured after administration. Whatever the truth of this tale might be, Ferrand subsequently became a well-known seller of guaiacum wood at seven gold crowns per pound (approx. $60), and accumulated a considerable fortune.

The substance enjoyed enormous popularity not only because of its relative efficacy (there was little else available) but also due to the impact of a book on *Morbus Gallicus* which was written in 1519 by Ulrich von Hutten, the German poet and reformer. His recounting of his travails with syphilis narrated his own experience whereby he had undergone salivation with mercury eleven times to no purpose; and how he had finally been cured completely in thirty days by a course of treatment by guaiacum. This early treatment, as it was developed in the sixteenth and the seventeenth centuries, is worthy of mention since it details yet another step in the long list of agents selected to cure the dreaded ravages of lues. First a decoction was made by boiling 1 lb

Jan van Der Straet (1570), also known as Stradanus, painted this depiction of a patient being treated with guaiac. The kitchen scene (right) demonstrates the guaiac bark being prepared by a workman whilst two women respectively weigh it and prepare the infusion. The patient (left) is in bed dutifully drinking the concoction, a flask of which is held by an assistant whilst the doctor, resplendent in his red gown, views the beneficial outcome with elegant assurance.

A guaiac pharmacological jar (inset) and the flower of the guaiac tree.

of the wood raspings in 8 or 10 pints of water down to 5 or 6 pints. After straining this off, another weaker decoction was made from the same wood. The syphilitic patient was prepared for his course of treatment by a few days spare diet, and by a few aperient doses. He was then placed in bed in a well-warmed room, and early every morning took half a pint of the first decoction warm. The dramatic temperature elevation that followed was accentuated by covering him with blankets and allowing sweating for two or three hours. Once recovered from this, he was dried and given a few biscuits with some almonds and raisins. The process was repeated in the latter part of the day, and continued twice a day for fifteen days, with only enough nourishment being provided so as to prevent the patient from collapsing. In the middle of the month a respite interval of one to two days was granted, and during that time the bowels were evacuated by an enema. Thereafter the treatment was renewed as before, but a rather more liberal diet was permitted with the second decoction taken as a drink as freely as the patient could be induced to swallow it. Gradually the usual habits of eating and drinking were resumed.

It is not surprising to learn that this treatment was soon accused of so reducing the strength of many patients that some never recovered from it, and it was actually in the process of being abandoned when Boerhaave revived it for a time as a remedy in syphilitic cases.

Ipecacuanha

Despite its importance as a critical remedy in the treatment of bowel disorders the precise origin of the agent is lost in the mists of time. Thus, several earlier allusions to ipecacuanha have been found, of which the first is an account from Brazil by a Portuguese friar written in a 1625 text by Purchas entitled *Pilgrimes*. The drug was referred to as *Igpecaya* and described as a remedy for the bloody flux. By 1686, however, it had been effectively introduced to European medicine when Louis XIV purchased its secret from Jean Adrien Helvetius after noting the remarkable cures of diarrhoea and dysentery that he had accomplished.

Helvetius, whose original name was Schweitzer, was the son of a Dutch quack, and had moved to Paris in an attempt to purvey his father's compounds amongst the aristocracy. Seeking to also further his own knowledge and acquire a degree of legitimacy, he had also enrolled himself as a student of medicine, and accompanied a physician of note, Afforty, in his attendance on a merchant called Garnier. The merchant, having recovered satisfactorily from his illness, sought to provide Afforty with the gift of a parcel of a new drug which he had received from Brazil. Although the physician was not tempted by the offer (preferring gold louis), Helvetius was more receptive to the idea of a novel agent and accepted it in lieu of mere gratitude. Undertaking his own study of it, he noted that the new compound was remarkably efficacious in the treatment of dysentery. Well-schooled in the arts of his father he placarded the corners of the streets with his

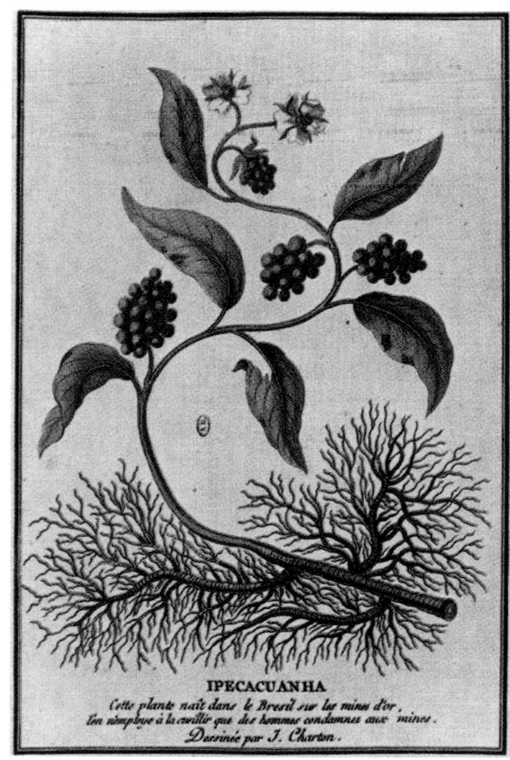

IPECACUANHA
Cette plante naît dans le Bresil sur les mines d'or,
on n'employe à la cueillir que des hommes condamnés aux mines.
Dessinée par J. Charton.

An early French drawing of the South American plant Cephaelis ipecacuanha*, from which ipecacuanha was derived. The agent was extracted by grinding the dried roots of either* C. ipecacuanha *or* C. accuminata *and was initially used for its expectorant and diaphoretic properties. The recognition that higher dosages resulted in emesis and purging subsequently led to its widespread usage in the treatment of poisoning.*

Society in general was extremely preoccupied with bowel evacuation and agents that augmented such activity were popular. The English cartoonists were especially sarcastic when depicting the utility of either such medications or the effects of enemas and considering them in a political or social context. In the engraving entitled "Idol worship or the way to Preferment," George II, King of England is depicted as having made his posterior into an idol for veneration by his subjects. Ipecacuanha could thus be regarded as a medication whose efficacy enhanced the performance of a regal activity.

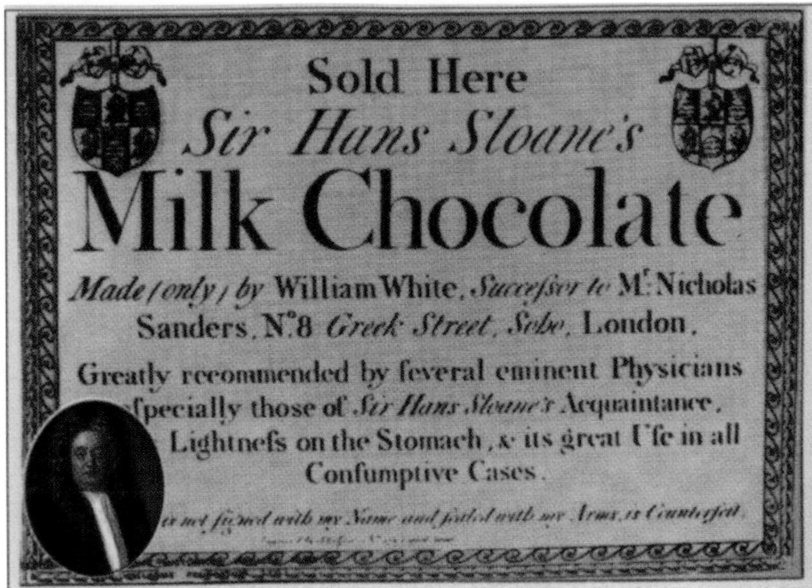

The introduction of ipecacuanha proved to be of remarkable efficacy in the treatment of dysentery. Sir Hans Sloane (inset) was a British physician and naturalist whose extraordinary collection of books, manuscripts, and curiosities formed the basis for the establishment of the British Museum in London. After having studied medicine in London, he traveled to France and received an MD degree from the University of Orange in 1683. While visiting Jamaica in 1687, he collected more than 800 new species of plants and published an elaborate Latin catalog on the subject in 1696. When created a baronet in 1716, he was the first medical practitioner to receive a hereditary title and became not only the physician to King George II but President of the Royal Society in 1727. On Sloane's retirement from active work in 1741, his library and cabinet of curiosity had grown to be of unique value and on his death he bequeathed his collection to the nation on condition that Parliament paid his executors £20,000. This bequest was accepted and became the basis of the collection that formed the British Museum when opened in 1759. Given his status and celebrity as well as his training as a physician, the attachment of Sloane's name to a particular product assured it of widespread public acceptance.

announcements of a new remedy, but cleverly refrained from indicating either the source or nature of the medication. Colbert, with his ear for even the most trivial of information, having heard of the success of Helvetius, mentioned the remedy to Louis XIV when the Dauphin was ill with dysentery. Fortune favored the young Dutch quack, who with the consent of the court physician, D'Aquin, was then permitted to treat the Dauphin. As a result of this huge success the king authorized D'Aquin and his confessor, the Père de la Chaise, to negotiate with Helvetius for the publication of his secret. With all due modesty the young opportunist sold the recipe for a thousand louis d'or, and successfully rebuffed the legal attempts of the merchant Garnier, who vainly sued for a share in the profit. Having succeeded in earning a reputation and a fortune, Helvetius embarked upon a successful medical career as Inspector General of the Hospitals of Flanders, and physician to the Duke of Orleans. The family fortunes waxed high as both his son and grandson prospered, the latter becoming a fashionable French poet and philosopher in the generation before the Revolution.

It appears from a treatise which Helvetius wrote that at first ipecacuanha was given in doses of 2 drachms, sometimes in decoctions and sometimes in enemas. Hans Sloane in England and Leibnitz in Germany wrote warmly in favor of the new remedy, but it was not till thirty years after it had been introduced that the dose was popularly reduced to some 4 to 10 grains. The fortuitous combination of ipecacuanha with opium as prepared by Dover had a considerable effect in ensuring its permanent adoption.

A depiction of a tapeworm of seemingly gigantic proportions surrounded by a verbal screed denouncing the abomination of the infestation and alluding to methods for cure. The identification of gastrointestinal parasites and their relationship to disease led to the search for agents such as kousso as remedies.

Kousso

Although the problem of worm infestation is not well-known in modern society and for the most part confined to developing countries, in ancient times parasitic worm infestation was a major health problem. Thus remedies to the disease were held in high regard. The first reports of the effectiveness of kousso were produced by Camé Brayer, a French physician named as residing in Constantinople about 1820. In fact, however, Bruce, the African traveler, and others had described the tree which bears the kousso flowers in Abyssinia (*Hagena Abyssinica*) and noted that the natives used these as worm medicine. Nevertheless the Brayer story is worth relating. The latter recounted that one day in a café he encountered a waiter extremely emaciated and suffering from severe abdominal pains from tapeworm. An old Armenian habitué of the café had informed the miserable waiter that he possessed a remedy which his son had brought from Abyssinia, and which he was certain would cure him. Brayer ascertained the successful result of the experiment and subsequently tested the remedy on other patients with similar felicitous results. Thereafter he sent some of the flowers to the German botanist Knuth, who having been unable to identify the species declared its novelty and named the tree *Brayera anthelmintica*. Despite the remarkable utility of the agent, it received little publicity and achieved no acclaim until about the year 1850, when a Frenchman offered the flowers in London for 35s. per ounce. As might be predicted, the excessive price garnered considerable attention for the remedy, which thereafter rose to a position of some prominence.

Philip, Duke of Orleans, after whom the city of New Orleans was named. As an individual of excessively debauched tastes and modest political skills it is likely that his physician, Helvetius, was kept well employed in ministering to the medicinal needs of his master.

Sarsaparilla

An agent of dubious medicinal value whose history has been clouded by its diffuse usage as a tonic, restorative and homeopathic remedy. Even the origin of the name of sarsaparilla is not agreed upon, with some authorities attributing it to *sarsa* – red, and *parilla* – a little vine. Littré believed that it derived it from *zarza* – a bramble, and *Parilla* – the name of a hypothetical Spaniard who initially helped to introduce it. The native Indians call it salsa, and the French follow this origin and call it salsepareille.

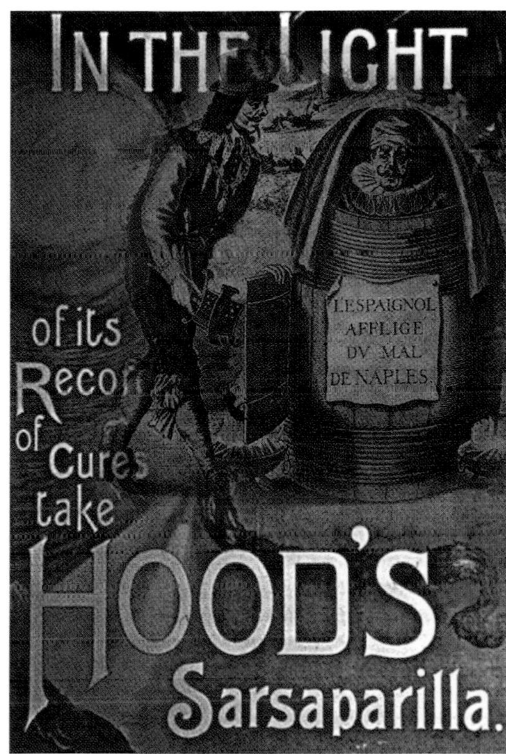

Sarsaparilla was initially considered useful in the treatment of syphilis but its efficacy was considerably augmented when used with either mercury or the sweating cure (inset).

It was introduced into Europe early in the sixteenth century, and soon acquired great fame, having been reputed to have effected the cure of the great Emperor Charles V, of gout. It appeared subsequently that it was really China root, another smilax, that had been administered to the Emperor, but it was called sarsaparilla, with the result that western medicine received the credit. Although sarsaparilla was initially much vaunted as a cure for syphilis, physicians soon discovered that it was much more effective whenever it was combined with mercurials.

Nevertheless, its advocates insisted that it was a wonderful sudorific, and for many years a "sweating cure" was common practice in Denmark and Sweden where it was reported to have achieved apparent success. Despite the fact that sarsaparilla possessed no sudorific properties whatever, it continued to be administered in long draughts in conjunction with other more effective medicines. This combination, to which was added vigorous exercise and heavy blankets, proved to be effective adjuncts of the cure and the associated sudorific result that ensued continued to be attributed to the effect of sarsaparilla. Even further misconceptions regarding the precise nature of the active agent further obfuscated the history of this so-called remedy. Thus the species which Linnaeus selected as the medicinal sarsaparilla and which he named *Smilax sarsaparilla*, fortuitously was the only one of some two hundred species which has never been employed in medicine at all! It is only found in North America and not further south than Virginia, whereas the Jamaica sarsaparilla which attained the highest medicinal reputation is grown only in Central America, while actual Jamaican-grown sarsaparilla was considered inferior and never deemed of value in Europe.

Corrosive Sublimate

Gerard L.B. van Swieten (1700-1772) was one of Boerhaave's most outstanding and faithful pupils and although not recognized for his creative skills, achieved fame not only for faithfully recording the lectures of Boerhaave, but for his administrative skill in reestablishing the potency of the medical school of Vienna. In 1736, chiefly through Boerhaave's influence, having been appointed professor of *materia medica* at Leiden, he was forced for religious reasons to relinquish the chair. Certain Protestants, opposed to the appointment of the Catholic van Swieten, invoked an old Dutch statute that forbade a Catholic to hold any public position, and thus in 1745 he accepted an offer as court physician to Maria Theresa (1717-780) and, a year

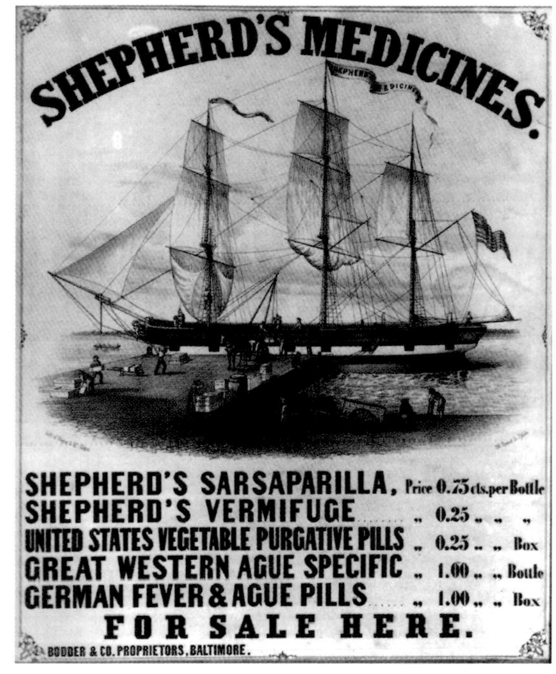

The lithograph depicts an American schooner (c. 1860) being loaded with drugs for export. Such was the much-vaunted efficacy of sarsaparilla as a cure for diverse diseases that it was the number one agent on a pharmaceutical listing of medicines prepared by the Shepherd pharmaceutical group and marketed by Bodder & Co. of Baltimore.

The protean manifestations of syphilis as well as the ubiquitous nature of the disease provided a fertile field for the development of quack remedies and false claims. Van Swieten (inset) was a powerful advocate of mercury dissolved in brandy as a cure and for obvious reasons this remedy achieved considerable popularity. Innumerable quacks each developed their own modifications of combinations of mercury and a variety of other metals and vegetable extracts for the treatment of syphilis. Given the high likelihood of failure, public ire directed against such individuals was often considerable as demonstrated in this 19th-century London cartoon.

Sylvius of Leiden, in the Netherlands, was so ardent a supporter of the use of opium that he believed the practice of medicine was not possible without its usage.

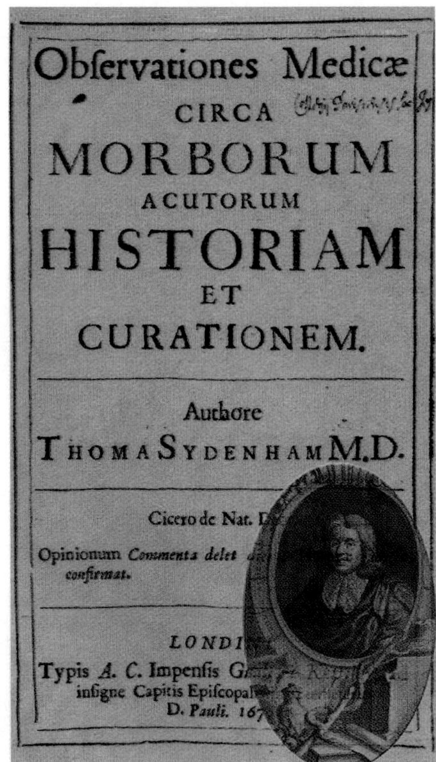

Observationes Medicæ
CIRCA
MORBORUM
ACUTORUM
HISTORIAM
ET
CURATIONEM.

Authore
THOMA SYDENHAM M.D.

Cicero de Nat. D

Opinionum *Commenta delet* ... *confirmat.*

LONDI

Typis *A. C.* Impensis G...
insigne Capitis Episcopal...
D. Pauli. 167

The much revered physician, Thomas Sydenham of London, stated with assurance "among the remedies which it has pleased almighty God to give to man to relieve his sufferings, none is so universal and so efficacious as opium!" Caveat emptor.

later, was appointed to the Chair of Medicine at Vienna. About 1754, van Swieten observed that the mercurial medications then in vogue for the treatment of syphilis were harmful, and began to experiment with various solutions of corrosive sublimate. During these investigations he indirectly learned from Antonio Nuñez Ribeiro Sanchez (1699-1783) that Russian surgeons were administering corrosive sublimate internally, without the appearance of excessive salivation, by dissolving 1 grain of bichloride of mercury in 2 ounces of brandy. Mercuric acetate, sulphate, and nitrate were also employed at this time. Van Swieten adopted the Russian prescription and it soon acquired the name of *liquor Swietenii*. He is also eponymously remembered by the *Febrifuge Swietenia*.

Opium

The ancients recognized two kinds of opium. The superior kind was called *opion*, and was the juice which exuded from the poppy head while it was growing; and the second quality, which was named *meconion*, was an extract made from the crushed heads and leaves of the poppy. Surprisingly enough for so well-known and widespread an agent, it appears that Hippocrates was not acquainted with the juice of the poppy. Although he refers to mecon, he attributes to it purgative as well as narcotic powers and may well have been describing some other plant. In either event his remedies rely very little on poppy or opium if he used either. On the other hand, Theophrastus was certainly aware of opium, and Dioscorides in his text clearly distinguishes between *opion* and *meconion*, providing a prescription for the famous *Dia-kodion* (made from the poppy head), the forerunner of the twentieth-century agent-syrup of poppies. His process was to macerate 120 poppy heads for two days in 3 sextarii (a sextarius was almost a pint) of rainwater, which was then boiled, strained, mixed with honey, and evaporated to a suitable consistence.

The use of opium in the Far East was not restricted to the management of disease. Indeed, opium became the cause of a disease (addiction) when used excessively. Such was its power that acquisition and abuse of the substance even led to war (the Opium Wars).

It is likely that the shopkeepers and traveling quacks made more use of opium in Rome than the regular physicians. Galen is emphatic in noting that he never used the drug except in very urgent cases, although he enthusiastically commended several confections such as *theriaca* which owed their efficiency to opium more than to any other ingredient. Indeed, it is likely that the efficacy of such remedies may be said to be more the reflection of their opium content, and that it was this agent that maintained the medicinal usage of such compounds for many subsequent centuries.

Paracelsus himself owed much of his success to the liberal fashion with which he dispensed opium to his patients, evidence that his contemporaries did not use it to any great extent. His followers were as enthusiastic as himself over the virtues of opium, and before long even the most conservative of practitioners were advocating it, and devising formulas for its suitable administration. Thus by about 1600, Platearius of Basle strongly recommended it for diverse illnesses, and in Holland, de la Boe (Sylvius), the eminent Dutch physician and mentor of Regnier de Graaf, said that without opium he would not practice. Indeed, such was its popularity and described efficacy that the eminent Van Helmont (*c.* 1640) used opium so frequently that he was widely referred to as the *Doctor Opiatus*. Similarly, the thoughtful and erudite Sydenham about 1680 noted, *"Among the remedies which it has pleased Almighty God to give to man to relieve his sufferings, none is so universal and so efficacious as opium."* Although many eminent physicians concurred with this viewpoint there were some, such as Stahl, who wrote a treatise entitled *De Imposturis Opii*, who demurred with vigor. Similarly, Hoffmann considered that the use of opium was greatly abused, and he believed his ether would fulfill and subsume its role in almost all instances.

Although its narcotic and analgesic effects had been long known, the adulteration of many other medications with opium reached a zenith in the eighteenth century. The apothecary shop of the time as dark, dismal, full of cobwebs, odoriferous canisters, and careless clerks, none mindful of the damage that inappropriate or wanton administration of medication might inflict. Particularly unfortunate was the method employed in dispensing narcotics, which were often surreptiously added to other, often useless medicines to amplify their efficacy. The picture which Thomas De Quincey (1785-1859) portrayed, concerning the circumstances surrounding his own addiction, are extremely enlightening and provide an exhilarating if depressing assessment of the circumstances surrounding his own addiction. *"... oftentimes lozenges for the relic of pulmonary affections found their efficacy upon the opium which they contain ... and under such treacherous disguise multitudes are seduced into a dependency which they had not foreseen upon a drug which they had not known; not known even by name or by sight: and thus the case is not rare that the chain of abject slavery is first detected when it has inextricably wound itself about the constitutional system."*

De Quincey listed the physiologic properties of opium as follows:

(1) to tranquillize all irritations of the nervous system;
(2) to stimulate the capacities of enjoyment; and
(3) under any call for extraordinary exertion ...
to sustain through twenty-four consecutive hours the else
drooping animal energies ...

Thomas de Quincey became an opium addict and documented in exquisite detail its effects upon his life by writing an extraordinary text: Confessions of an Opium Eater.

Although subsequent to the publication of the work of De Quincey's and the broader recognition of the problem, reforms were made in the dispensing of narcotics, the situation remained parlous. Indeed, the average eighteenth-century pharmacy was regarded with such aversion that many physicians who had the time or a capable assistant, preferred to dispense their own medications. This practice itself was, however, open to serious abuse and in England, pharmacists of the time also practiced medicine under a transparent and unethical evasion apropos of which De Quincey noted:

Unhappily my professional adviser was a comatose old
gentleman, rich beyond all his needs, careless
of his own practice, and standing under that painful necessity
(according to the custom then regulating medical
practice, which prohibited fees to apothecaries) of seeking his
remuneration in excessive deluges of medicine.
Me, however, out of pure idleness, he forebore to plague with
any variety of medicines. With simplicity he confined
himself to one horrid mixture, that must have suggested itself
to him when prescribing for a tiger.

As a result of the inclination of physicians to tout, as well as sell, their own medications, the role of the apothecary became still further degraded with the result that his practice became confined to the necessary position of catering to the kitchen-cupboard doctors and neighborhood busybodies. As might be predicted under the circumstances that prevailed, the majority of pharmacists yearned to concoct some witches' broth, which was usually compounded of the season's odds and ends and, after experimentation on some unsuspecting animal (to obtain a reasonable assurance of its non-lethal character) was ladled out to the spring cathartic trade. Included among the more humorous items stocked by these apothetaries were papers of white Greek earth, tins of dried millipedes, and bins of psyllium seeds.

Dover's powder dates from the late seventeenth century being named after Thomas Dover (1660-1742), pirate, member of the Royal College of Physicians, and author of a popular medical work for the laity entitled *Ancient Physician's Legacy to his Country*, London, 1733. A physician of the time, Silvester O'Halloran (1728-1807), writing in his text, *A New Treatise on the Different Disorders arising from the External injuries of the Head* (London 1783) said of Dover's powder, *"I would warmly recommend medicines of this kind, and particularly Dover's Powder. Indeed, I am so fond of it, that as it is seldom known, or prescribed in shops; I have always a quantity of it by me, ready prepared. This medicine, which is called Dover's Sweating Powder, has for its basis, opium and ipecacuanha, and is a powerful diaphoretic."*

The earliest use of opium and its relationship to the poppy may be found in the Sumerian records of Mesopotamia (5000 B.C.). The substance is also documented in Syrian medical tablets and the writings of Homer (c. 900 B.C.) as well as Hippocrates (c. 400 B.C.) who described extensive use of opium. Its introduction to Rome followed the conquest of the Eastern Mediterranean and by A.D. 130, physicians such as Galen were enthusiastic advocates of the virtues of opium. Opium-smoking began only after the early Europeans in North America discovered the Indian practice of smoking tobacco in pipes. Thereafter smokers began to mix opium with tobacco and smoking gradually became the preferred method of taking opium. The technique of opium-smoking had initially been introduced from Java into China in the 17th century and spread rapidly as European exposure, first via the Portuguese and then, the Dutch East India Company, introduced the habit to the West. Although the Chinese authorities were initially restrictive and prohibited the sale of opium, such edicts were largely ignored and China became an expanding and profitable market for the drug. The Western trading companies found the demand so voracious that the opium trade enabled them to acquire Chinese goods such as silk and tea without having to spend gold and silver. As a result of the widespread opium addiction in China and the Chinese government's attempts to prohibit the import of opium from British-ruled India, conflict developed with the British government that culminated in the Opium Wars. The Chinese defeat resulted in the legalization of the importation of opium in 1858 and remained a major problem until 1949 when the advent of the Communist government resulted in the eradication of the practice.

The recognition of salicylic acid as an anti-pyretic and anti-rheumatic led to its widespread marketing in both Europe and the United States by the end of the 19th century.

The Salicylates

In Europe, the primary source of salicylic compounds was willow bark and the agent was used as such in a variety of forms. Thus, the *Dublin Pharmacopoeia* listed the *Salix fragile* and *Salix alba*, the *London Pharmacopoeia* recognized *Salix caprea*, while the *Pharmacopeia of the United States* also mentioned a *Salix criocephala*. Surprisingly all these pharmacopoeias recommended the use of these substances as substitutes for cinchona, despite the fact that cinchona and *Salix* resemble each other only in antipyretic effect, unless poisonous doses are administered. On the other hand, the checkerberry (*Gaultheria*), which seems not to have been considered at all similar in its action to *Salix*, depends for its pharmacologic value upon the same chemical substance. Other plants containing salicylic acid, such as *Spiraea ulmaria* and *Andromeda leschenaultii*, occupied dubious positions, quite unrelated to those assigned to their chemical relatives. Thus, *Andromeda* was frequently used as a wash for the ground itch, to which the slaves of Georgia and the Carolinas were especially subject (ankylostomiasis).

This diverse utility of the botanical agent representing the salicylic compounds would have probably remained unchanged had it not been for the shift towards the chemical consideration of therapeutic agents. Indeed, if patients had been forced to rely upon the herbalists, it is more than likely that knowledge of the salicylic compounds would not have progressed beyond this generalized anecdotal experience. Thus, in the first *Pharmacopeia of the United States*, the checkerberry (*Gaultheria*) was listed in only a secondary classification although, as the grouseberry or deerberry it was quite popular among the people and the Indians who had long employed it under the name of "*pollom*." As such, it was widely utilized by the lay public in the treatment of asthma and it was also claimed to have anodyne properties.

Salicylic acid compounds were initially only available by extraction from willow bark. The application of pharmaceutical and chemical manufacturing processes, however, rapidly led to their production on a commercial basis with the use of potent marketing techniques to bring products to the attention of the consumer. One suspects that if the dog had its way the picture might have been entitled "Howard's End."

No clear understanding existed as to the explanation for the wide variety of plants that exhibited similar therapeutic properties. Finally, as a result of independent chemical investigations, it became apparent that the various species contained essentially the same substances. Thus in 1831, Leroux, a pharmacist at Vitry, isolated salicin from willow bark and shortly thereafter in 1838, Rafelle Piria (1815-1865) produced salicylic acid by the chemical decomposition of salicin. By 1843 Auguste Cahours had prepared salicylic acid from oil of *Gaultheria* and it was shortly afterward discovered that salicylic acid exists in the free state in *Spiraea* and *Andromeda*. A further masterful piece of work by Adolph W.K. Kolke (1818-1884), who as a student of Wohler, had been thoroughly imbued with his mentor's belief that organic substances are derived from inorganic material, demonstrated that by boiling phenol with caustic soda and carbon tetrachloride, he was able to produce salicylic acid. Aware of the fact that the surgeon, Lister, had been utilizing phenol as an antiseptic since 1867, the German surgeon, Karl Thiersch (1822-1895) in 1875 proposed that salicylic acid be afforded a formal surgical role believing that it too possessed antiseptic properties. Considerable credit is, however, due to C.E. Buss who, recalling the original use of willow, recommended salicylic acid as an antipyretic. Although its efficacy in this capacity was initially deemed to be limited, it gained considerable popularity as an antirheumatic and these properties were subsequently intensively investigated by Jean-Baptiste-Vincent Laborde (1830-1903) and Edme-Felix-Alfred Vulpian (1826-1887).

The poisonous effects of salicylic acid were perceived early and having been thoroughly investigated in the 1880s, led to a search for a compound with lower toxicity and higher therapeutic efficiency. Thus the observation of the analgesic and antipyretic properties of the salicylic compounds stimulated interest in the possible factors of those substances which were responsible for those particular effects. As a result of these investigations, a variety of substances were identified, including salol (phenylsalicylate) and aspirin (acetylsalicylic acid). Almost simultaneous with the interest in the salicylates agents was the physiologic focus on the subject of metabolism, and in particular the study of the mechanism of heat production and dissipation. Given the fact that salicylic compounds possessed a benzene ring, research was initially directed towards the aniline derivatives, but the first of the new synthetic antipyretics to be produced was a pyrazolon derivative (antipyrine) produced by Emile Knorr (1884-1937), and obtained by heating ethyl acetoacetate with phenyl hydrazine. Acetanilide was probably the first of the so-called coal tar antipyretics to be produced and, with the evolution of newer compounds, it became evident that an antipyretic action was a general characteristic of compounds that possessed a benzol or pyrazol ring, but if excessive ring modification was undertaken, the antipyretic effect was either lost or the substance acquired toxic characteristics. Furthermore, it became apparent that as the primary compounds became modified by the addition of various radicals, new characteristics, such as changes in solubility and chemical incompatibility, were produced. Similarly the relationship between the antipyretic action of quinine and willow bark was delineated such that the definite chemical basis became apparent (since quinine is a quinoline derivative), as did the great diversity between the two substances in other respects became explicable.

Fortunately the advances of the chemical school of thought occurred at the time when the therapeutic nihilism of the Viennese school had begun to

Lord Lister and his microscope. Apart from being a superb surgeon and an excellent scientist it was his introduction of the carbolic spray (bottom right) to operating rooms that transformed surgery. The subsequent diminution of sepsis revolutionized the development of surgery as much as the advances in anesthesia.

wane, and thus scientific input enabled major contributions to the understanding of the action and constitution of drugs. Since the aspirations of humankind change little with the passage of time but mostly alter in formulation and mode of expression, it remained the fervent belief that novel chemical techniques might enable pharmacology to support the development of specifics for various diseases or that it might be possible to prepare a single medicine against disease processes as a whole. Experience, perhaps cynicism, and the ebbing of religious zealotry allowed these ideas to be contemplated with less fervor than when initially advanced on a wide scale, some two centuries before.

Anesthesia

The use of analgesic and narcotic substances in medicine is a component of some of the earliest medical texts and practices. As such, it has evolved from wild berries, fermented grain, and poppy extracts through magnetism, mesmerism and alcoholic spirits to the use of gases and specific chemical agents. Ether (sulphuric ether) had not only been known as a chemical substance from the sixteenth century onward, but had been suggested as an inhalant for tuberculosis, although a sanatorium founded at Bristol, England for this purpose was a failure. In regard to its usage Coxe commented of ether as follows: *"when applied externally; it is capable of producing two very opposite effects, according to its management; for, if it be prevented from evaporating,... it proves a powerful stimulant and rubefacient, and excites the sensation of burning heat... On the contrary, if it be dropped on any part of the body, exposed freely to the contact of the air, its rapid evaporation produces an intense degree of cold..."*

With his usual creativity, Cullen employed it either as a rubefacient for toothache or as an analgesic to reduce hernias. Administration could be undertaken in two forms: either internally in doses varying from 20 drops upward and in various vehicles, or it could be given in the form of enemata. Nitrous oxide was isolated, in 1776, by Joseph Priestley and its peculiar effect when inhaled became known as the result of work by Humphry Davy (1778-1829) at the Bristol sanatorium, mentioned above. Davy, in fact, observed, *"As nitrous oxide in its extensive operation seems capable of destroying physical pain, it may probably be used with advantage during surgical operations in which no great effusion of blood takes place"* but did not actually attempt such an experiment. In 1824, Henry Hill Hickman (1800-1830), of England, actually succeeded in rendering animals unconscious by the inhalation of nitrous oxide but Coxe, in his commentary, failed to recognize its potential and focused on the "laughing gas" nature of the agent: *"Its respiration, when perfectly pure, when mixed with atmospheric air, produces the highest excitement of which the animal frame seems capable."*

Despite the seemingly benign nature of the gas and its analgesic properties, the subject of ether provided one of the most acrid controversies in the history of medicine. Much like the Four Horseman of the Apocalypse of pain, Horace Wells (1815-1848), William Thomas Green Morton (1819-1868), Charles Thomas Jackson (1805-1880), and Crawford William Long (1815-1878) each variously achieved immortality, suffering and fame from their contributions. Although the subject is cluttered by the innumerable texts written on these men and their claims, the general consensus is: that Long was the first to employ ether as an anesthetic agent on March 30, 1842; that Horace Wells, a dentist of Hartford, administered nitrous oxide while extracting teeth in 1844; that Morton consulted Jackson concerning a more

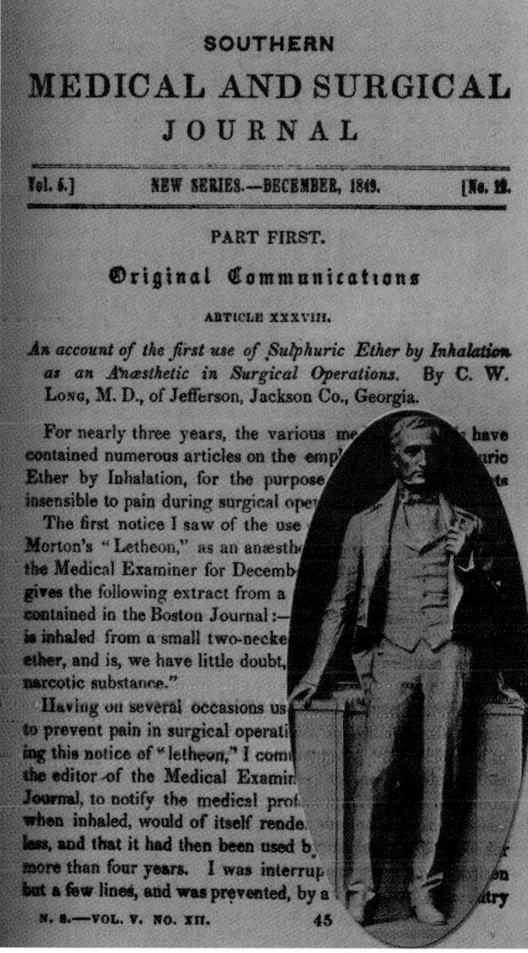

SOUTHERN
MEDICAL AND SURGICAL
JOURNAL

Vol. 5.] NEW SERIES.—DECEMBER, 1849. [No. 12.

PART FIRST.

Original Communications

ARTICLE XXXVIII.

An account of the first use of Sulphuric Ether by Inhalation as an Anæsthetic in Surgical Operations. By C. W. Long, M. D., of Jefferson, Jackson Co., Georgia.

For nearly three years, the various me
contained numerous articles on the emp
Ether by Inhalation, for the purpose
insensible to pain during surgical ope
The first notice I saw of the use
Morton's "Letheon," as an anæsth
the Medical Examiner for Decemb
gives the following extract from a
contained in the Boston Journal:—
is inhaled from a small two-necke
ether, and is, we have little doubt,
narcotic substance."
Having on several occasions us
to prevent pain in surgical operati
ing this notice of "letheon," I com
the editor of the Medical Examir
Journal, to notify the medical prof
when inhaled, would of itself rende
less, and that it had then been used b
more than four years. I was interrup
but a few lines, and was prevented, by a

N. S.—VOL. V. NO. XII. 45

Crawford Long (1815-1878) of Georgia described the inhalation of sulfuric ether as an anesthetic for surgical operations.

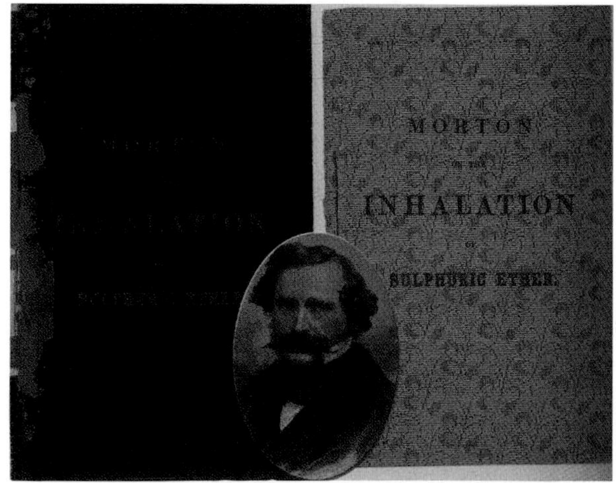

William Morton (1819-1868) claimed discovery of the use of sulfuric ether as an anesthetic agent.

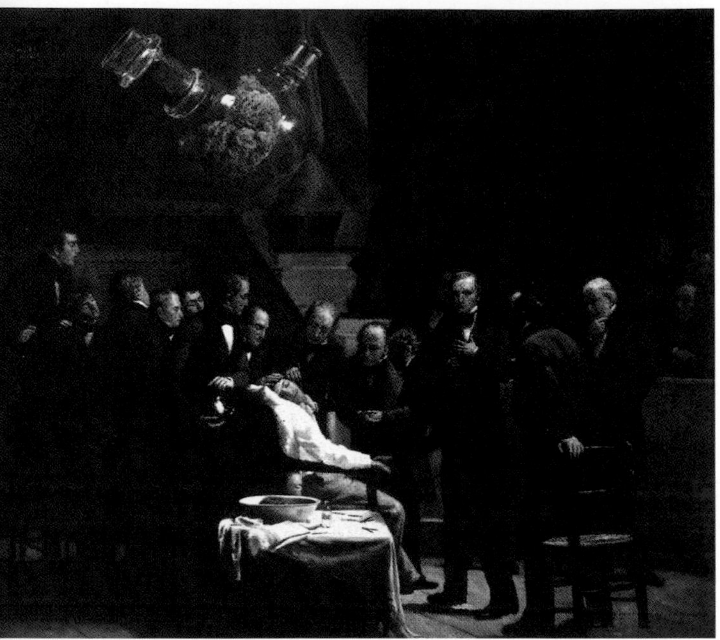

John C. Warren of the Massachusetts General Hospital operating on a patient anesthetized with an inhaler (inset) containing Morton's "letheon".

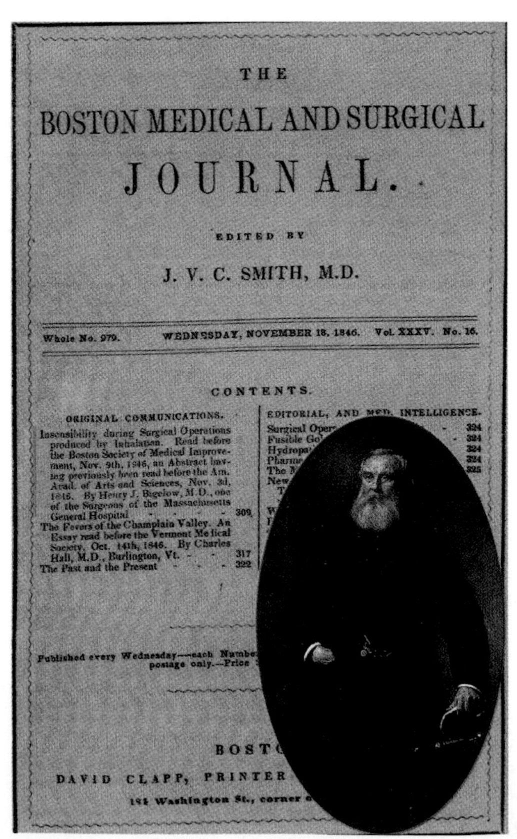

THE

BOSTON MEDICAL AND SURGICAL

JOURNAL.

EDITED BY

J. V. C. SMITH, M.D.

Whole No. 979. WEDNESDAY, NOVEMBER 18, 1846. Vol. XXXV. No. 16.

CONTENTS.

ORIGINAL COMMUNICATIONS.

Insensibility during Surgical Operations produced by Inhalation. Read before the Boston Society of Medical Improvement, Nov. 9th, 1846, an Abstract having previously been read before the Am. Acad. of Arts and Sciences, Nov. 3d, 1846. By Henry J. Bigelow, M.D., one of the Surgeons of the Massachusetts General Hospital - - - - - 309

The Fevers of the Champlain Valley. An Essay read before the Vermont Medical Society, Oct. 14th, 1846. By Charles Hall, M.D., Burlington, Vt. - - - 317

The Past and the Present - - - - 322

EDITORIAL, AND MED. INTELLIGENCE.

Published every Wednesday—each Number

DAVID CLAPP, PRINTER

The Boston Medical Journal of 1846 in which Henry Bigelow (inset) reported on the efficacy of anesthesia in surgery.

suitable anesthetic agent and, finally, that Morton himself successfully demonstrated the use of ether, in surgical operations, at the Massachusetts General Hospital in 1846.

Crawford W. Long was born in Danielsville, Georgia in 1815, studied medicine at the Universities of Transylvania and Pennsylvania and, after some graduate study in New York, returned to Georgia, where he established a rural practice. Early in 1842 some young men, in imitation of certain lecturers on chemistry who were then touring the country, inhaled ether as a form of amusement in the doctor's office. During these "frolics" Long observed that, while stuporose, the men frequently injured themselves without even realizing that they had done so. After due consideration he decided to try ether inhalation on a surgical case. A month or so later, on March 30, 1842, Long administered ether to James M. Venable and successfully removed a tumor from his neck. Unfortunately, he neglected to report his discovery until 1848 when he presented a lucid account of this operation at the annual meeting of the Georgia Medical Society. Although Long had never made any secret of the anesthetic value of ether and possessed sufficient documentary evidence to support priority claims, it was not until 1854, when Morton and Jackson endeavored to obtain financial aid from Congress, that this material became widely known, having been introduced by Senator Dawson of Georgia. Upon the publication of the evidence, Jackson examined the claims of Long at Athens, Georgia, and adjudicated that the Georgian be accorded the honor of priority publishing a statement to this effect in the April 11, 1861 issue of the *Boston Medical and Surgical Journal*. Subsequently in 1877, James Marion Sims (1813-1883) began his successful crusade for the universal recognition of Long as the discoverer of ether anesthesia, and the contributions of Crawford W. Long to anesthesiology achieved appropriate recognition.

Unfortunately, the tale of the other men involved in the introduction of anesthesia does not read as well, and for the most part their lives were filled with frustration and disappointment. Thus the young dentist, Horace Wells, committed suicide, William T.G. Morton died in unusual circumstances in Central Park in the wake of a neural disorder, and Charles Jackson died a raving lunatic in an insane asylum. Of these, Morton is worthy of more detailed consideration. Born in 1819 at Charlton, Massachusetts, he studied dentistry at the Baltimore College of Dental Surgery, and became a partner of Horace Wells. Unfortunately, this venture proved financially unsuccessful, and the partnership was dissolved in 1843, when each opened private offices. Morton wished to become a physician and in 1844, while practicing dentistry, enrolled as a medical student at Harvard. As a consequence of the distractions of the ether controversy he failed to complete his medical studies. On September 30, 1846, after a number of successful experiments on himself, he extracted the tooth of a patient who had been rendered unconscious by ether inhalation. Realizing the potential applications of his observation, Morton then sought a demonstration at the Massachusetts General Hospital and on October 16, in the narrow pit before the steep, wooden tiers of the old amphitheater, he successfully anesthetized a surgical patient of John C. Warren. Unfortunately, Morton engendered some discomfort in declining to announce the formula of what, at first, he termed "my preparation" and acquired a patent for it as

ACCOUNT

OF A

NEW ANÆSTHETIC AGENT,

AS A

SUBSTITUTE FOR SULPHURIC ETHER

REPUBLISHED BY RUSHTON, CLARK, & CO.,

CHEMISTS AND DRUGGISTS,

110 BROADWAY, AND 10 ASTOR HOUSE.

1848.

James Young Simpson, professor of Obstetrics at Edinburgh, was an early advocate of the use of chloroform as a substitute for sulfuric ether to facilitate childbirth.

"Letheon," on November 12, 1846, although everyone was soon aware that it was ether. Of interest is the fact that Oliver Wendell Holmes (1809-1894), a lawyer turned anatomist, though neither a surgeon nor a pharmacologist, is usually credited with the introduction of the term anesthetic, although the term anesthesia and its adjectival form were in common use throughout the eighteenth century.

Although chloroform was isolated in 1831 by three independent investigators, Justus von Liebig, Eugène Soubeiran (1793-1858) and Samuel Guthrie (1782-1848), it did not appear in pharmacopoeias or dispensatories until much later. The exciting report of the surgical application of ether inhalation reached England late in 1846 and the substance was immediately employed by individuals such as John Snow (1813-1858), one of the foremost of the early English anesthetists. His initial experiences with the agent from early 1847 until September of that year were published under the title of *On the Inhalation of the Vapour of Ether in Surgical Operations*, London, 1847. Not far behind their counterparts in London were the Scottish physicians and at approximately the same time as Snow was employing ether in London, James Young Simpson (1811-1870), professor of obstetrics of Edinburgh, was using "etherisation" during deliveries. Believing chloroform to be a more effective agent in obstetric practice, in November he substituted it for ether and, shortly afterward, published an *Account of a New Anesthetic Agent*, Edinburgh, 1847. As a consequence of so influential an opinion, chloroform soon became the favorite anesthetic of the English despite the relatively high mortality rate associated with its usage. Indeed, prior to the introduction of chloroform Snow had administered ether 152 times, but, at the request of the operating surgeons, over the course of the succeeding decade he administered chloroform 4,000 times and using ether on only a dozen occasions. Despite his apparent practice to the contrary Snow maintained that he preferred ether not only for its *greater pleasantness* but also because it is safer. "*I believe that ether is altogether incapable of causing the sudden death by paralysis of the heart, which has caused the accidents which have happened during the administration of chloroform. I have not been able to kill an animal in that manner with ether, even when I have made it boil, and administered the vapour almost pure. The heart has continued to beat after the natural breathing has ceased, even when the vapour has been exhibited without air; and in all cases in which animals have been made to breathe air saturated with ether vapour; at the ordinary temperatures of this country, they have always recovered if they were withdrawn from the vapour before the breathing ceased. Even in cases where the natural breathing had ceased, if the animal made a gasping inspiration after its removal from the ether it recovered. I hold it, therefore, to be almost impossible that a death from this agent can occur in the hands of a medical man who is applying it with ordinary intelligence and attention.*"

John Snow, one of the foremost of the early English anesthesiologists (and the delineator of the epidemiology of cholera – the Bow Street pump), wrote one of the first textbooks, Chloroform and other Anesthetics, *on the subject of anesthesiology.*

Snow conducted a series of meticulous pharmacologic studies on other anesthetic agents besides ether and chloroform and his text, *Chloroform and Other Anesthetics*, remains a classic in the history of anesthesiology. Among numerous agents of potential anesthetic interest that he evaluated was amylene (beta-isoamylene, trimethylethylene, or pentene) and its usage was initially proposed by him in 1856. Over the period of a year between November 1856 and July 1857 he administered it 238 times with only two fatalities, each of which exhibited the same pattern as that noted with chloroform whereby sudden cessation of cardiac action occurred. Snow's textbook *Chloroform and Other Anesthetics* sadly terminates with an unfinished section under preparation at the time of his death, describing the utility of ethyl chloride.

Despite the balanced remarks of Snow and the continued efforts of numerous investigators, almost a century of controversy as to the mechanism of the problems associated with the usage of chloroform would elapse before A. G. Levy in 1911 presented the physiologic solution of the problem.

Even in the very area of the country where ether had been first popularized by Crawford Long, chloroform had largely replaced ether and ironically its first use in America was by Paul Fitzsimmons Eve (1806-1877) of Augusta, Georgia. In examining the basis of these events Mettler, in 1939, wrote: "*Although Dr. C. W. Long had used ether as early as 1842 ... this substance was not exclusively used in Augusta [Georgia]. In 1849 the Augusta group had reported a series of sixty-four operations done under anesthetic agents. Of this number fifty-eight were done under chloroform alone although ether was used in the others. The reason for this indifference to ether seems to depend upon certain peculiar features. Apparently the indiscriminate use of ether by the population at large who employed it in the capacity of a drug placed the substance in a rather anomalous position in the eyes of the profession. Further the controversy about priority concerning the use of ether placed the substance in professional disfavor...*"

Another factor in the lack of popularity of ether was the generally unsatisfactory results which it gave at that time when administered by the method commonly employed. Some surgeons complained of the lack of depth of the anesthetic effect, but still more important reasons for its lack of use lay in anesthetic deaths resulting from it. Some of these were especially embarrassing and, in the case of the death of one of the medical students at the [Augusta] medical college, caused considerable unfavorable comment. Indeed, one wonders, in reading the reports of some of these deaths, if the substances used could really have always been pure ether. It is not to be wondered at if the medical men of the period in Georgia generally found in chloroform a more suitable agent than ether, about which so much strong emotional behavior was manifest.

The high regard for the efficacy of anesthetic agents was so great that even Queen Victoria consented to be anesthetized for the birth of the Prince of Wales. For years afterwards it was rumored that the subsequent licentious behavior of the Prince reflected his prenatal exposure to sulfuric ether.

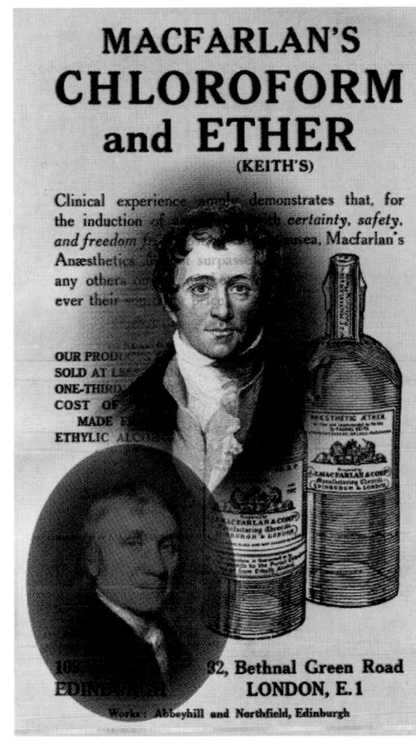

The resolution of scientific problems related to the elucidation of the chemical properties of gases had been considerably facilitated by the work of a number of scientists including Robert Boyle and Antoine Lavoisier. Of particular relevance to anesthesia was the work of Humphry Davey (center inset) who described the effects of nitrous oxide and Joseph Priestley (bottom left) who discovered oxygen.

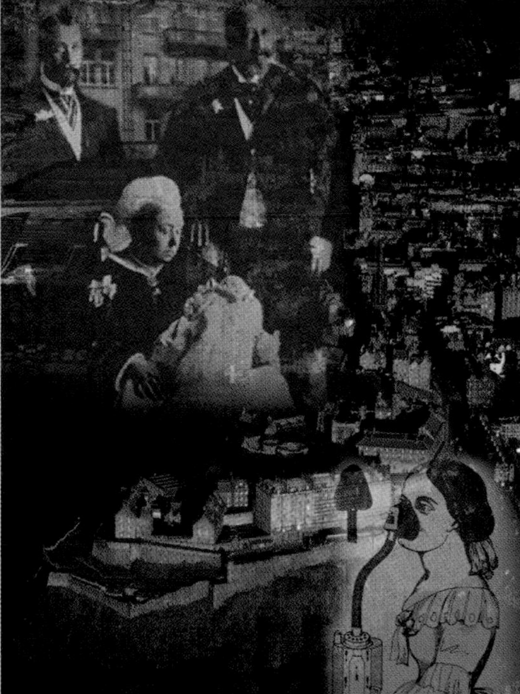

Section 9

From Herbs to Hypothesis

Eighteenth Century

From the sixteenth century onward, a certain amount of opposition had developed between the chemists and herbalists such that as late as 1646, Guy Patin had advised a medical student not to let himself *"be carried away in the current of so many promises as do the antidotaries who are destitute of experience. Nevertheless, it is necessary to know something of compositions for fear that the apothecaries* artis nostrae scandala et approbia, *can take the bar over you... Do not lose your time reading many of the moderns who only make books of our art from lack of practice, and from having too much leisure. Above all flee books on chemistry,* 'in quorum lectione oleum et perdes'."

The passage of time, however, resulted in a diminution of the tension. Thus, by the eighteenth century, the groups had reconciled their differences and considerably less animosity prevailed. This reflected the major advances made on the part of chemistry and those men who clung to the empiric use of simples, who though supported by the pragmatism of daily life, fell further behind as the century advanced. The change in the chemical viewpoint in this century was so extensive that it is not easy to fathom how it occurred with so little fanfare.

In the early eighteenth century the Epicurean enunciation of the indestructibility of matter had been virtually forsaken, forgotten, and the language of the "passions of the soul" was being used to express the behavior of particles of chemical substance while chemistry was still driven by the ephemereal concept of the phlogiston theory. The law of definite proportions, which would later be established by Carl Friedrich Wenzel (1740-1793) and Jeremias Benjamin Richter (1762-1807), was still unheard of and, while the quaternary theory of elemental constitution and the theory of the three principles had begun to fade into the mist of time, the modern conception of elements was still only partially formulated.

The advent of the chemical genius of Lavoisier had, by 1800, enabled a complete revision of such diffuse thought, and his insistence upon the authority of the balances vitiated the phlogiston theory and re-emphasized the law of the indestructibility of matter. Similarly, the initial introduction of the concept of animism by Stahl had metamorphosed into vitalism and vitalism had imbued those focused on chemistry to explore and define the distinction between "animal" and "general" chemistry. Carl Wilhelm Scheele (1742-1786), who prepared oxygen two years before Priestley (i.e 1771-72), and Antoine-François de Fourcroy (1755-1809) believed that *azote* represented the distinguishing mark of animal chemistry. By the end of the century Wenzel demonstrated that acids and bases combined in constant ratios, and this observation, together with Richter's extension of the principle into the law of definite proportions, forced scientists to reconsider the millennia-old observations of the venerable Democritus. Shortly thereafter, John Dalton (1766-1844) popularized the atomic theory that was in fact an extrapolation of the *tables des rapport* that had already been presented to the Académie des Sciences de Paris in 1718, by Etienne-François Geoffroy (1672-1731). In 1787, Lavoisier and Fourcroy in Paris

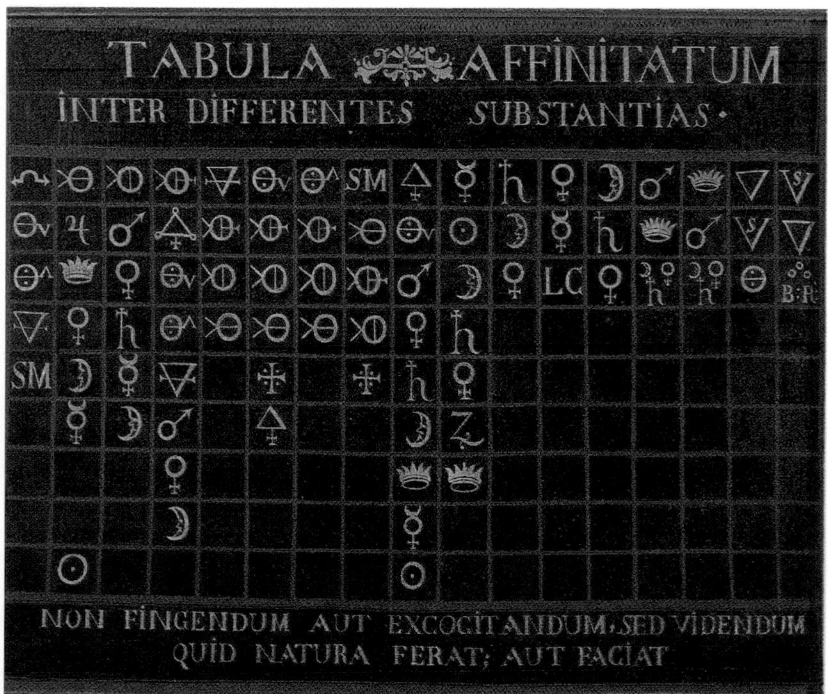

An early example of a table of affinities demonstrating the individual symbols used to describe metals, compounds and elements and their relationship to each other.

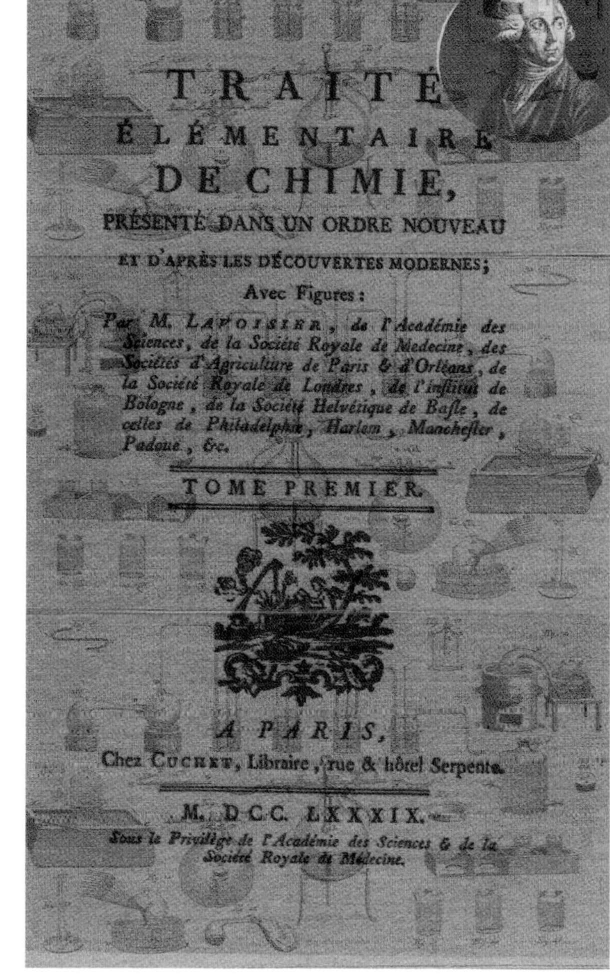

TRAITÉ ÉLÉMENTAIRE DE CHIMIE,
PRÉSENTÉ DANS UN ORDRE NOUVEAU ET D'APRÈS LES DÉCOUVERTES MODERNES;
Avec Figures:
Par M. LAVOISIER, de l'Académie des Sciences, de la Société Royale de Médecine, des Sociétés d'Agriculture de Paris & d'Orléans, de la Société Royale de Londres, de l'Institut de Bologne, de la Société Helvétique de Basle, de celles de Philadelphie, Harlem, Manchester, Padoue, &c.
TOME PREMIER.
A PARIS,
Chez CUCHET, Libraire, rue & hôtel Serpente.
M. DCC. LXXXIX.
Sous le Privilège de l'Académie des Sciences & de la Société Royale de Médecine.

The eminent French chemist, A. Lavoisier (inset), produced a detailed analysis of the basics of chemistry and in so doing laid the logical foundations for the development of the science of chemistry. The father of modern chemistry, Lavoisier was a brilliant experimenter and multifaceted intellect who was active in public affairs as well as in science. His work was instrumental in devising the modern system of chemical nomenclature and he was one of the first scientists to introduce quantitative procedures into chemical investigations. Indeed his experimental ingenuity, exact methods, and cogent reasoning, no less than his discoveries, revolutionized chemistry. Lavoisier developed a novel theory of combustion that led to the overthrow of the "phlogistic doctrine," which had dominated the course of chemistry for more than a century. His fundamental studies on oxidation demonstrated the role of oxygen in chemical processes and showed quantitatively the similarity between oxidation and respiration. In addition, he formulated the principle of the conservation of matter in chemical reactions and clarified the distinction between elements and compounds.

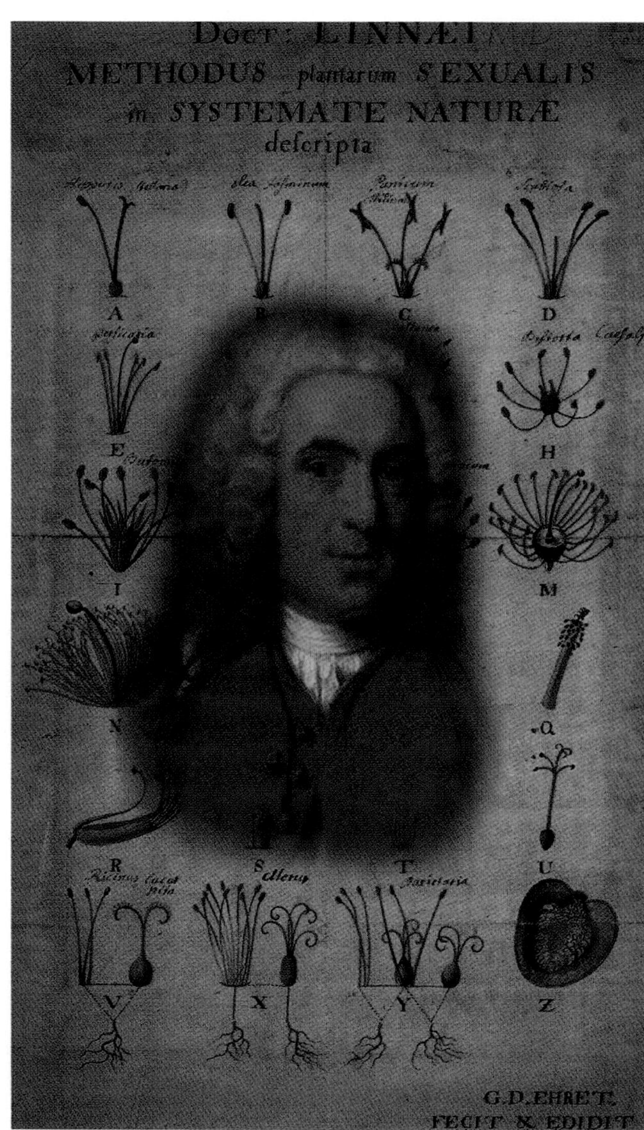

The establishment by Linnaeus (Uppsala, Sweden) of a logical classification of plants provided a fundamental basis for the delineation of different species. Cullen, who had been exposed to the work of Linnaeus during his training in Leiden, utilized the principles of the scheme to develop an artificial and abstruse taxonomy of drugs in the 18th century.

Xavier Bichat of Paris, France, was the first physician to provide a functional understanding of the different components of the body.

enacted a dramatic alteration in the nomenclature of chemistry with the production of a *Methode de nomenclature chimique*. A further major advance that reflected both a novel observation and the advent of a unique concept was the 1799 report of Alessandro Volta in regard to the generation of electricity. The demonstration that a constant source of electricity could be produced by chemical action simultaneously initiated the electrokinetic phase of physics, as well as establishing a significant interface between the disciplines of physics and chemistry.

As a consequence of the advances in chemistry and science in general, the previous focus on botanical therapeutic solutions altered dramatically as physicians viewed with enthusiasm the potential of acquiring substances that were either pure or might even be synthesized. Despite the fact that such goals and aspirations were enunciated over two centuries ago, progress towards their attainment has not been as swift as one might have anticipated. Indeed, the artificial taxonomy of drugs which is still employed is replete with archaic terminology such as cathartics, emetics, antispasmodics, antiseptics, and other curious phyla that represent the remains of a classification of the *materia medica* which was modeled after the fruitful and masterful botanical scheme of Linnaeus. A classic example of the use of such a botanical plan is represented by the system employed and published in London in 1772 by William Cullen.

Physiologic Action

Although the main advances in eighteenth-century pharmacology reflected progress in chemistry, it is apparent that this evolution was, in addition, a serious attempt to establish the physiologic basis of action of all forms of drugs. No specific individual can be identified as the originator of this physiologic technique in determining pharmacologic action since curiosity regarding the action of drugs had long been present and, in the efforts of investigators in the eighteenth century, are inextricably blended with the history of physiologic investigation. Actual studies of pharmacologic action were still hampered, however, by the supposition that chemicals might behave differently within the body to the actions manifested outside the body. A further archaic notion that persisted was the belief that individuals were still considered to be roughly divisible into certain types, each of which reacted diversely toward drugs. Thus it was considered necessary to not only discuss the temperaments but also the four ages of man. In his *Lectures on Materia Medica* Cullen stated:

> *In every person are appearances of a temperament peculiar to himself, though the Ancients only took notice of four, and some have imagined these were deduced from the theories of the four humours, or four cardinal qualities;... The two that are most distinctly marked, are the Sanguineous and Melancholic, viz. the temperaments of Youth and Age.*

He identified the *choleric temperament* as the period between the second and third ages of man but in regard to the *phlegmatic temperament* he maintained *"that it cannot be distinguished by any character of age or sex."* Cullen was aware through the medium of what he refers to as a "literary journal" that in 1755, Menghini had been able to produce convulsions with camphor. As a result of this information and considerations, he based his entire theory of pharmacologic action upon the belief that the most important and distinctive functions of the body were identified with the neural system. However, since knowledge of neural function and the pharmacologic action of medicines was so miniscule, he was forced to resort to utilizing the old humoral distinction between fluids and solids, and grouped his medicines into those which he supposed acted on fluids and those supposedly exerting their effects on solids. Medicines acting on solids were further subdivided into those exerting an effect upon moving solids and those working upon static solids. Similarly those acting on fluids were divided into alterants and evacuants, the first group being deemed to act upon moving fluids and the latter on static fluids. Each one of these main divisions was further subdivided into numerous classes which themselves, in turn, were subdivided to an absurd degree. This functional, albeit somewhat naive scheme, was largely an

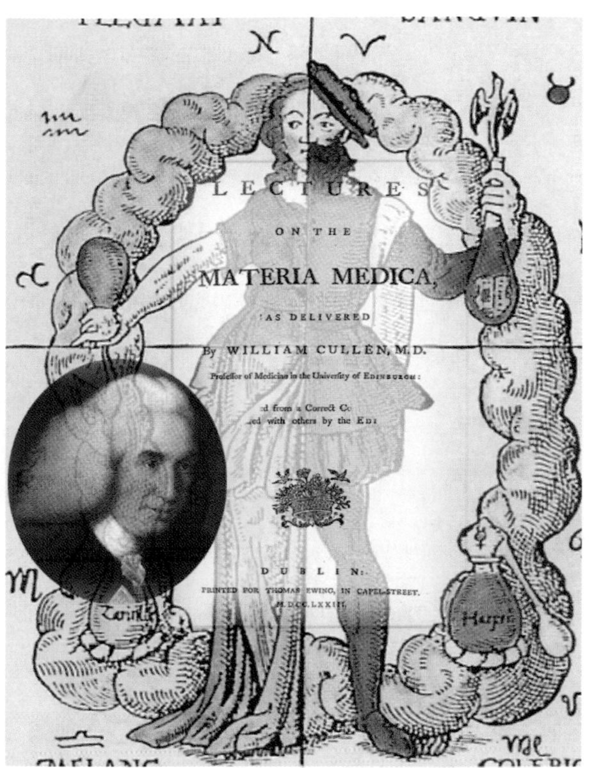

William Cullen (1712-90) was instrumental in founding the Medical School of Glasgow in 1744. During his long life he held the chairs of medicine and chemistry at both Glasgow and Edinburgh and was the first to lecture in the vernacular instead of Latin. An inspiring teacher and a modest clinician, he was particularly noted for his kindness in assisting needy students. He introduced few new remedies into practice and his critics claimed that "he failed to add a single new fact to medical science." Although his finest innovation was the use of hydrotherapy with rapid changes in temperature, he was particularly adept at developing descriptive classifications of disease processes and their therapy. In his synopsis "Nosologiae Methodicae" (1769) he divided diseases into fevers, neurosis, cachexias, and local disorders, even including gout amongst the neuroses and differentiating 34 different varieties of chronic rheumatism.

adaptation of the highly successful compromise therapy of his former teacher, Hermann Boerhaave (1668-1738). Based upon this classification, Cullen regarded belladonna as an anodyne and useful in dysentery, although he failed to note its midriatic action which apparently remained unobserved until Peter Johann Andreas Daries (*fl.* 1776) described this property. Thus, many materials classified in this schema appear to have been completely useless and almost as superfluous as the classification itself. Nevertheless, this conclusion fails to acknowledge that at that time, it was not yet evident that the actions of drugs were due to definite active principles, or that drugs acted on functional units (organs) of the body. Under such circumstances it is easier to understand the basis of Cullen's classification. A degree of appreciation that there was a more complex mechanism at work was provided by the iatrochemists or iatrophysicists who, by an extrapolation of the humoral theory, had assumed that drugs acted in a rather crude manner upon the blood and other fluids diluting or changing its degree of acidity or alkalinity. (The seventeenth-century hydrogen ion indicator was syrup of violets, which turned red in acid solutions [and green in alkaline]). Cullen, like many other investigators and authors, supposed that the physiologic effect of a drug might be directly related to its action on a specific organ (the pharmacologic corollary of structural pathology), but all recognized that the proof of the concept was too difficult to sustain.

Indeed, to move from the general concept of a broad humoral theory to the elucidation of specificity of both site of action and mechanism required a paradigm shift in thought. Early physicians had approached the concept of organic action by speculating on the manner in which poison operated and the most significant experimental research of this period, which tended to emphasize this necessary notion was the remarkable *Richerche filosofiche sopra il veleno della vipera*, Lucca, 1767, which summated the conclusions of the experiments undertaken by Felice Fontana on the venom of the viper and other poisons, in which he conclusively proved that the general symptoms were the result of action on particular organs. Such conclusions, while representing a major advance in pharmacologic theory, were also in a large part the product of alterations in anatomic as well as pathological concepts. Throughout the late eighteenth century individuals such a Xavier Bichat had been influential in deriving a systematic formulation of anatomy and with this change in viewpoint, the older pharmacologic views which themselves had become subject to other radical changes consequent upon the major advances in chemistry, ultimately collapsed, and classifications such as Cullen's became meaningless. The critical investigations that led to the elucidation of the effect of digitalis further fortified considerations in the organic and systemic action of drugs.

Nineteenth Century

Europe

In 1813 in Paris an important *Toxicologic Générale* was produced by Mathieu-Joseph-Bonaventure Orfila (1787-1853) and represented an example of the continuation of the technique employed by Fontana. L.N. Vauquelin (1763-1829), Orfila's sponsor, pointed out that it had been necessary for his young protégé *"to institute a series of researches very numerous and extremely delicate"* prior to presenting the manuscript before the Institut de France.

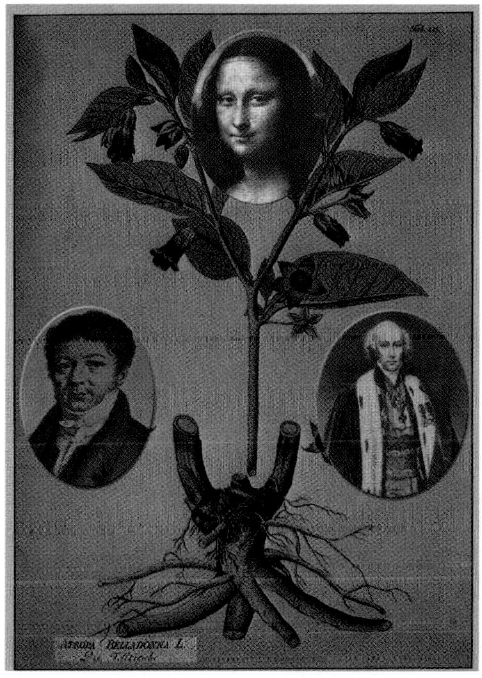

M. Orfila (right) and F. Magendie (left) made substantial contributions to the investigation of various drugs including Belladonna (center). The atropine effect of the plant (as documented by Da Vinci's Mona Lisa) was also widely utilized by women to amplify their pulchritude by augmenting pupillary dilatation.

The premature death of Bichat (1771-1802), at the age of 31 deprived the world of an innovative medical genius. By order of Napoleon his bust, along with that of his mentor Desault, was placed in the Hôtel Dieu. The novel analysis by Bichat of general anatomy as applied to physiology in medicine laid the stage for the development of cellular biology. Bichat studied anatomy and surgery under Marc-Antoine Petit, chief surgeon at the Hôtel Dieu in Lyons and in 1793 became a pupil, then assistant, of Pierre-Joseph Desault, surgeon and anatomist in Paris. After his teacher's death in 1795, Bichat completed the fourth volume of Desault's Journal de Chirurgie, adding a biographical memoir of its author. In addition to his observations at the bedsides of patients at the Hôtel Dieu, Bichat studied the postmortem changes induced in various organs by disease. Without knowledge of the cell as the functional unit of living things, he was among the first to visualize the organs of the body as being formed through the differentiation of simple, functional units, or tissues and developed this view in "Traité des Membranes" (1800; Treatise on Membranes). Although Bichat did not use the microscope, he distinguished twenty-one kinds of tissues that enter into different combinations in forming the organs of the body and his "Recherches physiologiques sur la vie et la mort" (1800; Physiological Researches on Life and Death) was followed by "Anatomie Générale" (1801). The first two volumes of "Anatomie Descriptive" were published in 1801-3, and the third completed by his pupils after his death.

François Magendie (1783-1855) of Paris utilized both physical and chemical procedures in his investigations and is regarded as the founder of modern experimental pharmacology. He regarded medicine as "science in the making" and sought to explain all observations in terms of physics and chemistry. In fact, Magendie considered pathology to be nothing more than "the physiology of the sick man"! Unfortunately, his brilliance was devoted more to the identification of isolated facts rather than the development of specific hypotheses and the derivation of generalizations. Magendie founded the first periodical devoted exclusively to physiology and made important contributions to the knowledge of bromine, iodine compounds, and alkaloids such as strychnine, morphine, veratrine, brucine, poperine, and introduced emetine into medical practice. He was the first to recognize the phenomenon of anaphylaxis although Edward Jenner had already observed this event in a number of inoculations as early as 1798.

Orfila's work was in actuality a comprehensive study of the pharmacologic action of a large number of materials found in the *materia medica* and his methods of experimentation clearly reflect the example and exhortation of Magendie. The text gives concise accounts of the pathologic lesions found after the death of animals and persons receiving lethal amounts of the various drugs, and is broadly divided into a consideration of mineral, vegetable, and animal poisons.

While the biologic or physiologic approach continued to yield important pharmacological information, and was often the only practical method, the overall direction of nineteenth-century pharmacology was more closely correlated with the progress of chemistry. In respect of this evolution, a number of landmarks provided defining examples of the dominance of chemical thought in influencing progress. The first of these was the formalization of the law of definite proportions through a version of the atomic theory that had initially been advanced by Dalton. Although the extrapolation of this concept reflected the contributions of many individuals, it was von Liebig and Wohler whose contributions to the development of organic chemistry that are most noteworthy. Thus in 1832 Justus von Liebig and Friedrich Wohler published a paper on benzaldehyde, and demonstrated that this substance contained a chemical grouping which acted as a unit in a long series of chemical combinations. Although this observation enabled the modern understanding of a radical, it was von Liebig's work on the natural alkaloids which dramatically denigrated the scientific standing of the herbal and botanic faction. This work further supported the critical observation published in 1828 by his associate Wohler, whereby it had been demonstrated that no sharp line of distinction existed between organic and inorganic substances. In this study, Wohler had shown that an aqueous solution of ammonium cyanate, when evaporated, was converted into urea (the Wohler synthesis) and had thus destroyed the fundamental basis for the contention that some mystical, distinguishing character attaches to organic materials and that these could not be prepared from inorganic materials without the intermediation of a living agent. As a consequence of the brilliance of von Liebig in perceiving an entirely different concept regarding the putative distinction between organic and inorganic material, that organic chemistry evolved into a scientific discipline that was so ably amplified by August Kekule (1829-1896) and his successors, who directed their attention to the benzene ring.

America

Given the increasing unpopularity of England in eighteenth-century colonial America, there was a considered effort on the part of most physicians to distance themselves from the fashions of English pharmacy and develop an independent body of thought. Thus, although the first *American Pharmacopeia*, a conservative, practical 32-page affair was compiled by William Brown (d. 1792) of Philadelphia and published in 1778, the United States contributions to pharmacology were of little overall significance. However, the growing interest in botany was considerable and was not confined to physicians, and one of the most popular texts of the period was that of Benjamin Smith Barton's (1766-1815) *Elements of Botany, or Outlines of the Natural History of Vegetables; Illustrated by 30 Colored Plates,* Philadelphia, 1804. Alexander Garden

The study of botany and medical matters in the United States for the most part reflected extrapolations of previous British or European work although it did contain observations novel to North America.

An early cartoon representing the skepticism with which most Americans viewed medicine and pharmacology. Death mixes the medications while the rotund and "well heeled" pharmacist generously doles out the therapy to the afflicted. The caption cynically notes "I have a secret art to cure each malady which men endure!" Caveat emptor.

An early 20th-century advert from the "New York Quinine and Chemical Works" identifying agents available for public consumption and linking them with the powerful icon of the Indian warrior. The latter group (those who had not already succumbed to the introduction of European smallpox) had of course themselves been decimated by another wonder drug of the colonists – whisky!

(1728-1792), of Charleston, introduced Carolina pink root (*Spigelia marilandica*) as a vermifuge in 1764 and John Mitchell (*c.* 1680-1768), an English physician and botanist who settled in Virginia, was the author of *A Botanical Treatise* which contained the description of several new genera of plants.

Similarly mercury, whose efficacy had been acclaimed by the group at Leiden, was a favorite remedy of colonial physicians, and James Thatcher (1754-1844) has noted of it:

> *... that, from about the first part of the 18th century, it has been the practice to administer mercury as an efficacious remedy in febrile diseases of every description. It was employed, not so much for its evacuating power, as with the intention of introducing it gradually into the system as an alterative. The fullest confidence was reposed in a moderate course of mercury in pleurisies and peripneumonies, esteeming it as the most efficacious attenuant and expectorant which the* materia medica *afforded. But the strongest prejudices against the use of mercury subsisted among all classes of people, and physicians were obliged to observe the utmost caution in its administration, as their popularity depended upon concealment. It was customary to give it the significant term of ponderous medicine, imagining that mercury acts upon the system by its ponderosity, destroying the too great siziness of the blood ... In various chronic diseases, a deobstruent course, in the form of Plummer's pills, was a favorite remedy.*

During the yellow fever epidemic in 1793, Benjamin Rush, whose training was indirectly derived from Leiden, resorted to mercury as a "sovereign" remedy. Thatcher wrote:

> *Influenced, probably, by the opinion and example of Dr. Rush, most of the learned physicians of the United States have declared themselves advocates for the mercurial mode of treatment. Being thus sanctioned by the highest medical authority and by general assent, the mercurial practice is now received and adopted by a majority of our practitioners as the safest and most successful method of cure, not only in the yellow fever, but also in typhus and other forms of malignant febrile affections.*

Even at moments in time when pharmacologic theory was at its most obscure, and there was little reason to select one drug in preference to another, physicians who attained the greatest success in the treatment of disease almost always endeavored to restrict their prescriptions to a small

Benjamin Rush (1745-1813) (inset) of Pennsylvania was of English Quaker stock and a graduate of Princeton (1760) and Edinburgh (1768). His graduating thesis was based on an investigation of "The coction of food in the Stomach." As such Rush may be regarded as one of the earliest gastroenterologists of America. Rush was the ablest American clinician of his time and his writing and reputation won him golden opinions abroad where he was regarded as the American Sydenham, although local admirers of dubious classical background had also referred to him as the Hippocrates of Pennsylvania. Despite the fact that Rush played a commendable part in treating the Philadelphia epidemic of yellow fever in 1793, his scheme of treatment may be regarded with some concern. He used large doses of calomel and jalap, copious blood-letting, a low diet, and abundant hydrotherapy both within and without. He believed that the cure of disease could be undertaken by the extraction of decayed teeth and also supported the massive use of arsenic in the treatment of cancer.

A depiction of a quack and his wagon passing through an American frontier town. By the time the duped patients realized that effects of the medication had failed to improve their disease the wagon and its proprietor were long gone!

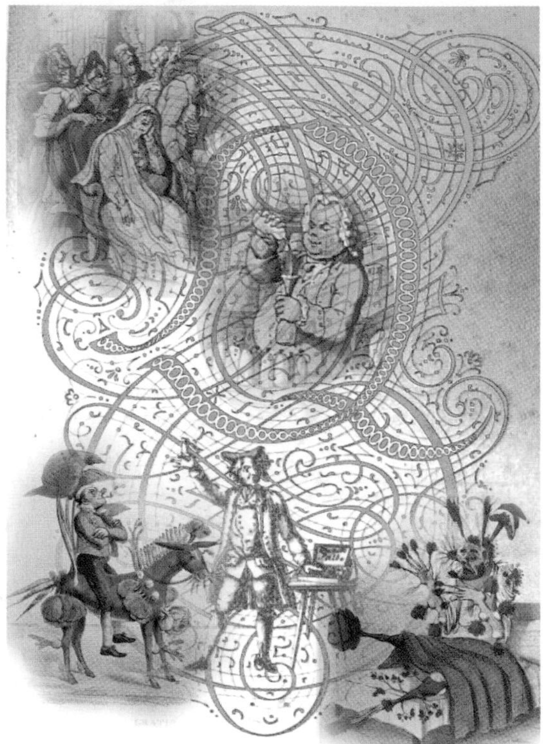

The nature of the evolution of American medical culture, with its proprietary medical schools, purchasable degrees, and entrepreneurial spirit, led to some abuses. A conglomeration of quackery, charlatanry, and sometimes even mysticism supervened as disreputable pharmacists and physicians often sought to enrich themselves without due regard to the welfare of their patients.

A collection of the diverse medicinal products available to the public. The exciting packaging attracted consumer attention and promised curative benefits that often failed to materialize.

number of drugs which were known to produce a fairly definite effect. It is a well-accepted dictum that the use of a large number of agents, exotic contents, and spectacular preparations for which a multitude of effects is claimed, has invariably been a sign of poor medical judgment. This maxim was especially evident in some of the medicine-related texts that were published in America in the early part of the nineteenth century. Thus, when a general convention composed of delegates from different parts of the United States was held at Washington on January 1, 1820, for the purpose of forming a *National Pharmacopoeia,* the men chosen for the preparation of this volume restricted themselves to a relatively small number of substances such that by the time a second edition was published in 1830, its *materia medica* still listed less than 300 substances.

In contradistinction, the young republic was flooded with books intended for family use and practically all contained sections known as herbals that listed interminable catalogues of weeds which the householder could prepare for his own delectation. The scope of such works may be gathered from some of the titles. Thus, parts of the *Domestic Medicine; or the Family Physician,* London, 1769, written by William Buchan (1729-1805), were combined with miscellaneous pearls to produce a masterpiece entitled, *Every Man His Own Doctor; or a Treatise on the Prevention and Cure of Diseases, by Regimen and Simple Medicines by William Buchan, M.D. To Which is Added, a Treatise on the Materia Medica; in Which the Medicinal Qualities of Indigenous Plants Are Given and Adapted to Common Practice. With an Appendix, Containing a Complete Treatise on the Art of Farriery. With Directions to the Purchasers of Horses; and Practical Receipts for the Cure of Distempers Incident to Horses, Cattle, Sheep and Swine – to all of Which Are Added, a Choice Collection of Receipts, Useful in Every Branch of Domestic Life – Making in All a Complete Family Directory,* New Haven, 1816. A similar prize, written by Samuel North (*fl.* 1820), *The Family Physician and Guide to Health,* Waterloo, 1830, which boasts *"A certain cure for a mad dog bite,"* gives an indication of the potential danger of such volumes. Almost as unrestrained in its claims are the suggestions contained in Daniel H. Whitney's (*fl.* 1825) *Family Physician,* Penn Yan, 1833, which, besides providing a formula for making an "exhilarating gas" (nitrous oxide) includes on the opposite page a recipe for an oyster pie as well as a description of the treatment of the gleet and Asiatic cholera. Lest their be any doubt on the subject Whitney notes *"It is altogether a mistaken notion that no man can amputate unless he has gone through a regular course of surgical studies."* Truly, Dr. Whitney had a deep and abiding interest in his patients and was committed to ensuring their comfort. Thus, in some brief notes on the subtleties of limb amputation, he has the grace to concede that during amputation of the arm, *"The patient may take 60 or 80 drops of laudanum if he has a mind to."* As the obvious fraudulent claims of some of these texts amplified, more of the family authors took refuge in anonymity, and with this device the books became even more ambitious in scope.

The snake oil salesman, whilst widely regarded as an icon of the American medical scene, was in fact little different from similar quackery that had existed in diverse European countries for centuries.

A wonderful example of such an all-encompassing book was the anonymous *Arts Revealed and Universal Guide,* Indianapolis, 1859, which included an herbal, provided a single cure (calcium phosphate and cod-liver oil) for consumption, scrofula, "general infantile atrophy," rickets, diarrhea, and tuberculosis, and also included directions on how to choose a wife, embroider on muslin, and clean *"Bed-ticks, however badly soiled."*

Samuel Thomson (1769-1843) was the most aspiring theorist among the authors of these *Family Physicians* and as such developed a very considerable public following while provoking a heated controversy with his more ethical colleagues. As was often the case in America at this time, he had not undergone any formal course of training but merely appropriated the title of doctor and as an outright quack had become one of the earliest promoters of rattlesnake oil. A highlight of his early career was provided by his successful evasion of a murder charge, and inspired by faith in his ability to withstand the system, since he had few scruples about his reputation as a "root doctor" when he took out a patent on a "system" of medicine. His global concept was, as might be predicted, extremely simple, and the so-called Thomsonian theory stated, *"That all diseases are the effect of one general cause and may be removed by one general remedy, . . ."* As regards this remedy he observed, *"that whatsoever course will restore or increase the natural internal warmth of the body, if not to exceed 100 deg. Fahrenheit, or the temperature of the blood, and remove all obstructions of the system, restore the powers of digestion, and promote a natural perspiration, is universally applicable in all cases of disease, and therefore may be considered as a general remedy."*

Thomson achieved this scenario by prescribing lobelia, which he called his Number I, but since lobelia was not always efficient he found it necessary to reinforce this with a second drug which he indicated as Number II. The original ingredient that comprised Number II was capsicum although sometimes ginger or black pepper might be included as well. In the event that this combination failed he would the introduce a Number III, and under serious circumstances a Number IV. Ultimately Thomson began to employ his drugs out of numerical order and adopted a pharmacologic theory not particularly different to his formally-trained colleagues.

An individual of some merit in the evolution of American therapeutic material was John Redman Coxe (1773-1864), who was born in Philadelphia, studied at Edinburgh and, later, became professor of chemistry and *materia medica* at Pennsylvania. In 1806 in Philadelphia he compiled the *American Dispensatory*, before the pharmacopoeia was published. *The American Dispensatory* was in fact little more than a compilation that consisted of material derived from the *London*, *Dublin* and *Edinburgh Pharmacopoeias* and as such proved to be somewhat disjointed. In 1858 these divergent works were outlawed in the British Isles and in 1864 supplanted by the *British Pharmacopoeia*, while in 1820 in America they became superseded by the *Pharmacopeia of the United States*. Some humor may be derived from a study of the text wherein it can be observed that one of the most ubiquitous phrases in American history "Yankee Doodle," is documented in the *Dispensatory*, (8th edition, 1830) where its therapeutic indications are listed under "Music".

The subject of lobelia was a prominent topic and in 1830, Coxe seemed disinclined to support its use. Although Thomson is generally credited with having introduced it into medicine (*New Guide to Health or Botanic Family Physician, Boston 1822*), earlier reports of its utility as a cure for asthma exist, and it was listed in the first *Pharmacopeia* of the United States. Coxe did not refer to Thomson by name but he apparently had him in mind when he wrote that lobelia had *"lately excited much speculation in the New England States."* Farther on he said, *"no rational practitioner will have recourse to it, but with the greatest precautions."* The first *Pharmacopeia of the United States* listed purple foxglove as *Digitalis purpurea*, the name which had been given the plant by Linnaeus. Digitalis was recommended externally for scrofulous tumors and, internally, for tachycardia, neural excitability, all forms of edema, aneurysms, hemorrhages, phthisis, to diminish the velocity of the circulation, asthma, and cardiac irregularities. Excessive doses of digitalis were noticed to produce vomiting, purging, vertigo, delirium, hiccup, convulsions, collapse, and death. Purkinje had noticed that visual disturbances occasionally followed its administration. Thus, though the cardiac and diuretic effects of the drug were known, it was apparently used in excessive doses and for many conditions for which it was not indicated.

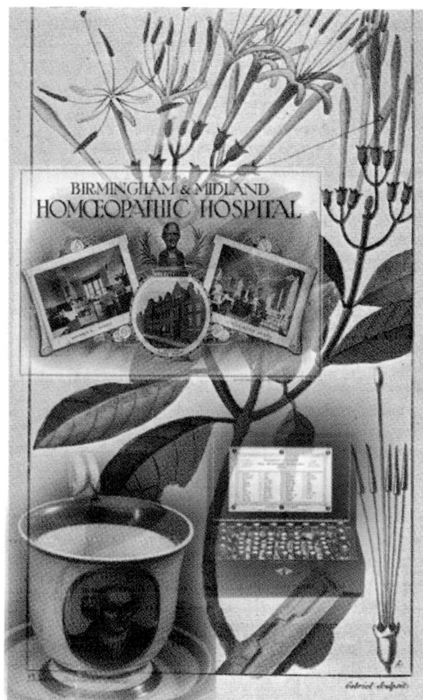

The development of homeopathy during the 19th century achieved widespread popularity. Although not significantly different from the theories pondered by Paracelsus, Hahnemann directed his arcana not against the cause of the disease but against symptoms or groups of symptoms. His therapeutic method was thus not a true isotherapy, nor were the isopathic systems that followed it quite the same as the treatment by sera, vaccines, bactrines, hormones and animal extracts which subsequently supervened.

Homeopathy and Therapeutic Nihilism

Although advances in the eighteenth century had greatly increased the potential number of substances theoretically available for the treatment of disease, so many of the botanical items were for practical purposes useless, that the study of *materia medica* and the practice of medicine had become arcane, complex, and almost unmanageable. Indeed, an assessment of the overall results obtained by eighteenth-century therapy was so dismal that when an almost as ineffective, useless, but much simpler system of therapeutics was advanced by Samuel Christian Friedrich Hahnemann (1755-1843) of Meissen, in his *Organon der rationellen Heilkunde*, it was accepted with enthusiasm by many patients and physicians. Despite original claims to the contrary, Hahnemann was not a quack or a fraud. Indeed, his theory was not essentially new but better defined and based upon three important tenets. Firstly, he held that disease depended upon a perversion of the purely spiritual vital powers and was entirely immaterial in its nature. Since it was logical to consider that the

The advantage of homeopathy from the point of view of a quack, was that the small quantities of medication required, considerably facilitated the mobility necessary for the marketing of such agents.

The burial place of Samuel Christen Fredrick Hahnemann (1755-1843), in the Père Lachaise cemetery in Paris. Born in Meissen, Germany, Hahnemann took his degree at Erlangen in 1779 and towards the end of the century as a result of experiments (often performed upon his own person), began to formulate the theories which characterized his system. In principle he revived the old Paracelsian doctrine of signatures, namely that diseases or symptoms of diseases are curable by those particular drugs which produce similarly pathological effects upon the body. He also believed the dynamic effects of drugs were amplified by administering them in infinitesimally small doses. His most remarkable belief was that most chronic diseases are only a manifestation of suppressed itch or "psora". The extreme popularity of Hahnemann's doctrines was probably due to the fact that they lessened the scale of drugs in use at that time. The success of his medical theories may be judged by the fact that he died a millionaire in Paris in 1843 and was buried amidst pomp and circumstance amongst the illuminati of the city.

Rudolf Buchheim (bottom right) held the first chair of pharmacology in Europe at the University of Dorpat (background). His pupil, Oswald Schmiedeberg (top left), succeeded him and after relocating to Strassbourg became regarded as one of the great experimental pharmacologists of his time.

spiritual could not be combatted by material remedies, Hahnemann turned to a spiritual power which he believed to be bound up in plants and liberated by dilution. He proposed that activity would therefore increase with dilution, and be the greater, the smaller the dose (*doctrine of potency*). This liberation of the principles exactly turned their action around, so that the action of his dilutions was, he stated, exactly the opposite of that of the concentrated drug, and could be used for the relief of such symptoms as the latter produced: *Similia similibus curantur*. This was the first tenet of Hahnemann. The second was that the nature of the disease being "*unseizable*", it was not subject to treatment, but that only its symptoms could be treated. Hence, homeopathy, in so far as it followed the original principles of Hahnemann, considered that there was no place for the medical sciences, such as physiology, anatomy, pathology, or chemistry. In essence anybody possessed of an indexed book of symptoms and their remedies would be able to practice it without elaborate study or preparation. The third dictum was, however, in marked contrast to the above, and proposed that medicinal treatment must be supported by dietetic and hygienic measures.

Basically, the claims of homeopathy as a rational system rested on the proof of the *similia similibus* theory and the doctrine of potentiation by dilution. Widespread acceptance proved difficult to obtain since most of its adherents refuted the relevance of scientific testimony, and based themselves purely on the quicksand of empirical experience. Other advocates of homeopathy chose rather to neglect the accumulated corpus of scientific experience which invalidated their theory and rather availed themselves of some marginal experimental facts which, by convoluted reasoning, were then woven into a matrix of specious support. Hahnemann himself based his fundamental work on the initial observation that large doses of drugs produced the opposite effects of moderate doses and in this respect he was for the most part correct. It was the subsequent leap of faith that was difficult to comprehend whereby it was assumed that infinitesimal doses would therefore follow suit and cause effects opposite to those of moderate doses!

Such was the fame of the physiologist, Claude Bernard, that even chocolate manufacturers sought to recognize his contributions in the hope that this would boost their sales. Ironically, it would transpire that the experimental work of Bernard in the elucidation of glucose homeostasis would be of fundamental relevance to the relationship between chocolate intake and diabetic therapy.

Although the principles underlying homeopathy were rigorously challenged, it was nonetheless evident that his work had exposed many earlier abuses. Thus, in 1833, a contributor to the *Organon der Heilkunde* exhibited a fine touch of rationality in noting that if Hahnemann's observations were themselves of no other practical value, one might still derive the following good from them. Thus, in the first place, when drugs were administered for long periods of time, they may themselves become responsible for the continuation of symptoms; and secondly, a superabundance of medication has really very little to recommend it and the simplest form of therapy must be the best, for, if good came from the minute doses prescribed by Hahnemann, how much more benefit might accrue from no doses at all. This latter comment may be regarded as a forerunner of the vogue of therapeutic nihilism that swept the third quarter of the nineteenth century. Initiated under van Swieten, in Vienna, it achieved complete fruition under Skoda and, in much the same fashion as the theory of Hahnemann, it represented an intellectual reaction generated by the frustration that had arisen at the inefficiency of the older therapeutics.

The Evolution of Pharmacological Strategy

Although Claude Bernard was a physiologist of genius and possessed of considerable pharmacological knowledge, he left few followers and failed to establish a French school of physiology and pharmacology. As a result, the lead in this area was subsumed by the German universities, where, with Teutonic thoroughness, the new information provided by experimental physiology became systematized and propagated, with the goal of "reducing" the science of life to a description purely in terms of physics and chemistry. In particular, the study of drugs received its greatest impetus at the University of Dorpat (now Tartu) in Estonia, where the first chair of pharmacology (under that name) was established in Europe. Since Dorpat was basically a German city in all but name, the university was filled with numerous outstanding individuals in science and medicine of whom Rudolf Buchheim (1820-79), a graduate of Leipzig, would become the first Chair of Pharmacology. Buchheim had learned much of his subject by translating an important new English textbook on drugs written by Jonathan Pereira (1804-53), physician and chemist in London. Buchheim studied the effects of the familiar drugs of the time – metals, purgatives, alkaloids, and alcohol, among others, and after construction of the pharmacological institute established a fine training program.

Although he cannot be credited with any major discovery, Buchheim did much to establish the science as a distinct discipline and his pupil, Oswald Schmiedeberg (1838-1921), succeeded him at Dorpat before in 1872 moving to Strassbourg. Fortunately for Schmiedeberg, Strassbourg University

A major contribution of early pharmacology was the scientific delineation of agents that could be used in anesthesia. John Warren (right) was amongst the first surgeons to utilize anesthetic agents in an operating room and even experimental surgeons such as Claude Bernard utilized the concept. Bernard, in fact, developed an anesthetic inhaler (bottom right). The subsequent dissemination of the concept and practice of anesthesia as well as the introduction of more sophisticated devices for gas administration (bottom left) proved of great benefit to surgeons throughout the world.

was undergoing a renaissance as Prussian politicians sought to establish it as a showplace of German culture in the newly-acquired (courtesy of the Franco-Prussian War) province of Alsace. As a result of the major resources placed at his disposal as well as his own skill and foresight, Schmiedeberg was thus able to establish a magnificent center for the development of experimental pharmacology.

It can be stated with assurance that at this institute were laid the foundations of modern pharmacology and with this, the basis established for the scientific elucidation of the mechanism and actions of drugs. Medicines in common use were investigated to discover how they acted on bodily tissues, and their putative therapeutic benefits were related, if possible, to demonstrable physiological facts. In this fashion numerous agents including chloroform and other anesthetics and narcotics, drugs such as nicotine and muscarine with actions related to the autonomic nervous system, digitalis, and heavy metals were all studied, with varying success. Of particular relevance was the establishment of the principle that such an investigation provided a critical background to the clinical use of drugs and served as an important basis by which more effective agents could be identified. Imbued with this spirit, pharmacologists trained by Schmiedeberg went elsewhere in Germany and further afield, and established either new departments of pharmacology or replaced the previous sections of *materia medica* (the study of the plants and minerals from which medicines were prepared). At the time of his retirement in 1918 Schmiedeberg had trained in excess of a hundred pupils, almost all of whom had established departments similar to his throughout the world, thereby in effect establishing a new science.

Far removed from the elegance of Alsace, amidst the forbidding grey buildings of Edinburgh, the science of pharmacology also developed strongly, evolving from a long-established discipline in *materia medica*. In this school, toxicology and forensic medicine were included with pharmacology and represented the practice of the French teachings. Notable teachers of the department included Robert Christison (1797-1882), who had studied in Paris under Magendie and Orfila and investigated the poisonous seeds of the tropical plant *Physostigma venenosum*, partly by self-medication. His successor, Thomas Fraser (1841-1920), isolated the alkaloid eserine or physostigmine from the plant and made the important observation that another alkaloid, atropine, blocked some of the actions of eserine.

Of particular relevance was the decision by Fraser to study the chemistry of drugs, particularly in respect of their interaction. As a result, Fraser collaborated with the organic chemist Alexander Crum Brown (1838-1922) in studying the antagonism between drugs and how chemical structure affected the ways drugs acted. Although by this time the approximate atomic composition of various alkaloids was known, it was not understood how even with almost identical formulae, in terms of the number of atoms present, similar pharmacological actions were not necessarily predictable. In order to further evaluate this issue, Crum Brown modified various alkaloids, including strychnine, codeine, morphine, and atropine, by attaching an additional methyl group to the contained nitrogen atom. Thereafter, Fraser was able to demonstrate that this change resulted in significant alterations in pharmacological effects. Despite the fact that the original alkaloids differed widely in their actions (strychnine was convulsant, morphine soporific, and atropine

Potent drugs prior to the nineteenth century

Drug	Plant	Recognition	Active principle
Wine	*Vitis vinifera*	Ancient Greece	Ethyl alcohol
Opium	*Papaver somniferum*	Ancient Greece	Morphine
Hemlock	*Conium maculatum*	Ancient Greece	Coniine
Mandragora	*Mandragora officinatum*	Ancient Greece	Hyoscine
Ma huang	*Ephedra spp.*	Ancient China	Ephedrine
Belladonna	*Atropa belladonna*	Middle Ages	Atropine
Ergot	*Claviceps purpurea*	Middle Ages	Ergotamine
Ipecacuanha	*Cephaelis ipecacuanha*	Brazil *c.* 1600	Emetine
Jesuit's bark	*Cinchona spp.*	Peru *c.* 1630	Quinine
Coca leaves	*Erythroxylon coca*	Bolivia and Peru *c.* 1688	Cocaine
Foxglove	*Digitalis purpurea*	England, 1775-85	Digitoxin

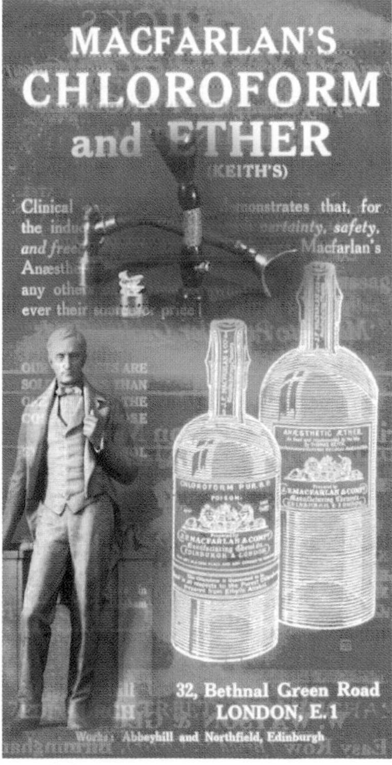

Crawford Long (1815-1878) of Danielsville, GA, a graduate of the University of Pennsylvania (1839) having previously noted accidentally some anesthetic effects of ether, removed a small cystic tumor from the back of the neck of the patient under its influence and subsequently used it in other cases between 1842 and 1843. Although these operations were certified and vouched for by contemporary physicians of his locality, Long published no reports of these results and in consequence individuals such as Welch misguidedly maintained "we cannot assign to him (Long) any influence upon the historical development of our knowledge of surgical anesthesia or any share in its introduction to the world at large." Fortunately the American Congress disagreed with this uncharitable assessment and a statue of Long (inset) was placed in the Capitol Building in Washington to memorialize his contributions to the subject.

In 1906, the Royal Society honored Perkin (center-left) and an eponymous medal commemorating his contributions was struck.

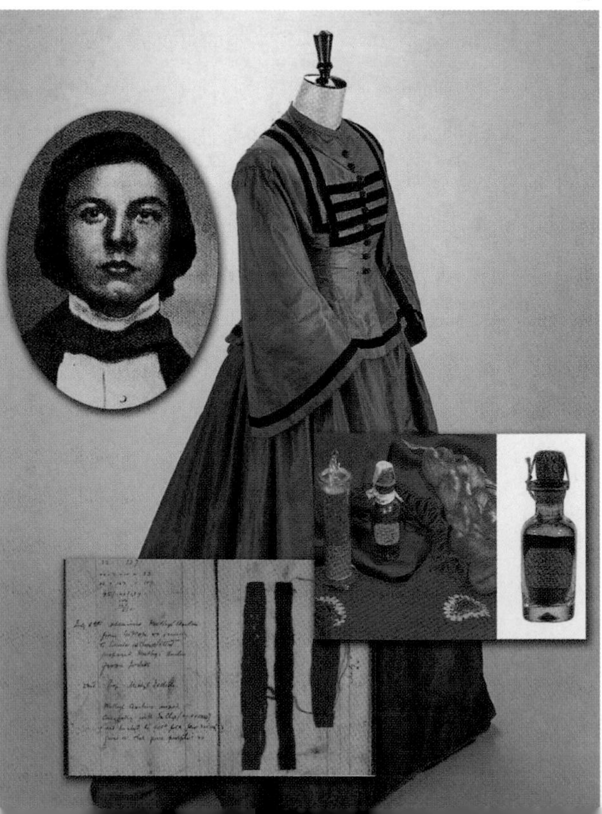

relieved colic), all the new compounds had acquired a new action, like that of curare, and caused paralysis. Indeed, on some occasions, they were even noted to have lost their own characteristic actions. Although Crum Brown and Fraser demonstrated that the presence of an ammonium-like structure, later known as an onium compound, consistently conferred curare-like action on any drugs to which it could be introduced, they were less successful in applying their discoveries to the invention of useful drugs. Indeed, curare and curare-like agents did not enter medicinal use for another seventy or eighty years. Nevertheless, their experiments were of fundamental importance as representing the first clear demonstration of a connection between chemical structure and pharmacological action.

The Application of Chemical Science to Medicine

It was the concept of biotransformation that engendered the next area of pharmacological investigation. This era was initiated by the English physician, Alexander Ure, in 1841, when he treated gouty patients with benzoic acid and noted that the urine contained crystals of hippuric acid. This observation was a surprise, since it was known that although hippuric acid was formed when benzoic acid combined with glycine, it was also known that the reaction did not occur when the components were juxtaposed at body temperature. Ure postulated that a chemical combination, of a kind that did not happen spontaneously, had occurred in the living organism. Schmiedeberg and others confirmed the observation and after further study proposed that this was a novel phenomenon and that the conversion was an example of "biotransformation". Further evaluation of this mechanism demonstrated that few drugs pass through the body unchanged, and that analysis of the chemical changes, which they undergo, might be important in interpreting their actions and their duration of action. Subsequent investigation of this area of drug chemistry led to the concept of detoxification and determined the degree of effectiveness of drug activity. Of interest was the observation that biotransformations with the opposite effect were also recognized as initially envisaged both by Buchheim at Dorpat and by Oscar Liebreich (1839-1908) in Berlin. Justus von Liebig (1803-1873) in 1832 had prepared chloral hydrate about the same time as chloroform and the fairly close resemblance between the two substances suggested that the body might convert chloral to chloroform and release the anesthetic gradually but effectively. In investigating this possibility both Buchheim and Liebreich noted that chloral hydrate did in fact produce sleep. Thus, in 1869, Liebreich published an account of his discovery and chloral hydrate became established as an agent useful in the induction of narcosis or sleep. Unfortunately, although correct in principle, the interpretation was flawed in that chloral actually undergoes "biotransformation" not to chloroform but to trichlorethanol, which is the active agent in producing sleep. A further major extrapolation of this concept has been in the introduction of the technique of developing drugs that are transformed before acting – "pro-drugs". Either the active substance is released gradually, without the dangers of a single large dose acting all at once, or the inconvenience of continuous infusion of the agent or the agent that is the active drug principle only, is released at the actual target site.

Another major advance in facilitating the interface of chemistry and medicine was the development of synthetic chemistry, whereby substances previously unknown to scientists or physiologists were produced. Consideration of the potential effects of such agents on humans were an obvious possibility. In this respect, among the earliest such agents evaluated were the volatile substances, such as nitrous oxide and ether, whose stupefying powers were apparent for thirty or more years before their practical application as general anesthetics between 1842 and 1846. In 1847 a different volatile substance, chloroform, was used on animals by M.J.P. Flourens (1794-1867), a colleague of Magendie and almost simultaneously in humans by J.Y. Simpson (1811-70) in Edinburgh. In spite of initial opposition, the use of nitrous oxide, ether, and chloroform extended widely, and their efficacy and utility prompted considerable investigation into similar, even more potent and effective agents. Similarly, the study of other volatile substances demonstrated different but still useful attributes such as the cardiac vasodilator properties of amyl nitrite and glyceryl trinitrate.

A further application of chemistry was the ability not only to synthesize agents but to produce them on a large scale applicable for commercial usage. Thus, when previously unknown substances identified in a laboratory were determined to have medicinal properties, it became both scientifically and fiscally attractive as well as necessary to produce them on a larger scale. Thus, while the existing traditional suppliers of drugs and medicines – druggists, apothecaries, pharmacists – were familiar with botanical and inorganic materials, they had little knowledge or experience in more elaborate organic chemistry and the rigorous processes required for mass production and quality control.

In order to encompass such difficulties, some wholesale businesses, notably Merck of Darmstadt, sent employees to laboratories where technical knowledge could be obtained, and embarked on the isolation of alkaloids that could be marketed as pure and more reliable medicines than cruder preparations from plants. This coincided with the realization of some chemists that their chemical skills were likely to have direct application to large scale manufacturing. Thus, innovative organic chemists, especially von Liebig in Germany, actively proselytized the industrial applications of their subject, including the extraction from raw materials of reactive ingredients and the

William Henry Perkin (1838-1907). In 1853 Perkin entered the Royal College of Chemistry London and studied with August Wilhelm von Hoffman. During this time he unsuccessfully undertook to synthesize quinine but obtained instead a bluish substance with excellent dye properties that later became known as aniline purple, Tyrian purple or mauve. In 1856 he filed a patent for the manufacture of this dye and by the next year, with the aid of his father and his brother, Thomas, had set up an aniline manufacturing plant near Harrow, London. Following the announcement by Liebermann and Graebe of their successfully synthesis of the red dye, alizarine, Perkin developed a cheaper procedure, obtained a patent for the process and held a monopoly on its manufacture for several years. In addition, his investigations covered the chemical spectrum including dyes, salicyl alcohol, and chemical flavoring. In 1874 he abandoned manufacture and devoted himself to research, studying not only chemical processes but investigating the optical rotation of various substances. In 1906 on the 50th anniversary of his discovery of mauve, he was knighted. The application of Perkin's contributions to organic chemistry allowed for the development of numerous novel agents, including the anti-pyretic analgesics and other dyes that exhibited anti-bacterial activity.

The application of chemistry to the development of pharmacological agents resulted in the transfer of the production of drugs from the modest individual laboratories of scientists to major pharmaceutical corporations.

synthesis of novel compounds with innumerable potential uses. An example was provided by the crystallization of pure plant alkaloids which represented a tiny and highly specialized component of such work. Chemical analysis of the new alkaloids indicated that they could be prepared synthetically, manufactured in large amounts and thus obviate cultivating medicinal plants, eradicate the problems of collecting and extracting the required drugs, as well as evade the problems associated with unpredictable yields.

Of particular interest were the events surrounding the 1856 attempts by the English chemist W.H. Perkin (1838-1907) to synthesize quinine. Although he failed utterly (it would only be achieved in 1940) in his objective (predictable given that the complexity of the quinine molecule far exceeded contemporary chemical knowledge) Perkin's synthesis produced a colored compound, that led to the synthesis of a dyestuff that he labeled as "mauvein".

The latter was widely developed for commercial usage and represented the foundation of the synthetic dyestuffs industry. Since good dyestuffs were valuable, organic chemistry advanced as new techniques were investigated to develop novel agents. As might also be expected, alternative uses for new compounds were examined, and with the passage of time the commerce of dyestuffs evolved into an industry that included not only fine chemicals but also medicinal substances among its products. Despite the difficulty experienced with quinine, other alkaloids proved less problematic and in addition, the increasing sophistication of organic chemistry enabled a better delineation of the structures of the simpler alkaloids with the result that their synthesis became realistic and indeed, in 1886 was achieved for coniine. Similarly, by 1900, even the more complex substances including atropine, cocaine, and nicotine, were all successfully synthesized. As a consequence of such scientific progress, the initial dream of Brown and Fraser to identify the relation of chemical structure to pharmacological activity that had been unattainable forty years earlier, now became an attainable reality, as did the possibility of synthesizing novel compounds that were simplified imitations of natural alkaloids. The earliest major group of compounds produced by the new chemical industry and found to have medicinal properties were the antipyretic analgesics (derived from coal tar) that included phenacetin, paracetamol, and several others that were subsequently discarded because of toxicity issues. Other examples of early synthetic drugs include the barbiturates and a variety of volatile anaesthetics. Interestingly enough, a number of compounds produced initially either in industry or in university laboratories, languished for decades prior to their medicinal applications becoming apparent. Thus aspirin, although synthesized in 1852, failed to have its medicinal properties recognized until 1899, and sulphanilamides too remained unrecognized from 1908 until the mid-1930s.

Justus von Liebig (top left) of Germany was not only an innovative organic chemist but actively proposed the industrial application of his discoveries. Thus, successful procedures initially developed in his laboratory were rapidly transferred to major manufacturing plants.

With the increasing sophistication of organic chemistry, compounds modeled on existing drugs that might have some adverse effects could be synthesized in an effort to generate agents that were equally or more effective as well as safe. A particularly good example of this strategy was the synthetic evolution of local anaesthetics that resembled cocaine. Thus, the hazardous properties of cocaine were obviated by the introduction of the more effective and chemically simpler agent procaine, in 1899.

Thus, by the beginning of the twentieth century, the application of chemical science to medicine had enabled the development of a number of potent synthetic drugs, some partially purified drugs and some active principles (in particular pure alkaloids). Notwithstanding the fact that their identification had for the most part been empirical and that the agents had not been developed primarily for medical usage, they represented the first elements of a new wave of therapeutically targeted probes that would evolve during the remainder of the twentieth century.

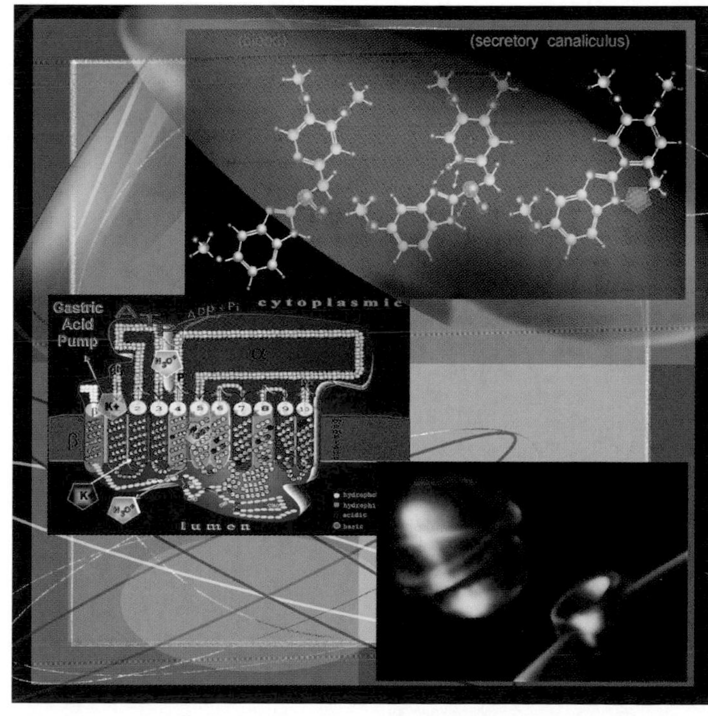

A proton pump inhibitor (top) (pro drug) targeting a cysteine moiety in the gastric H+/K+ ATPase (center) of the parietal cell. By the late 20th century, drug development had achieved such sophistication that chemists were able to identify targets at a molecular level and design agents capable of targeting either specific receptors (bottom right) or even synthesize "pro drugs" capable (after conversion) of selective function within a particular cell system.

Section 10

Current Therapeutic Strategies

For centuries disease had been a nebulous entity variously ascribed to divine influences, malignant spirits and noxious vapors. Giovanni Batista Morgagni (1682-1772) of Rome first defined the structural form of the damage to the body and Karl Rokitansky (1804-1878) of Vienna aligned the symptoms with the disease as Rudolf Virchow (1821-1902) of Berlin strove to relate the disease to a cellular dysfunction.

CHEMOTHERAPY

Subsequently Robert Koch (1843-1910) defined the concepts of the bacterial genesis of disease and Louis Pasteur (1822-1895) elucidated the mechanisms by which organisms function, as well as initiating the basis of bacterial eradication. As a consequence of the excitement accompanying the demonstration of the infectious etiology of many diseases, the principles of rigorous physiologic investigations were transiently relegated to the background as the interest in specifics reached its zenith, driven by the fervor for new cures. One individual, Paul Ehrlich (1854-1915), was in particular responsible for much of this enthusiasm and his interest in the subject had devolved from his cousin, Carl Weigert, who had instructed him in the technique of staining bacteria with aniline dyes. As a result of his own work and the research of Robert Koch, Ehrlich concluded that the staining of bacteria (and consequently all forms of cells) had its basis in a chemical union between the cell and the stain. Ehrlich supposed that the action of drugs on bodily organs was likely to involve similar fixation, and throughout his life he followed the principle "*Corpora non agunt nisi fixata*" (substances do not act unless they are fixed). This concept led him to propose "*that it might be possible to discover dyestuffs or other drugs whose chemical affinity for disease organisms was so great that the organism might be killed without damage to the host.*" As an early test of this thesis, he treated a small number of malarial patients with the dye methylene blue, which was known to stain (that is, be fixed by) the malaria parasite, and he showed that it had a modest therapeutic effect. The question that followed was: "*What substances in the tissues or what part of the antitoxin produced by the tissues combines with or fixes the dye or toxin?*" Ehrlich called the unidentified material a "receptor". The term was used in a similar sense, at about the same time, by the English physiologist J.N. Langley (1852-1925) for the material, which "received" nicotine and curare in the motor end plates of skeletal muscle. Despite the fact that knowledge of the chemical structure of tissues was inadequate for either Ehrlich or Langley to actually isolate and identify the specific receptors, the elucidation of the concept itself represented a fundamental advance.

Mittheilungen

aus dem

Kaiserlic... eitsamte.

KOCH, Robert
1843-1910
Zur Untersuchung von pathogenen Organismen,
in Mittheilungen aus dem Kaiserlichen Gesundheitsamte, Erster Band.
Berlin, Norddeutschen Buchdruckerei, 1881.

Berlin, 1881.
Druck und Verlag der Norddeutschen Buchdruckerei und Verlagsanstalt,

Much basic pharmacology evolved from attempts to identify receptor substances or structures, and to account for the quantitative aspects of drug action in terms of theoretical receptors. In his theoretical considerations to explain the action of chemotherapeutic agents, Ehrlich assumed a direct action of the substance, of its alteration product on the parasite and conceived of this action as being brought about by the avidity of certain "chemoceptors" in the cell of the parasite for certain groups contained in the chemical. By assuming these discrete affinities within the cell, the attempt was made to give more visible expression to certain phenomena which were observed in the reaction of microorganisms to chemicals containing certain groups in the molecule.

Based on his belief that cure could be effected under these conditions, Ehrlich spent the early part of his career evaluating and developing new biological remedies and deriving theories of their mode of action. In so doing he contributed considerably to both the resolution of practical problems as well as standardizing the remedies. He abandoned the notion of antitoxins and studied simpler substances, essentially products of chemical laboratories, both as drugs and as a basis for advancing knowledge of receptors. By the late 1890s Ehrlich became convinced that the identification of substances of

Robert Koch (1843-1910) provided the pivotal intellectual contributions that defined the bacterial genesis of disease.

Das
Sauerstoff-Bedürfniss
des Organismus.
Eine farbenanalytische Studie
von
Professor Dr. P. Ehrlich,

Berlin, 1885.
Verlag von August Hirs

The genius of Paul Ehrlich (1854-1915) initiated the identification of the first anti-bacterial therapy – Salvarsan.

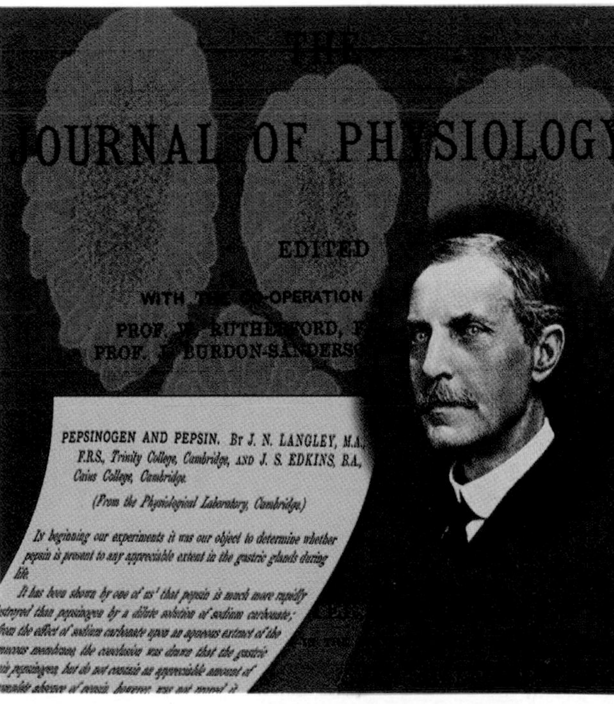

OURNAL OF PH SIOLOG

EDITED

PEPSINOGEN AND PEPSIN. By J. N. LANGLEY, M.A., F.R.S., Trinity College, Cambridge, and J. S. EDKINS, B.A., Caius College, Cambridge.
(From the Physiological Laboratory, Cambridge.)

J. Langley (inset) working with J. Edkins defined the physiology of pepsin. Langley also coined the word "oxyntic" to describe parietal cells and in addition utilized the term "receptor" to define the sites of action of nicotine and curare on skeletal muscle.

Paul Ehrlich (left) and Sahachiro Hata (originally of Tokyo) investigated the use of organic arsenical agents in seeking a cure for syphilis. Their discovery of Salvarsan was instrumental in leading to the subsequent development of a rational therapy for the disease.

known chemical composition would lead to the cure of microbial diseases and referred to this concept as chemotherapy. In a concerted attempt to achieve this goal he examined innumerable compounds for antiprotozoal and antibacterial activity. It was soon apparent that known antibacterial substances, such as phenol, were too poisonous [*organotropic* (toxic)] to be tolerated if administered as medicines, whereas tolerable agents such as quinine that were active against certain protozoa [*parasitropic* (lethal to the parasite)] were ineffective against bacteria. All substances which were therapeutically useful were also, to some degree, toxic to the host organism and as a result he was compelled to function within a narrow range of tolerated and lethal toxic effects and "*found it necessary to find some means of expressing the chemotherapeutic activity of compounds for purposes of comparison*." In an adroit method to overcome the therapeutic hurdle presented by the consideration of the risk-benefit ratio, Ehrlich therefore calculated for each new substance the ratio of the minimum curative dose to the maximum tolerated dose, and derived a novel expression of this ratio which he called the Chemotherapeutic Index.

Although he obtained some success against experimental infections with trypanosomes, protozoa of the family that cause sleeping sickness in rodents, malaria proved to be an unsatisfactory topic, because patients were uncommon in northern Europe, and no animal model of the disease existed. In the light of clinical reports that organic arsenical compounds were effective against trypanosomes, Ehrlich therefore focused on the chemistry and antimicrobial actions of such compounds and chose syphilis as his target. Since the organism that causes syphilis, the spirochaete *Treponema pallidum*, had recently been identified and it had been demonstrated that rabbits could be successfully infected, this seemed an ideal research area. This direction of research was to a large extent determined by the transfer of the technique to Ehrlich's laboratory by a Japanese scientist, Sahachiro Hata (1873-1938) of Tokyo. In conjunction they examined a number of antisyphilitic organic arsenicals, of which the one designated "606" appeared the most promising.

A late 19th-century portrayal of a young man of substance ruined by his unfortunate dalliance with the sylphlike "siren of syphilis."

As a result of the early promising experimental data, Ehrlich arranged for the compound to be made on a larger scale and instituted clinical trials both in Germany and elsewhere. The success of these studies led to Ehrlich's public announcement of the discovery of a "cure" for syphilis at the Congress for Internal Medicine held at Wiesbaden in April 1910. Early enthusiasm was, however, somewhat diminished by the recognition that "606" (later named "salvarsan" and arsphenamine) was unstable and the potency of successive batches unpredictable. In addition to the inherent drug difficulties, treatment was effective only by intravenous injection, required many months, and a substantial proportion of patients experienced serious toxic effects on the liver, bone marrow, or skin. As a result of intensive investigation, a more efficacious compound, "914" or neoarsphenamine, was introduced in 1913, and over the succeeding two decades would remain the principal drug in the treatment of syphilis.

The Development of Drugs from Physiological Agents

The late nineteenth century proved important from the perspective of pharmacology as physiologists began to delineate the regulatory mechanisms of function. Thus the work of Pavlov defined neural regulation and Bayliss and Starling elucidated the principles of the chemical regulation of secretory function as well as postulating even broader actions for this class of agents known as "chemical messengers". In order to better describe this novel

The main credit for establishing the science of bacteriology must be accorded to the French chemist Louis Pasteur (1822-1895) (right). It was Pasteur who, by a brilliant series of experiments, proved that the fermentation of wine and the souring of milk are caused by living microorganisms. His work led to the pasteurization of milk and solved problems of agriculture and industry as well as those of animal and human diseases. He successfully employed inoculations to prevent anthrax in sheep and cattle, chicken cholera in fowl, and finally rabies in humans and dogs. The initial bacterial studies of Robert Koch (left) inspired numerous physicians to define the specific bacterial causation of disease. A meticulous investigator, Koch discovered the organisms of tuberculosis, in 1882, and cholera, in 1883. By the end of the century many other disease-producing microorganisms had been identified.

group, the term "hormone" was adopted in 1905 by E.H. Starling (1866-1927) in connection with his observations on gastrointestinal chemical regulators. Within a decade physiologists had begun to postulate and sometimes demonstrate the existence of substances, which when released by specific cells or organs, had specific effects on other cells. Such information led to the description of the diffuse endocrine system by F. Feyrter and the notion of aggregations of such cells – the ductless glands. It was proposed that two kinds of substances were produced – one known as hormones was released into the bloodstream from certain ductless glands and acted on distant organs. The other kind was released at nerve endings and stimulated or inhibited other nerve cells, muscles, or glands. The action of the latter group was regarded as strictly localized and they were initially labeled as humoral transmitters, subsequently as local hormones and then finally as paracrine or neuracrine agents.

A series of studies of the effects of extirpation of glands such as the thyroid or the adrenals and replacement by extracts, led to the development of important therapeutic principles. Thus by 1891, extracts of thyroid gland had been used to treat myxoedema and adrenal extracts were shown in 1894 to raise the blood pressure of experimental animals. Subsequently John J. Abel (1857-1938) at Johns Hopkins University isolated from the adrenal gland an active principle, adrenaline, and its chemical identity was established and confirmed by synthesis. In 1890 Brown-Sequard claimed that testicular extracts possessed rejuvenating powers, and by 1900 the ovaries were recognized as a source of internal secretion although a further thirty years would elapse prior to the identification of the active principles involved in these phenomena.

As a result of the efforts of numerous investigators and a complex series of studies involving diverse endocrine glands, the novel science of endocrinology emerged and with this advent of a new discipline, hormones themselves became important as drugs; either to replace a deficiency of the natural secretion; to modify immune responses and check unwanted inflammatory reactions (cortisone and its congeners); or to modify healthy bodily functions, notably the reproductive cycle of women as a means of contraception. Furthermore, new drugs were developed which either acted like the natural hormones (e.g. the synthetic estrogen, stilboestrol) or stimulated the release of hormones (antidiabetic drugs), or prevented the release of hormones (analogues of somatostatin) or decrease glandular over-activity (e.g. thiouracil). Although the treatment of myxoedema with thyroid preparations was effective, considerable effort was expended in elucidating thyroid secretory regulation with the view to developing a more effective therapeutic strategy.

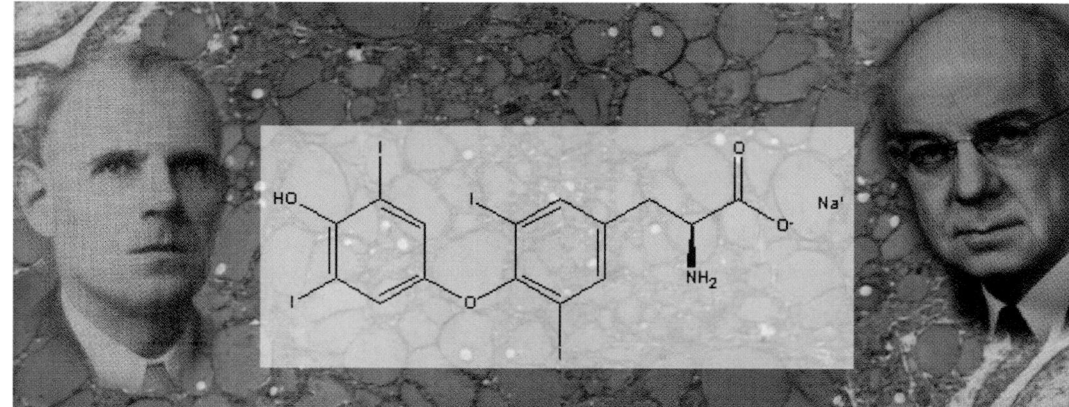

In 1915 E.C. Kendall and C.R. Harington of the Mayo Clinic were respectively responsible for the isolation, purification and synthesis of thyroxine.

Thus, in 1915, E.C. Kendall (1886-1972) at the Mayo Clinic isolated thyroxine and C.R. Harington (1897-1972) established its structure enabling the development of synthetic thyroxine, which proved as efficacious as the actual biological product. Although the identification of adrenaline from the adrenal medulla failed to benefit sufferers of Addison's disease (adrenal cortical insufficiency), the subsequent identification in 1930 of adrenal extracts that alleviated the consequences of adrenal deficiency led to the development of cortisone and formed the basis for the development of steroid therapy.

The most significant example of the extrapolation of a physiological agent into a therapeutic principle was provided in 1922 by the isolation from the pancreas of an agent that proved capable of reversing the sequela of diabetes mellitus. In fact, the critical role of the pancreas in preventing diabetes had been well recognized prior to the end of the nineteenth century by, amongst others, Bernard, von Mering, and Minkowski, and a number of attempts had been undertaken to isolate an antidiabetic principle. It was, however, the experiments of Frederick Banting (1891-1941) and Charles Best (1899-1978) in Toronto that resolved the issue.

Unfortunately the task of rendering insulin useful as a drug was complex, since it was a significantly more complex substance than

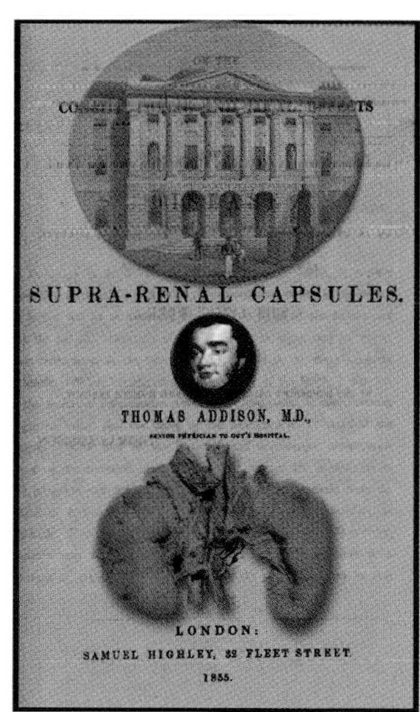

Thomas Addison of Guy's Hospital, London, in 1855 authored a monograph "On the Constitutional and Local Effects of Disease of the Suprarenal Capsules." His observation was prescient in that it proved to be the precursor to the study of the diseases of the ductless glands subsequently undertaken by Claude Bernard.

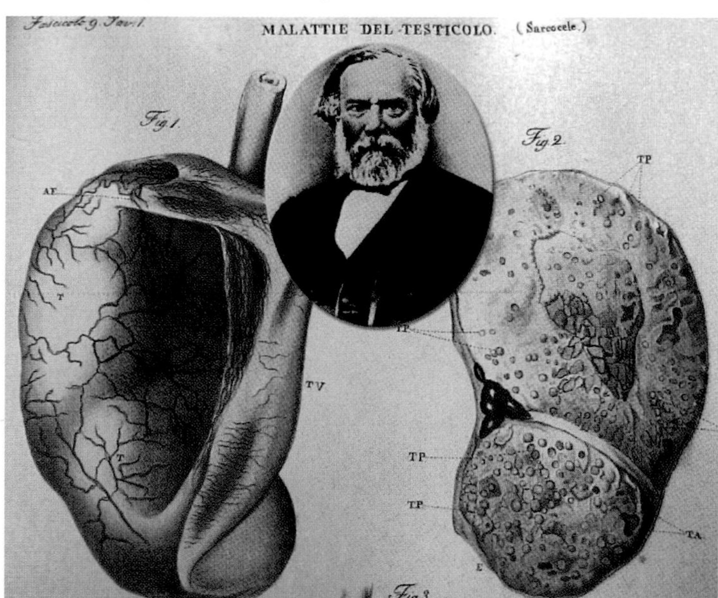

Charles Edouard Brown-Sequard (1817-94) (inset) was a native of Mauritius and led a peripatetic life as professor of medicine and physiology on both sides of the Atlantic (London, Paris, New York, and Boston). Having succeeded Claude Bernard as professor of experimental medicine at the Collège de France (1878) he was thereafter a professor in Harvard and Paris. As one of the principle founders of the Doctrine of Internal Secretions, he believed that the use of extracts of such glandular organs might have considerable therapeutic properties. Despite injecting himself with testicular extract (background), he was unable to convince others of the efficacy of this strategy.

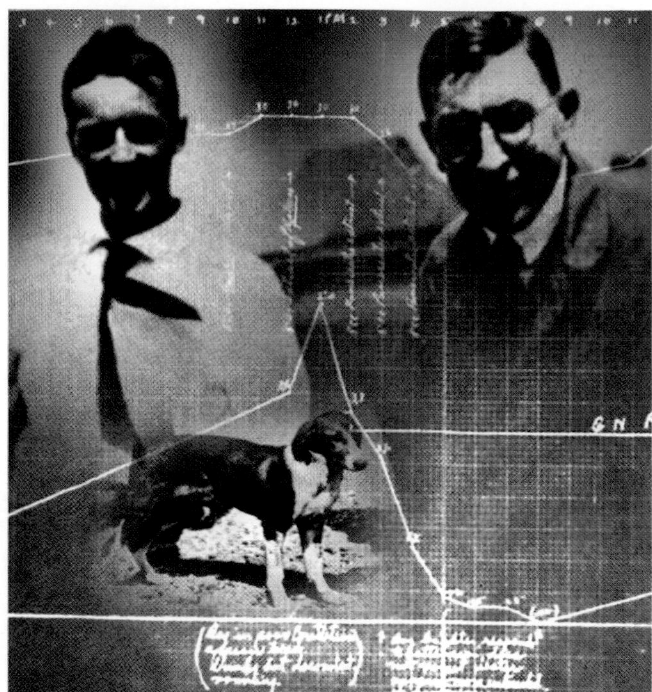

Charles Best (left) a medical student, and Fredrick Banting (right), an orthopedic surgeon of Toronto, identified the anti-diabetic principle known as insulin in 1922. Little acknowledgement was given to Marjorie (Dog# 33) (the one survivor out of 10 dogs) whose pivotal role in the experiments was barely acknowledged. Despite a pancreatectomy she survived (inset) after having received the crude pancreatic extract injections prepared by the two researchers. This experiment confirmed the existence of a pancreatic substance capable of regulating blood sugar. Some medical historians have considered Marjorie to be the most important dog in history.

At the turn of the century the pharmaceutical corporations recognized the importance of establishing professional relationships with great scientists who had previously confined their activities to universities. Thus individuals such as O. Loewi (left) and Henry Dale (right), who were more amenable to developing corporate relationships, directed their efforts towards not only pure science but the elucidation of the properties of agents that might have therapeutic potential.

either the thyroxine or the adrenal hormones and as a protein liable to digestion, thus rendering it orally ineffective. Furthermore, since the proteolytic pancreatic enzymes rendered its isolation and preparation difficult, the resources of a university laboratory were inadequate to generate enough of the substance for the massive patient population. The resolution of the practical aspects of the issue were resolved by the interface of the resources of the Connaught Laboratories in Toronto and of Eli Lilly in Indianapolis, and thereafter on judicious licensing of production to manufacturers in every part of the world. The outcome represented a major triumph of the application of science to medicine, and depended entirely on the conduct of experiments in animals, mostly dogs that were subsequently applied to organic chemistry and thereafter clinical trial. Nevertheless, problems still remained in that demand was greater than supply and quality an issue, until the elucidation of the structure of insulin in the 1950s enabled chemical synthesis of the molecule. The subsequent introduction of gene technology enabled microbial synthesis and in so doing, engendered a major therapeutic advance.

A further area of therapeutic advance derived from the study of neural transmission, since this was deemed to be an important area of regulatory function. Thus research concerned with the transmission of messages from nerve cells to other nerve cells and to muscles and glands on which nerves acted, focused for nearly a century on the mechanism of transmission, as controversy raged regarding whether the mechanism was by electrical impulses or pulses of chemically identifiable substances. Since adrenaline possessed actions similar to those of the sympathetic nerves, some scientists supported adrenaline as a transmitter; while the resemblance of the actions of muscarine to those of the vagus and other parasympathetic nerves prompted others to propose muscarine as the transmitter. Although neither supposition proved to be correct, O. Loewi (1873-1961) showed that the transmitter at vagal endings was probably acetylcholine, while H.H. Dale (1875-1968) and U.S. von Euler (1905-83) identified the principal transmitters as noradrenaline at sympathetic endings and acetylcholine at most other sites.

As a result of this elucidation of the neural transmitter conundrum, it then became feasible to develop a model whereby a comprehensive picture of the actions of a variety of agents [atropine (blocking muscarine-like actions of acetylcholine), eserine (delaying the destruction of acetylcholine and so imitating and enhancing its actions), curare (blocking non-muscarine-like actions of acetylcholine), ergotoxine (blocking certain actions of adrenaline)] could be incorporated into a global scheme of the mechanism of neural transmission. Unfortunately, despite the physiological advances represented by these observations there was little therapeutic benefit, although some drugs related to acetylcholine were developed for management of postoperative urine retention. In addition, ephedrine (long known in Chinese medicine) which chemically and pharmacologically resembled adrenaline, was shown to be beneficial in asthma. Nevertheless the delineation of the fundamental knowledge regarding the chemical basis of neural physiology prior to 1930 established a background which laid the foundation for many of the advances that occurred after 1950 and the cassation of global military conflict.

The Application of Science to Drug Development

Although there had been remarkable advances in the disciplines of physiology, chemistry, endocrinology and chemotherapy, pharmacology itself had remained relatively static despite its initial academic and industrial advance in Germany during the nineteenth century. The consequences of the First World War to a large extent hampered progress and the subsequent Nazi persecutions of the 1930s virtually destroyed the discipline as innumerable pharmacologists were either purged (murdered or incarcerated) or fled the country. In England between 1880 and 1930, although research on drugs flourished in physiological laboratories and in the state-supported National Institute for Medical Research, academic facilities were marginal and pharmacolgical education was entrusted to clinicians with no scientific training

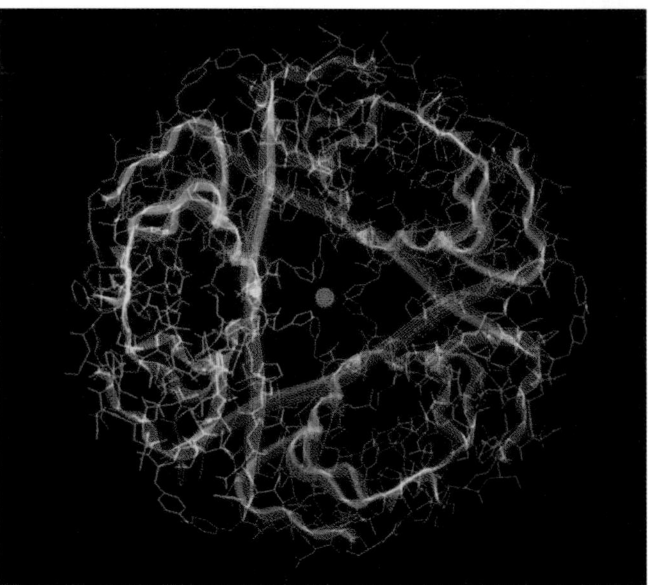

A three-dimensional reconstruction of the insulin molecule.

The advent of the Third Reich lead to a significant winnowing of the German intellectual ranks as great scientists were either purged based upon their genomic antecedents or fled the country of their own volition, fearing for their lives.

or interests. In 1932, a national society to oversee all the interests of British pharmacologists was founded and the subject gradually received wider recognition and acceptance. Although the British pharmaceutical industry was considerably less research-oriented than that in Germany, one firm, Burroughs Wellcome, as early as 1900, supported substantial research laboratories, interestingly named "chemical" and "physiological". In the eastern United States, as in Scotland, experimental pharmacology at the turn of the nineteenth century replaced the old curricula in *materia medica* but the western states lagged initially behind as issues of land acquisition and gold dominated the times. Indeed, given the nature of the evolving society and its heterogeneous population, opportunism and a flexible legal system led to early drug firms in America acquiring a bad reputation for their commercial practices. Indeed, the industry was held in such low esteem that the American Society for Experimental Pharmacology and Therapeutics, founded and dominated by Abel, initially was adamant in its exclusion of industrial pharmacologists from its membership. This state of affairs lasted until 1941, by which time industrial practices were deemed to have improved and the absence of such scientists considered to have diminished the effectiveness of the Society.

A number of scientific problems were specific to pharmacology, of which the most fundamental related to the mode of action of drugs, since prior to the turn of the twentieth century, it had been generally accepted that drugs acted diffusely throughout the body and not at specific sites. The recognition that there were, in fact, explicit sites of action generically referred to as receptors was accepted after the work of Langley but their identity remained obscure. It remained for Arthur Cushny (1866-1926), a pupil of Schmiedeberg and later successor to Fraser in Edinburgh, to elucidate the relation of optical activity to potency of drugs and define the geometrical properties of drug receptors. Prior to his seminal contributions, the mechanism by which drugs interacted with receptors and initiated a physiological effect, was unknown. His successor in the Edinburgh Chair of Pharmacology, A.J. Clark (1885-1941), subsequently published two classic monographs that not only delineated in detail the nature of drug receptors and the mode of action of drugs but also considered mechanisms by which drugs might block the actions of other drugs by competing for the same receptors.

Concomitant with the development of sophisticated assessment of receptor function was the introduction of sensitive techniques to identify and measure minute quantities of drugs using living tissues. Thus, the late nineteenth century had seen the introduction in legal matters of biological tests for organic poisons such as digitalis and similar poisons. Since chemical tests were too insensitive to identify potentially lethal quantities of digitalis, biological analysis proved not only sensitive but exceptionally specific and could distinguish digitalis from other cardio-active agents. Further biological tests were developed to provide estimates of the quantities of drug present and were also necessary for quality control of manufactured products: at first, antitoxins; and later, potent drugs of plant origin, such as digitalis or curare; as well as hormones and vitamins. The initial principles of rigorous assay methodology were established by Ehrlich, and their subsequent refinement utilizing sophisticated statistical methods reflected the contributions of J.W. Trevan (1887-1956) at the Wellcome Laboratories, and J.H. Gaddum (1900-65) at the National Institute.

Despite such refinements, the predominant focus of most pharmacologists was the investigation of familiar medicines with a view to the identification of methods by which the efficacy of the agent might be amplified. In general the approach was to attempt to relate a particular action to a known chemical structure, and then synthesize new compounds resembling the original substance. In the event that the novel agent appeared stable, further biological studies were undertaken to investigate the level of activity and determine safety. This operation of synthesis and screening became the principal activity of industrial pharmacological research and was applied to important alkaloids, including cocaine as a local anesthetic, eserine as an anticholinesterase, and atropine as a spasmolytic, and to physiological agents such as adrenaline and acetylcholine. Similarly, synthetic substances that demonstrated interesting physiological activity such as substituted ammonium compounds (autonomic ganglia blockade), provided a fruitful line of investigation and led to the introduction of a long sequence of hypotensive agents.

A British investigative laboratory at the turn of the 20th century featuring the Nobel Prize winners Ronald Ross (left and inset) and Sherrington (standing right). Sherrington was awarded the Nobel Prize for his contributions to neurophysiology and Ross received his Prize for the elucidation of the basis of malaria.

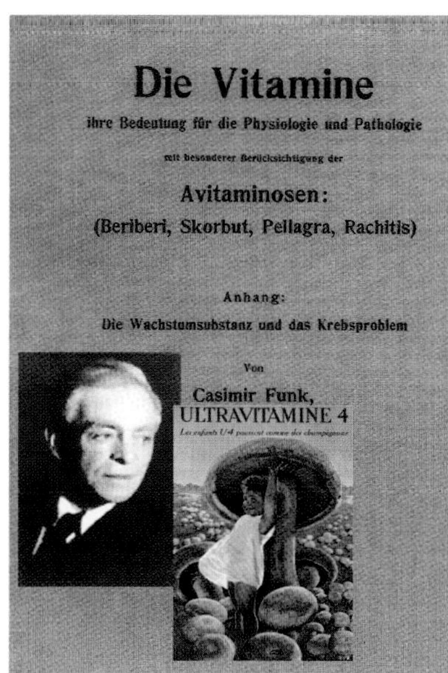

The contributions of Casimir Funk (inset) to the understanding of the critical nature of vitamins led to the development of replacement therapy and a substantial reduction of the incidence of a broad group of diseases (scurvy, rickets, beri beri, pellagra) known as "the deficiency diseases."

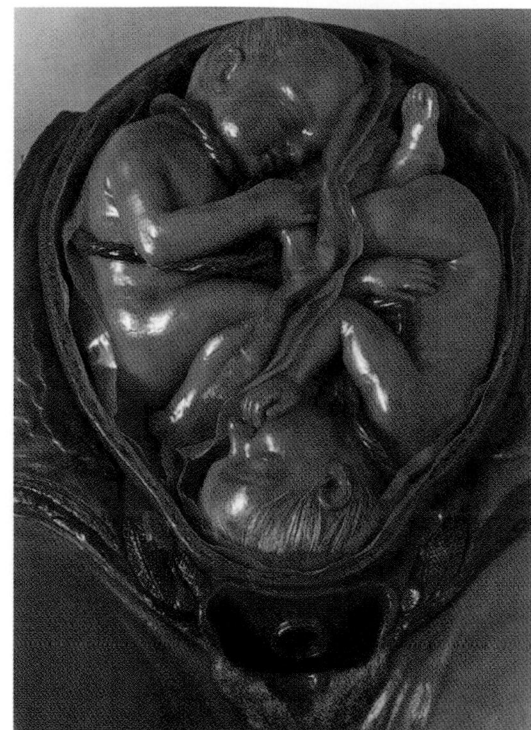

A model of a female uterus and fetuses from the museum collection of William Hunter in Glasgow. The search for effective agents capable of causing uterine contraction and cessation of postpartum hemorrhage was a critical focus for both pharmacologists and obstetricians at the turn of the 19th century.

Nevertheless, the critical flaw in the science of pharmacology lay in its inherent partition from clinical medicine in that the one group of laboratory-based persons (represented by scientists) perceived little common ground in the work of the other who were wholly devoted to issues of patient care on the clinical floor. A prime example of this dysfunctional relationship was provided by the attempts to identify the active principle of ergot employed in the control of postpartum hemorrhage. Thus, pharmacologists believed ergotoxine, which had been discovered in 1906 to be "the" active principle, whereas clinicians considered the watery extract of ergot to be responsible for uterine contraction. This argument was maintained for almost three decades and even further obfuscated by the discovery of yet another uterus contracting alkaloid, ergotamine. Only in 1933-5 was the problem finally resolved when clinical studies undertaken in collaboration with laboratory scientists determined that the clinically active principle of the watery extract was in fact yet another alkaloid, ergometrine or ergonovine. Collaboration, however, improved and the significant advances in therapeutics between the First and Second World Wars were in many instances a reflection of the application of concepts developed in physiological and biochemical laboratories that were applied and investigated by clinical scientists. In this fashion vitamins were discovered, mainly by biochemists and chemically-oriented nutritionists, and hormones entered clinical usage. Similarly physiological studies by Minot of the value of liver in some kinds of anemia led to trials in treatment of the hitherto fatal disease, pernicious or Addisonian anemia. The successful introduction of liver treatment and the subsequent isolation of intrinsic factor by Castle as well as the elucidation of vitamin B_{12} in the mid-1940s, represented the next major therapeutic advance after the introduction of insulin.

Alphonse Laveran (1845-1922) of Paris received a Nobel Prize in 1907 for identifying the parasites of malarial fever (1880) while an army surgeon in Algeria. His subsequent work on trypanosomiasis lead to the development of agents directed against both the Laveran plasmodia and trypanosomiasis.

Chemotherapy Redivivus

Although chemotherapy had initially been a term employed to denote the treatment of parasitic diseases with any chemical agent, with the passage of time it evolved into a concept that reflected more broadly the treatment of a disease with a chemical agent and thus embraced a far broader perspective of therapy. As such, chemical agents had been used in the treatment of disease for ages, and following the discoveries of Pasteur, Koch and others of pathogenic bacteria, germicides and antiseptics, attempts were made to disinfect the tissues with mercurial and other compounds. The application of this concept to surgery (disinfecting the tissues locally with phenol and related substances) by Lister had resulted in brilliant success and instigated a virtual renaissance in surgery at the turn of the twentieth century. Surprisingly and disappointingly, however, the early success of salvarsan, while demonstrating that microbes could be destroyed in patients by synthetic drugs, had not been followed by the anticipated identification of numerous other chemotherapeutic agents. To a large extent this represented the fact that there was little information that allowed the search to be focused, and as a result most discoveries were made empirically. Thus, although an acridine dye that inhibited trypanosomes was named "trypaflavine" and related acridines were found to be active against bacteria and adopted as antiseptics, in general their overall toxicity obviated systemic use. A major advance was the identification, in the laboratories of the Bayer Company, of compounds that destroyed protozoa and were in addition relatively harmless to humans. The work was conducted in extreme secrecy and even the chemical identity of the first important compound, "Bayer 205" or germanin for sleeping sickness, was not initially divulged. Thereafter two important antimalarials, Plasmaquin (pamaquine) and Atebrin (mepacrine in England and quinacrine in the US) were also discovered but none of these advances contributed to *antibacterial* chemotherapy, and even the most eminent of authorities in Britain and America continued to dismiss the concept of bacteria-targeted agents as an unrealizable dream.

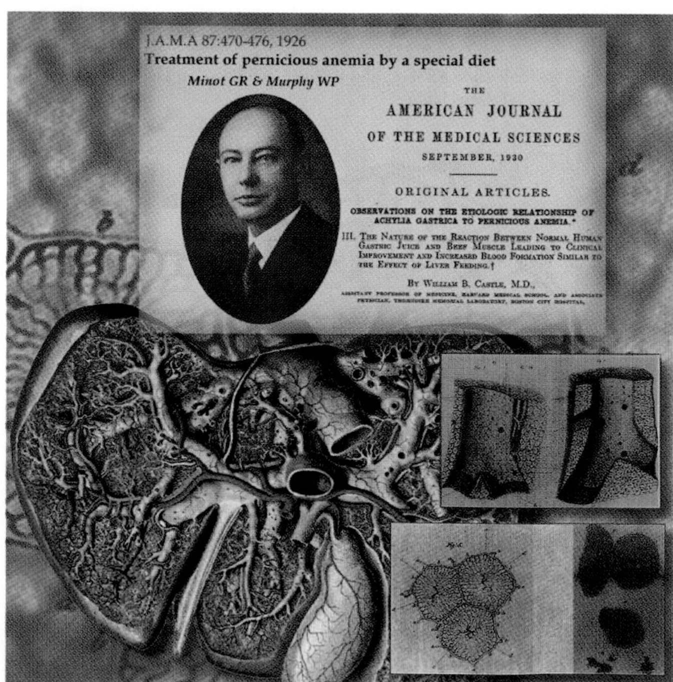

The description by G. Minot and W. Murphy of the basis of pernicious anemia led to the understanding of the critical role of the vitamin B_{12} in human metabolism. Their recognition that the ingestion of large amounts of liver was therapeutic formed the basis of treatment until the discovery of intrinsic factor by W. Castle and the subsequent synthesis of vitamin B_{12}.

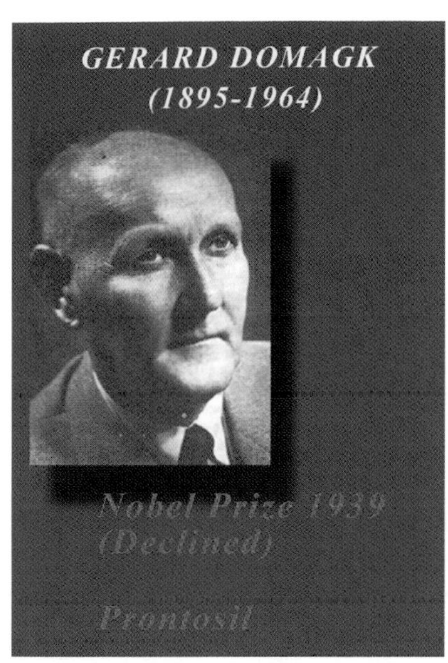

GERARD DOMAGK
(1895-1964)
Nobel Prize 1939
(Declined)
Prontosil

Gerhard Domagk identified a red dye (Prontosil) with anti-bacterial activities. Elaborations of this compound led to the development of the "sulpha" class of drugs that heralded a revolution in the management of sepsis. The Third Reich "persuaded" Domagk that acceptance of the Swedish Nobel Committee's recognition of his contributions would not be in his best interests.

Despite this universal English-speaking despondency, the German pharmaceutical establishment thought otherwise and Gerhard Domagk (1895-1964), who had joined the Bayer laboratories in 1927, avidly pursued the identification of potential antibacterial drugs, including a red dye later named "Prontosil". By 1935 Domagk had reported a Prontosil experiment in which mice infected with hemolytic streptococci were protected and as a result, clinical trials were widespread and the efficacy of the drug became well-accepted. Later in the same year, J. Tréfouël (1897-1977) and his colleagues at the Pasteur Institute in Paris demonstrated that a simpler compound, p-aminobenzenesulphonamide (sulphanilamide), liberated from Prontosil *in vivo* was equally effective. Sulphanilamide provided a model for the development of an entire series of novel compounds, each with a variety of advantages, that were described in the next decade. Within a decade, the mode of action of sulphanilamide was determined when the growth-promoting substance resembling sulphanilamide was identified in a yeast extract. Following this observation, a series of compounds were tested, and p-aminobenzoic acid (PABA) was identified as an agent that, like the yeast material, both supported microbial growth as well as counteracting the effects of sulphanilamide. Of particular relevance was the observation that the very species of microbe that depended on PABA for proliferation were identical to those sensitive to sulphanilamide! The elucidation of this phenomenon led to the recognition that the concept of competitive antagonism (between chemically-allied compounds as substrates for an enzyme system) could now be viewed in the more practical context of identifying agents that might have utility as novel pharmacotherapeutic agents. This discovery was therefore applied with vigor to the identification of specific metabolites essential to a pathogenic microbe, yet without any significant role in human physiology. As a result, numerous analogues were synthesized and tested for competitive blocking activity, and the most effective developed for medical purposes. Unfortunately, despite the validity of the principle, practical difficulties became obvious as time progressed (limited numbers of specific metabolites) and this avenue of exploration proved less felicitous than had been initially anticipated. Nevertheless, a substantial number of new drugs useful not only against bacterial and protozoal infections, but also for cancer chemotherapy, were identified in this fashion.

Fleming and Antibiotics

The search for alternative techniques to control microbial infections led to a reconsideration of a previously well-recognized phenomenon known as antibiosis. This concept had been identified by bacteriologists in the time of Pasteur (1822-95) and embodied the knowledge that prevention of growth or actual destruction of one species of microorganism could be achieved by substances produced by another species. Indeed, the fact that certain moulds possessed antibacterial property had been known in the 1870s and, in fact, the effects of some species of *Penicillium* had been utilized by Joseph Lister (1827-1912) in Edinburgh, who used a crude preparation to treat an infected wound. Nevertheless enthusiasm for the concept remained, and intermittent experiments with various extracts of moulds and bacteria were undertaken, such that by 1910 a preparation named pyocyanase, prepared from *Pseudomonas pyocyanea*, was actually commercially available but marginal efficacy led to its demise. Although Alexander Fleming (1881-1955) of St. Mary's Hospital in London, used the name penicillin to refer to the antibacterial matter produced by the mould that fell on his plate, he failed to isolate the unstable active principle of the compound.

The resolution of the substantial chemical problems necessary to engender pure active penicillin were surmounted by E.B. Chain (1906-79) and H.W. Florey (1898-1968) in Oxford early in the Second World War as part of a broad study of antibiotics. As a result of their efforts, adequate crude penicillin was produced in an academic laboratory to demonstrate that it was not only innocuous but highly effective. Since British resources were fully committed to other military needs, the further development of penicillin and the

H.W. Florey (top left), E.B. Chain (top right), and Alexander Fleming (bottom left) each provided significant contributions to the development of penicillin as an effective therapeutic agent. Much of the early research on the subject was undertaken at Oxford University (Bodleian Camera in background) where a plaque commemorates their achievement.

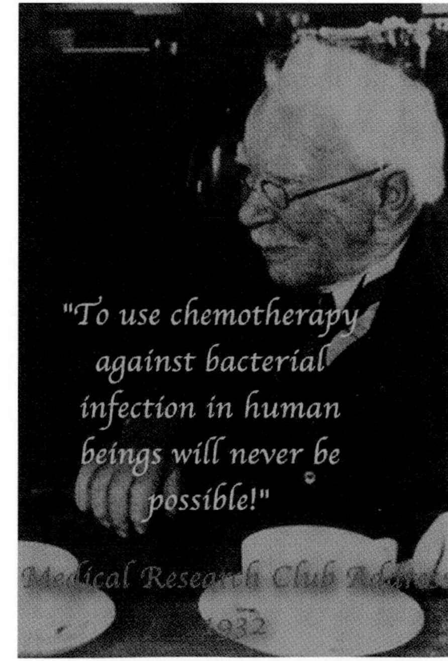

"To use chemotherapy
against bacterial
infection in human
beings will never be
possible!"

Sir Almroth Edward Wright (born in Dublin, 1861), an individual of unusual intellectual gifts, after a long and distinguished career became the director of pathology at St. Mary's Hospital, London. He not only devised a coagulometer but was also responsible for instituting typhoid vaccinations amongst the British Armed Forces in both India and South Africa. Although a firm believer in the concept of vaccination and possessed of a brilliant and independent mind, he utterly rejected the concept of chemotherapy as a rational form of treatment.

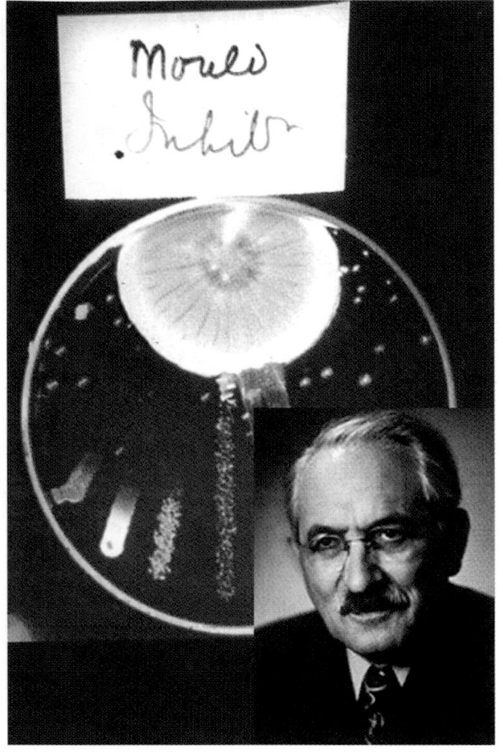

S.A. Waksman of Rutgers University, New Jersey, in 1943 identified streptomycin and in so doing revolutionized the therapy of tuberculosis. Waksman was also responsible for coining the term "antibiotic" to describe this class of drugs.

ability to generate it in large quantities depended on the substantial endeavors of American laboratories and manufacturers. It was apparent that there was more than one penicillin and that the chemistry was unexpectedly difficult, rendering large-scale synthesis problematic. Although many organisms insensitive to sulphonamides were sensitive to the original penicillins, the drug was degraded in gastric acid and effective only when injected. Furthermore, penicillins were rapidly excreted and thus required frequent dosing to maintain adequate antibacterial activity throughout a course of treatment. The efficacy of the agents was achieved by the development of modified penicillins that were insensitive to bacterial penicillinases, active by mouth and less rapidly excreted.

S.A. Waksman (1888-1973) at Rutgers University, New Jersey, in 1943 reported another fungal product, streptomycin, that was active against tubercle bacilli and other organisms and its clinical efficacy against tuberculosis was established by W.H. Feldman (b. 1892) and H.C. Hinshaw (b. 1902) at the Mayo Clinic. Unfortunately, resistant bacilli appeared with discouraging rapidity and in an attempt to counter this, American and Swedish studies in competitive antagonism led to the drug p-aminosalicylic acid (PAS), which although less potent than streptomycin was very effective when combined with it for preventing resistance. The success of penicillin and streptomycin served to stimulate a search for other antibiotics, and vast programmes were undertaken which yielded numerous antibiotics active against a wide variety of organisms. Although few were as innocuous as penicillin, their main merit lay in their broad range of activity against organisms (so making exact bacteriological diagnosis less critical), or against unfamiliar organisms or strains resistant to first-choice antibiotics.

Alexander Fleming being carried through the streets of Edinburgh by students of his alma mater after having been awarded the Nobel Prize (1945) for the discovery of penicillin.

Refined Drugs

Not only antibiotics, but also new drugs of all kinds, appeared after the Second World War. Human thirst for medicine was unquenched, and the pharmaceutical industry, greatly strengthened by advances in the sciences of chemistry, pharmacology, and all other subjects related to the manufacture and use of drugs, did its best to meet the demand. The principle of competitive antagonism gave a reasoned basis for seeking new drugs, and advances in the biochemistry of infectious organisms, of cancer, and other pathological processes showed enzymes worthy of attack and new models for chemists to modify. Pure, stable substances were more reliable and easier to store and use than tinctures and dried extracts, so that nearly all traditional and widely used remedies were gradually displaced (see Table).

The Evolution of Some Purified or Synthetic Drugs

Drug	Purpose or use	Decade
Nitrous oxide	General anesthetic	1840
Ether	General anesthetic	1840
Chloroform	General anesthetic	1840
Amyl nitrite	Angina pectoris	1860
Trinitron	Angina pectoris	1860
Phenacetin	Analgesic	1880
Novocain etc.	Local anesthetic	1900
Veronal etc.	Hypnotic	1900
Insulin	Diabetes mellitus	1920
Liver extract	Pernicious anemia	1920
Steroid hormones	Addison's disease	1930
	Disorders of reproduction	
Mepacrine	Malaria	1930
Prontosil, sulphonamides	Streptococcal infections	1930
Penicillin	Gram-positive infections	1940
Streptomycin	Tuberculosis	1940
Chloroquine	Malaria	1940
Nitrogen mustard	Blood-cell cancers	1940
Antifolates	Blood-cell cancers	1940
Cortisone	Anti-inflammatory	1940
Metonyms	Hypertension	1940
Chlorpromazine	Anxiety, schizophrenia	1950
Isoniazid	Tuberculosis	1950
Chlorothiazide	Diuretic	1950
Progestogen and oestrogen	Contraceptive (oral)	1950
MAO Inhibitors	Antidepressant	1950
Imipramine	Antidepressant	1950
Propranolol	Angina, hypertension	1960
Diazepoxides	Anxiety	1960
Allopurinol	Gout	1960
Cimetidine	Peptic ulcers	1960
Acyclovir	Herpes virus infections	1980
Omeprazole	Acid peptic disease	1980

The discovery by Waksman (inset) in 1943 of streptomycin dramatically altered the impact of the scourge of tuberculosis (illustration from the Carswell pathology textbook) on communities throughout the world. The recognition that early diagnosis and the institution of therapy led to cure, prompted major health advertising as governments sought to amplify the level of public awareness.

The design of clinical trials was greatly improved, particularly under the influence of A. Bradford Hill (1897-1991) and the authority of the Medical Research Council in Britain. Few drugs came into use without trials of some sort, and some drugs, especially against tuberculosis, were exceptionally well evaluated as soon as they became widely available. However, it did not follow that all the new remedies were of lasting benefit. Many were superseded within a few years of introduction by more recent discoveries that had some clear advantage, or were free from some obviously undesirable property. Other drugs were discredited after a brief period of enthusiasm, when unsuspected toxic effects appeared, or when evidence accumulated that their use was no more beneficial than their omission.

With the introduction of many new substances as drugs and their production and distribution on a wider scale, ill effects were observed from time to time and were, perhaps, an unavoidable price to pay for therapeutic successes. Drugs did not come into clinical use until they had been extensively assessed in animals, and many potential disasters were prevented in this way. However, tragedies occurred. Some were a consequence of ignorance on the part of manufacturers: for example, when a manufacturer of an elixir of sulphanilamide used ethylene glycol as a sweetening agent and over seventy deaths resulted before the sale of the medicine was stopped. Others arose when drugs had ill effects of a kind not previously recognized, notably the injury to the developing fetus caused by thalidomide.

The dramatic consequences of thalidomide toxicity led to the introduction of detailed drug development safeguards and the formalization of toxicity screening.

After the thalidomide tragedy, the toxicity of drugs was tested much more extensively in animals. The tests delayed the introduction of new drugs especially in the United States (the so-called "drug lag"): numerous drugs were not sanctioned there for months or years after they were freely in use in other parts of the world, despite available evidence of the life-saving value of some of them. The elaboration of formalized toxicity-testing in animals diverted resources from more useful ways of assessing toxicity, and the protracted poisoning of groups of animals probably contributed to the growth of protests, some more reasonable than others,

Paul Ehrlich in his study, February 26, 1909. His genius for research and extraordinary industry (note the modest collection of reading material) enabled him to make substantial contributions to the science of infectious diseases by expanding the domain of experimental pharmacology beyond the work of Pasteur and Koch. It has been said that his skill in improvising hypotheses to meet the opponents of his theories resembled that of Galen while his predilection for quaint and archaic Latin phrases was indistinguishable from that of Paracelsus.

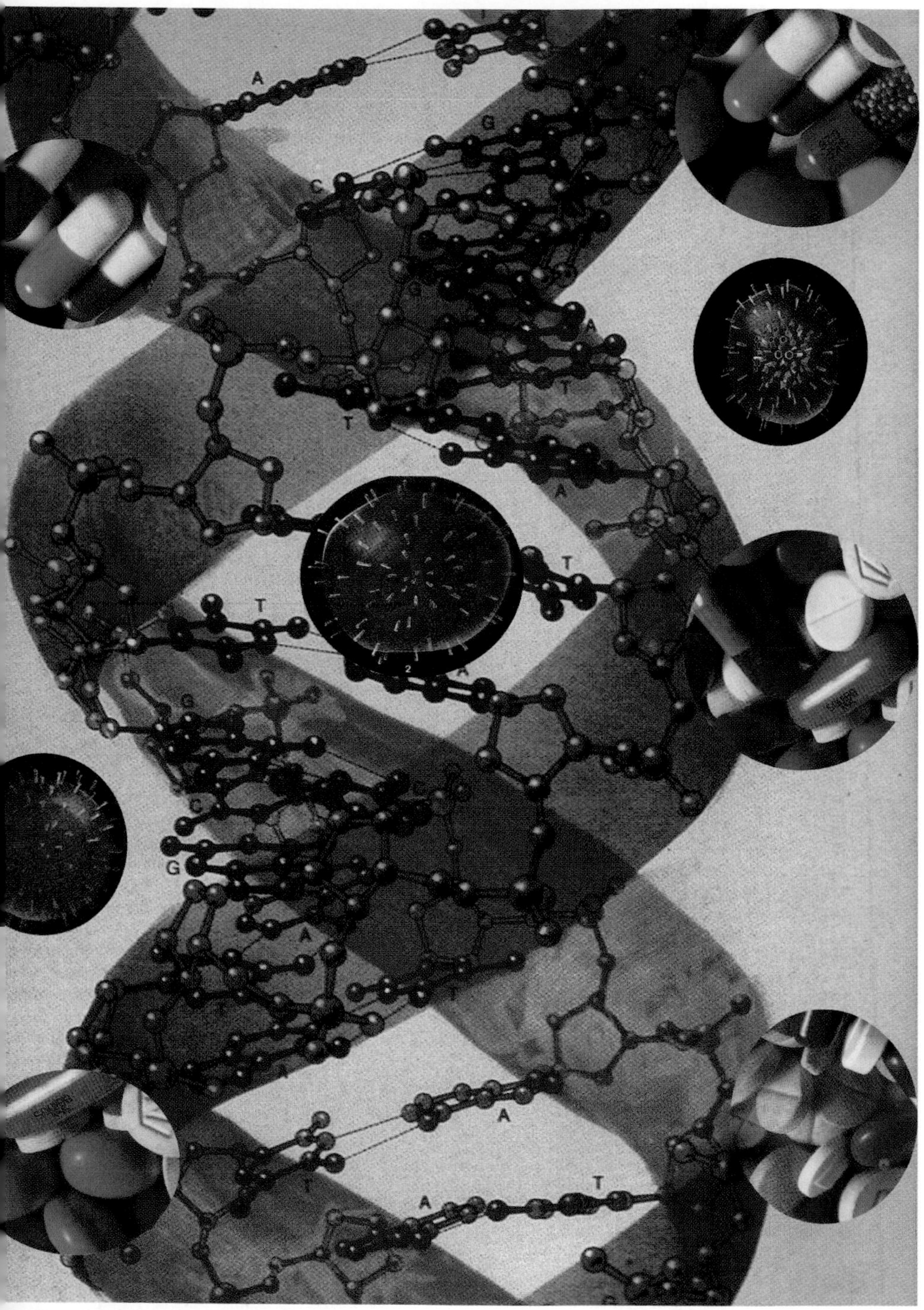

There is little doubt that the future of pharmacotherapeutic strategy will lie in the development of agents designed to access either molecular or genomic targets.

against experiments of any kind on animals, and a consequent check to innovation. Nor did elaborate ritual testing in animals prevent further tragedies, for example, with practolol and benoxaprofen.

Therapeutics has always suffered swings of fashion. The heroic treatments widely used in the eighteenth and early nineteenth century led to disillusion and a phase of therapeutic nihilism, which was well justified by discoveries of the extent of tissue damage in advanced disease and of the lack of real activity of most of the remedies in use. A crescendo of scientific discoveries, from antitoxins and early chemotherapy to penicillin and the drugs of the post-war era, brought the age of the pure drug and of "a pill for every ill." Once again, optimism was excessive and a sure foundation for new disillusion. Public understanding is not well-equipped to distinguish drugs that do more good than harm from inappropriate, ineffective, or misused drugs, and it is becoming fashionable to take refuge in hopes for "natural" remedies: that is, unpurified materials of uncertain potency and uncertain toxicity, and in systems of therapy such as homoeopathy, which contradict the most elementary scientific knowledge. There is ample historical evidence for the value of belief in a remedy as an aid to therapeutics, but belief in a remedy is no proof of its efficacy, and the history of drugs shows that the chemical identity of the remedy is fundamental to its curative powers.

Envoi

Nevertheless no simple definition of chemotherapy is entirely adequate since it does not fulfill the principles of the modern definition of chemotherapy, as the term was coined by Ehrlich. It is one thing to *treat* an infectious disease with a chemical agent, but a different one to cure it by destroying the organisms by such means. Thus the treatment of a bacterial infection like typhoid fever with mercuric chloride does not cure the disease, since a dose of the agent adequate to destroy the bacilli cannot be administered without engendering tissues and organ damage, which is what the real chemotherapy as proposed by Ehrlich sought to accomplish.

Paul Ehrlich (inset) deserves full credit for initiating the concept of the chemical targeting of pathogenic agents. The archer (Lyons, Musée des Beaux Arts) directs an abstract arrow at agents as yet unknown and in so doing embodies the surrealist philosophic concept of "The object unknown." Whether these will be pathogens, the immune system or the genome remains to be seen. Quo vadis!

The precise means by which a disease can be cured has, to a certain extent, lost its importance as long as the end result is accomplished without excessive danger to the patient. Thus few contemporary chemical agents can be considered as "specifics" and much of the significance pertinent to the old discussion of specifics has now been lost. Indeed, it is considered by most that there is little importance if a treatment is specific, provided that a definite therapeutic advantage can be attained and defined.

The older chemotherapeutic techniques were for the most part essentially detrimental, inasmuch as the earliest drugs all exerted some intrinsic injurious effects. As early as 1926, J.A. Kolmer in the *Principles and Practice of Chemotherapy* noted:

> *Under ideal conditions the medicine must not harm the body cells or produce toxic reactions at all, but since this is very difficult of actual attainment in the treatment of disease, the requirement may be made less stringent and to read that effects shall not be of a marked or serious character.*

The subsequent development of antibiotic substances, such as bacteriophage, gramacidin and, more particularly, penicillin and streptomycin, appeared to more closely approximate the ideal conditions that were sought by the purists. Such agents and their adverse effects were deemed most acceptable by patients who cared little for momentary discomfort if the treatment could provide a cure of a far greater evil. Nevertheless, the implication of toxicity which lies behind the vast body of chemotherapy, places a specific responsibility upon the physician to administer an effective treatment and never to allow the effects of the drug to outweigh the malignant characteristics of the disease whose cure is sought. Time has demonstrated that while the original proposal of Ehrlich was truly prescient in concept and noble in nature, it overall represented an oversimplification of a complex and multi-factorial biological situation. Ehrlich viewed disease as fundamentally caused by bacteria and failed to recognize the fact that the characteristics of a disease, even when proximally caused by a bacterial agent, are ultimately, to a great extent, determined by the reactions of the host and not merely by the nature of the parasite.

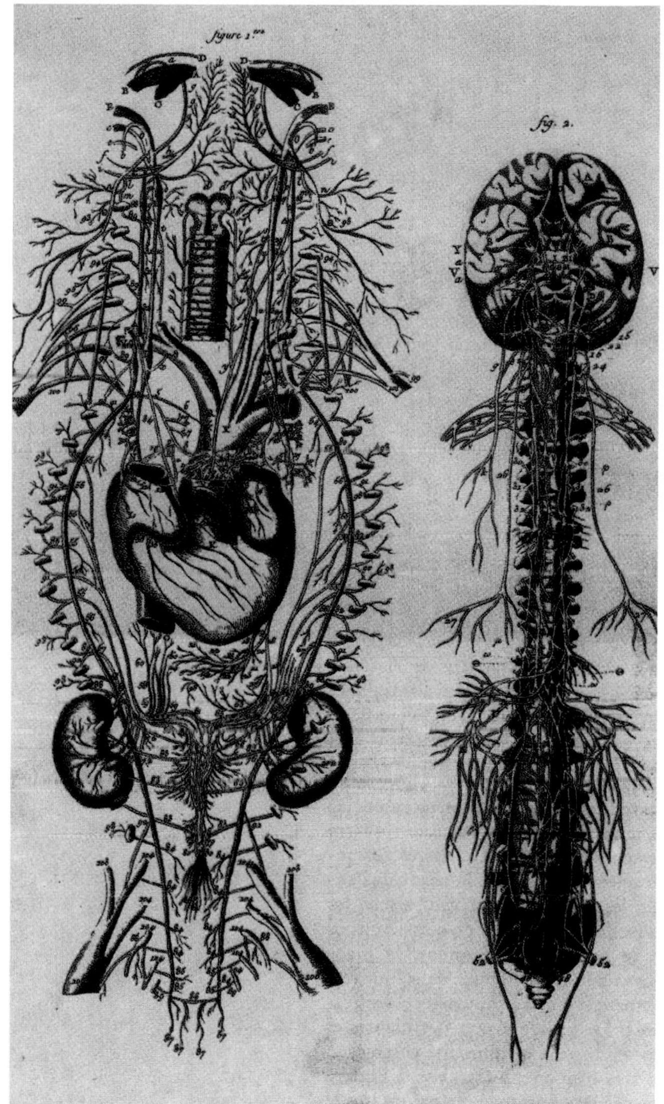

The central nervous system and its ability to regulate diverse organ functions throughout the body remains a primary target for therapy. Such an endeavor will require the development of agents of unique specificity and selectivity.

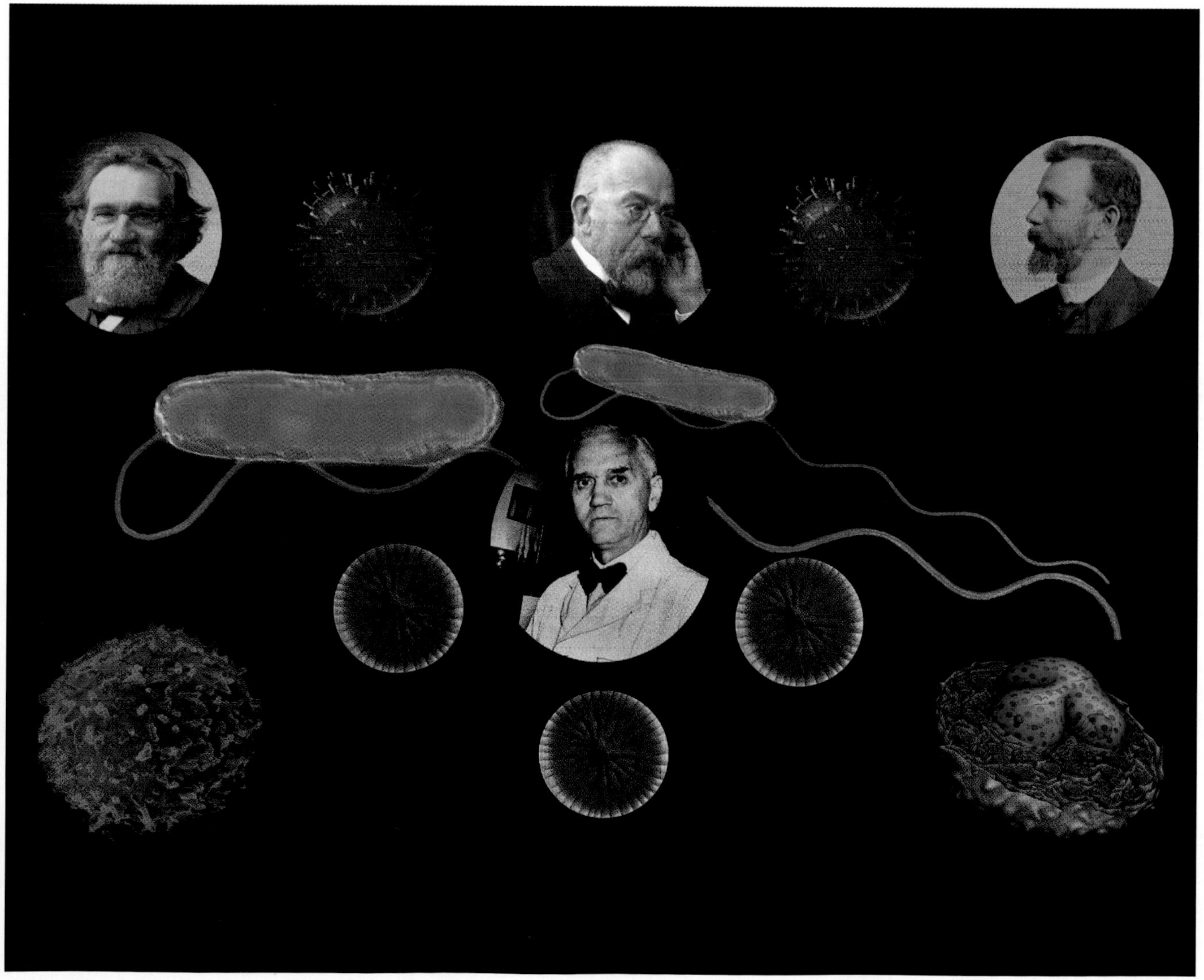

Robert Koch (center), and Paul Ehrlich (right) laid the foundation for the elucidation of bacterial cause of disease while Elie Metchnikoff (left) provided the basis for the development of the elucidation of the defense mechanisms of the body. Alexander Fleming (center) by the study of a fungal mould (sub-center) provided the initial information that led to the development of agents capable of inhibiting bacterial growth. There is little doubt that a future direction of bacterial therapy will lie in the development of agents capable of amplifying the immune response (T cell, bottom left) or altering intracellular mechanisms (bottom right) in order to facilitate protection against bacterial and viral pathogens (inset top).

SECTION II

The Early Development of Gastroenterology

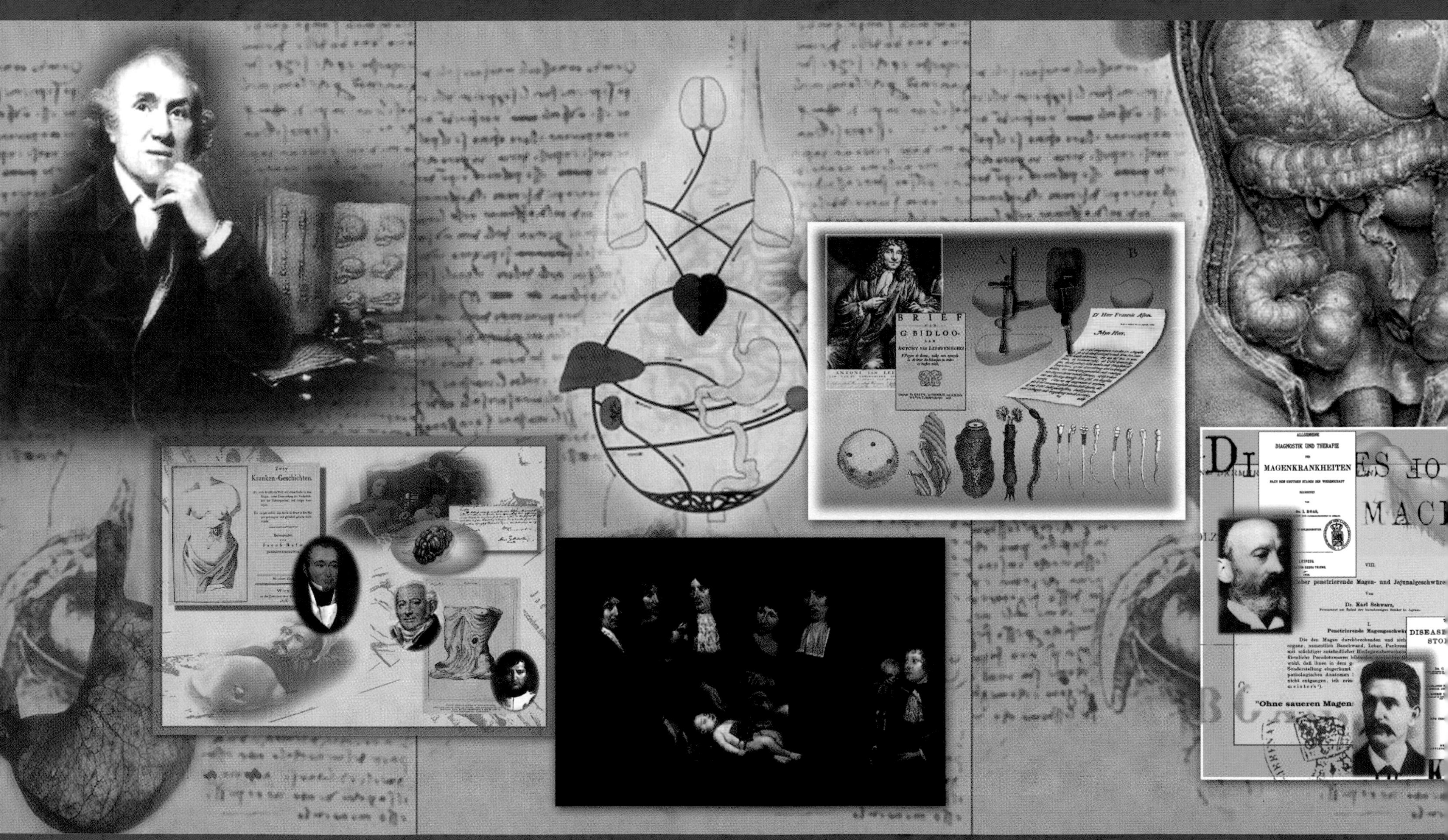

Introduction

Although man's earliest imaginings of disease related to divine influences such as the sun, moon and stars it soon became apparent that certain aspects of health related to diet. In this respect it was obvious that the ingestion of various types of food and drink and certain bodily activities were directly connected to feelings of good health.

The ingestion of certain substances not only promoted a sense of well-being but also engendered a sensation of satisfaction, whereas absence of water and food as well as lack of sleep and over-exercise generated perceptions of unhappiness and even discomfort. Since the majority of such sentiments related to the stomach it was little wonder that the abdomen became a site to which early man directed substantial attention. Although the heart and lungs were recognized to be vital, especially in terms of traumatic events and loss of life, it was the abdomen and the stomach in particular which played an on-going role in the perpetuation of feelings of good health and well-being. Indeed, for primitive man, the sensation of hunger and its abolition was as critical a response in early behavior as was the primal drive of sexual satiation and procreation.

Although the contributions of many individuals from the earliest of times will define the evolution of the discipline, its serious advance may be accepted as having proceeded from the beginning of the nineteenth century. Early physicians believed the liver to be the lord of the abdomen, if not the body, and the stomach to constitute if not the very soul of man, a source of great pleasure and therefore to be nurtured. The colon and anus were revered by the Egyptians and for thousands of years afterwards continued to be regarded as areas responsible for the origin of much disease and symptomatology. The gall bladder was considered as an organ of divination and the pancreas imagined to be the finger of God although considerable dispute raged over the precise site of the soul. Conjecture was replaced by the delineation of structure by Galen and Vesalius. Function was early explored by Erasistratus, and amplified over time by R. de Graaf, A. Haller, C. Bernard and numerous early physiologists. Disturbances in structure and function were described by G.B. Morgagni, amplified by K. Rokitansky and placed into a pathological framework by R. Virchow. From the time of W. Prout and W. Beaumont to the present, the subsequent progression in the elucidation of the physiology, pathology, and surgery of the digestive tract has been indebted to considerable enterprise and invention especially as regards the introduction of diverse biochemical, radiological and endoscopic advances. Such developments were, however, preceded by an ancient and lengthy foreground ranging from the Nile Valley and Kos through the mists of medieval and renaissance times to the intellectual potency of Europe at the turn of the twentieth century. Indeed, only the very barest of the actual early outlines of the history of the subject are known and in many instances only conjecture is possible in respect of man's earliest concepts of his gastrointestinal system.

The development of gastroenterology in the twentieth century owes a great debt to A. Kussmaul (1869), W. Leube, K. Ewald and I. Boas of Germany who may be regarded as the prime movers in the initiation of the discipline. Especial credit is, however, due to Ismar Boas of Berlin, who was the first to actually direct his attention to establishing a practice that specialized in gastro-intestinal disorders alone (1885). In this respect he not only established the first clinic devoted entirely to the discipline but also founded the first periodical (1896) dedicated to the subject. The American Gastroenterological Association was inaugurated in 1897, the German organization in 1914 and the British Society of Gastroenterology in 1937. It is thus almost a century since physicians dedicated themselves to the practice of gastroenterology as a specific and defined specialty. Although early skeptics such as F.T. Frerichs and H. Nothnagel were not understated in stressing the relatively backward condition of the subject in their time, the subsequent evolution of the discipline has laid to rest any initial concerns that may have been generated. The advent of endoscopy and radiology considerably

In a world illuminated only by fire and a hunger for knowledge, the pleasures of food and procreation were of paramount importance. Scenes from ancient Greek and Roman life attest to the commodious nature of the reclinium in the pursuit of digestive fulfillment. The finery and pomp devoted to dining exquisitely reflect the continuing recognition of the sensations of well-being accorded to gastric and limbic stimulation.

The concept of gases was a source of much scientific discussion and investigation. The relationship of the gas produced by chemical experimentation to human gaseous eruptions and their relationship to digestion were a source of considerable interest as well as mirth.

amplified the scope of gastroenterology while the development of newer modalities such as sophisticated biochemistry, computerized tomographic imaging, and ultrasound have further enhanced the breadth of the discipline. The more recent renaissance of gastrointestinal surgery prompted by the introduction of minimally invasive surgery has amplified the therapeutic spectrum and prompted further expansion of the field.

The Age of Osiris and Apollo

The stomach was regarded as a critical purveyor of pleasure, given its role in the assimilation of food and wine and the delightful sensations accompanying satiation. The further association of post-cibal sexual endeavors engendered by the mutual pleasures of the table and the *reclinium* served to further reinforce the critical nature of the abdomen in the enjoyment of life. Indeed the processing of specific foodstuffs such as honey, mushrooms, and diverse herbs by the stomach was even held to be a determinant in amplifying the limbic limits of lust. Thus, the pivotal role of this organ in the early pantheon of health was widely agreed upon and its optimal function a matter of serious concern to both princes and paupers. Indeed, the earliest of philosophers and poets from Omar Khayyam to Catullus noted that few feelings were more powerful than the considerations of pleasure invoked by food and wine and the effects of orgasm. The fact that almost as great a pleasure was derived by the evacuation of the bowels and the passage of gas further enhanced the importance of the digestive tract in the consideration of feelings of well-being. Such considerations led to an exquisite awareness of early man in the pleasures of emptying the bowel, and the sensations of relief related to this event resulted in much attention being devoted to such activities. The development of medical beliefs that this process was also of importance in ridding the body of noxious agents led to a significant focus on flatus and feces. Thus, even to this day purging and enemas are still considered of paramount importance in ensuring health and well-being in diverse cultures.

Thus, one of the most important physicians of the Egyptian Pharaoh was accorded the title of Shepherd of the Anus (1500 B.C.) and Egyptian medical doctrine held the anus and rectum to be the nexus of bodily function and health. Indeed, for two thousand years from the earliest tribes of Africa to the parlors of Versailles and San Francisco, the use of clysters, enemas, and suppositories has been regarded as a most salubrious method for the administration of therapy or the relief of distress.

Little, however, was known of illness and the signs of disease were reflected mostly in the observation of external events such as alterations in weight, vomiting, constipation, diarrhea and abdominal distention. Since the body was regarded as sacred and needed for the journey into the next life post-mortem examination was for the most part prohibited and the relations of these symptoms and signs to internal problems was not clear. The sacrifice of animals either for prophecy or food, and the determination of various abnormalities in their entrails led to the recognition that disease processes of individual organs could be related to certain symptoms and signs. Nevertheless, for many millennia, gastrointestinal disease in man was marked mostly by conjecture and derived by the extrapolation of abnormalities noted in sacrificial animals. Occasionally the fortuitous examination of individuals killed in battle, gladiatorial combat, or by execution might allow for the evaluation of the gastrointestinal organs. For the most part, however, disease process was regarded as either a manifestation of evil spirits, dangerous humors or as an indication of divine displeasure in response to some mortal failing. Indeed, for more than a thousand years the Church would perpetuate this dogma of disease as a terrestrial manifestation of divine retribution for the venal sins of the weak and flawed clay vessel which was man. Similarly, while the recognition of parasites and worms and their relationship to gastrointestinal symptoms was well accepted, such denizens of

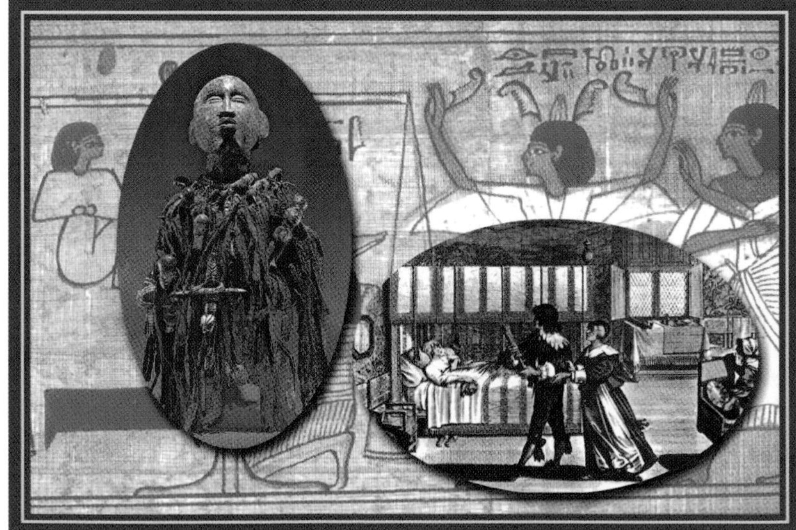

There was little therapy available for disease and outcome was believed to be in the hands of the gods. A talisman or herbal remedy combined with prayer was the best that a patient might expect. The Egyptians believed that the best one might do for the living was to prepare them for a wonderful afterlife. African tribes believed in protection from spirits by using exotic figures (left inset), while the Dutch considered that an appropriately administered enema (bottom right) would solve most medical problems.

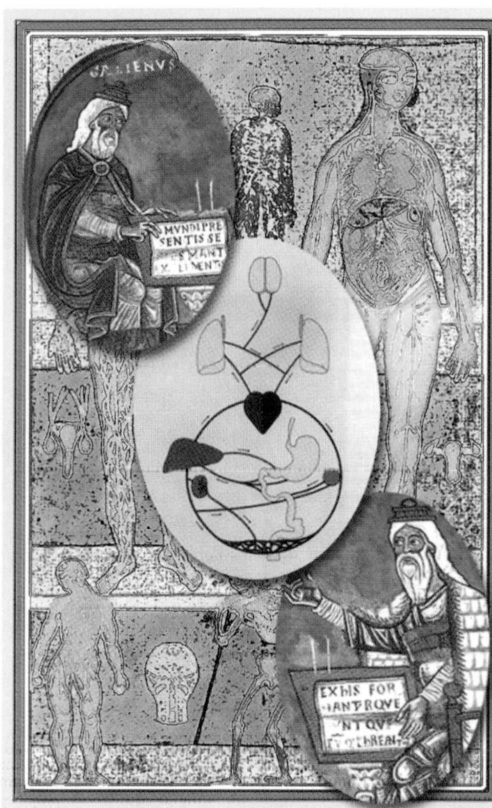

Galen had believed that the veins and lymphatics of the intestines carried chyle to the liver. This concept was disproved by the discovery of the lacteal vessels in 1622 by Gasparo Aselli of Cremona. Although Aselli believed that lymphatics passed to the liver, this error was subsequently rectified by the discovery of the thoracic duct and receptaculum chyli by Jean Pecquet and of the intestinal lymphatics and their connection with the thoracic duct by the Swede, Olof Rudbeck, in 1651.

the bowels were for the most part regarded by early physicians as manifestations of evil spirits that required to be cast out.

Digestion itself was regarded by Hippocrates (460-370 B.C.) as a process akin to cooking or *coction*. The process was referred to as *pepsis* and abnormalities of this process were variously grouped together as *dyspepsis, apepsis* and even *polypepsis* and connoted a variety of disease states generously regarded as representative of symptoms due to abnormalities in the state of "digestion". Given the observation that cooking was related to heat, the clinical symptoms of fever and sweating were thus also held to be related to abnormalities of internal coction. The conjectures of Galenic and Hippocratic teaching proposed that food be cooked or transformed in the different vats which represented various parts of the gut. Once its vital properties were released it was thereafter transported in vessels to different parts of the body, including the heart and lungs and liver, where it was imbued with another set of vital properties and rendered into a variety of *pneuma*. Aberrations of various aspects of this fanciful process were construed as being responsible for a wide variety of symptoms and signs related to the development of disease. Nevertheless, it was widely accepted and self-evident that good food and a sound digestion were absolute necessities to ensure a healthy and productive life. Indeed, the Roman sages adumbrated at some length upon the adage, *Homo est quod est* (Man is and becomes what he eats).

Abnormalities of digestion or sensations that were unpleasant and located in the abdominal cavity were initially regarded as the results of bad humors or possession by evil spirits or *archei*. Initial concepts of treatment included the avoidance of certain foods, the imbibition of various kinds of waters, and the extracts of herbs and roots. The development by Pedanius Dioscorides (A.D. 40-90) of a rational basis for herbal therapeutics was followed by the introduction of a diverse array of remedies, some possessed of known active substances and others simply divine inspirations of bizarre mixtures of *mithridatum*. The notion of the alchemic properties of certain elements prompted the use of metals and their combinations in a variety of suffusates or acids for the treatment of individual gastrointestinal diseases. Folk medicine was often valuable despite the arcane rituals associated with it, since it provided useful remedies which later investigation demonstrated to be based upon appropriate active substances. However, for many years, complex doctrines of punishing diets and absurd dogma relating to abstinence and penance were the dominant force in therapeutics. Thus, religious beliefs fostered the notion that pleasure and sin engendered disease as a divine punishment and that repentance by fasting and purging were necessary for cure. For the most part, however, the absence of any knowledge of the disease process itself led to the application of random agents, mostly soporifics or analgesics, which, while of little direct benefit, were of utility in effecting some symptomatic relief.

Acute circumstances involving the gastrointestinal tract were mostly manifestations of colic, emesis, hematemesis, diarrhea, and rectal bleeding but acute obstructions and ascites were well-described. For the most part little could be done about such events and the use of various sedatives, opiates, and even some prayer to relieve the misery of such victims was the accepted order of the day. In many circumstances poisoning was held to the cause of dramatic gastrointestinal symptoms and amulets, animal bezoars, or

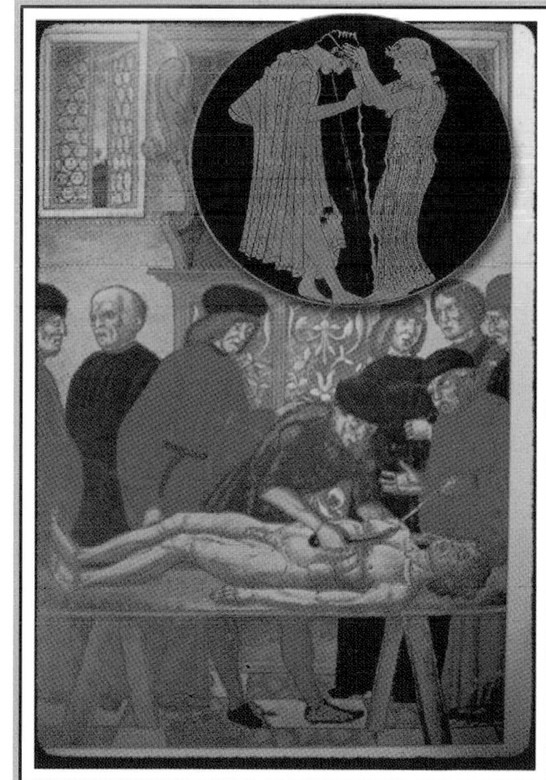

Knowledge regarding anatomy was usually obtained by post-mortem dissection. For the most part, information about the interior of the gastrointestinal tract was obtained by examining vomitus (inset), urine, or fecal matter.

In the 17th century the causes of dyspepsia were ill-understood and arcane texts still proposed diverse herbal remedies emanating from the work of Dioscorides (c. A.D. 60). Van Helmont, an Iatrochemist of Brussels (top right) believed that spirits (archei) resided in the stomach, while Paracelsus in Salzburg (center) railed against contemporary dogma, burnt medical books in public and proposed the presence of a acetosum ensurinum *(hungry acid) in the stomach.*

complex antidotes were employed to ward off such dire symptoms and their lethal consequences. Traumatic events involving war and assaults often led to perforation of the bowel, or evisceration, and although the early surgeons of Salerno in the thirteenth century had successfully sutured bowel there was little effective therapy that could be offered. In such instances, although the nature of the injury could be determined, there was little that could be done to ameliorate the problem. Early hemostasis was restricted to the use of goat milk (rennin) and spider webs while direct suture repair used horse hair, silk, or ant mandibles as a suture material. Overall, the therapy of gastrointestinal disease was little more than attention to modulation of diets, the use of various waters, and the introduction of specific herbal remedies for the alleviation of symptoms. The fact that the repertoire of symptoms for the gastrointestinal tract was relatively limited (nausea, vomiting, colic, diarrhea, constipation and distention) did not obviate the development of a myriad of extracts, elixirs, and homeopathic remedies, each guaranteed to alleviate all symptoms and fructify the life of the recipient.

The assessment of the relationship of the individual organs of the abdomen to digestion, as opposed to disease, was manifest in the imagery compounded by poets, philosophers, and dramatists over the years. Thus, the stomach was considered to be a source of energy and vigor and people of weak stomach were compared with those of poor character. Indeed, the image of Elizabethan times associated a big belly and a jovial personality with success and provided a stereotype of affluence best symbolized by Shakespeare's Falstaff. The ancient augers and soothsayers of Rome and Babylon were well aware of liver disease in animals and noted it to be an omen of poor portent. When considered in the context of the Galenic notion that the liver was the source of blood, people of weak character and cowardly behavior were considered to be "chicken-livered". Similarly, the bowels were felt to be the source of courage and conviction and men of "guts" and strong bowels were regarded as men of conviction, faith, and moral certitude. Indeed, oaths were sworn, "by my bowels" or even by "God's bowels", such was the power attributed to this lengthy piece of intestine. Similarly, the belief that a spiritual power resided within the abdomen was supported by the recognition that a sharp blow to the upper abdomen resulted in a cessation of breathing and collapse. This concept of a dominant Apollo-like presence – "solar plexus" – was given further weight by the early dissections of animals that disclosed the celiac collection of radiating nerves and ganglia, much like an image of emanating solar rays associated with the divine power of the sun.

Vesalius to Vienna

Indeed, it was the advent of dissection (A. Vesalius, 1514-1564) with the elucidation of precise anatomic structures and relationships, that first began to clarify the world of speculation and conjecture regarding the nature of the function of the abdominal organs and their relation to digestion. Although initially vivisection was confined to animals, criminals, or those killed in war or gladiatorial combat, a basic understanding of structure and the ability to relate it to function began to form in the early parts of the second millennium. It was apparent that the esophagus was a carrier of food, the stomach a vat for digestion and the bowels the site where "alteration" or digestion (*pepsis*) of foods occurred prior to absorption. Although the massive solid red liver was initially misconceived to be the source of blood, it was correctly recognized as vital to life. Despite much erroneous early speculation, the information derived gradually extended the understanding of the function of organs and allowed for speculation as to the role of nerves such as the vagus. Early Iatromathematic concepts propounded variously by the Italians G. Baglivi (1668-1706) and G. Borelli (1608-1679) as well as the Scotsman A. Pitcairn (1711-1791), even went so far as to propose that the entire digestive system was a mechanical device. Thus the teeth were considered scissors, the stomach a fermenting tank, and the intestines transport tubes directed to the septic tank of the cloaca.

The anatomic structure of the liver was well-known to ancient civilizations since its vagaries were utilized to predict the future. Numerous clay tablets and models have survived to attest to the importance which ancient civilizations of the Middle East ascribed to "hepatoscopy" as a form of prophecy. Observations were carefully recorded and correlation sought between previous events and future possibilities. The porta hepatis was known as the "gateway" and the insertion of the ligamentum teres as the "door to the palace". The gall bladder was designated "the bitter place".

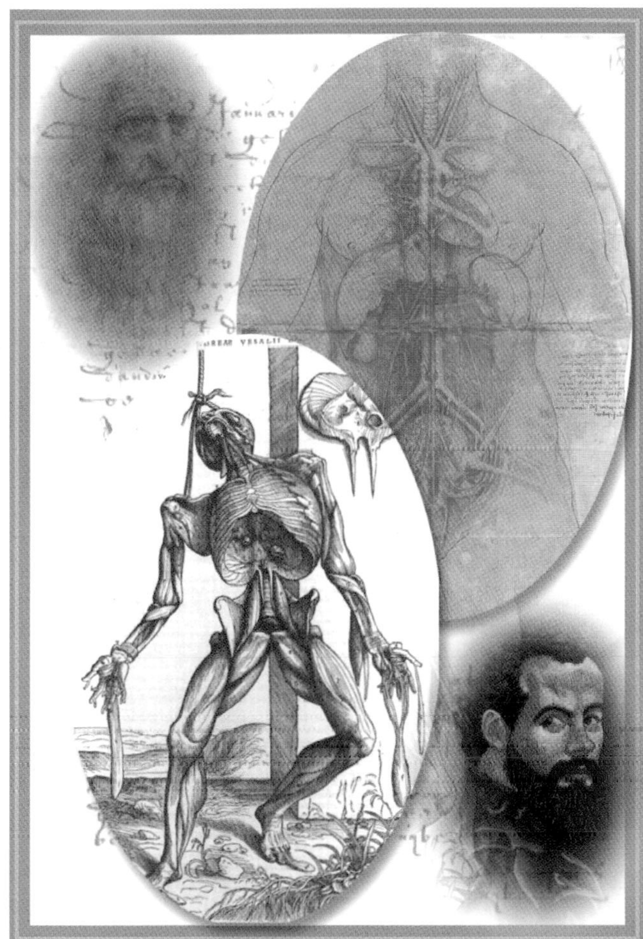

The inability to treat disease in a rational fashion for the most part reflected a relative lack of knowledge of the internal structure of the body and an almost complete absence of information pertinent to the elucidation of function. Initially, this had represented a superstitious belief that physicians could not meddle with the divine creation – man – and that to damage a body by studying it would leave the individual incapacitated and even without a soul in the afterlife. Thereafter, religious strictures forbade desecration of the property of God until the introduction of the "nosce te ipsum" concept. The drawings of Leonardo Da Vinci (top right) and the dissections of A. Vesalius (bottom left) provided a major impetus to the detailed understanding of structure and allowed a reasonable appreciation of the possible functional implications of different organs.

The subsequent introduction of the Iatrochemical doctrine (J. Van Helmont, 1577-1644, H. Boerhaave, 1668-1738) held that a variety of chemical agents were produced at each site and were variously responsible for the digestion and processing of food prior to its assimilation. Although the function of the liver was a source of disputation, T. Bartholin (1616-1680) unceremoniously dismissed the aged Galenic concept of blood formation and proposed a definitive role for the organ in digestion and detoxification. Similarly Regnier de Graaf (1641-1673) proved the pancreas to be a secretory gland although he erroneously supported F. de la Boe (Sylvius, 1614-1672) in the notion that it produced a digestive acid. G. Asselli (1581-1626) and thereafter F. Ruysch (1638-1723) delineated the course of the mesenteric lymphatics, defined their valves and thereby annihilated the vacuous notion propounded in 1650 by Louis de Bils of a circulatory cardio-mesenteric gyrus.

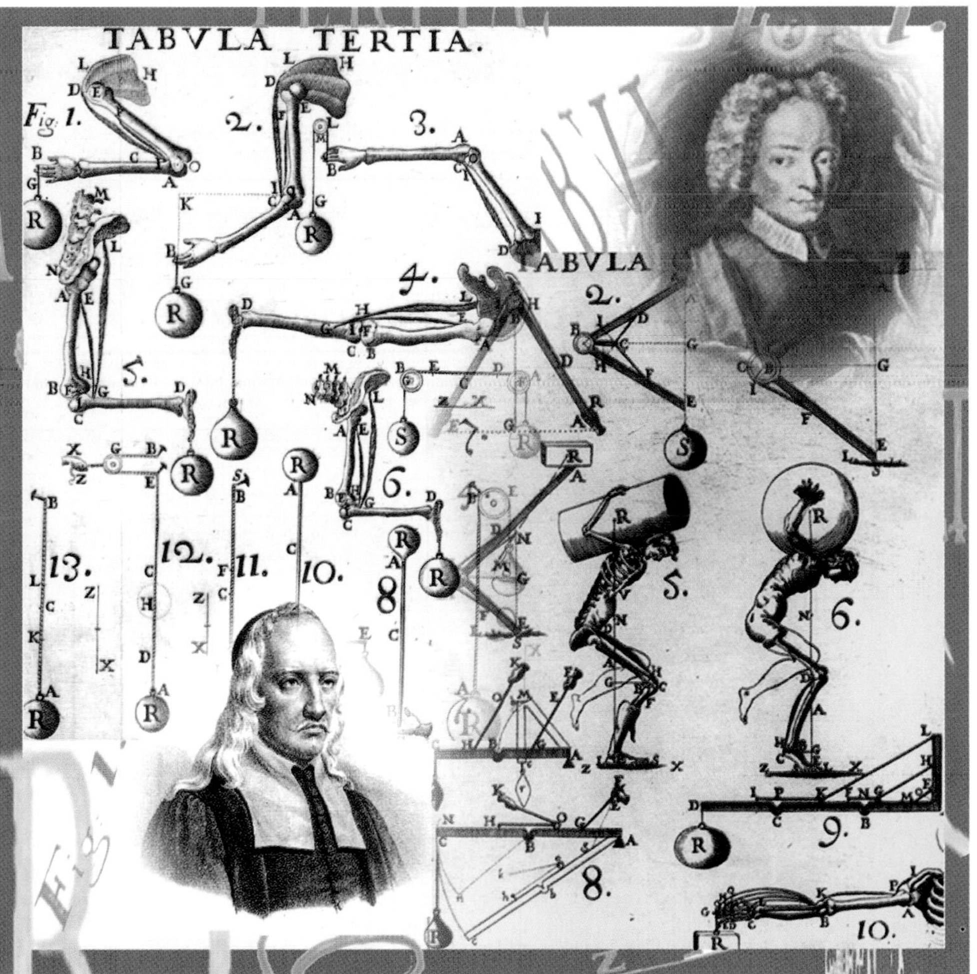

The Iatromathematical School maintained that all physiologic events should be regarded as fixed consequences of the laws of physics. Thus, the stomach was regarded as a mechanical mill responsible for grinding up its contents into chyme. Giorgio Bagilivi (1668-1706) (top right) was a pupil of Malpighi and the Chairman of Medical Theory at the Collegio Della Sapienza in Rome. In 1700, he was the first to distinguish between smooth and striated muscle. Baglivi referred to the stomach as a flask that possessed the muscular power of grinding food to facilitate digestion. His views were closely supported by G.A. Borelli (1608-1679) (bottom left) who, despite being a pupil of the enlightened Galileo, applied an extreme mechanistic view of human function to the process of digestion. The Iatromechanists considered that all human function could be interpreted within physical principles as an allegory of pistons, pulleys, weights, and joints. Garrison considered that "they pushed the mechanical allegory to the extent that they divided the human machine into innumerable smaller machines: likened the teeth to scissors, the chest to a bellows, the stomach to a flask, the viscera and glands to sieves, and the heart and vessels to a waterworks." Archibald Pitcairn, although a staunch proponent of the iatromathematical point of view, was concerned as to why the stomach, when it digested food, failed to digest itself. Did he perhaps dream of an acid and a barrier?

Thus, by the end of the eighteenth century, a good deal was understood of the basic elements of the digestive process, and it was apparent that the secretions of the ductile glands including the salivary, pancreatic, and hepatic, were critical participants in the processing of food. Indeed, the pancreas was often referred to as the salivary gland of the abdomen. It might be inferred that while the detailed Vesalian anatomical drawings that originated in Padua, Italy, had led to a clear understanding of structure, it was in the Netherlands that the first physiologic concepts of digestive function were satisfactorily addressed. Thus A. von Haller (1708-1777) of Bern (the author of more than 30,000 articles and dozens of books), whose seminal text on physiology was deemed by no less an authority than Sir William Osler (1849-1919) to represent the gateway to modern thought, was trained at Leiden. Indeed, the experiments conducted by Sylvius, F. Ruysch, T. Bartholin, N. Stensen (1648-1686), de Graaf, and A. van Leeuwenhoek (1632-1723) and the *Society Amstellodamensis* under the leadership of Gerhard Blasius (1626-1682), would provide the initial intellectual groundswell of thought that would lead towards the elucidation of gastrointestinal function.

F. Ruysch (top left) utilized his superb dissection and preservation skills to demonstrate the presence of lymphatic valves. Since lymph could not flow in the centrifugal direction proposed by the design (center) of de Bils, the observations of Bartholin were vindicated.

What remained was the need to firstly correlate function and particularly abnormal function with pathology, and secondly to develop a rational therapeutic approach. Clinicians such as Boerhaave of Leiden and subsequently his pupil G. van Swieten (1700-1772) in Vienna promulgated this doctrine widely and ensured that bedside teaching became a regular feature closely interfaced with not only didactic lectures but also postmortem correlations. Such individuals developed a clear understanding of the relationships of clinical symptomatology to specific gastrointestinal disease by constant attention to detail, and by teaching, sought to promote a rational understanding of disease, its causation and therapy.

The next major step in the understanding of the gastrointestinal tract involved the establishment of anatomic pathology as a tool whereby the causation of symptomatology might be directly linked to a disease state. The first definable pathologic information was provided initially by T. Bonet in his *Sepulchretum* of 1679, and thereafter by G.B. Morgagni (Padua, 1682-1771), by J. Cruveilhier (Paris, 1791-1873), by K. Rokitansky (Vienna, 1804-1878) and finally by R. Virchow (Berlin, 1821-1902). The meticulously detailed descriptions of innumerable cases (more than 30,000 from Rokitansky alone) produced information that enabled a precise correlation of the symptoms with the autopsy findings.

In this way the clinician became able to predict the underlying pathological process based upon the elucidation of the clinical presentation. So skilled and efficient were individuals such as J. Skoda (1805-1881) of the *Algemeine Krankenhaus* in Vienna that diagnosis became an obsession and therapeutic

Once the general concepts of anatomic structure and physiological function were established, attention was directed at the anatomic basis of disease – pathological anatomy. Morgagni (bottom left) was amongst the earliest to identify such events and his seminal descriptions provide some of the first images of organ pathology and its relationship to clinical symptomatology and disease. His observations were extended by Cruveilhier of Paris (right) and reached their acme with the work of Rokitansky (top left) in Vienna in the mid-19th century.

nihilism supervened. Cogniscent of the appalling lack of effective treatment, many physicians were quite satisfied with the establishment of a diagnosis and left the outcome to divine providence. The elaboration of the lenses introduced by van Leeuwenhoek and of the further development of microscopic design and achromatic lenses provided insight into the more subtle aspects of disease. The early clinical application of microscopic evaluation by Marcello Malpighi (1628-1694) in 1666 provided for the early delineation of the more detailed aspects of structure. Much later Rudolf Virchow would further extend such observations into the world of disease. Such studies led finally to the elucidation of the nature of the inflammatory process as defined by Eli Metchnikoff (1845-1916) and the concepts of new growth as considered by Theodor Schwann (1810-1882) respectively. This general amplification of the understanding of inflammation combined with the newer definitions of what constituted tumors or new growths led to a broader comprehension of the nature of abdominal disease process.

Anton van Leeuwenhoek of Delft (1632-1723) (top left), a draper and city hall janitor, fashioned 147 microscopes (background) with 4-19 lenses and provided information which revolutionized the world of science. In 1674 van Leeuwenhoek was the first to describe spermatozoa (bottom right) although his student Hamen had previously pointed them out to him. He also noted the existence of red blood corpuscles, discovered the striped character of muscle and was the first to see protozoa under the microscope in 1675. His identification of micro-organisms in the teeth and his accurate figurations of bacterial chains and clumps provided the information necessary to consider an extraneous cause for diseases of the human body. The amplification of the techniques originally described by van Leeuwenhoek laid the basis for the work of the bacteriologists Robert Koch (bottom left) and Ehrlich.

Bacteria and Chemistry

The subsequent contributions of Robert Koch (1843-1910), Louis Pasteur (1822-1895), T. Escherich (1857-1911) and K. Shiga (1870-1957) to the appreciation of a bacterial cause of gastrointestinal disease resulted in the development of knowledge designed to not only identify pathogens but also eradicate such agents. Nevertheless, this information was in many circumstances of little benefit to patients since it was either obtained postmortem or little appropriate therapy was available. Surgery was for the most part too quixotic to contemplate (no less an authority than Bernhard Naunyn [1839-1925] considered it to be nothing more than an autopsy *in vivo*) and Arbuthnot Wright believed targeted specific pharmacotherapy but a dream. The boundaries of the rational understanding of gastrointestinal disease and malfunction had, however, been breached and the doors of perception stood ajar as scientists, clinicians and surgeons focused on *"le milieu intérieur."* Of particular relevance was the widespread recognition that the days of superstition and global remedies were past. Thus by the early part of the twentieth century, there existed a clear realization that physicians needed to identify specific diseases, target their location, elucidate their causation, and develop appropriate agents to either ameliorate symptoms or preferably obliterate the process itself.

Although there was no uniform definition or agreement, the central belief of the vitalistic tradition was that the living organism could not be completely explained on the basis of chemical or mechanical facts. Most vitalists thought that an impassible difference existed between organic and inorganic worlds. For Bichat, living bodies possessed *"a permanent principle of reaction."* Each tissue and organ had its own special vital power that opposed the inorganic forces, and the vital powers maintained life by opposing the chemical forces that reduce the organism to inorganic elements. Bichat was able to describe the vital properties of tissues without rejecting their physical properties.

The vitalists in the generation following Bichat held more sophisticated interpretations in keeping with the new discoveries of chemistry and physiology. For Jons Jacob Berzelius (1770-1848), vital force, probably residing in the nervous system, directed the bodily processes. This nerve force prevented the organic compounds (composed of complex radicals and held together by electrochemical forces) from breaking down. Later in his career (1835), Berzelius characterized a catalytic force (forerunner of our present enzymatic catalysis) in chemical reactions; in the 1847 edition of his textbook on chemistry, he eliminated the term "vital force" but referred to the catalytic force.

Another contemporary of Berzelius with vitalistic principles was Johannes Muller (1801-1858), the founder of an important school of physiology. In his

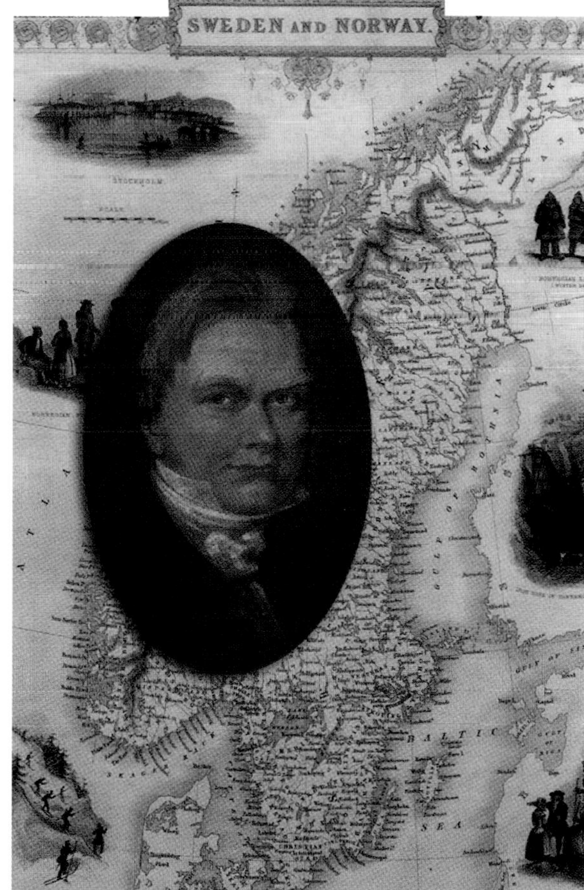

J. Berzelius (inset) of Stockholm was the undisputed leader of inorganic chemistry in the 19th century. Having discovered an entire range of elements and defined innumerable novel compounds and reactions, his pronouncements on matters of chemical validity were regarded as virtually sacrosanct and achieved Mosaic status.

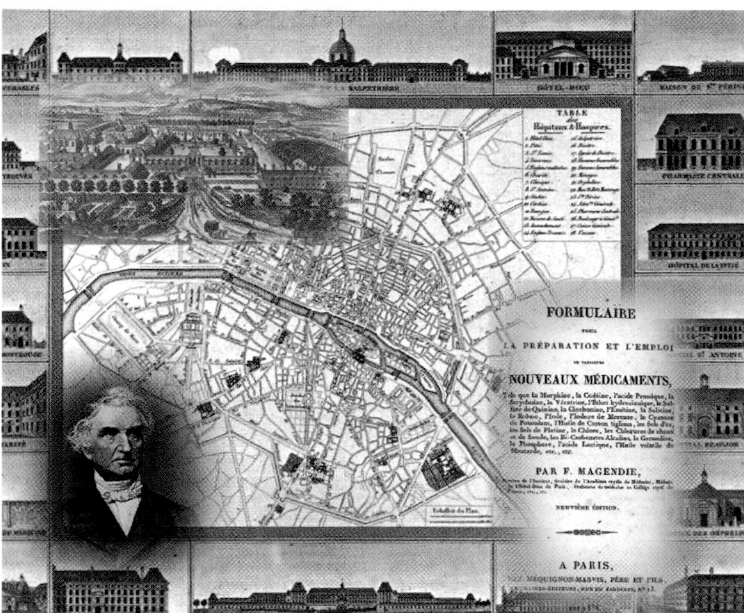

François Magendie was not only an extraordinary physiologist who first elucidated the role of the portal venous system in nutrient delivery but an exceptional teacher. His pupil Claude Bernard revolutionized the understanding of digestive physiology.

Elements of Physiology, Muller discussed the difference between organic and inorganic matter. He believed that organic bodies had "*proximate principles*" peculiar to them (1843) that were open to analysis but were not reproduced by experimental means. Organic matter tended to decompose, and only life itself prevented it from degrading into inorganic compounds.

Two other influential chemists were also vitalists: William Prout (1785-1850) and Justus von Liebig (1803-1873). Prout believed in a vital force residing in the nervous system that acted on individual molecules "*to effect its ulterior purpose*." Vital force was thus the cause and not the result of organization. As a believer in a form of vitalism who at the same time explained everything possible by the available facts of chemistry, von Liebig was a transitional figure during the long course of nineteenth-century vitalism. He made outstanding contributions to the progress of organic chemistry; in particular, the studies that he and Wohler undertook on benzyl derivatives established the concept of organic radical in chemical structure and reaction. Von Liebig was one of many attempting to elucidate the chemical basis of living processes. He did not separate, as others had, the organic and inorganic worlds, believing that the same laws and elements occurred in both. Von Liebig objected to a living force participating in chemical reactions but not to a vital force integrating organic processes. To him, vital force was a fact of nature, much like the law of gravity. Neither was explainable, but the effects of both were describable.

Naturphilosophie bore little resemblance to the empirical vitalism of Berzelius and von Liebig, but it was in reaction to these bizarre views that the group of mechanistic materialists, who sought to "*dissolve physiology into biochemistry and biophysics*," emerged. Karl Ludwig (1816-1895), Hermann von Helmholtz (1821-1894), Ernest von Brucke (1819-1892), and Emil du Bois-Reymond (1818-1896), all of whom studied under the vitalist Johannes Muller, maintained an anti-vitalist position. They wanted to establish physiology on a chemical-physical foundation.

Apart from the philosophic disputes, there evolved another line of investigations that utilized the techniques of organic chemistry to examine physiologic problems. This linkage of chemistry and physiology occurred in the studies of nutrition and digestion. Starting in the late eighteenth century, chemical discoveries came about with the development of technical innovations.

Before organic compounds could be studied, analytic methods had to be developed. Chemists began to employ solvent extractions, gaseous analysis, and new oxidizing procedures rather than old distillation methods of alchemic origin. Lavoisier was among the first to describe such a method, burning compounds with oxygen in a bell jar to determine the carbon dioxide and water formed. Joseph Louis Gay-Lussac (1778-1850) and Louis-Jacques Thenard (1777-1857) improved the technique by burning the sample in a combustion tube with oxidizing agents such as potassium chlorate (1810) and copper oxide (1815). Both Berzelius and von Liebig carried out organic analysis with minute care, with the latter perfecting standard techniques that lasted into the twentieth century. Jean Baptiste André Dumas (1800-1884) introduced a method of determining nitrogen inorganic material that made possible the study of a wide range of chemical phenomena.

In 1816, François Magendie (1783-1855) settled the question of the animal's requirement for nitrogen in a crucial experiment. To determine if a non-nitrogenous diet could support life, he fed dogs meals composed only of sugar and water. By the second week, the dogs grew weak, and by the third week, ulcerations of the eye appeared. After a month, the dogs died. Magendie not only demonstrated the effects of protein deficiency but also performed the first experimental model of vitamin A deficiency. His work, moreover, showed that the nitrogen requirement of animals must be derived from the diet. In other experiments, Magendie furnished proof that nutrients absorbed from the intestine were carried in the portal vein and not exclusively in the lacteals, as believed by most of his contemporaries. The recognition of the similar organic material in plants and animals led to the argument that nutrition of animals occurred by an incorporation of substances already existing in vegetable foods. This theory of nutrition was known as "animalization," a term proposed by Boerhaave and Haller. Von Liebig concluded that vegetable casein, albumen, and fibrin (gluten) were isomeric and identical with their animal counterparts. Dumas and Jean Baptiste Boussingault (1802-1887) advanced the concept of animalization by arguing that animals were unable to synthesize protein. For Dumas, the basic animal function was oxidation of foodstuff, a phenomenon akin to the chemical process of combustion. Such a notion was challenged by von Liebig who was convinced that animals could perform at least one synthetic function – converting fat from sugar and starch.

Digestion and Dogma

While debate revolved around the issues of animal nutrition and synthesis, students of digestion were beginning to discover new fundamental facts. For centuries, the assimilation of food was surmised to occur in two stages. First there was the formation of chyme (the production of the reaction of food with gastric acid). This was followed by the change of chyme into chyle, which took place in the intestine with absorption into the lacteals. The stomach was the

Jean Baptiste Van Helmont (1577-1644) (top right) with his son (bottom left). Van Helmont was the founder of the Iatrochemical School and proposed that gastric acid might be a mineral acid such as nitric or hydrochloric acid. By distilling salt and clay, he actually produced "spirits of sea salt" (hydrochloric acid) – spiritus salis marina – and demonstrated that it could be used to dissolve human kidney stones. His son posthumously published his major medical literary contribution, Ortus Medicinae, in 1648. The interest of the philosopher René Descartes (bottom right) in the stomach reflected his intellectual quest for the physical site of the soul. As a supporter of the Iatromathematical school, Descartes regarded the body as a material machine directed by a rational soul, which he believed to be located in the pineal gland. The consideration of the stomach as the source of the soul or the "solar plexus" was part of the widespread desire to identify the site of the human soul and the elucidation of its "secretion": the Holy Grail of philosophic physiology.

most important site of digestion, but just how gastric juices acted on food remained an age-old puzzle. After Van Helmont, many workers doubted the existence of any acid in the stomach under normal conditions. However, studies conducted in the nineteenth century refuted this notion.

	No. 1	No. 2	No. 3
	grs.	grs.	grs.
Muriatic acid in union with a *fixed alkali*†	·22	·95	1.71
———— *with ammonia*	1·56	·76	·40
———— in a *free or unsaturated state*	1·59	2·22	2·72
Total	3·27	3·93	4·83

William Prout (1785-1850) (right) was born in Horton, a remote village of Gloucestershire, England. Having studied at Guy's Hospital in London, he became a member of the Royal College of Physicians as well as a fellow of the Royal Medical Chirurgical Society. On December 11, 1823, at the Royal Society of Medicine, he presented his landmark paper "On the Nature of Acid and Saline Matters Usually Existing in the Stomach of Animals" (left). Prout identified hydrochloric acid in the gastric juice of numerous species, including humans, and quantified free and total hydrochloric (muriatic) acid (bottom). In addition, he related the amount of acid to the degree of dyspepsia and also proposed that chloride was secreted from the blood to the lumen by electrical means. In this hypothesis, Prout proposed (more than a century before it could be confirmed) that when gastric acid was secreted, the blood would become alkaline (postprandial alkaline tide). Apart from his definitive resolution of the nature of gastric acid, Prout was the first to propose that the atomic weights of all elements would be multiples of that of hydrogen (Prout's Hypothesis). A further major contribution to the science of gastroenterology was his classification, in 1827, of foods into the subgroups of carbohydrates (saccharinous), fats (oleaginous), and proteins (albuminous) for which he was awarded the Copley Medal.

In 1803, the American physiologist J.R. Young (1782-1804) of Philadelphia concluded after many experiments on animals and himself that digestion did not occur in the absence of the acid that was present in the gastric juice under normal conditions. He thought, however, the acid was phosphoric acid. He also noted that saliva and gastric juice flowed at the same time on stimulation. More remarkable were the investigations of William Beaumont (1785-1853), a surgeon in the United States Army. He began his classic studies in 1825 on Alexis St. Martin, who had sustained a gastric fistula after a gunshot wound. Over a period of eight years, Beaumont conducted two hundred and thirty-eight well-designed experiments on gastric secretion and motility. In his publication *Experiments and Observations on the Nature of the Gastric Juice and the Physiology of Digestion* (1833), he ended with fifty-one documented conclusions that on the whole hold true to this day. Beaumont stated that gastric acid "contains free Muriatic Acid and some other active chemical principles," hinting at the presence of enzymes. (Muriatic acid is the older term for hydrochloric acid.) He erred on two points: that gastric juice was not secreted unless food was present in the stomach, and that food caused gastric secretion by a mechanical action on the gastric wall. Beaumont's work was antedated by that of Jacob Helm of Vienna, who conducted similar observations on a woman with a gastric fistula. Helm's publication (1803), however, did not receive the notoriety that Beaumont's did.

The identity of the gastric acid was solved by William Prout, an unusual English physician who made important contributions to chemical physiology over a fifteen-year period and then disappeared into private practice. Prout showed in 1824 that free hydrochloric acid existed in stomachs. He was the first to divide food substances into three classes – sugars, fats, and proteins – and also proposed that atomic weights of elements were multiples of the atomic weights of hydrogen. At about the same time, over on the continent in Heidelberg, Friedrich Tiedemann (1781-1861) and Leopold Gmelin (1788-1853) carried out a series of classic experiments on the digestion of food by a variety of animals. Their analysis revealed the presence of both hydrochloric and acetic acids in gastric juice. They found that the gastric juice was always acid when food was present in the stomach, and that it dissolved a wide range of foodstuffs, including albumin, fibrin, gelatin, starch, and sugar.

Tiedemann and Gmelin suggested that digestion might be due to something more than acids alone, but the missing factor was not supplied until the work of Johann N. Eberle. In 1834, Eberle initiated research on digestive enzymes that indicated the existence of one or more ferments in gastric juice. He found weak hydrochloric acid or neutral gastric mucus alone did not dissolve organic substances, but that a mixture of both did. A year later, Theodor Schwann (1810-1882) together with Johannes Muller extracted

The French were considerably interested in digestion both at a scientific and epicurean level. R.A.F. Réaumur (1683-1757) (top left) studied the digestion of birds, particularly his own pet buzzard, (bottom left), in detail and concluded that their stomachs secreted acid that was necessary for digestion. The premature demise of his experimental model resulted in Réaumur's loss of interest in the subject of digestion, and he thereafter turned his skills to the development of a novel technique for strengthening steel. Anthelme Brillat-Savarin (1755-1826) (bottom right) studied digestion and its effect on the higher senses by compiling an exotic compendium of culinary information and dining etiquette. His reflections on the Physiology of Taste (background) and the relationship of food to human behavior are still regarded as definitive among those who believe that the gut-brain axis is modulated and amplified by a malolactic acid transduction system.

Johann E. Purkinje (top right) of Bohemia was a physiologist of genius. Although he initially trained as a preacher, he subsequently became a teacher before graduating in medicine at Prague in 1819. His original dissertation was on subjective visual phenomena and as a result he became a great friend of Goëthe who had written extensively on color and visual phenomena. Partly as a result of this relationship he was appointed professor of Physiology and Pathology at the University of Breslau in 1823. Although at first coldly received on account of prejudice against Slavs, he soon became a great favorite. As a microscopist Purkinje was the first to use the microtome, Canada balsam, glacial acidic acid and potassium dichromate. Amongst other things he discovered the sudoriferous glands of the skin, the Purkinje cells of the cerebellum, the lumen of the axis cylinder of nerves, and the ganglionic bodies in the brain. In 1823, well prior to the work of Francis Galton, he pointed out the importance of fingerprints and provided an accurate figuration of them. In 1834 with Gabriel Valentin, he co-authored the famous essay on ciliary epithelial motion. In 1839 he described the Purkinje fibers of cardiac muscle.

crude pepsin from gastric juice that converted albumin to peptones *in vitro*. The two noted that no gas evolved during pepsin digestion of food, thus dispelling the notion held for three centuries that digestion was a fermentation-like process. In the same year (1835), Eberle discovered that pancreatic juice had fat-splitting activity, and in 1844 Gabriel Valentin identified a starch-converting enzyme in pancreatic secretion while a year later in 1845, Louis Mialhe prepared a crude extract of salivary amylase.

Mechanisms and Maestros

The next milestone marked the start of the career of Claude Bernard (1813-1878), who began with the problem of digestion. Study of the stomach introduced him to the pancreas, then to the liver, and finally to the nervous system. On all three organs, Bernard made major discoveries. Starting in 1843, he noted gastric juice degraded cane sugar. From 1846 to 1856, he proved that pancreatic juice emulsified neutral fat (converting it into fatty acid and glycerol), changed starch into sugar, and completed the breakdown of protein after bile had inhibited peptic digestion. The next phase in the story of digestive enzymes, that of chemical purification, followed when organic chemists such as Berzelius and Emil Fischer (1852-1919) introduced the concepts of catalytic action and enzyme specificity. The first digestive enzymes purified were pepsin (Brucke, 1861), and trypsin (Kuhne, 1867). The interest in the process of digestion and nutrition renewed inquiry into the liver's role in all these activities. Such attention generated new knowledge of hepatic function in the intermediate metabolism of the body.

The study of enzymes also laid the foundations of modern biochemistry, for the pioneers performed both chemical and histological investigations. Johann E. Purkinje (1787-1869), who noted the inhibitory action of bile on pepsin, observed an analogy between the cellular structure of animals and that of plants (1837), calling granular substance in cells "protoplasm". It remained for Schwann to work out the details of the cell theory in a systematic manner.

The evolution of cell theory represented the product of two influences. First, there existed the tradition of microscopic investigations, which provided the empirical evidence. (The earlier observations of the cell were made with simple microscopes, but after 1840, the capabilities of compound microscope became fully exploited.) Second, the speculative doctrine of *Naturphilosophie* stimulated the search for the unity of matter and first principles. The cell theory that postulated a common generative element of plants and animals

Ernest Starling (top left) and William Bayliss (bottom left) were not only brothers-in-law but critical exponents of novel physiologic theories relating to the heart, intestine, and pancreas. In particular their elucidation of the hormonal regulation of pancreatic secretion provided the foundation for the development of an entirely new discipline of clinical medicine and physiology, namely endocrinology.

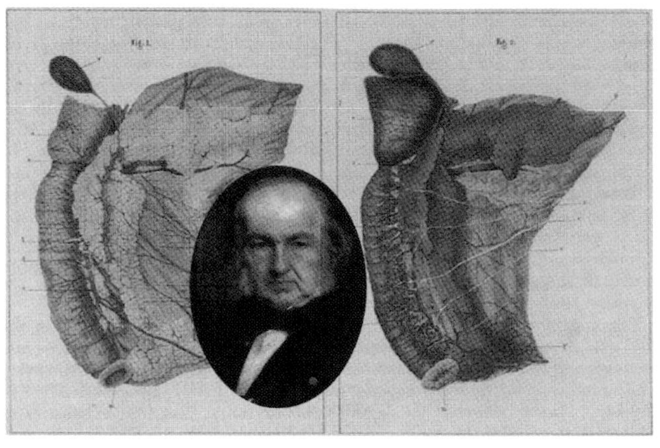

Claude Bernard (inset) provided unique insight into the mechanisms of glucose homeostasis and pancreatic function. His elucidation of the general principles of the physiology of digestion were to provide the scientific background against which digestive physiology was elucidated. His meticulous experimental work and drawings (pancreaticoduodenal relationship) remain to this time models of rigorous scientific investigation.

presented a structural and functional unit for all living things. Such a hypothesis was consonant with the thinking of the nature philosophers. Schwann, like Purkinje, believed that cells came into existence in an elementary substance called cytoblasteme (1839) and that there were chemical interactions between the cell and cytoblasteme. He wrote: *"All parts of the cell can be changed chemically during its growth. We should like to call the unknown cause of all these phenomena which can sum up under the name of metabolic phenomena of cells metabolic force."* Schwann's was thus the first usage of the term "metabolism" in its modern context.

By the second half of the nineteenth century dramatic advances in biological chemistry and science led to a major progression in the discernment of function. In particular, the elucidation of the nature of the diverse secretory products of the various parts of the gastrointestinal tract led to the exploration of the regulation of secretion. Ivan Pavlov (1849-1936) of St. Petersburg initially defined the neural regulation of secretory and motor function and was followed soon thereafter by the contributions of Sir William Bayliss (1860-1924) and Ernest Starling (1866-1927) of London, who identified chemical messengers and demonstrated their ability to excite response at a distance. An amalgamation of these contributions established the novel discipline of neuro-endocrinology of the gastrointestinal tract and opened an entire new vista of patho-physiology. The turn of the nineteenth century was marked by major developments in organ patho-physiology as J. Edkins (1863-1940) described gastrin and J. Langley (1852-1925) pepsin while A. Einhorn (1856-1917), J. Hemmeter (1864-1931) and F. Krause (1856-1937) variously explored gastric and duodenal secretion.

Boas and Berlin

This constellation of both medical and scientific advances expanded the horizons of understanding of gastrointestinal disease to the extent that when in 1896, Ismar Boas (1858-1938) of Berlin first proposed that gastroenterology be regarded as a separate discipline, his ideas were well received. The accumulation of gastrointestinal knowledge as well as the interest in the gut that had been engendered by the end of the nineteenth century fueled the concept that this area of medicine might be regarded as an area worthy of special focus. In this respect the Berlin physician Karl Ewald (1845-1915) and particularly his pupil Ismar Boas, were powerful leaders who influenced physicians in the establishment of gastroenterology as a separate discipline. Indeed, to Boas must be given the credit for founding gastroenterology and establishing the first journal devoted specifically to the topic. His establishment in Berlin of a clinic specifically for the management of gastrointestinal problems, was followed by the publication of a number of textbooks on the subject of the stomach that would attain almost biblical status. Boas emphasized the need for internal exploration of lumen of the gut and even in the light of the limited early instruments available predicted the future utility of endoscopy.

Prior to Boas' publication of the first textbook solely devoted to the new discipline of gastroenterology (in its entirety), *Diagnostik und Therapie der Magenkrankheiten*, printed in Liepzig in two parts between 1890 and 1893, only a few specialized discourses on organs or their disease had been printed. Boas' text inspired an explosion of literature and within a decade, a number of classic gastroenterological texts including those by K. Ewald and the American, J. Hemmeter, had been published. Focus on the subject as a whole, rather than specialized areas, had become the norm rather than the exception.

Therapeutic Advances

Gastrointestinal Surgery

Surgery is not only the oldest branch of medical science, but also the one most adapted to human nature, given the fact that it was the development of manual skills that raised initially raised humanity above the ranks of animals. Thus man, the artificer, was in all ages tempted to resolve problems by the employment of technical skills.

Amongst the medical tasks, the healing of wounds and the repair of bones were the ones that easily lent themselves to such applications. While reasoning and conceptions were entirely primitive, as were the notions of diseases, the healing methods occasionally produced quite admirable results in instances such as trephining skulls, amputation, setting broken bones, and even replacing noses. In general, however, broaching the cranial, thoracic and abdominal cavities was impossible up to the nineteenth century, given the predictable demise of the patient.

By the late nineteenth century the development of anesthesia and antisepsis had initiated a major upswing of surgery and the evolution of modern surgery had begun. In particular, it was the successes of abdominal surgery that played a leading role in gaining the confidence of the public in these operations and prepared the way for the magnificent achievements exhibited today by brain surgery, and cardio-thoracic surgery. In fact, in an age when abdominal operations are regarded as an everyday event and there is hardly an individual without a missing appendix or gall bladder it is, clearly, hard to understand the excitement occasioned by the word laparotomy fifty years ago.

As early as the turn of the twentieth century the news of an impending laparotomy was likely to cause widespread excitement in an institution.

Laparotomy, also referred to as celiotomy, was the term given to the intentional opening of the abdominal cavity by an incision. The predictably fatal consequences witnessed on battlefields and in gladiatorial contests had provided ample evidence of the outcome of entering the peritoneal cavity. As a result, surgeons confined themselves to suturing abdominal wounds or operating on hernias. Even the latter procedure had a devastating mortality if any bowel was involved since there was no understanding of how to effectively repair damage to so delicate a structure. While death was well recognized as an outcome, the nature of infection was not properly understood

Ivan Pavlov, by virtue of meticulous canine surgery and experimentation, was able to propound the theory of neural regulation which he termed "nervism".

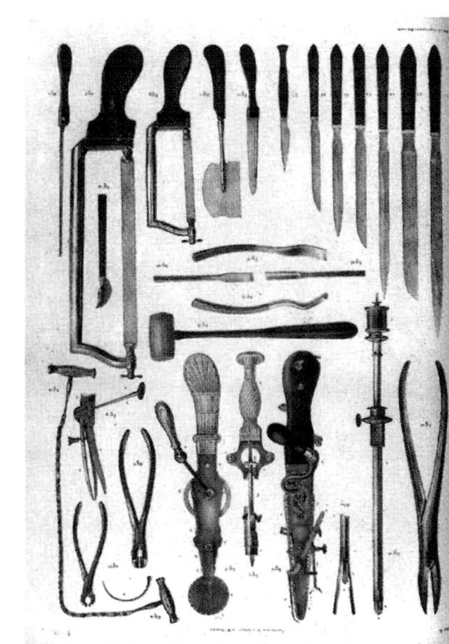

Surgical instruments have evolved from the earliest flints used for trephining to a diverse array of sophisticated implements. Early lancets for blood-letting were replaced by vascular clamps for hemostasis and a wide variety of complex mechanical devices for sewing, cutting, drilling, and crushing all became part of the armamentarium of the late 19th-century surgeon.

Ismar Boas (left) of Exin, Posen was the author of numerous texts on diseases of the stomach and intestines. His mentor, Karl Anton Ewald of Berlin (right), was one of the early authorities on the subject of digestion and developed intubation as a technique to explore the nature of the contents and function of the stomach. Together they devised the test breakfast and used this to assess gastric function. In 1885 Boas founded the first Polyclinic for gastrointestinal disease in Berlin and in 1895 established the first journal devoted entirely to the subject of gastroenterology, Archive fur Verdauungskrankheiten.

E. Polya was one of the great surgeons of Hungary and widely regarded throughout Europe and even the US for his contributions to gastric surgery. In his words: "An impending laparotomy on the next day in the Kovacs' clinic, the first surgical clinic in Hungary, was the chief topic of conversation on the previous day in the entire complex. On such a day Kovacs gave no lecture, the entire personnel was scrubbing the hall, where the operation was to take place on the following day. The operation hall was filled with the curious audience eager to watch the operation and all the benches were covered with sheets. Such an upheaval only occurred once, or twice a year, at the most, and therefore, when as a fourth-year student I enrolled with my unforgettable master Hertzel, I was most impressed. The chief theatre assistant, Sister Henrika of blessed memory, in reply to my inquiry as to the most frequent operation said: "laparotomy".

prior to the nineteenth century and the advent of R. Koch, L. Pasteur and J. Lister. Indeed, the concept of peritonitis was unknown before the end of the eighteenth century although references to "pussy" accumulations in the peritoneum had been known since the vey earliest medical literature.

It was, however, well-known from experience that the opening of the peritoneum, be it by accidental injury or during an operation, was very dangerous, although in some cases the patient might survive. There was no knowledge of why it went one way on a certain occasion and the other way on the next and the views regarding the serious consequences of laparotomy varied widely with the passage of time. The early physicians considered that the life giving *"spiritus animalis"* (soul spirit) would depart through the abdominal wound and were wary of "tapping" the fluid contents of the abdominal content. Others were concerned at the loss of "body heat" and such thoughts led them to consider the advice of Roger of Salerno who proposed that intestines prolapsed on account of injury should have a dog or a cat placed on them to keep them warm. As a result of the known mortality and the varied other concerns, it remained almost taboo to enter the abdomen until the 1850s. There were, however, some interesting exceptions. Thus the Indian Susutra recommended in cases of obstruction of the bowel the opening of the abdominal cavity and the swollen intestine. The Talmud refers to Caesarean section and even to excision of the spleen. Hippocrates recommended the opening of abscesses of the liver and even the usually thoughtful Erasistratus suggested the idea of opening the diseased liver in cases of cirrhosis of the liver in order to be able to apply medicaments.

Thus in the course of history there exists the odd reference to laparotomies and survival, with such events being generally regarded as some sort of miracle. Yet the public perception not much more than one hundred years ago is illustrated by the fact that during the years 1856-7 a great disputation occurred in the Medical Academy of Paris for five months, as to whether the operation of cysts of the ovaries was permissible. Amongst the many contributors to this disputation, only one, P. Cazeaux, actually spoke in favor of it. In London in 1850 no less a personage than Sir W. Lawrence, surgeon of St. Bartholomew Hospital and physician to Queen Victoria, raised the question with the Royal Medical and Surgical Society. He asked: *"whether the venerable association can afford to permit and continue the disputation about the eradication of ovarian cysts, without placing in jeopardy the authority and prestige of the medical faculty?"* In Philadelphia in 1849, when Dr. Washington Atlee announced that he intended to excise ovarian cysts, he was attacked by his colleagues. One even proposed that the police intervene, while another called on his patient to persuade her not to undergo the operation, because if the operation were undertaken she would be dead within twenty four hours. Finally, when the operation had succeeded, a third professor wrote a fulminating article to the effect stating that *"no amount of success can justify the immorality of a surgeon cutting open the abdomen of any women!"* This vitriolic condemnation of opening the abdomen was not held among primitive peoples and Caesarean section had been widely practiced from even biblical times. A traveler by the name of Felkin, reported the performance of this operation in a village called Kahura in Uganda in the early nineteenth century. Cowle in 1785 reported a Negro woman having become so fed up with the pain of childbirth that she grabbed a knife and cut into her own abdomen so deeply, that she even injured the buttock of her offspring. Only after she had pulled out the infant and the placenta did she call a Negro veterinarian, who somehow managed to suture her abdomen.

Ancient Indian medicine described the removal of the offspring by laparotomy from women who died in childbirth and the Romans even promulgated a law ordering this. During the Middle Ages the Church required it. It was alleged the Julius Caesar was born this way; that is why he was named CAESAR, not, as suggested by the widespread use of the words, was the operation named after him *sectio caesaria*. According to Pliny the Elder, Scipio Africanus was also born in this manner and, as the legend would have it, so were also Bacchus and Aesculapius.

The Talmud also speaks of a child being able to be born through the abdominal wall of his mother, in order that both mother and infant may stay alive, but whether such operation was actually performed on a live woman is not known. According to history, the first Caesarean section on a live woman was performed by Jacob Nufer (a pig castrator) of Siegershausen, Thurgau, on his own wife, who thirteen midwives and several lithotomes had failed to deliver. Both mother and child survived, and the woman subsequently had several more children *per via natura*, including twins. It is recorded that the child lived to the age of seventy-seven!

The introduction of the surgery of ovarian cysts met with even more resistance, than the Caesarean section. Although there were few conditions in the eighteenth century that could cause more chronic misery than an ovarian cyst so huge as to inhibit breathing and movement, their removal was a source of great controversy. When Robert Houston attempted the first ovariotomy for such indications in 1701, there was little chance of success. Ephraim McDowell of Kentucky who undertook the first successful ovarian cyst operation on Christmas Day 1809, was told by his teacher, the famous John Bell of Edinburgh, that ovarian cysts were incurable. *"Any surgical intervention would lead unavoidably to peritonitis and death."* Although no less a

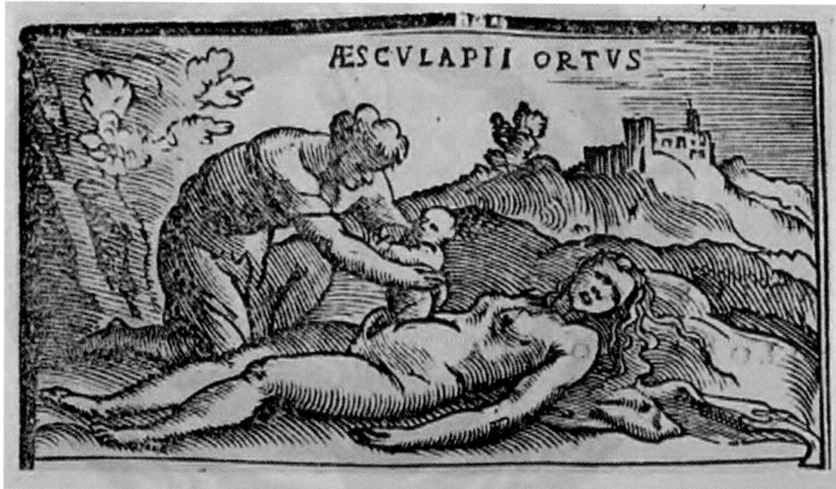

The first desperate attempts to operate on the abdomen were inspired by the desire to save the child of a dying mother. In the reign of the Roman king Numa, the Caesarean operation was supported by law. Thus the Lex Regia stated: "Si mater pregnas mortua sit, fructus quam primum caute extratihur" *(If a pregnant mother die the child [fruit] must first be removed). The procedure was thus legally obligated in order to save the child in the case of death of a pregnant woman. Although it is reported that Julius Caesar was born in this manner, it is highly unlikely, since even at the time of the Gallic Wars it is noted that he was writing letters to his mother. The first successful attempt at Caesarean section on a living woman was reported to have been undertaken by Jacob Nufer, a sow gelder, in 1500.*

surgeon and scientist than John Hunter raised the question in 1787, as to *"why should women not survive the removal of the ovary, seeing, that animals survive it very well,"* he too came to the conclusion that ovarian cysts should not be operated upon.

The consequence of the removal of ovarian cysts was the development of the surgery of the uterus. Often the diagnosis of ovarian cysts would lead at surgery to the identification of tumors of the uterus (myomas), and naturally attempts to remove these took place. The first such case was recorded in 1815 (R. Getaus, Faenza). Kimball in 1853 was the first to diagnose a uterine tumor and remove it together with the uterus. Complete hysterectomy was first performed by Conrad John Martin Langenbeck, professor at Gottingen, who was one of the most skilled surgeons of his time. Thus the early advance into the abdomen was mainly driven by issues relating to gynecology and obstetrics, which although relatively difficult operations, did not approach the challenge produced by addressing the hollow visceral structures of the stomach and bowel. At this stage a number of such areas of pathology were variously addressed by surgeons.

Although rational therapy had advanced somewhat, the early twentieth century exhibited few defined forms of pharmacological intervention and opiates, analgesics, mercury, belladonna and various liquors were the mainstays of therapy. In this milieu of therapeutic stasis the development of anesthesia (G. Morton) and antisepsis (Lord Lister) provided considerable impetus for surgeons to enter the abdominal cavity with a degree of safety not previously available. Whereas previously surgery of the gut had been limited to dramatic interventions undertaken *in extremis* and with a generally dubious outcome, the peritoneal cavity could now be entered with relative impunity. In Vienna and Berlin, T. Billroth (1829-1894), J. von Mikulicz-Radecki (1850-1905), B. von Langenbeck (1810-1887), and C. Langenbuch (1846-1901), respectively, pioneered esophago-gastroduodenal and gall bladder surgery as well as training a new generation of surgeons skilled in the techniques of resection and anastomosis. Baron B. Moynihan (1865-1936) did likewise in England, while in France J. Pean (1830-1898), H. Hartmann (1860-1952) and M. Jaboulay (1860-1913) amplified the work of T. Kocher (1841-1917) of Bern and A. von Eiselsberg (1860-1925) of Vienna. In the United States W. Halsted (1852-1922), C. Fenger (1840-1902), A. Berg (1872-1950), W. Mayo (1861-1939), and A. Ochsner (1896-1981) epitomized the advance of the New World and surgery became a major consideration in the management of gastrointestinal disease. Indeed, such was the triumph of surgery that by the middle part of the century L. Dragstedt (1893-1975) and vagotomy, and Mayo and gastrectomy, were as synonymous with peptic ulcer disease as B. Sippy (1866-1924) and white medicine.

The advent of Prontosil (G. Domagk) followed by the era of antibiotics introduced by Sir A. Fleming (1881-1955) and H. Florey (1898-1968) heralded a cornucopia of pharmacotherapeutic agents specifically targeted for the amelioration of gastrointestinal symptoms. Thus, surgery slowly relinquished its primacy as powerful drugs capable of controlling infection, decreasing inflammation, inhibiting secretion, and regulating motility were introduced. Nevertheless the major issues in the gut remained that of access and the identification of disease site and type. Thus, while physical diagnosis and detailed history taking, combined with clinical experience and knowledge of pathology often generated a working diagnosis, the nature and the site of the lesion were for the most part unknown until either operation or autopsy was undertaken.

At the turn of the century, a number of concepts were considered with a view to facilitating diagnosis by providing imaging access to the interior of the abdomen. These included roentgen rays and endoscopy. The latter technique had some proponents that supported viewing the gastrointestinal tract using the orifices of the mouth and anus while the former considered a direct view of the peritoneal cavity to be advantageous. The latter endeavor was known as laparoscopy and although initially used

Obstetric and gynecological problems led to the development of some of the earliest abdominal surgical procedures as physicians sought to save the lives of both young women and babies.

In the era before the introduction of acid suppression, chronic peptic ulceration resulted in considerable morbidity and mortality. The only effective remedy for intractable pain and complications, such as perforation, bleeding, and gastric outlet obstruction, was surgery. The results, however, were so terrible that many eminent physicians (Naunyn) regarded surgery as little more than an autopsy in vivo. The introduction of anesthesia (inhaler) by William Morton (top left) allowed for surgery to be performed in an unhurried fashion on a patient protected from pain. The subsequent advent of antisepsis (carbolic spray), as introduced by Lord Joseph Lister (top right), significantly decreased infectious complications and facilitated the performance of cautious and meticulous surgery. In addition, advances in hemostatic technique (the first-time use of gloves) as instituted by William Halsted of Baltimore (bottom right), and technical efficiency as promulgated by Berkley Moynihan of Leeds (bottom left), facilitated the development of relatively safe gastric surgery. Nevertheless, the morbidity of postgastrectomy syndromes engendered by such operations resulted in patients being cured of their peptic ulcer only to acquire a series of lifetime disabilities. Thus, the consequence of the anatomic and physiologic derangement attendant upon gastric resection, pyloric ablation, and a variety of gastrojejunal and duodenal anastomoses were as debilitating if not worse than the original disease. Theodore Billroth (center), who undertook the first successful gastrectomy, was not only a surgeon, but a fine musician, music critic and excellent poet.

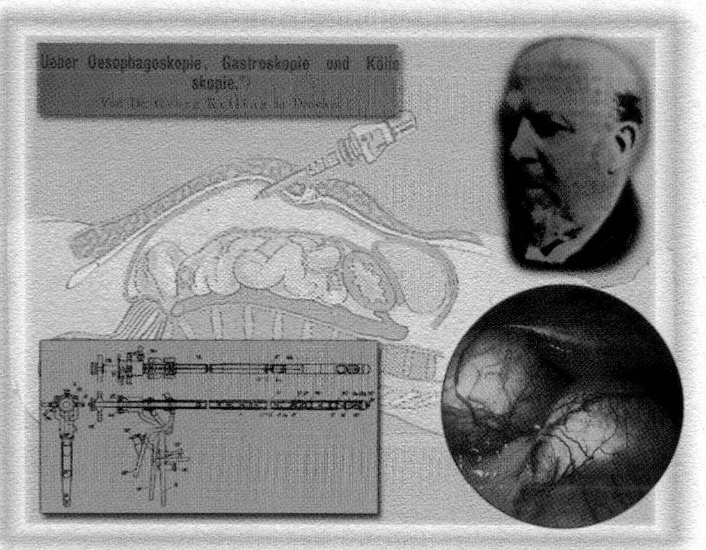

George Kelling (top right) of Dresden, although better remembered for his contributions to the establishment of laparoscopy, played a role in the evolution of gastroscopy. The Kelling gastroscope (bottom left) was a masterpiece of engineering craft but its utility was limited due to its complexity. The outer tube carried a lamp and the distal part of the tube possessed a segmental flexibility and could be straightened by a complicated mechanism when introduced in the stomach, after which a straight optical system was inserted via the outer tube. The tip of the instrument was slightly angled (bottom left) since this was thought to facilitate a more detailed inspection of the antrum than a straight instrument. Although Kelling examined more than thirty patients and published his observations, the device was poorly received by his colleagues and no other physicians adopted its usage.

principally for diagnostic means, was also considered as having potential therapeutic application. Unfortunately the lack of adequate technology limited its utilization in this capacity. However, the advances in biotechnology that occurred during the twentieth century led to a renaissance of laparoscopy such that by 1990 it had once again become not only a substantial diagnostic tool, particularly amongst gynecologic surgeons, but also an important asset to gastrointestinal surgeons. The subsequent advance of laparoscopic surgery under the marketing banner of "minimally invasive surgery" attracted both patients and surgeons alike. Some surgeons perceived it as a valuable technique in specific areas such as cholycystectomy while others touted it as a technique capable of replacing almost all conventional open surgery. As usual in surgery, the lack of controlled studies, as well as the technical zealotry of some proponents, led to overenthusiastic application, initially with high complication rates as learning curve problems and hubris abrogated judgement and common sense in some instances. The advent of individuals and societies to monitor training and to provide oversight on application has led to some degree of therapeutic balance, although in some areas territorial imperative and naive enthusiasm rather than clinical logic and rationale still obfuscates the issues.

Minimally Invasive Surgery

The first documented laparoscopy was undertaken in 1901 by Dimitri Oskarovich Ott of St. Petersburg using a gynecological head mirror, external light source, and speculum to perform the procedure, who described the intervention as "ventroscopy". Thereafter although numerous others descriptors including peritoneoscopy, celioscopy, and organoscopy were utilized to describe the procedure, the term laparoscopy has gained the widest acceptance.

In 1902, George Kelling of Dresden, who was an early pioneer both in esophagoscopy and gastroscopy, examined the peritoneal cavity of a dog using the Nitze cystoscope and becoming the first to introduce the technique as a gastrointestinal diagnostic procedure.

By 1910 he had undertaken a number of successful diagnostic laparoscopies on humans and utilized the term "*Koelioskopie*" to describe the methodology for safely inducing a pneumoperitoneum as well as the location and appropriate technique of port placement. Later in the same year, Hans Christen Jacobaeus of Stockholm coined the term "laparoscopy" which has subsequently become the accepted terminology used to describe almost all varieties of this form of intervention. More recently, the use of the generic term "minimally invasive surgery" has supplanted laparoscopy, particularly when utilized to describe the diverse therapeutic applications of the procedure. Jacobaeus was enthusiastic about the utility of the procedure, and in his initial experience with forty-five patients reported its successful application in the diagnosis of cirrhosis, tuberculous peritonitis, metastatic tumors, and even Pick's disease. In 1911 at John Hopkins Hospital, Bertram Bernheim similarly described his early experiences with laparoscopy but chose to refer to the procedure as "organoscopy". Bernheim, like his predecessors, noted the restrictions of current instrument design and in particular commented upon the limited angle of vision of 90° imposed by the use of a cystoscope as a laparoscopic instrument. This limitation in design was addressed by Kremer in 1927 and resulted in modification of the instrument to a forward-viewing device. Subsequently in 1929 Kalk further adapted the lens system to increase the viewing angle to 135° (81).

In spite of the fact that laparotomy was a dangerous procedure, its use as a diagnostic tool was widespread and there was little impetus for surgeons to develop an alternative. Thus, regardless of the unique clinical possibilities that could have evolved from the development of laparoscopy, its widespread use was not embraced by the medical community. Indeed, instrument design would remain essentially unchanged for the next thirty years, apart from some design modifications introduced in the 1930s by John C. Ruddock

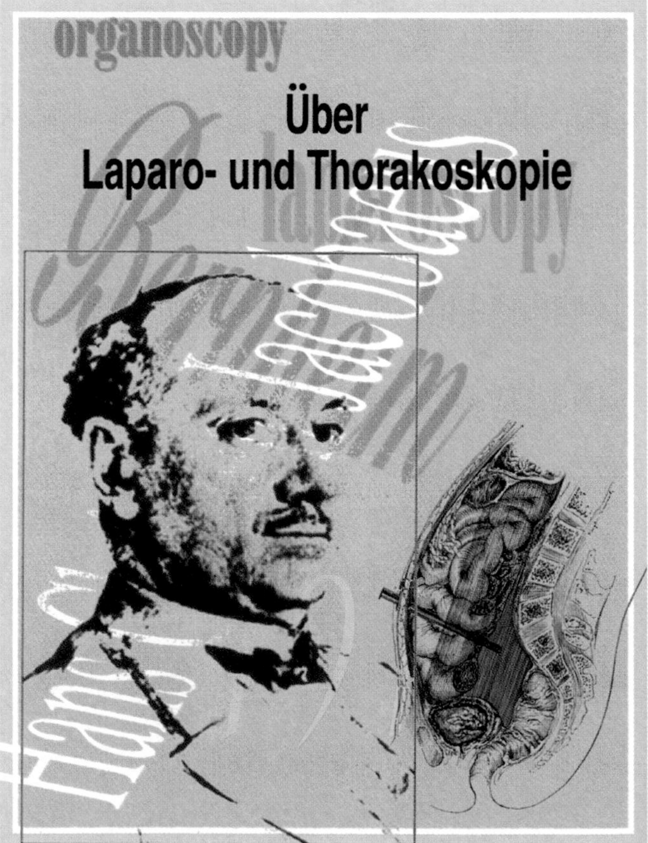

In 1910 Hans Christen Jacobaeus of Stockholm (left) published two cases of visceral exploration: one thoracic and one abdominal, and designated his technique as thoraco-laparoscopy (Über Laparo-und Thorakoskopie). The methods he used were less advanced than Kelling who had described a separate needle with filtered air to produce the pneumoperitoneum, preferring to use the trocar for this purpose. Although Jacobaeus reported on 115 laparoscopies in 1912 and described cirrhosis, metastatic disease, and tuberculous peritonitis, he thereafter abandoned the procedure and devoted his attention to thoracoscopic lysis of tuberculous lung lesions. The logic of the latter procedure proposed that lysis would permit complete lung collapse after artificial pneumothorax induction and thereby ensure healing!

In 1948 E.B. Benedict developed the Operating Gastroscope. A major advantage of this instrument was that it obviated the need for a piggyback biopsy device by incorporating both a biopsy forceps and a suction tube within the housing of the gastroscope itself. Critics of the instrument claimed that the addition of the extra channels necessary for the suction and biopsy not only increased the diameter to 14 mm but also generated a somewhat unwieldy shape and posed a disadvantage. Benedict vehemently defended his instrument by claiming that the advantage it offered by generating diagnostic certainty more than justified any of the putative shortcomings.

(Los Angeles) and Edward B. Benedict (Boston), who were enthusiastic supporters of the technique.

In 1934 Ruddock collaborated with ACMI to modify the McCarthy cystoscope and developed a fore-oblique visual system that greatly facilitated viewing the peritoneal cavity. Ruddock termed his device a "peritoneoscope" and subsequently published details of five hundred patients who he had successfully investigated. Of particular relevance was his claim that use of the instrument had not only increased his clinical diagnostic accuracy from 63.9% to 91.7% but also avoided the expensive and dangerous necessity of a diagnostic laparotomy. Benedict, who was already an avid supporter of the utility of gastroscopic biopsy for the acquisition of diagnostic information, took a similar strong position in support of laparoscopy. Both he and Ruddock were enthusiastic in advocating its extensive use in the diagnosis of gastrointestinal disease as well as noting its obvious gynecological applications. Nevertheless the relatively clumsy nature of the instruments, as well as the limited visibility of some areas of the peritoneal cavity, hindered the widespread acceptance of this technique.

Such concerns were, however, to some extent mollified by the advance of technology, and in 1952 when N. Fourestier introduced the use of a quartz light rod to replace the distal lamp in the bronchoscope, its application to laparoscopy was readily apparent and the use of this novel method of light transmission in diverse endoscopic instruments, including laparoscopes, not only drastically improved illumination but also obviated the heat and electrical problems associated with the previous use of a distal lamp. The quartz light rod also facilitated the development of color cinematography and television imaging in the peritoneal cavity, thereby considerably facilitating diagnosis. However, despite its utility, the quartz rod exhibited a number of unfortunate limitations including high price, fragility, and the need to position the light source in close proximity to the external eyepiece. While improvements in these areas were under critical examination, the entire matter became moot in 1957 when B. Hirschowitz introduced the fiber optic bundle. Indeed, the subsequent widespread introduction of fiber optic technology to laparoscopy, combined with the development of flexible tip instruments, initiated a renaissance of the technique.

In 1981 Robert A. Sanowski reported that modification of a pediatric Olympus endoscope for use as a laparoscope enhanced visualization of the peritoneal cavity, and proposed that the endoscope might be readily applicable to laparoscopy without major modification. Such studies were, however, superceded by the development of instruments designed specifically for diagnostic and therapeutic application within the peritoneal cavity. In this respect corporate instrument-makers played a substantial role in promoting a gastrointestinal surgical renaissance by developing novel instruments that facilitated the interface of the disciplines of endoscopy and surgery. Indeed,

PERITONEOSCOPY
JOHN C. RUDDOCK, M.D., F.A.C.P., Los Angeles, California
91.7%
Surgery, Gynecology and Obstetrics 65 (1937):623-39

Ruddock of Los Angeles became a major proponent of laparoscopy. To facilitate peritoneoscopy, as he preferred to call it, Ruddock modified a McCarthy cystoscope, redesigned the trocar and biopsy instruments and utilized local anesthesia. In 1937 he documented his initial experiences with 500 patients. By the end of his career he had reported more than 2,500 cases with excellent results and low complication rates. Of particular interest was his early successful collaboration with R. Hope utilizing the peritoneoscope to diagnose ectopic pregnancy.

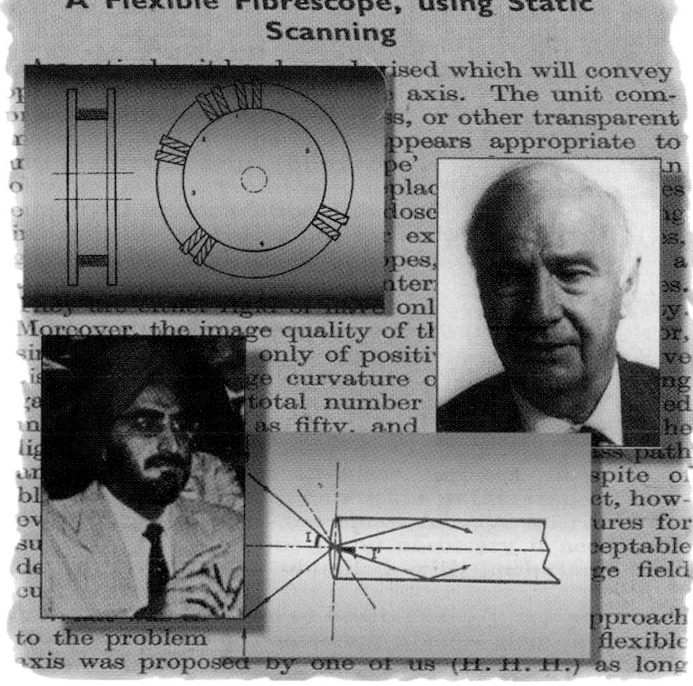

H. Hopkins (right) and his student N.S. Kapany (left) developed the theoretical basis of fiber optic technology. The application of this technology to gastroscopy by Basil Hirschowitz in 1957 introduced the era of fiber optic endoscopy.

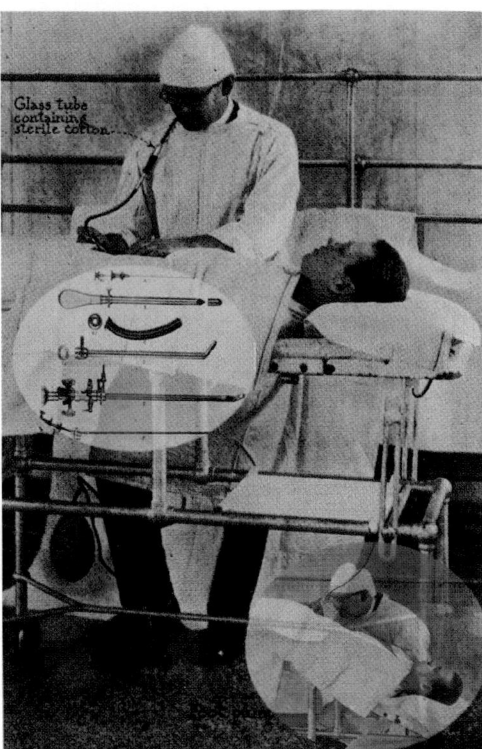

O. Nadeau of Chicago (top) (c. 1925) undertakes laparoscopy on a patient under local anesthesia. The collage of instruments is representative of the diverse array available for examining the peritoneal cavity and abdominal viscera. Nadeau himself referred to the technique as "Endoscopy of the Abdomen" and bemoaned the fact that the method was seldom used in the US, though popular in Europe.

the introduction of technology that had been chiefly utilized for intraluminal diagnostic and limited therapeutic purposes (hemostasis, dilation, polypectomy, stone retrieval, and sphincterotomy) to an extramural or transperitoneal application, provided gastrointestinal surgeons with a major impetus to almost re-invent their specialty. In the era of obsession with cost containment, early discharge from hospital consequent upon "keyhole" surgery has provided considerable incentive for the rapid and widespread adoption of minimally invasive surgery as the technique of choice.

The recent rapid introduction of diverse technical modifications has considerably advanced the application of therapeutic laparoscopy. Indeed, the development of multiple-port laparoscopy has virtually supplanted laparotomy in many instances. Furthermore, the introduction of charge-coupled devices (CCD) with greater optical discrimination, flexible instruments, staplers, retractors, suction devices, bipolar cautery, clips, and implantable meshes has expanded the surgical horizon enabling almost all techniques previously considered as operations of the open domain to be undertaken as laparoscopic procedures. Modifications in therapeutic technique have further amplified the ability of the surgeon to improve the "open operations" and optimize the use of therapeutic or minimally invasive surgery. In addition, the adaptation of diagnostic instrumentation such as biopsy forceps and ultrasound probes for passage via the trocar port into the peritoneal cavity, has further enhanced the diagnostic spectrum of the technique. The more recent development of robotic devices (Da Vinci and Zeus) that can function as extensions of the hands of the surgeon within the peritoneal cavity has produced a dramatic advance in surgical capability. Their extraordinary sensitivity and technical accuracy has facilitated the expertise of the operating surgeon by electronically and mechanically transferring the wrist movement beyond the port site to the operative area. Thus, a surgeon seated at an electronic three-dimensional interface can undertake the procedure from a control station distant from the patient with a degree of precision and vision hitherto undreamed of. Although such instruments are currently bulky and expensive, their obvious advantages suggest that the introduction of the concept is a portent of the paradigm shift that will occur in gastrointestinal surgery. The concept of long-range surgery – telesurgery – is becoming a similar reality. A further potentially useful development has been the application of laparoscopic intervention as a synchronous support system for difficult intraluminal endoscopic procedures such as polypectomy, anastomotic or stricture dilation and hemostasis. Thus, lesions may be either immobilized from the serosal side to facilitate intra-luminal access or observed to assure no transmural damage occurs. Under such circumstances appropriate therapeutic laparoscopic intervention may be introduced in an expeditious fashion and avoid post-procedure concerns regarding integrity of the bowel wall.

The development of laparoscopic surgery has initiated a "renaissance" of intra-abdominal surgery. Whether the advantages conferred by the limited abdominal incisions will outweigh its technical limitations remains to be judged.

Although almost any diagnostic or therapeutic procedure that has been considered at open surgery can be contemplated or has been undertaken laparoscopically, it is evident that not all are necessarily of appropriate efficacy to warrant unequivocal acceptance. Indeed in many instances, either inadequate data has been accumulated or insufficient time has elapsed to allow adequate evaluation. Diagnostic techniques such as biopsy and ultrasound have clearly proven to be safe and efficacious. Similarly, the use of the laparoscope to evaluate and stage neoplastic diseases such as the pancreas may be of some use in detecting peritoneal seeding and avoiding an unnecessary laparotomy. The development of very small diameter flexible laparoscopes may even further advance the diagnostic utility of the procedure. A puncture incision and local anesthesia will enable inspection of any area of the peritoneal cavity to identify any covert cause for an acute abdomen or the basis for any undetermined post-operative event. Such a technique has proven of considerable benefit in critically-ill patients in intensive care units or after major trauma when transport to radiographic facilities for investigation or an unnecessary laparotomy might be deleterious.

There is, however, considerable debate as to which laparoscopic procedures offer advantages over open procedures. Complications for the laparoscopic

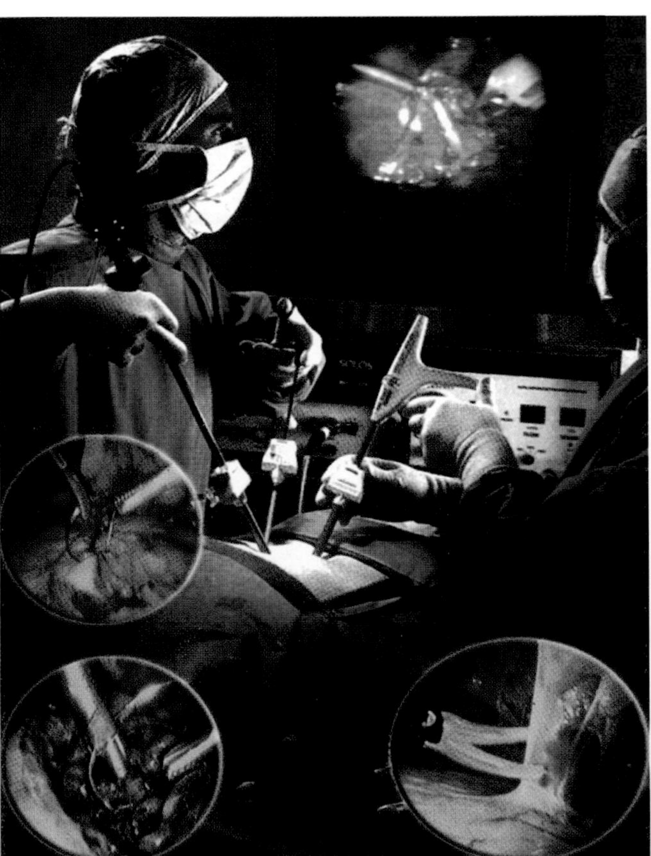

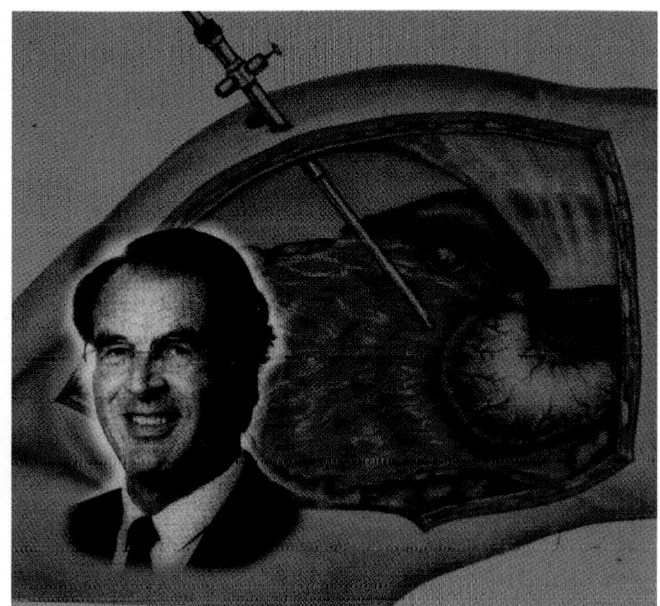

Until the advent of anesthesia, antisepsis and hemostasis, the vast majority of surgery was either confined to repair of traumatic injury or events relating to obstetric problems. Caesarean section in particular was one of the earliest forms of surgery perfected, since its utility to save the life of a child was undeniable. Hans Semm (inset), although originally trained as an obstetrician, was one of the first surgeons to recognize the potential therapeutic applications of laparoscopic surgery.

interventions are often higher than in open operations since surgical expertise is still relatively limited in some areas, and furthermore, ideal instrumentation is as yet unavailable or still under development. Indeed, one of the major impact areas has been the need to significantly reconfigure surgical training programs. It has been necessary to not only add a new tier of technical training for young trainees but to devise teaching modules to train mature surgeons never previously exposed to such technology and deficient in the visual and motor skills necessary for its implementation.

At the close of the twentieth century cholycystectomy and gastric fundoplication have become widely acceptable laparoscopic operations in terms of efficacy and safety. Colectomy for benign disease is similarly considered appropriate but concerns regarding port site metastatic seeding and adequate cancer resection make colectomy for malignant disease still somewhat controversial. Laparoscopic appendectomy may be useful under certain circumstances but cost-benefit analysis considerations, as well as issues of operative time and outcome, renders its widespread acceptance uncertain at this time. Similarly, hernia surgery is currently under evaluation as costs of equipment and time of hospitalization are weighed against the incidence of recurrence and the safety of the procedure in patients with other co-morbid diseases. Splenectomy, gastrojejunostomy, vagotomy, jejunostomy and even gastrectomy and pancreatectomy have all been reported but such applications are restricted to individuals or centers of excellence and are not routinely undertaken. Nevertheless, they confirm the possibility that all previously acceptable open interventions may become feasible.

While almost every known surgical procedure can or has been performed, the techniques and instrumentation currently available are in their infancy and considerable development will be necessary to ensure the successful transfer of surgery into the micro-invasive mode. Nevertheless the impact of endoscopic advance has been nothing less than dramatic in altering the way in which both patients and surgeons now consider the management of gastrointestinal disease. Reduced costs of hospitalization have pleased administrators as well as patients and insurance-payers. Similarly the diminution of discomfort, incision size, length of hospital stay, and early return to productivity, have impacted favorably upon patients, families, and employers.

The cycle whereby diagnostic laparotomy in the early part of the century was supplanted by endoscopy and laparoscopy has now attained full circle whereby laparoscopy has evolved from a diagnostic procedure into one with major therapeutic applications. Issues regarding the extent of training and expertise that are required to differentiate those individuals capable of undertaking diagnostic versus therapeutic procedures are still matters that require resolution. Recapturing the intrepid spirit of the early pioneers of surgery, a new generation of surgeons thwarted by the depredations of their territory inflicted by new drugs, interventional radiology, and endoscopy, applied themselves to the applications of laparoscopic technology in the abdomen. Thus within a decade, laparoscopy, with the synergy of biotechnology, has developed from a humble and relatively cumbersome diagnostic procedure in the early 1980s to become within a decade the perceived state-of-the art technique for a wide variety of operations including appendectomy, cholecystectomy, hernia repair, fundoplication, splenectomy, colectomy and gastrointestinal anastomoses.

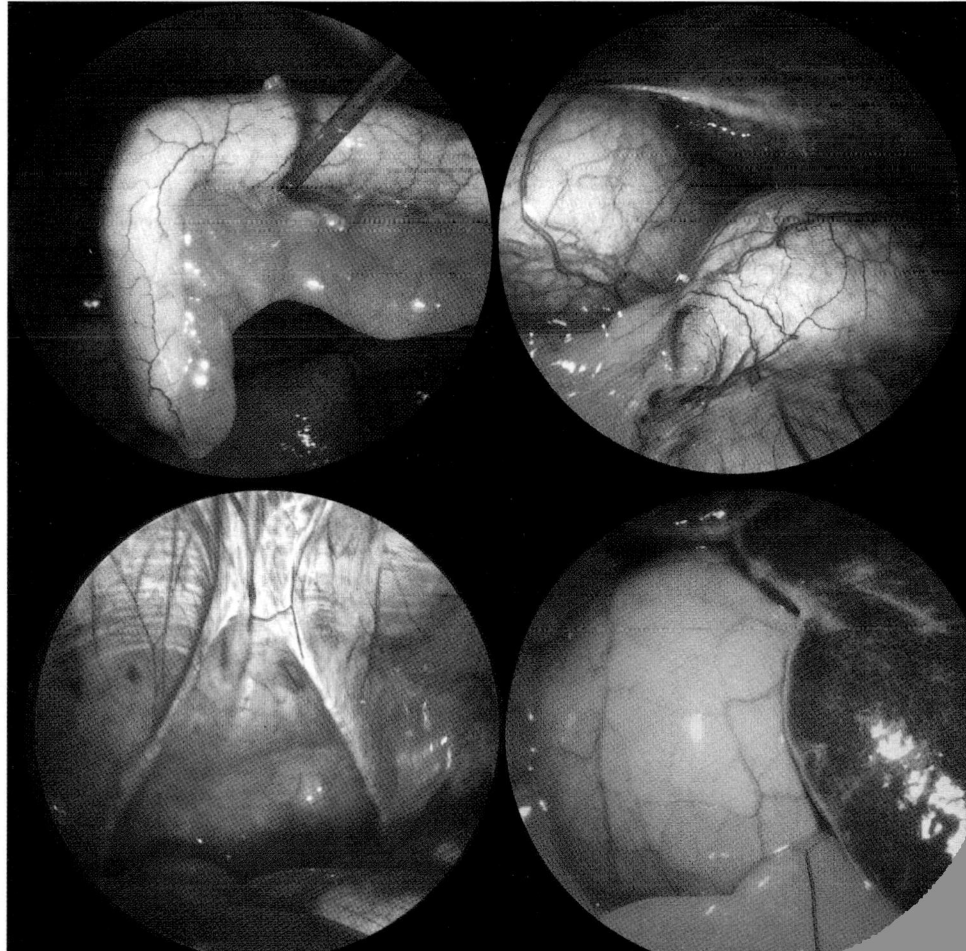

The applications of laparoscopic surgery to the management of diverse intra-abdominal disease processes have become ubiquitous.

SECTION 12

Imaging the Abdomen

The advent of W. Roentgen (1845-1923) and his X-rays prompted W. Cannon (1871-1945) to study motility while bismuth and barium facilitated the skills of G. Bucky (1880-1963), G. Holzknecht (1872-1931) and R. Carman (1875-1926) in the diagnosis of gastrointestinal ulcers and tumors. For the first time the concept of the diagnosis of abdominal disease became a reality and the early endoscopists with their rigid instruments vied with radiologists to identify the source of intra-abdominal problems.

ROENTGEN AND X-RAYS

The concept of investigating the gastrointestinal tract by an alternative, indirect method was provided following the discovery of X-rays and the observation that ingested radio-opaque material could be visualized. In seven weeks of furious experimentation between November 8 and December 26, 1895, W. Roentgen (1845-1923) in Wurzberg, using Hittorf-Crookes tubes, Ruhmkorff coils, and barium platinocyanide screens, conclusively documented that rays emitted from a cathode tube were able to alter a photographic emulsion and produce X-rays.

The first public demonstration of the properties of X-rays before a scientific body occurred soon thereafter on January 23 of the following year. Roentgen gave generous credit to his predecessors in the investigation of cathode rays and in particular, acknowledged the contributions of Hertz, Leonard, and Crookes. Albert von Kolliker, the famous anatomist, and an intellectual force of the time, was present and volunteered to be a subject for the demonstration of an X-ray picture of the hand. At the successful conclusion, von Kolliker stated that *"in 48 years as a member of the Society, I have never attended a meeting with a presentation of greater significance in either medicine or natural science."* As a scientist of considerable international standing, this statement considerably amplified the acceptance and impact of Roentgen's discovery.

Although Roentgen deserves full credit for his observations, his invention could not have taken place without the contributions of many scientists who had toiled in this area before him. The evolution of the identification of X-rays involved an appreciation of the concept of radiant matter (Helmholtz, Sir Joseph John Thompson and Sir Olivier Lodge), elucidation of magnetism, electricity (Faraday), batteries, electromagnetic induction (Maxwell and Hertz), and the development of cathode rays (Crookes) and vacuum tubes.

Early Attempts

Attempts to study the gastrointestinal tract using radiological techniques began soon after Roentgen's report of X-rays. On March 26, 1896, Wolf Becher undertook the first experimental

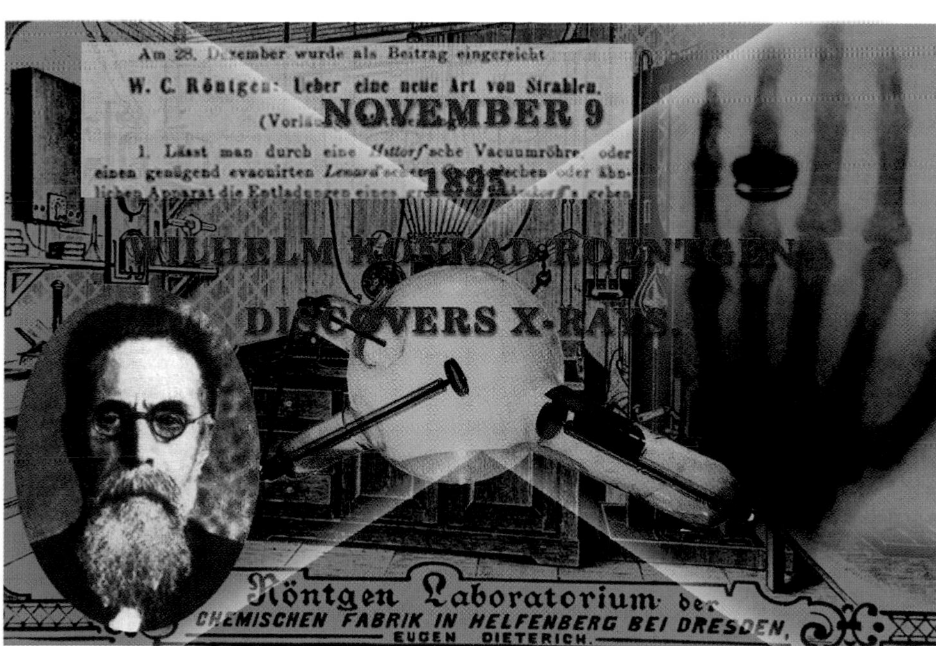

Wilhelm Konrad Roentgen was born in Lennep in the Rhineland, the child of a German father and a Dutch mother. Educated at Utrecht, he was regarded as a dreamer, indifferent student, and difficult child. Having studied with Clausius at Zurich he subsequently became an assistant to A. Kundt and accompanied him to Wurzburg. In 1895, while experimenting with a Crookes tube, he produced strange and accidental shadows of solid objects. His subsequent demonstration that this novel radiation could pass through most substances and provide the shadows of internal organs and bones was first communicated to the Wurzburg Society on December 28, 1895. Roentgen modestly called the phenomena X-rays. However, upon the motion of Kolliker, who predicted their usefulness in medicine and surgery, they were subsequently named Roentgen rays. In 1901 Roentgen was awarded the Nobel Prize.

In 1600, William Gilbert, physician to Elizabeth I of England, published "De Magneti" (bottom left) and in so doing, provided the foundation for the subsequent investigations of the phenomena of magnetism that led to the concept of electricity. The extrapolation of these observations culminated in the discovery of X-rays. James Clerk Maxwell Atkins (bottom right), a Scottish physicist had developed the electro-magnetic theory of light. Von Helmholtz (top left) confirmed this concept and proposed to his student Hertz (top right), a cousin of Sir Arthur Hurst [sic Hertz], the eminent British gastroenterologist that he further investigate the phenomenon. By use of a receiving resonator Hertz substantiated these theoretical proposals. This work was further extrapolated by Philip Lenard, a pupil of Hertz and led to the construction of a vacuum tube with a thin aluminum window in the glass wall of the bulb at the point where the cathode rays were focused. The evacuated Lenard tube (center) was utilized to provide the first quantitative measurements of cathode rays.

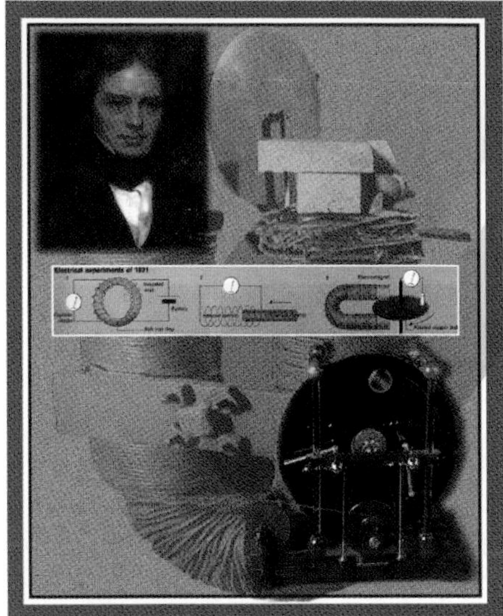

In 1831 the British scientist, Michael Faraday (top left), elucidated the relationship between electrical and magnetic forces. His work moved beyond the electrostatic production of electricity (right, top and bottom) and led to the identification of the principle of electromagnetic induction and the construction of induction coils and transformers (center and left) adequate to produce electrical currents of high voltage. Heinrich Daniel Ruhmkorff, a Parisian mechanic, utilized Faraday's electro-induction principles to construct an improved induction coil (Ruhmkorff coil) that W. Roentgen utilized to produce X-rays. An additional contribution of Faraday was his recognition that a differential electrical potential applied to two points in an electrolyte solution resulted in negatively charged particles moving towards the positive terminal while positively charged ones traveled towards the negative terminal. He designated these charged particles as ions (derived from the Greek for travelers), or carriers of electricity and was the first to use the words anode and cathode.

radiological gastrointestinal study in white mice and guinea pigs and successfully opacified the stomach and a portion of the intestine by the injection of *"liquor plumbi subacetic"*. He noted *"the property of such solutions (salts of various metals) in being impermeable to X-rays offers a means of obtaining photographs of the internal hollow organs of animals through the use of Roentgen's procedures. One need only to introduce into a hollow organ the solution of the metal salt in such an amount that the walls of the organ are somewhat distended."*

One month later (April 30, 1896) Carl Wegele proposed the introduction of a thin metal wire into the lumen of a long pliable Boas gastric tube to determine radiographically the position of the tube as it bent around the greater curvature and moved towards the pylorus. E. Lindemann on April 22, 1897 published the first radiographic image of the stomach using this technique and stated with some degree of pride *"we have here an adequately reliable method for determining the boundaries of the stomach."* This was deemed of considerable importance clinically since *"ptosis"* was regarded as a major cause of abdominal disorders. A variety of techniques were thereafter developed to demonstrate the inferior gastric margin, and Max Einhorn attempted to trans-illuminate the stomach after introducing a capsule containing a small amount of radium bromide. In June of 1896, John C. Hemmeter introduced the use of an intragastric deglutible elastic rubber bag that after swallowing, could be filled with the plumbic acetate solution until the entire gastric cavity was occupied and thus be definable by X-rays. The site of the stomach in relation to the umbilicus could then be noted and the plumbic acetate thereafter removed using a stomach pump. Unfortunately, the plumbic acetate was noted by Hemmeter to have a corrosive effect on the bag and he subsequently suggested that a solution of bone powder might be *"a proper substance with which to distend the intragastric bag"* before obtaining a radiogram.

Am 28. December wurde als Beitrag eingereicht

W. C. Röntgen: Ueber eine neue Art von Strahlen.

(Vorläufige Mittheilung.)

In 1896, W. Roentgen (left) discovered X-rays. Their application to the study of the gastrointestinal tract by individuals such as G. Holznecht (right) enabled the used of bismuth and barium to define the mucosal surface of the upper gastrointestinal tract.

In September of 1896, Straus used gelatin capsules containing a radio-opaque material to identify the greater curvature of the stomach by means of a fluoroscope. A year later in 1897 (April 20), Rumpel was the first to obtain radiographs of a segment of the gastrointestinal tract opacified by a bismuth solution. He utilized a 5% suspension of bismuth subnitrate (300 ml) which was introduced via tube into a dilated esophagus and then observed fluoroscopically. Although it had been inadvertently noted that the bismuth compounds widely employed in the treatment of dyspepsia in the late nineteenth century were of use as a contrast medium, little had been done to capitalize on the observation. In 1897 George Pfahler noted the presence of bismuth in the stomach on a photographic plate but sadly failed to appreciate the potential significance of his observation. *"I did not follow through and failed to show the value of bismuth meals in the study of the gastrointestinal tract."* Charles Leonard in 1897 was more ingenious and washed out a patient's stomach prior to instilling an ounce of bismuth, whereupon he observed the condition of gastroptosis. Leonard pursued these observations and at a scientific meeting later that year reported, *"by filling the organ with opaque liquids, as emulsions of bismuth in the stomach... their exact area can be readily determined."* David Walsh, who subsequently became the first honorary secretary of the Roentgen Society of London, had also noted in 1897 that after a patient had taken some bismuth *"a faint outline of the stomach and colon with some coils of small intestine and sigmoid flexure were visible."*

Hermann Rieder (1858-1932) used bismuth compounds initially mixed in food or water to produce radiographs of the digestive tract. The so-called "Rieder meal" became the definitive study for the assessment of the stomach and even the small intestine. Rieder developed the technique of "bio-roentgenography" which was defined as "the preparation of a sufficient number of successive roentgenograms of an organ *in situ* during the course of a single cycle of its characteristic movements."

Walter Bradford Cannon (1871-1945) utilized bread soaked in warm water and mixed with bismuth subnitrate to study peristalsis in the stomach of a cat and produced the first manuscript on the subject, "The Movements of the Stomach Studied by Means of Roentgen Rays" in the American Journal of Physiology, 1898. The illustrations for his classic paper were obtained by placing toilet paper over the fluoroscopic screen and tracing an outline of the stomach at specific time-points after the bismuth meal (background).

By 1901 Francis H. Williams had already published a text which defined the conditions necessary for adequate radiological examination of the gastrointestinal tract and noted the opportunities that radiology provided in the diagnosis of gastrointestinal disease. Indeed, given the potential dangers of endoscopy and the limited viewing capacity of the early instruments, radiological diagnosis was regarded as by far the most promising technique.

By 1904-05 Hermann Rieder had further increased the diagnostic power of digestive tract X-rays by development of a pure thick paste of bismuth – the "Rieder meal". Its widespread use allowed for a sharp delineation of the stomach, small intestine, and even part of the colon. His subsequent introduction of "*Bio-Roentgenography*", whereby a number of successive roentgenograms of an organ were acquired during the course of a single test, allowed for an evaluation of its characteristic movements.

Holzknecht and the evolution of contrast

Since Roentgen had discovered simultaneously both the fluorescent and the photographic effect of X-rays a major controversy in gastrointestinal radiology revolved around the respective gastrointestinal merits of the two techniques. Although there was considerable support for the Rieder technique of bio-roentgenography, Guido Holzknecht of Vienna became an important proponent of fluoroscopy. To his mind it proved *"a virtually endless number of pictures, all of equally good quality, which are very definitely superior to the indistinct... distorted radiographs."*

The popularity of fluoroscopy was further supported by the evolving school of "*symptom complexes*", also known as the Continental School. This method

H. Gunther and the first published barium study of the stomach and proximal small intestine (1910).

The application of X-rays to the study of the gastrointestinal tract by individuals such as G. Holzknecht (inset) enabled the use of bismuth and barium to define the mucosal surface of the upper gastrointestinal tract.

The radiology examining room at a Philadelphia hospital (c. 1920). Fluoroscopy was considered the most useful study but the dangers of excessive radiation exposure were initially unrecognized.

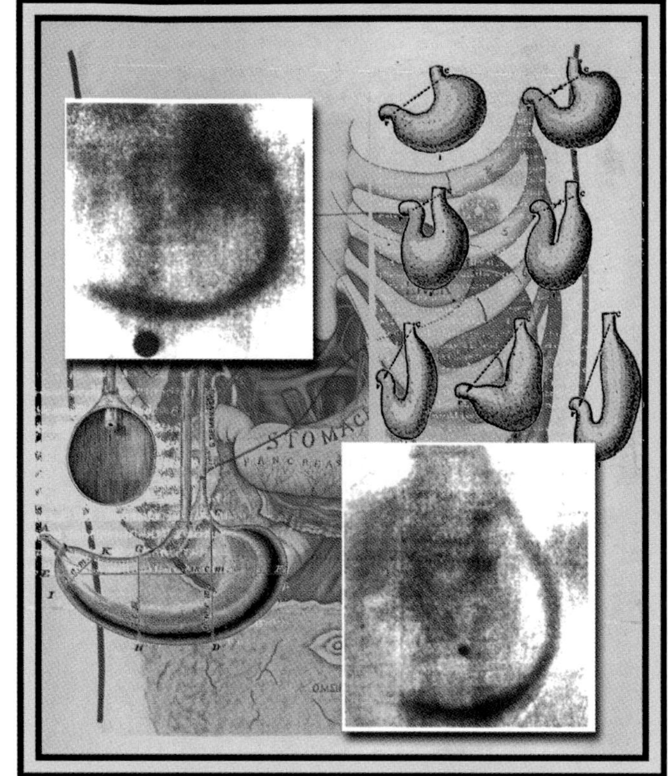

At the end of the 19th century a diagnosis of visceroptosis was considered of considerable relevance in the elucidation of gastrointestinal symptomatology. The introduction of X-rays considerably facilitated the diagnosis of gastroptosis (Glenard's disease), an abnormally low position of the stomach. The opaque gastric tube is evident, outlining the margin of the greater curvature of the stomach and lying above a coin placed over the umbilicus (top left). In a second patient (bottom right) the position of the greater curvature lies 5 cm below the umbilical coin indicating "a sinking of the stomach due to atony without dilatation."

of indirect diagnosis stressed the need for palpation of the opacified areas under fluoroscopic control. To facilitate this procedure, Holzknecht had developed a wooden spoon, a *"distincter"*, that enabled him to exert pressure on the abdomen without actually placing his hand in the irradiated field. A wide variety of the *symptom complexes* described combined, in their definition, the indirect signs of gastrointestinal disease and the appearances perceived on fluoroscopic observation, and the discipline became an important part of the gastrointestinal diagnostic process. To a large extent the popularity of fluoroscopy was dictated by the inadequate power sources and sub-optimal intensifying screens available for abdominal radiographic pictures. Such, however, was the advance of technology that by 1903, Rieder and his colleagues could rely on a series of photographic plates each taken with the diminished exposure time of 15 to 20 seconds. Thus, controversy continued to rage between the proponents of the various techniques. Although Rieder, as the protagonist of roentgenography, survived unscathed, Holzknecht, a protagonist of roentgenoscopy (fluoroscopy), subsequently died of roentgen-induced cancer.

Cannon and motility

The contributions of W.B. Cannon to gastrointestinal radiology began as a first-year student at Harvard, when he and a follow student, Albert Moser, studied the swallowing mechanism of animals after ingestion of a radio-opaque substance. They experimented with both dogs and geese and, at the meeting of the American Physiological Society in Boston of December 29, 1896, demonstrated the phenomenon of deglutition in a goose swallowing capsules containing bismuth subnitrate. Having studied the esophagus, they thereafter turned their attention to the activity of the stomach. By April 1897, Cannon had devised an experimental technique whereby bread soaked in warm water and mixed with bismuth subnitrate could be used to evaluate the gastric peristalsis of a cat.

The subsequent extrapolation of this work to humans laid the basis for the recognition that central mechanisms, particularly emotion, and the consideration of various kinds of foods prior to eating vigorously altered the nature of gastric activity.

As has been noted, the early radiological examinations were uncomfortable for both the patient and the radiologist involved, being laborious, tiring, and not without some personal danger. One of the most unpleasant techniques developed for the examination of the stomach was Turcke's *"gyromele"*, an instrument composed of a mop at the end of a long cable rotated by an old-fashioned eggbeater mechanism. In many respects it was not dissimilar to the *"magenkratzer"* used by Heister for "gastric cleaning". A bismuth salt emulsion was initially applied to the mop prior to introduction into the stomach, thereby coating both it and the esophagus with radio-opaque material. By 1916, the methodology still left much to be desired and Hurst noted that *"until recently the esophagus was outlined for this (contrast) examination by the insertion into its lumen of sounds, bougies, rubber tubes filled with shot, chains, by inflation of rubber bags filled with bismuth..."*. Although bismuth subnitrite was widely used in the early days of gastrointestinal radiology, it was soon apparent that it was sub-optimal, since it was reduced to a highly toxic nitrate compound in the stomach and bismuth salts were expensive. Paradoxically,

KLINIK

DER

LEBERKRANKHEITEN

VON

DR. FRIED. THEOD. FRERICHS,

1858.

The ability to visualize the interior of the abdomen using X-rays and radio-opaque substances allowed for the identification of the precise site of the viscera. Alterations in position of intra-abdominal organs were presumed to result in symptoms and even disease. Frerichs in his textbook on liver diseases noted that dramatic deformations of the liver could be accounted for by the extreme pressure placed upon the organ by the use of fashionable whalebone corsets.

Russell D. Carman (1875-1926) was the head of the section of Roentgenology at the Mayo Clinic and a powerful proponent of the use of fluoroscopy for diagnosis. He and Lewis Gregory Cole of New York, an advocate of plate radiography, argued bitterly as to the relative merits of the two techniques. Cole utilized between 50 or 60 plates in a technique that he termed "serial radiography". Carman, on the other hand, preferred to use fluoroscopy, which he enhanced by direct palpation of the abdomen during the examination. In a dramatic and tragic situation, Carman, while demonstrating the technique of gastric fluoroscopy using himself as the subject, was noted by the students to have a seriously distorted gastric shadow on the fluoroscopic screen. When his dismayed associates laid the final films on his desk, Carman pronounced the diagnosis as he had done many of thousands of times before: "Cancer of the stomach. Inoperable!"

although the neutralization of gastric hydrochloric acid by bismuth carbonate was considered unacceptable and a disadvantage, it may well have conferred considerable therapeutic benefit to patients with peptic ulcer disease. Substitutes for bismuth included the insoluble salts of heavy metals, especially those of iron, the thorium compounds, and zirconium oxide. Unfortunately, the majority of these agents were either expensive or tasted so appalling that patients were unable to tolerate them. In 1910, Carl Bachem and H. Gunther proposed the use of "barium sulfate" administered in the form of a chocolate drink. Since barium sulfate was tasteless and odorless, they noted that when mixed with some sort of food *"it is quite agreeable to take."* In the United States, the advent of the First World War and the lack of adequate sources of bismuth, to a certain extent prompted the subsequent shift from bismuth to barium as the agent of choice.

Interpretation

Despite substantial progress in the diagnosis of gastrointestinal disease using Roentgen technology, many physicians and surgeons (in particular) remained skeptical. At the 1914 combined meeting of the Gastrointestinal Society and the Medical Section of the American Medical Association, it was asserted the early diagnosis of gastric ulcer by X-rays was impossible.

Surgeons stated that a positive X-ray diagnosis of a gastric ulcer could be relied upon but doubted whether a negative diagnosis could be regarded as certain. As a result, the surgical policy was to ignore negative X-ray findings if the clinical symptoms suggested the presence of an ulcer. The controversy persisted until Louis Gregory Cole of New York agreed to evaluate the patients of a New York City surgeon, George Emerson Brewer. Of the 27 patients who underwent radiographic examination after referral to Cole, the negative diagnosis was a 100% correct and in a further 11 cases, a positive diagnosis was correct in 9. Cole declined to comment on 5 cases because of incomplete observation and thus produced a correct interpretation in 89% of cases.

Cole subsequently became embroiled in a major dispute with Russell D. Carman, head of the Section of Roentgenology at the Mayo Clinic, who supported the use of fluoroscopy. The prodigious volume of the Mayo Clinic provided Carman the opportunity to perform more than 50,000 X-ray examinations annually and he affirmed with confidence that the combination of fluoroscopy and direct palpation of the abdomen was superior to multiple individual static Roentgen plates.

Although Cole and Carman hotly debated the issue of whether serial radiography as practiced by Cole was more effective than fluoroscopy as practiced by Carman, no final conclusion as to this issue was reached. Time has demonstrated the position of both Carman and Cole to have their respective merits since adequate radiological evaluation of the gastric duodenal area requires both a series of films and thorough fluoroscopic examination.

Contrast radiology of the upper gastrointestinal tract proved to be of considerable benefit in allowing symptoms of dyspepsia to be directly linked to peptic ulceration. Since little adequate medical therapy existed prior to the introduction of the histamine 2 receptor antagonist class of drugs, many patients underwent gastrectomy (background – Billroth's first resection) to obviate bleeding, perforation or intractable pain. Endoscopic evaluation of peptic ulcer disease considerably advanced the ability of physicians to determine the efficacy of treatment and even manage bleeding.

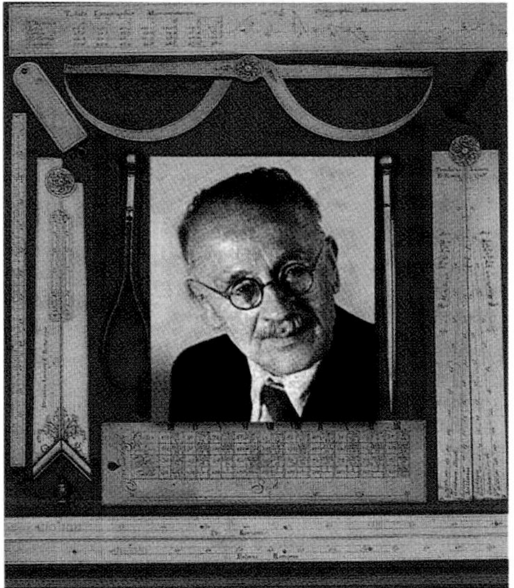

J.H. Radon, the Austrian mathematician, whose original work provided the scientific basis for the development of computerized axial tomographic scanning.

Computerized Axial Tomographic Scanning (CT Scan)

In 1972 Godfrey Hounsfield of EMI Limited in London, introduced the concept of computer tomography. The principle of CT had initially evolved from the work of an Austrian mathematician, J.H. Radon , while working on equations relating to the nature of gravitational fields. In 1917 he demonstrated that the image of a three-dimensional object could be reconstructed from an infinite number of two-dimensional projections of the object. The derivations of Radon were extrapolated during the 1950s and '60s, and the mathematical calculations modified for a finite number of projections and applied to several imaging problems including electron microscopy, holographic interferometry, and solar astronomy. In 1961, Oldendorf examined a similar concept when he explored the potential of producing images from the transmission projections produced with gamma rays from an iodine 131 source. The scintillation detector that he constructed measured the intensity of radiation transmitted through an object rotating between the source and the detector.

In a completely separate venue, Alan M. Cormack of Cape Town, South Africa, in the early 1950s had become interested in the changes in radiation therapy dose distribution caused by inhomogeneous regions of the body. Recognizing that such changes could be predicted if the distribution of the attenuation coefficients displayed as gray scale image were known across the body region of interest, he sought to further explore this concept. Thus in 1964, Cormack was able to publish his first experimental results in which the attenuation coefficients of a slice of an object were reconstructed from a series of angular projections obtained at 7.5° increments. Although his publication received little attention, the combination of his observations and Hounsfield's work would result in the award of the 1979 Nobel Prize for medicine for both Cormack and Hounsfield.

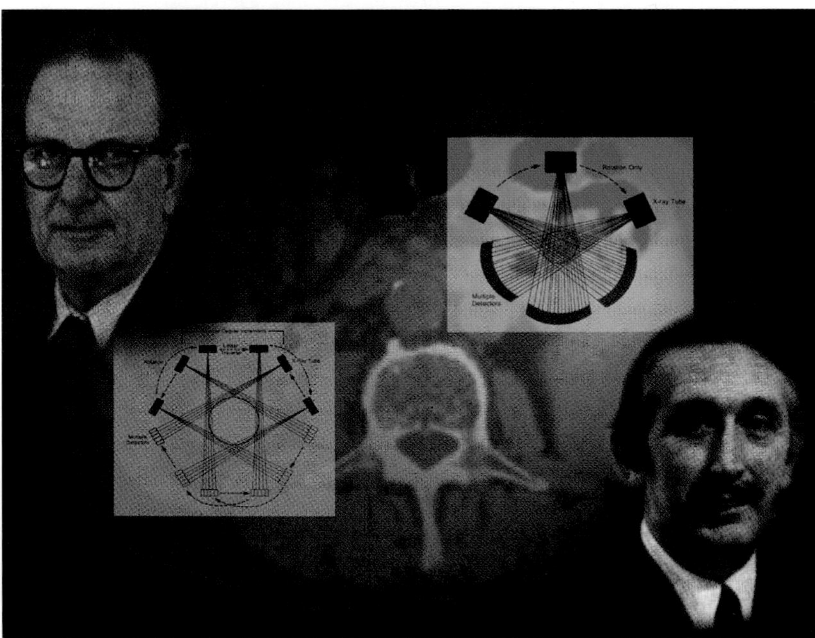

Alan M. Cormack (left) of Cape Town had directed his attention to the changes in radiation therapy dose distribution caused by differences in the "density" of different areas of the body. The exploration of this concept led to the publication of the methodology to determine the attenuation coefficients of a "slice" of an object that could be derived by reconstruction of the images of a series of angular projections. ("Representation of a function by its line integrals with some radiological applications", J. App Phys 1964). Godfrey Hounsfield (right) recognized the implications of the work of Alan Cormack. Aware of the limitations of conventional X-rays, he established the methodology for evaluating the attenuation of X-ray beams and developed a technique that enabled a computerized tomographic reconstruction of a particular area. The combination of this work, with that of G. Hounsfield, resulted in their being awarded the Nobel Prize for medicine in 1979.

In his Nobel Prize lecture, Hounsfield noted the capabilities of conventional X-ray methods displayed three main limitations. *"First, it is impossible to display within the framework of a two-dimensional X-ray picture all the information contained in the three-dimensional scene under view. Thus, objects situated in depth, that is the third dimension, superimpose, causing confusion to the viewer. Secondly, conventional X-ray cannot distinguish between soft tissue and thirdly, when conventional X-ray methods are used, it is not possible to measure, in a quantitative way, the separate densities of the individual substances through which the X-ray rays pass. Computer tomography, on the other hand, measures the attenuation of X-ray beams passing through sections of the body from hundreds of angles and then, from evidence of these measurements, a computer is able to reconstruct pictures of the body's interior... The technique's most important feature is its enormously greater sensivity."*

The first clinical prototype of the EMI head scanner was installed in the Atkinson Morley Hospital in London in early 1972 and within a year, units were available in North America. Although the EMI scanner was originally designed primarily for the brain, a United States dentist, Ledley, was intrigued with the possibility of applying the technique to other regions of the body and obtained support to construct the first whole body scanner. This clinical unit was called the ACTA scanner and installed at the University of Minnesota in 1973. Unfortunately, anatomical motion remained a significant problem in applications of the scanner to regions other than the head and the extremities. Subsequent to the first generation CT scanners, major technical advances have resulted in increasing speed of scanning and imagery construction. For the most part, this has been accomplished by simultaneously acquiring data through more extensive detector arrays. Thus, second generation scanners used a complicated translator to obviate mechanical motion and a fan beam with multiple angles, allowing for a single translation across a patient. The development of third and fourth-generation systems allowed for the use of rotation only and limited the necessity of back-and-forth translation whilst facilitating a continuous smooth motion. In fourth-generation systems, the doctor array was modified into a stationary circle structure and only the X-ray tube rotated through a circle within the array. As a result of such modifications and the use of 1,200 to 2,400 detectors, individual slices could be obtained in 2 to 4 seconds. Subsequent variations on the fourth-generation design included the ultra-fast CT scanners used for imaging the heart.

Nuclear Magnetic Resonance

The birth of the twentieth century resulted in the discovery of X-rays by Wilhelm Konrad Rontgen, and the quantum theory. Peter Zeman (1865-1943), a Dutch physicist, had noted that magnetic fields effected atomic phenomena and demonstrated that the optical spectrum of the sodium atom could be effected by placing the atom in a strong magnetic field. The implication that atoms possessed a magnetic field required that the quantum theory be adapted to describe the behavior of an atomic nucleus immersed in a strong magnetic field. Otto Stern (1888-1969) and Walter Gerlock (1889-1979) demonstrated in 1924 the existence of the intrinsic magnetic moment of the atoms and subsequent research by Isadore Rabi

(1898-1988) led to the first direct measurement of nuclear magnetic resonance (NMR) in atomic and molecular beams in 1938. As a result of their contributions, the Nobel Prize for physics was awarded to Stern in 1943 and to Rabi in 1944 for their work on atomic and nuclear magnetic phenomena. In 1946, two separate research teams first reported NMR in solid material. The first comprised Felix Bloch, Wilfred Hanson, and Martin Packard and the second, Edward Purcel, Henry Torry, and Robert Pound. Bloch and Purcel were subsequently awarded the Nobel Prize for physics in 1952 and the basis of their work allowed for the evolution of the discipline as a substantial diagnostic technique.

The Bloch equations became the basis of all analyses of NMR experiments and provided the rationale for the development of substances that could be used as contrast agents for NMR. The subsequent extrapolation of the work of Bloch by Nicholas Bloembergen, a Dutch physicist, working with Purcel in Boston, allowed for the development of the theory of nuclear magnetic relaxation. Bloembergen subsequently became a recipient in 1981 of the Nobel Prize for physics for his contributions to the development of the laser spectroscopy. The need to sustain the NMR signal over extended periods of time for the measurements of NMR phenomena resulted in Irwin Hahn developing the spin echo in 1950, and this technique was subsequently improved in 1954 by Herman Carr and Edward Purcel. Additional advances allowed for the quantitation of water content and the NMR signatures "T1 and T2." These signatures were later applied to the identification of free and bound water in living cells and the identification of lipid signals.

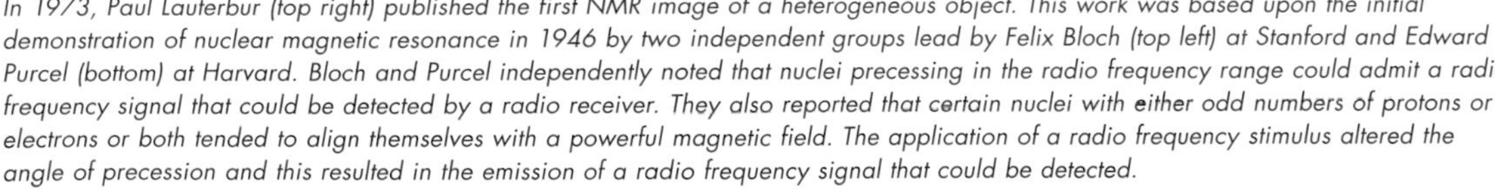

In 1973, Paul Lauterbur (top right) published the first NMR image of a heterogeneous object. This work was based upon the initial demonstration of nuclear magnetic resonance in 1946 by two independent groups lead by Felix Bloch (top left) at Stanford and Edward Purcel (bottom) at Harvard. Bloch and Purcel independently noted that nuclei precessing in the radio frequency range could admit a radio frequency signal that could be detected by a radio receiver. They also reported that certain nuclei with either odd numbers of protons or electrons or both tended to align themselves with a powerful magnetic field. The application of a radio frequency stimulus altered the angle of precession and this resulted in the emission of a radio frequency signal that could be detected.

Paul Lauterbur amplified the work of Leon Saryn in compiling the NMR spectra of different body tissues. Having noted that even normal tissues differed markedly amongst themselves in NMR relaxation times, he proposed that there might be some way to non-invasively demonstrate such quantitative differences within the body. With this goal in mind, Lauterbur enunciated a principle upon which a technique might be based that coded spatial coordinates by known magnetic shapes and derived this information to generate a true image. Although this manuscript was initially rejected by *Nature* since it was *"not of sufficiently wide significance for inclusion"*, (*Nature* had also rejected the first paper describing the Krebs cycle!) Lauterber reconfigured the manuscript and on March 16, 1973, it was finally published. Although he originally derived the name Zeugmatography from the Greek word zeugma (meaning the result of joining together), this term failed to win acceptance and NMR remained the technical term.

In 1971, Raymond Damadian introduced the concept of using the NMR technique for detecting neoplasms by demonstrating that the relaxation constants (T1 and T2) of water (that is hydrogen) were significantly longer in malignant tumors than in corresponding tissues. Damadian was prescient in suggesting that NMR should be present in operating rooms as an aid to identify malignant disease in excised tissues! In 1974, the first image of a biological specimen (a mouse) was obtained at the University of Aberdeen in Scotland. The mouse's organs were visible, and the darkest areas in the image were corresponding to edema around a neck fracture. In 1976, Damadian published the first NMR image of a live animal with a tumor surgically implanted in the anterior chest wall and, in 1977, obtained the first human image of a cross-sectional visualization through the chest at the level of the eighth thoracic vertebrae.

Since the field-focusing NMR technique of Damadian was time-consuming, Mansfield and his associates at the University of Nottingham in England developed a procedure to sample a region of one line (rather than a point) at a time. Using this procedure, a plane region of tissue could be sampled by incrementally moving the data acquisition line and in 1976, Mansfield was able to publish images of a finger and subsequently, in 1978, the abdomen itself. The main problem, however, was the existence of motion artifact, but in 1980, Moore and Henshaw, employing a new technique with alternating magnetic radiants, produced substantially more useful pictures of the forearm and the human brain. Although MR imaging was initially very prolonged and required the patient to be motionless for up to an hour, the development of fast-imaging techniques facilitated rapid examination and allowed studies of the chest and abdomen during both respiration and in the presence of peristalsis. Fast-imaging techniques incorporated small flip angles and

R. Damadian designed the first NMR scanner used to study humans in 1988 at the University of Aberdeen. (Left to right: R. Damadian, L. Minkhoff, and M. Goldsmith)

The first image produced by the Aberdeen prototype NMR device in 1979 was a cross section through the chest (bottom right). Although, initially NMR appeared particularly useful in demonstrating intracranial pathology (top right) its utility in the diagnosis of abdominal conditions became apparent.

Ernest Rutherford (top center), the fourth of twelve children from Nelson on South Island, New Zealand, evolved into one of the great physicists of the century. He named his only daughter Ione as a reflection of his interest in the ionic components of gases. The modest laboratory of Rutherford at Cambridge (below) was the site where Hans Geiger (his research assistant) developed a method to count radioactive particles and by 1911 Rutherford had acquired enough information to develop his initial theory of atomic structure known as the Rutherford atomic model.

gradient-focusing to produce images in less than one second. In addition, MR angiograms became available, and enabled the delineation of vascular structures and assessment of perfusion. Its further development in the last quarter of the twentieth century has greatly facilitated the study of intra-abdominal disease process.

Isotopic Imaging

Prior to 1932, the use of radioactive materials in many biological studies was limited, since the only radioactive isotopes available with naturally-occurring forms were present in only minute quantities in biological systems. The demonstration in 1919 at the Cavendish laboratories in Cambridge, England, by Ernest Rutherford, of the existence of positively charged nuclear particles known as protons was to inaugurate a new era. By 1931, Ernest O. Lawrence at the University of California Radiation Laboratory developed the first cyclotron and, by 1933, was able to effect nuclear transformations and accelerate protons, deuterons, and alpha particles. This work was amplified by the announcement on Feb 10, 1934, by Irene Curie and her husband Fréderic Joliot, who demonstrated that alpha particles' bombardment of certain elements produced new radioelements "radioactive isotopes". George Hevesy, a Hungarian physicist working in Denmark played a major role in developing the use of artificially-produced isotopes in diagnostic medicine. By 1936, Hevesy had demonstrated that certain isotopes exhibited selective localization in particular tissues, and could thus be utilized to study flow and metabolic properties in specific organs. A second major breakthrough was the subsequent development of the scintillation scanner (scintiscan) by Benedict Cassen in 1949 at the University of California Los Angeles. This technique enabled the identification of SPECT scanning. The subsequent use of a variety of isotopes to identify the thyroid, spleen, kidney, and pancreas proved to be of considerable medical relevance. The linkage of isotopes to white blood cells by M. Thakur enabled the identification of infection and abscess sites. Further modification of techniques of isotope production and the labeling of metabolic substrates such as glucose, facilitated the development of PET scanning. Thus, by the early 1980s a wide variety of isotopes tagged to different carriers had been utilized to identify lesions, bleeding, blood flow, diffusion, or metabolic activity.

By the mid 1980s, the identification of neoplastic lesions had evolved from shadows on plain radiography plates to more specific identification using CAT scan and NMR technology. Additional imaging modalities available included angiography and ultrasound, but all such techniques basically used contrast agents or alterations in density to differentiate between healthy and diseased tissue. The demonstration of the over-expression of the somatostatin type 2 receptor (SSTR2) on neuro-endocrine tumors (NETs) of the gut and pancreas facilitated the development of an imaging technique that identified tumors based upon the expression of receptor density as opposed to tumor size of mass. Using an isotope (Indium 111) linked to a somatostatin congener, E. Krenning and his colleagues in Rotterdam were able to identify a wide variety of gut NETs (both primaries and metastases), including carcinoids, gastrinomas, glucagonomas and vipomas by gamma camera scanning. In a further extrapolation of this technique the usage of higher dosages of the isotope and even other isotopes, including yttrium and lutetium, was extrapolated to enable the delivery of therapeutic levels of radiation to the lesion.

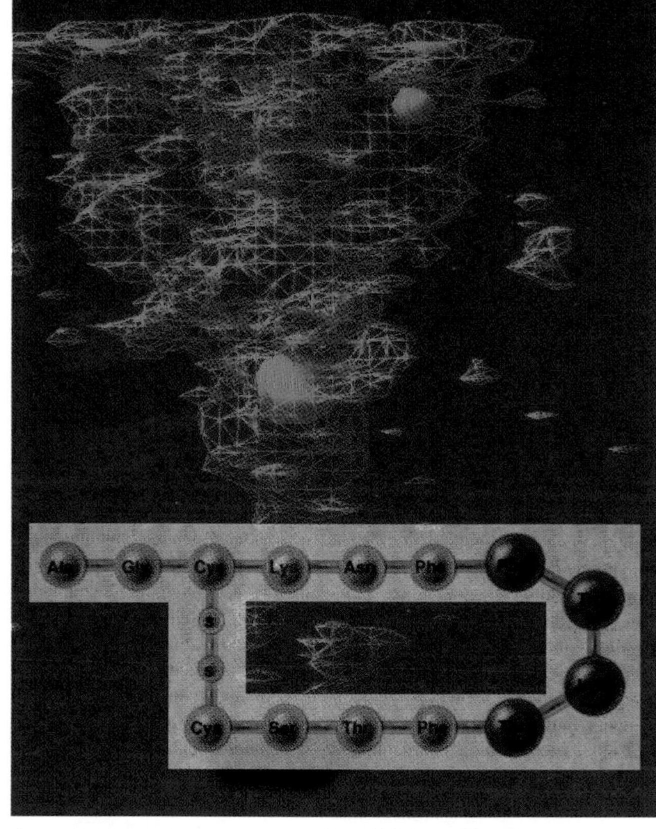

A somatostatin receptor scintigram. Indium^{111} labeling of the somatostatin congener (Octreotide) enabled identification of lesions expressing somatostatin subtype 2 receptors. The high specificity and sensitivity of this diagnostic test was such that it challenged the use of CT scan in the diagnosis of gastrointestinal neuroendocrine tumors.

Endoscopy

Early attempts to penetrate the darkness had not moved far beyond the pharynx or the anus and rectum. Although the use of specula was well known both by the early Romans and Egyptians, the limitations imposed by inadequate lighting or instrument design rendered visibility more than a hand's breadth or a candle-length within the natural orifices of the body impossible.

The introduction of blind tubes and probes of varying designs and construct provided little diagnostic benefit, although they were of some marginal therapeutic utility in displacing obstructing foreign bodies. In the early nineteenth century, the use of gas lamps and candles with reflectors by P. Bozzini (1773-1809) of Frankfurt, P. Segalas (1792-1875) of Paris, as well as F. Cruise of Dublin and J. Fisher of Boston, allowed for some egress into both the upper and lower gastrointestinal tract. In particular, the use of such devices to visualize the urethra and bladder, as well as the rectum and vagina, provided some measure of diagnostic information as well as the opportunity for therapy such as lithotripsy and cautery. Fortunately, by the mid-nineteenth century, engineering techniques had improved to the point that longer tubes capable of direct passage into the esophagus and stomach were available, although their rigidity and the lack of appropriate lens and lighting systems, rendered their utility both limited and their usage somewhat dangerous.

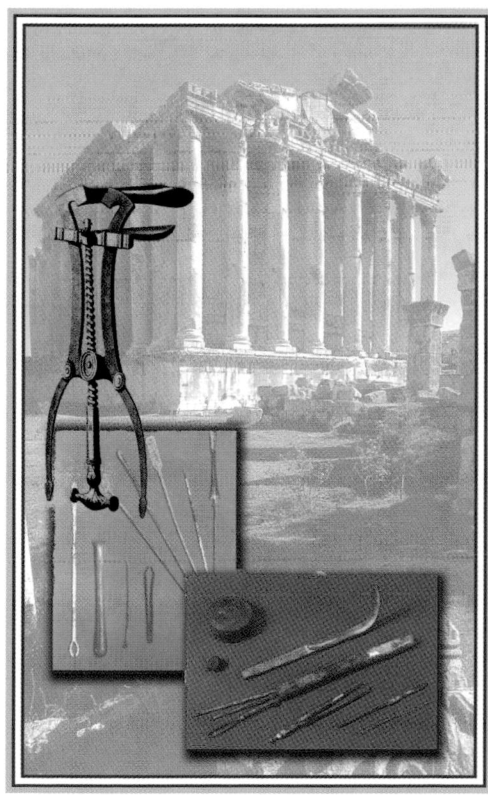

Examples of ancient Roman surgical implements (wound probes and lancets) as well as a speculum from the ruins of Pompeii. Most medical thought was originally of Greek and Alexandrian origin since the Romans thought little of physicians. Ideologues such as Pliny and Cicero considered medical art to be little more than "Greek puffery" practiced by foreigners and rogues more skilled in the art of poisons than cures. The assimilation of Greece by the Roman Empire led to the slow acceptance of Grecian medical ideology. The speculum (top left) recovered from the House of the Surgeon in Pompeii (c. A.D. 62-79) attests to the early fascination and skill in seeking to visualize the interior of the body. Its design would remain almost unchanged until the early 20th century.

Credit must be given to Philip Bozzini of Frankfurt for first using a lighting device to look within the bladder, and to A. Kussmaul (1822-1902) of Freiburg for attempting to visualize the esophagus and the stomach. Subsequent extrapolations of urological instruments developed by A. Desormeux (1830-1894) and Segalas of Paris, enabled M. Nitze (1848-1906) and thereafter, von Mikulicz of Vienna, to progress in the exploration of the bladder, esophagus and stomach respectively. The ensuing productive relationship that developed among engineers, skilled optical instrument-makers, and physicians, facilitated collaborations that led to the emergence of the early science of endoscopy. Despite frustration at the problems posed by rigidity, inadequate lighting, and poor lens systems, it was apparent to the physicians of the turn of the of the twentieth century that exploration of both the lumen of the gastrointestinal tract and the interior of the peritoneal cavity represented critical goals. Such endeavors were well-supported by the contributions of the optical, scientific and engineering schools of Vienna, Paris, and Berlin, while the introduction of appropriate illumination by T. Edison of New Jersey greatly facilitated the internal exploration of the gastrointestinal tract.

The first successful endoscope (lichtleiter) was designed by Philip Bozzini (1773-1809) (top right) of Frankfurt in 1805. The ingenuity and skill of the design are reflected in the detailed structural design blueprints and provide a thought-provoking legacy to the subsequent evolution of endoscopic design. The original lichtleiter (bottom right) is preserved in the American College of Surgeons Museum in Chicago. A. Kussmaul (bottom left) was the first physician to attempt to use a rigid scope to visualize the stomach.

Roentgen in Wurzberg developed the X-ray machines that provided internal vision of not only body cavities but also, with the advent of bismuth and barium, the very interstices of the gut lumen itself. Similarly, the early contributions of von Mikulicz, J. Leiter (1830-1892), and Nitze in Vienna, in the development of rigid endoscopes, were amplified and extended by T. Rosenheim (1860-1910), W. Sternberg, G. Wolf (1873-1938) and finally

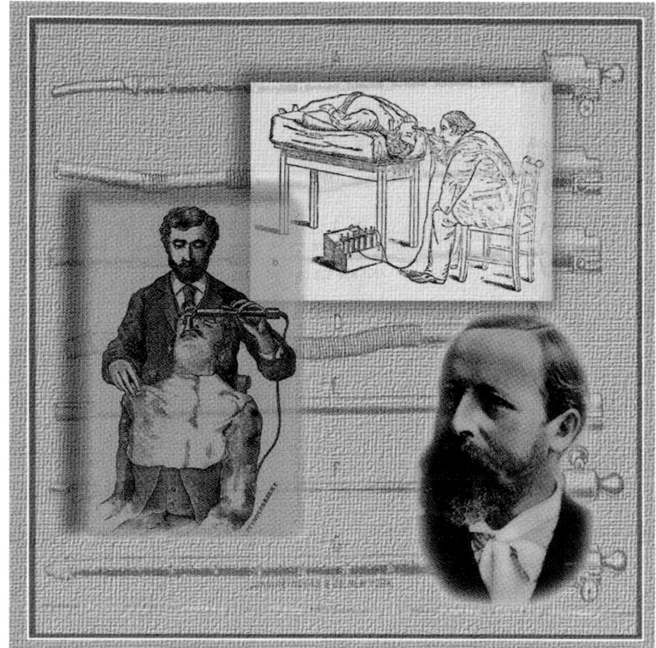

J. von Mikulicz, although a surgeon, was one of the first physicians to recognize the utility of endoscopy and played an important role in the development of both a functional esophagoscope and gastroscope.

Antoine Desormeux (1815-1881) of Paris (top) was responsible for the introduction of the first effective endoscope (bottom) and his painted illustrations (right) provided critical and novel documentation of pathology. Prior to his contributions the future of endoscopy appeared to have been relegated to obscurity by the use of clumsy and unacceptable instruments.

Rudolf Schindler (1888-1968), who not only introduced novel lens systems but for the most part overcame the problems of flexibility and illumination. The subsequent application of H. Hopkins (1918-1994) and N. Kapany's work on optics, and the development by Basil Hirschowitz and Larry Curtiss of the flexible fiber optic endoscope, enabled the design of instruments that would allow the illumination and vision of the farthest reaches of the bowel.

Thus, in almost a century, the physician had moved from the orifice of a hard steel tube illuminated by candle or gas-light, to a charge-coupled device and video endoscopic monitoring. Biochemistry has advanced from a nebulous area to one of exactitude, and tissue diagnosis from organ-based necropsy material to percutaneous biopsy and histological evaluation. The imagery of disease has shifted from clinical features to radiology, ultrasonography, axial tomography, and magnetic resolution imagery. Non-visible wavelength light has both diagnostic and therapeutic potential and robotic devices may soon replace endoscopists and surgeons alike.

Ultrasonography

Historical development

L. Spallanzani (1729-1799), while professor of Natural History in Pavia in 1794, noted that bats were able to navigate in the dark, and conducted the first perspicacious observations on sonar. Perceiving that they flew without striking obstacles, he proposed that their guidance system was auditory rather than visual, and since he could hear no sound, he concluded that it was beyond human auditory perception! The next contributions to the subject were by the Curie brothers, Pierre and Jacques, who in 1880 discovered the piezoelectric effect whereby mechanical pressure on quartz generated an electric charge. Application of an oscillating current across the crystal resulted in contraction and expansion of the crystal and the generation of sound waves that could be recorded. Their fundamental observations led to the principle

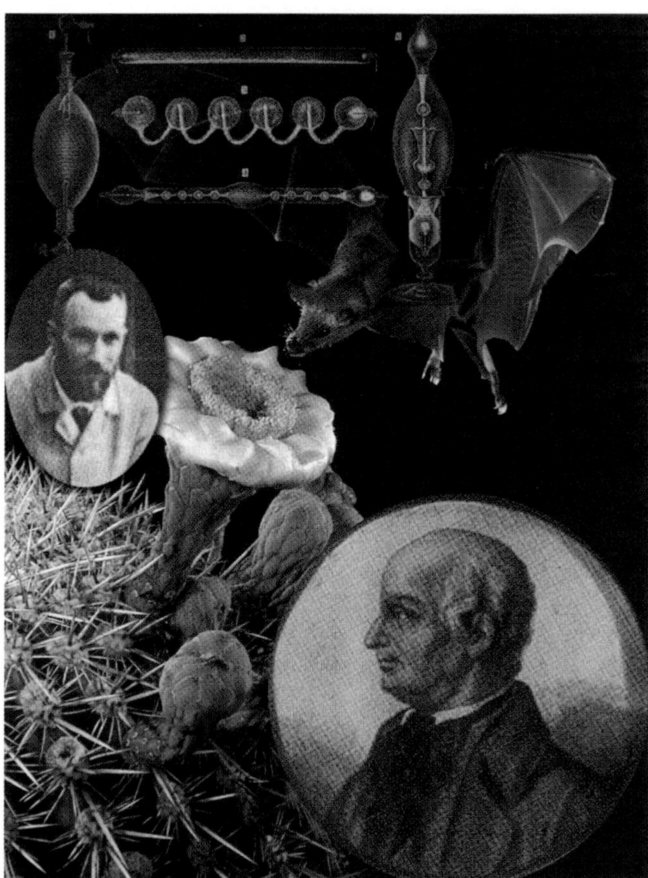

In 1794 L. Spallanzani (inset right bottom) of Pavia, noted that bats could navigate in the dark and concluded that they possessed an auditory guidance system. The Curie family dominated late 19th-century science. In 1880, Pierre (inset left) and Jacques Curie identified the piezoelectric effect that would lead to the development of ultrasonic transducers.

of ultrasonic transducers and detectors. Strangely enough, it was the sinking of the Titanic in 1912 that was to be the basis for the further pursuit of this phenomenon. Appalled by the event and fearful lest a similar disaster befall a French vessel, the government of France proposed that an attempt be undertaken to devise a method whereby a device to detect underwater objects might be developed.

As a result of such maritime concerns, Paul Langevin of France was supported by the French government in World War I to develop the use of high frequency waves for the detection of submerged enemy submarines. Elaboration and modifications of this system lead to the introduction and use of Sonar (*Sound Navigation and Ranging*). The observation by Langevin that ultrasound beams (sonic waves) also destroyed small fish, led to the application of using high intensity ultrasound for cancer treatment, especially in Germany. Similar applications of ultrasound in physical therapy were utilized for their proposed tonic, restorative, and balancing effects. The detection of these waves, and retrieval of information from their passage through an object, played no role in this process.

A number of modifications of the equipment facilitated imaging and enhanced its sensitivity to the point that it could be considered for medical usage. In 1941, Donald Sproule of England developed a system in which a second non-generating transducer detected returning echoes in the interval between generated pulses. In 1944, Floyd Firestone of the United States patented the reflectoscope, in which the same transducer could identify the echoes returning in the interval between generated pulses. Most of the work of this type was, however, based on an interaction between military or industrial personnel, and it was only in 1947 that ultrasound became applied to medical diagnosis. The Austrian physician, Karl Dussik, and his physicist brother, Friederich, introduced hyperphonography by means of a through transmission technique that produced echo pictures of what they interpreted to be the ventricles of the brain (ventriculograms). It subsequently transpired that this technique had actually failed to image the ventricles, but merely showed variations in attenuation caused by the overlying skull. In 1949, George Ludwig of the *United States Naval Military Research Institute* using a similar method to the flaw detection approach, was able to identify gallstones and foreign bodies which had been artificially embedded in tissues. By 1950, John J. Wild of the University of Minnesota had utilized ultrasound to measure the thickness of intestinal wall and demonstrated that different echo patterns could be obtained from each of the individual layers. Of particular significance, however, was his observation that echoes produced by tumor-invaded tissue were distinguishable from those produced by normal tissue. The demonstration that such echo changes identified tumor tissue that could not be detected by the standard palpation or inspection was of critical clinical significance. Wild's proposal that ultrasound might not only detect differences between malignant lesions and normal tissues, but that the technique might identify tumor-invaded tissues earlier than any other technique then available was regarded as of considerable relevance.

Further development of his technique, in collaboration with John M. Reid, led to the development of a two-dimensional B-mode scanning system for the breast. This technique allowed Wild to analyze the echo patterns and identify malignant tissue as opposed to normal surrounding structures. At almost the same time, further development was undertaken by Douglas Howry in collaboration with Roderick Bliss in Colorado. Although initially a laundry tub was used, they subsequently graduated to a metal cattle-watering trough, and thereafter, the scanning tank was constructed of the rotating ring gear of a B29 gun turret! Following Ludwig's initial attempts in 1949, Howry and Bliss, using a *Somascope*, succeeded in demonstrating gallstones within a freshly excised gall bladder. By 1952 they had reported successful ultrasonic visualization of soft tissue structures such as the kidney, liver, and spleen in living subjects. Chou Yung Chang of China had also made this observation by detecting space-occupying lesions in the liver and the kidney during his attempts to destroy ureteral calculi with ultrasound beams. Although the first transducer probes for entry into the body had originally been designed and used by Wild in the 1950s, trans-rectal and trans-vaginal scanning did not achieve full recognition until the mid 1970s. Thus, in 1974, Watanabe reported the development of an *"ultrasonic chair"* whereby a thin rigid probe containing an ultrasonic transducer was passed through the seat of the chair into the anus and the rectum. The first prototype of the mechanical sector-scanning instruments for endoscopic ultrasound that had been introduced in the early 1980s displayed only 180° images. The subsequent introduction of a 360° image endoscope, the GF-UM3, provided the first commercially available echo-endoscope, although initially there were few practitioners with the requisite expertise to utilize it. Initially designed to facilitate ultrasound imaging of the pancreas, EUS has become extremely useful in the identification of intramural lesions, and the determination of the nature of intramural masses. In addition, the development of EUS-directed fine-needle aspiration (FNA) cytology has enabled this technique to become an important tool in the staging of gastrointestinal cancer.

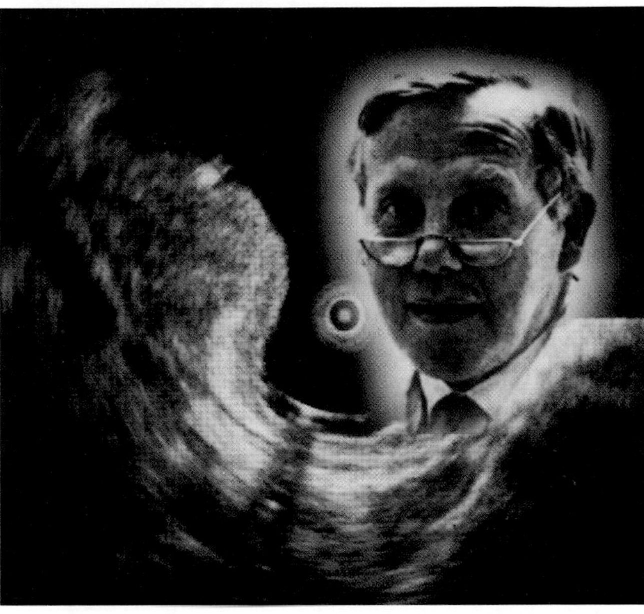

John J. Wild (inset) of the University of Minnesota was the first to determine that ultrasound could be used to measure the thickness of the intestinal wall and demonstrate that different echo patterns denoted specific abnormalities in tissue. His observation that ultrasound could differentiate between normal tissue and a malignant lesion was subsequently applied to the development of endoscopic ultrasound. Detection of an abnormality could be further verified by the additional usage of fine needle aspiration.

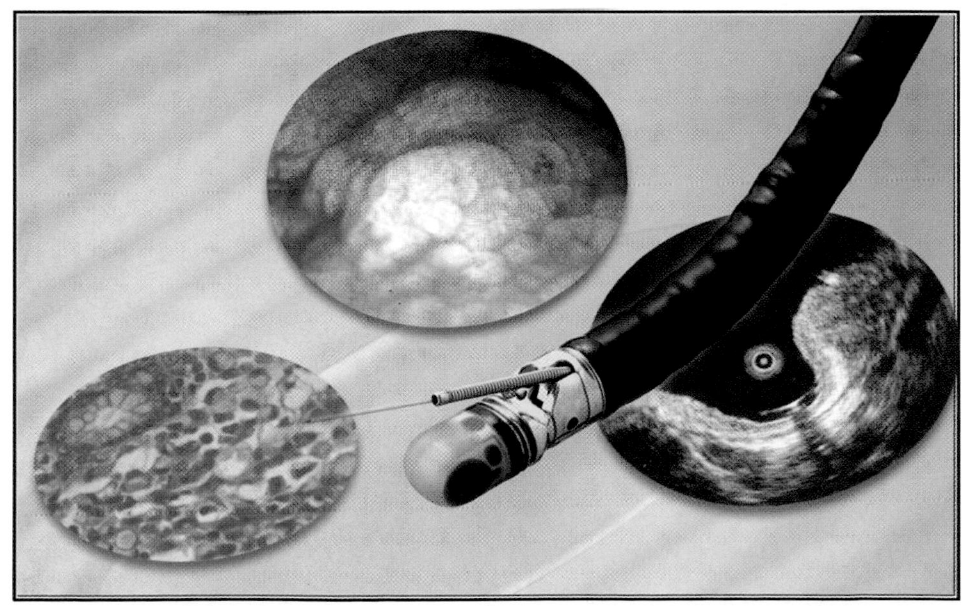

The state of the art (c. 2002) endoscopic ultrasound device with fine needle aspirator. The visual image is at the top (center), the fine needle aspirate at left and the ultrasonographic image at right.

Section 13

The esophagus

Esophagus

The esophagus has for long languished as an organ not highly regarded by any group and little understood by either laymen or physicians. To some extent, this reflects its course through three different anatomical territories – the neck, mediastinum, and abdomen and the reluctance of the medical specialists of each group to claim the organ as their own. Even its name is poorly understood and much conjecture exists regarding the origin of the term.

Although derived from an old Homeric term for the gullet, the meaning became transmuted to reflect a combination of swallowing and food, thus becoming interpreted as "a tube that conveys food". Aristotle claimed that the name derived from its narrowness and length, and some etymologists have linked the origin of the word to an osier twig, since the old Greek term could also be translated as an "eater of osiers". Whether this reflected the early usage of such flexible branches in the treatment of esophageal obstructions is not recorded.

Nevertheless, the esophagus claimed early medical attention, given the propensity of foreign bodies to obstruct it, and the rapid onset of symptoms once ingress of fluids or liquids into the stomach was impaired.

Obstruction

Blind tubes were initially used for the removal of foreign bodies from the esophagus by either extraction or by forcing them into the stomach. In 1493, Johannes Arculanus, professor at Bologna and Padua, described a short, perforated lead tube for the purpose of clasping foreign bodies such as fish bones. By the seventeenth century, however, these instruments had evolved a range of modifications such as an elaborately carved silver tube with an attachment of small sponges at the lower end. Hildanus, who designed the device, described it as follows:

> *"a hollow silver bent tube the size of a swan's feather about a foot and a half in length. This tube, which is perforated throughout its length and has a sponge the size of a hazelnut securely attached at its end, is introduced in the esophagus and is utilized with much success in extracting fish bones, small bones, and other foreign objects."*

Foreign bodies that could not be extracted, however, were dislodged directly into the stomach.

Hieronymus Fabricius ab Aquapendente (1537-1619) of Padua, in addition to advocating the latter course, was also interested in artificial feeding, and designed a silver tube covered with the intestine of a sheep, which was introduced through the nose into the stomach. Once in place, the tube was withdrawn and the intestine left in place as a conduit. This device subsequently evolved into catheters of leather that were both easier to introduce, as well as of a greater length. John Hunter (1728-1793) of London undertook the next important contribution in this area, and described the use of syringe attached to a hollow bougie or flexible catheter of sufficient length, such that it might be introduced into the stomach and *"convey stimulating matter into it without affecting the lungs."* Initially conceived as useful in reclaiming drowning victims, this was amplified in a second essay in 1793, *"A Case of Paralysis of the Muscles of Deglutition Cured by an Artificial Mode of Conveying Food and Medicines into the Stomach."*

Hunter also developed a hollow flexible tube that could be used for the introduction of medicaments, as well as food to treat a 50-year-old man with depression, anxiety, and hypochondriasis. The device was introduced by the patient himself to administer flower of mustard and tincture of valerian tube twice-daily into his own stomach. The procedure was described as follows:

A variety of 16th-century devices developed and used by Arculanus, Scultetus, Hildanus and Aquapendente (right) for the extraction of foreign bodies from the esophagus.

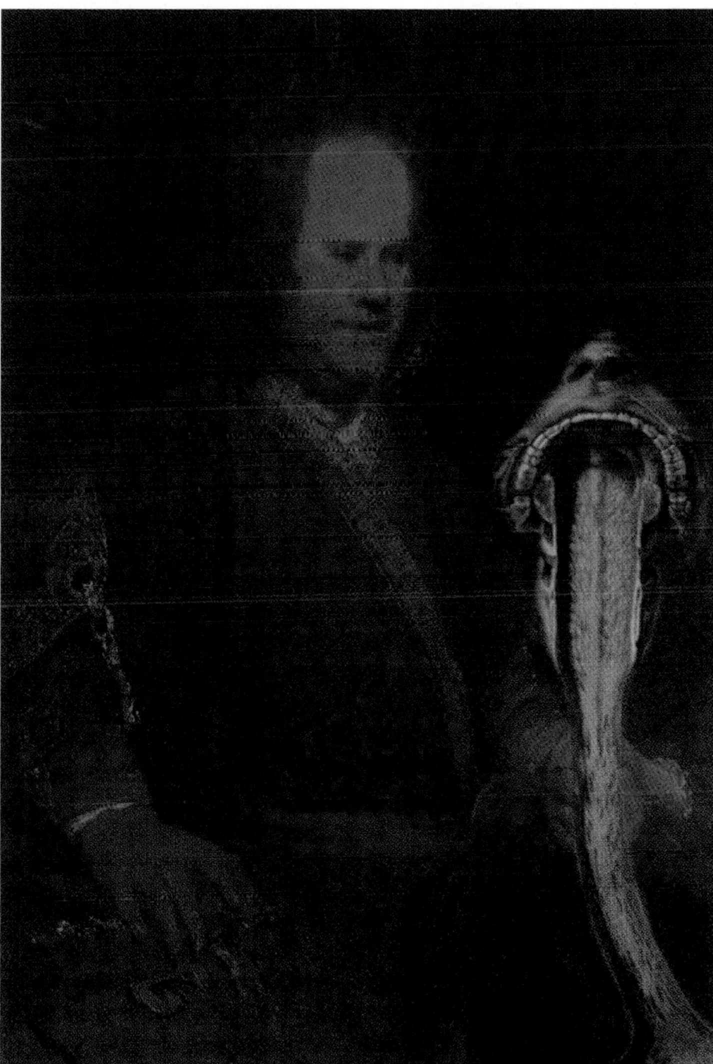

As a result of his astute clinical observations in respect of the condition of the ruptured esophagus of the Dutch Admiral, Baron van Wassenaar, the name of the eminent Leiden physician, H. Boerhaave (background) has become inextricably linked with both the condition and the organ.

John Hunter of London (1728-1793) was the first surgeon scientist and intellectually explored the structure and function of the body in almost every species available, leaving in excess of 50,000 specimens at his death. His friend Sir Joshua Reynolds painted the portrait (top left) (Courtesy of the Hunterian Museum of the Royal College of Surgeons of London). In the background is an injected specimen of the stomach from the Hunterian collection and the foreground instruments are of the type utilized to "sound" the esophagus. On March 21, 1776, Hunter delivered a paper entitled "Proposals for the recovery of persons apparently drowned." In this essay, Hunter amplified Boerhaave's suggestions by describing the use of a syringe attached to the hollow bougie of a flexible catheter of sufficient length such that it might be introduced into the stomach and "convey stimulating matter into it without affecting the lungs."

> *"a fresh eel skin of rather a small size, drawn over a probang and tied up at the end, where it covered the sponge, and tied again close to the sponge, where it fastened to the whale bone, and a small longitudinal slit was made into it just above this upper ligature. To the other end of the eel skin was fixed a bladder and wooden pipe, similar to what is used in giving a clyster, only the pipe was large enough to let the end of the probang pass into the bladder without feeling up the passage. The probang thus covered was introduced into the stomach and the food and medicines put into the bladder and squeezed down through the eel skin."*

The long-term compliance and success of the procedure is not recorded!

Visualizing the Esophagus

A. Kussmaul of Freiburg deserves the credit for the first, albeit unsuccessful, attempt at visualizing the esophagus and the stomach. His experimentation in 1868 laid the foundation for the later work of J. von Mikulicz of Vienna, Chevalier Jackson (1865-1958) of Philadelphia and R. Schindler of Munich.

As the esophagus was more difficult to traverse than the urethra, physicians interested in exploration of the upper gastrointestinal tract required help both with instrument design and the mode of introduction. As might have been predicted, they therefore turned to engineers and sword-swallowers. As early as 1865, Kussmaul had directed his attention to the problem of access to the stomach, initially with the object of effecting decompression in cases of obstruction. Convinced of the clinical relevance of this goal, he had initiated a renaissance of the gastric tube at the clinic in Freiburg.

Initially, he had undertaken direct esophagoscopy using a tube-shaped speculum to which he had attached the endoscope of Desormeaux for illumination. His concern with patient safety led him to enlist the services of a sword-swallower to help him with the development of a technique that might be safe. After a careful study of a sword-swallower introducing his sword, Kussmaul made a number of design modifications of the original instrument and used two special tubes, each of 47 cm length, one round with a diameter of 13 mm and the other elliptical. Although the sword-swallower successfully introduced the tube in his usual upright position, the examination, however, was unsatisfactory due both to the inadequacy of illumination and the copious amount of fluid obstructing the field of visibility. Although Kussmaul demonstrated the introduction of the tube at the medical section of the Society of Naturalists in Freiburg, and even sent his sword-swallower with the tubes for study at the surgical clinic in Zurich, he failed to publish a report. Difficulties with toleration by patients of the rigid instrument and sub-optimal visualization, however, dimmed Kussmaul's initial enthusiasm and, sadly for the discipline of endoscopy, despite having identified esophageal pathology on a number of occasions, he failed to further pursue this area in any great detail. After the initial contributions of Kussmaul, the development of gastroscopy became closely associated with esophagoscopy.

Johann von Mikulicz (1850-1905), the leading pupil and collaborator of Billroth in Vienna, played the next major role in the evolution of endoscopy. Apart from his other widespread interests in disease, von Mikulicz was particularly involved in the surgical management of diseases of the gastrointestinal tract. Although the chest cavity was inviolate to surgeons of his time, the esophagus remained a surgical challenge that could not be ignored, particularly since it represented the roadway to the stomach. Cogniscent of ongoing experiments to evaluate the interior of the bladder by the urologist Max Nitze (1848-1906) and Fritz Leiter (instrument-maker), as well as the work of Kussmaul, von Mikulicz developed a particular interest in the subject of endoscopy and especially the area of the esophagus.

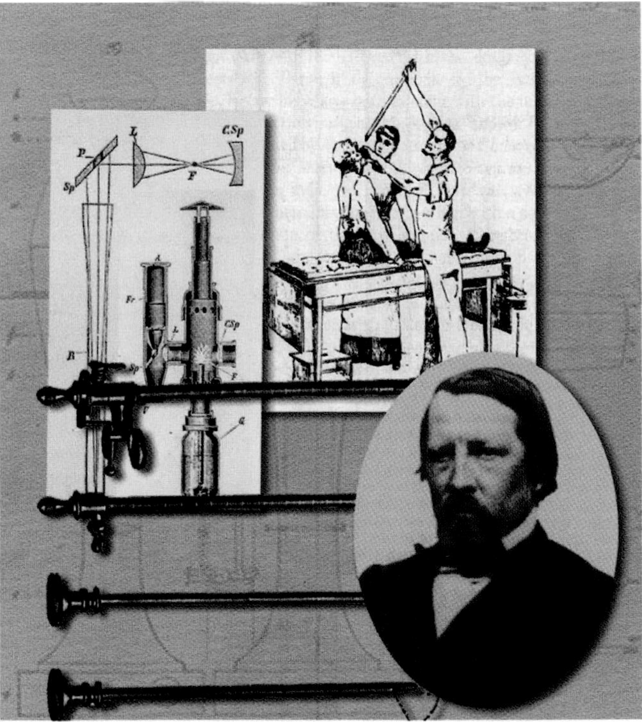

Adolf Kussmaul (1822-1902). His contributions include: being the first to a) treat gastric obstruction with a stomach tube (1867); b) treat gastric ulcer with bismuth (1868); c) attempt esophagoscopy and gastroscopy (1869); d) diagnose mesenteric embolism during life (1867).

The urologist Max Nitze (1848-1906) (right) and Fritz Leiter (top), an instrument-maker of Vienna together designed and produced the first effective cystoscope. Their collaboration dissolved after acrimonious disagreements in regard to the optimal design for a gastroscope. With the departure of Nitze to a position in Berlin, Leiter collaborated with Mikulicz in the development of endoscopes for the esophagus and stomach.

Initially skeptical of the technique, von Mikulicz recognized that illumination would remain the problem and, at the insistence of Leiter (who had parted company with Nitze), undertook the evaluation of the esophagus in 1880. In addition to the skills of the instrument-maker, he also sought the help of an elderly woman with a proclivity for swallowing instruments, as well as studying the passage of instruments in cadavers. In this way he was able to determine that apart from a slight resistance at the level of the larynx, the only condition necessary to ensure successful esophagoscopy was that the head of the patient be held firmly in a sword-swallower's position. Von Mikulicz' esophagoscope had a diameter of 11 to 13 mm and was closed by a knob-like head of a stylet or mandarin placed in the lumen of an instrument prior to its usage. Once the instrument had been successfully introduced to the lower level of the esophagus, the stylet was withdrawn and replaced with a thin flat rod that contained an insulated wiring system and minute conduits utilized for the purpose of cooling the lighting element. At its proximal end, the wire was connected to a Bunsen battery and its terminal end possessed a "u" shaped platinum wire that could be brought to incandescence behind a glass window. The light source or "glow bulb" was then cooled by water that flowed in the tiny circuits surrounding the platinum loop. The advantage of this component was that it only occupied a small space within the tube that left considerable room available for visualization of the lumen of the esophagus.

Von Mikulicz provided clinical observations regarding the esophagus of considerable interest and which attest to his highly-developed skills. For example, he noted that in a normal organ, the mucosa appeared the same throughout, being a uniform pale red traversed intermittently by tiny blood vessels, and commented that the uniform smoothness of the mucosa produced a glaring effect that made visualization difficult. He also reported some interesting pathological observations and described in detail foreign bodies, cancer, and esophageal compression due to lung disease and aortic aneurysm.

Von Mikulicz was aware that the stomach required examination but difficulties with instrument design precluded adequate development of this technique. On the other hand, Chevalier Jackson (1907) of Philadelphia, an early esophagoscopist of considerable skill, proposed that the stomach could be quite adequately and safely examined utilizing open tubes. His proposal, however, met with little general acceptance, since it was evident that few possessed the formidable skills necessary to obtain the superlative results that he claimed.

Nevertheless, Jackson, an oto-rhino-laryngologist, using an open tube devoid of any optical system and differing only from an esophagoscope in its increased length, became adept at inspection of the stomach. Narcosis was employed and the patient maintained in a recumbent position through out the procedure. Although there was no apparatus for inflation of the stomach, visibility was good, since residual gastric fluid could be removed by continuous suction through a narrow tube attached to the outer surface of the instrument.

Despite Jackson's enthusiasm (he was a man of considerable conviction and unquestionable endoscopic skill), the subsequent development of endoscopes over the next two decades followed the principle of a rigid tube through which an optical system was passed.

Chevalier Jackson of Philadelphia (top right), apart from his talents as a sculptor, writer, and painter was an esophagoscopist of virtuoso-like skill. Able to maneuver the rigid esophagoscope with the dexterity of a maestro he developed a wide range of instruments (center) for the extraction of foreign bodies (top left). Innumerable children (patients from his ward) (bottom) were saved by his therapeutic endeavors and to this day the manufacture of the size/shape configurations of toys in the USA is measured against the huge collection he removed over his career. Given his consummate skill with the rigid endoscope, he asserted that it was adequate for gastroscopy and initially criticized the efforts to introduce bent or flexible devices.

Esophageal Rupture

While impairment to swallowing food constituted a problem, it paled in comparison to the events consequent upon rupture of the esophagus. The classic description of this entity reflects the clinical acumen and erudition of Hermann Boerhaave of Leiden. Undoubtedly the leading physician of the age, Boerhaave was the founder of the "Eclectic School" and it was largely due to efforts that Leiden achieved considerable fame as a medical center.

Boerhaave was born on 31 December 1668 in the parsonage at Voorhout near Leiden, the son of the minister of the local Dutch Reformed Church. After education by his father and later at the grammar school, Boerhaave entered the University of Leiden in 1684 with the intention of becoming a minister.

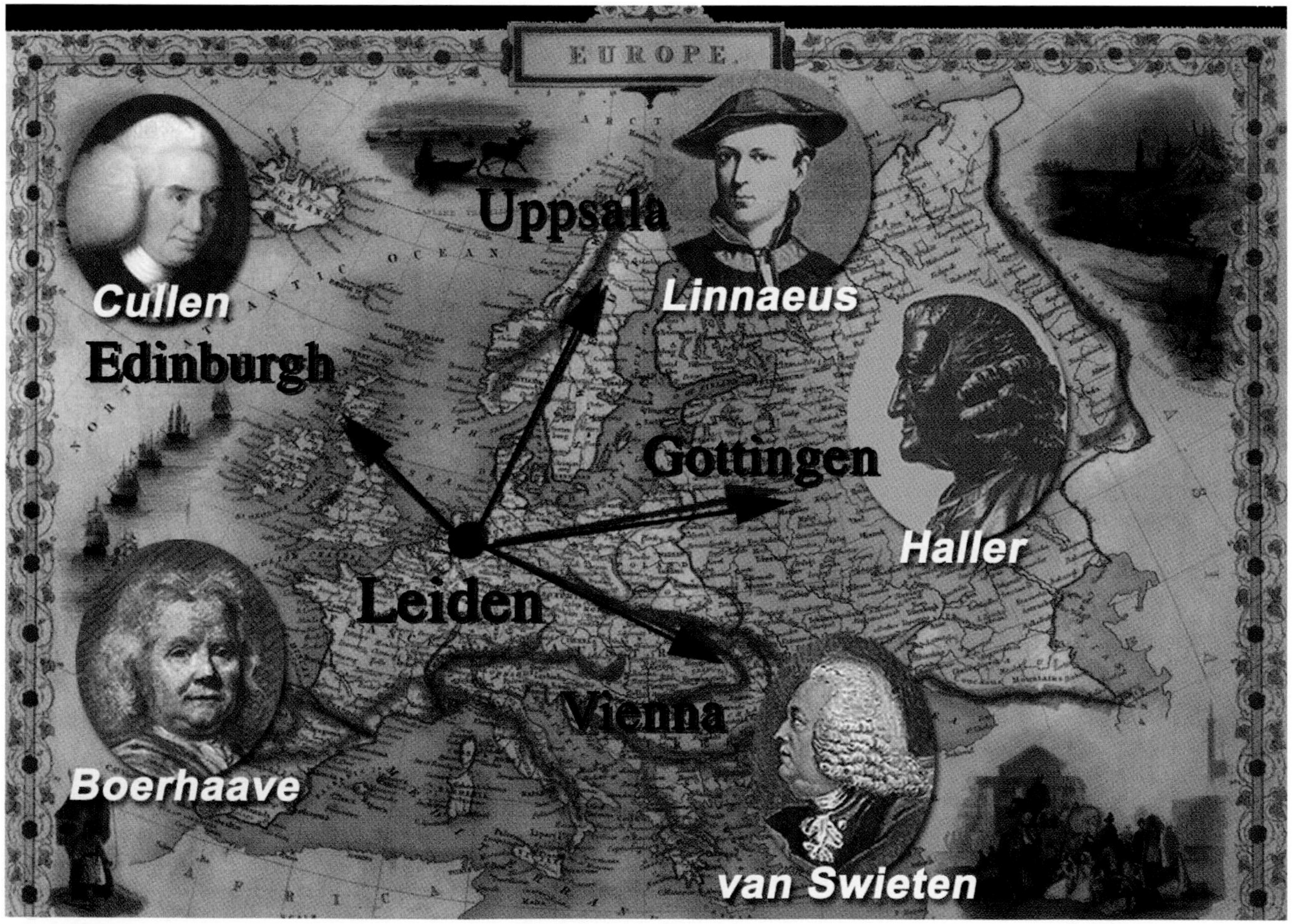

Although Boerhaave contributed little to clinical medicine outside of his oral instruction, hundreds of students traveled to Leiden from all parts of Europe during his tenure from 1714 to 1738. Included in the list of his pupils are illustrious names such as Haller, Gaub, Linnaeus, Cullen, Pringle, van Swieten and de Haen. Many of these subsequently became leading physicians in their own countries such as Sweden, Germany, Austria, and Scotland and thus further augmented the influence of Boerhaave and the Leiden School of Medical thought. Indeed, the motto "Simplex Veri Sigillum" – simplicity is the sign of truth, by which Boerhaave lived, perhaps most accurately sums up the direction which scientific research undertook during his tutelage.

He continued his classical studies, reading philosophy, natural history, and divinity before graduating after six years as a Doctor of Philosophy. At this stage, he decided that he would in addition, graduate in medicine, and to this end adopted an unusual method. Thus, while holding a temporary post in the university library he read the works of all the great medical men written, starting with Hippocrates and ending with Sydenham, as well as those of the anatomists, and occasionally attended a dissection by Anton Nuck, the professor of Anatomy. Indeed, there exists no evidence that Boerhaave ever attended a formal medical lecture in the University of Leiden! Having thus prepared himself in his own manner, he wrote a thesis for his M.D. degree, and having presented it, not at Leiden but at Harderwyck, graduated M.D. of that university in July 1693.

For the next seven years, Boerhaave practiced as a physician in Leiden and also taught mathematics privately. In 1700, the University of Leiden approached Boerhaave to assume the responsibilities of Charles Drelincourt, the professor of Medicine whose position they had not been able to fill although he had passed away in 1697. Thus, on 18 May 1701, Boerhaave was formally appointed to this post, and accepted the title of "lector". Despite his relatively limited exposure to university life, Boerhaave rapidly gained acclaim as a lecturer not only on physiology, but also general pathology and the elements of symptomatology and therapeutics.

In the autumn of 1707, Boerhaave published his *Institutiones Medicae*, and in the autumn of 1708 (dated 1709) his *Aphorismi de Cognoscendis et Curandis Morbis*. These two small books, which were, in fact synopses of his lectures, were enormously successful, being repeatedly revised in successive editions and translated into many languages. Boerhaave was, however, a relatively poor writer, and the numerous sets of students' manuscript notes, and the commentaries of Haller and Van Swieten, reveal how far his spoken word exceeded the printed text. Nevertheless, these two books remained standard medical textbooks until long after their author's death.

In 1714, Boerhaave was named Rector Magnificus of the University and succeeded Govert Bidloo (1649-1713), who had passed away in the previous year. Although Bidloo and Frederik Dekkers (1648-1720) had been responsible for most of the teaching, their interest had waned towards the end of their careers. As a result, Boerhaave, who was particularly interested in teaching and who was in his own right a commanding presence, earned a great reputation as a clinician and bedside teacher. In 1718, the professor of Chemistry, Jacobus Le Mort, who had not always been *persona grata* with the university authorities, died, and Boerhaave was appointed professor of Chemistry in addition to his other two chairs. Since Boerhaave had been delivering private lectures on chemistry since his earliest days, and was known to have undertaken considerable experimental work in chemistry, the choice of Le Mort's successor was never in doubt. As a result of this appointment, Boerhaave continued to carry out all the duties of these three chairs for eleven years until 1729, when following an illness, he resigned from the chairs of Botany and Chemistry. He did, however, retain the Chair of Medicine, and continued to lecture on the Institutes and on practical and clinical medicine until his death in 1738. At the end of 1737 Boerhaave began to suffer from dyspnoea, and by April 1738 his condition had declined with the development of anasarca, such that he perished on 23 September 1738.

Baron van Wassenaar

Apart from his contributions as a teacher, his most masterful skill was his ability to relate clinical symptomatology to anatomical findings that he subsequently confirmed at post-mortem. In this respect, his most significant contribution to gastroenterology was made in the description of the ruptured esophagus of his friend and patient, Baron Johannes Wassenaar of Rosenbergh, in the neighborhood of Leiden. Wassenaar was a good friend of Boerhaave and occupied the substantial position of Admiral of the Republic and Dikereeve of Rhineland, and Boerhaave who had previously treated his gout, knew him to be a glutton who took little exercise. On the 29th of October, 1723, at half past twelve at night, the Admiral's son called Boerhaave from his residence to the home of the Baron, where he found him sitting upright in bed, bent forward and complaining of acute shortness of breath and pain in his chest. The clinical story, as it emerged, was that the Baron had some three days previously partaken of a copious dinner together with friends and afterwards in good health, gone horse-riding with his son. Later that evening he had felt somewhat dyspeptic and as was his habit, had taken three small cupfuls of a gentle emetic. When this failed to produce the required effect, he took four more cupfuls but on attempting to vomit, had uttered a terrible cry on account of *"a violent pain in his chest."* Wassenaar described a sensation of *"something having broken or torn"* and declaring instantly that he was dying, began to pray to God and to resign himself to his will. In the following hours he took four doses of olive oil (each about 28 grams) and later drank six ounces of beer. Prior to the arrival of Boerhaave, the patient had been treated by Dr. De Bye but despite the use of clysters and venesection, no improvement had been noted. Boerhaave prescribed a second venesection, soft drinks and warm compresses, but all to no avail, and the following day the Baron died in great distress.

Boerhaave, in the presence of Dr. De Bye and three other interested gentlemen, undertook the autopsy. The examination of the corpse revealed the presence of subcutaneous emphysema in addition to a large amount of air in the abdominal cavity. When the chest was opened, a tremendous rush of air escaped and Boerhaave was able to identify the rancid odor of the duck meat that had constituted the major content of the Baron's last meal (three days earlier). The lungs had completely collapsed and were floating on liquid that filled the entire chest on both sides equally. During the examination of the left pleural cavity, a finger-sized tear was found in the lower end of the esophagus. Boerhaave's conclusion was that the esophagus, which had been previously healthy, had been spontaneously torn by the violent vomiting induced by the emetic taken by the Baron. He considered the disease to be incurable. The clarity of his meticulous description of the symptoms and pathological findings of the condition led to the eponymous recognition of his contributions to the clinical delineation of the entity.

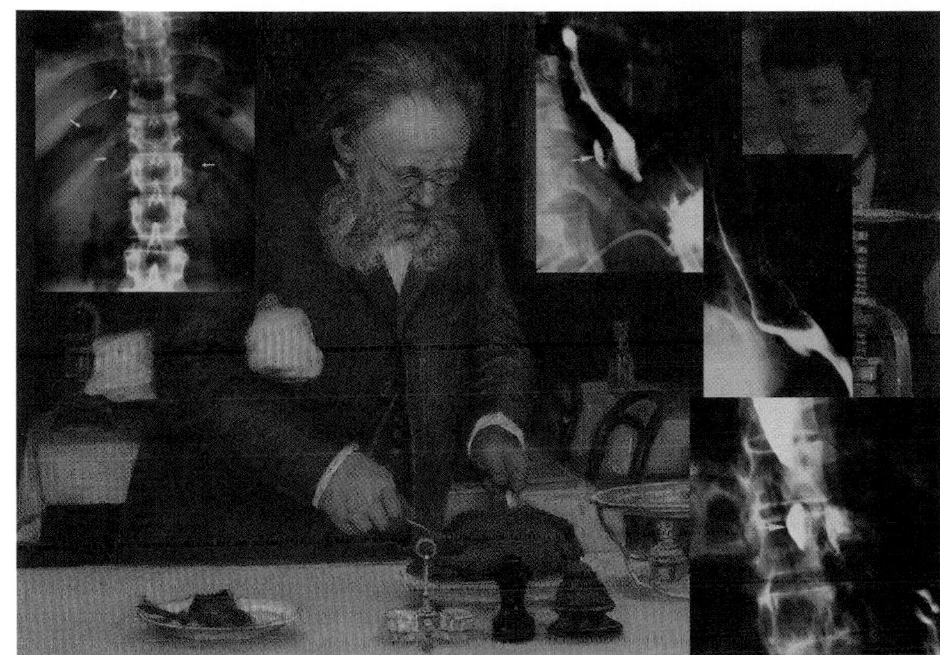

The ingestion of a large amount of duck followed by self-induced vomiting led to rupture of the esophagus. Boerhaave correctly identified the pathology at postmortem and indeed in many instances this still occurs. The advent of contrast radiology facilitated the diagnosis of ruptured esophagus (inset).

Johannes Wassenaar was a noted admiral of the redoubtable Dutch Fleet. Unfortunately, his proclivity for over-indulgence led to his demise from a ruptured esophagus. Although he is little remembered, his physician, Boerhaave, attained fame for describing the late Admiral's medical condition.

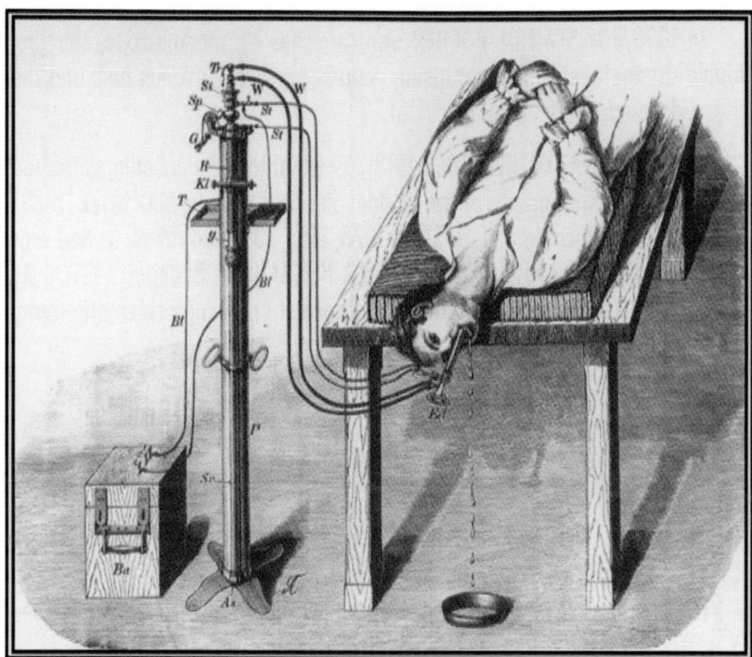

The Mikulicz esophagoscope proved to be of considerable utility and novel information in regard to esophageal conditions was obtained. Its rigidity, however, required considerable caution during introduction and the extended head position (right) was rendered even more incommodious by problems with inadequate pharyngeal anesthesia and excessive salivary secretion. The complex electrical apparatus for lighting (left) designed by Leiter was ingenious but cumbersome, in that it required a water cooling system to sustain the platinum lighting elements and a large Bunsen battery to provide power for illumination. Having successfully developed an esophagoscope (1880) and a less effective gastroscope (1881) during his association with Billroth in Vienna, von Mikulicz subsequently became the department chairman in Cracow (1882) and then Breslau (1890). These moves and the loss of close contact with Leiter led to a more sustained focus on administration and technical surgery with little further upper gastrointestinal endoscopic development work. Ironically Mikulicz would perish of a gastric neoplasm in 1905 after undergoing an exploratory laparotomy which proved him to have inoperable disease.

Esophagitis

History

The first description of the disease by Galen was accurate, although somewhat incomplete. Nevertheless, he duly noted that although difficulties with swallowing may be due to tumors or paralysis, the esophagus when inflamed hinders swallowing by itself, acting as a hindrance due to the associated excruciating pain. In 1884, Morell Mackenzie defined esophagitis as an *"acute idiopathic inflammation of the mucous membranes of the esophagus giving rise to extreme odynphagia and often to aphagia."* It was this anglicized description that was utilized to qualify the disease known as "esophagitis" which had first been described by John Peter Frank in 1792. Although similar observations had been made previously by Boehm in 1722, who described an acute pain *"reached down even to the stomach and which was accompanied by hiccup and a constant flow of serum from the mouth"*, the latter had not defined the condition as accurately. Honkoop published a thesis on inflammation of the gullet in 1774 and in 1785, Bleuland, a physician himself, was struck down with the disease and carefully recorded the details of his illness. The first reports of the condition of "esophagitis" in children originated with Billard, who in 1828 published a statement regarding the ailments of newborns. In 1829, Mondière wrote a thesis describing his own severe personal experiences with esophagitis and, in addition, collected much of the extant material on the subject. His laborious compilation represents more industry than discrimination, but the thesis provides a good overview of early nineteenth-century thoughts on the esophagus. Indeed, it is from the work of Mondière that much of the literature sources of esophageal diseases were drawn for the next century. These included Velpeau's *The Esophagus – A Dictionary in Four Volumes*, Follin's essay Considerations of Esophageal Disease and Copland's *Dictionary*. In 1878, Knott in Dublin published *The Pathology of the Esophagus* and included in it the cases of esophagitis described by Roche, Bourguet, Broussais, and Paletta as well as some original illustrations of diseases of the organ. In 1835, Graves of Dublin made some observations on the disease but thereafter confined his attentions to the thyroid. The subject was further illuminated by communications from Hamburger, Padova, Laboulbène and a number of other distinguished physicians of the time.

Sir Morell Mackenzie

Although Mackenzie regarded the condition to be of unknown etiology, he carefully defined the chief symptom as excruciating burning or tearing pain – odynphagia – induced by any attempt to swallow or any movement of the laryngeal muscles. He also noted that such patients developed considerable thirst but were unable to achieve relief by drinking, since the pain was so severe. In adults, he reported that there was a constant expectoration of frothy saliva and although patients might not always have a fever, they often became delirious. Mackenzie believed the lesion to represent a diffuse catarrhal inflammation of the mucosa of the upper end of the gullet, and felt the diagnosis was based upon the history of extreme pain and the absence of pharyngeal inflammation on examination!

Although the description by Mackenzie of esophagitis is very different to that now recognized to represent the contemporary understanding of the disease, his is the first lucid attempt to define the subject. His text, *Diseases of the Throat and Nose*, contains a fascinating and detailed analysis, as well as classification of esophagitis, but sometimes fails to accurately distinguish between disease of the lower and upper end of the gullet. In the twentieth century, the term esophagitis has become referable almost solely to an entity involving the lower part of the gullet. Nevertheless, Mackenzie recognized

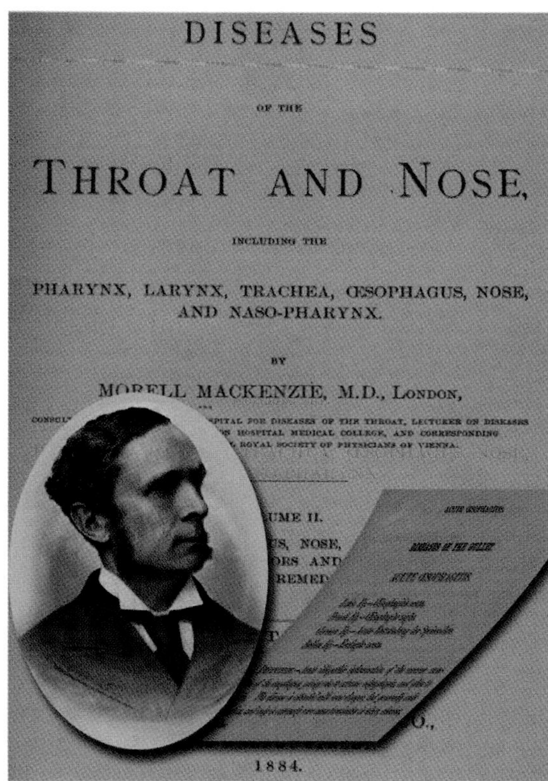

DISEASES
OF THE
THROAT AND NOSE,
INCLUDING THE
PHARYNX, LARYNX, TRACHEA, ŒSOPHAGUS, NOSE, AND NASO-PHARYNX.
BY
MORELL MACKENZIE, M.D., LONDON,
1884.

Although Sir Morell Mackenzie is most often remembered for the debacle regarding the tragic demise of the German emperor (Frederick III of Prussia) from laryngeal cancer, his contributions to the early literature of the esophagus were both thoughtful and substantial.

that the inflammatory conditions of the upper part of the gullet were specific and included diphtheria, thrush, tuberculosis, syphilis, actinomycosis, and corrosive damage. Some of the associated non-specific conditions (myalgia, general hyperaesthesia) alluded to by Mackenzie, are no longer recognized but as late as 1900, all inflammatory conditions effecting the gullet were still regarded as varieties of "*esophagitis*".

Early Treatment

Of particular interest were the treatments proposed in the management of this vexatious condition. It was considered mandatory that the organ be maintained in a state of absolute rest. Thus, feeding was undertaken by nutrient enemata and morphia administered by hypodermic injection to facilitate resolution of inflammation and abolish pain. Poultices were applied along the upper part of the spine or if the pain was particularly severe, anodyne embrocations such as oleate of morphia or belladonna liniments were rubbed into the back. Mondière, following the French practice of the time, believed in venesection and cupping as well as leech applications (12 to 30 at a time). Counter-irritation by the application of mustard poultices or moxas was also widely recommended. By 1884, Mackenzie was, however, able to declare that bleeding or even the local abstraction of blood was little value and that he himself had found counter-irritation to be of no effect. He favored derivatives and especially recommended the use of extremely hot *pediluvia*. Bleuland used blisters "*loco dolenti*" between the shoulders with success and Pagenstecher reported the use of hydrochloride of ammonia to great advantage. This agent had long been a favorite of German and Dutch physicians and was used as a remedy for many different kinds of disease. Mackenzie was adamant that the passage of bougies was dangerous and should never be attempted, since it was likely to cause rupture of the esophagus. Once convalescence commenced, the patient could be changed from liquid to a solid diet gradually and if pain returned, immediate return to a liquid diet should once again be undertaken.

Pathology

Despite the attention to the gullet provided by Mackenzie, the disease was not commonly recognized and little known about it. In 1906, Wilder Tileston carefully defined at least 12 different types of ulceration which included carcinoma, corrosive, foreign bodies, acute infectious diseases, decubitus, aneurysms, catarrhal inflammations: those associated with diverticulum, tuberculosis, syphilis, varicose, and ulcers due to thrush. Tileston was particularly drawn to the disease that he referred to as "*peptic ulcer of the esophagus*" that he claimed exactly simulated the behavior and appearance of chronic gastric ulcer. He noted that although a rare entity, it had initially been described by Albers in 1839 and thereafter sporadically noted by pathologists. No less an authority than Rokitansky had concurred that peptic ulcer of the lower esophagus was a real and definable entity and represented the aftermath of gastric juice in the gullet. Nevertheless, when Tileston reviewed the literature as far as 1906, there had only been 44 clear-cut examples of the condition published. The ulcers described were usually single and often associated with chronic peptic ulcer in the stomach or the duodenum. They were large penetrating lesions sometimes 6 to 8 cm in length that lay "*above the cardiac sphincter*" and although often longitudinal might also encircle the entire gullet.

The patients were elderly and many had no symptoms referable to the esophagus until their admission to the hospital. Death usually occurred from perforation into a large vessel, the pericardium, the mediastinum, or the pleural cavity, although some died of pneumonia. Of interest was the fact that few exhibited symptoms of esophageal obstruction. Tileston further reported that the histology of such ulcers was identical to that of chronic gastric ulcer and that the adjacent mucosa was gastric in type. He assumed it to be "ectopic" since it lined the lower part of the gut in the mediastinum.

Barrett and Hurst

The understanding of ulceration of the esophagus and esophagitis itself became further obfuscated with the advent of radiology and esophagoscopy at the turn of the twentieth century. The use of these diagnostic tools enabled the identification of a variety of esophageal lesions, particularly ulcers and inflammation at the lower end of the gullet, not previously apparent to clinicians. Thus, by the 1920s, it was apparent that pathologists, clinicians, and endoscopists, while assuming that they were describing the same entity when they referred to peptic ulcer of the esophagus or esophagitis, were each unclear as to the exact nature of the disease process. In 1929 Chevalier Jackson, a virtuoso esophagoscopist, reported 88 cases in 4,000 consecutive endoscopies, while Stewart and Hartfall in the same year claimed that they were able to identify only 1 example of esophagitis in 10,000 consecutive autopsies. The subsequent reports of Lyall (1937), Chamberlin (1939), Dick and Hurst (1942), provided further insight into the nature and occurrence of these lower esophageal lesions. The further substantial contributions by Allison and Johnstone of Leeds (1943, 1946, and 1948) left little doubt that the authors were confident in their ability to recognize and diagnose "peptic ulcer of the esophagus" or "esophagitis". Norman Barrett believed that the early descriptions of ulcer by Tileston, Stewart, and Lyall differed significantly from those identified by clinicians such as Allison. He felt that the former were "*rare and of little clinical significance*" whereas the latter were "*common and important entities*." He further proposed that this confusion had arisen because the pathology of the former had been tacked onto the symptomatology of the

Esophagitis is a relatively novel term and the condition was previously called either cardiodynia, gastralgia, or noxious dyspepsia. Given the limited understanding of the problem, the therapy proposed was either leaching, cupping, or venesection.

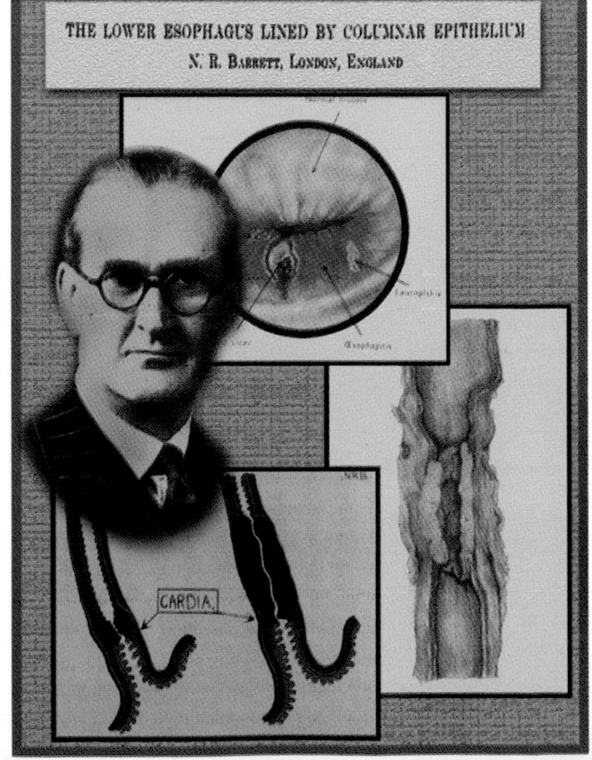

A series of drawings from the publications of Norman Barrett illustrating his clear recognition of the relationships between esophagitis, ulceration, herniation, and the development of neoplasia.

A. Winkelstein is credited with having proposed the term esophagitis in 1935 to describe acid peptic disease of the esophagus.

latter. Indeed it was Barrett's opinion that the condition described by Allison actually represented "reflux esophagitis" and that this was the best name for the lesion that had been so clearly described by Allison in 1948.

The assessment of the situation at the lower end of the esophagus by Allison was prescient. He was of the opinion that chronic esophageal ulcers could develop into lesions similar to gastric ulcers, and noted that the features of the esophageal ulcers that complicate reflux esophagitis are that they are situated in esophagus and represent digestion of the squamous epithelium. Allison opined that these lesions arose in areas of general acute inflammation and manifested initially as erosions that could either heal or persist depending upon the amount of gastric juice that had access to the gullet. Such areas remained as superficial defects for a considerable period of time in the majority of individuals but eventually, when the site had become significantly scarred, they burrowed through the muscularis. It was Barrett's proposal that the stricture of the esophagus generated by this chronic inflammation had been mistakenly regarded as the esophagus, whereas it was in fact a patch of stomach partially enveloped by peritoneum that had been drawn up by scar tissue into the mediastinum. Barrett therefore concluded that it was this stomach which was the site of the chronic gastric ulcer, and that the ulcers that had been described in the lower gullet were in truth gastric and not esophageal, and that they were located below the stricture. In his opinion, such ulcers arose in the esophagus in islets of ectopic gastric mucosa themselves or as a consequence of the secretion of acid into the gullet by such islets. The history of these ectopic islets of gastric mucosa in esophagus is actually quite intriguing. Although first described by F.A. Schmidt in 1805, the observation was overlooked until Schridde in 1904 reported that microscopic ectopic islets were present in 70% of all gullets and always situated in the post crycoid region. Taylor of Leeds in 1927, in examining 900 cases, had identified in 6, at the top of the gullet, areas large enough to be visible with the naked eye. Terracol in 1938 reported similar lesions at the top of the gullet while Rector and Connerly (1941) identified in infants 56 examples at the upper end and 7 somewhat lower down. Barrett did not believe that these isolated islets secreted acid or if they did, the volume was of such paucity that it could not cause ulcers. Indeed he claimed *"nor were there any reports of ulcers associated with such islets."*

The final conclusion that Barrett arrived at in his provocative but seminal comments on esophagitis, was that the word had now become a blunderbuss term and was being used to cover many different pathological lesions. He believed that its usage should always be qualified by the descriptive adjective, "reflux esophagitis" and that this condition was common and could produce ulceration of the esophagus and stricture formation. He further believed that this particular lesion was separate to the condition regarded by pathologists as "peptic ulcer" of the esophagus, that he felt to be an example of a congenital short esophagus. In the latter, there was neither evidence of general inflammation, nor stricture formation, but a part of the stomach extended up into the mediastinum and even into the neck, and it was in this type of stomach that a typical chronic gastric ulcer could form.

Although there is much debate in regard to who first noted reflux esophagitis and what its precise etiology might be, the contributions of A. Winkelstein require consideration. In 1935 in the Journal of the American Medical Association, Winkelstein noted, *"one cannot avoid the suspicion that the disease in these five cases is possibly a peptic esophagitis i.e. an esophagitis resulting from the irritant action on the mucosa of free hydrochloric acid and pepsin."* Indeed, it was the culmination of Winkelstein's proposal and Allison's later concept of a *"chronic reflux"* of gastric contents that finally assured the place of the term "reflux esophagitis" in the literature. The subsequent arguments as to whether anatomical and mechanical factors such as a hiatus hernia were responsible engendered much discussion. In 1968, E.D. Palmer cast considerable doubt on the relationship between hiatus hernia and esophagitis. In a 22-year prospective study, he reported that many patients with hernias had neither reflux symptoms nor esophagitis, and that many other patients had esophagitis in the absence of a hiatus hernia. At this stage, the role of the lower esophageal sphincter became an area of critical relevance in establishing the primary mechanism of reflux disease. The further expansion of the gastroesophageal horizon of disease was proposed in 1962, when J.H. Kennedy implicated reflux symptoms in the production of pulmonary symptomatology and, in 1968, Cherry and Margulies suggested that laryngeal abnormalities might be second to gastroesophageal reflux. By 1990, Sontag had demonstrated that more than 80% of asthmatics exhibited reflux and the disease of GERD had assumed almost epidemic proportions. Indeed,

Sir Arthur Hurst (1879-1944) was born in Bradford, England. The great physicist, Henrich Rudolf Hertz, was his father's cousin. In 1908 Hurst (the name change reflected British sensitivities to Germanic origins) published a detailed account of the movement of the stomach, intestine, and colon, having been influenced by the pioneer X-ray studies of W.B. Cannon. Having been appointed to the staff of Guy's Hospital at the age of 27, he established himself as a general physician with a special interest in gastroenterology. Hurst was particularly interested in ulcer disease, achalasia, and constipation and wrote definitively on these and diverse gastrointestinal subjects. In 1936 Hurst established the Gastroenterologic Club, (subsequently the British Society of Gastroenterology) and at its first meeting in 1937, was elected President.

epidemiological studies indicated that up to a third of the people in developed countries such as the United Kingdom and the United States suffered from the disorder.

Medical Therapy of Dyspepsia and Heartburn

The early history of the treatment of esophagitis is essentially the same as the treatment of dyspepsia in general, since there was no clear understanding of the difference between esophagitis and gastric or duodenal disease. Indeed, even to this day, acid peptic disease as a generic description, provides a broad target for all therapy directed at either neutralizing secreted acid or suppressing acid on the basis of the consideration that this will both ameliorate symptoms and promote ulcer healing.

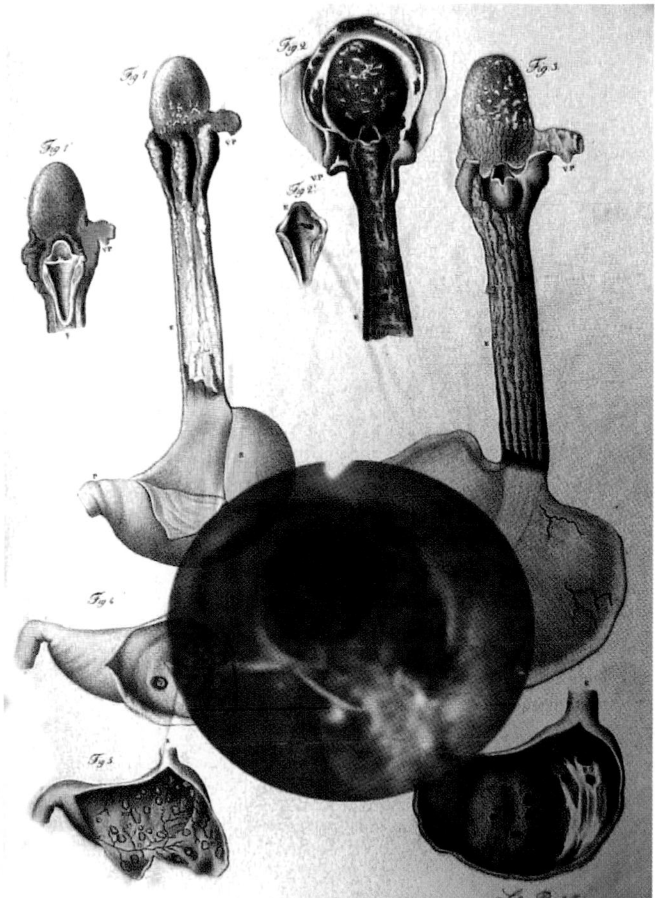

The precise nature of esophageal disease and its relationship to the reflux of acid and pepsin was ill-understood until the early 20th century. It was at first considered to be a component of pharyngitis and laryngitis! A century later this concept reappeared as a novel consideration!

Wilhelm Leube (1842-1911) in 1875 intubated the stomach and explored the nature of digestion by developing a "test breakfast".

The foundations of dyspepsia or heartburn therapy were laid in ancient times when wood ashes, powdered coral, seashell, or chalk ($CaCo_3$, calcium carbonate) was used to relieve dyspepsia, long before it was realized that acid-induced ulceration was responsible for the pain. The subsequent complex regimens of the late eighteenth and early nineteenth centuries reflected the primitive state of medical knowledge and included changing of environment, abstruse diets, mercury, silver or bismuth salts, alkalis, purging, vomiting, and blood-letting. In France, leeches were applied to the upper abdomen to treat dyspepsia, and Johnson in 1831 recommended soda, magnesia, and chalk for pain in the stomach due to acidity. The concept of "resting the bowel," introduced by Leube in Germany in 1876, was used extensively for ulcer-related disorders (although this was speculative since no visualization of the stomach was yet available) and was gradually displaced by the frequent-feeding regimen of Sippy in Chicago in 1915.

Sippy's disciplinarian and obsessive regimens prescribed not only diets and accompanying antacids, but emphasized strict timing and progression by clearly-enunciated principles of strict acid neutralization. He also advocated testing the gastric contents for acid and removing them by stomach tube before bedtime. As a result of such considerations, a large variety of antacids

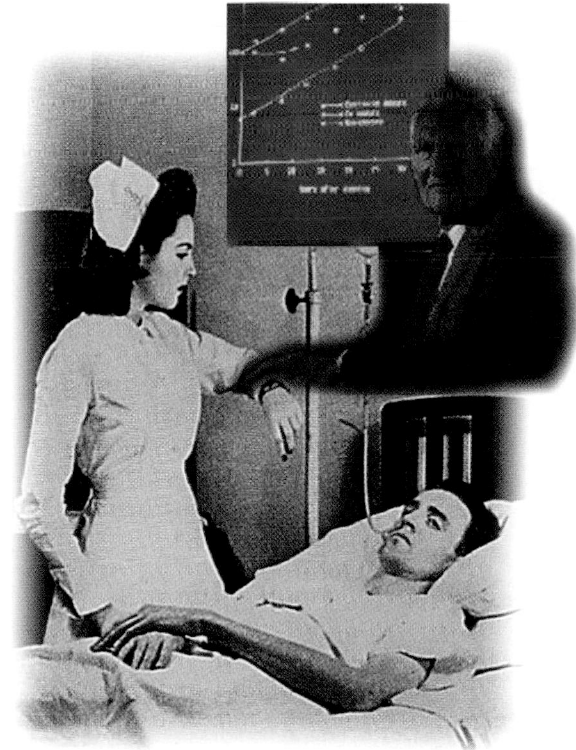

Richard Doll (top right) in the 1950s proposed that ulcers could be cured by instilling milk in a continuous fashion through a nasogastric tube into the stomach of the patient.

Sir Francis Avery-Jones (left) and his student Basil Hirschowitz both contributed significantly to the advancement of the diagnosis and therapy of peptic ulcer disease.

(NaHCo$_3$, and salts of calcium, magnesium, and aluminum) were tested both *in vitro* and *in vivo*, and prescribed for symptoms to be taken with hourly feedings between 7:00 a.m. and 9:00 p.m. The milk/alkali drip of Winkelstein applied the principle of continuous neutralization for initial treatment of symptomatic ulcer.

The rigid requirements of this therapy for as long as 12 to 18 months, led to Kinsey and Zollinger's recommendation, in 1966, for surgery in order to free the patient from "*the abstemious existence required by strict medical therapy*." It was not until the early 1930s that Meulengracht's principle of early feeding after gastrointestinal bleeding replaced Leube's ill-conceived treatment. Bland diets, which avoided "rough" and spicy foods, were based on the concept that white foods (e.g., milk, porridge, mashed potatoes) were more benign, and this notion lasted until the late 1960s. Although Wangensteen credited William Hunter in 1784 as the first to advise the use of milk in the treatment of peptic ulcer, this suggestion may be noted as far back in time as Celsus and the ancient Greek writers.

With the enthusiastic support of the patent medicine sector of the marketplace, diverse other therapies included synthetic resins, gastric mucin, vegetable mucins (Okrin), cabbage juice, vitamin C, high-fat diets, protein hydrolysates, pectin, powdered duodenal mucosa, and a number of parenteral agents, each achieved some degree of support and success. Various non-specific protein products were injected in the 1920s and early 1930s to evoke an "immune reaction" and even pepsin injections to provoke pepsin antibodies; pituitary extract, histidine (Larostidine), parathormone, insulin, and even histamine were administered. In a masterful summation of the subject, Avery-Jones in 1952 was able to amass no less than 56 different regimens, 89 drug preparations, and 19 nonpharmaceutical remedies, each that had enjoyed its "*moment in the sun of therapeutic bliss*."

A cartoon depicting the desperation of a dyspeptic patient faced with the infinite therapeutic possibilities presented to him by his physicians and pharmacist.

No serious relief was possible since the principles of a controlled clinical trial had not yet been established, and were only introduced by Doll in the early 1950s. Spontaneous healing (placebo responses) and the rapid subsidence of symptoms, confused the interpretation of all the uncritical open trials of symptom treatment. Thus bed rest, a vacation, elevation of the head of the bed, weight-loss regimes, and light, white foods were all considered optimal treatment.

Bed rest, often in hospital, was considered essential to remove the patient from the environment in which the disease occurred or relapsed. Anticholinergics (antispasmodics) were used to reduce pain and make acid easier to control, while in Europe, a phenobarbital was widely used in the treatment of many disorders felt to have a psychological component. Psychotherapy became popular in the 1940s and 1950s, as it did for many other illnesses, including ulcerative colitis.

With the introduction of the randomized clinical trial, it became possible to examine various treatments for gastric and duodenal ulcer, although evaluation of esophagitis was difficult, if not impossible. The somewhat improved radiological techniques provided modest objective evidence for adequate statistical analysis, and enabled Doll to conclude that diet did not significantly affect healing, but that bed rest was effective. Of particular interest was a study that examined treatment with diet, phenobarbital, and stilbestrol, and demonstrated clear benefit only from estrogen. Its feminizing effects were, however, considered a significant disadvantage and stilbestrol never reached general use for peptic ulcer. Irrespective of the therapy used, it was apparent that at least 75% of patients relapsed in 5 years and 48% required surgery.

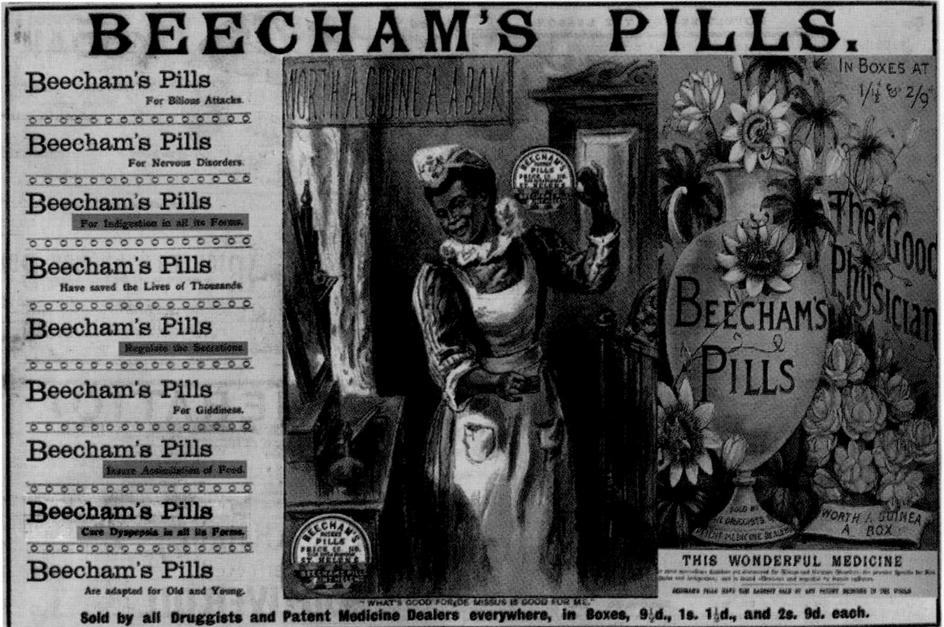

An advert demonstrating the efficacy of Beecham's pills in the management of innumerable complaints, including a variety of gastrointestinal problems such as dyspepsia.

A later controlled trial showed benefit from antacids in healing duodenal ulcer, and antacids remained the mainstay of ulcer treatment until cimetidine.

Although belladonna had been used in clinical practice for many decades for control of "stomach spasms", the introduction of synthetic anticholinergics (late 1950s) resulted in further interest in this treatment. However, efficacy in healing was not uniform and use of anticholinergics fell, at first gradually and then rapidly, after the introduction of cimetidine. The subsequent demonstration by Hammer of cholinergic receptor subtypes and the introduction of a specific drug, pirenzepine, resulted in a brief revival of interest in the subject but efficacy was less than the H2 antagonists, and pirenzepine faded from clinical use in peptic ulcer. Carbenoxolone, an extract of licorice, was shown in the early 1960s to promote healing of gastric ulcers without affecting pH but, because of its aldosterone-like side effects and lower efficacy, carbenoxolone was finally abandoned for acid peptic disease therapy. In general, the agents that were most widely used for symptom relief prior to the introduction of the H2 receptor antagonist class of drugs, were antacids. Although at first shown to be as effective as cimetidine, when used in high doses they were subsequently recognized to be less effective and the introduction of proton pump inhibitor agents largely relegated antacids to a supporting role for rapid relief of heartburn and dyspepsia symptoms.

A medieval depiction of the cultivation of the licorice plant. Herbalists and physicians from the time of Dioscorides onwards had been aware of the soothing effect of licorice extracts on dyspepsia.

Sucralfate, another drug without effect on acid secretion, was developed in Japan and introduced into clinical practice around 1980. Although demonstrated to have an efficacy equal to that of other effective agents in ulcer healing, its mode of action was uncertain and, with the advent of the PPI class of drugs, its use waned. Bismuth (colloidal bismuth suspension), unlike sucralfate and carbenoxolone, has a definite place as an effective ulcer-healing drug because of its effectiveness in *H. pylori* related disease. Its utility in symptoms deriving from esophagitis is, however, uncertain. Although bismuth had been used for dyspepsia for centuries, it first claimed interest in the 1970s, not only because it was effective, but also because of apparently lower relapse rates. In recent years, a possible explanation of the latter findings might be the suppression of *H. pylori*, which is sensitive to bismuth.

Owen Wangensteen of Minnesota was an innovative surgeon who in 1932 had proposed decompression of obstructed bowel that lead, in 1934, to Thomas Miller and William Abbott of Philadelphia inventing a tube for this purpose. In the 1960s Wangensteen proposed that peptic ulcers (especially bleeding lesions) could be treated by gastric freezing, using perfused balloons (inset) inserted into the stomach.

Among the interesting nonsurgical treatments for decreasing acid secretion were gastric irradiation and gastric freezing. Irradiation of the stomach was first used by Bruegel in 1917, and numerous studies of radiation injury and specific experiments on gastric irradiation showed a decrease in acid secretion. Ricketts reported that 90% of gastric ulcers healed with medical treatment plus radiation versus 60% without radiation. Similar results were obtained in duodenal ulcer and recurrences of duodenal and gastric ulcers in a one to ten-year follow-up were reduced from 70% to 33%. Indeed, gastric irradiation was used as late as 1970 for patients with "surgical" ulcers who were considered poor surgical risks.

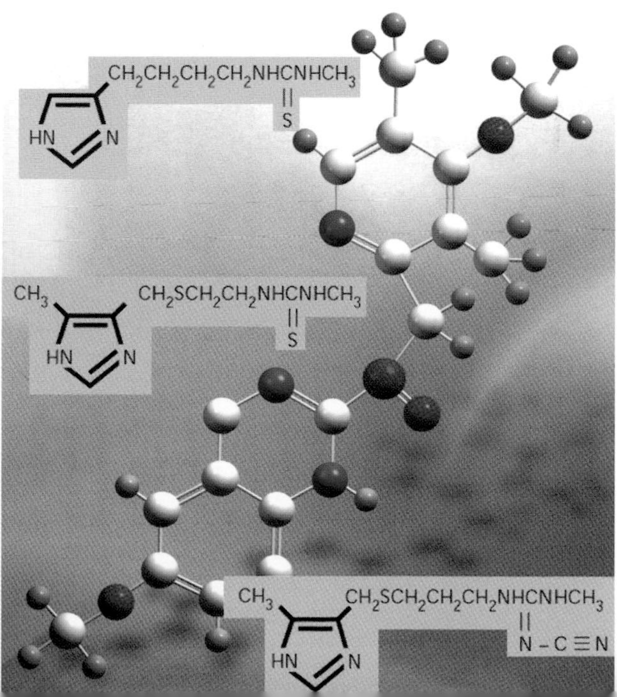

The molecular structures of a variety of histamine 2 receptor antagonists and a proton pump inhibitor (center).

Philip Allison of Leeds, England, was one of the first surgeons to recognize the potential role of a hiatus hernia in reflux esophagitis and to treat it successfully by surgical repair.

Receptor and Pump-directed therapy

A new era of ulcer treatment was initiated by the development of histamine H2 receptor antagonists by James Black. Although metiamide, the first H2 blocker used clinically, caused agranulocytosis, the development of cimetidine led to the accumulation of considerable evidence of its safety and efficacy, and it soon became one of most widely used drugs in the world. As a result, by 1981, within two years after the introduction of cimetidine, Wyllie was able to document a sharp (38%) decline in the number of operations for duodenal ulcer in the United Kingdom. Unfortunately, while effective in the management of GERD, high dosages were necessary to control symptoms and cessation of therapy led to rapid relapse. The introduction of omeprazole in the 1980s, with its more effective acid suppression, led to a considerable improvement in GERD management, but in many instances relapse would follow cessation of therapy. Neverthless, the PPI class of drugs dramatically improved the ability of patients with esophagitis to remain symptom-free and the long-term usage of such agents became considered appropriate for the management of GERD.

As a result, the surgical technique of fundoplication, which had already been considered by most to have an unacceptably high morbidity and even mortality, as well as a significant failure rate, fell into general disrepute. The advent of laparoscopic surgery has re-opened this issue to a certain extent, since the minimally invasive nature of the operation has lent some credence to claims that it is now safer and more effective. Considerable controversy, however, surrounds the issue, since the "learning curve" concept has hampered uniform results, and overzealous application of the operation by surgeons hungrily seeking the lost acid peptic disease target have confounded a rigorous evaluation of the efficacy of the procedure. Since the principle of the operation is the same as for the failed open fundoplication, there seems little to support its re-introduction except in individuals with obvious lower esophageal sphincter dysfunction, unavailability of PPIs, or inability to tolerate an acid-suppressive medication.

Surgery for Hiatus Hernia and Esophageal Reflux

Winkelstein in 1935 first defined the essential clinical picture of reflux and suggested that the esophagitis resulted from the action of digestive gastric juice. This concept did not gain wide understanding until the classic publications of Allison and Barrett, who concluded that reflux esophagitis was common and could cause ulceration and stricture. Although it was recognized that a mechanism existed for preventing reflux, it was not until manometric studies that the anatomically inconspicuous sphincter was found to be a functioning reality. Thus, most surgical repair procedures were directed at reducing the hernia and reconstructing the hiatus. Allison was of the firm belief that the hiatus hernia played a pivotal role in reflux, but this was for many years a point of considerable controversy. Hiatal hernia was not diagnosed in life before the introduction of contrast radiology in the first decade of the twentieth century, thus the Mayo Clinic could record only 30 diagnosed cases between 1900 and 1925 and 211 between 1925 and 1937. Since surgical dogma held that a hiatal hernia was an anatomic abnormality, analogous to an inguinal hernia, it became axiomatic in some circles that it required anatomic repair in its own right. The first recorded repair of hiatal hernia was in 1919 by the Italian surgeon Soresi. Subsequent refinements of surgical technique to improve the operation included crural approximation and even phrenic nerve division, to allow the diaphragm to rise and thereby change the pressure relationship between the stomach and the esophagus. Eventually, the high recurrence rate of the Allison operation led to a

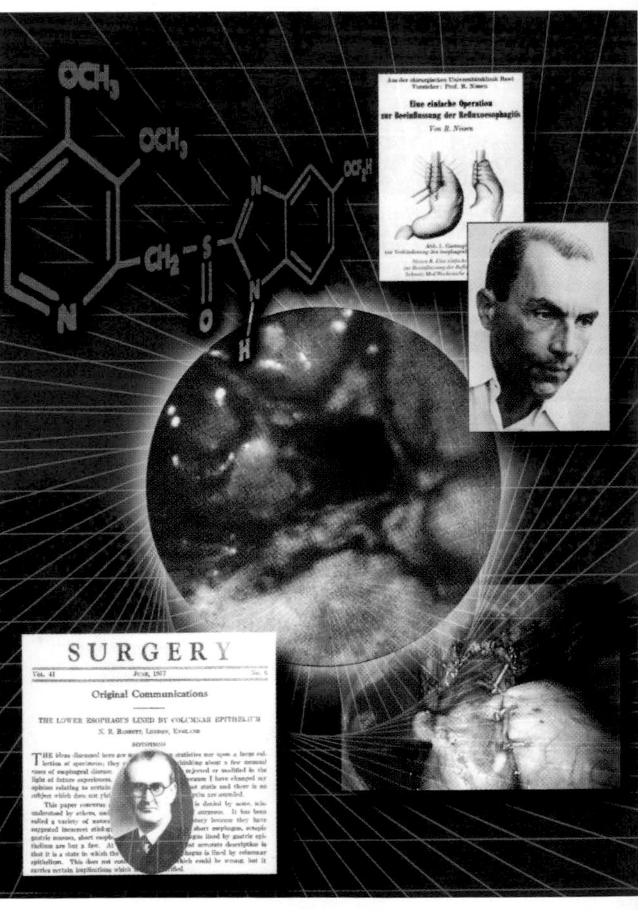

Norman Barrett (bottom left) was prescient in directing attention to the subject of peptic esophagitis and for initiating a reconsideration of its pathogenesis. Rudolf Nissen (top right) described the operation of fundoplication for the treatment of reflux disease. Esophagitis (center) in the late 20th century is treated either by acid suppressive therapy (top left) or laparoscopic fundoplication (bottom right).

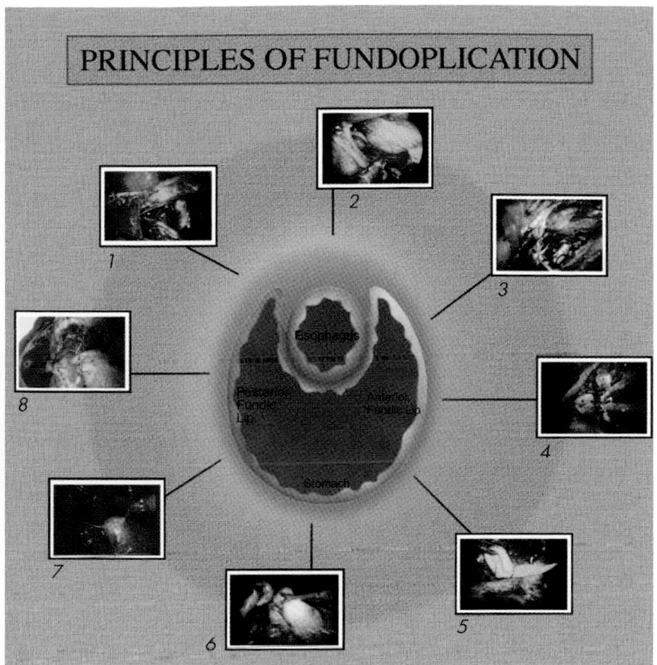

The most commonly performed antireflux procedure is the laparoscopic Nissen fundoplication. The essential elements of this procedure are illustrated in a clockwise fashion.

1. *Crural dissection with the identification and preservation of the vagal nerves.*
2. *Circumferential dissection of the esophagus.*
3. *Suture closure of the crura.*
4. *Division of the short gastric vessels and fundic mobilization.*
5. *Traction of the greater curve of the fundus behind the esophagus.*
6. *Creation of a short, loose fundoplication over the esophagus containing a 60 F bougie.*
7. *Suture of the two fundic lips to each other and to the anterior gastric wall.*
8. *Completed procedure with wrap sutured over the lower esophagus.*

search for newer surgical methods in the late 1960s. Amongst the alternative explanations considered was the original proposal by Barrett of the existence of a "short esophagus". This entity was proposed to be a congenitally short esophagus containing acid and pepsin-secreting mucosa, which was believed to be a cause of esophagitis, ulceration, and stricture and susceptible to malignant degeneration. Resection with jejunal or even colonic substitution was sometimes recommended for such complications.

The unacceptable failure rate of hiatal hernia repair as described by Allison, and the recurrence of symptoms, led to the development of a series of permutations and commutations of the operations of fundoplication by Nissen, Belsey, Hill, Toupet, and a host of surgeons inclined to believe that operating on the gastro-esophageal junction might resolve the problem. In principle, all the procedures shared some common elements, including a gastric fundic wrap (various degrees of wrap were each considered critical) around the lower esophagus. The Hill posterior gastropexy repair was introduced in 1967 and, like the former two, was also modified by later experience. All procedures had overall satisfactory results confirmed by manometry and in recent years, 24 hours pH probe of reflux. However, they none were without problems and in 10% to 15% of patients relapse, dysphagia, and difficulty in belching, were major issues. The morbidity of the procedure was about 15% even in experienced hands, mortality as high as 1% to 2% and long term effectiveness decreased with time to 70% to 80% depending on the degree of care with which patients were studied. Even in those operations regarded as a success, the majority of patients were noted to take acid suppressive medications to suppress symptomatology. The advent of laparoscopic fundoplication appears to have done little to alter the balance of opinion that for the vast majority of patients, pharmacotherapy remains the safest and most efficacious form of therapy.

Esophageal Surgery

With the spread of antisepsis, larger and more complex operations were undertaken. This was particularly apparent in surgery of the esophagus, that for years had been regarded as beyond surgical reach. Although Billroth had resected the esophagus in 1872, the procedure was rarely undertaken because of its mortality. The commonest problems of the esophagus were posed by strictures due to caustic ingestion in children. Although benign, they resulted in death from inanition. In cases of such "benign" constrictions, a stomach fistula not only permitted the feeding of the patient, but also enabled dilation to be undertaken. In cases where this was not possible, other surgical alternatives were considered. In this manner, the formation of a "gullet in front of the ribcage" viz. the formation of a tube running under the skin of the ribcage, was first considered. A connection of the stomach with the gullet thus enabled food taken by mouth to bypass the strictured area and reach the stomach. Henry Bircher of Switzerland (1894), who extended the work of Victor Hacker of Graz, Austria, successfully developed this operation. The latter had undertaken much work in esophageal surgery and had pioneered the concept of connecting the cervical esophagus to the stomach using a skin tube. Subsequently Cesar Roux of Lausanne improved this procedure by constructing the connecting tube placed under the skin out of the small intestine.

George Gray Turner (1877-1951) was a master surgeon with a particular interest in the esophagus. Turner was one of the first to resect the thoracic esophagus and replace it with an anti-thoracic intestinal tube anastomosis. The inset is of his patient Joseph Wright, 59 years of age, enjoying a meal of poached egg, bread and butter, tea and some pears on the 206th day after the first operation.

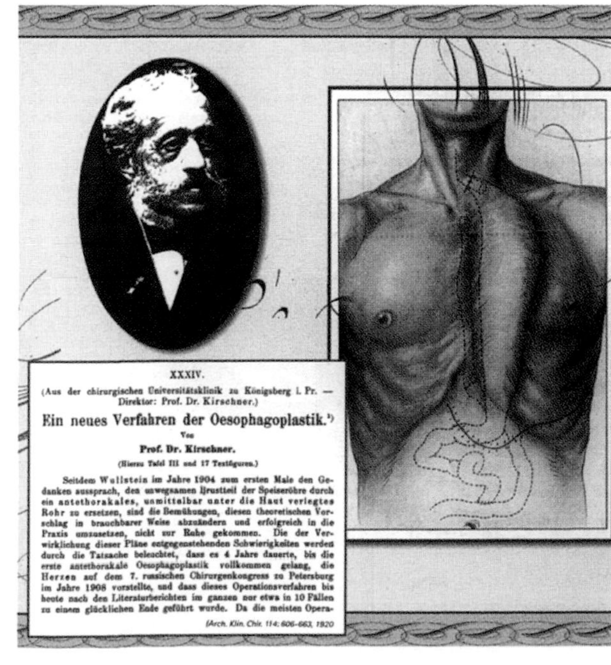

XXXIV.

(Aus der chirurgischen Universitätsklinik zu Königsberg i. Pr. — Direktor: Prof. Dr. Kirschner.)

Ein neues Verfahren der Oesophagoplastik.[1]

Von

Prof. Dr. Kirschner.

(Hierzu Tafel III und 17 Textfiguren.)

Seitdem Wullstein im Jahre 1904 zum ersten Male den Gedanken aussprach, den unwegsamen Brustteil der Speiseröhre durch ein antethorakales, unmittelbar unter die Haut verlegtes Rohr zu ersetzen, sind die Bemühungen, diesen theoretischen Vorschlag in brauchbarer Weise abzuändern und erfolgreich in die Praxis umzusetzen, nicht zur Ruhe gekommen. Die der Verwirklichung dieser Pläne entgegenstehenden Schwierigkeiten werden durch die Tatsache beleuchtet, dass es 4 Jahre dauerte, bis die erste antethorakale Oesophagoplastik vollkommen gelang, die Herzen auf dem 7. russischen Chirurgenkongress zu Petersburg im Jahre 1908 vorstellte, und dass dieses Operationsverfahren bis heute nach den Literaturberichten im ganzen nur etwa in 10 Fällen zu einem glücklichen Ende geführt wurde. Da die meisten Opera-

(Arch. Klin. Chir. 114: 606-663, 1920

Esophageal replacement was a formidable issue. The development of techniques for the construction of a subcutaneous gastric or small intestinal bypass into the neck alleviated the problem. Although numerous individuals were responsible for the evolution of this procedure, the work of Kirschner (frontispiece) and Langenbeck (inset) was regarded as pivotal in the development of the operation.

SECTION 14

The Stomach and Duodenum

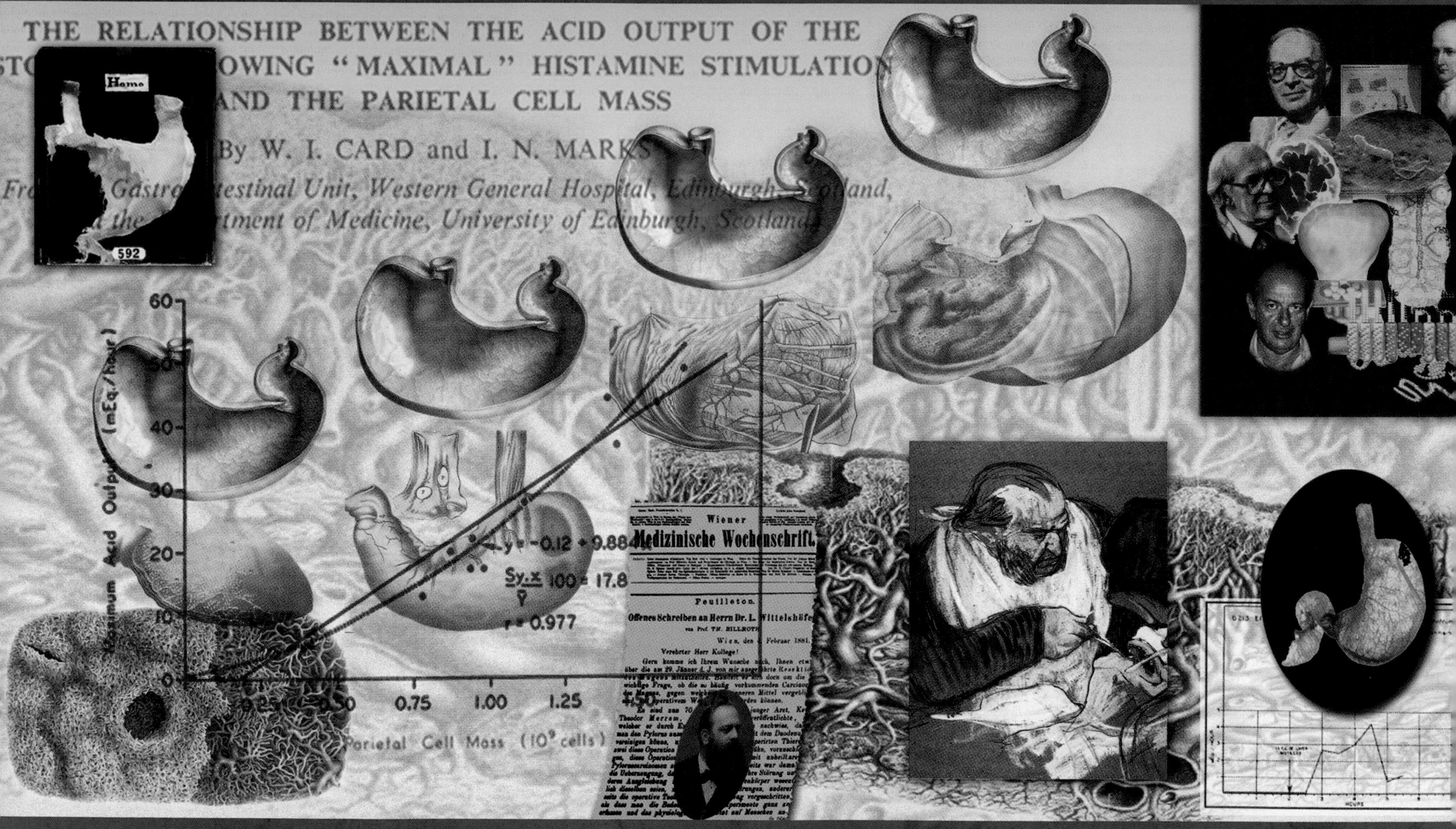

Stomach and Duodenum

The digestive tract and stomach, before Leonardo Da Vinci and Andreas Vesalius, remained simply an object of ill-understood function and was regarded as a mere repository of food and, possibly, some spiritual powers. Ancient concepts are best suggested by the terminology employed by Shakespeare and dramatists of his time.

Thus, in keeping with Greek and Roman usage, the stomach (*ventriculus*) was equated with the belly (*venter*) as noted in the parable about *"the belly and the members"* in *Coriolanus* or the episodes of *Falstaff* and *Justice Greedy* (Massinger). Indeed, the stomach was most often characterized as involved with gluttony or drinking by the Elizabethans, whereas the Persian poets such as Saadi, noted that an empty belly supported mental and spiritual activity. Later thoughts on the stomach suggested that the entire gastrointestinal tract was associated with pluck and courage (*"guts"*). But apart from these literary allusions little was known about the organ itself.

Vesalius had beautifully illustrated the anatomy of the organ and depicted its relationship to other intra-abdominal structures especially the "wandering nerve" or vagus. However, the precise functional significance of this observation would require almost four centuries before the investigations of Pavlov would further define the functional significance of neural regulation. Descriptions of the coats or layers of the stomach added little to the elucidation of function, and the use of animals or fish as experimental models further obfuscated issues, as the pyloric ceca became confused with elements of the pancreas by Regnier de Graaf and his colleagues. The introduction of microscopy to the study of the stomach reflected the contributions of van Leeuwenhoek to the improvement of lens design. G. Bidloo and H. Boerhaave applied his techniques early in the eighteenth century to the study of gastric glands and, in Bidloo's text, are the earliest examples of microscopic anatomy. Subsequently, Camillo Golgi while working with Bizzozero in Pavia, demonstrated that these glands considerably alter their morphology as the resting stomach enters the secretory mode.

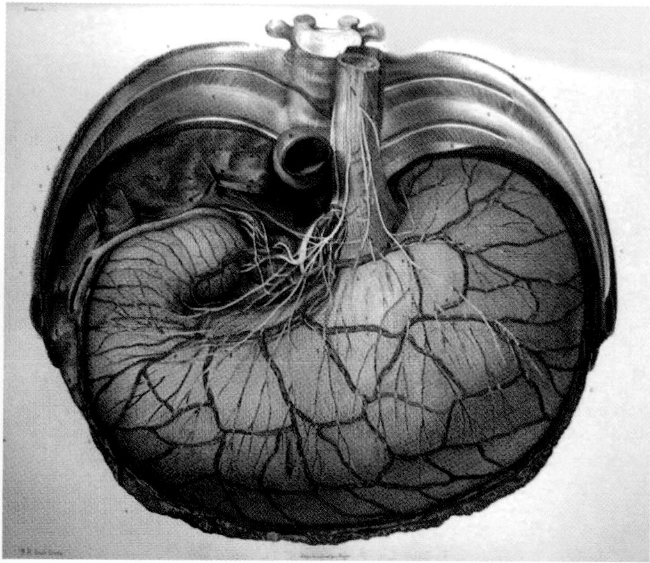

An 1832 illustration of the stomach, esophagus, and duodenum by J.P. Bougery of Paris. Originally trained as a painter by no less a personage than Jean-Louis David, the portraitist of Napoleon, Bougery was to find himself unemployed after the defeat of Napoleon and the subsequent loss of patronage. He, therefore, turned his considerable skills to anatomic illustration.

It is, however, of particular interest to note that in addition to these cell types, Heidenhain identified a "third" type of cell in the form of minute oval elements found adhering to the external surface of the epithelial tube (gastric gland) (1868-70). These cells were particularly conspicuous in preparations made with bichromate solutions, in which they stained a deep yellow color and occupied a parietal position on the surface of the glands in both the rabbits and numerous other animals studied by Heidenhain. Given their staining characteristics and location, it is possible, therefore, to presume that in 1868, Heidenhain had identified chromaffin cells (EC) in the gastric mucosa. A further careful perusal of his writings and drawings suggests that two years later, in 1870, he may in addition have noticed the existence of the ECL cell.

Gastric Acid

The early Greeks were not aware of acids in the modern chemical sense, but were able to identify them as bitter-sour liquids. Diocles of Carystos (*c.* 350 B.C.) was able to specify sour eruptions, watery spitting, gas, heartburn and epigastric hunger pains radiating to the back (with occasional splashing noises and vomiting) as symptoms of illness originating in the stomach. Approximately three hundred years later, Celsus (30 B.C. – A.D. 25) recognized that certain foods were acidic and recommended that *"if the stomach is infested with an ulcer, light and gelatinous food must be used and everything acrid and acid is to be avoided"*.

A millennium later, opinions ranged from there being no acid in the stomach at all, to it originating from the pancreas. Physicians of the fifteenth and sixteenth centuries felt that any acid present in the stomach was the result of putrefaction or fermentation, and did not in any way reflect an active secretory

Aurelius Cornelius Celsus of Rome was not a physician but an aristocrat of the noble family of Cornelii and lived during the reign of Tiberius Caesar. His classical work, De re Medicina, *was one of the first medical books to be printed and, although ignored by the Roman practitioners of his day and slighted as "mediocre" by Quintilian, he remains one of the authorities of his time. He wrote on medicine in much the same spirit in which Virgil considered veterinary matters in the* Third Book of the Georgics. *Celsus provided medical assistance free to the members of his country estate as would be expected of a wealthy Roman aristocrat. So highly rated was his writing that he was considered the Cicero of Medicine, and the eight books that constitute* De re Medicina *are masterpieces of precise literary style. The first of the four texts deals with diseases that may be treated by diet and alteration of lifestyle, whereas the last four describe those amenable to drugs and surgery. Celsus believed that nutritive enemata were important in treating abdominal problems, and provided a diffuse and exotic list of herbal remedies that might be used to remove stomach discomfort and other digestive ailments.*

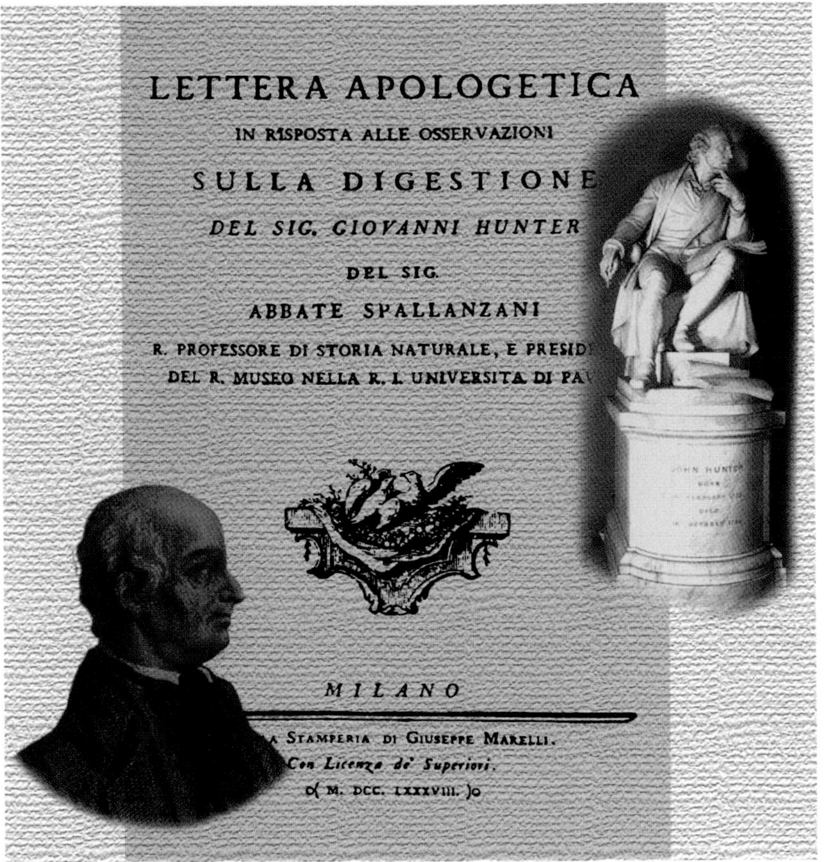
LETTERA APOLOGETICA
IN RISPOSTA ALLE OSSERVAZIONI
SULLA DIGESTIONE
DEL SIG. GIOVANNI HUNTER
DEL SIG.
ABBATE SPALLANZANI
R. PROFESSORE DI STORIA NATURALE, E PRESID
DEL R. MUSEO NELLA R. I. UNIVERSITA DI PA
MILANO
A STAMPERIA DI GIUSEPPE MARELLI.
Con Licenza de' Superiori.
M. DCC. LXXXVIII.

L. Spallanzani (1729-1789) (bottom left) was a physiologist of considerable skill and insight. His proposal that the stomach produced acid was the source of an acrid debate between he and John Hunter (top right) of London. The matter was amicably settled by a suitably diplomatic letter of apology (background).

process of the body or the stomach itself. In the sixteenth century, Paracelsus (1493-1541), an alchemist-physician and a proponent of chemical pharmacology and therapeutics, however, believed intimately that there was acid in the stomach and that it was necessary for digestion. His proposal that gastric acid was of extra-corporeal origin was of course wrong, but nonetheless, he recognized the importance of chemistry and its relation to disease, and rejected Galenism and the mysticism of humors and health. The Iatrochemical views propounded by Paracelsus, and thereafter by J.B. Van Helmont (1577-1644) and others, were strongly opposed by the Iatromathematical School, which maintained that all physiologic happenings should be treated as fixed consequences of the laws of physics. The disciples of this school of thought favored the view that the stomach was little more than a mechanical mill, grinding up its contents into chyme, and their approach to the acid question is exemplified by Mobius, who denied the existence of gastric acid. Caring little for the new science of chemistry, their postulates fermented in corporeal cul-de-sacs, fading into such sterile eccentricities as the proposal by Pitcairn, that the entirety of medical practice could be based on mechanical principles. Ingenious methods for obtaining gastric juice (sponges, hollow tubes and even emesis), as well as the demonstration and recognition of vegetable dyes to determine acidity or alkalinity, substantially aided the investigation of the precise nature of gastric juice. Such agents possessed the property of color change when exposed to appropriate acids or alkalis and thus facilitated identification of the nature of the material being tested. At this time, while there was some agreement that acid was indeed present in the stomach, there was considerable disagreement about both the chemical nature of the acid, as well as whether it was primarily secreted by the stomach or derived in some way from ingested food.

In 1760, Reuss found that, even with preliminary alkalization of the stomach, the ingestion of a meal of meat and vegetables resulted in secretion of acid. The vomit had an acid taste and turned an infusion of campanules a *"feuilles-rondes"* red. Gosse, in 1783, repeated the studies more elegantly. He had, as a child, developed the faculty of aerophagy and self-induced emesis, whereas Reuss required taking an emetic. By inducing emesis at specific times after eating, Gosse was able to obtain "pure" gastric juice. In his studies he was unable to identify acid or alkaline gastric juice. In 1780, Lazzaro Spallanzani (1729-1799), who was the professor of Natural History in Pavia, published his extensive observations in this area. He had used the methods of Réaumur upon fish, frogs, snakes, cattle, horses, cats, dogs and even himself, and asserted that gastric juice was probably neutral. Spallanzani was however, uncertain about his findings regarding the acidity of gastric juice, and therefore undertook collaborative studies in an effort to resolve this question. Thus in 1785, in conjunction with Carminati, professor of Medicine at Pavia, they first detected the acidity of the contents of a meal.

Spallanzani was advised to test birds on a meat-free diet; he also found marine acid in the juice squeezed from sponges fed to five ravens that were fed on vegetables for 15 days. Later, Brugnatelli in 1786, and Werner in 1800, found the contents of the stomachs of sheep, cats, fish and birds to be acid. Despite the relatively clear evidence produced by Spallanzani and his colleagues that there was acid in the stomach and that it was hydrochloric acid, considerable controversy persisted. Indeed, many of the investigators of this area, including no less a scientist than John Hunter, reversed their thoughts a number of times during the study of the subject. Thus, even among the minds of the most eminent physicians of the day, confusion reigned, not only as to the presence of acid, but as to the exact nature of the substance.

Initial human studies

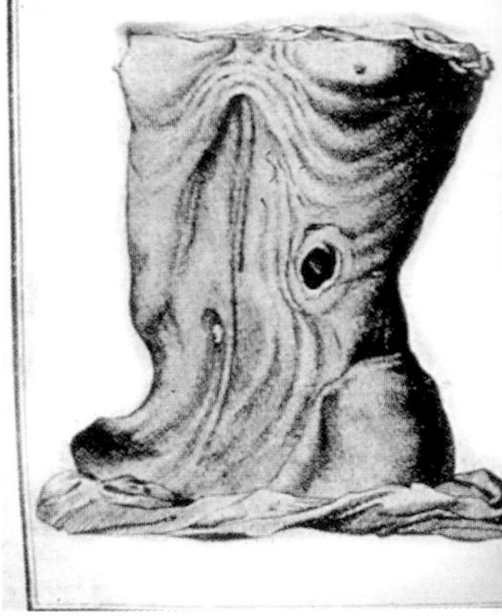

Studies of gastric fistula patients yielded some, albeit mixed, information about gastric acid in humans. In 1797, Jacob Anton Helm of Vienna studied a 58-year-old woman, Theresa Petz of Breitenwaida (left), who had a spontaneous gastric fistula and used a hired person, Zyriak Sieddeler, and himself, with his own brother as a control. Helm undertoook meticulous studies of digestive processes, but did not measure acid, nor was he able to demonstrate a change in the color of dye to indicate the presence of acid in the gastric juice. Four years later, in 1801, Rouilly transferred to the care of Dupuytren and Bichat in Paris a patient, Madeline Gore (right), with a gastric fistula. Gore's gastric juice was analyzed by Clarion, a professor of chemistry, who thus can be credited with attempting the first quantitative assessment of this secretion. Clarion found neither acid nor alkali and concluded that gastric juice was identical with saliva. This conclusion remained dogma for years in the French medical profession so that, even in 1812, when Montnegre reported acid in fasting and meal-stimulated gastric juice, he attributed this acid to the digestion of food and saliva.

The Contributions of William Prout

William Prout (1785-1850) provided the final resolution as to the exact nature of acid produced by the stomach in 1823. A brilliant physician with diverse interests outside of medicine, Prout was productive in the fields of chemistry, meteorology, and physiology as well as clinical medicine. In addition, he was one of the first scientists to apply chemical analysis to biologic materials. Prior to Prout, the exact nature of the gastric acid had been a controversial issue and altough Johann Thölde had first described the acid known as hydrochloric acid, although it had also been called muriatic acid for many years, its presence in the stomach was debated. In fact, even Prout at an earlier stage of his studies into the nature of acid, had, like Young of Philadelphia, believed phosphoric acid as the acid agent of the stomach.

Unfortunately, however, Prout's observations were not readily accepted across La Grande Manche. Physiologists as eminent as Claude Bernard were of the opinion that lactic acid (a product of fermentation) was the gastric acid present in gastric contents, while some such as Montnegre even believed that there was no gastric secretion of acid. The French Académie des Sciences determined to resolve the exact nature of acid in the stomach, and in 1828 established an essay contest for which they offered a prize of 3,000 francs for the solution to the problem. A panel of distinguished judges was selected to evaluate the essays and one year later, the prize was awarded jointly to Leuret and Lassaigne of Paris, and Tiedemann and Gmelin of Heidelberg. Leuret and Lassaigne declared that the acid in gastric juice was lactic, whilst Tiedemann and Gmelin confirmed Prout's earlier observations that it was hydrochloric acid. When asked to share the prize, the Germans, offended by the contradiction provided by the judges, declined and withdrew from the competition. At this time, J. Berzelius of Sweden was regarded as the ranking authority on chemistry in Europe and his arbitration on the matter was anxiously awaited by the authors. Thus Wöhler, in a letter of May 17, 1828, reported to Berzelius how gratified Tiedemann and Leopold Gmelin were to have noted in the *Årsberättelser* 7, 297, his deprecatory comments regarding the "*unbedeutende Arbeit*" of Leuret and Lassaigne.

F. Tiedemann (top) and L. Gmelin (center) of Germany correctly identified that gastric acid was hydrochloric in nature. Despite this the French scientists, Leuret and Lassaigne, were jointly awarded a prize by the French Academy of Science for determining that it was lactic acid.

Berzelius indeed may have been too smug in this comment on the work of Leuret and Lassaigne since he himself had previously reported that gastric acid was lactic! Despite this error, the contributions of Leuret and Lassaigne were not inconsequential, since in separate canine experimental studies, they were the first to demonstrate that acid introduced into the duodenum elicited the secretion of pancreatic juice and bile. Although they failed to explore the mechanism in detail, their observations preceded those of Pavlov and Starling. This is explored further in the next section. Nevertheless, the animal experimental data failed to provide conclusive evidence regarding the human physiology of digestion until the contributions of William Beaumont and his patient Alexis St. Martin almost half a world away from the sophistication of nineteenth century Europe.

Alexis St. Martin, a French voyageur who on June 6, 1822 suffered a musket wound to his left upper abdomen at Fort Mackinac. William Beaumont, the military physician at the fort, saved his life and thereafter studied the gastric fistula that resulted from the wound. The subsequent observations laid the foundations of human gastric physiology.

III. *On the nature of the acid and saline matters usually existing in the stomachs of animals.* By William Prout, M. D. F. R. S.

Read December 11, 1829.

That a free, or at least an unsaturated acid usually exists

On December 11, 1823, at the Royal Society of London, Prout presented his landmark paper, "On the Nature of Acid and Saline Matters Usually Existing in the Stomach of Animals." This presentation was unique in two ways. First, Prout had specifically identified hydrochloric acid in the gastric juice of many species (man, dog, rabbit, horse, calf and hare), and second, he was able to quantify the free and total hydrochloric acid and chloride present. The human gastric juice was obtained from patients at Guy's Hospital who were under the care of the surgeon Astley Cooper. In addition to demonstrating the presence of hydrochloric acid in diverse animals, Prout was also able to determine that the same acid was present in dyspeptic patients, and that the amount of this acid appeared to be related to the degree of dyspepsia. The acid was measured by neutralization with a potash solution of known strength and the chloride by titration with silver nitrate. So advanced were his ideas that he proposed that chloride may be secreted from blood to lumen by electrical means and that, when gastric acid was secreted, the blood would become alkaline (now recognized as the post-prandial alkaline tide). Indeed, more than 100 years were to elapse before his subsequent proposal was confirmed.

William Beaumont (bottom right) was the first individual to study gastric digestion in a rigorous fashion. His patient, Alexis St. Martin, received a gunshot wound at Fort Mackinac and survived with a gastric fistula (bottom left) which Beaumont studied for almost 10 years. St. Martin was a somewhat unwilling subject and in order to maintain his experimental services Beaumont was forced to negotiate a contract with him (center).

William Beaumont and Alexis St. Martin

William Beaumont (1785-1853) was born in Lebanon, Connecticut, and having trained in medicine by apprenticeship, thereafter became a military doctor. In 1819, after a brief period in practice, his former colleague, Joseph Lovell, who had now become surgeon-general, offered Beaumont a commission, and he was assigned to Fort Mackinac on the island of Michel Mackinac at the junction of Lakes Huron and Michigan. As the only physician within three hundred miles Beaumont was busy, and in addition to his military medical responsibilities, was often involved in managing the trauma consequent upon the frequent brawls among Indians and fur traders. One such event resulted in his care of a young man with a musket-induced gastric fistula. Despite his background as a surgeon and no formal training in physiology, Beaumont seized the opportunity to study the patient, A. St. Martin, in a manner similar to that previously utilized by Helm of Vienna and Rouilly of Paris to investigate their patients. Albeit unschooled in experimentation and the sophistication of chemistry, Beaumont meticulously studied the physiologic basis of human digestion and produced a classic text on the subject in 1833.

On the morning of June 6, 1822, a 19-year-old-French Canadian voyageur, Alexis St. Martin, was accidentally shot in the left upper abdomen and chest. Beaumont was called to see the victim and hearing the extent of the disastrous wound pronounced the chances of survival to be slim, remarking: "*The man cannot live 36 hours; I will come and see him by and by.*" Surprisingly, St. Martin survived the initial catastrophe and with the active care provided by Beaumont, had largely recovered after about ten months, although a gastric fistula remained. By this stage, the ill and unemployed St. Martin was penniless and the county authorities, refusing further support, proposed transporting him fifteen hundred miles back to his birthplace in Canada. Beaumont opposed the proposal, fearing both for the safety of his patient and the loss of his human experimental model. Thus in April 1823, Beaumont moved St. Martin to his own home, where he remained for almost two years under constant care and attention while also being studied. In 1824, Beaumont had sent his commanding officer (Surgeon General Lovell) a manuscript detailing his observations concerning the gastric fistula of St. Martin and the results of his preliminary considerations on the nature of digestion. It was published in the *Medical Recorder* as "A Case of Wounded Stomach" by Joseph Lovell, Surgeon General, USA. The oversight of Beaumont's omission as an author was, however, soon remedied and Beaumont instated as a co-author.

At this stage, Beaumont, having recognized the unique opportunity that St. Martin's gastric fistula presented for formal study, began his epic investigation into gastric function and digestion. Given his lack of knowledge of science, he enlisted the aid of Robley Dunglison (professor of Medicine in Philadelphia) and Benjamin Silliman (professor of Chemistry at Yale) to support his investigations. In 1826, his first paper was published, but unfortunately further studies were curtailed by a military transfer to Fort Niagara and the simultaneous disappearance of St. Martin back to Canada. Despite significant effort to locate his difficult patient, it took until 1829 for Beaumont to locate St. Martin and arrange employment at the American Fur Company at Fort Crawford on the Upper Mississippi River where Beaumont was then stationed. During the next two years, although many successful experiments were performed, St. Martin and his family, having become homesick and discontented, returned to Canada.

Studying St. Martin had by now become an obsession for Beaumont, and he even attempted to arrange to travel to Europe with him for further scientific investigation. Although this proposed trip failed, he was, with the help of Lovell, able to enlist St. Martin in the United States Army to forestall any further episodes of abscondment, which would henceforth be regarded as desertion. Thereafter, Beaumont entered into a formal written agreement with St. Martin as his "human guinea pig". In return for allowing the study of his stomach and digestion, St. Martin was to receive board, lodging, and an annual stipend. Despite being an unpleasant and dissolute person to work with, St. Martin was studied by Beaumont without further interruption until November 1, 1833. At this stage, he again disappeared into Canada and Beaumont was never able again to work with him. St. Martin died at the age of 83 and, in fact, outlived his physician, Beaumont, by several years. William Osler actually sought to obtain the stomach for study but so adamantly opposed were the family, that a militia was organized to protect the body and the local priest advised Osler to defer the matter lest he come to harm.

Despite the incontrovertible evidence produced by Prout, Tiedemann, Gmelin, and Beaumont as late as 1885, some German physiologists still had not fully accepted that hydrochloric acid was the critical acid secreted by the stomach. Thus, the doyens of German gastroenterology, K. Ewald and I. Boas (1858-1938), reported that all acid present in the stomach at the beginning of a meal was lactic. It was their theory that hydrochloric acid gradually replaced the lactic acid during eating, with the result that, by the end of a meal, only hydrochloric acid was evident!

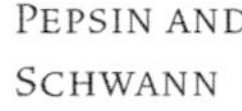

Pepsin and Schwann

The story of pepsinogen begins essentially in the Berlin laboratory of J. Muller, where Theodore Schwann had been asked by Muller to attempt to subject the physiological properties of either an organ or a tissue to physical measurement. Schwann initially developed a muscle balance, and became the first to establish the basics of the tension-length diagram. Thereafter, whilst successfully measuring secretion from the gastric gland, he stumbled upon a proteolytic enzyme, whose properties he characterized, and soon thereafter, in 1836, published. In this paper he described a water-soluble factor in gastric juice which digested egg-white and named it "pepsin", after the Greek word for digestion.

Three years after the initial identification of pepsin by Schwann, Wasmann was able to isolate the protein and thereby establish the premise for protein digestion. In 1854, the possibility of a pro-enzyme, pepsinogen, was formally postulated by Epstein and P. Grützner, but the first evaluation of the protein products of gastric digestion were only described by Meisner in 1859. Heidenhain, during his tenure, was able to describe the secretory mechanisms of proteolytic zymogens with the gastric lumen and noted that pepsin was secreted by the "*Hauptzellen*". The observations of Heidenhain were further extended by W. Kuhne, who theorized that since the stomach itself was not self-digested, that gastric ferments must be produced as inactive protein precursors (e.g. pepsinogen). Indeed, such was the prescience of Kuhne in defining this area of physiology that he developed the term "zymogen" to describe such precursors, and was the first to use the term "enzyme", having identified the proteolytic pancreatic enzyme, trypsin, in 1868. His influence on the evolution of gastrointestinal physiology was substantial and a number of English physiologists, including Starling and Langley, worked in his laboratory.

John Langley

Although the initial contributions to the discovery of pepsin were those of Schwann, his genius led him variously into fermentation, neural cell morphology, the single cell theory of disease and the design of underwater diving apparatus. It therefore remained for Langley of Cambridge in the 1880s to formalize the study of pepsinogen and the mechanisms of its secretion. Langley's introduction to the gastric gland was driven by chance, since his initial assignment by his mentor, Foster (the first chairman of Physiology at Cambridge) had been to evaluate the effects of the drug, *jaborandi*, on the heart. In pursuit of this goal, by 1874 his work had led him towards the investigation of its effects on secretion. After an initial prelude in the submaxillary gland, Langley addressed the regulation of secretion in the stomach, which he would pursue for the better part of the next twenty years.

Using the salamander as a model, he undertook histological studies of the gland structure in activity and rest and checked the interpretation of the appearance of killed and stained cells with that of direct observation of living gland cells. He correlated these findings with the effect of nervous

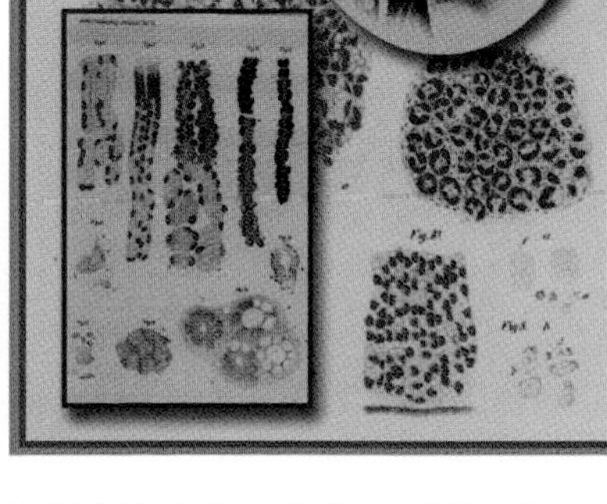

Rudolph Heidenhain, Professor of Physiology at Breslau, was amongst the first to conduct classic research on the structure of the gastric gland and the secretory apparatus of the stomach. Eight years into his tenure Heidenhain began a systematic study of glands, which would occupy him for almost the next thirty years. His observations led him to the conclusion that the "Labzellen" (rennin cells) were distinct from a second type of cell which he termed a "Hauptzelle" and which formed the complete lining to the gland. Since he felt the "Labzellen" were more peripheral, he therefore renamed them as "Belegzellen". These two types of cells subsequently were referred to as the parietal (Belegzellen) and the chief cell (Hauptzelle) respectively.

Theodore Schwann (center) and his mentor Mueller (top) the eminent physiologist. Schwann not only discovered pepsin (bottom right) and described fermentation, but also established the basis of muscular contraction. He received the Sydenham Prize for his elucidation of the "Single cell theory of disease" and was regarded as one of the eminent scientists of his time. Unfortunately, an argument with J. von Liebig precluded his obtaining a post in Germany and he moved to Lièges in Belgium, where he incidentally designed the first underwater diving apparatus for use in coal mines, while scientifically directing his attention to exploring the role of bile in digestion.

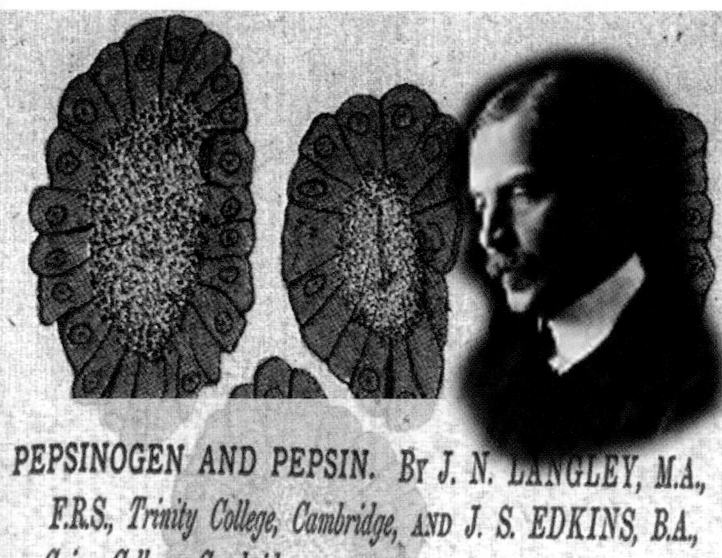

PEPSINOGEN AND PEPSIN. By J. N. LANGLEY, M.A., F.R.S., Trinity College, Cambridge, and J. S. EDKINS, B.A., Caius College, Cambridge.

John Langley of Cambridge not only coined the term oxyntic to identify the role of the acid secreting cells but established the secretory regulation of pepsinogen.

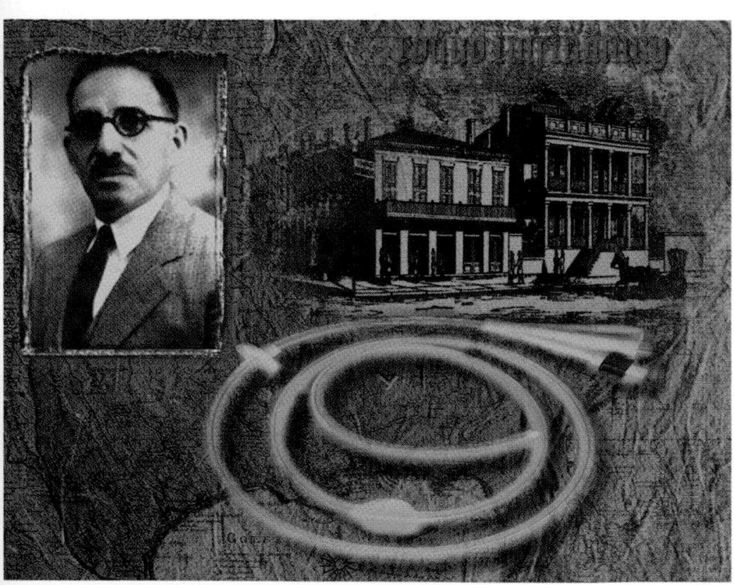

A.L. Levine was originally trained as a rabbi before his forced induction into the army of the Russian Czar led him to emigration and a career as a distinguished gastroenterologist in New Orleans, Louisiana. His introduction of the Levine tube provided the primary method of access to the stomach for generations of gastroenterologists prior to the advent of the Hirschowitz gastroscope.

influence on the glands, and linked these observations to chemical estimations of the changes in the quality of pepsinogen secretion under different circumstances. Indeed, his drawings and sketches, although now over a hundred years old, attest to his clear understanding of the nature of zymogen secretion and the general mechanisms of its stimulation. In addition, Langley was so impressed with Heidenhain's contribution that he was to borrow and translate his terms for the cells in the stomach into English as "border" and "chief" cells, respectively, and also coined the term "oxyntic" to identify the role of the acid-secreting cells. In a series of publications between 1879 and 1882, he established the basic morphology and secretory characteristics of the pepsin-forming glands of the stomach and esophagus and was, in addition, able to correct Heidenhain, by demonstrating that contrary to previous reports, gland cells became less granular as secretion took place. Langley demonstrated that granules were stored up during rest and discharged during secretion in not only the pancreas, but also the stomach and salivary glands and that during this event, a chemical change in the zymogen occurred. To quote:

> *"The fresh gastric glands contain no pepsin; they do however contain a large quantity of pepsinogen; consequently the granules of the chief cells consist wholly or in part of pepsinogen."*

The Evaluation of the Stomach

Although esophagoscopic endoscopy would naturally lead onto gastric endoscopy, the danger of perforation with rigid instruments and the limited visibility provided by the mirror and lens systems, left some physicians dissatisfied. Thus, the turn of the nineteenth century led to the development of a number of interesting and innovative devices designed to provide further information about the stomach.

The Development of the Stomach Tube

The concept of access to the interior of the gut had long fascinated both patients and their physicians. At first, the requirements were simple and based upon the need to either remove *per os* foreign objects that had become lodged, or to open up the lower passages when feelings of distention and obstruction were perceived to be present. Thus, early attempts at medication were targeted at either promotion of emesis or acceleration of defecation, and purges and clysters were the order of the day.

With time, however, the frustration and impatience of physicians with such unpredictable intervention led to efforts to gain more direct access to the interior of the gut. The ingenious development of a diverse variety of tubes was first aimed at therapy either for removing blockages, dilating strictures, or providing sustenance. After recognizing the limitations of the finger or the feather, the concept of using tubes to enter the alimentary tract represented the initial early and important impetus in promoting access to the interior. At first, these were rigid and introduced blindly, but the discovery of more pliable agents, functional light sources, and thereafter lenses, led to increased flexibility and better visibility. Thus, therapeutic applications initially preceded diagnostic usage and, only after the advent of fiber optic technology, was parity regained. The evolution of the science of endoscopy was thereafter determined by the introduction of light sources, lenses, mirrors, and flexibility as physicians have moved from blind bougies to flexible fiber optics.

Emptying the Stomach

It had long been recognized that a full stomach generated a feeling of discomfort and in many cases, inhibited the eating of food and interfered with exercise. This was particularly disadvantageous in early history when large complex banquets were the custom and post-prandial exotic activities an important part of social intercourse. While emetics were initially employed to generate gastric emptying, nausea, and incomplete voiding accompanied low dosages, while excessive usage culminated in ongoing emesis despite the stomach having already been emptied. A simple introduction of the finger into the back of the throat was deemed immodest and from the time of the Emperor Claudius, dinner guests were either provided with a "*pinna*" or a vomiting feather at the completion of each banquet course.

A modification of the Rose Garden of Heliogabalus by Sir Alma Tadema. Gargantuan meals of the Lucullian school of Roman cuisine culminated in massive gastric distention and precluded further ingestion as well as limiting the aptitude for post-cibal debauchery. A discerning host would therefore provide peacock feathers for posterior pharyngeal stimulation and the initiation of emesis thereby allowing a guest to proceed with the further activities of the evening. The exquisite meals of lark tongues, Caspian caviar, ostrich brain and Falernian wine provided by the Roman Emperor Heliogabalus culminated in a variety of digestive sensations. These ranged from ethanol-induced languor to an ecstatic gastric epiphany or even demise. Should there be any perception on the part of the Emperor that the guests were unhappy, hidden ropes supporting the roof of the tent were pulled and the diners suffocated beneath many tons of rose petals. Those who survived might avail themselves of the peacock feathers provided to stimulate self-emesis and thereafter resume further gluttony.

A further utility of such self-induced emesis was in the rapid evacuation of covertly administered poisons. The application of such ingenuity to obviate the effects of covertly administered poison was circumvented by Agrippina, who poisoned the Emperor Claudius by applying the agent to the feather itself! In the fourth century A.D., the master physician Oribasius described a number of methods utilized to produce emesis. These included swinging an individual in a suspended bed; goose feathers dipped in iris or cypress oil, and a variety of herbal combinations. More direct intervention included a *digital vomitorium* that consisted of a long feather glove, 10 to 12 inches in length, of which the lower two-thirds were filled with wood fiber while the upper third remained empty to receive the directing finger of the physician. Presumably this novel device might be regarded as the earliest form of *gastric sound*. Although the utility of such instruments decreased as Roman gluttony abated, they were still of some use to physicians who were employed to protect royal personages from would-be poisoners. By the sixteenth century, Hieronymus Mercurialis had described a more elegant device for the induction of vomiting. This *lorum vomitorium* had initially been described for the treatment of opium poisoning by Scribonius Largus in the first century and consisted of a leather strap treated with a nauseating tannic acid-containing substance. The combination of the strap and the chemical, when introduced into the esophagus, resulted in emesis.

A wide variety of tubes, dilators, probangs, and whalebone-based devices were developed over the course of centuries. Thus, the hollow sounds and graspers of Sculetus and Arculanus were replaced by the dilators of T. Willis and the eel skin-covered contraptions of W. Hunter as physicians sought access to the esophagus and stomach. A late seventeenth century example of the most dramatic type was the "*magenkratzer*".

A Magenkratzer or Magenraumer (mid 17th-18th century). *Desperate to alleviate the ill-understood symptoms of dyspepsia, even notable physicians such as L. Heister supported rigorous brushing of the stomach with a view to attaining a state of gastric cleanliness. Such was the Germanic regard for gastric cleanliness that even in the early 20th century a "good" gastric cleansing with a brush might still be obtained at many spa clinics (background).*

Early devices

Magenkratzer

The first mechanical devices, or stomach brushes to cleanse the stomach, were recorded in the seventeenth century and despite their almost fearsome description, achieved great popularity. A stomach brush usually consisted of either a long smooth flexible arched whalebone, 2 to 3 feet in length, tipped with an ivory button to which a tuft of silk cord, horse hair, or linen was firmly attached. Introduction of the instrument was normally facilitated by slight bending and carefully soaked in water, as well as the imbibing of copious quantities of diluted brandy prior to the introduction. Once through the mouth and esophagus into the stomach, appropriate cleaning maneuvers were undertaken. Copious vomiting (of the brandy and gastric residue) usually ensued and was regarded as tangible evidence of gastric emptying and cleansing. For a time, these devices were often found hidden in monasteries or convents where usage was regarded as a sacred secret or "*arcanum*". Such instruments proved so effective in the hands of certain physicians, that they were proposed for usage in even healthy individuals as a prophylactic measure by which means a long life could be attained and all stomach troubles avoided. Indeed, the concept acquired such vogue that men of considerable medical stature, including L. Heister, supported outrageous statements made by the likes of Socrates who claimed "*it appears as if death had laid aside its scythe and instead has had the stomach cleanser placed in its hands.*"

Although gastric brushing caused certain problems, a number of reports clearly detailed its effectiveness in the cure of chronic gastric ailments.

This is ascertained by both Rumsey in 1694, an English physician who wrote glowingly of its effectiveness, as did Sobierus of Paris. In the same decade, the Danish King was so impressed with reports of its efficacy that he commanded a royal demonstration to evaluate its utility. One report even documents the complete cure of a Russian aristocrat who was repetitively treated in a convent for *"over fatigue and the excessive abuse of alcohol"* and is worthy of further consideration. In this instance the *"magenkrauser"* was applied to his stomach until the organ was entirely cleansed of mucous, bile, and a clotted foul-smelling purulent material had been discharged per mouth. The heroic treatment was continued on a daily basis for eight days with intermittent nutrition of eggs, soup, and softened chicken to assuage the nutritional requirements of this poor soul, with the result that at the end of two weeks, the treatment was pronounced a complete success.

Such digestive therapy was not limited to rich Europeans and is described in the journals of Dapper, who traveled with the Dutch West Indies fleet in 1673. In them, he describes a novel treatment personally witnessed amongst the South American Indians.

> *"The Tapagus, a Brazilian tribe, have a remarkable method of cleansing the stomach. They pass a rope made of padded sharp leaves down the throat and into the stomach and then turn and twist it until vomiting and a bloody discharge occurs. The rope is then withdrawn and the stomach is cleansed."*

It is probably not surprising that prolonged usage of gastric cleansing treatment resulted in some poor results. Esophageal perforation, gastric bleeding, and even the development of carcinoma in the stomach, led to the eventual termination of this technique in both Europe and the Americas.

Aspiration pumps

Stomach pumps for the removal of noxious substances were the next technological innovation in the field. An analysis of the literature of the time suggests that while Hunter had been interested in this possibility, it was Monro *tertius* who first introduced the application in 1797. This was followed by the work of Baron G. Dupuytren (1777-1835) and C. Renault of Paris who, in 1803, not only suggested the use of a flexible tube of sufficient length to reach the stomach, but also connected it to a syringe to aspirate swallowed poison. P.S. Physick (1768-1837), who had been a pupil of Hunter, first introduced the application in America in 1812. The unfortunate and contentious rival claims of pump priority (though not technological priority) established in England in 1822 and 1823 may be regarded as modifications of a general principle that had been earlier established by Hunter.

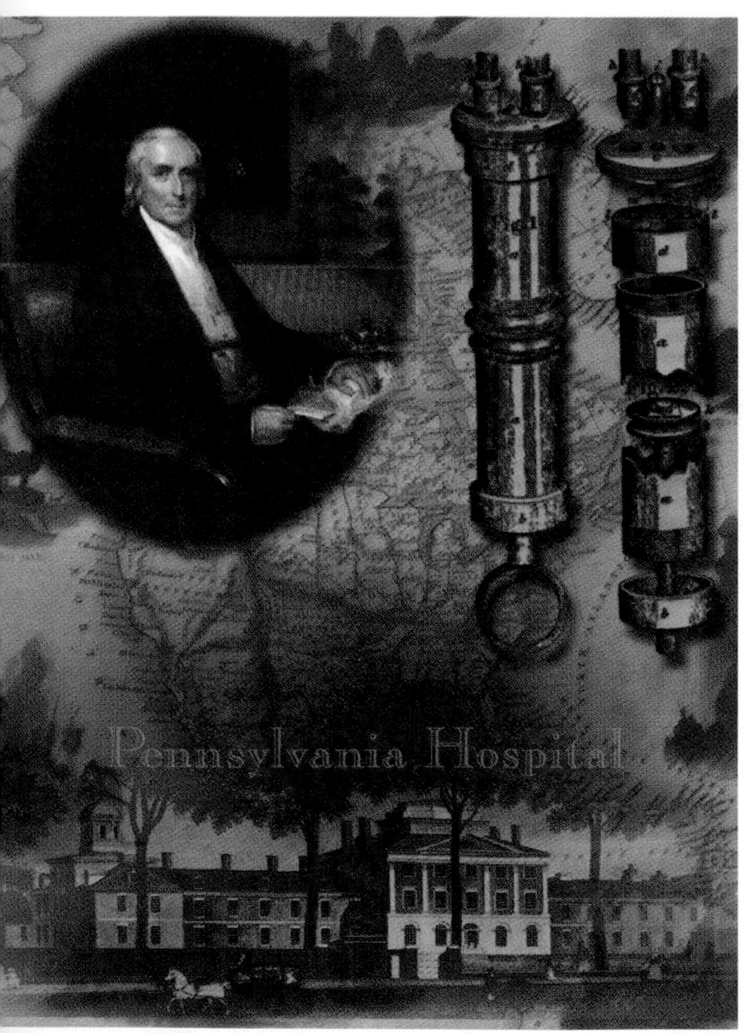

Although the eminent medical historian Fielding Garrison was of the opinion that Philip S Physick (1768-1837) (top left) "wrote nothing of consequence" *posterity has nevertheless accorded to him the honorific of "Father of American Surgery". An Edinburgh graduate of 1792 and a pupil of John Hunter, he subsequently became Professor of Surgery at the Pennsylvania Hospital in Philadelphia. In 1812 he published* "An Account of the New Mode of Extracting Poisonous Substances from the Stomach" *and in so doing claimed to have described a novel method of treatment. A year later he was forced to recant this claim when it became apparent that Monro of Edinburgh was the rightful author. Nevertheless, he was the first American to use a syringe and tube to wash out the stomach in a case of poisoning. Since the case described was that of twins accidentally overdosed with laudanum by their mother and one died, his mortality was 50 percent. The syringes and pumps (top right) used for the purpose of extracting gastric contents underwent a series of modifications and a number of London physicians including Bush (1822), Jukes (1822), and Mathews (1826), each laid their claim to priority of the invention.*

In his inaugural medical thesis, *"Disputatio Medica Inauguralis de Dysphagia"*, A. Monro (1773-1859) provided the first description of the use of a tube and syringe in cases of poisoning. In it, he proposed that a tube could be utilized not only for the extraction of poison from the stomach, but also for the introduction of food into the stomach of individuals with severe dysphagia and an inability to swallow. His observations, were, however, to a large extent based upon the work of his father Monro *secundus*, who had employed a flexible tube to remove fermenting fluids and gasses from the stomach of distended cows in 1767.

Alexander Tertius Monro (1773-1859) (bottom right) was the third successive member of the Monro family to hold the Chair of Anatomy in Edinburgh. His thesis "Disputatio Medical Inauguralis de Dysphagia" *elegantly described the design and use of a tube, syringe, siphon and expendable mouth-piece/tongue depressor (left) that had been designed to empty the stomach of ingested poison. This device represented an extrapolation of a similar piece of apparatus first utilized by his father to decompress Highland Angus cattle suffering from alfalfa-induced acute gastric distension.*

Physick, who was a professor of Surgery at the University of Pennsylvania and a former student of J. Hunter, provided the American contribution. The gastric contents of two three-month old twins, who had accidentally been given an overdose of laudanum, were washed out utilizing a large flexible catheter. This was accomplished after firstly injecting a drachm of diluted ipecac into the stomach with a syringe and then withdrawing the fluid contents of the stomach repeatedly with warm water. Only one of the children was saved, however; but Physick noted the tragic length of time that had elapsed between imbibing the laudanum and the aspiration.

These observations were published in 1812 in an article entitled "Account of the New Mode of Extracting Poisonous Substances from the Stomach." Interestingly, Monro *tertius* was disingenuously acknowledged the following year with the following statement, *"I, therefore, am happy in having called the attention of the profession to a mode of treatment not before used in this country, at least within my knowledge; but I have now an act of justice to perform, in describing the merit of the invention to Dr. Alexander Monro, Jr. of Edinburgh who published it in his inaugural thesis in A.D. 1797. Of this circumstance I was entirely ignorant when I sent you my paper."*

Such machinations were but a part of the full-fledged academic squabble that subsequently developed regarding the priority of the discovery of the stomach tube. In May 1822, E. Jukes, an English surgeon, published a paper in the London Medical and Physical Journal entitled "New Means of Extracting Opium from the Stomach," in which he described an instrument called a "stomach pump" for *"removing by mechanical agency, poison from the stomach."* This consisted of a flexible tube two-and-a-half feet in length and a quarter-of-an-inch in diameter, tipped with an ivory globe containing several perforations. An elastic bottle filled with warmed water was attached to the other end. Following successful introduction of the tube into the stomach, the water could be forced in and out. Jukes initially experimented on dogs into whose stomachs he had introduced laudanum, which was thereafter irrigated until the water cleared, but to confirm the efficacy of his treatment, he himself swallowed ten drachms of laudanum and allowed his colleague, a Mr. James Scott, to undertake a successful lavage. This performance was repeated in public at Guy's Hospital to the wonder of Sir Astley Cooper (1768-1841).

Unfortunately for Jukes, very similar observations had been published in the same journal two months previously by F. Bush, who although utilizing a flexible tube to enter the stomach, employed a syringe rather than a wash bottle to generate a wash. Bush termed his apparatus a *"gastric exhauster"*. As a result of the widespread acceptance of the efficacy of the device, an acrimonious debate regarding primacy immediately ensued. Unfortunately for Jukes and Bush, gastric aspiration using a similar mechanical device had previously been described by D. Evans in 1817 (although not published until 1823). A bivalve syringe system that represented a design advance, since it obviated the need for repetitive removal of the syringe during the process of gastric lavage, was thereafter demonstrated by a W. Reed. This was followed, in 1825, by Weiss' small, sophisticated pump which had the advantages of being used for the emptying of the stomach of poisons, water from drowned persons, or for the presentation of enemata. The latter design became widely used throughout Europe and Weiss was lauded (wrongly) as the inventor of the stomach pump. In 1826, Mathews also described a syringe and provided certificates from three other physicians supporting his primacy. In a publication entitled *"Description of an Improved Instrument for Extracting Poison from the Stomach with some Statements tending to establish the Validity of Dr. Physick's title to the credit of having invented the Stomach Tube,"* Mathews spared no-one and criticized Jukes, Bush, Evans, and Reed, for falsely claiming priority for the discovery. At this stage, Physick became re-embroiled in the saga and claimed that after initially recommending the introduction of the tube into the stomach as early as 1802, he had thereafter, in 1805, demonstrated the insertion of a tube covered with elastic gum. He alleged that such a tube had not originated in London but had been acquired in Paris and brought to America by his nephew, Dr. John Dorsey. As a result of this unfortunate series of events, the issue of the primacy of discovery of the gastric pump and its usage, waxed and waned for years as the various protagonists vied with each other for recognition.

Sir Astley Cooper (top right) was the doyen of British surgery during the early 19th century and, apart from his sartorial elegance, recognized as an individual of quixotic intellectual genius. Guy's Hospital (background), where he practiced has long been the recipient of widespread acclaim as the origin of numerous medical and scientific advances. Wittgenstein, Bright, Addison, Hodgkin, Gull and a host of intellectual illuminati have graced its portals. In 1822, Scott and subsequently Reed demonstrated the use of a Gastric Exhauster (left) to Cooper and convinced him of its efficacy. As a footnote, it is worth commentary that William Prout also worked at Guy's and his first description of the presence of hydrochloric acid in human gastric juice (1823) presumably reflects his access to the material provided by these demonstrations.

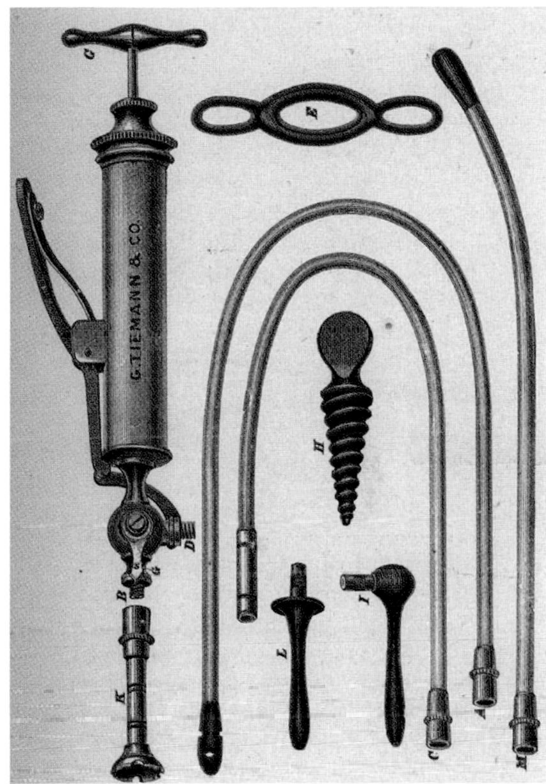

An example of a stomach pump available from a New York Surgical Supply catalogue during the early 20th century.

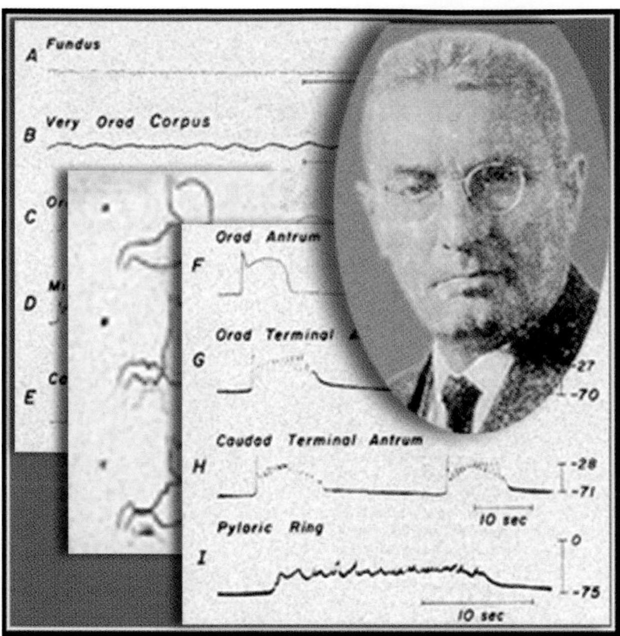

A. Carlson during his chairmanship of the Department of Physiology at the University of Chicago, made substantial contributions to the physiology of digestion and peristalsis. A brilliant and rigorous investigator originally from the Gothenberg area of Sweden, Carlson had begun his life in America by training as a religious minister. Using the Hemmeter method for studying gastric contractions he developed the basis for the physiological study of the regulation of gastrointestinal motility. It was his lifetime custom when addressing speakers at physiological meetings to rise from his seat with the question, "What is the evidence?"

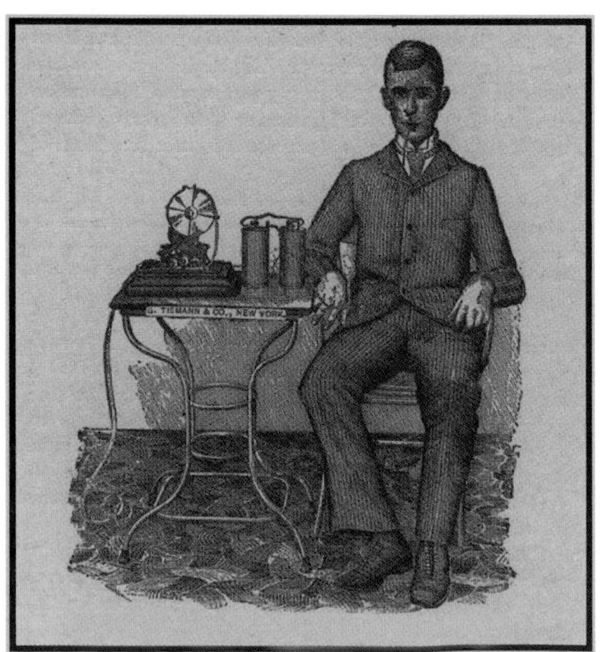

The Gastrograph designed by J.C. Hemmeter of Baltimore as a test for measuring gastric peristalsis. The patient swallowed a stomach-shaped elastic bag connected by a thin rubber tube to a kymograph. Once in place the bag was filled with air and then connected with a water manometer to the kymograph. Movement of the stomach altered the pressure within the bag and enabled a record of gastric peristalsis to be derived.

Gastrodiaphany (Gastrodiaphanoscopy)

Ismar Boas in his 1907 textbook, *Diseases of the Stomach* wrote: *"even though transillumination or illumination of the human stomach is not applicable to general practice, these methods are of much of interest. They point towards the road which, when improvement and simplification have taken place, would have to be followed."* In the same text he also stated *"gastroscopy has hither to been found only of slight practical use that it might undoubtedly play as an important role in the future provided it is simplified as cystoscopy has done in the diagnosis of the diseases of the bladder."*

Cazenave in 1845 was the first to devise the technique of diaphanoscopy in order to view the inner urethral walls. He employed a funnel-shaped metallic tube, which was introduced into the urethra by means of a mandarin. The light, which was reflected from a lamp and made more powerful by means of a glaciating lens, was directed against the lower surface of the penis. In this manner it was possible to plainly see the inner wall of the urethra in spite of the thickness of the tissue. In 1860, two groups, Czermak and Gerhardt, and Störk and Voltolini, similarly sought to transilluminate the larynx with sun and gaslight. In the same year, Fonssagrives reported on the transillumination of the cavities of the human body by means of Geissler's tubes. It is, however, to Julius Bruck, a dentist in Breslau, who the credit should be given for employing galvanic light for transillumination in 1867. The platinum coil was brought to a white heat by current provided by an atttached Middeldorp battery. Using an instrument similar to the vaginal speculum, he was able to explore the rectum in the male and the vagina in the female, and thereby transilluminate the neighboring portions of the bladder with some degree of success. One year later in 1868, Milliot successfully transilluminated portions of the abdominal cavity (in animals) by means of a light generated within a glass tube which had been introduced into the stomach or colon. The light was obtained from two thin and platinum wires placed within the tube that were connected to the electrodes of the battery. In 1868 Dr. Lazarowicz utilized a similar device while in 1889, M. Einhorn of New York, stimulated by the work of Voltolini on electrical transillumination of the larynx, undertook to perform transillumination of the stomach. He utilized a Nelaton tube, to the lower end of which was attached an Edison hard glass incandescent lamp containing carbon filaments.

The Gastrograph

Einhorn constructed an apparatus to assess the mechanical function of the stomach in the living patient. Prior to developing the device, he had utilized laparotomized experimental animals to determine the appropriate site of placement and mode of introduction. The apparatus consisted of a ball, electric cells, and a ticker. The procedure consisted of swallowing the ball and its connected wires and thereafter monitoring the movements of the stomach. Once placed in the stomach, the motions of the former, which were caused by active and passage motions of the stomach, could be recorded. Einhorn labeled the apparatus as a gastrokinesograph or a gastrograph and stored the information to provide objective record of the alterations in the motility of the stomach.

J.C. Hemmeter of Baltimore devised a slightly different but equally ingenious method for also testing gastric peristalsis. The essential part of the apparatus consisted of a deglutible elastic stomach-shaped bag of very thin rubber attached to an esophageal tube. Since the stomach-shaped pouch only adopted the shape of the stomach when it was blown up and occupied little space when collapsed, it could be introduced without difficulty. Once the bag was in place in the stomach, it was filled with air and connected either with a water manometer or tambour on the Ludwig kymograph.

Thus, the slightest contraction of the gastric muscle layer compressed the elastic intragastric bag and distended the tambour, to which a glass bulb ink pin was attached, to record the gastric peristalsis on the kymographion. Similarly, a pen connected to a chronometer indicated seconds on the record by small dots so that it was possible to determine the time, occurrence, and duration of gastric peristalsis. Subsequently, A.J. Carlson utilized the Hemmeter-Moritz method for studying the normal contractions of the stomach and was able to deduce at least three different rhythms.

These included periods of powerful rhythmic contractions altering with periods of relative quiescence (the 32 rhythm). Carlson also described a second rhythm of constant uniformity of about 20 seconds, which increased in intensity during periods of powerful rhythmical contractions of the fundus. The last rhythm type was that of powerful episodic contractions identical with the "hungry contractions" that had also been noted by both Cannon and Washburn. Hemmeter commented that *"in making studies on the kymograph on the gastric motility only such patients are taken as have become accustomed to the stomach tube as the nausea and vomiting first attending the initial introduction of the tube make an exact record impossible."* His opinion summarized the difficulty of utilizing apparatus of this kind to determine gastric function.

Gastrogalvinization

The concept of inducing direct electrization of the stomach reflected the belief in the early, middle, and late nineteenth century that the application of electricity to a damaged part was of therapeutic benefit. The *Handbuch der Electrotherapie* stated that *"the first maxim to observe is the treatment* in loco morbio", that is the application of electricity to the morbid part itself… *"there is no*

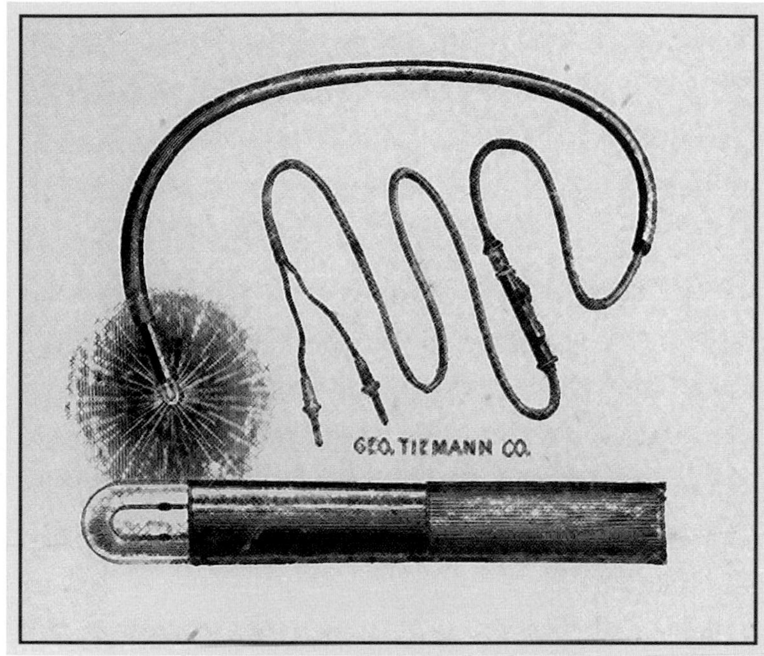

Max Einhorn of New York sought to illuminate the interior of the stomach by introducing a tube to which an incandescent lamp was attached. By viewing the brightly illuminated stomach in a dark room, its size, shape, and masses in its anterior wall could be appreciated. Gastrodiaphany, however, failed to gain widespread acceptance.

doubt that it is best in the great majority of cases to operate directly on the diseased spot." Indeed, so well regarded was the therapy, that authorities including Pepper of Philadelphia, Kussmaul, and Canstatt, proposed that dilation of the stomach could be combatted by direct electrization. This was achieved by the introduction of one electrode into the stomach itself and the other into the stomach region. No less an individual than Duchenne was the first to make use of this method! In 1877, Kussmaul began to practice direct electrization of the stomach using a copper wire which ended in an olive point fastened to the cut-off end of a gastric tube. In several patients with dilation of the stomach, Kussmaul introduced this electrode into the stomach holding the other ordinary electrode in his own hand. Although in individuals with thin abdominal walls the contraction of the stomach was directly visible, not all physicians were as convinced of the efficacy of the indirect method of gastric electrostimulation. Thus, in 1881 Balduino Bocci, in experiments on animals, was persuaded "*that the indirect faradization of the stomach through the abdominal walls produced in the stomach even when applied in a very energetic way, phenomenon of very little importance and of dubious curative effect!*" Since direct faradization of the stomach on the other hand showed all the above-mentioned physiological effects, Bocci enthusiastically recommended the use of direct electrization of the stomach for therapeutic purposes. This proposal of gastric electrization was further advanced by G. Bardet in 1884, who filled the entire stomach with water to facilitate the passage of the electric current between the stomach wall and the electrode, thus establishing contact for the entire organ.

Einhorn facilitated the process of internal direct electrization by constructing an electrode on the same principle as the stomach bucket. He named this device "*the deglutible stomach electrode*". The electrode, once swallowed, reached the stomach without further artificial aid and the silk thread of the bucket was represented in the electrode by a very fine (1 mm) rubber tube through which an even finer soft conducting wire ran to the external battery.

After an extensive study of the physiological effects of direct electrization of the stomach, he published a number of papers, which concluded that direct faradization of the stomach with the positive electrode increased gastric secretion whereas with the negative pole electrode within the stomach, gastric secretion was diminished. In individuals with severe and "*obstinate gastralgia*", he regarded this therapy as "*the sovereign means*" for combatting the disease. In fairness, it must be stated that Einhorn was quite honest in concluding that he had little understanding of what role was played by faradization. He was uncertain whether it functioned as a gastric sedative or stimulant, but concluded in pragmatic fashion that a great variety of "*gastric neuroses*" depended on an "*imperfect innervation of the stomach and that electricity improves this innervation thereby reliving the cause of the conditions.*"

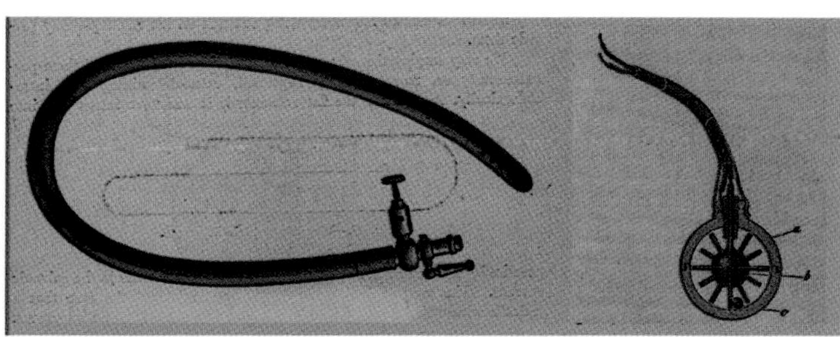

The Einhorn mechanical gastrograph. *The ball consisted of two hollow metallic hemispheres that were screwed together. Within the large one and attached to the upper hemisphere, but perfectly insulated from the same at the attachment, was another ball provided with spikes radiating in all directions, but not touching the inside walls of the hemispheres. Another very small platinum ball (c) lay within the large ball and could be freely moved in all directions knocking at the spikes. Two insulated wires – one connected to the hollow ball and the other to the spike ball were encased in a very fine thin rubber tube forming the cable and separated at the end into two branches attached to a battery. When the platinum ball touched the spikes an electric circuit was completed. When, however, the ball moved away and ceased to touch the spike, the current was broken. On connecting the "ticker" with the battery and the ball, each motion of the latter was recorded on a strip of paper.*

The concept of "electric therapy" as a remedial modality was considered seriously in many reputable medical establishments. For a period of time, its efficiency in the cure of pulmonary tuberculosis was widely accepted.

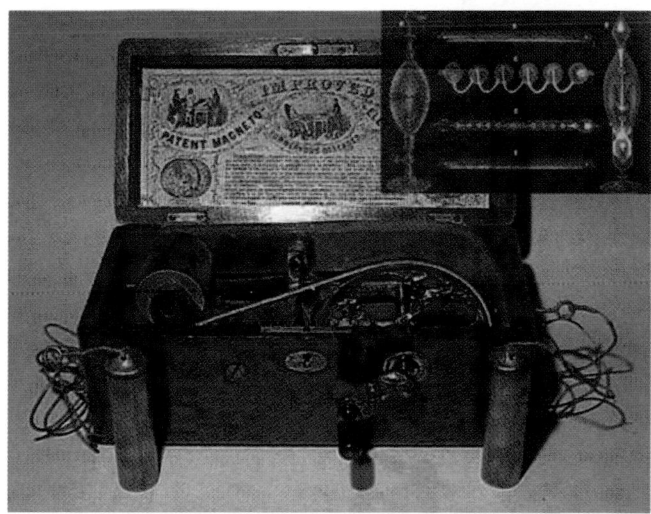

The commercial availability of batteries and a variety of cathode ray tubes led to the widespread usage of such devices in the administration of "electrical" therapy. For the most part this constituted optimistically unrealistic expectations of both patients and physicians but in some circumstances it was pure gimmickery or charlatanism.

Gastroscopy

Von Mikulicz in 1881 provided the nexus of endoscopic development within the nineteenth century by developing a unifying concept that embraced the three critical components of an endoscope, namely an electric light source, an optical system, and a tubular endoscope body. In the early part of the twentieth century, although Hans Elsner, Theodore Rosenheim, and Sussman of Berlin made further progress, rigidity, and a lack of illumination continued to be problematic issues. Most gastroscopists accepted these limitations and by 1922 there were five well-accepted models available: Sussman, Loening-Stieda, Elsner, Schindler, and Kausch, and until 1932 the field was dominated by rigid endoscopes. At that stage, Rudolph Schindler (1888-1868) in conjunction with George Wolf, a Berlin instrument-maker, introduced the semi-flexible endoscope and revolutionized gastroscopy. This device remained the prototype of all instrument design until the introduction of the fiberoptic endoscope by Basil Hirschowitz in 1957.

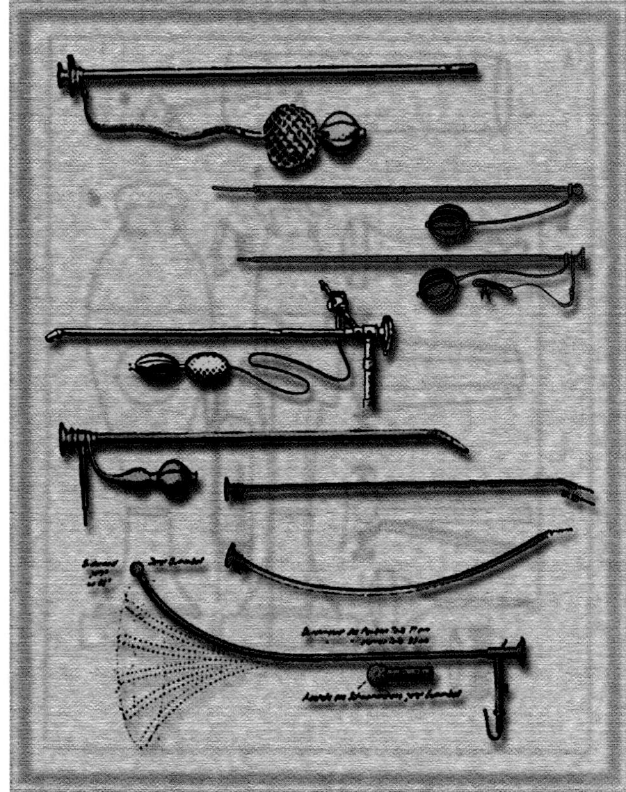

Some examples of the diversity of gastroscopes available between 1911-33. The Elsner scope (1911) (top) was the most widely used prior to the introduction of the Schindler rigid gastroscope (second from the top) in 1922. The Sternberg instrument (third from the top) introduced in 1923 was claimed to have a size advantage (9 mm as compared to 11 mm of the preceding two) as well as better visibility, but patient fatalities diminished its appeal. The Korbsch instrument of 1926 (third from bottom) had an even smaller diameter of 8.5 mm but was supplanted in 1932 by the Schindler flexible instrument (second from bottom). The disadvantage of its relatively large diameter (12 mm) was far outweighed by the unique introduction of flexibility. Korbsch subsequently produced an elastic metal instrument (1933) of smaller diameter (bottom) but the Schindler design became the accepted gastroscope of the decade.

The Schindler modification of the Elsner rigid gastroscope introduced in 1922, and modified by others, was the most extensively used instrument of the decade up to 1932, when the Schindler-Wolf semi-flexible gastroscope first became a reality. Most of the fundamental observations of gastroscopy were undertaken with this device and its contributions to the understanding of various diseases of the stomach probably make this instrument one of the great bio-technical devices of the century.

Despite his early success and acclaim, it was apparent to Schindler that the potential problem of stomach perforations and esophageal tears with rigid instruments would be the rate-limiting factor in the development of the discipline. The first attempts to construct a flexible gastroscope were based on the awareness that an optical image could be conducted by a number of movable prisms. Schindler, who had acquired more than a decade of experience in both instrument use and design, was not slow in perceiving what needed to be done. Collaboration with George Wolf (1873-1938), a Berlin instrument-maker who had considerable familiarity with the field, resulted in the construction and patenting (German patent #662,788; U.S. patent #1,995,196) of a flexible gastroscope in 1932 (after six versions). Although the first version of the new gastroscope was flexible in its entire length, it was apparent that it was more satisfactory to have only the distal half flexible while the ocular half was maintained rigid and straight. This adaptation facilitated introduction of the instrument into the stomach, and also simplified the design of the optical system.

The flexible part was also made elastic and could straighten itself, and the rubber fingertip was retained and modified from the original rigid instrument to facilitate safe passage. The final model of the instrument consisted of a straight rigid proximal part and a distal flexible segment that contained a number of lenses of short focal length, capable of transmitting the optical image even when the instrument was flexed. As a result of these dramatic advances, the gastroscope became widely used in different countries, and culminated in a rapid, almost explosive, spread of the

R. Schindler's seminal text, Lehrbuch und Atlas der Gastroskopie.

Rudolf Schindler of Munich had during his military service become intrigued with the prevalence of the vague diagnosis of gastritis amongst the soldiers. Frustrated by his inability to adequately visualize the stomach, he devised a rigid gastroscope (1922) and published his findings "Problems and Techniques of Gastroscopy with a description of a new Gastroscope." (Arch. VerdauKr., *1922, 30, 133-66). A year later (1923) he published a book,* Lehrbuch und Atlas der Gastroskopie, *that was unique in its color pictures (center) and descriptions of gastric pathology. Schindler personally supervised the hand-painted illustrations and the cost of the color plates for the text was underwritten by the generosity of a former patient, Mrs. Morse of Chicago. After his forced immigration to the United States in 1934, this text was translated with the aid of Walter L. Palmer of the University of Chicago and in 1937 published as* Gastroscopy, The Endoscopic Study of Gastric Pathology.

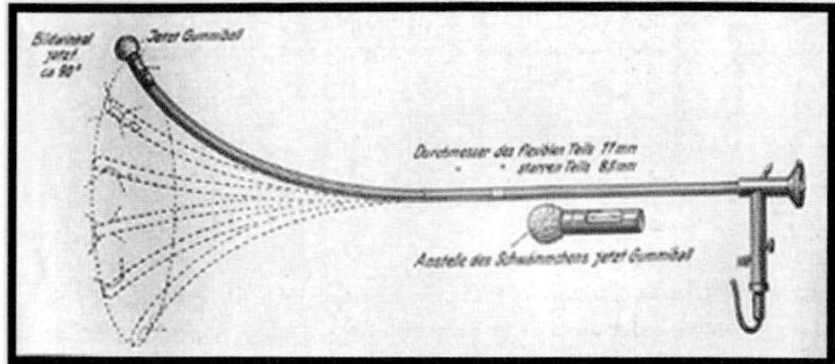

The Schindler-Wolf Semi-Flexible Gastroscope c. 1932. *The relationship between Schindler and Wolf reflected the belief of both parties in the need for a flexible gastroscope. The design parameters sought were a thin flexible tube whose length and flexibility would not only enable lenses to be mounted in such a fashion that flexion would not interfere with vision but provide adequate length to examine the stomach.*

gastroscopic method that had languished for so long in the netherworld of unfulfilled discoveries. It consisted of a straight open outer tube introduced into the stomach with an obturator on whose tip a long (8 cm) rubber-finger had been implanted to ensure safe guidance during introduction. Once the stomach had been safely reached (in 80%-95% of patients), the optical tube that carried the lamp was then utilized to replace the obturator. Driven by the belief that gastroscopy would provide a unique diagnostic window to the resolution of gastric disease, Schindler displayed such enthusiasm and commitment to the subject that by 1923, he had already published an atlas of gastroscopy, *Lehrbuch und Atlas der Gastroskopie*.

Unfortunately the work of Schindler in Germany was halted by the advent of the Third Reich, and his incarceration in Dachau led him to the conclusion that emigration was the only possible salvation. Fortunately Marie Ortmayer, a gastroenterologist at the University of Chicago, obtained Schindler a faculty appointment and with the generous support of some former patients, both he and his family escaped Nazi Germany in 1934. Schindler subsequently established gastroscopy in the United States and, in 1941, became the founder of what is now the American Society for Endoscopy.

During his lifetime Schindler produced more than one hundred and seventy manuscripts and five books. The *Lehrbuch* had been published in 1923 and his classic monograph on gastroscopy was published in 1937. This was followed, in 1957, by the widely accepted *Synopsis of Gastroenterology* which detailed not only the contributions of endoscopy but placed Schindler's own views in perspective. He recognized the special merit of gastroscopy in the early detection of gastric disease, but fully accepted the necessity for the interface between both radiology and gastroscopy in the accurate and early diagnosis of stomach disease. At his death in 1968, his exemplary record as a skilled gastroenterologist and innovator deservedly earned him the sobriquet of "*The Father of Gastroscopy*".

Biopsy

The necessity of gastric biopsy to confirm visual pathology identified either by radiology or gastroscopy, was recognized to be an important necessity. Schindler, himself, provided considerable support for this endeavor, since he believed that the use of laparotomy and exploratory surgery were unduly dangerous for the acquisition of a tissue diagnosis. As early as 1940, a forceps for tissue sampling that could be successfully used in combination with the Schindler semi-flexible gastroscope had been devised by Bruce Kenamore. These forceps, however, were not actually a true component of the gastroscope but were clamped onto the shaft of the endoscope ("piggyback") and could therefore only be utilized in conjunction with it. As might be predicted, the instrument was subject to mechanical problems and failure.

In 1948, Edward B. Benedict who, in collaboration with the American Cystoscope Makers Corporation, had developed a fully operational gastroscope for the acquisition of gastric tissue, overcame the Kenamore problem. This device consisted of an operating gastroscope in which both a biopsy forceps and a suction tube had been incorporated (within the housing of the gastroscope itself). Although the addition of the extra channels necessary for the suction and biopsy in Benedict's operating gastroscope increased the diameter to 14 mm, this became the instrument of choice and remained in use until the early 1960s. Nevertheless some endoscopists criticized

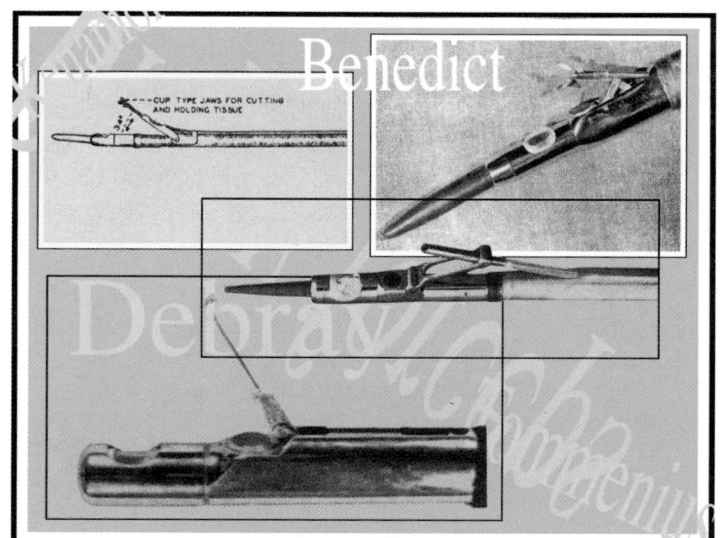

E.B. Benedict in 1948 was instrumental in recognizing that the gastroscope could be used not only for visual purposes but to obtain biopsy material for histological examination. Unfortunately, the addition of an extra channel rendered the scope more cumbersome and difficult to pass, with the result that biopsy was viewed negatively by some gastroenterologists.

Rudolf Schindler *(1888-1968). A brilliant man possessed of a formidable intellect and occasionally irascible nature, Schindler was an intriguing amalgam of sophistication, high intellect, and exotic eclecticism. A product of two cultures and two centuries, he saw and dared what few had done before. Resilient, innovative, consumed by curiosity, and gifted with extraordinary insight and perspicuity, he strove and succeeded in extending the boundaries of diagnosis. None who worked with him would ever forget him and whether he engendered love, admiration or sometimes – even frustration, his outstanding contributions would forever change the way physicians viewed* "le milieu intérieur". *A worthy first president of the American Gastroscopic Club Schindler might rightfully claim, as did Newton of Hooke* "that I saw further by standing on the shoulders of the giants who had gone before me."

Benedict's device, and patients, since its large diameter and oval cross-sectional design (banana shape) rendered it uncomfortable and difficult to use. Benedict defended his instrument by claiming that any potential shortcomings were offset by a degree of diagnostic certainty. Benedict maintained that while gastroscopy itself should not be regarded as a routine diagnostic procedure, if a gastroscopic examination were to be performed, it could not be regarded as complete unless the gastroscopist had some means of biopsy readily available.

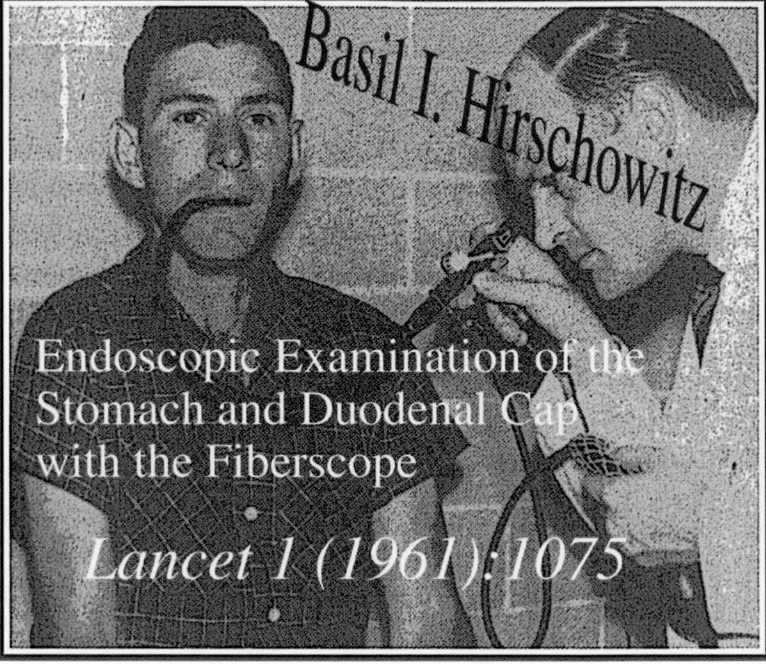

B. Hirschowitz endoscoping a patient (c. 1961). In 1959 Hirschowitz moved to Birmingham, Alabama, as Director of the Gastroenterology Unit and much as Birmingham, England, had flourished under the intellectual influence of the Lunar Society (Priestley, Watt, Galton, Bolton, Darwin, etc.), so the endoscopic cognoscenti flocked to his doors. In an epic Lancet article of 1961 that assessed the utility of the ACMI 4990 (the model T of fiber optic endoscopy) Hirschowitz claimed to the horror of the Schindlerian Luddites and other inflexible conservatives of the establishment that "the conventional gastroscope is obsolete on all counts." He was right!

Fiber Optic Gastroscopy

The rate-limiting factor, however, at this stage of endoscopy, was the critical spacing of the optical lenses, which affected both the flexibility as well as the visual acuity of the instrument. Aware of the advances in fiber optics that had been made by Hopkins and Kapany of the Imperial College, London, Basil Hirschowitz attempted to relate the potential applications of fiber optics to endoscopy. The first step in this venture was the need to perfect the fibers by producing a glass-coated fiber with the optical qualities adequate for gastroscope bundles; this was achieved between 1954-57. Despite the obvious potential of this application to gastroscopy, numerous optical and medical instruments, manufacturing corporations declined to participate in the venture.

Hirschowitz demonstrated his new gastroscope that he called a "fiberscope" at a meeting of the American Gastroscopic Society on May 16, 1957, at Colorado Springs. This presentation was remarkable since the President of the Society, J.T. Howard, actually yielded the podium and declined to give his Presidential address in favor of Hirschowitz. Howard's statement: "*I shall forego my prerogative of boring you with a Presidential address so that Dr. Hirschowitz may at half past 8 o'clock tell you about what I understand to be a new principle of gastroscopy. I hear that fiber glass conducts light around corners and that Dr. Hirschowitz has used this material in a new type of gastroscope*" would usher in an entirely new era of medical and gastroenterological practice. Acceptance of the device, however, was not as rapid as might have been predicted. Initial reports comparing the fiberscope and the conventional gastroscope were guarded in their pronouncements and noted that, while the fiberscope provided a better view of the duodenum, the gastroscope resulted in a better quality visual image! The first marketable prototype, the Hirschowitz ACMI 4990 fiberscope, was detailed in a 1961 article in the Lancet entitled "The Endoscopic Examination of the Stomach and Duodenal Cap with the Fiberscope." This seminal publication was the harbinger of a new world of gastroscopy and documented the introduction of what would prove to be one of the greatest contributions of gastroenterology to the world of medicine. Hirschowitz commented within the publication that it was his considered opinion that "*the conventional gastroscope has become obsolete on all counts.*"

Despite these early optimistic predictions, the ACMI Hirschowitz FO-4990 gastroduodenoscope proved less than ideal in its ability to pass the pylorus into the duodenum. One report in the *American Journal of Digestive Diseases* in 1966 stated that they had been "*unable to enter the duodenum with certainty in any examination*" in 1,000 fiberscope examinations. Nevethless, with the passage of time, gastroenterologists came to recognize the unique advance that fiberoptic endoscopy had conferred upon them. Indeed, such was the enthusiasm of the field that in much the same way as computer technology in

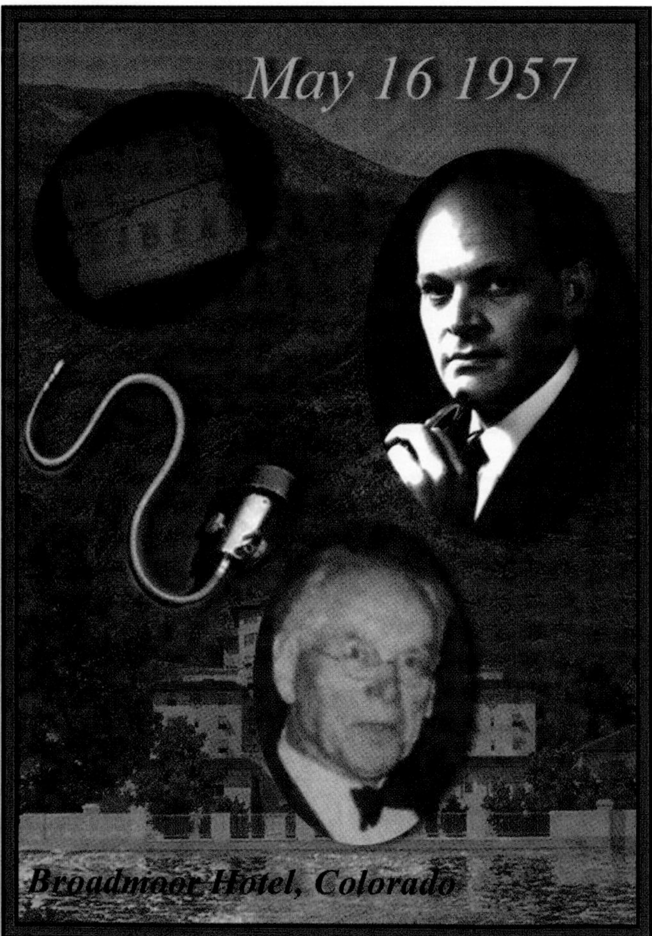

The meeting of the American Gastroscopic Society of May 16, 1957, at the Broadmoor Hotel, Colorado (background) was presided over by John Tilden Howard (bottom) and enshrined an epic moment in the history of endoscopy. With a masterful display of humility and prescience, Howard yielded the podium and graciously eschewed the privilege of delivering his Presidential Address to enable B. Hirschowitz (right) to present the first demonstration of the fiberscope to the Society. Due to a major snowfall, less than forty persons witnessed the early morning (8:30 a.m.) presentation of the instrument (center left) and a subsequent demonstration of its capability to transmit an image (top left). Few present may have realized that they had witnessed the dawn of a new era.

the 1990s altered on an almost monthly basis, endoscopy in the 1970s generated technical advances at such a pace that gastroenterologists were barely able to stay abreast of the new possibilities.

Percutaneous Endoscopy Gastrostomy (PEG)

A wide variety of procedures had been developed in the late nineteenth and early twentieth centuries to provide access to the stomach.

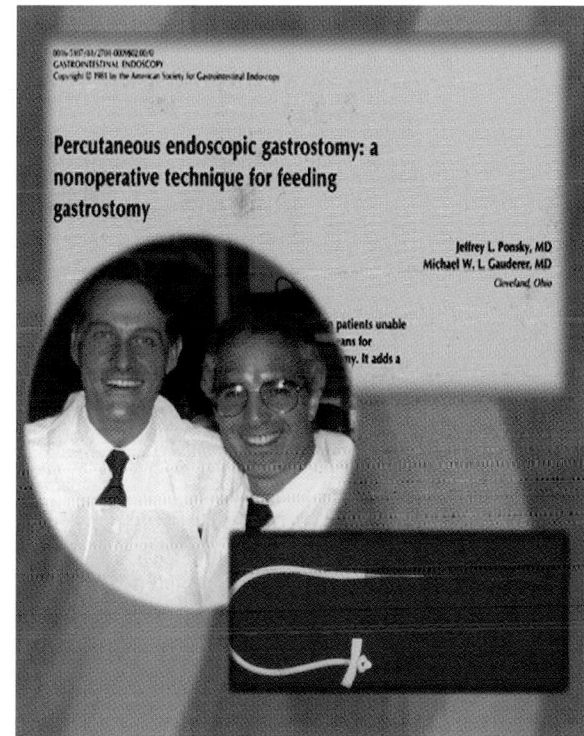

J. Ponsky and M. Gauderer in 1980 conceived and perfected a novel technique to obviate the need for open surgical construction of a gastrostomy. As a result of its safety and efficacy, the standard technique of open operative gastrostomy (like peptic ulcer surgery) has for the most part faded from the armamentarium of the general surgeon.

The surgical procedures had supplanted the chronic use of stomach tubes and were of particular utility in feeding patients who could not swallow, or decompressing stomachs of those with pyloric obstruction. The earliest percutaneous acess to the human stomach was provided by either incidental trauma or disease. Thus, Jacob Helm of Vienna reported his experience of studying the digestion of Theresa Peitz in 1803 when she presented with a spontaneous gastric fistula. Subsequently William Beaumont studied Alexis St. Martin in 1822 after the latter had acquired a musket-induced gastric fistula and in 1843, Nicolas Blondlot successfully constructed a canine gastrostomy for the formal study of gastric secretion. His work was based upon knowledge of Madelaine Gore, a patient with a gastric fistula, studied by Clarion and Dupuytren in Paris in 1801. Although the Russian physiologist, W. Bassow, was the first to propose the utility of the human gastrostomy, Charles Sedillot in 1849 was the first to successfully undertake the procedure. Thereafter, A. Vernuil (1876), Charles Richet (1878) and K. Lennander (1908), variously demonstrated the efficiency of the procedure to either provide nutrition or drain and obstructed stomach, and popularized the operation. Over the next three decades, gastrostomy became regarded as a popular and useful technique, and a wide variety of surgical modifications were developed in the early twentieth century to provide long-term access to the stomach. Such operative procedures supplanted the chronic use of stomach tubes and were of particular utility in feeding patients who could not swallow, or for the decompression of stomachs obstructed by pyloric pathology. Despite being a relatively modest surgical technique, the morbidity and mortality was substantial, given the infirmity of the patient population that required such intervention.

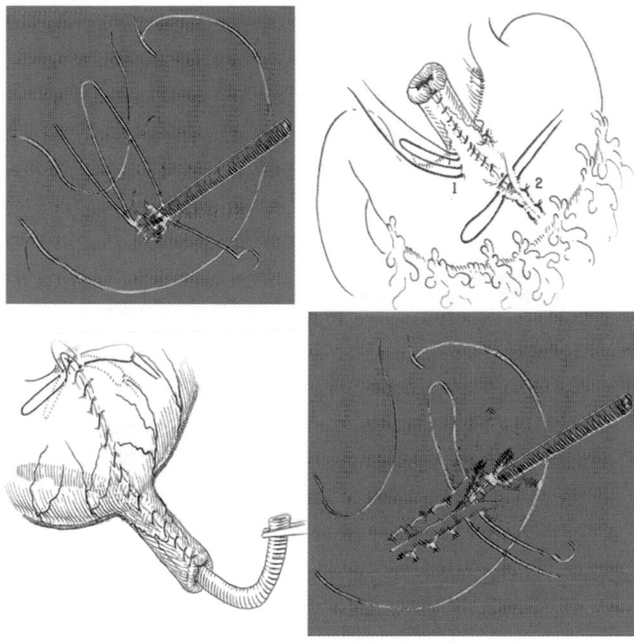

For almost a century continual access to the stomach in cases of gastric outlet obstruction or esophageal disease could only be attained by the construction of a gastrostomy. A wide variety of such stomas have been devised (each with its proponents and critics). All, however, require major surgical intervention and were associated with a substantial morbidity and mortality.

In 1980, Jeffrey Ponsky and Michael W.L. Gauderer described an *"incisionless gastrostomy"* that had been developed for long-term internal feeding of pediatric patients at the Children's Hospital in Cleveland. So effective and safe has this procedure become that in 1990, it was estimated to be the second most common indication for upper endoscopy in hospitalized patients in the United States. Indeed, the efficacy of the maneuver has been such that surgical gastroscopy has virtually become a technique of the past.

Mucosal Barriers

The question of why the stomach does not autodigest itself was often posed and the Iatromathematician, Archibald Pitcairn, asked: *"Why upon the digestion of food upon the stomach, which is as easily digestible as the food, yet the stomach itself should not be dissolved?"* No reasonable answer was forthcoming and the pundits, such as John Hunter, could only perseverate upon the existence of a putative vital force that maintained the gastric wall intact under the circumstances of digestion. The invocation of *"vital spiri"*, however, was of little satisfaction and

Archibald Pitcairn (inset) was prescient in posing the question as to why the stomach digested only food and not itself. This answer would only be forthcoming centuries later with the elucidation of the unique tight junction properties of the gastric mucosa.

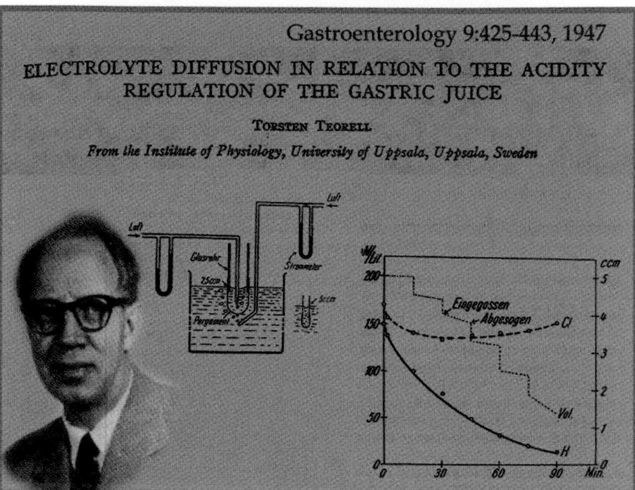

Gastroenterology 9:425-443, 1947

ELECTROLYTE DIFFUSION IN RELATION TO THE ACIDITY REGULATION OF THE GASTRIC JUICE

Torsten Teorell

From the Institute of Physiology, University of Uppsala, Uppsala, Sweden

Torsten Teorell was the first to scientifically delineate the barrier properties of the gastric mucosa.

represented a regression to pre-Paracelsian views on the nature of digestion. Issues such as the existence of a "*locus minoris resistentia*" were entertained to explain ulceration and embraced the concept that this was indeed local digestion of the stomach mucosa. Further reflection on the matter resulted in the recognition that the stomach wall itself must harbor an intrinsic "force" capable of resisting digestion. Indeed, the attractive concept that a breakdown of such an intrinsic mechanism might be responsible for the development of ulcers or even neoplasia, became a source of considerable speculation.

In the early 1930s, the issue had arisen as to whether acid was neutralized within the lumen or after diffusion into the mucosa in the interstitial fluid. Torsten Teorell suggested that the back-diffusion of H^+ ions through the mucosa in exchange for Na^+ ions might define the permeability characteristics of gastric mucosa. An alternative hypothesis was that the bicarbonate content of gastric secretion might be responsible for neutralization of some of the acid. Nevertheless, the ability of the stomach to retain the acid it secreted under normal circumstances without digesting itself, produced a compelling consideration to define the concept of the existence of a "gastric mucosal barrier". Teorell began the delineation of the barrier properties by demonstrating that ionized organic acids but not ionized mineral acids would disappear rapidly from the gastric contents by diffusing into the mucosa. Whilst not fully resolving the issue, his concept of a diffusion process in the mucosa had, by 1947, initiated the formal evaluation of the intrinsic mechanisms available to deal with back diffusion of acid into the interstitium of the stomach.

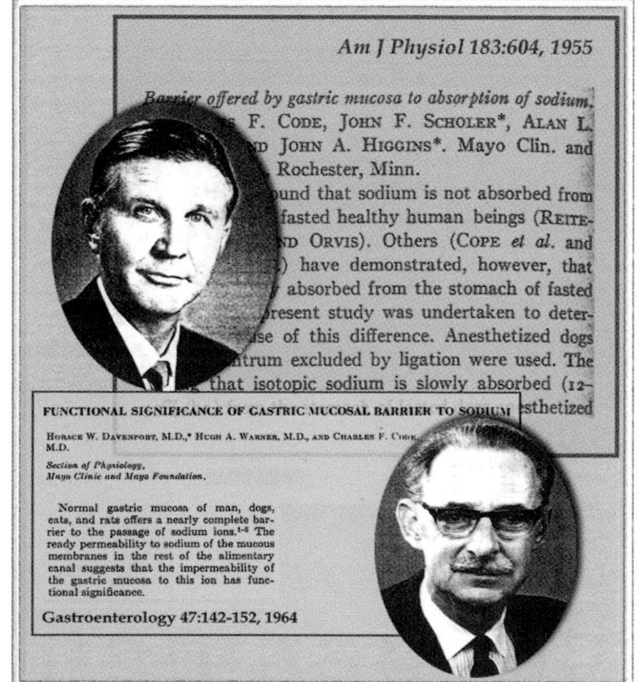

Am J Physiol 183:604, 1955

FUNCTIONAL SIGNIFICANCE OF GASTRIC MUCOSAL BARRIER TO SODIUM

Horace W. Davenport, M.D.,* Hugh A. Warner, M.D., and Charles F. Code, M.D.

Section of Physiology, Mayo Clinic and Mayo Foundation.

Normal gastric mucosa of man, dogs, cats, and rats offers a nearly complete barrier to the passage of sodium ions.[1-6] The ready permeability to sodium of the mucous membranes in the rest of the alimentary canal suggests that the impermeability of the gastric mucosa to this ion has functional significance.

Gastroenterology 47:142-152, 1964

Charles Code (top left) and Horace Davenport (bottom right) were responsible for a series of rigorous scientific studies, which defined the functional significance of the gastric mucosal barrier. They established that the "barrier" represented a generalized function common to a polarized epithelial system and that a wide variety of ingested agents were capable of acting as "barrier breaking" substances.

The first formal usage of the term "barrier" arose in 1955 in the work of Davenport and Code, who had published a series of experiments under the title "The Functional Significance of Gastric Mucosal Barrier to Sodium." Davenport in later work examined this concept further, by seeking to evaluate the effects of damage with various agents including eugenol, fatty acids, and alcohol and was able to prove that back diffusion into the mucosa of acid occurred under such conditions. He provided further substantiation of his observations of increased mucosal permeability by demonstrating anatomical evidence of damage to the surface epithelial cells and underlying tissues including vessels. Considerable substance was thus provided for the important association of barrier-breaking and its relationship to acute mucosal ulceration and stress bleeding. Following the initial contributions of Davenport, an immense and tedious body of work was now undertaken by diverse investigators who variously identified the noxious effects of hypoxia, acid, bile salts, aspirin, non-steroidal anti-inflammatory agents, prostaglandins, and numerous other agents on the integrity of the barrier. This achieved little except to support the existence of the mucosal barrier and the ability of a variety of agents to break it, but failed for the most part to establish either the precise site or mechanism of the phenomenon. The more recent usage of sophisticated techniques to investigate cell function has determined the relevance of tight junctions and identified the specific property of the apical membrane of the gastric mucosal cells as being of vital importance in maintaining barrier function.

Further experiments in this area were designed to identify the physical site of this uptake zone, and resulted in the proposal that it was the mucous layer that construed the barrier function. Proof for this, however, was difficult to obtain, although evidence of surface mucous barriers on the skin of fish was well-recognized. Thus, support for the alternate proposal that bicarbonate secreted by the gastric mucosa neutralized acid and thus created a biochemical barrier, still remained strong. Further elaboration of this line of work generated much discussion about the "unstirred layer" and held that under such conditions, even a modest concentration of bicarbonate would produce a barrier of both functional and physical significance to acid.

An electron microscope image demonstrating the tight junction structure of the gastric mucosa.

Measurement of Acid

Early measurements of gastric acid were qualitative and mostly involved the use of indicator dyes or litmus preparations; however since W. Prout first measured muriatic acid in 1823, definitive quantification became possible, and a number of techniques were introduced. In the latter part of the nineteenth century, however, a confusing terminology developed around the inability to adequately quantify low levels of gastric acid secretion. Thus, the term achylia was used by M. Einhorn to describe the absence of both enzymes and acid in the stomach, while achlorhydria was used to denote the absence of free acid as determined by Topfer's reagent.

The latter term, however, may have been misleading, given the fact that very low levels of acid secretion may have been obscured by bicarbonate secretion. This biochemical confusion spilled over into the clinical arena and the use of the term "hypochlorhydria", to denote low levels of acidity, further obfuscated the assessment of the secretory status of the stomach. In 1952, Card and Sircus proposed that any gastric pH more than 6.0 should be denoted as an "anacidity". This resulted in an evolution of the definition of achlorhydria to be a persistent failure of intragastric pH to fall below 6.0 in the presence of any stimulation of gastric acid secretion. The subsequent evolution of quantitative measurements of gastric acid secretion played a pivotal role in the resolution of the role of histamine as an acid stimulant, as well as providing further information necessary to define the physiology of acid secretion. In this respect, the development of the augmented histamine test by Andrew Kay of Glasgow was particularly useful in the establishment of the precise relationship of histamine to acid secretion in humans. This work amplified that of Popielski, who had initially experimentally established the relationship in the second decade of the twentieth century, and G. Katsch who had undertaken similar studies in Germany in 1925. Kay measured the ability of histamine to stimulate acid secretion at a dose of 0.1 mg/10 kg of body weight and derived the values for maximal acid secretion in a number of different groups of patients while administering mepyramine maleate to block the systemic effects of histamine. Wilfred Card and I.N. Marks of the Western General Hospital in Edinburgh subsequently determined the dose response curves for acid secretion in human subjects in response to intravenous infusions of histamine.

Marks and Card then applied their method of estimating parietal cell mass to gastrectomy specimens of patients with duodenal ulceration, chronic gastric ulceration, or carcinoma of the stomach, and established that the maximal acid output correlated with the parietal cell mass. Thereafter, Marks, working with Simon Komarov and Harry Shay at the Fels Research Institute of Temple University of Philadelphia, was able to correlate the maximal

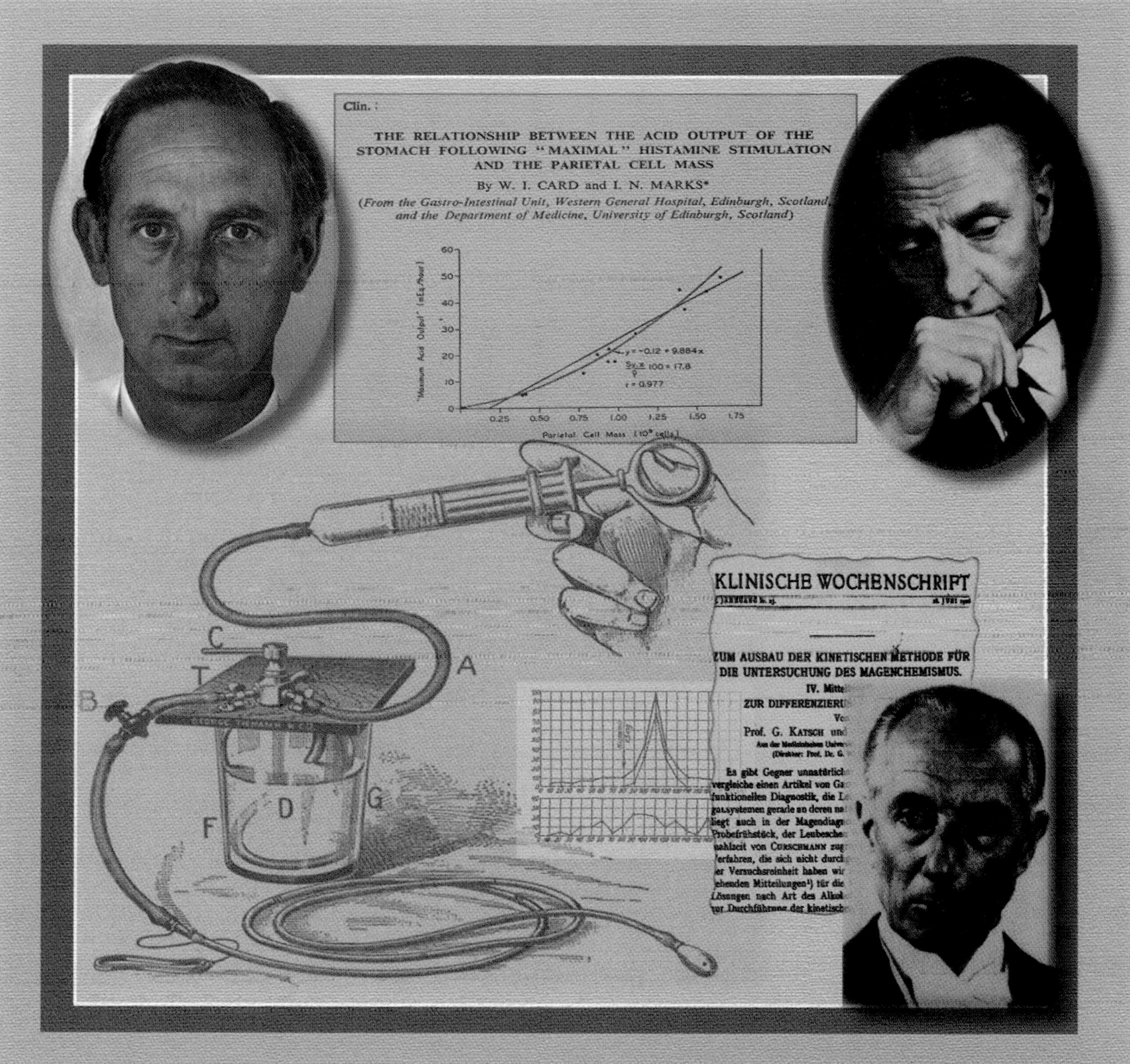

The utility of the "blind tube" was epitomized by its application to the elucidation of gastric secretory function. Gerhard Katsch of Greifswald (1887-1961) (bottom right) introduced quantitative gastric function tests (1925) with caffeine or histamine (kinetic method) to evaluate gastric secretory capacity. By 1960, I.N. Marks (top left) of Cape Town and W. Card (top right), working in Edinburgh, had successfully defined the relationship of the parietal cell mass to the acid secretory capacity of the stomach. Such studies led to the proposal that surgery for peptic ulcer disease might be tailored to the acid secretory capacity of an individual patient.

Sir Andrew Watt Kay of Glasgow was instrumental in developing the histamine stimulation test of gastric acid secretion as a diagnostic tool with predictive application in defining the extent of gastric surgery.

secretory response of dogs to the estimated total parietal cell mass of each stomach. The subsequent development of an analog of histamine (3-beta-aminoethyl pyrazole) by C.E. Rosière was particularly useful, since it enabled stimulation of acid secretion without generating the side effects of histamine. The widespread availability of the standardized augmented histamine test was useful both for experimental studies and for the evaluation of the therapeutic efficacy of various medical agents and surgical procedures.

Acid suppression

The role of histamine antagonists

It had long been recognized that acid and ulcer were related and the Schwartz dictum of "*no acid, no ulcer*" was widely accepted. The exploration of the pathogenesis of peptic ulcer disease suggested a further corollary, namely that hyperchlorhydria (hyper acidic secretion) might play a pivotal role. Since histamine has been identified as a critical secretory agent, the exploration of the pharmacology of histamine evoked considerable attention with the objective of identifying appropriate blocking agents. Indeed, it was proposed that the identification of such drugs would likely alter the natural history of the disease. Nevertheless, by 1950, numerous antihistaminic agents (produced by modification of the imidazole ring) had been studied without identification of an agent effective in the inhibition of acid secretion. In 1966, A.S.F. Ash and H.O. Schild of the University College, London, stated with some degree of frustration: *"At present, no specific antagonist is known for the secretory stimulant action of histamine in the stomach."* They suggested the symbol H1 for receptors that are specifically antagonized by low concentrations of anti-histaminic drugs (H1 receptor antagonists were first synthesized by Boivet in the 1950s), and proposed that another class of histamine receptors existed, which might mediate the acid secretory action of histamine.

The first series of gastric-specific histamine receptor antagonists were soon thereafter synthesized in Welwyn Garden City, U.K., at a site of a stately home occupied by the Smith, Klein and French pharmaceutical corporation. Although the site had been initially used for development of diving gear during WW II since it possessed a deep pond, SK & F had acquired it for research purposes. At this stage, Sir James Black, a pharmacologist working for the pharmaceutical corporation, provided an observation of considerable significance. After synthesizing and testing "*about 700 compounds*" his group in 1972, announced that a compound burimamide, which possessed an imidazole ring with a side chain much bulkier than that of histamine, was a potent suppresser of acid secretion. By focusing on the side chain rather than the imidazole group itself, they were able to generate a drug which antagonized the responses to histamine that were not antagonized by drugs acting on the H1 receptor. Included in these responses were the inhibition of the secretion of acid. The screen used by this group was inhibition of histamine-induced acid secretion in the perfused rat stomach in the Gosh-Schild preparation, an eminently suitable screen for the discovery of a gastric targeted anti-histaminic. Black therefore proposed that there existed a homogenous population of non-H1 receptors that he chose to term "H2" receptors. It was evident that burmamide inhibited pentagastrin-stimulated as well as histamine-stimulated acid secretion and Black suggested that H2 blockade might resolve the long-debated question of whether histamine was the final common mediator of acid secretion. Metiamide and cimetidine followed this first success, and cimetidine was introduced for treatment of acid-related diseases in 1977. George Sachs (originally of Edinburgh and later to be responsible for critical advances in the field of parietal cell proton pump inhibition) noted that James Black, the project leader, Bill Duncan, the site director and Bryce Douglas, the head of research of SK & F (based then in Philadelphia), were all Glaswegian Scots.

During the 1980s, the H2 receptor antagonists became first-line therapy in peptic ulcer disease and led to an improvement in quality of life for a large number of patients. It was found to be superior to any other form of medication at the time, giving good inhibition of nighttime secretion and lesser inhibition of daytime acid secretion. After the first successes with the short acting H2 receptor antagonists, considerable effort was next expended on identifying compounds which were longer-acting, hence relatively irreversible or insurmountable, in order to improve the acid inhibitory profile of this class of drug. The SK & F patent was bypassed by a group of chemists working at Allen and Hanbury led by David Jack, also from Glasgow. The imidazole ring was exchanged for a furan, and a small side chain modification was made. This generated ranitidine, famotidine with a thiazole ring, and nizatidine.

Sir James Black (left) of Aberdeen, Scotland, developed the family of histamine antagonist drugs which specifically blocked the gastric H2 receptor. These agents initially revolutionized the treatment of acid related diseases and for the most part obviated the need for surgery.

It was soon apparent that the introduction of the H2 receptor antagonist class of agents revolutionized the management of acid peptic related disease and provided a major increase in the quality of life for innumerable patients. The recognition that further improvement in the regulation of the acid secretory process would yield better clinical results, especially for erosive esophagitis, led to further efforts to amplify acid suppression. Thus the identification of the proton pump as the final step in the pathway of parietal cell acid secretion provided a unique opportunity for better control of parietal cell secretion.

The Development of Proton Pump Inhibitors

The concept that drove the development of alternatives to H2 receptor antagonists was the recognition that these would have limited efficacy. Indeed, it seemed that inhibition of the pump itself would be a more effective way of controlling of acid secretion. Although work towards this end began at SK & F in Philadelphia, it was terminated with the launch of cimetidine.

The development of the first of this series of drugs was due to a combination of serendipity, mechanism, and conviction that the ATPase was the best target for control of acid secretion. A compound, pyridine-2-acetamide had been acquired by a company, Hassle, in Goteborg, Sweden, for possible use as an antiviral agent. Although this compound was found ineffective, it surprisingly was noted to possess some anti-secretory activity. Modification to a pyridine-2-thioacetamide in order to improve its anti-viral efficacy proved ineffective, although it retained its anti-secretory activity. In 1973, SK & F announced the development of cimetidine, the world's first clinically useful H2 receptor antagonist. Based on the structure of cimetidine structure, a benzimidazole ring was added to the anti-secretory drug (pyridine-2-thioacetamide) based on the belief that the mechanism of action of these forerunners was H2 antagonism. Anti-secretory activity was retained. Finally the sulfide was modified for stabilization to a sulfoxide and timoprazole was born.

This compound had rather remarkable anti-secretory properties: it inhibited gastric acid secretion whatever the stimulus. In experimental studies, it inhibited secretion in isolated gastric glands irrespective of the stimulus, but was relatively acid-unstable and showed inhibition of iodide uptake by the thyroid and was thymotoxic. The first polyclonal antibody against the H^+,K^+-ATPase reacted with cells in the stomach, but also mysteriously with the thyroid and thymus. This suggested that perhaps the ATPase was the target of timoprazole. By 1977, a compound, picoprazole, had been made which retained the core structure of timoprazole. It was shown that this compound inhibited the gastric H^+,K^+-ATPase only when this ATPase was making acid, and that there was a lag phase before inhibition of transport activity occurred. Since the compound was a weak base, a number of steps that were thought to result in inhibition of ATPase activity and acid secretion were determined. These included accumulation of the compound in the acid space of the isolated gastric vesicle during H^+ transport (or the parietal cell canaliculus) followed by conversion to an active compound. It was postulated that this class of compound acted as prodrugs that only reacted with the ATPase after acid-catalyzed conversion to an active form, perhaps the sulfenic acid. Later, it was proven that this active form in solution was a rearranged planar tetracyclic compound containing a highly reactive sulfenamide group.

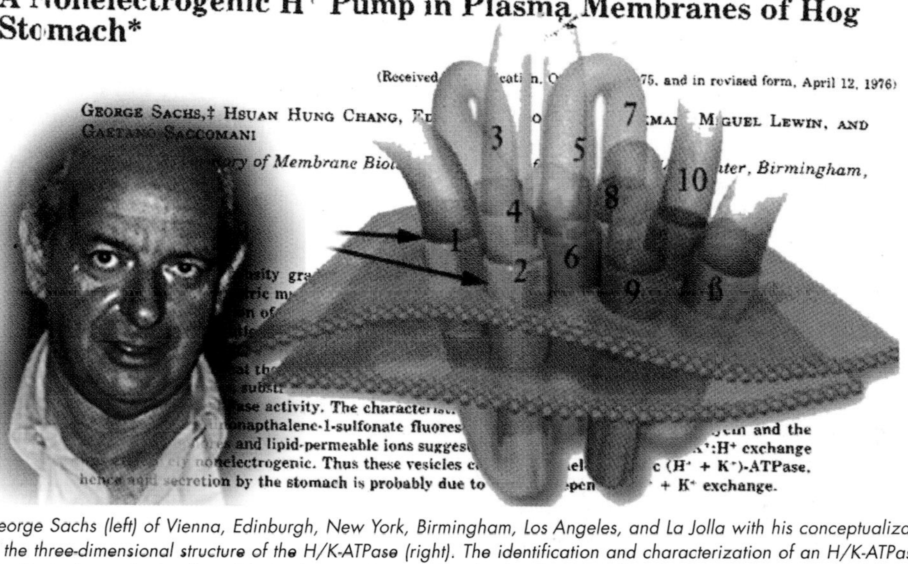

George Sachs (left) of Vienna, Edinburgh, New York, Birmingham, Los Angeles, and La Jolla with his conceptualization of the three-dimensional structure of the H/K-ATPase (right). The identification and characterization of an H/K-ATPase specific to the parietal cell provided a therapeutic target for the development of acid suppressive agents. Modification of the initial PPI drug structure abrogated concerns that it might interfere with thyroid or thymic function.

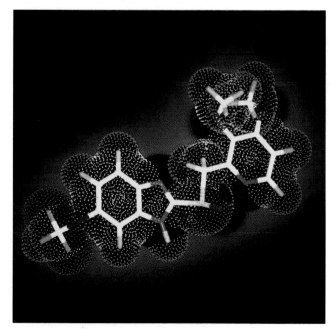

In order to optimize the acid stability of the parent compound and to generate absolute selectivity for accumulation in the acid space of the parietal cell, omeprazole was synthesized in 1979 and became the compound that was launched in 1988 at the Rome World Congress of Gastroenterology. The name coined for this class of drug was proton pump inhibitor (PPI). Following publication in 1981 of the first of a series of papers on the mechanism of action of these drugs, a variety of derivatives were synthesized that also led to the introduction of other drugs including pantoprazole, with generally similar properties to this first clinically effective PPI. The next generation of drugs which suppress gastric acidity will most likely be acid pump antagonists. While the PPIs have a unique mechanism of action based on their chemistry, acid pump antagonists have a structural specificity for their target, the K^+ binding region of the H^+,K^+-ATPase. Although they have been actively pursued for almost fifteen years, thus far none has reached the market place. They promise a more rapid onset of inhibition than the proton pump inhibitors and an inherent stability that will allow design of more flexible formulations.

The molecular structure of the proton pump inhibitor drug, Pantoprazole.

Theodore Billroth (1829-1894), the pioneer in gastric surgery, developed two procedures to which his name was eponymously attached. The Billroth I (upper) had a high mortality on account of the leakage from the lesser curve anastomosis (angle of sorrow). The Billroth II (lower) was safer since the gastrojejunostomy did not leak with the frequency of the gastroduodenostomy of the Billroth I. On the other hand, the anatomic reconfiguration often led to the development of dramatic postoperative symptomatology.

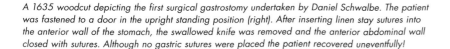

Gastric Surgery

Until the mid-nineteenth century, the techniques of surgery were mostly confined to the extremities and usually related to the management of trauma. No surgeon would reasonably consider the violation of a body cavity prior to the introduction of anesthesia and antisepsis. Even under the latter conditions, both the morbidity and mortality were such that incursions into the peritoneal cavity were undertaken with considerable trepidation.

Even Galen was aware that the injuries to the stomach were relatively less dangerous than the injuries to the intestines. For the most part, this reflected the fact that due to the bactericidal properties of the gastric juice, few bacteria were present compared to the large and small bowel.

Gastrostomy

Florian Mathias, imperial surgeon in Prague, performed the first recorded gastric procedure in 1602 on a 36-year-old peasant. This individual, who was accustomed to earn free beer and a few pennies in an inn by inserting a long knife into his throat and drinking down the beer past it, on this occasion swallowed the knife as well. Although this initially resulted in no particular discomfort it subsequently caused severe pain, presumably as the point began to erode through a part of the gastric wall. Mathias applied plasters to the spot where the point of the knife could be felt under the skin and fifty-one days after the knife had been swallowed, successfully incised and extracted the 21 cm long blade with full recovery of the patient.

A considerably greater feat was performed by Daniel Schwalbe in 1635 on a 22-year-old waiter. This individual, while attempting to relieve his dyspepsia by using an 18 cm long knife to tickle his throat and induce vomiting, inadvertently swallowed the blade. Although he reported no serious symptoms, the medical faculty at Konigsberg decided that the knife should be removed from the stomach. Schwalbe, having fastened the patient to a door in an upright standing position, operated upon the unfortunate in the presence of the faculty and the medical students.

A 1635 woodcut depicting the first surgical gastrostomy undertaken by Daniel Schwalbe. The patient was fastened to a door in the upright standing position (right). After inserting linen stay sutures into the anterior wall of the stomach, the swallowed knife was removed and the anterior abdominal wall closed with sutures. Although no gastric sutures were placed the patient recovered uneventfully!

In this case, there were no adhesions between the stomach and the abdominal wall, and the free abdominal cavity was opened up at surgery. Having identified the stomach, Schwalbe exposed it by inserting a curved needle and linen for traction and at the point where he could palpate the knife made an incision, and removed the object. Of note is the fact that he did not suture the gastric incision and allowed the stomach to fall back into the abdomen before suturing the abdominal wall with five stitches. Quite surprisingly, the patient recovered from the first open gastrostomy. For the most part, the early reports of stomach surgery reflected the consequences of either military action with war wounds or incidental trauma. A therapeutic gastrostomy was reported in 1819 to remove a silver fork that had been *"inadvertently"* swallowed by a 26-year-old female servant. Jacques Mathieu Delpech (1777-1832) of Montpellier confirmed the diagnosis of a penetrating fork upon noting a red inflamed mass on the anterior abdominal wall five months after the fork had been ingested. He was a shrewd enough clinician to persuade a colleague, Cayroche of Mende, to remove this foreign body (May 1, 1819) via an anterior abdominal incision. Despite this feat, Delpech was subsequently assassinated by a former patient who believed that a varicocele operation had rendered him impotent.

A patient of particular physiological interest was that of the traumatic gastrostomy of the Canadian voyageur Alexis St. Martin. Although the biological significance of the gastrostomy has been described earlier in this text, the possibility of using it for therapeutic purposes was never fully

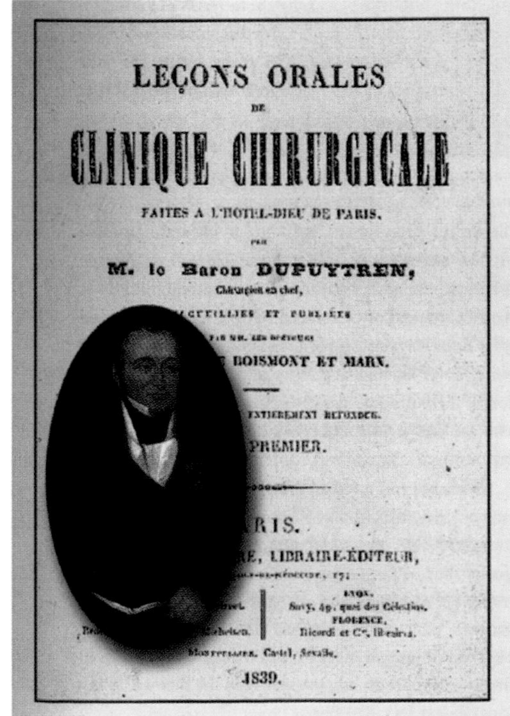
LEÇONS ORALES

DE

CLINIQUE CHIRURGICALE

FAITES A L'HOTEL-DIEU DE PARIS,

PAR

M. le Baron DUPUYTREN,

Chirurgien en chef,

BOISMONT ET MARX.

PREMIER.

RIS.

E, LIBRAIRE-ÉDITEUR,

1839.

G. Dupuytren, although revered as a surgeon and teacher, was much disliked by his colleagues for his arrogance and immodesty. His technical skills were legendary, as were his powers of observation. Although he was well aware of gastroduodenal ulceration and its sequelae, he did not perceive operative intervention as feasible.

explored by William Beaumont. In 1837, Christian Egeberg, a surgeon in Baerum, Norway, drew attention to the fact that patients with cancer of the esophagus could be maintained in reasonably good health by gastrostomy. The first gastric fistulas were made for instructive purposes on dogs by the Russian Bassow in 1842 and thereafter by the French physiologist Blondlot. Charles Sedillot performed the first gastrostomy on a human (the patient died) in November 13, 1849, and proposed the name gastrostomy. A similar fate met the next twenty-seven patients who perished from peritonitis. Credit is due to Sidney Jones, surgeon of St. Thomas Hospital in London, for undertaking the first successful gastrostomy (the twenty-ninth patient). This individual survived for forty days after the operation!

Despite random contributions by diverse practitioners, the principal contributions in gastric surgery at that time emanated from the work of Dupuytren of Paris. Few surgeons have evoked more controversy and divergent opinions. He was variously known as *"the first of surgeons and the least of men"* or a *"genius but of unprecedented unkindness and coldness"*. Born on October 5, 1777, to a family of modest means, his extraordinary intelligence was apparent from an early age. In 1802, at the age of 25, he was appointed to the Hotel Dieu, and by 1815, he was chief surgeon, a post he held until his death some twenty years later. Despite the fact that he dressed with appalling taste and that his personal habits left much to be desired, he was highly regarded not only as a teacher but also as a surgeon of extraordinary intellectual and technical proficiency. His workload was extraordinary and it is reported that at the apogee of his career, he would see some 10,000 private patients a year. Although Dupuytren's fame as a surgeon and teacher was prodigious, he wrote little and most of his work is recollected by renditions of his lectures in notebook form. The majority of his teachings were collated in a book entitled *Lecons Orales* and published by his students. His teachings cover a diverse range of conditions ranging from ano-rectal problems to chronic bleeding, arterial aneurysms, urinary calculi, and cataract management. Amongst his most notable contributions are his observations on duodenal ulceration. Although Curling, in 1841, had called attention to the connection between cases of burn and acute ulceration of the duodenum, it was Dupuytren who had first made this observation. In 1836, he drew attention to the congestion of various mucous membranes in the alimentary canal in the early stages of burns. He described in detail the ulceration and bleeding of the stomach and duodenum consequent upon such an event, some five years before Curling provided the definitive description of duodenal ulceration associated with cutaneous burns.

Resection and Anastomosis

Overview

Once gastrostomy had been accomplished, the concept of resecting the stomach was next considered. Charles Tivadar Daniel Merrem wrote in his dissertation, published in Giessen in 1810, that he had excised the part of the stomach nearest to the pylorus of three dogs. Of the three only one died of peritonitis; one lived for twenty-two days, but perished due to unceasing vomiting. The dissection demonstrated that the peritoneum was undamaged and that the suture at the site of the resection of the stomach had healed well. Although the third dog was well for twenty-seven days, it was stolen and could thereafter no longer be observed. Merrem's experiment demonstrated that resection of the stomach could be achieved and that the resection wound heal without any special problems. In spite of this, for many decades the operation of Merrem was spoken of as an item of curiosity or even folly, and even the usually genial Johann Dieffenbach (1792-1847) of Konigsberg was fond of referring to it as *"Merrem's dream"*. In 1874, two pupils of Billroth, Karl Gussenbauer, who later became professor of surgery in Lièges, Prague, and Vienna and Alexander Winiwater, later professor in Lièges, demonstrated by experimental work in dogs that the operation could be successfully performed.

Jules Pean, a Parisian surgeon, was the first to perform a gastrectomy on a human (April 8, 1879); the second being undertaken by Ludwig Rydygier, then a practicing surgeon in Kulm, later professor of surgery in Cracow and Lemberg.

Christian Albert Theodore Billroth (1829-1894) was born in Pomerania of Swedish stock and became renowned as a music critic, scholar, and surgeon. Appointed Professor of Surgery at Vienna in 1867, he became the most distinguished surgeon of his time and attracted to his clinic post-graduate students from all over the world. Many of his trainees became chairmen of surgery at different European centers and his surgical influence dominated gastrointestinal surgery for almost half a century. Numerous gastrointestinal surgical advances of the 20th century occurred under his stewardship while the Vienna General Hospital (top) achieved international status as the greatest teaching center of the time.

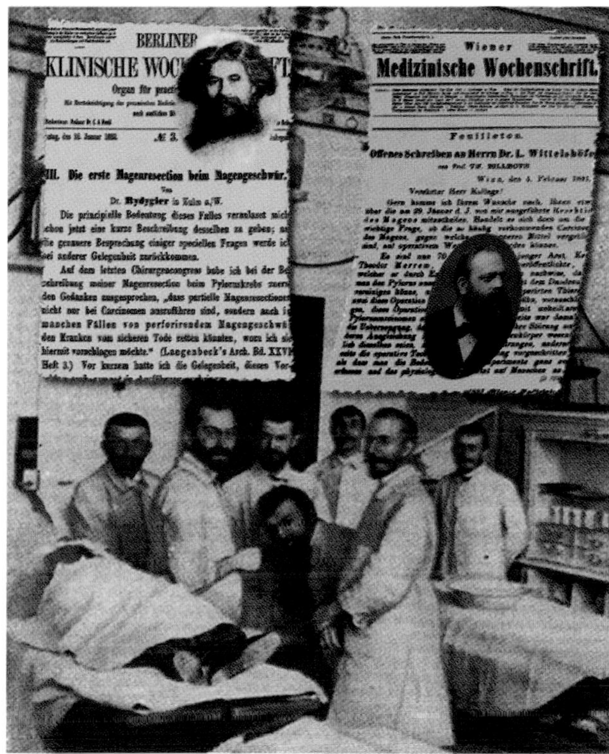

Billroth and von Mikulicz in the Vienna General Hospital Clinic.

On November 16, 1880, Ludwig Rydygier of Chelmo preceded Billroth in undertaking the first gastrectomy (top left). Unfortunately his patient perished! The journal article that documented the first successful gastrectomy undertaken by Billroth, (top right) was annotated by the journal editor, "and hopefully the last!"

Karl G. Gussenbauer (1842-1903) a physician's son from Obervallach, Austria, was one of Billroth's most brilliant trainees. Having obtained a medical degree in 1866, he subsequently became interested in skeletal muscle trauma and the lymphatic spread of malignant tumors. In addition, he described with Billroth the first laryngectomy (1874) and undertook animal studies on partial gastrectomy in 1876. After becoming Professor of Surgery in Prague (1878-1894), he returned to become the new head of the Second Surgical Clinic of surgery in Vienna (1894-1903) at the death of Billroth. In 1894, he became the first German-speaking foreigner from Austria to be elected to the German Surgical Society as well as co-editor of "Langenbeck's Archive" with A. von Eiselsberg.

Von Mikulicz and Billroth in the operating room at the General Hospital, Vienna (c. 1886). Early in 1881 Billroth successfully resected the pyloric tumor of Theresa Heller (background). The resected specimen (left) and the autopsy specimen (right) may both still be seen at the Josphinum Museum in Vienna. L. Rydygier's (top right) gastric resection (1880) had taken place before that of Billroth but unfortunately his patient failed to survive.

Unfortunately, both of these patients died, and it remained for Billroth in Vienna to successfully undertake the first resection of the stomach on a young woman with pyloric obstruction due to a neoplasm in 1881. Unfortunately, she too perished a few months later from metastatic disease. In the course of time the technique of gastrectomy underwent many modifications and became a common procedure for most of the twentieth century, as the definitive cure for peptic ulcer disease. In addition, it was amplified considerably as a radical operation used in the management of gastric cancer. Charles Schlatter of Zurich first carried out a complete removal of the stomach with complete success in 1897, and the concept that survival without a stomach was possible, attained medical reality. In 1881 Anthony Wolfler, while an assistant to Billroth (later professor of Surgery in Graz and Prague), during an operation for a tumor obstructing the pylorus, found that it was irresectable. At the suggestion of Charles Nicoladoni, who was an assistant at the operation (later professor of Surgery in Innsbruck and Graz), Wolfler established a communication (gastroenterostomy) between the stomach and the small intestine. This enabled food to bypass the obstructed pylorus and enter the small intestine, as well as obviating the dramatic symptoms of obstruction and the vomiting of stagnant material.

Gastrectomy

The first gastrectomy was performed by Jules Émile Pean of Paris. Born in 1830 to the family of a miller, Pean attended medical school in Paris in 1855, and in 1868, after training with Denon Villiers and Nelaton, was awarded a doctor of medicine degree in surgery. Pean's reputation as a clinician and a surgeon was prestigious. Although his initial contributions to abdominal surgery were in the area of ovarian cystectomy in 1867, he undertook the first successful splenectomy during a laparotomy for an ovarian cyst in which incidental damage to the spleen had occurred. A further major contribution in 1868 was the development of a special hemostatic clip made by Gueride that he successfully utilized for hemostasis. On April 8, 1879, Pean undertook what was to be his most epic contribution to surgery by resecting a pyloric gastric cancer. The operation lasted 2 1/2 hours and the patient initially recovered successfully.

Unfortunately, over the subsequent three days, the patient received two blood transfusions of 50 and 80 ml, and died on the fifth postoperative day prior to a further transfusion. Although the cause of death is unknown, the recognition of blood groups did not occur for some forty years later and it seems likely that either sepsis or transfusion incompatibility may have contributed to this fatality. Nevertheless, to Pean goes the credit for having undertaken the first (albeit unsuccessful) gastrectomy.

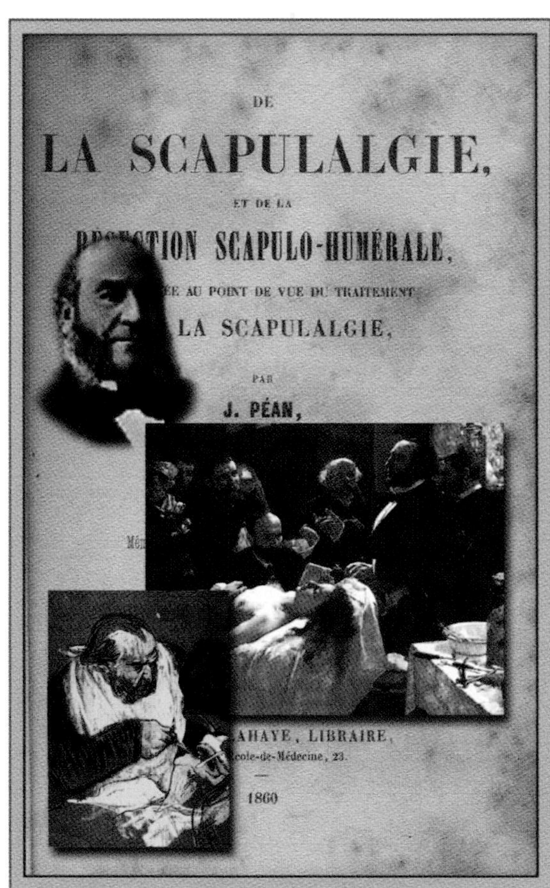

J. Pean was a surgeon of considerable technical virtuosity as well as being a renowned gourmand and socialite. Toulouse-Lautrec portrayed him operating (bottom left) and the depiction of his demonstration of the vascular clamp that he designed hangs in the Musée D'Orsay (center). In 1879, Pean was the first to resect a pyloric tumor but unfortunately the patient perished.

On November 16, 1880, Ludwig Rydygier of Chelmo, performed the second documented but also unsuccessful gastrectomy. Like Pean, he undertook a partial resection of the pre-pyloric portion of the stomach in a patient with gastric cancer. Some two months later in Vienna, Billroth became the first surgeon to successfully undertake a gastrectomy. This third reported gastrectomy was also for a pyloric tumor but in this instance the patient, Theresa Heller, survived to be discharged home three weeks postoperatively. The cumulative operative survival from gastrectomy in the two decades following Pean's initial operation rarely exceeded 50%. As a result of the substantial mortality involved in gastrectomy in the pre-antiseptic era, lesser procedures were usually contemplated in an attempt to deal with diseases of the stomach thought to require surgical intervention.

The most popular operation was the gastroenterostomy pioneered by Mathieu Jaboulay of France, but Von Mikulicz of Vienna and Wolffler were also protagnists of the procedure. Jaboulay was born on July 5, 1860, and educated in the Lyons area, where he achieved wide renown as a surgeon of considerable intellectual and technical skill. One of his early accomplishments had been to remove the vagi, coeliac ganglion, and sympathetic chains of the upper abdomen in an attempt to deal with the discomfort induced by the lightning pains of *tabes dorsalis*. His later development of the gastroenterostomy procedure to obviate problems generated by the gastric outlet obstruction (some consequent upon vagotomy) achieved widespread popularity in Europe. Indeed, gastroenterostomy remained the standard of choice for the first two to three decades of the twentieth century as the preferred surgical treatment of either peptic ulcer or gastric neoplasia. Thereafter, better techniques developed to ensure the safety of the anastomosis after gastric resection, and with the advent of Listererian antisepsis the era of the gastrectomist supervened.

M. Jaboulay (seated center) achieved legendary status at the Hôtel Dieu of Lyons. This photograph of Jaboulay operating was taken by Harvey Cushing who had visited Lyons during his tour of French surgical clinics en route to work with T. Kocher in Bern. The lack of masks, gloves, and the formal suit of the principle surgeon (MJ) reflect the current woeful state of surgical antiseptic technique. Although Anton Wofler (1850-1917) of Vienna had first introduced the operation of gastroenterostomy in 1881, the technique devised by Jaboulay was subsequently widely utilized.

The early use of gastrectomy in peptic ulcer disease focused on the management of complications such as obstruction and bleeding. Initial problems related to the leakage of the anastomosis between the duodenum and the gastric remnant led to the popularization of the gastrojejunal anastomosis known as the Billroth II. The significant disturbances in physiology consequent upon this procedure (dumping syndromes, afferent and efferent loop syndromes) were thought tolerable as compared to the invariable mortality associated with a leak from a Billroth I type anastomosis. In order to obviate the development of such symptomatology, a great number of modifications of the procedure involving the construction of valves or different bowel loop lengths, were introduced almost to no avail.

Vagotomy

Although the role of the vagus in the regulation of gastrointestinal secretion and motility was incompletely understood, there was general awareness of the fact that it might in some way be implicated in gastric disease processes. The first

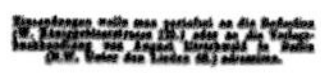

BERLINER
KLINISCHE WOCHENSCHRIFT.
Organ für practische Aerzte.
Mit Berücksichtigung der preussischen Medicinalverwaltung und Medicinalgesetzgebung nach amtlichen Mittheilungen.
Redacteur: Professor Dr. C. A. Ewald. Verlag von August Hirschwald in Berlin.
Montag, den 16. Januar 1882. № 3. Neunzehnter Jahrgang.

III. Die erste Magenresection beim Magengeschwür.
Von
Dr. Rydygier in Kulm a./W.

Die principielle Bedeutung dieses Falles veranlasst mich, schon jetzt eine kurze Beschreibung desselben zu geben; auf
die genauere Besprec … en Fragen werde ich
bei anderer Gelegenh …
Auf dem letzten … habe ich bei der Beschreibung meiner … Pyloruskrebs zuerst
den Gedanken ausges … elle Magenresectionen
nicht nur bei Carcin … nd, sondern auch in
manchen Fällen … n Magengeschwür
den Kranken vom si … könnten, wozu ich sie
hiermit vorschlagen m … ck's Arch. Bd. XXVI
Heft 3.) Vor kurzen … genheit, diesen Vorschlag auch zuerst … ingen.

The first report of a gastric resection for a gastric ulcer by Ludwig Rydygier of Kulm (Chelmo) was published in 1882, although the operation had been undertaken in 1880. The patient did not survive the procedure.

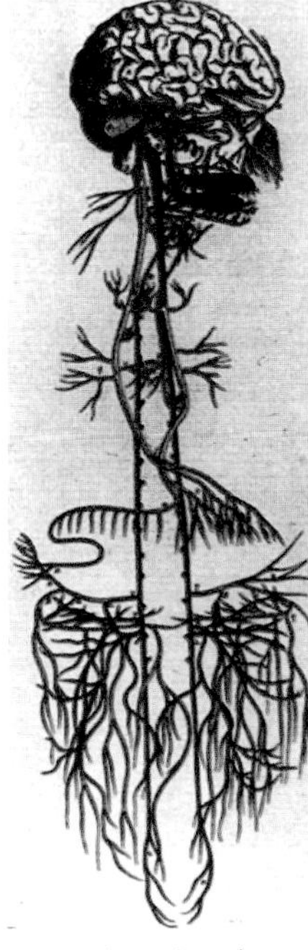

The wandering nerve (vagus) as depicted by Vesalius at Padua in his monumental anatomical text of 1543.

The early part of the 20th century represented the glory days of gastric surgery where surgeons such as the Mayo brothers of Rochester were acclaimed for their heroic surgical efforts in the treatment of peptic ulcer disease (inset).

vagotomy upon a human was conducted by Jaboulay, who undertook this in the process of excising the celiac plexus of a man suffering from the lightning pains of *tabes dorsalis*.

A few years later, Exner similarly divided the vagi in a number of patients afflicted with tabes, but presciently noted that a percentage of these individuals subsequently suffered from the effects of gastric atony. As a result of this observation, he thereafter combined vagotomy with a gastrojejunostomy to promote gastric emptying. In time, other surgeons, including Kuttner, Borchers, and Podkaminsky, attempted vagotomy on patients for a variety of diagnoses that ranged from dyspepsia to gastric ptosis and neurasthenia. Thus by 1920, the results of 20 sub-diaphragmatic vagotomies for treatment of gastric ptosis were reported by Bircher who commented upon decreased acidity and, curiously, improved tonus in 75% of his patients. Some years later, Alvarez in reviewing the work of Bircher, concluded: *"His vagotomies were probably incomplete because, aside from some lowering of acidity, he did not seem to obtain the usual effects of a complete nerve resection."*

Latarjet

The outcome of these early clinical vagotomies inspired André Latarjet of Lyons to further evaluate the procedure. Latarjet made the most detailed investigations into the anatomy of the vagi to date and applied his findings to the surgical patients he treated. The eponymous attribution of the anterior and posterior vagal nerves of the gastric lesser curve, attest to his profound influence and excellent work in this area. André Latarjet was born on August 20, 1877, in Dijon and studied medicine in Lyons. Because of financial pressures, Latarjet was forced to choose between a career in surgery or anatomy. Since a surgical practice was difficult to establish in the hospitals of Lyons, and Latarjet was not financially able to support himself in private practice, he chose a career based principally in anatomy. As an anatomist, he never relinquished his initial dedication to surgery, and together with Raymond Grégoire in Paris, became one of the principle proponents of a field later known as applied anatomy. His research was initially directed broadly towards the innervation of the abdominal organs and over a period of twenty years, he wrote extensively on nerves of the colon, biliary tract, and the pelvis in both men and women. The detailed study of the hypogastric and sacral plexuses in females resulted in the development of a surgical treatment for dysmenorrhea (*operation de cotte*). Probably his most important contribution relates to the work undertaken with his colleague Pierre Wertheimer. In 1921 Wertheimer completed his thesis *"De l'Enervatione Gastrique"*. This study documented both anatomical and experimental work in regard to the vagal innervation of the stomach and reported that cutting the vagus nerves significantly impaired gastric motility and emptying as well as producing a substantial inhibition of acid secretion. The subsequent publication, in 1923, of the surgical studies in which vagotomy and a drainage procedure were utilized, resulted in the international recognition of Latarjet's contributions and his eponymous attribution to the gastric vagi. Unfortunately, Latarjet never formally confirmed that vagotomy was a successful therapy for peptic ulcer disease, although his studies of acid inhibition and radiological measurements of delayed gastric emptying provide clear evidence of its potential efficacy.

The principal difference between the work of Latarjet and his predecessors was his decision to perform vagotomy in a systematic manner for patients with dyspepsia. His operation, first reported in 1921, entailed denervation of the greater and lesser curvatures and the suprapyloric region, with partial circumcision of the serosa and muscularis down to the level of the submucosa. He designed this operation to sever all the extrinsic nerves to the stomach and pylorus, leaving intact the large branch of the right gastric nerve that accompanies the left gastric artery to the celiac plexus. In 1922, Latarjet reported his results on twenty-four patients to the French Academy of Surgery. Like Exner before him, he found delayed gastric emptying in many of these vagotomized patients and as a result, later added a gastrojejunostomy to this operation. He explained *"Indeed, in all of our cases, gastroentero-anastomosis was done at the same time as denervation, either for reasons of promoting mechanical order or to avoid the possibility of an aggravated ulcer evolution as a consequence of the prolonged journey of food in a stomach which has been rendered hypotonic by denervation."*

In 1922, Latarjet (top left) reported his results on twenty-four patients to the French Academy of Surgery. Like Exner before him, he found delayed gastric emptying in many of these vagotomized patients and, as a result later added a gastrojejunostomy to this operation. He explained, "Indeed, in all of our cases, gastroentero-anastamosis was done at the same time as denervation, either for reasons of promoting mechanical order or to avoid the possibility of an aggravated ulcer evolution as a consequence of the prolonged journey of the food in a stomach which has been rendered hypertonic by denervation." *Almost thirty years later, Lester Dragstedt of Chicago would come to a virtually identical conclusion.*

Almost thirty years later, Lester Dragstedt of Chicago would come to a virtually identical conclusion.

As early as 1927, Charles Mayo was aware that operations not based on sound physiologic principles have no place in the surgical repertoire. "*If anyone should consider removing half of my good stomach to cure a small ulcer in my duodenum, I would run faster than he.*" Since one theory of ulcerogenesis popular during the 1920s was that ulcers were caused by gastric stasis, skeptics proposed that the excellent results of his procedure might be attributed to the concomitant gastroenterostomy – not the vagotomy.

Dragstedt

On 18 January 1943, Dragstedt performed a sub-diaphragmatic vagal resection upon a patient with an active duodenal ulcer and so, ushered in the modern era of vagotomy. Born in Anaconda, Montana, of Swedish immigrant parentage, Dragstedt had first trained as a physiologist with A. Carlson in Chicago before accepting the invitation of D. Phemister to join his department of surgery at Rush University. Given his basic training in science, he brought a different focus to his research on the pathogenesis of peptic ulcer disease and was fascinated by the work of John Hunter and Claude Bernard that showed that normal stomachs do not digest themselves. He recognized that "*pure gastric juice as it is secreted by the fundus of the stomach, has the capacity to destroy and digest various living tissues, including the wall of the jejunum, duodenum, and even the stomach itself. It does not do this under normal conditions because the usual and appropriate stimulus to gastric secretion is ingestion of food. This dilutes and neutralizes the gastric juice and decreases its corrosive powers.*" Dragstedt further postulated that most mucosal damage takes place at night when people do not eat, and that this nocturnal acid secretion was of nervous origin (an observation of some prescience). He disagreed with his colleagues who speculated that ulcers were caused by diminished mucosal resistance to injury. The key to understanding ulcerogenesis, he reiterated, was acid secretion and, in support of his theory, presented two stimuli of acid hypersecretion: neural and hormonal. In citation of his own experiments, he demonstrated clear evidence that neural stimulation caused increased output of gastric acid. From this generous theoretic background, Dragstedt set out to provide a surgical cure for patients with peptic ulcer disease. The operation he initially proposed was a total vagotomy much like that originally undertaken by Latarjet some decades earlier. The first patient to receive a Dragstedt vagotomy was a 35-year-old man who had a bleeding ulcer, necessitating multiple blood transfusions despite medical therapy. The young man underwent a bilateral vagotomy by way of a left thoracotomy approach and his abdominal pain immediately subsided. Dragstedt, always the physiologist, intermittently instilled 0.1 normal hydrochloric acid into the stomach of the patient for the next couple of weeks. For the first eight days, he was able to reproduce the abdominal pain of the patient. On the ninth day, however, acid infusion no longer caused discomfort. Dragstedt took this to indicate that the ulcer had healed!

Dragstedt went on to perform more than 200 vagotomies during the next four years because of its physiologic basis and clinical success. Since one-third of these patients developed gastric stasis severe enough to necessitate a gastro-enterostomy as a secondary procedure, an abdominal approach to the vagi was developed in order to perform the procedures simultaneously. Initially, the drainage procedure of choice was a gastroenterostomy but during the next decade, the technique of pyloroplasty was perfected and became the drainage method of choice. Later, as the role of the antrum in the physiology of gastric secretion became better understood, vagotomy combined with antrectomy was the procedure used to reduce the secretion

A. Carlson (bottom left) was Dragstedt's (right) physiology mentor. Dragstedt recognized that hormonal stimulation could also account for acid hypersecretion. First, he cited the work of Pavlov in which acid secretion had been elicited in response to food introduced into denervated gastric pouches. Next, he admitted the validity of the theory of Edkins, but only after he conducted his own experiments. In these studies, Dragstedt excised and transplanted the antrum from a denervated stomach of a dog to its abdominal wall and found markedly reduced gastric secretion. When the antrum was re-implanted with the duodenum, normal gastric secretion resumed. With these studies, he not only confirmed Edkins' findings, but also established a fundamental observation – that gastrin secretion did not take place in an acid environment. Thus, Dragstedt recognized and described the existence of a feedback mechanism dependent on mucosal pH for the control of secretion of gastrin. In so doing he produced physiological proof of the antral regulation of acid secretion which could be utilized to support the rationale for the introduction of the surgical operation of antrectomy.

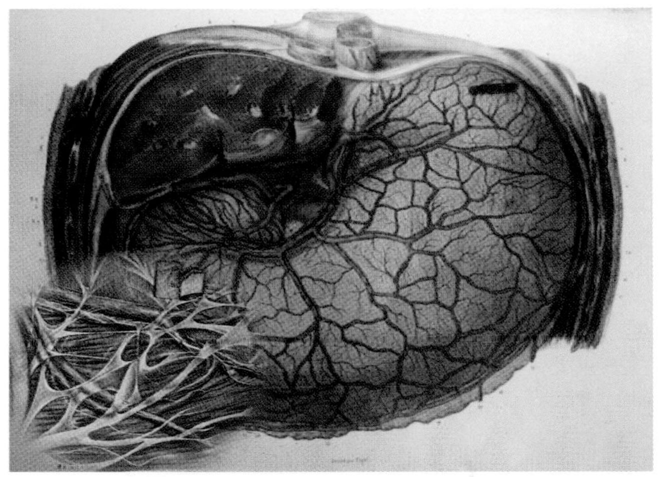

The regulation of pyloric function was ill-understood (inset bottom left – a microscopic dissection of pyloric neural innervation) and the sequela of vagotomy resulted in gastric outlet obstruction unless a concomittant gastroenterostomy or pyloroplasty was undertaken.

Lester Dragstedt (left) and his brother Carl (c. 1918). A.R. Carlson, the doyen of gastric physiology at the University of Chicago, trained both as physiologists. It is of interest that Carlson utilized the services of a local surgeon (J. Moorehead) to teach all his students the art of experimental surgery. Carl became a well-recognized pharmacologist and undertook substantial investigative work in the physiology and pharmacology of histamine. Lester, although trained as a physiologist, became a surgeon and, in addition to introducing vagotomy to North America, established the antrum as an endocrine regulatory mechanism of acid secretion.

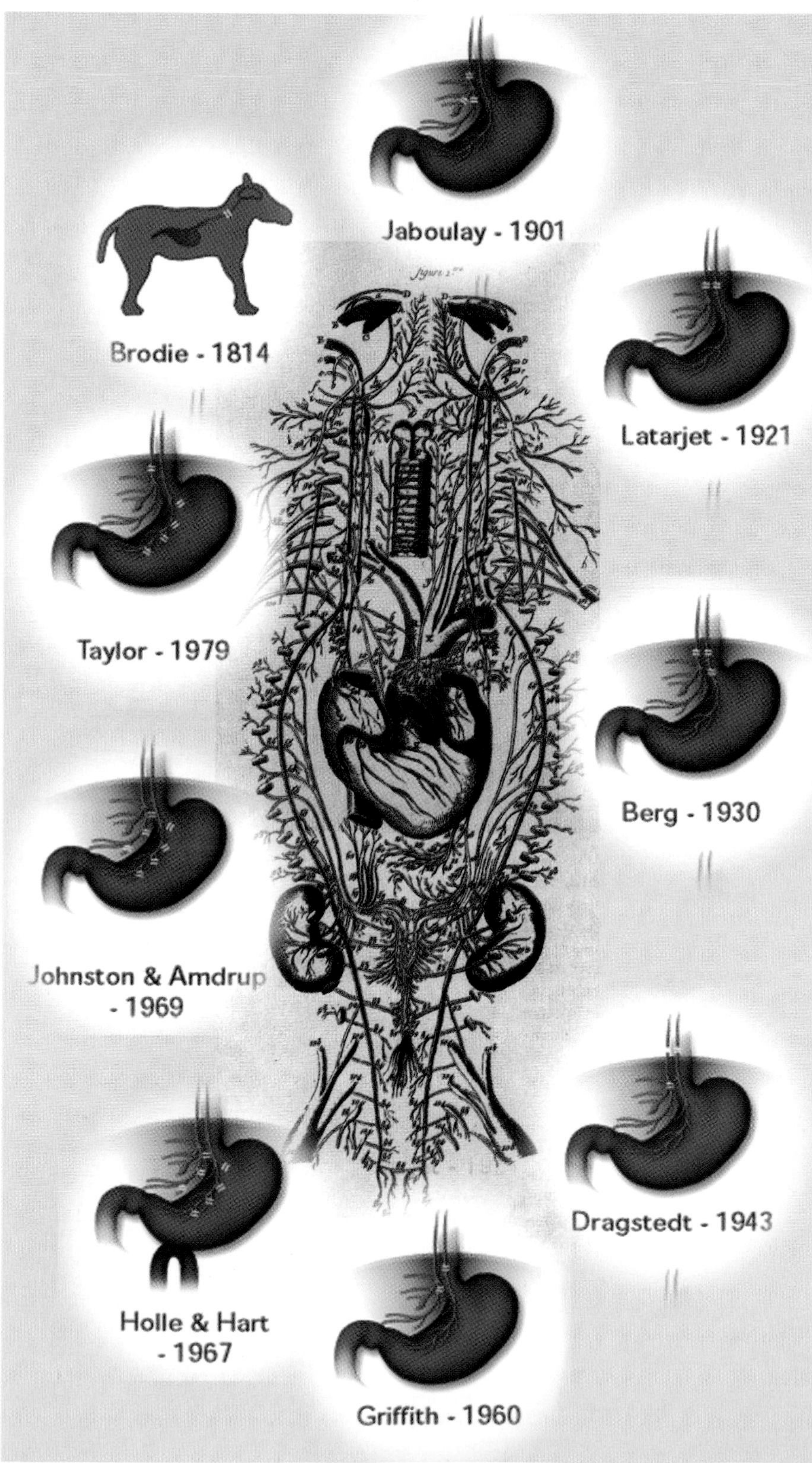

of gastric acid maximally. Despite the clinical success of Dragstedt and his physiologic arguments favoring vagotomy for peptic ulcer disease, his medical and surgical colleagues in general resisted his methods. Nonetheless, a number of pioneering surgeons dared to try his techniques on patients with difficult ulcers. Such surgeons as Grimson and Ruffin from Duke University, Walters from Rochester, Minnesota, and Moore from Massachusetts General Hospital, performed about 200 vagotomies. Their findings were presented at the Central Surgical Association meeting in Chicago in February 1947. By this time, surgeons from the Mayo Clinic, a relatively conservative institution, had performed about 80 of the Dragstedt procedures that they termed a "gastric neurectomy" and observed with concern that *"the results are inconstant, variable and in most cases unpredictable."* The most serious complication they encountered was gastric stasis. In an attempt to establish a reasonable answer, the American Gastroenterological Association formed the National Committee on Peptic Ulcer in 1952. In a 200-page report, the committee concluded that gastro-enterostomy was the operation of choice for peptic ulcer disease and emphasized, *"It should not be concluded from this study that gastro-enterostomy plus vagotomy is superior to gastroenterostomy alone"*. Fortunately, not all surgeons were persuaded and the usefulness of vagotomy continued to be investigated.

Gradually, more favorable reports appeared. In 1952, Farmer and Smithwick from Boston University recommended that vagotomy be combined with hemigastrectomy for treatment of duodenal ulcer disease. Refinements in operative technique also yielded better results. By 1956, Weinberg and his colleagues from the Veterans Hospital in Long Beach, California, described an improved single layer pyloroplasty. The single layer method contrasted with the double layer closure of the Heinecke-Mikulicz procedure, which the authors contended could *"cause an infolding of the tissues which constricts the lumen and thus jeopardizes the patency of the canal."* They reported their results using a single layer pyloroplasty on more than 500 patients and found a 5% recurrence rate and a 5% rate of side effects. They attributed their success to the elimination of the retrograde movement of food seen with gastro-jejunal anastomoses.

Nevertheless, it was apparent that better methods of preventing gastric stasis were necessary to obviate the side effects of truncal vagotomy. Griffith and Harkins published the theoretic basis for a more selective vagotomy in 1957. They further defined the gastric vagal anatomy and performed a partial vagotomy in ten dogs. They incised the branches of the nerves of Latarjet, which were thought to *"supply clusters of parietal cells"*. As a result, they concluded that the cephalic phase of gastric secretion was eliminated and these dogs experienced minimal to no gastric stasis. Even though they proposed that *"clinical application appears feasible"*, ten years elapsed before the first selective vagotomy was performed upon a human. Holle and Hart performed the first highly selective vagotomy in 1967. Their procedure was combined with a pyloroplasty. By 1969, it became apparent that a drainage procedure was unnecessary. The technique was further developed to selectively denervate the fundus whilst retaining antral innervation to facilitate gastric emptying, and the term parietal cell vagotomy utilized to describe operative procedure. Experience from Britain, Scandinavia, and the United States, demonstrated only seventeen deaths after 5,539 highly selective vagotomies and proudly documented decreased dumping, gastritis, and duodenal reflux, as compared with the more traditional operations. Although the initial ulcer recurrence rate was reported at about 5%, a result similar to that after truncal vagotomy and drainage, subsequent authors reported substantial increases in recurrence rates over time, even after the learning curve for this procedure had been overcome.

Unfortunately, the therapeutic relevance of vagal section soon became overshadowed by the introduction of acid suppressive agents in the mid-1970s, and by 1985, the use of the procedure had significantly declined in developed countries. In 1993 at a conference at Yale University School of Medicine held to memorialize Lester Dragstedt, the first American surgical scientist, a consensus was reached that vagotomy was no longer a relevant therapeutic procedure in the management of peptic ulcer disease. Indeed, except in conditions of dire emergency, surgical vagotomy should not be considered any more as a means of inhibiting acid secretion.

Numerous individuals had undertaken a wide variety of vagotomies in an attempt to both study vagal function and treat peptic ulcer disease. Early attempts at vagotomy alone had resulted in pyloric dysfunction requiring the addition of gastric drainage procedures. Although such operations resulted in technical success, recurrent ulceration was also the problem. More extensive procedures involving partial gastrectomies and antrectomy were introduced but the morbidity from surgical complications and post-gastrectomy syndromes diminished enthusiasm for such procedures. Selective operations that sought to dennervate the parietal cell mass without interfering with the innervation of the antrum, pylorus and other gastrointestinal organs proved to be of merit but their efficiency was subsumed in the mid-1970's by the introduction of effective acid suppressive medication.

Gastric Freezing

A novel method, which vanished in much the same fashion as vagotomy, was proposed by Wangensteen. In 1962 Wangensteen delivered the Moynihan lecture at the Royal College of Surgeons on the topic "The stomach since the Hunters-gastric temperature and peptic ulcer." He discussed Moynihan's contribution to gastric surgery and outlined the history of gastric secretion and the progression of knowledge of acid peptic diseases. He then presented the case for, and the methodology of, gastric freezing, using a specially designed balloon and a coolant pump for *"the control of the peptic ulcer diathesis."* Gastric freezing was widely practiced for a few years throughout the U.S. until endoscopy began to reveal the extent of the serious mucosal damage with its inevitable complications, as well as its lack of benefit.

Bettarello in 1985, felt that five events defined the present treatment of acid peptic disease: fiber optic endoscopy, which enabled routine examination and precise assessment of therapeutic results, prospective double blind trials, continuous pH monitoring to assess efficacy of acid suppression, new drugs such as HZ blockers, proton pump inhibitors, sucralfate, prostaglandins, bismuth preparations, pirenzepine, and reduction of relapse by long-term therapy.

Helicobacter Pylori

Although the association between *Helicobacter pylori* and ulcers was discovered by Robin Warren in 1979, and the organism was cultured by Barry Marshall in 1982, resulting in their seminal publications in *Lancet* in 1983, the historical origins of its discovery are rooted in the latter half of the nineteenth century. It was during this period that the eminent German bacteriologist, Robert Koch, proved scientifically that bacteria were the cause of certain diseases. Almost simultaneously, the Frenchman Louis Pasteur, having been galvanized by Koch's contributions, was in the process of developing vaccines against the microbes causing cholera and rabies. In Sicily, in a small home-made laboratory in Messina, the émigré Russian, Elie Metchnikoff, had discovered phagocytosis, thus initiating an entirely new vista of biological investigation: host defense mechanisms.

Early observations

Careful analysis of gastric contents revealed that under fasting conditions, the normal stomach contained mucus, a few bacilli and some yeast cells, whilst in stagnant gastric contents, obtained from patients with gastric disease, bacilli, micrococci, yeast, and fungus could readily be seen. Such early observations supported speculations regarding a putative causative role of these "foreign bodies" in gastric pathology. It was, however, unclear to the early gastric bacteriologists whether a specific organism was the cause of a gastric disease entity or whether it was simply an abnormal accumulation of organisms in the stomach itself which culminated in gastric disturbances.

One of these first gastric bacteriologists was the German, G. Bottcher, who along with his French collaborator, M. Letulle (1853-1929), demonstrated bacterial colonies in the ulcer floor and in its mucosal margins. Their convictions in regard to the disease-causing potential of ingested organisms were that ardent that by 1875, they attributed the causation of ulcers to such bacteria. This view was, however, not popular. Indeed, in spite of an 1881 report by the pathologist, E. Klebs, of a bacillus-like organism evident both free in the lumen of gastric glands and between the cells of the glands and the tunica propria with corresponding *"interglandular small round cell infiltration"*, the "bacterial hypothesis" fell into disuse. Bottcher was, however, probably the first to report the presence of spiral organisms in the gastrointestinal tract of animals, although spiral organisms were already well known, and had been described as early as 1838 by Ehrenburg. In 1889, Walery Jaworski, professor of Medicine at the Jagiellonian University of Cracow, Poland, was the first to describe in detail spiral organisms in the sediment of washings obtained from humans. Amongst other things, he noted a bacterium with a characteristic spiral appearance that he named *Vibrio rugula*. He suggested that it might play a possible pathogenic role in gastric disease. Jaworski supposed that these "snail" or "spiral" cells were only to be found in rare cases.

However, I. Boas, already a luminary for his gastrointestinal contributions and for the discovery of the "Oppler-Boas" lactobacillus, found these cells quite constantly in all "fasting" gastric contents containing hydrochloric acid. Further detailed analysis by Boas' assistant, P. Cohnheim, indicated that such "cells" could be induced by the reaction of bronchial or pharyngeal mucus and hydrochloric acid. This led to the suggestion that Jaworski had consistently observed: acidaltered myelin and that similar secondary structures, threads, and small masses could also be induced by these simple chemical reactions. Cohnheim and Boas therefore inferred from their experiments that Jaworski's "cells" were most probably the product of gastric mucus and acid chyme.

The observations of Bottcher and Letulle had suggested a causative bacterial agent in ulcer disease and by 1888, Letulle was actively searching for this postulated entity. A few years earlier in 1881, the Scottish surgeon and bacteriologist, Alexander Ogston (1844-1929) had identified *Staphylococcus pyrogenes aureus* both in acute and chronic abscesses. Letulle was never able to experimentally discriminate between these different agents and was therefore not able

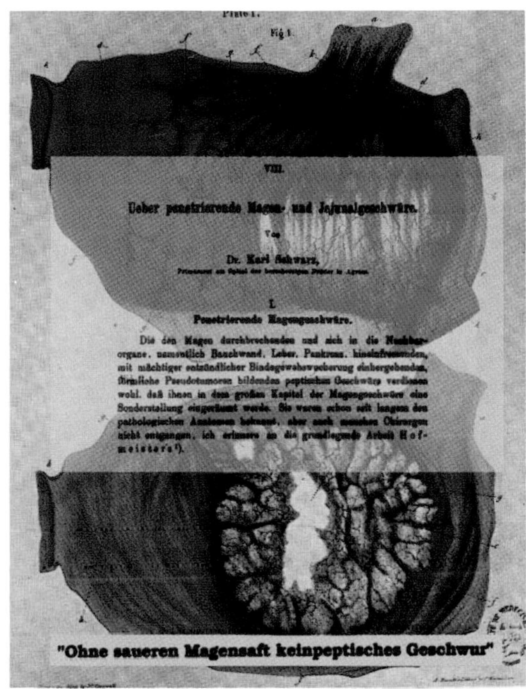

The 19th century doctrine of Karl Schwartz "that without gastric acid there could be no peptic ulceration" remained a credo that blinded gastroenterologists for more than a century. Despite good collateral evidence that bacteria might play a role, this suggestion was disdained.

Although the discovery of Helicobacter pylori *is credited to R. Warren and B. Marshall, a number of other people were influential in exploring gastric bacteria. Clockwise from top left: G. Bizzozero, H. Salomon, E. Klebs, E. Rosenow, B. Marshall, R. Warren, J. Edkins, M. Letulle, W. Jaworski, and I. Boas.*

A late 19th-century drawing of gastritis. Although well-catalogued and interminably described, the subject is still ill-understood by pathologists and gastroenterologists alike.

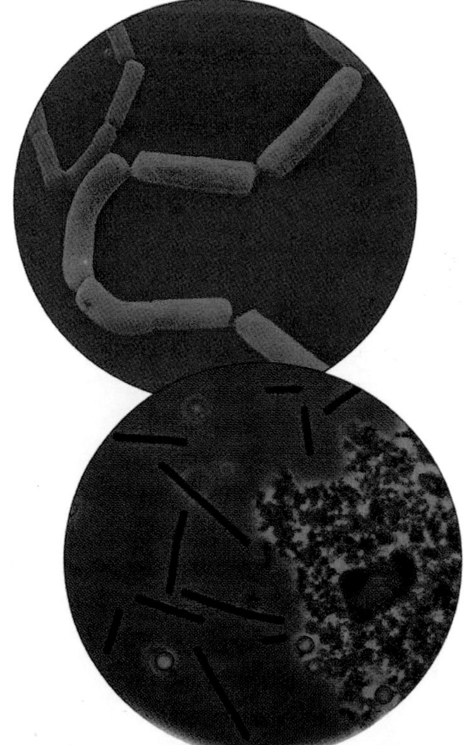

The identification of bacteria in the gastric mucosa led to considerable debate as to their pathogenic relevance. Dogma unfortunately overruled scientific observation until the advent of R. Warren and B. Marshall.

to conclusively prove a role for bacteria in ulcer disease. Nevertheless, the experimental work of Letulle inspired a number of other scientists to follow his lead and similar results were attained with *Lactobacillus*, diphtheria toxin, and *Pneumococcus*.

In a time frame contiguous to these sophisticated experiments, the Italian anatomist G. Bizzozero (1846-1901) was busily engaged in the extensive study of the comparative anatomy of vertebrate gastrointestinal glands with his adept and capable pupil, the future Nobel Prize winner, Camillo Golgi. In the specimens of the gastric mucosa of six dogs, Bizzozero noted the presence of a spirochete organism in the gastric glands and both in the cytoplasm and vacuoles of parietal cells. He commented that this organism affected both pyloric and fundic mucosa, and its distribution extended from the base of the gland to the surface mucosa. Although he neglected to ascribe any clinical relevance to these observations, he did, however, remark upon their close association with the parietal cells.

Three years later, in 1896, in a paper entitled "Spirillum of the mammalian stomach and its behavior with respect to the parietal cells," Hugo Salomon reported spirochetes in the gastric mucosa of dogs, cats and rats, although he was unable to identify them in other animals, including man. In this early paper, Salomon undertook a series of somewhat bizarre experiments in which he tried to transmit the bacterium to a range of other animal species by using gastric scrapings from dogs. He failed to transmit it to owls, rabbits, pigeons, and frogs; however, the feeding of gastric mucus to white mice resulted in a spectacular colonization within a week, as evidenced by the series of drawings of infected gastric mucosa reproduced in the original paper. The lumen of the gastric pits of the mice was packed with the spiral-shaped bacteria, and invasion of the parietal cells was also noted. Almost two decades later, in 1920, Kasai and Kobayashi successfully repeated these experiments, and using spirochetes isolated from cats, demonstrated pathogenic results in rabbits. Histological examination indicated both hemorrhagic erosion and ulceration of the mucosa in the presence of masses of the spirochetes.

The Twentieth Century

By the beginning of the twentieth century, physicians involved in the treatment of gastrointestinal disease were generally familiar with some infective processes of the digestive tract: the ulcerative processes of typhoid fever, a variety of dysenteric conditions, and tuberculosis. In 1906, Krienitz identified spirochetes in the gastric contents of a patient with a carcinoma of the lesser curvature of the stomach, and commented that upon microscopic examination, three types of spirochetes, including *Spirochete pallidum*, could be identified. He did not address the question of etiology. Spirochetal dysentery, as well as the presence of spirochetes in the stool of healthy individuals were known, and Muhlens and independently, Luger and Neuberger, had all reported these organisms to be evident in the stomach contents of patients with ulcerating carcinomas of the stomach. The latter authors also noted the rarity of these organisms in the gastric mucosa and gastric juice of healthy individuals. Experimental biology, however, dominated gastric research and in the same year, Turcke had undertaken an experiment in which he fed broth cultures of *Bacillus coli* to dogs for a number of months. This resulted in the development of chronic gastric ulceration. In an attempt to establish cause and effect, he thereafter cultured *B. coli* from the feces of ulcer patients, which

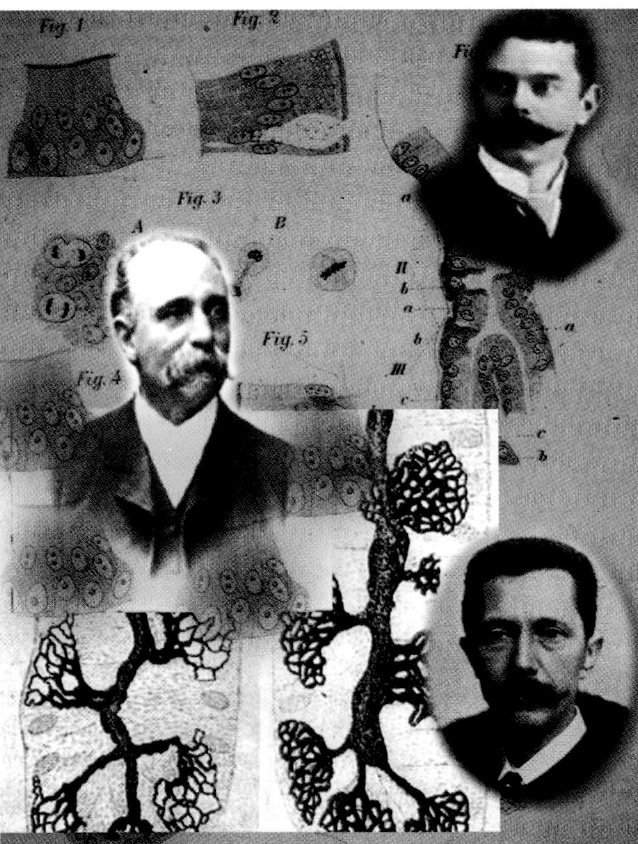

Camillo Golgi (left) was the first to depict the differences between the resting (left) and stimulated (right) gastric glands. His mentor, Giulio Bizzozero (bottom right) was able to differentiate large parietal cells whose stained mitochondria produced a granular appearance from chief cells that possessed a flat peripheral nucleus. In addition, he noted a novel cell in the neck of the glands of the acid-secreting part of the stomach as well as organisms adherent to the surface of the gastric cells. Although he proposed that the chief and surface epithelial cells might be produced by proliferation of the neck cells, he did not further explore the nature of the organisms and turned his attention to the discovery of blood platelets. H. Salomon (top right) in 1896 noted spirochetes in some animals but failed to confirm the observation.

were then injected intravenously into dogs, without effect. However, when the animals ingested the microorganism, every single dog reacted with a spectrum of non-specific gastric and duodenal alterations, which Turcke loosely called "ulcers". When Gibelli attempted to repeat this work, he could not confirm the results obtained by Turcke.

In Cincinnati, Ohio, the American bacteriologist, E.C. Rosenow, over a decade from 1913 to 1923, vehemently maintained that ulceration of the stomach could be reproduced in laboratory animals by *Streptococcus*. He isolated this bacterium from foci of infection in humans with ulcer disease and injected the culture into a wide range of animals including rabbits, dogs, monkeys, guinea pigs, cats, and mice. Based upon these observations, Rosenow postulated that "*gastric ulcer producing* Streptococci" had a selective affinity for the gastric mucosa and produced a local destruction of the glandular tissue. He further proposed that consequent upon such damage, ulcers would thereafter form, given the autolytic capacity of gastric acid. Rosenow thought that the reservoir for these bacteria were carious teeth, and advanced the idea that a hematogenous bacterial invasion would result in the formation of an ulcer.

A British cartoon of the 19th century alluded to the public awareness of the diverse organisms present in water. It also drew attention to the confusion that existed in the medical field as to the source of bacteria in the human gastrointestinal tract.

One of the early scientific interests of L.R. Dragstedt was the causation of gastro-duodenal ulceration, although he would subsequently (1943) achieve renown as the surgeon who established the "physiological" rationale for vagotomy as a treatment for duodenal ulcer disease. As early as 1917, as a young physiologist, he had attempted to define the different mechanisms by which gastric juice could affect healing of acute gastric and duodenal ulcers. Aware of Rosenow's work, and the question of the importance of the virulence of different bacterial strains in determining the chronicity of ulcers, he attempted to isolate and culture any bacteria he could find in the silver nitrate-induced ulcers of five experimental Pavlov pouch dogs. Bacteriologic examination revealed *Streptococcus, Staphylococcus* and *Bacillus* species, which were similar to those types of bacteria isolated from clinical ulcers in man. Fifteen years later, at the Mount Sinai Hospital, A. Berg utilized partial vagotomy to reduce "secondary" infections in ulcer margins. Soon thereafter, however, he turned his attention to the colon and along with his collaborator, Burrell Crohn, become more famous for his role in the discovery of the etiology of this disease.

John Edkins, of London, had made a significant contribution to the elucidation of gastric physiology by the discovery of gastrin. Although the scientific doyens of the time declared it to be humbug, time would vindicate Edkins. Motivated by his disappointment in the investigation of gastrin, Edkins still maintained his enthusiasm for the exploration of gastric patho-physiology. In contrast to the inoculation mode of experimental studies, he proceeded to investigate how the host itself might affect the prevalence and location of the spirochete organisms in different parts of the stomach. The organisms were named *Spirochete regaudi*, after Regaudi who considered that the organisms of the gastric mucus layer of cats were morphologically analogous to the syphilis spirochete.

In 1925, Hoffman investigated whether the causative agent of ulcer disease was a member of the bacillus family by the injection of 5 cc of gastric contents from a peptic ulcer patient into guinea pigs. He successfully produced gastric ulcers from which he recovered gram-negative, fine slender rods which, when inoculated into another guinea pig, once again produced the same lesions. He modestly named his organism "*Bacillus Hoffmani*", but it was evident after further study that the lesion-producing capabilities of this bacterium were non-specific. In 1930, Saunders demonstrated that the streptococcus organism isolated from peptic ulcers in humans was of the alpha variety, and identified specific antibodies against this agent in serum from patients. However, he was unable to produce ulcers in animals by injecting the inoculum, and proposed that laboratory animals do not spontaneously form gastric ulcers, since they exhibited an innate resistance to this organism.

Based to a certain extent on the recognition of the widespread scourge of luetic disease, at around the beginning of the Second World War, spirochetes returned to gastric prominence. J.L. Doenges observed the organisms to invade the gastric glands of every single one of the *Macacus* rhesus monkeys he studied and to be present in 43% of human gastric autopsy specimens. In contrast to the monkey, the organisms appeared to be difficult to identify in human gastric mucosa and only 11 of the 103 specimens showed appreciable

In 1926 the Nobel Prize in medicine was awarded to Johannes Andreas Grib Fibiger for the subsequently refuted discovery that gastric carcinoma in rats was caused by the nematode Spiroptera carcinoma. *Johannes Fibiger was born in Silkeborg, Denmark, in 1867 and received a medical degree in 1890 from the University of Copenhagen where he subsequently also earned a doctoral degree in bacteriology. At 33 years of age he was named Director of the Institute of Pathological Anatomy of the University of Copenhagen and held this position until 1928 when he died. In 1907 Fibiger noted, while studying gastric papillomas in three wild rats, the presence of nematodes which he believe to be the cause of the tumors.*

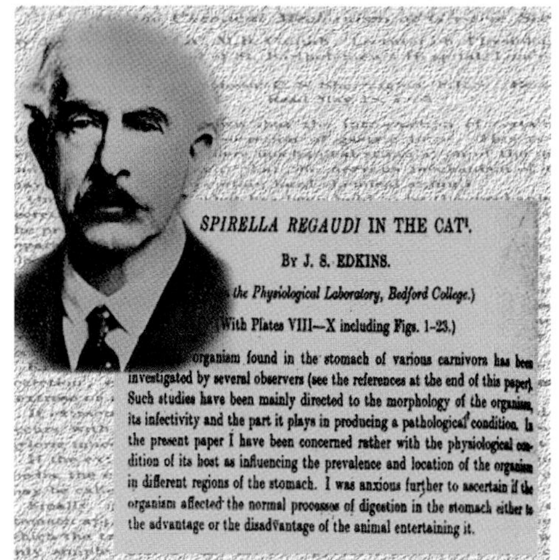

SPIRELLA REGAUDI IN THE CAT[1].

By J. S. EDKINS.

(… the Physiological Laboratory, Bedford College.)

(With Plates VIII—X including Figs. 1-23.)

… organism found in the stomach of various carnivora has been investigated by several observers (see the references at the end of this paper). Such studies have been mainly directed to the morphology of the organism, its infectivity and the part it plays in producing a pathological condition. In the present paper I have been concerned rather with the physiological condition of its host as influencing the prevalence and location of the organism in different regions of the stomach. I was anxious further to ascertain if the organism affected the normal processes of digestion in the stomach either to the advantage or the disadvantage of the animal entertaining it.

The frontispiece of J.S. Edkins' communication documenting his investigations on spiral organisms present in the gastric mucosa of cats. Apart from his epic manuscript documenting the existence of a novel antral stimulant of acid secretion-gastrin (1905), Edkins had studied pepsin with Langley, defined the effects of phosgene on lung function, and developed chemical techniques for destroying weevils without damaging flour. His investigation of the presence of bacteria in the gastric mucosa and the changes they underwent during digestion were, like his studies of gastrin, unappreciated during his lifetime.

Adolf Kussmaul (1822-1902). Apart from his respiratory observations, his gastroenterological contributions included: being the first to a) treat gastric obstruction with a stomach tube (1867); b) treat gastric ulcer with bismuth (1868); c) attempt esophagoscopy and gastroscopy (1869); d) diagnose mesenteric embolism during life (1867).

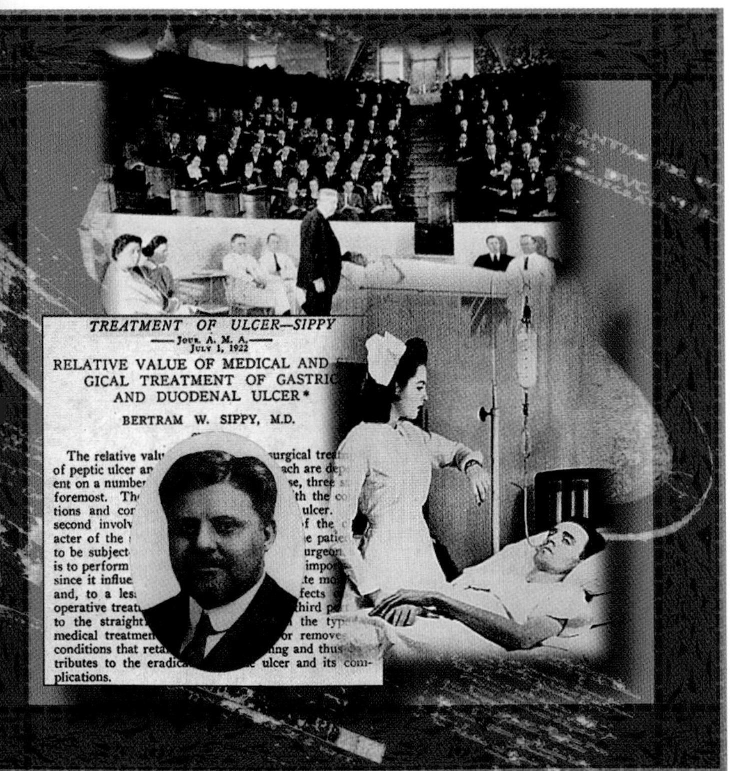

numbers of spirochetes. These reports prompted Freedberg and Barron in 1941 to further investigate the presence of spirochetes in the gastric tissue of patients who had undergone partial resection surgery. Both authors were familiar with the methods of identifying the organism, and used the silver staining method of Da Fano, which they had previously successfully used (but not published) to identify spirochetes in dogs. In spite of such expertise, they were not able to identify the organisms, although they could demonstrate that spirochetes were more frequently present in ulcerating stomachs as compared to non-ulcerated stomachs (53% vs. 14%). Based upon their own difficulties with adequate identification, and the apparent histological differences noted in Doenges' observations in the *Macacus mucosa*, they concluded that no absolute etiopathologic role for these organisms could be defined. It is with almost tragic irony that one reads that, in the report of the discussion of this paper, Frank D. Gorham, of St. Louis, Missouri, he noted: "*I believe that a further search should be made for an organism thriving in hydrochloric acid medium (and variations of hydrochloric acid are normal in all stomachs) as a possible factor of chronicity, if not an etiologic factor, in peptic ulcer.*" Of interest is that Gorham also wrote that he had, over the previous ten years, successfully treated patients who had refractory ulcer disease with intramuscular injections of bismuth! Although Gorham may have seemed to be ahead of his time, as early as 1868, A. Kussmaul had advocated the use of bismuth subnitrate for the treatment of gastric ulcer. In fact, the oral use of bismuth for gastrointestinal symptoms was well accepted, and as early as the late eighteenth century, reports of the therapy had begun to appear in the English literature. In fact, R. Sazerac and C. Levaditi had already successfully exploited the antibacterial properties of bismuth in 1921 when they reported the cure of experimental syphilis in rabbits.

Whilst ammonia was noted in gastric juice as early as 1852, it was not until 1924 that Luck discovered gastric mucosal urease. His subsequent work and the work of others, especially the Dublin biochemist, E.J. Conway, who specialized in investigations of the redox mechanism of acid secretion, confirmed the presence of gastric urease in a number of mammals. O. Fitzgerald (Conway's medical colleague postulated a clinical role for urea in gastric physiology, and proposed that gastric urease functioned as a mucosal protective agent by providing ions to neutralize acid. This led to a number of studies in which the ingestion of urea-containing solutions was utilized to alter histamine-stimulated gastric acid secretion. Notwithstanding the unpleasant side effects of this administration (diarrhea, headache, polyuria, painful urethritis), Fitzgerald further applied his hypothesis by treating ulcer patients with this regimen in 1949. Although he charitably summarized his results as "*in general, satisfactory*", no further therapeutic studies were undertaken with this particular agent.

Acid Protection by Internal UREASE

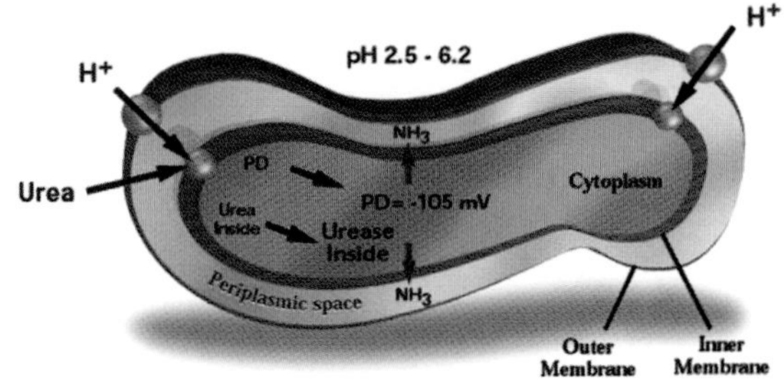

Acid protection by internal urease (courtesy of G. Sachs, 1999). By 1954 gastric urease-containing tissue suspensions were demonstrated to contain urea-splitting organisms. This led to the suggestion that gastric urease might actually be of bacterial origin. Preliminary feeding of antibiotics (penicillin and terramycin) to animals resulted both in reduced expiration of $^{14}CO_2$ from intra-peritoneally injected ^{14}C-urea, as well as the abolition of urease activity in mucosal homogenates. Similar studies with analogous results were also performed in controls and subjects with uremia. These observations, whilst establishing that gastric urease was of bacterial origin, failed to initiate an investigation of the relationship between urease-containing bacteria and ulcer disease. Indeed the prevailing notion by the end of 1955 was that neither the bacterial gastric urease nor the bacteria played any essential role in gastric pathology!

The negative results of Freedberg and Barron, the ambivalent results of Doenges, and the fact that the gastric urease story was still being unraveled, prompted E.D. Palmer, in the early fifties, to investigate spirochetes in human gastric samples. He obtained gastric mucosal biopsies from 1,180 subjects using a vacuum tube technique, but using standard histological techniques, failed to demonstrate either spirochetes or any structures resembling them. Although Palmer did not attempt to identify the organisms with the more reliable silver stain, he concluded (confidently) that the results of all previous authors could be best explained as a postmortem colonization of the gastric mucosa with oral cavity organisms. He also postulated that such spirochetes were normal commensals of the mouth, and essentially debunked the concept of bacterial involvement in peptic ulcer disease. Palmer's work may thus be credited with the envious distinction of setting back gastric bacterial research by a further thirty years.

In 1975, Steer, while studying polymorphonuclear leukocyte migration in the gastric mucosa in a series of biopsy material obtained from patients with gastric ulceration, identified bacteria in close contact with the epithelium and suggested that white cells migration was a response to these bacteria. In this seminal contribution, he not only clearly demonstrated bacterial phagocytosis, but provided electron microscopic images consistent with ingestion

Dr. Bertram Sippy of Chicago (bottom left) devised a complex dietary regimen of bland food that included hourly feedings of milk, eggs, and purée as well as the administration of large quantities of calcium and sodium bicarbonate. In addition, he proposed that particularly severe nocturnal dyspepsia could be relieved by regular gastric aspiration. Although cumbersome and likely to generate obsessive–compulsive disorders, this strict regimen was of some benefit and particularly efficacious when compared with the outcome of current surgical intervention far acid peptic disease. Many physicians (top center) enthusiastically attended lectures by Sippy to learn more of his novel therapeutic techniques. An alternative dietary therapy developed by Richard Doll proposed hospital admission for up to three weeks with continuous nasogastric milk infusion with and without alkali. Cynics proposed that the excessive use of milk accelerated coronary artery disease and that any putative therapeutic benefit was actually derived from the bed rest, the charm of the nursing staff, and the Freudian benefits of the acquisition of milk. This treatment soon fell into disregard except among unusual sects of medical practice.

of a *Helicobacter*. Steer also attempted to isolate and culture the organism, but being unfamiliar with micro-aerophilic techniques, succeeded only in growing and identifying *Pseudomonas aeroginosa*.

By 1980, reports concerning a disease entity broadly referred to as *"epidemic gastritis associated with hypochorhydria"* had been published. These observations coupled with Steer's findings of an apparent association between "active gastritis" and a gram-negative bacteria, suggested that the simultaneous occurrence of bacteria in the stomach and peptic ulceration might represent more than a correlatable epi-phenomenon. Robin Warren, a pathologist at the Royal Perth Hospital, had for many years observed bacteria in the stomach of people with gastritis. Although convinced that they somehow played a role in gastric disease, in the light of the prevailing dogma of acid-induced ulceration and the sceptiscm of his colleagues, he had been reluctant to discuss this controversial observation in the wider gastroenterological community.

In 1982, as a young gastroenterology fellow in Perth, Australia, Barry Marshall was looking for a project to complete his fellowship. The iconoclastic hypothesis of Warren attracted Marshall, who persuaded Warren to allow him to investigate this further in the appropriate clinical setting. Later in the year, Marshall submitted an abstract detailing their initial investigations to the Australian Gastroenterology Association. It was flatly rejected, along with a handful of other abstracts on the same subject prepared by him. Young and unfazed, and seeking an alternative audience for the work, Marshall submitted the same abstract to the International Workshop of Campylobacter Infections, where it was accepted. Although the audience was skeptical of Marshall's and Warren's results, some members became interested enough to attempt to repeat some of their observations. Soon after this meeting, both Warren and Marshall published their initial results as two modest letters in the *Lancet*. In the introduction to his seminal article on an S-shaped *Campylobacter*-like organism, Warren noted both the constancy of bacterial infection, as well as the consistency of the associated histological changes, which he had identified in 135 gastric biopsy specimens studied over a three-year period. He commented that these microorganisms were difficult to see with hematoxylin and eosin, but stained well in the presence of silver. Furthermore, he observed the bacteria to be most numerous in an "active chronic gastritis", where they were closely associated with granulocyte infiltration. It is a mystery, he wrote, that bacteria in numbers sufficient to be seen by light microscopy were almost unknown to clinicians and pathologists alike! He presciently concluded, *"These organisms should be recognized and their significance investigated."* Koch's second postulate states that *"the germ should be obtained from the diseased animal and grown outside the body."* In the same issue of the *Lancet*, Marshall described the conditions necessary to fulfill this requirement.

In order to substantiate that the micro-organism was actually a disease-causing agent, it was necessary to demonstrate that it could colonize normal mucosa and induce gastritis (Koch's third and fourth postulates). To prove pathogenicity, Marshall, looking back in time for guidance, decided to be his own guinea pig. Marshall, who had a histologically normal gastric mucosa and was a light smoker and social drinker, received, per mouth, a test isolate from a 66 year-old, non-ulcer dyspeptic man. Over the next fourteen days, a mild illness developed, characteristic of an acute episode of gastritis, and was accompanied by headaches, vomiting, abdominal discomfit, irritability and "putrid" breath. The infectivity of the agent was thereafter successfully confirmed, when after ten days, histologically proven gastritis was endoscopically documented. The disease process later resolved on its own accord by the fifteenth day. Marshall went on to describe the urease of the organism and recognized its role in enabling survival of the organism in acidic media. Subsequent work demonstrated that eradication of the organism reduced recurrence of duodenal ulcer to the level found with maintenance therapy with histamine 2 receptor antagonists, and acceptance of this organism as causative, in association with acid, is now universal. More recently the entire genomes of two organisms, one pathogenic, the other not, have been released. This had led to a considerable amount of work aimed at generating a complete biological picture of the organism, and hopefully will lead to new and different drug targets.

Of particular interest was the observation that *H. Pylori* was associated with the development of lymphoid follicles in the stomach, and that such histological changes could even progress to neoplasia. Indeed, the description of MALT lymphomas of varying degrees of malignancy, led to a renaissance of the old belief that infection and malignancy were related. This conclusion was further bolstered by complex epidemiological and statistical analyses that purported to demonstrate that geographical areas of *H. Pylori* infection exhibited a far greater incidence of gastric cancer. So dramatic was this information considered, that the World Health Organization declared the bacteria to be a Class 1 pathogen, and many physicians declared world-wide eradication of the organism as a certain means by which the holy grail of peptic ulcer disease obliteration might be achieved. Few remembered that an organism responsible for the cause of gastric cancer had already been previously discovered in the twentieth century.

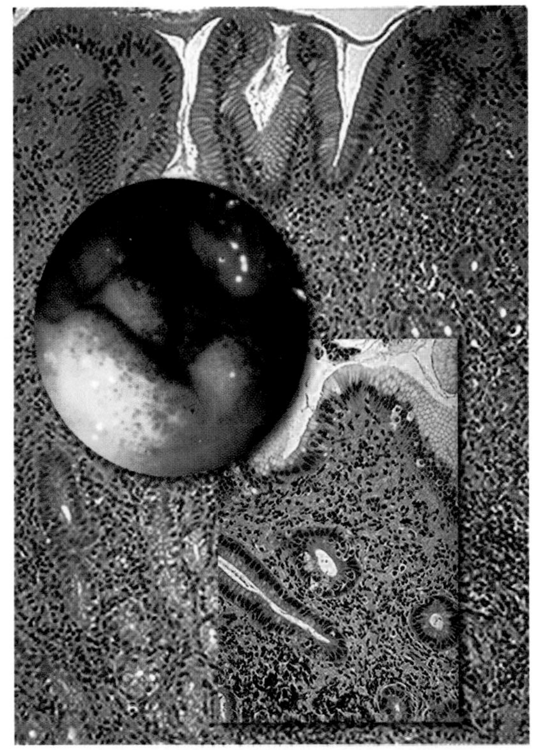

The concept that a pathogenic organism could be associated with neoplasia had been previously recognized in a number of circumstances. The recognition that H. pylori *was associated with a novel group of diseases known as the MALT lymphoma generated considerable scientific and clinical interest.*

Robin Warren (bottom right), a pathologist at the Royal Perth Hospital in Australia, had long been convinced that the bacteria that he noted in the gastric biopsies of patients with gastritis were relevant to the condition. In 1982 Barry Marshall, a gastroenterology fellow, working with Warren, was able to demonstrate the clinical relevance of Campylobacter *in the pathogenesis of the condition previously known as acid peptic disease.*

Section 15
Exocrine pancreas

Exocrine Pancreas

Early Concepts

The derivation of the word pancreas, or sweetbread, originated with Homer, who broadly used the term to describe edible animal flesh. Herophilus named the organ for its meaty or fleshy character, and the term was used both by Aristotle and Rufus of Ephesus, although it was the opinion of Vesalius that the ancients had not adequately distinguished between the mesenteric glands and the pancreas itself.

Although it is believed that the Greeks were the first to recognize the pancreas as a distinct organ, arcane references in the even earlier Babylonian Talmud refer to a structure designated by the rabbis as the *"finger of the liver"*. Galen provided a modest description of the organ, but neither he, nor Hippocrates and Erasistratus, were able to identify a relationship to disease. About 300 B.C., Herophilus of Chalcedon, one of the first scholars to have the opportunity to dissect humans, described the pancreas in his diverse deliberations on the structures and functions of the body. Since the ancient anatomists regarded the pancreas as unusual, given that it had no cartilage or bone present, they considered it to be literally *"all flesh or meat."* Thus Rufus of Ephesus (*c.* A.D. 100) named the organ pancreas (Greek *pan*: all and *kreas*: flesh or meat). Andreas Vesalius, in his monumental seven books of anatomy, referred to the pancreas in the fifth book as a *"glandulous organ or kannelly body of substance growing in the neather pannicle of the caule (omentum)."* Despite his anatomic skill, he possessed little understanding of its function, and his illustrations deal chiefly with its vascular structure. Vesalius considered the pancreas to provide a protective function (*Schutzorgan*) for the stomach. A subsequent translation of the Vesalian anatomy text by the London astrologer, Nicholas Culpepper, in 1653, first used the lay term "sweet bread" to describe the organ.

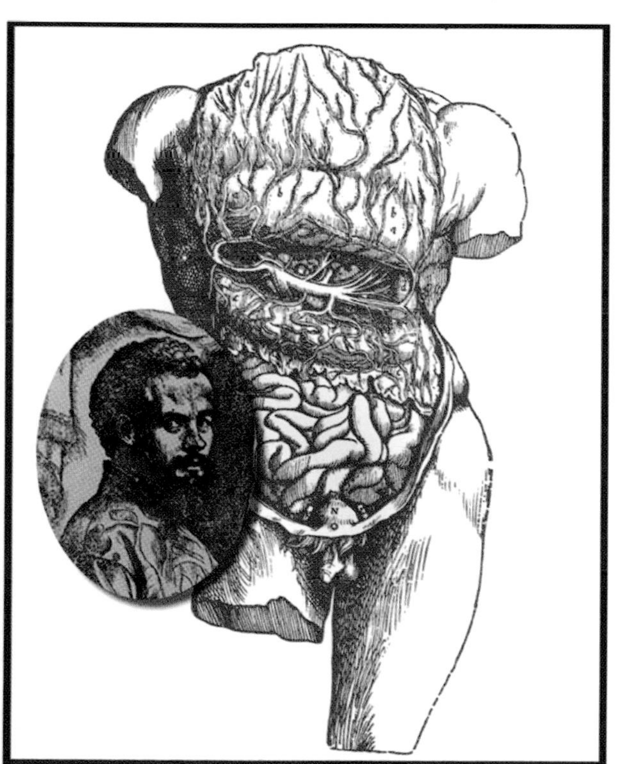

Andreas Vesalius (inset) (1514-1564) was one of the first anatomists to depict the pancreas. Despite a relatively accurate assessment of its structure there was little appreciation of its function. Vesalius referred to it as a "kannelly body" and considered it to act as a "cushion" for the stomach. Subsequent concepts of its function embraced the prescient notion that it was an abdominal salivary gland.

Since little was known of the function of the organ, initial attention was directed to the subject of the duct and the structure of the gland. Thomas Wharton (1610-1673) of York (also a lecturer at Gresham College) was among the first to undertake a systematic study of the glands of the body. His text *Adenographia Sive Glandularum Totius Corporis Descriptio* not only identified and named the thyroid gland, but commented upon the general similarity between the structure of the pancreas and the submaxillary gland. In 1642, Johann Georg Wirsung, the prosector to Veslingus in Padua, was the first to describe the main duct of the human pancreas, although rumor holds that his student, M. Hoffmann, had informed him of the presence of such a duct in a rooster a year previously. The function of this duct, however, was utterly misunderstood, since contemporary views considered that "chyme" from the duodenum ascended into the pancreas to provoke secretion of a *"sharp juice not unlike to the gall."* It remained, however, for the anatomist Sommering (1755-1830) to first employ the vernacular term *Bauchspeicheldrüse* (abdominal salivary gland) in the medical and scientific literature. Subsequently, in his 1797 thesis on the salivary system, von Siebold of Jena presciently considered that the three glands might be regarded as analogous to the pancreas. Indeed, as a result of this work, the pancreas was, until the late nineteenth century, considered as an abdominal salivary gland.

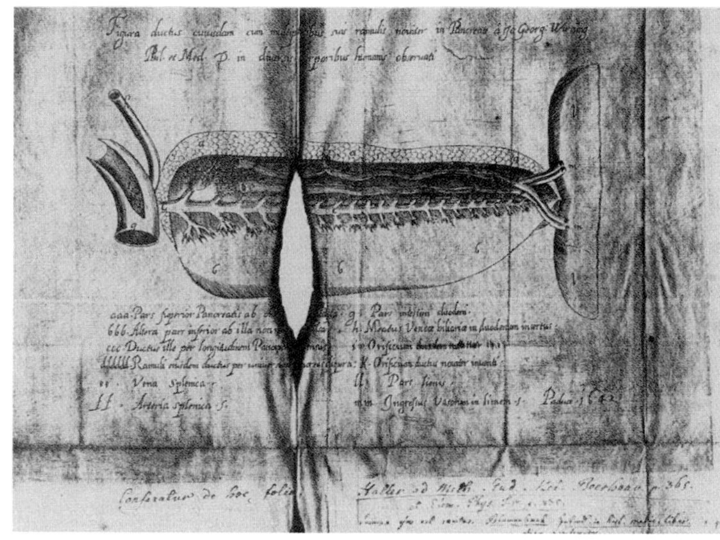

On March 2, 1642, Wirsung first identified the pancreatic duct and, being unaware of its function, engraved his findings on a single copper plate of which he sent seven impressions to the most famous anatomists of Europe seeking their opinion regarding the function of the ductal structure. His request for information was met with deafening silence!

Regnier de Graaf focused his brilliance not only on the elucidation of pancreatic function but the delineation of the human ovarian cycle. His contributions to reproductive physiology led to the eponymous attribution to him of the nomenclature of ovarian follicle.

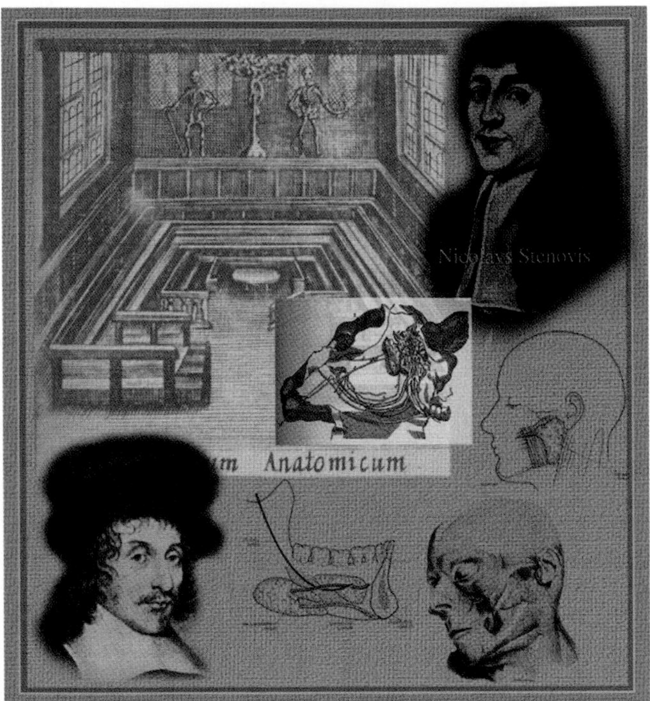

The anatomic significance of Wirsung's discovery (1642) opened a new consideration of the drainage of glandular structures which subsequently lead to Thomas Wharton's (bottom left) discovery of the submaxillary duct in 1656 and thereafter Stensen's identification of the parotid and lacrymal ducts in 1662. Wirsung's contribution was also responsible for stimulating Regnier de Graaf to cannulate the pancreatic duct of the dog in 1664 and facilitate the further exploration of the role of the pancreas in digestive physiology.

Johann Georg Wirsung

Johann Georg Wirsung was born in Augsburg on July 3, 1589, and studied anatomy in Paris under Professor Jean Riolan, and subsequently in Altdorf under Professor Kaspar Hoffmann. On November 8, 1629, he enrolled at Padua University and graduated from the Sacro Collegio on March 23, 1630, with a Doctorate in Philosophy and Medicine. This rapid progress reflected the fact that he had already studied at the universities of Paris and Altdorf, but desired to have degree conferred upon him by the University of Padua since it was recognized as a far more prestigious institution. At this time, the foreign students of Padua University were divided into 31 "nations" and Wirsung joined the German Nation of Artists on November 8, 1629, when he enrolled.

As a young graduate, he was strongly supported by Johann Wesling, the Professor of Anatomy at Padua. While working under his direction on March 2, 1642, during the autopsy of Zuane Viaro della Badia, a 30-year-old man guilty of murder and executed by hanging in the Piazza del Vin on the previous day, Wirsung discovered a duct in the pancreas. Since the dissection was undertaken privately at the San Francesco Hospital, Professor Wesling and the Register of the Deceased provided confirmation of the event. Present at the dissection were Thomas Bartholin (1616-1680) of Denmark and Moritz Hoffmann (1622-1698) of Germany. Five years after the death of Wirsung, Moritz Hoffmann, in fact, claimed to have discovered the pancreatic duct in a turkey rooster in September of 1641, and to have informed Wirsung, who then sought to identify this duct in man. Most reliable authorities refuted Hoffmann's claim and he never published anything on the subject.

Wirsung had no understanding of the function of the pancreatic duct, but recognized its significance and sought further information. He therefore personally engraved his findings on a single copper plate and made seven identical impressions that he then sent to famous anatomists throughout Europe, seeking their opinion as to the function of the ductal structure. These authorities included Dr. Ole Worm of Copenhagen (brother-in-law of Thomas Bartholin), Kasper Hoffmann of Altdorf and Jean Riolan of Paris. In addition, the pictures were also sent to Professor Severino of Naples and to anatomists at Gena, Hamburg, and Nuremberg. As might have been predicted, none of the authorities at the various institutions were able to offer any specific insight as to the function of the duct. Worm thought it might be involved in lymphatic drainage. Riolan, having no answer, did not reply, and Hoffmann believed it was somehow related to chyle transport.

A plaque (right) depicting the contributions of Wirsung at the University of Padua. The stamma decorating the walls of the Medical School of Padua (left) attest to the diverse origins of the students who attended the institution. Indeed, the early history of the development of medicine is virtually memorialized within the dissecting room and Aula of Padua.

Unfortunately, almost a year later, midnight on August 22, 1643, as Wirsung returned home late one evening and while standing in the doorway of his residence talking to neighbors, he was assassinated with arquebus by a Belgian student, Jacques Cambier. Indeed, no less an authority than Morgagni (1728) who had become Chief Professor of Anatomy in Padua in 1715, related the events: *"In the year 1643 when Wirsung died we found the following facts of his fate written down by his fellow citizens and friends: the 22nd of August was the fatal day for the most noble, most excellent and famous man, Johann Georg Wirsung, doctor of philosophy and medicine, the honorable member of our famous nation (German). As usual; at about the 24th hour of the night he was conversing at the door of his house with some of his fellow tenants when he was shot by Jacques Cambier for private revenge of unknown reason with a big firearm which is usually called a carabine, where upon he was pierced by the bullet, lost a large amount of blood, and at once gave up his mind repeating the words: 'I am dead, oh Cambier, oh Cambier!"*

Fortunately, the colleagues and friends of Wirsung did not forget his discovery and van Horne, professor of Surgery and Anatomy in Leiden, in 1685 honored his colleague by applying the name "*Wirsungianus*" to the duct.

Sylvius and de Graaf

The nature of the functional role of the pancreas was first investigated by Franciscus de le Boe (Sylvius) of Amsterdam, who proposed that digestion was a multi-step process divided into three principal stages. The first involved fermentation by saliva in the mouth and the stomach, while the second involved the pancreas. In the elucidation of this issue, a brilliant pupil, Regnier de Graaf of Delft, ably supported Sylvius. De Graaf ingeniously developed a method for the direct investigation of the nature of pancreatic juice utilizing canine pancreatic fistula through which he inserted feather quills into the pancreatic ductal orifices to obtain *succus pancreaticus*. Both de Graaf and Sylvius believed that the function of pancreatic juice was to *effervesce* with bile, and that the combination of acids and alkalis which occurred were a critical component of digestion. They further postulated that pancreatic juice exhibited a dual function by both "*attenuating the mucous lining of the gut as well as initiating segregation of the useful food elements*." Unfortunately, de Graaf's conclusion that pancreatic juice was acidic was incorrect, and reflected not only the relatively limited chemical knowledge of the time, but the fact that some of the experiments were undertaken in fish, and the complex gastric pyloric ceca were mistaken as part of the pancreas. Nevertheless, emboldened by his pancreatic contributions, de Graaf ventured forward to his seminal work on ovarian structure and function. By the end of the

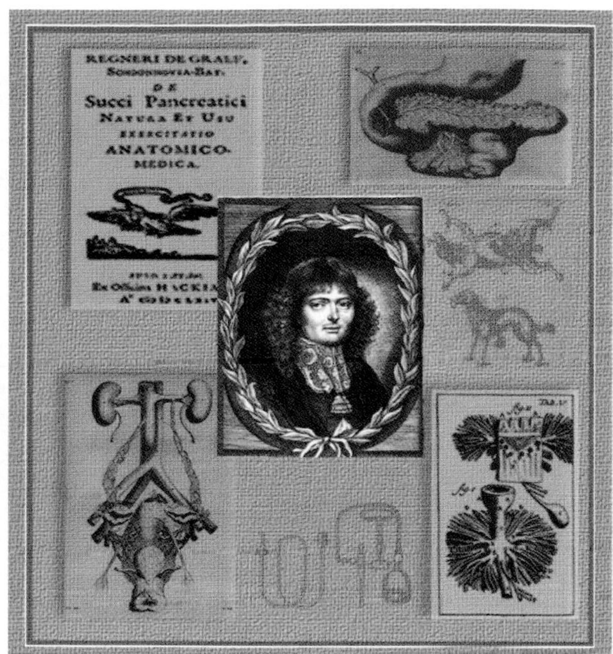

Regnier de Graaf (1641-1673) was the first to scientifically address the nature of pancreatic secretion. In order to facilitate his studies he developed an ingenious method for the creation of canine pancreatic fistulas (inset) and was thereby able to elucidate the nature of pancreatic juice. His publication (top left) De Succi Pancreatici (1662) defined the nature of the juice and detailed the preparation of the canine fistula model. He is also credited with the anatomical investigations of the female reproductive system (bottom left), but the tragic early demise of de Graaf precluded his further elucidation of pancreatico-follicular function.

seventeenth century, Johann Bohn revised Sylvius' doctrine and successfully demonstrated that the pancreatic juice was not acid. Sylvius maintained that the third stage of digestion represented the passage of chyle into lymphatics, which was then conveyed to the venous system by the thoracic duct, which bore it to the right side of the heart. His innovative theories on digestion were subsequently modified by the discovery of Peyer's patches and the duodenal glands named after Johannes Conrad Brunner (also known as the Swiss Hippocrates).

During the eighteenth century, Albrecht von Haller (1708-1777) studied pancreatic physiology (and almost everything else including botany, astronomy, color spectra, and poetry). He noted the close relationship of the pancreatic duct to the bile duct and with his customary perspicacity proposed that pancreatic juice and bile interacted in the process of digestion. Further eighteenth-century contributions included that of Giovanni Domenico Santorini, professor of Anatomy and Medicine in Venice. Girard published his identification of the accessory duct of the pancreas in *Observationes Anatomicae* (1742) many years after Santorini's demise, since the latter was concerned that the Venetian authorities would consider his work heretical. In 1806 Meckel provided a detailed description of the embryology of the pancreas and, in 1861, Goette initiated the study of the comparative anatomy of the pancreas.

Further elucidation of pancreatic physiology was provided by Willy Kuhne (1837-1900) of Germany, who identified trypsin and evaluated its role in the digestion of protein. In 1815, Alexander Marcet (1770-1822) identified lipase. Between 1849 and 1856 Claude Bernard (1813-1878) of Paris investigated pancreatic physiology in detail and conclusively demonstrated its clinical relevance to digestion as a whole. Over a seven-year period, Bernard unified the concepts of pancreatic digestion, demonstrating that gastric digestion "*is only a preparation act*" and that pancreatic juice emulsified fatty foods splitting them into glycerin and fatty acids. In addition, he demonstrated the power of the pancreas to convert starch into sugar, and its solvent action upon the "*proteides that have not been cleaved in the stomach*." Further work by Eberle in 1843 demonstrated that pancreatic juice emulsified fat, and, a year later Valentin demonstrated its activity on starch.

The regulation of pancreatic secretion was a vexatious question, which Ivan Petrovich Pavlov (1849-1936) and his pupils addressed with vigor at the turn of the nineteenth century. Dolinski, a pupil of Pavlov, noted that acid introduced into the duodenum stimulated pancreatic secretion, and interpreted this as indicative of a local neural reflex. In 1902, Bayliss and Starling of University College, London, demonstrated that this phenomenon was in fact not a neural reflex, but the effect of a chemical messenger or regulator. They termed the substance a hormone (derived from the Greek *hormonos* – I arouse to excitement) and proposed the putative agent in the duodenal mucosa be called *secretin*. Yet another of Pavlov's pupils, Chepovalnikov, demonstrated that pancreatic juice acquired and exerted a powerful solvent action on *proteids* only after contact with either the duodenal membrane or extracts thereof. This observation enabled him to deduce that the duodenum produced a unique enzyme (enterokinase) responsible for the activation of pancreatic juice.

Pancreatic Disease

Since the anatomic location of the organ was not well-known and its physiological functions ill-defined, pathological conditions of the pancreas were difficult to delineate. Thomas Willis in 1674 noted the urine of diabetics to be "*wonderfully sweet as if it were imbued with honey or sugar*." These subtle observations marked the beginning of the clinical correlation of pancreatic disease

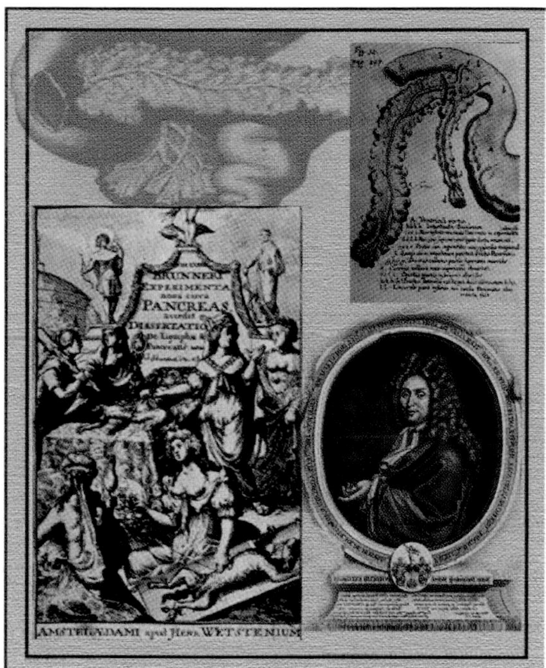

Johannes Konrad Brunner studied the secretion of both the pancreas and duodenum. He considered the duodenal glands to be the main source of digestive juice secretion, whereas Peyer proposed that Brunner's gland and his own patches were adjuncts to digestion, producing a "fortifying secretion" for the pancreatic juice as it descended through the digestive tract. Brunner based his belief on the subsidiary nature of the pancreas after having successfully pancreatectomized a number of animals, which survived for long periods of time. In 1682 he presented this work in "Experimenta Nova Circa Pancreasa" Although Brunner noted that his pancreatectomized dogs survived for up to a year despite polyuria, polydypsia, and bulimia, he unfortunately failed to identify the presence of sugar in the urine. Indeed, his fixation on the issue of digestion precluded him from successfully defining the pancreatic relationship with polydypsia and its association with diabetes.

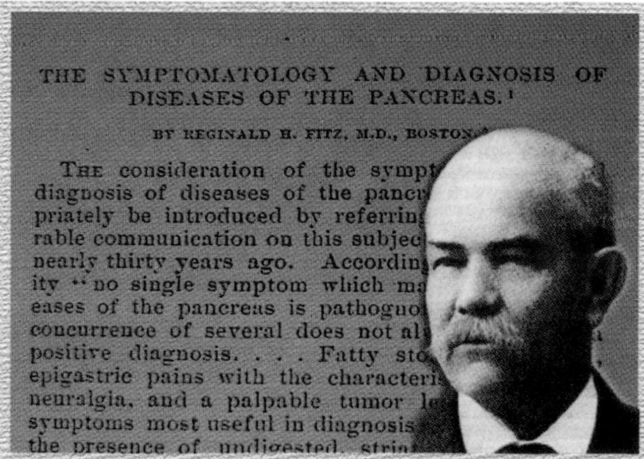
THE SYMPTOMATOLOGY AND DIAGNOSIS OF DISEASES OF THE PANCREAS.¹

BY REGINALD H. FITZ, M.D., BOSTON

The consideration of the symp diagnosis of diseases of the panc priately be introduced by referrin rable communication on this subjec nearly thirty years ago. Accordin ity "no single symptom which m eases of the pancreas is pathogno concurrence of several does not al positive diagnosis. . . . Fatty st epigastric pains with the characteri neuralgia, and a palpable tumor l symptoms most useful in diagnosis the presence of undigested strin

Reginald Fitz was initially educated at Harvard and thereafter spent two years in Europe where he studied at hospitals in Paris, London, Glasgow, Vienna, and Berlin. During this period of time he was exposed to the work of Classen in Germany who had contributed substantially to the elucidation of pancreatisis. In addition, he had studied with Rudolf Virchow, and had become aware of the relevance of cellular pathology. On his return to Boston in 1870 he introduced the use of the microscope to Harvard Medical School. Apart from his seminal contributions to appendicitis in 1886, in 1889 he produced a definitive work on pancreatitis that represented the first logical assessment of the pathology and management of the disease process in America. Fitz subsequently became the Shattuck Professor of Pathological Anatomy at Harvard University.

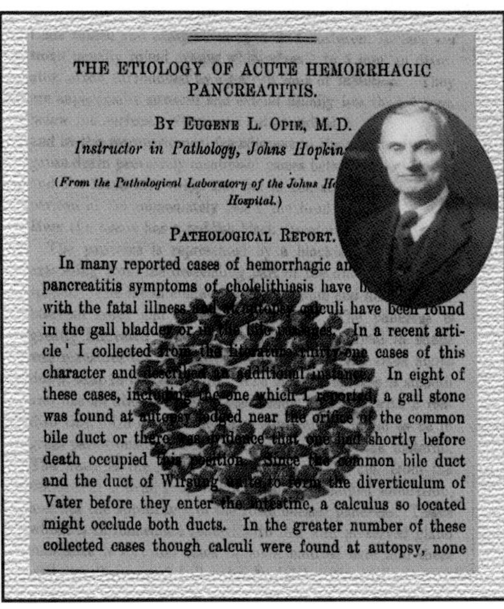

THE ETIOLOGY OF ACUTE HEMORRHAGIC PANCREATITIS.

BY EUGENE L. OPIE, M. D.

Instructor in Pathology, Johns Hopkin[illegible]

(From the Pathological Laboratory of the Johns H[illegible] Hospital.)

PATHOLOGICAL REPORT.

In many reported cases of hemorrhagic a[illegible] pancreatitis symptoms of cholelithiasis have [illegible] with the fatal illness [illegible] calculi have been found in the gall bladder [illegible]. In a recent article[1] I collected [illegible] cases of this character and [illegible]. In eight of these cases, [illegible] a gall stone was found at [illegible] near [illegible] the common bile duct or [illegible] shortly before death occupied [illegible] common bile duct and the duct of Wirsung [illegible] the diverticulum of Vater before they enter [illegible], a calculus so located might occlude both ducts. In the greater number of these collected cases though calculi were found at autopsy, none

E. Opie in 1901 proposed the "common channel theory" of pancreatitis and implicated gallstones in the pathogenesis of the disease.

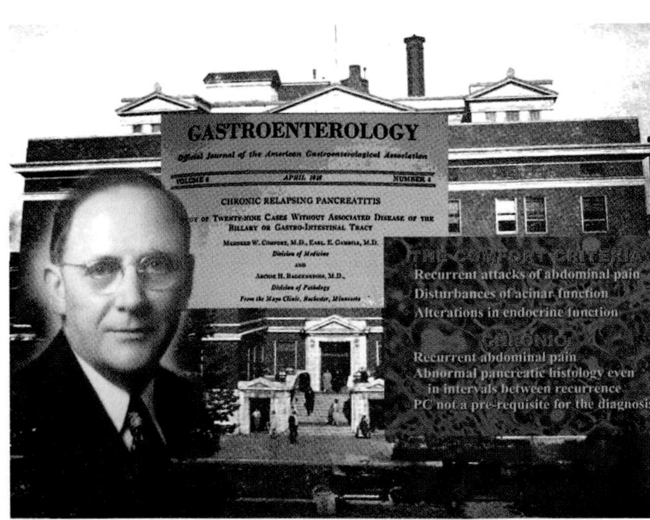

In 1946, Comfort at the Mayo clinic (background), published a clinical paper that provided the first coherent assessment of the nebulous concept of chronic pancreatitis.

and diabetes, but no specific relationship was recognized until 1788, when Thomas Cawley broadly alluded to such a disease entity. Descriptions of pancreatic abnormalities from antiquity refer mostly to *"scirrhous"* disease, without any specific identification of pathology. In Germany, Friedrich and Claasen were prominent in establishing the role of alcohol in pancreatitis and defined its clinical and pathological sequel in the 1880s. Subsequently, Reginald Fitz of Boston, who had studied with Claasen, defined the signs and symptoms of pancreatitis and categorized the disease in terms of its gangrenous, hemorrhagic, and suppurative forms. His reflections on the nature and causes of the disease were published in the *Boston Medical and Surgical Journal* of 1889, and have remained little changed in the centuries since their initial proposal. Opie in 1901, further elucidated the pathogenesis of the pancreatitis and proposed a *"common channel"* hypothesis whereby acute pancreatitis was the aftermath of the flow of infected bile into the pancreatic duct when the common bile duct. He proposed that this clinical circumstance occurred when a gallstone became impacted in the ampulla of Vater and caused obstruction.

Archibald, in 1919, experimentally demonstrated that spasm of the sphincter of Oddi increased biliary pressure and culminated in the development of acute pancreatitis, and provided further credence for this theory. Although alcohol and gallstones remain the common denominator of the etiology of acute pancreatitis to this day, Rich and Duff in 1936 proposed that a combination of pathological vascular changes and local pancreatic enzyme damage were responsible for the pathogenesis. The diagnosis of acute pancreatitis, which had initially been purely clinical, was subsequently supported by the work of R. Elman of St. Louis, who in 1929, described the quantitative determination of blood amylase using a viscometer. Subsequent investigation has concluded that the cytokine cascade of acute pancreatitis may be a consequence of disorganized intracellular trafficking of the zymogen granules.

Early Observations on Pancreatitis

The identification of the etiology of chronic pancreatitis has frustrated physicians since the very earliest observations of the entity. Initially, the pathological examination of the pancreas was the most defining focus in the diagnosis, with clinical assessment of the patient as the only available diagnostic tool for the physician. As early as 1788, Cawley became the first to suggest a link with lifestyle and pancreatic disease. His patient, *"a 34-year-old man accustomed to free living and strong corporeal exertions in the pursuit of country living,"* was noted to have extensive pancreatic disease at autopsy. One of the earliest reports of pancreatitis was by Edwin Klebs, who reported a case of hemorrhagic pancreatitis in 1870. This was followed by many scattered reports throughout the medical literature, without much focus toward a diagnosis before the patient's demise. At the turn of the nineteenth century Mayo-Robson presumed the etiology to be due to bacterial infection, however, the distinction between acute, sub-acute, and chronic was still controversial. Others physicians, including Reginald Fitz, felt that the underlying insult was the hemorrhage of the pancreas, which resulted in necrosis of the gland as evidenced at autopsy. This assessment resulted in some prejudicial views, since cases described by pathologists represented advanced and fatal forms of pancreatitis. Thus, many early attempts at classification resulted in contradictions, as physicians and pathologists differed on the nature of the process and in addition, lacked scientific data to address the question of etiology.

In 1946, Comfort provided a significant analysis of the clinical entity of chronic pancreatitis and in so doing, produced the seminal manuscript on the subject that has for fifty years remained the critical commentary on the disease. Although there had been references to the relationship between alcohol and chronic pancreatitis, there were no clinical studies, and proof remained anecdotal until Comfort described in detail the connection between alcohol abuse and chronic pancreatitis. His study added considerable credibility to the much earlier description of the "drunkard's pancreas" by Friedrich in the eighteenth century. The criteria utilized by Comfort to characterize the diagnosis included recurrent attacks of abdominal pain, disturbances of acinar function, and alterations in endocrine function. During the last fifty years, despite the fact that much has been learned from studies of alcoholic pancreatitis, the definitive mechanisms are for the most part obscure. The relative increase in the diagnosis of pancreatitis probably reflects a wide variety of factors, including increased awareness, greater diagnostic skill and more sophisticated technology, as well as an increase in alcohol consumption. Considerable debate has centered round the question of whether pancreatic lithogenesis is a diagnostic criterion of chronic pancreatitis or whether it merely represents a correlatible epiphenomenon. Prior to the twentieth century, pancreatic stones were thought of as exceedingly rare. Indeed, the correlation between the mere presence of pancreatic calculi and the diagnosis of chronic pancreatitis itself remains debated. Thus, in the condition of "senile pancreatitis", described by Amman, the relationship between the presence of idiopathic asymptomatic pancreatic calculi found in the elderly suggests that the chronicity and calculi may not necessarily occur *pari passu*. There is, however, little disagreement that pancreatic stones may obstruct the ducts and play a part in the development of pancreatic pain. This observation has resulted in efforts to remove stones either by medical dissolution or by mechanical intervention. Thus lithotripsy, endoscopic sphincterotomy with or without stent placement, and a wide variety of ductal and pancreatic surgical techniques have been proposed to eliminate calculous disease of the pancreas.

In 1959, Zuidema labeled dietary factors as an additional etiologic agent and proposed that the entity known as "tropical pancreatitis" in underdeveloped countries was associated with the standard low protein, fat-deficient diet prevalent in such areas. Subsequent reports have suggested that the Cassava root (manioc) might be the agent implicated in tropical pancreatitis, but rigorous confirmation of this theory is still required. Despite considerable attention to the identification of the basis of chronic pancreatitis, approximately 30% of patients diagnosed with the disease still are regarded as idiopathic with no known evidence of any associated disease or inciting event.

In the absence of minimal evidence for etiology, the identification of a mechanistic explanation of the disease process has been similarly frustrating. Various theories have been propounded to explain the pathology, and include the necrosis-fibrosis concept of Kloppel, the obstruction theory of Sarles, the toxic metabolic hypothesis of Bordalo, and the oxidative stress hypothesis of Braganza.

The Evolution of Management

The definition of chronic pancreatitis and its classification has changed with the advance of biochemical and scientific technology over the last fifty years. The natural history of chronic pancreatitis, with the development of endocrine and exocrine insufficiency, leading to diabetes and steatorrhea, provide further supportive clinical evidence. There exist no pathognomonic criteria for the disease but rather a constellation of symptoms and signs corroborated with radiographic, ERCP, and biochemical data.

Despite numerous attempts, no particular classification system has proved entirely satisfactory and the field of chronic pancreatitis has been troubled in the area of categorization. Recent attempts include the Marseilles (morphologic criteria) and Cambridge (imagery of the ductal system) classifications, but neither has adequately resolved the dilemma. Overall, the definition and clinical pictures of both acute and chronic pancreatitis intertwine, and separation often remains obscure. Since no definitive treatment exists, the evolution of therapy has perforce been directed at dealing with the symptomatic manifestations of the disease.

Medical Treatment

Pain

The first and predominant treatment regime of pancreatitis was pain control, although in the early part of the twentieth century, the lack of accurate diagnosis often resulted in treatment delay. For the most part, measures employed included high dosage opiates, especially morphine. Other strategies included the use of calomel to lessen distention, and as a potential intestinal antiseptic. Overall, the extent of the medical treatment in the early part of the century included little more than observation, although in dire circumstances such as shock, hot saline enemas were advocated. The dominant therapy, however, relied upon pain management, thus the introduction of intravenous agents greatly enhanced the ability to ameliorate acute discomfort. Orr in 1950 established the efficacy of the epidural technique, and its application to the management of pancreatic pain proved quite efficacious. Although pain relief was predominantly a pharmacotherapeutic strategy, in 1946, Fontaine achieved some moderate success by resection of splanchnic nerves to relieve the pain associated with chronic pancreatitis and, as a result, a wide variety of neural denervations enjoyed some vogue.

Exocrine Deficiency

Aside from pain, complaints of chronic diarrhea and fatty stools proved to be issues of considerable discomfort to individuals with chronic pancreatitis. Complaints varied from simple "unrest in the abdomen" to major and even uncontrollable attacks of diarrhea. Although exocrine function *per se* had not been studied in detail, Fles in 1868 reportedly used oral extracts of pancreas to relieve the steatorrhea associated with the disease. In 1902, Salomon effectively used a more defined role of diet and "fresh pancreas" with moderate success. This substitution of exocrine production, or *organotherapy*, was the precursor of later efforts to "cool" the pancreas to both alleviate pain and restore exocrine function. Although the oral supplementation of zymogens has proved to be highly beneficial in the symptomatic management of disordered digestion, rigorous data regarding the effects of "pancreatic cooling" has not been forthcoming. Similarly, the usage of subcutaneous Octreotide (an analog of somatostatin) that inhibited acinar secretory activity, has been without significant benefit in decreasing the progress of the disease although some amelioration of pain has been claimed.

Endocrine Deficiency

The progressive pancreatic fibrosis associated with the inexorable progress of chronic pancreatitis culminates in diabetes in approximately 15% of patients. Although the overt manifestations of diabetes are not usually evident until the destruction of approximately 90% of the gland, subtle alterations in glucose homeostasis may predate such events by many years. The early institution of appropriate dietary and pharmacotherapeutic (insulin) measures thus became an important prophylactic strategy in stabilizing the adverse metabolic events noted during the evolution of chronic pancreatitis.

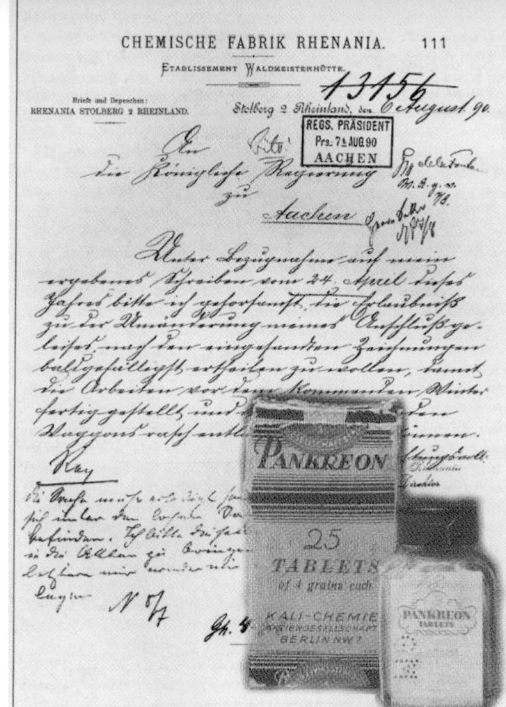

The recognition that some of the long-standing effects of pancreatic dysfunction could not be ameliorated by surgery and that in addition, surgery of the pancreas was dangerous, directed attention to pharmacotherapy. Rhehania pancreatin was developed in 1897 to augment pancreatic function and subsequently Franz Thomas and Wilhelm Weber further addressed the utility of a "pancreatic extract". By 1900, Matthias Gockel was able to publish his clinical experience with the substance and Pankreon soon became regarded as a critical agent in the management of pancreatic and gastric disorders.

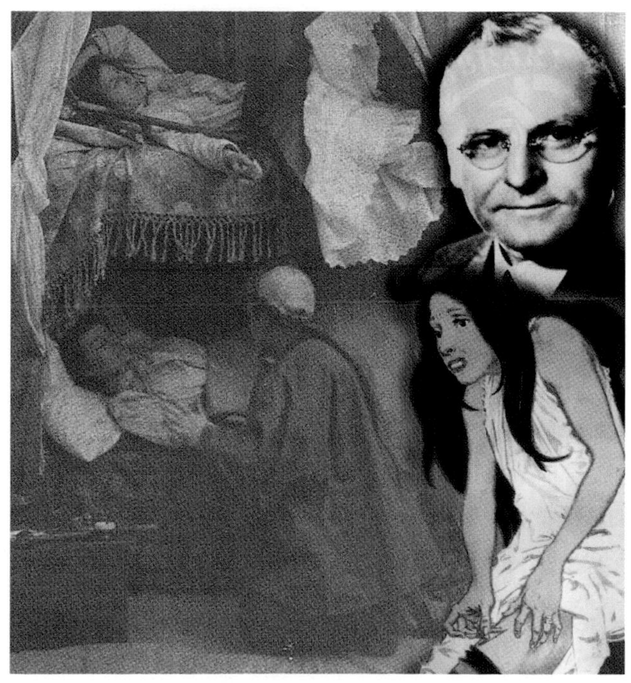

The invention of a hypodermic syringe by Orr (top right) facilitated the use of morphine to alleviate pain and suffering. Unfortunately the social consequences were not appreciated for some years and led to widespread abuse of narcotic agents (bottom right).

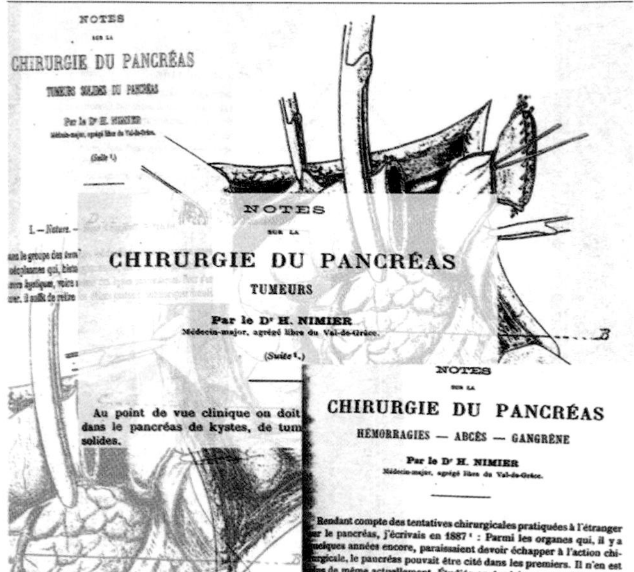

H. Nimier of Paris, France, wrote extensively on the subject of pancreatitis and described in detail the diverse operative techniques available for dealing with the disease.

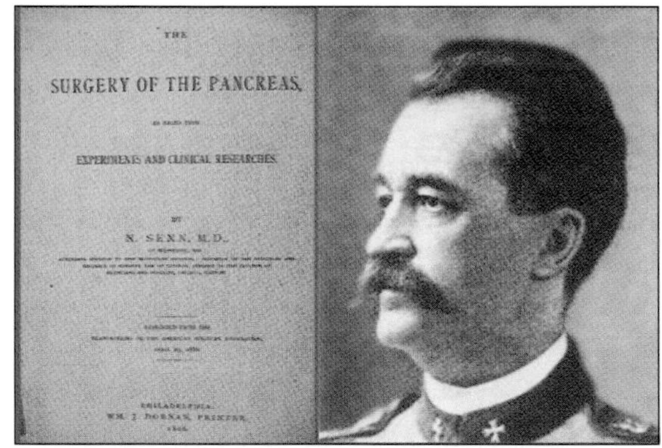

Nicholas Senn of Chicago was an early pioneer of experimental surgical research and his contributions to the evolution of pancreatic surgery were particularly noteworthy. Despite his enthusiasm for the area, his evaluation of contemporary work in the field led him to a pessimistic conclusion regarding the viability of pancreatic surgery. As a prescient and thoughtful individual he cautioned his colleagues as to the utility of surgery for pancreatic disease. Little has changed!

Surgical Strategy

The development of a rationale for surgical intervention in chronic pancreatitis has been hindered by numerous difficulties. Firstly, there was little appreciation of pancreatic disease itself. Secondly, the inflammatory condition of acute pancreatitis was often so violent and rapidly terminal that little explicit surgical therapy other than simple exploration, incision, and drainage was ever possible. The notion that various gradations of this disease process were related or even amenable to specific therapy, was to a large extent obviated by the technical difficulties encountered in operating upon the pancreas itself. Nevertheless, when faced with the relentless progress of the disease and the ravages inflicted by pain, narcotics, and organ dysfunction, physicians have been driven to seek a therapeutic, albeit symptomatic intervention. Thus, despite the lack of any discernable cause for chronic pancreatitis, surgeons have, since the latter part of the nineteenth century, applied themselves vigorously and in diverse fashions to the treatment of the disease. The solutions seemed initially obvious. Thus, a damaged and dysfunctional gland causing pain might be best removed. Needless to say, the technical aspects of this endeavor soon resulted in reconsideration of this concept. Biliary or pancreatic calculi capable of causing both pain and obstruction should be extracted, but this obvious remedy appeared to be relatively ineffective. The obvious target of a sphincter in "spasm" or fibrosed, was attractive as a solution, but its ablation once again appeared to effect little relief. The observation of a massively dilated duct system suggested that drainage would bring relief, but neither disease amelioration nor pain abeyance appeared either to be predictable or occur with any acceptable regularity. Indeed, for the most part the surgery of chronic pancreatitis has today come to rest in the hands of stalwarts determined to do what best they can, fully aware of the absolute limitations of their procedures, and those who confine their activities to the elimination of pain effected by means of nerve injection or ablation.

Aware of the problems of pancreatic disease, Nicholas Senn in 1886 commented in one of his earliest papers, "The surgery of the pancreas, as based upon experiments and clinical research," on what he recognized as a vexatious problem. Senn demonstrated that experimental extirpation of the pancreas in animals was *"invariably followed by death,"* although prior separate experiments by both Brunner and von Mering had not drawn so absolute a conclusion. Nevertheless, it was evident to most surgeons of any experience that the vast majority of pancreatic surgery (whether major or minor) resulted in fatal consequences.

The general advances in surgery of the late nineteenth and early twentieth centuries heralded the introduction and refinement of surgical treatment for pancreatic disease but, as might have been predicted, there were misadventures. Intervention in pancreatic disease was regarded as extremely dangerous and even the most experienced of the gastrointestinal surgeons, such as Mayo-Robson of Leeds, advocated the surgical approach of "waiting until collapse of the patient with presumed pancreatitis" before surgery was undertaken. In fact Mayo-Robson – an arbiter on such matters – maintained that *"until collapse no surgery [was] justifiable."* Out of therapeutic strategies of this type would grow the justifiably cynical medical comments of men such as Naunyn, who described such surgery as little more than an autopsy *in vivo*! The lack of technical expertise and knowledge limited the ensuing surgery to

Robert C. Coffey during his early surgical career at Portland, Oregon, proposed that chronic pancreatitis could be treated by pancreatoenterostomy for drainage of the duct combined with pancreatic resection of irreversibly damaged components of the gland.

a mere evacuation of the septic material and, given the non-availability of antibiotics and the primitive state of knowledge of fluid and electrolyte balance, the outcome was invariably fatal. Indeed, the early twentieth century tenet of Kocher seemed most applicable when directed to the subject of pancreatic surgery: *"A surgeon is a doctor who can operate and knows when not to."*

The Origins of Pancreatic Surgery

In order to understand the limitations of surgery for chronic pancreatitis and the difficulty in developing a rationale for such intervention, a brief diversion into an assessment of the evolution of pancreatic surgery is helpful. The inaccessibility of the organ to both diagnosis and intervention, coupled with an almost complete absence of its function and pathology, rendered interfering with it worrisome. Early experimental pancreatic surgery originated in 1673, when Regnier de Graaf constructed pancreatic fistulas on dogs to determine the nature of pancreatic secretion. These experiments laid the foundation of pancreatic physiology and initiated further interest in the organ that had previously been inaccessible. His publication, *"De Succi Pancreatici"*, detailed the nature of pancreatic juice and described the technical requirements needed to create the fistula. A decade later, Johannes Conrad Brunner (1683) expanded de Graaf's work by undertaking a series of partial resections of canine pancreas that were published as "Experimenta Nova Circa Pancreas".

Resection

Other than the occasional acute dramatic incision and drainage of acute pancreatitis, the field of formal pancreatic surgery remained quiescent for over two hundred years. Although the literature in the late nineteenth century periodically alluded to isolated cases of resection and extirpation, no specific intervention for pancreatic disease was contemplated or described. At the turn of the nineteenth century, more intrepid surgeons including Trendelenburg, Halsted, and Codvilla, began to report pancreatic resections and suggest the possibility in formal intervention in "tumorous" disease processes that afflicted the organ. In 1898, William S. Halsted of Baltimore resected the first carcinoma of the "duodenal papilla and diverticulum Vateri" and in so doing demonstrated that pancreatic surgery was a feasible, albeit risky, proposition. Almost simultaneously, Alessandro Codvilla undertook an "en bloc" resection of the pancreas and duodenum, becoming, in all likelihood, the first to perform a pancreaticoduodenectomy. An appreciation of the inherent risks associated with the presence of jaundice, as well as the recognition of the appalling prognosis of pancreatic cancer, led to the development of a two-stage operation to first relieve the "cholemia" and thereafter removal of the tumor. In 1907, A. Desjardins described an experimental two-stage operation for resection of the pancreas based on his cadaveric resections, and in the following year, L. Sauvé devised a one-stage operation and noted the loss of exocrine function as a necessary evil. Neither Sauvé nor Desjardins had the temerity to undertake these procedures in patients! Apart from the magnitude of the procedure itself, a major surgical problem was presented by the anastomotic sites and even in the experimental setting, limited results and certain mortality were associated with leakage. In 1909, Kausch was able to document the successful re-implantation of the pancreas via pancreatico-enterostomy after ampullary resection for carcinoma. Fearful surgeons, although unaware of the precise nature of the problem, proposed that the reason for the anastomotic failures were due in part to the inherent nature of the pancreatic juice, which caused leakage with resultant fatality. As a result of the high mortality and morbidity of intervention, the development of pancreatic surgery was slow and most surgeons refrained from undertaking such procedures. As a result, isolated case studies dominated the literature and no definable approach could be discerned. Nevertheless, isolated successful procedures led to a degree of progress.

At the turn of the 19th century more intrepid surgeons, including F. Trendelenburg from Breslau (left) and A. Codvilla from Bologna (right) began to report pancreatic resections and suggest the possibility of formal intervention in "tumorous" disease processes that afflicted the organ.

Although Santorini (left) described the duct that bears his name, in the 18th century little effective pancreatic surgery was undertaken prior to the 20th century. Substantial contributions to the development of pancreatic surgical therapy were undertaken by (left to right) Moynihan, Mayo-Robson, Trendelenburg, Courvoisier, Whipple, Fortner and Beger. Nevertheless, outcome in most instances, particularly for neoplastic disease, was not far different from that initially noted by Hippocrates and his colleagues on the island of Kos (background), millennia previously.

Evarts A. Graham reported the first successful *"as nearly a total resection of the pancreas as possible"* in an infant suffering from hypoglycemia in 1934, and in so doing, inspired the future efforts of Allen O. Whipple in undertaking radical pancreatic excisional surgery. Thus in 1935, Whipple published *"Treatment of Carcinoma of the Ampulla of Vater"* and laid the groundwork for modern pancreatic surgery. The operation was a two-staged procedure that initially involved a posterior gastro-enterostomy and anterior cystogastrostomy. Three to four weeks later, the second stage, that included excision of the descending duodenum with V-shaped excision of the pancreatic head and over-sewing of the pancreatic ducts, was undertaken.

Shortly thereafter, Alexander Brunschwig published his experience, documenting the *Resection of the Head of the Pancreas and Duodenum for Carcinoma*. This description was the first radical resection of a carcinoma in the head of

Zur operativen Behandlung der Pankreas-Cysten.

Von

Dr. Carl Gussenbauer,

Professor der Chirurgie in Prag.*)

(Hierzu Taf. XIII. Fig. 1, 2.)

M. H.! Im letzten Semester kan
kreascyste … handeln, ur
fahrung … wie mi
opera … Feld d
Pa … Erla
nä … sch
B … A
V … z
f … h
a …
… ter
kr … bel
tob … er
Biere … belkeit
nachde … ntwein g
brechen. … er noch
mit ziemliche … Vom zweiten
nicht mehr krank und brachte er die nächs
zu. Nach Ablauf dieser Frist bemerkte e
schwellung, die in weiteren zwei Wochen
Hervorwölbung der Magengegend bewirkte.
minderte sich sein Appetit, nach den Mahlz

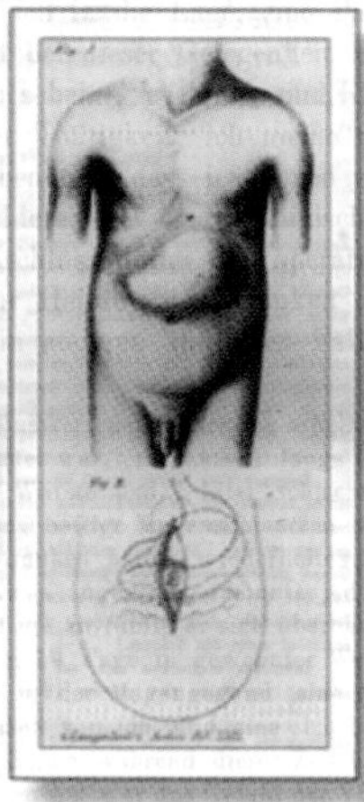

Karl Gussenbauer, a former pupil of Billroth, was the first to describe a successful technique for the management of pancreatic pseudocysts.

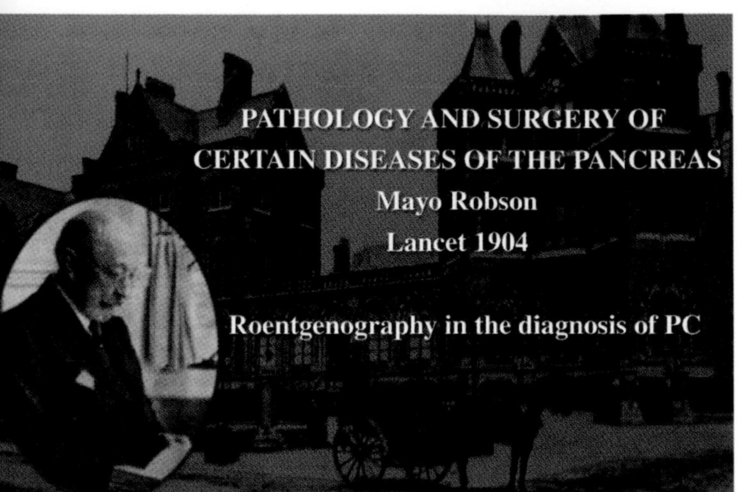

Sir Mayo-Robson (Leeds, England) (left) had initially proposed in the latter part of the 19th century that diseases of the pancreas should be non-operatively managed but thereafter became the first surgeon to perform a transpancreatic stone extraction early in the 20th century.

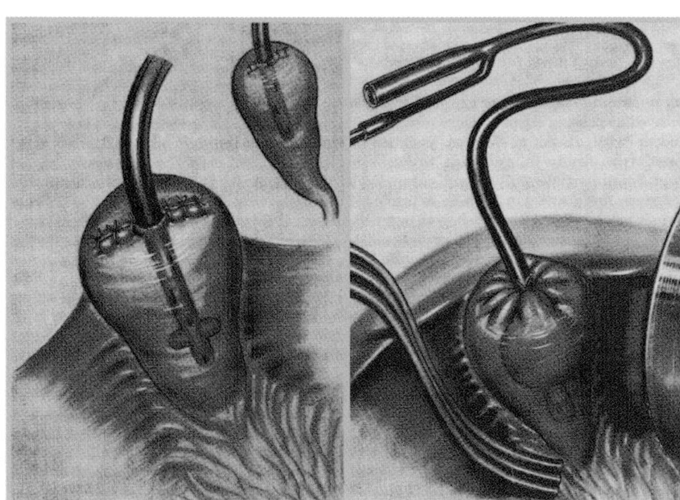

Cholecystostomy was proposed by many as a reasonable procedure to drain the biliary system and thus prevent recurrent pancreatitis. It was certainly safer than any currently available form of pancreatic surgery.

the pancreas, and demonstrated that the complete removal of the duodenum could be undertaken without consequence. In so doing, Brunschwig was the first to confirm Lester R. Dragstedt's proposal that the extirpation of the duodenum was compatible with life. Despite the rigorous efforts of Brunschwig and Whipple, the first total pancreatectomy is actually credited to Eugene W. Rockey, who in 1942 undertook this atypical procedure under circumstances where the carcinoma had spread throughout the entire pancreas and no other method of treatment was possible. Unfortunately, the patient died a couple of weeks after the operation, due to a presumed biliary anastamotic leak. A further issue in the danger of pancreatic surgery was presented by the problems of excessive bleeding. As a result of prolonged biliary obstruction, the resultant hemostatic diathesis rendered major surgery hazardous. The discovery of vitamin K, its biological effects, and the profound relationship to hepatic function by Henrick Dam, initiated a major strategic evaluation of pancreatic surgery. The entire concept of hemostasis in patients with jaundice was reviewed and as a result, hemostasis in pancreatic surgery was addressed from the biliary obstructive perspective.

Thus, improvement of hepatic function consequent upon relief of biliary obstruction, became a critical issue in defining a resolution of the bleeding. Armed with this knowledge, Whipple was able to successfully perform a one-stage procedure later that year, modifying the two-stage procedure by re-anastamosis of the pancreatic duct into an enterostomy. By 1940, sufficient experience had been developed in pancreatic carcinoma and resection that other diseases and other areas of the pancreas could be considered amenable to intervention.

Sphincterotomy

As early as 1884, Langenbuch of Berlin proposed that biliary disease was related to sphincter stenosis, and actually proposed division of the muscle fibers as a method of treatment. In 1901, Eugene L. Opie described the common channel theory as a mechanism of pancreatitis secondary to bile reflux and in so doing, was the first to provide a rationale linking biliary disease to pancreatic pathology. E. Archibald provided the critical experiments that established a definitive link between the resistance of the sphincter and pancreatitis in 1913. Proof of concept was demonstrated by application of the theory when sphincteric ablation by Archibald of a patient with recurrent pancreatitis was reported to have successfully relieved the symptoms. An extrapolation of this concept led to the notion that long-standing sphincter dysfunction (stenosis) might be an etiological factor (reflux of bile into the pancreas) in the development of chronic pancreatitis, and that the condition could be ameliorated by sphincterotomy. Support for this notion was provided by the work of Henry Doubilet and Ralph Colp, who in 1935 undertook a series of studies which confirmed the theories of Archibald. Although the classic initial sphincterotomy was credited to Archibald in 1919, the most active proponents of this concept were Henry Doubilet and John H. Mulholland, who pursued the subject over the course of many years. In 1956, they published the "*Eight-Year Study of Pancreatitis and Sphincterotomy*." In addition to performing a sphincterotomy, they mandated the surgical removal of the gall bladder due to alteration of dynamics of the biliary tree. Unfortunately, the efficacy of sphincterotomy did not live up to these miraculous claims. A further diversion on the sphincterotomy odyssey was based upon a fanciful notion that sphincter spasm reflected the effects of acid from the stomach. Thus, removal of acid by gastrectomy would decrease secretory function of the pancreas, diminish spasm, and relieve pain. This theory accorded well with the then current ill-conceived understanding of the basis of chronic pancreatitis, and Colp thus became a proponent of gastrectomy as a means of treating pancreatic disease of the "chronic pancreatitic type." The introduction of endoscopic retrograde cholangio-pancreatography in 1968 by a surgeon, McCune, failed to excite initial interest in chronic pancreatic disease, but subsequent advances in the development of sphincterotomy by Claasen and Kawai led to a further re-examination of the clinical efficacy of sphincterotomy. P. Cotton was an early adept in the application of this novel modality to the treatment of pancreatitis, culminating not only in the relief of putative obstruction by papillotomy, but the introduction of stents and even the extraction of calculi, which were deemed to play a role in obstruction and pain.

The Extraction of Pancreatic Calculi

In 1891, A. Pearce Gould was the first to remove pancreatic calculi from the duct of Wirsung. Almost a decade later in 1902, the first diagnosis and transduodenal surgical removal was undertaken by B.G. Moynihan of Leeds. In 1908, A.W. Mayo-Robson, also of Leeds, performed the first transpancreatic stone extraction. For the most part, such surgical expeditions were random occurrences and not part of a recognizable management strategy. Indeed, the entity of chronic pancreatitis was barely recognized at that time. A more interesting anecdote was provided by the interesting case of a baroness with an epigastric abscess, which after surgical drainage by Capparelli, resulted in the development of a pancreatic fistula that produced hundreds of stones, as observed over the subsequent six-year period.

Ductal Drainage

After the failure of sphincterotomy to adequately improve the condition of chronic pancreatitis, it was proposed that the problem might lie with the inability of the former procedure to adequately decompress and allow drainage of a damaged and/or dilated distal ductal system. This inadequacy of sphincterotomy was accepted by many surgeons, who thereupon embarked upon the development of strategies designed to adequately address the presumed distal component of the disease. In 1909, Robert C. Coffey reported the effects of a variety of experimental techniques utilizing pancreatico-enterostomy and established the possibility of pancreatectomy and pancreatic anastamosis as a viable procedure. A report in 1921 by Walter Ellis Sistrunk was deemed important, since it claimed that the successful achievement of a direct drainage procedure on the "pancreas proper" without complication had resulted in an improvement in the diabetic condition. In 1954, Merlin K. Duval and Robert M. Zollinger separately, and almost simultaneously published their innovative descriptions of experience using a caudal pancreatico-jejunostomy. Duval stated that he did not accept Opie's common channel theory as *sine qua non* of pancreatitis, and claimed that current information confirmed the presence of a bi-directional flow of pancreatic juice. Driven by this reasoning, Duval (1954) proposed and implemented the procedure of caudal pancreatico-jejunostomy drainage as an alternative treatment for chronic pancreatitis. In his published experience, he gracefully acknowledged that the final result would require the "tincture of time" before definitive conclusions could be drawn.

In 1958, Puestow proposed an extension of the efficacy of drainage by opening the dilated duct of Wirsung lengthwise (filleting), and anastamosing the filleted duct to a loop of jejunum that had been similarly treated. This mechanical arrangement was proposed as beneficial, since each ductal branch was now able to drain directly into a new widely patent jejunal lumen, rather than a single narrow distal anastamosis.

Biliary

Despite the conclusion of the majority that a pancreatic drainage problem was the crux of the issue in chronic pancreatitis, some surgeons clung steadfastly to the concept of biliary tract disease as the *modus operandi* in chronic pancreatitis. A body of literature therefore accumulated during the mid-twentieth century as attempts at relief were directed at the purported biliary component. Thus cholycystostomy, cholycystectomy, common bile duct exploration, bile duct drainage, and sphincterotomy, continued to be explored as avenues by which the disease could be dealt with.

Excisional Surgery

Since the progress in the surgery of pancreatic carcinoma had resulted in a drastic reduction in morbidity and mortality, it was soon accepted that an "excisional cure" for a malignant disease might have considerable merit if applied to even a "benign disease" such as chronic pancreatitis. Thus, in 1946 O.T. Clagget performed a total pancreatectomy for chronic pancreatitis and in so doing, became the first of a long line of surgeons who would undertake extensive and radical surgery for this "benign" condition. Unfortunately, the complications of the procedure and the severe metabolic consequences for the most part, persuaded the majority that this course was less than effective and the procedure did not gain widespread acceptance. A further problem noted was that even in those who survived the operation and could come to terms with the disastrous metabolic sequelae, "phantom pain" still remained a major issue. Indeed, the concept of a diabetic with no exocrine pancreatic function and dependent upon narcotics for pain relief, proved to be a daunting specter for even the most hardened pancreatic surgeon.

In 1965, William J. Fry and Charles G. Child realized that the superfluity of surgical operations for the cure of pancreatitis were a result of the lack of an ideal treatment. Seeking to ameliorate this state of affairs, they proposed an alternative to complete resection and reported the results following a 95% distal pancreatectomy. The rationale for their procedure was well-conceived, and addressed many of the concerns raised by the previous attempts to derive a solution for the surgical management of chronic pancreatitis. They proposed a procedure that would encompass the strong points of the previous excisional techniques, yet obviate the disadvantages. The operation (95% distal pancreatectomy) entailed removal of the spleen, the uncinate process, and the body and the tail of the pancreas, i.e., the majority of the diseased tissue, and was designed to be technically easier, reduce postoperative complications, and have a higher success rate. Regrettably, this surgery also failed to absolutely attain its objectives and provided a further reminder that the surgical therapy for chronic pancreatitis remained an enigma. Although Whipple's original two-stage pancreaticoduodenectomy spared the pylorus, he subsequently revised this, and included removal of the distal stomach and entire duodenum in the one-stage procedure. A significant portion of these patients developed jejunal ulceration. Given the limited life expectancy of a patient with pancreatic carcinoma, this was acceptable but in the more chronic condition of pancreatitis, the issues of mucosal ulceration were significant in a population of this type. However, W. Traverso questioned the rationale of not preserving the pylorus for a benign condition, and in 1978, applied this technique of preservation of the pylorus to patients with chronic pancreatitis with acceptable results.

Another refinement of the pancreaticoduodenectomy (the duodenum preserving resection of the head of the pancreas [DPRHP]) was proposed by Hans G. Beger in 1985. Beger, having presciently noted the distinct nature of the discrete inflammatory mass in the head of the pancreas in some patients, devised a technique specifically designed to deal with this apparent subset of patients with chronic pancreatitis. It is of interest that this group of patients had been emphasized as early as 1925 by Mallet-Guy; however, no surgical

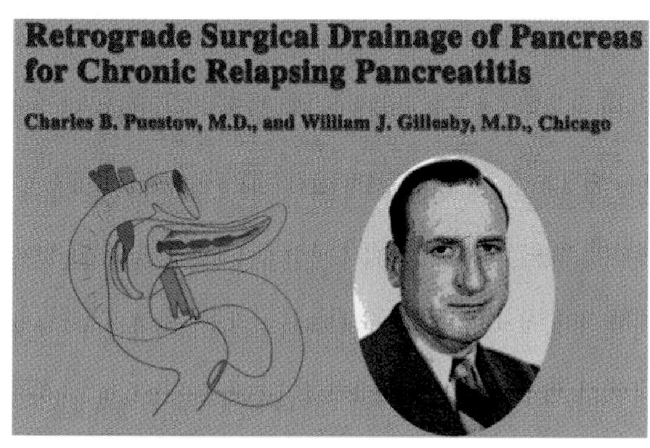

G. Puestow in 1958 termed the procedure a lateral pancreatico-jejunostomy, and based upon early enthusiastic reports as to its efficacy, it soon achieved a prominent role in the treatment of chronic pancreatitis associated with ductal disease. A criticism that had been leveled at the Puestow procedure was that it necessitated a splenectomy as well as mobilization of the pancreas itself to enable a distal pancreatectomy. In 1960 Robert E. Rochelle therefore proposed a judicious modification that retained the spleen and simply anastomosed the jejunum to the intact pancreas.

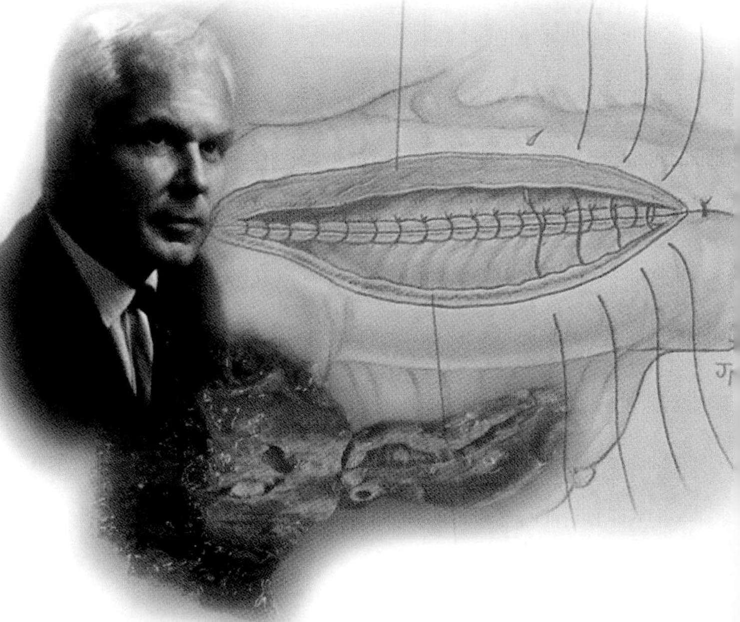

Merlin K. Duval (left) in 1954 described an innovative technique for the procedure of caudal pancreaticojejunostomy. He proposed that this procedure would not only decompress the gland but in addition obviate the deleterious effects of pancreatic calculi (bottom).

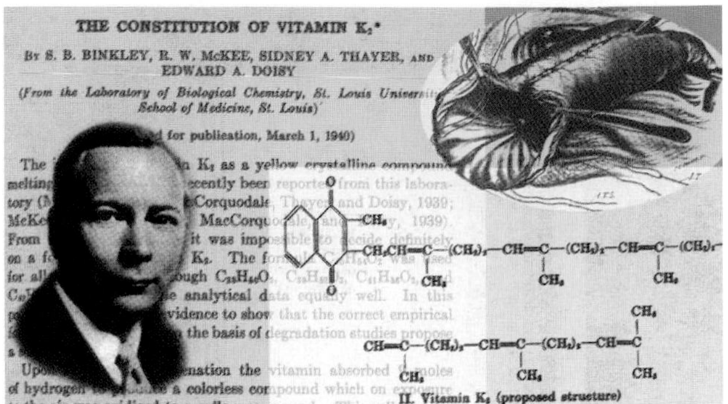

Technical advances in surgery considerably benefited the outcome of pancreatic resection. A major advance, however, was the discovery by H. van Dam (inset) in 1939, and the subsequent synthesis in 1940 by K. Doisy, of vitamin K. This enabled adequate blood coagulation in patients with longstanding obstructive jaundice. Van Dam, whose work had been undertaken in Denmark, shared the Nobel prize in 1943 with Doisy of St. Louis. Van Dam had called the substance Vit K because of its effect on "Koagulation".

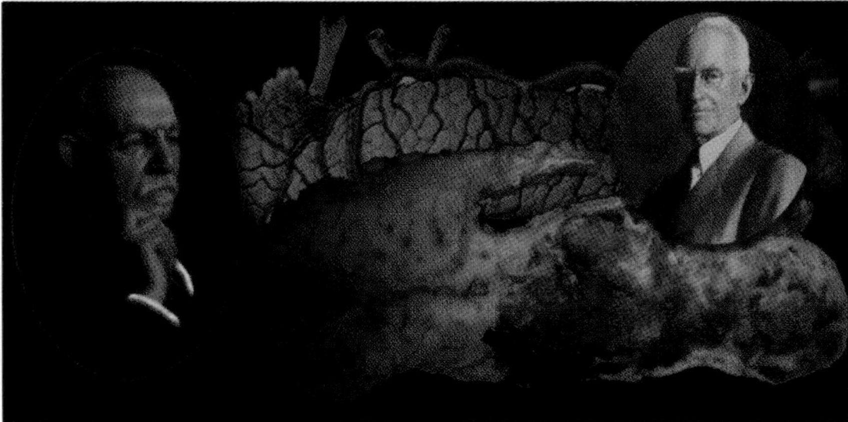

William S. Halsted (left) in 1898 resected the first carcinoma of the "duodenal papilla and diverticulum Vateri" and in so doing demonstrated that pancreatic surgery was a feasible, albeit risky, proposition. Whipple (right) in 1935 undertook radical pancreatic excisional surgery which laid the groundwork for modern pancreatic surgery.

refinements resulted from his astute observations until the advent of Beger. The proposed surgical goal of this limited resection was relief of pain, decrease of the local complications due to the inflammation, as well as avoidance of the dramatic effects of exocrine and endocrine dysfunction that accompanied massive resection. Beger, in fact, questioned that this disease might well represent a separate entity within the broad spectrum of chronic pancreatitis. Dissatisfied with the results of available surgery, Frey proposed a further modification and introduced the combination of local head resection (LRH) of the pancreas, with a lateral pancreatico-jejunostomy. This operation was designed for a specific subset of patients who had both discrete pancreatic head disease and multiple irregular segments of the pancreatic duct, and initially appeared to have some advantage.

Pancreatic Neoplasia

Given the fact that initial descriptions of pancreatic pathology all fell under the generic heading of *scirrhous*, it has been difficult to separate early descriptions of what may have been chronic pancreatitis from patients with cancer. It is probable that Morgagni (1682-1771) was the first to recognize the condition although he noted that Bonet in 1679 had previously described five cases in his text, *Sepulchretum*. In his usual impeccably detailed fashion Morgagni described a variety of autopsy findings that were consistent with a pancreatic neoplasm. These included a patient with jaundice due to obstruction of the common bile duct *"as if a ligature had been made upon it... this contraction seemed to have been bought by a scirrhous and even cancerous tumor of the neighboring pancreas."* Despite the recognition of cancer as an entity in other organs, prior to the eighteenth century, some physicians were of the belief that the pancreas did not develop cancer. This confusion was further amplified by the centuries-old difficulty in differentiating between the sequelae of chronic pancreatitis and cancer of the pancreas itself. Thus, Mondière in the late eighteenth century commented on patients whom he considered to have perished of cancer of the pancreas, but these were not proven. In 1835, Bigsby was able to collect twenty-eight cases of pancreatic cancer from the literature, although once again the validity of the diagnosis had not been established in all. In 1858, J.M. Da Costa of Philadelphia provided the records of thirty-five autopsies of what he claimed to be pancreatic carcinoma, but was only able to provide a microscopic diagnosis of an adenocarcinoma in one. By the end of the nineteenth century, Bard and Pick had distinguished between ductal and acinar cell cancers as well as noting the possibility that the islet cells themselves might be the source of neoplasia. Such pathological distinctions were, however, not of direct clinical relevance given the absence of an understanding of the concept of hormones and the possibility of lesions producing symptoms other than those referable to mass effect.

Jacob M. Da Costa (1833-1900) of Philadelphia was an accomplished pupil of Trousseau. In 1858 he assembled the first American autopsy series of pancreatic carcinoma and in1864 wrote a definitive treatise on diagnosis.

In 1882, Trendelenburg was probably the first to successfully excise a solid tumor of the pancreas, which was subsequently diagnosed as a spindle cell carcinoma. Unfortunately, this patient died shortly after discharge. In 1883, Gussenbauer, a pupil of Billroth, became the first to diagnose a pancreatic cyst preoperatively and treat it successfully by marsupialization, although Bazeman (1882) had in fact resected a pancreatic cyst under the impression that it was ovarian in origin. In 1887, Kapeller described the first cholecystojejunostomy performed as a palliative procedure for cancer of the pancreas in a patient who survived fourteen-and-a-half months. In 1894, Biondi removed a tumor that arose from the head of the pancreas, and although a bilious and pancreatic fistula developed, it healed in twenty-five days and the patient was reported well eighteen months after surgery. In 1893, Menier published an extensive review of pancreatic diseases including solid tumors, cysts, and pancreatitis, and proposed that many of them would be amenable to surgical therapy. Spurred on by such exhortations, Codvilla in 1898 performed a block excision of the major part of the duodenum and the head of the pancreas for carcinoma of the pancreas. The pylorus was closed, the termination of the duodenum invaginated and the transected common duct ligated. A Roux-en-Y

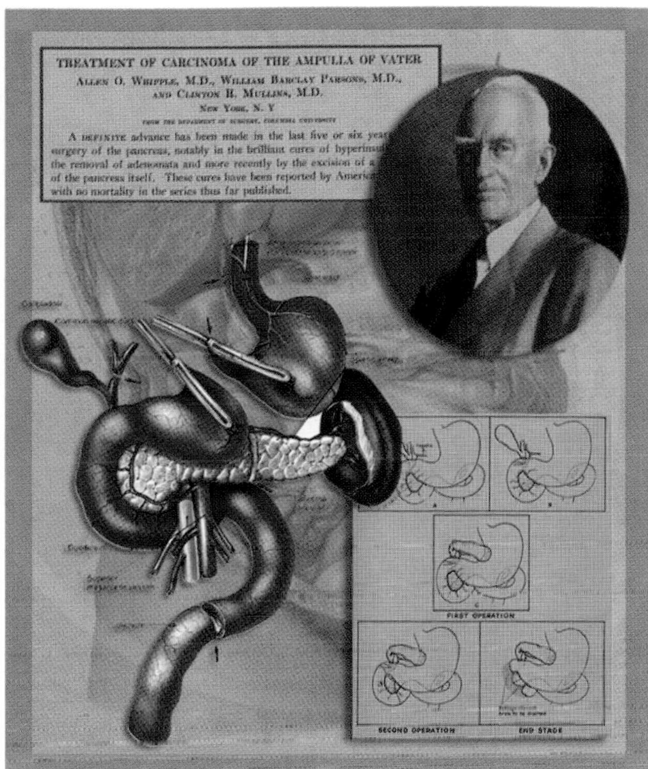

Allen Whipple successfully resected the pancreas and duodenum for adenocarcinoma in 1934 and although the first patient only survived days, the "resection barrier" had been broken and surgeons enthusiastically rallied to extend the new frontier. Improvements in technique and the need to provide palliation for pancreatic disease led to the optimistically unrealistic adoption of this "radical" procedure not only for neoplasia but also the "benign" process of chronic pancreatitis.

gastroenterostomy was performed and a "button" cholecystenterostomy constructed for biliary drainage. Unfortunately, the patient died after twenty-four days and the autopsy revealed disseminated metastases.

The first successful removal of the cancer of the ampulla, with excision of a segment of duodenum and a portion of the pancreas around the ampulla, was undertaken by William S. Halsted in 1898. The pancreatic and common duct were implanted into the repaired line of incision of the duodenum, but stenosis of the common duct developed after three months and the patient died six months later. Autopsy revealed recurrent carcinoma in the head of the pancreas and the duodenum. In the next decade, a number of surgeons including Kehr, Coffey, Sauvé, and Desjardins, proposed a variety of major operations to remove the head of the pancreas and the duodenum. While some of these were performed in one stage and others in two stages, all were associated with considerable mortality and a substantial morbidity.

In 1912, W. Kausch was the first to carry out a successful partial pancreaticoduodenectomy in two stages. He implanted the stump of the resected pancreas at the distal end of the resected duodenum and the patient survived nine months before developing acute cholangitis and dying. In 1914, G. Hirschel performed a one-stage partial pancreaticoduodenectomy for an ampullary carcinoma and connected the common bile duct to the duodenum by means of a rubber tube. Although the jaundice was ameliorated, the patient only survived a year. In 1922, O. Tetoni reported a successful partial pancreaticoduodenectomy undertaken in two stages. In the first, a gastrojejunostomy was undertaken, the common bile duct divided and its end connected to the lower part of the duodenum. One month later, the second stage included resection of the duodenum and included the head of the pancreas beyond the limits of the ampullary tumor. The stump of the pancreatic head was then implanted into the lower end of the transected duodenum and the patient reported as cured. Lester R. Dragstedt of the Laboratory of Physiology provided scientific support for this surgery and to whom the State University of Iowa experimentally demonstrated that dogs could survive total duodenectomy, and the physiological consequences of the operation might therefore be tolerable to humans. In February 1935, A.O. Whipple undertook a two-stage operation for carcinoma of the ampulla, which consisted of a cholecystojejunostomy initially, and thereafter, a total duodenectomy with resection of the head of the pancreas. Other contributions to major pancreatic surgery at this time were provided by Hunt, Illingworth, and Orr, who each described and undertook a variety of modifications of this two-stage procedure with varying degrees of morbidity and mortality.

In 1937, however, Alexander Brunschwig became the first to report a two-stage wide resection of the head of the pancreas, together with practically the entire duodenum, for carcinoma of the head of the pancreas. Although the patient survived the operation, lymph node metastases were evident and death from carcinomatosis occurred two-and-a-half months later. By 1940, Whipple and Nelson had gained further experience, and refined the procedure to the extent that they were able to successfully undertake one-stage pancreaticoduodenectomy. By 1945, Whipple could, based upon his own extensive work, advocate the one-stage procedure as the operation of choice for pancreatic carcinoma. He judged his experience to be substantial and noted that in his initial eight two-stage procedures, the mortality had been 38%, whereas in the subsequent nineteen one-stage procedures, the postoperative mortality was only 31%!

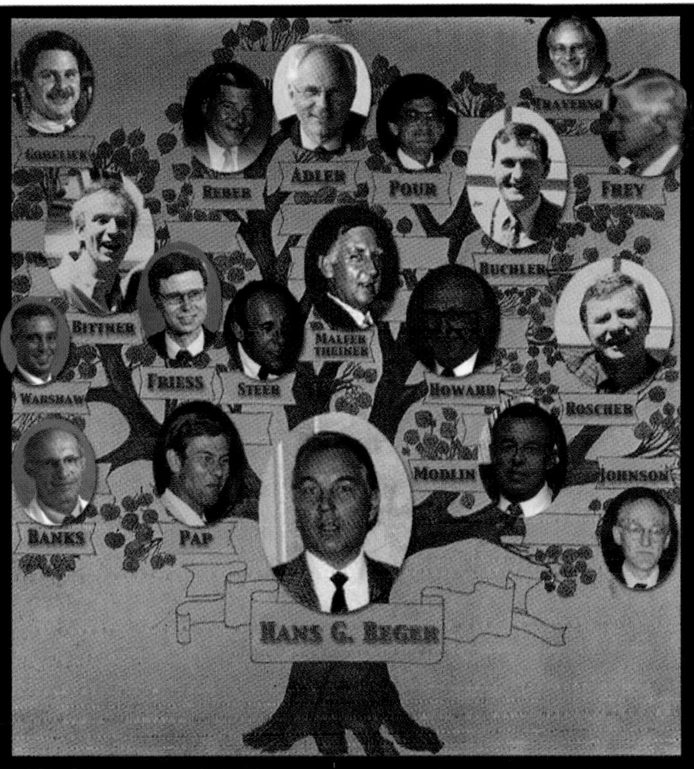

Hans G. Beger of Ulm made significant contributions to the evolution of pancreatic surgery in the late 20th century. In 2001 the pancreatic cognoscenti gathered to record their appreciation of a lifetime dedicated to the application of scientific principles to the elucidation of pancreatic disease.

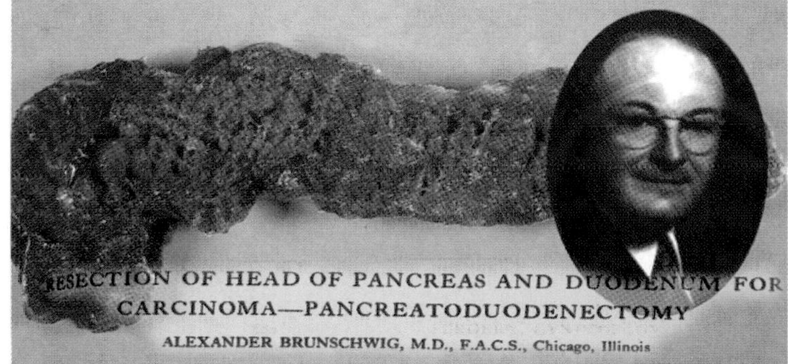

Alexander Brunschwig undertook the first "successful" pancreatico-duodenectomy for carcinoma of the pancreas on January 8, 1937. The patient died on April 30, 1937.

Section 16
gut neuroendocrine system

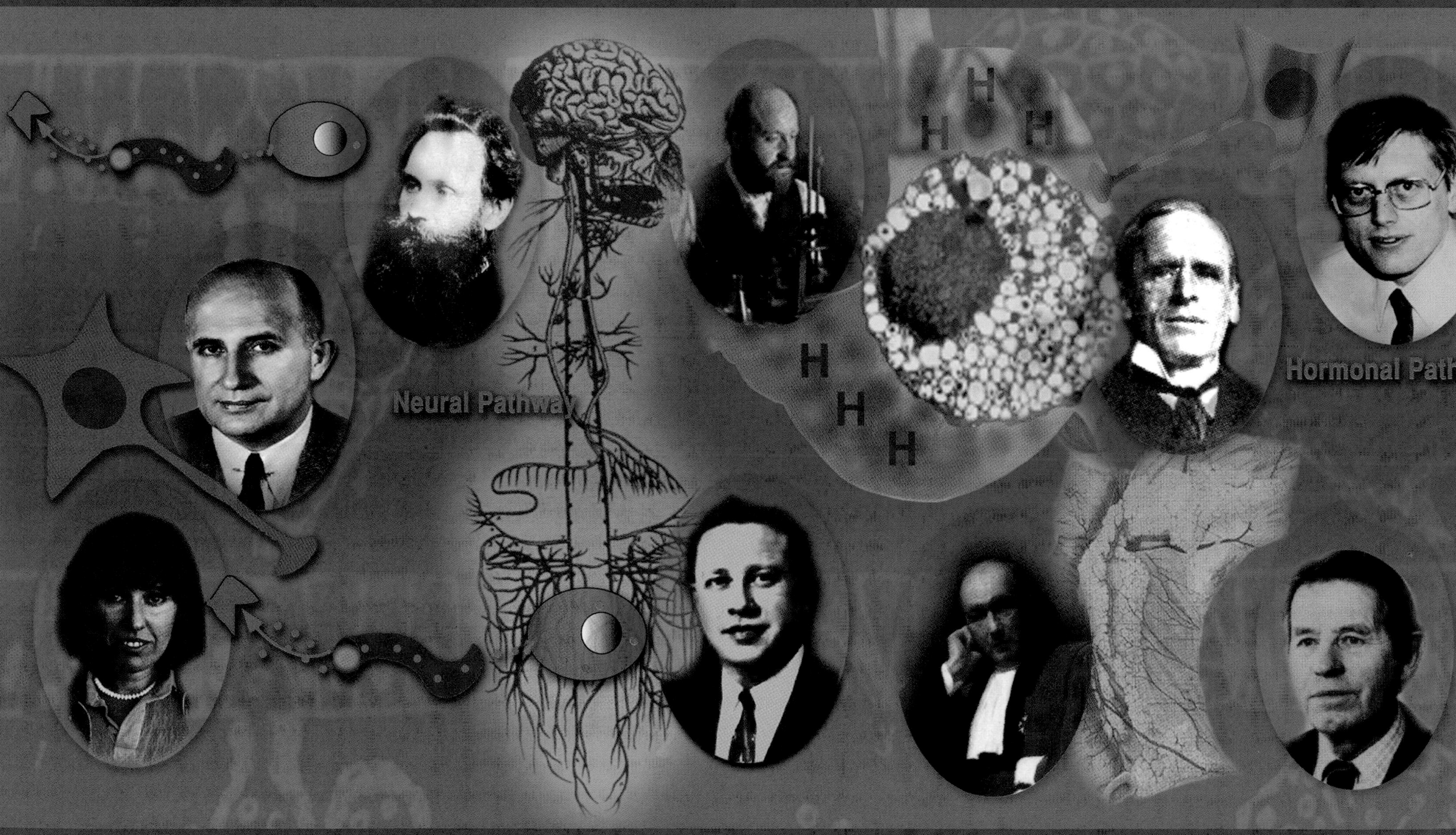

Gut Neuroendocrine System

Gastrointestinal Neuro-endocrinology

The majority of the glands and tissues that form the endocrine system were recognized by the end of the nineteenth century. Although they were initially described and studied individually, like other organs they were later grouped together as the ductless glands and regarded as the source of internal secretions. The gonads were recognized in prehistoric times, with the testes being the most obvious given their location, while the ancient Egyptians later identified the ovaries. Galen described the pituitary in the second century and Andreas Vesalius of Padua, the thyroid in 1543.

By the mid-seventeenth century Thomas Wharton had included the thyroid, suprarenals, and pancreas, amongst the glands of the body in his classic *Adenographia* published in 1656. Nevertheless, the function of the endocrine glands were unknown and the subject of much speculation until 1776, when Albrecht von Haller described the thyroid, thymus, and spleen, as glands without ducts that poured substances into the circulation. Claude Bernard in 1855 demonstrated this effect experimentally by describing sugar, which enters the portal vein as an internal secretion, and bile as an external secretion of the liver. He similarly listed the adrenals, thyroid, lymphatic glands, and spleen, as further sources of internal secretion. Although the effects of castration had been recognized from early days, it was John Hunter of London who in 1786 proposed that an internal secretion from the testes was responsible for the development of secondary sex characteristics.

Similarly, Thomas Addison of Guy's Hospital, London, provided evidence that the absence or destruction of an endocrine gland causes disease, when in 1855 he published his work *"On the constitution and local effects of disease of the supra renal capsules."* Theodore Kocher, professor of Surgery at Bern, confirmed this principle in 1883 when he described the condition of *"cacahexia strumipriva"* that supervened after total extirpation of the thyroid gland in man. In 1890 George Oliver, a general medical practitioner from Harrogate, England, extracted a potent vasoconstrictor from the adrenal medulla together with Edward Schäfer (later Sharpey-Schäfer), professor of Physiology at University College, London. The active principal, epinephrine, or adrenaline, was isolated in 1897 and in 1901 became the first internal secretion chemically identified.

Although the physiological climate of this time was dominated by Ivan Pavlov of St. Petersburg, who believed that the nervous system controlled all bodily activities, the concept of the ductless gland effects were still regarded as important by some. Thus, Bayliss and Starling in a discovery *"breathtaking in its elegant simplicity"* noted that acid in the gut stimulated secretion of the pancreas when both organs were denervated. They concluded that since acid introduced directly into the circulation failed to cause this response, whereas injection of the jejunal mucosa extract did, that the action of acid on the gut was the effect of a chemical reflex and proposed the name "secretin" as the hypothetical chemical messenger involved. This new class of chemical substances was grouped together under the term "hormone" by Starling and the use of the colloquation, endocrine, which had previously been attributed to the islets of Langerhans in 1893 by Eduard Laguesse of France, was utilized to describe this discipline of medicine. As a result, the consideration of nervism as the only regulatory mechanism of the body waned as the science of endocrinology achieved dramatic prominence. Thus, in subsequent years more endocrine tissues and numerous hormones were identified, and their functions and complex interrelationships explored. The Leydig cells of the testes, the Kulchitsky cells of the gut, the islets of Langerhans, the parathyroid glands, and the pituitary, were thus all recognized as endocrine organs over a relatively short period of time. Thyroxin was isolated from the thyroid by Edward Kendall of the Mayo Clinic in 1914, and in 1921 Fredrick Banting, an orthopedic surgeon and physiologist of London, Ontario, extracted insulin from the pancreatic islets. In 1931 Walter Langdon Brown of London, England, described the pituitary as *"the leader in the endocrine orchestra,"* and the endocrine glands were regarded as sharing not only a common mode of action, but to be functionally interdependent. Thus, the endocrine system became regarded as an integrated mechanism for the control of body functions in a fashion that complimented nervism, or the regulation of the nervous system, as proposed by Pavlov. The particular interrelationship between nerves and endocrine cells was of considerable interest in the regulation of gut, motor, and secretory activity. In 1911, Walter Cannon, professor of Physiology at Harvard University, Boston, using adrenaline as

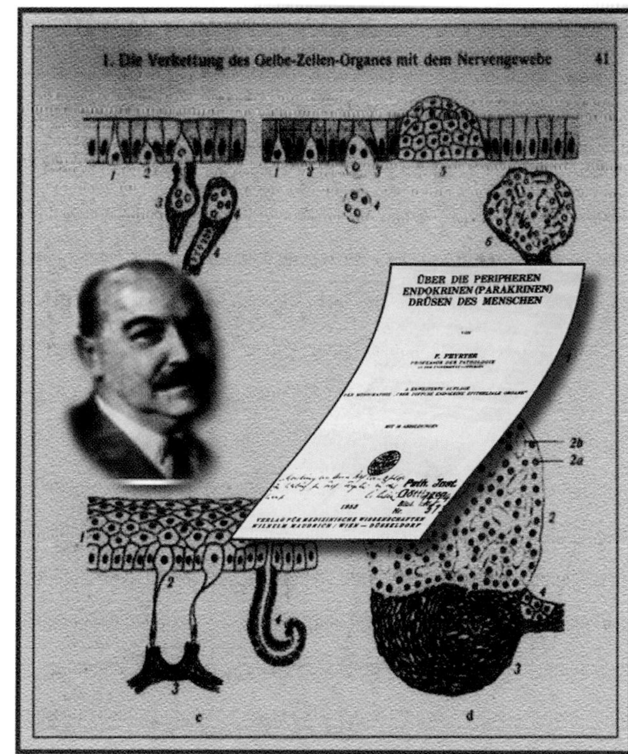

In 1930 F. Feyrter of Gdansk proposed the existence of a diffuse system of neuroendocrine cells in the gastrointestinal tract.

P. Masson (1880-1959) described in detail the characteristics of the cells that formed the basis of the diffuse neuroendocrine system (background).

an example, demonstrated that the adrenal medulla functioned not only as an endocrine gland, but also as part of the autonomic nervous system. In 1921 Otto Loewi, a pharmacologist at Graz, Austria, established the chemical nature of nerve transmission, and in the 1930s the secretory cells in the hypothalamus were demonstrated to exert neuro-hormonal control over the anterior pituitary. Thus, feedback mechanisms were identified and central nervous system regulation became a recognized part of hormonal regulation. As regards the gastrointestinal tract, Pierre Masson, a pathologist in Montreal, had suggested in 1914 that the Kulchitsky cells in the gut formed a diffuse endocrine organ and later in 1928 described them as being of neural origin.

In the early 1930s, the Austrian pathologist, Fredric Feyrter, of Gdansk, Poland, described a system of *helle zellen* (clear cells) which were distributed widely in tissues, but were most prominent in the gastrointestinal tract and the pancreas, and proposed that such cells were the source of hormones that acted locally. This concept, later to be recognized under the terminology paracrine, was subsequently linked to a similar concept that related interaction to nerve cells under the term neuracrine. The conglomeration of these investigations over a period of three decades led to the conclusion that the nervous and endocrine systems were inseparable, and in the gut formed an interwoven syncytium responsible for regulatory function. The summation of these thought processes was consummated and finally extended in the 1960s by Everson Pearse, a histochemist in London, who demonstrated that the cells described by Masson and Feyrter shared important functional characteristics with cells in many of the major endocrine glands, as well as in the hypothalamus. Thus, all were concerned with the metabolism of amines and the production of peptides and were thus conveniently described by the acronym APUD (amine precursor uptake and decarboxylation). While the hypothesis of Pearse failed to completely resolve the cell lineage of the diffuse endocrine system, his work, together with that of Steven Bloom and Julia Polak, confirmed the concept of a single neuroendocrine system which pervaded the tissues of the body and was particularly conspicuous in the gastrointestinal tract.

Pavlov and the Vagus

The modern era of the study of vagal physiology was initiated and dominated by Ivan P. Pavlov (1849-1938) of St. Petersburg. Although he achieved considerable recognition for his investigation of conditioned reflexes, his methods and the results of his observations on vagal function, laid the foundation for the subsequent study of the nervous control of gastrointestinal function. Although B. Brodie of London had, a century earlier, identified some of the general effects of vagal nerve function, it was Pavlov and his students who, over the course of three decades, scientifically delineated the role of the vagus in both pancreatic and gastric physiology.

As a graduate of the Medico-Chirurgical Academy in St. Petersburg, Russia, in the late nineteenth century, the scientific philosophy of Pavlov had been greatly influenced by the work of Lister and Pasteur. Thus, when given the opportunity to create a laboratory for physiologic studies, he established an operating suite for animals that was, in fact, superior at that time to most European facilities used for operations upon humans! Indeed, the care given to the animals in Pavlov's laboratory was exemplary and combined with his own ambidextrous and superb surgical skills, considerably facilitated his experimental studies. Pavlov's theory of "*nervism*" was a momentous postulate for the times in which he lived, and he was fond of explaining it as "*a physiological theory which tries to prove that the nervous system controls the greatest possible number of bodily activities.*" Using this proposal as a basis, Pavlov sought

Ivan Petrovich Pavlov (top right) was the son of a Russian priest and a pupil of both Heidenhain and Ludwig. He became director of the Institute for Experimental Medicine at St. Petersburg in 1890 and in 1904 received the Nobel Prize for his investigations into the neural regulation of gastrointestinal secretion. The success of Pavlov's work was in a large measure due to his remarkable surgical skills. A brilliant thinker as well as an ambidextrous surgeon, his development of a diverse variety of gastric and pancreatic fistulas allowed him to elucidate the neuro-regulatory mechanisms of gastric and pancreatic secretion. Boris Babkin (left) was a pupil of Pavlov and responsible for introducing much of his physiological thought into North America. A brilliant physiologist and a keen linguist, he translated Pavlov's work into English.

to prove the hypothesis that the neural regulation of gastric secretion (nervism) was mediated via the vagus nerves.

Initially, he examined the work of his predecessors and recognized that most of their experiments used cervical separation of the vagi. With this protocol, Pavlov observed that most of the body functions of the animals *"came to a standstill."* In his book, *The Work on the Digestive Glands* (first published in Russian in 1897 and translated into English in 1902), Pavlov analyzed the work of Schiff from 1867. Although the contributions of Schiff have been credited with being *"characterized by great originality of minutiae of experimental procedure,"* Pavlov concluded that Schiff *"made no detailed comparison of the secretory activity of the stomach before and after vagotomy."* The first studies performed in his newly created modern operating rooms generated canine surgical models with diverted cervical esophagi to evaluate the cephalic phase of gastric function. Oral feeding was undertaken, while gastric output was measured and up to 700 milliliters of the *"purest gastric juice"* was secreted by the stomachs after this sham feeding. After subdiaphragmatic vagotomy sham-feeding induced gastric secretion of gastric juice was dramatically reduced. *"It is obvious,"* Pavlov concluded, *"that the effect of feeding was transmitted by nervous channels to the gastric glands."* Electrical excitation of the vagi of the dogs, and the observation of increased gastric secretion, provided final confirmation of this observation.

Bayliss, Starling, and Secretin

While the central regulation of gastric digestive activity was initially delineated by Pavlov, the discovery by W.M. Bayliss (1860-1924) and E.H. Starling (1866-1926) in 1902 of the hormone secretin, and the establishment of the concept of "chemical messengers", ushered in a new era of gastrointestinal physiology. Indeed, the description of the stimulatory effect of secretin on pancreatic secretion would not only establish the hormonal basis for the regulation of gastric secretion, but also directly inaugurate the field of endocrinology. The work on the movement and innervation of the intestine and on the nature of the peristaltic wave (1898-1899) led Bayliss and Starling on to what was probably their most fecund investigation, the concept of the existence of "chemical messengers". In actuality the story of secretin, however, had begun as early as 1825, when F. Leuret and J.-L. Lassaigne wrote that they had: *"opened the abdomen of a living dog: incised the first part of the small intestine along its length; applied vinegar diluted with water to the villi. Instantly a serous liquid was produced in abundance... At the same time the openings of the biliary and pancreatic ducts were dilated, and bile and pancreatic juice flowed for several minutes... If an acid stimulates duodenal secretions and dilates the ducts of the liver and pancreas, chyme ought to do the same thing, for it is always acid."*

Although Leuret and Lassaigne are more often remembered for their ill-fated studies demonstrating that gastric acid was lactic in spite of W. Prout (1823) and L. Tiedemann and L. Gmelin's proof that it was hydrochloric, the relevance of this seminal observation was, for the most part, ignored.

Seventy years later in 1895, I.L. Dolinski, a student of I. Pavlov in St. Petersburg, rediscovered the fact that acid in the duodenum stimulates pancreatic secretion. Dolinski, as an acolyte of the "master of nervism", believed that the nervous apparatus of the pancreatic gland was responsive to specific irritants, including acid and fat, and had postulated that such a neural reflex could be proven. This proposal reflected the firmly held belief of the time that all glandular secretion was nerve-operated, and was for the most part based on the work of C. Ludwig, who had initially demonstrated this phenomenon in salivary glands in 1851. Pavlov had inherited, and thereafter expanded, the

Ernest Starling (top left) and William Bayliss (bottom center) were not only brothers-in-law but critical exponents of novel physiologic theories relating to the heart, intestine, and pancreas. In particular, their elucidation of the hormonal regulation of pancreatic secretion provided the foundation for the development of an entirely new discipline of clinical medicine and physiology, namely endocrinology. Sir Charles Martin (right) was a witness to their initial seminal experiments.

ARCHIV FÜR DIE GESAMMTE PHYSIOLOGIE DES MENSCHEN UND DER THIERE. ACHTER BAND. BONN, 1874.

E. Pfluger was the editor of his own journal (Archiv der Physiologie), which provided him a forum to air his sometimes controversial views on medical and surgical subjects. He criticized the conclusion of Starling that a chemical regulator existed, claiming that the pancreas had not been denervated.

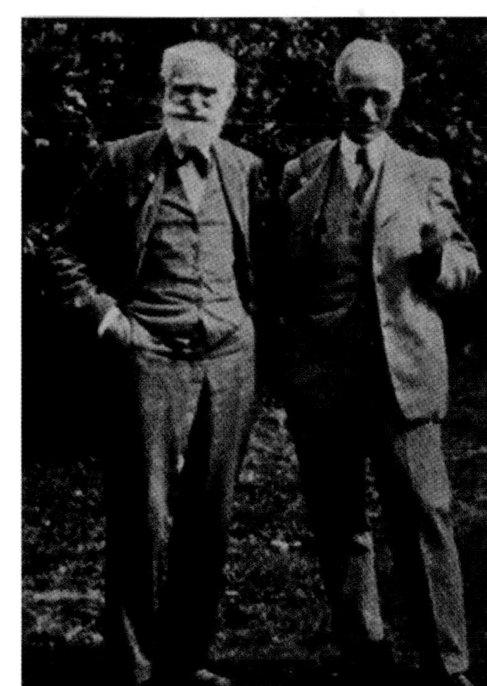

Pavlov and Cushing, 1929. Harvey Cushing had defined neurosurgery as a unique discipline following an "arbeit" with Kocher in Berne in 1901. Pavlov's interest in surgery prompted Cushing to let him use the surgical cautery device recently devised by Bovie. He signed his name on the piece of steak which is still preserved in the Cushing Surgical Collection at Yale.

Bayliss (right) demonstrating an experiment on a dog at University College to Henry Hallett Dale and E.H. Starling (both far left). Considerable controversy fueled by the anti-vivisectionist movement arose surrounding the experimental work of Bayliss and Starling. In a court case for libel, Bayliss was adjudged the victor and donated the settlement to the physiology research fund.

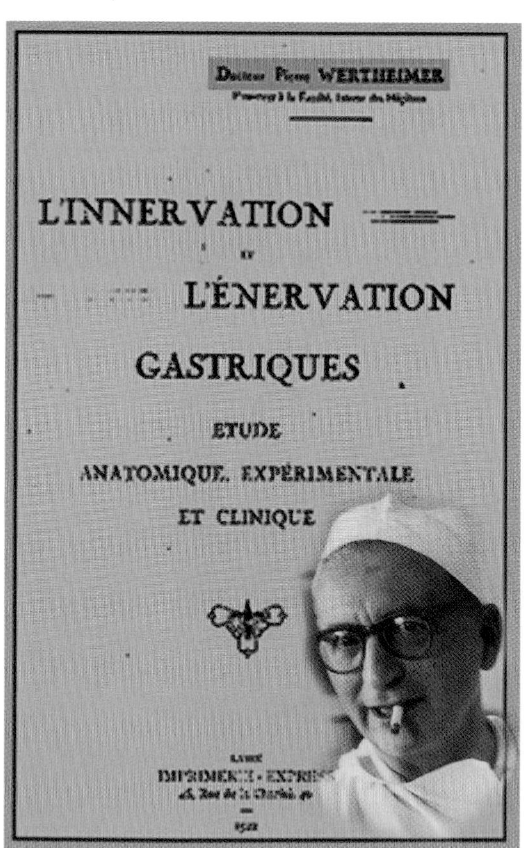

Docteur Pierre WERTHEIMER

L'INNERVATION

et

L'ÉNERVATION

GASTRIQUES

ETUDE

ANATOMIQUE, EXPÉRIMENTALE

ET CLINIQUE

Pierre Wertheimer in 1921 had written a thesis describing the innovation of the stomach. He believed implicitly that the secretory process was regulated by a neural mechanism.

doctrine of "nervism" – the belief that all physiological responses are mediated by the nervous system. Since the pancreas was regarded by physiologists of the time as the equivalent of an abdominal salivary gland, Pavlov proposed that the pancreatic response to acid in the duodenum was regulated by a local neural reflex. Given this background to the issue of the regulation of pancreatic secretion, L. Popielski in Pavlov's laboratory was given the task of elucidating the nervous connections between the mucosa of the upper small intestine and the pancreas that had previously been postulated by Dolinski. In all these experimental scenarios, Popielski noted that the pancreas secreted when he infused hydrochloric acid or acetic acid in the duodenum. Applying the dogma of "nervism," he therefore concluded that if the central and autonomic nervous systems are unnecessary for reflex regulation of pancreatic secretion, that control must be the function of local nerves connecting the intestine and pancreas. These nerves, he thought, were processes of the 25 to 30 nerve cells he found in several ganglia contained within the pancreas. Unfortunately, the exposure to the bias of Pavlov's beliefs led Popielski to an erroneous conclusion that a peripheral reflex through these nerves. Indeed, the exhaustive experiments described, quite clearly indicate the need to have considered the presence of a chemical reflex.

The next stage of the saga of the identification of a "secretin" took place in Lille, France, in 1901, where P. Wertheimer had developed an interest in the role of nerves in both physiological and pathological processes. Indeed, his subsequent work with A.R. Latarjet would explore the effects of innervation and denervation on numerous gastrointestinal and gynecological organs, and finally lead to the development of vagotomy for the treatment of acid peptic disease. Wertheimer conducted a series of experiments to further investigate Popielski's thesis. He found that despite cutting the junction of the pylorus and duodenum, ablating the celiac and mesenteric plexuses, sectioning the vagi as well as the thoracic sympathetic chains, and destroying the spinal cord in a curarized dog, he could not abolish the pancreatic secretory response to acid in the duodenum. Wertheimer, accepting only neural regulation as an explanation for these phenomena, concluded that the response to acid in the jejunum was mediated by the abdominal sympathetic ganglia – a reflex operating in nerves directly connecting the duodenum with a center in the pancreas itself.

Since Bayliss had been interested in secretion since 1890, he engaged Starling in studying the mechanisms by which acid introduced into the upper intestine was followed by secretion of pancreatic juice. As the first step in evaluating the question, they therefore decided to repeat the work of Wertheimer. Thus, on January 16, 1902, they performed their crucial experiment witnessed by Starling's friend, Charles Martin. A loop of jejunum was tied off and carefully denervated in order that its only connection with the rest of the body remained the mesenteric vessels. Dilute HCl introduced into the loop of jejunum resulted in a steady flow of pancreatic juice, just as it had previously done in the control experiment when introduced into the intact duodenum. The mucosa was then scraped from some jejunum, ground with 0.4% HCl, filtered and injected intravenously, and within minutes a free flow of pancreatic juice ensued. In the same set of experiments, they then demonstrated that the active substance was not destroyed by boiling, and that it was absent from the lower ileum. This further supported the observation that the introduction of acid to this area of the bowel did not to lead to any secretion of pancreatic juice. As Martin afterwards wrote:

> *"I happened to be present at their discovery. In an anesthetized dog, a loop of jejunum was tied at both ends and the nerves supplying it dissected out and divided so that it was connected with the rest of the body only by its blood vessels. On the introduction of some weak HCl into the duodenum, secretion from the pancreas occurred and continued for some minutes. After this had subsided a few cubic centimeters of acid were introduced into the enervated loop of jejunum. To our surprise a similarly marked secretion was produced. I remember Starling saying: "Then it must be a chemical reflex." Rapidly cutting off a further piece of jejunum he rubbed its mucous membrane with sand in weak HCl, filtered and injected it into the jugular vein of the animal. After a few moments the pancreas responded by a much greater secretion than had occurred before. It was a great afternoon."*

Six days after their first experiment, Bayliss and Starling read a paper before the Royal Society describing their work. They published the same story in the March 22, 1902 issue of the *Lancet* and a longer summary in German in the February 1, 1902 issue of *Centralblatt fur Physiologie*. This paper provoked Wertheimer to perform the experiment of irritating the jejunal mucosa with mustard oil and thereafter re-injecting the collected venous blood. On two occasions, this stimulated pancreatic secretion and as a consequence Wertheimer unwillingly edged towards accepting a hormonal hypothesis. E. Pfluger (1829-1910) who edited his own *Archives* (*Pfluger's Archives*) was, however, still unconvinced. In a more critical analysis, he suggested that the denervation performed by Bayliss and Starling had not been complete, and that the effect was non-specific, since it was well recognized that the extracts of many tissues stimulated glands to secrete.

Bayliss and Starling completed their work in March 1902 and when their complete paper was published in the September issue of the *Journal of Physiology*, they apologized for the long delay, citing the need to completely validate their novel proposal. The interval, however, also provided the opportunity to cite Wertheimer and Pfluger and in so doing, to rebut their criticisms. In a masterful riposte, they agreed that denervation had probably not been complete, and intimated: *"that it does not matter whether the nerves were all cut or not; the only fact of importance is that it was the belief that all nerves were cut that caused us to try the experiment of making an acid extract of the mucous membrane that led to the discovery of secretin."*

Pavlov, after some inner turmoil, accepted the evidence presented in support of the existence of the chemical control of pancreatic secretion. His compatriot, B. Babkin (1877-1950), summarized the conflict thus: *"Pavlov radically changed his opinion about the new fact discovered by the English physiologists probably in the fall or winter of 1902-03 after reading Bayliss and Starling's complete and excellent paper on secretin in the* Journal of Physiology *(1902)... I think it was in the fall of 1902 that Pavlov asked V.V. Savich to repeat the secretin experiments of Bayliss and Starling. The effect was self-evident. Then, without a word, Pavlov disappeared into his study. He returned half-an-hour later and said: "Of course, they are right. It is clear that we did not take out an exclusive patent for the discovery of truth."*

"We are dealing here with a problem which, betraying, as it does, an intimate relationship between nerve excitation and excitation by chemical messengers, promises by its solution to throw a most interesting light on the nature of the nerve process and of excitatory processes in general."

In the same lecture, he also considered the possible role of sex hormones, the anti-diabetic hormone of the pancreas, and a probable gastric hormone (gastrin), which had recently been proposed by J. Edkins (1863-1940). The discovery of histamine by H.H. Dale (1875-1968) in 1910, as well as the demonstration that extracts from other tissues had a similar physiological effect to gastrin, led many to seriously question the validity of Edkins' observation. As a result, gastrin, although originally acknowledged and accepted, subsequently fell into disfavor, and a further half-century was required before Simon Komarov (1892-1964) produced incontrovertible proof of its existence.

Sir Henry Hallett Dale was a rigorous scientist and received the Nobel Prize for his investigation of acetylcholine. He was of the erroneous opinion that the studies undertaken to demonstrate the presence of gastrin were flawed and that the acid secretory activity reported by Edkins represented contamination of the extract with histamine.

Having effectively rebuffed the critique of their European counterparts, Bayliss and Starling demonstrated remarkable alacrity at not only following up their discovery, but also expanding the applications. Such was the impact, that Bayliss was elected to the Royal Society in 1903. In 1904, they gave a joint Croonian lecture to the Royal Society and also published in German one account of the chemical co-ordination of bodily functions. It was Starling, however, who was most effective in placing the work in the broader scientific domain and expanding upon its possible extrapolation. In 1905, at the suggestion of William B. Hardy, he used the general name of *"hormone"* from the Greek "to excite" to describe the chemical messengers as a class of agents. In his Croonian address to the Royal College of Physicians, he took the opportunity to outline his concepts of what the general outlines of endocrinology might become. As examples, he utilized the then recent studies of adrenaline by J.N. Langley (1852-1925) in 1901, and by H.K. Elliot (1877-?) in 1904. Starling also adumbrated upon his considerations of the theory of humoral transmission in the following words:

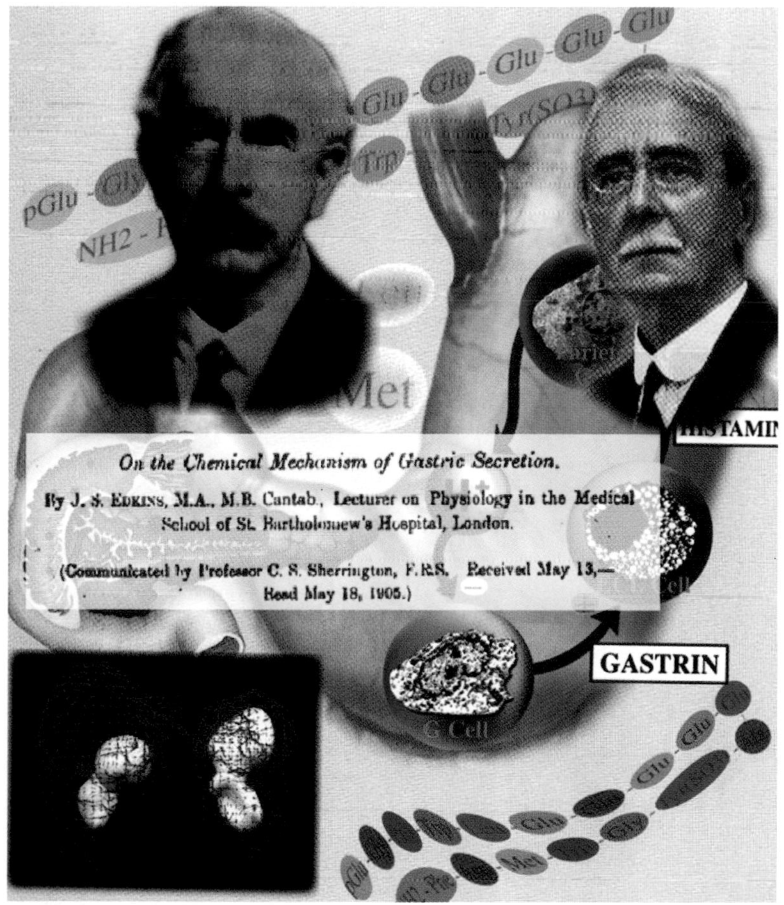

Glu-Glu-Glu-Glu-Glu
pGlu
NH2
Met
On the Chemical Mechanism of Gastric Secretion.
By J. S. Edkins, M.A., M.B. Cantab., Lecturer on Physiology in the Medical School of St. Bartholomew's Hospital, London.
(Communicated by Professor C. S. Sherrington, F.R.S. Received May 13,—Read May 18, 1905.)
GASTRIN
G Cell

J.S. Edkins (top left) and the frontispiece of his epic communication of 1905 documenting the existence of a novel antral stimulant of acid secretion-gastrin which was sponsored by C.S. Sherrington of Liverpool (right). Apart from his fundamental observations in regard to gastrin, Edkins worked with Langley on the study of pepsin, defined the effects of phosgene on lung function and developed a chemical technique for destroying weevils without damaging flour. He was a fine oarsman, a superb croquet player, and president of the British Croquet Association from 1935 to 1937. As the Chairman of Physiology at Bedford College for Women from 1914 and 1930, Edkins was responsible for training the majority of women physiologists in England.

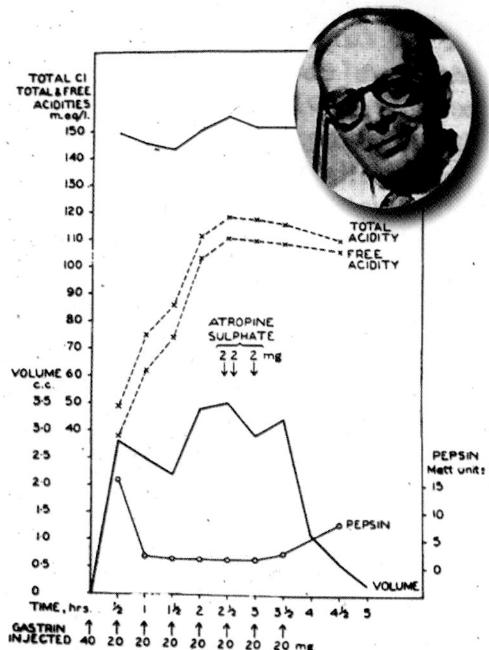

The graph from the original publication (1942) of S.A. Komarov (inset) in Rev. Can. Biol. *The demonstration of the acid response of anesthetized cat to an intravenous injection of histamine free antral mucosal extract and the effect of atropine on the response confirmed the existence of "gastrin" and vindicated Edkins.*

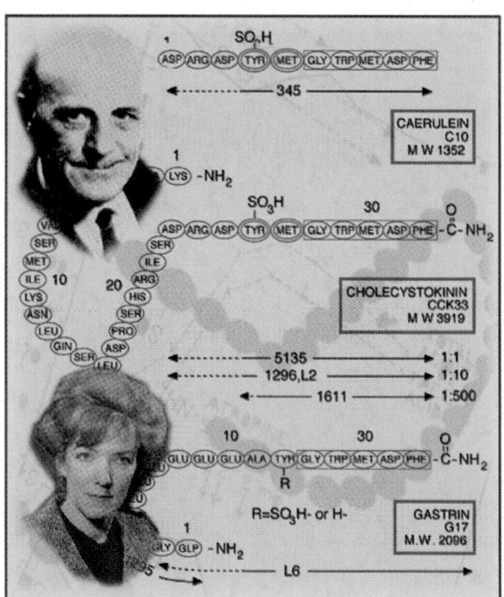

Rod Gregory of Liverpool was responsible with Hilda Tracy for the elucidation of the structure of gastrin in 1962.

John Edkins and Gastrin

The observations of Bayliss and Starling stimulated John Sidney Edkins, a physiologist working with Sherrington, to evaluate the control of gastric secretion. Even prior to the presentation of the data regarding secretin, Edkins had harbored the idea that absorbed peptones might liberate a chemical messenger, but had lacked the support to pursue the matter. His deliberations in this area led him to conclude that since there was now evidence for an agonist for pancreatic secretion, there might well be a "*gastric secretin*". He thus proposed that there might be in the gastric mucosa, a pre-formed substance that is absorbed into the portal stream and returned to the circulation to stimulate the fundic oxyntic glands was a critical hypothesis. On May 18, 1905, he obtained sufficient evidence to make a preliminary communication to the Royal Society on this matter. In a modest paper titled "On the Chemical Mechanisms of Gastric Secretion", he described how various extracts of antral mucosa potently stimulated gastric secretion in anesthetized cats.

It was unfortunate for Edkins that a large number of distinguished investigators, including H.H. Dale, provided substantial and "*apparently incontrovertible*" evidence in support of the theory that the active principal in his antral extract was histamine. More than a quarter of a century was to elapse before Simon Komarov, a Russian émigré in Canada, in 1938 recognized the sad trick that nature had played on Edkins. In antral mucosa, there is both histamine and a protein-like substance with a bioactivity that mimics the action of histamine on gastric acid secretion. Komarov, a meticulous chemist, undertook the task of demonstrating the existence of gastrin. After numerous tedious repetitions of precipitation, extraction, salting out, and further extraction, a powder that was a protein in nature was obtained. Komarov said it was free of choline and "organic crystalloids", but could say nothing further about its chemical nature. Since the product did not lower the blood pressure of anesthetized cats when injected intravenously, he reasoned that it therefore did not contain histamine and he believed that he was justified in calling it gastrin.

> *"In all cases without exception the pyloric preparation, injected in quantities equal to 5 gm of mucosa, elicited a copious secretion of gastric juice, which was characterized by high acidity and low peptic power and which was not affected by atropine even in large doses."*

Rod Gregory and his assistant Hilda Tracy of Liverpool were the first to devise a method of extracting gastrin using trichloro-acetic acid in acetone. Early in his career, Gregory had worked at the Mayo Clinic and, having mastered German, read all the early physiology texts in the original. Despite the fact that he was a British citizen working in Liverpool, he was on good terms with his American counterparts and thus received a substantial grant from the US Public Health Service. This support enabled him on his return to the United Kingdom to purchase numerous items of capital equipment necessary to fully undertake the isolation and characterization of gastrin. In addition, he and Tracy signed a contract with a Liverpool firm that made pork pies and as a result, were able to acquire, for extraction purposes, up to six hundred hog antrums weekly for six months. Despite this huge load of material, the system worked well enough that by the end of eighteen months they had accumulated hundreds of milligrams of pure gastrin.

In collaboration with George W. Kenner, a Manchester and Cambridge-trained peptide chemist, who was then the head of the Department of Organic Chemistry at Liverpool, they set out to identify the structure of gastrin. On Christmas Day 1962, Gregory and Tracy noted that they had identified not one, but two gastrins, that they imaginatively proceeded to name Gastrin I and Gastrin II. Of interest was the observation that the tyrosine on Gastrin II was sulfated. Gregory subsequently presented this work on April 26, 1962, at a meeting in New York at which Simon Komarov was chairman.

It now remained to fully determine the precise clinical and biological relevance of gastrin. In 1958, Solomon Berson and Rosalyn Yalow had published a manuscript documenting the use of radio immunoassay (RIA) to measure plasma insulin. Using this principle, James McGuigan in 1967 developed a similar strategy to devise an RIA for gastrin by developing a double antibody technique, and was able to measure gastrin in human serum.

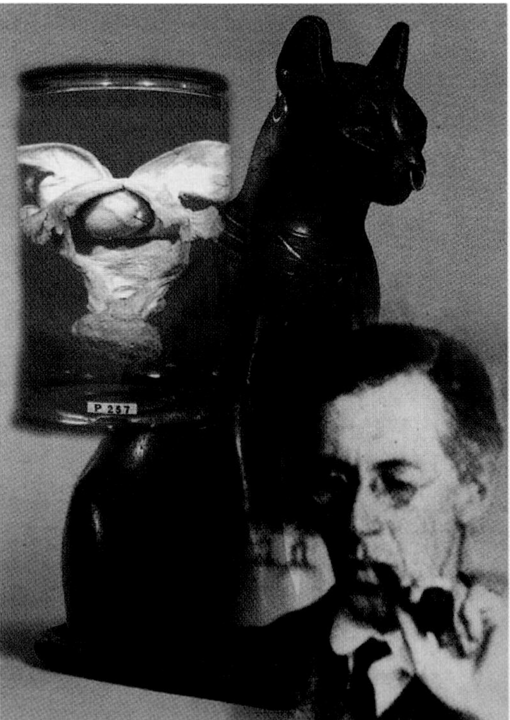

Henry Hallett Dale (right) in 1911 identified the effects of ergot [histamine] in cat uteri.

Histamine and Henry Hallet Dale

In 1911, H.H. Dale, while working with the chemist George Barger, applied Kutscher's silver method to a specimen of ergot dialysatum and *"isolated a few centigrams of the picrate of an intensively active base, which produced a characteristic action on the cat's non-pregnant uterus in a minute dose."* Barger and Dale identified the base as beta-imidazolylethylamine, and compared it with an authentic sample that had been obtained by the putrefaction of histidine. Many years later in his life, commenting on the early days of histamine research, Dale wrote:

> *"Beta-1 as we called it, is, of course, the now almost too familiar histamine; and this was always the obvious name for it. Somebody, however, had objected to its use, as infringing his trademark rights in a name to which its resemblance was, in fact, only distant. Later somebody called it histamine and then the road was clear."*

In fact, the supplement of the *Oxford English Dictionary* attributes the first use of the term *"histamine"* to the Journal of Chemistry, c.iv, 1913.

Dale worked extensively in the area of the pharmacological and physiological actions of histamine between 1910 and 1927, but despite an exhaustive evaluation of its properties, failed to detect its role in promoting acid secretion by the glands of the stomach. This unique property of stimulating acid secretion was to be discovered by Leon Popielski, a student of Pavlov. After leaving Pavlov's laboratory in 1901, Popielski had been placed in charge of the military bacteriological laboratory in Moscow, where his initial work was on the mechanism by which intravenous injection of Witte's peptone (a peptic digest of fibrin) caused a fall of blood pressure. This research continued after he had become the Professor of Pharmacology at the University of Lemberg, and Popielski believed that he had identified a substance, *"vasodilantine"*, as a component of Witte's peptone distinct, from histamine or choline. On October 28, 1916, in the course of experiments on the effect of the injection of an extract of the pituitary gland upon gastric secretion, Popielski injected 32 mg of beta-imidazolylethylamine hydrochloride sub-cutaneously into a dog with a gastric fistula. Over the next 5.75 hours, the dog secreted 937.5 ml of gastric juice, having a maximum acidity of 0.166 N. Because similarly stimulated secretion was unaffected by section of the vagus or by atropine, Popielski concluded that beta-imidazolylethylamine acted directly on the gastric glands to stimulate acid secretion. Unfortunately, the First World War delayed the publication of Popielski's paper describing these results until 1920.

The key protagonist in the elucidation of the role of histamine and its clinical relevance in gastric secretion would be Charlie Code. Code had grown up in Winnipeg and received a M.D. degree from the University of Manitoba in 1933 before joining Frank Mann at the Mayo Clinic. Thereafter he obtained support to study in London, where he first worked with Charles Lovatt Evans at the University College of London and later, with Sir Henry Dale at the National Institutes for Medical Research. There, Code demonstrated that 70%-100% of histamine in unclotted blood is in the white cell layer and that clotting liberates 60%-90% of this into the serum. He further determined that granular lymphocytes contained most of the histamine in the buffy coat, and that the white cells leaving the marrow carry histamine with them. Although Code, on his return to the Mayo Clinic in 1937, continued to work with Frank Mann as his first assistant at the operating room table, he remained fascinated by the effect of histamine and its bioactivity.

Since its rapid disappearance from the blood made it difficult to study, he developed a technique of suspending histamine in beeswax that could be injected subcutaneously. The biological test for the effectiveness of histamine liberation was to measure the gastric acid secretion of the animal, and in order to facilitate this a number of "pouch models" were constructed.

It soon became apparent to the group that with increasing doses of histamine and increasing acid secretion, duodenal ulcers could be initiated not only in dogs but in a number of other animal species, including chickens, woodchucks, calves, monkeys, and rabbits. Code concluded that the experiments incriminated gastric juice as the factor in the production of peptic ulcer, and noted the relationship of histamine to this event. A series of meticulous studies conducted over many years led to his determination of the critical role of histamine in the stimulation of parietal cell acid secretion. In addition, Code proposed the existence of an intermediate cell that he called

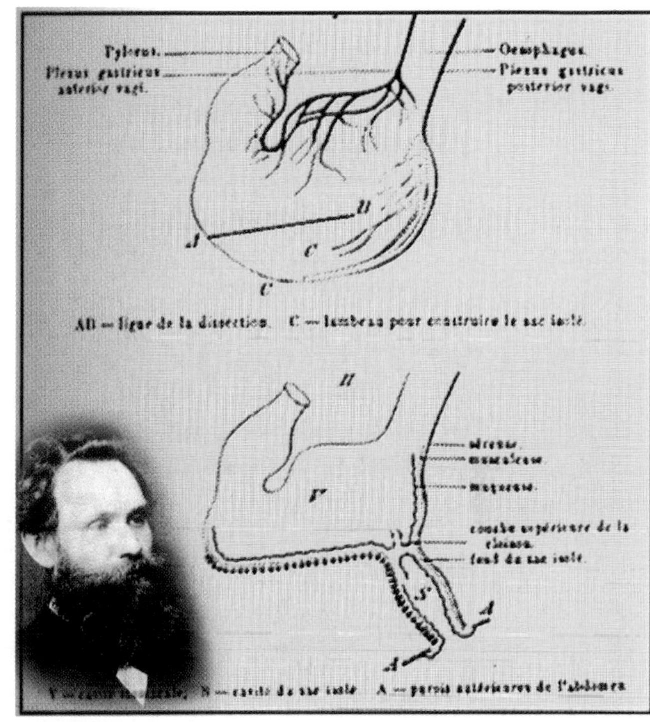

The creation of a variety of gastric fistulas enabled Ivan Pavlov to study gastric acid secretion and neural reflexes. By virtue of meticulous canine surgery (he was totally ambidextrous) and experimentation Pavlov was able to propound the theory of neural regulation which he termed "nervism".

J. PHYSIOL LXX, 1930

THE INACTIVATION OF HISTAMINE.

BY C. H. BEST AND E. W. McHENRY

(From the Department of Physiological Hygiene, University of Toronto.)

THE transient effects produced [illegible] [in]travenous or subcutaneous injection of small or moderate [illegible] [hista]mine suggest that the body may possess an efficient [illegible] [eliminatio]n or inactivation of this substance. When histami[ne] [illegible] intravenously, relatively large amounts can be adm[illegible] appearance of the characteristic signs which the [illegible] [o]f small quantities to the same animal produce. It [illegible] [tha]t very little histamine is found in the urine even aft[er] [illegible] injection of large doses of the substance [Oehme, 191[illegible]] [illegible] [possibili]ty that the amine may be eliminated by passage from th[e] [illegible] [in]to the intestine has not been investigated.

Charles Best, having participated in the discovery of insulin (1922) subsequently investigated the physiology of histamine.

Beiträge
zur mikroskopischen Anatomie der Bauchspeicheldrüse.

INAUGURAL-DISSERTATION,
zur
ERLANGUNG DER DOCTORWÜRDE
in der
MEDICIN UND CHIRURGIE
vorgelegt der
MEDICINISCHEN FACULTÄT
DER FRIEDRICH-WILHELMS-UNIVERSITÄT
ZU BERLIN
und öffentlich zu vertheidigen
am 18. Februar 1869
von
Paul Langerhans
aus Berlin.

OPPONENTEN:
G. Loeillot de Mars, Dd. med.
O. Soltmann, Dd. med.
Paul Ruge, Stud. med.

BERLIN.
Buchdruckerei von Gustav Lange.

In his medical student doctoral thesis (1869), Paul Langerhans of Berlin described microscopic structures in the pancreas, which he termed "Zellhauschen" (little heaps of cells). Despite the seminal nature of this observation he attributed no function to these cells and it remained for E. Laguesse (in 1893) to propose their relationship to diabetes and generously name them after Langerhans.

a "histaminocyte" responsible for the regulation of gastric histamine secretion. Indeed, the validity of his observations were borne out by the subsequent identification of the histamine subtype 2 receptor on the parietal cell and the profound inhibitory effects of the histamine subtype 2 class of antagonists in generating acid suppression.

The Pancreatic Islets

In 1869, Paul Langerhans, while a medical student, published his inaugural thesis "*Contributions to the Microscopic Anatomy of the Pancreas*", and utilizing staining and transillumination became the first to note the differences between the exocrine and endocrine pancreas. In 1882, Kuhne and Lea noted the complex capillary network which embraced the collection of islets, and in considering the physiological implications, failed to divine the relationship to glucose homeostasis. Laguesse eponymously attributed the islet structures that Langerhans had identified to him in 1893. In 1902, the latter further amplified the histological characteristics of these micro-organs by studying the atrophied pancreas after duct ligation and proposed a putative relationship with diabetes.

The regulation of pancreatic secretion was a vexatious question, which Ivan Petrovich Pavlov (1849-1936) and his pupils addressed with vigor at the turn of the nineteenth century. His pupil, Dolinski, noted that acid introduced into the duodenum stimulated pancreatic secretion, and interpreted this as indicative of a local neural reflex. In 1902, Bayliss and Starling of University College, London, demonstrated that this phenomenon was in fact not a neural reflex, but the effect of a chemical messenger or regulator.

The subsequent integration of the neural and hormonal mechanisms provided by the two schools of physiological thought regarding the modulation of gastrointestinal function proved to be a major contribution to twentieth-century gastroenterology. Further work on pancreatic juice itself was produced by yet another of Pavlov's pupils, Chepovalnikov, who demonstrated that pancreatic juice acquired and exerted a powerful solvent action on proteids only after contact with either the duodenal membrane or extracts thereof. This observation enabled him to deduce that the duodenum produced a unique enzyme (enterokinase), responsible for the activation of pancreatic juice.

Diabetes

Although the relationship between the pancreas and diabetes is seemingly self-evident at this time, it was only in 1889 that Joseph von Mering and Oscar Minkowski noted that extirpation of the pancreas of a dog resulted in diabetes. This observation had escaped Brunner, who almost two centuries previously had resected the canine pancreas and, despite noting the onset of polydypsia in the surviving animals, had failed to relate it to diabetes. A vignette of interest in the Mering-Minkowski experiments was the seminal observation of an astute laboratory attendant, who noted that the urine of the pancreatectomized dogs attracted flies, whereas the urine of the non-pancreatectomized animals exhibited no such muscophilic effect. Although Langerhans had initially described the islets of the pancreas in 1869, it remained for M.E. Laguesse to suggest that they were related to the genesis of diabetes. This proposal was supported by Eugene Opie, who described hyaline changes in islets of diabetic patients, and Sobelow and Schulze. The latter investigators demonstrated that although ligation of the pancreatic duct atrophied the exocrine component of the pancreas, the islets remained unchanged and diabetes did not supervene. Similar observations were subsequently made by both W.G. MacCullen of Johns Hopkins and Moses Baron of Minnesota. The latter succinctly noted that in instances of pancreatic disease without islet involvement, no diabetes was evident.

In 1922, Frederick Banting, working with Charles H. Best at the University of Toronto, Canada, responded to Baron's observations on the relationship

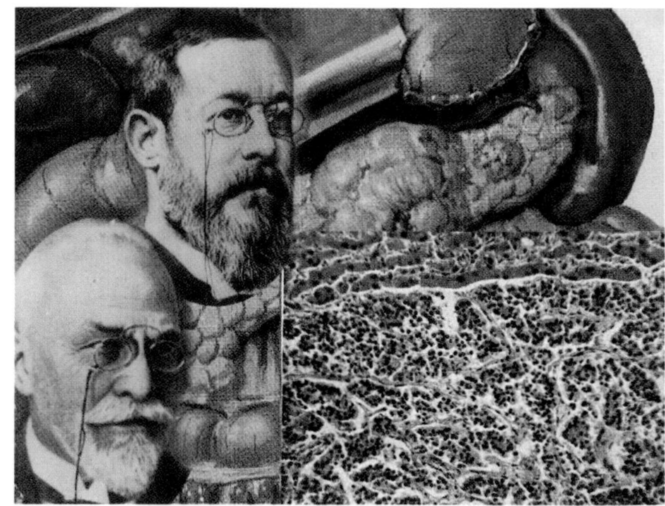

Von Mering (right) and Oscar Minkowski in 1889 noted that extirpation of the pancreas of a dog resulted in diabetes. This dramatic observation resulted from the astute observation of a laboratory attendant who noted that the urine of the pancreatectomized dog attracted flies!

between islet cell damage and diabetes. Their relatively simple two-phase experiment provided information that earned Banting a Nobel Prize and forever altered the management of diabetes. Having initially ligated the pancreatic duct of a dog, they waited ten weeks before sacrificing it, and producing a crude preparation of "*islets and isletin*" in Ringer's solution from its atrophic pancreas. This extract was then injected into a second dog that had been pancreatectomized some days previously and thereafter allowed to lapse into diabetic coma. As a result of the insulin (*isletin*) injection, the dog recovered from its coma and the clinical relevance of insulin became apparent. Subsequently, J.B. Collip standardized insulin, and the widespread use of this agent in the treatment of diabetes revolutionized the management of the disease.

Pancreatic Transplantation

Although the discovery of insulin had significantly advanced the management of diabetes, the morbidity of lifelong injections, and the advance of the disease process, fueled the consideration of alternative modes of therapy. In the late 1920s, Gayet and Guillaumie had demonstrated that a transplanted pancreas could successfully regulate the blood glucose level in human subjects and diabetic dogs for periods of up to twelve hours. By 1936, Bottin could report animal survival for more than seven days after pancreatic homografts but rejection, together with leaks and sepsis, obviated longer efficacy. In 1959, Brooks and Gifford used radiation in an attempt to decrease pancreatic exocrine leak and pancreatitis and in 1962, Dejode and Howard transplanted a pancreas with an attached duodenal cuff to control pancreatic drainage. A variety of surgical modifications to assure graft survival and decrease leakage were undertaken over the next decade, but overall long-term graft survival was not feasible. In the 1960s and 1970s, a variety of operations were undertaken in humans by W. Kelley and R. Lillehei, but problems with vascular perfusion, graft rejection, and failure of islet function rendered these results dismal. The concept of islet cell transplantation was rendered feasible by advances in scientific technique that allowed for the isolation and purification of adequate numbers of functional islets.

Thus by 1965, Moskalewski had utilized collagenase to generate intact islets from guinea pig pancreas and Lacy, Ballinger, and Lucy, were able to demonstrate that isolated adult islets could produce long-lasting amelioration of experimentally-induced diabetes in rats. Although administration of the islets via the portal vein was proposed as an effective method of generating micro-islet function of the liver, islet viability and rejection significantly diminished any long-lasting beneficial effects.

Gastroentero-Pancreatic Tumors

Islet Cell Tumors

Although Bard and Pick in 1888 had proposed that the islet cell was a potential candidate for the development of neoplastic lesions, it was 1908 before A.G. Nichols became the first to report a solitary adenoma of the pancreas arising directly from the islet tissue. The lesion was noted at autopsy as a small round flattened nodule located on the anterior side of the pancreas, approximately at the junction of the middle and the terminal third. Other reports included that of Cecil in 1909, who while studying the islets of Langerhans and diabetes, noted an "enormous adenomatous hypertrophy of an islet of Langerhans." Over the next decade, several reports of islet cell adenoma were generated both in Europe and America, but the functional

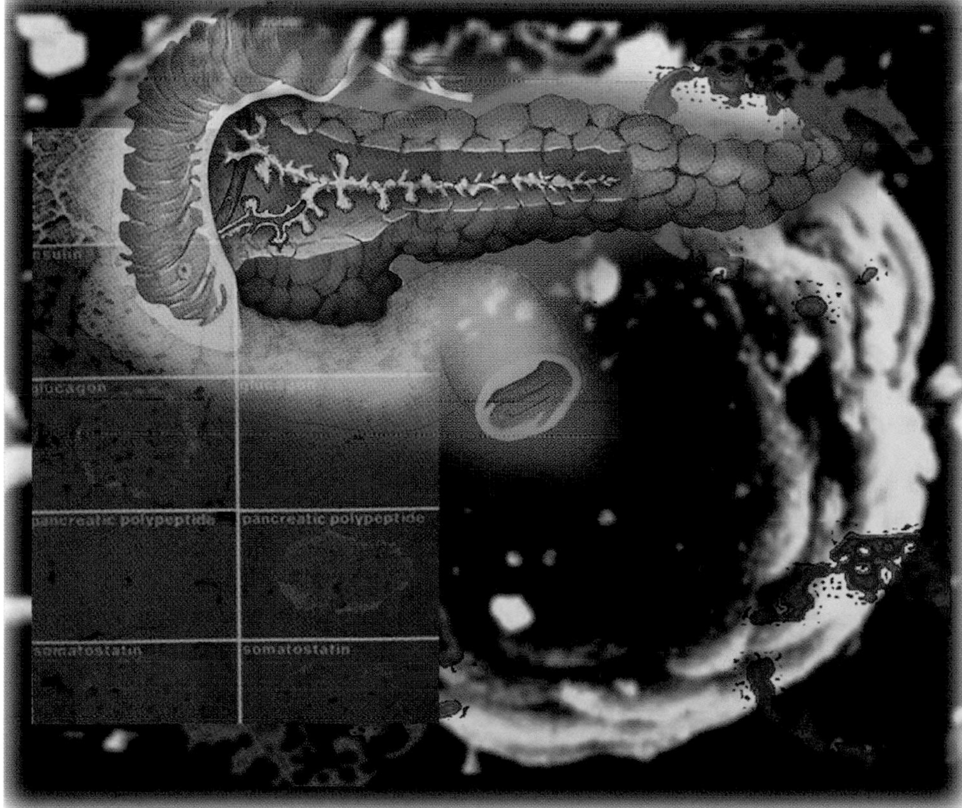

Cells in a pancreas (top). An electron micrograph of an isolated islet (right) demonstrates complex neural elements as well as an internal portal system. The identification of a wide variety of peptide and amine chemical regulators produced by individual islet cells (left) is an indication of the complex regulatory nature of the system and its importance in metabolic homeostasis.

Charles H. Best (left) and Frederick Banting discovered insulin in 1922. Although Banting was an orthopedic surgeon it was his original idea that led to the elucidation of the pancreas as the source of insulin. Best, a medical student, was not recognized by the Nobel Prize Committee but Banting generously shared his prize money with the brilliant young student. It is not recorded what Marjorie, the dog on whom the first successful experiment was undertaken, received as an award for her contributions to science!

Roscoe Graham of Toronto, on the Ides of March in 1929, undertook the first successful resection of a pancreatic insulinoma.

S.R. Bloom (top right), J. Polak (left), and A. Pearse (bottom right) of the Hammersmith Hospital, London, were instrumental during the 1970s in establishing the concept of the Apudoma and elucidating the peptide secretion and histopathology of neuroendocrine tumors of the gut.

effects of such lesions were not noted. However, in 1927, Russell M. Wilder reported the first case of hyperinsulinism in a 40-year-old physician whose episodic unconsciousness was related to hypoglycemia. The unsuccessful surgical attempt at removal undertaken in December 1926, revealed metastatic disease of the liver, lymph nodes, and mesentery. Histology indicated a striking resemblance to the cells at the islets of Langerhans and alcoholic extracts of the "cancer" tissue injected into rabbits generated hypoglycemia. On March 15, 1929, Roscoe R. Graham of Toronto undertook the first successful removal of an islet cell tumor from a 52-year-old woman suffering from repeated hypoglycemic episodes of coma and convulsion. Successful enucleation of the tumor from the body of the pancreas resulted in cure. Recognition of the disease allowed Whipple in 1938 to describe an eponymous clinical triad for the diagnosis of insulinoma and by 1950, the literature contained descriptions of more than four hundred such patients.

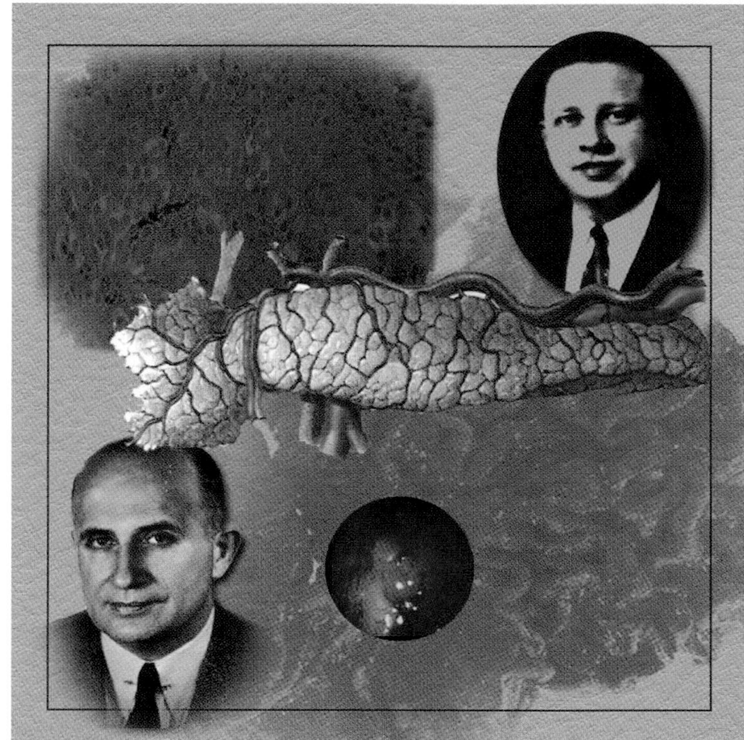

In 1995, R. Zollinger (left) and E. Ellison identified the relationship between non-beta islet cell tumors of the pancreas and a peptic ulcer diathesis. The subsequent identification of gastrin as the cause of the increased acid secretion and the trophic effect on the gastric mucosa, led to a further understanding of the secretory and trophic roles of peptide hormones. Although gastrinomas were initially believed to be of pancreatic origin, the subsequent identification of the duodenum (center) as a major site of the tumor led to reconsideration of the biology of the disease process.

In 1955, Zollinger and Ellison proposed that lesions of the non-beta islet cells might have the capacity to produce an "ulcerogenic humoral factor" and reported two patients with jejunal ulceration and pancreatic non-beta islet cell tumors. Having duly noted the massive gastric hypersecretion, it remained for Rod Gregory to subsequently isolate and identify gastrin as the causal agent of the "Ulcerogenic Syndrome". In 1958, Verner and Morrison similarly reported a non-beta islet cell syndrome associated with diffuse diarrhea and hypokalemia that Said and Mutt subsequently identified as due to tumor secretion of vasoactive intestinal polypeptide (VIP). The identification of VIP in neural tissue and the recognition that a similar series of clinical symptoms could occur with adrenal or sympathetic chain tumors, resulted in the elucidation of the Vipoma syndrome. Further work by S. Bloom, J. Pollak, and R. Mallinson, led to the identification of a number of different endocrine tumors of the pancreas including glucagonoma, somatostatinoma, and pancreatic polypeptidoma. Such lesions were recognized to sometimes form part of the Multiple Endocrine Neoplasia Type I syndrome (MEN I), and the concept of linked neural, endocrine and gastrointestinal disease attained widespread acceptance by the 1970s.

Carcinoid Disease

In 1867, Langerhans first described a tumor of the gut that, on later review, seems almost certain to have been a carcinoid lesion. Otto Lubarsch of Breslau provided the first detailed description of such a tumor in 1888, when he reported autopsy findings on a patient with multiple carcinoids of the ileum. Two years later, William Ransom of Nottingham described in detail a patient with diarrhea and wheezing secondary to an ileal carcinoid tumor with liver metastases, thus providing the first identification of the classical symptomatology of the carcinoid syndrome. At about this time, the development of diverse staining techniques enabled numerous additional endocrine cell types, including Nussbaum cells, Ciaccio cells, Schmidt cells, Feyrter cells, and Plenk cells, to be identified, and aroused a widespread interest in their location, function, and relation to disease. Given the distinct histological appearance and particular staining properties, these cells could be codified as enterochromaffin, argentaffin, argyrophil, pale or yellow cells and recognized simply as being morphologically different to other intestinal mucosal cells.

The first appendiceal neoplasm that may have been a carcinoid tumor was reported by L. Glazebrook in 1895. He noted during the autopsy of a 55-year-old man who had died of a cerebral hemorrhage, a primary appendiceal tumor, *"the size and shape of a pigeon's egg"* found in the anterior wall about three inches from the appendiceal base. Microscopic evaluation demonstrated that the tumor consisted of nests of irregular cuboidal and cylindrical cells, and no metastases were evident. In 1907, Siegfried Oberndorfer, noting the *"benign course of the tumors that resemble carcinomas"* first coined the term *"karzinoid"* to describe these tumors. He first used this diminutive at the German Pathological Society meeting of the same year in Dresden, where he sought to signify his appreciation of the more benign biological and clinical course of the lesions of this type.

Ciaccio introduced the term "enterochromaffin" in the same year and six years later, Kull noted that the gastrointestinal tract contained cells with a morphology similar to that of chromaffin cells. Since they were unable to reduce silver nitrate (i.e. lacked argentaffinity), he proposed that such cells be considered as the progenitors of the EC cell. A year later (1914), Gosset and Masson of Montreal demonstrated the argentaffin-staining properties of the carcinoid tumors and proposed that such lesions were derived from the enterochromaffin-cells or Kulchitsky's cells, which had been earlier discovered in 1897 by Nikolai Kulchitsky within the crypts of Lieberkhun in the intestinal mucosa.

Subsequent studies have, to a large extent, confirmed this proposal. Masson, in addition, suggested that the cells formed a "diffuse endocrine gland" in the intestines, but misguidedly some fourteen years later, proposed that these cells were neuracrine and that they originated in the intestinal mucosa before subsequently migrating to the nerves. In the 1930s, Friederich Feyrter of Gdansk, Poland, also described a diffuse endocrine organ that included the gastro-enteropancreatic (GEP) argentaffin cells as well as a number of argyrophilic cells. The ability to stain EC and non-EC cells of the gastrointestinal tract (using silver nitrate) was developed by Dawson in 1948, while the endogenous substance which reduced silver and chromium, 5-hydroxytryptamine, was identified by Erspamer and Asero. In 1963, Williams and Sandler initially classified carcinoid tumors according to their site of origin in the gut as fore-gut, mid-gut, or hind-gut, but this grouping has, for the most part, been replaced by a histological classification based on the cell of origin and the nature of the secretory product. The term carcinoid is now generally considered archaic, since it is understood to represent a spectrum of very different neoplasms, which originate from different neuroendocrine cell types and produce diverse biochemical agents.

Initially, carcinoid tumors were resected as widely as possible since it was evident that even if metastatic, that this would represent the best means of ameliorating the unpleasant sequelae of the secretion of the diverse biogenic amines and peptides responsible for the symptomatology. Unfortunately, resective techniques were relatively ineffective, and pharmacotherapy was directed either at the specific symptoms including diarrhea, flushing, and bronchospasm or the causal agent(s) using antiserotinergic agents. While of some benefit, each agent was rarely effective in the long term and patients required polypharmaceutical intervention to maintain even minimal comfort. The discovery of the ovine inhibitory peptide, somatostatin, by Guillemin and Schally (1977) led rapidly to the elucidation of the somatostatin receptor subtype and the development of a receptor agonist capable of activating the system. Since neuroendocrine cells expressed significant numbers of such receptors, the further development of a long-acting anologue (Octreotide) resulted in a substantial decrease in symptomatology and also life expectancy. The addition of an isotope ($Indium^{111}$) to the molecule, enabled the development of a sensitive and sophisticated isotopic study (Octreoscan) that greatly facilitated the diagnosis of both primary and secondary neuroendocrine tumors. A subsequent extrapolation of this concept led to the introduction of somatostatin receptor analogues complexed with other isotopes (Yttrium, Lutetium), capable of delivering therapeutic dosages of irradiation to the tumor sites when administered intravenously. Thus, somatostatin receptor expressing lesions (the majority of NETs) could be diagnosed with an SST receptor scan, have their symptoms controlled with Octreotide (inhibitor of tumor amine and peptide secretion) and irradiated by somatostatin receptor specific targeted intravenous irradiation. Surgery was reserved for mechanical problems of obstruction, perforation and bleeding and hepatic resection to a large part replaced by percutaneous hepatic embolization techniques although very occasionally, transplantion was deemed to be of some merit.

The original drawings by S. Oberndorfer from the 1907 Frankfurt Journal of Pathology. *His prescient recognition of the difference between this disease (karzinoid) and cancer laid the basis for the understanding of the unique nature of neuroendocrine tumors of the gut.*

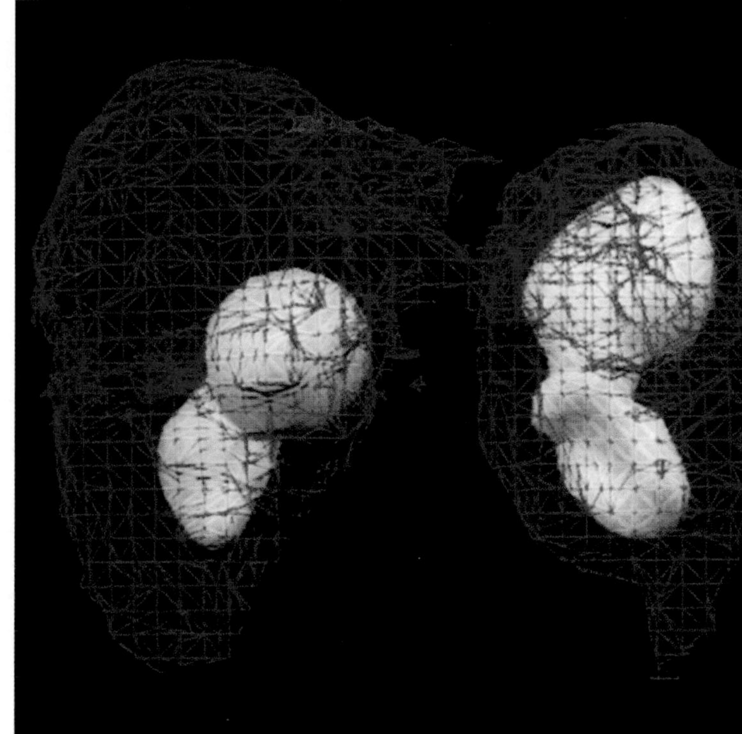

A somatostatin receptor scintigram demonstrating a gastrinoma in the head of the pancreas. The identification of the increased expression of somatostatin receptors on neuroendocrine tumor cells allowed for the development of a unique and specific isotopic diagnostic test. Thus linkage of the isotope indium to the somatostatin analog (Octreotide) enabled detection of neuroendocrine tumors by use of gamma camera scanning.

SECTION 17

The Hepato-Biliary Tract

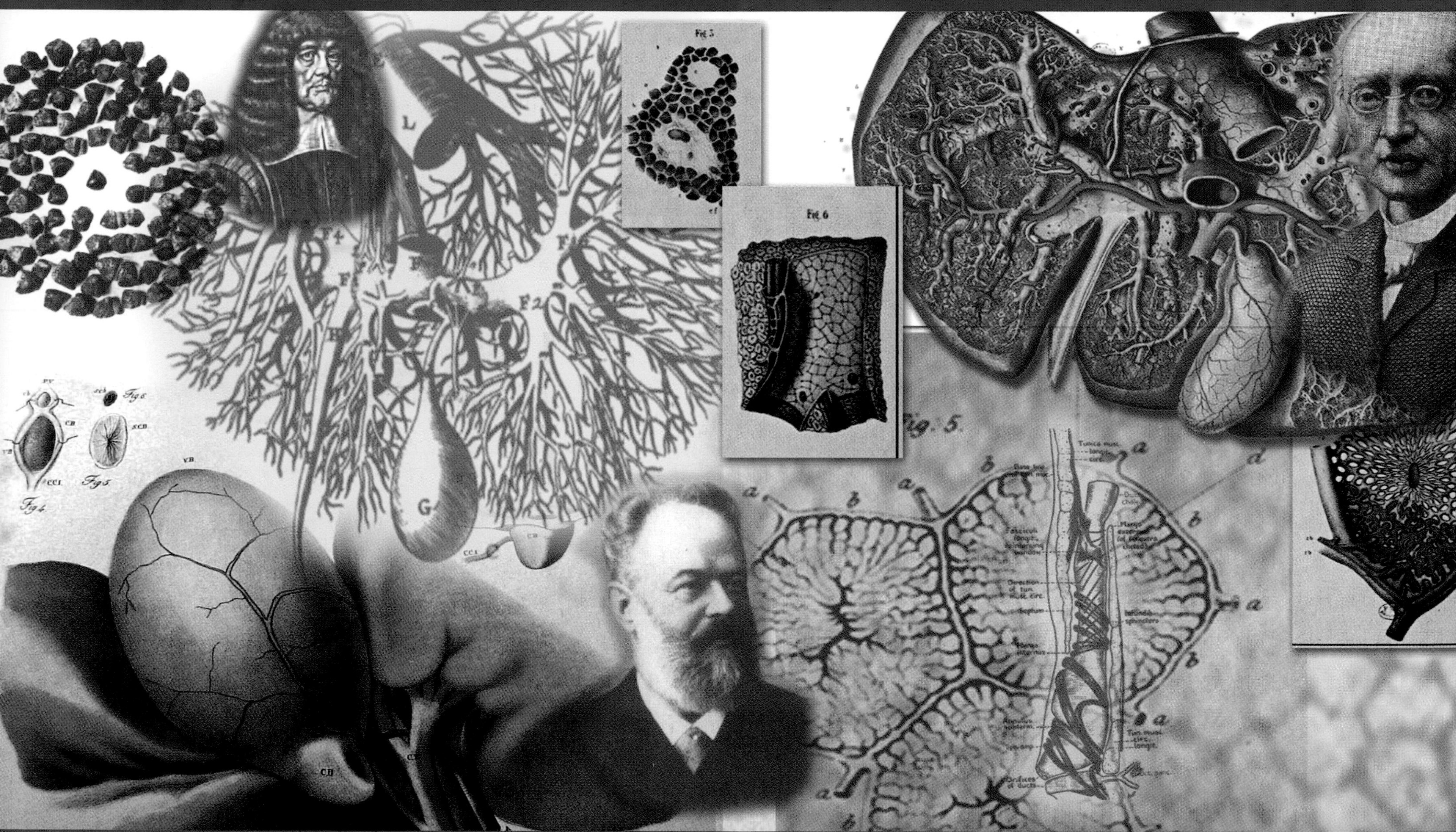

The Liver

The preoccupation of ancient people with the liver provides a long and interesting tale of belief in its ability to not only predict the future, but its role as the preeminent vital organ of the body. During antiquity, it was considered to be one of the most important organs, and variously regarded as harboring either the soul, the life spirit, or being the source of blood. The Mesopotamians considered it to be the seat of the soul and the very center of life and used it both to define the future and predict the outcome of disease.

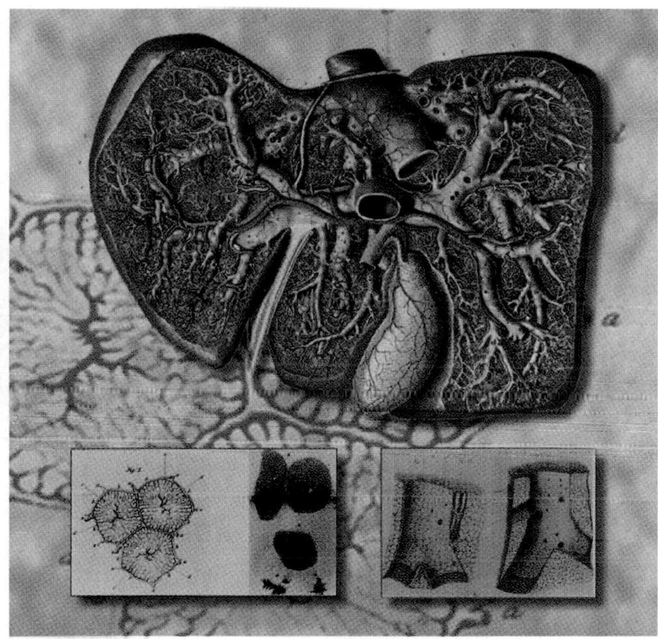

F. Kiernan in The Anatomy and Physiology of the Liver, *published in 1833, provided the first detailed drawings of the portal triad. The large perforated vessel (right) is the portal vein accompanied by a smaller artery and bile duct. The triangular spaces (portal triads) subsequently became known as Kiernan's spaces and Kiernan, himself, wrote,* "the lobules constitute the secreting portion of the liver. A lobule is apparently composed of numerous minute bodies of yellowish color (imparted to them by the bile they contain) and are various forms, connected with each other by vessels. These minute bodies are the acini of Malpighi." *Kiernan disposed of the prevalent idea of the time that two types of lobules (red or yellow) existed which had been termed "cortico medullary substance" by Antoine Ferrein of Montpellier. The Kiernan concept of lobular organization of the liver became the accepted model of hepatic microstructure and has lasted almost 200 years.*

During the Assyrian civilization, hepatoscopy was regarded as a skill of considerable importance, and individuals capable of interpreting the shape of the liver, its lobes, and the markings on its surface were highly regarded and became personages of considerable influence in the political system.

A widespread belief existed for many centuries that the liver was the repository of life. Indeed, ancient poetry and writings referred to it as the seat of emotions and vitality. Thus, in demotic Greek the word liver (*hepar*) was used in place of the word heart. Similarly, the expression "hit in the liver" was equivalent to the phrase "struck in the heart" and was interpreted as a mortal wound. In the Old Testament the words liver and life are often juxtaposed. Thus in Psalms VII, 5 it is recorded *"let him tread down my life to the earth and drag my liver to the dust."*

The need to predict the future required a careful examination of the liver, and interpretations were based on the number of different parameters. Thus, enlargement or protrusion of a portion of the liver indicated power and was favorable. Conversely, an area of softness or contraction indicated weakness and was regarded as an omen that boded ill. Even the minutest variations of the morphology were recognized and were particularly prevalent, since liver disease abounded amongst the sheep of the Tigris and Euphrates valleys. In this context, it is worth noting that liver divination marked the initial stages in the study of anatomy, since to develop appropriate and precise interpretation novel terminology needed development to facilitate description of the pathological features of the liver. For purposes of both education and consistency of interpretation, clay models demonstrating the gall bladder, porta hepatis, the umbilical vein, right and left, quadrate, caudate lobes, and the pyramidal process were constructed.

The portal triads noted on cutting the liver surface were variously designated in Assyrian scripts as either "weapons", "paths", or "holes". Similarly, the

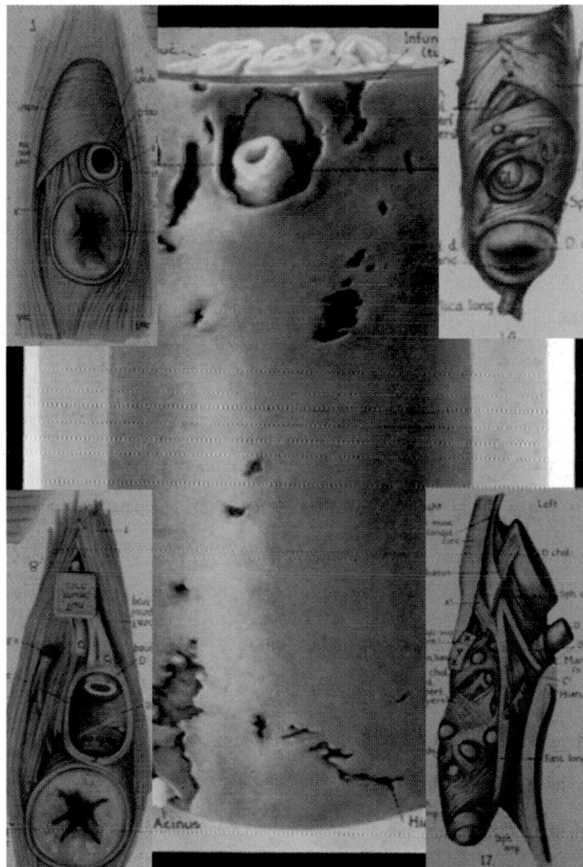

The anatomical nature of the insertion of the common bile duct into the duodenum is of considerable clinical relevance given its close relationship to the pancreatic duct and the association between biliary disease and pancreatitis. Although well-defined anatomically, the regulation of sphincteric function (Oddi) is ill understood and nebulous concepts of dyskynesia continue to cloud the precise delineation of aspects of biliary disease.

The anatomic structure of the liver was well-known to ancient civilizations since its vagaries were utilized to predict the future. Numerous clay tablets and models have survived to attest to the importance which ancient civilizations of the Middle East ascribed to "hepatoscopy" as a form of prophecy. Observations were carefully recorded and correlation sought between previous events and future possibilities. The porta hepatis was known as the "gateway" and the insertion of the ligament arteries as the "door to the palace". The gall bladder was designated "the bitter place".

port hepatis was known as the gate, the *incisura* and *"umbilicalis"* as the "door to the palace", while the gall bladder was called the "bitter part" and the common bile duct the "outlet". Indeed, the concepts embodied in Babylonian hepatic structure provided a fundamental assessment of liver anatomy that would remain unsurpassed until the advent of Vesalius in the sixteenth century.

Even the Greek philosophizers and physicians deemed the liver to be of considerable importance and Galen (of Phrygia and later Rome), following the commentaries of Plato, went so far as to establish the liver as the site of the vegetative part of the soul. The Alexandrian intellects and physicians considered the liver to be the source of the heat of the body and believed that nourishment in the form of chyle reached it from the blood, thus enabling the liver to be the main source of blood formation. There were various considerations as to what bile might represent. Overall, it was considered a waste product of the process by which absorbed food underwent conversion into blood by the liver. In other centers of erudition, bile was considered to be an important product of the liver and the contents of the gall bladder were often used in therapeutic admixtures to provide strength and potency. For those physiologists more concerned with the concept of its circulation, the liver was regarded as the center of the venous system from which blood was distributed to the various parts of the body.

Further confusion as to the role of the liver was engendered by the controversy regarding the discovery of lacteals and the thoracic duct in the seventeenth century. Thus, despite the argument regarding lymphatic valves and the fanciful notion of a "gyrus", it was apparent to the experimentalists of Amsterdam (Sylvius, Blasius, Ruysch and van Horne) that chyle moved from the abdominal *cisterna chyli* into the thoracic duct and then, into the venous circulation. Bartholin in 1657 was not reticent in pointing out that under these circumstances, chyle could not be regarded as providing nourishment for the liver. Although now regarded as a relatively obvious piece of information, this dramatic re-interpretation of liver function led to widespread skepticism and controversy. Bartholin rendered the coup de grace, himself, by writing an epitaph to the liver (see caption page 287), and thus ended centuries of hepatic hegemony (Bartholin, *Vasa Lymphatica*, Copenhagen, 1653).

Subsequently in 1669, Glisson gave his name to the capsule of liver and together with Wepfer and Malpighi, described the glandular structure of the organ and confirmed the role of the lacteals in transmitting intestinal nutrients to the circulation. In so doing, they supported the position of Bartholin and confirmed that since the liver was bypassed by the chylous circulation it should now be relegated to an inferior position as a simple manufacturing site for bile.

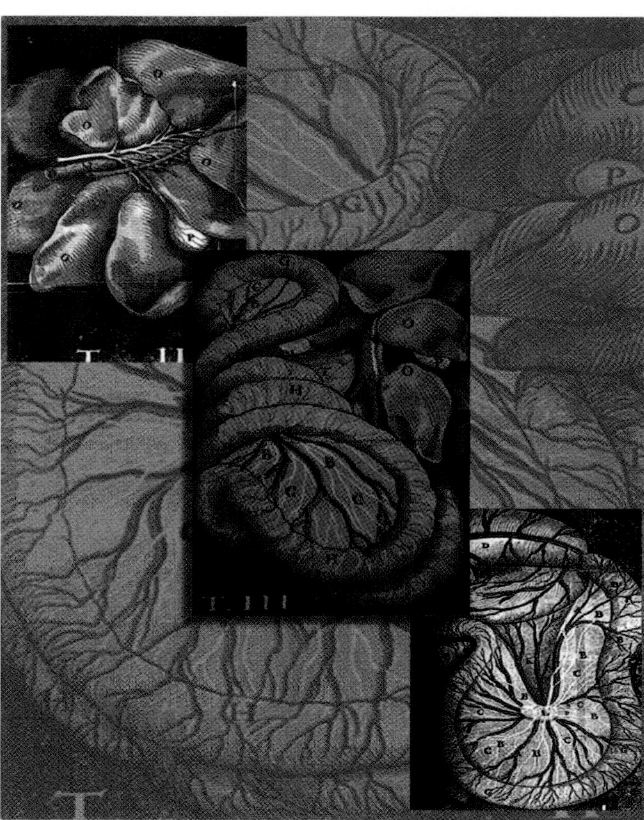

Galen had believed that the veins and lymphatics of the intestines carried chyle to the liver. This concept was disproved by the discovery of the lacteal vessels (drawing inset) in 1622 by Gasparo Aselli of Cremona. Although Aselli believed that lymphatics passed to the liver, this error was subsequently rectified by the discovery of the thoracic duct and receptaculum chyli by Jean Pecquet, and of the intestinal lymphatics and their connection with the thoracic duct by the Swede, Olof Rudbeck, in 1651.

Possessed of a mind unfettered by doctrine (note the lymphatic flow and lacteals coursing from the breasts of the nubile women bearing his name) Bartholin did not hesitate to deride the fanciful notion that the liver was a blood-forming organ. Herewith a translation of his epitaph to the liver. "Halt, traveler: In this tomb lies buried the chief, cook, and ruler of the body, who has buried many people – known for generations but unknown to science – the liver, who secured grandeur of name by tradition and has kept it by repute. It has been digesting for so long that it at last by a cruel command it has digested away. Go, traveler, without bile and leave bile to the liver so that you may jest well without it. Pray for It."

During the nineteenth century, the further refinement of chemical methodology lead to major advances in the study of bile and the delineation of its metabolic and digestive role. Thus by 1826, the old Galenic concept of the liver being a main organ in the nutritional system had once again achieved popularity as the biochemical work of F. Tiedemann became accepted. T. Schwann, as well as Claude Bernard, recognized its important digestive role and the use of experimental biliary fistula enabled elucidation of the function of bile in fat absorbtion. L. Gmelin had developed a test to identify bile pigments in 1826 and, after prolonged study of the nature of bile cells by a number of individuals, W. Kühne in 1858 isolated and measured bilirubin in blood. In 1846, F. Magendie demonstrated that the portal vein was the recipient of considerable venous influx from the gut and together with L. Gmelin, confirmed the potential central role of the liver in human metabolic function. Claude Bernard in 1853 produced a masterful thesis on the novel functions of the liver relating to its ability to form and store glycogen and, in an epoch-making series of studies, he demonstrated experimentally that the body (liver) could not only degrade chemical substances but was able to synthesize them. In 1877, N. Eck used the experimental model of the Eck fistula to further evaluate the chemical function of bile and to study its relationship to digestive function. S. Rosenberg demonstrated that the amount of ingested fat is an important regulator of bile production, while W. Bayliss and E. Starling outlined the role of secretin in stimulating bile secretion. J.L. Bollmann and F.C. Mann studied the effects of total hepatectomy on the formation of urea and provided important physiological information regarding the extrahepatic production of bile pigments. B.E. Lyon (1850-1950) was the first to use a chemical cholagague to study gall bladder disease and thus used physiological information to elucidate the management of pathology. In 1926, Minot and Murphy demonstrated that the liver also contained a major blood-forming factor and further confirmed the multiple metabolic functions of the liver in the maintenance of body hemostasis. Indeed, the ability of ingested liver to cure the then fatal disease of pernicious anemia was regarded as further evidence of its vital role in the sustenance of life.

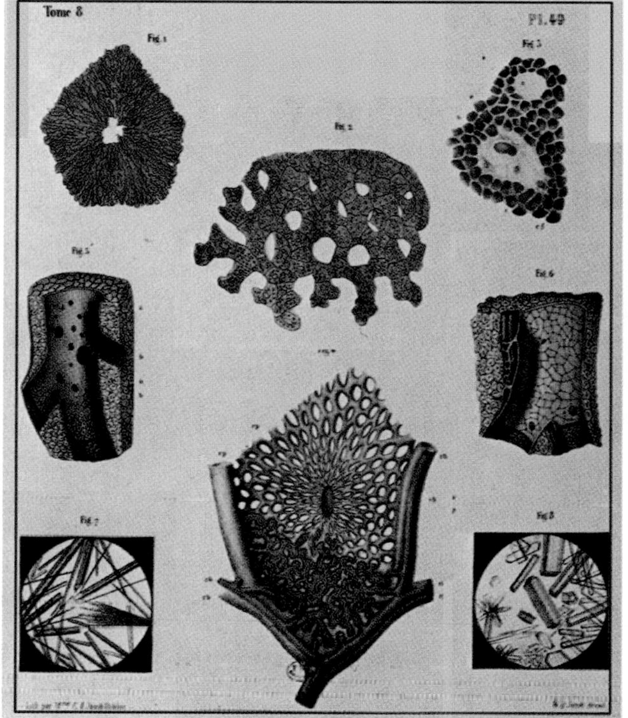

A series of 19th-century microscopic drawings depicting the cellular architecture of the portal triad, bile ducts, and bile crystals. F. Kiernan in 1833 was the first to accurately characterize the lobular architecture of the liver and note the relationship between the cells, bile ducts, and vasculature.

Disease of the Liver

Although no clear evidence is available except that evident in old cuneiform scripts and disintegrated mummies, it is likely that ancient Egypt and Mesopotamia were major sites of liver disease, particularly of a parasitic nature. In Greco-Roman antiquity, much indirect evidence is available to support the fact that physicians were aware of jaundice, cirrhosis, abscess, and hepatitis. Indeed, the accounts of jaundice by Aretaeus and Caelius Aurelianus (*c.* A.D. 400) are excellent examples of the general features of

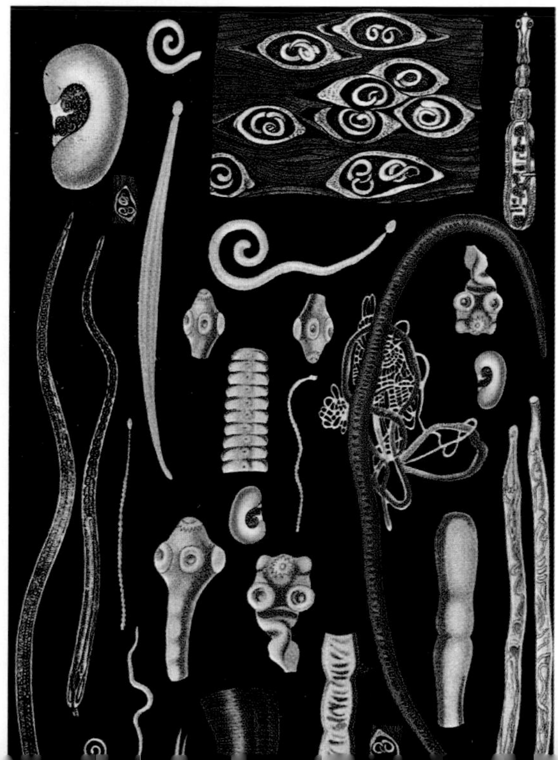

The advent of histology provided for a major amplification in the identification of parasites and enabled the demonstration of their pathological effects on the different gastrointestinal organs. A diverse variety of parasites were identified once microscopes became available. Prior to that, liver disease due to parasites could usually only be identified at autopsy.

liver disease. All of the extant Arab literature in medicine dealt in considerable of detail with hepatic disease, but since their religion forbade dissection and autopsy, only broad clinical descriptions of problems are available.

Icterus

In the fifth century B.C. Hippocrates had produced an excellent description of icterus and recognized the poor prognosis of individuals with yellow discoloration and a hard liver. Rufus of Ephesus in first century A.D. had advanced further in his thinking and divided jaundice into three types: that associated with fever; that related to hepatic abscess and jaundice due to obstruction of the bile duct. Galen in the second century A.D. wrote that an effusion of yellow bile was related to stone in the biliary tree, but also noted that disease could be unrelated to the liver and that conditions such as snakebite might result in the development of jaundice. Aretaeus in the second century A.D. was of the opinion that jaundice arose not only from the liver but also the spleen, kidney, colon, and stomach. He was the first to relate the symptom of itching to jaundice and like Galen, believed that such symptoms were due to the failure of the spleen to remove black bile from the blood. Rhazes in the ninth century opined that jaundice originated from obstruction of the bile ducts while Avicenna, in his *Canon* of A.D. 1000, commented that jaundice from duct obstruction was different to other kinds of jaundice.

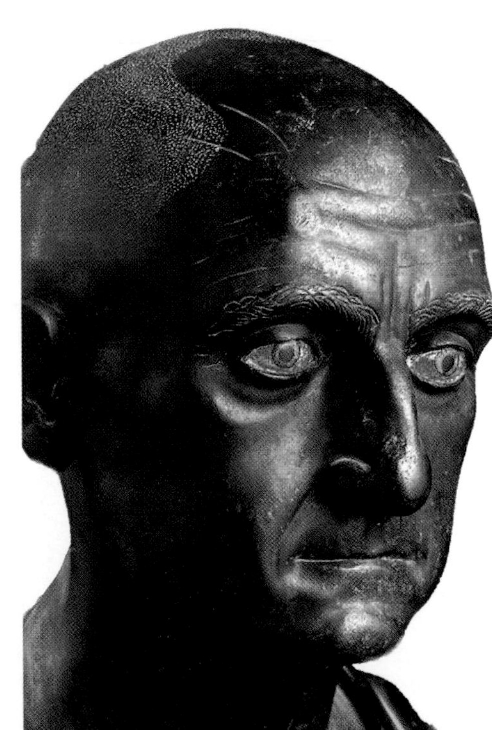

It was long recognized that an excess of bilirubin (jaundice) was associated with serious illness. In clay tablets from Mesopotamia circa 3000 B.C. the condition is well described: "when a man suffers from jaundice of the eye line and his disease rises in the interior of his eyes, the water of the interior of his eyes is green like copper... his interior parts being raised, return food and drink. The disease dessicates this man's entire body: he will die." *Although the Mesopotamians did not specifically recognize jaundice as related to underlying liver disease, the Bible notes that a yellow discoloration of eyes is a sign of the disease.*

Thomas Willis in 1673, demonstrating his usual intellectual prescience, recognized not only obstructive jaundice but also what are now regarded as either retention or regurgitation as causes. He wrote: *"The cause of the Jaundies to consist chiefly in this, that the choler being sever'd in the liver is not by reason of the ways being obstructed... but that it must of necessity regurgitate into the mass of blood to proceed... when... the choler is more plentifully separated or discharged forth by the ordinary ways."*

The clinical sign of jaundice was a source of considerable anxiety for the people of ancient times and evoked both fear and loathing. Thus, an eleventh century Anglo-Saxon text stated: *"From gall disease that is from the yellow jaundice, cometh great evil; it is of all disease most powerful when there wax within a man unmeasured humours; these are tokens: that the patient's body all becometh bitter and yellow as good silk; and under the root of his tongue there may be swart veins and pernicious, and his urine yellow."*

The word jaundice did not enter usage in English lnguage until the 14th century. Etymologically it derives from "jaundis" (Middle English), "jaunisse" (Middle French), "galbinus" (Latin), "jaune" (French), "galbos" (Celtic) and "ghel" (Indo-European). All the roots of these words mean the color yellow. In fact, the synonym icterus is traceable back to the Greek word "iktis" which was derived from the name for the yellow-breasted Marten that in ancient Greece was kept as a household pet; or to "iktepos", the gold Oriole, the sight of which was supposed to cure jaundice, and to "iktivos", a kite with yellow eyes.

It is probable that the first individual to identify bilirubin as the chromogen in bile was Thenard who, in 1827, shortly after the Battle of Waterloo, worked with the yellow magma removed from the dilated biliary tract of an elephant that had died in the Paris zoo. After drying 500 grams of the powdery material that was insoluble in water, he treated it with HCl and noted its change to a green color. Although Thenard believed that this green color was derived from an impurity in the mucus of bile, his description of a second orange pigment in the elephant material was probably the first isolation of relatively pure unconjugated bilirubin. In 1826 F. Tiedemann and L. Gmelin used nitric acid to promote the oxidative conversion of bilirubin to biliverdin and observed the change of colors. In 1840, J. Berzelius resolved the formula for bilirubin and called the substance "cholephyrrine". A year later, he also identified biliverdin from an ox and in 1845, Scherer isolated biliverdin from humans. The green pigment was later crystallized by Küster in 1909 and purified by Barcroft and Lemberg in 1932.

T. Bonet in his *Sepulchretum* of 1679 described numerous *"jaundice producing conditions"*, but as late as the eighteenth century, the ancient Galenic theories of hepatic function would still be utilized to explain hepatic disease. By the early nineteenth century, however, Laennec's description of cirrhosis (1819), and Bright's (1836) as well as Rokitansky's (1842) contributions, had produced a substantial new amount of clinical pathologic information which allowed for a better understanding of hepatic disease.

F.T. Frerichs in 1860 produced his classic monograph on liver disease and, by focusing attention on the subject in a formal fashion, facilitated the development of a substantially better understanding of hepatic pathology. In 1875, V.C. Hanot using microscopic technology, was able to provide considerable further pathological detail on the underlying processes of hepatic dysfunction. As a result of the fusion of biochemical and pathological information,

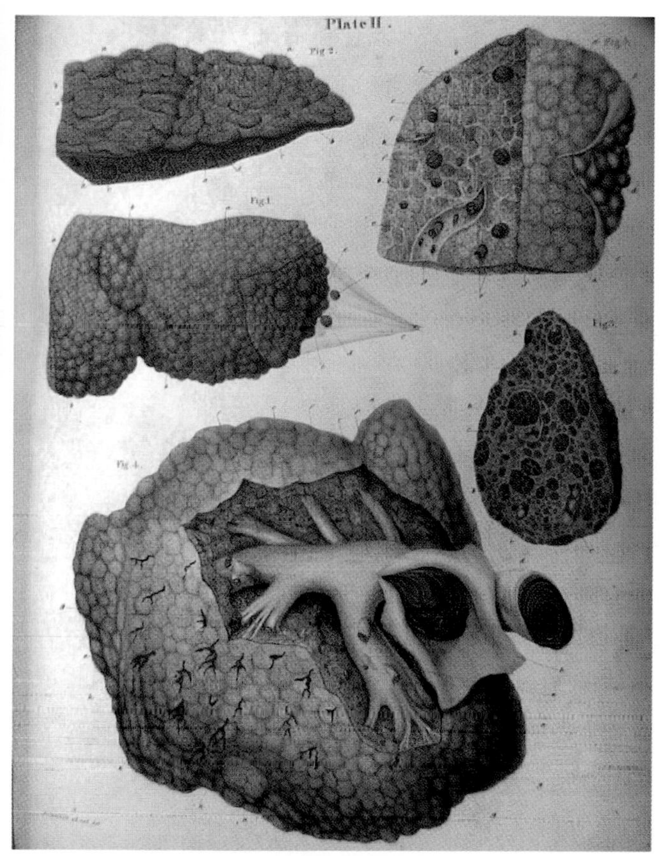

A Carwell illustration of a cirrhotic liver with a portal venous thrombosis. Galen also noted that "heavy wine which heats up the intestine... will increase the obstruction of blood vessels... and therefore it will increase the damage to the liver when inflammation and scirrhous already exist. After the liver, the spleen can also be damaged by this sweet wine."

jaundice became recognized as a common denominator clinical manifestation of serious liver disease. A. Weil, who described the relationship of parasitic infestation to jaundice (*Leptospirosis*), highlighted the role of extrinsic disease in the development of hepatic pathology in 1886. L. Lucatello, who first described hepatic biopsy, provided a considerable advance in the assessment of hepatic pathology in 1895, but the technique failed to gain widespread acceptance until many years later. As a result, the widespread introduction of this diagnostic technique did not occur until 1939 with the report of P. Iverson and K. Roholm. Correlations of hepatic pathology with biochemical function were first established reliably by Hijmans van den Bergh in 1913, and subsequent to this contribution, innumerable biochemical assessments of parenchymal function appeared.

Cirrhosis

It is worthy of note that the first commentary on cirrhosis is reflected in the Hippocratic aphorism of the fourth century B.C.: *"in cases of jaundice it is a bad sign when the liver becomes hard."* Although a similar remark is apparent in the writings of Celsus (A.D. 100), as far back as the third century B.C., Erasistratus had noted that cirrhosis was associated with ascites. He considered that the basis of the fluid accumulation was: *"a chronic and scirrhous inflammation of the liver or the spleen which prevented the assimilation of the food in the bowels and its distribution through the body, that changes to water, which, being refrigerated is deposited between the intestines and peritoneum."*

Galen was somewhat more sophisticated in his clinical assessment of the situation and noted: *"The liver offers a clearer diagnostic picture when it becomes scirrhous because scirrhous is harder than inflammation and under such conditions the patient is losing much weight. When in the course of disease the mass of the scirrhous becomes heavier, the diagnosis by palpation will present with greater difficulties because of the presence of an abundance of water effusion. Such a condition could not arise without the involvement of the liver."*

It was well-known in antiquity that the "hard state" referred to the consistency of the cirrhotic liver whereas scirrhous was used more to describe carcinoma. Thus Aretaeus the Cappadocian, a contemporary of Galen, had the following to say in regard to the evolution of a cirrhotic liver: *"but if after the inflammation, the liver does not suppurate, the pain does not go off, its swelling, changing to a "hard state", settles down into scirrhous; in which case, indeed, the pain is not continued, and when present is dull; and the heat is slight; there is loss of appetite; delight in bitter taste, and dislike of sweets; they have rigors; are somewhat pale, green, swollen about the loins and feet, forehead wrinkled; belly dried up, or the discharge is frequent. A cap of these bad symptoms is dropsy."*

Aretaeus thus indicates that cirrhosis may evolve from hepatitis and carcinoma from cirrhosis. Little further was added to the assessment of cirrhosis until the Middle Ages, when a salt-poor diet was introduced in the treatment of ascites.

By the seventeenth and eighteenth centuries, pathological anatomy had allowed for the postmortem identification of a cirrhotic liver. Thus Vesalius (1543), Tulp (1652), Bonet (1679), and Morgagni (1769), all produced reasonable descriptions of the disease process. Of particular interest is the description by Vesalius of an autopsy of a lawyer who died during a meal. The abdomen was found to be full of blood from a ruptured portal vein and the liver pale, indurated, and studded with nodules. Although Morgagni introduced the term "tubercle" to denote a nodule in the liver, he did not

Although better remembered for his anatomic contributions, Vesalius accurately described a cirrhotic liver found at the autopsy of a lawyer. He failed to comment upon whether this represented an occupational disease.

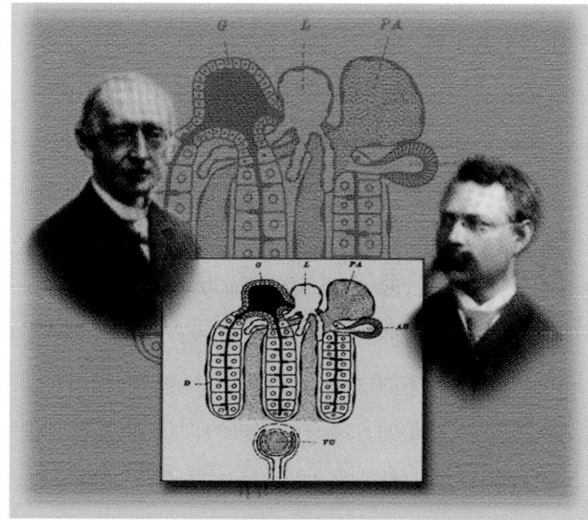

Theodore von Frerichs (left) is regarded as the father of Hepatology, based upon his systematic and scientific contributions to liver disease. His monumental two-volume book on liver disease included an atlas with his own drawings of morphological findings. Josef Disse (right) delineated the basis of normal liver anatomy and defined the spaces named after him.

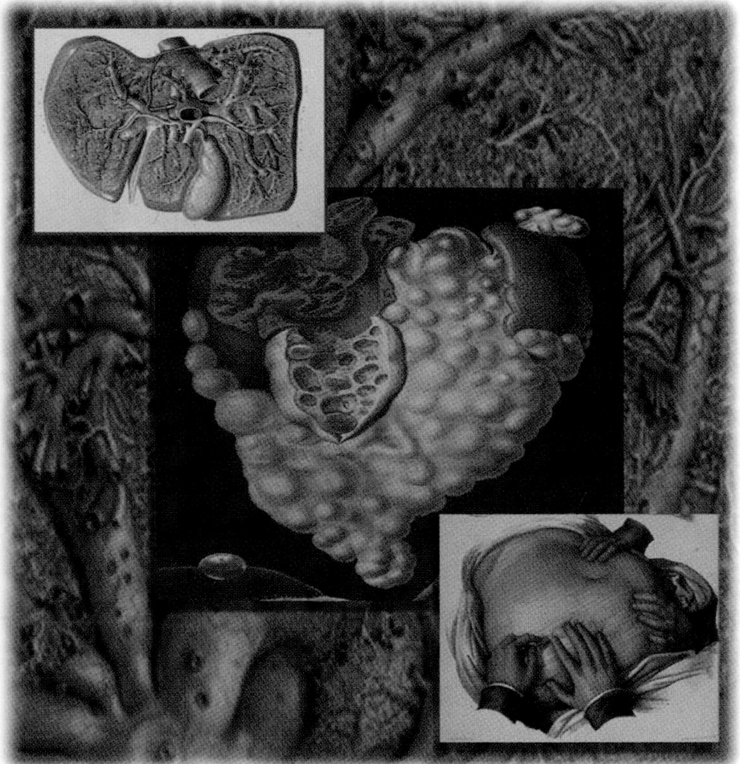

Although the clinical and pathological descriptions of cirrhosis have been apparent since the time of Galen, the fundamental basis of the pathology still remains uncertain. The diagnosis of cirrhosis was usually made by the clinical detection of ascites, palpation of hard liver, and the presence of icterus. Despite the fact the clinical and pathological description of cirrhosis has been well-known for many centuries, the fundamental basis of the pathology still remains uncertain.

differentiate between cirrhotic nodules and those due to neoplasia. In 1685 John Brown, a London surgeon, was the first to describe and publish an illustration of cirrhosis.

Although William Harvey in 1616 had reported the presence of "*a gray liver, retracted and hard*" in a postmortem examination of a person who had perished of ascites, he had failed to define in detail the nature of the condition. By the end of the eighteenth century, Matthew Baillie had established cirrhosis as a nosological entity in pathology (1793) and in his text, *Morbid Anatomy*, he described the disease in detail. "*The tubercles which are formed in this disease occupy generally the whole mass of the liver and are placed very near each other, and are of a rounded shape; they give the appearance of everywhere of irregularity to its surface. If a section of the liver be made in this state, its vessels seem to have a smaller diameter than they have naturally. It very frequently happens that in this state the liver is of a yellow color, arising from the bile accumulating in its substance; and there is also water in the cavity of the abdomen which is yellow from the mixture of bile.*"

Baillie not only described the anatomic-pathological nature of cirrhosis but noted the relationship of alcohol intake to cirrhosis. "*This disease is hardly ever met within a very young person, but frequently takes place in persons of middle or advanced age: it is likewise more common in men than women. This seems to depend on the habit of drinking more common in one sex than the other; for this disease is most frequently found in hard drinkers...*"

The consequences of the "gin plague" (1720-1750) resulted in a widespread awareness of alcoholic cirrhosis in England, and the massive consummation of cheap and contaminated spirits at this time was well documented in the writings of Henry Fielding and the characters of William Hogarth.

The over-indulgence of gin related to a surplus of corn crops on the continent and in England, and in an attempt to stabilize the price of the grain commodity, Parliament promoted distilling and consumption of spirits. As a result of the repeal of the old laws governing distillation and the lowering of taxes related to the buying and selling of alcohol, cirrhosis became widespread and was known in England as either "gin liver" or "gin drinker's liver".

Boullard in 1826 considered the yellow granulation to consist of disorganized hepatic parenchyma, but much controversy arose as to the exact nature of the cirrhotic process. Andral in 1829 proposed that the red substance containing blood vessels was converted to fibrous tissue and that this accounted for the atrophic portions of the liver. Hope in 1834 endorsed the concept of hypertrophy of the white substance, but further complicated the matter by stating that there was in addition "*an interstitial deposition in that substance, connected with a lesion of secretion.*" Becquerel in 1840 proposed an alternative hypothesis, stating that the primary lesion in cirrhosis was an infiltration of the yellow substance by an "*albumino fibrinous material*" that secondarily compressed the red substance. A more sensible approach, however, was adopted by J. Cruveilhier, who proposed that it was fibrous tissue which resulted in cirrhosis, causing atrophy in one area while the remainder grew in order to compensate for the atrophy. Subsequent to his proposals, F. Kiernan of England in 1833 described the appropriate hepatic microanatomy which enabled a better understanding of the disease process.

R. Carswell in 1838 demonstrated that cirrhosis depended on the growth of interlobular connective tissue, and E. Hallman (1839) in Germany became the first to examine cirrhosis microscopically, noting nodules of liver cells surrounded by fibrotic bands. By 1842, K. Rokitansky had begun to refer to cirrhosis as a "granular liver". Von Oppolzer claimed that the early gestation of cirrhosis included partial obliteration of the small portal veins due to inflammation and compression by enlarged bile ducts. F.T. Frerichs of Freiburg, in 1861, supported the concept of new capillaries growing into the scar tissue of the liver and referred to the condition as "chronic interstial hepatitis" rather than cirrhosis. In his description of the vascular lesions of cirrhosis, he provided the first clear recognition of the important impact of the disease process on the portal venous system. Over the next forty years, considerable discussion took place in regard to both vascular alterations

Leon Jean-Baptiste Cruveilhier (1791-1874), despite having initially left medical school because of his disgust with autopsies, ultimately became one of the finest pathologists of his time. Although not an eloquent teacher, he was a fine researcher and writer and many of his initial observations are still relevant. In 1829 he wrote the Pathological Anatomy of the Human Body *and described in detail the pathology of hepatic cirrhosis.*

As a result of a decrease in alcohol tax, a massive over-production and consumption of gin resulted in an epidemic of cirrhosis. "Gin liver" became one of the commonest clinical diagnoses of the 18th century and numerous cartoons and caricatures of the time, from Hogarth to Rowlandson, attest to the vices and diseases of the inebriati.

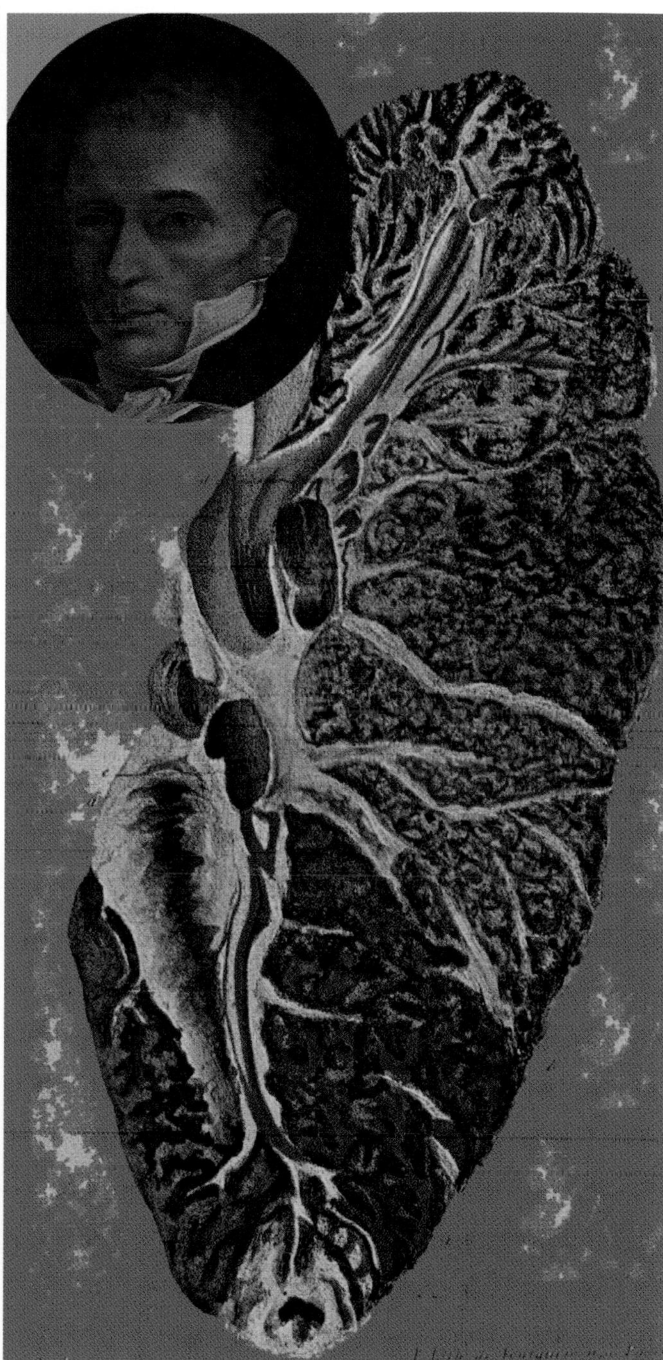

Some 25 years after the publication of Baillie, Laennec, the discoverer of the stethoscope, formally introduced the name cirrhosis. He stated: "This type of growth belongs to the group of those which are confused under the name scirrhous. I believe we ought to designate it with the name cirrhosis because of its color." Laennec coined the term from the Greek word kirrhos, meaning orange yellow, and thought that the disease was due to a new growth that resulted in normal liver tissue reabsorbing and diminishing in size. The case that Laennec described was the postmortem of a 45-year-old man who died of a hemorrhagic pleurisy and was found to have ascites and liver cirrhosis.

and the nature of the development of nodular hyperplasia. R. Kretz in 1905 affirmed the regenerative aspects of cirrhosis and proposed that the nodular appearance of the liver was a consequence of asymmetric degeneration and regeneration of liver cells. By 1911, F.B. Mallory had written the definitive paper entitled "Cirrhosis of the Liver" and placed the disease on solid footing as a clinico-pathological syndrome. "*To the clinician the term cirrhosis usually means a chronic, progressive, destructive lesion of the liver combined with reparative activity and contraction on the part of the connective tissue. This contraction of the connective tissue may lead to obstruction of bile ducts causing more or less jaundice and to interfere with the flow of the blood through the blood vessels resulting in portal congestion and ascites*." In 1928, A.H. McIndoe produced exquisite vascular injection models of the hepatic circulation.

Alcohol

Although the deleterious affects of alcohol had been well recognized since time immemorial, it was only in the eighteenth century that it became accepted that alcohol was responsible for the development of both a fatty liver and cirrhosis. Thus, Thomas Addison in 1836 drew attention to the relationship between fatty liver and alcohol and wrote that patients with fatty liver may be diagnosed when their skin "*presents a bloodless and almost semi-transparent and waxy appearance.*" About the same period, J. von Liebig (1842) attempted to provide a chemical explanation for the development of the fatty liver. He drew a powerful analogy between the force feeding of geese with grain to produce *foie gras*. Although fatty livers had been previously noted in wasting diseases, particularly tuberculosis, F. Magendie and Lereboullet (1853) and others had demonstrated dietary variations increased the amount of hepatic fat in animals. R. Virchow in 1860 stated that fatty livers were pathological and distinguished fatty degeneration from fatty infiltration. To further confuse the issue, French clinicians including F. Trousseau (1870) proposed that steatosis in an enlarged liver was an early component in the development of alcoholic cirrhosis. Further support for the dietary origin of cirrhosis was provided by the experimental work of J. von Mering and O. Minkowski, who in 1889, demonstrated that in animals without a pancreas with experimental diabetes mellitus, increased hepatic fat deposition occurred. G. von Hoppe-Seyler in 1902 believed that gastric disturbances were responsible for the generation of toxic substances that then induced cirrhosis in the liver. Taking a similar position, O. Lubarsch in 1907 proposed that it was the absorption of toxins from the gastrointestinal tract that caused the cirrhosis, and that alcohol facilitated the absorption of such toxic substances. By the turn of the twentieth century, it was

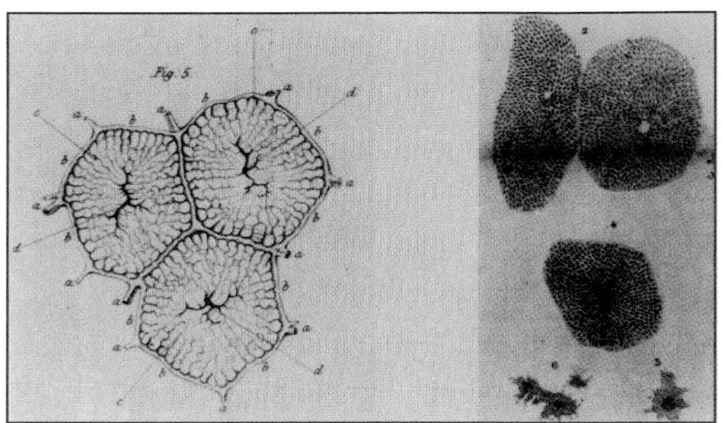

The Kiernan model of lobular formation of the liver. Kiernan was amongst the first histologists to appreciate the cellular construct of the hepatic lobule and propose a rational basis for the functional anatomy of the liver.

The "Vanitas" genre of Dutch art depicted the emblems of mortality and warned the viewer of the fragility of life. Thus bitter lemons, half burnt candles, empty wineglasses, and timepieces all numbered the days of human existence and pointed out the evanescent nature of life. Wine carried a special connotation. While its euphoric properties were much appreciated, its deleterious effects on health were recognized as allied to the "human condition".

A self-portrait of the ebullient Rembrandt with his beloved wife, Saskia. Although the exciting social effects of alcohol were well recognized in the 17th century, it was not then apparent that excessive consumption resulted in severe liver disease and ascites. In fact, the flagon of beer held by Rembrandt was probably healthier than the lead-contaminated drinking water of Amsterdam.

UNTERSUCHUNGEN
ÜBER DEN
DIABETES MELLITUS
NACH
EXSTIRPATION DES PANKREAS.
VON
O. MINKOWSKI,

Aus dem Laboratorium der medicinischen Klinik zu Strassburg i. E.
SONDERABDRUCK.

LEIPZIG,
...G VON F.C.W.VO...
1893.

J. von Mering (1849-1908) (left) and Oscar Minkowski (1858-1931). Their recognition that pancreatic resection led to diabetes provided the basis for the elucidation of the condition. In 1889 at the University of Strassbourg, they attempted to disrupt fat digestion in dogs by removal of the pancreas, the only organ known to secrete a fat-degrading enzyme, and discovered that the dogs developed diabetes. This led Minkowski to postulate that the pancreas was the site of secretion of an "antidiabetic" substance. Von Mering subsequently became medical director in Halle and with Emil Fischer developed (1902-05) the barbiturates barbital, veronal, and proponal. Minkowski taught at the universities of Strassbourg (1882-1904), Cologne (1904-05), Greifswald (1905-09), and Breslau (1909-26). At Strassbourg in 1884, he investigated the biochemical basis of diabetes and found (1884) that beta hydroxybutyric acid, with a concomitant decrease in blood bicarbonate, is the cause of diabetic acidosis, and proved that diabetic coma was accompanied by a decrease in the amount of CO_2 dissolved in the blood, and introduced alkali therapy to counteract it. By removing the liver from birds, he demonstrated in 1885 that the organ is responsible for the manufacture of bile pigments and the site of uric acid formation.

well accepted that alcohol had no specific action on the liver except to promote fatty change.

J.M. Hershey and S. Soskin (1931) proposed that a preventative precursor in raw pancreas was lethicin, but D.L. McLean and C.H. Best in 1934 demonstrated that choline was the active agent. V. du Vigneaud, in 1940, demonstrated that a labile methyl group present in choline, casein, cystine, or methionine allowed each of the chemicals to function as a lipotrophic agent. Thus, a deficiency of lipotrophic agents and experiments with choline deficiency models further supported Laennec's original hypothesis that cirrhosis was due to a dietary deficiency condition provoked by an excessive indulgence of alcohol. By the turn of the century, the major interest in bacteria, provoked by the work of R. Koch and his colleagues, stimulated considerable enthusiasm to identify an infectious cause of cirrhosis. Syphilis was the first candidate, followed by malaria and thereafter schistosomiasis. The subsequent identification of hepatitis and its related viral etiology promoted even further interest in the possibility of an initiating infective agent.

Viral Hepatitis

The concept of infectious jaundice has long plagued physicians. Indeed, for almost two millennia the catch-all phrase "bilious fever" covered a multitude of ill-understood diseases associated with icterus. The further uncertainty about viral hepatitis is reflected in the terminology, which over time has included at least twenty-one different designations. Up to 1937, the terms "catarrhal jaundice," "epidemic jaundice," and "infectious jaundice" were used. Then the terms "infective hepatitis" (preferred in England, 1939) or "infectious hepatitis" (US, 1943) replaced catarrhal jaundice. In 1943, the terms "homologous serum jaundice" and "serum hepatitis" appeared. To gain some understanding of the evolution of thought on the subject, it is necessary to reflect on the manner in which icterus was considered over time.

Given the lack of knowledge at the time, it is admirable that the Hippocratic writers and their successors postulated that yellow bile was the cause of jaundice with fever. In addition, they noted that the disease often occurred in epidemics and could end fatally. The humoral concept of yellow bile was extended to cover other clinical entities that featured icterus as a sign and in which it was considered that the primary lesions were neither hepatic nor biliary. Thus the term "bilious fevers" was used to describe diverse illnesses that probably included malaria, typhoid fever, and typhus, as well as viral hepatitis.

With the demise of the vacuous notion of humoral pathology in the eighteenth century, thoughtful physicians such as Boerhaave (1721) considered jaundice to be a disorder of the liver and biliary tree, and proposed that

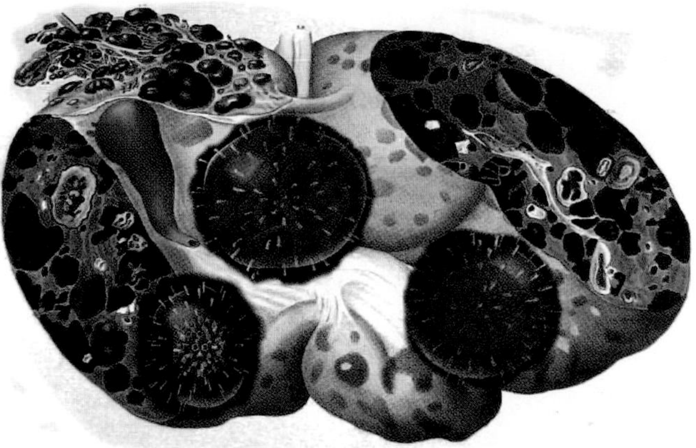

A depiction by the anatomic artist, Bougery, of a liver with melanoma secondaries. Prior to the identification of virus particles (inset), hepatic disease had been considered to be either due to tumors, infection, or fibrosis.

icterus was a consequence of a hepatitis-linked duct obstruction. The observations of Morgagni (1761) also supported the mechanical theory of jaundice.

During the nineteenth century, controversy arose as to whether jaundice was solely a hepatic phenomenon or due to other diseases as well. The identification of infectious diseases such as typhoid fever, led to a decline in the use of the generic term "bilious fever" as a catch-all diagnosis for uncertain entities. On the other hand, appreciation of other causes of febrile jaundice such as pneumonia, septicemia, Weil's disease, scarlet fever, relapsing fever, and even phosphorus poisoning, enhanced the difficulty of delineating acute viral hepatitis.

JO. BAPTISTÆ
MORGAGNI
P. P. P. P.
DE SEDIBUS, ET CAUSIS
MORBORUM
PER ANATOMEN INDAGATIS
QUINQUE.

VENETIIS,
MDCCLXI.
EX TYPOGRAPHIA REMONDINIANA.
SUPERIORUM PERMISSU, AC PRIVILEGIO.

G.B. Morgagni (1682-1771) was one of the most profoundly learned men of his time, not only in science, but in the literature of science. No less than five popes sought his care and his contributions to medicine and pathology in particular reflect his genius. Of his 15 children, 8 daughters became nuns, while the sons, who were similarly as intellectually endowed as their father, each made substantial scientific contributions. Morgagni's text On the Seats and Causes of Disease *published in Venice in 1771, laid the foundation of modern pathology.*

Friederich Theodor von Frerichs (1819-1885) taught initially at Breslau and subsequently was director of the Charité Hospital in Berlin (1859-1895). He devoted much of his career to the elucidation of hepatic disease. Frerichs was the founder of German experimental pathology, whose emphasis on the teaching of physiology provided the scientific foundation of clinical medicine. His contributions to general biochemistry led to improvement in the diagnosis and treatment of both diabetes and liver disease. His student Paul Ehrlich, inspired by the exacting skills of his mentor, was awarded the Nobel Prize in 1908.

The concept of catarrhal jaundice arose around 1825, when the proponents of the disease believed to be biliary obstruction was the mechanism of jaundice. For Broussais (1832) of France , "*Jaundice almost always depends upon gastroduodenitis or hepatitis, and is removed by the application of leeches.*" On the contrary, Andral (1829) attributed the icterus to an inflammation ascending from the duodenum and obstructing the biliary ducts. This emphasis on obstruction partly reflected the spirit of "anticontagionism" current at the time, and ignored the infectious nature of diseases. It is noteworthy that a number of significant thought leaders of the time, including Stokes (1833), Budd (1845), Frerichs (1861), Bamberger (1864), and Virchow (1865), all accepted the causal role of duodenitis and gastroenteritis and the disease became referred to as catarrhal jaundice.

The pathogenesis of this entity assumed a more contemporary appearance with the description of serous hepatitis which both Rossle (1930) and Eppinger (1937) considered to be a "capillaritis". They proposed that the intralobular edema and the capillary permeability were due to damage by toxins absorbed from the intestines, with the exuded serum deposited as albuminous material in the spaces of Disse. Keschner and Klemperer (1936) preferred the term "primary hepatic edema" to serous hepatitis, and described the changes as focal and inconstant, interpreting the intact areas as representative of a compensated phase of the serous inflammation, and the involved area as the decompensated phase (Zinck, 1941).

Although the diagnosis of catarrhal jaundice was long considered as a sporadic disease, by the early nineteenth century, there emerged a distinct separation from other infectious causes of jaundice as Weil's disease and relapsing fever were defined. Weil (1886) described a peculiar acute infectious disease accompanied by icterus, splenomegaly, and nephritis in four patients, and resolved the diverse etiologies that had been attributed to this entity (ictère grave essentiel, fièvre bilieuse, biliose typhoid, and icterus typhosus). Inada and Ido (1915) of Japan subsequently isolated the causative organism. Another infective jaundice – louse-borne relapsing fever – was also resolved at about this time when Obermeir discovered the responsible organism in 1868.

The contagious aspects of epidemic jaundice were first appreciated by Pope Zacharias (eighth century A.D.), who advised in a letter to St. Boniface, archbishop of Mainz, that patients be segregated from healthy persons. To Cleghorn, however, belongs the credit of providing the first reliable reference to epidemic jaundice. He wrote of its prevalence on Minorca during the summer of 1745. Although Thomas Sydenham (1624-1689) had already identified the clinical features of the disease, it was Herlitz of Gottingen who introduced the term "*icterus epidemicus*" in 1791.

Epidemic jaundice actually became best recognized as a military disease in the seventeenth and eighteenth centuries, but its full impact and clear symptoms were not appreciated until the nineteenth century, when army physicians such as Frohlich (1879) reported its high incidence and low mortality. During the American Civil War (1861-1865), the Union army sustained 41,569 reported cases of jaundice with 161 deaths among a total of just over 2 million troops. Similar epidemics attacked both the civilian and military population during the Franco-Prussian War of 1870, and the French referred to the disease as "*jaunisse des camps*" while the Germans named it "*Soldatengelbsucht*." The Japanese navy reported large numbers of hepatitis cases in its war with Russia

A Christmas Day celebration during the American Civil War. Although trauma was the chief medical issue and amputation (inset) the defining surgical procedure of the conflict, epidemic jaundice resulted in considerable morbidity and even mortality.

R. Virchow (1821-1902), the father of cellular pathology, and his collection of anthropological specimens. Virchow was an individual of extraordinary intellectual brilliance and political sagacity and his career spanned the disciplines of pathology, public health, and anthropology. He is regarded as the founder of cellular pathology and was a major advocate of the cell theory. namely that cells arose from each other in a continuous series of generations (omnis cellula e cellula) (where a cell arises there a cell most have previously existed). His belief that evolution was a flawed concept and that certain skeletal characteristics were indicative of higher development led to considerable debate and his anti-evolutionary views on anthropology were not accepted by many, in particular his former student, Haeckel. The latter argued that ontogeny recapitulates phylogeny and in fact coined the term ecology in 1866. Unfortunately Haeckel's attempt to describe human evolution in racial terms was later adopted by the Nazi regime and utilized as a pseudo-scientific basis to justify the proposal of Aryan supremacy.

(1904-1905), as did the German navy in World War I. The Teutonic explanation for this phenomenon was attributed to hunger that had weakened the usually staunch German livers. During World War II, large epidemics occurred amongst Allied troops in the Middle East theaters, and over 5 million cases occurred among the German armies and civilians alone. An amplifying factor in the case of the Allied troops was certainly provided by the practice of giving pooled plasma to the wounded, and plasma-associated hepatitis accounted for about one-fourth of all cases of jaundice.

In 1886, Louis Kelsch (1841-1911) clarified the relationship of catarrhal jaundice, acute yellow atrophy, and epidemic jaundice by analyzing clinical and epidemiological data currently available, and concluded that they were all forms of the same disease as Frohlich had already suggested somewhat earlier. Nevertheless, the authors of most standard German medical texts prior to World War I maintained an ambivalent attitude toward the three entities. In his analysis of thirty-four epidemics of jaundice, Hirsch (1886) declared some were due to infections and others to gastroduodenitis. Conversely Stadelmann avoided the problem in his monograph "Der Icterus" (1891) by omitting any discussion of epidemic jaundice, while Quincke and von Hoppe-Seyler (1899) supported the concept of catarrhal jaundice propagated by Virchow and Frerichs.

Although Ewald (1913) raised doubts as to the nature of the obstructive element in catarrhal jaundice, he offered no new thoughts on the pathogenesis. Naunyn (1911) replaced the concept of an obstructive catarrh with the proposal of infectious cholangitis; thus expanding the earlier view of Strumpell (1883), who had differentiated catarrhal jaundice from acute yellow atrophy. Eppinger (1922), who autopsied four icteric soldiers killed in World War I, found no obstruction but *"an acute destructive hepatitis,"* and concluded that the disease represented a milder and nonfatal form of the massive necrosis in acute yellow atrophy.

Although Eppinger was well aware of the identity of catarrhal jaundice and acute yellow atrophy, he refuted the concept that they were of infectious origin. In his classic textbook *Die Leberkrankheiten* (1937), Eppinger was prescient in distinguishing two clinical and histologic types of hepatitis, the hepatocellular and cholangitic forms. He noted that the first was more common than the second, and characterized by jaundice of short duration with considerable evidence of deranged liver function. The second type exhibited jaundice of longer duration (2 to 4 months) with features that mimicked obstructive jaundice. The concept of cholangitic hepatitis was particularly seminal and initiated the concept of cholangiolitic cirrhosis later proposed by Watson and Hoffbauer in 1946.

Similarly, this proposal also instigated Popper in the 1950s to consider the entity of cholangiolitis or intrahepatic cholestasis. A similar ambivalence toward catarrhal jaundice prevailed among the English and Americans. Thus, although Cockayne (1912) recognized the composite nature of hepatitis – which was clearly infectious in nature – he considered that epidemic jaundice was transmitted by an airborne route. On the other hand, traditionalists such as Osler differed, and in the first edition of his famous textbook of medicine, Osler (1892) placed catarrhal jaundice among "diseases of the bile-passages," explaining that the disease was *"due to swelling and obstruction of the terminal portion of the duct."*

Bernhard Naunyn (1839-1935) (as sketched by Harvey Cushing during his 1901 visit to Heidelberg) considered jaundice to represent a form of infectious cholangitis. Naunyn was specifically interested in the metabolic applications of pathology, especially as they related to the liver and the pancreas. His training with Frerichs contributed considerably to his interests in hepatic disease.

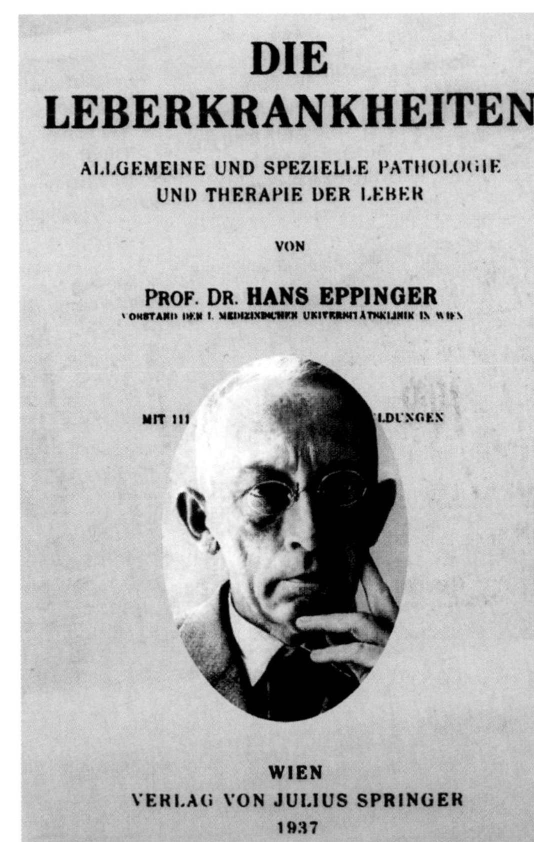

DIE
LEBERKRANKHEITEN

ALLGEMEINE UND SPEZIELLE PATHOLOGIE
UND THERAPIE DER LEBER

VON

PROF. DR. HANS EPPINGER
VORSTAND DER I. MEDIZINISCHEN UNIVERSITÄTSKLINIK IN WIEN

MIT 111 LDUNGEN

WIEN
VERLAG VON JULIUS SPRINGER
1937

Hans Eppinger of Vienna contributed significantly to the study of hepatic disease and proposed that there existed two separate types of hepatitis, namely a hepatocellular and a cholangitic form. His illustrious scientific contributions were subsequently clouded by well-founded allegations of involvement with the Nazi organization.

Sir William Osler in his study. His definitive text on medicine was held in high regard and considered a sound opinion on most medical subjects. Osler mistakenly regarded "catarrhal jaundice" as a disease of the bile passages and did not consider it an infectious problem.

Although the earliest recorded epidemic of serum (type B) hepatitis struck shipyard workers in Bremen in 1883 (Liirman, 1885), it must have been present before the nineteenth century, its survival ensured by the practices of venesection, scarification, and tattooing. Following extensive vaccinations with glycerinated lymph of human origin against smallpox of 1,289 employees, 191 developed jaundice after intervals of several weeks to six months. In contrast, none of the 500 new unvaccinated employees became icteric. Liirman's clear description leaves little doubt about the long-incubation hepatitis. Jern in 1885 reported a similar epidemic of post-vaccinal jaundice that occurred in Merzig in 1883. Further incidents involving syringe-transmitted jaundice were common in venereal disease clinics when salvarsan (arsphenamine) was introduced for the treatment of syphilis (1909). Similarly Flaum in 1926 reported outbreaks in Sweden in 1925 among diabetics attending a laboratory for blood tests. Although both Stokes (1920) and Ruge (1932) entertained the possibility of blood-borne hepatitis, the idea did not germinate until the 1940s. At around this time, numerous reports of the disease occurring under different but similar conditions were present in the literature. Thus, Findley reported jaundice following accidental exposure to infective serum in a laboratory worker, and hepatitis complicated the use of yellow fever vaccine, while Beeson in 1943 noted its occurrence after whole blood transfusion. The development of parenteral therapy of tuberculosis and of rheumatoid arthritis with gold compounds, development of new vaccines, and the use of convalescent serum for infectious diseases, all contributed to the rise of serum hepatitis in the 1930s and 1940s.

McDonald (1908-1918) was the first to postulate a virus as the cause, and as a result, during the first half of the twentieth century, there were numerous efforts to detect the specific etiology of viral hepatitis. After examining outbreaks in Sweden (1926, 1927), Bergstrand ascribed the parenchymal necrosis to chemical damage potentiated by either a bacterial or viral infection but despite careful investigation, Blumer (1923), Brugsch (1933), and others were unable to detect a bacterial pathogen. Although Loeper, Barber, and Propert in the 1930s suggested that a hepatotrophic virus was involved, as late as 1940 Lainer maintained categorically that hepatitis was due to toxins and not an icterogenic organism!

The advent of techniques for viral culture facilitated study of the issue, as did World War II, when military needs accelerated the necessity to understand the disease. In 1942, after inoculation of yellow fever vaccine containing human serum, 28,505 American soldiers in the African theater developed jaundice, with 62 deaths. Despite the American incentive to resolve the problem, it was in Japan that the first experimental transmission of hepatitis was achieved, when Yoshibumi and Shigemoto (1941) gave filtered samples of blood, urine, and pharyngeal secretions from infected patients to children. Voegt (1942) in Germany carried out similar experiments in volunteers, as did Cameron (1943) in Palestine. In fact, the work of Voegt confirmed the

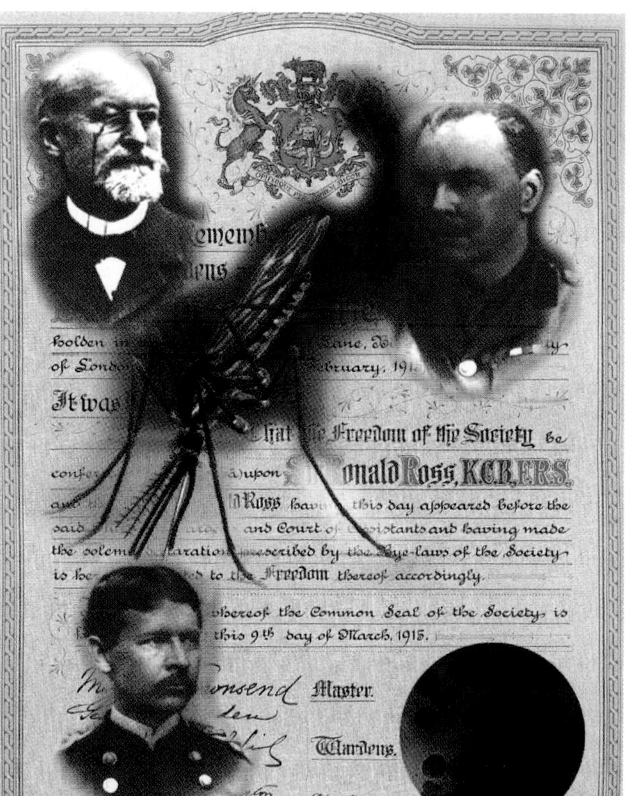

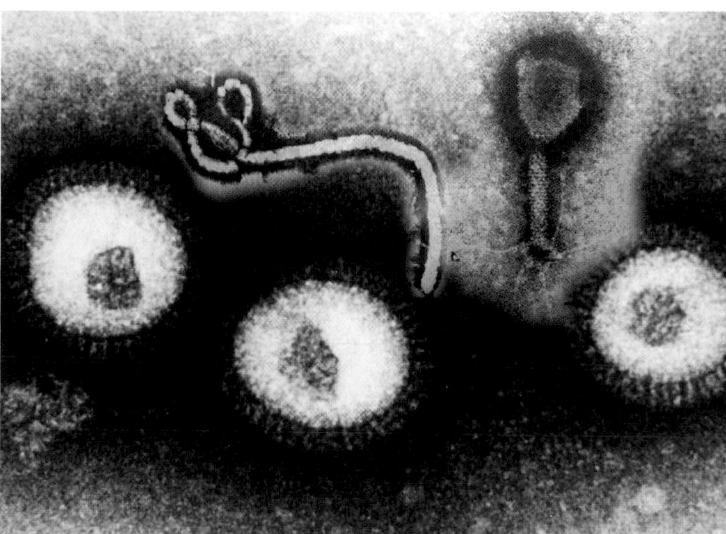

The identification of a variety of different virus particles led to the consideration of their relationship to hepatitis.

An initial difficulty in elucidating the problem of viral hepatitis lay with the fact that other diseases, such as malaria and yellow fever, which did not directly involve the liver, also caused jaundice. Sir Ronald Ross (top right) received the Nobel Prize for defining the basis of malaria. Laveran of France (top left) played an important part in defining the parasite (bottom right) and Lazar (bottom left) of the U.S. Medical Corp perished in Cuba as a victim of yellow fever during his study of the disease. In the background is the commemorative diploma of the Royal Society of Apothecaries awarded to Ross who had many years earlier failed their examination!

23. PRIMARY HEPATIC CARCINOMA AND HEPATITIS B INFECTION. A SUMMARY OF RECENT WORK.
Blumberg BS, Larouze B, London WT, Lustbader ED, Saimot G, Payet M
Inst. Cancer Res., Fox Chase Cancer Center, Philadelphia, PA
Prevention and Detection of Cancer. Part II. Detection. Vol. 2 Cancer Detection in Specific Sites. Proceedings of the Third International Symposium on Detection and Prevention of Cancer held in New York NY April 26 to May 1 1976Nieburgs HE, ed. New York, Marcel Dekker, Inc., 1303-2456 pp., 1980.

The role of hepatitis B in the pathogenesis of primary hepatic carcinoma (PHC) was evaluated. There is evidence that in many patients th[illegible]ression of events leading to PHC may include i[illegible]patitis B virus, development of hepatitis[illegible]hepatitis to chronic hepatitis, and po[illegible] collected in West Africa were us[illegible]tive model which can be used to [illegible]f individuals proceeding from o[illegible] were three groups of patients wit[illegible] B, and Mali) and one with chro[illegible] group was selected for each of [illegible]stablished on clinical grounds and [illegible]ated alpha-fetoprotein (AFP). Hepa[illegible]HBsAg) was determined by radioi[illegible]Bs was determined by direct hema[illegible]tis B core (HBc) and AFP were an[illegible]n methods. In every case the frequ[illegible]c were higher in the disease gro[illegible] in each of the groups the frequ[illegible]ys higher than that of HBsAg. T[illegible]ad much higher levels of alpha-fetopro[illegible]ith chronic liver dis-

Baruch Blumberg was born in 1925 in New York City and educated at the Flatbush Yeshiva where he studied the Talmud before attending Far Rockaway High School. After completing medical school at the College of Physicians and Surgeons of Columbia University in 1947, he became interested in genetic polymorphism following studies undertaken at Moengo in Northern Surinam. Although his initial studies related to the variation in response to infection with Wuchereria Bancroftia, *he subsequently became interested in the study of inherited polymorphisms which culminated in the discovery of the hepatitis B virus and his award of a Nobel Prize in 1976.*

existence of anicteric hepatitis, which had been previously proposed by Mende (1810) and accurately described by Eppinger (1922).

Despite their relatively limited scope, the transmission studies did, however, establish the viral etiology of hepatitis. Subsequent studies undertaken by MacCallum and Bradley in England (1944), and by Havens (1944) and Neefe (1944) in America, thereafter characterized two filterable agents responsible for the two types of hepatitis. The two diseases, similar clinically and pathologically, differed on epidemiological grounds and were variously referred to as infectious and serum hepatitis (Neefe 1946), type A and type B hepatitis (MacCallum, 1947), and MS-1 and MS-2 hepatitis (Krugman 1967). The prophylactic effect of gamma globulin for type A hepatitis was noted in 1945 (Stokes and Neefe, 1945; Havens and Paul, 1945). After numerous failures to isolate or grow the viruses, however, the study of hepatitis lapsed into an arid period.

In 1965 a serendipitous discovery by B. Blumberg, a geneticist interested in the genetic basis of polymorphism, of a serologic marker for type B hepatitis, re-ignited the further elucidation of viral hepatitis. Blumberg wondered if patients receiving multiple transfusions might develop antibodies against polymorphic serum proteins. The blood of one patient reacted with inherited antigenic specificities on the low-density lipoproteins, a system that Blumberg termed Ag. In 1963, he examined the reactions of hemophiliac sera that did not commonly have antibodies against the Ag antigen and noted that one hemophiliac serum precipitated one of twenty-four test sera in a panel. Since this specimen was quite unlike any of the other Ag precipitins and came from the blood of an Australian aborigine, the reactant in the aborigine serum became known as Australia (Au) antigen. Serendipity favored Blumberg, since if he had examined only sera of normal Americans (which have a 0.1% positivity against Au antigen), as opposed to sera of Australian aborigines (with a 20% positive reaction), he might have never made this discovery. Since Au antigen was found initially in patients with leukemia, Down's syndrome, and leprosy, the possibility of a marker for leukemia was entertained. However, the conversion from negative to positive reaction in one patient with Down's syndrome and in a laboratory worker, led, in 1966, to the hypothesis that Au antigen was associated with viral hepatitis. In fact, the specificity of the marker for type B hepatitis was subsequently confirmed by Prince (1968) and Okochi (1968) and Blumberg received the Nobel Prize in 1976.

The Au antigen particles were subsequently demonstrated by Bayer (1968) in serum by electron microscopy and, in 1970, Dane identified larger particles now regarded as the viron of type B hepatitis. Additional antigenic determinants of the Au antigen were suggested (Levene and Blumberg, 1969) and defined (LeBouvier, 1971; Bancroft et al., 1972), and the identification of other antigen/antibody systems related to hepatitis B virus followed over the next five years antigen/antibody (Magnius 1972) and delta antigen/antibody (Rizzetto 1977). The careful studies of hepatitis epidemics in a mental institution, by Krugman and colleagues (1960s), defined the existence of two immunologically distinct hepatitis viruses that they called MS-1 and MS-2.8. It soon became clear that one represented type B virus and the other type A virus. The transmission of the latter by Deinhardt in 1967 to marmoset monkeys caused hepatitis, and facilitated studies of this infection. The type A virus was visualized on electron microscopy in stools of patients (Feinstone 1973), and propagated in cell culture *in vitro* by Provost and Hilleman in 1979. A third human hepatitis virus, a non-A and non-B type, was first suggested by Havens in 1956 and subsequently by Mosley in 1966, who had noted that some cases of hepatitis had an incubation period between that of type A and type B disease. In 1974, Prince, in a study of post-transfusion hepatitis, confirmed the existence of this third virus.

The marker for viral hepatitis confirmed the previous proposal of Jones and Minot in 1923 that the infection might culminate in the development of cirrhosis and even liver-cell carcinoma (Sheldon and James, 1948). Furthermore, the development of different types of vaccine against viral hepatitis (Krugman 1971; Maupas, 1976; Szmuness 1980), enabled some degree of therapeutic control to be developed of what had previously been an ill-understood and nebulous entity.

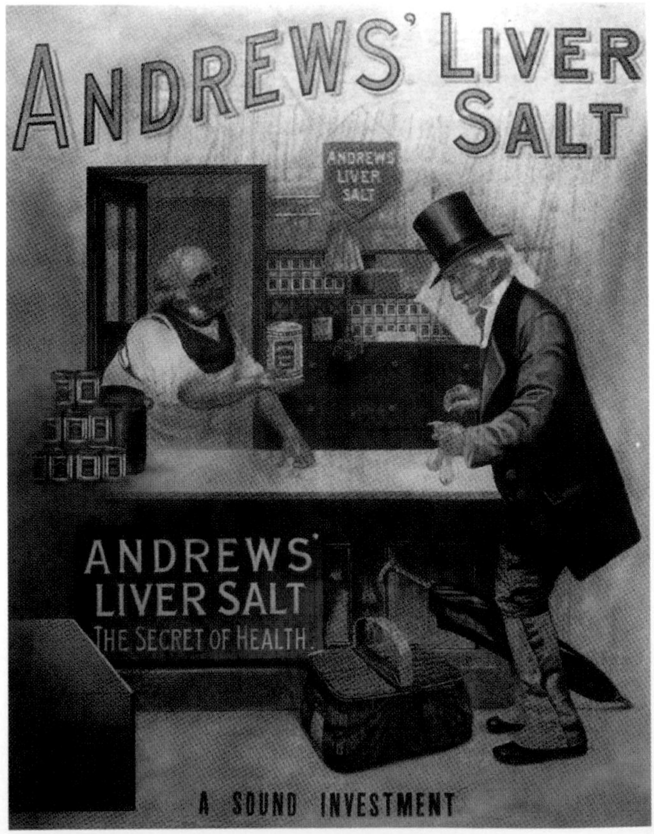

The widespread uncertainty as to the specific cause and appropriate therapy for liver disease led to the development of numerous remedies of dubious efficacy. The remedy offered by the pharmacist appears to have had little effect on his own condition.

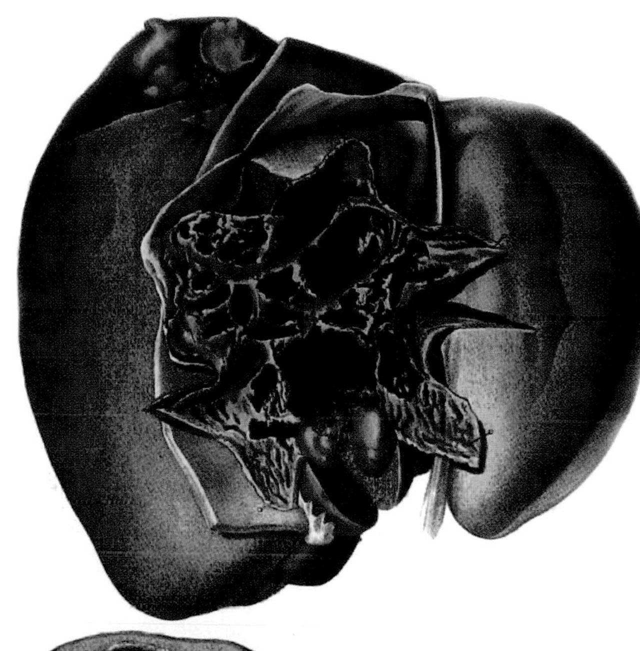

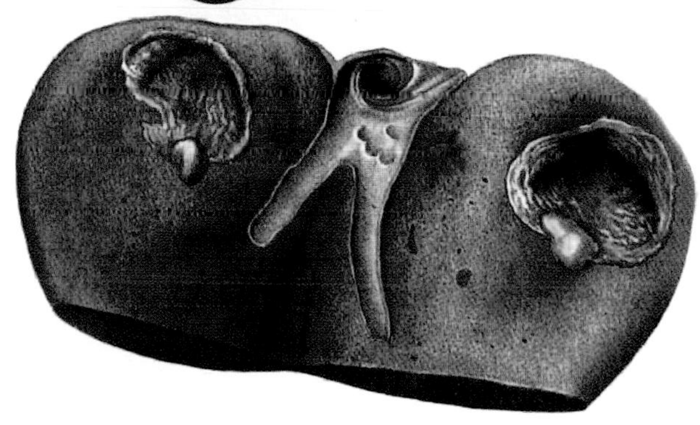

A 19th-century Carswell pathological drawing of multiple hepatic tumors. The recognition that infective disease might lead to neoplasia was of particular relevance to the long-term prognosis of viral hepatitis.

The general management of infectious and toxic hepatitis initially was broad and included bed rest, avoidance of hepatotoxins, and a high-protein, high carbohydrate diet. The rationale for the latter proposal lay with the reasoning that *"a high glycogen content in the liver cell acted as a protective substance for the essential cell proteins and lessened necrosis."* The era of high-protein diets lasted until the late 1950s, by which time it had become apparent that protein overload had little effect upon the morbidity and mortality of patients with chronic liver disease and on the contrary, might even precipitate hepatic coma. A fad regarding the use of specific amino acid mixtures was thereafter promulgated, chiefly by J. Fisher, but rigorous analysis of the data and evidence of only marginal clinical efficacy led to a loss of enthusiasm.

The introduction of purified adrenal hormones into everyday practice, by Hench in 1949, marked a pivotal point in the history of liver therapy, although as Eppinger had proposed, their usage in liver disease as early as 1937 in purified preparations were unavailable. Clinicians reacted swiftly to the availability of adrenal hormones for the treatment of acute viral hepatitis, and conflicting claims for benefits resulted. A dramatic response in comatose patients with hepatitis was claimed by Wildhurt (1951) and Ducci and Katz (1952) using cortisone therapy, but controlled trials failed to support the contention efficacy. The overwhelmingly fatal course in fulminant hepatitis forced the utilization of alternative heroic measures including hemodialysis, peritoneal dialysis, exchange blood transfusion, cross-circulation, total body washout, hemoperfusion with artificial exchange columns or membrane, and even extracorporeal liver perfusion (Eiseman 1965). Few met with any predictable success although recently liver transplantation has proved of some utility.

Despite the relatively disappointing results with corticosteroid therapy, it proved to be of some use in the treatment of chronic active hepatitis, although the end point – mortality rate – was not much different in the treated and untreated groups. The status of corticosteroids for treating alcoholic hepatitis became a subject of debate, but most studies failed to demonstrate any efficacy.

The high incidence of serum hepatitis during World War II enlisted the attention of the U.S. Army, and scientific efforts of that time resulted in much of the present understanding of viral hepatitis. A notable advance was Stokes and Neefe's demonstration in 1945 that gamma globulin prophylaxis attenuated the severity of type A hepatitis. The subsequent discovery by Blumberg of the marker for type B hepatitis in 1965 led to the demonstration that immune

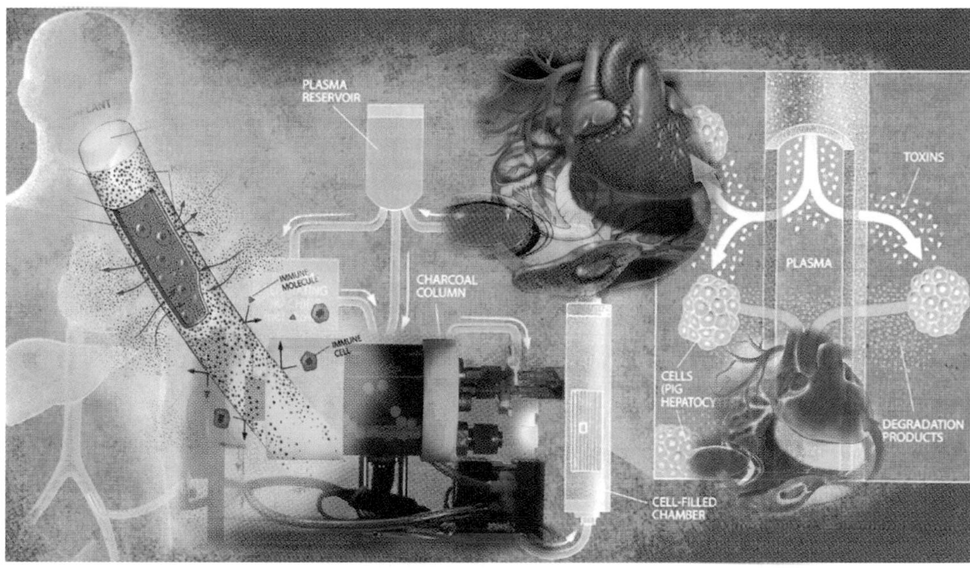

The age of biotechnology has spawned the development of numerous devices capable of substituting for organ and cell function. The quest for an artificial liver, however, remains the Holy Grail of hepatology.

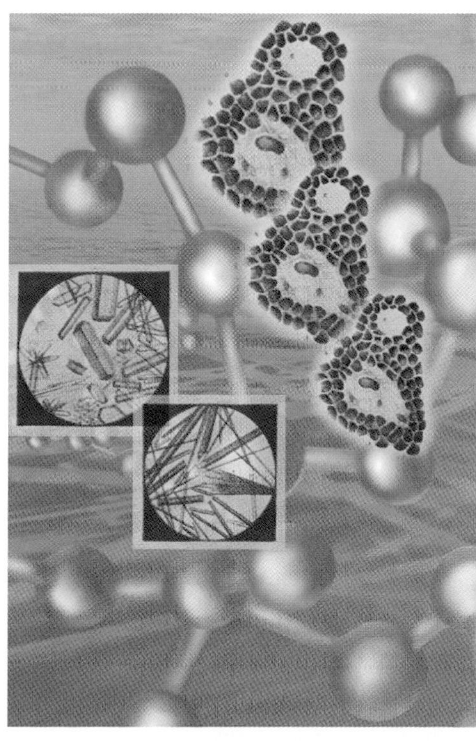

Although considerable information has accrued in regard to hepatic metabolic function, much is still unknown in regard to both its synthetic and detoxification mechanisms. The mechanisms whereby proteins are constructed and other metabolites degraded remain a source of major investigative interest.

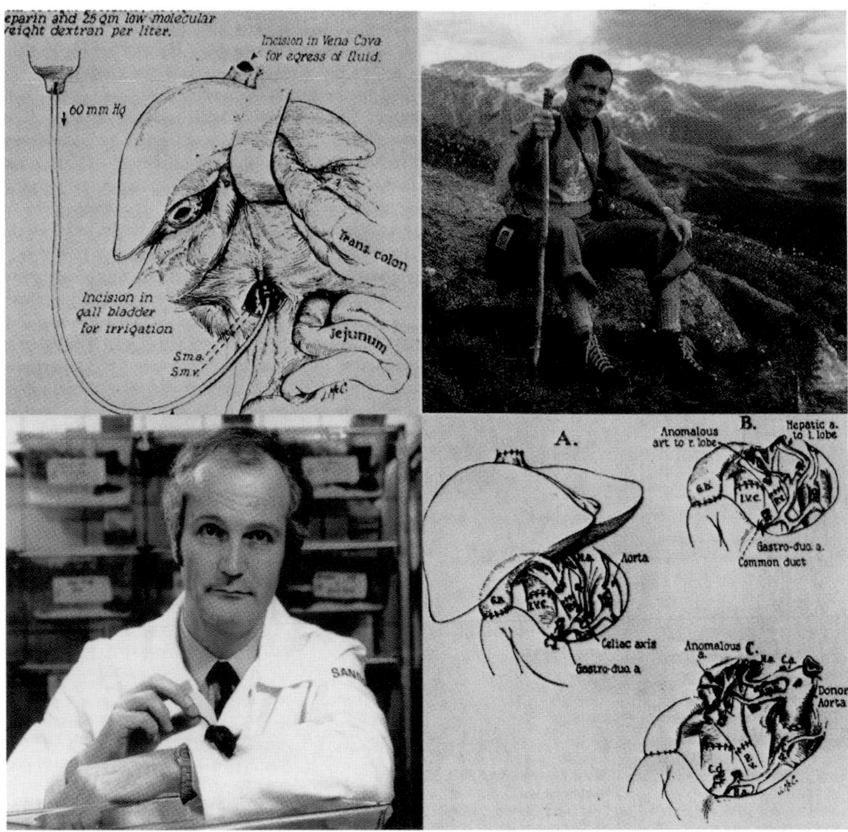

A major advance in the therapy of hepatic disease was hepatic transplantation (inset) introduced by T. Starzl (sitting) in 1963. The success of the admirable technical accomplishment, however, often remained dubious and unpredictable until the discovery of cyclosporine by Bordet (bottom left) of France.

globulin was also effective for preventing or attenuating infection with this virus. More recently, the development of specific vaccines directed against the individual hepatitis viruses, has led to a major therapeutic advance.

A major advance in the annals of hepatic therapeutics and surgery was provided by the successful introduction of liver transplantation. Although Welch in 1955 had undertaken the first attempts in heterotopic transplantation of the liver in dogs, the difficulties of maintaining vascular inflow and adequate biliary drainage soon forced abandonment of this procedure. In 1959, Starzl in Denver, successfully undertook orthotopic liver transplantation and thereafter in 1963, he performed the first successful liver grafting in man. Thereafter Calne, at Cambridge and King's College Hospital in England, further advanced the subject and the long-term survival of recipients became noteworthy.

Hepatic Echinococcus

The concept of parasitic disease of the liver was well known from autopsy material, but there was no form of therapy available although accidental opening of a hydatid cyst of the liver had been reported in the seventeenth century. A systemic approach to the disease was initiated by the innovative French surgeon Recamier (1794-1856). In 1825 he reported his experience, based upon the premise that successful evacuation of a hydatid cyst would be possible only after joining the abdominal wall with the visceral peritoneum of the cyst in order to prevent peritonitis. In order to facilitate the procedure, Recamier employed quicklime prior to the operation to establish adhesions between the hydatid sac and its surroundings. Having arbitrarily determined that the adhesions were sufficiently matured, he successfully drained the cyst. It is reported that this method was subsequently used by Maylley and Dodard in 1668, but thereafter fell into disrepute, since failure to obtain adequate adhesive response led to intra-abdominal cyst spillage and death.

Nevertheless, the success of Recamier produced its imitators for operating upon other afflictions of the liver, and even early gallstone surgery employed the technique of inducing a "walled off" effect initially followed by a definitive procedure at a later time. After the introduction of asepsis, such techniques were mostly abandoned and replaced by laparotomy. By the end of the nineteenth century, standardized operations became elaborate as the concepts of hemostasis and antisepsis provided some measure of safety, thus by 1877, Sanger reported total excision of the hydatid cyst in and in 1883, Croft similarly confirmed his positive experience with the technique. Surgery proved so effective that four years later, Loreta in 1887, was able to report the first hepatic resection for echinococcus.

The dramatic intervention of surgery, and its high morbidity, led to a search for nonoperative methods for the treatment of hydatid cysts, and as a result diverse agents including iodine preparations, mercury, and even common table salt were tried. A more exotic technique, electropuncture of the cyst, was reported by Guerault in 1857 based upon his belief that electrolysis would kill the echinococcus organism but this, like other indirect methods of treatment, had no success. Treatment of multilocular echinococcus cysts was described by Buhl for the first time in 1852, but was far more difficult than

Jean Recamier (1794-1856) of Paris, France, was the first surgeon to successfully operate upon a hepatic hydatid cyst. He used the principle of marsupialization to successfully accomplish the extirpation of the parasite.

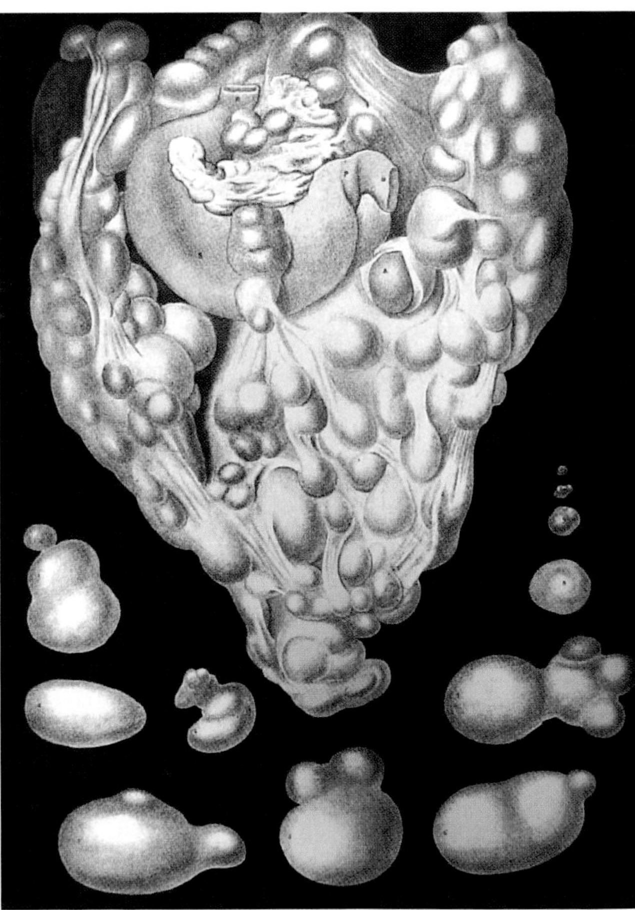

A pathological specimen demonstrating hepatic hydatid disease culminating in extensive involvement of the peritoneal cavity with daughter cysts.

the treatment of unilocular echinococcal cyst. Nevertheless, in 1896, Brunsl successfully resected a portion of the liver for echinococcus alveolaris. Even a century later, the treatment of parasitic liver cysts has changed little, and excision of the cyst remains the only reasonable therapy.

Corset Liver and Wandering Liver

The exigencies of nineteenth-century fashion resulted in the development of significant anatomical distortions of the waist and even spine. In some women, the exaggeration of high fashion produced dramatic contortion of the liver and provided surgeons with difficulty in establishing whether symptoms were related to hepatic pressure effects or structural aberrations of the liver. Since it was thought not unreasonable that the monstrously contorted livers might be a good reason for the cause for complaints, and since ladies could not be induced to abandon their foundation garments, the surgeons (as might be predicted) took out the scalpel. Indeed, no less a savant than Billroth (1829-1894) carried out ventrofixation of a corset lobe in 1884! Other surgeons were less inhibited in their response and actually undertook complete resection of corset lobes. Few successful reports exist to document the efficacy of this therapy.

An even more exotic disease was provided by descriptions of the wandering liver, which appeared to be a "*forme frust*" of the visceroptosis mania which afflicted both medical and surgical diagnosis at the turn of the twentieth century. Such was the belief in this condition – known as Glenard's disease – that eminent surgeons including Kolliker (1906) and Eugene Bircher in 1918 operated on what they described as genuine wandering livers. The most likely explanation is that these livers had been pressed low into the abdominal cavity by corsets. No validated description of a genuine wandering liver (unlike the wandering spleen), has ever been noted at autopsy examination. Indeed, in most circumstances a suspected "wandering liver" has proved to be either a tumor or other disease that has deceived the clinicians.

The use of complex corsets to define the waists of women was a fashion statement that led to major alterations of hepatic architecture as can be noted from the pathology insets (left and right). These abnormalities were at one stage believed to be responsible for disease, and surgery was even undertaken in a misguided attempt to remedy the disorder.

Portal Hypertension

The ancient world had noted that liver damage was associated with other abdominal abnormalities, particularly fluid collection. Thus, a study of the Ebers Papyrus (1600 B.C.) reveals that the ancient Egyptians were aware of the relationship between ascites and liver disease. Given the prevalence of schistosomiasis in Egypt, it is likely that parasitic disease may have been the cause. More than ten centuries later, Erasistratus of Alexandria (300 B.C.) commented on the presence of ascites with hardness of the liver. The occurrence of splenomegaly in diseases of the liver was later reported by physicians as diverse as Vesalius, Boerhaave, and Bianchi.

The early clinical, and the later morphologic, descriptions of cirrhosis as undertaken by Bonet, Morgagni, Rokitansky, and Skoda, recognized ascites as an integral component of the disease complex.

In 1689, Stahl had described a syndrome of portal hypertension that was associated with his theory of plethora. The vague disease involved the portal and splenic veins and the hemorrhoidal venous plexuses, and Stahl reported epistaxis and the salutary effects of rectal hemorrhages in alcoholic individuals. Subsequently in 1751, Kremff observed engorgement of the portal vein in patients who vomited blood and Morgagni (1769) recorded a case of thrombosis of the portal vein in a young man who presented with hematemesis and splenomegaly. Almost a century later, Le Diberder and Fauvel (1857-1858) in France and Power (1840) in America recognized the entity of esophageal varices. Meanwhile, both Retzius (1835) and Sappey (1859) published descriptions of the portacaval anastomotic circulation, while

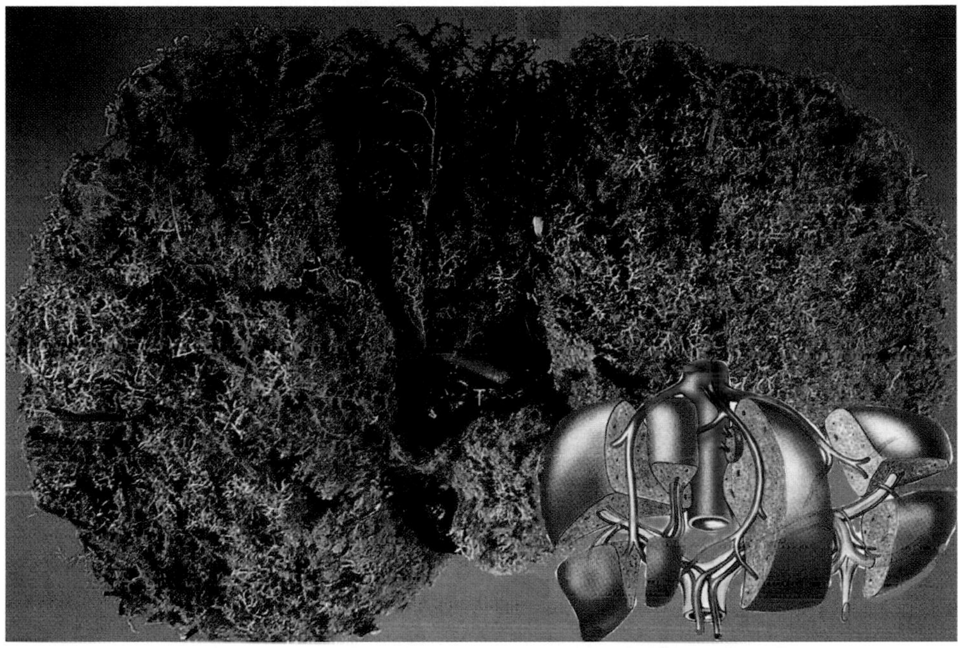

An injection specimen of the liver demonstrating (in green) the portal venous circulation. The elucidation of the complex vascular architecture of the individual hepatic segments (inset) provided critical information necessary to facilitate surgical intervention in hepatic pathology.

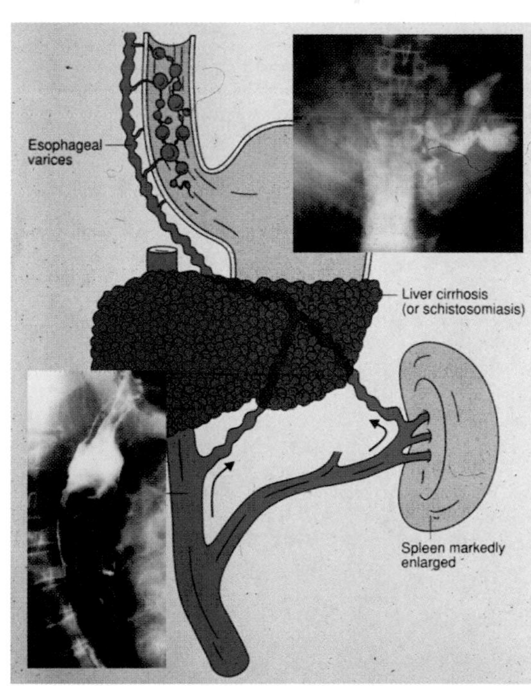

Portal hypertension led to the development of esophageal varices and the lethal complication of hemorrhage. Despite their identification by either an upper GI series or endoscopy, little definitive therapy was available for their management.

LO SPERIMENTALE

GIORNALE MEDICO

ORGANO DELL' ACCADEMIA MEDICO-FISICA FIORENTINA

DIRETTO DAI PROFESSORI

D. BAJARDI, G. BANTI, G. BUFALINI, G. CHIARUGI, F. COLZI, G. FANO, A. FILIPPI, P. GROCCO, A. LUSTIG, G. MYA, G. PELLIZZARI, E. PESTALOZZA, G. ROSTER

COMU... VISTE

STABILIMENTO TIPOGRAFICO FIORENTINO

Via San Gallo, 33

1894

Banti in 1883 documented a syndrome that included splenomegaly, hepatic enlargement, and anemia, which culminated in gastrointestinal bleeding. This was initially considered as a separate disease process until later recognized to be part of the protean manifestations of cirrhosis and portal hypertension.

CONCLUSIONS BASED ON SIXTY CASES OF FATAL GASTRO-INTESTINAL HEMORRHAGE DUE TO CIRRHOSIS OF THE LIVER.

BY R. B. PREBLE, A.B., M.D.,

CHICAGO, ILL.

...wing brief clinical and post-mortem notes of four new cases ...ro-intestinal hemorrhage—three from my hospital experience ...indly furnished me by Dr. R. B. Olson—will serve as an ... To these four cases fifty-six collected from the literature

R.B. Preble of Chicago in 1900, was amongst the first to note the relationship between cirrhosis, the development of portal hypertension, and gastrointestinal bleeding.

Raikem (1848) commented upon other features of portal hypertension – including the formation of collateral circulation and ascites – attributing the pathogenesis to an inflammation of the portal vein. In his definitive monograph on the liver, Frerichs (1860), who identified splenomegaly as a regular component of portal hypertension, referred to the case of Fauvel (1858) as the only recorded one of bleeding varices. The focus of physicians of this time period with the secondary manifestations of portal hypertension (splenomegaly and anemia), led to the development of splenic anemia, a term first proposed by Gretsel in 1866.

In 1883, Banti published the first systemic treatise on the syndrome, then known as hepatosplenopathy, which was to subsequently bear his name. Banti maintained that the disease ran a chronic course, progressing in three stages. The first was the anemic phase, with splenomegaly, leucopenia, and occasional gastrointestinal hemorrhage; the second was a transitional stage with oliguria, urobilinuria, hepatomegaly, and increased gastrointestinal bleeding; and finally came the ascitic stage, with cirrhosis and death from hemorrhage or hepatic insufficiency. He proposed that the pathognomonic lesion was splenic in origin and comprised a thickening of the reticulum around the central arteries of the follicles. The precise etiology of this splenopathy was much debated and included a range of organisms. Banti himself suggested a toxic cause, believing that the spleen was the organ principally affected, and that the liver was secondarily damaged by a toxin released by the spleen. This proposal was not accepted in Europe, although in England and America it was considered credible mostly by the fact that Osler, as one of the most influential clinicians of the time, supported it. Indeed, his articles "On Splenic Anemia" (1900 and 1902), document the coexistence of splenomegaly and anemia in forty-five cases. Osler, however, did not consider that the disease was a primary splenic disorder , but simply a "chronic splenic anemia" plus features of cirrhosis of the liver.

Treating the putative disease of "splenic anemia" was an interest of surgeons, who claimed that cure could only be effected by performing splenectomy or omentopexy. And indeed, notable wielders of the scalpel, including Cushing (1898), Halsted (1901), and Mayo (1902), insisted that splenectomy was useful in alleviating recurrent hematemesis.

Reconsideration of the fundamental basis of the problem occurred at the turn of the century. Thus, Gilbert in 1899, deduced that portal vein pressure must be high in the patient with ascites after obtaining pressure readings of ascitic fluid as high as 400 mm of saline, and introduced the term "portal hypertension". The observations in terms of increased pressure were subsequently confirmed by Villaret (1906) and Pichancourt (1913) in patients with ascites.

At that stage, doubts about Banti's hypothesis began to appear when investigators explored the relationship of the hepatic vasculature to portal vein pressure. Thus, Herrick in 1907 conducted perfusion studies that correlated the intrahepatic increase of vascular resistance to the cirrhotic process and demonstrated the backflow of portal venous flow secondary to arteriovenous shunting. Similarly, Dock and Warthin in 1904, on the basis of their clinical studies, thought that the congestion of the portal vein accounted for the congestive splenomegaly. They concluded that splenic anemia was not a primary disease but secondary to the portal vein thrombosis. The case was virtually closed by 1920 when Eppinger, and subsequently Klemperer (1928), reported the splenic changes of Banti's disease were produced by cirrhosis and thrombosis of the splenic vein. Confusion about the pathogenesis of Banti's syndrome persisted until the 1950s, and the English standard textbooks of medicine treated it with ambivalence. The myth of splenic anemia was finally exorcised when radiological and hemodynamic studies in the early 1950s refuted Banti's concept of the disease.

The connection between the esophageal varices of portal hypertension and cirrhosis was poorly understood until Preble of Chicago (1900) published his autopsy series of sixty patients with cirrhosis and fatal gastrointestinal hemorrhage. He noted that esophageal varices occurred in 80% of

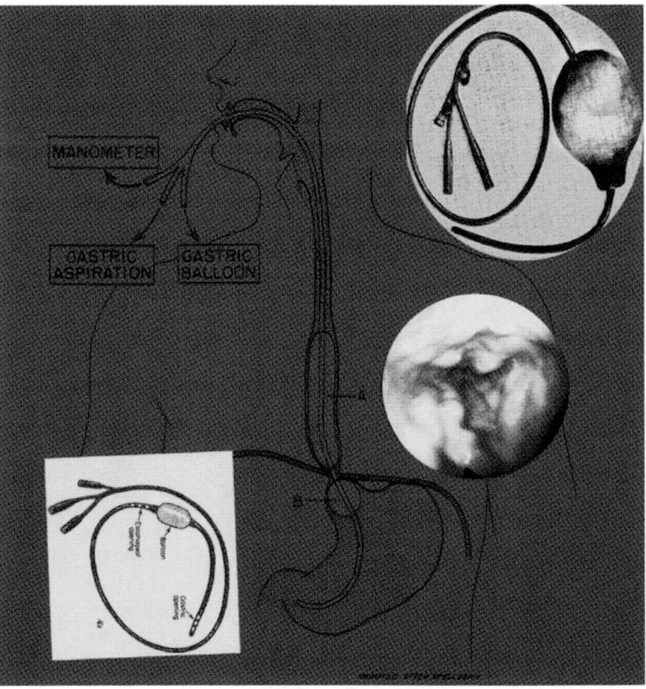

The development of a collateral venous circulation at the lower end of the esophagus resulted in esophageal varices. The combination of acid peptic reflux and the increased venous pressure in the submucosal plexus often culminated in fatal bleeding. A number of balloon tubes were designed in an optimistically unrealistic effort to compress the varices and control hemorrhage.

VASCULAR LESIONS OF PORTAL CIRRHOSIS*

ARCHIBALD H. McINDOE, M.B., Ch.B. (N.Z.)
Fellow in Surgery, The Mayo Foundation
ROCHESTER, MINN.

In the last two years the most distinct advance made in the treatment for ascites of portal cirrhosis has been the introduction of the newer diuretics. Keith and Whelan[1] have shown that following the intravenous administration of merbaphen combined with the simultaneous use of ammonium chloride or ammonium nitrate, the ascites can be well controlled for long ...

3. Blumenau, Ernst: Ueber Todesursache bei Lebercirrhose, Arch. f. Verdauungskr. 27:1, 1921.

Archibald H. McIndoe of New Zealand, while a fellow at the Mayo Clinic in 1928, defined the physiological basis of portal hypertension. Presumably disappointed at the therapeutic possibilities available for the mangement of cirrhotic disease, he turned to plastic surgery and became a war-time legend for his reconstructive skills employed in the treatment of military victims.

the cases and proposed that the varices developed in response to the blockage of the portal vein, with the obstruction following from the loss of elasticity of the cirrhotic liver. His observations were supported by the respective work of a number of other investigators (Heller, 1904; de Josselin de Jong, 1912; Enderlen and Magnus Alsleben, 1914), who all correlated portal hypertension with the formation of esophageal varices and ascites. All four authors attributed the epistaxis seen in cirrhosis to the elevated portal pressure. Thus Enderlen wrote: "*If the hepatic cirrhosis antedates the thrombosis and as a consequence of the compromised intrahepatic circulation the esophageal veins are dilated, then overfilling of these veins must lead to rupture and immediate esophageal hemorrhage. If cirrhosis is not present, hemorrhages occur much later and are less dramatic.*" The importance of portal venous stasis in the development of congestive splenomegaly was recognized by Warthin (1910) and by Eppinger (1920), who coined the term "*Staungsmilz*" in his treatise on hepatolienal disease.

A definitive comment, "Vascular Lesions of the Portal Cirrhosis", was produced in 1928 by McIndoe, who concluded that portal vein pressure is high in cirrhosis with the hemodynamic changes evolving in stages. McIndoe suggested the use of an Eck's fistula as a means of relieving portal hypertension. The use of the term portal hypertension was given further credence by McMichael (1931, 1934) who extended the concept by relating it to the thickening and narrowing of the portal or splenic vein.

Congestive splenomegaly, according to McMichael, might be explained on the basis of increased portal pressure, reasoning by analogy with pulmonary hypertension. In 1930, Carnot reported the initial measurement of portal venous pressure in animals, and shortly thereafter in 1936, Rousselot published the first determination of pressure in the human portal system. This data was subsequently confirmed in 1937 by Thompson (working with Whipple) in New York. Both groups measured splenic vein pressure of patients with congestive splenomegaly during laparotomy. Thereafter hemodynamic studies of the portal circulation accelerated with the introduction of hepatic vein catheterization (Warren and Brannon, 1944), a method for measuring hepatic blood flow (Bradley et al., 1945), and the technique for measuring hepatic wedge pressure (Friedman and Weiner, 1951; Meyers and Taylor, 1951; Sherlock et al., 1953).

The repetitive demonstration of hypertension led to surgical enthusiasm to decrease the pressure in the belief that this would ameliorate hemorrhage. Indeed in America, many of the pioneer investigations were performed by surgeons seeking to rationalize the therapy. Thus, the revival of surgical therapy for portal hypertension (Blakemore and Lord, 1945; Whipple, 1945) led, in addition, to an increased recognition of disorders with elevated portal pressure other than cirrhosis. One consequence of the detailed evaluation of the problem was the development of sophisticated radiological examinations as the need for accurate anatomical diagnosis increased. Such procedures included celiac angiography (Seldinger, 1953), splenoportography (Abeatici and Campi), umbilical vein catheterization (Gonzales Carbalhaes, 1955), and hepatic venography (Tori, 1953). During the 1960s, shunt surgery became popular as a method to control the high incidence of variceal hemorrhage in patients with cirrhosis, and a diverse range of procedures were introduced as each surgeon claimed advantages for a novel technique. As a result, several cooperative studies involving groups of medical centers were mounted to define the efficacy of shunt procedures. The overall analysis of the mortality and complications, especially hepatic encephalopathy, drastically tempered the enthusiasm for shunt surgery in patients with hepatic cirrhosis. As a result of the disappointing surgical outcomes, the use of pharmacological agents that decreased portal venous pressure was considered a more reasonable approach. Thus, vasopressin was initially demonstrated to provide considerable relief in acute situations and the subsequent introduction of the somatostatin analogue, Octreotide provided evidence that long-term pharmacological control of portal hypertension might be a feasible therapeutic option.

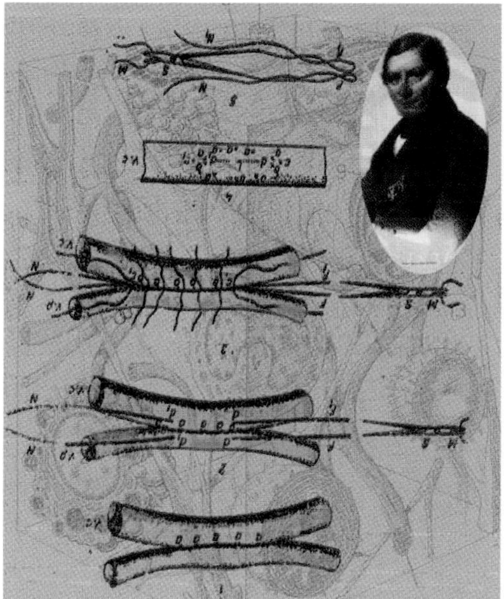

Nikolai Vladimirovich Eck (1849-1902) surgeon, bureaucrat, and mining engineer was born in St. Petersburg, the only son of Vladimir E. Eck, a distinguished physician and professor of medicine at the Military Medical Academy in St. Petersburg. As might have been predicted, Eck, whose family personified social prominence and political influence, undertook his postgraduate training at the First Medical Institute in St. Petersburg, of which his father was the director. In 1877 Eck described the surgical creation of a fistula between the inferior vena cava and the portal vein in a dog and suggested that this operation might be of use in humans for the treatment of ascites. Some fifty years would elapse before A.O. Whipple reported his experience with Eck's operation and initiated the nebulous surgical era of the portacaval shunt as a treatment for portal hypertension. It is of interest that in 1882 (three years before Billroth), Eck successfully resected a cancerous stomach. Because of his substantial interest in other areas such as mining and geology, history has depicted Eck as an erratic individual in search of an unknown destiny. Indeed, for thirteen years he was divorced from medicine and surgery, although it was during this period that he undertook the only clinical portacaval shunt of his career (of note: it was successful!). Eck's little known connection with I.P. Pavlov was substantial, and even at this time the "Eck-fistula" is referred to in St. Petersburg as the "Eck-Pavlov shunt".

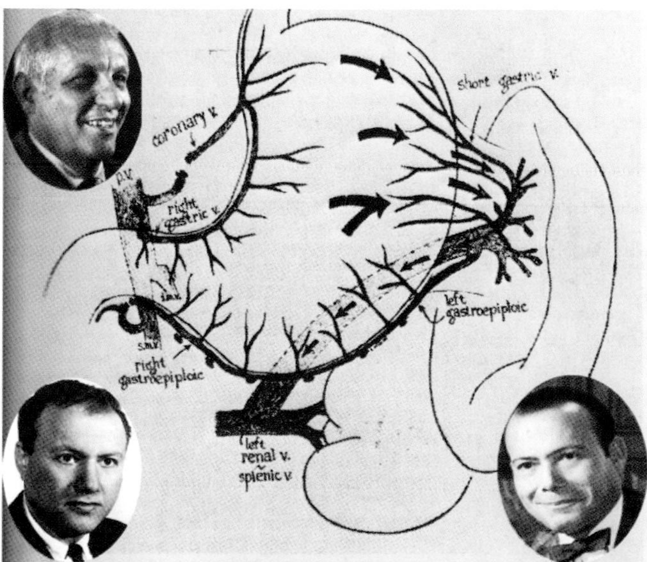

Innumerable surgical procedures were proposed in an attempt to decompress portal hypertension. In general these were described as "shunts". The morbidity and mortality of such operations was considerable and the depressing long-term outcome in most cases of cirrhosis resulted in little enthusiasm for this therapeutic strategy. Dean Warren (top left), Marshall Orloff (bottom left) and Robert Zeppa (bottom right) each contributed considerably to the development of surgical strategies aimed at decreasing portal venous pressure.

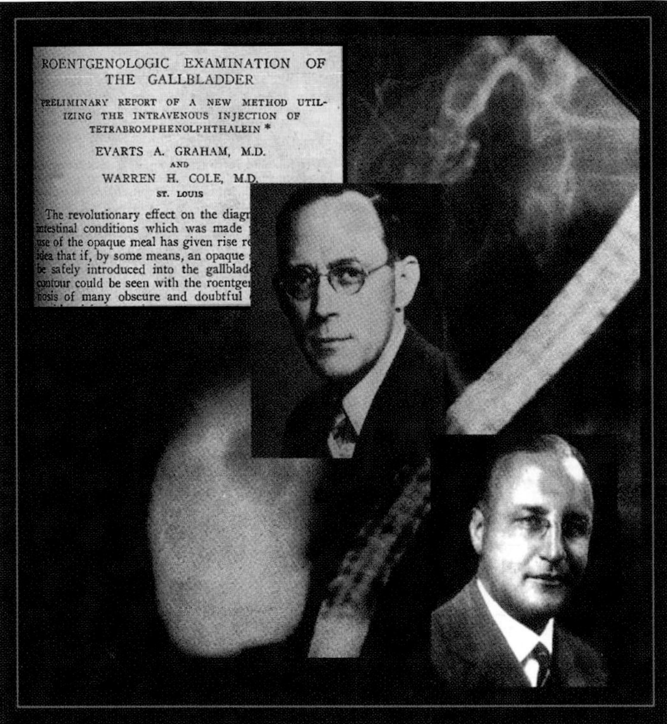

Evarts Graham (1883-1957) (bottom), Professor of Surgery at Washington University, St. Louis, and later the organizer and first chairman of the American Board of Surgery, convinced Warren H. Cole (top), a first-year resident, to spend a research year working on the problem of visualizing the gall bladder. Graham proposed that an iodine or bromine derivative of phenopthalein, because of the high atomic number of halogen, might be radiographically visible in the gall bladder once it had been excreted by the liver. After four-and-a-half months of complete failure, Cole achieved the first successful cholecystogram in a dog. To his horror, the experiment could not be successfully repeated until it was realized that the chance failure of the animal caretaker (Bill) to feed the one dog had resulted in a positive study. Forty years later Cole recalled, "I must have injected as many as 200 dogs and rabbits without obtaining a single gall bladder shadow! After the one successful study I earnestly sought to repeat it, ...finally in desperation I called the animal caretaker and asked him if the treatment of that dog had been in anyway different... Bill hesitated a bit, but stated he could think of nothing different in that dog. When I told him that the dog showed exactly the thing we were looking for his expression of apprehension changed and he meekly stated: 'Well, Dr. Cole there was one thing different. I forgot to feed that dog the morning he was injected!'"

Ascites

Hippocrates associated liver disease with dropsy and stated *"when the liver is full of fluid and this overflows in the peritoneal cavity so that the belly becomes full of water, death follows."* Erasistratus of Alexandria noted that a hard liver and dropsy were related, and proposed that ascites is formed by the leakage of fluid into the peritoneal cavity. Galen felt the problem was due to suppression of hemorrhoids or imperfect evacuation with the accumulation of cold humors. Aretaeus of Cappadocia proposed: *"dropsy sometimes is occasioned suddenly by a copious cold draught when on account of thirst much cold water is swallowed and the fluid is transferred to the peritoneum."*

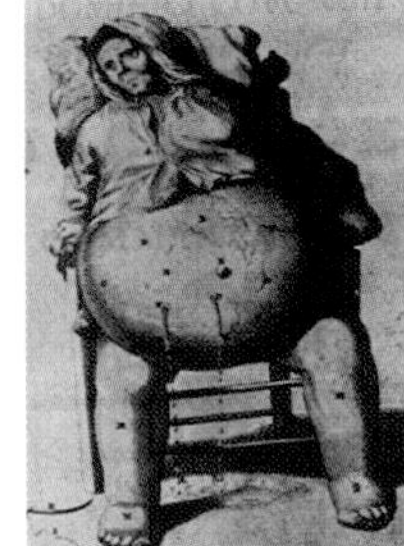

A garish caricature of the morbid consequences of cirrhosis and ascites. The drainage technique depicted was developed by Dekkers in 17th century Holland, to help relieve discomfort.

As early as the first century A.D. both Celsus and Hippocrates had proposed paracentesis for the relief of ascites. Celsus used a lead or bronze tube with the collar about the middle to avoid fluid loss in the patient's abdomen, but preferred medical therapy including long walks and the application of *"fatty figs bruised with honey"*. Paul of Aegina in the seventh century A.D. proposed dehydration as well as paracentesis, but suggested that the latter be undertaken slowly *"lest having evacuated the vital spirit with the fluid the patient be killed."* In the fourteenth century, John of Gaddesden advocated salt-poor bread for the use of treatment of dropsy and in 1728, John Lower, an Oxford physiologist, was the first to produce experimental ascites in dogs by ligating the thoracic segment of the inferior vena cava. By the early nineteenth century, the clinical detection of ascites was well advanced and R. Bright noted that obstruction of the venous system could be the basis of some ascitic effusions. He used cirrhosis of the liver with its obstruction of the portal vein as a classic example of this situation. P. Charcot of Paris (1881) astutely noted that ascites would not develop if venous collaterals were present, and implicated portal hypertension in the developing of the condition. Ernest Henry Starling in 1895 provided a considerable contribution to the physiological understanding of ascites by defining the nature of colloid osmotic pressure. In 1928, A.H. McIndoe opined that hepatic insufficiency was considerably more dangerous than ascites and that once jaundice appeared, it was likely that vascular compromise of the hepatic parenchyma had occurred. Subsequent to the evaluation of the hemodynamic factors involved in the development of ascites, hypoalbuminemia, and thereafter excessive intraabdominal lymph secretion, were recognized as further issues involved in the genesis of the disease. The demonstration of sodium retention in the 1940s by E.B. Farnsworth and the relationship to increased anti-diuretic hormone secretion and excessive aldosterone production, led to the development of spironolactone diuretics to antagonize the effects of aldosterone. At least three separate theories were developed in regard to the basis of the sodium and water problems in the development of ascites. These included the oldest concept (endocrine changes secondary to the intra-abdominal fluid secretion that resulted from portal hypertension); the second or renal theory (impaired renal ability to excrete salt and water). The third or lymphatic theory maintained that the primary cause of cirrhotic ascites was increased lymph flow into the abdominal cavity due to the portal hypertension and hyperdynamic splenic blood flow.

The Gall Bladder

The significance of the gall bladder and its ductular system was a source of considerable debate in antiquity. Although many physicians considered it to be only useful as a source of omens and predictions, others believed that its presence was vital to sustain life, and bile was variously regarded as poisonous, a vital spirit, or of considerable importance in maintaining health and potency. In some cultures, it was the main focus of hepatoscopy and in certain cities and cults, even regarded as the seat of the soul.

The early anatomists described it accurately but had little idea of its function, although A. Haller had, in 1736, proposed that it played a role in the digestion

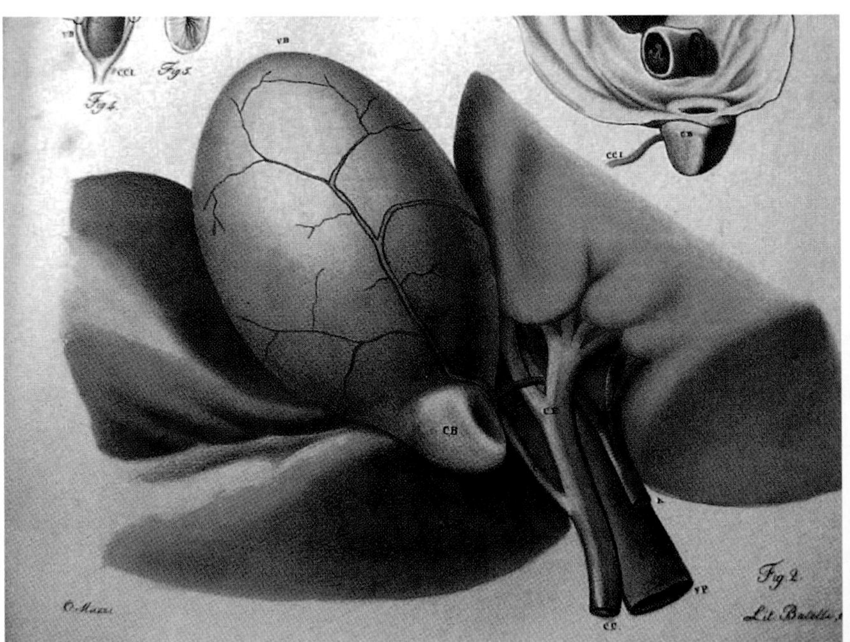

An anatomical illustration of the gall bladder and its principal vessels.

BERLINER
KLINISCHE WOCHENSCHRIFT.
Organ für practische Aerzte.
Mit Berücksichtigung der preussischen Medicinalverwaltung und Medicinalgesetzgebung nach amtlichen Mittheilungen.
Redacteur: Professor Dr. C. A. Ewald.
Montag, den 27. November 1882. № 48.

I. Ein Fall von Exstirpation der Gallenblase wegen chronischer Cholelithiasis. Heilung.
Mitgetheilt von
Dr. Carl Langenbuch,
dirig. Arzt am Lazarus-Krankenhause in Berlin.
Die Gallenblase ist nach einstimmigem Urtheil der modernen Autoren, wie Frerichs[1]), Schüppel[2]) u. A., der eigentliche Bildungsherd der Steine und nur verhältnissmässig selten entstammen diese den Gallengängen. Lediglich die Gallenblasensteine sollen uns hier interessiren. Es ist von ihnen sogleich zu beachten, dass neueren Forschungen zufolge, solche von 1 Ctm.

On the 15th of July 1882, Carl Langenbuch operated upon a 43-year-old accountant who for sixteen years had suffered so badly from biliary colic that he had become a morphine addict. After 5 days of preliminary enemas, Langenbuch removed the gall bladder without difficulty and noted the presence of two cholesterol stones. One day after the surgery, the patient had no fever or pain and smoked a cigar. He was allowed to walk on the 12th day and after 6 weeks discharged from the hospital. The lengthy hospital stay reflected the current belief that removal of the gall bladder was incompatible with life!

of fat. In 1720, A. Vater was the first to describe the ampulla and thereafter in 1887, Ruggero Oddi of Perugia described the sphincter and its function. Although this mechanism had been previously been recognized by Francis Glisson in 1654, the contributions of Oddi represented a significant advance in attempting to elucidate the physiological role of the sphincter in digestion. The earliest examples of gallstones were demonstrated in an Egyptian mummy from 1500 B.C. but apart from a passing mention of the subject by Alexander of Tralles (525-605 A.D.), there is little clear evidence that their relationship to disease was recognized.

The fact that gallstones may be formed was known since the fourteenth century and indeed the first description of these was attributed to Gentilis di Foligno, who died of the plague in Perugia in 1349. During the next centuries, when dissections became more frequent, stones, although previously mostly thought to be in the urinary bladder, were found more common in the gall bladder, paricularly in developed countries. For the most part, gallstones were obtained postmortem and used like bezoars as talismans capable of exerting powerful therapeutic effects themselves. A. Benivieni (1443-1502) was the first to relate the presence of gallstones with clinical and pathological findings in 1507. Thereafter, numerous individuals including G.B. Morgagni as well as J. Muller and B. Naunyn, to cite a few, produced important information and detail regarding the relationship of gallstones to hepatic disease and their ability to produce jaundice by duct obstruction. The correct diagnosis of the symptoms produced by stones, however, remained an enigma, and a considerable interest in gall bladder disease and duct obstruction was evident in the early nineteenth century, as frustration with the postmortem identification detection of such stones grew. The French surgeon, J.-L. Petit, as early as 1837 had proposed that in cases of gall bladder disease, the organ should be drained. Fortunately, the introduction of safe and effective surgery to effect cure of gall bladder disease was not possible until more than a century later, when Marion Sims performed the first planned cholecystostomy in 1878. Thereafter, in 1882 C.J.A. Langenbuch (1846-1901) of Berlin undertook the first successful cholecystectomy. Unfortunately, the clinical symptomatology was such that in many incidences, misdiagnoses occurred until the introduction of appropriate radiological techniques in 1924 by E.A. Graham and W.H. Cole.

Although A. Buxbaum had, as early as 1898, been able to demonstrate the presence of gallstones, the development of reliable techniques for the clinical identification of such pathology required a further twenty years and the development of appropriate radio-opaque dyes.

Stone Removal

The first gallstone was removed from a live person by William Fabry, a surgeon in Bern, known under the name of Fabricius Hildanus (1618). Cornelius Stalpart van der Wyl, a surgeon in The Hague, also performed these operations and there is record of two operations from the eighteenth century in which gallstones were removed from abscesses caused by ruptured gall bladders that contained stones. The first deliberate operation to deal with gallstones was carried out by Jean-Louis Petit of Paris in 1743. He considered such surgery permissible only in cases where the gall bladder adhered to the wall of the abdomen, and used a trocar through which he inserted long pliers to discharge the contents of the gall bladder and extract the stones from the bladder.

Since there was great anxiety in opening the abdominal cavity, much effort was directed to generating adhesion of the expanded gall bladder to the peritoneum of the anterior wall of the abdomen. In order to achieve this end, stimulants were applied to the skin of the frontal wall of the abdomen. Bloch, a Berlin physician, advocated the use of radishes, onions, and even the notorious aphrodisiac, Spanish fly, for this purpose! Others made an incision in the abdominal wall as far as the peritoneum and then placed various stimulants into the wound. August Gottlieb Richter (1742-1812) of Gottingen,

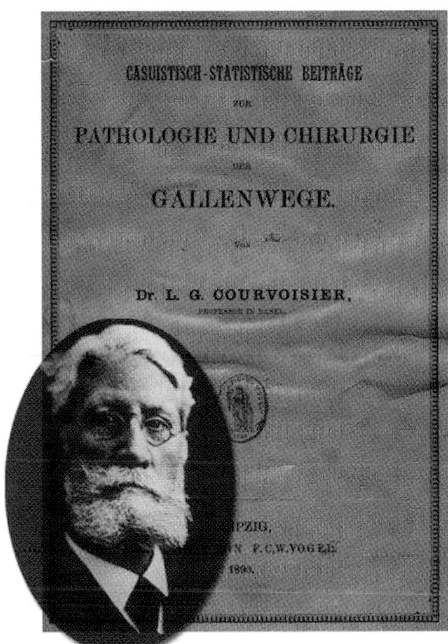

CASUISTISCH-STATISTISCHE BEITRÄGE
ZUR
PATHOLOGIE UND CHIRURGIE
DER
GALLENWEGE.
VON
Dr. L. G. COURVOISIER,
PZIG,
N F.C.W.VOGEL
1890.

L. Courvoisier of Geneva, Switzerland, pioneered much of the early surgery of the gall bladder and the biliary system.

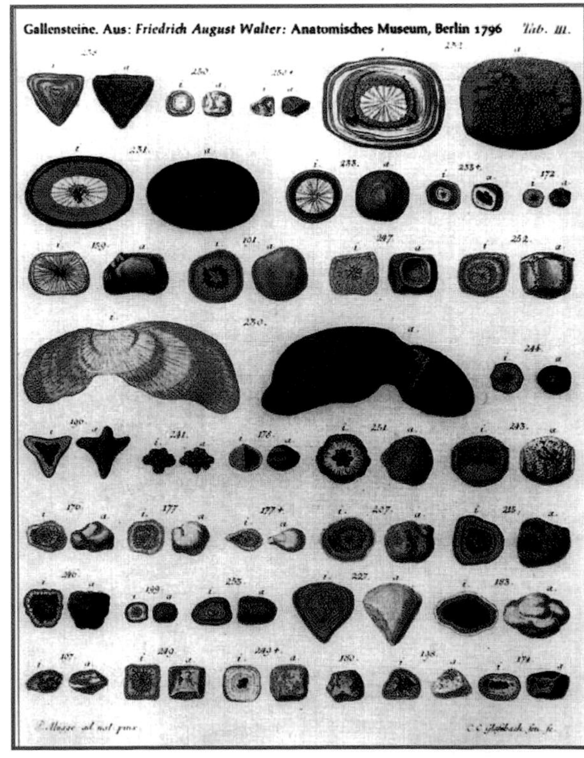

A collection of gallstones assembled by Friedrich August Walter and exhibited in the Anatomic Museum of Berlin in 1796.

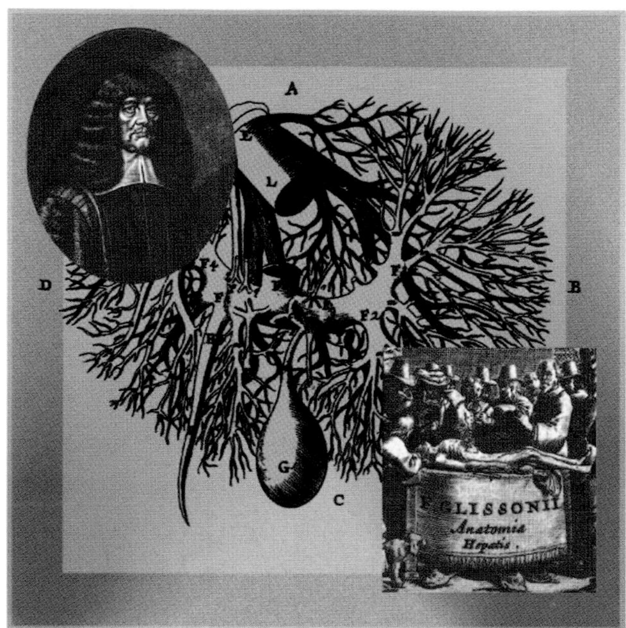

Francis Glisson, Regius Professor of Physic at Cambridge and Reader of Anatomy at the College of Physicians in London, contributed substantially to knowledge of the liver and bile ducts. Glisson believed that the primary function of the sphincter was to prevent chyle from flowing into the bile duct, rather than to regulate the flow of bile into the intestine. Indeed, Glisson was of the opinion that this function was governed by another sphincter at the neck of the gall bladder. "In the same place where the cystic passage is joined to the gall bladder, it is finished with a fibrous ring; by which it happens that the bile cannot of its own accord flow out; and from there does not move unless a light pressure has been given, or on account of an extraordinary fullness (which amounts to the same)... for the decree of nature seems to be that in bodies possessing favorable health this vesicle is always found full!" Indeed, Glisson felt that the gall bladder was filled at least in part by ducts that emanated from the cavity of the liver.

advocated the crushing of the stone in order to facilitate their elimination through a smaller opening, and proposed that the adhesion of the peritoneum to the gall bladder could be achieved by leaving the inserted trocar in the gall bladder. More in keeping with current surgical principles was a procedure recommended in 1859 by Thudichum, who proposed opening that abdominal cavity and palpating the gall bladder to determine whether it contained any stones. Should this be the case, the gall bladder should be sutured to the wall of the abdomen and once adherent, opened after six days and the stones removed. This operation in this form was only performed in 1882 by Francis Konig, professor of Surgery in Gottingen and later in Berlin.

In 1867, Bobbs in Indianapolis operated in the belief that he was dealing with an ovarian cyst. He identified a large gall bladder that he opened and removed the stones before proceeding to suture the bladder to the abdominal wall. This was the first singlestage gall bladder operation, albeit an unintended one. In 1877, Marion Sims, a gynecologist in New York, performed this operation deliberately, but the patient died in eleven days. William Williams Keen of the USA, and Lawson Tait of Birmingham, also proceeded along the lines of the gall bladder while Theodor Kocher of Bern preferred to place tampons around the gall bladder and only opened it after six days when it had already adhered to its surroundings.

Despite the obvious evidence that the diseased gall bladder needed to be removed, numerous physicians were of the opinion that survival would not be possible without the organ! The fact that dogs were known to survive the removal of the gall bladder without any harmful effects was demonstrated by Zambeccari as far back as 1630, and was confirmed by Teckoff, a student in Leiden in 1667, and by Herlin in 1767. The latter was, in fact, the first to advocate the removal of the gall bladder in cases of gallstone complaints. However, this operation on a human was only performed more than a century later by Charles Langenbuch, a surgeon in Berlin, on July 15, 1882. Despite a stay of more than a month in hospital, his patient recovered.

As a result of this success, this procedure soon became widely accepted and Courvoisier first performed the procedure in France in 1885, followed soon thereafter in the US in 1887. In England, however, the operation was strongly opposed by Lawson Tait, who regarded it as a complete absurdity! Indeed, Lawson Tait considered that Marion Sims had already written everything that could be written about gall bladder surgery and its stones, and therefore considered the "experimentation of Langenbuch" to be completely superfluous! The problem of stones in the duct system itself became the next issue that required resolution. Langenbuch was aware of the problem, and wisely stated that in such cases, the bile ducts required exploration (choledochotomy) and stone removal. Although Hermann Kummel of Hamburg performed the first choledochotomy in 1884, the patient died and it remained for Louis Theodore Courvoisier of Switzerland to successfully undertake the procedure shortly thereafter. Knowsley Thornton in 1889 introduced the operation to England, while the German surgeon Hans Kehr was instrumental in disseminating the technique as well as drainage of the liver ducts, throughout Europe.

John Nussbaum Nepomuk (1880) was the first to consider the elimination of severe jaundice caused by tumors blocking the principal bile duct by connecting the gall bladder with a part of the intestine, by forming a permanent opening between them. This allowed the obstructed bile to reach the intestines in a normal way by bypassing the obstruction. This idea was brought to fruition by Alexander Winiwater, an assistant of Billroth, and later professor of Surgery at the University of Lièges (1882). He established a somewhat unsatisfactory communication between the gall bladder and the colon, and the procedure was never really accepted. In 1887 Kapeller, as well as Monastirsky, used single-stage operations to connect the gall bladder with the small intestine. F. Terrier, professor of Surgery in Paris, used the duodenum, and in 1892 the Viennese surgeon, Robert Gersuny, also a pupil of Billroth, connected the obstructed gall bladder to the stomach (cholecystogastrostomy). As a result of such an anastomosis between the gall bladder and the intestine, or the gall bladder and the stomach, it was noted that the good general state of health of the individual, even in cases of malignant tumors, was restored. As Jean-Louis Petit remarked two hundred years ago of the surgical treatment of jaundice and liver disease: *"their ailment went unrecognized and there was no surgeon, who would have been prepared to relieve their suffering."*

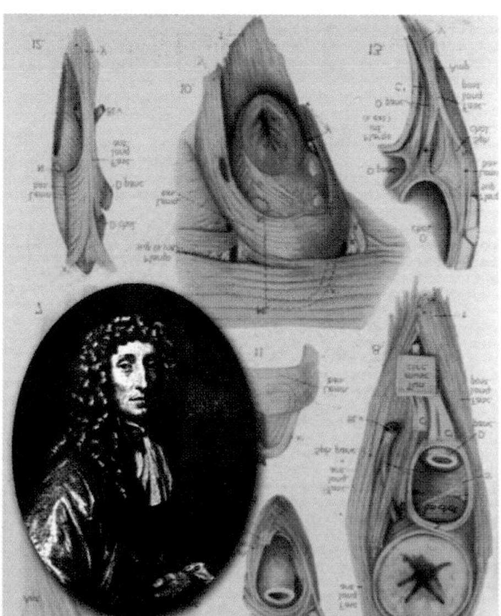

Govert Bidloo of Leiden was, in addition to being the personal physician of William III of England, an anatomist of considerable distinction. His early work defining the bile duct and choledochal sphincter demonstrated a substantial knowledge of bile duct anatomy.

Lawson Tait of Birmingham, although amongst the first to successfully remove an appendix, subsequently became a vehement opponent of cholecystectomy.

The Sphincter of Oddi

Early recognition of such a structure began with Vesalius, who in his *Fabrica* (1542) referred to the ancient controversy as to where the meatus of the bile vesicle was inserted. Even in his day, he wrote, some physicians still thought it was divided into two portions: one inserting into the stomach, the other into the intestine. However, Vesalius noted, some of those defending that assertion had never personally observed the organs. He, himself, by dissection was able to confirm *"that not the smallest portion of the bile vessicle was extended into the stomach except in one oarsman of a pontifical trireme."*

An important question at this stage was the nature of the anatomic relationship of the bile duct to the intestinal wall. In 1561, in his *Observationes Anatomica*, Fallopius established that the common bile duct took an oblique course through the intestinal wall. Roughly one hundred years later (in 1654), Francis Glisson In his *Anatomica Hepatis*, gave what is thought to be the first description of a sphincter mechanism at the orifice of the common bile duct, however, history has somewhat overlooked Glisson's discovery. In his *De Meatu Cystico* (1681), Glisson presented considerable further discussion of the sphincter and the gall bladder.

In 1685, Govert Bidloo of Leiden (physician to William III of England) produced what is probably the first pictorial representation of the union of the pancreatic duct (ductus pancreaticus) and the bile duct (ductus biliarius) within the membranes of the intestine. It is unclear exactly when the theory originated which proposed that gall bladder filling is initiated by contraction of a special muscle at the distal of the common bile duct in the duodenum.

Vesalius described the gall bladder and also the common bile duct in some considerable detail, noting that "the course of the vessicle is divided in two, one portion ascending to the liver while the other travels down a little obliquely and is implanted in duodenal jejunum." *At this junction, he added,* "there are two little membranes which hang loosely at each side of the orifice, easily yielding to the weight of the in-flowing bile and obstructing the way lest anything can flow back into the passage (meatus)."

After the contributions of Bianchus, interest in the regulatory mechanism of Glisson's sphincter faded. Haller discussed the effects of peristalsis on the common bile duct in *Selected Disputations* (1748), although it seems probable that he borrowed the ideas from earlier work by Seeger. Subsequently, in his *Elementa Physiologicae* (1757), he asserted that the primary issue was the transfer of force between the intestine and the intramural portion of the duct. Indeed, in his own estimate, this was sufficient explanation for the regulation of flow and the question was not really raised again until 1887, when Oddi took up the problem.

The Ampulla of Vater

In 1720, Abraham Vater, professor of Anatomy at Wittenburg, presented the first description of the tubercle or diverticulum that was later to be named the ampulla of Vater. Of particular note was the fact that he appeared to recognize that there was no simple combination of the pancreatic and bile duct, but that they were fused in a complex fashion and ended as an elevation of the mucosa (later referred to as an ampulla). Vater considered this tubercle to be made up of branches of the two organs mingled, and to consist of branches of the two organs mingled. Utilizing the technique of injection developed by Frederick Ruysch, he delineated the ampulla as having two orifices. He furthermore provided extensive descriptions of his injections and dissections, and also commented on the lack of a spiral valve in the cystic duct that had been described by Heister.

Contributions of Oddi

Like the sphincter itself, much of Oddi's life is shrouded in mystery. Little biographical information is available and that which can be found, is often contradictory and open to interpretation. Ruggero Oddi was baptized as Ruggero Ferdinando Antonio Guiseppe Vincenzo after being born in 13 Brushchi Street in Perugia at about 1:00 a.m. of July 20, 1874.

Oddi enrolled in the Faculty of Medicine and Surgery of the University of Perugia in 1883 and it was there that he undertook his first innovative work. There, as a 23-year-old medical student in the fourth year of this training, Oddi described the choledochal sphincter in a paper written in French and published in the 1887 volume of *Archives Italiennes de Biologie*.

In 1887, Oddi published his "D'une disposition à sphincter spéciale de l'ouverture du canal choledoche" in *Archives Italiennes de Biologie*. Having thus demonstrated the presence of such a sphincter, it still remained for Oddi to determine its physiological properties. In the manuscript *"Sulla tonicita dello sfintere del coledocho"* (1888), he addressed the problem of determining the

ANNALI
DELL' UNIVERSITÀ LIBERA
DI PERUGIA

DI UNA SPECIALE DISPOSIZIONE A SFINTERE
ALLO SBOCCO DEL COLEDOCO
RICERCHE
DI
RUGGERO ODDI

The life of Oddi is the fascinating story of a brilliant young man from a modest background who reached the heights of academic physiology and medicine only to become involved in a tormented existence of drugs and scandal resulting in an early and ignominious demise in Tunisia. Despite his initial meteoric rise to a position of power and acclamation in Italian university physiology, he perished alone, disillusioned and unremembered. His peregrinations led him from his birthplace in Perugia to Belgium, the Congo River Basin, Spain and finally back to Italy before his last passage to Tunis and death in the French Foreign Legion.

Oswald Schmiedeberg (1838-1921) was one of the leading German pharmacologists of the 19th century. Born in Courland, he becam professor at Dorpat in 1870 and thereafter Strassbourg in 1872. He investigated the action of poisons on frogs' hearts with Ludwig, discovered hippuric acid synthesis in the kidneys in1876, and thereafter identified sinistrin and histozyme. Of particular interest is his determination of the true formula of histamine in 1896 from the posthumous notes of Miescher. In addition, he undertook considerable work in the study of muscarinic agents, digitalis, and ferritin, crystallizing these observations in his textbook, Elements of Pharmacology *published in 1883.*

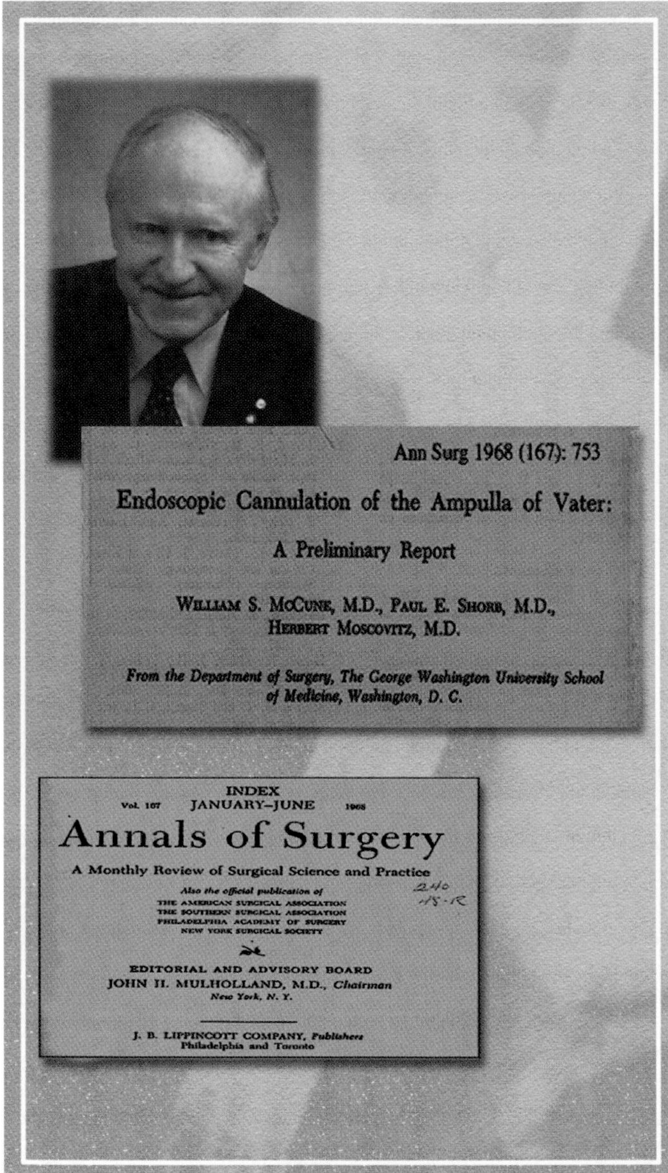

Ann Surg 1968 (167): 753
Endoscopic Cannulation of the Ampulla of Vater:
A Preliminary Report
William S. McCune, M.D., Paul E. Shorb, M.D.,
Herbert Moscovitz, M.D.
From the Department of Surgery, The George Washington University School of Medicine, Washington, D. C.
INDEX
Vol. 167 JANUARY–JUNE 1968
Annals of Surgery
A Monthly Review of Surgical Science and Practice
Also the official publication of
THE AMERICAN SURGICAL ASSOCIATION
THE SOUTHERN SURGICAL ASSOCIATION
PHILADELPHIA ACADEMY OF SURGERY
NEW YORK SURGICAL SOCIETY
EDITORIAL AND ADVISORY BOARD
JOHN H. MULHOLLAND, M.D., Chairman
New York, N. Y.
J. B. LIPPINCOTT COMPANY, Publishers
Philadelphia and Toronto

William S. McCune (1909-1998), a surgeon at George Washington University, Washington, D.C. published his initial observations with endoscopic retrograde cannulation of the ampulla of Vater in the Annals of Surgery *in 1968. Unfortunately the potential of the technique failed to capture surgical interest and as a result the management of biliary disorders thereafter became (for the most part) the eminent domain of endoscopists.*

resistance of the sphincter, and in subsequent papers, turned to questions of its nervous control. In the following year, Oddi transferred to the *Reale Istituto Superiore di Perfezionamento* in Florence, where at the age of 25 on July 2, 1889 he was awarded the degree in Medicine and Surgery. Although his graduation thesis was, as might be expected, on "Common Bile Duct Sphincter Tone", in addition, he defended two oral theses on the subjects, respectively, "Ataxia" and "Antipyretics". In 1893, having obtained a government scholarship, he moved to Strassburg and worked with the brilliant German pharmacologist, Oswald Schmiedeberg.

During his sabbatical in Strassburg, Oddi succeeded in isolating chondroitin sulfate from coamyloid. This work was to form the basis for his inaugural lecture at the Genoa Royal Academy in 1894. At the age of 29 in 1894, he was appointed Acting Director of the Physiological Institute of Genoa. In 1897, Oddi published a monograph titled, "The Physiotherapy of the Biliary Tree," which summarized the studies undertaken between 1887 and 1894.

Oddi retained the Chairmanship of Physiology for almost seven years until almost 1901, when in a series of catastrophic and ill-understood events, he was removed from this position, left Italy and sought employment in Brussels. Theories abound as to what events transpired to initiate the implosion of this brilliant man's scientific career. It may well have been a marital problem since it is known that his wife disappeared, or more likely, the malign influence of Stefano Capranica, his mentor, who was a known cultist. During his time in Brussels, Oddi became depressed and a serious drug addict. These problems were somewhat alleviated by a Belgian physician, Mersh. The latter converted him to Indian mysticism, and in addition, treated him with a homeopathic preparation, Vitaline (glycerine, sodium borate, ammonium chloride and alcohol).

In 1901 Oddi transferred to Boma in the Belgian Congo, and became a physician in the Belgian Colonial Service. In this capacity he traveled on the Congo riverboats for a short period of time before once again succumbing to narcotics and being repatriated to Belgium. A brief period of practice in Spain was followed by a return to live in the small town of Torgiano near Perugia. Then on the 15th of November in 1905, he returned to Perugia and took up residence at 15 Via Bonazzi, close at the home where he had been born. During the six years that he stayed Perugia, he practiced as a homeopathic doctor and widely advocated the use of Vitaline. Following a patient problem, he was charged with abusive use of medical products (Vitaline) and tried for voluntary manslaughter. In 1906, in an attempt to rationalize his therapy, Oddi wrote a pamphlet entitled *"New Therapy for Infectious Diseases and Malignant Terminal Diseases. Methods for Their Prevention and Treatment. Gatchkowski's Vitaline."*

The events that led to his leaving Perugia in 1911 and seeking passage to Tunisia are unclear. Although it has been assumed that he intended to join the Foreign Legion, that organization still maintains the utmost secrecy concerning its records, and no evidence in support of this romantic suggestion has been obtained. Nevertheless, whatever the motivation for his presence in Tunis, he died there on March 22, 1913 at the age of 49. The site of his burial place is unknown, as are his final thoughts and reflections.

Endoscopic Retrograde Cholangiopancreatography (ERCP)

As a result of the improved flexibility of instruments and better visibility, novel opportunities for the examination of the gastrointestinal tract presented themselves to physicians. In 1966, W.C. Watson of Glasgow reported in *Lancet* his observations of the ampulla of Vater, and concluded that endoscopic examination might be helpful in the diagnosis of biliary and pancreatic disorders. Although he did not discuss his technique, his suggestions were instrumental in the development of an entirely new diagnostic application of endoscopy. In 1965, a pair of radiologists, Rabinov and Simon, utilizing a fluoroscopically-guided catheter, reported the successful per oral cannulation of the papilla of Vater, thus rendering pancreatography a non-operative technique. They noted that since the ampulla could not be regularly visualized fluoroscopically, even by use of barium, the technique was arduous and required blind probing of the medial duodenal wall. The situation was problematic, since the surgical method of pancreatography was dangerous and difficult, requiring not only a laparotomy but also duodenotomy while the radiological technique was clumsy, blind, and time-consuming. In contradistinction endoscopy had obvious potential advantages in terms of direct visualization.

In 1968, William S. McCune of George Washington University reported in the *Annals of Surgery* his experience with successful endoscopic cannulation of the ampulla of Vater.

McCune had employed considerable ingenuity to attach a cannula housing onto an Eder fiber optic duodenoscope, and was thus able to directly visualize the papilla during the cannulation procedure itself. He commented that *"the technique is not easy and requires considerable experience"*, thus presaging the feelings of endoscopists to this very day. Indeed, the initial success rates of McCune and his colleagues for cannulation with this makeshift instrument were less than 50%. By 1970, however, technical modifications to the duodenoscope greatly simplified the procedure, and expert endoscopists were able to claim cannulation rates approaching 90%. The development of different endoscope models and techniques were especially supported by the work of several innovative Japanese gastroenterologists including Itaru Oi,

T. Takemoto, T. Kondo, and Kunio Takagi, and considerably aided by a number of instrument-makers, including Machida and Olympus.

Thus, by 1972 Jack Vennes and Steven E. Silvis were able to publish information pertaining to their first eighty attempts at cannulation, and the procedure entered the domain of acceptability in the United States. In 1978, Vennes received the Schindler award from the American Society of Gastrointestinal Endoscopy in recognition of his contributions to this important new development in gastrointestinal endoscopy.

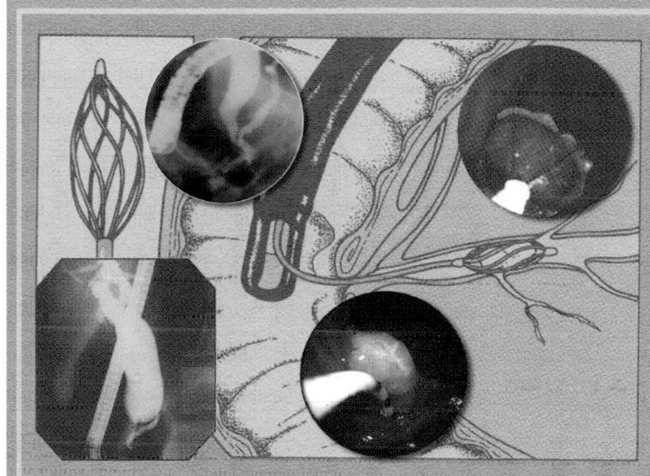

Once the papilla could reliably be cannulated for diagnostic purposes, a wide variety of devices were implemented to broaden the therapeutic horizon. The sphincters of Oddi and Boyden were breached by papillotomes; balloons, baskets, stents and coils as a new generation of endoscopists and instrument makers colluded to transluminally supplant the hepato-biliary surgeon. Few would remember the work of the urologist Joaquin Albarran who in Paris in 1897 had mastered the ureter with almost precisely the same strategies!

L. Demling and M. Classen initially conceived the concept of a therapeutic application in 1973, recognizing the major barrier that an intact papilla of Vater constituted for the introduction of therapeutic devices. In order to open the papilla, they developed a high frequency diathermy snare – *the Demling-Classen probe*. This device consisted of a Teflon catheter containing a thin steel wire that could be protruded to allow for the development of "bow string" that served as a diathermy knife. An additional advance of this probe was the ability to instill contrast medium at the time of the papillotomy, and therefore ensure appropriate positioning. At almost the same time K. Kawai of Japan (1973) described a papillotomy device consisting of two diathermy blades of 2 mm length at the tip. This method was particularly useful in instances where the stone was impacted in the ampulla.

Although ERCP became widely recognized as an important diagnostic modality, it was apparent that the procedure could be associated with potentially serious complications. A survey conducted in 1974 by the ASGE revealed that the complication rate was at least 2.2%, and therefore significantly higher than for any other currently practiced endoscopic technique. Since post-ERCP problems included serious events such as pancreatitis, cholangitis, instrument injuries, and sepsis, recommendations were provided in an attempt to decrease these complications. Despite the criticisms of those who noted the unacceptably high complication rate, the utility of the procedure in diagnosing pancreatic and hepato-biliary disease provided strong support for its further usage. With the subsequent advent of appropriate training courses and the development of guidelines, as well as added experience, the complication rate decreased to within acceptable limits.

As endoscopists became more familiar and comfortable with the technique of ERCP as a diagnostic tool, the possibility of therapeutic intervention became a reality. The earliest procedure introduced was that of endoscopic papillotomy using electrocoagulation. Subsequently, the removal of biliary calculi was undertaken, and a wide variety of techniques and instruments introduced to facilitate this process. Thus, all the procedures to extract stones from the common bile duct initially used by surgeons were therefore adapted by endoscopists and instrument-makers. The 1975 report by David Zimmon and his colleagues in the *New England Journal of Medicine*, describing successful stone removal after endoscopic papillotomy, would thereafter open an entire new field of therapeutic endeavor for endoscopists.

Further advances in the use of chemical dissolution and mechanical, electrohydraulic or pulsed dye laser lithotripsy, have facilitated the successful management of even the largest and most intractable of biliary calculi. In addition, the design and placement of catheters impregnated with high-energy isotopes (Yttrium 90 or Iridium 192) has raised the issue of even more novel therapeutic possibilities. The likelihood of combined procedures involving both percutaneously-introduced steerable catheters by interventional radiologists, used in conjunction with trans-sphincterically passed forceps to grasp and manipulate such tubes, may result in the development of intraluminal biliary or hepatic surgery in the future.

K. Kawai (left) of Japan and M. Classen (right) of Germany at the twenty-fifth anniversary meeting (Kohler, Wisconsin, 1968) to celebrate the introduction of papillotomy. Their independent successful development of the concept of the technique and instrumentation in 1973 was responsible for an extraordinary advance in biliary and pancreatic therapeutic intervention.

The early experience and innovative development of ERCP and papillotomy by a number of Japanese endoscopists played a prominent role in the worldwide implementation of the techniques. In particular K. Kawai, T. Takemoto, I. Oi, T. Kondo, and K. Takagi were preeminent in advancing the field.

Section 18
Small Bowel

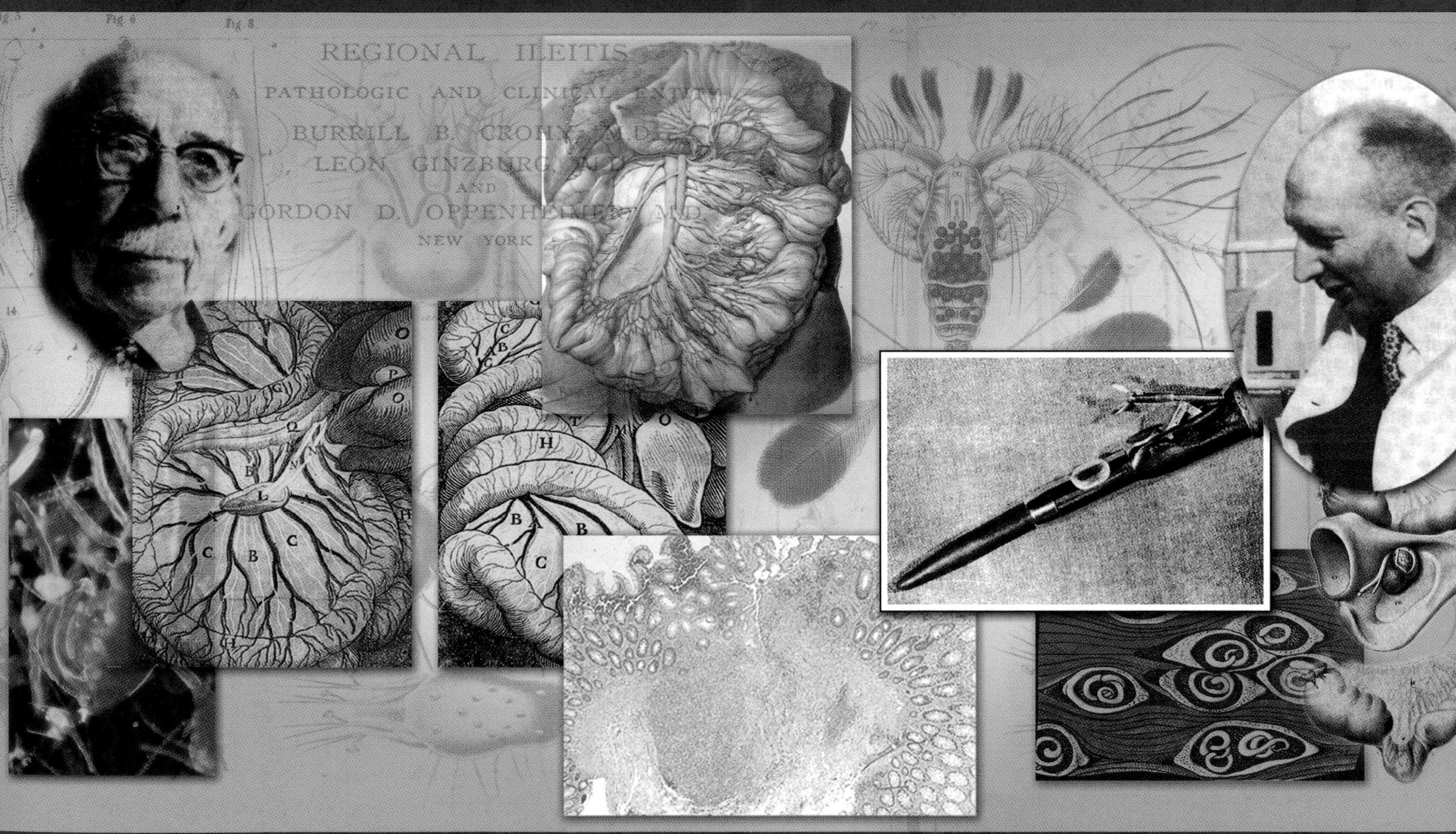

Small Bowel

Anatomy

The original use of the word intestine is derived from "*intus*" meaning internal or within, but when used in the plural, was taken to refer to the "guts" or internal organs. In the medical sense it was first used by Celsus, who in *De Medicina* referred to "*intestinum tenue et crassum*." The origin of the word "gut" is not as clear, although in Latin "*guttus*" was a narrow-necked jug and "*guttar*" referred to the throat.

In Anglo-Saxon, gut meant a drain or channel, while the common origin of both words may derive from the Aryan "*ghud*", meaning to pour. After the fourteenth century, the word gut was generally regarded as inclusive of the alimentary tract between the pylorus and anus.

The first part of the small intestine was referred to as "duodenum" since it was estimated by Herophilus to be 12 fingerbreadths in length. This Greek terminology was subsequently translated into Arabic, and thereafter into "barbarous Latin" from the *Canon of Avicenna* by Gerard of Cremona as duodenum, meaning twelve (the correct translation would have been *duodecim digitorum*).

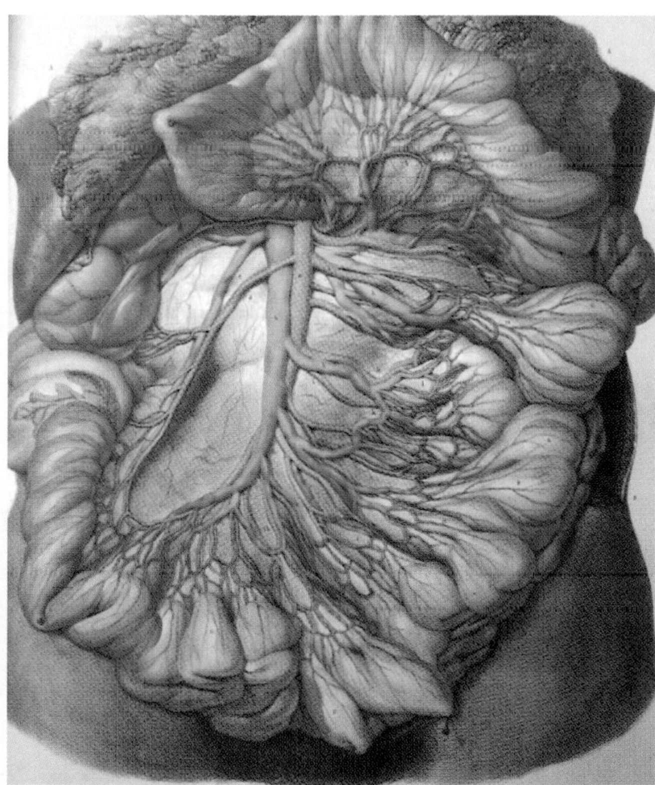

An early 14th-century illustration of the small bowel and its vasculature by J.P. Bougery of Paris. The proximal portion was named duodenum since it was 12 fingers (duo decima) in length and the jejunum, so called since it is the Latin term for empty. The term "ileum" was designated for the latter part of the small bowel since it meant to twist or writhe (Greek derivation).

The portion of the small intestine that followed the duodenum was noted by the ancients as always being empty even after death. So apparent was this observation that even Aristotle commented upon it. The basis of the name "jejunum" is a derivation of the Latin translation of vacant, since this part of the intestine was always empty and regarded as the hungry part of the gut. In fact, jejunum was the first breakfast among the Romans. Galen is credited with declaring it to be "fasting" and this became translated into Latin as "*jejunus*" *jejeunum intestinum quia ubique est vacuum* (the jejunum is that part of the intestine that is always empty). The term was first popularized by Celsus and, by the fourteenth century, had appeared in the English literature.

In contradistinction, "*intestinum ileum*" meant the colicky part of the gut, since it was always in contraction and derived from the Greek, meaning "to twist". Hence the ileum was regarded as the twisted gut. Galen did not distinguish between the two parts of the small intestine, and it was known by him as "*tenue*" or "*gracile*" and the name retained as *vasa intestini tenuis*. Although Galen was responsible for using the term "*ileum*", he used it mostly in the pathological sense. The first recognized use of the term appears in a 1618 text entitled *Anonymous Introduction to Anatomy*.

The division between the ileum and the colon was known as the ileo-cecal valve. It was first observed by Diocles and various early anatomists, and recorded by Fallopius in an unpublished manuscript, *Anatomia Simiae*, that currently resides in the Göttingen library. This report of 1553 not only identified the bowel, but noted its action in delaying the passage of food into the colon. Vidius, a pupil of Fallopius, proposed that the valve function was to delay the passage of material through the intestine, and similarly, Varolius was aware of the action of this valve and considered it an invagination of the

Nicholas Tulp (right), leader of the Surgeons Guild of Amsterdam, portrayed in Rembrandt's Anatomy Lesson *demonstrating the flexors of the fingers, was one of the first to describe the ileo-cecal valve (inset).*

Herophilus of Alexandria (4th century B.C.) was regarded as the father of scientific anatomy. He was amongst the first to practice human vivisection and, having been taught by Praxagoras became an astute observer, differentiating the cerebrum from the cerebellum, describing the fourth ventricle of the brain, distinguishing the parotid and submandibular gland and delineating the duodenum. In addition, he was the first to measure the pulse using a water clock.

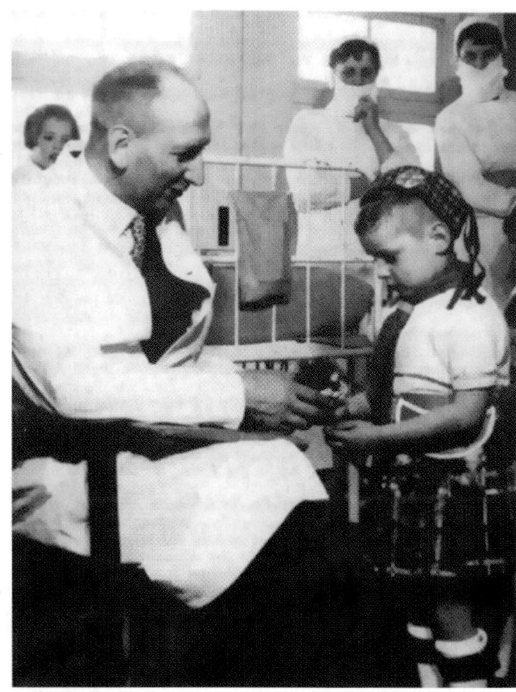

W.K. Dicke of the Netherlands provided the clinical and scientific information fundamental to the elucidation of the diagnosis and therapy of celiac disease. Dicke was recognized as an outstanding clinician, scientist, and administrator possessed of exceptional personal qualities. Born in 1905 in Dordrecht, it was as a relatively young pediatrician in The Hague in 1936 that he first became alerted to the etiology of celiac disease. It is claimed that the statement from a young mother that her celiac child's rash improved rapidly when she removed bread from the diet, directed his attention to the possible etiology of the condition. In addition, he noted that the health of many celiac children improved significantly during the bread scarcity prevalent in the Netherlands during the war.

ileum into the cecum. A detailed description of the structure is contained in his work, *De Resolution Corporis Humani,* published in 1591. Subsequently, in 1592, Caspar Bauhin of Basel published *Theatrum Anatomicum,* and claimed to have previously described the valve in Paris as early as 1579. The Dutch physician Tulp subsequently redescribed the ileo-cecal valve in the seventeenth century and it thus variously became known as the valve of Tulp or Bauhin.

Celiac Disease

The background and precise nature of celiac disease was ill-understood for almost 2,000 years until Dicke of the Netherlands noted the remarkable decline of the disease during the war when bread was unavailable. It is, however, likely that the condition was known as early as the second century A.D. since Aretaeus the Cappadocian described in detail a condition that seems quite likely to have been celiac disease. The 1856 translation of his work by Francis Adams on behalf of the Sydenham Society reads as follows: *"the stomach being the digestive organ labors in digestion when the diarrhea seizes the patient. If this diarrhea does not proceed from a slight cause of only one or two days duration, and if, in addition, the patients general condition be debilitated by atrophy of the body, the celiac disease of a chronic nature is formed."*

Aretaeus further commented that the illness predominantly affected adults and, in particular, women, but made little mention of its relationship to children. It is possible that the high infant mortality rates of the time precluded the identification of this disease as separate to other debilitating infectious diseases then prevalent. As was the custom of the time, many illnesses were considered as representative of abnormalities in digestion, and thus Aretaeus proposed that *"pepsis"* (digestion) be augmented by support of the patient by prevention of chilling and restoration of heat. In addition, he provided homeopathic advice including exercise, massage, and even emetics and purges if all else failed. Of interest is Aretaeus' suggestion that *"drinks be taken before meals, for otherwise bread is very little conducive to trim vigor."* His description of the disease, however, was reasonably accurate, and he claimed that the inability to adequately digest failed to convert the food into its *"proper chyme"* leaving the work of digestion *"half finished"*. As a result of this flaw in the digestive process *"the food then being deprived of this operation is changed to a state which is bad in color, smell, and consistence. For its color is white and without bile, it has an offensive smell and is flatulent; it is liquid and wants consistence from not being completely elaborated."*

The disease, as such, was little apparent in the literature thereafter, as more dramatic medical problems captured the attention of physicians. Indeed, little further was written on the subject of celiac disease for almost 2,000 years and it lay concealed within a myriad of gastrointestinal problems such as dysentery, parasitic disease, and tuberculosis. In 1699 a Dutch physician, Vincent

Aretaeus the Cappadocian (2nd-3rd century A.D.) came nearer than any other Greek to the spirit and method of Hippocrates and ranked next to the father of medicine in the graphic accuracy and fidelity of his pictures of disease, of which he provided the classic accounts of pneumonia, pleurisy, diabetes, tetanus, elephantiasis, and diphtheria. In addition, he supplied what is clearly one of the earliest descriptions of celiac disease.

Ketelaer, wrote a text, *De Aapthsis nostratibus, seu Belgarium Sprouw,* that although it describes the oral apthous ulceration associated with sprue, devoted little attention to its intestinal manifestations. In 1759, William Hillary of Yorkshire produced the first description of tropical sprue in *Observations on the Changes of the Air and the Concomitant Epidemical Diseases of the Island of Barbadoes*. Thereafter Manson in China in 1880, and Van der Burg in Java, made major contributions by delineating the clinical features of tropical sprue.

Probably the next significant contribution to the subject was provided in October 1887 when Dr. Samuel Jones Gee lectured on the subject of "On the celiac affection", and subsequently published his observations in the St. Bartholomew's Hospital report of 1888. Gee drew attention to the fact that the disease affected all ages and particularly children between the ages of one and five years. He similarly reiterated Areteaus' earlier observations, noting: *"the feces being loose, not formed but watery; more bulky than the food taken which seemed to account for; paling color as if devoid of bile; yeasty, frothy, and appearance probably due to fermentation, stinking, stench often very great, the food having undergone putrefaction rather than concoction."*

Not surprisingly, he proposed that the best form of treatment would be to regulate the diet, and quite presciently instructed that the allowance of farinaceous foods should be minimal, although he supported the use of thin toasted bread and rusks (a well-versed Victorian dietetic remedy). As was the custom of the time, he proposed a variety of diets to treat children afflicted

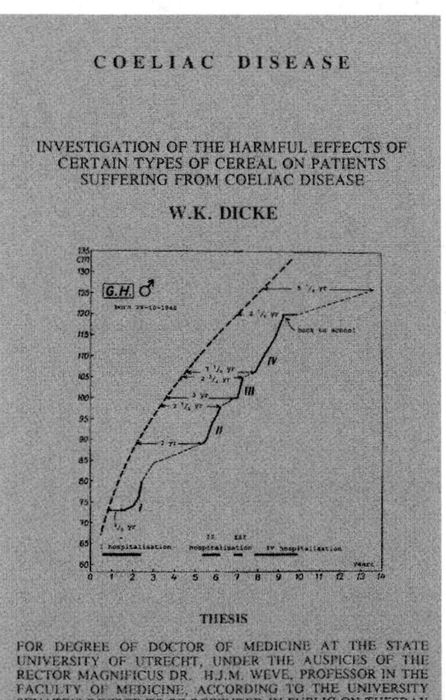

COELIAC DISEASE

INVESTIGATION OF THE HARMFUL EFFECTS OF CERTAIN TYPES OF CEREAL ON PATIENTS SUFFERING FROM COELIAC DISEASE

W.K. DICKE

THESIS

FOR DEGREE OF DOCTOR OF MEDICINE AT THE STATE UNIVERSITY OF UTRECHT, UNDER THE AUSPICES OF THE RECTOR MAGNIFICUS DR. H.J.M. WEVE, PROFESSOR IN THE FACULTY OF MEDICINE, ACCORDING TO THE UNIVERSITY SENATE'S DECREE TO BE DEFENDED IN PUBLIC ON TUESDAY 30 MAY 1950 AT 4 P.M.

Dicke's 1950 doctoral thesis on Celiac disease with the growth chart of one of his young patients (inset).

with the disease process. One in particular has remained a source of interest to the gastroenterological fraternity. Gee claimed that *"a child who has fed upon a quart of the best Dutch mussels daily, throve wonderfully but relapsed when the season for the mussels was over; next season he could not be prevailed upon to take them. This is an experiment I have not yet be able to repeat...but if the patient can be cured at all, it must be by means of diet."*

A year later R.A. Gibbons contributed two papers on the "Celiac affection in children" to the *Edinburgh Medical Journal,* and described four patients managed according to the dictates of Gee. Although Gibbons undertook post-mortem studies of his patients (Gee's diet was obviously less than efficacious), he was able to demonstrate no obvious abnormalities. As a result, he contented himself by claiming that the disease represented *"a functional disturbance of the nervous supply of the liver, pancreas, glands of Brunner, and the follicles of Lieberkuhn, possibly also those of the stomach and salivary glands."*

The manifestations of celiac disease continued to remain an issue of considerable concern to physicians of the turn of the century. Thus in 1903, Dr. W.B. Cheadle published in the *Lancet* a copy of a lecture, which he had delivered in the previous year at St. Mary's Medical School. Although Cheadle was able to add little to the understanding of the disease process, he somewhat changed the focus by publishing his description of it under the title of *Acholia*. He noted that although there was no jaundice, *"the stools are as white as though of obstructive jaundice when the bile is absolutely shut out from the intestine."* Of particular note, however, was his important observation that the stools contained an excess of fat and that this could be quantified by fat estimation.

The advent of the late nineteenth and early twentieth century focus on microbiology and the influence of this discipline, resulted in considerable attention being directed to bacteria as the cause of diverse disease processes. Thus, in 1908 when C.A. Herter published his text *"Infantilism from Chronic Intestinal Infection"*, he proposed that celiac disease was due to an inflammation of the intestine caused by the persistence and overgrowth of intestinal flora derived during nursing. He claimed to have identified *bacillus bifidus* and *bacillus infantilis* in such patients and therefore proposed that the term *"intestinal infantilism"* be utilized to describe the condition. Although this notion was subsequently demonstrated as flawed, Herter's observations regarding the disposal of food constituents by the gut were important. Thus, his report that, in such patients, proteins and fats were well-handled but that carbohydrates were badly tolerated, is still regarded as a seminal and fundamental contribution to the understanding of celiac disease.

Unfortunately, little progress was made in the further evaluation of the problem in 1918. C.F. Still, in his Lumleian lectures on the subject, to the Royal College of Physicians of London, was able to add no new information. Six years later in 1924, Sidney Haas, writing in *The American Journal of Diseases of Children,* reported his successful management of celiac disease using a banana diet. Having successfully treated patients with anorexia nervosa using this fruit, he concluded that the anorexia of celiac disease might be similarly amenable to banana therapy which he claimed to function as some kind of *"hormone"*. The initial rationale of the therapy was based upon evidence emanating from Puerto Rico, where it had been noted that town dwellers on this island who ate bread suffered from sprue, whereas farmers who lived on bananas were protected from the disease process. Even during the Second World War, children with celiac disease were provided with an extra ration of bananas.

Although Haas had been prescient in recognizing that celiac disease was connected to carbohydrate metabolism, he had failed to identify the critical role of gluten. This observation was elegantly derived by Willem Karl Dicke of the Netherlands, and subsequently became the basis of his medical thesis. On May 30, 1950, *"Celiac Disease – An Investigation of the Harmful Effects of Certain Types of Cereal on Patients Suffering from Celiac Disease,"* was successfully defended by Dicke, and his proposal soon received international acceptance. In a modest 97-page monograph, Dicke, with extraordinary accuracy and skill, delineated the clinical and biochemical basis of celiac disease, and proposed a successful therapy. Born in 1905 in Dordrecht, it was as a relatively young pediatrician in The Hague in 1936 that he first became alerted to the etiology of celiac disease. It is claimed that the statement from a young mother that her celiac child's rash improved rapidly when she removed bread from the diet, directed his attention to the possible etiology of the condition. In addition, he noted that the improvement of the condition of many celiac children seemed to be associated with the scarcity of bread in The Netherlands during the war. Thus in 1941, he published a brief report in *"Het Nederlands Tijdshrift voor Geneeskunde"*. In this article, he proposed that a wheat-free diet be utilized in place of either the Haas' *"banana diet or the Fanconi vegetable"* diet. In 1950, his thesis detailed meticulous dietary studies of children with celiac disease and demonstrated unequivocally that a strict

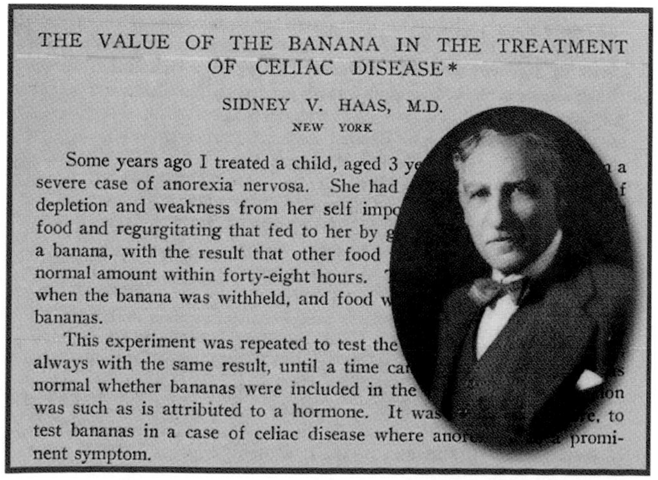

THE VALUE OF THE BANANA IN THE TREATMENT OF CELIAC DISEASE*

SIDNEY V. HAAS, M.D.
NEW YORK

Some years ago I treated a child, aged 3 y... a severe case of anorexia nervosa. She had ... depletion and weakness from her self imp... food and regurgitating that fed to her by ... a banana, with the result that other food ... normal amount within forty-eight hours. ... when the banana was withheld, and food w... bananas.

This experiment was repeated to test the... always with the same result, until a time ca... normal whether bananas were included in the ... was such as is attributed to a hormone. It was ... to test bananas in a case of celiac disease where ano... promi- nent symptom.

Sidney Haas in 1924 claimed that celiac disease could be successfully treated using a banana diet. Although the clinical and scientific evidence provided by Dicke was unequivocal, Haas as late as 1963, continued to propound the success of his banana diet. He claimed, "that Dicke's demonstration was an excellent achievement scientifically and of immense value for the study of the celiac syndrome, but clinically it was a possible disservice since he ignored other carbohydrates as etiological factors."

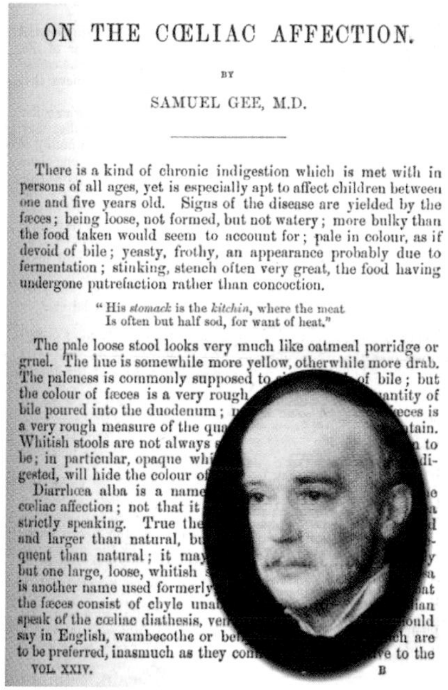

ON THE CŒLIAC AFFECTION.

BY

SAMUEL GEE, M.D.

There is a kind of chronic indigestion which is met with in persons of all ages, yet is especially apt to affect children between one and five years old. Signs of the disease are yielded by the fæces; being loose, not formed, but not watery; more bulky than the food taken would seem to account for; pale in colour, as if devoid of bile; yeasty, frothy, an appearance probably due to fermentation; stinking, stench often very great, the food having undergone putrefaction rather than concoction.

"His *stomack* is the *kitchin*, where the meat
Is often but half sod, for want of heat."

The pale loose stool looks very much like oatmeal porridge or gruel. The hue is somewhile more yellow, otherwhile more drab. The paleness is commonly supposed to ... of bile; but the colour of fæces is a very rough ... quantity of bile poured into the duodenum; ... fæces is a very rough measure of the qu... tain. Whitish stools are not always ... to be; in particular, opaque wh... di-gested, will hide the colour o...

Diarrhœa alba is a name ... cœliac affection; not that it ... strictly speaking. True the ... and larger than natural, bu... quent than natural; it may ... but one large, loose, whitish ... is another name used formerly ... the fæces consist of chyle una... speak of the cœliac diathesis, ve... say in English, wambecothe or be... are to be preferred, inasmuch as they co... to the

VOL. XXIV. B

In 1888 Dr. Samuel Jones Gee of St. Bartholomew's Hospital, London, published an excellent and still viable clinical description of celiac disease under the title "On the Celiac Affection".

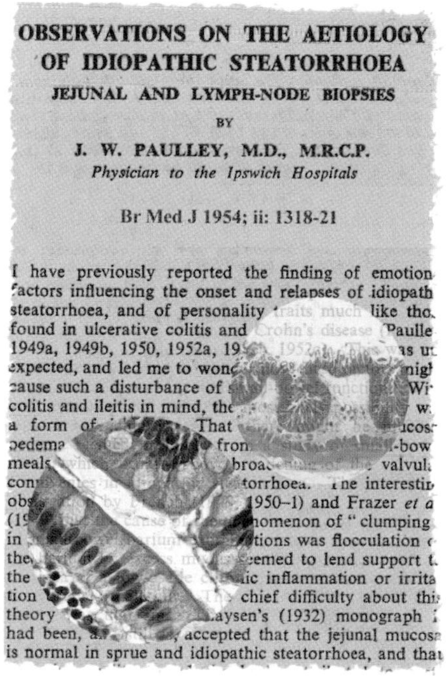

OBSERVATIONS ON THE AETIOLOGY OF IDIOPATHIC STEATORRHOEA

JEJUNAL AND LYMPH-NODE BIOPSIES

BY

J. W. PAULLEY, M.D., M.R.C.P.
Physician to the Ipswich Hospitals

Br Med J 1954; ii: 1318-21

I have previously reported the finding of emotion... factors influencing the onset and relapses of idiopath... steatorrhoea, and of personality traits much like tho... found in ulcerative colitis and Crohn's disease (Paulle... 1949a, 1949b, 1950, 1952a, 19... 1952...). This was un-expected, and led me to wond... migh... cause such a disturbance of ... Wi... colitis and ileitis in mind, the ... w... a form of ... That ... mucos... oedema ... from ... -bow... meals ... broa... valvul... con... torrhoea. The interestin... obs... 1950–1) and Frazer *et a*... (19... nomenon of "clumping... in ... tions was flocculation ... the ... seemed to lend support t... the ... ic inflammation or irrita-tion ... chief difficulty about thi... theory ... aysen's (1932) monograph ... had been, ... accepted that the jejunal mucosa is normal in sprue and idiopathic steatorrhoea, and that

In 1954, some seventy years after the classic description of the clinical manifestations of celiac disease provided by Gee, J.W. Paulley of Ipswich Hospital, London, noted with dismay that the normal appearance of the human jejunum was virtually unknown. Given the absence of any then-available technique whereby the organ might be biopsied during life, only a laparotomy could provide such information. In 1955 M. Shiner developed a viable jejunal biopsy system and two years later W. Crosby described the Crosby capsule.

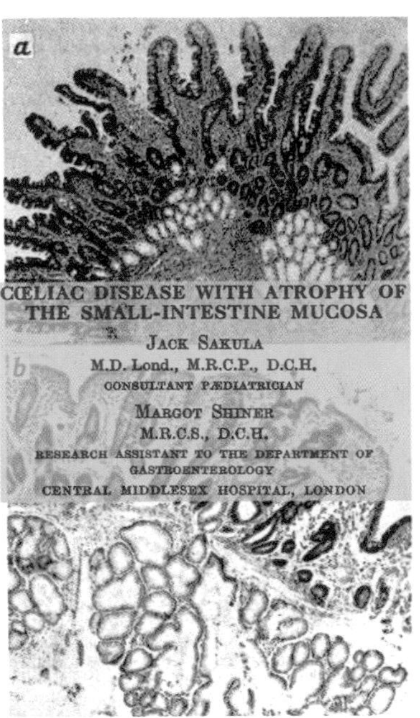
CŒLIAC DISEASE WITH ATROPHY OF THE SMALL-INTESTINE MUCOSA

JACK SAKULA
M.D. Lond., M.R.C.P., D.C.H.
CONSULTANT PÆDIATRICIAN

MARGOT SHINER
M.R.C.S., D.C.H.
RESEARCH ASSISTANT TO THE DEPARTMENT OF GASTROENTEROLOGY
CENTRAL MIDDLESEX HOSPITAL, LONDON

The development of a small intestinal biopsy system by M. Shiner in 1956 led to the subsequent establishment of the histological characteristics of celiac disease in conjunction with I. Doniach and J. Sakula in London.

regimen of wheat-free diet had a favorable and normalizing affect on such patients. Based on this work, as well as several supportive biochemical studies undertaken at The Netherlands Central Institute for Nutritional Research in Utrecht and at the Wilhelmina Children's Hospital, Dicke concluded that wheat flour, but not well-purified wheat starch, were the causes of the anorexia, increased fecal output, and steatorrhea observed in such patients.

The development of, and introduction of, the gluten-free diet, and the consequent dramatic improvement in the prognosis of the disease, rapidly achieved international acceptance. In a subsequent publication with van de Kamer and Weyers, Dicke published that the alcohol soluble or the gliadin component of the water insoluble protein or gluten moiety of wheat, produced the fat malabsorption in patients with celiac disease. As a consequence of his contributions, The Netherlands Society for Gastroenterology instituted the Dicke medal to reward pioneering work in gastroenterology and made Dicke himself the first recipient.

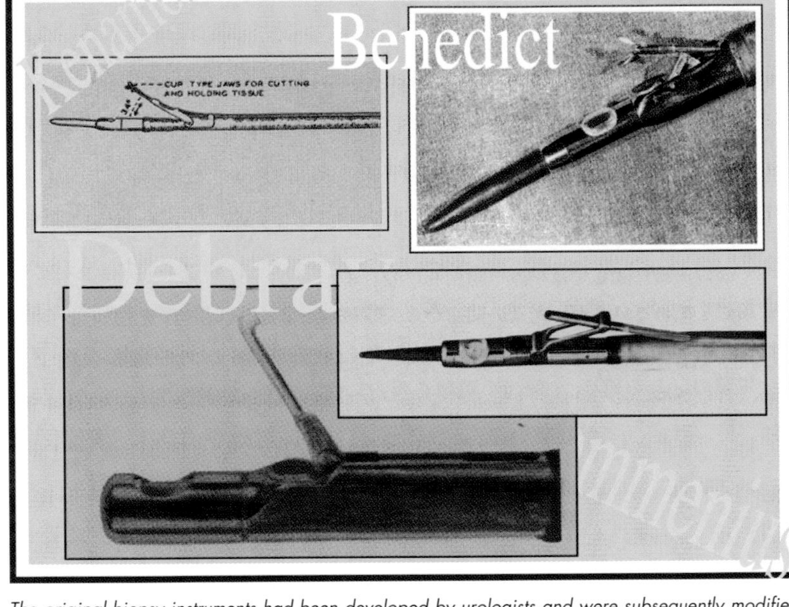

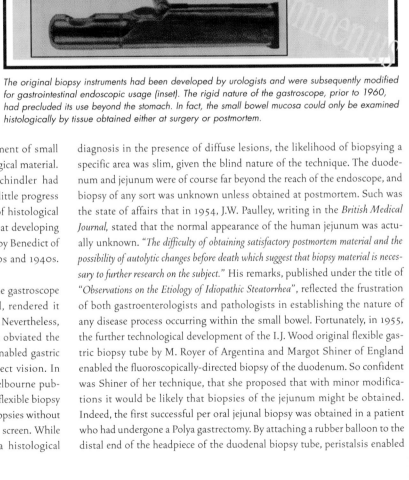

The original biopsy instruments had been developed by urologists and were subsequently modified for gastrointestinal endoscopic usage (inset). The rigid nature of the gastroscope, prior to 1960, had precluded its use beyond the stomach. In fact, the small bowel mucosa could only be examined histologically by tissue obtained either at surgery or postmortem.

BIOPSY

A potential problem, however, in the diagnosis and management of small bowel disease, was the lack of the availability of jejunal histological material. Although the development by R. Schindler had allowed visualization of the stomach, little progress had been made with the acquisition of histological material for diagnosis. Early attempts at developing biopsy techniques had been proposed by Benedict of Boston and Kenamore in the late 1930s and 1940s.

Unfortunately, the modifications of the gastroscope to accommodate the biopsy channel, rendered it clumsy and even more difficult to use. Nevertheless, such material was valuable in that it obviated the need for diagnostic laparotomy and enabled gastric biopsies to be undertaken under direct vision. In 1949, I.J. Wood and R.K. Doig of Melbourne published in *Lancet*, the design of a simple flexible biopsy tube which could be used for gastric biopsies without the use of the gastroscope or an X-ray screen. While this enabled the establishment of a histological diagnosis in the presence of diffuse lesions, the likelihood of biopsying a specific area was slim, given the blind nature of the technique. The duodenum and jejunum were of course far beyond the reach of the endoscope, and biopsy of any sort was unknown unless obtained at postmortem. Such was the state of affairs that in 1954, J.W. Paulley, writing in the *British Medical Journal*, stated that the normal appearance of the human jejunum was actually unknown. "*The difficulty of obtaining satisfactory postmortem material and the possibility of autolytic changes before death which suggest that biopsy material is necessary to further research on the subject.*" His remarks, published under the title of "*Observations on the Etiology of Idiopathic Steatorrhea*", reflected the frustration of both gastroenterologists and pathologists in establishing the nature of any disease process occurring within the small bowel. Fortunately, in 1955, the further technological development of the I.J. Wood original flexible gastric biopsy tube by M. Royer of Argentina and Margot Shiner of England enabled the fluoroscopically-directed biopsy of the duodenum. So confident was Shiner of her technique, that she proposed that with minor modifications it would be likely that biopsies of the jejunum might be obtained. Indeed, the first successful per oral jejunal biopsy was obtained in a patient who had undergone a Polya gastrectomy. By attaching a rubber balloon to the distal end of the headpiece of the duodenal biopsy tube, peristalsis enabled

Intraluminal Biopsy of the Small Intestine

The Intestinal Biopsy Capsule

WILLIAM H. CROSBY, LT. COL., MC, U. S. ARMY and HEINZ W. KUGLER

THE NEED FOR JEJUNAL BIOPSY in Puerto Rico prompted a… ing intraluminal specimens of t… vation of the biopsy knife by… because of the cable's rigidity… spring-activated knife were stu… were considered, but it was fi… mechanism. On this principle… structed and successfully used to obtain the biopsy material.

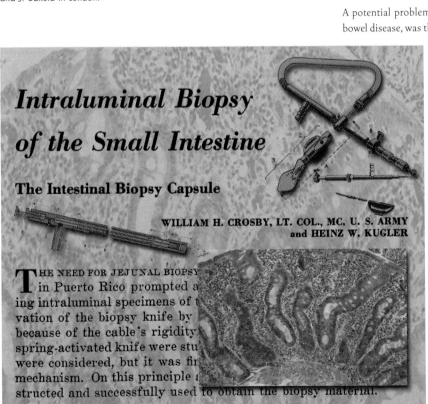

In 1957 Crosby and Kugler published in the American Journal of Digestive Diseases *the first successful series of intraluminal biopsies of the small intestine using a device that subsequently became known as the "Crosby capsule".*

the device to be propelled through the duodenum into the jejunum, where a biopsy could be taken.

Despite its success, the Shiner biopsy tube was cumbersome, and as a result Lt. Col. W.H. Crosby of the United States Army improved the design. As part of the American army sprue team stationed in Puerto Rico, Crosby was aware of the need of a more flexible instrument to obtain jejunal biopsies. Together with H.W. Kugler, he therefore developed a series of modifications including a spring-loaded knife, a timer, solenoids, and magnets before settling on an air pressure mechanism for biopsy. In 1957, Crosby and Kugler published in the *American Journal of Digestive Diseases* the first successful series of intraluminal biopsies of the small intestine, using a device which subsequently became known as the Crosby Capsule.

Crohn's Disease

Few conditions have provided as much controversy and speculation as the non-specific ileitis involving the terminal ileum and parts of the colon. Issues have been raised as to whether it is even one disease, what its cause might be, and even what it should be called. Some felt that terminal ileitis might create a feeling of foreboding amongst patients and preferred regional ileitis, while others still use the eponymous attribution. Although the disease ultimately bears the name of the man (Burrell Crohn) who was responsible for documenting it, his colleagues L. Ginzburg and G.D. Oppenheimer were intimately involved in its delineation. A name not often included is that of Alexander Berg, the surgeon who was responsible for the first successful resections performed in the early cases, but whom declined inclusion in the authorship of the original manuscript.

There is little known about the earliest reports of the condition, and although Soranus of Ephesus described a Crohn's-like proctitis, most of the conditions involving rectal bleeding and weight loss reported by the early Greek and Alexandrian physicians, were probably various forms of parasitic disease or dysentery. The postmortem of a 34-year-old man recounted by G.B. Morgagni in 1769 in *De Sedibus et Causis Morborum* refers to an inflamed terminal ileum and colon with ulceration stricture and large mesenteric lymph nodes. Although this was probably intestinal tuberculosis, the description is consistent with non-specific enteritis and has long been regarded as one of the earliest possible reports. In the subsequent two centuries, a number of descriptions of diseases of this kind appeared under synonyms which included "*non-specific granuloma of the intestine*" and "*chronic cicatrizing enteritis*." No less a personage than Louis XIII was felt to suffer from an anal variant of the disease process and much speculation has accrued regarding the royal posterior and its management. In 1813, C. Combe and W. Saunders, writing in the *Medical Transactions of the College of Physicians* (London) reported a case of stricture and thickening of the ileum that they had demonstrated at the Royal College of Physicians of London. In so doing, they may have provided the first verifiable documentation of the disease. A similarly well-described case was that of J. Abercrombie, who in 1828 in *Pathological and Practical Researches on Diseases of the Stomach and Intestinal Tract and Other Viscera of the Abdomen,* reported a 13-year-old girl with inflammatory thickening of the terminal ileum, proximal colonic involvement, and skip lesions. In 1859, Samuel Wilks proposed that idiopathic colitis should be considered as a disease different to that of specific epidemic dysentery. Subsequently he and W. Moxon (1875) in *Lectures on Pathological Anatomy,* described "*severe acute ileitis in the shape of the thickening of the whole of the coat including the* valvulae conniventes." They noted the condition to be evident in a circumscribed patch from 6 in. to 2 or 3 ft. in the ileum and "*the whole wall was thick with inflammatory lymph, the microscope showing a generalize charging of the whole tissue with pyoid corpuscles.*" In 1882, N. Moore, in the *Transactions of the Pathological Society of London,* was amongst the first to describe the microscopic and macroscopic features of Crohn's disease in a patient with intestinal obstruction, and reported on the presence of chronic inflammatory cell infiltrates. In 1905, R. Wilmanns' contribution to *Beiträge zur klinischen Chirugie* documented a case of inflammation of the ileo-cecal valve in which resection of the involved segment resulted in cure of the intestinal obstruction. The surgeons A.W. Mayo-Robson and B.G.A. Moynihan of Leeds, in 1907 and 1908, respectively, reported their experience with chronic inflammatory masses causing intestinal obstruction. A year later, H. Braun adumbrated further in the *Deutsche Zeitschrift für Chirugie* upon the origin of chronic inflammatory disease of the large intestine, and proposed that tuberculosis, syphilis, and actinomycosis were separate diseases from idiopathic chronic inflammatory changes and could be distinguished by microscopic examination of the resected bowel.

Sir Kennedy Dalzeil of Edinburgh, who described "chronic intestinal enteritis" in 1913 in the British Medical Journal.

In 1913, Sir Kennedy Dalzeil described the entity of chronic intestinal enteritis in the *British Medical Journal.* He reported nine patients (two fatalities) with the disease, and noted involvement of the jejunum, middle and lower ileum, as well as the transverse and

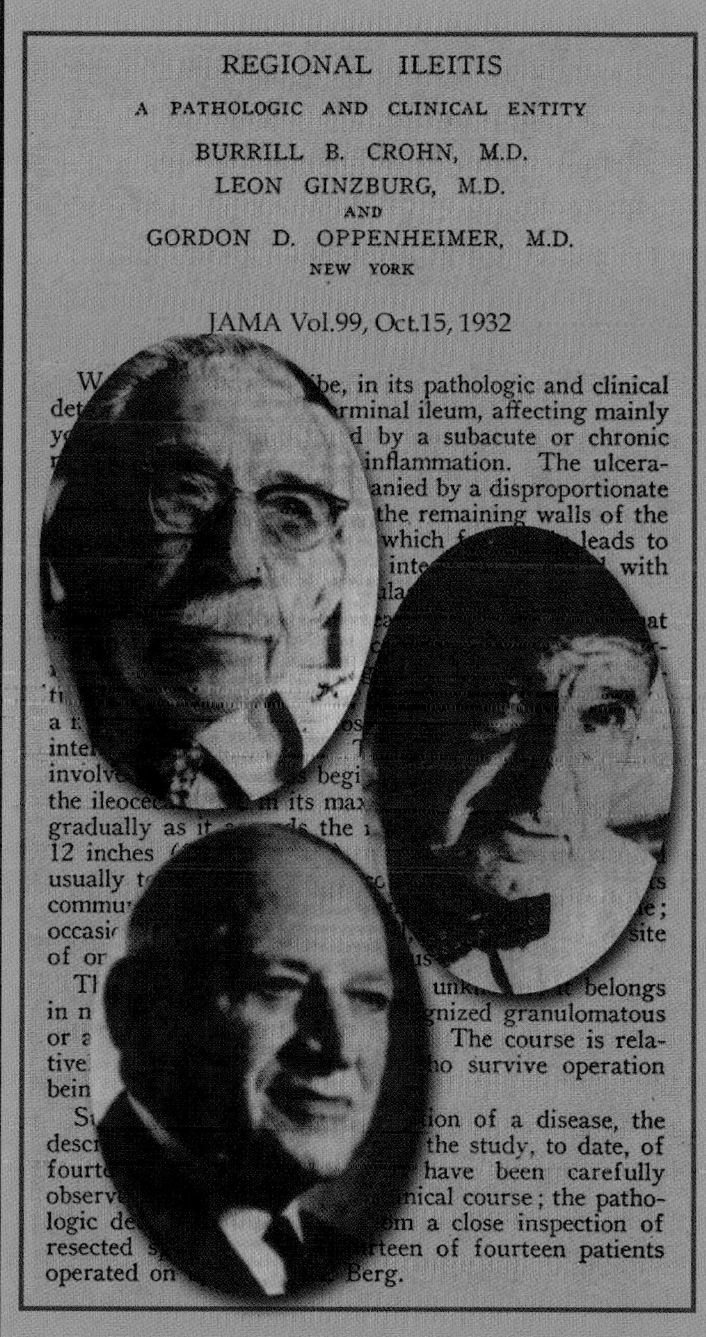

REGIONAL ILEITIS

A PATHOLOGIC AND CLINICAL ENTITY

BURRILL B. CROHN, M.D.
LEON GINZBURG, M.D.
AND
GORDON D. OPPENHEIMER, M.D.
NEW YORK

JAMA Vol.99, Oct.15, 1932

In 1932 B. Crohn (top left), L. Ginzburg (right), and G.D. Oppenheimer (bottom) of Mount Sinai Hospital, New York, defined the condition of regional ileitis.

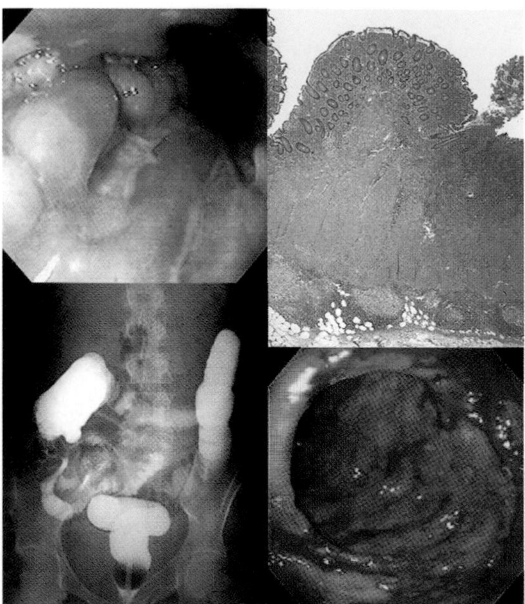

The endoscopic, histological, and radiological manifestations of Crohn's disease.

sigmoid colon. *"The effected bowel gives the consistency and smoothness of an eel in a state of rigor mortis and the glands, though enlarged, are evidently not caseous."* Dalzeil considered the prognosis to be generally poor unless the disease was localized and could be treated surgically. *"As far as I am aware, the prognosis is bad except in cases where the disease is localized and even then seems to be rather hopeless unless operation be had recourse to."* Of interest is the preoccupation at this time of physicians to differentiate the disease from tuberculosis, which was already well-recognized as capable of mimicking almost every known condition.

In 1914, A. Lawen published in the German surgical literature his proposal that claimed the existence of an entity which he termed *fibroplastic appendicitis*. He maintained that chronic inflammation was initiated in the appendix and thereafter spread to the cecum, ileum, and ascending colon. Lawen classified this condition into three groups: namely, inflammatory tumors of the cecum and adjacent colon; inflammatory tumors originating in the appendix and involving the abdominal wall or surrounding intestine and omentum; and lastly, inflammatory tumors originating in the appendix but remaining localized to the appendix, cecum, colon, and terminal ileum. He further noted the importance of differentiating this condition from intestinal tuberculosis. The origin of the disease was the source of much speculation and, in 1927 Razzaboni proposed that a virus might be the etiologic agent, although little rigorous evidence was produced in support of this suggestion.

Mt. Sinai Hospital, New York

In 1923, Moschowitz and Wilensky, in the *American Journal of Medical Sciences,* produced an overview of non-specific intestinal granulomas. They described the presence of the giant cells and their resemblance to hyperplastic ileo-cecal tuberculosis, but emphasized the unknown etiology of this disease process, given the absence of bacteria and caseation. Indeed, their analysis of the contemporary literature of ileo-cecal tuberculosis led them to conclude that in many instances, this pathology was novel and represented a simple inflammatory process and not tuberculosis itself. Their conclusions were thus consistent with the original proposals of Lawen in regard to the nature of fibroplastic appendicitis.

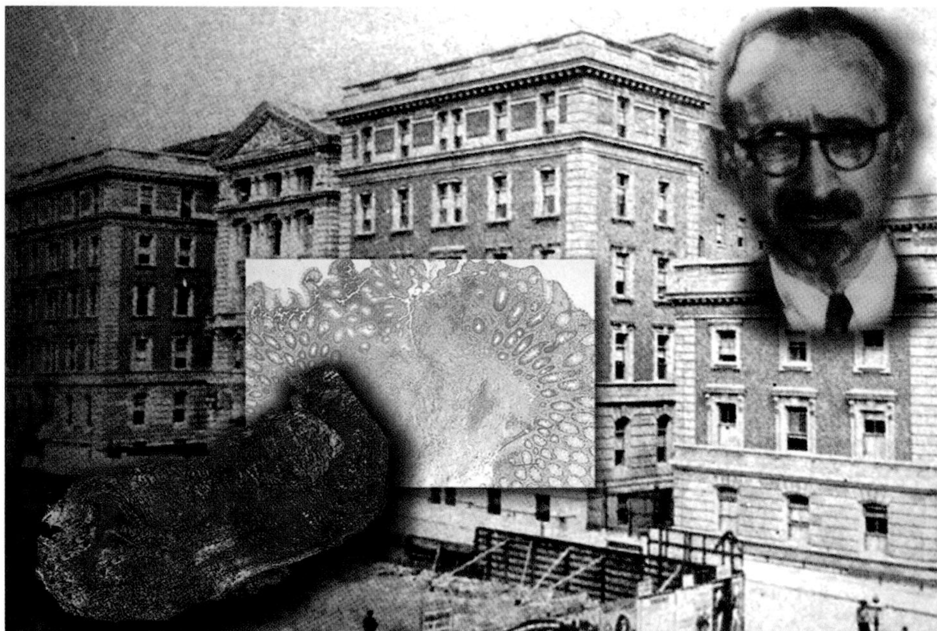

Alexander Berg, the Chief of Surgery at Mount Sinai Hospital in New York, declined authorship in the original manuscript describing regional ileitis, indicating that his contributions in undertaking a resection of the bowel were minimal and did not merit recognition. A decade previously (1920) Berg had noted the presence of bacteria in stomachs he had resected for peptic ulcer disease and proposed that a bacterial origin for gastro-duodenal ulceration should be considered!

In 1932 however, Burrell Crohn, Leon Ginzburg, and Gordon Oppenheimer published their paper entitled "Regional Ileitis: a Pathological and Clinical Entity" in *The Journal of the American Medical Association*. They described their experiences with fourteen cases of terminal ileitis, which they termed a pathologic and clinical entity. A series of meticulous clinico-pathological studies subsequently laid the basis for the establishment of a "novel" disease process. Although its exact nature is still far from being understood, Crohn's original article described a disease *"affecting mainly young adults, characterized by a subacute or chronic narcotizing and cicatrizing inflammation."* A detailed evaluation of the clinical presentation, as well as the complications including stenosis, fistula, and perforation were provided and illustrated by both radiological and histological data. The Sinai group believed the treatment at that stage to be *"purely palliative and supportive"*, although in certain instances surgery was appropriate. They declared the disease to exhibit a relatively optimistic course: *"the course is relatively benign, all the patients who survive operation being alive and well."*

Subsequent progress in the elucidation of regional ileitis involved the assessment of its course, a delineation of its histological profile, and a consideration in regard to whether the colonic form was different to the ileal component. Thus in 1951, H. Rappaport, in one hundred patients with regional ileitis, noted that in more than half there existed a similar, but less severe disease in the colon. He asserted that primary small intestinal regional enteritis appeared to be a disease distinct from segmental nonspecific granulomatus disease, which was limited to the colon. This data was supported by histological criteria documenting the absence of the sarcoid-like granulomas in the colonic disease form. Indeed, the absence of these granulomas, even in regional enteritis, suggested to Rappaport and his colleagues that there existed a heterogeneous etiology for the entire process. A year later, C. Wells, writing in the *Annals of the Royal College of Surgeons of England,* proposed that certain types of ulcerative colitis closely resembled regional enteritis of the small intestine, and suggested that segmental colitis might represent a colonic form of Crohn's disease without an associated ileitis. S. Warren and S.C. Sommers subsequently (1954) noted that regional enteritis was restricted to the small intestine in almost 85% of individuals but in 10%, skip areas of involvement co-existed in the large intestine.

A significant advance in the thought processes relating to this disease process was provided by Brian Brooke in 1959 in a *Lancet* article. He considered that regional enteritis was not limited to small intestine and that not all idiopathic colitis was ulcerative. The basis for his observations was derived from information contained in the Birmingham Crohn's disease register. His second proposal, namely that ulcerative colitis and Crohn's disease of the colon should be differentiated from each other because they varied in their response to medical therapy and in progress after surgery, was of critical clinical importance. Brooke was prescient in his recognition that Crohn's disease recurred after total colectomy and ileostomy, whereas in the instance of ulcerative colitis, such procedures were usually curative. Further observations in the early 1960s by Basil Morson and Sir H.E. Lockhart-Mummery provided further information on the histological and clinical nature of the disease process, but shed little light on its etiology. Although little progress has been made in defining the etiology, the development of a number of different anti-inflammatory agents, including steroids, has considerably facilitated therapy. Similarly, the development of appropriate surgical procedures has greatly improved the quality of life of many individuals suffering from regional ileitis.

Diarrhea, Parasites, and Bacteria

It is likely that the earliest symptom appreciated as being of gastrointestinal significance was abdominal pain. Almost certainly this would have been followed by an appreciation that vomiting and diarrhea were similarly related to gut function. The recognition that something ingested might engender emesis was relatively straightforward, but the recognition of the causation of diarrhea was more complex. Intuition suggested that contamination of food might be involved, and certainly decomposed products were obvious, but the understanding of toxins and invisible organisms awaited the development of the microscope, bacteriology, and the science of chemistry. However, for centuries prior to this, most diarrheal diseases were generically referred to as dysenteries and if associated with bleeding, as bloody dysenteries.

An ancient Greek depiction of a physician seeking to define the site of abdominal pain. The trust implicit in the gaze of the young patient belies his unawareness of the lack of therapy for any diagnosis that might be entertained.

Indeed, diarrhea, or dysentery, is one of the oldest diseases known to mankind, and references to this uncomfortable and dangerous condition are found in the most ancient writings of antiquity. In fact, the modern word "cholera" derives from the Hebrew *cholira*, and in II Chronicles XXI, 19, the first recorded references to this disease bear witness to the fact that "*Jehoram died of an incurable flux lasting two years*." Later in the Bible it is recorded that in Acts XXVIII, 8, the intractable diarrhea besetting the father of Publius is described, as is probably the first recorded psychiatric approach to the treatment of the problem, when Paul cured the venerable patient with the laying-on of hands.

Hippocrates commented extensively on diarrhea and noted the influence of weather: "*For when suffocating heat sets in all of a sudden, while the earth is moistened by vernal showers ... men's bellies are not in an orderly state, for it is impossible, after such a spring, but that the body and its flesh must be loaded with humors. Dysenteries are also likely to occur...*". Hippocrates was also aware of different types of this illness and that diarrhea could accompany other diseases: "*when they are set with fever*" or "*with inflammation of the liver*", and commented that under such circumstances the prognosis might be worse. Similarly, he noted that cases "*attended with blood and scrapings of the bowels*" (bacillary dysentery?) enjoyed a better prognosis. In addition to these observations, Hippocrates noted the relationship of diarrhea with teething, as well as the significance of anuria in severe diarrhea: "*those who pass from below humors and scarcely urinate... are sickly.*"

In the third and fourth centuries immediately following the birth of Christ and the beginning of the disintegration of the Roman Empire, very little was written on either medicine or diarrhea. Of this period, only the writings of the Talmudists, and the excellent textbook on pediatrics by Soranus, comment upon the subject. The Talmudists stressed that sudden changes in living habits, particularly overeating, were apt to cause diarrhea and Rabbi Samuel stressed the importance of fluids: "*He who eats without drinking, eats blood from his own body ... and this is the beginning of diarrhea.*" The sages considered that diarrhea or dysentery was a severe illness and Rabbi Joseph wrote that he wished to die of this disease, for the suffering associated with it was so great that it would surely absolve its victim from the tortures of hell in the afterworld.

The early erudition of the Arab physicians led to the development of important information regarding the management of gastrointestinal disease. Many of their therapeutic recommendations in respect of the management of intestinal disorders are still adhered to almost five centuries later.

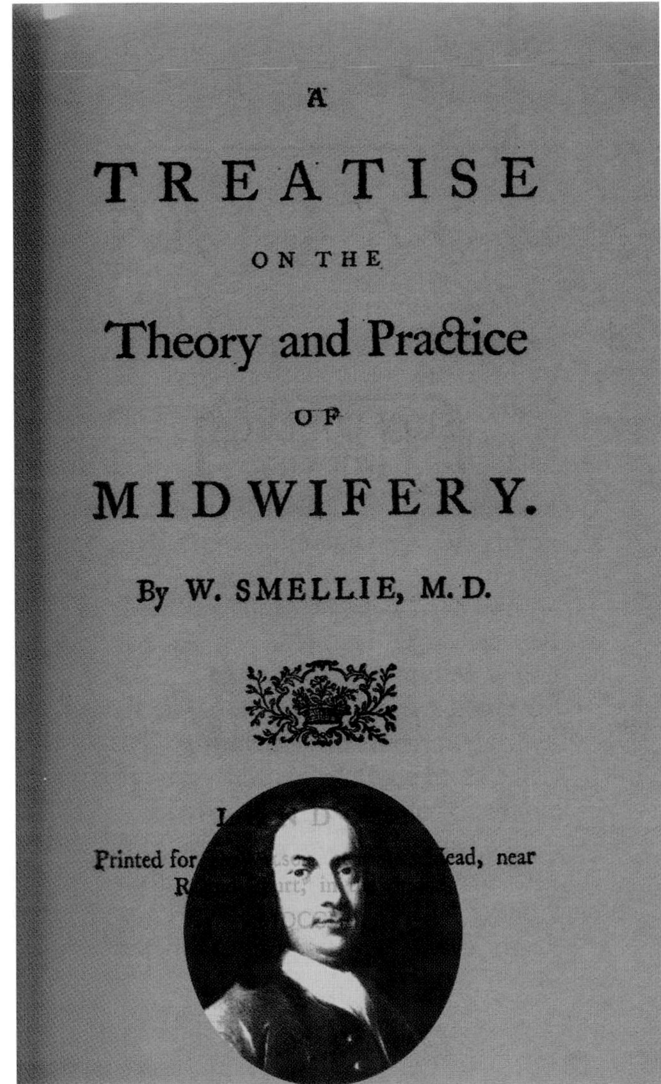

A

TREATISE

ON THE

Theory and Practice

OF

MIDWIFERY.

By W. SMELLIE, M.D.

Printed for … ead, near

William Smellie (1697-1762) of Lanark, Scotland, was the first to teach obstetrics and midwifery on a scientific basis. After twenty years of practicing in Lanark, Smellie moved to London where he established a teaching course for midwives and medical students. To facilitate education he would deliver poor women free of charge, if his students were allowed to attend the delivery and thus learn the principles of the practice of obstetrics. In addition to being a superb teacher, he developed an obstetric forceps, described and detailed the mechanism of labor, and provided much useful information in regard to the post-natal care of babies.

Although descriptions of early therapy appear odd to us today, the treatment recorded by the Talmudic scholars remained essentially unchanged for over a thousand years. They advised external applications to the abdomen – usually heat of some sort, or irritants such as wine and oil, as well as cupping to the navel. In the diet, they advised old apple or grape wine or lemons, and to drink much water. In severe cases of tenesmus, as with the daughter of Rabbi Ascher, pepper seeds in wine were administered. It is possible that the rabbis were aware of the contagiousness of dysentery. While it was a holy duty to visit the sick, they advised against visiting patients with diarrhea and eye diseases and despite the age-old objection of religious admonition against tampering with the bodies of the deceased, the rabbinate advocated fumigation for the corpses of victims of diarrhea.

The concept of the origin of the problem was, however, not generally appreciated, although it is likely that much of the Hebraic dietary code evolved from rabbinical observations of illness.

During the Greek period, Soranus of Ephesus (*c.* 98-117) wrote a pediatric text consisting of twenty-three chapter headings, amongst them, *On flux of the Belly*. The latter is notable in that it contains the first description of the fingernail test for purity of milk. This test continued in use for over 1,600 years, and was repeated almost verbatim in the first English book on diseases of children, written by Thomas Phaer in 1515: *"That mylke is goode that is whyte and sweete; and when ye droppe it on your nayle and do move your finger, neyther fleteth abrod at every stiring nor will hange faste upon your nayle, whex ye turn it downeward, but that whvche is betwene bothe is best."* This ancient test for the palatability of milk is repeated even as late as 1752 in W. Smellie's *"Treatise on the Theory and Practice of Midwifery."*

The disintegration of the Roman Empire was followed by the Dark Ages, unenlightened for medicine as well as it was for other sciences and arts. Medical writing was confined chiefly to the Arab physicians who devoted themselves to translating the ancient Greeks and in so doing, perpetuated the ancient Galenic concepts. The translations were later reintroduced into Europe by Hebrew authors, who retranslated the Arabic into Latin. One of the best known manuscripts on pediatrics of this period, *Liber de Passionibus Puerorum Galeni*, was attributed to Galen but in reality was more a compendium of many classic medical essays gathered together during the sixth to the ninth centuries. Indeed, the text contained little new regarding the treatment of diarrhea. However, Rhazes (852-932), a Persian of a somewhat later period, in referring to diarrhea, bridged the ancient with the most modern, by attributing the disease to teething, to catching cold (parenteral infection) and to spoiled milk. A compatriot of Rhazes, Avicenna, attributed diarrhea to teething, reaffirmed the need for belly fermentations and fruit seeds, but added two new ideas. The first was the advice to *"drink five grains of kids' rennet in cold water…"* In fact, this suggestion to ingest the secretion of a glandular organ was repeated in succeeding literature on the subject until the modern era, and forms an interesting background to contemporary use of pancreatic extracts in chronic diarrhea. The other admonition was, *"… instead of milk let him take… some barley soaked in water."* The prohibition of milk and the use of barley water are little different to contemporary therapy in many parts of the world.

In the first printed book on pediatrics, written by Paulus Bogellardus in 1472 and published in Padua, the subject of diarrhea formed an extensive part of the text but mostly quoted Galen, Avicenna, and Rhazes. A significant

The ancient Jewish physician/rabbis were well aware of the potentially harmful effects of certain kinds of food. A complex set of dietary laws was thus developed to protect the populace from infection or infestation. Although some of the edicts of "Kashrut" reflected mysticism and superstition, many even to this day demonstrate a sound understanding of the principles of food hygiene.

In 1886 Theodore Escherich (left) described Bacillus coli. *Subsequently Kiyoshi Shiga in 1897 identified the cause of dysentery* (Shigella).

contribution, however, was the suggestion that some cases of diarrhea would be cured if the baby is fed *"goat's milk diluted with cool water."* The second printed book on pediatrics, by Bartholemus Metlinger (Augsberg 1473), considered the etiology of dysentery as teething, and proposed that the treatment should be "skimmed – oat's milk, also almond milk diluted with heated water."

The father of pediatrics in England, Thomas Phaer, earned his title by writing *The Boke of Children* in 1584, but the text was little more than another compilation of the classic authors, and its chief importance is historical, since its existence illustrates the Renaissance tendency to translate the classic authors into the vernacular. The ideas of Phaer in regards to the etiology of diarrhea were conventional and his treatment standard, although it is interesting that he stressed abstention from milk for two-hour periods during the disease and then advised heating it when its use was resumed. Subsequently, neither Robert Penells nor Franciscus Sylvius (Amsterdam, 1674) (Sylvan fissure and aqueduct) added anything new to the subject. In France, Simon de Vallembert (1565) publisheded a treatise, "Cinq Bares de la manière de nourrier et souvener les infants des leur naissance." Although he had little novel to add to the subject, his description of the different forms of the illness is worthy of consideration: *"food is passed much as when eaten [the Greek, lientery]; the condition is accompanied by skinning of the intestines [the Greek, dysentery]; and lastly, neither of these two [called diarrhea by the Greeks]."*

The descriptive state of diarrhea remained in place for thousands of years and only the vague concept of spoiled food or bad milk attested to any thoughts of etiology. Despite any real understanding of contamination or contagion, the consideration of parasites as a source of disease had, however, long been apparent given the observation of worms in the stools.

Although initially considered to represent infestation by an evil spirit, the recognition that such agents were themselves responsible for disease, led to more determined efforts to identify causative agents.

In this respect, the development of the microscope and the subsequent work of Koch, Pasteur, Cohnheim, and Escherich would prove to be of fundamental importance.

Studies of parasites that were identified, first in the skin and thereafter the gut, led to an understanding of the biological processes involved in their diseases. They were regarded as organisms living in or on another animal and, in obtaining food from the host, might or might not cause damage. Their presence certainly conferred no benefit. The diverse parasites identified in man included bacteria, viruses, fungi, protozoa and metazoa (multicellular organisms) as well as worms.

As a result of the widespread prevalence, an almost separate scientific discipline arose to deal with the effects of the association of two organisms. The term "parasite" is derived from the Greek word meaning "situated beside" and was used in ancient times to describe people who ate beside or at tables of others. In spite of this "social" background of the word, scientists have used the term to define parasites as organisms residing on, or within, another living organism. Parasites may, therefore, be organisms that are either animals or plants, including a diversity of species such as bacteria, yeasts, fungi, algae, viruses, protozoa, helminths, and arthropods. From a biological point of view, parasitology may thus be defined as a branch of ecology in which one organism constitutes the living environment of another.

From the medical point of view, parasitism and potential harm to the host have become synonymous. Further restriction of the domain of parasitology occurred between the seventeenth and nineteenth century where parasitology became the science dealing with zooparasites, that is organisms that belong to the animal kingdom. Thus

Francisco Redi (inset) (1626-1697) of Arezzo, Italy, refuted the current dogma that grubs and maggots developed spontaneously in decaying matter. The decline of the theory of spontaneous generation as well as the observation by Leeuwenhoek of bacteria, led to the conclusion that disease processes could be transmitted by living agents (bacteria, fungi, parasites). The further use of histology facilitated the identification of the different lifecycle forms of parasites in various hosts and the subsequent elucidation of a wide variety of parasitic diseases that involved humans.

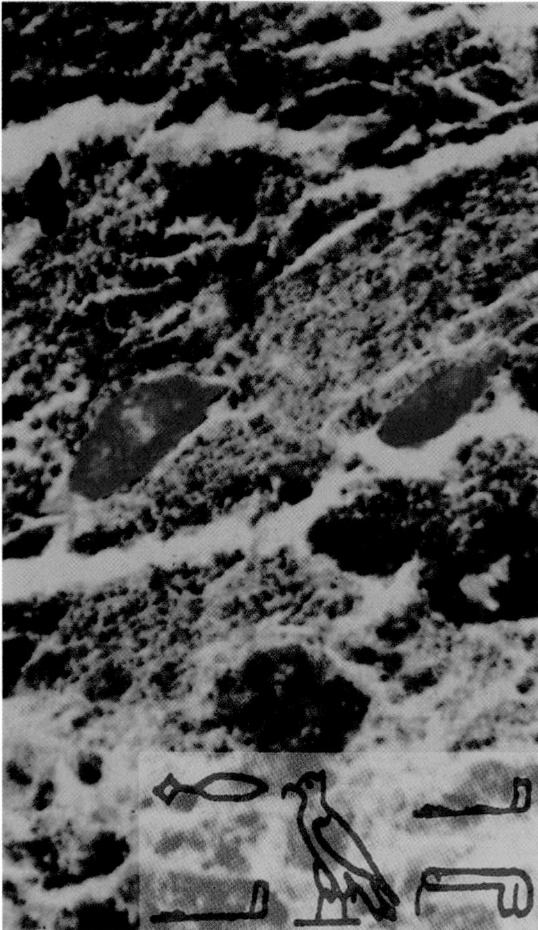

Photomicrograph of a liver section from "Nakht", a mummy of a 14-year-old ancient Egyptian. The 3,000-year-old body was found in Thebes and despite the dried soft tissue structures, two Schistosoma haematobium *eggs with the characteristic terminal spine can be identified (blue). The bottom right insert is a hieroglyphic description of a urinary tract-related syndrome included in the Ebers Papyrus. The discharge from the penis (bottom right) refers to haematuria, a characteristic feature of* Schistosomiasis.

parasites such as bacteria, viruses, and fungi, that have been classified as of plant origin, are dealt within the discipline of microbiology.

Anthony van Leeuwenhoek was credited with seeing the first protozoon using a simple microscope, and between 1674 and 1716, he described many free-living protozoa and also the first parasitic protozoan, *Eimeria stiedai*. In 1681, van Leeuwenhoek described the first human parasitic protozoon by the identification of *Giardia lamblia* in his own diarrheic stools. The major discoveries of parasitic protozoa were, however, delayed until the nineteenth century, when trypanosomes, amoebas, and malaria parasites were identified. Indeed, prior to the 1870s, worms or flukes had comprised almost all known parasites. In retrospect, evidence for several worm infections have been found in ancient Egyptian mummies (1210-1000 B.C.), reflecting the long-standing relationship between man and parasites. The Ebers Papyrus of 1550 B.C. indicates that in ancient Egypt, at least four worm infections were recognized, including *Ascaris lumbricoides, Taenia saginata, Dracunculus medinesis* (guinea worm), and *Schistosoma haematobium* (bilharzia). The papyrus also includes information on arthropods such as fleas, flies, and lice. More recently, evidence was obtained from examining tissue sections of ancient Egyptian mummies that *Trichinella spiralis* existed as an infection during that period. Worms also were mentioned by Assyrian, Babylonian, and Greek physicians.

The two most prominent historical discoveries of worms occurred in 1379 (*Fasciola hepatica*) and in 1558 (*Cysticercus cellulosae*), but it was not until the eighteenth and the first half of the nineteenth century that many species of worms and arthropods were identified and classified. Thus, by the latter part of the nineteenth century and early twentieth century, a consolidation of the discoveries of many human parasites had occurred, and in general the identification of their life cycle, and recognition of their related disease syndromes had been established.

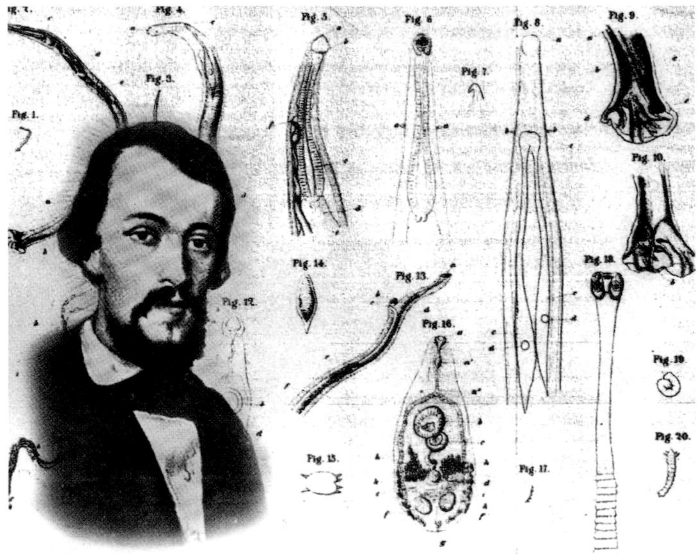

Theodore Maximilian Bilharz (left) was a young German pathologist from the University of Tübingen who, as a pupil of Karl von Siebold, had developed an interest in helminthology. As a result, in 1815 he accompanied Professor Wilhelm Griesinger of Kiel, who had been appointed director of the Kasr-el-Aini Medical School in Cairo, to Egypt. Here he described the Schistosoma haematobium *(background). Unfortunately, the Cairo medical school failed to prosper and Bilharz and Griesinger returned to Germany after two years. In 1862, on an expedition to Massawah with the Duke of Saxe-Coburg-Gotha, Bilharz contracted typhus and perished at the age of thirty-two.*

The three major groups of organisms recognized as falling within the scope of parasitology are protozoa, helminths, and arthropods, of which only the former two directly impact upon the gastrointestinal tract. The three vary greatly in biological characteristics and historically, there is little justification for including them in a single group, except that they are all zooparasites. Biologically, however, they are quite different: protozoa are unicellular organisms that share with bacteria and viruses the capability of dividing and multiplying within their mammalian host. In contrast, worms are multicellular, all adults can be seen by the naked eye, and may reach huge dimensions, for example, some tapeworms may reach ten meters in length. Furthermore, worms generally cannot multiply within the mammalian host; to increase the worm population in a specific host,

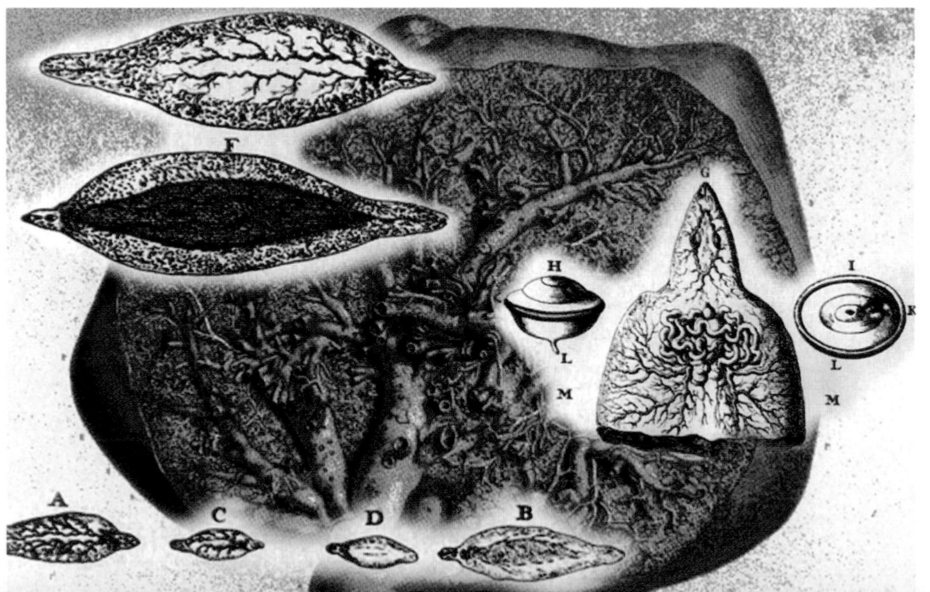

The liver fluke (Clonorchis sinensis) was recognized to be a major source of liver disease in the East. In 1911 Harujiro Kobayashi discovered the second intermediate host of the liver fluke and in so doing facilitated the eradication of the disease. Indeed, the elucidation of the trematode worm diseases was to a large extent the province of Japanese bacteriologists and microbiologists. Thus, in 1904 S. Katsurada had discovered Schistosomium japonicum and in 1914 K. Nakaga had identified the intermediate host of Paragonimus westermanii. *Similarly, the migratory course of human ascaris was demonstrated by S. Yoshida and the experimental production of cancer from continuous stimulation noted by K. Yamagawa and K. Ichikawa in 1915.*

re-exposure must occur. The third group of zooparasites, the arthropods, represent a heterogeneous collection of vectors of disease which may be bacterial, viral, or protozoan, or they themselves may parasitize mammalian hosts causing varying degrees of discomfort or disease.

The host-parasite relationship is a dynamic process and although the host may exhibit several natural (innate) and acquired protective mechanisms, the complex structure of zooparasites, in contrast to bacteria and viruses, poses a significant challenge to host immune responses. Furthermore, not all of these responses are protective and in fact, protective immunity is the exception rather than the rule, following a specific parasitic infection. Successful survival of parasites has dictated that several mechanisms of evasion of host protective mechanisms have been developed to ensure their propagation. Thus, parasites may evade the host immune response either by simple mechanisms such as intracellular location, or by more elaborate processes involving changing their antigenic structure or altering the host responses in a way that favors their survival. A by-product of some host responses is a chain of immunopathological reactions that ultimately results in significant morbidity. Whether diseases such as ulcerative colitis or Crohn's disease represent examples of such events is a matter of considerable controversy.

The prevalence, intensity, and clinical significance of parasitic infections vary in different parts of the world. They are generally more prevalent in warm climates, in less developed areas, and in the socially deprived sections of any given society. Environmental and economic factors are prominent among those responsible for endemicity of parasitic infections in many parts of the world. Attempts to control the major parasitic infections have yet to demonstrate the effectiveness of any given strategy. In the 1940s and 1950s, vector control and chemotherapy were thought to be the effective measures against the spread of malaria. Short-term successes were achieved, but soon drug resistance developed in the mosquito vectors and in the parasite. Newer tools, whether chemotherapeutic or immunological, are therefore needed to bring about containment of these major health problems. Furthermore, their close relationship to socio-economic development, and the role of cultural factors, must be taken into consideration in formulating control strategies. Although initial studies were aimed at eliminating the vectors, the evolution of bio-medical sciences has led to the development of tools that are now being applied to the study of human parasites. It is likely that the identification of specific pharmacotherapeutic probes, and the introduction of antiparasitic vaccines and new methods of controlling these infections, will become the ideal therapeutic pathway.

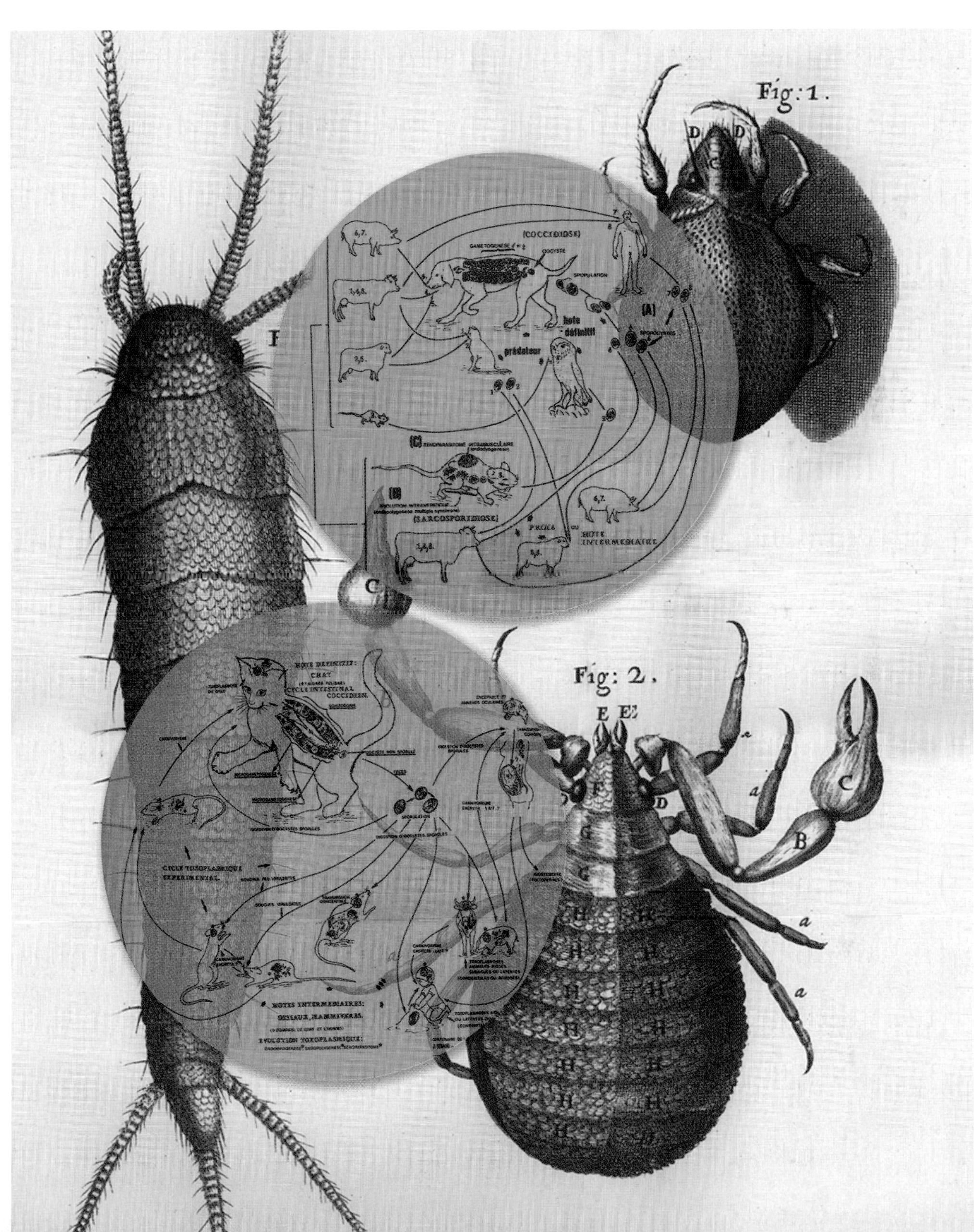

The advent of histology considerably increased the ability of gastroenterologists to identify gut parasites. As a result of the information available, the lifecycle of individual pathogens could be traced and appropriate public health and therapeutic measures instituted.

Section 19

Large Intestine and Rectum

The Large Intestine

The colon has, since time immemorial, been an object of both medical and social concern, as the passage of gaseous and noxious effluent constantly remained a source of concern as well as humor. The ancient Egyptians believed that the very essence of life resided in the anal area, while even thousands of years later in the elegant and sophisticated city of Vienna, Sigmund Freud asserted that issues relating to the colon and fecal retention were as pertinent to the health of the mind as the body. Although the physicians of the Nile Valley maintained that health depended upon a clean colon, their notion extended far beyond the immutable secrets of Thebes and Luxor, such that throughout history, both the physician and the patient have exhibited an obsessional requirement to clean the bowels by purgatives, cathartics, or enemata.

Indeed, emptying of the bowel is regarded to this day as one of the most salubrious of sensations recordable across all cultures. Given the fact that medications were often unpalatable or the patient too ill to swallow and retain them, the nether route of administration attained widespread popularity and acceptance amongst both physicians and patients. Enema administration became regarded not only as an appropriate medical intervention but indeed, a requisite daily exercise necessary to ensure maintenance of good health. Thus, self-administration devices were *de rigueur* amongst the upper classes of France and England during the eighteenth and early nineteenth centuries, and the elegance of design and workmanship of the device, highly prized as acceptable items connoting social status.

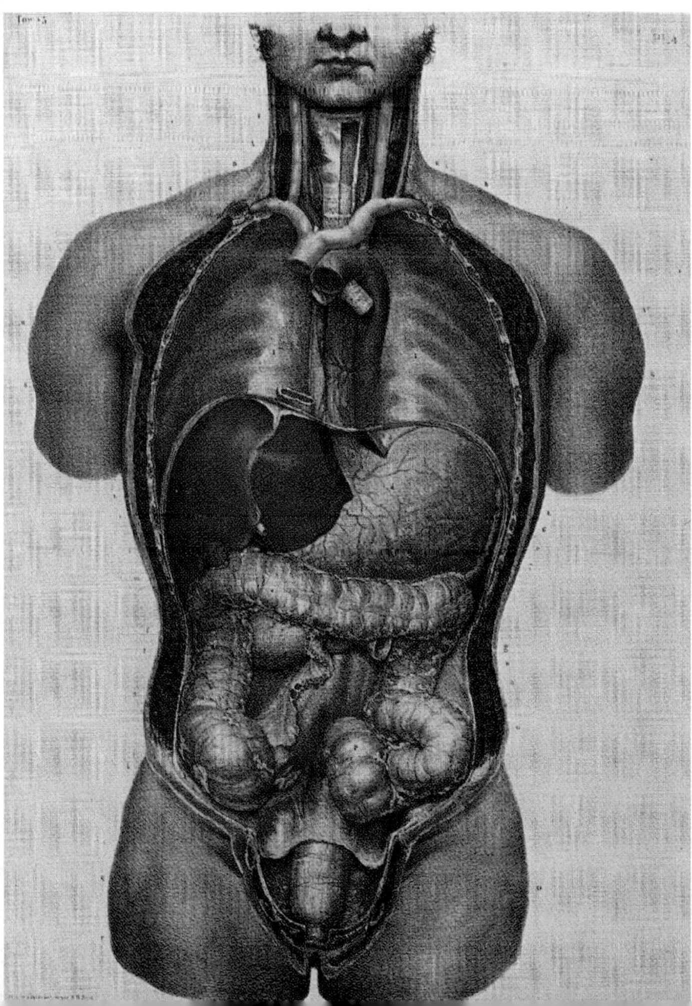

Given the early lack of knowledge of the interior of the system, a considerable preponderance of attention was paid to external manifestations, thus bleeding or prolapsed hemorrhoids figure amongst the earliest descriptions of disease and therapy. Therapy ranged from ointments to pessaries and even cautery. Excision was a dramatic intervention, and particularly so prior to the developement of analgesia and anesthetic agents. A particular problem was also posed by the difficulty of adequate visibility of the area, and thus early considerations were directed at the development of specula whose utility was amplified first by mirrors, and subsequently candles, lamps, and eventually even lenses. Turcke is believed to have been the first to X-ray the rectum in order to confirm the position of metallic tubes that he had inserted. The first radiographic observations of the colon were, however, recorded by Walsh (*c.* 1905) who identified a faint outline in an abdominal radiograph of a patient receiving therapeutic bismuth. Unfortunately, he and numerous other radiologists of the time failed to recognize the potential value of this observation in obtaining contrast studies of the large intestine.

Disturbances of bowel function, when associated with pain or obstruction, led to obvious discomfort, rapidly apparent by way of either distention or loss of flatal or fecal effluent. The dreaded disease of

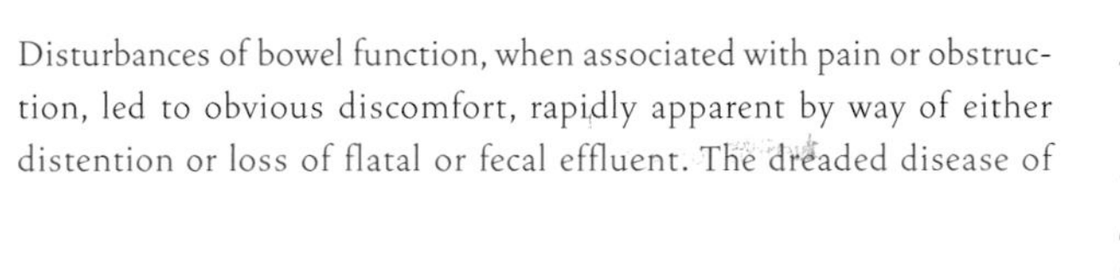

Bougery's 19th-century anatomic illustration of the colon, rectum, and upper abdomen. Although substantial topographic information was available, little was known of the physiology of the colon.

A considerable impetus to the advance of endoscopy at the turn of the 19th century was provided by progress made in the area of electricity and illumination. Thus, sunlight and candlelight, augmented by mirrors and lenses, was supplanted by first gaslight, and thereafter electrical heated carbon and platinum filaments. In addition, unwieldy and clumsy batteries were replaced by more efficient power sources and large lamps supplanted by miniature bulbs suitable for intra-cavity illumination.

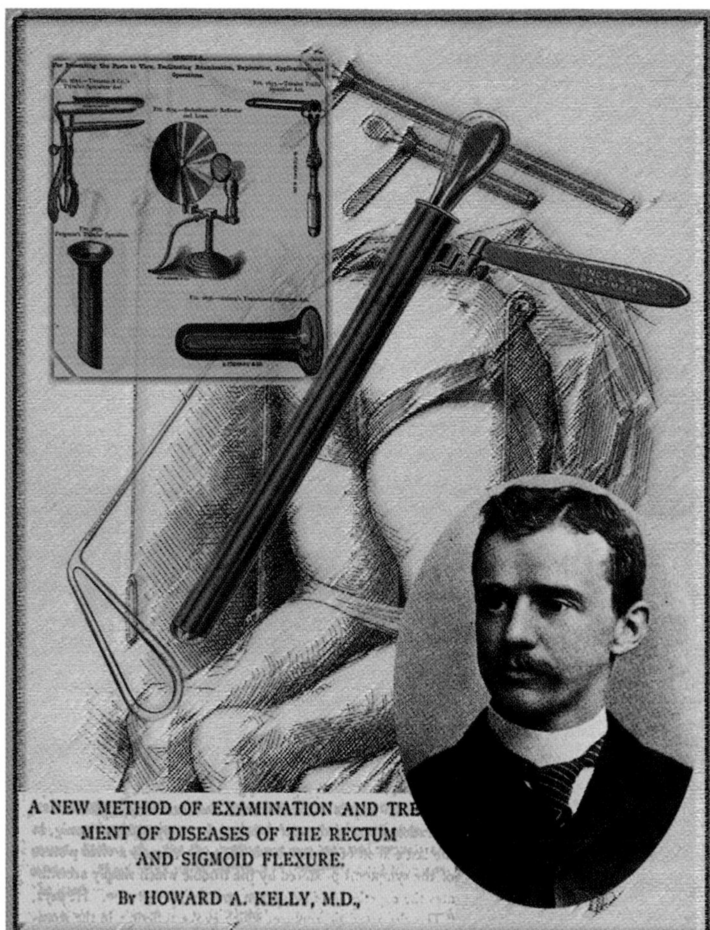

A NEW METHOD OF EXAMINATION AND TRE-
MENT OF DISEASES OF THE RECTUM
AND SIGMOID FLEXURE.
By HOWARD A. KELLY, M.D.,

In 1895, Howard Kelly, Professor of Gynecology and Obstetrics at Johns Hopkins University, published in the Annals of Surgery *the detailed description and drawings of the instruments that he had devised for procto-sigmoidoscopy. Kelly claimed that a kitchen table was adequate and that the knee chest position allowed the use of either sunlight or lamplight using a head mirror. The long sigmoidoscope (center oblique) permitted ingress to 30 cm and visibility could be improved by use of the "fecal scooper" (center vertical) or the cotton-tipped applicator (left vertical) to remove mucus. A graded conical sphincter dilator (top left) was useful for stricture management and by notation of the gradations therapeutic progress could be assessed.*

appendicitis was completely misunderstood for years, and in a world deficient of antibiotics and surgery, resulted in extensive loss of life. However, by the early 1900s, the prohibition against surgery declined to the extent that reasonable intervention became possible. Large bowel obstruction, however, remained the bane of physicians, as surgery represented a formidable challenge, given the problems of sepsis and the difficulties associated with resection and anastomosis. Thus, the most critical challenges in the development of large bowel therapy related firstly to the advance of methods to amplify visibility, and secondly, to the evolution of techniques that could be used to safely resect obstructions or inflammatory masses or neoplastic masses, and facilitate the restoration of bowel continuity.

Imaging the Colon

The first formal opaque enema examination of the colon was undertaken in 1904 by Schule, who published radiographs of patients who had received 300 to 400 ml of an oily suspension of bismuth subnitrate administered in the knee/chest position. By 1910, Georg Fedor Haenisch had described a more sophisticated fluoroscopic technique for the examination of the colon utilizing a novel horizontal fluoroscopy table – the *trochoscope* – and the retrograde instillation of a mixture of bismuth carbonate, *bolus alba*, and water. A decade later in 1923, A.W. Fischer first utilized the double contrast technique and noted with enthusiasm that *"the contours and lumen of the intestine are very clearly recognizable, so that any stenosis or tumor is certain not to pass unnoticed."* By the 1930s, Kirkland and Weaver of the Mayo Clinic had further modified and improved Fischer's double contrast examination of the colon to produce radiographs that were able to detect the very smallest of intra-luminal tumors. The subsequent use of gastrografin enemas, and the introduction by Cook and Margulis of the silicon foam enema for the examination of the rectum and the sigmoid, produced novel information but was superceded by the introduction of colonic endoscopy.

Although a variety of endoscopic devices and tubes had been inserted into the colon for centuries prior to the introduction of X-rays, little visibility was possible beyond the rectum due to lighting problems and the inability of rigid tubes to circumvent the recto-sigmoid flexure. The ability to pass a flexible tube as far as the cecum had been demonstrated as early as 1928 by H.C. Hoff. Although this blind procedure was of little diagnostic use to endoscopists, it did indicate that transmission of a device from the anus to cecum was possible. F. Matsunaga utilized a modified gastro-camera to intubate the colon but the procedure was difficult, and provided only limited information. However, the advent of the Hirschowitz gastroscope in 1957 paved the way for applications of a similar type to the colon, and by the early 1960s, both the Machida and Olympus Corporations had developed prototype models for colonic examination.

In 1963, Robert Turell of New York reported his experiences in the *American Journal of Surgery* with colonoscopy, and detailed his use of a Hirschowitz gastroscope adapted to function as a colonoscope. Despite his pioneering efforts with a "flexible fiber optic colonoscope", Turell expressed reservations about the application and development of the flexible instrument for colonoscopic use. Nevertheless, market versions of these devices were introduced in 1965.

Luciano Provenzale and Antonio Revignas of Cagliari University, Sardinia, Italy, reported the first total colonoscopy in a human subject in the same year. In a highly innovative fashion, their subject was induced to swallow a long polyvinyl tubing, which over a period of days emerged from his anus.

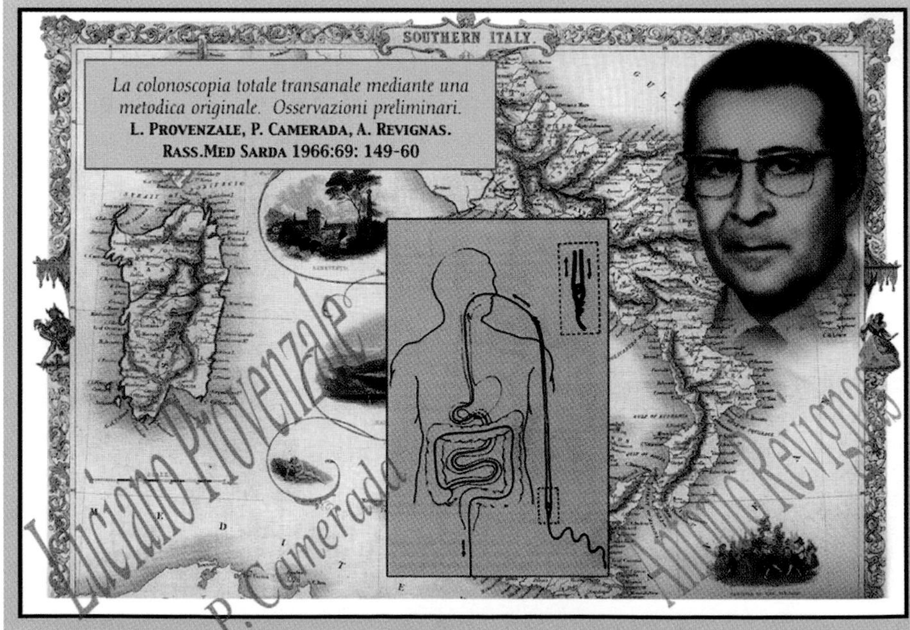

Although the island of Sardinia (left) had languished in relative obscurity since the departure of the Carthaginians, the innovative contributions in 1966 of Luciano Provenzale (right) and Antonio Revignas of the University of Cagliari to the development of colonoscopy once again reminded the world of the power of the heirs of the Caesars. Using the 1955 technique of Blankenhorn for end-to-end intestinal intubation with a small caliber swallowed tube, they positioned a pulley system of thin polyvinyl tubing arranged in tandem in the digestive tract and attached it to a lateral viewing, non-steerable Hirschowitz gastroscope. The application of a light pulling or pushing force enabled the gastroscope to progress endolumenally in a retrograde fashion along the length of the colon (center).

William Wolff (right) and Hiromi Shinya (left) (c. 1975) of the Beth Israel Hospital, New York (background), were not only instrumental in developing safe and effective colonoscopy but convincingly demonstrated that polypectomy was not only a feasible procedure but safe and effective. Although the concept of polypectomy was initially criticized, the publication of a series of carefully documented patient studies and reviews (top left) led to the widespread acceptance of therapeutic colonoscopy. There is little doubt that their contributions dramatically impacted upon the issues of colon cancer surveillance and prophylaxis.

Provenzale and his colleague then attached the tubing to a side-viewing Hirschowitz gastroscope and gently pulled it northwards through the entire colon up to the cecum. Although this succeeded in its goal of achieving total colonoscopy, the technique was generally regarded as unacceptable for routine usage.

In May of 1967, Bergein F. Overholt, working in conjunction with the Eder Instrument Co., developed a flexible fiber-optic sigmoidoscope whose application he presented at the ASGE meeting in Colorado Springs, Colorado. Convinced that better illumination, adequate flexibility, and deeper penetration would all be to the advantage of both the endoscopist and the patient, Overholt enthusiastically generated the supporting data and within two years, reported favorably on the newly introduced Olympus colonoscope. By 1970, a longer version of this instrument had been introduced, which possessed the additional feature of a four-way tip deflection that facilitated negotiation of the colonic flexures. Further modifications of the short and long colonoscope resulted in modifications of the flexibility, as well as the introduction of omni-directional viewing with four-way tip deflection. Some adepts still proposed a place for the rigid sigmoidoscope, but by the late 1970s, almost all endoscopists had concluded that fiber optic sigmoidoscopes or colonoscopes were superior in almost all circumstances.

The ability to place a wire snare into an endoscope considerably amplified the utility of the endoscope as a therapeutic device. One of the applications of the use of such a reconfigured endoscope was the successful removal of colonic polyps with a wire loop snare in the biopsy channel of a fiber optic colonoscope. This was undertaken at the Beth Israel Hospital in New York by William I. Wolff and Hiromi Shinya. Within a year, they were able to report a further three hundred polypectomies with minimal complication rates and zero mortality. The recognition that polyps represented pre-cancerous lesions and that polypectomy might now be safely undertaken in many circumstances without resort to laparotomy or colectomy was regarded, not surprisingly, as a dramatic advance by some.

More cautious individuals and some surgeons with a vested interest in colectomy, however, insisted that colonoscopic polypectomy was being practiced over-enthusiastically and that bleeding, perforation, and gas explosions were, or could be, common complications. Such conclusions were not supported by the available data, and were effectively rebuffed by the publication, in 1973, in the *New York State Journal of Medicine*, in which Wolff noted that he had undertaken sixteen hundred polypectomies without complication. Therapeutic endoscopy realized through polypectomy was unanimously vindicated as a procedure that had come of age.

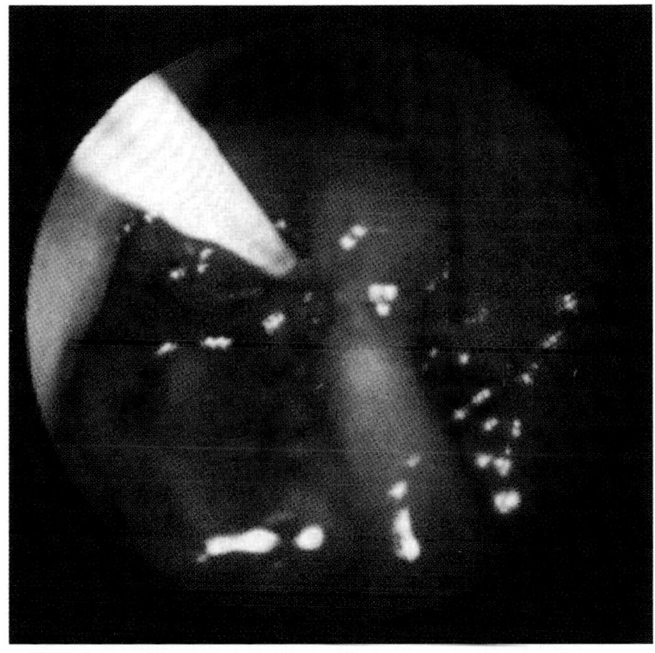

The technique of endoscopic polypectomy for the most part replaced laparotomy and colonic resection and greatly facilitated early diagnosis of gastrointestinal neoplasia.

APPENDICITIS

Although now regarded as an organ of only modest medical and surgical interest, a hundred years ago, inflammation of the appendix was a highly morbid condition often leading to death. The elucidation of the pathogenesis of the disease process and the development of a rational therapeutic strategy remains an important milestone in the successful management of patients presenting with abdominal pain. The history of appendicitis includes examples of considerable resistance to change, prescient but unacceptable early observations, and emotional support of ofteninsupportable views leading finally to the development of an acceptable therapeutic strategy.

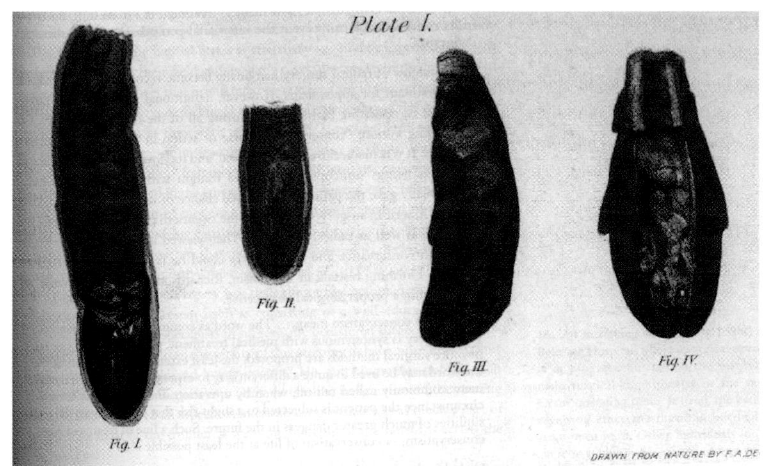

A series of pathological drawings depicting appendiceal disease. Despite its diminutive size and its lack of function, extraordinary medical attention has been directed at this vestigial organ.

IOANNIS
FERNELII
AMBIANI
De luis Venereæ curatione
perfectiſſima
LIBER,
FERNEL
M. D. LXXIX.

Jean Fernel was born in Montdidier in 1497 and attended school at Cleremont before entering the College of St. Barbe at Paris in 1516 where he studied philosophy and eloquence. In 1519 he became a Master of Arts, a student of mathematics, and in 1530 at the age of 33 acquired his degree in medicine. Disinterested in the subject he focused chiefly on mathematical work and became the first to determine the exact measurement of a degree of the meridian as well as other contributions in mathematical and astronomical research. Unfortunately, despite his intellect he was unable to support his family by research in science and at the advanced age of 38 undertook the practice of medicine, thereafter rapidly achieving a considerable reputation.

Although the appendix was not much referred to in early anatomical studies (since these were mostly undertaken in animals that did not possess the vestigial organ), by 1889 almost 2,500 articles or books relevant to the subject had been published. By 1950, this number had risen to more than 13,000 and the subject of appendicitis, appendiceal abscess, antibiotics, and surgery had become major issues amongst both gastroenterologists and surgeons.

Background

Although the physician-anatomist, Berengario Da Carpi, was the first to describe the appendix in 1521, Leonardo Da Vinci had clearly depicted the organ in his anatomic drawings that date back to 1492. By 1543, the work of Andreas Vesalius (*De Humani Corpis Fabrica*), although clearly delineating the existence of the appendix, failed to discuss the organ in any detail in the text. The publication of the drawings by Leonardo Da Vinci of the peritoneal cavity in the eighteenth century, and thereafter the work of Morgagni published in 1719, provided further details of the gross anatomy of the appendix. Unfortunately, some confusion arose at this time since the word "cecum" was often used interchangeably to describe the vestigial organ. While considerable current interest is devoted to the appendix, acute inflammation of the appendix appears to be an age-old disease and evidence of its existence can be demonstrated in Egyptian mummies of the Byzantine Era. The first description of appendicitis is that of Jean Fernel, published in 1544.

Such was his success that he became chief physician to the Dauphin of France, and garnered further acclamation upon the latter's accession to the throne as King Henry II, being appointed the first Court Physician and doctor to Catherine de Medici. At the delivery of her first child, she paid him a fee of $10,000 and instructed the court purser to pay him a like sum upon the birth of each succeeding child.

In book 6, chapter 9, of *The Causes and Signs of Diseases in the Intestines*, Fernel described a case of a 7-year-old child with acute appendicitis and perforation. Since he used the term "*cecum intestinum*", controversy has existed as to whether the diagnosis actually was a perforated appendicitis. Nevertheless, Fernel's description of the symptomatology and the autopsy finding with a perforation above "the obstructed place" at the base of the appendix are consistent with perforation and death from peritonitis. A similar case published by von Hilden, a German surgeon, in 1652 is somewhat dubious but the account of Lorenz Heister of 1711 presented a very clear description of perforated appendix and appendicitis.

In this text, Heister described the appendix as the seat of acute inflammation and drew attention to the surgical significance of such disease.

In November of 1711, Heister, while dissecting the body of a criminal, noted the small bowel to be diffusely erythematous, and commented that even the smallest vessels were filled with blood "*as if they had been injected with red wax after the manner of Ruysch.*" In phraseology that carries weight even three centuries later, he noted,

> *"when I was about to demonstrate the situation of the great guts, I found the vermiform of process of the cecum pre-naturally black adhering closer to the peritoneum than usual. As I now was about to separate it, by gently pulling it asunder the membranes of this process broke not withstanding the body was quite fresh and discharged two or three spoonfuls of matter. This instances may stand as a proof of the possibility of inflammations arising and abscesses forming in the appendicular as well as in other parts of the body, which I have not observed to be much noticed by other writers; and when in practice we meet with a burning and pain where this part is situated we ought to give attention to it."*

In 1759, M. Mestivier of Paris reported an autopsy on a 54-year-old man who died shortly after surgical drainage of a right lower quadrant abscess. Despite the surgeon having opened the abdomen and drained the pus, the patient subsequently perished and, at the autopsy, Mestivier noted that the abdomen was sprinkled with gangrenous sloughs and that the vermiform appendix had been penetrated by a pin! Unfortunately, the report of Mestivier regarding a foreign body perforation of the appendix resulted in the erroneous belief that appendicitis was often caused by such perforations. Almost a decade later in 1767, John Hunter described a gangrenous appendix encountered at the autopsy of a Colonel Dalrymple, but failed to pursue the subject with his usual vigor. Of particular interest is the report of James Parkinson in 1812 in respect of disease of the *appendix vermiformis*. At autopsy, he described an ulcerated and perforated appendix with an aperture sufficient to insert a crow quill.

Thomas Guy (1644-1724) founded Guy's Hospital in London and in so doing established one of the great medical centers of the 19th century. Thomas Addison (adrenal disease) (top right), Thomas Hodgkin (lymphoma) (bottom right), and Richard Bright (nephritis) (bottom left) had all opined that the appendix was the cause of most inflammatory processes in the right iliac fossa. Given the high morbidity and mortality of surgical intervention and their training as physicians, they opposed any consideration that Sir Astley Cooper of Guy's (top left), one of the finest surgeons of the time, contemplate surgical intervention.

D. LAURENTII
HEISTERI
SERENISS. BRUNSUICENS. ET LUNEBURG. DUCIS
Consiliarii Aulici & Archiatri, Medicinæ, Chirurgiæ ac Botanices in Regia atque Ducali Academia Julia, quæ Helmstadii est, Profess. Publici, Academiæ Scientiar. Cæsareæ Regiæque Londinensis atque Berolinensis Collegæ
INSTITUTIONES
CHIRURGICÆ,
IN QUIBUS

Heister was born in Frankfurt in 1683 and after studying initially at Giessen and Wetzlar, travelled to Holland where he became a docent in Amsterdam and taught surgical courses using cadavers. In 1708 he received a medical degree at Harderwyk and enrolled in the Dutch army as a surgeon. Relinquishing his military obligations after a year he thereafter continued his studies in Strassbourg, Paris, and London before accepting a Professorship of Surgery at Altdorf in Franconia in 1710. After ten productive years at Altdorf he moved to the University of Helmstedt where he remained until 1758, dying at the age of 75. An extraordinarily industrious man and indefatigable student, his reputation was such that during his lifetime he declined professorships at Göttingen, Kiel, Würzberg, and St. Petersburg. His major opus, Institutiones Chirurgicae and Chirurgische Warnehmungen, *is the source of the first authoritative account of appendicitis.*

Parkinson had attended John Hunter's lectures in surgery and was regarded as a reformer, a radical, and known to be a member of several secret political societies. Although he is best remembered for his 1817 "Essay on Shaking Palsy" he also authored several political and medical pamphlets including *Revolution without Bloodshed* as well as *Hints for the Improvements of Trusses*.

The French consideration of appendicitis was significantly inhibited by the fact that the premiere surgeon of the time, Baron Guillaume Dupuytren, did not accept the appendix as a cause for right lower quadrant inflammatory disease, but believed that the cecum itself was the origin. Thus, when Louyer-Villermay demonstrated the presence of gangrenous appendix in the autopsies of two young men in 1824, there was little enthusiasm for its acceptance as a novel disease process. Indeed, when François Melier subsequently added a further six autopsy descriptions, the Royal Academy of Medicine in Paris exhibited little interest. It is noteworthy that as early as 1827, Melier had suggested that the disease might be ameliorated by early surgical intervention. Nevertheless, the primacy of Dupuytren as the Chief of Surgery at the Hôtel Dieu prevailed, and Melier's suggestion fell upon deaf ears. A further confounding problem of the era was the confusion provided by an abundant literature seeking to define the differences between the putative entities of *typhlitis* and *perityphlitis*.

Nevertheless, in 1839 Bright and Addison (of Guy's Hospital), in their text *Elements of Practical Medicine*, clearly described the symptomatology of the appendicitis, and opined that the appendix was the cause of most of the inflammatory processes described as arising in the right iliac fossa. Since both were physicians (internists), they failed to propose surgical intervention. Thomas Hodgkin (also of Guy's Hospital) had similarly commented on the clinical symptomatology of appendicitis, but likewise failed to support surgical intervention. Thus, while knowledge of the appendix and appendicitis was clearly widespread by the mid-nineteenth century, the dangers of abdominal surgery, the lack of adequate anesthesia, and problems with sepsis prohibited enthusiasm for a surgical remedy.

Surgical Treatment

The advent of anesthesia in 1846, and the introduction of antisepsis by Lister in 1867, produced a more acceptable environment for the consideration of surgery. Thus, on June 18, 1886, at the first meeting of the Association of American Physicians at Washington, D.C., Dr. Reginald H. Fitz read a paper entitled "Perforating Inflammation of the Vermiform Appendix: with Special Reference to its Early Diagnosis and Treatment." In a monumental contribution to the subject, Fitz emphasized that most inflammatory disease of the lower quadrant began in the appendix, and urged early surgical removal of the organ as the only treatment likely to yield a favorable outcome.

Fitz was the first to actually use the term appendicitis and in so doing, was in fact criticized by the classically-educated audience for the use of a word consisting of a Greek suffix and a Latin stem. As a result of his pathological contributions to the study of the appendix, the terms *typhilitis* and *perityphilitis* declined in usage, and much of the confusion around the disease was abolished.

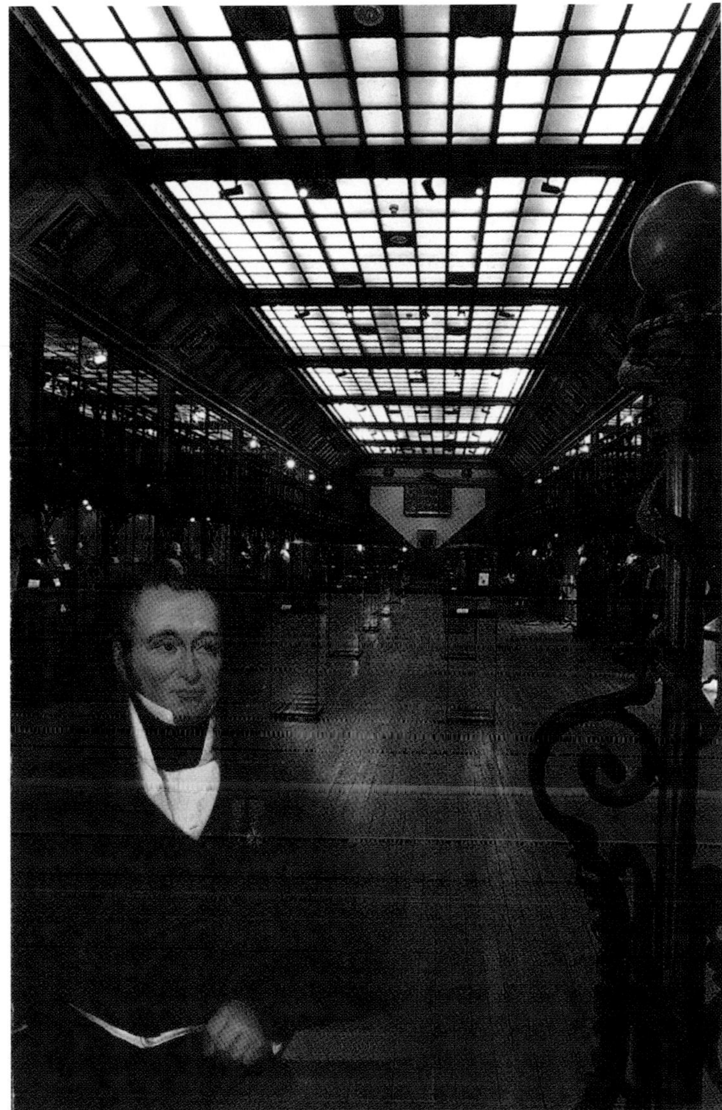

Guillaume Dupuytren (1777-1835) (inset) was an individual of Olympian personality. In Paris (background – Medical History Museum of the Sorbonne) he was regarded as "nobody's friend" and tolerated no rival, pursuing any who aspired to that eminence with vindictive hatred. As an individual he was hard, cold, unscrupulous, contemptuous, and overbearing and more respected than beloved. Amongst his colleagues he was known as "the first of surgeons and the least of men", but such was his fame that when he traveled abroad he was treated as a prince. His "absolute" decision that the appendix was not the cause of an inflammatory mass in the right lower quadrant thus prevailed and the suggestions of thoughtful surgeons such as Villermay and Melier were disregarded.

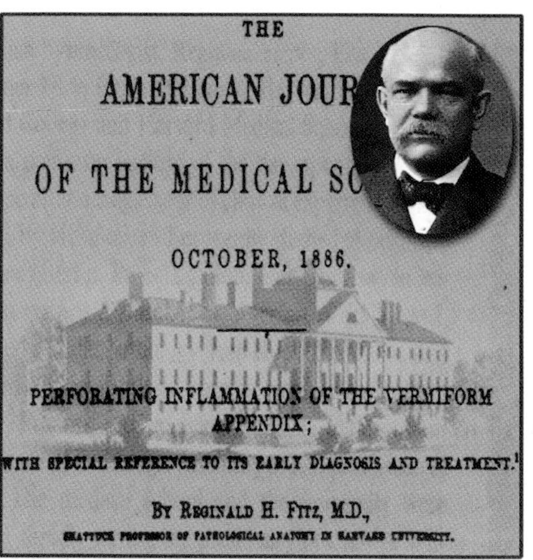

THE

AMERICAN JOUR

OF THE MEDICAL S

OCTOBER, 1886.

PERFORATING INFLAMMATION OF THE VERMIFORM APPENDIX;

WITH SPECIAL REFERENCE TO ITS EARLY DIAGNOSIS AND TREATMENT.[1]

BY REGINALD H. FITZ, M.D.,

SHATTUCK PROFESSOR OF PATHOLOGICAL ANATOMY IN HARVARD UNIVERSITY.

As the Shattuck Professor of Pathological Anatomy at Harvard University, Fitz represented the 9th generation of Fitzs in America and was descended from the original 1639 settlers of the Massachusetts Bay Colony. Named after the British hymnologist, Reginald Heber, Fitz was educated at Harvard and thereafter spent two years in Europe where he studied at hospitals in Paris, London, Glasgow, Vienna, and Berlin. As a student of Rudolf Virchow, he was fully aware of cellular pathology and on his return to Boston in 1870 introduced the use of the microscope for study at Harvard Medical School. Apart from his seminal contributions to appendicitis in 1886, in 1889 he produced a definitive work on pancreatitis and in so doing assured himself of a place in the pantheon of gastrointestinal pathology.

Lawson Tait of Birmingham was one of the first surgeons to successfully remove a gangrenous appendix (1880). Despite his technical skill he spoke critically of antisepsis and believed gallbladder surgery to be utterly unwarranted.

Ironically, after having convinced the Association of American Physicians that the frequent abscesses in the right iliac foci were not due to *typhilitis*, *perityphilitis*, or *epityphilitis* but to perforation of the vermiform appendix, Fitz himself would perish in 1913 as a consequence of a perforated gastric ulcer.

Surgical Evolution

Claudius Amyand, a Huguenot refugee and founder of St. George's Hospital in London, is attributed with the first surgical removal of appendix in December 1735. He operated on an 11-year-old boy with a longstanding scrotal hernia and a fecal fistula of the thigh. Having opened the hernia through a scrotal incision, he noted an appendix wrapped in omentum and perforated by a pin with a resultant fecal fistula. Amyand amputated the omentum and appendix, opened the fistula, and a satisfactory recovery ensued. No further accounts of such surgery occurred for a further century, with abdominal pain and inflammation being for the most part treated by opium administration. This therapy had been initially introduced by C. Stokes of Dublin in 1838, and was regarded as the standard therapy based on its ability to relieve pain, inhibit peristalsis, and presumably allow localization of the inflammatory process.

The strategy was first challenged in 1848 when Henry Hancock, the President of the Medical Society of London, presented a paper describing the successful treatment of a 30-year-old woman with acute peritonitis, drained via a right lower quadrant incision. The subsequent removal of a fecolith from the wound, two weeks after the operation, was followed by recovery of the patient. Similarly, in 1867, Willard Parker of New York reported his experiences with four patients whom he had treated over ten years with successful drainage of appendiceal abscesses.

Although Lawson Tait of Birmingham successfully removed a gangrenous appendix from a 17-year-old girl in 1880, he failed to report the procedure until 1890, concentrating his activities mostly on gynecological surgery. Abraham Groves of Fergus, Ontario, undertook a similar case of unreported successful appendectomy in 1883. Groves, educated at the University of Toronto, was a friend of William Osler and highly regarded as a clinician and scholar. Despite the fact that the 12-year-old boy who he operated upon on May 10, 1883, recovered successfully, Groves failed to mention the condition until its inclusion in his autobiography, published in 1934. A series of further reports of appendectomy included a failed instance by von Mikulicz in 1884, a successful intervention by Kronlein of Zurich in 1885, and an additional success by Charter Symonds of London in 1885. In America, R.J. Hall performed the first appendectomy at the Roosevelt Hospital in New York in 1886, while Henry Sands, an assistant to Willard Parker, reported operating on a patient with appendicitis and removing two fecoliths. It is of interest that McBurney, a subsequent major contributor to the subject of the management of appendicitis, was an assistant to Sands. In 1887, Thomas G. Morton of Philadelphia reported a successful appendectomy with the drainage of an abscess in a 27-year-old patient. Sadly for Morton, both his brother and son would die of acute appendicitis. By 1889, McBurney had published the first of several important papers on the subject of appendicitis, and his clinical description of the process would assure him a place in the history of the disease.

Sir Frederick Treves was widely known for his work on surgical anatomy, intestinal obstruction, appendicitis, and peritonitis. In addition to his important contributions to the evolution of surgery, he was instrumental in saving the life of King Edward VII in 1902 by undertaking a timely appendectomy.

In 1889, Dr. Edward Cutler reported his successful experiences with a number of patients with appendicitis, and described one of the first instances of an appendectomy for unruptured acute appendicitis. By this stage, the level of enthusiasm for surgical intervention had considerably increased, and attention was now directed not only to the type of surgery, but its timing. Thus, by 1898 Bernays had reported seventy-one consecutive appendectomies without death and, in 1904, John B. Murphy of Chicago reported a personal experience of 2,000 appendectomies. A.J. Ochsner of Chicago, in 1902 published a text on the management of appendicitis and advocated non-operative treatment in circumstances where evidence of spreading peritonitis could be determined.

Technique

Although timing of the operation was an issue of considerable debate, even more attention was directed to the nature and site of the incision. Although the earliest incisions were simply for drainage of the most inflamed, tender, or fluctuant areas, the most commonly-used incision at the turn of the century was that described by William Henry Battle of St. Thomas' Hospital in London in 1897. This constituted a vertical incision through the lateral edge of the right rectus sheath, and often resulted in denervation of the rectus muscle with subsequent incisional hernia formation. In 1894, Dr. Charles McBurney of New York described the lateral muscle splitting or "grid iron" incision at almost the same time that an identical incision was described by Lewis L. McArthur of Chicago. Unfortunately for McArthur, the presentation of his paper at the Chicago Medical Society of June 1894 was postponed due to time constraints, and the prior publication of McBurney's manuscript in the *Annals of Surgery*, in July 1894, resulted in priority being incorrectly

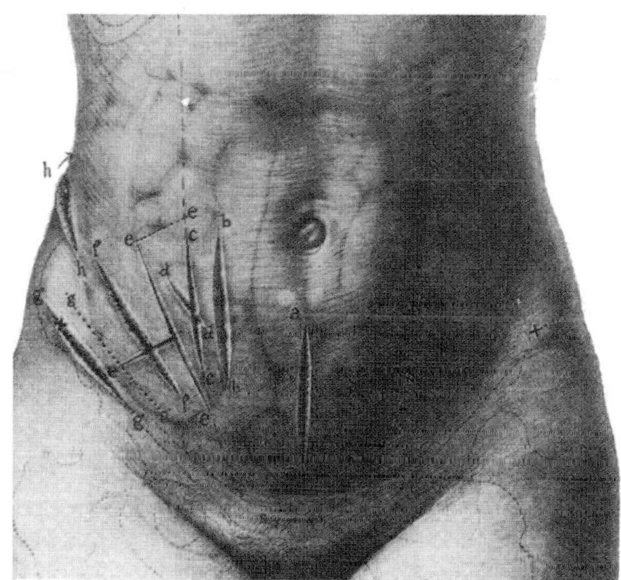

An early 20th-century diagram depicting the wide variety of abdominal incisions proposed to facilitate appendectomy. A similar complex and amarinthine debate regarding the best placement of "port sites" engaged surgical minds of the 21st century.

ascribed to the former. Despite McBurney's generous and open acknowledgement of McArthur's primacy, the term "McBurney incision" has remained in common usage. Two years later in 1896, J.W. Elliot of Boston advocated a transverse skin incision but this excited little attention until 1905, when A.E. Rockey of Portland, Oregon, once again proposed a transverse skin incision with vertical division of the muscle layers for lower abdominal operations.

The question of how to deal with the appendix and cecum at surgery remained a subject of considerable controversy for many years. Simple ligation of the appendix and amputation at the cecum often led to perforation and fistulas. In 1895, G.R. Fowler described a "cuff" method and R. Dawbarn, at about the same time, proposed the use of a "purse-string" suture with inversion of the unligated stump of the appendix into the cecum. The further elucidation of the diagnosis and management of appendicitis was facilitated by the introduction of antibiotics and the development of ultrasonography and CT scan technology. Early diagnosis and surgical removal, whether by open or laparoscopic technology, decreased morbidity and mortality to almost negligible figures except in countries with limited health care facilities. The widespread use and development of major antibiotics obviated both the local and systemic sequelae of sepsis, and the dreaded disease of the nineteenth century, typhylitis, had within a century evolved into a simple and routine diagnosis and operation often undertaken by the most junior physicians.

Of particular interest is the operation performed upon King Edward VII by Sir Frederic Treves. Edward was the first male child of Queen Victoria, and given his irresponsible behavior, was little thought of in terms of subsequent regal responsibilities. On the death of Queen Victoria in 1901, the coronation of Edward VII was scheduled for June 26, 1902. On June 14, the King developed abdominal discomfort and was examined by Sir Francis Laking, the physician-in-ordinary to the monarchy. By midnight, the abdominal pain had worsened to the extent that Laking summoned Sir Thomas Barlow as his consultant on the following morning, seeking to confirm his diagnosis. Despite his declining condition, the King proceeded by carriage to Windsor on Monday the 16th, but such was his ill health, that on the 18th Sir Fredric Treves was asked to examine him. At this stage, the clinical presentation was of swelling and tenderness in the right iliac foci with elevated body temperature. Fortunately, these findings appeared to improve over the next 48 hours and by Monday, June 23, Edward felt sufficiently recovered to travel to London to host a large dinner party for the coronation guests.

As a result, a relapse occurred and by ten o'clock the next morning, Sir Fredric Treves, Sir Thomas Smith, Lord Lister, Sir Thomas Barlow, and Sir Francis Laking, all agreed that an operation was necessary. Edward, however, was unwilling to delay his coronation and declined to have the procedure, preferring, as he told his physician, to attend the coronation rather than a surgery. When Sir Fredric Treves informed him "*then Sir you will go as a corpse,*" the King capitulated, and the operation was undertaken in a room at Buckingham Palace on June 24 at 12:30 p.m. Anesthesia was provided by Sir Fredric Hewitt, and a large abscess opened and pus evacuated. The appendix was not removed, and Edward made an uninterrupted recovery and the coronation took place some weeks later. Although Treves was not an advocate of early operations for appendicitis, he nevertheless was successful in his therapy of King Edward and as a result of the successful outcome, was made a Baron. Ironically, the daughter of Treves would subsequently die of acute appendicitis.

ILLNESS OF THE KING.

OFFICIAL ANNOUNCEMENTS.

CORONATION POSTPONED.

The appendicitis of King Edward VII was successfully treated by the surgical intervention of Sir Frederick Treves. The delay of the coronation is reported to have cost the British government many millions of pounds and represents one of the first documented instances of lost revenue based upon delay of therapeutic intervention. Treves also achieved considerable fame for a series of erudite travel books as well as his documentation and care of his famous patient "the Elephant Man."

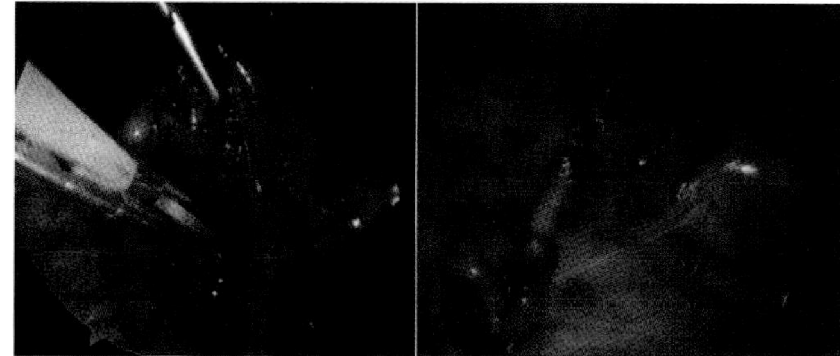

Laparoscopic appendectomy. Although appendectomy had become a standard operation in the 20th century, the advent of laparoscopic surgery led to a belief that this methodology offered considerable advantages. The fact that surgical excision had become the definitive therapy in a pre-antibiotic era failed to affect the dogma that only excision could result in cure.

Ulcerative Colitis

Introduction

It is uncertain when it actually became apparent that there was a difference between the wide variety of dysenteries and a more specific disease entity that could be characterized as ulcerative colitis. Certainly the recognition by Koch of bacteria and their relationship to specific disease entities was an important advance, but the wide variety of gut flora obfuscated the identification of causal pathogens for many decades. Indeed, it can be inferred from the historical texts that the idiopathic inflammatory bowel diseases (IBDs), ulcerative colitis and Crohn's disease, are, as J. Kirsner noted, "old" rather than "new" diseases. Matthew Baillie, in his 1793 *Morbid Anatomy of Some of the Most Important Parts of the Human Body,* provided enough descriptive material for B. Morson to conclude that *"patients were dying from ulcerative colitis during the latter part of the eighteenth century."* The first "impact" description of "ulcerative colitis" by Samuel Wilks of London in 1859, concerned a 42-year-old woman who died after several months of diarrhea and fever. Autopsy demonstrated a transmural ulcerative inflammation of the colon and terminal ileum, originally designated as "simple ulcerative colitis," but a century later identified as Crohn's disease. The 1875 case report of Wilks and Moxon of extensive ulceration and inflammation of the entire colon in a young woman who had succumbed to severe bloody diarrhea, also was labeled "simple ulcerative colitis." By 1907, 317 patients had been admitted to seven London hospitals with an inflammatory and ulcerative disease of the colon.

Sigmund Freud (inset) and the legendary couch in his study at Maresfield Garden, London. Despite having been evicted from Vienna by the Nazis, Freud's teachings generated such widespread interest that psychoanalysis was even applied to the management of patients with ulcerative colitis.

A 19th-century color illustration of a colon demonstrating the severe inflammatory changes of ulcerative colitis.

Although precise details of all were not available, almost half of the patients perished from perforation of the colon and peritonitis, hemorrhage, and complications including "nephritis, infective endocarditis," sepsis, hepatic abscess, fatty liver, and pulmonary embolism.

At the turn of the twentieth century, similar clinical reports emanated from both Europe and the United States. Thus in 1902, R.F. Weir performed an appendicostomy in a patient to facilitate colonic irrigation with a 5% solution of methylene blue alternating with a 1:5000 solution of silver nitrate or of bismuth, presumably to eliminate an "infection." J.P. Lockhart-Mummery of London, in 1907 diagnosed carcinoma of the colon in 7 of 36 patients with ulcerative colitis and recommended use of the recently-developed electrically illuminated proctosigmoidoscope to facilitate diagnosis. Awareness of the condition resulted in an increased number of reports of ulcerative colitis from France, Germany, Italy, and England, during the early years of the twentieth century, and ulcerative colitis was a major subject of the 1913 Paris Congress of Medicine. During the second quarter of the twentieth century, A.F. Hurst of London implicated an organism *"related to* B. dysenteriae," as being the causative agent, and recommended as treatment, daily irrigations of the colon with dilute solutions of silver nitrate or tannic acid, and the intravenous administration of a *"polyvalent anti-dysenteric serum."*

During the 1930s through the 1950s, etiologic speculation was rampant and included food and pollen allergy, deficiency of an "intestinal protective substance," and a wide variety of aerobic and anaerobic intestinal bacteria, as well as an underlying psychiatric disorder (the so called "ulcerative colitis personality").

Given the current vogue for Freudian intervention, many patients actually underwent extensive psychiatric scrutiny and prolonged psychotherapy without apparent sustained benefit. The introduction of the sulfanilamide agents in 1938 facilitated treatment, and similarly, management improved with the availability first of penicillin in the 1940s, and subsequently ACTH adrenal steroids and their related compounds in 1950. Thus by 1951, Kirsner of Chicago was able to document the complete clinical and radiologic reversibility of ulcerative colitis in a group of patients who had responded promptly and consistently to therapy.

Pathologic descriptions of ulcerative colitis, almost from the beginning, emphasized the diffuse, predominantly mucosal and submucosal involvement, typically beginning in the rectum and rectosigmoid, limited to the left colon in some patients but in others, advancing to involve the entire colon. In 1933, Buie and Bargen of the Mayo Clinic implicated vascular *"thrombotic phenomena"* as the pathologic basis for ulcerative colitis, and in 1937 Bargen actually went so far as to designate the disease as *"thrombo-ulcerative colitis."* Despite the fact that a review of one hundred and twenty surgical patients and sixty autopsied cases by S. Warren and S.C. Sommers of Boston in 1949 re-emphasized the mucosal involvement, none of the prevailing etiologic hypotheses seemed acceptable. However, the focus on a vascular pathogenesis was further accentuated in 1954 when Warren and Sommers reclassified 10% of their 1949 series as *"colitis gravis"* with inflammatory necrosis of arteries, veins, or both, leading to vascular occlusions and infarction of a part or all of the adjacent colon. However, the presence of a *"damaging substance"* in the fecal stream was acknowledged as a significant possibility, as had been suggested by P. Manson-Bahr in 1943, and even earlier by B. Dawson at the 1909 London Symposium. Nevertheless, the search for a luminal pathogen proved frustrating. Thus, a series of studies in the 1950s by Kirsner included the repeated instillation of fecal discharges from patients with severe active ulcerative colitis into self-retaining canine ileo-colonic pouches constructed in dogs, but met with negative results. Similarly, direct intramucosal injection of fecal filtrates from ulcerative colitis also failed to induce inflammation of the rectum in monkeys. R.T. Stoughton in 1953 isolated a substance which was thought to possibly be a proteolytic enzyme probably originating in the gut microflora (bacterial endotoxin), from fecal filtrates of patients with ulcerative colitis. Since it was demonstrated to be capable of digesting epidermal cells even after the skin has been fixed in formalin, it was considered a likely candidate agent until the *"acantholysis"* was noted to also occur with fecal extracts from individuals without any evidence of colonic disease.

Little more progress was made in defining the etiology of the disease and clinicians could do little but content themselves with a description of the pathology as provided by Morson. *"In active ulcerative colitis, the mucous membrane shows diffuse infiltration with chronic inflammatory cells, mainly lymphocytic and plasma cells but also eosinophils. There is also a variable degree of vascular congestion and intra-mucosal hemorrhage. The epithelium shows goblet cell depletion and reactive hyperplasia, and some of the tubules contain an accumulation of polymorphonuclear leukocytes, so called crypt abscesses. With remission, the first change is restoration of the goblet cell population, accompanied by a reduction in the amount of inflammation and the disappearance of crypt abscesses. The mucous membrane may return entirely to normal but if there have been repeated attacks of severe colitis, atrophy will develop as judged by a reduction in the number of epithelial tubules per unit area, loss of their parallelism and failure of the bases of the crypts to reach down to the mucularis mucosae. Although none of these features are specific for ulcerative colitis, together they create a characteristic histological picture."*

The histopathologist, Basil Morson of London (c. 1960), was responsible for focusing attention on the criteria necessary to confirm the diagnosis of ulcerative colitis as well as the issues related to its neoplastic transformation.

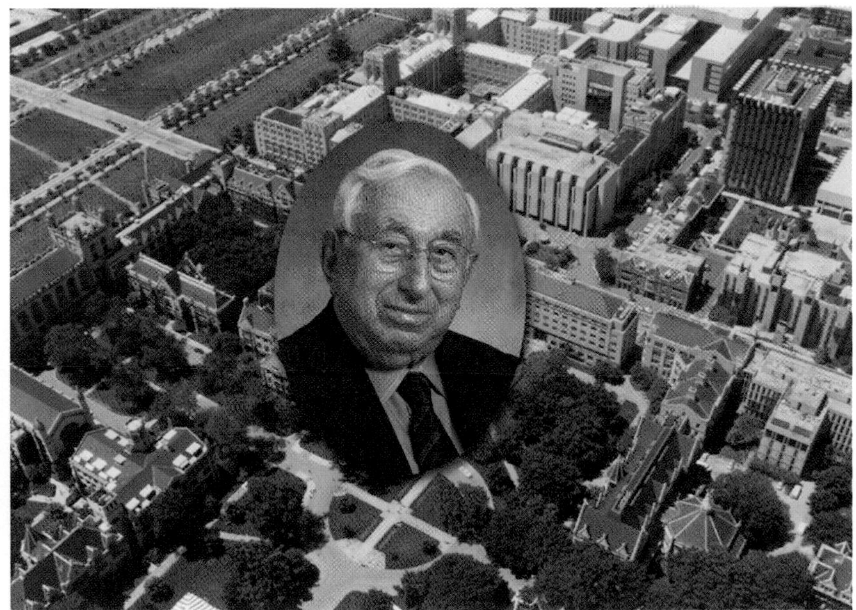

Dr. Joseph B. Kirsner of the University of Chicago played a prominent role in the elucidation of inflammatory bowel disease. His thoughtful evaluation of the problems related to ulcerative colitis led to the establishment of numerous investigative centers throughout North America.

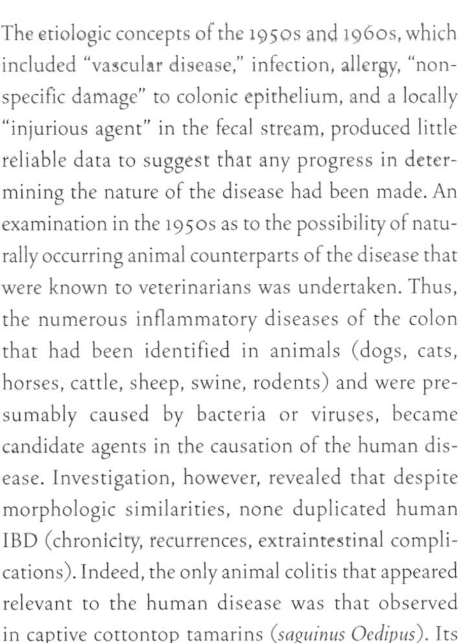

The etiologic concepts of the 1950s and 1960s, which included "vascular disease," infection, allergy, "non-specific damage" to colonic epithelium, and a locally "injurious agent" in the fecal stream, produced little reliable data to suggest that any progress in determining the nature of the disease had been made. An examination in the 1950s as to the possibility of naturally occurring animal counterparts of the disease that were known to veterinarians was undertaken. Thus, the numerous inflammatory diseases of the colon that had been identified in animals (dogs, cats, horses, cattle, sheep, swine, rodents) and were presumably caused by bacteria or viruses, became candidate agents in the causation of the human disease. Investigation, however, revealed that despite morphologic similarities, none duplicated human IBD (chronicity, recurrences, extraintestinal complications). Indeed, the only animal colitis that appeared relevant to the human disease was that observed in captive cottontop tamarins (*saguinus Oedipus*). Its

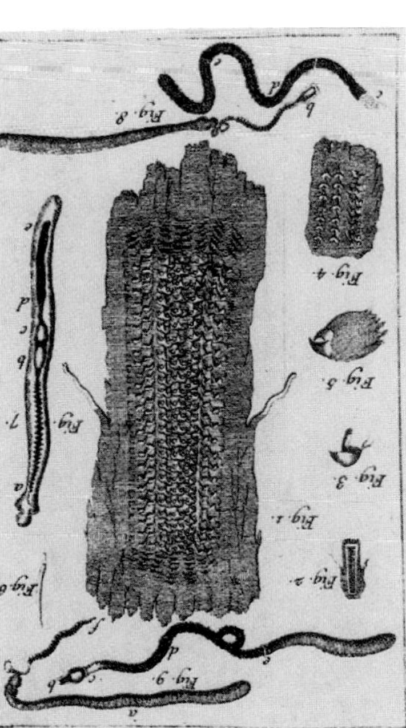

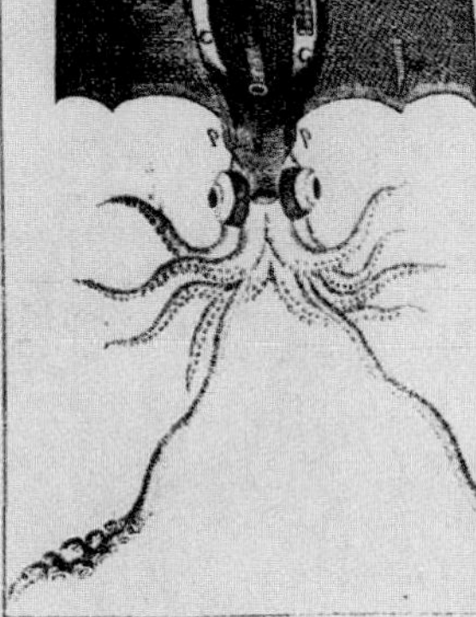

The identification of diverse parasites led to the suggestion that as yet unidentified pathogens might be the cause of inflammatory bowel disease.

The elucidation of the disease or diseases broadly classified as ulcerative colitis has been difficult since few experimental models for study exist. The only relevant animal colitis model available is the disease identified in captive cotton-tailed tamarin monkeys from South America. These animals are part of the marmoset New World monkey species and although primarily insect-eaters, take fruit as well as other small animals. Of interest is the fact that the females of the species generally bear twins. While tamarins normally exhibit little colonic disease, it appears to only affect those in captivity. The issue of a stress response or infestation by agents not present in the tropical jungle has been raised as etiological agents. An examination of the taxonomy of the marmoset and tamarin families broadly classified as part of the Leontopithecus *genus provides little clue as to why these animals might develop an acute colonic infection. Of further interest is the fact the catarrhine family or Old World monkeys which also form part of the* Cercopithecidae*, do not exhibit this disease even when maintained in captivity.*

clinical and histologic features were almost identical in that it responded to sulfasalazine and if untreated, was complicated by colonic carcinoma. Furthermore, since the colitis was absent among the wild cottontop tamarins of the Colombian rain forest, the findings suggested an environmental (e.g. infection, "cold stress") as a cause for the colitis of the captive tamarins.

Although numerous attempts were made during the 1920s through 1960 to reproduce ulcerative colitis in animals (rabbits, guinea pigs, hamsters, dogs, mice, rats), none succeeded. The diverse methodologies employed included the induction of nutritional deficiencies (vitamin A, pantothenic acid, pyridoxine, folic acid), the local application of Shiga and staphylococcal toxins to colonic explants in dogs, vasoconstriction induced by adrenalin hydrochloride, the intraperitoneal infusion of lipopolysaccharide, intravenous injection of staphylococcus toxin, and the administration of the enzymes, collagenase and lysozyme, intrarectally and intra-arterially. In some circumstances, the small and large intestine were readily damaged by these manipulations, but the lesions healed rapidly and in no fashion resembled the human condition. In 1969, ulcerations in the right colon were produced in guinea pigs and rabbits given orally a 5% aqueous solution of carrageenan, a sulfated polysaccharide of high molecular weight extracted from red seaweed (*chondrus crispus, euchema spinosum*). The reaction was enhanced immunologically by a component of the outer cell wall of *Bacterioides vulgatus*, inhibited by the addition of metronidazole, and was not reproducible in germ-free animals. Although the inflammatory reaction mimicked ulcerative colitis (mucus depletion, diffuse inflammation and pseudopolyps), granulomas also developed. Similar findings were also obtained by the topical colonic application of a variety of compounds including (4% to 10% acetic acid, trinitrobenzene sulfonic acid in 50% alcohol), orally administered drugs (indomethecin, mitomycin-c), as well as inhibition of fatty acid oxidation-induced colonic injury, but none reproduced human ulcerative colitis.

Treatment

In 1938, a study of 871 patients with ulcerative colitis suggested physical fatigue and emotional distress are as "predisposing circumstances" and as a result, psychotherapy was regarded as an important form of treatment. However, by the mid-1940s Dr. Nana Svartz, a Swedish rheumatologist, became the first physician to use sulfasalazine to treat ulcerative colitis and the compound soon became the most widely prescribed drug for people with the disease. The subsequent development in the 1950s of adrenocorticotrophic hormone (ACTH) and cortisone led to their utilization as the standard treatments for IBD. With the advent of relatively effective pharmacotherapy the emphasis on the role of psychogenic factors began to diminish. Nevertheless, uncontrollable disease required surgical management, and in 1954 B.N. Brooke, who had been responsible for developing the ileostomy, concluded that there were three distinct forms of colitis with more than one cause.

The confusion regarding the precise nature of the disease and whether there was more than one type was further obfuscated by clinicians in the U.S. acknowledging that Crohn's disease could also affect the colon, as had been previously reported in England. The advent of the concept that an immune disorder might be the cause of the disease led to the utilization in the 1960s of immunosuppressive drugs, such as 6-mercaptopurine and azathioprine. The positive results led to clinical enthusiasm and such agents were recognized as effective in treating Crohn's disease. Thus by the early 1970s, an immune target was considered the most promising avenue of investigation and the search for agents capable of modulating the immune reaction became the focus of therapeutic research. Currently unresolved in the genesis of the disease are the contributions of genetic components and the role of smoking. Despite advances in medical therapy, a substantial number of patients still required surgery and the development in 1969 by Dr. Nils Kock, a Swedish surgeon, of the continent ileostomy ("Kock pouch"), was regarded as a major advance, since it eliminated the need for an external pouch. Unfortunately, the patency of the pouch and complications related to it, led to disenchantment with the result that alternatives were sought.

THE MANAGEMENT OF AN ILEOSTOMY
INCLUDING ITS COMPLICATIONS

B. N. Brooke
M.Chir. Camb., F.R.C.S.
Reader in Surgery in the University of Birmingham

An ileostomy must work perfectly if the surgical treatment of ulcerative colitis is not to fall into disrepute; the closest attention must therefore be paid to the minutiæ of technique and to subsequent care.

The ileum should be divided and the ends separated so that the functioning stoma presents as a terminal vent about 1–$1^1/_2$ in. long (Hardy et al. 1949). A loop ileostomy is still regarded by some surgeons as justifiable in a *serious case (Lahey 1951); but it should be avoided if* possible, because an ileostomy bag cannot be applied effectively to it. Where a primary colectomy without pre-existing ileostomy is done, the terminal ileum forms the stoma, and the same principles apply.

Ileostomy Bags

Generally an ileostomy acts after meals and during the night, though some of the contents of the small bowel may be voided at any time. It must not be thought that one type of bag suits all patients—indeed a few prefer the old rigid cup appliance—but usually the Koenig-Rutzen type of bag is most favoured, and most makes of bag act on the same principle of adherence to the skin, from the simple disposable type to the more complicated kind in two pieces with an adherent flange and removable bag.

The cement or glue is not always satisfactory, but this is occasionally the fault of the patient, who is unaware that it should not be applied

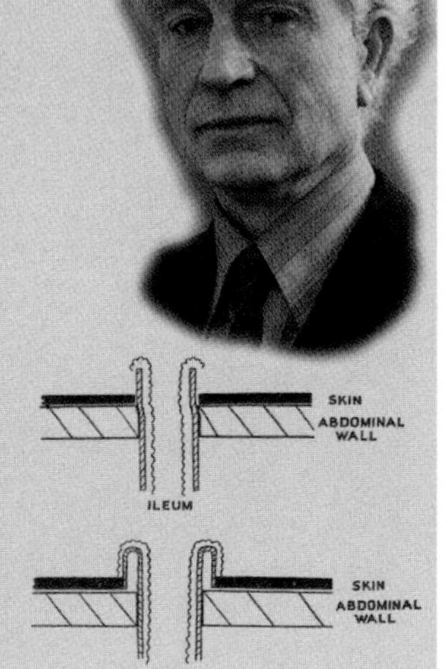

The English surgeon, Brian Brooke, was responsible for developing an improved ileostomy procedure that substantially augmented the quality of life of patients who underwent a pan-proctocolectomy as therapy.

Intra-abdominal "Reservoir" in Patients With Permanent Ileostomy

Preliminary Observations on a Procedure Resulting in Fecal "Continence" in Five Ileostomy Patients

Nils G. Kock, MD, Goteborg, Sweden

...ring recent years much prog-
...ress has been made in creating
...l functioning ileostomies in pa-
...nts after panproctocolectomy.
...he development of the adherent
...tomy bag has to a great extent
...ted the care of these patients.
... of all the progress in man-
... of the ileostomy and in
... the fact that most of the
...ts are very pleased with the
...stomy after a long disabling dis-

troublesome skin irritation. Some patients do not tolerate the glue used for fixation of the bag and for these patients the management of the skin is laborious and time-consuming. Skin irritation seems to be one of the most frequent late complications of ileostomy and occurs, at least occasionally, in 26% to 70% of patients.[1-3] For many patients the presence of odor and its control can be a significant problem.

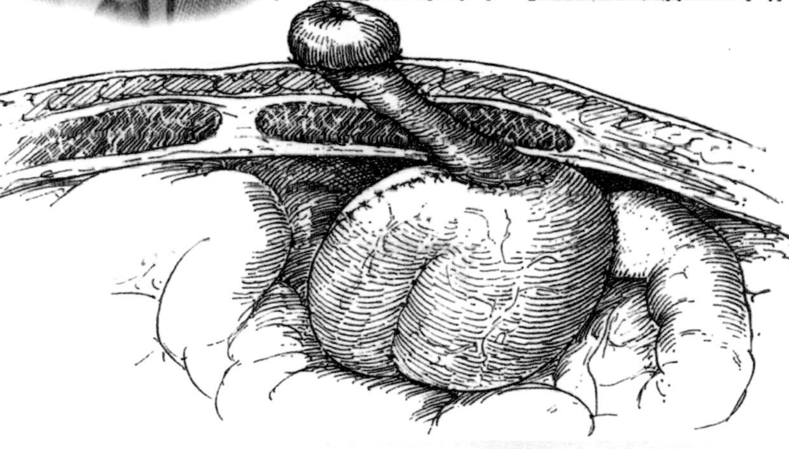

g/Vol 99, Aug 1969 Intra-abdominal "Reservoir"/Kock 223

Nils Kock of Gothenburg, Sweden, in 1959 developed a continent ileostomy pouch, which allowed patients to discard the ileostomy bag. Unfortunately, technical problems with the long-term management of the pouch led to discontinuation of this procedure.

Modifications of the ileoanal anastomosis or "pullthrough" procedure were undertaken, and construction of an internal pouch subsequently became an acceptable alternative to the external ostomy. In 1988, the first 5-ASA drug received FDA approval for the treatment of ulcerative colitis but despite substantial efficacy, failed to resolve all instances of the disease. At this stage, there remain more questions than answers regarding the genesis of the disease and the ideal method to treat it. The possibility that the use of genetic technology may provide a more appropriate molecular target remains to be determined.

Obstruction

Although surgery of the colon and rectum had originally developed to manage either trauma or obstruction induced by tumor, increasing technical skill and safety allowed its application to other conditions. Thus the treatment of diverticular disease, Hirschprung's disease, inflammatory bowel disease, and prolapse of the rectum, moved from the province of medical therapy into the surgical arena. It was, however, in the management of obstruction that the greatest progress was made. Although the clinical description of intestinal obstruction with its distention, vomiting, and failure to pass feces and flatus may be noted in the earliest of literature, there was little except homeopathic remedies that could be directed at its remedy. Prior to the advent of anesthesia and antisepsis, treatment was expectant and mortality almost uniform. In the case of obstruction due to strangulated hernias, Astley Cooper and others would suspend the patient in the upside-down position on an attendant's shoulders as a preliminary to taxis and reduction.

Sydenham of London favored opium as a universal panacea and even two centuries later, this form of therapeutic nihilism was defended as reasonable by Hugh Owen Thomas of Liverpool. The use of mobile metallic mercury had long been favored, given the concept that the freely flowing substance would make its way past an obstruction and re-establish intestinal continuity. Indeed, this method was widely advocated, since mercury had achieved a substantial reputation as a therapeutic agent. In one recorded instance, the French surgeon Pilloré, using a cecostomy, had met with some success but the 21 lbs of metallic mercury that also had been administered to his patient resulted in demise. Physicians as eminent as Begin, Broussais, and Dupuytren, had all vainly attempted to intervene in intestinal obstruction. Purges, enemas, ice packs, electrical stimulation, leeches, and even the use of esophageal sounds, were of little use and even colostomy, while an

I.

Stuhlträgheit Neugeborener in Folge von Dilatation und Hypertrophie des Colons.

Casuistische Mittheilung von

Prof. Hirschsprung, Kopenhagen

in der Gesellschaft für Kinderheilkunde Berlin 1886.

Ich erlaube mir, dieser sachkundigen Versammlung zwei
pathologische Präparate aussergewöhnlicher Art nebst gan
kurzgefassten Krankengeschichten vorz... ist mein
Hoffnung, möglicherweise dadurch B... Beob-
achtungen oder einschlägige Beme... ielen
Anwesenden Collegen hervorzuruf...
Ich werde Ihnen sofort d...
Wie Sie sehen, ist es ein Dick...
sionen, dass es Sie gewiss übe...
er von einem Kinde herrührt,
alt war. Als der Unterleib
paar enorm ausgedehnte Da...

Harald Hirschsprung (1830-1916) was born in Copenhagen, the son of a wealthy tobacco merchant. On May 11, 1861, he presented his doctoral thesis in gastroenterology on the topic of achalasia of the esophagus and small bowel and in 1870 was appointed as a neonatal physician and the first pediatrician in Denmark to the Queen Louisa Hospital for Children. Despite being a poor speaker he was an enthusiastic teacher and often presented his lectures on Sunday mornings between 9 a.m. and 11 a.m. Although the Queen of Denmark (after whom the hospital had been named) had requested that a biblical text be placed above each bed, Hirschsprung insisted that the children preferred pictures of animals and as a result the Queen thereafter refused to enter the hospital. In 1886 at the Berlin Congress for Children's Diseases, Hirschsprung presented a lecture on constipation associated with dilation and hypertrophy of the colon (inset). He concluded his lecture by stating "It appears unquestionable that the condition is caused in utero, either as a developmental abnormality or as a disease process". Although his conclusions were controversial, the issue was resolved in 1901 when Tille recorded an absence of ganglion cells in the colonic wall of individuals with Hirschsprung's disease. This was confirmed by Bretino in 1904 and finally resolved conclusively in 1949 by Bodian, who had reviewed a large number of autopsy specimens at the Hospital for Sick Children, London. It is worthy of note that Hirschsprung also developed the technique of controlled hydrostatic pressure to manage intussusception and thus avoided the previous high mortality related to surgery.

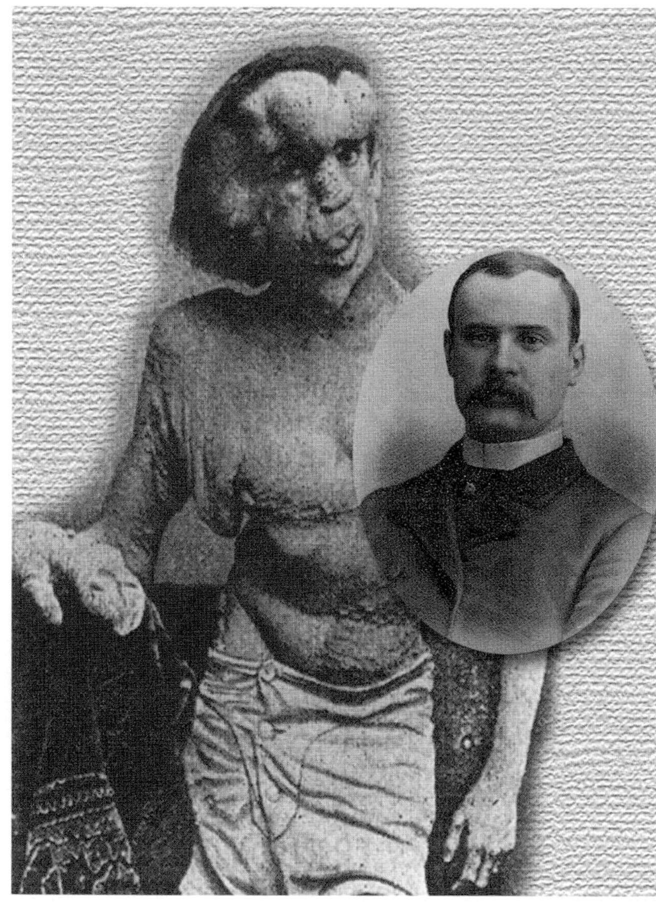

Frederick Treves (inset) was widely known for his work on surgical anatomy, intestinal obstruction, appendicitis and peritonitis. In addition to his important contributions to the evolution of surgery, he was instrumental in saving the life of King Edward VII in 1902 by undertaking an appendectomy. As surgeon to the British army in the Transvaal War (Boer) he made important contributions to military surgery and wrote fascinating travel sketches of the area. His care and concern for the "Elephant Man" earned him a place of distinction as a man of both intellectual skill and exquisite human sensitivity.

Joseph Carey Merrick (left) was born Aug. 5, 1862, in Leicester, England, and as a disfigured person entertained a brief career as a professional "freak" before becoming a celebrity patient of London Hospital from 1886 until his death in 1890. Merrick was initially confined to a workhouse at the age of 17, but escaped after four years and joined a freak show in 1883. Although Merrick's mother was slightly crippled his parents and brother appeared normal. He was normal until about the age of five but thereafter exhibited signs of a strange disorder that resulted in overgrowths over much of the skin and bony surfaces. In particular, his head became enormous with large bags of brownish spongy skin hanging from the occiput and across his face. In addition, the deformation of his jaws rendered him incapable of showing facial expression or speaking in a comprehensible fashion. Although his left arm was normal, the right arm was discolored and grotesque, ending in a 12-inch wrist and a finlike hand. The legs imitated the deformed arm, and a defective hip caused such disability that Merrick could walk only with the aid of a stick. While on exhibition, he was discovered by Frederick Treves, and admitted to London Hospital where he remained until the age of 27, when he died in his sleep of accidental suffocation (April 11, 1890). The disorder from which Merrick suffered was long thought to be a severe case of neurofibromatosis, but more recently it has been concluded that he probably suffered from an extremely rare disease known as the Proteus syndrome.

obvious remedy, usually proved fatal due to leakage and peritonitis, when employed. Percutaneous intestinal puncture had been proposed in 1756 and as late as 1880 was still used by the Boston physicians, Blake and Bigelow, although such patients usually perished of sepsis and inanition.

The operative treatment of intestinal obstruction was first proposed by Sir Fredrick Treves of London Hospital, who wrote: "*It is less dangerous to leap from the Clifton suspension bridge, 250 to 275 ft. above the Avon River near Bristol, than to suffer from acute intestinal obstruction and decline operation.*" Treves believed that the use of the stethoscope allowed for some differentiation between small and large bowel obstruction, but such a distinction could not be accurately or reliably ascertained prior to the 1930s.

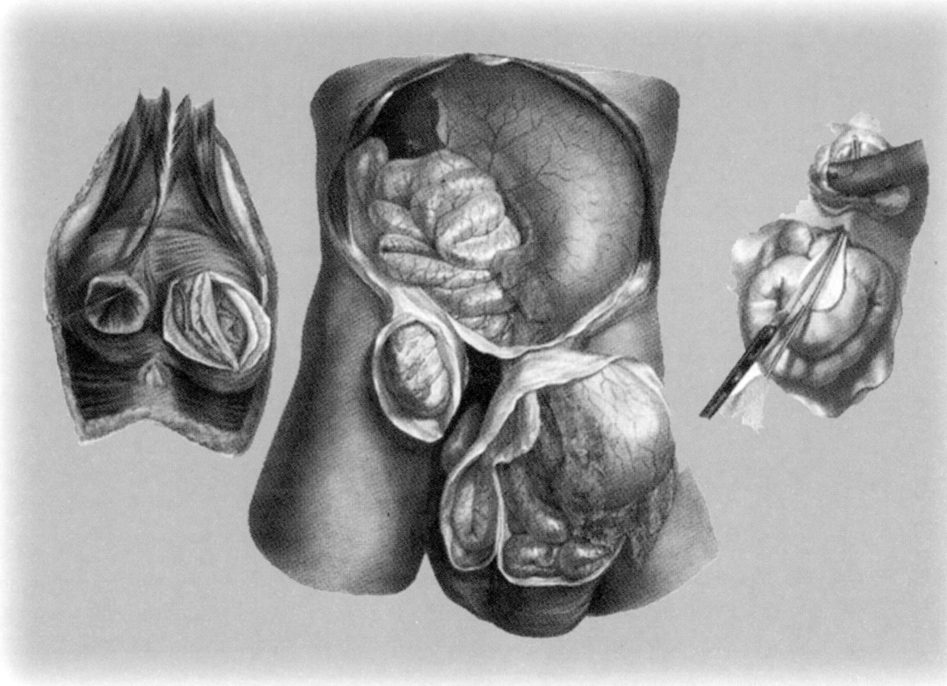

Bowel obstruction due to a hernia. In the early management of intestinal obstruction (uniformly considered fatal) treatment had focused on the use of opiates, mercury, and expectancy. The repair of strangulated hernias, although undertaken, was associated with major morbidity and mortality due to peritonitis, gangrene and sepsis. Physicians were thus hesitant to allow surgeons to operate and ignored commentary by luminaries such as Lawson Tait, who complained: "Is it not better to perform exploration before rather than after death?"

Heschl, the successor of Rokitansky as the professor of pathology at the Allgemeine Krankenhaus in Vienna, proposed that the ileo-cecal valve might act as a check valve and preclude regurgitation of the distended colon back into the ileum. Hence, for a period of time, some physicians believed that small and large bowel obstruction were completely separate events.

The development of the intestinal or nasogastric tube facilitated the diagnosis of obstruction, as well as being of considerable therapeutic value. In 1883, at a meeting of the British Medical Association, Lawson Tait of Birmingham, in his usual forthright fashion, protested the protracted palliative management of intestinal obstruction, commenting: "*was it not better to perform exploration before rather than after death*?" His frustration reflected the prevailing medical view that it was better to ease the patient into oblivion with sedatives and opium rather than permit operation. Substantial interest in the surgical relief of intestinal obstruction was provided in 1885 when Greves of Liverpool invited Mr. Pue, a local surgeon, to operate on a patient with obstruction. The division of a loop of ileum close to the cecum, resulted in the patient's survival. Such enthusiasm, however, for intervention was tempered by the reports of Madelung of Rostock and von Mikulicz of Breslau at the German Surgical Congress of 1887. They noted that in their experience, early operative invention for intestinal obstruction resulted in a high operative mortality rate and urged caution. Indeed, as late as 1929, C. Jeff Miller of the New Orleans Charity Hospital reported that the mortality rate for small bowel obstruction was 65% and for obstruction of the colon 88%. By 1930, the important role of decompression, whether achieved by indwelling duodenal suction or by aseptic operative decompression, had demarcated the first significant advances in the reduction of mortality and the management of intestinal obstruction. The turn of the twentieth century, with the introduction of sophisticated diagnostic technology, better understanding of metabolic homeostasis and improved surgical technique and postoperative care, has left the previously dreaded specter of bowel obstruction a mere shadow of itself.

Colostomy

Although the first proposal that an enterostomy or colostomy be considered as a formal procedure was made by Littré (1658-1726), the operation would not be performed for another sixty-six years until undertaken by the French surgeon, Pilloré. Pilloré made a lower transverse incision to enter the abdomen and thereafter, having created a transverse incision of the cecum, sutured it to the edges of the wound. Unfortunately the patient perished twenty days after the operation from erosion of the intestine due to large quantities of mercury, which had been previously administered in the fond belief that this would ease the obstruction. Duret, who undertook a left ileal colostomy in the case of imperforate anus in a three-day-old child, is accorded credit for the first successful elective colostomy in 1793. It is noteworthy that the patient survived until the ripe old age of forty-five years.

Although the concept of a colostomy made obvious sense, the operation met with little success in its initial stages. Dessault (1744-1795) of the Hôtel Dieu in Paris, performed a similar operation on a two-day-old child in 1774, but having omitted to suture the edge of the bowel to the wound, the patient died.

In 1810 Callisen, professor of Surgery at Copenhagen, described his experience with colostomies and Freer, a surgeon of Birmingham in England, performed the first colostomy in the United Kingdom in 1815. By 1826, Philip Syng Physick (1768-1837) of Philadelphia had written a paper describing colostomy under the title of "An operation for artificial anus" and the inimitable Dupuytren (1777-1835) of Paris had extended the procedure by developing a clamp for the exteriorized bowel. Although this technique was highly regarded and widely practiced for a period of time as a result of the great surgical reputation of Dupuytren, it was associated with considerable morbidity and mortality. Its further evolution, however, was considerably amplified by the French surgeon, Amussat (1856), who had been greatly influenced by the tragic death of his friend, Broussais, who perished of intestinal obstruction due to a carcinoma of the rectum. After evaluating the technique and results of colostomy as currently practiced, Amussat recognized that the fatalities were due to peritonitis, and therefore proposed that a lumbar colostomy should be undertaken. As such, the technique developed by Amussat was both logical and eminently clinically sensible. First he determined the location of obstruction by rectal examination and when the exact site of the tumor could not be determined, punctured the distended bowel with a small trocar. He proposed that the operation should be undertaken on the right side if the tumor was proximate to the site of operation, on the left side or when the obstruction was either distant from the anus or if its precise site could not be determined. A true diplomat and scholar, Amussat cautiously noted that the operation he proposed was difficult and required considerable skill. *"An artificial anus, it is true, is a grave infirmity but it is not insupportable. To be able to practice it a surgeon ought to fear to be surprised by pressing occasion and he should prepare himself by repetitions of the operation upon the cadaver."*

While most attention was directed to the construction of a colostomy for rectal obstruction, some surgeons actually attempted to excise the lesion itself. Jacques Lisfranc (1790-1847) of La Pitié Hospital in Paris, was the first to perform a successful peritoneal or posterior resection of the rectum in 1826. By 1833, he had reported nine cases and proposed that only those lesions palpable on digital examination should be removed. The procedure as described by him was more an anal excision, and only palliative, since the majority of the patients reported, died of general carcinomatosis within two years. Nevertheless, physicians were now fully aware that conditions of the bowel and the rectum were amenable to surgical intervention. Formal attention was therefore devoted to the subject of the anus and the rectum, and in the first half of the nineteenth century, several textbooks were variously published by John Kirby, John Hawship, Fredrick Salmon, William White, Thomas Copeland and George Calvert. The 1810 text of Copeland described cancer of the rectum in terms not much different to those employed by John of Arderne. In 1836, Bushe published the first American textbook on rectal diseases. Of particular relevance was the establishment by Fredrick Salmon (1796-1868) in 1835 of a seven-bed infirmary known as "Infirmary for the relief of the poor afflicted with the fistula and other diseases of the rectum." In 1854, this institution was renamed St. Mark's Hospital and over the next century, established itself as a center for the treatment and investigation of colorectal disease.

With the advent of colostomy as an acceptable and successful operation, surgeons then turned their interests to methods whereby colostomy might be avoided. Thus, the treatment of intestinal wounds, resection of bowel, and the suturing of intestines, became an area of considerable interest. In 1812, Benjamin Travers (1783-1858) reported on his work with intestinal repair: "An inquiry into the process of Nature in repairing injuries of the Intestines", and demonstrated the successful experimental use of intestinal sutures.

A triumvirate of Parisian surgeons of the 19th century: Amussat (top left), Emile Littré (top right) and Dupuytren (center) were responsible for the major initial advances in the development of enterostomy and colostomy.

Jacques Lisfranc (1790-1847), a surgeon at La Pitié Hospital, was responsible for the development of numerous novel surgical procedures including partial foot amputation, disarticulation of the shoulder joint, laparotomy in women and amputation of the cervix uteri. In addition, although he was one of the first individuals to undertake a posterior excision of the rectum, he had little enthusiasm for the operation, given the high rate of local recurrence. His feud with Dupuytren was celebrated in Parisian medical circles, who little admired him because of his aspersions against his many colleagues, although they disliked Dupuytren even more for his extraordinary arrogance and incredible surgical skill.

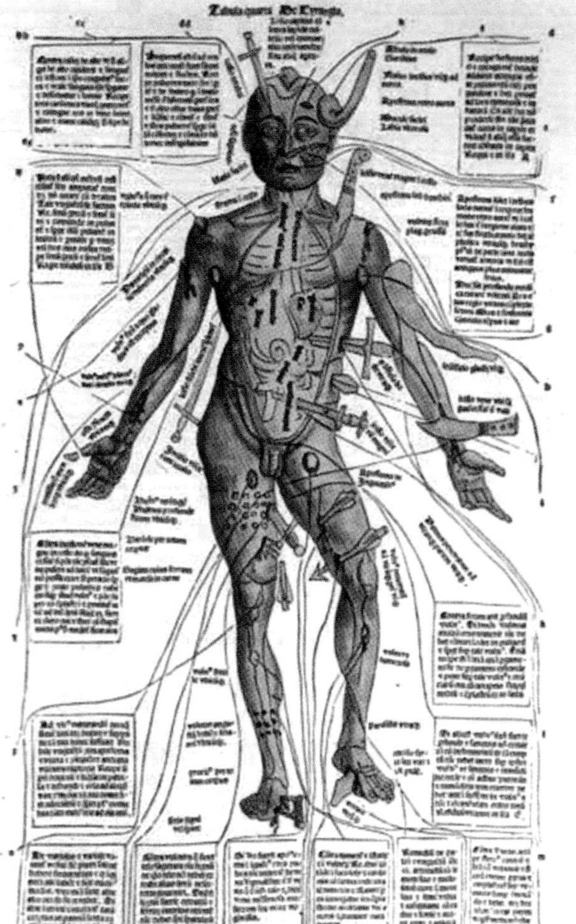

A detailed diagram of the diverse injuries known to physicians of the Middle Ages. Although considerable advice was available as how best to manage the damage inflicted by arrows, swords, and blunt objects, it was well recognized that penetrating wounds of the head, chest, and abdomen were invariably fatal. Most therapy involved excision of arrowheads, suturing of bleeding vessels and cauterization of wounds. Only in unique circumstances could a laceration of the bowel be considered for therapy. Nevertheless, animal hair and even plant fibers were utilized to close wounds of the intestines. The use of cat trachea as a stent had been proposed as early as the 13th century.

Resection and Anastomosis

While gall bladder surgery reflects a history of less than two hundred years, the origins of surgery of the intestines recapitulates many thousands of years of vain experiment and fruitless intervention. Thus sepsis, soilage, and the lack of sutures, defeated even the most ardent of surgical enthusiasts. Intervention ranged from the attempts of the Samhita of Susruta (second century A.D.) who effected intestinal suturing utilizing large red ants, to Galen's use of hairs drawn from the tails of horses.

Given the frequency of abdominal wounds and the use of spears, daggers, and swords, the question of managing prolapsed or perforated intestines had exercised the minds of surgeons since ancient times. It was well recognized that something had to be done and in particular, the need to replace the prolapsed abdominal viscera was obvious. The problem of suturing the intestine was less easily addressed. It was the teaching of Abukaszim that raising the pelvis of the patient could facilitate the relocation of the intestines in cases of injuries to the lower abdomen. Almost two thousand years later a similar position was advocated by Friederich Trendelenburg, professor of Surgery in Leipzig, for the purpose of operating within the pelvis, and nowadays almost all abdominal procedures undertaken for gynecologic surgery are carried out in this position. The concept of actually enlarging the abdominal incision to replace abdominal contents was initially advocated by Rhazes, and thereafter supported in the writings of both Celsus and Galen. Subsequently the Alsatian army surgeon, Hans von Gersdorff (*c.* 1450-1530) (dubbed "*Schyllhans*", cross-eyed Johnny), of Strassbourg popularized the notion that if the intestine prolapsed into the abdominal wound and could not be put back, the wound should be extended to ensure complete replacement prior to suturing the abdominal wall.

This proposal was far more effective than the suggestion that the intestines be punctured and their contents drained prior to replacement. Indeed, this concept was surprising, since it had been accepted since very ancient times that feces harmed the peritoneum, and that the flow of excrement into the abdominal cavity was dangerous.

In fact, it was the acceptance of these considerations that had been responsible for the earliest attempts to suture intestines. The failure of reliable intestinal repair led to the recognition that the abdominal cavity could be prevented the peril of the influx of excrement by leaving the damaged intestine outside the abdominal cavity. Although this created an unpleasant situation, since leaking feces would soil the body, it was preferable to an internal leak with peritonitis and death. The concept of an artificial anus was unattractive but in desperate circumstances there was often little alternative.

The history of the suturing of intestines provides one of the most interesting chapters of surgery and undying proof of the creativity of physicians. A wide variety of fibers of animal (hair) and plant origin were tried as threads before the use of silk thread and catgut, which are still in use. The primary concern apart from leakage was the problem posed by constriction of the intestine. In order to avoid this problem, a number of diverse measures were advocated. Roger Frugardi (twelfth century) sutured the intestine over a tube made of elderpith while William of Saliceto used animal gut inserted into the two cut ends of the intestine (endo-prosthesis) to support the suture. The four masters (thirteenth century) used the trachea of an animal over the sutured ends of the intestine and indeed, this technique proved so effective that it was renewed by Duverger as late as 1744. Sabatier in 1760 proposed the formation of an internal tube by rolling a membrane and united the two

*The jaws of the ant species (*Eciton burchelli*) were regarded as an appropriate method for securing wound opposition in the intestine. In South America the leaf cutting ant (*Atta cephalotes*) was used by local shamans to effect wound closure.*

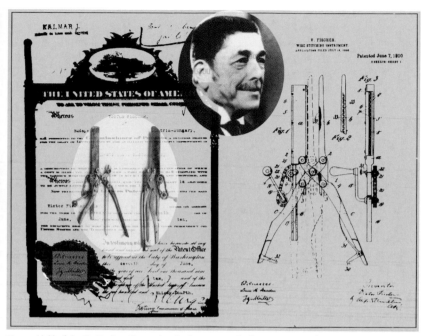

Humer Hultl of the St. Rochas Hospital in Budapest was the first surgeon to design a successful stapling device for intestinal anastomosis (inset). Although the original patent (inset) was held by him for many years, subsequent design modifications superseded the earlier device which was heavy, clumsy to use, and required to be hand-loaded.

ends of the intestine over this. Experienced surgeons such as Frederick Treves supported this technique and even Thienot, as late as 1899, applied his name to this procedure. Similarly, William Halsted of Baltimore accepted this idea and his least favorite pupil, Cushing, in 1898 even advocated the suturing of the ends of intestines over inflatable rubber balloons. Lanfranco and Purman and other older surgeons declared these aids dispensable and the concept soon fell into disfavor.

At about the beginning of the nineteenth century, it became apparent that the healing of intestinal sutures was dependent on the cohesion of the serous and mucous membrane surfaces of the two ends of the intestine. As a result it was realized that for healing of the sutures, the intestine could only be effected if sutures provided adequate apposition of these two layers. Credit for the recognition of this critical observation is due to two Parisian surgeons, Antoine Jobert de Lamballe and Antoine Lembert. Jobert reported his procedure in 1824, Lembert in 1826. Although Ramdohr had described a similar procedure to that of Jobert in 1727, a surgeon of Wolfenbuttel, it was inferior in respect of safety and accuracy. Overall the Lembert technique was more acceptable, since it did not penetrate the mucous membrane of the intestine and in fact, the procedures in use today remain very similar to the original procedure described by Lembert. Despite such advances, it is worth noting that the method of suturing described by Celsus (two thousand years previously) also emphasized the contact of the serous membranes of the edges of the intestinal wound! Even at the juncture of the twenty-first century, with more than a hundred methods for suturing intestines available, the useable ones are all based on the principle of Jobert and Lembert, viz. the securing of contact between the serous membranes. A number of alternative devices for intestinal apposition were developed, including the Murphy button as proposed by the Chicago surgeon John Benjamin Murphy in 1892, and the Senn plate. By the first two decades of the twentieth century, although suturing was still the standard technique, T. Hertzel of Budapest had developed the first automatic stapling device and the subsequent advance of this technique would dramatically alter intestinal anastomosis.

J.B. Murphy of Chicago in 1892 described the Murphy button (inset). This device was utilized to hold the two ends of the intestine together and functioned both as a stent and as a mechanism to maintain intestinal apposition. The two telephones (a rarity at the beginning of the 20th century) on his desk suggest the nature of his working habits.

In ancient times, sutures of intestines were used exclusively for the treatment of accidental injuries and remarkably, in spite of the imperfections of the sutures, many successes were recorded. As noted by Felix Platter (1536-1614), professor in Basle, most were due to the good fortune of the development of adhesions around the damaged intestines that resulted in the leaking contents of the intestines being evacuated outward and not inward. Subsequent external fistulas would often heal, whereas an internal leak resulted in sepsis and death. The principle beneficiaries of the advance of intestinal sutures were those operated on for strangulated hernia, since the development of strangulated bowel had previously been a death sentence. The earliest advances in this area reflected the contributions of François de la Peyronie (1678-1747) of Montpellier, who worked diligently on the promotion of better training for surgeons and founded, in 1731, the Académie de Chirurgie of Paris.

Once the precedent for successful bowel resection had been established, operations were undertaken for other causes, including obstruction and tumors. The first such procedure was performed by Balthasar Anselme Richerand in Paris in 1829 but the patient did not survive. Thereafter, Reybard (1793-1863) of Lyons was the first to excise a colon cancer (1833) with survival. This operation was repeated forty-two years later in Germany by Karl Thiersch of Leipzig, but his patient had died. As might be predicted,

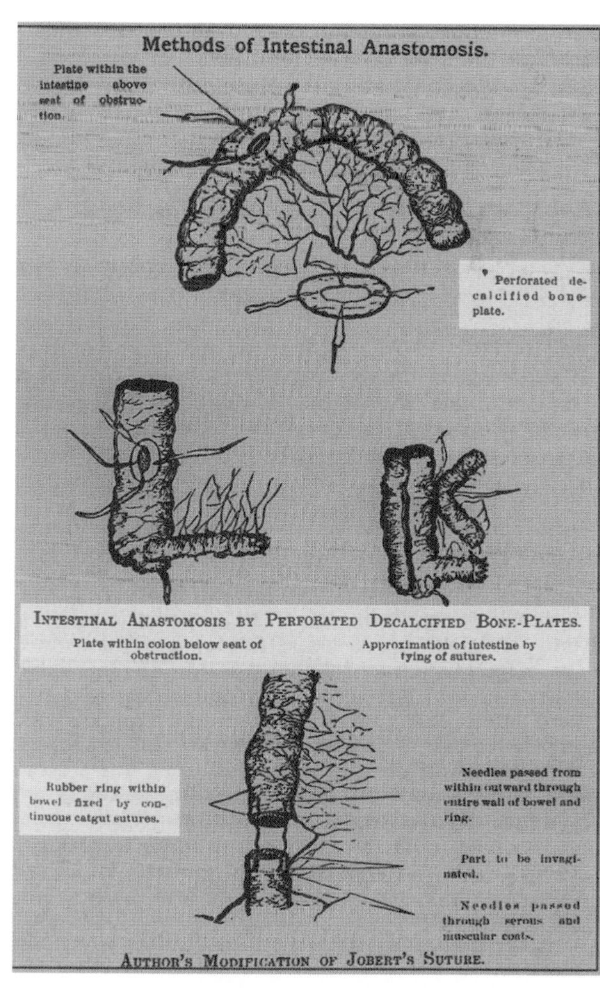

Numerous devices were considered in an attempt to provide safe intestinal anastomosis. These ranged from the use of animal tracheas as stents to perforated decalcified bone plates or rubber rings.

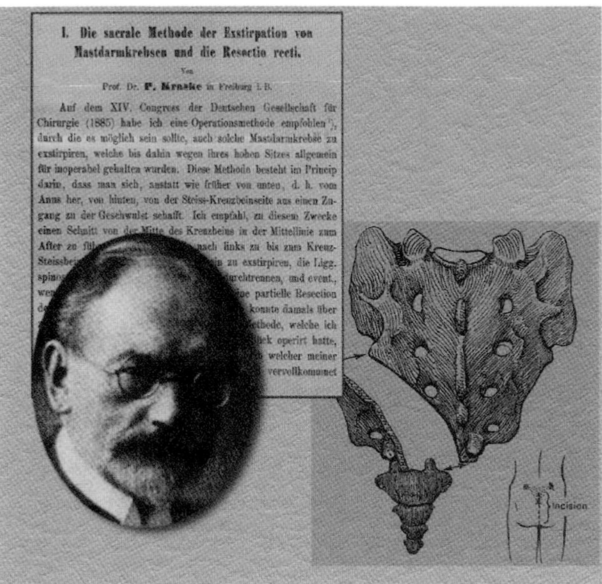

I. Die sacrale Methode der Exstirpation von Mastdarmkrebsen und die Resectio recti.

Von

Prof. Dr. P. Kraske in Freiburg i. B.

Auf dem XIV. Congress der Deutschen Gesellschaft für Chirurgie (1885) habe ich eine Operationsmethode empfohlen, durch die es möglich sein sollte, auch solche Mastdarmkrebse zu exstirpiren, welche bis dahin wegen ihres hohen Sitzes allgemein für inoperabel gehalten wurden. Diese Methode besteht im Princip darin, dass man sich, anstatt wie früher von unten, d. h. vom Anus her, von hinten, von der Steiss-Kreuzbeinseite aus einen Zugang zu der Geschwulst schafft. Ich empfahl, zu diesem Zwecke einen Schnitt von der Mitte des Kreuzbeins in der Mittellinie zum After zu fü... nach links zu bis zum Kreuz-Steissbe... zu exstirpiren, die Ligg. spino... urchtrennen, und event., we... e partielle Resection d... konnte damals über ... thode, welche ich ... k operirt hatte, ... welcher meiner ... vervollkommnet

The Kraske technique of rectal excision. In 1885 Kraske, at the 14th Congress of the German Surgeons, presented his major contribution to the field. He described in detail his posterior resection of the sacrum, extensive excision of the rectum, and anastomosis of the bowel to the anus.

Karl Thiersch (1822-1895) underwent his surgical training at Munich before becoming professor of Surgery initially at Erlangen (1854) and subsequently Leipzig in 1887. Thiersch was a gifted surgeon and a great pioneer of Listerism. His contributions included the study of epithelial cancer, the healing of skin wounds, and technical improvements in skin grafting. Although his results with resection of the colon were disappointing, he described a successful perianal stitch to control rectal prolapse.

the mortality for colon resection at the beginning of the twentieth century fluctuated between 70% to 80%. The subsequent development of colonic lavage, colostomy, the early antibiotics and better anastomotic techniques reduced this to under 10% by the 1940s. More familiarity with anastomotic options and particularly with the construction of stomas, resulted in the development of numerous methods for restoring the continuity of the intestines after the removal of smaller, or larger sections of the small intestine, or the colon. The once-feared procedure of enterotomy for the removal of a foreign body or the establishment of lateral communications between intestines (enteroenteroanatomosis) as well as the construction of temporary, or permanent, intestinal fistulas became common practice by the 1920s. A particular challenge was, however, provided by lesions of the anus and rectum. Since the trans-anal excision of rectal tumors was difficult and often incomplete, rectotomy had been used, but this often resulted in disastrous leakage.

The surgery of intestinal obstruction where there was no external hernia was late in development, since diagnosis was difficult and abdominal exploration risky. Hilton almost succeeded with such a case practice (obstruction by a band) as early as 1846, but for many years after this, cases of intestinal obstruction were left to die in the hands of physicians. Towards the end of the nineteenth century, such cases began to be handed over to surgeons and Treves made clear the possible causes which might lead to such obstruction. Unfortunately, for many years the results of surgery for obstruction were poor, since cases were generally referred for surgery too late and operations upon toxic and dehydrated patients with septicemia produced unsatisfactory results. In 1912, Hartwell and Hoguet showed the importance of replacing fluid lost by vomiting, and in 1923 Haden and Orr demonstrated the metabolic problems resulting from a loss of chlorides. Intravenous replacement led to a rapid improvement in mortality and in 1953 Wangensteen demonstrated the beneficial effect following decompression of the small intestine line by means of a small rubber tube swallowed into the stomach and allowed to pass into the small bowel. Aspiration of intestinal and gastric contents led to a great improvement. Conservative management of intestinal obstruction became possible and surgery was only necessary in situations involving strangulation.

When resection of distended in obstructed large bowel was attempted, it was soon found that similar methods to those used in cases of resection of small gut were inapplicable. Sutures did not hold and peritonitis resulted. It was found necessary to develop methods of external drainage of the bowel as to close the resulting fistula at a later date. Von Mikulicz, Paul, and Bloch each independently devised techniques whereby the affected portion of the bowel was brought outside the abdomen, the loop excised, and temporary bowel drainage instituted.

Rectal surgery of a minor character had been performed for many centuries, but the major operation of excision of the rectum for cancer only became possible after the introduction of anesthesia and antisepsis. Those surgeons who first made the attempt, adopted the perennial route and even under such circumstances, were only able to undertake a limited excision. Of particular note in the development of this procedure are the names of Cripps, Allingham, and Langenbeck, though each described different aspects. In 1874, Kocher advised removal of part of the sacrum to facilitate approach to the rectum and in 1886, Paul Kraske of Freiburg developed this technique and the sacral approach which is still known by his name.

As early as 1883, Czerny had tried a combined abdominal and perineal approach and after him, numerous surgeons in a variety of different countries tried to expand this technique. Miles, however, was the first individual to develop the abdomino-perineal method to a high degree of technical efficiency. Grey-Turner first practiced and Gabriel subsequently extended, the usefulness of starting excision from the perineum and then finishing through the abdomen. Finally, the work of Devine demonstrated that results were better when the operation was performed by two surgeons working simultaneously – one from the perineum and the other through the abdomen.

A METHOD OF PERFORMING ABDOMINO-PERINEAL EXCISION FOR CARCINOMA OF THE RECTUM AND OF THE TERMINAL PORTION OF THE PELVIC COLON.

BY W. ERNEST MILES, F.R.C.S. ENG., L.R.C.P. LOND.,

SURGEON TO THE CANCER HOSPITAL ... AND TO THE GORDON HOSPITAL ... RECTUM, VAUXHALL ...

REMOVAL of the rectum ... perineal operation was first ... Since ... several othe... Chalt... Challot, W... Re... Gant, Math... have empl... edure and ... as I have ... ject, howe... have failed in ... e eradication of ... rectum, whereby ... se, above the field ... entirely obviated.

W.E. Miles (1869-1947). Born in Trinidad and educated at Queen's Royal College, Port-of-Spain, at which his father was headmaster, Miles undertook his clinical training at St. Bartholomew's Hospital and St. Mark's Hospital for Diseases of the Rectum. In 1899, he was appointed to the Royal Cancer Hospital, where in 1907 he introduced the abdominoperineal resection for rectal carcinoma. Not only a doyen of rectal surgery, Miles was a keen horse-racer and maintained a box at Ascot where he was highly regarded as an equinophile.

Ano-rectal Disease

The Ebers Papyrus of *c.* 1700 B.C. provides more than thirty-three prescriptions or recipes for treatment of anal and rectal disease. These include liniments, enemas, ointments, and suppositories, as well as prescriptions for vermifuges and cathartics. Similarly, the Beatty Medical Papyrus of the twelfth and thirteenth centuries B.C. consists almost entirely of methods and remedies for the treatment of anal, rectal, and colonic disease. Its prescriptions contain ingredients such as myrrh, honey, flour, ibex fat, and rectal injections with honey and sweet beer. The conditions described include pruritus am, painful swelling (thrombosed hemorrhoids) and prolapsed rectum.

Between 460 and 377 B.C., Hippocrates wrote a number of dissertations on the subjects of *"On fistula"* and *"On hemorrhoids."* He proposed treatment of the disease by ointments, enemas and suppositories, but in an advance on Egyptian medicine, also discussed surgical treatment. This included cutting, excising, sewing, binding and cautery of hemorrhoids. The directions given to the surgical novice for treatment of such conditions using cautery were: *"force out the anus as much as possible with the fingers, make the irons red hot, and burn the pile until it be dried up and as that no part may be left behind... You will recognize the hemorrhoids without difficulty, for they project on the inside of the gut like dark colored grapes and when the anus is forced out they spurt blood."* In addition to hemorrhoids, Hippocrates described the relationship between ano-rectal abscess and fistula and his treatment using a stent or ligature remains in practice to this day in various somewhat updated forms. In addition to surgery, however, Hippocrates proposed the use of astringent dressings as well as suppositories to control bleeding.

The Egyptians had a profund respect for the anus, believing it to be both a portal of pleasure as well as a source of serious disease. The Ebers Papyrus (background) detailed many prescriptions to be administered via the nether orifice and the most senior and respected of the physicians (right) to the pharoah was graciously entitled "Shepherd of the Anus".

Although skilled in the management of anorectal conditions, Hippocrates believed that all wounds of the intestines were fatal. Despite the Susruta (sixth century B.C.) Hindu writings, which advised the closing of wounds of the intestine with the pincers of black ants, most early Middle Eastern and Western physicians had concluded that gut wounds were fatal. Thus, in the Bible (Judges 2:3:22), when Eglon was attacked by Ehud, *"he could not draw the dagger out of his belly and the dirt came out."* Although Greek medicine was transmuted to the Romans after their conquest of Athens, even Galen could contribute little to the management of ano-rectal disease. Celsus, who was in effect little more than an assimilator (albeit a very fine one) of information, as late as A.D. 50, proposed that wounds of the intestine should be sutured in all layers and suggested that the knife and ligature be used to treat anal fistulas. During the Byzantine period, Paul of Aegina, in the seventh century A.D. recounted a slightly more sophisticated method for the management of hemorrhoids and anal fistulas, proposing the use of frequent clysters to clean the intestine before everting the anus and using a strong ligature to tie off the hemorrhoids. Leonides avoided the ligature, preferring to first cauterize the hemorrhoids before excising them with a scalpel. Maimonides (1135-1204), in his treatise on hemorrhoids, proposed a light diet and the frequent usage of baths. By the close of the twelfth century the preoccupation with ano-rectal disease had diminished somewhat as surgeons began with some temerity to approach the bowel itself.

Roger Frugardi (Roger of Salerno) proposed that intestinal wounds could be sutured over a stent provided by either the trachea of a large bird or a hollow elder twig. More particularly, however, the School of Salerno proposed hygiene as one of the most important issues in the treatment of bowel disorders and the *regimen sanitatis Salerni* was widely used. Indeed, an English translation of one of their dictums by Sir John Harrington (godson of Queen Elizabeth I and inventor of the modern water closet) makes interesting reading. *"Great harmes have grown and maladies exceeding, By keeping in a little blast of wind:*

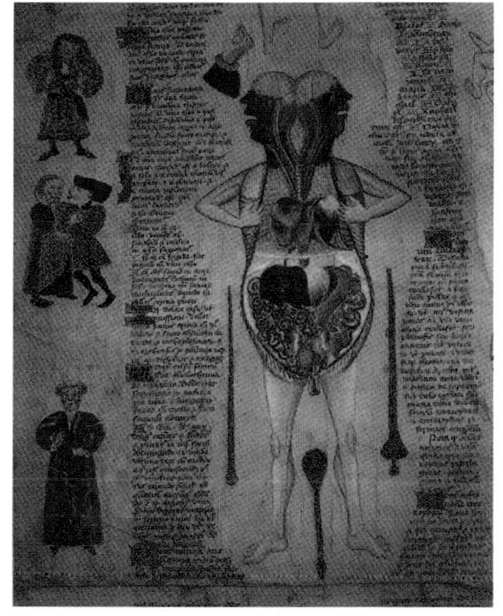

Early English medicine, particularly as practised by John of Arderne, focused heavily on the management of ano-rectal disease.

The French medical practise of educating patients in the efficacy of self-administered enemas, achieved widespread popularity. The resistance of the young woman to the entry of her suitor raises questions in regard to both her technique and motivation!

St. Fiacre was a 7th-century acolyte. Originally the patron saint of gardeners, he subsequently became the patron saint of hemorrhoid sufferers. The inn at which numerous patients were treated for their hemorrhoid disease stood opposite the church commemorating St. Fiacre and was named after him. As a result, the numerous horse-drawn carriages waiting for their patients to be treated outside this Parisian establishment eventually became known as fiacres.

So cramps and dropsy Colleagues have their breeding and mazed brains for want of venting behind!"

The influence of the Church and its relationship to health was such that by the Middle Ages, almost all diseases had acquired a patron saint. Thus, the seventh century acolyte, St. Fiacre, who was the patron saint of gardeners, eventually became the patron saint of those with hemorrhoids. Indeed, so popular was his beneficence in Paris that an inn was actually named after him and a statue erected in his honor. The horse-drawn carriages that waited for their patrons outside the inn eventually became known as *fiacres*.

In the fourteenth century, the dominant influence on ano-rectal disease was provided by John of Arderne, who served in the Hundred Years' War under the Duke of Lancaster, John of Gaunt. On discharge from the army, he established a practice in ano-rectal disease and developed a great reputation, becoming immensely rich in the process. Nevertheless, he insisted that his followers be charitable and live a chaste life, providing them with strict rules of conduct which would ensure their health. Arderne was advanced for his time and wrote extensively on appropriate follow-up of patients, reporting both his successes and failures. Although he was effective in the treatment of ischio-rectal abscesses and fistulas and described their care in great detail, he recognized the inadequacy of treatment for rectal cancer. "*I never saw nor heard of any man that was cured of cancer of the rectum but I have known of many that died of the aforesaid sickness.*" His description of the condition is noteworthy. "*Bubo is an apostm breeding within the anus in the rectum with great hardness but little aching. This I say, before it ulcerates, is nothing else than a hidden cancer, that may not in the beginning of it be known by the sight of the eye, for it is all hidden within the rectum; and therefore it is called a bubo, for as bubo, that is an owl, is always dwelling and hiding so that this sickness lurks within the rectum in the beginning but after passage of time it ulcerates and eroding the anus comes out.*"

Although the sixteenth century provided surgery with Andreas Vesalius and Ambroise Paré (1510-1590), they contributed little of interest to the management of intestinal disease, although Paré did produce a text dealing with wounds of the intestine under the title of *The Gut*. "*When the guts are wounded the whole body griped and pained, the excrements come out of the wound, where at often times the guts break force with great violence.*" His description of an enterocutaneous fistula was accurate but unfortunately, he could provide no adequate therapy. Given the inability to safely enter the peritoneal cavity, intestinal surgery languished well into the seventeenth century until Felix operated on Louis XIV and with this success, initiated the renaissance of French surgery. In 1685, Louis XIV developed a small but painful lump in the rectum. Despite numerous remedies the court doctors and apothecary failed to successfully cure the condition and as a last resort his surgeon, Charles François Felix, was summoned. Felix explained to Louis how the surgery would bring relief, and thereupon proposed that a date six months in the future be set for the operation. This provided Felix with the opportunity to practice on more lowly patients, of whom it is rumored a substantial number perished under his knife as he perfected his technique. It is reported that they were buried at night, to keep news from reaching the public ear!

Finally on November 18, 1686, Felix had the temerity to perform the operation at Versailles in the presence of Madame de Maintenon and the court medical staff. Fortunately for both himself and the King it proved a complete success. As Louis recovered, his sycophantic courtiers paraded around Versailles with bandaged bottoms to show their sympathy with the King's

Given the lack of sanitary facilities in Versailles and the debauched lifestyle that he lived, it was little surprise to the surgeon, C.F. Felix (top left), that King Louis XIV developed a perianal abscess. The successful incision and drainage of the royal posterior is claimed by many to have provided the initial impetus for the development of French surgery.

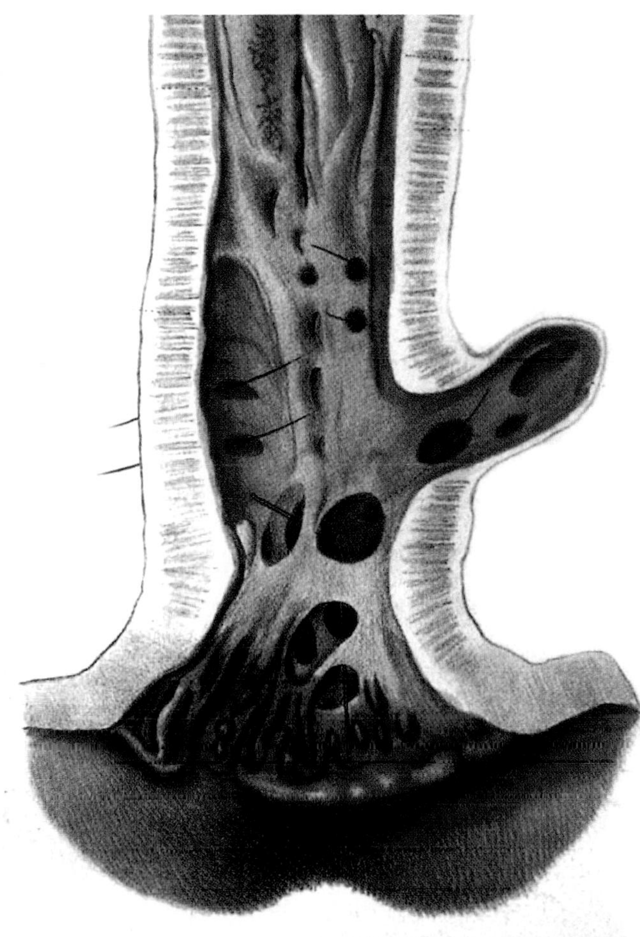

The management of rectal fistula was both difficult and dangerous prior to the introduction of anesthesia and antisepsis. Perianal operations often culminated in death from septicemia or uncontrollable hemorrhage. Those who were fortunate enough to survive operative intervention were often rendered incontinent due to the difficulty in appreciating the anatomy.

posterior discomfort. In recognition of his services to the royal posterior, Felix received 300,000 livres, which represented a sum equivalent to three times the annual salary of the chief physician. In addition, he was ennobled and cynics of the time referred to the year 1686 as *L'Année de la Fistule*.

By the eighteenth century Morgagni (1682-1771) had not only described the crypts and columns of the anus, but also proposed an operation for cancer of the rectum. Indeed, in 1739 Fajet performed a posterior resection of the rectum, but the subsequent uncontrollable sacral anus proved impossible to deal with and as a result, the procedure evoked considerable criticism. The aftermath of this catastrophe served to focus more attention on the development of a colostomy procedure, since much experience had been inadvertently gained in this area by virtue of accidental fistulas caused by either trauma or disease. In the early eighteenth century, Lorenz Heister produced a report on "*The spontaneous or operative creation of an external intestinal fistula in injuries or gangrene of the bowel*." In it he proposed that in the case of a damaged intestine it should be "*stitched to the external wound either by continued or interrupted suture for by this means the patient may not only be saved from instant death but there have been instances where the wounded intestine has been so far healed that the feces which used to be voided per anum have been voided by the wound in the abdomen.*" Heister went on to describe a series of techniques whereby bowel that had been inadvertently damaged might be fashioned into a colostomy, stating quite pragmatically: "*it is surely far better to part with one of the conveniences of life than to part with life itself. Besides the excrements that are voided by this passage are not altogether so offensive as those that are voided per anum!*"

Frederick Salmon (right) in 1835 established a seven-bed infirmary in London, known as "The infirmary for the relief of the poor afflicted with a fistula and other diseases of the rectum." When the institution was enlarged, the new benefactor insisted that it be called St. Andrew's Hospital of the Lower Intestine since it was located in the parish of St Andrew's. Salmon declined and accepted an offer to locate the hospital in the parish of St Luke's, provided it could be called "The Fistula Hospital". The benefactors objected, claiming that it would be "difficult to raise public funds for an institution with this name." Since the parish already contained a St Luke's Hospital, a compromise was reached by renaming the institution St. Mark's Hospital for Fistula. The new name was determined by designating the opening day as August 25, 1852 – St. Mark's Day! Over the next century St. Mark's established itself as an epicenter for the study of colorectal disease.

Rectal prolapse had been well recognized since the earliest medical literature and Hippocrates had even described it: "*eversion of the gut takes place in middle aged persons having piles, of children affected with stone and in protracted and intense discharge of the bowel, and in old persons having mucous concretions (Scybale).*" Although the first therapy involved the application of fomentations and reductions, curative treatments included cauterization, excision and even incision. By 1843, Chelius was able to record a list of more than a half dozen notable surgeons who had described a surgical methodology for dealing with the condition. Thus Heister (1745), Copeland (1814), Hawship (1820), Bushe (1827), Senn (1828), Dupuytren (1831) and Velpeau (1841), had all provided detailed information as to their surgical techniques.

Section 20

quo vadis

To document the past is to define the present and thereby illuminate the paths necessary to secure the future. The evolution of therapy from the early days of herbs and roots to the current molecular strategies, is a tale of fascination intertwined with both frustration and despair, yet replete with great advances, examples of inspiration and moments of pure genius and exaltation. Despite great advances, there is much that is as yet unknown and many diseases still evade not only definition but also effective cure.

Nevertheless, progress has been heartening and the same human spirit that imbued men with the courage to round the Cape of Storms and cross the Atlantic still endures. Few things can be spoken of with certainty, in particular the future, but in respect of progress one may be sure that physicians and scientists will undoubtedly continue to scale the steep slopes of the vast mountain of human illness. If death is the ultimate point on the human horizon and the scientifically measurable end point of life, then man's quest for the understanding of the infinity of life obligates members of society to seek health during their brief journey into oblivion. A consideration of the gut as the internal roadway towards health and understanding may be a quixotic notion, but provides a focus on disease and its therapy since it is certain that we are and become what we eat!

In 1896 Ismar Boas founded the discipline of gastroenterology and established the first journal devoted entirely to the subject. The subsequent century has seen extraordinary advances in many different areas and transposed the discipline from a relatively humble place in medicine to a position of critical importance. Numerous different sub-specialties including radiology, nuclear medicine, endoscopy, biochemistry, and surgery have coalesced to produce a complex matrix within which present-day gastroenterologists function. At the turn of the nineteenth century, diagnosis was vague, pathology barely visible, and therapy almost non-existent. A century later the darkness surrounding gastrointestinal disease has, in many areas, been illuminated by the identification of the pathological basis for the disease and the introduction of effective therapy. Nevertheless, there still remain huge areas of uncertainty, some of which are so large they constitute the gastrointestinal equivalent of celestial black holes. One wonders what Hippocrates, Galen, Avicenna, Maimonides, Sydenham, Boas, and their brethren might have thought of the future if they had stood at the brink of a new millennium.

Clearly, the major issues are the early identification of gastrointestinal neoplasia and the development of techniques to ablate and eradicate the problem. It is evident that early diagnosis provides the only reasonable hope of cure, and that currently, major surgery is little more than palliative and, in many circumstances such as pancreatic or hepatic neoplasia, provides little more than occupational therapy for surgeons and a glimmer of hope for patients. For the level of diagnosis required, imaging modalities of the gut, while useful, are still relatively crude and diagnosis is still at a microscopic level, only marginally advanced from that reported by Virchow in Berlin more than a century ago. Thus, larger lenses and more vivid stains supported by proliferative markers or mitotic abnormalities still represent little more than the feeble graspings at an early diagnosis. The world of pattern recognition needs replacement by the development of instruments capable of surveying individual mucosal cells using either non-visible wavelength light and fluorophores or laser capture microscopes to isolate individual cells and determine their genetic profiles. Areas to be evaluated may be selected by the use of devices, which are self-propelled within the lumen of the gastrointestinal tract or the peritoneal cavity, and may be robotically guided in order to identify and sample specific areas. Once an abnormality is detected, therapy will be delivered intravenously or transluminally by site-specific probes targeted to particular regions of the molecular structures responsible for unregulated proliferation.

An alternative possibility is that detection of disease may be replaced by prediction of disease. Thus, further evaluation of the human gene and the evolution of the science of proteonomics will facilitate the identification of individuals prone to a particular disease and define the genetic abnormalities inherent in the development of the disease process. The evolution of molecular medicine as applied to gastrointestinal disease will result in early diagnosis, genetic engineering, or the introduction of targeted probes to delete effected cells. A second possibility is that once the genomic determinants of a disease are known, internal sensing devices may be implanted to provide real time assessment of cellular events or plasma sensing of the message determinants of impending dysfunction.

While the early part of the century devoted itself to "Nervism" and the Pavlovian doctrine of regulation, much of the subsequent fifty years were devoted to the elucidation of the chemical regulation of cell function. This obsession with regulation has resulted in the failure to examine sensation or elucidate visceral pain or identify the cellular pathogenesis inherent in

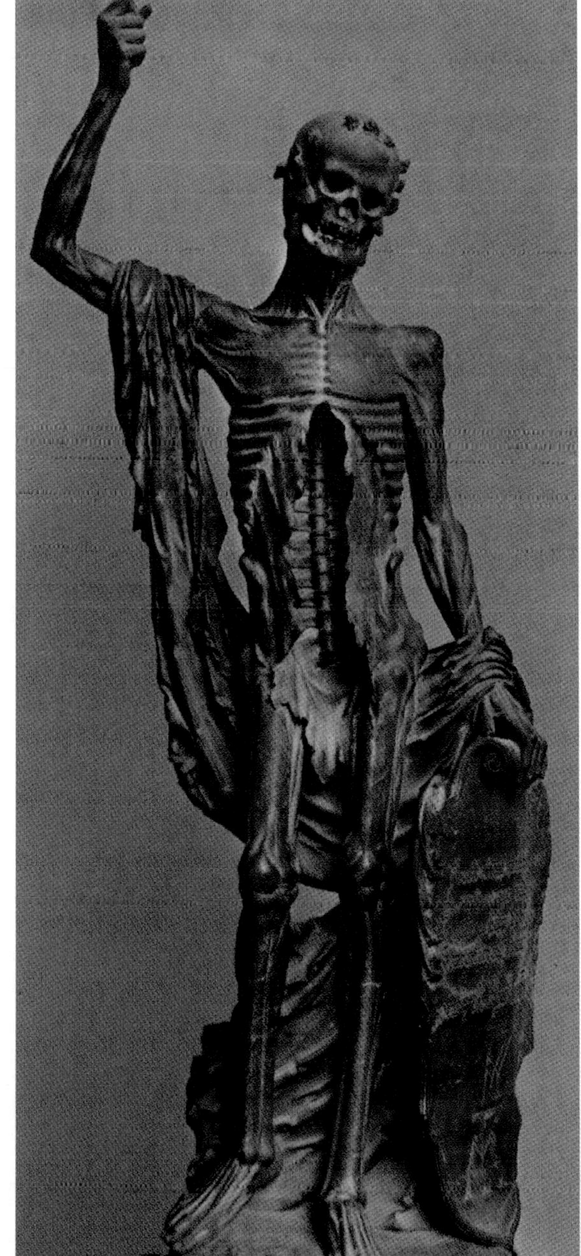

Despite considerable advances in management, numerous gastrointestinal diseases are incurable and the majority of therapy is symptomatic. The grim visage of mortality still remains the icon of disease as it intones: "Look carefully, oh physician, I was what you are; you will be what I am...!" *Mors vincit omnia.*

disordered peristalsis has. As a consequence, non-infectious diseases of the gut are currently regarded somewhat as a medieval taxonomy and referred to as "the irritable bowel syndrome." This heterogeneous group colloquation represents the last refuge of the intellectually destitute and represents a number of utterly ill-understood disease processes for which little physiological or pathological information is available. This area requires investigation at a fundamental level since it is, at present, a diagnostic quagmire much remindive of the ludicrous visceroptosis syndromes of the early twentieth century. Arguments in regard to diet, laxatives, psychoactive drugs, and dubious promotility agents need to be put aside until the formal basis of the neural and myoelectric circuitry of the gut is elucidated and the appropriate therapeutic targets defined.

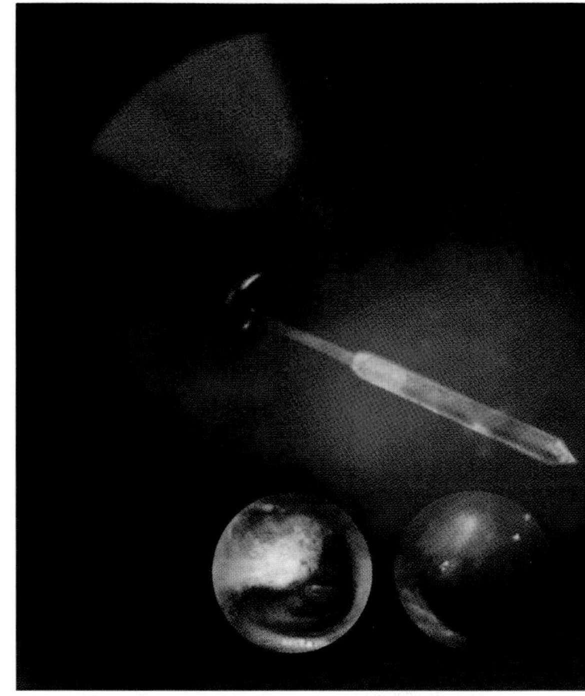

The advent of novel biotechnology in the management of disease is well-exemplified by the utility of photodynamic therapy. Such intervention represents the successful fusion of aspects of the disciplines of physics, endoscopy, biochemistry, cell biology, and oncology in the treatment of neoplasia.

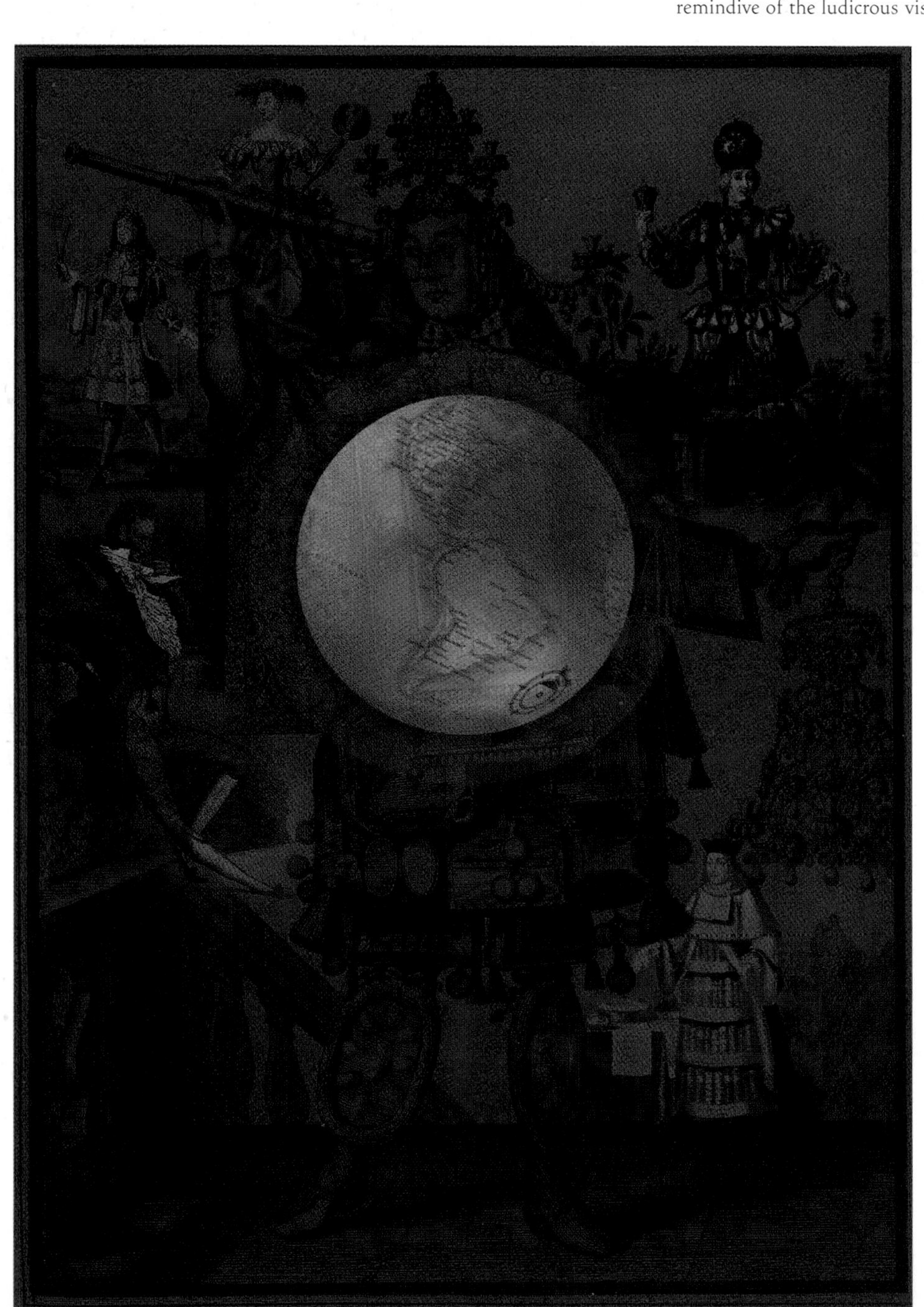

The fanciful and seemingly absurd notions and posturings of surgeons, physicians, and pharmacists of the past appear humorous today. It is likely that our own modest efforts will be similarly viewed by future generations.

The question of mucosal immunology requires considerable further investigation and the relationship between gut bacteria and gut mucosal cells, which has been virtually unexplored, requires considerable amplification. Whether agents present in the food are responsible for abnormal antigen presentation, or actual damage needs exploration, as does the entire concept of the pathobiology of that nebulous entity currently known as the mucosal barrier. Much as twenty-first century computers have been provided with "virus scans" to prohibit the introduction of damaging materials to the system, it seems necessary to consider the introduction of a similar process for ingested and imbibed agents.

A major target of therapy is the venerable lord of the abdomen, the liver. The pathophysiology of hepatic parenchymal injury and fibrosis that result in cirrhosis is an important target for the hepatologist. The centuries-old threadbare terminology of chronic inflammation and fibrosis needs replacement with a serious understanding of what constitutes damage and repair in individual organs. Indeed, the entire regulation of the constellation of agents, which are grouped together as growth factors, requires definition and characterization in much the same way as the blood coagulation cascade was defined. Therapy needs to be developed that will identify damage-inducing agents and modulate their pathogenic effects as well as regulate the obscure self-perpetuating mechanisms of fibrosis. The current focus on the sequelae of such events has been clearly demonstrated to have little more than a palliative, albeit marginal, effect on outcome.

While the etiology of gallstones has been to a large extent appreciated and techniques developed to destroy the concretions, there is a critical requirement to developed prophylactic therapy prior to the onset of cholecystitis or pancreatitis. The latter disease itself still remains an unsolved mystery shrouded in superstition and quasi-scientific explanations of its pathogenesis. Extraordinarily complex and detailed arguments as to whether it should be operated upon, when, and how, need to be shelved in favor of a focused search for the etiological mechanisms and the cellular targets necessary to inhibit the process. In respect of gallstones, it seems obvious that surgery only deals with the end product of the underlying disorder and that attention should be focused on the hepatocellular component of the crystallization equation or the ileal bile salt receptors. The prophylaxis of biliary concretions would obviate much morbidity and result in a considerable diminution in health expenditure.

The anatomical basis of the arterial and venous systems of the body and even the portal system of the gut, have been clearly defined but almost no attention has been paid to the lymphatic system. The obvious physio-pathological significance of a completely separate absorption and transport system bypassing the liver and feeding directly into the systemic venous circulation requires careful consideration. Might not the etiology of some pulmonary disease be a consequence of direct access of ingested agents to the pulmonary parenchyma by way of lymphatic transport? Indeed, why does a system exist that is designed to specifically bypass hepatic metabolism and directly enter the systemic circulation? The agents transported, and their possible implications whether nutrient or immunological, require identification and resolution in order to define the pathologic implications. Might the gut lymphatic absorption and transport system not be a thoroughfare of therapeutic relevance?

At a purely mechanical level the seemingly simple issue of sphincteric function remains a conundrum. While the assessment of neural and hormonal regulation has provided much useful information, a clear understanding of the mechanism of sphincter function and even dysfunction is almost utterly lacking. Crude techniques of surgical resection, ablation or wrapping need to be refined and replaced with the appropriate pharmacological agents capable of altering tone and specifically regulating sphincter activity. The therapy of esophageal reflux disease needs not only the development of rapid-acting acid suppressive agents but specific muscle-targeted agents capable of restoring normative sphincteric function, whatever that is! In this vein it might be noted that the blind spot of an infective disorder that obviated the elucidation of acid peptic disease still exists in the inability of physicians to consider pepsin as a viable therapeutic target.

The ultimate therapeutic evolution will almost certainly be the safe replacement of damaged or failing components of the gastrointestinal system. An intermediate goal may be the use of artificial organ support, but the consideration of organ cloning and xenografts are both relevant areas of focus. In the current time frame, the elucidation of the precise immunological mechanisms of rejection and the development of agents to ameliorate such responses are the most critical areas of endeavor.

There is little doubt that since the first musings of Man as to the nature of coction, pepsis, and dyspepsis, much has been learned. The consideration of abdominal pain and its diverse causations have advanced to the point that physicians have shed light on what was once a dark plain and provided succor to many who would previously have suffered and perished. Nevertheless, there are many issues that require resolution and great questions that still seek answers. The evolution of therapy is an endless road that requires not only commitment but also a dedication to the art that is medicine. If the secret of happiness is knowledge and the secret of knowledge an inquiring mind, then no physician can fail to join the eternal quest to not only understand but to heal and provide comfort to those in distress.

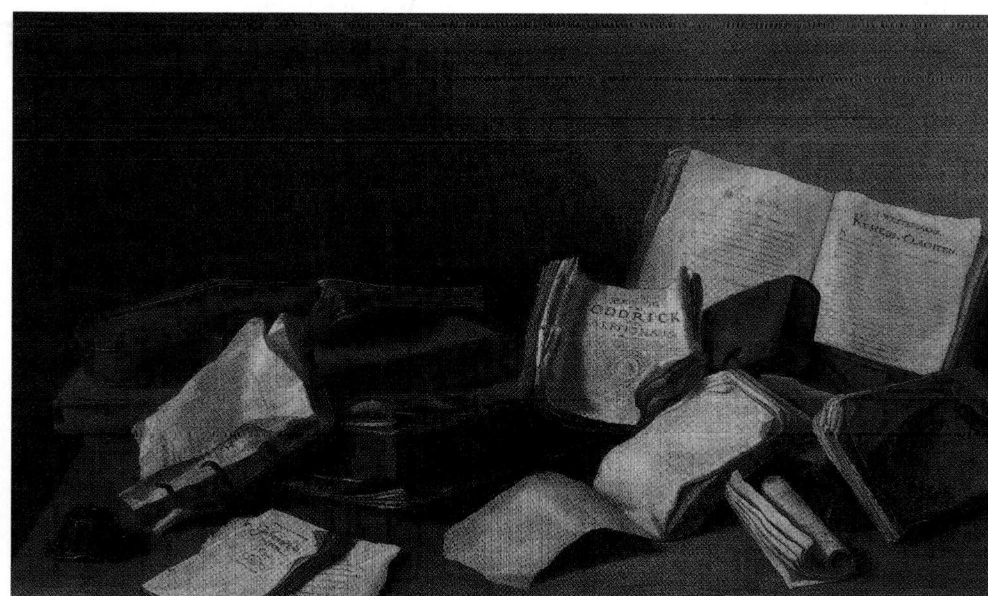

Therapy as accepted today may have little relevance in the near future, yet current knowledge could never have been attained without access to past information. Indeed, as so eloquently noted: "The moving finger writes; and having writ moves on: nor all your piety nor wit shall lure it back to cancel half a line!" *(Omar Khayyam, Naishapur, 1110 A.D.).*

It is likely that the determination of the molecular basis of disease will lead to the development of definitive therapeutic interventions. The visions of the poetic seer, Blake, probably best encapsulate the future of molecular medicine as defined in human terms:

"To see a World in a Grain of Sand
And a Heaven in a Wild Flower,
Hold Infinity in the Palm of your Hand
And Eternity in an Hour."

Auguries of Innocence
William Blake, 1801

Name Index

Subject Index

References

1. Early Concepts of Health and Disease

Albutt, T.C. *The Historical Relations of Medicine and Surgery to the End of the Sixteenth Century.* New York: Macmillan and Co., Ltd., 1905.

Breasted, J.H. *The Edwin Smith Surgical Papyrus.* Birmingham: The Classics of Medicine Library, 1984.

Castiglioni, A. *Storia della medicina.* From the Italian and edited by E.B. Krumbhaar, 2nd edition. New York: Alfred A. Knopf, 1947.

Cumberledge, J. *Science, Medicine, and History*. London: Oxford University Press, 1953.

Garrison, F.H. *Contributions to the History of Medicine.* New York: Hafner Publishing Co., 1966.

Huang ti nei ching su wen: the Yellow Emperor's Classic of Internal Medicine. Birmingham: The Classics of Medicine Library, 1988.

The Genuine Works of Hippocrates. Translated from the Greek with a Preliminary Discourse and Annotations by Francis Adams. New York: W. Wood, 1891.

Majno, G. *The Healing Hand.* Cambridge: Harvard University Press, 1991.

Morton's Medical Bibliography: An Annotated Checklist of Texts Illustrating the History of Medicine. 5th edition. Edited by J. Norman. Brookfield: Gower, 1991.

2. Rome and its Physicians

Brockbank, William. *Ancient Therapeutic Arts.* Springfield: Thomas, 1954.

Dioscorides Pedanius of Anazarbos. *The Greek Herbal of Dioscorides*. Edited by R.T. Gunther. Oxford: Oxford University Press, 1934.

Friedenwald, H. *The Jews and Medicine.* Baltimore: John Hopkins Press, 1967.

Garrison, F.H. *Contributions to the History of Medicine.* New York: Hafner Publishing Co., 1966.

Mettler, Cecilia Charlotte. *History of Medicine: A Correlative Text, Arranged According to Subjects.* Philadelphia: Blakiston Co., 1947.

3. Medieval Pharmacology

Biedermann, H. *Medicina Magica.* Birmingham: Gryphon Editions, 1978.

Crawfurd, Sir Raymond H.P. *Plague and Pestilence in Literature and Art.* Oxford: Clarendon Press, 1914.

Rawcliffe, Carole. *Sources for the History of Medicine in Medieval England.* Kalamazoo: Medieval Institute Publications, 1995.

Rubin, Stanley. *Medieval English Medicine.* New York: Barnes & Noble Books, 1974.

The Medical Writings of Moses Maimonides. Edited by S. Muntner and F. Rosner. New York: Gryphon Editions, 1997.

Wear, Andrew. *Knowledge and Practice in English Medicine, 1550-1680.* New York: Cambridge University Press, 2000.

Wootton, A.C. *The Chronicles of Pharmacy.* Boston: Milford House Inc., 1910.

4. Dogmas and Delusions

Alchemy and the Occult: A Catalogue of Books and Manuscripts from the Collection of Paul and Mary Mellon Given to Yale University Library, compiled by Ian MacPhail. New Haven: Yale University Library, 1977.

Christison, Sir Robert. *A Treatise on Poisons in Relation to Medical Jurisprudence, Physiology, and the Practice of Physic.* From the 4th Edinburgh edition. Philadelphia: Barrington & Haswell, 1845.

Darby, John Custis. *Science and the Healing Art, or A New Book on Old Facts.* Louisville: J.P. Morton and Company, 1880.

De Rola, S.K. *The Golden Game.* London: Thames and Hudson, 1988.

English Hospitals, 1660-1948: A Survey of their Architecture and Design. Edited by Harriet Richardson. Swindon: Royal Commission on the Historical Monuments of England, 1998.

Greenberg, A. *A Chemical History Tour.* New York: J. Wiley & Son, Inc., 2000.

Hooke, Robert. *Micrographia, or, Some physiological descriptions of minute bodies made by magnifying glasses: with observations and inquiries thereupon.* London: Printed by Jo. Martyn, and Ja. Allestry, Printers to the Royal Society, and are to be sold at their shop at the Bell in S. Paul's Church-yard, 1665.

Mettler, Cecilia Charlotte. *History of Medicine: A Correlative Text, Arranged According to Subjects.* Philadelphia: Blakiston Co., 1947.

Roob, Alexander. *The Hermetic Museum: Alchemy and Mysticism.* Cologne: Taschen America Llc., 1997.

Siraisis, N.G. *Medieval and Renaissance Medicine.* Chicago: University of Chicago Press, 1990.

Walsh, J.J. *The Popes in Science.* New York, 1908.

5. Alchemist Physicians

Brockbank, William. *Ancient Therapeutic Arts.* Springfield: Thomas, 1954.

Mathison, Richard R. *The Eternal Search: the Story of Man and his Drugs.* New York: G.P. Putnam, 1958.

Paracelsus. *Four treatises of Theophrastus von Hohenheim, called Paracelsus.* Translated from the original German, with introductory essays, by C. Lilian Temkin, George Rosen, Gregory Zilboorg, and Henry E. Sigerist. Baltimore: The Johns Hopkins Press, 1941.

Porter, Roy. *The Biographical Dictionary of Scientists.* 2nd edition. New York: Oxford University Press, 1994.

Rawcliffe, C. "God, Mammon, and the Physician: Medicine in England before the College." *Journal of the Royal College of Physicians of London* 2000;34(3):266-72.

6. Magic, Fraud and Therapy

Bauer, William Waldo. *Potions, Remedies, and Old Wives' Tales.* Garden City: Doubleday, 1969.

Carlino, A. *The Books of the Body.* Chicago: University of Chicago Press, 1994.

Crawfurd, Sir Raymond H.P. *The King's Evil.* Oxford: Clarendon Press, 1911.

Singer, Charles Joseph. *Early English Magic and Medicine.* London: Oxford University Press, 1920.

Singer, Charles Joseph. *From Magic to Science: Essays on the Scientific Twilight.* New York: Dover Publications, 1958.

7. Administration of Therapy

Health and Healing in Early Modern England: Studies in Social and Intellectual History. Edited by Andrew Wear. Brookfield: Ashgate, 1998.

Lucia, Salvatore Pablo. *A History of Wine as Therapy.* Philadelphia: Lippincott, 1963.

Metcalfe, Richard. *The Rise and Progress of Hydrotherapy in England and Scotland.* London, 1906.

Modlin, I.M. "The Surgical Legacy of Arris and Gale." *Journal of Medical Biography* 1996;4:191-99.

Snow, J. *On Chloroform and Other Anesthetics.* London: John Churchill, 1858.

The Collected Essays of Sir William Osler. Birmingham: Classics of Medicine Library, Gryphon Press, 1985.

8. Agents and Remedies

Addison, Thomas. *A Collection of the Published Writings of the Late Thomas Addison, M.D., Physician to Guy's Hospital.* London: The New Sydenham Society, 1860.

Chaplin, Arnold. *Medicine in England During the Reign of George III.* London, 1919.

Cowen, David L. and Helfand, William H. *Pharmacy: An Illustrated History.* New York: Abrams, Inc., 1988.

Drugs and Narcotics in History. Edited by R. Porter and M. Teich. New York: Cambridge University Press, 1995.

Hahnemann, S. *The Homeopathic Medical Doctrine.* Dublin: W.F. Wakeman, 1833.

Singer, Charles. *The Herbal in Antiquity and its Transmission to Later Ages.* London, 1927.

Sloan, A.W. *English Medicine in the Seventeenth Century.* Durham: Durham Academic Press, 1996.

Wootton, A.C. *Chronicles of Pharmacy.* London: Macmillan and Co., Ltd., 1910.

9. From Herbs to Hypothesis

Beaumont, William. *Experiments and observations on the gastric juice, and the physiology of digestion.* Plattsburgh: F.P. Allen, 1833.

Bollet, Alfred J. *Plagues & Poxes: The Rise and Fall of Epidemic Disease.* New York: Demos Publications, 1987.

Chaplin, Arnold. *Medicine in England During the Reign of George III.* London, 1919.

Dennis, Frederic Shepard. *The History and Development of Surgery during the Past Century.* New York, 1905.

Fissell, Mary Elizabeth. *Patients, Power, and the Poor in Eighteenth-century Bristol.* New York: Cambridge University Press, 1991.

Fulton, John F. *Selected Readings in the History of Physiology.* 2nd edition. Springfield: Thomas, 1930.

Holmes, F.L. *Claude Bernard and Animal Chemistry: The Emergence of a Scientist.* Cambridge: Harvard University Press, 1974.

Morgagni, Giambattista. *The seats and causes of diseases investigated by anatomy: in five books, containing a great variety of dissections, with remarks, to which are added very accurate and copious indexes of the principal things and names therein contained.* Translated from the Latin of Morgagni by Benjamin Alexander, M.D. London: A. Millar, and T. Cadell, his successor, 1769.

Rogal, Samuel J. *Medicine in Great Britain from the Restoration to the Nineteenth Century, 1660-1800: An Annotated Bibliography.* New York: Greenwood Press, 1992.

Stirling, William. *Some apostles of physiology; being an account of their lives and labours, that have contributed to the advancement of the healing art as well as to the prevention of disease.* London: Waterlow and Sons, Limited, 1902.

Weatherall, Mark. *Gentlemen, Scientists, and Doctors: Medicine at Cambridge 1800-1940.* Rochester: Boydell Press, 2000.

Youngson, A.J. *The Scientific Revolution in Victorian Medicine.* New York: Holmes & Meier Publishers, 1979.

10. Current Therapeutic Strategies

Bast, T.H. *The Life & Time of Adolf Kussmaul.* New York: Paul B. Hoeber Inc., 1926.

Clinical aspects of genetics: the proceedings of a conference held in London at the Royal College of Physicians of London, 17th – 18th March, 1961. Edited by F. Avery Jones. Philadelphia: 1961.

Garrison, Fielding Hudson. *An Introduction to the History of Medicine, with Medical Chronology, Suggestions for Study and Bibliographic Data.* 4th edition. Philadelphia: W.B. Saunders Company, 1929.

Hemmeter, J.C. *Diseases of the Stomach.* Philadelphia: P. Blakiston's Son & Co., 1902.

Jackson, C. Gastroscopy: report of additional cases. *J Amer Med Assn* 1907;49:1425-8.

Kussmaul, A. *Memoirs of an Old Physician.* New Delhi: Amerind Publishing Co., 1981.

Leiter, J. *Elektro-endoskopische Instrumente.* Wien: W. Braumuller & Son, 1880.

Lister, Joseph. *The Collected Papers of Joseph, Baron Lister.* Oxford: The Clarendon Press, 1909.

Mann, R.D. *Modern Drug Use.* Boston: MTP Press, 1984.

McCune, W.S., Shorb R.E., Moscovitz H. "Endoscopic cannulation of the ampulla of Vater: a preliminary report." *Ann Surg* 1968;167:753.

Ponsky, J.L., Gauderer, M.W. Percutaneous endoscopie gastrostomy: a nonoperative technique for feeding gastrostomy. *Gastrointest Endosc* 1981;27(1):9-11.

Provenzale, L., Revignas, A. "An original method for guided intubation of the colon." *Gastrointestinal Endoscopy* 1969;16(1):11-17.

Reuter, Hans Joachim. *Philipp Bozzini and Endoscopy in the 19th Century.* Stuttgart: Max Nitze Museum, 1988.

Ringleb, O. "Zur Erinnerung an Philipp Bozzini." *Zeit Urol* 1923;17:321-30.

Schindler, R. *Lehrbuch und Atlas der Gastroskopie.* Munich: J.F. Lehmans, 1923.

Schindler, R., Ortmayer, M. "Classification of chronic gastritis with special reference to the gastroscopic method." *Arch Intern Med* 1936;57:959-78.

Senn, Nicholas. *Principles of Surgery.* Philadelphia: F.A. Davis, 1890.

The Growth of Gastroenterologic Knowledge During the Twentieth Century. Edited by Joseph B. Kirsner. Philadelphia: Lea & Febiger, 1994.

The Surgical Papers of William Stewart Halstead. Baltimore: The John Hopkins Press, 1934.

11. The Early Development of Gastroenterology

Beaumont, William. *Experiments and observations on the gastric juice and the physiology of digestion: facsimile of the original edition of 1833, together with a biographical essay by Sir William Osler.* Cambridge: Harvard University Press, 1929.

Bernard, C. "Du suc pancréatique et de son rôle dans les phénomènes de la digestion." *Arch Gen Med* 1849;19:60-81.

Billroth, T. "Offenes schreiben an Herrn Dr. L. Wittelshofer." *Wien Med Wochenschr* 1881;31:161-5.

Cooper, Astley. *Surgical Essays.* London: Cox, 1818-19.

Gastroenterology in Britain: Historical Essays. Edited by Bynum, W.F. London: Wellcome Trust, 1997.

Kirsner, J.B. "The origin of 20th century discoveries transforming clinical Gastroenterology." *Am J Gastroenterol* 1998;93:862-71.

Langley, John Newport. *Pepsin-forming Glands.* London, 1881.

Modlin, I.M., Lawton G.P. "Observations on the Gastric Illuminati." *Perspectives Biol Med* 1996;39(4)527-43.

Moynihan, Berkeley. *Duodenal Ulcer.* Birmingham: The Classics of Medicine Library, 1991.

Mueller, J. "Versuche über die künstliche Verdauung des geronnen Eiweisses." *Arch Anar Physiol wiss Med,* 1836.

Nitze, M. "Eine neue Beobachtungs-nod Untersuchungsmethode für Harnrohre, Harnblase und Rektum." *Wien Med Wschr* 1879;24:650.

Prout, William. "On the nature of the acid and saline matters usually existing in the stomach of animals." *Philos Trans* 1824;114:45-49.

Schwann, F.T. "Über das Wesen des Verdauungsprocesses." *Arch Anat Physiol wiss Med* 1836;90-138.

Stirling, William. *Some apostles of physiology; being an account of their lives and labours, that have contributed to the advancement of the healing art as well as to the prevention of disease.* London: Waterlow and Sons, Limited, 1902.

12. Imaging the Abdomen

Becher, W. "A proposal for the use of Roentgen procedures in medicine." *Deutsch Med Wschr* 1896;22:28.

Benedict, E.B. "Examination of the stomach by means of a flexible gastroscope: a prelimary report." *New Engl J Med* 1934;210:669-74.

Cannon, W. "Early use of the roentgen rays in the study of the alimentary canal." *J Amer Med Assoc* 1914;62:1-3.

Davis, A.B. "Rudolf Schindler's role in the development of gastroscopy." *Bull Hist Med* 1972;46:150-70.

Desormeaux, A.J. "De l'endoscope, instrument propre à éclairer certaines cavités intensivement de l'économie." *Comptes rendues de l'Académie des sciences* 1855;40:692-93.

Haubrich, W.S. "History of Endoscopy." In *Gastroenterologic endoscopy.* Michael V. Sivak, Philadelphia: Saunders, 1987.

Hirschowitz, B.I., Curtiss, L.E., Peters, C.W., Pollard, H.M. "Demonstration of a new gastroscope, the 'fiberscope'." *Gastroenterology* 1958;35:50-53.

Hounsfield, Sir Godfry Newbold. "Computerized transverse axial scanning (tomography)." *Brit J Radiol* 1973;46:1016-22.

Lauterbur, P. "Image formation by induced local interactions: Examples employing nuclear magnetic resonance." *Nature* 1973;242:190-91.

Modlin, I.M. *A Brief History of Endoscopy.* Milan: Multi Med, 2000.

Morrissey, J.F., Yoshihisa, T., Thorsen, W.B. "Progress in Gastroenterology: Gastroscopy – A review of the English and Japanese literature." *Gastroenterology* 1967;53:456-76.

Oi, I., Takemoto, T., Kondo, I. "Fiberduodenoscope: direct observation of the papilla of Vater – A preliminary report." *Endoscopy* 1970;3:101-03.

Reuter, M.A., Reuter, H.J., Engel, R.M. *History of Endoscopy.* Stuttgart, 1999.

Roentgen, W.C. "Über eien neue Art von Strahlen (Vorlaufige Mitteilung), Sitzber." *Phys Med Ges Wurzburg* 1895;132-41.

Segalas, M. "Description of an instrument for inspecting the urethra and bladder." *Lancet* 1826;11:603-04.

Wallace, D.M. "New lamps for old." *Proc R Soc Med* 1973;66:455-58.

Wallace, F.J. "Fiber optic endoscopy." *J Urol* 1963;90:324-34.

Wild, J.J. "Progress in the technique of soft tissue examination by IS MC pulsed ultrasound." In: *Ultrasound in Biology and Medicine.* Edited by E. Kelly, Washington. D.C.: American Institute of Biological Sciences, 1957.

Williams, Francis H. *The Roentgen Rays in Medicine and Surgery.* New York: McMillian Company, 1901.

13. The Esophagus

Allison, P.R. "Peptic ulcer of the Oesophagus." *J Thorac Surg* 1946;15:308.

Barrett, N.R. "Chronic peptic ulcer of the Oesophagus" and "Oesophagitis", *Brit J Surg* 1950;38:175-82.

The Growth of Gastroenterologic Knowledge During the Twentieth Century. Edited by Joseph B. Kirsner. Philadelphia: Lea & Febiger, 1994.

Mackenzie, M. *Diseases of the Throat and Nose, Vol II.* Philadelphia: P. Blankston, Son & Co., 1884.

Modlin, I.M. *A Brief History of Endoscopy.* Milan: Multi Med, 2000.

Modlin, I.M., Farhadi, J. "Rudolf Schindler – A Man for All Seasons." *J Clin Gastroenterol* 2000;v.31:(2):95-102.

14. The Stomach and Duodenum

Bircher, E. "Die Resektion von Aesten der N. Vagus zur Behandlung gastrischer Affektionen." *Schweiz Med Wochenschr* 1920;50:519-28.

Black, J., Duncan, W., Durant, C., et al. "Definition and antagonism of histamine H_2 receptors." *Nature* 1972;236:385-90.

Boas, I.I. *Diagnostik und Therapie der Magendarmkrankheiten.* Leipzig: G. Thieme, 1890.

Card, W., Marks, I. "The relationship between the acid output of the stomach following 'maximal' histamine stimulation and the parietal cell mass." *Clin Sci* 1960;19:147-63.

Code, C., Scholer, J. E. "Barrier offered by gastric mucosa to absorption of sodium." *Am J Physiol* 1955;183:604.

Dragstedt, L. "Section of the vagus nerves to the stomach in the treatment of peptic ulcer." *Ann Surg* 1947;126:687-708.

Ewald, O. *Klinik der Verdauungskrankheiten.* 3 Vols. Berlin: A. Hirschwald, 1879-1902.

Gussenbauer, C., Winiwater, A. "Die partielle Magenresektion; eine experimentelle operative Studie." *Arch kim Chit* 1876;19:347:80.

Heidenhain, R.P. "Über die Pepsinbildung in den Pylorusdruesen." *Pflueg Arch ges Physiol* 1878;18:169-71.

Jones, Francis Avery, Gummer, J.W.P., Lennard-Jones, J.E. *Clinical Gastroenterology.* 2nd edition. Edinburgh: Blackwell Scientific, 1968.

Kidd, M., Modlin, I.M. "A century of *Helicobacter pylori*. Paradigms Lost – Paradigms Regained." *Digestion* 1998;59:1-15.

Koch, R. *Untersuchungen ueber die Aetiologie der Wundinfektionskrankheiten.* Leipzig: FCW Vogel, 1878.

Kocher, E. Th. "Über die Radicalbehandlung des Krebses." *Deutsch Z Chir* 1880;13:134-66.

Latarjet, A. Résection du nerf de l'estomac: technique opératoire; résultats cliniques. *Bull Acad Natl Med Paris* 1922;87:681-91.

Mikulicz-Radecki, Johann von. "Chirurgische Erfahrungen über das Darmcarcinom." *Arch kim Chir* 1903;69:28-47.

Modlin, I.M., Sachs G. *Acid-related Diseases.* Konstanz: Schnetztor-Verlag GmbH, 1998.

Modlin, I.M. *From Prout to the Proton Pump.* Konstanz: Schnetztor-Verlag GmbH, 1995.

Polya, E.A. "Zur Stumpfversorung nach Magenresektion." *Zbl Chit* 1911;38:532-5.

Rutkow, J.R. *Surgery: An Illustrated History.* St. Louis: Mosby-Year Book, in collaboration with Norman Pub., 1993.

Rydydgier, L. "First extirpation of carcinomatous pylorus: Death after 12 hours." *Deutsch Z Chir* 1881;14:252-60.

Sawyer, Sir J. Clinical lecture on the treatment of gastralgia. London, 1887.

Sedillot, C. "Opération de gastrostomie pratique pour la première fois le 13 novembre 1849." *Gaz med Strasbourg* 1849;9:366-77.

The Growth of Gastroenterologic Knowledge During the Twentieth Century. Edited by Joseph B. Kirsner, Philadelphia: Lea & Febiger, 1994.

Warren, J.R., Marshall, B. "Unidentified curved bacilli on gastric epithelium in active chronic gastritis." *Lancet* 1983;1:1273-75.

15. Exocrine Pancreas

Banting, F.G., Best, C.H. "The Internal Secretion of the Pancreas." *Journal of Laboratory and Clinical Medicine* 1922;7(5):465-80.

Bartholin, I. *De lacteis thoracicis in homine brustique.* Hafinae: M. Martzan, 1652.

Brunner, J.C. *De glandulis in intestino duodeno hominis deectis.* Heidelberg: C.E. Buchta, 1687.

Howard, J.M., Hess, W., Traverso, W. "Johann Georg Wirsung and the pancreatic duct: the prosector of Padua, Italy." *J Am College Surg* 1998;187:201-11.

Langerhans, P. "Beitraege zur mikroskopischen Anatomie der Bauchspeicheldruese." Berlin: Gustav Lange, 1869. English translation by Morrison, H., *Bull Hist Med* 1937;5:259-97.

Modlin, I.M., Hults, C., Kidd, M., Hinoue, T. "A brief history of chronic pancreatitis in *Chronic Pancreatitis*." Buchler M.W. and Freiss H. (eds). Blackwell, Berlin, Germany, 2001:3-21. Nyhus, L.M. Surgical sketch on Wirsung.
World J Surg 1999;23(5):528.

Opie, E. *Disease of the Pancreas, its Cause and Nature.* Philadelphia: J.B. Lippincott, 1903.

Rudbeck, Olof. "Nova exercitatio anatomica, exhi hens ductus hepaticos aquosos, et vasa glandulorum serosa, 1653." English translation in *Bull Hist Med* 1942;11:304-39.

Schmid, S.W. Buchler, M.W., Kidd, M., Modlin, I.M. "Acute pancreatitis" in: *Evidence-based Gastroenterology.* Irvine J.E., and Hunt R.H. (eds). BC Decker Inc., Ontario, Canada 2001:422-33.

Whipple, A.D. "Treatment of carcinoma of the ampulla of Vater." *Ann Surg* 1935;102:763-79.

Zollinger, R.M., Ellison, E.H. "Primary peptic ulcerations of the jejunum associated with islet cell tumors of the pancreas." *Ann Surg* 1955;142:709-28.

16. Gut-Neuroendocrine System

Babkin, B.P. *Die aussere Sekretion der Verdauungsdruesen.* Berlin: J. Springer, 1914.

Bayliss, W., Starling, F. "Preliminary communication on the causation of the so-called 'peripheral reflex secretion' of the pancreas." *Lancet* 1902;2:810-13.

Best, C., McHenry, F. "The inactivation of histamine." *J Physiol Lond* 1930;70:349-72.

Code, C. "Histamine and gastric secretion." In: *Histamine.* Edited by G. Wolstenholme and C. O'Conner. Boston: Little, Brown & Co., 1956.

Dale, H. *Adventures in Physiology.* London: Pergamon Press, 1953.

Edkins, J. "The chemical mechanism of gastric secretion." *J Physiol Lond* 1906;34:133-44.

Gregory, R., Tracey, H. "The preparation and properties of gastrin." *J Physiol Lond* 1959;149:70-71.

Komarov, S. "Gastrin." *Proc Soc Exp Biol Med* 1938;38:514-16.

Mann, F.C., Ballman, J.L. "Experimentally produced peptic ulcer: Development and treatment." *JAMA* 1932;99:1576.

McGuigan, J. "Gastric mucosal intracellular localization of gastrin by immunofluorescence." *Gastroenterol* 1968;55:315-27.

Modlin, I.M., Kidd, M., Marks, I., Tang, L. "The pivotal role of John S. Edkins in the discovery of Gastrin." *World J Surgery* 1997;21:226-34.

Modlin, I.M., Schmid, S.W., Tang, L.H., Farhadi, J., Buchler, M. "Endocrine Tumors of the Pancreas." *Pancreatic Tumors: Achievements and Prospective.* 2000;332-53.

Modlin, I.M., Kidd, M. "Ernest Starling and the discovery of secretin." *J Clin Gastroenterol* 2001;32:187-92.

Pavlov, I. *The Work of the Digestive Glands.* London: Griffin, 1902.

Pearse, A. "The cytochemistry and ultrastructure of polypeptide hormone-producing cells of the APUD series and the embryologic, physiologic and pathologic implications of the concept." *J Histochem Cytochem* 1969;17(5):303-13.

Starling, E.H. The Croonian Lectures on the chemical correlation of the functions of the body. *Lancet* 1905;2:339-41,423-5,501-03,579-83.

Welbourn, R.B. *The History of Endocrine Surgery.* New York: Praeger, 1990.

17. The Hepato-Biliary Tract

Browne, J. A remarkable account of a liver, appearing glandulous to the eye. *Phil Trans* 1685;15:1266-8.

Burnett, James Compton. *The Diseases of the Liver: Jaundice, Gall-stones, Enlargements, Tumours, and Cancer: and their Treatment.* 2nd edition Philadelphia: Boericke & Tafel, 1895.

Frerichs, Friedrich Theodor. *Klinik der Leberkrankheiten.* Braunschweig: F. Vieweg, 1858.

Glisson, Francis. *Anatomia hepatis: Cui praemittuntur quaedam ad rem anatomicam universe spectantia.* London: Typis Du-Gardianis, impensis Octaviani Pullein, 1654.

Graham, E., Cole, H. "Roentgenologic examination of the gallbladder." *J Amer Med Assoc* 1924;82:613-14.

Kidd, M., Modlin, I.M. "Frederick Ruysch – Depictor of the surreality of death." *J Med Biog* 1999;7:69-77.

Laennec, R.I. *De l'auscultation mediate.* Paris: J. A. Brosson & J. S. Chude, 1819.

Langenbuch, C. "Em Fall von Exstirpation Jet Gallen blase wegen chronischer Cholelithiasis." *Berl kim Wschr* 1882;19:725-7.

Modlin, I.M., Ahlman, H. "Oddi: The Paradox of the Man and the Sphincter." *Arch Surg,* 1994;129:549-56.

Muraskin, William A. *The War against Hepatitis B: A History of the International Task Force on Hepatitis B Immunization.* Philadelphia: University of Pennsylvania Press, 1995.

Naunyn, B. *Klinik der Cholelithiasis.* Leipzig: E.C.W. Vogel, 1892.

Oddi, R. "D'une disposition à sphincter spéciale de l'ouverture du canal choledoque." *Arch Iral Bid* 1887;8:317-22.

Ross, I. Clunies. *Liver Fluke Disease in Australia: Its Treatment and Prevention.* Melbourne: H.J. Green, Government Printer, 1928.

Sherlock, Sheila. *Diseases of the Liver and Biliary System.* Oxford: Blackwell Scientific Publications, 1955.

The Liver and its Diseases. Edited by Schaffner, F., Sherlock, S., and Leevy, C.M. New York: Intercontinental Medical Book Corp, 1974.

18. Small Bowel

Ballantyne, G.H., Leahy, P.F., Modlin, I.M. (eds). *Laparoscopic Surgery.* W.B. Saunders, Philadelphia, PA; 1994.

Begos, D.G., Modlin, I.M., Ballantyne, G.H. A Brief History of Intestinal Surgery. *Col Rect Surg* 1994;7:133-57.

Chapman, John. *Diarrhoea and Cholera: Their Nature, Origin, and Treatment Through the Agency of the Nervous System.* 2nd edition. London: Trubner, 1866.

Crohn, B.B., Ginzburg, L., Oppenheimer, G. "Regional ileitis: a pathologic and clinical entity." *JAMA* 1932;99:1323-9.

Crosby, W.H. "Intraluminal biopsy of the small intestine." *Am J Dig Dis* 1957;2:236-41.

Dalzeil, K. "Chronic interstitial enteritis." *Brit Med J* 1913;ii:1068-70.

Fitz, R.H. "Perforating inflammation of the vermiform appendix: with special reference to its early diagnosis and treatment." *Am J Med Sci* 1886;92:321-46.

Fowler, G.R. *A Treatise on Appendicitis.* 2nd edition. Philadelphia: J.B. Lippincott Company, 1900.

Gee, S. "On the coeliac affection." *St. Barth Hos. Rep* 1888;24:17.

Hall, R. "Arthur Hedley Clarence Visick FRCS 1897-1949." *Annals of the Royal College of Surgeons of England* 1986;68(3):147.

Halsted, W.S. "Circular suture of the intestines: an experimental study." *Amer J Med Sci* 1887;94:436-61.

Jaboulay, H. "La gastro-enterostomie. La jejunoduodenostomie. La résection du pylore." *Arch Prov Chir* 1892;1:1-22.

McBurney, C. "The incision made in the abdominal wall in cases of appendicitis, with a description of a new method of operating." *Ann Surg* 1894;20:38-43.

Meckel, J.E., "Ueber die Divertikel im Darmkanal." *Arch Physiol (Halle)* 1809;9:421-53.

Murphy, J.B. "Cholecysto-intestinal, gastro-intestinal, entero-intestinal anastomosis, and approximation without sutures." *Med Rec* (N. Y.) 1892;42:665-76.

Treves, F. "Inflammation of the vermiform appendix." *Lancet* 1902;1:815-18.

Woelfler, A. "Gastro-Enterostomie." *Zbl Chit* 1881;8:705-08.

19. Large Intestine and Rectum

Bernier, Olivier. *Louis XIV: A Royal Life.* Garden City: Doubleday, 1987.

Hirschprung, H. "Stuhltraegbeit Neugeborener in Folge von Dilatation und Hypertrophie des Colon." *Jahrb f Kinderh* 1887;27:1.

Jones, Sir Francis Avery. *Management of Constipation.* Oxford: Blackwell Scientific Publications, 1972.

Kelly, H.A. "A new method of examination and treatment of diseases of the rectum and sigmoid flexure." *Ann Surg* 1895;21:468-78.

Kraske, P. "Die sacrale Methode der Extirpation von Mastdarmkrehses und die Resectio recti." *Berlin klin Wschr* 1887;24:899-904.

Miles, W.E. "A method of performing abdomino-perineal excision for carcinoma of the rectum and of the terminal portion of the pelvic colon." *Lancet* 1908;2:1812-13.

Turell, R. "Fiberoptic coloscope and sigmoidoscope: preliminary report." *Amer J Surg* 1963;105:133.

Wolff, W.I., Shinya, H.A. "A new approach to colonic polyps." *Ann Surg* 1973;178:367-76.

20. Quo Vadis

Christopher the Armenian. *Peregrinaggio di Tre Giovani Figliuoli del Re di Serendippo.* Venice, 1557.

Modlin, I.M., Kidd, M., Sandor, A. Perspectives on Stem Cells and Gut Growth: Tales from a Crypt – From the Walrus to Wittgenstein in *The Gut as a Model in Cell and Molecular Biology.* Edited by F. Halter, D.J. Winton and N.A. Wright. Kluwer Academic Publishers, London UK 1997;94:121-34.

Remer, Theodore G. *Serendipity and The Three Princes, from the Peregrinaggio of 1557.* Norman: University of Oklahoma Press, 1965.

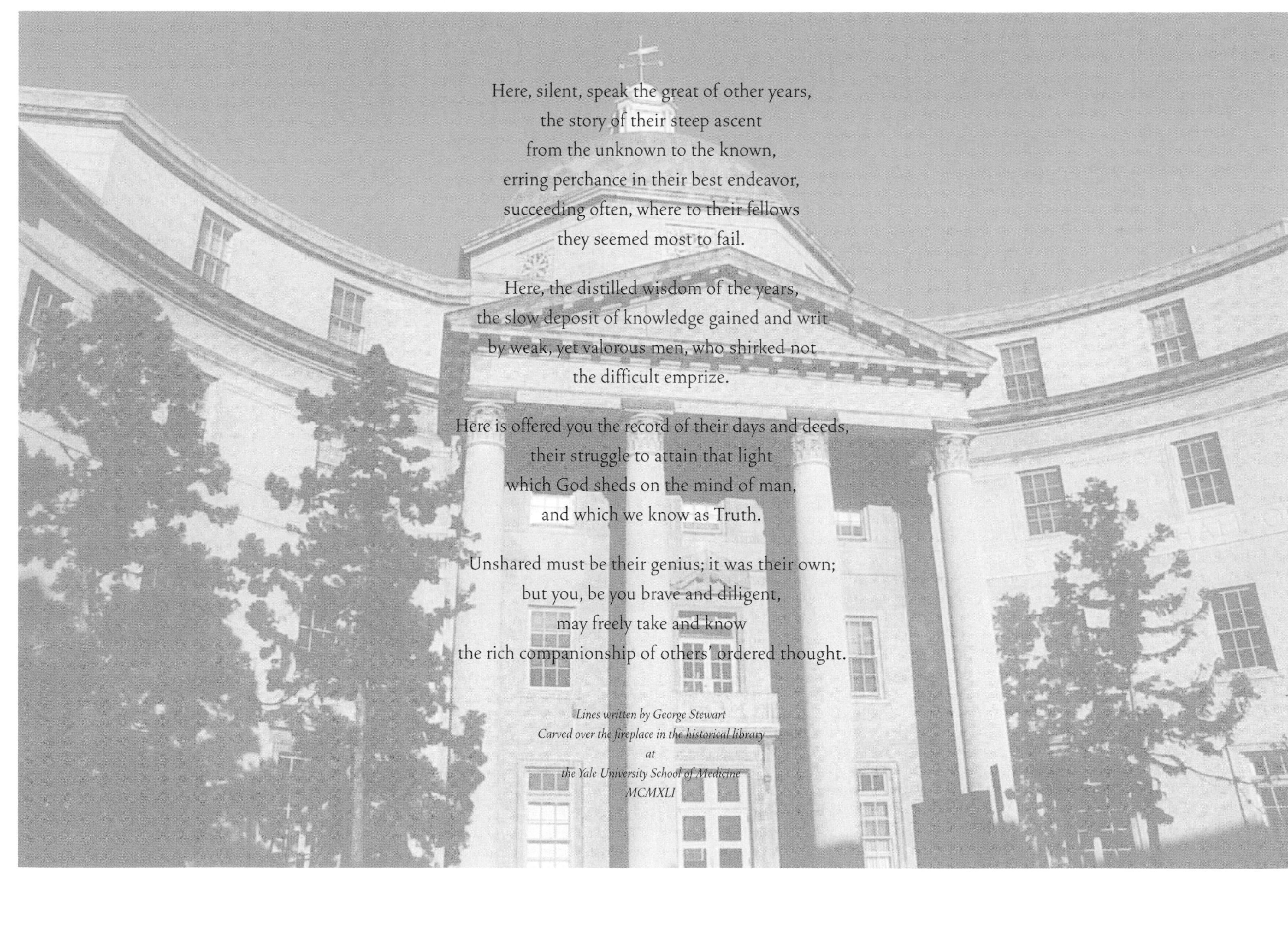

Here, silent, speak the great of other years,
the story of their steep ascent
from the unknown to the known,
erring perchance in their best endeavor,
succeeding often, where to their fellows
they seemed most to fail.

Here, the distilled wisdom of the years,
the slow deposit of knowledge gained and writ
by weak, yet valorous men, who shirked not
the difficult emprize.

Here is offered you the record of their days and deeds,
their struggle to attain that light
which God sheds on the mind of man,
and which we know as Truth.

Unshared must be their genius; it was their own;
but you, be you brave and diligent,
may freely take and know
the rich companionship of others' ordered thought.

Lines written by George Stewart
Carved over the fireplace in the historical library
at
the Yale University School of Medicine
MCMXLI

Ismar Boas

THE FOUNDER OF THE DISCIPLINE
OF GASTROENTEROLOGY

"My greatest joy always was, and is even now, my scientific activity and the furtherance of my speciality, for the foundation of which I feel responsible..."

Ismar Boas, 1928

BORN MARCH 28, 1858 EXIN, PRUSSIA
PERISHED MARCH 15, 1938 VIENNA, AUSTRIA
A VICTIM OF THE ANSCHLUSS.